MAN IN ADAPTATION
The Cultural Present

MAN IN ADAPTATION

The Cultural Present

SECOND EDITION

EDITED BY Yehudi A. Cohen LIVINGSTON COLLEGE, RUTGERS UNIVERSITY

ALDINE PUBLISHING COMPANY / New York

Second edition published 1974 by
Aldine Publishing Company
200 Saw Mill River Road
Hawthorne, New York 10532
Second printing, 1980

Library of Congress Catalog Card Number 74-169511
ISBN 0-202-01109-7 cloth
        0-202-01110-0 paper
Printed in the United States of America

For
Rhoda

CONTENTS

PREFACE TO
SECOND EDITION

THIS BOOK CONTAINS 39 selections, with interpretations and editorial essays, that are intended to serve as an introduction to cultural anthropology from the point of view of the processes of adaptation. These selections are organized to provide coherence for the study of man's cultural evolution, from his social beginnings to the present. The book is a companion volume to *Man in Adaptation: The Biosocial Background* and *Man in Adaptation: The Institutional Framework*.

In preparing the second edition of this volume, I have been more explicit than before in focusing on the sociopolitical aspects of adaptation in the organization and evolution of human societies. This revision of *The Cultural Present* has resulted from my own and others' experiences in using it in teaching anthropology to beginning and advanced students and from theoretical advances in the study of cultural adaptation during the past few years. These experiences have helped to sharpen and give direction to the anthropological study of adaptation. I believe I have made this point of view clearer, helping us to understand where man has come from, what his present condition is, and where he may be headed.

To this end, two fundamental changes have been made in the book's organization. First, this volume is now divided into two major parts. The first deals with stateless societies. It includes hunter-gatherers, stateless cultivators and pastoralists and pastoralist chiefdoms. The second part deals with state societies. It includes cultivators and industrial people living under centralized political systems.

The reader who is familiar with the first edition will quickly notice the other organizational change: the relinquishment of the distinction between horticulture and agriculture, which are now grouped as "cultivating." The separation of these two stages of sociocultural development has tended to produce more confusion than clarity among students and created unexpected difficulties for many teachers. I am grateful to the many students and teachers who brought this to my attention.

There are two further reasons for my greater explicitness in focusing on political aspects of adaptation. First, I began organizing the first edition of *The*

Cultural Present in late 1964 and early 1965, when the first major incidents of student activism began at Berkeley. At that time, no one could have foreseen the directions it would take. I completed that work during the summer of 1967, while dozens of American cities were struck by violence, riots, and burnings. Only during the next two years did the politicization of American universities—and other groups that had been politically inactive—become evident. While no science should be made an instrument of political partisanship, anthropology—and especially the frame of reference provided by the concepts of adaptation and evolution—can make a unique contribution to increasing our understanding of the storms and strife surrounding us. Anthropology has contributed (albeit slightly) to civilized man's increasing self-consciousness and knowledge of himself during the past half century by providing information about different life-styles in different parts of the world. This self-consciousness and knowledge can be further increased by illuminating the role of political institutions in cultural adaptation and evolution.

Second, research since the publication of the first edition of *The Cultural Present* has, I believe, made it possible to expand the concept of adaptation to include more than the relationships maintained by groups with their natural habitats. This is particularly highlighted by new insights into pastoralism, especially pastoralists who are characterized by centralized political systems. But it is also underlain by new and sharpened concepts of hunting-gathering, the transition to horticulture, and the origin of the state. These investigations now require that we include social pressures—in addition to ecological ones—in the habitat to which people must adapt. While this expanded concept of adaptation is most clearly reflected in the sections dealing with centralized cultivators and pastoralists, its ramifications extend throughout the book, substantively as well as taxonomically.

Students of social change may wish to reflect on the possibility that these two sets of changes are somehow related. While the political ferment in American society (and others) and the intellectual changes in anthropology may seem at first glance to be independent of each other, the idea that a culture represents a set of interrelated parts suggests that they may be of a piece. Our views of the organization of social relations in general have been shaken during the past few years, but it is neither wise nor possible to say more about the relationships among these changes at present. These are important questions for further discussion and study.

Most of the selections deal with stable social systems as they have been observed by anthropologists and others, although greater attention is paid in this edition to transitional periods in the evolutionary process. The selections dealing with stable systems have been arranged to present a picture of the sweep of man's evolution and adaptations from his tribal beginnings to the present. Even the most stable social system represents but a passing moment in the unfolding history of man's search for more and more viable relationships with his milieus and, as a consequence, with his fellows. A culture—and culture generally—is a changing system, one that is constantly in flux. Of course, not all cultures change at the same rate. Some change so slowly that they give the impression of absolute stability, while others change very rapidly.

My purpose here is to focus on the concept of adaptation, instead of presenting an encyclopedic and exhaustive compilation of readings that reflect my personal tastes or the standards of current popularity. In making these selections I was guided by at least five criteria.

1. As I combed the anthropological literature I was primarily concerned with the relevance of a piece to the theme of adaptation. Many illuminating and elegant articles, which could easily be included in any collection of anthropological readings, were excluded because they dealt with other problems. In several instances I found it necessary to go beyond the traditional boundaries of anthropology in search of selections that would throw needed light on different facets of adaptation.

My bias in selecting and organizing these readings is clearly evolutionary. Although it is difficult to study the processes of human adaptation without an evolutionary perspective, some anthropologists feel that such a separation can be made, and my intent is to draw attention to a point of view around which anthropological materials can be organized rather than to present or to defend an argument. Hence, wherever it was feasible and whenever a choice existed, I chose a selection that dealt with the problem of adaptation instead of one that was devoted simply to an evolutionary argument, so that attention can be focused on the processes of adaptation without necessarily adopting the evolutionary point of view.

2. I have selected papers that are empirically grounded: that is, papers that can be considered to be within the "case-study approach."

3. In choosing among alternatives that were relevant to the theme of adaptation and within the case-study approach, I allowed some of my personal tastes to intrude. Where choices had to be made, I elected to include selections that were well written and displayed imagination.

4. The reader will note that this book is one of three volumes. *Man in Adaptation: The Biosocial Background* deals with the processes of adaptation in biology, language, prehistoric cultures, and man's first civilizations. *Man in Adaptation: The Institutional Framework* considers six spheres of behavior— marriage and the family, law and social control, religion and magic, values and ideologies, personality, and the arts—within an evolutionary and adaptational frame of reference. The present volume and *The Institutional Framework* thus cut across and complement each other. This volume is organized around descriptions of total social and cultural systems and the levels of technological and political development that the particular cultures exemplify; the major aspects of each way of life are here conceived as part of a strategy of adaptation. *The Institutional Framework* focuses instead on the particular institutional, psychological, and intellectual activities around which the various strategies of adaptation described here are organized. Nevertheless, the three volumes have been organized so that they can stand separately.

5. Finally, I have attempted to highlight the major methodological problems in the analysis of human evolution and behavior. If these problems were not

made explicit in the selections, I have tried to point them out in my editorial introductions. I have not tried to present a complete inventory of methodological problems and their solutions, discussing only those that seemed to be most relevant to the problems at hand.

■ The editorial introductions appear in sans serif type (as here) and are off from the text of the selections themselves by squares like those preceding and ending this paragraph. To assist the reader who wishes to explore more thoroughly the topics that are covered in this book, I have included suggestions for further reading at the end of each introduction to sections and selections. Whenever possible, I have included books published in inexpensive paperback editions. ■

The final form of this book reflects in certain ways the economic realities with which I have been confronted by my publisher. Many more selections were eligible for inclusion according to my criteria, but I had to limit the scope of the book to keep its price within the reach of many readers (and there were a few instances in which permission to reprint could not be secured). For the same reason, and following the custom of all other introductory collections in anthropology, I have omitted footnotes and bibliographical references in most cases; the reader who wishes to consult the sources that were used by the authors of these selections can easily refer to the original publications. Throughout the book, the accents and diacritical marks that normally appear in certain foreign names and phrases have been deleted at the request of the publisher, for reasons of economy and simplicity. Similarly, a number of tables, charts, and illustrations that appeared in the original articles have been deleted where they were not essential to the flow of the argument; all such omissions have been marked with ellipses in the usual way. With these few exceptions, the selected articles and passages are reprinted without abridgement. In a few cases where authors used highly technical terminology, I have supplied definitions in footnote form.

Although it is customary in prefaces and forewords to express the most important kinship obligations last, I want to reverse this form and note my obligation for the atmosphere created and sustained by my wife, Rhoda Cohen, which has made this book possible. The work on this book and on its companion volumes often continued late into the night and into weekends and holidays. My family has repeatedly assured me that there never was need to apologize for this, and, were it otherwise, I doubt that the work would have been completed. Further, the initial organization of this volume was undertaken jointly with my wife; she brought several items to my attention that might otherwise have escaped my notice, and the diagram in Selection 3 is hers. In a sense, then, this book is as much hers as it is mine.

This work began around 1962, when a friend gave me a copy of Sir P. B. Medawar's *The Future of Man* (New York: Basic Books, 1960). I found the ideas in the book very exciting as I explored their relevance for the study of social organization. As time passed, I noticed that I was relying more and more on the ideas and implications of Medawar's book in my teaching and in my research. When some of my students expressed their appreciation for this point of view, especially in introductory courses, and asked for further readings about adaptation, I began to think of collecting a small group of selections.

From the time I received Medawar's book to the time I completed this preface, I have amassed many special intellectual debts. One aspect of adaptation in modern society is the steady attenuation of culturally provided mechanisms for repaying or reciprocating such obligations, and unfortunately there is no way in which I can properly express my sense of debt to the more than forty scientists whose work is represented here. I want not only to thank them for their courtesy in allowing me to reprint their work and for their patience as we corresponded about this project, but also to express my admiration for the quality of thought and the excitement of imagination that became more and more evident every time I read and re-read each paper. I have learned much from each of them.

My deepest thanks go to the anonymous readers of Aldine Publishing Company and to Walter Goldschmidt and Robert A. Manners who went out of their way to make helpful suggestions and to offer their encouragement. Many times I went back to read their reassurances that this was a worthwhile project. To Alexander J. Morin, Publisher of Aldine, I offer a nonritual salute for his work, assistance, and emboldening words, which were above and beyond the call of duty. There are many points where I no longer know where his ideas leave off and mine begin, and some ideas in this book are exclusively his. His patience in the face of one delay after another on my part was in itself an important source of reassurance for me.

I also take this opportunity to express my appreciation to Robert McC. Adams, Harumi Befu, Robin Fox, Chet Lancaster, Richard B. Lee, Jay Ruby, William C. Smith, and Frank R. Vivelo, from whom I benefited greatly in discussing this project and who also brought valuable references to my attention. I express special thanks to James L. Gibbs, Jr. who graciously found time to help me with several difficult problems during his own gruelling schedule of work. As usual, David A. Fredrickson has been a leavening influence, and many of my formulations owe much to conversations with him. I also acknowledge a great intellectual debt to J. Ralph Audy, who clarified several difficult problems for me. Denise O'Brien and Katherine Branstetter brought some important selections to my attention, as did Vera-Mae Fredrickson who also helped me clarify some details.

A BALLAD OF TELEOLOGIES

JOHN CIARDI

Says Father Malthus, "I'm delayed
but not denied. The table's laid
for the last tuber, I'm afraid."

Says Father Marx, who have the Law,
"I must confess I'm left in awe:
it comes to more than I foresaw."

INTRODUCTION

CULTURE IS MAN'S MOST important instrument of adaptation.[1] A culture is made up of the energy systems, the objective and specific artifacts, the organizations of social and political relations, the modes of thought, the ideologies, and the total range of customary behaviors that are transmitted from one generation to another by a social group and that enable it to maintain life in a particular habitat. Although a capacity for culture is not the exclusive property of *Homo sapiens,* only human culture evolves. Correlatively, as far as we know, man is the only animal capable of self-consciousness with respect to his cultures—the only animal able to blush, laugh at himself, and think of himself as a culture-bearer in third-person terms. It is man's culture that has enabled him to free himself from the restrictions or limitations of his genetic constitution and his natural milieus. The evolution of man's adaptations, as embodied in his cultures, is one of the themes that lend coherence and continuity to his historical development.

A person who confronts for the first time the vast amount of material that makes up the discipline of anthropology can easily be overwhelmed. He can soon become bogged down in apparently unrelated details, methods, problems, findings, and interpretations; he may conclude—as have some anthropologists—that the discipline is but a thing of shreds and patches to which every investigator has made his own whimsical and impetuous contributions, which serve only to satisfy his own curiosity. The newcomer to anthropological materials may find the vast panorama of human cultures interesting mainly because it is spiced with differences, exotic customs, and quaintnesses. In the absence of an overview of man and his works, it is easy to conclude that human cultures are little more than a hodgepodge of unrelated patterns.

The purpose of this book is to provide a guided introductory tour to cultural and social anthropology. It is selective, focusing on the role of adaptation in man's attempts to construct his patterns of social relations and to free himself from the limitations of his habitats. As every traveler knows, different guides stress their own interests and themes, and this holds true in anthropology and

---

1. This introduction and the introductions to the two companion volumes, *Man in Adaptation: The Biosocial Background* and *Man in Adaptation: The Institutional Framework,* are organized in parallel and are to some degree repetitive. Nevertheless, I suggest that the reader of the three volumes also read each of the introductions because they differ in emphasis and will serve to recapitulate the setting for the subsequent discussions.

1

in other fields. Other anthropologists would stress different themes, and other points of interest would attract the attention and excite the imagination of different guides and audiences.

I have focused on the concept of adaptation in bringing these selections together because this concept provides a unifying theme that enables us to compare different cultures, from man's most primitive groups to the huge metropolitan areas in modern civilizational states. Thus we can bridge the seemingly disparate interests of anthropologists. I do not contend that adaptation is the only unifying theme in anthropology but only that it is one way of making sense out of the many different things that anthropologists do.

Anthropology, in addition to being a scientific discipline, is a point of view about man's history and his culture. Perhaps one way of conceptualizing this point of view is to assert that the Australian aborigine is as important for an understanding of man and his works as is contemporary Western civilization. A corollary of this assertion is the axiom that even the most stable social system represents but a moment in man's history. To understand man's achievements of the present and to develop hypotheses about the directions in which he might be headed the forces that have led him from his cultural past must be appreciated. I include in this history the changes that now seem to be taking place in our own institutions and ideologies and that in another century (or less) will be evaluated by the same standards that we now apply to the transition from hunting-gathering to horticulture or from the European Middle Ages to industrialization.

Underlying the anthropological study of man is the principle that there is a reality, or several realities, to which man must adapt if he is to survive, reproduce, and perpetuate himself. Populations must adapt to the realities of the physical world; they must do this not only in terms of acquiring a livelihood, constructing shelter, and designing clothing, but they must maintain a proper "fit" between their biological makeup and the pressures of the various habitats in which they seek to live. However, there comes a point in the evolution of human societies—as in the emergence of nation-states or other modes of centralized political authority—when political elements in the habitat become at least as important as natural factors such as rain, climate, soils, and barriers (mountains and rivers), and to which people must adapt. Likewise, centralized political modes represent energy systems that—like bows and arrows, digging sticks or hoes, plows, steam, or electricity—provide limits and potentials for man's exploitation of the natural habitat and for the development of certain kinds of social relationships. In other words, it is necessary for us to shift our focus in studying the evolution of man's adaptations from physical to political elements in the habitat when we consider politically integrated societies.

Local social groups must adapt their organizations of social relations to these political forces, and vice versa, if there is to be order, regularity, and predictability in patterns of cooperation and competition and if the groups are to survive as viable units. Thus the institutions of society also must be seen as an integral part of a society's adaptation. When an individual is born he enters a world he did not make but with which he must come to terms. He must learn to live with the established means of coping with the natural habitat, with institutions, fore-ordained value systems, and the like if he is to succeed socially and biologically.

Every culture has its standards of social success, just as organic nature has its standards of success in terms of physical survival and reproduction. Neither set of standards can be considered solely an achievement of the moment; both are products of history. This book is a collection of studies that deal, from the point of view of adaptation, with man's cultural evolution.

Everything man does takes place in a context of institutions. By institution I mean here an organization of social relations—a stable grouping of persons whose activities are designed to meet specified challenges or problems, whose behavior is governed by implicit or explicit rules and expectations of each other, and who regularly use special paraphernalia or symbols in these activities. Social institutions are the principal focus of modern anthropology because they are the frames within which man spends every living moment. From his birth to his death, man does nothing outside the institutions of his society.

When we study adaptation in anthropology we are concerned with populations, not with individual organisms or persons. More specifically, we study institutions as instruments of adaptation because without institutions there can be no human adaptation, and the study of man's cultural evolution is inseparable from the study of the evolution of his institutions. The study of individual adaptation involves very different concepts. In a later essay (Selection 3), I will discuss the nature of the adaptive unit in man.

A population's adaptation is its *relationship* to its habitat. The concept of adaptation is historical: When we say a population is adapting we mean that it is altering its relationship to its habitat to make that habitat a more fit place in which to live or to make itself more fit to live in that milieu. To take an analogy from biology, the growth of a coat of fur by a population of mammals in a cold climate is adaptive because it alters the animals' relationship to the habitat. Similarly, the historical process in which the Eskimos' unique clothing developed, enabling each man to live in a private quasi-tropical climate, is adaptive because it altered the relationship of the group to the habitat. A change that does not affect the population's relationship to its milieu, such as embroidery on a parka or a moccasin, is not an adaptation.

The adaptation achieved by a population of mammals is the result of genetic mutation. In man, however, adaptation is achieved by means of culture. The point of view that is taken in this book is that human adaptation is the result of the energy systems that are harnessed by a group and the organizations of social relations in the group that make it possible to use its energy systems effectively. Among nonhumans, adaptations are achieved by the breeding population. We focus on this group in the study of biological adaptation because it is the vehicle for the gene pool, and we analyze the gene pool because it is the mechanism of biological evolution. Among humans, cultural adaptations are achieved by the social group; this group carries the culture, and it is the culture that is the mechanism of evolutionary change in man.

Thus, when we say that a human group is adapted to its habitat, we mean that it has achieved and maintains a viable relationship with its habitat. This adaptation assures the group's survival, reproduction, and efficient functioning, in the sense of "doing its job in nature." The achievement of this type of viable relationship always results from modifications in the habitat through changes in the group's energy systems and its organizations of social relations over a long period of time; it is never achieved in one generation. The historical aspect of the process of adaptation is underscored by the phenomenon of cultural evolution, by which I mean the process of sequential and largely nonrepetitive change that we see in culture. The fact of evolution demonstrates that adaptation also has taken place; if adaptation had not characterized man, cultural evolution could not have occurred.

I have avoided the use of the word *environment* because of my conviction that much more terminological rigor is necessary in the study of adaptation than has characterized it heretofore. Several parts make up an environment, and it is necessary to distinguish among them. By *environment* I mean the total system of components that interact with each other and that characterize a group or population. (I am using *environment* in much the same way that many persons use *ecosystem,* but I prefer the former because it is more inclusive.) The physical or natural habitat is only one component of an environment, although it is of primary importance. In the study of biological adaptation, the species that occupies a habitat must be regarded as a distinct component of the environment because it alters the habitat by the use that it makes of it; each species places its unique stamp on the habitat that it seeks to exploit by altering the "balance of nature" in it. The same considerations apply to man but in a still more complex way, since human organizations of social relations—especially political institutions—constitute still another component in the environment.

The adaptation of man is accomplished principally by cultural means, through the harnessing of new sources of energy for productive ends and through the organizations of social relations that make it possible to use these energy systems effectively. Without an effective organization of social relations to which it is wedded, a source of energy has nothing more than potential. Examples of such potential sources of energy are the bow and arrow, the spear, the digging stick or hoe, the plow and draft animals, steam, and electricity. Whenever groups of people introduce a new source of energy into a habitat and harness that energy, they create a new environment. Among the most important adaptive accompaniments of a new source of energy as a component of the environment are changes in the organizations of social relations that make it possible to use the potential energy.

Thus *habitat* and *environment* overlap to a considerable extent. But an environment contains more than a habitat and a group and its adaptation; it also contains the adjustments among the elments of the adaptation. Adaptation and adjustment must be regarded as distinctive processes. Adaptation refers to the processes by which a population or group alters its relation to its habitat. Especially in human societies, however, some changes in a group's customary behavior do not appreciably affect its relations with its habitat, and these changes must be considered separately from adaptive changes. A very good example of this is the development of linguistic variations with a group that speaks the same language (for example, "boid" instead of "bird"). Another example of adjustive change is found in the sphere of etiquette, when men abandon the ritual of doffing their hats to women. Yet the development of equal rights for women and changes in the familial division of labor in caring for children must be regarded as adaptive because they alter the organization of social relations in the group's relationship with the habitat.

Adaptation must be distinguished from *adjustment* not only for purposes of clarity but also because even the adjustments within an adaptation alter the group's environment—however subtly—when it is conceived as a total system of components. Thus the use of "boid" denotes the continued existence of social-class differences in a society, and a system of social classes (or castes) appears to be an important aspect of adaptation in societies that rely on advanced agriculture or industrialization; but such organizations of social relations can function effectively without linguistic differences. Changes in male-female etiquette denote important changes in the roles of women in the division of labor in society and in their political status, but these roles are not directly affected by relinquishments of ritual postures. The abandonment of such rituals may reinforce the new roles that are enjoyed by women, but they do not produce them.

As in other aspects of anthropological inquiry, when we study adaptation in anthropology we are concerned with social groups, not with individual persons, and these groups (organizations or institutions) are not directly observable; they are abstractions from the observed behavior of individuals. More specifically—and to place this in realistic perspective—we speak about the institutions of a society, but we study individuals. There are two principal reasons for this, and they are closely related to each other. The first is a practical consideration; the second reason is theoretical.

On the practical side, it is difficult, if not impossible, to study *all* the members of a tribe or community, to say nothing of a nation, in order to learn about their economic activities, kinship relations and family behavior, religious beliefs and practices, legal involvements, political activities, and the like. Hence the investigator chooses a sample he considers representative of the entire group; then, after studying it, he tries to present a picture of the group as a whole with respect to the problem he is trying to understand and the way of life he is trying to portray. Sometimes an anthropologist, although living with a group for an entire year or even longer, might not have the opportunity to observe a birth, a marriage, or a funeral, and in such cases he has to rely on the verbal accounts of a few individuals (or "informants," as they are usually called by anthropologists). Anthropologists have to adapt to the realities of the world in which they work, abstracting or generalizing from a relatively small number of informants for the entire group about which they are speaking.

Even the theoretical reason is closely tied to practical expediency. Adaptation is a process, a relationship between an item of behavior and its source; it is also an abstract principle that refers to the sweep of institutions that are changing in a particular direction. No single institution—not even a single society—can give direct evidence of the evolution of man's cultural adaptations. The familistic organization of a nomadic band cannot tell us about the exigencies of the habitats of the hunters and gatherers who produced that social system. The development of specialized legal personnel, such as lawyers and mediators, cannot tell us about the increasing impersonality and complexity of nation-states that underlie the changes in their institutions for the maintenance of law and order. The organization of English society in the thirteenth century or of peasant communities in contemporary Mexico cannot tell us directly about the evolution of community structure, even though each is a special case of sociocultural evolution.

To portray the system of a particular group, the anthropologist seeks to abstract from the information gathered from the representatives of that group, a set of principles that help explain the phenomena he has found: the relationships and family organization, a system of social stratification, a legal organization, or a political structure. In this book we will examine sequences of cultural patterns (or strategies of adaptation) as a means for understanding the underlying principles in sociocultural evolution.

The adaptations that man has achieved are the most advanced of all forms of life because he has a set of specialized tools of adaptation that are unparalleled by those of other forms: his culture. Man's culture is an adjunct to the human architecture, superimposed on his genetically determined organ systems. Thus culture has made man's instruments of adaptation even more specialized than his physiological tools. Viewed in the context of the total evolution of life, man's culture is a revolutionary addition to his architecture and his most powerful instrument for adaptation. Through his cultures man is now able to adapt himself to different habitats long before genetic mechanisms could do this for him; he does not have to await genetic modifications in his constitution.

The central concern of this book is with the organizations of social relations that enable people in different societies to make effective use of the energy potentials in their habitats, rather than with specific items of custom and behavior. We will not be concerned with such matters as whether people put rings in their ears or in their noses or whether they symbolize marriage by exchanging rings or small dishes of rice and saki. We will be concerned with phenomena such as the varieties of power relationships, the allocation of resources and of access to the means of production, with inheritance, family organization, settlement patterns, and the like, as aspects of adaptation.

The systematic study of man's evolution in an adaptational framework is relatively new. As a result, many problems—largely methodological but also conceptual—remain on this frontier of the science. One of the greatest challenges facing us is the establishment of rigorous methods for the study of adaptation. Presently, as in every new scientific development, we are still largely restricted to intuition, hunch, and insight. While these qualities of thought are indispensable for any science, no matter how mature, we need to systematize our procedures of investigation so that we can know where to look for evidences of adaptation and so that we can more fully replicate each other's investigations.

At present, our procedures in the study of adaptation can be described as follows. In the course of his readings, an anthropologist is struck by the changing family organization of a particular society. While thinking about the overall context of this change, he recalls having read that the soils on which this group depended have been seriously depleted in nutrients or that a change has been made in taxation policy making each person, rather than the community as a whole, responsible for the payment of taxes. Hypothesizing a relationship between the changes in family organization and those in either the ecological or political habitat, he then looks for instances of other societies in the historical record in which soil depletion or the inauguration of individual taxation has occurred in order to learn whether this is usually followed by the adoption of this particular family organization. If this turns out to be the case, he will feel justified in explaining the change in family organization in terms of adaptation.

Or, to take a slightly different procedure, an anthropologist interested in the evolution of, say, legal systems might start out with the assumption that every sequential change in the legal sphere of human society is due to changes in technological or political organization. Thus, for example, he will try to correlate legal changes with the adoption of a sedentary way of life in place of a nomadic one (or vice versa) or with the breakdown of autonomous walled cities and their integration into a nation-state. If he finds that fundamental changes in legal systems consistently follow changes in people's relationship to the habitat, he will be justified in casting his hypotheses in an adaptational frame of reference.

But the two procedures just mentioned begin with specific questions about certain institutions. Other starting points are more formal and rely less on rules of thumb. As discussed by Betty J. Meggers in *Amazonia: Man and Culture in a Counterfeit Paradise* (Chicago: Aldine-Atherton, 1971), "a particular culture can be selected and the manner in which it is articulated with its habitat can be analyzed; or . . . a certain kind of environment can be chosen and the variability in cultural adaptation within its boundaries can be examined through time and space." Meggers used the second procedure in her analysis of cultural adaptation in Amazonia; it is one of the best and most systematic studies of adaptation. A similar procedure was employed by John W. Bennett in *Northern Plainsmen: Adaptive Strategy and Agrarian Life* (Chicago: Aldine, 1969), which is a fine study of the relationships among different agrarian strategies, the Canadian Great Plains ecology, and Canadian political policies. Other anthropologists whose work is represented in this volume, focus on input-output analyses (the work or caloric energy expended to produce a given amount of food); they concentrate on variables such as energetics (the group's exchange of energy with the habitat), population, nutrition, health, spacing, technology and knowledge, and the interrelationships of these variables in ritual systems and other social activities. Others have been exploring the utility of comparative or cross-cultural methods for the study of adaptation; the nature of cross-cultural research is discussed in the introduction to Section I, Hunting-Gathering. While we can look forward to important methodological advances in the study of adaptation during the next few years, the various approaches, like those just mentioned, probably will complement each other rather than stand as exclusive alternatives.

The reader who wishes to become more familiar with the methods being explored by students of adaptation can begin with *Adaptation in Cultural Evolu-*

tion: An Approach to Medical Anthropology (New York: Columbia University Press, 1970), by Alexander Alland, Jr. This book focuses on disease-related behavior and attempts to show how the data derived from this area of study can be applied to the study of adaptation generally. Two papers that rely heavily on statistical methods are "Social Evolution and Structural-Functional Analysis: An Empirical Test," by George L. Buck and Alvin L. Jacobson (*American Sociological Review,* 33 [1968]: 343-55) and "Ascertaining, Testing, and Interpreting Sequences of Cultural Development," by Robert L. Carneiro (*Southwestern Journal of Anthropology,* 24 [1968]: 354-75).

PROLOGUE: THE CONCEPT OF CULTURE: EVOLUTION AND ADAPTATION

THE PURPOSE OF THIS section is to introduce the reader to the concept of culture. Plausible and seemingly easy to attain, it is a difficult goal because anthropologists attribute a great variety of meanings to the term. For some anthropologists, culture is an abstraction that refers to everything the people in a particular group do. For others, culture is not only an abstract concept but a very real force that affects the physical and mental behavior of the members of a group. Anthropologists conceptualize culture in other ways too, but there are at least seven points of agreement among all of them, and it is these that we will emphasize.

First, *culture* in the anthropological sense refers to the full *range* of behavior in a group, not just to literature, music, drama, and art. Second, all aspects of each group's culture—aesthetics, law, language, religion, personality patterns, therapeutics, kinship, attitudes toward equality and change, and the like—are closely interwoven into a pattern that is unique to each group. This feature of culture is emphasized by Geertz in Selection 1. Third, cultures change as a result of contact between groups and of forces within a group, such as technological innovation, that create new challenges and problems. This is the principal theme in Selections 2 and 3, by Greenberg and Cohen, respectively.

Fourth (as Geertz stresses in Selection 1), every culture is a set of symbols. The importance of this fact lies in the postulate that people in their daily lives respond to cultural symbols rather than to objective reality. For example, people respond in particular ways to *flags* rather than to pieces of cloth that are cut to specific proportions and decorated with specifically arranged colors. People do not respond indiscriminately to members of the opposite sex; instead, they define each other as attractive or unattractive according to the symbolic definitions provided by their group. A painting by Rembrandt is not merely an object whose material components (canvas, stretcher, and pigments) are worth only a few pennies; it is also a symbolically defined object to which people in various groups respond in a socially appropriate manner.

But symbols are more than objects or acts to which people respond; they are also ties that bind people to each other. Examples of ties that bind are religious rituals and language, which is the most complex system of symbols in every human group. Every word in a language is itself a symbol; at the same time, a common language provides an important social bond for the members of many groups—such as ethnic groups in complex industrial societies—and linguistic differences provide a basis for divisiveness among tribes as well as in a modernizing society, as in India.

Dress, hair styles, and adornment provide another example of symbolic activity with far-reaching implications. In every social group there are appropriate modes of dress and body decoration appropriate to each sex and to people at different ages; ordinarily, we take such things for granted. In the United States and other industrial societies, men have in recent years been adopting the hair styles and adornment that traditionally have been regarded as feminine. Part of the volatility in the reactions to this has been the complaint that "you cannot tell the difference between the boys and the girls any more." While this is hyperbole, there is an element of truth in it. Why are these styles changing and why are there extremely emotional reactions to the change? Not only had men and women dressed distinctively in the past but they also maintained different lifestyles. Men went "out" to work and women stayed "in" to care for house, meals, laundry, and children. When women did go out to work, they earned less than men and rarely had access to prestigious jobs and positions of authority. To a large extent, these practices were rooted in a technology in which most labor involved strenuous activity requiring masculine musculature.

But as we move into a technology based on electronically controlled production, women can write computer programs, work in steel mills, pilot airplanes (there is, in fact, very little that they cannot do) on equal terms with men. At the same time, men who celebrate this equality of status feel that they can do most things that women traditionally did. Furthermore, this is being expressed legally, in laws forbidding sexual discrimination in hiring and wage policies. Changes in dress, hair styles, and adornment symbolize these changes in the organization of social relations. In their opposition to the symbolic changes, conservative people are also—though indirectly—expressing their opposition to the fundamental social changes. Thus even symbols in dress and hair styles can provide important clues in deciphering political reactions. In Selection 6 we read about another kind of symbolization of material things (stone axes) that help maintain social separateness between the sexes.

Fifth, all social life takes place in groups. The concern of anthropology is with the behavior of social aggregates rather than of individuals as such. There are two aspects to this feature of culture. The first, which is directly relevant to the study of adaptation (and to which we will return below), is that the adaptations that have been achieved in a particular culture are maintained by the *group*, not by individuals acting as independent or discrete agents. In the study of biological adaptation, the deme or reproducing group is regarded as the adaptive unit by virtue of its perpetuation of a particular gene pool. In the study of cultural adaptation, the social group must be regarded as the adaptive unit.

All cultural adaptations—modes of acquiring a livelihood, family organization, social control, settlement patterns and the use of space, and religion—

refer to complex group relationships even though they are acted out by individuals. Merely to say that all social activities are carried out in groups, however, is insufficient. That no group exists independently of others is a characteristic of human society. It is always necessary to speak of a group as existing vis-a-vis others. For example, there can be no such group as a family unless there are several families, each maintaining itself in relation to—and being maintained by—other families through a web of reciprocal obligations, rights, duties, and privileges. Similarly, no man in any society provides for his family independently of intricate patterns of cooperation and mutual assistance with others, and usually these relationships are highly formalized. When a youngster is taught how to hunt or fish or work at a machine, he is taught not only the mechanical skills involved but also how to conduct these activities in cooperation with others. Thus all cultural phenomena are made up of socially shared activities and must be regarded as properties of the group and not of individuals alone.

A corollary aspect of the fact that all social life takes place in groups is that everything people do is done with or in reference to others. Ideally, every statement about the activities of a particular individual in a particular society must be phrased in terms of the other persons with or in relation to whom he does something. From an anthropological point of view, to say merely that married people in a particular society are permitted to engage in sexual behavior is not sufficient. Instead, it is necessary to specify with whom they may engage in such relations, under what conditions and in what ways, and to note the circumstances in which such behavior is forbidden or disapproved.

When an anthropologist describes the characteristics of a given culture, however, he does not mean to suggest that every person in the group behaves in the ways described. Instead, an anthropological portrayal of a culture, technically referred to as an ethnography, is a profile of the behavior that is most characteristic of the members of the group. Furthermore, behavior in a group can vary from one situation to another, depending on the culture's symbolizations of the different situations. Consider, for example, our contemporary Western culture's definition of feminine modesty. A pretty young coed may think nothing of parading about a beach in a bikini (which in another context would be defined as underclothing), but might be distressed if, while she was riding a bicycle around campus, the wind blew her skirt above the level that is considered acceptable in this situation. A professor is supposed to be a lecturer, but not (his family says) at the dinner table. "Thou shalt not kill" is not an absolute rule; it is appropriate only in various socially defined situations.

Sixth, every culture has a range of permissible behavior, not a set of inflexible rules about how each activity must be conducted. Except for incest, every culture provides its members with alternatives in practically every sphere of behavior. There are alternative ways of being polite, of expressing affection, of being angry, of wooing and being wooed, of rewarding and disciplining children, of being cooperative and competitive. However, as will be seen below (in Selection 3), an increase in alternatives in particular spheres of social life (for example, in the variety of available occupations) does not occur randomly or fortuitously; such increase is an important aspect of adaptation and cultural evolution.

A seventh point of agreement among anthropologists is that every culture is learned by means of specific cultural techniques and procedures. These techniques are cultural and not biological. It is clear from anthropologists' investigations in every area of the world that there is no relationship between the biological characteristics of a group—such as skin pigmentation, hair texture, eye shape, and stature—and its patterns of culture). In every society there are patterned means for shaping the minds of the growing members of the group. A ubiquitous feature of the teaching of culture is the inculcation of values (the group's ideas of what is desirable and undesirable) and motivations. Similarly, the young are taught how to respond to different pressures that are designed to maintain conformity (such as ridicule, shame and guilt, threats of ostracism, and coercive power). People must be taught *how* to act independently and cooperatively and in which situations one or the other kind of behavior is appropriate, which individuals and groups to identify with and which to regard as alien and hostile, how to select culturally provided alternatives and how to make use of them, when to treat others as equals, and the like. The socialization (or culturalization) of the individual is always designed to make him into a person who will function effectively in his society.

While all anthropologists agree that every culture is learned, events during the past few years have thrown many of our formulations about this into confusion. Part of almost every generalization about the ways in which a culture is learned was the assertion that this learning involved transmission from generation to generation, elders teaching skills and social behaviors to the young. What is often referred to as the "generation gap" makes it doubtful that such simple descriptions can suffice. If a culture is transmitted from one generation to another, how can we account for the radical changes now going on in the United States and elsewhere and the sharp differences between generations in symbol systems, values about work and wealth, sexual standards, family and household organization, drugs, religion, and protest? Surely these new and emerging standards have not been transmitted from the older to the younger generations, at least not in any simple and direct way.

Modes of upbringing are designed to satisfy an individual's biological needs for food, water, warmth, and comfort. Children also need love, diversity, and amusement—but how much do they need? Is there a biologically determined minimum of each that all groups must provide if their children are to grow fully? These are important questions because they go to the heart of one of the central problems in anthropology: Where does biology leave off and culture begin? Which needs are basically biological and which are culturally generated? This problem underlies still others, which increasingly preoccupy anthropologists —especially those who believe significant biological bases exist for many aspects of social behavior, such as male solidarity and dominance, social stratification, social control, language, and family organization.

Many anthropologists believe there are biological (genetically transmitted) predispositions for these phenomena but that their social forms (their institutionalized expressions) vary among societies and change over time in response to pressures in their strategies of adaptation. These variations among groups and over time are what we are concerned with in this book. For example, we will see that social ranking is characteristic of even the simplest societies and that patterns of stratification tend to become increasingly complex as societies advance technologically. When we combine this observation with the clearly observable hierarchies of social superordination and subordination that we find in almost all prehuman primate groups, we can speculate that man is predisposed to organize his social relations hierarchically but his particular cultural adaptations maximize or minimize this predisposition. Similarly, man appears to be biologically predisposed to gregariousness, but the forms taken by the social relations in which he expresses this predisposition will vary from society to society and over time as aspects of his cultural adaptation.

It is important to bear in mind that man is a biosocial being—that nothing in life is ever wholly biological or wholly cultural. Everything in man that is biological, even his patterns of breathing and sleeping, is always culturalized, always suffused with symbolism and culturally approved ways of achieving gratification. The first exposure an infant has to his society is in connection with the gratification or the frustration of his biological needs. The socially patterned ways of treating these needs are among the foundations for all subsequent social learning. Similarly, everything that is cultural is part of man's biological adaptation, an aspect of his attempts to insure biological survival. In this book we are primarily concerned with this reciprocal relationship.

An increasing number of anthropologists question the familiar concept that all social behavior is learned; they feel that we must search for the biological underpinnings of human organizations of social relations, maintaining that some aspects of human behavior—such as mother-child bonds, relations between the sexes, and the maintenance of group order and conformity—are part of our genetic inheritance, evolutionary outgrowths from our nonhuman past. Many anthropologists are convinced that the human neonate is not born a blank slate on which only cultural inputs are written; instead, they are investigating the biological (genetic) "programs" that set limits and provide potentials for human social organization. But we still do not know what this programming consists of, what is written on the slate before cultural inputs begin.

Another major problem in contemporary anthropology is the division among those subscribing to positions of "cultural materialism" and "cultural symbolism," though the differences between the two are sometimes more apparent than real. Simply put, the materialist point of view asserts that cultural phenomena must be approached exclusively by the strategies of natural science and that every cultural activity—no matter how esoteric or seemingly (to us) irrational—must be seen as having a natural cause. (The most eloquent exponent of this point of view is by Marvin Harris in his books, *The Rise of Anthropological Theory* [New York: Crowell, 1968] and *Culture, Man, and Nature* [New York: Crowell, 1971].) Selections 4, 9, and 23 provide clear expositions of this point of view, and this is also the point of view predominating in Selection 3. Cultural symbolism can be generally described as a line of research based on the axiom that the causes and dynamics of a way of life are to be sought in a group's "world view," in its symbolic definitions of reality. Thus family and household relations and the division of labor are to be explained in terms of the symbolization of sexual status and roles; political relations are explainable in terms of perceptions of age and authority; the individual's place in the social order is seen as an aspect of the religious system, and so forth. This is an oversimplification, but it points to the major direction taken by anthropologists working within this mode; it is the substance of Selection 1 by Clifford Geertz, who is probably its most eloquent exponent.

By and large, anthropologists who adopt the materialist approach tend also to be inclined toward evolutionary considerations. Those who adopt the symbolic mode tend to be nonevolutionary in their research.

Cutting across the materialist and symbolic modes is still another conceptual dichotomy, generally referred to among anthropologists by the terms *etic* and *emic*. Basically, these approaches—again most clearly formulated by Marvin Harris, in *The Nature of Cultural Things* (New York: Random House, 1964)—refer to an underlying question in all anthropological research: Is a culture to be described from the point of view of its bearers (emic) or in terms of the categories and conceptual framework of the observer (etic)? While an emic approach has many appealing features, there are advantages and disadvantages in both.

The emic approach—the inside view of a culture—tries to get away from the taint of ethnocentrism, to avoid the imposition of the ethnographer's values on the culture of the people being studied. While advocates of this approach are trying to develop appropriate techniques for it, it is unlikely that we will ever be able to capture a cultural experience genuinely in "native" terms. Furthermore, cultures vary widely in the principles according to which they are organized, and the emic approach fails to provide the standardized information that is necessary for making cross-cultural comparisons.

The etic approach similarly gains and suffers in comparison with the emic. This mode does provide a basis for comparing cultures when observers use the same categories—such as political organization, energy input and output, population density, legal institutions, and technology. But the etic approach presupposes that an investigator's biases (his culture's categories and values) are equally applicable to all cultures; in fact, however, the extent of their applicability is one of the things the observer is supposed to be investigating. For example, many anthropologists concerned with institutionalized religion in tribal societies regard it as an aspect of political control and an ideological superstructure of economic strategies and relations. While I, too, maintain this position, I must constantly remind myself that it is an outsider's point of view which members of tribal groups may find alien, if not abhorrent, and that ways must be found to determine whether (and to what extent) it is a valid category or merely my particular bias.

The consensus among anthropologists seems to be that because of the advantages and disadvantages of each approach, a balance must be struck between the two. One of the benefits of the debate between proponents of the two modes is that anthropologists are asking each other to specify whether their observations are emic or etic, and this has led to a healthy self-consciousness, forcing ethnographers to make their theoretical biases more explicit.

All anthropologists agree that cultures are changing systems, but they disagree about the principles that govern the nature of cultural change. Some maintain that culture evolves in lawful regularity and that there are discernible patterns and principles in the development of culture from the days of man's appearance on the evolutionary scene to the present time. This is the position taken in Selections 2 and 3, and I will attempt to explicate some of these principles and regularities as we proceed with the case-study materials. However, some anthropologists, although in no way denying that all cultures change, are skeptical of the hypothesis that the changes that have characterized the total span of human culture can usefully be viewed in terms of regularity. Still other anthropologists are willing to entertain the evolutionary point of view only as a tentative hypothesis, which they feel has yet to be tested conclusively.

Another source of disagreement among anthropologists centers around this question: What is the role of the individual innovator in cultural change? Some students of human culture maintain that every culture has a life of its own and is largely independent of the will and innovative genius of the individuals who "carry" it. This is often referred to as "cultural determinism." Those who hold this position maintain that culture is not subject to rational, conscious, or deliberate control; a culture changes, but people cannot change their culture deliberately, except by the accident of drastic and violent revolution.

How do anthropologists who subscribe to this position interpret important historical figures such as Genghis Khan, Popes Leo XII and John XXIII, Franklin Roosevelt, Freud, and Garibaldi? Some people in and outside anthropology contend that their effects on history "would have happened anyway." From this point of view the uniqueness of these persons lay in the fact that they responded with acuity of vision and mind to the pressures and potentials of their times. Responding to challenges that were already present when they came on the scene, in most cases they applied solutions that also were already present and moved history only by crystallizing available ends and means, as—perhaps—others could not. They did not change their cultures; they did not even serve as catalysts for change; instead, it is hypothesized, they were agents of history who made use of intellectual and other means of action and applied them in unusual ways.

The alternative point of view differs in emphasis; it is not one of outright disagreement. Proponents of the hypothesis that the individual does—or at least can —serve as a catalyst of change use two separate but related arguments. First, there have been instances in which gifted and visionary persons have transformed their cultures, as in the present-day "cargo cults" of the South Pacific. These cargo cults start in a small, primitive society when an innovator heralds the arrival of a vessel loaded with a cargo of European wares; this influx, he prophesies, will be accompanied by a complete transformation of the social organization, including the disappearance of the whites or their reduction to the status of servants. The prophecy of the innovator is said to have been inspired by a supernatural revelation, and the arrival of the cargo is attributed to a supernatural agency. In many cases the prophecies have indeed been followed by profound transformations in the local culture, which would not have occurred had it not been for these unusual prophets. These events suggest that individuals can serve as moving forces in cultural change.

Another—and to be more plausible—argument in favor of the contention that an individual can play a major role in cultural change can be stated as follows: One of the consequences of the growth of knowledge, of which the science of human culture is an important part, is that the more man knows about physical and social nature the more he is able to control his physical and social milieus. The more man knows about the forces of history the less he needs to be passively subject to them. Thus, although the radical innovator may have had a small place in primitive societies, he has an important role to play in contemporary and future societies by virtue of the current and future state of knowledge. As Margaret Mead put it in *Continuities in Cultural Evolution* (New Haven: Yale University Press, 1964):

There is little doubt that among our living population as mankind is constituted—without resort to controlled eugenic manipulation—there is a sufficient number of highly gifted individuals who, given the proper cultural conditions in which to work, could go on to make the necessary innovations [to assure the survival of the species] (p. 247).

In any event, in the words of Robert Coles ("Dialogue Underground: II," by Daniel Berrigan, S.J., and Robert Coles, *The New York Review* [March 25, 1971] 26:

Those who have to initiate and brave the hardship and dangers of social change often are as fearful and apprehensive (naturally so) as they are bold and courageous. How *can* they know what will happen until they go and test and try both themselves and the society they wish to change? Often they are surprised by the possibilities for change that they find both in individuals and in the political system—all of which means that they are *part* of the world they are confronting and thus heir to the assumptions that world possesses about, say, human nature and the nature of political protest. Do you see what I mean, how such ironies constantly plague us?

To what degree are people conscious of the adaptive changes they introduce, especially those—like the establishment of nation-states—that have far-reaching consequences? As the eminent historian Marc Bloch observed in his analysis of the adoption of the basic social forms of medieval Europe (*Feudal Society*, Chicago: University of Chicago Press, 1961, p. 148):

In yielding thus to the necessities of the moment . . . generations of men had no conscious desire to create new social forms, nor were they aware of doing so. Instinctively each strove to turn to account the resources provided by the existing social structure and if, unconsciously, something new was eventually created, it was in the process of trying to adapt the old.

In considering the merit of the cultural deterministic view it is helpful to bear in mind that this notion of the individual's relationship to his culture is only one of several "deterministic" points of view that have gained currency at one time or other in Western intellectual history. In addition to cultural determinism, the broader deterministic philosophy has included concepts such as the "rational man" hypothesis of many economists, the hypotheses of Marx and Engels about the relationship between control of the instruments of production and social stratification in social evolution, and the traditional Christian belief that God set the world into motion and all history is a reflection of His preconceived scheme.

Greenberg, who discusses the deterministic point of view in Selection 2, refers to it as a body of "creationist" or "catastrophist" theories and beliefs. Without analyzing each theory separately, he observes that the data uncovered by archeologists, historians, linguists, and ethnologists require the abandonment of such points of view and their replacement by what he calls the "transformationist" point of view. The latter is the foundation of modern evolutionary studies, and it is the approach that is followed in this book.

It must also be made clear that these two points of view are not the only alternatives in the study of the individual's relationship to his culture. For example, Geertz rejects both in Selection 1. His is a theoretical position subscribed to by many anthropologists. While I disagree with Geertz's rejection of the evolutionary perspective, it is a point of view that warrants careful attention.

The three essays in this section represent different ways of viewing human culture, but I do not believe they are mutually exclusive. Instead, emphasizing different aspects of culture, each shades off into the other.

The extent to which anthropologists have different conceptualizations of culture can be appreciated very quickly by consulting *Culture: A Critical Review of Concepts and Definitions,* by Alfred L. Kroeber and Clyde Kluckhohn (New York: Vintage Books, 1952, 1963). This thick volume details the many ways in which anthropologists think of culture.

In addition to the books by Marvin Harris cited in the text, the reader can consult one of Harris' most important papers in which he applies the materialist approach to an important social and ecological problem: "The Cultural Ecology of India's Sacred Cattle" *(Current Anthropology,* 7 [1966]: 51-66). For another application of this approach—widely regarded as the most convincing thus far— see Roy A. Rappaport's *Pigs for the Ancestors: Ritual in the Ecology of the a New Guinea People* (New Haven: Yale University Press, 1968) and "Ritual Regulation of Environmental Relations among a New Guinea People" *(Ethnology,* 6 [1967]: 17-30; reprinted as Selection 15 in *The Institutional Framework*). *Theory in Anthropology,* edited by Robert A. Manners and David Kaplan (Chicago: Aldine, 1968) is a source book of articles describing various aspects of anthropological Theory, including the materialist and symbolic approaches. *Culture Theory,* by David Kaplan and Robert Manners (Englewood Cliffs, N. J.: Prentice-Hall, 1972) is an excellent up-to-date analysis of the principal theoretical trends in the discipline.

1. THE IMPACT OF THE CONCEPT OF CULTURE ON THE CONCEPT OF MAN

CLIFFORD GEERTZ

Reprinted from John R. Platt (Ed.), New Views of Man, *by permission of the University of Chicago Press (Copyright © 1965). Clifford Geertz is Professor of Anthropology at the Institute for Advanced Studies in Princeton, N.J. He has conducted extensive research in Indonesia and Morocco, particularly on problems of economic development, comparative religion, and urbanization. He is the author of* The Religion of Java, Peddlers and Princes: Social Development and Economic Change in Two Indonesian Towns, Agricultural Involution, The Social History of an Indonesian Town, *and* Islam Observed: Religious Development in Morocco and Indonesia.

■ A Pomo Indian once said to an anthropologist: "What is a man? A man is nothing. Without his family he is of less importance than that bug crossing the trail, of less importance than spittle or turds."

Geertz also begins with the question, What is a man? His analysis is from the point of view of an anthropologist, however, rather than through the lenses of a particular culture. Implicit in Geertz's essay is an assertion that the anthropological concept of culture has had an influence on the concept of man as profound as the psychoanalytic concept of the mind or the Marxian interpretation of economic and political behavior. Geertz maintains that the question What is man? is meaningless without an explicit statement of the culture in which he participates. According to this view, it is not possible to generalize about the nature of man and apply the result equally to a nomadic Pomo and to a sedentary person who participates in a modern industrialized social system. Each is a unique being.

We do not have to agree entirely with this view of man and culture to appreciate its provocativeness. Geertz suggests that each culture is dominated by "control mechanism"—a unique set of regulating ideas—that shapes the individual into a unique kind of human. Every culture, he maintains, is made up of a set of symbolic devices for the control of behavior, for giving the individual a set of life goals, and for giving him a set of definitions of himself and of others. In one sense Geertz views culture at a lower level of abstraction than Kroeber because he ties it directly to the individual's subjective experience of the world in which he lives. From another point of view,

Geertz's conceptualization of culture is more abstract than Kroeber's because he focuses on its symbolic rather than its material content.

Another very important point in this selection is that man's biological constitution is as much a product of his capacity for culture as his capacity for culture is a product of his biological nature. Geertz maintains that culture is not a characteristic of man that was superimposed on his biological structure; instead, biological and cultural evolution went hand in hand and the development of human culture contributed greatly to the direction of human biological evolution. In these terms, man's capacity for the symbolic organization of life and his biological constitution are to be seen as aspects of each other rather than as opposed processes.

Geertz has spelled out this view of culture more fully in several published papers, of which two are most illuminating: "The Transition to Humanity" (in *Horizons of Anthropology,* edited by Sol Tax [Chicago: Aldine Publishing Company, 1964]), and "The Growth of Culture and the Evolution of Mind" (in *Theories of the Mind,* edited by Jordan Scher [New York: The Free Press, 1962]). Also relevant is *The Myth of the Machine,* by Lewis Mumford (New York: Harcourt, Brace, 1967). ■

I

TOWARD THE END of his recent study of the ideas used by tribal peoples, *La Pensée Sauvage,* the French anthropologist, Lévi-

Strauss, remarks that scientific explanation does not consist, as we have been led to imagine, in the reduction of the complex to the simple. Rather, it consists, he says, in a substitution of a complexity more intelligible for one which is less. So far as the study of man is concerned, one may go even farther, I think, and argue that explanation often consists of substituting complex pictures for simple ones while striving somehow to retain the persuasive clarity that went with the simple ones.

Elegance remains, I suppose, a general scientific ideal; but in the social sciences, it is very often in departures from that ideal that truly creative developments occur. Scientific advancement commonly consists in a progressive complication of what once seemed a beautifully simple set of notions but now seems an unbearably simplistic one. It is after this sort of disenchantment occurs that intelligibility, and thus explanatory power, comes to rest on the possibility of substituting the involved but comprehensible for the involved but incomprehensible to which Lévi-Strauss refers. Whitehead once offered to the natural sciences the maxim: "Seek simplicity and distrust it"; to the social sciences he might well have offered "Seek complexity and order it."

Certainly, the study of culture has developed as though this maxim were being followed. The rise of a scientific concept of culture amounted to, or at least was connected with, the overthrow of the view of human nature dominant in the Enlightenment—a view that, whatever else may be said for or against it, was both clear and simple—and its replacement by a view not only more complicated but enormously less clear. The attempt to clarify it, to reconstruct an intelligible account of what man is, has underlain scientific thinking about culture ever since. Having sought complexity and, on a scale grander than they ever imagined, found it, anthropologists became entangled in a tortuous effort to order it. And the end is not yet in sight.

The Enlightenment view of man was, of course, that he was wholly of a piece with nature and shared in the general uniformity of composition which natural science, under Bacon's urging and Newton's guidance, had discovered there. There is, in brief, a human nature as regularly organized, as thoroughly invariant, and as marvelously simple as Newton's universe. Perhaps some of its laws are different, but there *are* laws; perhaps some of its immutability is obscured by the trappings of local fashion, but it *is* immutable.

A quotation that Lovejoy (whose magisterial analysis I am following here) gives from an Enlightenment historian, Mascou, presents the position with the useful bluntness one often finds in a minor writer:

The stage setting [in different times and places] is, indeed, altered, the actors change their garb and their appearance; but their inward motions arise from the same desires and passions of men, and produce their effects in the vicissitudes of kingdoms and peoples.

Now, this view is hardly one to be despised; nor, despite my easy references a moment ago to "overthrow," can it be said to have disappeared from contemporary anthropological thought. The notion that men are men under whatever guise and against whatever backdrop has not been replaced by "other mores, other beasts."

Yet, cast as it was, the Enlightenment concept of the nature of human nature had some much less acceptable implications, the main one being that, to quote Lovejoy himself this time, "anything of which the intelligibility, verifiability, or actual affirmation is limited to men of a special age, race, temperament, tradition or condition is [in and of itself] without truth or value, or at all events without importance to a reasonable man." The great, vast variety of differences among men, in beliefs and values, in customs and institutions, both over time and from place to place, is essentially without significance in defining his nature. It consists of mere accretions, distortions even, overlaying and obscuring what is truly human—the constant, the general, the universal—in man.

Thus, in a passage now notorious, Dr. Johnson saw Shakespeare's genius to lie in the fact that "his characters are not modified by the customs of particular places, unpractised by the rest of the world; by the peculiarities of studies or professions, which can operate upon but small numbers; or by the accidents of transient fashions or temporary opinions." And Racine regarded the success of his plays on classical themes as proof that "the taste of Paris . . . conforms to that of Athens; my spectators have been moved by the same things which, in other times, brought tears to the eyes of the most cultivated classes of Greece."

The trouble with this kind of view, aside from the fact that it sounds comic coming from someone as profoundly English as Johnson or as French as Racine, is that the image of a constant human nature independent of time, place, and circumstance, of studies and professions, transient fashions and temporary opinions, may be an illusion, that what man is may be so entangled with where he is, who he is, and what he believes that it is inseparable from them. It is precisely the consideration of such a possibility that led to the rise of the concept of culture and the decline of the uniformitarian view of man. Whatever else modern anthropology asserts—and it seems to have asserted almost everything at one time or another—it is firm in the conviction that men unmodified by the customs of particular places do not in fact exist, have never existed, and most important, could not in the very nature of the case exist. There is, there can be, no backstage where we can go to catch a glimpse of Mascou's actors as "real persons" lounging about in street clothes, disengaged from their profession, displaying with artless candor their spontaneous desires and unprompted passions. They may change their roles, their styles of acting, even the dramas in which they play; but—as Shakespeare himself of course remarked—they are always performing.

This circumstance makes the drawing of a line between what is natural, universal, and constant in man and what is conventional, local, and variable extraordinarily difficult. In fact, it suggests that to draw such a line is to falsify the human situation, or at least to misrender it seriously.

Consider Balinese trance. The Balinese fall into extreme dissociated states in which they perform all sorts of spectacular activities—biting off the heads of living chickens, stabbing themselves with daggers, throwing themselves wildly about, speaking with tongues, performing miraculous feats of equilibration, mimicking sexual intercourse, eating feces, and so on—rather more easily and much more suddenly than most of us fall asleep. Trance states are a crucial part of every ceremony. In some, fifty or sixty people may fall, one after the other ("like a string of firecrackers going off," as one observer puts it), emerging anywhere from five minutes to several hours later, totally unaware of what they have been doing and convinced, despite the amnesia, that they have had the most extraordinary and deeply satisfying experience a man can have. What does one learn about human nature from this sort of thing and from the thousand similarly peculiar things anthropologists discover, investigate, and describe? That the Balinese are peculiar sorts of beings, South Sea Martians? That they are just the same as we at base, but with some peculiar, but really incidental, customs we do not happen to have gone in for? That they are innately gifted or even instinctively driven in certain directions rather than others? Or that human nature does not exist and men are pure and simply what their culture makes them?

It is among such interpretations as these, all unsatisfactory, that anthropology has attempted to find its way to a more viable concept of man, one in which culture, and the variability of culture, would be taken into account rather than written off as caprice and prejudice and yet, at the same time, one in which the governing principle of the field, "the basic unity of mankind," would not be turned into an empty phrase. To take the giant step away from the uniformitarian view of human nature is, so far as the study of man is concerned, to leave the Garden. To entertain the idea that the diversity of custom across time and over space is not a mere matter of garb and appearance, of stage settings and comedic masques, is to entertain also the idea that humanity is as various in its essence as it is in its expression. And with that reflection some well-fastened philosophical moorings are loosed and an uneasy drifting into perilous waters begins.

Perilous, because if one discards the notion that Man, with a capital "M," is to be looked for "behind," "under," or "beyond" his customs and replaces it with the notion that he, uncapitalized, is to be looked for "in" them, one is in some danger of losing sight of him altogether. Either he dissolves, without residue, into his time and place a child and perfect captive of his age, or he becomes a conscripted soldier in a vast Tolstoian army, engulfed in one or another of the terrible historical determinisms with which we have been plagued from Hegel forward. We have had, and to some extent still have, both of these aberrations in the social sciences—one marching under the banner of cultural relativism, the other under that of cultural evolution. But we also have had, and more commonly, attempts to avoid them by seeking in culture patterns themselves the defining elements of a human existence which, although not constant in expression, are yet distinctive in character.

II

Attempts to locate man amid the body of his customs have taken several directions, adopted diverse tactics; but they have all, or virtually all, proceeded in terms of a single overall intellectual strategy: what I will call, so as to have a stick to beat it with, the "stratigraphic" conception of the relations between biological, psychological, social, and cultural factors in human life. In this conception, man is a composite of "levels," each superimposed upon those beneath it and underpinning those above it. As one analyzes man, one peels off layer after layer, each such layer being complete and irreducible in itself, revealing another, quite different sort of layer underneath. Strip off the motley forms of culture and one finds the structural and functional regularities of social organization. Peel off

these in turn and one finds the underlying psychological factors—"basic needs" or what-have-you—that support and make them possible. Peel off psychological factors and one is left with the biological foundations—anatomical, physiological, neurological—of the whole edifice of human life.

The attraction of this sort of conceptualization, aside from the fact that it guaranteed the established academic disciplines their independence and sovereignty, was that it seemed to make it possible to have one's cake and eat it. One did not have to assert that man's culture was all there was to him in order to claim that it was, nonetheless, an essential and irreducible, even a paramount ingredient in his nature. Cultural facts could be interpreted against the background of non-cultural facts without either dissolving them into that background or dissolving that background into them. Man was a hierarchically stratified animal, a sort of evolutionary deposit, in whose definition each level—organic, psychological, social, and cultural—had an assigned and incontestable place. To see what he really was, we had to superimpose findings from the various relevant sciences—anthropology, sociology, psychology, biology—upon one another like so many patterns in a *moiré*; and when that was done, the cardinal importance of the cultural level, the only one distinctive to man, would naturally appear, as would what it had to tell us, in its own right, about what he really was. For the eighteenth-century image of man as the naked reasoner that appeared when he took his cultural costumes off, the anthropology of the late nineteenth and early twentieth centuries substituted the image of man as the transfigured animal that appeared when he put them on.

At the level of concrete research and specific analysis, this grand strategy came down, first, to a hunt for universals in culture, for empirical uniformities that, in the face of the diversity of customs around the world and over time, could be found everywhere in about the same form, and, second, to an effort to relate such universals, once found, to the established constants of human biology, psychology, and social organization. If some customs could be ferreted out of the cluttered catalogue of world culture as common to all local variants of it, and if these could then be connected in a determinate manner with certain invariant points of reference on the subcultural levels, then at least some progress might be made toward specifying which cultural traits are essential to human existence and which merely adventitious, peripheral, or ornamental. In such a way, anthropology could determine cultural dimensions of a concept of man commensurate with the dimensions provided, in a similar way, by biology, psychology, or sociology.

In essence, this is not altogether a new idea. The notion of a *consensus gentium* (a consensus of all mankind)—the notion that there are some things that all men will be found to agree upon as right, real, just, or attractive and that these things are, therefore, in fact right, real, just, or attractive—was present in the Enlightenment and, probably, has been present in some form or another in all ages and climes. It is one of those ideas that occur to almost anyone sooner or later. Its development in modern anthropology, however—beginning with Clark Wissler's elaboration in the nineteen-twenties of what he called "the universal cultural pattern," through Bronislaw Malinowski's presentation of a list of "universal institutional types" in the early forties, up to G. P. Murdock's elaboration of a set of "common-denominators of culture" during and since World War II— added something new. It added the notion that, to quote Clyde Kluckhohn, perhaps the most persuasive of the *consensus gentium* theorists, "some aspects of culture take their specific forms solely as a result of historical accidents; others are tailored by forces which can properly be designated as universal." With this, man's cultural life is split in two: part of it is, like Mascou's actors' garb, independent of men's Newtonian "inward motions"; part is an emanation of those motions themselves. The question that then arises is, Can this halfway house between the eighteenth and twentieth centuries really stand?

Whether it can or not depends on whether the dualism between empirically universal aspects of culture rooted in subcultural realities and empirically variable aspects not so rooted can be established and sustained. And this, in turn, demands (1) that the universals proposed be substantial ones and not empty categories; (2) that they be specifically grounded in particular biological, psychological, or sociological processes, not just vaguely associated with "underlying realities"; and (3) that they can convincingly be defended as core elements in a definition of humanity in comparison with which the much more numerous cultural particularities are of clearly secondary importance. On all three of these counts it seems to me that the *consensus gentium* approach fails; rather than moving towards the essentials of the human situation, it moves away from it.

The reason the first of these requirements —that the proposed universals be substantial ones and not empty or near-empty categories —has not been met is that it cannot. There is a logical conflict between asserting that, say, "religion," "marriage," or "property" are empirical universals and giving them very much in the way of specific content, for to say that they are empirical universals is to say that they have the same content, and to say they have the same content is to fly in the face of the undeniable fact that they do not. If one defines religion generally and indeterminately —as mans most fundamental orientation to reality, for example—then one cannot at the same time assign to that orientation a highly circumstantial content, for clearly what composes the most fundamental orientation to reality among the transported Aztecs, lifting pulsing hearts torn live from the chests of human sacrifices toward the heavens, is not what comprises it among the stolid Zuñi, dancing their great mass supplications to the benevolent gods of rain. The obsessive ritualism and unbuttoned polytheism of the Hindus expresses a rather different view of what the really real is really like from the uncompromising monotheism and austere legalism of Sunni Islam. Even if one does try to get down to less abstract levels and assert, as

Kluckhohn did, that a concept of the afterlife is universal or, as Malinowski did, that a sense of Providence is universal, the same contradiction haunts one. To make the generalization about an afterlife stand up alike for the Confucians and the Calvinists, the Zen Buddhists and the Tibetan Buddhists, one has to define it in most general terms, indeed —so general, in fact, that whatever force it seems to have virtually evaporates. So, too, with any notion of a "sense of Providence," which can include under its wing both Navaho notions about the relations of gods to men and Trobriand ones. And as with religion, so with "marriage," "trade," and all the rest of what A. L. Kroeber aptly called "fake universal," down to so seemingly tangible a matter as "shelter." That everywhere people mate and produce children, have some sense of mine and thine, and protect themselves in one fashion or another from rain and sun are neither false nor, from some points of view, unimportant; but they are hardly very much help in drawing a portrait of man that will be a true and honest likeness and not untenanted "John Q. Public" sort of cartoon.

My point, which should be clear and I hope will become even clearer in a moment, is not that there are no generalizations that can be made about man as man, save that he is a most various animal, or that the study of culture has nothing to contribute toward the uncovering of such generalizations. My point is that such generalizations are not to be discovered through a Baconian search for cultural universals, a kind of public-opinion polling of the world's peoples in search of a *consensus gentium* that does not in fact exist, and, further, that the attempt to do so leads to precisely the sort of relativism the whole approach was expressly designed to avoid. "Zuñi culture prizes restraint," Kluckhohn writes; "Kwakiutl culture encourages exhibitionism on the part of the individual. These are contrasting values, but in adhering to them the Zuñi and Kwakiutl show their allegiance to a universal value; the prizing of the distinctive norms of one's culture." This is sheer evasion, but it is only more apparent,

not more evasive, than discussions of cultural universals in general. What, after all, does it avail us to say, with Herskovits, that "morality is a universal, and so is enjoyment of beauty, and some standard for truth," if we are forced in the very next sentence, as he is, to add that "the many forms these concepts take are but products of the particular historical experience of the societies that manifest them"? Once one abandons uniformitarianism, even if, like the *consensus gentium* theorists, only partially and uncertainly, relativism is a genuine danger; but it can be warded off only by facing directly and fully the diversities of human culture, the Zuñi's restraint and the Kwakiutl's exhibitionism, and embracing them within the body of one's concept of man, not by gliding past them with vague tautologies and forceless banalities.

Of course, the difficulty of stating cultural universals which are at the same time substantial also hinders fulfilment of the second requirement facing the *consensus gentium* approach, that of grounding such universals in particular biological, psychological, or sociological processes. But there is more to it than that: the "stratigraphic" conceptualization of the relationships between cultural and noncultural factors hinders such a grounding even more effectively. Once culture, psyche, society, and organism have been converted into separate scientific "levels," complete and autonomous in themselves, it is very hard to bring them back together again.

The most common way of trying to do so is through the utilization of what are called "invariant points of reference." These points are to be found, to quote one of the most famous statements of this strategy—the "Toward a Common Language for the Areas of the Social Sciences" memorandum produced by Talcott Parsons, Kluckhohn, O. H. Taylor, and others in the early forties—

in the nature of social systems, in the biological and psychological nature of the component individuals, in the external situations in which they live and act, in the necessity of coordination in social systems. In [culture] ... these "foci" of structure are never ignored. They must in some way be "adapted to" or "taken account of."

Cultural universals are conceived to be crystallized responses to these unevadable realities, institutionalized ways of coming to terms with them.

Analysis consists, then, of matching assumed universals to postulated underlying necessities, attempting to show there is some goodness of fit between the two. On the social level, reference is made to such irrefragable facts as that all societies, in order to persist, must reproduce their membership or allocate goods and services, hence the universality of some form of family or some form of trade. On the psychological level, recourse is had to basic needs like personal growth—hence the ubiquity of educational institutions—or to panhuman problems, like the Oedipal predicament—hence the ubiquity of punishing gods and nurturant goddesses. Biologically, there is metabolism and health; culturally, dining customs and curing procedures; and so on. The tack is to look at underlying human requirements of some sort or other and then to try to show that those aspects of culture that are universal are, to use Kluckhohn's figure again, "tailored" by these requirements.

The problem here is, again, not so much whether in a general way this sort of congruence exists but whether it is more than a loose and indeterminate one. It is not difficult to relate some human institutions to what science (or common sense) tells us are requirements for human existence, but it is very much more difficult to state this relationship in an unequivocal form. Not only does almost any institution serve a multiplicity of social, psychological, and organic needs (so that to say that marriage is a mere reflex of the social need to reproduce, or that dining customs are a reflex of metabolic necessities, is to court parody), but there is no way to state in any precise and testable way the inter-level relationships that are conceived to hold. Despite first appearances, there is no serious attempt here to apply the concepts and theories of biology, psychology, or even sociology to the analysis of culture (and, of course, not even a suggestion of the reverse exchange) but merely a placing of supposed facts from the cultural and subcultural levels side by side so as to induce a vague sense that some kind of relationship between them—an obscure sort of "tailoring"—obtains. There is no theoretical integration here at all but a mere correlation, and that intuitive, of separate findings. With the levels approach, we can never, even by invoking "invariant points of reference," construct genuine functional interconnections between cultural and noncultural factors, only more or less persuasive analogies, parallelisms, suggestions, and affinities.

However, even if I am wrong (as, admittedly, many anthropologists would hold) in claiming that the *consensus gentium* approach can produce neither substantial universals nor specific connections between cultural and non-cultural phenomena to explain them, the question still remains whether such universals should be taken as the central elements in the definition of man, whether a lowest common denominator view of humanity is what we want anyway. This is, of course, now a philosophical question, not as such a scientific one; but the notion that the essence of what it means to be human is most clearly revealed in those features of human culture that are universal rather than in those that are distinctive to this people or that is a prejudice we are not necessarily obliged to share. Is it in grasping such general facts—that man has everywhere some sort of "religion"—or in grasping the richness of this religious phenomenon or that—Balinese trance or Indian ritualism, Aztec human sacrifice or Zuñi rain dancing—that we grasp him? Is the fact that "marriage" is universal (if it is) as penetrating a comment on what we are as the facts concerning Himalayan polyandry, or those fantastic Australian marriage rules, or the elaborate bride-price systems of Bantu Africa? The comment that Cromwell was the most typical Englishman of his time precisely in that he was the oddest may be relevant in this connection, too: it may be in the cultural particularities of people—in their oddities—that some of the most instructive revelations of what it is to be generically human are to be found; and the main contribution of the science of anthropology to the construction—or reconstruction—of a concept of man may then lie in showing us how to find them.

III

The major reason anthropologists have shied away from cultural particularities when it came to a question of defining man and have taken refuge instead in bloodless universals is that, faced as they are with the enormous variation in human behavior, they are haunted by a fear of historicism, of becoming lost in a whirl of cultural relativism so convulsive as to deprive them of any fixed bearings at all. Nor has there not been some occasion for such a fear: Ruth Benedict's *Patterns of Culture,* probably the most popular book in anthropology ever published in this country, with its strange conclusion that anything one group of people is inclined toward doing is worthy of respect by another, is perhaps only the most outstanding example of the awkward positions one can get into by giving oneself over rather too completely to what Marc Bloch called "the thrill of learning singular thinks." Yet the fear is a bogy. The notion that unless a cultural phenomenon is empirically universal it cannot reflect anything about the nature of man is about as logical as the notion that because sickle-cell anemia is, fortunately, not universal it cannot tell us anything about human genetic processes. It is not whether phenomena are empirically common that is critical in science—else why should Becquerel have been so interested in the peculiar behavior of uranium?—but whether they can be made to reveal the enduring natural processes that underly them. Seeing heaven in a grain of sand is not a trick only poets can accomplish.

In short, we need to look for systematic relationships among diverse phenomena, not for substantive identities among similar ones. And to do that with any effectiveness, we need to replace the "stratigraphic" conception of the relations between the various aspects of human existence with a synthetic one; that is, one in which biological, psychological, sociological, and cultural factors can be treated as variables within unitary systems of analysis. The establishment of a common language in the social sciences is not a matter of mere coordination of terminologies or, worse yet, of coining artificial new ones; nor is it a matter of imposing a single set of categories upon the area as a whole. It is a matter of integrating different types of theories and concepts in such a way that one can formulate meaningful propositions embodying findings now sequestered in separate fields of study.

In attempting to launch such an integration from the anthropological side and to reach, thereby, an exacter image of man, I want to propose two ideas. The first of these is that culture is best seen not as complexes of concrete behavior patterns—customs, usages, traditions, habit clusters—as has, by and large, been the case up to now, but as a set of control mechanisms—plans, recipes, rules, instructions (what computer engineers call "programs")—for the governing of behavior. The second is that man is precisely the animal most desperately dependent upon such extragenetic, outside-the-skin control mechanisms, such cultural programs, for ordering his behavior.

Neither of these ideas is entirely new, but a number of recent developments, both within anthropology and in other sciences (cybernetics, information theory, neurology, molecular genetics), have made them susceptible of more precise statement as well as lending them a degree of empirical support they did not previously have. And out of such reformulations of the concept of culture and of the role of culture in human life comes, in turn, a definition of man stressing not so much the empirical commonalities in his behavior, from place to place and time to time, but rather the mechanisms by whose agency the breadth and indeterminateness of his inherent capacities are reduced to the narrowness and specificity of his actual accomplishments. One of the most significant facts about us may finally be that we all begin with the natural equipment to live a thousand kinds of life but end in the end having lived only one.

The "control mechanism" view of culture begins with the assumption that human thought is basically both social and public—that its natural habitat is the house yard, the market place, and the town square. Thinking consists not of "happenings in the head" (though happenings there and elsewhere are necessary for it to occur) but of a traffic in what have been called, by G. H. Mead and others, significant symbols—words for the most part but also gestures, drawings, musical sounds, mechanical devices like clocks, or natural objects like jewels—anything, in fact, that is disengaged from its mere actuality and used to impose meaning upon experience. From the point of view of any particular individual, such symbols are largely given. He finds them already current in the community when he is born, and they remain, with some additions, subtractions, and partial alterations he may or may not have had a hand in, in circulation there after he dies. While he lives he uses them, or some of them, sometimes deliberately and with care, most often spontaneously and with ease, but always with the same end in view: to put a construction upon the events through which he lives, to orient himself within "the ongoing course of experienced things," to adopt a vivid phrase of John Dewey's.

Man is so in need of such symbolic sources of illumination to find his bearings in the world because the nonsymbolic sort that are constitutionally ingrained in his body cast so diffused a light. The behavior patterns of lower animals are, at least to a much greater extent, given to them with their physical structure; genetic sources of information order their actions within much narrower ranges of variation, the narrower and more thorough-going the lower the animal. For man, what are innately given are extremely general response capacities, which, although they make possible far greater plasticity, complexity, and on the scattered occasions when everything works as it should, effectiveness of behavior, leave it much less precisely regulated. This, then, is the second face of our argument: Undirected by culture patterns —organized systems of significant symbols —man's behavior would be virtually ungovernable, a mere chaos of pointless acts and exploding emotions, his experience virtually shapeless. Culture, the accumulated totality of such patterns, is not just an ornament of human existence but—the principal basis of its specificity—an essential condition for it.

Within anthropology some of the most telling evidence in support of such a position comes from recent advances in our understanding of what used to be called the descent of man: the emergence of *Homo sapiens* out of his general primate background. Of these advances three are of critical importance: (1) the discarding of a sequential view of the relations between the physical evolution and the cultural development of man in favor of an overlap or interactive view; (2) the discovery that the bulk of the biological changes that produced modern man out of his most immediate progenitors took place in the central nervous system and most especially in the brain; (3) the realization that man is, in physical terms, an incomplete, an unfinished, animal; that what sets him off most graphically from nonmen is less his sheer ability to learn (great as that is) than how much and what particular sorts of things he *has* to learn before he is able to function at all. Let me take each of these points in turn.

The traditional view of the relations between the biological and the cultural advance of man was that the former, the biological, was for all intents and purposes completed before the latter, the cultural, began. That is to say, it was again stratigraphic: Man's physical being evolved, through the usual mechanisms of genetic variation and natural selection, up to the point where his anatomical structure had arrived at more or less the status at which we find it today; then cultural development got underway. At some particular stage in his phylogenetic history, a marginal genetic change of some sort rendered him capable of producing and carrying culture, and thenceforth his form of adaptive response to environmental pressures was almost exclusively cultural rather than genetic. As he spread over the globe he wore furs in cold climates and loin cloths (or nothing at all) in warm ones; he didn't alter his innate mode of response to environmental temperature. He made weapons to extend his inherited predatory powers and cooked foods to render a wider range of them digestible. Man became man, the story continues, when, having crossed some mental Rubicon, he became able to transmit "knowledge, belief, law, morals, custom" (to quote the items of Sir Edward Tylor's classical definition of culture) to his descendents and his neighbors through teaching and to acquire them from his ancestors and his neighbors through learning. After that magical moment, the advance of the hominids depended almost entirely on cultural accumulation, on the slow growth of conventional practices, rather than, as it had for ages past, on physical organic change.

The only trouble is that such a moment does not seem to have existed. By the most recent estimates the transition to the cultural mode of life took the genus *Homo* over a million years to accomplish; and stretched out in such a manner, it involved not one or a handful of marginal genetic changes but a long, complex, and closely ordered sequence of them.

In the current view, the evolution of *Homo sapiens*—modern man—out of his immediate pre-*sapiens* background got definitively underway nearly two million years ago with the appearance of the now famous Australopithecines—the so-called ape men of southern and eastern Africa—and culminated with the emergence of *sapiens* himself only some one to two hundred thousand years ago. Thus, as at least elemental forms of cultural, or if you wish protocultural, activity (simple toolmaking, hunting, and so on) seem to have been present among some of the Australopithecines, there was an overlap of, as I say, well over a million years between the beginning of culture and the appearance of man as we know him today. The precise dates—which are tentative and which further research may alter in one direction or another—are not critical; what is critical is that there was an overlap and that it was a very extended one. The final phases (final to date, at any rate) of the phylogenetic history of man took place

in the same grand geological era—the so-called Ice Age—as the initial phases of his cultural history. Men have birthdays, but man does not.

What this means is that culture, rather than being added on, so to speak, to a finished or virtually finished animal, was ingredient, and centrally ingredient, in the production of that animal itself. The slow, steady, almost glacial growth of culture through the Ice Age altered the balance of selection pressures for the evolving *Homo* in such a way as to play a major directive role in his evolution. The perfection of tools, the adoption of organized hunting and gathering practices, the beginnings of true family organization, the discovery of fire, and most critically, though it is as yet extremely difficult to trace it out in any detail, the increasing reliance upon systems of significant symbols (language, art, myth, ritual) for orientation, communication, and self-control all created for man a new environment to which he was then obliged to adapt. As culture, step by infinitesimal step, accumulated and developed, a selective advantage was given to those individuals in the population most able to take advantage of it—the effective hunter, the persistent gatherer, the adept toolmaker, the resourceful leader—until what had been a small-brained, protohuman *Homo australopithecus* became the large-brained fully human *Homo sapiens*. Between the cultural pattern, the body, and the brain, a positive feedback system was created in which each shaped the progress of the other, a system in which the interaction among increasing tool use, the changing anatomy of the hand, and the expanding representation of the thumb on the cortex is only one of the more graphic examples. By submitting himself to governance by symbolically mediated programs for producing artifacts, organizing social life, or expressing emotions, man determined, if unwittingly, the culminating stages of his own biological destiny. Quite literally, though quite inadvertently, he created himself.

Though, as I mentioned, there were a number of important changes in the gross anatomy of genus *Homo* during this period of his crystallization—in skull shape, dentition, thumb size, and so on—by far the most important and dramatic were those that evidently took place in the central nervous system; for this was the period when the human brain, and most particularly the forebrain, ballooned into its present top-heavy proportions. The technical problems are complicated and controversial here; but the main point is that though the Australopithecines had a torso and arm configuration not drastically different from our own, and a pelvis and leg formation at least well launched toward our own, they had cranial capacities hardly larger than those of the living apes—that is to say, about a third to a half of our own. What sets true men off most distinctly from protomen is apparently not overall bodily form but complexity of nervous organization. The overlap period of cultural and biological change seems to have consisted in an intense concentration on neural development and perhaps associated refinements of various behaviors—of the hands, bipedal locomotion, and so on —for which the basic anatomical foundations —mobile shoulders and wrists, a broadened ilium, and so on—had already been securely laid. In itself, this is perhaps not altogether startling; but, combined with what I have already said, it suggests some conclusions about what sort of animal man is that are, I think, rather far not only from those of the eighteenth century but from those of the anthropology of only ten or fifteen years ago.

Most bluntly, it suggests that there is no such thing as a human nature independent of culture. Men without culture would not be the clever savages of Golding's *Lord of the Flies,* thrown back upon the cruel wisdom of their animal instincts; nor would they be the nature's noblemen of Enlightenment primitivism or even, as classical anthropological theory would imply, intrinsically talented apes who had somehow failed to find themselves. They would be unworkable monstrosities with very few useful instincts, fewer recognizable sentiments, and no intellect: mental basket cases. As our central nervous system— and most particularly its crowning curse and glory, the neocortex—grew up in great part in interaction with culture, it is incapable of directing our behavior or organizing our experience without the guidance provided by systems of significant symbols. What happened to us in the Ice Age is that we were obliged to abandon the regularity and precision of detailed genetic control over our conduct for the flexibility and adaptability of a more generalized, though of course no less real, genetic control over it. To supply the additional information necessary to be able to act, we were forced, in turn, to rely more and more heavily on cultural sources—the accumulated fund of significant symbols. Such symbols are thus not mere expressions, instrumentalities, or correlates of our biological, psychological, and social existence; they are prerequisites of it. Without men, no culture, certainly; but equally, and more significantly, without culture, no men.

We are, in sum, incomplete or unfinished animals who complete or finish ourselves through culture—and not through culture in general but through highly particular forms of it: Dobuan and Javanese, Hopi and Italian, upper-class and lower-class, academic and commercial. Man's great capacity for learning, his plasticity, has often been remarked, but what is even more critical is his extreme dependence upon a certain sort of learning: the attainment of concepts, the apprehension and application of specific systems of symbolic meaning. Beavers build dams, birds build nests, bees locate food, baboons organize social groups, and mice mate on the basis of forms of learning that rest predominantly on the instructions encoded in their genes and evoked by appropriate patterns of external stimuli: physical keys inserted into organic locks. But men build dams or shelters, locate food, organize their social groups, or find sexual partners under the guidance of instructions encoded in flow charts and blueprints, hunting lore, moral systems, and aesthetic judgments: conceptual structures molding formless talents.

We live, as one writer has neatly put it, in an "information gap." Between what our body tells us and what we have to know in order to function, there is a vacuum we must fill ourselves, and we fill it with information (or misinformation) provided by our culture. The boundary between what is innately controlled and what is culturally controlled in human behavior is an ill-defined and wavering one. Some things are, for all intents and purposes, entirely controlled intrinsically: we need no more cultural guidance to learn how to breathe than a fish needs to learn how to swim. Others are almost certainly largely cultural: we do not attempt to explain on a genetic basis why some men put their trust in centralized planning and others in the free market, though it might be an amusing exercise. Almost all complex human behavior is, of course, the vector outcome of the two. Our capacity to speak is surely innate; our capacity to speak English is surely cultural. Smiling at pleasing stimuli and frowning at unpleasing ones are surely in some degree genetically determined (even apes screw up their faces at noxious odors); but sardonic smiling and burlesque frowning are equally surely predominantly cultural, as is perhaps demonstrated by the Balinese definition of a madman as someone who, like an American, smiles when there is nothing to laugh at. Between the basic ground plans for our life that our genes lay down—the capacity to speak or to smile—and the precise behavior we in fact execute—speaking English in a certain tone of voice, smiling enigmatically in a delicate social situation—lies a complex set of significant symbols under whose direction we transform the first into the second, the ground plans into the activity.

Our ideas, our values, our acts, even our emotions, are, like our nervous system itself, cultural products — products manufactured, indeed, out of tendencies, capacities, and dispositions with which we were born, but manufactured none the less. Chartres is made of stone and glass. But it is not just stone and glass; it is a cathedral, and not only a cathedral, but a particular cathedral built at a particular time by certain members of a particular society. To understand what it means, to perceive it for what it is, you need to know rather more than the generic properties of stone and glass and rather more than what is common to all cathedrals. You need to understand also—and, in my opinion, most critically—the specific concepts of the relations between God, man, and architecture that, having governed its creation, it consequently embodies. It is no different with men: they, too, every last one of them, are cultural artifacts.

IV

Whatever differences they may show, the approaches to the definition of human nature adopted by the Enlightenment and by classical anthropology have one thing in common: they are both basically typological. They endeavor to construct an image of man as a model, an archetype, a Platonic idea or an Aristotelian form, with respect to which actual men—you, me, Churchill, Hitler, and the Bornean headhunter—are but reflections, distortions, approximations. In the Enlightenment case, the elements of this essential type were to be uncovered by stripping the trappings of culture away from actual men and seeing what then was left—natural man. In classical anthropology, it was to be uncovered by factoring out the commonalities in culture and seeing what then appeared—consensual man. In either case, the result is the same as tends to emerge in all typological approaches to scientific problems generally: the differences among individuals and among groups of individuals are rendered secondary. Individuality comes to be seen as eccentricity, distinctiveness as accidental deviation from the only legitimate object of study for the true scientist: the underlying, unchanging, normative type. In such an approach, however elaborately formulated and resourcefully defended, living detail is drowned in dead stereotype: we are in quest of a metaphysical entity, Man with a capital "M," in the interests of which we sacrifice the empirical entity we in fact encounter, man with a small "m."

The sacrifice is, however, as unnecessary as it is unavailing. There is no opposition between general theoretical understanding and circumstantial understanding, between synoptic vision and a fine eye for detail. It is, in fact, by its power to draw general propositions out of particular phenomena that a scientific theory—indeed, science itself—is to be judged. If we want to discover what man amounts to, we can only find it in what men are: and what men are, above all other things, is various. It is in understanding that variousness—its range, its nature, its basis, and its implications—that we shall come to construct a concept of human nature that, more than a statistical shadow and less than a primitivist dream, has both substance and truth.

It is here, to come round finally to my title, that the concept of culture has its impact on the concept of man. When seen as a set of symbolic devices for controlling behavior, extra-somatic sources of information, culture provides the link between what men are intrinsically capable of becoming and what they actually, one by one, in fact become. Becoming human is becoming individual, and we become individual under the guidance of cultural patterns, historically created systems of meaning in terms of which we give form, order, point, and direction to our lives. And the cultural patterns involved are not general but specific—not just "marriage" but a particular set of notions about what men and women are like, how spouses should treat one another, or who should properly marry whom; not just "religion" but belief in the wheel of karma, the observance of a month of fasting, or the practice of cattle sacrifice. Man is to be defined neither by his innate capacities alone, as the Enlightenment sought to do, nor by his actual behaviors alone, as much of contemporary social science seeks to do, but rather by the link between them, by the way in which the first is transformed into the second, his generic potentialities focused into his specific performances. It is in man's *career*, in its characteristic course, that we can discern, however dimly, his nature, and though culture is but one element in determining that course, it is hardly the least important. As culture shaped us as a single species—and is no doubt still shaping us—so too it shapes us as separate individuals. This, neither an unchanging subcultural self nor an established cross-cultural consensus, is what we really have in common.

Oddly enough—though on second thought, perhaps not so oddly—many of our subjects seem to realize this more clearly than we anthropologists ourselves. In Java, for example, where I have done much of my work, the people quite flatly say, "To be human is to be Javanese." Small children, boors, simpletons, the insane, the flagrantly immoral, are said to be *ndurung djawa*, "not yet Javanese." A "normal" adult capable of acting in terms of the highly elaborate system of etiquette, possessed of the delicate aesthetic perceptions associated with music, dance, drama, and textile design, responsive to the subtle promptings of the divine residing in the stillnesses of each individual's inward-turning consciousness, is *sampun djawa*, "already Javanese," that is, already human. To be human is not just to breathe; it is to control one's breathing, by yoga-like techniques, so as to hear in inhalation and exhalation the literal voice of God pronouncing His own name—*hu Allah*. It is not just to talk; it is to utter the appropriate words and phrases in the appropriate social situations in the appropriate tone of voice and with the appropriate evasive indirection. It is not just to eat; it is to prefer certain foods cooked in certain ways and to follow a rigid table etiquette in consuming them. It is not even just to feel but to feel certain quite distinctively Javanese (and essentially untranslatable) emotions — "patience," "detachment," "resignation," "respect."

To be human here is thus not to be Everyman; it is to be a particular kind of man, and of course men differ: "Other fields," the Javanese say, "other grasshoppers." Within the society, differences are recognized, too—the way a rice peasant becomes human and Javanese differs from the way a civil servant does. This is not a matter of tolerance and ethical relativism, for not all ways of being human are regarded as equally admirable by far; the way the local Chinese go about it is, for example, intensely dispraised. The point is that there are different ways; and to shift to the anthropologist's perspective now, it is in a systematic review and analysis of these—of the Plains Indian's bravura, the Hindu's obsessiveness, the Frenchman's rationalism, the Berber's anarchism, the American's optimism (to list a series of tags I should not like to have to defend as such)—that we will find out what it is, or can be, to be a man.

We must, in short, descend into detail, past the misleading tags, past the metaphysical types, past the empty similarities to grasp firmly the essential character of not only the various cultures but the various sorts of individuals within each culture if we wish to encounter humanity face to face. In this area, the road to the general, to the revelatory, simplicities of science lies through a concern with the particular, the circumstantial, the concrete, but a concern organized and directed in terms of the sort of theoretical analyses that I have touched upon—analyses of physical evolution, of the functioning of the nervous system, of social organization, of psychological process, of cultural patterning, and so on—and, most especially, in terms of the interplay among them. That is to say, the road lies, like any genuine quest, through a terrifying complexity . . . .

2. LANGUAGE AND EVOLUTION

JOSEPH H. GREENBERG

Reprinted from Betty J. Meggers (Ed.), Evolution and Anthropology: A Centennial Appraisal *(Washington, D. C.: Anthropological Society of Washington, 1959). Joseph H. Greenberg is Professor of Anthropology, Chairman of the Committee on African Studies, and Acting Chairman of the Committee on Linguistics at Stanford University. One of his major interests has been the classification of languages, such as those of Africa and, more recently, the non-Austronesian languages of the Pacific. He has worked extensively in theoretical linguistics on the universals of language. He is the author of* Languages of Africa *and* Essays in Linguistics. *and the editor of* Universals of Language.

■ Geertz, in the preceding selection, strongly rejected an evolutionary perspective for the study of culture. Why do other anthropologists maintain, with equal strength, that an evolutionary perspective is necessary? What advantage is there in this point of view? As a matter of fact, how do we know that cultural evolution has taken place?

The concept of evolution is an abstraction; it is inferred from observations made under a variety of conditions and is used to explain relationships among observed phenomena. No one has ever observed cultural evolution directly—any more than culture itself, mutation, biological inheritance, democracy, or totalitarianism have been observed directly. All of these concepts are intellectual constructs and are intended to explain the relationships that are assumed to exist among a series of phenomena. (This is not intended to render aid and comfort to those who insist that evolution is "merely a hypothesis," which usually means "it should not be taught in our schools." The concept of evolution is no more a "mere hypothesis" than the concept of "table," which also is an abstraction from a series of observed phenomena.) When we speak of cultural evolution we refer to its manifestations, just as we do when we speak of physical gravity.

The concept of evolution is a theoretical framework, a convenient tool with which we try to understand how man arrived at advanced agricultural and industrial stages of cultural development from a past that began with nomadic hunting and gathering. It may seem gratuitous, but it is nevertheless essential to point out that the first men did not plow, sail across oceans, live in metropolises, or plan the colonization of other planets and the ocean floors. Many millennia were required to achieve the mastery over the habitat that is represented by these achievements; and each achievement was accompanied by significant changes in the human relations by which people organize social life. Similarly, cultural evolution will continue as long as man survives.

Everyone agrees that man began his cultural career as a nomadic forager and that industrial society represents his most recent cultural achievement. Disagreement centers on the question whether successive degrees of mastery over the habitat emerged sequentially in time, according to regular and discernible principles. Did different degrees of mastery over the habitat "just happen" or did they develop in a manner that reflects cultural design?

The selections in this book are organized to illustrate such a design, and this evolutionary perspective enables us to read order into what might otherwise be a hopeless jumble of unique cultures. This is the theme of Selection 2, by Greenberg, which is divided into two parts. In the first part Greenberg introduces us to the concept of evolution, which, he maintains, is a product of evidence. In the second part he applies the concept of evolution to the study of language. For our purposes in this context, the study of language in evolutionary perspective provides an excellent model for analysis of the evolution of other aspects of culture. (The place of language in biological and cultural evolution is examined in Part IV of the accompanying volume.)

The notion of stages or levels of cultural development in sequences of time is at the heart of an evolutionary perspective. When students of evolution disagree with each other (in contrast with their disputes with those who entirely reject an evolutionary perspective) their arguments usually center around the nature of these sequences. Unless one is careful, the concept of sequences in time—the postulate of stages of cultural development—can be a serious trap. When we speak of sequences of cultural stages we do not mean that these stages were arranged in a straight line or that each culture has gone through the same pattern of change. As Greenberg stresses, the relevant imagery for evolution is a branching tree, not a straight line. The importance of this is that all levels or stages of cultural development could—in fact do—occur simultaneously. Africa, for example, contains nomadic hunters and gatherers (such as the Pygmies of the Congo), cultivators who use the hoe or digging stick (including neighbors of the Pygmies), plow cultivators (in Ethiopia and elsewhere), long-distance traders (in the Sudan), and industrial societies (in South Africa and elsewhere). Each of these may be adaptive to its own habitat (see Selection 3); and none may have grown from another in any systematic way.

As these examples suggest, not every culture has participated fully in the sweep of evolution. In the terminology of Marshall Sahlins and Elman Service in *Evolution and Culture* (Ann Arbor: University of Michigan Press, 1960), it is useful to distinguish between "general evolution" and "specific evolution." General evolution refers to the changes that have taken place in human culture as a whole; specific evolution denotes the transformation of a particular culture from one stage of mastery over the habitat to another, each with its characteristic technology, essential institutions, ideologies, and customary behaviors. This process of change is adaptive in the sense that it provides the group with a greater degree of mastery over its habitat than it enjoyed before. The change can result from accretions in knowledge and techniques within the society itself or from the introduction of new technological procedures from other societies. The focus of this book is on general rather than specific cultural evolution, and each of these stages of development will be referred to as a strategy of adaption for which particular cultures will serve as illustrations.

Finally, the concept of cultural evolution should not suggest that only one path can be taken to reach any particular stage. We will see that the same type of family or household organization can occur in vastly different stages of cultural development. Complex states

generally arise in connection with cultivation by means of plows or terracing, but they can also develop in societies whose people gain their livelihoods by cultivation with hoes or digging sticks or by herding. Urbanization can emerge under varying conditions and from various backgrounds. Nevertheless, as this books seeks to show, one interpretation of the total human record is that there have been successive stages of mastery over the habitat as a result of increasingly effective ways of exploiting a greater range of the energy sources in a habitat.

Several sources can be consulted by the reader who wants to broaden his familiarity with the concept of cultural evolution, in addition to *Evolution and Culture* and the volume from which Greenberg's selection was taken. A very important collection of papers that deal with various aspects of evolution is *Evolution after Darwin*, Vol. 2: *The Evolution of Man*, edited by Sol Tax (3 vols.; Chicago: University of Chicago Press, 1960). One of the earliest and still one of the most germane works dealing with the relationship between technology and social organization is *The Material Culture and Social Institutions of the Simpler Peoples* by L. T. Hobhouse, G. C. Wheeler, and M. Ginsberg (London: Chapman and Hall, 1915). Among the first and clearest expositions of the importance of energy systems in the study of adaption and evolution are Leslie White's *The Evolution of Culture* (New York: McGraw-Hill, 1959) and *The Science of Culture* (New York: Grove Press, 1958). Together with White's work the reader should consult Julian H. Steward's *Theory of Culture Change* (Urbana: University of Illinois Press, 1955), which established the framework for the concept of levels of sociocultural development, and Elman R. Service's *Primitive Social Organization* (New York: Random House, 1962). ■

THE GREAT ACHIEVEMENT of Darwin in the *Origin of Species* was to establish on a firm and generally accepted basis the interpretation of differences among species as arising gradually through processes of change from other species rather than once and for all by an original creative act. Of the factors of change by which new species might develop, the most prominent in Darwin's theory, but by no means the only one, was the perpetuation through natural selection of those variations best suited for survival in the struggle for existence. As has often been noted, the theory that species evolve in the course of time was not invented by Darwin. It was, indeed, a familiar notion to the biologists of the preceding half-century but it was not until the careful and impressive marshalling of evidence in its behalf by Darwin in his classic work and, in particular, the advancement of natural selection by him as an explanatory principle that it became plausible to more than a minority of biological scientists.

In view of these historical developments, any consideration of Darwinian evolution must carefully distinguish the theory that species develop from other species, which is an assertion concerning the history of life-forms, from the theory of natural selection which asserts that natural selection has played a major role in producing this result. The specification and analysis of such ambiguities assumes crucial importance when the term evolution is applied to a set of phenomena as radically different from the biological as language.

There is a further ambiguity lurking in the phrase "theory of evolution," partly allied to the distinction just mentioned, but of even more fundamental importance. In the first of two senses of evolution, which in this aspect may be called transformism, it may be contrasted with creationism as the opposing doctrine. In the second sense, which is quite distinct, it may be considered synonymous with advance or progress.

The transformationist meaning of evolution arises from the considerations involved in any class of phenomena in which the investigator is confronted with the existence of a variety of kinds or species. In such instances, there are two alternative types of theories to account for the existence of distinct kinds. According to the creationist view, each kind is a fixed type that can only vary within certain fixed bounds in the entire course of its existence. Each kind is defined by reference to certain constant and unchanging characters that constitute, in the terminology of scholastic logic, its essential or definitional predicates. Variations may occur

with respect to the other characters, which are therefore accidental rather than essential. Further, this essence is a formal cause which explains the existence of the species.

Differences among species are explained according to this doctrine as issuing from distinct creative acts. Species can be created or destroyed but they cannot, by changing their essential characteristics, give rise to other and new species. It is not necessary that all kinds should have been created at the same time or that all should survive indefinitely. When confronted with fossil evidence indicating that the species of different geological epochs were, in general, different, the creationist necessarily denied that any links of development connected similar but distinct species in successive periods. The theory adopted was that called "catastrophism," namely that by a series of cataclysms, earlier species had been destroyed and were replaced by more recent ones through new creative acts.

The evolutionary theory of transformation of species, as opposed to creationist beliefs, maintains that there are no fixed bounds to specific change. Therefore earlier species give rise to later ones by a process of developmental change. The fact that, in the instance of life-forms, species fall into coherent larger groupings, the genera, and that these in turn may be grouped into distinct families, and so on, in an ordered hierarchy receives its distinctive transformationist explanation. Such groupings had long been noted and had been codified by Linnaeus in his great systematic work, which appeared more than a century before Darwin's *Origin of Species*. According to transformationist theory, those species that belong to the same genera are the differentiated descendants of a single ancestral species, their resemblances being explained as the result of common descent. The resemblances among those genera which belong to the same family are explained in turn by the theory that the species ancestral to each genus are the descendants of a still earlier species ancestral to the family as a whole, and similarly with larger and higher groupings. Fossil forms are, then, either such ancestors of existing groupings or additional lines of descent from them which have become extinct without leaving descendants.

The model of evolution that thus emerges is a branching tree, the varieties of today are like twigs which, as they sprout, become the species of tomorrow. These in turn likewise put forth new twigs, some of which perish while others survive and produce new differentiated descendants. Hence the transformationist theory may fittingly be called that of branching evolution.

The creationist and transformationist views are not merely two philosophic theories between which the observer chooses on the basis of predilection or metaphysical inclination. Given sufficient data we can decide between them for any particular group of phenomena. Thus the theory of catastrophism posited by the creationists was eventually abandoned because it was not supported by the geological evidence. Further, it was the ability of the transformationist theory to account for the coherence of generic and higher classificational groups which, it appears, first aroused in Darwin the conviction that species were not fixed, unchangeable types. For being struck by the number of distinct species on certain islands, which in the creationist view would be separate creations, and at the same time by their resemblance to the species of the nearest mainland, the theory forcibly presented itself to Darwin that whether by migration or whether by geographical continuity at a former period when a land bridge existed, what was originally the same species on island and mainland must during the subsequent period of isolation have developed into separate but related species. This would explain at once their distinctness and their close resemblance, both of which, as Darwin noted, are inexplicable by the creationist theory.

What is argued here is not that the evolutionary transformationist view is necessarily the correct explanation as opposed to the creationist in every instance, but that the question can be decided on the basis of certain kinds of evidence and that, in the case of biological species, this evidence was decisive in favor of the transformationist theory.

The foregoing definition of evolution as transformaiton of species, in which meaning it is the logical opposite of creationism, is to be distinguished from evolution in the sense of progress in the course of evolutionary change. Because of the ethical implications of the term "progress," it might be better to employ the word "advance" for purposes of scientific discussion. By advance will be meant the theory that more complex, internally differentiated and efficiently adapted forms make their appearance in general in the later stages of evolutionary change. The ethical judgment that this occurs and is good may be called the doctrine of progress.

The distinctness of the theories of evolution as transformism and evolution as advance is indicated, among other evidences, by the fact that certain scientists have held one while rejecting the other. As was pointed out by the eminent geologist Lyell, who distinguished these two theories by the names "transmutation" and "progress," it is quite possible to hold the creationist and progressive views at the same time. For example, those biologists in the earlier part of the nineteenth century who adhered to the catastrophist version of creationism maintained that each successive creation marked an advance over the previous one in the sense described above.

The particular mechanism of evolutionary change to which Darwin attached major significance and whose plausibility was a primary factor in the spectacular success of his theory was, of course, natural selection. Now, as Darwin states repeatedly, the descendants of a particular life-form are, through the agency of natural selection, likely to be more efficient than their ancestors. There is, therefore, implicit in the notion of natural selection the theory of the inevitability of continuous advance in the series of life-forms. It is true, moreover, as an empirical fact, that the paleontological evidence, as we go back in time, becomes increasingly confined to forms of simple and relatively undifferentiated structure and of limited range of adaptation to environment. It was precisely one of the recommendations of the theory of natural selection that it helped to make this temporal advance intelligible.

However, it is a well-known fact of the history of biology that the status of natural selection as a major factor in evolution has been less secure than the acceptance of the reality of evolution in the sense of transformation of species. Likewise the concept of advance has tended to remain a vague and generally unsatisfactory notion to many biologists. Thus George G. Simpson states, "Whether recent man is to be considered more complex and more independent than a Cambrian trilobite will be found subject to qualification and definitions." Among the difficulties here are that efficiency of adaptation is always relative to a particular environment while the environment itself changes in the course of time, and that there are many scales of efficiency so that, of two species compared, one may have superiority in one respect and the other in some other respect and these scales are, strictly speaking, incommensurable. For these reasons the definition of evolution as transformation appears to be more fundamental than the definition in terms of advance.

It is one of the contentions of this paper that the theory of evolution as transformation applies *mutatis mutandis,* and with relatively minor modifications both to linguistic and biologic change. This agreement was noted both by biologists and linguists in the period immediately following the publication of *Origin of Species.* Thus Darwin himself remarks in *The Descent of Man,* a later work, that "the formation of different languages and of distinct species and the proofs that both have been developed through a gradual process are curiously parallel."

In linguistic science, the creationist view is represented by the Biblical account of the Tower of Babel, according to which all language differences were created at the same time by the confusion of tongues. This theory was superseded by the transformationist account much earlier than in the instance of biology. Thus Max Mueller, an outstanding

linguistic scholar contemporary with Darwin, in spite of his opposition to Darwin's views regarding the animal descent of man, was able to say that "in language, I was a Darwinian before Darwin," while August Schleicher, another leading linguist of the period, in a published lecture "Die Darwinsche Theorie und die Sprachwissenschaft," spelled out this parallel in detail.

The event that marks most clearly the triumph of transformism over creationism in linguistic science was the recognition that the resemblances among the languages we now call Indo-European are to be explained as a result of common inheritance with differential change from an extinct ancestral form of speech. The acceptance of this theory is usually, but somewhat arbitrarily, dated from a statement by Sir William Jones substantially to this effect in 1786. In fact, both in the case of the Semitic and Finno-Ugric languages, this explanation had been current even earlier. Thus the recognition of transformism in linguistics substantially antedates the first modern statement of this theory in biology by Lamarck in 1801.

Probably the chief factor in the early acceptance of this type of explanation in linguistics as compared with biology is the vastly more rapid rate of change in language. The common-sense objection to transformism in biology, namely, that actual changes in species had never been observed in historic times and that, to all appearances, species were fixed types, appears to have been the most powerful single factor in the general rejection of evolution by biologists in the period preceding Darwin. Language, within the realm of individual experience and unaided by records of its past, seems fixed no doubt, but not to the same degree. Older people can recall vocabulary items and idioms which were current in their youth but are no longer heard. On occasion, they may even have noted phonetic changes. Thus the older generation of New Yorkers remembers when the *oi* diphthong in such words as "hurt" was general and accepted among educated speakers and has witnessed its replacement, at least among educated speakers, within an individual life-span.

These changes, apparently small within the lifetime of a single person, display powerful cumulative effects in periods of time well within the scope of written records. Thus, Anglo-Saxon exhibits differences from modern English comparable with those of modern German. If Anglo-Saxon and modern English were spoken contemporaneously they would undoubtedly rank as separate languages. It was possible, then, actually to observe in this historically well-attested instance the change of one language into another.

In general, languages ancestral to existing groups of genetically related languages, which would correspond to the fossil evidence of biology, take us back to periods before the existence of written records. However, in the well-known instance of Latin, there are abundant records of a language which, through a series of locally different variants, has given rise to the existing diversity of Romance local dialects and standard languages. In view of these known facts, it was not too audacious a step to assume that in similar fashion an ancestral language had once existed bearing the same relation to the existing branches of Indo-European that Latin held in relation to Romance speech-forms. It became a mere historical accident that Latin was attested in written form whereas the Indo-European Ursprache, which was spoken before the existence of writing in the area of its occurrence, could not be known through direct evidence of this kind.

The nature of the parallel between the evolution of languages and species, which so struck both linguists like Mueller and Schleicher and natural scientists like Darwin and Lyell, refers to the conception of evolution as transformation of kinds. The transmission of physical characters by the genetic mechanism corresponds to the transmission of language from one generation to the next or one population to another by learning. In both cases, variations arise, some of which are perpetuated. In both instances geographic isolation, whether complete or imperfect, leads to the perpetuation of locally different variants. Difficulties of determining where a variety ends and a species begins, difficulties that were important factors in Darwin's disillusionment with the creationist theory, resemble the linguist's difficulties in defining language as opposed to dialect. Ultimately these variant descendants became distinct enough to be ranked indisputably as separate languages or species. The parallelism is further indicated by the metaphor of the branching tree common to both disciplines.

The status of transformist explanations of linguistic similarities was further enhanced by the successful reconstruction of essential features of the ancestral language through systematic comparison of features of the descendant languages, notably in the instance of Indo-European where, as is the rule, the ancestral language was not known from written records. This enterprise received a great impetus through the discovery, which was not long in coming, that in certain respects, particularly in regard to the sound system, changes were not haphazard but rather showed a surprising degree of regularity. This discovery of the regularity of sound changes, first announced in the specific instance of the consonantal changes of Germanic as compared to Sanskrit, Greek and Latin by Rask and Grimm and which came to be known as Grimm's law, aided greatly in making comparative linguistics the most systematic in its method and reliable in its results of all the reconstructive historical sciences dealing with man in his sociocultural aspects.

Just as transformism in the analogue of genetic relationship, so the creationist view of fixed species is implied in the use of classificational criteria with typological rather than genetic validity. Typological classifications have their legitimate uses provided it is made clear that they have no necessary historical implications. The distinction between genetic and typological classification rests on the criteria employed in classification, and here again there is a parallel between biology and linguistics. In the terminology of biology, we wish to distinguish between homologies, or similarities that are the outcome of true common descent, and analogies which result from convergence, generally through similarity of function, and which are irrelevant to genetic classification.

In language it is characteristically resemblances involving sound without meaning or meaning without sound that provide the basis for typological classifications. An example of the former is a classification of languages into tonal and non-tonal, in which all languages will fall into one class or the other regardless of the presence or absence of concrete sound-meaning resemblances. For example, the tone languages of West Africa, Southeast Asia and indigenous Mexico will fall into one typological class and even languages closely related to any of these will be in the other nontonal group if they differ in regard to the particular typological criterion employed. An example of a criterion of meaning without sound is the use of sex gender as a principle of language classification: in certain languages there are morphemes, that is sequences of sound, with the meaning "masculine" and "feminine," while in the nonsex gender languages they are absent.

The use of any such criteria for supposed genetic classification—and they continue to be widely employed in certain areas—requires the unstated assumption that certain features like the essential as opposed to the accidental attributes of the creationists are fixed and define the species or, in this instance, the language family. Thus when a writer on southeast Asia states that Annamite cannot belong to the Austroasiatic family of languages because it is tonal whereas the other recognized members of the family are not, he is assuming that a nontonal language can never evolve into a tonal one. If this statement were true, we would have two or more languages at the beginning and each would have one of its essential attributes tonality or nontonality and would be incapable of losing tonal structure if it possessed it or acquiring it if it did not. This is the precise analogue of the notion of fixed species.

What decides the case for real historical connection is the existence of resemblances in both sounding and meaning, such as exist between English and German in basic vocabulary and specific morphemes with grammatical function. Cognate forms are therefore the methodological equivalent of homologies in biology. Because of the arbitrariness of the relation between sound and meaning in language, in that any sequence of sounds is capable of any meaning, these provide a precise parallel to the nonadaptive character of biology.

It seems, at first blush, a much more important thing to say regarding a language that it is tonal or has gender than that the word for "nose" is *nase* and this perhaps accounts for the persistence of such criteria which, on the face of it, seem to involve more impressive resemblances. Darwin, in his discussion of the criteria of biological classification, notes likewise that it is not the functionally important characters that are significant for classification but rather an accumulation of apparently trivial nonadaptive details:

It might have been thought (and was in ancient times thought) that those parts of the structure which determined the habits of life and the general place of each being in the economy of nature would be of high importance in classification. Nothing could be more false.

Once it is realized that a classification based on gender or nongender is similar in principle to a biological classification into flying and nonflying animals and that a Semitic language which ceases to be triliteral does not cease to be a Semitic language by descent any more than a bat ceased to be a mammal when it began to fly, then typological classification can resume its legitimate place without giving rise to the confusions that have marked this type of endeavor in the past.

The distinction between the fact of evolution as specific change and the mechanism of survival of the fittest was pointed out in an earlier section of this paper. Darwin himself extended the parallel between language and biology in this instance also. The new linguistic forms that arise continually in any language community are likened to variations, only the fittest of which survive and become incorporated in the linguistic heritage. Again Lyell, in his elaborate comparison of languages to biological species, notes the spread of specific languages over wide areas followed by their later differentiation into separate languages and the extinction of the other languages spoken in these territories. This sequence of events resembles closely the biological processes of adaptive radiation and extinction of species. Natural selection as applied to language would then involve an intralinguistic struggle for survival among forms within the language and a battle among languages in which some spread and produce decendants while others perish.

Regarding the intralinguistic struggle, linguists would probably agree that many changes are functionally indifferent and that while certain changes make for greater efficiency there are likewise certain outcomes of normal linguistic processes of change, such as grammatical irregularities and semantic ambiguities, which are functionally negative. Taking linguistic change as a whole, there seems to be no discernible movement toward greater efficiency such as might be expected if in fact there were a continuous struggle in which superior linguistic innovations won out as a general rule.

Similarly, it can be seen that one language succeeds another, not because it is more advanced as a language, but for extra-linguistic reasons of military, economic or cultural superiority of its speakers. Nor has any people ever perished because of the inadequacy of its language. This is not to say that there are not important differences between languages that have been the object of literary cultivation and those that have not, or those which possess an extensive technical vocabulary and those lacking in this regard. However, such differences are but a reflection of nonlinguistic differences. They affect nothing basic in the language itself; any language is capable of literary elaboration or technical expansion if nonlinguistic circumstances encourage or require it.

Any attempt to show the existence of evolutionary advance in language development must rest on a typological basis. The linguistic typology prevalent in the nineteenth century which in its most common version involved a threefold classification into isolating, agglutinative and inflective is an instance of such a typology. For such a typological analysis to prove the existence of evolutionary advance in language requires, in addition to a methodologically valid typological procedure, the proof of two further premises. The first of these is that, when the types are arranged in some given order, it can be demonstrated or at least made probable that there was once a time in which all languages belonged to the most "primitive" of these types. Following this, there should be a stage in which the next most advanced type existed alongside survivals of the earliest type, and so on. This is similar to the requirement that for stone tools to be considered a more primitive stage of technology than metal tools we must demonstrate that there was once a period in which stone tools existed while metal tools had not yet made their appearance.

The other requirement is a proof that the criteria employed in distinguishing the typological classes are not irrelevant to the actual uses to which language is put so that the criteria for the more advanced types involve characteristics that can be shown in some manner to be adaptively superior to the criteria which distinguish languages lower on the scale of evolutionary advance.

The well-known nineteenth century typology alluded to above was in its most commonly accepted form considered by almost all of its adherents to be a typology of evolutionary advance. In fact, this typology failed on all three grounds mentioned. It was not a methodologically valid typology, since the criteria were never clearly stated in such a manner that they might be applied reliably to all languages. Further, there was no proof of the chronological sequence concerned and there was no proof that isolating languages, such as Chinese, were any less efficient in expressing thought than inflective languages such as Sanskrit.

Those who posit a number of stages in the development of thought and endow these stages with historical reality in addition to conceptual validity will generally seek support from the data furnished by language. That is, they will tend to see in language at once the reflection of varous stages of mental development and a kind of evidence in language, by this very fact, of the validity of their analogies. Implicit in all such attempts is a typology defining these stages and such a typology must satisfy the requirements discussed above. One example is the approach of Levy-Bruhl which in setting up two polar types of mentality, pre-logical and logical, uses evidence from language in support of this thesis. His attempts and those of similarly oriented writers have generally used linguistic evidence in such a fashion that virtually all linguists find them unconvincing. The issue is, however, of some significance because in certain other disciplines the naivete of such employment of linguistic evidence is not always realized.

From the discussion thus far it may seem that the positive contribution of Darwinism to linguistic science is minimal. Our results might be summarized as follows: The concept of evolution can be analyzed as involving two major but independent components. The first of those, the notion of transformation of kinds, is valid but was well established in linguistics prior to Darwin. The second component, that of progress or advance, is not valid in the instance of language and its application whether under the flag of Darwinism or under other influence has led to no positive results.

Yet one question remains—the origin of language itself in the evolutionary process—and it is precisely the success of Darwin's ideas in the biological science that makes this problem in the end unavoidable not only for linguistics, which it would appear chiefly to concern, but for the other sciences that deal with man as well. For, by any definition of emergence, language is a major instance of the appearance of something essentially new in the course of evolution, comparable in its significance only to such other basic emergents as life itself or intelligent behavior.

Darwin himself sought to bridge the gap by showing that human language is but a further elaboration of germs already found in animal behavior. Max Mueller, on the other hand, saw the difference as so great that he rested his argument against the possibility of human descent from other animals on the possession of language by man:

... it becomes our duty to warn the valiant disciples of Mr. Darwin that before they can claim a real victory, before they can call man the descendant of a mute animal, they must lay regular siege to a fortress which is not to be frightened into submission by a few random shots; the fortress of language, which as yet stands untaken and unshaken on the very frontier between the animal kingdom and man.

Today, presumably, no scientist would accept this as a refutation of the Darwin theory. We distinguish between the evidence for the truth of a fact and the theories designed to account for the fact. If the linguist cannot furnish a satisfactory theory of the origin of language, this does not invalidate the other evidence for the descent of man from forms of life that did not possess symbolic behavior. It rather poses a problem for the sciences dealing with man to explain how language could have arisen in the course of evolutionary development.

The fundamental role of language in making possible that accumulation of learned behavior which we call culture and which is the distinctively human mode of adjustment is appreciated by all anthropologists and social scientists in general. At the present time, however, it is probably more usual to phrase this difference between man and other species in terms of symbolic as distinct from merely sign behavior, with the understanding, no doubt, that language is by far the most important type of human symbolic behavior. It would seem, however, that this view of language as merely one, even if the most important kind of symbolic behavior, tends to obscure the particular and unique functions of linguistic compared to other types of human symboling. Among nonlinguistic human symbols we may distinguish first certain individual symbols. Some of those are found in every human community. An example is the sending of flowers at a wedding, which would be generally stated to have a symbolic significance. It is true that only human communities have symbols of this kind, but they are clearly isolated in that they do not fit into any system of multiple related symbols. A more elaborate instance of a nonlanguage symbol is a set of traffic lights since this is a system of several symbols, red, green, and, it may be, amber. However, in distinction to language, the number of messages is finite and, indeed, extremely small.

The subordinate status of such symbols in respect to language is of a more fundamental nature than their mere isolation or finiteness, for it is a subordinate status shared even with such elaborate and infinite systems as those of mathematics. Language has a unique role which results from its generality of reference and ontogenetic priority in the life history of the individual. For example, in descriptions of Navaho religion we learn that certain colors symbolize certain cardinal directions, i.e. black symbolizes north. We take this to be a direct explanation of the symbol, but in fact we have described it by another symbol, the Navaho word for "north." If we do not know what this means we may translate into English. The infinite regress of explaining symbols by other symbols must have a conclusion, the point at which understanding is reached. If this is itself a symbol system it is always some language, which is thus the ultimate level of explanation. If this also fails we must resort to nonsymbolic behavior such as pointing or the like. This even applies to such complex and elaborate systems as mathematics. We all learn some language before we learn mathematics and mathematics is ultimately explainable in ordinary language but not vice versa.

It is conceivable in certain instances that a nonlinguistic symbol might be learned without language actually being employed. Thus, by standing on a corner and noting the events associated with the different traffic signals an observer might discover the system involved. It is unlikely that the reasoning involved could be carried out before language was mastered. I do not believe that any fond parent of a pre-language child would risk the experiment. Even if such learning were pos-sible, it would still be true that such a system could not occur in a community without language and that verbal behavior figured indispensably in its invention, its establish-ment, and the diffusion of the necessary knowledge concerning it in the community. In other words, non-linguistic symbols always arise through some kind of concerted action and pre-arrangement which depends on lan-guage. To cite another illustrative example, the symbol system "one if by land and two if by sea," which functioned in connection with the ride of Paul Revere, was a pre-arrange-ment agreed on by means of language. The relevance of these considerations in the pres-ent connection is that since all other symbols have language as a precondition, the evolu-tionary problem of the origin of symbolic behavior resolves itself into the problem of the genesis of language. Once language exists, the conditions for the existence of the other kinds of symbols are fulfilled.

The question then, which will be consid-ered here in only a few of its numerous aspects, is the difference between sign be-havior, which is pre-linguistic intelligent be-havior, and linguistic behavior, which is behavior mediated by the symbol system we call language. We may define a sign, A, as a state of affairs that is evidence to an organ-ism of another state of affairs, B, not si-multaneously experienced but associated with it by temporal contiguity in the past. Then A is a sign of B, or we may say that A means B. In these terms, classical or instrumental conditioning is easily restated in the language of sign theory. In the instance of Pavlov's experiment, the bell (A) is a sign of food (B) to the dog. That this relation indeed holds is indicated to the observer by the organism's response of salivation to the conditioned stim-ulus. Thus salivation itself becomes a sign to the observer that the bell is a sign of food for the dog. In such cases, we may say that the bell as a sign has a meaning functionally equivalent to a sentence in language such as "food will be offered." Such a sign, which is equivalent to a sentence in language, may be called "complete."

The difference between sign and symbol is usually described in terms of the arbitrariness and conventionality of the latter. However, the connection between the bell and the food is conventional also and the two are without casual connection. For sign behavior all that is required is that the sign and thing signified should have been regularly associated in the previous experience of the organism. In many discussions of language learning, the symbolic counterpart of the sign is some single word, which is isolated from its context in a sentence and is therefore incomplete. The question is then raised how this word becomes associated with the thing it signifies. The paradigm is still that of sign learning and this is not disguised by the superficial difference that the physical sign vehicle is a sequence of articulate sounds. This is no doubt a stage in the human acquisition of language. In principle it would appear that animals are capable of such responses. It should also be obvious that the fact that a parrot speaks or responds to what to the human is a whole sentence does not make it any the less a single sign.

The difference between a symbol such as a sentence and a sign such as the bell of Pavlov's experiments is that the symbol analytically specifies the situation to which it refers. Particular parts of the sentence refer to particular aspects of the situation, whereas the bell is a unitary sign for an unanalyzed situation. The meaning of a sentence cannot be explained in every instance by past experience in which, like the bell, it has been associated with the state of affairs it describes. When we have mastered language, we can respond appropriately to a sentence we have never heard before and which cannot therefore have any association with our experience, or we can construct such a novel sentence.

How is this feat accomplished? The key, I believe, is the first postulate of Bloomfield's set, that in every speech community some utterances are partly alike both phonetically and semantically. For example, the utterances "Take the apple!" and "Take the banana!" are partly alike in sound and meaning. What is

different phonetically between the utterances refers to what is different about the two situations and what is the same refers to what is constant. If we now take the sentence "Drop the apple!" the contrast between this situation and the one correlated with "Take the apple!" confirms our analysis of "take." All this has doubtless been facilitated by experience during the period in which the child learns such words as "apple" and "banana" as isolates, not yet as parts of symbols, i.e., sentences. The evidence that analysis has taken place is the ability, having learned the three sentences, "Take the apple!" "Take the banana!" and "Drop the apple!" now to understand or reproduce the new sentence "Drop the banana!" without previous experience of it. It is this power that language possesses of analyzing experience and then combining the parts isolated by analysis into new syntheses that enables us to talk of past and remote future experience, to entertain hypotheses, tell lies and talk grammatical nonsense. Initially, however, there must have been coordination between linguistic and nonlinguistic events in the experience of the learner. Let us imagine a community of schizophrenics each continually verbalizing in detached fragments having no reference to the immediate situation, with no internal sequential connections nor with connections to what others are saying! Then it is obvious that even the most talented observer unacquainted with this language could never acquire it by considering the linguistic behavior of its speakers.

The rules by which novel utterances are understood or constructed involve an analysis into classes of words and smaller meaningful units, rules of combination and rules of semantic interpretation. This analysis is what is called grammar. The ability to carry out grammatical analysis would then seem to be one of the things that distinguishes man from other animals. It involves what for want of a more suitable term might be called "multiple abstraction." At the same time that the learner abstracts one element from its context and associates it with some aspect of the situation, he is likewise analyzing other parts of the utterance in similar fashion. We might therefore call language a 3-ring, or more accurately an *n*-ring abstraction circus since there is no upper limit to the length of sentences. To carry all this out, man must moreover compare what is in his immediate experience with past sentences and the situations associated with them.

It would seem then that, as might have been anticipated, language does involve a new skill of which other animals are incapable. Yet, this skill can still be understood as a stage that depends on the sign skills occurring in pre-language behavior. It is hoped that the present analysis of the basic essentials of symbolic behavior, while it renders full justice to the status of language as an evolutionary emergent, may also serve to make this emergence appear understandable so that, even as Darwin believed, no conceptually unbridgeable gap separates man from his nonhuman ancestors.

3. CULTURE AS ADAPTATION

YEHUDI A. COHEN

Yehudi A. Cohen is Professor of Anthropology, Livingston College, Rutgers University. He has conducted field work in Jamaica, Okinawa, and Israel. His principal interests are political anthropology, cultural evolution, culture and personality, religion, and cross-cultural research. He is the author of The Transition from Childhood to Adolescence *and* Social Structure and Personality: A Casebook. *He was the 1955 recipient of the Socio-Psychological Award of the American Association for the Advancement of Science.*

■ Culture is understandable as an abstraction that is known through its manifestations. In Geertz's terms, it is a set of symbolizations by which man's mind is shaped. But it can also be conceptualized more concretely, and this is the point of view of Selection 3, which regards culture as man's most important instrument of adaptation—that is, as an extension of his physiology and as an artificial instrument for maintaining a viable relationship with human habitats. Culture is part of man, and man can have no existence without it. Man creates it, uses it, and is affected by it. Culture has largely replaced the mechanisms of natural selection and genetic mutation as the instrument by which life is maintained in the milieus that man seeks to exploit. Moreover, culture changes, and with every change in a group's culture the people in the group undergo modifications in their psychological makeups and social relations in order to make use of the new form of culture.

The following essay, which was prepared for this volume and has not appeared elsewhere, has been revised for this edition; it is intended to serve as an introduction to the organization of the remaining parts of this book. My emphasis in this selection is on man's attempts to achieve increasing freedom from the limitations of his habitats through his adaptations. Although the advantages of this for the species are readily apparent, it is necessary to point out that adaptation is not necessarily synonymous with advantages for all of the members of a group; distinct disadvantages accrue to some members of a group with every advance in adaptation. These drawbacks are not unimportant but they will largely be overlooked in the attempt to conceptualize the evolution of culture in terms of adaptation.

Among the important works that underlie the study of cultural adaptation are Karl Marx's *Capital* (New York: E. P. Dutton, 1951-57); Friedrich Engel's *The Origin of the Family, Private Property, and the State;* Herbert Spencer's *Principles of Sociology* (New York: Appleton, 1923-25); and more recent works: *The Evolution of Urban Society,* by Robert McC. Adams (Chicago: Aldine, 1966); *Peasants,* by Eric R. Wolf (Englewood Cliffs, N.J.: Prentice-Hall, 1966); "The Origins of New World Civilization," by Richard S. MacNeish *(Scientific American* [November 1964], 211 [5]: 29-37); *Oriental Despotism,* by Karl Wittfogel (New Haven: Yale University Press, 1957) (in my opinion effectively rebutted by Adams); *Trade and Market in the Early Empires,* edited by Karl Polanyi, Conrad Arensberg, and Harry Pearson (New York: The Free Press, 1957); *Dahomey and the Slave Trade,* by Karl Polanyi (Seattle: University of Washington Press, 1966); and *Courses Toward Urban Life,* edited by Gordon R. Willey and Robert J. Braidwood (Chicago: Aldine, 1962). In *The Dynamics of Modernization* (New York: Harper and Row, 1966), C. E. Black seeks to show that accretions in knowledge, science, and technology have been some of the most important factors in the modernization of contemporary nations. Although his argument is slightly overdrawn, his book should be consulted by those who are interested in contemporary sociopolitical developments. ■

INTRODUCTION

IN THIS PAPER I SEEK to conceptualize culture in terms of adaptation and to understand the processes of culture change from an evolutionary perspective. My point of departure is the observation that human existence has been characterized by a succession of levels of adaptation. Each level is distinct and can be thought of as a particular way of life; each provides man with different capacities for "doing his job in nature." These capacities are social as well as technological.

Adaptation in man is the process by which he makes effective use for productive ends of the energy potential in his habitat. The most elementary source of energy, at least as far as man is concerned, is muscular. Reliance on this source—in the use of bows, spears, bludgeons, hoes, and digging sticks—is basic to the food quest in many human societies and has immediate consequences for the organization of social relations. We may contrast muscular energy with sources of extrapersonal energy such as draft animals (used for drawing plows), water (for irrigation or transportation), chemicals, steam, and electricity. Whenever people introduce a new energy system into their habitat their organizations of social relations—that is, their institutions—also change, so that the latter will be appropriate to the exploitation and efficient use of the energy source on which they rely.

An important factor in the organization of social relations of different societies is the extent to which extrapersonal energy replaces muscular energy. Thus far in cultural evolution, extrapersonal energy has not entirely displaced muscular energy. The use of a plow requires muscular energy, though less than a hoe or digging stick. Similarly, the control of production by electronic means in contemporary industrial society has not eliminated all muscular energy.

Every culture is a special case of the adaptive process in general and of a particular level of adaptation; every culture is a special case of the complex ways in which people make effective use of their energy potentials. Thus a culture must first be defined in terms of specific sources of energy and their social correlates. Every culture can be conceptualized as a strategy of adaptation, and each represents a unique social design for extracting energy from the habitat. Every strategy of adaptation requires appropriate organizations of social relations; no energy system can be effective in human society without groups that are designed for using it. A very simple example will illustrate the point.

Factory work, in which exclusive reliance is placed on, say, electrical energy and that is devoted to the manufacture of a product to be sold for a profit, requires a very special type of personnel organization. The personnel recruited for the factory's tasks should be evaluated in terms of their abilities to do their respective jobs, not in terms of their relationship by blood or marriage to each other or to the factory manager. The labor force of the factory should, ideally, be composed only of the number of people necessary to produce the product, maintain the plant, acquire raw materials, and ship and sell the finished product. Such an organization could not function effectively or for very long if the people in it were recruited only because they were relatives of the owner.

A culture includes a technology and the institutions appropriate to that technology. It can be defined as the artifacts, institutions, ideologies, and the total range of customary behaviors with which a society is equipped for the exploitation of the energy potentials of its particular habitat.

ADAPTATION AND FREEDOM FROM HABITATIONAL LIMITATIONS

The concept of adaptation—the key mechanism in the evolutionary process—was originally developed in the study of biological evolution. In discussions of the relationship of organisms to their habitats, the term *adaptation* refers to success, measured by the ability of populations to survive and reproduce. Thus a population of organisms is considered to have achieved an effective relationship with a habitat—to be adapted to that habitat —if it has been able to perpetuate its form of life. Evolution occurs because no adaptation is permanent because no habitat remains unchanged. New adaptations must be developed if effective relationships with altered habitational conditions are to be maintained.

Similarly, adaptation in man refers to fitness for reproduction and survival. However, adaptation in man does not take place through genetic mutation but, rather, through man's ability to make use of energy potentials in the physical habitat. In the record of successive strategies of cultural evolution each level of adaptation refers to a quantitative increase in the ability to sustain and perpetuate life. At each successive stage of cultural evolution man is better adapted for the survival of his group—that is, the survival of his adaptive unit—and, in turn, of the species as a whole.

The record of human evolution also suggests that man's cultural adaptations have increasingly freed him from the limitations of his habitats. He has accomplished this by harnessing increasingly effective sources of energy and by shaping his institutions to meet the demands of each energy system so that he can make maximum use of it.

In the study of adaptation, the key variables are people's harnessed energy systems, not only (or necessarily) the amount of food and other goods available to them. For example, some hunter-gatherers (like the !Kung Bushmen [Selection 4] and the Mbuti) enjoy a greater abundance of food than their horticulturist neighbors; we nevertheless speak of the latter as representing a higher level of development because horticulture is a strategy based on more efficient energy systems. Hence we are going to speak of levels of technological development, each successive level representing a strategy of cultural adaptation in which there are more efficient means of exploiting the energy resources available to a group. The concept of levels of technological development and adaptation refers not only to techniques but also to the configurations of institutions and social relations that are appropriate to the effective use of each particular energy system, so that we will speak more generally of "sociotechnological levels."

Several elements can be evaluated in determining the degree in which freedom from habitational limitations has been achieved by a particular group. One such element is the nature of the diet over an annual period. An abrupt shift in diet from one season to another, as occurs in many hunting-gathering groups, connotes close control over people's lives by the vicissitudes of the habitat. In contrast, the ability of the members of a society to subsist on essentially the same diet during the entire year, regardless of seasonal variations and the exigencies of different milieus, points to a high degree of freedom. Perhaps one of man's greatest achievements is that he can eat fresh strawberries for dessert at Christmas dinner while a blizzard rages outside.

A second element is the proportion of people who must engage in the food quest. At lower levels of technological development —particularly, among hunter-gatherers, horticulturists, and pastoralists—every man and usually every woman must be a producer. In societies at later stages, such as those relying on plow agriculture, food production becomes an occupational specialization, fewer and fewer people producing food for more and more people engaged in nonfood-producing activities. In modern industrial farming, each farmer produces enough food to feed about 45 people; for instance, there are now only about 4½ million farmers and farm managers in the United States.

People do not work less hard or fewer hours per year as a result of technological advance. Actually, the contrary is true. In an analysis of energy inputs and outputs, Marvin Harris found (*Culture, Man, and Nature,* New York: Crowell, 1971) that the annual average number of hours worked by food producers from hunting-gathering to industrial levels has steadily increased. For example, and again to take only extremes, a !Kung Bushman works about 810 hours a year compared to the average wage-earner's 1,714 hours in the contemporary United States (and the latter figure may be an underestimate). While this is a neat empirical demolition of the myth of our leisurely society —notice how much less time homemakers seem to have with the introduction of each labor-saving device—it must also be remembered, as Harris observes, that the returns are greater with each increase in amount of effort expended. The !Kung get an average of 9.6 calories for each calorie expended in working effort; in the contemporary United States, the average ratio is 210 to 1.

A third element is the ability of the members of a group to make substitutions in their diet. Freedom from the limitations of the habitat is minimal among hunter-gatherers because drought, flood, or pestilence (in addition to human predation) can destroy their entire food supply. If a natural catastrophe destroys the wild tubers and fruit on which they subsist or if the small animals they hunt are wiped out or do not follow their normal migratory patterns, few substitutions can be made. At the other extreme of sociocultural evolution, if a natural catastrophe wiped out the herds of cattle and the hogs that make up a large part of the diet of a contemporary industrial society, many dietary substitutions could be made, with little (if any) effect on the quality of the diet or on the ongoing institutions of society.

Fourth, a direct correspondence exists between reliance on domesticates (instead of wild-ranging animals and wild-growing foods) and people's freedom from the limitations of their habitats. As will be seen when we turn to the cultures of cultivators, the proportion of domesticates in the total diet has important social consequences. One of the most significant features of industrial man's freedom from habitational limitations is that wild-ranging and wild-growing foods and animals are important only as luxury items and objects of sport, because domesticated plants and animals make up almost his entire diet.

A fifth element is knowledge about cause and effect in nature. Sometimes the simplest insights can produce radical transformations in man's relationship to the food-producing milieu and, as a result, in his institutional organizations. For example, both the Washo Indians of western Nevada (in the area of Lake Tahoe) and the Kwakiutl of the northwest coast of North America relied heavily on fishing for their subsistence. The Kwakiutl had a fairly complex social organization (by foraging standards) that involved relatively dense and permanent settlements, stratification, and chieftainship (see Selection 6). The Washo were characterized by a very simple social system based on small bands that split up and recombined seasonally. (A concise description of the Washo is provided by James Downs in *The Two Worlds of the Washo,* New York: Holt, Rinehart and Winston, 1966.) One of the noteworthy differences between the two groups is that the Kwakiutl learned how to preserve fish, but the Washo never stumbled onto this important bit of knowledge. Hence, the Kwakiutl were able to amass huge surpluses of fish on which they subsisted for a large portion of the year after the fishing season had ended. Unlike the Washo, they did not have to disperse into small bands in search of other wild foods, and they were able to supplement their fish diet with animals and plants.

Sixth, the greater the mastery over nature the smaller is the element of fortuitousness in social life. The adaptive importance of modern man's supermarkets is in the certainty that when he walks into such an establishment he will find all the food that is regarded as necessary for the maintenance of a consistent diet throughout the year. In contrast, one of the indexes of the relatively low level of adaptation of hunter-gatherers is that fortuitousness plays a dominant role in the organization of their social relations. If the migratory small animals on which they subsist are absent during the normal hunting season or if wild-growing plants are in short supply, their territory will be uninhabitable because it cannot sustain life. If large numbers of animals should be available, a drive can be organized under the direction of a chief (whose authority is temporary and is not recognized in any other situation). If there are not enough animals for such a large social undertaking, a drive is not possible, and not even a temporary chieftainship can emerge.

Fortuitousness in the food-producing milieu also gives rise to fortuitousness in interfamilial social relations in many hunting and gathering societies. Relationships are not haphazard, but the frequency with which families can unite into larger groups is largely controlled by habitational exigencies. As mastery over nature increases, the food supply becomes more certain and, correspondingly, interfamilial social relationships become more stable and predictable.

A seventh index of man's success in freeing himself from the limitations of his habitats is his increasing freedom from seasonal variation in his cultural behavior. In many primitive societies, especially among hunter-gatherers and low-level cultivators, "seasonal cultures" are apparent. We can observe an annual cycle of winter and summer cultures with entirely different organizations of social relations prevailing during each period. Core institutions, such as those intended to maintain order and stability, are suspended at the end of a six-month period and replaced by entirely different sets of institutions, even though the personnel may be the same. Although seasonal cultures are most obvious in societies at the lowest levels of technological development, they are sometimes found among more advanced cultivators, as in thirteenth-century England (see Selection 31). I am told by friends who have lived among agriculturists of the American Ozark region that this area also is characterized by the seasonal suspension of some of its important institutional configurations.

Seasonal cultural variations are matters of degree; they are not all-or-nothing swings in the cultural pendulum, and it cannot be said simply that groups are or are not characterized by a seasonal culture. The greater the mastery over the food-producing resources in the habitat, the more its people will tend toward a year-round or annual culture. (The brief cessations of work that occur on sabbaths and vacations in technologically advanced societies are not to be equated with the seasonal suspension of institutions in simpler societies.) The weaker the mastery over the milieu—that is, the more a group governed by natural seasonal cycles—the greater the tendency of a group's culture to vary seasonally.

Why is there a strong correspondence between lower levels of sociotechnological adaptation and seasonal cultural variations?

Why does the evolutionary record give strong evidence supporting the hypothesis that advancing technology tends to give rise to year-round cultural patterns? One reason, of course, is that the adaptive splitting up of groups in hunting-gathering societies holds down population pressure on available resources. Because an institution is a group of persons whose activities are designed to meet particular ends, the recurrent dispersal and congregation of groups makes it impossible for them to participate in the same activities throughout the year.

However, seasonal fragmentation of groups cannot tell the entire story. There are cultivator groups, like the Cherokee Indians and thirteenth-century Englishmen, that do not fragment seasonally and cyclically but nevertheless display seasonal-cultural variations. For these, a purely physical explanation seems to be insufficient, and fuller explanation is to be sought at an entirely different level of analysis, namely, in the relationship between modes of thought (which are often referred to as "cognitive orientations") and levels of technological development.

I suggest that people whose technology makes their food consumption directly dependent on the cycles of nature—those whose acquisition of food depends on the cycles of plant and animal activity and on the seasonality of rainfall and temperature—follow the rhythm of nature in their ways of thinking about the world as well as in their physical activities and the organization of their social relations. One of the reasons why modern industrial man can conceive of maintaining his institutions without interruption throughout the year is that his relations with the habitat have become increasingly free of seasonal cyclicality and variation. As they work and eat, so do people think and live. It is not possible to appreciate contemporary industrial social systems without bearing in mind that people may eat exactly the same breakfast and lunch 365 times a year (although they may rebel at the thought of having the same dinner so often).

Geertz questions this [handwritten marginal note]

THE DYNAMICS OF CULTURAL EVOLUTION AND THE UNIT OF ADAPTATION

I have stressed that the total record of human evolution suggests that from his beginnings, man has sought to free himself from the restrictions and limitations of his habitat. This is the mainspring of cultural evolution, most of which has occurred during less than one per cent of human history. However, it must be borne in mind that although people may welcome technological innovations that provide them with increasing mastery over their habitat, they tend to resist the necessary accompanying changes in their organizations of social relations. It is in the social sphere that people tend to exhibit their greatest conservatism, and this is one of the reasons that cultural evolution seems to have been a slow process.

There are three other sources of cultural evolution, in addition to technological innovations: contact between groups and the resulting dissemination of information and techniques, population growth, and political innovations (especially the development of centralized states). None of these is distinctive; all of them tend to occur simultaneously. This is especially true of the relationship between population growth and political development, as Carneiro makes clear in Selection 27. However, population size and political development are themselves dependent on other factors, such as the level of technological development and (as Carneiro stresses) habitational considerations.

Every major technological advance in the course of cultural evolution—cultivation by means of a digging stick or hoe, plowing, terracing, large-scale centralized irrigation, domestication of large herds of animals, machines driven by steam or electricity—was discovered independently in a few places, but spread from its center of development to neighboring groups. This spread of technology continued until it was halted by a natural barrier—an ocean, mountains, a desert, or a habitat in which the new system of produc-

tion was useless. Simple examples are the barriers presented by an arctic region to the spread of cultivation techniques or by a hinterland to the spread of an ocean-fishing technology.

Anthropologists generally refer to the spread of cultural elements from one group to another as "diffusion" and "borrowing." These terms are used not only to refer to the spread of material elements of culture but also to the spread of all other aspects of culture. Perhaps 80 percent or more of the elements in any culture may have been borrowed from others. Thus human groups add to their stores of knowledge and productive techniques not only by themselves but, more importantly, by contact with other groups.

The borrowing and transmission of cultural elements between groups is an integral feature of culture. All groups (with the possible exception of the Eskimo and the Australian aborigines) have been in contact with other groups throughout their histories. Sometimes groups were in direct contact even though they were separated by thousands of miles and all travel was by foot or by canoe (a fact that is often forgotten by people who have become accustomed to travel by car, train, or airplane). In premodern times such contact was always personal; individuals from different groups introduced each other to new ways. In modern times diffusion often is impersonal—by radio, television, films, books, and newspapers—and these media have accelerated the rate at which culture diffuses. Later in this book we will see that contact between groups is not always so peaceful as these examples suggest; often, an entire way of life is changed as a result of conquest by an alien and stronger society.

Largely because of the inevitability of diffusion and borrowing most societies in a common geographical area are at approximately the same level of cultural development. This is not always the case, however, as the contiguity of cultivators and herders or the !Kung Bushman and their cultivator neighbors attests. Sometimes neighboring groups display different levels of adaptation because their respective habitats will not accommodate each other's technology; this often appears to be the case with neighboring herders and cultivators. In other instances, traditionalism or animosity between neighboring groups can raise barriers to diffusion and borrowing. As Oliver demonstrates in Selection 20, important cultural differences between neighboring groups at the same level of adaptation may result from their different historical backgrounds.

Cultural borrowing does not occur at random or fortuitously. The adoption of a new technology, ceremonial pattern or religion, legal system, or mode of etiquette reflects a decision (usually implicit rather than explicit) that people cannot treat lightly or allow to happen without direction. Chaos would result if every new technique, idea, or custom was adopted by a group every time someone learned about it or independently discovered it. Order, regularity, and stability are the hallmarks of social life, and they must govern the introduction and adoption of new cultural elements. Hence, cultural evolution requires decision-making and decision-implementing within the group, viewed as a unit of adaptation.

The intimate relationship between a level of exploitation of the habitat, and the behavior appropriate to that level rests on the apparent purpose of life itself: to sustain and perpetuate life. Man's foremost concern, like that of any other animal, is to secure enough food from his habitat—enough for individual survival and for the reproduction of the group. In every society mature adults spend more time and energy in the acquisition and preparation of food than in any other single activity. It therefore is in no way surprising that productive activities occupy a position of primacy in human institutions and modes of thought. People must organize their social relationships and activities and even their thought processes in ways that will make their productive activities effective; otherwise their societies will not survive.

A hunter hunts not only with bow and arrow or rifle; he must also organize his social relations with his fellow hunters so that he can effectively find, stalk, and kill his prey. His kill must then be prepared and be divided among his dependents. He must have additional sources of food for safety and for adequacy of diet, and for this purpose there must be a division of labor in his society ensuring that his women will collect berries, tubers, and nuts. Similarly, a factory worker works not only at a machine. His productive activities are organized around networks of other people who make certain that his tools and other resources are available when they are needed, who pay him his wages, and who produce and make available food into which his wages can be converted. All of this involves a particular type of family organization as well as a complex merchandising system.

The importance to the rest of the culture of the organization of productive activities is repeatedly underscored by the findings of modern archeological and ethnological research: The adoption of a new source of energy by a society is invariably followed by changes in the institutional configurations of its culture. The reason for this can be clearly and simple exemplified. The average adult man is capable of exerting energy that is equal to about one-tenth of a unit of horsepower; hence a man who relies only on his own physical energy is restricted to a very low level of output. The division of labor in a society of men at this technological level must be relatively simple and unelaborated, and there is no centralized control over production because everyone is equal as a producer. Correlatively, in such a society there is no centralized control over the distribution of food and other commodities.

As the people in a society begin to use increasingly efficient extrapersonal sources of energy—animals, water power, steam, electricity, and other fuels—they develop specializations in the division of labor. These specializations inevitably lead to the establishment of a hierachy in productive activities: For reasons to be discussed, a few men assume positions of dominance in organizing and supervising the activities of those who do the bulk of the manual work. A corollary of the development of centralized control over productive activities is an increasing centralization of control over distribution.

Because all productive activities in all societies at all levels of adaptation take place in groups, in an organized, systematic, and predictable manner, all of these activities rest on decisions that must be made about the allocation, use, and distribution of energy. Men do not simply go out to hunt, plant, tend animals, construct terraces or irrigation networks, build factories or work in them as if they were a random agglomeration of Robinson Crusoes. Each of these activities, as well as the distribution of the resultant wealth, requires that decisions be made regularly about what directions men will take to hunt animals, how land will be allocated, which plots of land will be opened to cultivation, where animals will be driven for grass and water, where terraces or irrigation networks will be built, and where factories will be erected and how they will have access to sources of power. Similarly, decisions have to be made about who will engage in each of these activities (about how labor will be divided, allocated, and organized) and about the distribution of income (about the criteria according to which each person, family, and household will be awarded a share in the social product).

Thus decision-making and implementation are central features of every adaptation, of every strategy for exploiting the energy potentials of a particular habitat. Obviously, people are not always fully aware that they are making and implementing decisions, nor are they aware of the mechanisms by which they do so, any more than people are fully aware of the rules of grammar that govern their languages. Nevertheless, no significant change can occur in a culture, neither in its technology nor in its institutions or ideologies, without an accumulation of decisions (conscious or unconscious, deliberate or inadvertent) that permits its adoption.

In the evolution of human culture, therefore, we shall consider the unit of adaptation to be the largest and most inclusive group that makes and implements decisions with respect to the exploitation of energy potentials in the habitat. Thus, among nomadic hunter-gatherers, the band (or camp) is usually the unit of adaptation. Among some cultivators, it is a small, local group of kinsmen, and among other cultivators it is the community (territorially conceived). Among some pastoralists (herders of domesticated animals), it is the tribe or tribal segment, and among others it is a kin group that is a component of the tribe. Among industrial workers and some advanced cultivators (such as plow-agriculturists or those who rely on centralized irrigation networks), it is the nation-state. As man advances toward a single worldwide community, the species as a whole—through the political representation of the world community, as in the United Nations or a more effective successor—will have to be regarded as the adaptive, the decision-making, and the implementing unit.

Each level of adaptation has an appropriate organization of decision-making and implementing institutions. Whenever man changes his environment by harnessing and introducing a new source of energy, he alters these institutions. This complex set of events provides focal constancy for our understanding of the evolution of human culture, conceptualized as successive strategies of adaptation.

As societies change in their adaptive level, different individuals and groups in the adaptive unit stand in new relationships to the process of decision-making. One of the features of the evolution of social organization is that at each successive level the individual participates in a larger group (band, lineage, community, tribe, nation, civilization, world community) in which the decision-making centers are more and more distant from him. In some societies, such as those with peasant classes, an individual responds to units that are very close to him (such as the local community) and to those that are very distant (such as the central state); in such cases, each group tends to regulate different aspects of life. (This is discussed more fully in the section on centralized cultivators.) One of the consequences of the succession of levels of adaptation is that the individual has decreasing access to the decision-making and implementing mechanisms of his society.

POLITICAL INSTITUTIONS AND TECHNOLOGICAL DEVELOPMENT

We have focused on two of the variables that underlie human strategies of adaptation: technology and habitat. To round out this picture, we must consider the third: political organization. This will complete the foundation for a taxonomy of successive strategies, in which the most general distinction is between stateless and state societies.

The adoption of an evolutionary perspective in the study of adaptation requires a clear-cut set of hypotheses about priorities in change. Do some aspects of culture necessarily depend on prior change in other aspects? Are there changes that automatically set others into motion? Anthropologists who reject an evolutionary point of view tend to give negative answers to these questions; similarly, a denial of priorities in cultural change necessarily leads to the abandonment of an evolutionary point of view. The difficulties of "chicken and egg" propositions have plagued students of history and society in their attempts to untangle the skein of social change. Is change in the institutional structure of society always the result of technological change? Does the sequence of events always go in that direction, or is it possible for institutional change to give rise to technological change? Can the nontechnological institutions of leadership, authority, and decision-making underlie a society's adaptations by stimulating technological change? These are among the central questions in modern anthropology, which we are far from having answered definitely. Nevertheless some tentative answers and lines of inquiry can be provided. Once we accept the axiom that necessary priorities in social change exist, our attempts to organize the record of human evolution leads to a consideration of the re-

lationship between political organization and technological development. The two are inseparable.

Institutionalized leadership, police, and legislative or administrative offices are not necessary for a society to carry on political activities. Many societies at different stages of evolutionary development have political activities that take place in the absence of institutions, which are among man's responses to social complexity, to population density, urbanization, impersonality in social relationships, and the like.

For brevity and purposes of illustration I will distinguish between "stateless societies" and "state societies" in discussing whether nontechnological forces can be the source of societal adaptation. A stateless society is one in which the checks, balances, and controls over behavior that are prerequisite to social life are exercised through local institutions at the community level, without the intervention of supracommunity centers of authority. Local autonomy is the key factor in the maintenance of order and conformity and in the resolution of disputes; the locus of this autonomy may be in the corporate kin group where emphasis is on the rules of kinship relationships, in the community territorially conceived, or in sodalities that cross-cut the two. Local autonomy is expressed in many ways in a stateless society: in economic self-sufficiency, self-protection (including the right to feud and to wage war), the administration of land tenure, and the application of juridical controls.

The concept of the state is inseparable from that of the nation. A nation is a society occupying a limited territory, made up of many subgroups—communities and regions, classes and sometimes castes, ethnic and sometimes linguistic groups, economic and other specialized groups, a diversity of daily cycles and life styles—all of which are centrally controlled in some measure by a set of interlocking agencies or bureaucracies that are themselves more or less differentiated. These agencies constitute the state. They are under a single person—President of the United States, Chairman of the People's Republic of China, England's monarch—who is the empirical representation of the state. This person is not necessarily the one with the greatest individual power; nor is he or she concerned with day-to-day control of the society, which is in the hands of the agencies that constitute the state. In these terms, "nation" is the territorial representation of the society, and "state" is its political representation. Thus nation-states are always and by definition more complex than stateless societies.

There are several types of states and stateless societies, and I do not want to suggest that a simple dichotomy between the two reflects political realities in human society; the different types have to be carefully distinguished in empirical research. However, I am adopting this artificial polarization of political organization for heuristic purposes, to illustrate various processes in the technological and economic spheres of society. If I wished to analyze processes in political organization, such a dichotomy would be meaningless.

Societies characterized by state organizations do not represent a distinct level of technological development. Hunting-gathering is known only among stateless societies, and industrialization is associated exclusively with nation-states. With these exceptions, there is no direct or necessary relationship between the degree of political integration achieved in a society and its level of technological development.

Nevertheless, the distinction between stateless and state societies can only be appreciated in terms of the principle that technology is the fulcrum of adaptation in stateless societies, in which there is no central political organization that unites local groups (villages, kin groups, and regions) under a single ruler. In nation-states, however, adaptation is underlain by political institutions. In stateless societies the quest for food is the overriding force in social organization, and almost all of their institutions are geared to the demands of the technology. This is made evident by the ethnographic data for hunter-gatherers and stateless cultivators and pas-

toralists. In these societies, each local group is autonomous in decision-making and implementation in all spheres of production and consumption. Limitations on the amount of food produced are established by considerations of personal energy, technology, ecology (for example, rainfall, fertility of the soil, migrations of fish), and need; a family in a stateless society will produce as much food as it needs within the limits imposed by the amount of manpower, the nature of available exploitative energy, and the physical habitat. Such a group may well seek to produce a surplus, but only against an increase in the numbers of persons who have to be fed or the loss or incapacitation of productive members of the group. People in such societies do not produce a surplus for a distant political authority—a superordinate king, nobility, or temple.

Even in relatively complex stateless societies such as chiefdoms, the source of economic and political authority is local, and no superordinate or centralizing organization exists. A chiefdom can be characterized as a society in which many centers coordinate their own social, political, and religious life independently; it has centralized leadership, but integration takes place within each separate nucleus, not within the society as a whole. Each nucleus splits recurrently, usually every generation, and the people strongly resist all attempts to unify the entire society under a single leadership. Similarly, economic activity is coordinated in each nucleus and there is socioeconomic specialization, but chiefdoms lack the institutions that bind the entire society into a permanent socioeconomic entity. Each neighboring chiefdom is autonomous and refuses to recognize the political and economic authority of any larger organization. Chiefdoms do not have legalized force to back up the demands of local chiefs for tribute, a large proportion of which is redistributed to the populace at large. Chiefdoms probably represent a transitional stage between stateless and state societies. The best known society organized into chiefdoms is that of the Trobriand Islanders and the Nyakyusa of Tanzania.

Distribution, like production, is locally regulated in stateless societies. The flow of goods is controlled exclusively by local institutions: kinship, friendship, neighborliness, and the like. No distant political or controlling economic authority requires regular payments of taxes or other forms of tribute. Nor does any distant authority regulate the distribution to a local cultivator of seed, implements, draft animals, and other sources of exploitative energy. Also there is no central agency to control and regulate marketing, exchange, or barter within the society as a whole or with other societies; instead, exchange is made in face-to-face relationships.

But the sequence of priorities in adaptation is reversed in societies that are integrated into nation states. Adaptation in such societies can best be understood if technological advance is seen as a product of—or at least as stimulated by—the political institutions that unify the society into a single entity. This must be qualified, of course, by the observation that nation-states can only develop among people who have the potential for producing surpluses and for making the technological advances that state systems precipitate. These potentials are to be sought not only in a group's technology but also in its habitat. For example, hunter-gatherers and cultivators who continue to rely on wild foods and animals do not have the technological and social means for the creation of state systems, nor could such systems develop in the arctic, in the barren regions of Nevada and California, or in the South African desert.

A state organization creates a new environment, one that is unknown in stateless societies, and the development of state organization is a watershed in cultural evolution. It is one of the achievements that has increased man's freedom from the restrictions of his habitat, because it makes possible the harnessing of more efficient sources of energy. The goals of a state organization are not only to centralize decision-making and implementation but also to exploit physical energy potentials in the service of the society as a whole. One of the characteristics of states is that they employ rational and future-oriented planning in decision-making and implementation in almost all spheres of social organization—the harnessing of energy systems, the advance and control of technology, economic policies, and the rest. This can be seen most clearly in state-sponsored construction of large-scale irrigation networks, in long-range trade, and in economic advance in the face of poverty of natural resources (as in modern Japan and Israel).

State systems are linked to technological advances and social policies that have profound repercussions for the organization of social relations throughout the society. Once established—usually by force—the state becomes the most important group in the society. Those who speak in its name are the only ones who are in constant touch with all the other groups in the nation. As a result, the state becomes the most significant element in the habitat to which people in local groups must adapt. States are constantly issuing orders, formulating new policies, embarking on and stimulating new economic ventures, exploiting and harnessing new sources of energy, entering into different kinds of relations with different nations. Each of these has consequences at every level of the society, and these consequences increase geometrically because the state has to respond in turn to the changes that it has produced at local levels and thus produces still other changes. The results affect family and household organization, sexual standards, education, production and trade, religion, architecture and art, law, recreation, and almost every other aspect of human activity. This feedback relationship is described for Japan by Befu in Selection 28.

State organizations do not give rise to identical cultural patterns in all societies or even in a continuing society at different historical periods. For example, ancient Egypt was characterized by very different cultural patterns during the Middle and the New Kingdoms even though both were based on large-scale irrigation networks, trade, military activities, and elaborate systems of social stratification. Among the many factors that underlay the reorganization of cultural elements between the New Kingdom and the Middle Kingdom were changes in values among the nobility as a result of greater concentration of wealth in their hands. Changes in foreign policy and fluctuations of fortune in international affairs also played important parts in changing patterns of life within the level of adaptation achieved by ancient Egypt.

Let us take an example that is closer to home. American society achieved an industrial level of adaptation within the first two decades of the twentieth century, but significant changes in the culture at this level have resulted from successive realignments of its elements: American society of the 1970s is very different from that of the 1930s. Without trying to understand all the reasons for these differences within the society's basic adaptation, we need only consider the impact on the society of changes in the media of mass communication, in transportation, in the diffusion of formal education to larger segments of the population, and in the registration of social and political dissent. (Each of these, incidentally, is either stimulated or controlled by the central government.) The similarities between the two periods can be attributed largely to the constancy of the level of adaptation, though we now seem to be moving into a post-industrial stage of adaptation; the differences can be understood, in part, in terms of new relationships among cultural elements.

Statelessness does not refer only to the absence of a set of unifying political institutions in a society; it constitutes a set of limiting conditions for technological advance because there is no stimulus for the production of gross deployable surpluses in such societies. States, however, encourage the harnessing of more efficient extrapersonal sources of energy in the interest of the production of surpluses, largely for the benefit of the ruling classes. The political institutions of a state embody only the potentials for such technological advance and do not guarantee that it will occur, but technological advance is always severely limited in the absence of a unifying state.

The history of irrigation perhaps provides the clearest and best-known example of the harnessing of extrapersonal sources of energy by states. Although many stateless cultivators use irrigation ditches, the ditches are always small in scale, and each cultivator digs and maintains his own. Moreover, the ditches are not tied to a system of centralized political controls. By contrast, large-scale irrigation networks or centrally regulated viaducts represent a qualitatively different adaptation because they provide a measure of freedom from ecological pressures (such as localized droughts or flooding) that is not afforded by localized or private ditches. Large-scale irrigation networks make it possible for people to divert water from one region to another, to regulate the volume of water that is supplied to an individual farmer or to a region, and to store water. As a result, the farmer can increase the yield of his soil, assure the appearance of his crops, and thus increase the certainty of his survival—the essence of adaptation.

Almost all students of social evolution agree that the development of large-scale irrigation networks is one of the greatest human achievements. Recent evidence indicates that the construction of these networks has always followed the integration of a society into a nation-state by centrally unifying political institutions; they do not seem to have preceded the formation of states. (The clearest statement of this point of view is by Robert McC. Adams in *The Evolution of Urban Society* [Chicago: Aldine, 1966].) The reasons for the stimulation of irrigation networks by states are not yet clear (and not all states accomplished this). Yet we can speculate that one aspect of the genius of the men who have established nation-states and caused these networks to be built was their awareness that large populations can be centrally controlled if they must depend for water on the agencies that build, maintain, and regulate the irrigation systems. There are many gaps in our knowledge of how rulers gained such power—aside from conquest—but we can surmise that once this dependence is established—and it is a simple matter to secure conformity and obedience if the threat of withholding water is easily carried out—it is a short step to the regulation of the supply of seed and draft animals, the control of trade and exchange, and centralized monetary control. Once developments in knowledge and technology reach the point at which man can create new fuel systems or other new sources of energy, there is only a quantitative difference between a state that stimulates the construction of large-scale irrigation networks and one that subsidizes the development of rocket fuels, supersonic aircraft, artificial foods, and other materials that facilitate the perpetuation of life. Such a state also underwrites the growing wealth of the ruling classes, as well as the standard of living of the masses.

In societies that have been unified into nation-states, production as well as consumption tends to be strongly influenced, if not dominated, by the central political institutions. Centralized authorities in agricultural societies often stimulate production by decreeing how much land will be cultivated, which crops will be planted, and who will get water and seed. The principles that underlie these activities also are found in industrial societies—for example, in decisions about who will receive electricity, natural gas, or atomic energy, or in government control of access to waterways and air space. Centralized political institutions frequently control distribution directly through marketing systems, or in their absence, by establishing standards of exchange and equivalences. The classes that control these institutions are inseparable from the business apparatuses in which it is decided which products will be consumed domestically and which will be used in intersocietal trade. These groups stimulate production of the surpluses they control to underwrite their standard of living, and they redistribute the surpluses to welfare-program recipients and to others who do not directly produce wealth, such as members of their bureaucracies.

Not all states control local economies in these ways, but the important fact is that such centralized direction is found only in nation-states. In this sense the sequence of priorities in the process of adaptation is reversed in societies that are integrated into nation-states. To put this in terms that are closer to the theme of this essay, we can say that institutional change underlies technological change in nation-states by stimulating technological development; nontechnological institutions (such as political organizations) are the basis for adaptation in these societies.

A TAXONOMY OF CULTURAL ADAPTATIONS

Our taxonomy of successive strategies of adaptation will broadly distinguish between stateless and state societies. Within that dichotomy, the materials of this book will be organized around a taxonomy of four major technological and social designs of human society: hunting-gathering, cultivation, pastoralism, and industrialization. Cultivation and pastoralism are represented in both stateless and state societies; hunting-gathering is found exclusively within stateless societies, and industrialization appears only in state societies.

I defined culture as the artifacts, institutions, ideologies, subjective perceptions, and total range of customary behaviors with which a society is equipped for the exploitation of the energy potentials of its particular habitat. But a taxonomy of levels of cultural development denotes more than a strategy of mastery over the habitat. Every culture is also a unique environment.

Many scientists phrase questions about adaptation in terms of man's alterations of his physical and social environments. Thus there is often an explicit or implicit premise that we must learn how man is able to achieve different densities of population and settlement patterns, freedom from the restrictions of the habitat, the amelioration and elimination of disease, and different degrees of social complexity, all in terms of man acting on the environment. What too often is neglected is the corollary questions: What is the effect of each of these adaptations on man himself? How is man shaped by the shapes he imposes on his habitats? How is man shaped by the shapes he imposes on his habitats? What (for example) are the effects on people of different densities of population? Of compact or dispersed and of horizontal or vertical settlement patterns? Of environmental noise, dietary variety, architectural styles, large or small communities or no communities at all (as in many modern metropolitan areas)? Of reliance on muscular energy or extrapersonal sources of energy?

These questions are important because man shapes himself as he shapes his environment. Either set of questions without the other deals with only half the process of adaptations, and therefore is incomplete. Anthropologists, as well as novelists and others, have often been able to depict with great sensitivity the shapes imposed on human nature in a particular society, but with few exceptions, this task has been neglected in comparative studies of adaptation. It is a task for the future, and its performance will depend on the availability of empirically grounded studies. Meanwhile, in considering the following taxonomy and the case studies organized around it (in the remaining sections of this book), the reader should bear in mind that each strategy of adaptation creates a unique environment for the individual. Every culture presents the individual with a self-contained world, not merely a set of tools with which to exploit a habitat.

Hunting-gathering refers to a particular energy system that represents the first level of cultural adaptation achieved by man about which we have systematic information. In its simplest form, hunting-gathering is a technique of extracting a livelihood from the habitat by an almost exclusive reliance on muscular energy: collecting wild-growing foods and hunting with bows and arrows, spears, bludgeons, nets, weirs, and the like. Typically, hunter-gatherers are nomadic, usually living in small groups that move around a lot. Depending on habitational factors (especially the availability of food), their groups range in size from a few to about twenty-five families and in some habitats rarely reach a density of more than one person per square mile; groups larger than 50 may exhaust the available resources, though

in western California there were groups of about 100.

Although the importance of kinship in social relations among hunter-gatherers is less than at more advanced levels of adaptation, it is customary for a married pair to settle in a camp in which at least one spouse had a parent, sibling, or (later in life) a married child. Also depending on habitational factors, several camps may congregate periodically. Among the !Kung Bushmen (Selection 4), for instance, congregations will occur at water holes during the dry season. Among some Eskimo groups, especially those that rely almost exclusively on seals for survival in the winter (after the caribou leave the territory), this season is the time of large encampments in extended igloo communities. Seals keep open many breathing holes, and large hunting parties—each man at a water hole with a harpoon—have the best chances for a speedy catch. Among other people, such as the Shoshonean Indians (Selection 5), several camps will congregate during the summer when food is more abundant. The same families do not always come together, and the composition of the larger groups from one year to the next is somewhat unpredictable. These larger encampments provide a time and place for acquiring spouses, gossiping, visiting with distant relatives, and conducting ceremonials.

Degrees of nomadism and sedentism among hunter-gatherers vary, related primarily, though not entirely, to the availability of food. Generally, the scantier the natural supply of food, the smaller the bands and the greater their nomadism. In desert or desert-like regions and also on the arctic wastes, camps may consist of only two or three families, each group requiring up to 20 square miles to provide enough food for its members. In temperate regions population density and sedentism increases slightly with every increase in the availability of food. As Suttles shows in his analysis of exploitative activities and social organization among Northwest Coast Indians (Selection 7), there is a direct correspondence between variety of resources, density of population, and complexity of social organization.

A clear distinction has to be made between nomadic hunter-gatherers and hunter-gatherer-fishermen; the latter are more or less sedentary or at least have permanent bases that are left during periodic shortages. Both strategies of adaptation share one important thing: In both, people are not responsible for the presence of the food on which they subsist; essentially they merely stoop to pick up what is available and can do nothing to replenish the stock or find dietary substitutes if drought, flood, pestilence, or human predation destroy their food supply. The permanent villages of hunter-gatherer-fishermen sometimes number up to 100 people, as in western California. Among many of these groups, residents disperse during the summer or other periodic shortages, returning in the winter. These permanent villages—often headed by chiefs—are made possible by the availability of fish, removing the need to chase wild animals to satisfy protein requirements; hunting plays a very small role in these groups' subsistence. Though chiefs are generally without coercive power to enforce decisions in these groups, they enjoy very high rank and prestige; among the Pomo of northwest California, for example, chiefs often are provided with food by members of their villages. In some cases, certain activities may not be undertaken without the chiefs' permission. For example, among the Yokuts of California, a group of men first had to secure the village chief's consent if they wished to execute someone for a particularly heinous offense.

Cultivation is the second strategy of adaptation we will discuss. It, too, has several varieties—many more than hunting-gathering, in fact—that are based on combinations of technological and political elements. Each of these varieties has unique social consequences.

The first cultivators were horticulturists, people using as their principal means of production a hoe or digging stick to plant seeds, roots, or tubers. They generally tend small garden plots and, like hunter-gatherers, rely primarily on muscular energy in their exploitative activities. This type of cultivation represents an important advance, its continued reliance on muscular energy notwithstanding: Cultivators are responsible for presence of the cultivated food on which they subsist. But reliance on a hoe or digging stick generally sets a limit on productivity, in part because the horticulturist does not turn over the topsoil. Furthermore, the horticulturist's methods of clearing and preparing the soil—especially when he cuts the covering brush and burns it (called *swidden* or *slash-and-burn* cultivation)—often lead to rapid exhaustion of the soil, requiring that he shift his cultivated plots every few years.

The development of horticulture in the course of cultural evolution used to be called the "Neolithic Revolution" by anthropologists. That horticulture evolved slowly and gradually is now known from archeological research; it did not burst forth in a "revolutionary" eruption. Most hunter-gatherers (like the !Kung Bushmen) practice, or at least know about, some of the techniques of horticultural cultivation, but domesticated plants make up a very small part (less than 10 per cent) of their diets.

Perhaps the single most important consequence of the adoption of a cultivating strategy of adaptation is the development of the notion of exclusive rights over land; this was probably intended to protect investments of time and effort in particular plots with a view to future returns. But these rights are not always vested in individuals or even households; sometimes they reside in corporate kin groups, such as lineages or clans.[1]

To understand this variability among cultivators, it is necessary to appreciate the basic principle that every increase in the amount of cultivated food and in the amount of time devoted to farming—and every corresponding decrease in reliance on wild or hunted foods—has direct consequences in social

---

1. A corporate kin group usually is politically and judicially autonomous. It is a landowning group that exists in perpetuity, a ceremonial group, and a primary or face-to-face group in which an individual is responsible to and for the other members of the group and the latter are responsible to and for him. Corporate kin groups are almost always exogamous; that is, members of the group are forbidden to marry each other.

organization. The most evident of these is in the degree of sedentism and in political organization. Stateless people who begin cultivating while continuing to rely on hunting and gathering for most of their food are not fully sedentary, though they may have permanent or semipermanent settlements they leave for part of the year to hunt and gather wild foods, returning for the harvest. Their political organization is weak and amorphous. (This pattern is illustrated by the Pima Indians of the American Southwest [Selection 11].)

Social complexity increases as cultigens occupy a steadily greater place in the diet. With decreasing reliance on hunting and gathering, settlements become more fixed, relationships among households become closer and more permanent, kin organizations begin to coalesce and take on corporate attributes, and the authority of clan elders or chiefs in enforcing decisions and resolving disputes becomes stronger. (This is exemplified by the Papago, who are neighbors of the Pima [see Selection 11].) Population densities increase at first slowly, then take off more abruptly as the food supply becomes more certain and hunting and gathering are mostly supplanted by farming. High population densities among stateless cultivators are often accompanied by ideologies that assume people are going to be residentially stable, but even when settlements are permanent, individuals and families may change their village and sometimes their kin-group affiliations. Among hoe and digging-stick cultivators, the division of labor is organized by sex: Men clear the bush, hunt, fight, and tend domesticated animals, while women do the basic work of cultivation.

When cultivators come to rely almost entirely on farming for protein, their social and political organizations exhibit still greater variety and complexity. Villages become even more compact and more densely populated; the Yako villages of Nigeria, for example, contained several thousand persons and had a density of about 230 persons per square mile (see Selection 13). Political organization often becomes complex under these conditions, and headmen may have a considerable amount of power. In societies relying almost entirely on domesticated food, political institutions range from considerable weakness and amorphousness (as among South American tribes and in highland New Guinea) to highly complex state systems (as in Polynesia).

Plows and draft animals, large-scale and centrally controlled irrigation networks, and terracing require specific organizations of labor to maintain and protect these sources of energy; moreover, each involves its own modes of distributing resources and products. (Mechanical tractors, sowers, and reapers are tools of industrialism, to be discussed below.) The use of a plow depends entirely on the use of draft animals, but this involves more than domestication: Such beasts must be in adequate and reliable supply for the entire community. The importance of this consideration can be seen in medieval English records in which most disputes and manorial regulations involved the allocation of draft animals to the members of the village. Similarly, social relationships that center on the ownership and use of draft animals are pivotal in such diverse agricultural societies as contemporary Mexico and India. In all such societies the maintenance of dependable supplies of livestock for draft purposes requires specialized groups of persons to care, protect, breed, and oversee the distribution of the animals.

Thus the change from hoe to plow in the course of cultural evolution involves a change in social organization as well as in technology. Many pastoralist societies—for example, those in East Africa—have great numbers of domesticated animals, practice limited horticulture, and sometimes know about plows, but have not converted their domesticates into draft animals. Similarly, many grain-growers, such as the Pueblo Indians of the American Southwest, have domesticated animals but have not developed livestock that can be used for draft. Here, as always, changes in social organization lag behind the possibilities of technological innovation.

Terracing and large-scale irrigation networks are particular kinds of social systems as well as feats of engineering. Not only does each require the organization of labor for construction, each also demands appropriate institutions for regulation, protection, and repair. Such a technology also and inevitably involves specializations in production (including crafts), the development of markets or other means of trade, urbanization, the bifurcation of rural and urban value systems, and the like.

These advanced techniques of cultivation are thus intimately related to drastic changes in the political organization of society, especially the development of centralized political systems and clearly defined social classes. But these complex political systems did not have the same consequences everywhere. For example, in precolonial sub-Saharan Africa, the central state (where it existed) had very limited control over local populations, and farmers—who relied on hoes and digging sticks—retained almost complete control over their land and other aspects of their social organization. The power—and often the terror—of the state may have extended to the most distant hamlet, but the power of the clan chiefs was not destroyed. In Polynesia, where people also subsisted by horticulture (supplemented by fishing), the power of the central rulers was close to absolute, affecting labor, production, consumption, and most other spheres of life.

The strongest and most complex nation-states, however, emerged in those societies whose adaptive struggles rested on plow agriculture, large-scale and centralized irrigation, and terracing. There are several well documented examples of these relationships. The most ancient is provided by Mesopotamia, in which the movement to centralized political control is exemplified in the Code of Hammurabi (see *Man in Adaptation: The Institutional Framework*). Another well known example is ancient China; the course of centralized controls there was marked by a shift from a feudal organization—with a tenuous balance between local and central power—to a more effectively entrenched national gov-

ernment, exemplified in an elaborate bureaucracy to which people were (ideally) recruited by competitive examination. One of the best documented illustrations of this evolutionary process in England, in which the effectiveness of centralization (even during the feudal period) was facilitated by its "territorial circumscription," to use Carneiro's terminology in Selection 27.

Regardless of the technology on which people rely or their level of political development, the advantages of more advanced technologies (like plows or terracing) should not be overestimated. The productivity of many stateless cultivators relying on hoes or digging sticks outweighed that of many state cultivators using more advanced technologies. This parallels my earlier observation that food is sometimes more plentiful for hunter-gatherers than for horticulturalists and illustrates the importance of placing the study of adaptation in an evolutionary framework. Taken alone, the concept of adaptation can easily be restricted to levels of productivity, and this is the viewpoint of many students of the subject. But the significance of adaptational change is altered when they are viewed in evolutionary perspective, because each stage is then seen as an outgrowth of one and a precursor of another: It is part of an historical flow, a step in man's course toward freeing himself increasingly from reliance on muscular energy.

Thus, in the last few thousand years before agriculture, both hunting and gathering became much more complex. This final adaptation, including the use of products of river and sea and the grinding and cooking of otherwise inedible seeds and nuts, was worldwide, laid the basis for the discovery of agriculture, and was much more effective and diversified than the previously existing hunting and gathering adaptations" (S. L. Washburn and C. S. Lancaster, "The Evolution of Hunting," in *Man the Hunter*, edited by R. B. Lee and I. DeVore, Chicago: Aldine, 1968, p. 295).

No level of adaptation can be understood in terms of itself, but only as having come from somewhere (an earlier stage) and being headed elsewhere (a later stage whose seeds have already been planted). Plow-agriculturists, for example, may not always have developed a higher standard of living than stateless cultivators using hoes, but their importance in human history is that their organizations of social relations set the stage for industrialization. Similarly the evolutionary importance of industrialization is that it is setting the stage for the institutions of what may be called a "post-industrial" strategy of adaptation.

Pastoralism is a technology devoted to gaining a livelihood from large herds of domesticated animals. Sustenance may be derived from the herds themselves (milk, meat, blood) or from the use of the domesticated animals as instruments of production (as among North American Indians who used horses to hunt bison). The several varieties of pastoralism also are strategies of adaptation that must be distinguished in terms of technology and political organization; these varieties depend largely on habitational circumstances, as can be seen in the differences among East African, North American, and Asian pastoralists.

While most pastoralists are without centralized controls, there are significant instances in which they have been organized in chiefdoms. Thus, like all other levels of sociotechnological development, each of the varieties of pastoralism is a particular kind of social organization as well as a particular system of production. The essential element of pastoralism is transhumance, a settlement pattern in which herders seasonally drive their animals from lowland areas of permanent villages and fields to highland pastures. Transhumance differs from nomadism in that the pattern of movement is from fixed settlements to highland pastures and back again, whereas nomads usually move not between fixed points but over a wide territory in search of food. After transhumant people complete a move, they remain relatively stationary until the next season, unless there is a shortage of water and food in the highlands; nomads generally remain stationary only for very brief periods. The entirely different patterns in the movements of pastoralists and nomadic foragers result in different organizations of social relations.

The distinctive political organization of pastoralists is evident in two major and overlapping spheres: the maintenance of order and conformity (including the resolution of disputes) and the decision-making and implementing mechanisms by which their migrations are governed. Among pastoralists without centralized controls, each household or small group of households must respond to minute changes in climate, water, and fodder and decide more or less autonomously when and where to move to find the best grazing for its herd. In pastoralist chiefdoms, however, these decisions are made by headmen. As Salzman observes in Selection 17, such centralized decisions are possible only when resources (such as water and grass) are predictable and plentiful. However, as seen in Selection 18, ecological factors alone are insufficient to give rise to centralization among pastoralists. Centralization among pastoralists is almost always an adaptation to political and economic pressures exerted by the governments of the nation-states of which they are a part; stateless pastoralists are not subject to such pressures. Among centralized pastoralists, people in authority not only regulate relationships among herding camps in the exploitation of the habitat but also those between the herders and settled villagers. More research is needed to learn whether Salzman's hypotheses are applicable to other strategies of adaptation or whether they are unique to pastoralists.

Pastoralism is based on the mutual dependency of man and domesticated animals. Its basic requirement is that the animals be pastured, grazed, and protected; but although pastoralists can control the migrations of their animals, the availability of water is entirely beyond their control. Cattle herders usually subsist on dairy products; they rarely eat meat, except under very special circumstances, because the herds are their capital.

Many pastoralists practice a measure of horticulture, but cultivation is always a secondary source of food at this level of technological development. Rarely, if ever, do cultivated plants make up more than a small proportion of pastoralist diets, usually less than 15 percent. The pasture, grazing, and protection of large herds of animals require distinctive systems of social relations, and pastoralism is a sociotechnological system that is suited to particular kinds of habitats. It requires a unique way of life, involving particular attitudes toward land as well as mechanisms that provide for flexibility in the organization of social relations. For the latter, pastoralists rely on kinship relations as heavily as do many cultivators, but the two systems make very different uses of the principles of kinship.

Industrialism is the last strategy of adaptation I will discuss. (Other strategies—such as mercantilism—intervene between agriculture and industrialism, but they will not be dealt with here.) Industrialism, like other adaptations, is as much a unique social organization as it is a technology. The use of extrapersonal energy in complex forms requires its own organizations of social relations, centering upon man's relationship to the machine.

For example, one of the outstanding differences between agriculture and industrialism is that machines are movable but land is not. Correspondingly, man in an industrial society follows the machine; if he can better survive and better support his family by moving to a different machine in a different locality he does so, largely without regard to other people. He holds his position in relation to his source of subsistence through an impersonal system that pays for the use of his labor power rather than through a group of kinsmen and by inheritance. The intellectualized goal of an industrial society is to run itself like the machines upon which it is based. The organization of a factory is supposed to rest entirely on rational considerations of profit, efficiency, and production—not, as with the working unit in a preindustrial society, on considerations of consumption.

Several difficulties confront the anthropologist who tries to understand industrialism as a strategy of adaptation, to say nothing of the post-industrial stage that seems in the offing. First, the system is a relatively new level of development in cultural evolution. We have a perspective down thousands of years of history in generalizing about preindustrial adaptations, but industrialism is still in the process of maturing and forming the organizations of social relations appropriate to itself. Industrialism is the only strategy of adaptation that is inseparable from state organization, and it is closely related to the emergence of a world community. It is tied to very complex intersocietal political developments that are still at an early stage of their history. A corollary of these considerations is that there has not been enough time for local variations of the strategy to develop. Although a worldwide industrial pattern appears to be emerging, each nation will place its own stamp on its own local application.

Second, and perhaps as a result of their comparative newness, we do not have systematic, empirical studies of industrial cultures as such. There are many studies of particular communities in industrial societies, but an industrial society is not simply an extension of the community. To study such a society it is necessary to study the nation (or region or economy) as a single entity rather than as an arbitrarily defined collection of social segments. Because of the apparent emergence of an intersocietal or world order, it also is necessary to study the effects of participation in the international system on the nation or region that is being studied. The organization of social relations in Peoria, Illinois, for example, is not a self-contained system; it is profoundly affected by events and decisions in New York, Washington, Moscow, Peking, and the United Nations. Some anthropologists are now developing the methodologies appropriate to such inquiries.

This, then, is the outline of the taxonomy according to which we will organize our data. It is, in part, an expedient device; it will be added to below, in the context of other purposes.

CULTURAL ADAPTATION AND CULTURAL ADJUSTMENT AS ASPECTS OF EVOLUTION

In the study of cultural change it is insufficient to say only that culture changes or evolves. Culture changes and evolves because of changed environments; more specifically, culture changes and evolves because of the changes man makes in his environments.

An environment, whether an amoeba's or that of a human group, is a system of interrelated parts. Nothing can take place in an environment entirely by itself, independently of all the other elements in it. These include energy systems and technology and the organization of social relations that makes it possible to exploit them, as well as values, modes of cognition, personality characteristics, and the like; these must be regarded as intrinsic aspects of environments as much as the earth's topography.

Man subsisting by horticulture, for example, changes the chemical composition of the topsoil when he deforests it and burns its trees and brush. Not only has he organized his social relations appropriately to carry out these activities, but his alteration of the organic bed of the soil may sometimes lead to its exhaustion after two or three crops. When this happens he must abandon previously cultivated tracts of land and open new ones. This in turn leads to a particular value system about property and boundaries that is very different from the values of a society in which cultivators deliberately fertilize fallowed tracts and return to them frequently, and from the values of a society that builds factories or other permanent structures. Similarly, when industrial man overcrowds his cities he changes himself by self-protectively disregarding other people and treating them as objects. This reinforces his attitude toward his environment, as something little more than a series of objects to be manipulated and added to.

I stress this point because an important tradition in anthropology has deemed it sufficient to discuss any particular facet of culture in terms of itself, without relating it to anything else. Thus many monographs and essays deal with political organization, law, economics, religion, and personality as subjects that are unrelated to any other aspect of an environment. The best of these studies may be enormously useful, but all of them run the risk of obscuring change and variation, cause and consequence, priorities and relationships among phenomena in a society as a whole. Such an approach makes it difficult to establish meaningful taxonomies of cultural phenomena.

Yet one cannot simplistically say that everything is related to everything else; such an approach is conducive neither to sanity nor explanation. All elements in an environment are interrelated but they are related in different ways. For example, the elaborate concepts of property that are developed by many pastoralists in relation to their cattle are inseparable from the exploitation of cattle as a source of food. At the same time, some cattle pastoralists express their deep attachment to their beasts by giving each a personal name. Are we to regard the naming of cows as much a part of the pastoralist adaptation as property concepts?

If we do, we run the risk of making anthropology consist of undiscriminating descriptions of the variant customs and behavior of people rather than a science of learning the laws and principles that govern the evolution of culture and the organization of society. In the former alternative, everything in a culture is equally relevant to every question. In the latter, it is necessary to distinguish among different types of relationships in a culture to ascertain priorities and sequences of change. The distinction between cultural adaptation and the phenomenon I call cultural adjustment is a means to this end. Cultural adaptation refers to major alterations in the relationship of societies to their habitats that result in different levels of adaptation—from foraging to industrialism. Cultural adjustment refers to the "homeostatic" changes that occur within a society at a given level of adaptation; these changes result in a better "fit" or articulation between the group's technology

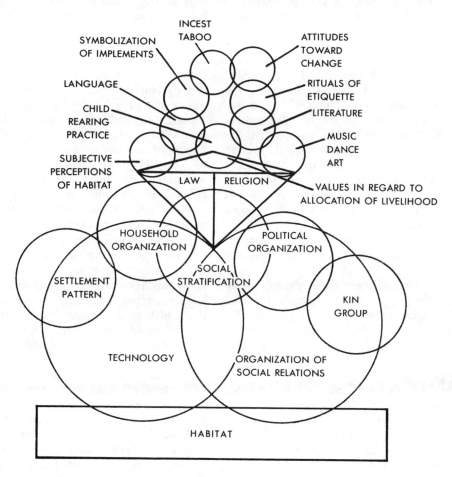

FIGURE 3.1

HIERARCHY OF CULTURAL ADAPTATIONS AND ADJUSTMENTS

and its institutions, ideologies, and customary behavior. Adjustments represent conservative forces, not forces for evolutionary change; they equip a society for better exploitation of the energy potentials it has harnessed within the limits of its level of cultural evolution. Differences in cultural adjustments can thus account for at least some of the variations among societies at the same level of evolution.

Cultural adjustments can be conceptualized as "back-up" institutions (a term suggested by Paul J. Bohannan and Karan Huckleberry in "Institutions of Divorce, Family, and the Law," *Law and Society Review,* 1 [1] [1967]: 81-102). Back-up insti-

tutions are not directly or materially tied to a society's maintenance of an adaptive relationship with its habitat. They are, however, important instruments for maintaining an even tenor in daily social life. People work at gaining a livelihood, participating in a political system, engaging in kin relations, and living by a system of status relations; these activities occupy the major portion of an adult's time and energy but they are not all that people do. People also organize their worlds intellectually; they sing and dance and respond to other esthetic symbols; they make sexual choices according to prescribed rules, attach symbols to the implements they use (see, for example, Selection 6), greet each other, and otherwise behave in ways that express attitudes and status relationships. They bring up their children in ways that will guarantee at least a modicum of household stability and prepare them for adult life. They speak in ways that will ensure communication. None of these activities is actually part of the adaptive process but they "back up" a group's adaptations, inasmuch as a serious breakdown in the group's adjustments would affect the integrity of its adaptations. Correlatively, a fundamental change in a group's adaptations would have repercussions throughout its cultural adjustments.

One of the clearest examples of adjustments within a culture is provided by the subjective perceptions of the habitat that characterize a group. People do not simply exploit a habitat. Rather, perceptions of the physical habitat and of social relations are organized in conceptual categories that are appropriate to the group's overall strategy of adaptation. They enable the group to maintain relationships with the habitat and in the social realm in an orderly, predictable, and ongoing manner. These categories of ideas and perceptions represent an important aspect of a culture's superstructure; they rest on the substructure of technology and its appropriate organization of social relations—the adaptive strategy. While a group's subjective perceptions of the habitat represent part of the culture's superstructure, they have consequences for the organization of social relations. Consider, for example, the perceptions of affluent whites in our society who see their habitat as endangered by pollution—though they used to look at belching smokestacks as symbols of progress. Poor blacks see it as endangered by social and economical oppression. This has important consequences for the society as a whole. Concern with pollution is usually phrased in terms of smog, detergents, industrial waste, noise, air quality, and the like, rather than in terms of people who are producing these things, who are using machines and harnessing energy in particular ways and who maintain particular relationships with

their society. Does this mode of approaching the world—in terms of things rather than social relations—provide a screen to divert attention from a needed reorganization of relations among racial and ethnic groups?

Perceptions of the physical habitat and of social relations are always organized in conceptual categories. Before about 1960, most Americans tended to regard industry in rather beneficent terms, and this set of values distinguished between industry *per se* and those who profited most from it. (Marxists who spoke about the alienation fostered by industry were usually lone voices.) People gladly accepted industrialism and the authority of those who controlled industrial empires. All this changed when industry began to be seen as a pollutant; during the same period workers began to rebel against industrial routine and many people, especially in the younger age groups, began to reject traditional values that had been deemed appropriate to an industrial strategy. More research is needed to determine which was cause and which was consequence.

Another example of subjective perceptions of the habitat can be seen among the Mbuti Pygmies of the Congo forest: Half the men are net-hunters and the other half are archers. No discernible reason for this difference exists today, though it may have been adaptive at the time of its historical development. Each group now regards the other as quaint; but when they visit each other, the archers become net-hunters and vice versa quite proficiently. The net-hunters perceive the short honey season as a time of plenty, while the archers see it as a time of scarcity, and "each group takes appropriate measures to meet the perceived situation, the net-hunters splitting into small units, and the archers congregating into larger ones" (Colin Turnbull, "The Importance of Flux in Two Hunting Societies," in *Man the Hunter,* edited by R. B. Lee and I. DeVore, Chicago: Aldine, 1968, p. 134; reprinted as Selection 6 in *The Institutional Framework*).

A group's organized subjective perceptions are closely related to the ways in which their productive and social relations are organized.

Because of their perceptions, Mbuti net-hunters split up into small units during the short honey season; the archers group themselves into larger units. In the example of contemporary American industry, changes in perceptions of the habitat and in attitudes to work may herald a shift in the organization of productive labor and other social relations.

Anthropologists have been unable to determine in what degree subjective perceptions of the habitat grow out of existing technology and institutions or influence them. In any case, these perceptions shade off into values, "personality," language, symbolization of implements, and aesthetics (see Figure 3.1).

Are some aspects of a group's cultural adaptations more important than others? Do some adjustments play a more important back-up role than others? Much more research is needed to learn the answers to these questions, but I suspect—on purely intuitive grounds—that the answers are affirmative. I have tried to show this in Figure 3.1 by the positions I have assigned various adaptive and adjustive institutions. To represent my contention that the technological institutions of a society and its organization of labor are its most important means of adaptation. I have placed these institutions closer to the habitat than other adaptive institutions. Similarly, I have placed some adjustive institutions close to adaptation to suggest that they are more important in their back-up functions than are others. For example, I hypothesize that changes in a group's values about the allocation of a livelihood—or about religion, law, or cognition—will exert a stronger effect on the adaptive institutions than changes in language, incest taboos, or the rituals of etiquette.

Although adjustive institutions represent conservative forces in a culture, nonetheless there is more room for variation among them than in the adaptive institutions, which can display less variability over time within a society at a particular level of evolution and among societies at the same level. Adjustive institutions that are somewhat removed from a society's adaptive institutions—those that have a lesser back-up role—will have less effect on the group's adaptations than those that are closer to the base of technology and the organization of labor.

For example, several years ago Leopold Pospisil reported a deliberate change in the incest taboos of the horticulturist Kapauku Papuans of the central highlands of New Guinea. A chieftain who was noted for his collection of the choicest women in his marriages (polygyny is very desirable in this society) coveted a very pretty lass who happened to be his cousin. Traditionally, such a marriage had been defined as incestuous by the Kapauku, and the people were outraged; but their anger soon simmered down and the marriage was recognized as legitimate. This led to other changes in the incest taboos and, in turn, to other changes in the Kapauku culture. Nevertheless, the Kapauku remained horticulturists under a weakly organized political system in which each local group maintains autonomy. There was no change in their strategy of adaptation or in their level of cultural evolution.

This observation leads to the more general and very important question: How do we explain the rate of cultural evolution and, in particular, the discrepancy between technological possibilities and social actualities? For example, most foragers knew the elementary principles of horticulture—clearing land, planting seeds, tending crops, and harvesting. Why didn't they go directly to a level at which domesticates constituted a higher proportion of their diet? Why didn't low-level horticulturists go to a level at which these cultigens made up most of their food supply? Why don't pastoralists rely more heavily on cultivated plants? The food supply is certainly more dependable at higher levels of technology, and life is safer and group survival more certain. Why, then, does man appear to have inched his way forward in gaining mastery over his habitat, teetering for many generations on the brink of new adaptations, instead of making the larger jumps that appear to have been possible?

At the same time, the rate of change appears to have been speeding up. Empirical data show us that approximately 2,000 years were needed between the first tentative experiments in the domestication of plants and animals and the effective domestication of even 10 percent of the diet. However, only about 230 years elapsed between the discovery of the atmospheric one-way steam engine and the first artificially controlled nuclear fission chain reaction. The rate of urbanization reflects a similar acceleration: Thousands of years elapsed between the initial appearance of small urban centers in Mesopotamia and the residence in cities during the nineteenth century of a significant portion of the European population, but the rate of urbanization between 1850 and 1900 was much higher than it was between 1800 and 1850, and the rate between 1950 and 1960 was twice that of the preceding 50 years.

While anthropologists are still some way from understanding the reasons for these lags and accelerations in the rate of cultural change, the axiom that every technology is also a particular kind of social system, although it is descriptive rather than explanatory, can serve as a starting point. Cultural evolution involves not only changes in sources of energy but also alterations in social institutions, and the evolutionary record suggests that more time is required to effect the latter than the former. The transition from one level of adaptation to another requires the harnessing of new energy sources *plus* changes in settlement patterns, political institutions, household and family organization, religion, education, and the like. So long as these organizations of social relations, with their accompanying sets of personal values, modes of cognition, and motivations, were limited to local, autonomous groups, change was likely to be slow. Groups of this kind—kin groups, ethnic enclaves, corporate cities, autonomous regions —are almost invariably traditional and conservative in the extreme.

The development of state organizations, which I have described as a watershed in cultural evolution, had profound consequences in speeding up the rate of cultural change. States are able to catalyze technological advances and changes in social relations by assigning specialists to these tasks and by developing and reallocating economic surpluses that can be used for these purposes. Further, one of the consequences—and also one of the means—of centralized political control in state organizations is the weakening of traditionally conservative, locally autonomous groups; the state generally regards such groups as competitors for the loyalties of individuals and seeks to eliminate them. Thus, states are able simultaneously to encourage change in positive ways and to subvert resistance to it.

These consequences were apparent even in the earliest agricultural states, but they have been greatly accelerated in industrial societies. Changes in the material aspects of life have been dramatic during the most recent stages of cultural evolution, but the resistance displayed toward changes in the organization of social relations suggest that the intensity of feeling that was once spread over many generations may now be condensed into one lifetime. It remains to be seen whether societies so challenged can endure.

I have stressed that cultural adaptation is the process by which man makes effective use of the potential energy in his habitat for productive ends. Cultural evolution—the successive strategies in the organization of social relations by which people make use of harnessed energies—is a product of man's attempts to free himself from the limitations of his habitats.

As we turn to the case-study materials, which have been organized according to the taxonomy of cultural adaptations discussed above, we will see illustrations of the relationships between the adaptive (decision-making) unit and strategies for exploiting energy potentials in particular habitats, the involvement of these strategies with political organization, and the interdependence of adaptations and adjustments. We will also see that while cultural evolution is a gradual process, the rate of evolutionary change appears to be speeding up as man gains increasing mastery over his habitat and creates increasingly complex political systems. Each cultural advance makes the next one easier to achieve, though none of them are inevitable.

PART ONE: STATELESS SOCIETIES

INTRODUCTION

WE DISTINGUISH BROADLY between stateless and state societies. Every society, regarded as a political system as well as a unit relying on a particular technology, is a unique system of organizing access to sources of energy—land, water, labor, tools of production, seed and fertilizer, and the like. In a stateless society, access to resources and energy systems and their control are organized locally, without the intervention of centers of authority outside the community. An important feature of this access and control is the underlying premise that every member of the group has rights of access to available and exploitable resources. This in turn is based upon another premise of social life in stateless societies: most members of a group have essentially equal status in their relations with each other and with the habitat. In other words, stateless societies tend to be more or less egalitarian.

Egalitarianism as an adaptive principle is most clearly observable among nomadic hunter-gatherers. In these groups, every member of a camp has equal rights to hunt and gather within its territory; no person can gain control over others because there are no resources over which he can exercise exclusive rights. The ideological expression of this is that no one in a hunting-gathering group has special authority to tell anyone else what to do. This is not to say that such groups are without status systems; different individuals have different measures of prestige and influence over others and are more sought after as hunting or marriage partners by virtue of their ability and other personal attributes. But this prestige does not provide them—or anyone—with authority, with the legal or rightful power to command others to act in particular ways. The exceptions to this rule are specific and limited, as when an Eskimo organizes and leads a caribou hunt or (as described in Selection 5) when a Shoshonean Indian owns a net that others share during a rabbit hunt.

Among hunter-gatherer-fishermen who achieve a degree of sedentism, like the Northwest Coast fishermen (Selection 7), a pattern of "seriation" emerges the touchstone of which is a more or less hereditary office of chieftainship that is often usually honorific, rudimentary, and almost devoid of authority. There are variations in this pattern even among Northwest Coast fishermen, depending largely on habitational factors, but no matter how precise social distinction may become, each status position in these egalitarian societies is occupied by only one person. In contrast, in the nation-state, any number of people—as many

71

as millions—may occupy a single status, especially at the lower reaches of society. This development is explored in *The Evolution of Political Society*, by Morton H. Fried (New York: Random House, 1967).

These principles continue to apply in cultivating strategies of adaptation, though with important modifications or elaborations. Among cultivating societies organized along stateless lines, order and conformity, regularity in productive relationships, and the smooth flow of goods in the course of distribution and consumption are maintained by autonomous networks of people who are attached to each other by ties of kinship, by trade relationships (which may also be hereditary), by friendship, neighborliness, and the like. Rules are important in the organization of these networks and their relationships with each other, for example concerning marriage, feasting and other ceremonials, and feuding. Economic and political relationships are conducted through institutions that are locally based and in which positive and negative sanctions are applied directly in face-to-face interactions.

The most significant change in political organization seen among completely sedentary cultivators is in connection with the allocation of resources, especially land. Here control over land moves from the household to larger units, such as groups of households, lineages, and clans. These groups are not only economic and political units in their control of access to resources but also religious and ceremonial units, since they validate their control by means of religious ideology. Although there are chiefs, they are without power or authority. Control over resources is exercised by the group as a whole; this group may be a lineage, clan, or some other kin group, and its exclusionary policies are directed toward members of other groups, not to anyone within the group. Effective and direct control over land is generally exercised by those who cooperate regularly in productive activities and participate in common religious ritual.

The allocation of land is the central problem for all cultivators; the principles underlying this apportionment are integral features of a group's political organization. But the rules of allotting land do not grow in the abstract or in the minds of political theorists; they must, instead, be seen as aspects of the technology used in exploiting the habitat. When farming rests on hoes or digging sticks, every man can make and carry his own implements; as long as he can find a few men to help him clear an unclaimed and unused plot of land, he can pretty much go and do as he pleases and allocative rules must account for this. But as soon as a strong organization is able to gain monopolistic control over any indispensable resources—whether land or instruments of production—a man is subject to its political authority and there is a change in the rules by which resources are allocated.

But even when a cultivator controls his own instruments of production in a stateless horticultural society, he is not completely free of political authority. Control over land in stateless societies is inseparable from political organization because without a group's permission to use land, a man and his household cannot live there; the group that allocates land also has complete control over its membership. Theoretically, this also means that the group can banish a nonconformist by the simple expedient of refusing him access to any of its land for cultivation. In this way, citizenship has a distinct economic base. Nominally, allocation of land rights is in the hands of a chief (or council) as representative and spokesman of the group, and the group expresses its will through him; sometimes, however, citing his prerogative as the community's principal representative with the ancestors, he may act independently. In any event, however, he has little coercive authority, and his status largely depends on his ability to maintain a following in addition to his hereditary status.

Chiefdoms are neither stateless nor state societies in the fullest sense of either term; they are on the borderline between the two. Having emerged out of stateless systems, they give the impression of being on their way to centralized states and exhibit characteristics of both. They continue to show features of statelessness in that local groups—though larger than in truly stateless societies—frequently split and always retain autonomy in economic and jural relationships. The basic unit of productive activity continues to be the household but, heralding a nation-state organization of social relations, villages are joined in larger cooperative networks for purposes of production and consumption. At this stage of cultural development groups begin to produce surpluses; they do so under the impetus of their chiefs, who are obligated to redistribute the tributes they collect to the households that contributed them. These redistributions generally occur during ceremonial feasts. As we will see, surpluses in nation-states are also redistributed by those who speak in the name of the state, with the principal difference that they are generally redistributed to people who do not produce food, such as bureaucrats and indigents.

How are law and order maintained in stateless societies in view of the absence of coercive institutions such as police? These societies illustrate the fundamental errors of views of "human nature" to explain social life. For example, Thomas Hobbes, author of *Leviathan*, argued in the seventeenth century that man in a "state of nature" lived in a state of anarchy that conflicted with the wish to live—endless war of all against all, aggression and insecurity, inability to keep the fruit of one's labor because everyone has a right to everything, and an absence of justice and injustice. The only way people may live together, Hobbes maintained, is for them to form a coercive political order; this alternative to the "anarchy" of a "state of nature" was for him a logical outgrowth of the "law of nature" according to which man desired to live.

For Jean Jacques Rousseau of the eighteenth century, author of *The Social Contract*, organized social life sets men apart and makes them enemies. In *Emile*, he wrote that "the greatest good is not authority, but liberty." Community life, he maintained, entailed a complete surrender of all individual rights. A logical outgrowth of this concept was his idea that the state entailed only one supreme power to which everyone was subordinate; he thus excluded any balance or equilibrium of powers. Rousseau's view of the incompatibility of individual rights and the sovereignty of political institutions led to his famous idea of the social contract, in which individuals surrendered rights by consensus in a tradeoff for the rights they merely seem to have surrendered.

Like Hobbes, Rousseau began with an axiomatic "state of nature." In the light of this it may be said that one of anthropology's singular contributions to thought has been the empirical demonstration that there is no such thing. However, these ideas are still with us, both in political theories and in the rhetoric of politics. Hobbes' ideas appear in modern dress in the underlying premises of positions like "law-and-order" while Rousseau evokes ideas such as people's actions are forced on them by the political system and that no one can be held accountable for acts that others regard as detrimental to the common weal. If anthropology has one lesson to teach it is that the institutions by which people live rest on the bedrock of their relationships with the habitat, on the sources of potential energy that they have been able to harness. *Homo sapiens* cannot be characterized in any single set of terms.

In hunting-gathering groups, the maintenance of law and order has to be viewed against the background of their strategy of adaptation: the necessity for groups to split up recurrently to keep down pressure on available resources, the fact that neither groups nor individuals have exclusive rights to resources, the related fact that there are no chiefs with the power or authority to enforce decisions, and the strong emphasis on kinship in daily social relationships. When disputes break out among nomadic hunter-gatherers, one or both partners to an argument pack up and go to join another camp, and this technique fits well with their ecological realities. Owning few articles and having no deep attachment to any territory, they are able to split off from each other with considerable ease when necessary. But splitting off from the camp is generally a last resort. All hunting-gathering societies have a variety of techniques, usually symbolic in form, for trying to keep tensions within reasonable bounds. These techniques may include witchcraft and sorcery, joking and ribaldry, and competitive singing in which the parties to a dispute defend their positions and the assembled members of the community judge who is the victor (as among some Eskimo groups). Only when such techniques fail, when feelings get out of hand and violence breaks out, will people leave for another camp, for several hours or months or permanently.

Because local groups among hunter-gatherers do not have exclusive rights over resources and because every member of a local group has an equal right to hunt and gather over a territory, there are no chiefs or other authorities who can enforce decisions by threatening to withhold access to resources. Individuals may try to settle quarrels, but whether they succeed depends entirely on their prestige and the willingness of the disputants to abide by their recommendations. Authority of this kind develops only at more advanced levels of adaptation, when it becomes possible for the head or representative of a group to deprive people of resources or access to them. Among hunter-gatherers, then, every man has to settle his own disputes and each seeks to enforce resolutions at best he can.

The legal systems of stateless cultivators are quite different, because cultivation makes different demands on people and because the institutional requirements by which people live are changed by this technological development. The most important difference between hunter-gatherers and cultivators is in their relationship to land; in horticultural societies, groups acquire exclusive rights to land and individuals are given rights to use portions of this territory. These rights are secured through membership in the group—usually based on considerations of kinship—and both rights (to land and to membership in the group) are inherited. This is inevitably reflected in the legal system.

Sedentism, the investment of personal energy in tracts of land, and the commingling and inheritance of group membership and rights in land lead to the development of rules of property in cultivators' legal systems to an extent never found among hunter-gatherers. At the same time, the fact that cultivable land is generally in limited supply means that ultimate control over its distribution to individuals and households must be vested in the groups—such as lineages and clans—that have exclusive rights to it. This is one of the most important factors in the development of chieftainship or headmanship among cultivators; and whether the head of a kin group ever exercises his right to deprive members of access to land, this theoretical power is basic to his authority in resolving disputes or punishing transgressions. Very often this power is cast in magical or religious terms, and this reflects the commingling of legal, religious, kin, and economic institutions in stateless cultivating societies.

In summary, stateless societies represent a very complex concept; their authority structures and means for maintaining order and conformity, however, are diffuse and characterized by very simple apparatuses of government. There are "offices," but no enduring hierarchies of authority in the sense in which we know them in a nation-state. Headmen, where found, inherit their positions, but they rarely have the means or right to enforce decisions; their leadership—whether for warfare or coordination of productive activities—rests on the willingness of others to follow them, and this in turn depends largely on their personal qualities. Sometimes, as among North American Plains Indians, a group may have several headmen or chiefs who have overlapping areas of authority.

There are several sources, in addition to Fried's book cited in the text, that can be consulted by the reader who wants to read more about stateless societies. Most of these sources are British; American anthropologists are relative latecomers to the study of political systems. Moreover, most of these sources pay only scant attention to the overall adaptive strategies in which particular political systems are set. *African Political Systems,* edited by Meyer Fortes and E. E. Evans-Pritchard (London and New York: Oxford University Press, 1964, paperback edition), first published in 1940, contains case studies of three stateless and five state societies; it is generally regarded as the cornerstone of modern anthropological studies of political organization. *Primitive Government,* by Lucy Mair (Baltimore: Penguin, 1962) is a more discursive attempt to show that all societies exhibit systems of government and law; the book provides a very clear distinction between the diffuseness of authority in a stateless society and the principle of "sovereignty" in more complex political systems. *Tribes without Rulers,* edited by John Middleton and David Tait (London: Routledge and Kegan Paul, 1958) focuses on six segmentary African societies. (This concept is discussed in Selection 14.) *Government and Politics in Tribal Societies,* by

I. Schapera (London: Watts, 1956), ranges from hunter-gatherers to early African nation-states.

Two books by Max Gluckman are especially noteworthy: *Custom and Conflict in Africa* (Glencoe, Illinois: The Free Press, 1955) focuses on the ways in which order and conformity are maintained in tribal society and on the incompatibilities of the different groupings that command allegiance in stateless societies. *Politics, Law and Ritual in Tribal Society* (New York: New American Library, 1968, paperback edition), like Schapera's book, spans stateless and state societies; these two eminent anthropologists are in sharp disagreement on many important issues. *Political Anthropology,* edited by Marc J. Swartz, Victor W. Turner, and Arthur Tuden (Chicago: Aldine, 1966) and *Local-Level Politics,* edited by Swartz (Chicago: Aldine, 1968) present case studies of political organization ranging from tribal to modern societies, as does *Comparative Political Systems,* edited by Ronald Cohen and John Middleton (Garden City, N.Y.: Natural History Press, 1967).

I.
HUNTING-
GATHERING

OF WHAT SIGNIFICANCE to us are hunter-gatherers? They are thought to represent the longest-surviving strategy of adaptation in the 600,000 years of *Homo sapiens'* existence; all subsequent strategies, it is believed, were developed during the latter one percent of human history. They are thus part of our heritage and of our humanity. One aspect of this record is that foragers represent man's closest cultural link to nonhuman primates. But these similarities should not be exaggerated, though they enable us to see the biological bases of social behavior that may have been inherited from our nonhuman past and distinguish them from these foundations in uniquely human ways.

Hunter-gatherers are important because they illustrate what men are capable of when they live by a strategy of adaptation that rests almost exclusively on muscular energy. Foragers are more closely governed by the limitations inhering in their technology than people at any other level of technological development. This is illustrated by the similarities in their organization of social relations, which cross-cut habitats of scarcity and abundance, mild and harsh milieus, nomadic and sedentary ways of life. The variations in this strategy show us the ways in which the organization of social relations is an aspect of man's attempts to make effective use of the energy systems at his disposal under different conditions.

Although there is greater homogeneity within this level of adaptation than any other, there is nevertheless enough variation among foragers to demonstrate the sensitivity of their social organization to their habitational exigencies, especially in the size of their groups and in their political organization. Thus, camps tend to be larger among the !Kung Bushmen (Selection 4) than among the Great Basin Shoshonean Indians (Selection 5), and Eskimo seal hunters often have camps larger than either of these groups. Although the Shoshoneans and the Northwest Coast Indians (Selection 7) rely on muscular energy and are not responsible for the presence or absence of the food on which they subsist, the simplicity of social organization among the Shoshoneans and its relative complexity among the people of the Northwest Coast can be understood in terms of differences in the natural availability of food as well as in differences in available formal knowledge. These relationships can be seen in even sharper focus within the Northwest Coast area itself, where variations in the availability of food produced corresponding differences in social organization.

From hunter-gatherers we can begin to understand the relationship between technological mastery of a habitat and settlement patterns, social stratification, group segmentation, and property relationships. We are able to begin tracing the ways in which, for example, cultural uses of space, culminating (for the moment) in the modern metropolis, respond to the energy systems people have been able to harness in different habitats. We see this by comparing nomadic and relatively sedentary hunter-gatherers, as well as by comparing hunting-gathering to other adaptations. Similar processes can be observed in connection with social stratification, the fragmentation and cohesiveness of groups, and property relationships.

One of the principal features of cultural evolution is the increases in socio-economic complexity that accompany advances in mastery over the habitat. A criterion of this complexity is the amount of differentiation that characterizes the organization of roles in a group. "Differentiation" refers here to the degree to which roles are separated from each other, and this may be gauged by whether the performance of one role is independent of others. Economic speciali-zation is an example of role differentiation; another is the separation of church and state officials and their jobs. The obverse of differentiation is "commingling." When the performance of political, religious, kinship, and educational roles (for example) are dependent on each other—for instance, when a man holds political office because he is an excellent provider and the oldest member of his kin group and when he is also the religious representative of the group—we say these roles are "commingled." Another criterion of social complexity, one that is easily measurable, is the amount of occupational choice available to people in a society. Occupational choice is closely tied to role differentiation and both accompany advances in adaptation. A modern youth in turmoil over his choice of occupation is experiencing one aspect of life in a culture at the highest level of adaptation achieved thus far by man.

The relative lack of social complexity among foragers is reflected in their commingling of roles and the almost complete absence of occupational choice. Almost every socially relevant task is (or can be) performed by almost every person; chieftainship, which is largely devoid of power and authority, is the only noteworthy exception. Similarly, in a nomadic hunting-gathering society every man is a hunter and every woman is a gatherer; few alternatives are open to an individual. In a fishing society every man is a fisherman; this is true even of chiefs or shamans and their families.

But such terms as differentiation and commingling are only abstractions applied by the anthropologist; what are the real elements in the lives of nomadic hunter-gatherers? The following profile, which is fleshed out in the selections that follow, is an excellent starting point.

"We make two basic assumptions about hunters and gatherers: (1) they live in small groups and (2) they move around a lot. Each local group is associated with a geographical range but these groups do not function as closed social systems. Probably from the very beginning there was communication between groups, including reciprocal visiting and marriage alliances, so that the basic hunting society consisted of a series of local "bands" which were part of a larger breeding and linguistic community. The economic system is based on several core features including a homebase or camp, a division of labor—with males hunting and females gathering—and, most important, a pattern of sharing out the collected food resources.

"These few broadly defined features provide an organizational base line of the small-scale society from which subsequent developments can be derived. We visualize a social system with the following characteristics. First, if individuals and groups have to move around in order to get food there is an important implication: the amount of personal property has to be kept to a very low level. Constraints on the possession of property also serve to keep wealth differences between individuals to a minimum and we postulate a generally egalitarian system for the hunters.

"Second, the nature of the food supply keeps the living groups small, usually under fifty persons. Large concentrations of population would rapidly exhaust the immediate resources, and members would be forced to disperse into smaller foraging units. It is likely, as Mauss observed, that several bands would come together on a seasonal basis, resulting in a division of the year into "public" and "private" periods. Because of the small size of the living groups and the wide variance of family size, bands wax and wane in numbers. It is probably necessary between bands in order to maintain food-gathering units at an effective level.

"Third, the local groups as groups do not ordinarily maintain exclusive rights to resources. Variations in food supply from region to region and from year to year create a fluid situation that can best be met by flexible organizations that allow people to move from one area to another. The visiting patterns create intergroup obligations, so that the hosts in one season become the guests in another. We think that reciprocal access to food resources would rank as equal in importance with exchange of spouses as a means of communication between groups. It is likely that food may antedate women as the original medium of exchange.

"Fourth, food surpluses are not a prominent feature of the small-scale society. If inventories of food on hand are minimal, then a fairly constant work effort has to be kept up throughout the year. Since everyone knows where the food is, in effect the environment itself is the storehouse; and since everyone knows the movements of everyone else, there is a lack of concern that food resources will fail or be appropriated by others.

"Fifth, frequent visiting between resource areas prevents any one group from becoming too strongly attached to any single area. Ritual sites are commonly associated with specific groups, but the livelihood of the people does not depend on such sites. Further, the lack of impediments in the form of personal and collective property allows a considerable degree of freedom of movement. Individuals and groups can change residence without relinquishing vital interests in land or goods, and when arguments break out it is a simple matter to part company in order to avoid serious conflict. This is not to say that violence is unknown; both homicide and sorcery are found among a number of current hunter-gatherers. The resolution of conflict by fission, however, may help to explain how order can be maintained in a society without superordinate means of social control" ("Problems in the Study of Hunters and Gatherers," by Richard B. Lee and Irven De Vore, in *Man the Hunter,* edited by R. B. Lee and I. De Vore, Chicago: Aldine, 1968, pp. 11-12).

One of the focal points of the nomadic foraging social system is the individual's need to have hunting partners on whom he can rely for assistance and support. The sentiments and obligations of kinship provide the basis of these alliances within the group, which are indispensable in the hazardous occupation of hunting by means of such rudimentary tools as spears and bows and arrows. In addition, kinship provides the basic lines along which food is distributed (though sharing is not confined to kinsmen); this too is important, especially in times of scarcity. As a result of these requirements and almost without exception, a married pair in a hunting-gathering group settle in a camp in which at least one spouse has a blood relative.

Although hunter-gatherers almost invariably are governed by egalitarian ideologies, they are not without social ranking. A hierarchial arrangement of people appears to be an inevitable accompaniment of society at even the lowest levels of adaptation. It is difficult to avoid noting the fact that social groups among nonhuman primates also are governed by ranking arrangements in which dominance and inferiority are clearly recognized by members of the groups. What is the basis of this parallel between nonhuman and human societies? Is a capacity for social ranking an aspect of our genetic programming from our nonhuman past? (This subject is more fully discussed in *Man in Adaptation: The Biosocial Background.*)

As a hypothesis, I suggest that successive levels of adaptation in man tend to increase this tendency, as in the elaborate systems of stratification that are found in agricultural and industrial societies. But once stated, this hypothesis must be qualified immediately; I do not intend it to provide aid and comfort for the so-called Social Darwinists. Although most human societies are characterized by patterns of ranking, many temper these patterns with ideologies of egalitarianism. In most preagricultural societies, chiefs are regarded as first among equals.

Another important qualification is that it is erroneous to equate the class and caste systems of agricultural and industrial societies with the ranking systems of hunter-gatherers and many horticulturists. The building blocks of systems of stratification in technologically advanced and politically complex societies are groups: classes and castes. These groups are ranked in terms of dominance and social inferiority; the higher the group in the social scheme the greater the access of people in that group to privilege and power. One of the characteristics of a system of stratification is that all members of a particular class or caste tend to be regarded and treated equally by people in other strata; all the members of the lowest class will tend to regard and treat all the members of the nobility in roughly the same way, and vice versa.

A system of social stratification in a technologically advanced and politically complex society has many more individuals than class or caste statuses; millions of people can be organized into as few as 15 or 20 statuses within such a system. In hunting-gathering groups, however, there generally are as many statuses as individuals; each person, rather than a class or caste, is ranked relative to other individuals. (Suttles uses the term "seriation" in this connection in Selection 7.) The same thing is true of most stateless horticultural societies.

Furthermore, and in marked contrast to the systems of stratification in politically complex societies, ranking (or "seriation") in a hunting-gathering group does not confer unequal access to privilege or power. It generally bestows little more than prestige, by which is meant social influence. It means that a man of high rank will be sought out as a friend or partner; his opinions will be heeded, although he is without power to enforce them; he will tend to have his choice of the most desirable girls in the group; and people will readily come to his assistance and follow him on his exploits. Although systems of social class and caste can be regarded as aspects of social ranking, not all ranking is expressed in classes or castes.

The reader who wants to learn more about foragers should first consult *Man the Hunter,* referred to in the text. This indispensable work contains many excellent reports of research among hunter-gatherers throughout the world as well as discussions of the newest concepts in this field of study. Archeological studies are also important for an understanding of this level of adaptation, which cannot be appreciated fully from either ethnographic or archeological data alone. The reader will find the following archeological works worthwhile: *African Ecology and Human Evolution,* edited by F. Clark Howell and François Bourliere (Chicago: Aldine, 1963); *Social Life of Early Man,* edited by Sherwood L. Washburn (Chicago: Aldine, 1961); *Back of History: The Story of Our Own Origins,* by William Howells (Garden City, N.Y.: Doubleday, 1954); *Prehistory and the Beginnings of Civilization,* by Jacquetta Hawkes and Leonard Wolley (New York: Harper and Row, 1963); and *An Introduction to American Archeology* (Vol. 1: *North and Middle America,* Vol. 2: *South America),* by Gordon R. Willey (Englewood Cliffs, N.J.: Prentice-Hall, 1966). *Man in Adaptation: The Biosocial Background* contains an excellent discussion of the Bushmen of the Kalahari Desert of southern Africa, by Philip Tobias.

Two good studies of adaptation among hunter-gatherers will provide the reader with insight into the ways in which anthropologists view institutions as attempts to come to terms with the habitat: *The Ainu: A Study of Ecology and the System of Social Solidarity between Man and Nature in Relation to Group Structure,* by Hitashi Watanabe *(Journal of the Faculty of Science,* University of Tokyo, Section 5, Volume 2, Part 6, 1964) and *The North Alaskan Eskimo: A Study in Ecology and Society,* by Robert F. Spencer (Smithsonian Institution: Bureau of American Ethnology, Bulletin 171 [Washington, D.C.: U. S. Government Printing Office, 1959]). Several briefer descriptions of hunter-gatherers which, while not directly devoted to processes of adaptation, help to provide a fuller picture of this way of life. Two of these by Colin Turnbull deal with the Mbuti Pygmies of the Congo: *The Forest People: A Study of the*

Pygmies of the Congo (Garden City, N.Y.: Doubleday, 1962) and "The Mbuti
Pygmies: An Ethnographic Survey" *(Anthropological Papers, American Museum
of Natural History,* 50 [1965] Part 3: 139-282). A well-known work, describing a hunting-gathering group that apparently does not conform to the general
picture of sharing and cooperativeness, is *Nomads of the Long Bow: The Siriono
of Eastern Bolivia,* by Allan R. Holmberg (Garden City, N.Y.: Natural History
Press, 1970). A useful brief monograph is *The Eskimo of North Alaska,* by
Norman A. Chance (New York: Holt, Rinehart and Winston, 1966). An
unusual marriage system is described in *The Tiwi of North Australia,* by C. W.
M. Hart and Arnold R. Pilling (New York: Rinehart and Winston, 1960).

As we turn to examples of ethnological field research, it is necessary to consider the methods by which anthropologists gather their data. We cannot provide
a detailed or complete outline of the methods of anthropology, but the following sketch should give the newcomer a sense of some of the ways in which
anthropologists gather their data and an indication of some of the changes in
anthropological methodology that have taken place in recent years. Three
questions must be answered: How do anthropologists study culture? How do
they gather their data? How do they interpret data?

The basic research procedure for a cultural anthropologist is to select a
group of people and go to live with them, usually for a year or more. The
standard method in what is generally called "field work" is "participant observation": the anthropologist observes everything possible by using his eyes and
ears (and sometimes his nose). But he is not a passive observer; he constantly
asks his "informants" why they do the things he observes and why they fail to
do other things, and he seeks to validate what one person tells him in what he
learns from others. Sometimes he conducts interviews with selected informants.
An ethnographer might spend an entire day tracing an informant's genealogy,
from which he learns not only the kinship terminology of the group but the appropriate behavior for people who stand in different kinship relations. He learns
the rules of marriage, forbidden sexual relationships, the household composition, and many other features of the culture.

He also learns by systematizing the events and observations of his personal
life in the society. For example, one of his most instructive experiences will
be finding a place to live. In the course of trying to get people to build or sell
or rent a house he learns about the rules of property, the nature and role of
money, the organization of labor, techniques of procrastination, incentvies to
work, customs in house-building, and the like. Many anthropologists have been
"adopted" by a member of the community or by a secret society, receiving a
kinship or pseudo-kinship status and thereby entering into an intricate round
of reciprocities, rights, and obligations. The field worker must secure food for
himself, and, whether people in the society he is studying get their food by
foraging or in a supermarket, this is another aspect of participation by which
he learns a great deal about the organization of social relations in the group.
His goal in all such activities is to take part in as much of the culture as

possible without compromising himself or influencing the nature of the material he is trying to gather.

Anthropologists vary greatly in their feelings about the people they study. Some individuals everywhere are simply and basically unlikable, and sometimes an entire culture may strike an anthropologist as uncongenial. There also are persons who are extraordinarily likable and cultures that are entirely compatible with the anthropologist's values. When an anthropologist responds to a society in either of these ways—and it must be remembered that often he is cut off from contact with his own society—he is faced with the problem of maintaining his objectivity. The greatest danger—although this has rarely happened—is "going native," completely adopting a native way of life and identifying so closely with the people he is studying that he loses perspective about them and his capacity to generalize about their behavior in scientific terms.

Basically there are two types of ethnological field research. In one, the ethnographer seeks to learn as much as possible about an entire culture within a limited amount of time. Such research had priority among most anthropologists for a long time because the impact of Western culture was rapidly transforming the traditional cultures of primitive and peasant peoples and there was urgent need to "salvage" these cultures for the record before they were lost to history. Once these cultures were recorded, an increasing number of anthropologists could devote themselves to a second type of field research, which is oriented toward specific problems rather than whole cultures.

There are several types of problem-oriented ethnological research. In one, a limited aspect of a culture—law, religion, political organization, or psychological processes—is selected and examined in detail, to an extent not possible when the goal is the description of an entire culture. Another type is a product of the impact of Western culture on primitive and peasant societies: the restudy of societies to learn what adaptive responses they have made to the influences of the West on their cultures. These restudies provide "before and after" pictures; they not only give us detailed pictures of transformed cultures, they enable us to gain more insight into the processes of change and adaptation. For example, there are many societies whose cultures were recorded in the later nineteenth and early twentieth centuries and then studied again in the 1950s and 1960s.

Methods and techniques of collecting data vary considerably, depending on the nature of the problem being investigated. The basic procedures of participant observation and the genealogical method have not been abandoned but the formulation of new types of problems and hypotheses has led to the adoption and refinement of new anthropological techniques. For example, to some anthropologists cameras and tape recorders are as important as pencil and paper. Using these and other techniques, anthropologists have borrowed heavily from concepts developed by political scientists, legal scholars, sociologists, biologists, and others. As we have turned our attention to the study of whole nations, we have had to learn to use questionnaires and other large-scale survey techniques, archival research, selected and formal interviews of brief duration, and the like. The investigation of personality dynamics and psychological processes in different cultural contexts has led other anthropologists to use modified versions of some of the tests and techniques of clinical psychology, such as the Rorschach and Thematic Apperception tests, figure drawing, and life histories.

In an era in which precision, quantification, and laboratory procedures have become ideals, the methods employed by anthropologists sometimes seem slip-shod and unreliable to other scientists. Some anthropologists have been rather bumptious and disdainful with respect to quantification and method; others, per-haps captivated by the quasi-mythical precision of a missile countdown, have tried wholesale adoption of the procedures of computer technology. But both of these extremes are unsatisfactory for anthropology. No method should be-come so confining that an investigator loses sight of his subject matter, and no scientist should allow himself to adopt an undisciplined and devil-may-care attitude toward his collection of data.

A well-known anthropologist once suggested that anthropology can be as precise a science as astronomy, but (aside from his failure to ask whether this is desirable) his assertion is based on a fundamental error. Anthropology is the study of culture; culture is a characteristic of the human species; and the methods by which people and their works are studied must be different from the procedures by which celestial actions are investigated. Nor is anthropology one of the arts, though there is an art to doing "good" anthropology just as there is an element of art in the "hard" sciences. Attempts to ape astronomy and other natural sciences interfere seriously with the tasks of anthropology.

An ultimate test of a scientific method is its ability to yield results that can be replicated by independent investigators. By this criterion anthropology has fared about as well as most other disciplines. Two types of studies support this assertion.

First, several societies have been studied by two or more anthropologists who have worked independently of each other and at different times. To be sure, this replication has sometimes resulted in more disagreement than agreement—there are similar instances in all sciences, including physics and chemistry—but in most cases there has been a high degree of concurrence among such independent observers. Wide disagreements can be attributed to the fact that anthropologists studied a culture at different times and therefore under different conditions. For example, the Hopi Indians of the American Southwest have been characterized in two different ways: Some anthropologists have seen them as peaceful and harmonious, living with a minimum of coercion; others have noted that their child-rearing practices are repressive and the adults are constrained and see the Hopi as anxious, mistrustful, and full of suppressed hostility. Analyses of these contrasting pictures has revealed that the former qualities emerge when the Hopi are relatively free from serious pressure; the latter become apparent when they are under stress, as from drought, flood, sickness, or pressure from white Americans.

The second basis on which it can be said that the methods of anthropological field research generally produce reliable data is the results produced by cross-cultural investigations, which brings us to another important method in the anthropological armamentarium. In a comparative or cross-cultural study an investigator selects a sample of societies throughout the world and compares them in terms of a hypothesis. Usually he must use data that have been collected by other people. Scores of large-scale cross-cultural studies have been conducted to date and many have yielded statistically significant results, which suggests a considerable degree of reliability in the primary data collected by anthropologists.

For example, let us say an anthropologist who is conducting a cross-cultural study of divorce hypothesizes that divorce occurs most often in societies or in groups within societies that are characterized by poverty and economic deprivation. He must assume that anthropologists generally have been accurate in reporting economic standards of living and rates of divorce. If the hypothesis is borne out by the data, this can be taken as an indirect indication that the data from different societies are comparable and accurate. If the hypothesis is not borne out, either the hypothesis is wrong and is based on faulty theory or the original data are inconsistent and unreliable. The latter assumption is not untenable in itself but the great number of substantiated cross-cultural hypotheses suggest oherwise.

Finally, the distinction between the data of anthropology and interpretations of these data. The data of anthropology are made up of what people in different societies do—for example, in a particular society people gain their livelihood by cultivation with digging sticks and by hunting and that in another society people acquire all their food by purchasing it with money they get from selling their labor in an open market. Any statement about adaptation in connection with either of these modes of gaining a livelihood is an interpretation or hypothesis—for example, egalitarianism is an adaptation to hunting-gathering or elaborate systems of stratification and inequality are adaptations to an industrial system. Data and interpretation represent two different levels of abstraction and should never be confused. Very few of the case materials in this book deal with adaptation as such; most of the hypotheses about the significance of these data for the study of adaptation will appear in my introductory essays.

As noted, anthropologists vary in their feelings about the people they study. A benign view of life as a cultural anthropologist is in the late Hortense Powdermaker's autobiographical *Stranger and Friend: The Way of an Anthropologist* (New York: Norton, 1966); her field work ranged from the Melanesian island of Lesu and contemporary Zambia to Hollywood and a community in the American South, and her account of her own work is sincere and personalized. At the other extreme is a hair-raising account of field work in South America: *Yanomamo: The Fierce People,* by Napoleon Chagnon (New York: Holt, Rinehart and Winston, 1968, especially pp. 1-18). In my view, the best general discussion of field work (covering the ground between these extremes) is "Ethnography: Method and Product," by Gerald D. Berreman, in *Introduction to Cultural Anthropology: Essays in the Scope and Methods of the Science of Man,* edited by James A. Clifton (Boston: Houghton Mifflin, 1968).

A review of the nature of cross-cultural research, types of cross-cultural studies, and some of the methodological problems involved is in my own paper, "Macro-Ethnology: Large-Scale Comparisons," in *Introduction to Cultural Anthropology,* edited by James A. Clifton. This paper also contains an original study that illustrates cross-cultural anthropological research. An excellent introduction to the method of historical reconstruction (and germane to the study of adaptation) is Robert McC. Adams' *The Evolution of Urban Society* (Chicago: Aldine, 1966). This book is based almost entirely on archeological investigations, but it contains many hypotheses and interpretations that are indispensable to the cultural anthropologist. Another example of historical reconstruction, based on documentary materials and direct observations by other anthropologists, is Karl Polanyi's *Dahomey and the Slave Trade* (Seattle: University of Washington Press, 1966).

In the last few years, reflecting anthropologists' growing concern with methodology, several good books and collections of essays have appeared. Eight of these are reviewed in *American Anthropologist*, 73 (6) (1971): 1435-46. The reader who wants to pursue the question of methodology, especially in field work, can judge from these brief reviews which books he wants to look into.

4. WHAT HUNTERS DO FOR A LIVING, OR, HOW TO MAKE OUT ON SCARCE RESOURCES

RICHARD B. LEE

Reprinted from Man the Hunter *(Chicago: Aldine. Copyright 1968 by the Wenner-Gren Foundation for Anthropological Research, Inc.). Richard B. Lee is Associate Professor of Anthropology at the University of Toronto. He is particularly interested in problems of human ecology, social evolution, capitalism and socialism, and he has conducted long-term field research among the Zu/wa (!Kung) Bushmen of Botswana. He edited (with Irven DeVore)* Man the Hunter *and* Studies of Bushmen Hunter-Gatherers.

■ We begin with the !Kung Bushmen of Botswana in South Africa. They represent a hunting-gathering strategy of adaptation in a beneficent habitat. Prior to the field research of Richard Lee and a few other young anthropologists who have been trail-blazing in the study of adaptation, hunter-gatherers were regarded as living very precariously. This, as Lee demonstrates, is not always true.

Carefully analyzing !Kung caloric input in relation to their energy output, Lee shows that they make out very well indeed, even when suffering from drought. The basis of their subsistence is wild-growing foods, 50 per cent of which (by weight) is made up of mongongo nuts. These nuts are drought resistant and are nutritionally remarkable; for example, 300 nuts (a person's average daily consumption) yield about 1,260 calories and 56 grams of protein. This wild-growing diet is supplemented with hunted meat.

But Lee's principal concern is with the group's organization of social relations, and he describes the sensitivity of !Kung social organizations to habitational factors. During droughts, many camps assemble at the few remaining waterholes; here scarcity leads to sharing rather than to group splits, as among the Shoshonean Indians (Selection 5) or to competition, as often happens among us. We also see here that the population of a hunting-gathering camp is constantly shifting, an important strategy in reducing the pressure on available resources. Lee's documentation of the fluidity of !Kung camps—which seems applicable to all hunter-gatherers—is an important step in the revision of the accepted model of this level of sociotechnological development.

This selection is also important in illustrating an important change in anthropological field methods and theory. As a result of the research of Lee and other ecologically oriented field workers, it is no longer possible to say merely that hunter-gatherers do or do not have "enough" to eat or that camps are "large" or "small." Instead, there is growing emphasis on such procedures as weighing food and people, counting heads repeatedly over extended periods of time, measuring hours and days spent working, and carefully clocking the distribution of particular foods in a camp. Such procedures are rapidly providing more rigorous standards for theories of adaptation.

The reader who wishes to explore further should consult the other papers in the volume from which this selection is taken, as well as Lee's more quantitative analysis of the themes explored here: "!Kung Bushman Subsistence: An Input-Output Analysis," in *Contributions to Anthropology: Ecological Essays,* edited by David Damas (Bulletin 230, National Museums of Canada, Anthropological Series No. 86, Ottawa, 1969). An important essay on hunter-gatherer population size and hunting territories is "The Size of Algonkian Territories: A Function of Ecological Adjustment," by A. Irving Hallowell *(American Anthropologist,* 51 [1949]: 35-45). "Habitat, Culture, and Archaeology," by George I. Quimby, in *Essays in the Science of Culture in Honor of Leslie A. White,* edited by Gertrude E. Dole and Robert L. Carneiro (New York: Crowell, 1960; reprinted as Selection 28 in *Man in Adaptation: The Biosocial Background),* seeks to relate archaeological and ethnological data among northeastern North

American hunter-gatherers. Also relevant are two articles by James B. Birdsell: "Some Environmental and Cultural Factors Influencing the Structuring of Australian Aboriginal Populations" (American Naturalist, 87 [1953]: 171-207) and "On Population Structure in Generalized Hunting and Collecting Populations" (Evolution, 12 [1958]: 189-205). ■

THE CURRENT ANTHROPOLOGICAL VIEW of hunter-gatherer subsistence rests on two questionable assumptions. First is the notion that these peoples are primarily dependent on the hunting of game animals, and second is the assumption that their way of life is generally a precarious and arduous struggle for existence.

Recent data on living hunter-gatherers show a radically different picture. We have learned that in many societies, plant and marine resources are far more important than are game animals in the diet. More important, it is becoming clear that, with a few conspicuous exceptions, the hunter-gatherer subsistence base is at least routine and reliable and at best surprisingly abundant. Anthropologists have consistently tended to underestimate the viability of even those "marginal isolates" of hunting peoples that have been available to ethnographers.

The purpose of this paper is to analyze the food getting activities of one such "marginal" people, the !Kung Bushmen of the Kalahari Desert. Three related questions are posed: How do the Bushmen make a living? How

easy or difficult is it for them to do this? What kinds of evidence are necessary to measure and evaluate the precariousness or security of a way of life? And after the relevant data are presented, two further questions are asked: What makes this security of life possible? To what extent are the Bushmen typical of hunter-gatherers in general?

BUSHMAN SUBSISTENCE

The !Kung Bushmen of Botswana are an apt case for analysis. They inhabit the semi-arid northwest region of the Kalahari Desert. With only six to nine inches of rainfall per year, this is, by any account, a marginal environment for human habitation. In fact, it is precisely the unattractiveness of their homeland that has kept the !Kung isolated from extensive contact with their agricultural and pastoral neighbors.

Field work was carried out in the Dobe area, a line of eight permanent waterholes near the South-West Africa border and 125 miles south of the Okavango River. The population of the Dobe area consists of 466 Bushmen, including 379 permanent residents living in independent camps or associated with Bantu cattle posts, as well as 87 seasonal visitors. The Bushmen share the area with some 340 Bantu pastoralists largely of the Herero and Tswana tribes. The ethnographic present refers to the period of field work: October, 1963-January, 1965.

TABLE 4.1
NUMBERS AND DISTRIBUTION OF RESIDENT BUSHMEN AND BANTU BY WATERHOLE*

Name of Waterhole	No. of Camps	Population of Camps	Other Bushmen	Total Bushmen	Bantu
Dobe	2	37	—	37	—
!angwa	1	16	23	39	84
Bate	2	30	12	42	21
!ubi	1	19	—	19	65
!gose	3	52	9	61	18
/ai/ai	5	94	13	107	67
!xabe	—	—	8	8	12
Mahopa	—	—	23	23	73
Total	14	248	88	336	340

*Figures do not include 130 Bushmen outside area on the date of census.

The Bushmen living in independent camps lack firearms, livestock, and agriculture. Apart from occasional visits to the Herero for milk, these !Kung are entirely dependent upon hunting and gathering for their subsistence. Politically they are under the nominal authority of the Tswana headman, although they pay no taxes and receive very few government services. European presence amounts to one overnight government patrol every six to eight weeks. Although Dobe-area !Kung have had some contact with outsiders since the 1880's, the majority of them continue to hunt and gather because there is no viable alternative locally available to them.

Each of the fourteen independent camps is associated with one of the permanent waterholes. During the dry season (May-October) the entire population is clustered around these wells. Table 4.1 shows the numbers at each well at the end of the 1964 dry season. Two wells had no camp resident and one large well supported five camps. The number of camps at each well and the size of each camp changed frequently during the course of the year. The "camp" is an open aggregate of cooperating persons which changes in size and composition from day to day. Therefore, I have avoided the term "band" in describing the !Kung Bushman living groups.

Each waterhole has a hinterland lying within a six-mile radius which is regularly exploited for vegetable and animal foods. These areas are not territories in the zoological sense, since they are not defended against outsiders. Rather they constitute the resources that lie within a convenient walking distance of a waterhole. The camp is a self-sufficient subsistence unit. The members move out each day to hunt and gather, and return in the evening to pool the collected foods in such a way that every person present receives an equitable share. Trade in foodstuffs between camps is minimal; personnel do move freely from camp to camp, however. The net effect is of a population constantly in motion. On the average, an individual spends a third of his time living only with close relatives, a

third visiting other camps, and a third entertaining visitors from other camps.

Because of the strong emphasis on sharing, and the frequency of movement, surplus accumulation of storable plant foods and dried meat is kept to a minimum. There is rarely more than two or three days' supply of food on hand in a camp at any time. The result of this lack of surplus is that a constant subsistence effort must be maintained throughout the year. Unlike agriculturalists who work hard during the planting and harvesting seasons and undergo "seasonal unemployment" for several months, the Bushmen hunter-gatherers collect food every third or fourth day throughout the year.

Vegetable foods comprise from 60-80 per cent of the total diet by weight, and collecting involves two or three days of work per woman per week. The men also collect plants and small animals but their major contribution to the diet is the hunting of medium and large game. The men are conscientious but not particularly successful hunters; although men's and women's work input is roughly equivalent in terms of man-day of effort, the women provide two to three times as much food by weight as the men.

Table 4.2 summarizes the seasonal activity cycle observed among the Dobe-area !Kung in 1964. For the greater part of the year, food is locally abundant and easily collected. It is only during the end of the dry season in September and October, when desirable foods have been eaten out in the immediate vicinity of the waterholes, that the people have to plan longer hikes of 10-15 miles and carry their own water to those areas where the mongongo nut is still available. The important point is that food is a constant, but distance required to reach food is a variable; it is short in the summer, fall, and early winter, and reaches its maximum in the spring.

This analysis attempts to provide quantitative measures of subsistence status including data on the following topics: abundance and variety of resources, diet selectivity, range size and population density, the composition of the work force, the ratio of work to leisure time, and the caloric and protein

TABLE 4.2
THE BUSHMAN ANNUAL ROUND

	Jan.	Feb.	Mar.	April	May	June	July	Aug.	Sept.	Oct.	Nov.	Dec.
SEASON	SUMMER RAINS		AUTUMN DRY			WINTER DRY			SPRING DRY		FIRST RAINS	
Availability of Water	Temporary summer pools everywhere			Large summer pools			Permanent waterholes only					Summer pools developing
Group Moves	Widely dispersed at summer pools			At large summer pools				All population restricted to permanent waterholes				Moving out to summer pools
Men's Subsistence Activities	1. Hunting with bow, arrows, and dogs (Year-round)											
	2. Running down immatures						Trapping small game in snares				Running down newborn animals	
	3. Some gathering (Year-round)											
Women's Subsistence Activities	1. Gathering of mongongo nuts (Year-round)											
	2. Fruits, berries, melons						Roots, bulbs, resins				Roots, leafy greens	
Ritual Activities	Dancing, trance performances, and ritual curing (Year-round)				Boys' intiation[1]							[2]
Relative Subsistence Hardship	Water-food distance minimal						Increasing distance from water to food				Water-food distance minimal	

[1] Held once every five years; none in 1963-64.
[2] New Year's: Bushmen join the celebrations of their missionized Bantu neighbors.

levels in the diet. The value of quantitative data is that they can be used comparatively and also may be useful in archeological reconstruction. In addition, one can avoid the pitfalls of subjective and qualitative impressions; for example, statements about food "anxiety" have proven to be difficult to generalize across cultures.

ABUNDANCE AND VARIETY
OF RESOURCES

It is impossible to define "abundance" of resources absolutely. However, one index of *relative* abundance is whether or not a population exhausts all the food available from a given area. By this criterion, the habitat of the Dobe-area Bushmen is abundant in naturally occurring foods. By far the most important food is the Mongongo (mangetti) nut (*Ricinodendron rautanenii* Schinz). Although tens of thousands of pounds of these nuts are harvested and eaten each year, thousands more rot on the ground each year for want of picking.

The mongongo nut, because of its abundance and reliability, alone accounts for 50 per cent of the vegetable diet by weight. In this respect it resembles a cultivated staple crop such as maize or rice. Nutritionally it is even more remarkable, for it contains five times the calories and ten times the proteins per cooked unit of the cereal crops. The average daily per-capita consumption of 300 nuts yields about 1,260 calories and 56 grams of protein. This modest portion, weighing only about 7.5 ounces, contains the caloric equivalent of 2.5 pounds of cooked rice and the protein equivalent of 14 ounces of lean beef.

Furthermore the mongongo nut is drought resistant and it will still be abundant in the dry years when cultivated crops may fail. The extremely hard outer shell protects the inner kernel from rot and allows the nuts to be harvested for up to twelve months after they have fallen to the ground. A diet based on mongongo nuts is in fact more reliable than one based on cultivated foods, and it is not surprising, therefore, that when a Bush-

man was asked why he hadn't taken to agriculture he replied: "Why should we plant, when there are so many mongongo nuts in the world?"

Apart from the mongongo, the Bushmen have available 84 other species of edible food plants, including 29 species of fruits, berries, and melons and 30 species of roots and bulbs. The existence of this variety allows for a wide range of alternatives in subsistence strategy. During the summer months the Bushmen have no problem other than to choose among the tastiest and most easily collected foods. Many species, which are quite edible but less attractive, are bypassed, so that gathering never exhausts *all* the available plant foods of an area. During the dry season the diet becomes much more eclectic and the many species of roots, bulbs, and edible resins make an important contribution. It is this broad base that provides an essential margin of safety during the end of the dry season when the mongongo nut forests are difficult to reach. In addition, it is likely that these rarely utilized species provide important nutritional and mineral trace elements that may be lacking in the more popular foods.

DIET SELECTIVITY

If the Bushmen were living close to the "starvation" level, then one would expect them to exploit every available source of nutrition. That their life is well above this level is indicated by the data in Table 4.3. Here all the edible plant species are arranged in classes according to the frequency with which they were observed to be eaten. It should be noted that although there are some 85 species available, about 90 per cent of the vegetable diet by weight is drawn from only 23 species. In other words, 75 per cent of the listed species provide only 10 per cent of the food value.

In their meat-eating habits, the Bushmen show a similar selectivity. Of the 223 local species of animals known and named by the Bushmen, 54 species are classified as edible, and of these only 17 species were hunted on a

TABLE 4.3
!KUNG BUSHMAN PLANT FOODS

Food Class	Part Eaten								Total number of species in class	Totals (Percentage)	
	Fruit and Nut	Bean and Root	Fruit and Stalk	Root, Bulb	Fruit, Berry, Melon	Resin	Leaves	Seed, Bean		Estimated contribution by weight to vegetable diet	Estimated contribution of each species
I. PRIMARY Eaten daily throughout year (mongongo nut)	1	—	—	—	—	—	—	—	1	c.50	c.50[1]
II. MAJOR Eaten daily in season	1	1	1	1	4	—	—	—	8	c.25	c.3[2]
III. MINOR Eaten several times per week in season	—	—	—	7	3	2	2	—	14	c.15	c.1
IV. SUPPLEMENTARY Eaten when classes I-III locally unavailable	—	—	—	9	12	10	1	—	32	c.7	c.0.2[3]
V. RARE Eaten several times per year	—	—	—	9	4	—	—	—	13	c.3	c.0.1
VI. PROBLEMATIC Edible but not observed to be eaten	—	—	—	4	6	4	1	2	17	nil	nil
TOTAL SPECIES	2	1	1	30	29	16	4	2	85	100	—

[1] 1 species constitutes 50 per cent of the vegetable diet by weight.
[2] 23 species constitute 90 per cent of the vegetable diet by weight.
[3] 62 species constitute the remaining 10 per cent of the diet.

regular basis.[1] Only a handful of the dozens of edible species of small mammals, birds, reptiles, and insects that occur locally are regarded as food. Such animals as rodents, snakes, lizards, termites, and grasshoppers, which in the literature are included in the Bushman dietary, are despised by the Bushmen of the Dobe area.

RANGE SIZE AND POPULATION DENSITY

The necessity to travel long distances, the high frequency of moves, and the maintenance of populations at low densities are also features commonly associated with the hunting and gathering way of life. Density estimates for hunters in western North America and Australia have ranged from 3 persons/ square mile to as low as 1 person/100 square miles. In 1963-65, the resident and visiting Bushmen were observed to utilize an area of about 1,000 square miles during the course of the annual round for an effective population density of 41 persons/100 square miles. Within this area, however, the amount of ground covered by members of an individual camp was surprisingly small. A day's round-trip of twelve miles serves to define a "core" area six miles in radius surrounding each water point. By fanning out in all directions from their well, the members of a camp can gain access to the food resources of well over 100 square miles of territory within a two-hour hike. Except for a few weeks each year, areas lying beyond this six-mile radius are rarely utilized, even though they are no less rich in plants and game than are the core areas.

Although the Bushmen move their camps frequently (five or six times a year) they do not move them very far. A rainy season camp in the nut forests is rarely more than ten or twelve miles from the home waterhole, and often new campsites are occupied only a few hundred yards away from the previous one. By these criteria, the Bushmen do not lead a free-ranging nomadic way of life. For ex-

ample, they do not undertake long marches of 30 to 100 miles to get food, since this task can be readily fulfilled within a day's walk of home base. When such long marches do occur they are invariably for visiting, trading, and marriage arrangements, and should not be confused with the normal routine of subsistence.

DEMOGRAPHIC FACTORS

Another indicator of the harshness of a way of life is the age at which people die. Ever since Hobbes characterized life in the state of nature as "nasty, brutish and short," the assumption has been that hunting and gathering is so rigorous that members of such societies are rapidly worn out and meet an early death. Silberbauer, for example, says of the Gwi Bushmen of the central Kalahari that "life expectancy . . . is difficult to calculate, but I do not believe that many live beyond 45." And Coon has said of the hunters in general:

The practice of abandoning the hopelessly ill and aged has been observed in many parts of the world. It is always done by people living in poor environments where it is necessary to move about frequently to obtain food, where food is scarce, and transportation difficult . . . . Among peoples who are forced to live in this way the oldest generation, the generation of individuals who have passed their physical peak is reduced in numbers and influence. There is no body of elders to hand on tradition and control the affairs of younger men and women, and no formal system of age grading.

The !Kung Bushmen of the Dobe area flatly contradict this view. In a total population of 466, no fewer than 46 individuals (17 men and 29 women) were determined to be over 60 years of age, a proportion that compares favorably to the percentage of elderly in industrialized populations.

The aged hold a respected position in Bushman society and are the effective leaders of the camps. Senilicide is extremely rare. Long after their productive years have passed, the old people are fed and cared for by their children and grandchildren. The blind, the senile, and the crippled are respected for the special

1. Listed in order of their importance, the principal species in the diet are: wart hog, kudu, duiker, steenbok, gemsbok, wildebeeste, springhare, porcupine, ant bear, hare, guinea fowl, francolin (two species), korhaan, tortoise, and python.

ritual and technical skills they possess. For instance, the four elders at !gose waterhole were totally or partially blind, but this handicap did not prevent their active participation in decision-making and ritual curing.

Another significant feature of the composition of the work force is the late assumption of adult responsibility by the adolescents. Young people are not expected to provide food regularly until they are married. Girls typically marry between the ages of 15 and 20, and boys about five years later, so that it is not unusual to find healthy, active teenagers visiting from camp to camp while their older relatives provide food for them.

As a result, the people in the age group 20-62 support a surprisingly large percentage of nonproductive young and old people. About 40 per cent of the population in camps contribute little to the food supplies. This allocation of work to young and middle-aged adults allows for a relatively carefree childhood and adolescence and a relatively unstrenuous old age.

LEISURE AND WORK

Another important index of ease or difficulty of subsistence is the amount of time devoted to the food quest. Hunting has usually been regarded by social scientists as a way of life in which merely keeping alive is so formidable a task that members of such societies lack the leisure time necessary to "build culture." The !Kung Bushmen would appear to conform to the rule, for as Lorna Marshall says:

It is vividly apparent that among the !Kung Bushmen, ethos, or "the spirit which actuates manners and customs," is survival. Their time and energies are almost wholly given to this task, for life in their environment requires that they spend their days mainly in procuring food.

It is certainly true that getting food is the most important single activity in Bushman life. However, this statement would apply equally well to small-scale agricultural and pastoral societies too. How much time is *actually* devoted to the food quest is fortunately an empirical question. And an analysis of the work effort of the Dobe Bushmen shows some unexpected results. From July 6 to August 2, 1964, I recorded all the daily activities of the Bushmen living at the Dobe waterhole. Because of the coming and going of visitors, the camp population fluctuated in size day by day, from a low of 23 to a high of 40, with a mean of 31.8 persons. Each day some of the adult members of the camp went out to hunt and/or gather while others stayed home or went visiting. The daily recording of all personnel on hand made it possible to calculate the number of man-days of work as a percentage of total number of man-days of consumption.

Although the Bushmen do not organize their activities on the basis of a seven-day week, I have divided the data this way to make them more intelligible. The work-week was calculated to show how many days out of seven each adult spent in subsistence activities (Table 4.4, Column 7). Week II has been eliminated from the totals since the investigator contributed food. In week I, the people spent an average of 2.3 days in subsistence activities, in week III, 1.9 days, and in week IV, 3-2 days. In all, the adults of the Dobe camp worked about two and a half days a week. Since the average working day was about six hours long, the fact emerges that !Kung Bushmen of Dobe, despite their harsh environment, devote from twelve to nineteen hours a week to getting food. Even the hardest working individual in the camp, a man named =oma who went out hunting on sixteen of the 28 days, spent a maximum of 32 hours a week in the food quest.

Because the Bushmen do not amass a surplus of foods, there are no seasons of exceptionally intensive activities such as planting and harvesting and no seasons of unemployment. The level of work observed is an accurate reflection of the effort required to meet the immediate caloric needs of the group. This work diary covers the mid-winter dry season, a period when food is neither at its most plentiful nor at its scarcest levels, and the diary documents the transition from better to worse conditions (see Table 4.2). During the fourth week the gatherers were mak-

TABLE 4.4
SUMMARY OF DOBE WORK DIARY

Week	(1) mean group size	(2) adult-days	(3) child-days	(4) total man-days of consumption	(5) man-days of work	(6) meat (lbs.)	(7) average work week/adult	(8) Index of Subsistence Effort
I (July 6-12)	25.6 (23-29)	114	65	179	37	104	2.3	.21
II (July 13-19)	28.3 (23-27)	125	73	198	22	80	1.2	.11
III (July 20-26)	34.3 (29-40)	156	84	240	42	177	1.9	.18
IV (July 27-Aug. 2)	35.6 (32-40)	167	82	249	77	129	3.2	.31
4-week Total	30.9	562	304	866	178	490	2.2	.21
Adjusted Total[1]	31.8	437	231	668	156	410	2.5	.23

[1]See text.

KEY: Column 1: Mean group size $= \dfrac{\text{total man-days of consumption}}{7}$.

Column 7: Work week = the number of work days per adult per week.

Column 8: Index Subsistence Effort $= \dfrac{\text{man-days of work}}{\text{man-days of consumption}}$ (e.g., in Week I, the value of "S" = .21, i.e., 21 days of work/100 days of consumption or 1 work day produces food for 5 consumption days).

TABLE 4.5

CALORIC AND PROTEIN LEVELS IN THE !KUNG BUSHMAN DIETARY, JULY-AUGUST, 1964

Class of Food	Percentage Contribution to Diet by Weight	Per Capita Consumption		Calories per person per day	Percentage Caloric Contribution of Meat and Vegetables
		Weight in grams	Protein in grams		
Meat	37	230	34.5	690	33
Mongongo Nuts	33	210	56.7	1,260 ⎫	
Other Vegetable				⎬	67
Foods	30	190	1.9	190 ⎭	
Total All Sources	100	630	93.1	2,140	100

ing overnight trips to camps in the mongongo nut forests seven to ten miles distant from the waterhole. These longer trips account for the rise in the level of work, from twelve or thirteen to nineteen hours per week.

If food getting occupies such a small proportion of a Bushman's waking hours, then how *do* people allocate their time? A woman gathers on one day enough food to feed her family for three days, and spends the rest of her time resting in camp, doing embroidery, visiting other camps, or entertaining visitors from other camps. For each day at home, kitchen routines, such as cooking, nut cracking, collecting firewood, and fetching water, occupy one to three hours of her time. This rhythm of steady work and steady leisure is maintained throughout the year.

The hunters tend to work more frequently than the women, but their schedule is uneven. It is not unusual for a man to hunt avidly for a week and then do no hunting at all for two or three weeks. Since hunting is an unpredictable business and subject to magical control, hunters sometimes experience a run of bad luck and stop hunting for a month or longer. During these periods, visiting, entertaining, and especially dancing are the primary activities of men. (Unlike the Hadza, gambling is only a minor leisure activity.)

The trance-dance is the focus of Bushman ritual life; over 50 per cent of the men have trained as trance-performers and regularly enter trance during the course of the all-night dances. At some camps, trance-dances occur as frequently as two or three times a week and those who have entered trances the night before rarely go out hunting the following day. Accounts of Bushman trance-performances have been published in Lorna Marshall and Lee. In a camp with five or more hunters, there are usually two or three who are actively hunting and several others who are inactive. The net effect is to phase the hunting and nonhunting so that a fairly steady supply of meat is brought into a camp.

CALORIC RETURNS

Is the modest work effort of the Bushmen sufficient to provide the calories necessary to maintain the health of the population? Or have the !Kung, in common with some agricultural peoples, adjusted to a permanently substandard nutritional level?

During my field work I did not encounter any cases of kwashiorkor, the most common nutritional disease in the children of African agricultural societies. However, without medical examinations, it is impossible to exclude the possibility that subclinical signs of malnutrition existed.

Another measure of nutritional adequacy is the average consumption of calories and proteins per person per day. The estimate for the Bushmen is based on observations of the weights of foods of known composition that were brought into Dobe camp on each day of the study period. The per-capita figure is obtained by dividing the total weight of foodstuffs by the total number of persons in the camp. These results are set out in detail elsewhere and can only be summarized here. During the study period 410 pounds of meat were brought in by the hunters of the Dobe camp, for a daily share of nine ounces of meat per person. About 700 pounds of vegetable foods were gathered and consumed during the same period. Table 4.5 sets out the calories and proteins available per capita in the !Kung Bushman dietary from meat, mongongo nuts, and other vegetable sources.

This output of 2,140 calories and 93.1 grams of protein per person per day may be compared with the Recommended Daily Allowances (RDA) for persons of the small size and stature but vigorous activity regime of the !Kung Bushmen. The RDA for Bushmen can be estimated at 1,975 calories and 60 grams of protein per person per day. Thus it is apparent that food output exceeds energy requirements by 165 calories and 33 grams of protein. One can tentatively conclude that even a modest subsistence effort of two or three days work per week is enough to provide an adequate diet for the !Kung Bushmen.

THE SECURITY OF BUSHMAN LIFE

I have attempted to evaluate the subsistence base of one contemporary hunter-gatherer society living in a marginal environment. the !Kung Bushmen have available to them some relatively abundant high-quality foods, and they do not have to walk very far or work very hard to get them. Furthermore this modest work effort provides sufficient calories to support not only the active adults, but also a large number of middle-aged and elderly people. The Bushmen do not have to press their youngsters into the service of the food quest, nor do they have to dispose of the oldsters after they have ceased to be productive.

The evidence presented assumes an added significance because this security of life was observed during the third year of one of the most severe droughts in South Africa's history. Most of the 576,000 people of Botswana are pastoralists and agriculturalists. After the crops had failed three years in succession and over 100,000 head of cattle had died on the range for lack of water, the World Food Program of the United Nations instituted a famine relief program which has grown to include 180,000 people, over 30 per cent of the population. This program did not touch the Dobe area in the isolated northwest corner of the country, and the Herero and Tswana women there were able to feed their families only by joining the Bushman women to forage for wild foods. Thus the natural plant resources of the Dobe area were carrying a higher proportion of population than would be the case in years when the Bantu harvested crops. Yet this added pressure on the land did not seem to adversely affect the Bushmen.

In one sense it was unfortunate that the period of my field work happened to coincide with the drought, since I was unable to witness a "typical" annual subsistence cycle. However, in another sense, the coincidence was a lucky one, for the drought put the Bushmen and their subsistence system to the acid test and, in terms of adaptation to scarce resources, they passed with flying colors. One can postulate that their subsistence base would be even more substantial during years of higher rainfall.

What are the crucial factors that make this way of life possible? I suggest that the primary factor is the Bushmen's strong emphasis on vegetable food sources. Although hunting involves a great deal of effort and prestige, plant foods provide from 60-80 per cent of the annual diet by weight. Meat has come to be regarded as a special treat; when available, it is welcomed as a break from the routine of vegetable foods, but it is never depended upon as a staple. No one ever goes hungry when hunting fails.

The reason for this emphasis is not hard to find. Vegetable foods are abundant, sedentary, and predictable. They grow in the same place year after year, and the gatherer is guaranteed a day's return of food for a day's expenditure of energy. Game animals, by contrast, are scarce, mobile, unpredictable, and difficult to catch. A hunter has no guarantee of success and may in fact go for days or weeks without killing a large mammal. During the study period, there were eleven men in the Dobe camp, of whom four did no hunting at all. The seven active men spent a total of 78 man-days hunting, and this work input yielded eighteen animals killed, or one kill for every four man-days of hunting. The probability of any one hunter making a kill on a given day was 0.23. By contrast, the probability of a woman finding plant food on a given day was 1.00. In other words, hunting and gathering are not equally felicitous subsistence alternatives.

Consider the productivity per man-hour of the two kinds of subsistence activities. One man-hour of hunting produces about 100 edible calories, and of gathering, 240 calories. Gathering is thus seen to be 2.4 times more productive than hunting. In short, hunting is a *high-risk, low-return* subsistence activity, while gathering is a *low-risk, high-return* subsistence activity.

It is not at all contradictory that the hunting complex holds a central place in the Bushman ethos and that meat is valued more highly than vegetable foods. Analogously, steak is valued more highly than potatoes in the food preferences of our own society. In both situations the meat is more "costly" than the vegetable food. In the Bushman case, the cost of food can be measured in terms of time and energy expended. By this standard, 1,000 calories of meat "costs" ten man-hours, while the "cost" of 1,000 calories of vegetable foods is only four man-hours. Further, it is to be expected that the less predictable, more expensive food source would have a greater accretion of myth and ritual built up around it than would the routine staples of life, which rarely if ever fail.

ESKIMO-BUSHMAN COMPARISONS

Were the Bushmen to be deprived of their vegetable food sources, their life would become much more arduous and precarious. This lack of plant foods, in fact, is precisely the situation among the Netsilik Eskimo, reported by Balikci. The Netsilik and other Central Arctic peoples are perhaps unique in the almost total absence of vegetable foods in their diet. This factor, in combination with the great cyclical variation in the numbers and distribution of Arctic fauna, makes Eskimo life the most precarious human adaptation on earth. In effect, *the kinds of animals that are "luxury goods" to many hunters and gatherers, are to the Eskimos, the absolute necessities of life.* However, even this view should not be exaggerated, since most of the Eskimos in historic times have lived south of the Arctic Circle and many of the Eskimos at all latitudes have depended primarily on fishing, which is a much more reliable source of food than is the hunting of land and sea mammals.

WHAT HUNTERS DO FOR A LIVING: A COMPARATIVE STUDY

I have discussed how the !Kung Bushmen are able to manage on the scarce resources of their inhospitable environment. The essence of their successful strategy seems to be that while they depend primarily on the more stable and abundant food sources (vegetables in their case), they are nevertheless willing to devote considerable energy to the less reliable and more highly valued food sources such as medium and large mammals. The steady but modest input of work by the women provides the former, and the more intensive labors of the men provide the latter. It would be theoretically possible for the Bushmen to survive entirely on vegetable foods, but life would be boring indeed without the excitement of meat feasts. The totality of their subsistence activities thus represents an outcome of two individual goals; the first is the desire to live well with adequate leisure time, and the second is the desire to enjoy the rewards, both social and nutritional, afforded by the killing of game. In short, *the Bushmen of the Dobe area eat as much vegetable food as they need, and as much meat as they can.*

It seems reasonable that a similar kind of subsistence strategy would be characteristic of hunters and gatherers in general. Wherever two or more kinds of natural foods are available, one would predict that the population exploiting them would emphasize the more reliable source. We would also expect, however, that the people would not neglect the alternative means of subsistence. The general view offered here is that gathering activities, for plants and shellfish, should be the most productive of food for hunting and gathering man, followed by fishing, where this source is available. The hunting of mammals is the least reliable source of food and should be generally less important than either gathering or fishing.

In order to test this hypothesis, a sample of 58 societies was drawn from the *Ethnographic Atlas*. The basis for inclusion in the sample was a 100 per cent dependence on hunting, gathering and fishing for subsistence as rated in Column 7-11 of the Atlas. The *Ethnographic Atlas* coding discusses "Subsistence Economy" as follows:

A set of five digits indicates the estimated relative dependence of the society on each of the five major types of subsistence activity. The first digit refers to the gathering of wild plants and small land fauna; the second, to hunting, including trapping and fowling; the third, to fishing, including shell fishing and the pursuit of large aquatic animals; the fourth, to animal husbandry; the fifth, to agriculture.

Two changes have been made in the definitions of subsistence. First, the participants at the symposium on Man the Hunter agreed that the "pursuit of large aquatic animals" is more properly classified under hunting than under fishing. Similarly, it was recommended that shellfishing should be classified under gathering, not fishing. These suggestions have been followed and the definitions now read: *Gathering*—collecting of wild plant, small land fauna and shellfish; *Hunting*—pursuit of land and sea mammals; *Fishing*—obtaining of fish by any technique. In 25 cases, the subsistence scores have been changed in light of these definitions and after consulting ethnographic sources.

In the Old World and South American sample of 24 societies, sixteen depend on gathering, five on fishing, while only three depend primarily on mammal hunting: the Yukaghir of northeast Asia, and the Ona and Shiriana of South America. In the North American sample, thirteen societies have primary dependence on gathering, thirteen on fishing, and eight on hunting. Thus for the world as a whole, half of the societies (29 cases) emphasize gathering, one-third (18 cases) fishing, and the remaining one-sixth (11 cases) hunting.

On this evidence, the "hunting" way of life appears to be in the minority. The result serves to underline the point made earlier that mammal hunting is the least reliable of the subsistence sources, and one would expect few societies to place primary dependence on it. As will be shown, most of the societies that rely primarily on mammals do so because their particular habitats offer no viable alternative subsistence strategy.

THE RELATION OF LATITUDE TO SUBSISTENCE

The peoples we have classified as "hunters" apparently depend for most of their subsistence on sources *other* than meat, namely, wild plants, shellfish and fish. In fact the present sample over-emphasizes the incidence of hunting and fishing since some three-fifths of the cases (34/58) are drawn from North America (north of the Rio Grande), a region which lies entirely within the temperate and arctic zones. Since the abundance and species variety of edible plants decreases as one moves out of the tropical and temperate zones, and approaches zero in the arctic, it is essential that the incidence of hunting, gathering, and fishing be related to latitude....

Hunting appears as the dominant mode of subsistence *only* in the highest latitudes (60 or more degrees from the equator). In the arctic, hunting is primary in six of the eight societies. In the cool to cold temperate latitudes, 40 to 59 degrees from the equator, fishing is the dominant mode, appearing as primary in 14 out of 22 cases. In the warm-temperate, subtropical, and tropical latitudes, zero to 39 degrees from the equator, gathering is by far the dominant mode of subsistence, appearing as primary in 25 of the 28 cases.

For modern hunters, at any rate, it seems legitimate to predict a hunting emphasis only in the arctic, a fishing emphasis in the mid-high latitudes, and a gathering emphasis in the rest of the world.[2]

THE IMPORTANCE OF HUNTING

Although hunting is rarely the primary source of food, it does make a remarkably stable contribution to the diet. Fishing appears to be dispensable in the tropics, and a number of northern peoples manage to do without gathered foods, but, with a single exception, *all* societies at all latitudes derive at least 20 per cent of their diet from the hunting of mammals. Latitude appears to make little difference in the amount of hunting that people do. Except for the highest latitudes, where hunting contributes over half of the diet in many cases, hunted foods almost everywhere else constitute 20 to 45 per cent of the diet. In fact, the mean, the median, and the mode for hunting all converge on a figure of 35 per cent for hunter-gatherers at all latitudes. This percentage of meat corresponds closely to the 37 per cent noted in the diet of the !Kung Bushmen of the Dobe area. It is evident that the !Kung, far from being an aberrant case, are entirely typical of the hunters in general in the amount of meat they consume.

CONCLUSIONS

Three points ought to be stressed. First, life in the state of nature is not necessarily nasty, brutish, and short. The Dobe-area Bushmen live well today on wild plants and meat, in spite of the fact that they are confined to the least productive portion of the range in which Bushmen peoples were formerly found. It is likely that an even more substantial subsistence base would have been characteristic of these hunters and gatherers in the past, when they had the pick of African habitats to choose from.

Second, the basis of Bushman diet is derived from sources other than meat. This emphasis makes good ecological sense to the !Kung Bushmen and appears to be a common feature among hunters and gatherers in general. Since a 30 to 40 per cent input of meat is such a consistent target for modern hunters in a variety of habitats, is it not reasonable to postulate a similar percentage for prehistoric hunters? Certainly the absence of plant remains on archeological sites is by itself not sufficient evidence for the absence of gathering. Recently-abandoned Bushman campsites show a similar absence of vegetable remains, although this paper has clearly shown that plant foods comprise over 60 per cent of the actual diet.

Finally, one gets the impression that hunting societies have been chosen by ethnologists to illustrate a dominant theme, such as the extreme importance of environment in the molding of certain cultures. Such a theme can be best exemplified by cases in which the technology is simple and/or the environment is harsh. This emphasis on the dramatic may have been pedagogically useful, but unfortunately it has led to the assumption that a precarious hunting subsistence base was characteristic of all cultures in the Pleistocene. This view of both modern and ancient hunters ought to be reconsidered. Specifically I am suggesting a shift in focus away from the dramatic and unusual cases, and toward a consideration of hunting and gathering as a persistent and well-adapted way of life.

2. When severity of winter is plotted against subsistence choices, a similar picture emerges. Hunting is primary in three of the five societies in very cold climates (annual temperature less than 32° F.); fishing is primary in 10 of the 17 societies in cold climinates (32°-50° F.); and gathering is primary in 27 of the 36 societies in mild to hot climates (over 50° F.).

5. THE GREAT BASIN SHOSHONEAN INDIANS: AN EXAMPLE OF A FAMILY LEVEL OF SOCIOCULTURAL INTEGRATION

JULIAN H. STEWARD

Reprinted from The Theory of Culture Change: The Methodology of Multilinear Evolution *(Urbana: University of Illinois Press, 1955). At the time of his death in 1972, Julian H. Steward was Graduate Research Professor of Anthropology and a member of the Center for Advanced Studies at the University of Illinois. His research interests covered North American and South American Indians, comparative studies of hunting and gathering societies, especially of the Great Basin, cultural evolution, and the modernization of traditional societies. He was also the author of* Sociopolitical Groups of the Great Basin, *and co-author and editor of* Handbook of South American Indians, The People of Puerto Rico, Native Peoples of South America *(with Louis C. Faron), and* Contemporary Transformations in Traditional Societies.

■ The Shoshonean Indians of the North American Great Basin—described by Steward in this selection—represent a different variation from the !Kung on the overall strategy of hunting-gathering. In contrast to the !Kung, the central fact about the Shoshoneans is the severe limitation of natural resources in their habitat. Because of the scarcity of animals, the diet of the Shoshoneans depended more on gathering than on hunting, and this limited the groups into which Shoshoneans could band. It was difficult for them to maintain large aggregates of people because of the vast areas required to support each person, and it was more efficient for families to work separately in gathering wild foods.

While the Shoshoneans, like the !Kung, exhibit fission and fusion in their camps, they do so under different conditions. The Shoshoneans had larger encampments during times of plenty, splitting up during times of scarcity. This had important consequences for other aspects of their social relations, especially in decision-making.

What was the adaptive (decision-making) unit among these people? The strategy of adaptation represented by the Shoshoneans is perhaps best understood in terms of a hypothesis that the nature of the adaptive unit changed seasonally, according to the availability of resources and other factors. During the winter months the family was the adaptive unit, in the sense that it was completely autonomous in decision-making and implementation. During the summer season the multi-family band, which was able to congregate because enough food was concentrated in one area, was the adaptive unit. During the summer, Steward notes, it was possible for one man to assume leadership if he owned a net for a drive and if there were enough animals to warrant a hunt. If these fortuitous factors were absent, decision-making probably remained at the family level.

Thus, as Steward observes, unpredictability was an important feature of the Shoshonean habitat. Fortuitousness was the basis of their adaptation. Hence interfamily associations also were erratic and largely unpredictable. The property system developed by the Shoshoneans also was an aspect of their adaptation, as was their limited form of cooperation.

The delicate equilibrium achieved by the Shoshoneans with their habitat is highlighted by Steward's description of the consequences of the introduction of the horse. Domesticated animals, especially in large numbers, exert pressure on the land because they must be fed, and on the organization of social relations because they must be cared for and protected. This posed a serious problem for the Shoshoneans inasmuch as horses subsisted on the same flora the people themselves depended on.

For many Shoshonean groups the horse at first was useless as a source of energy and as an instrument of food acquisition; it was eaten. Under different habitational conditions the horse became valuable as an instrument of production. It was useful for those who lived near the buffalo ranges, and for a while it became important in the lives of the Western Shoshoni and Northern Paiute when their landscape was radically altered by the introduction of a new feature: the invading European and his culture, which provided worthwhile objects for raids But the Shoshoneans were no match for the Europeans; their culture was destroyed almost overnight. (The postscript at the end of this Selection was prepared by Professor Steward for this book in 1967; it was written in light of the conference published as *Man the Hunter,* edited by R. B. Lee and I. De Vore.)

The reader who wants to study the western North American foragers should consult *Handbook of the Indians of California,* by A. L. Kroeber (Berkeley: University of California Press, 1925); *The Two Worlds of the Washo,* by James Downs (New York: Holt, Rinehart and Winston, 1966); *Paiute Sorcery,* by Beatrice B. Whiting (New York: Johnson Reprint Corp., 1950); and *Archaeological Researches in the Northern Great Basin,* by Luther S. Cressman and others (Washington, D.C.: Carnegie Institution, 1942). One of the earliest attempts to relate patterns of social organization to adaptations to different habitats was Kroeber's *Cultural and Natural Areas of Native North America* (Berkeley: University of California Press, 1940). ∎

THE TYPES OF CULTURES and processes of development illustrated in this chapter are arranged in a sequence of successively higher levels of sociocultural integration. This does not imply a unilinear evolutionary sequence of cultural development. Since particular cultures have unlike configurations and element content resulting from their distinctive origins, histories, and ecological adaptations, many different local or areal types of culture may represent the same level of sociocultural integration. Thus, the Shoshonean Indians of the Great Basin and the Eskimo illustrate an essentially family level of integration, although their respective ways of life and cultural types differed quite profoundly. Every level could be exemplified by several different cultures, some representing cross-culturally recurrent types and other unique developments.

The Shoshonean-speaking Indians—the Ute, Western Shoshoni, and Northern Paiute of western Colorado, Utah, Nevada, and eastern Oregon and California—acquired most of their hunting and gathering techniques from other peoples, but their general adaptation to the intermontane steppes and deserts was so distinctive that they constitute a special culture area usually called the Great Basin or Basin-Plateau area. In a quantitative sense, this culture was extremely simple. An "element list," which breaks the culture down into details such as basket weaves and shapes, religious beliefs, social practices, and other details, includes a total of about 3,000 items. By comparison, the U.S. forces landing at Casa Blanca during World War II unloaded 500,000 items of material equipment alone. The total "elements" of modern American culture would probably run to several million.

Shoshonean culture, however, is of interest for the nature of its organization as much as for its quantitative simplicity. Virtually all cultural activities were carried out by the family in comparative isolation from other families. A contrast with modern America helps clarify this point. In the United States today, people are highly specialized workers in an economic system geared to national and international patterns; education is increasingly standardized and the community or state takes over this function from the family when the child is six years old or younger; health practices are dictated largely by research carried out on an international scale and in part administered by the state and community; recreation more and more involves the consumption of products made by national organizations; religious worship is carried on in national or international churches. These growing functions of the community, state, and nation increasingly relieve the family of functions it performed in earlier historical periods. It is perhaps difficult to imagine that a family, alone and unaided, could obtain virtually all the food it consumed; manufacture all its clothing, household goods, and other articles; rear and train its children without assistance; take care of its sick except in time of crisis; be self-sufficient in its religious activities and, except on special occasions, manage its own recreation. Why this was so in the case of the Shoshoneans is explainable largely in terms of their cultural ecological adaptations.

Owing to the nature of the natural environment of the Great Basin area and to the simple hunting and gathering techniques for exploiting it, it was inevitable that the individual family or at the most two or three related families should live in isolation during most of the year. "Family" in this case signifies the nuclear, biological or bilateral family, consisting of mother, father, and children. Unlike many primitive peoples, the Shoshoneans were not organized in extended family or lineage groups, and although, as we shall see subsequently, the immediate family was frequently enlarged through plural spouses and different families were closely allied by marriage, the functioning unit was the nuclear family, augmented only by a grandparent, aunt, or uncle who otherwise would be homeless.

ENVIRONMENT AND RESOURCES

The natural resources which were exploitable by Shoshonean culture were so limited that the population was extremely sparse. In the more fertile portions of this area there was perhaps one person to five square miles, while in the vast stretches of nearly waterless terrain the ratio was one to fifty or even one hundred square miles. The mean for the whole area was between one person to twenty or thirty square miles.

The territory once inhabited by the Shoshonean Indians is extremely arid, but technically most of it is classified as "steppe" rather than true "desert" although there are large areas devoid of vegetation. The country consists of large arid valleys lying between mountain ranges which run north and south. These valleys are from five to twenty miles wide and twenty to eighty miles long. The greater portion of the Shoshonean habitat lies within the Great Basin, a vast area of interior drainage between the Wasatch Mountains of

Utah and the Sierra Nevada Range of California and Oregon, but it also includes portions of the Columbia River Plateau of Idaho and eastern Oregon and the Colorado River Plateau of eastern Utah and western Colorado.

The flora and fauna of all these areas are very similar. There are several biotic zones, which set the basic conditions for a society equipped only with very simple hunting and gathering techniques. In the valleys, which lie between 4,000 and 6,000 feet elevation, the low rainfall—five to twenty inches a year—together with high evaporation supports a predominantly xerophytic vegetation, that is, such drought-resisting plants as sagebrush and greasewood. This vegetation has very limited value to human beings or animals. Plants bearing edible seeds and roots occur in some abundance immediately along the stream banks, but, except in favored areas, such as the piedmont of the Wasatch Mountains and the Sierra Nevada Mountains, the streams are small and widely spaced. In the Great Basin, the streams end in saline marshes or lakes. In the vast sandy areas between the streams, the quantity of edible plants depends directly upon rainfall, which varies from year to year and from place to place. These plants only afforded small quantities of food for the Indians, and they could not support game in herds comparable to the bison of the Great Plains or the caribou of the far north. The two species of greatest importance to the Indians were antelope and rabbits. These not only supplied meat and skins, but the communal hunts in which they were sometimes taken were among the few collective cultural activities. The numbers of both species, however, were limited, and the hunts were infrequent.

It is impossible to estimate the quantitative importance of different animal foods in the valley zone, but the Shoshoneans probably ate more rats, mice, gophers, locusts, ants, ant eggs, larvae of flies which breed in the salt lakes, snakes, and lizards than large game. In the rivers, such as the Owyhee, John Day, Crooked, Snake, Truckee, Carson, Walker, and Humboldt rivers, fish were an important supplement to other foods, but the runs were seasonal, the quantity did not compare with that of fish in coastal rivers, and the fish were evidently not suited for preservation and storage.

The zone of pinon and juniper trees lies between about 6,000 and 8,000 or 9,000 feet. This zone is largely restricted to the flanks of the mountain ranges since most valleys lie below this altitude. The juniper had little value to the Indians except for its wood, but the pinon (*Pinus monophylla* in the north, *Pinus edulis* in the south), which occurred throughout the Shoshonean area to a little north of the Humboldt River in Nevada, yielded pine nuts which were the most important of all food species. North of the pinon area, the seeds of certain other species of pines were eaten, but they were a relatively minor item in the diet. Since there was greater rainfall in the pinon-juniper belt than in the valleys, this zone afforded more seeds, roots, and grasses, and it had more game, especially deer. But it constitutes only a small portion of the total area, and the growing season is short. A few mountain ranges rise above 8,000 or 9,000 feet into the zone of the ponderosa pine, where vegetation is lush and where mountain sheep as well as deer were hunted.

The Shoshonean tribes were of necessity gatherers of vegetable foods and lower forms of animal life rather than hunters. They utilized nearly a hundred species of wild plants. The more important of these yielded small, hard-shelled seeds, which were collected in conical basketry containers, roasted with live coals in shallow baskets, ground on flat stones or metates, and eaten from basketry bowls. In the higher altitudes and latitudes where rainfall is greater, roots were relatively more important as food. When seeds and roots would not be had, especially in early spring, leafy vegetables or greens from many plants were eaten.

SOCIALLY FRAGMENTING EFFECT OF THE CULTURAL ECOLOGY

All of the plant and animal foods had in common the extremely important character-istic that the place and quantity of their occurrence from year to year were unpredictable, owing largely to variations in rainfall. A locality might be very fertile one year and attract large numbers of families, but offer little food for several years thereafter. Few localities had foods in sufficient quantity and reliability to permit permanent settlements. Throughout most of the area, the families were concerned predominantly with warding off potential starvation by moving from place to place. These movements were determined by reports from friends or relatives about the probable quantities of foods to be had. Families from different localities would assemble at places where food was temporarily plentiful, but, owing to the impossibility of storing large quantities of food for the future, they soon dispersed to seek elsewhere.

The typical Shoshoni family living in the pinon area of Nevada traveled alone or with one or two related families during the spring and summer, seeking seeds, roots, various small mammals, rodents, insects, larvae, and other edible items. In the late summer when a family heard reports that the pine nuts seemed very promising in a certain portion of a mountain range, it arranged its travels so as to arrive in that locality in late October or early November, when the first frosts would have opened the cones and made the nuts ready to harvest. Other families who had also been foraging for food within a radius of perhaps twenty to thirty miles of that locality came there for the same reason.

In gathering the pine nuts, each family restricted itself by common understanding to a limited area, because there were so many pine nuts in the locality as a whole that no one could gather them all before they dropped and because each family could harvest more if it worked alone. The different families remained from several hundred yards to a mile or more apart. Each gathered pine nuts as rapidly as it could and stored them in earth caches. If the harvest was good, it might support the family throughout most of the winter.

The winter encampment consisted of perhaps twenty or thirty families within easy visiting distance of one another. Early spring generally found the people suffering more or less acutely from hunger. The families then had to go their separate ways to forage for greens, game, and any other foods they could find. Throughout spring and summer, the migrations of a particular family, although limited in general to the terrain it knew well, were determined almost week to week by its knowledge of available foods. It might learn that sand grass seeds were promising in one place, rabbit numerous elsewhere, fly larvae abundant in a certain lake, and antelope ready for a communal hunt under a shaman or medicine man over in the next valley.

Although the pine nut was perhaps the most important factor in determining the whereabouts of the winter encampment and which families would be associated in it, most other foods had a very similar effect in causing seasonal variations in interfamilial contacts. Owing to yearly and local variations in rainfall, the whereabouts of other wild seed and root crops and animal resources was unpredictable. Rabbits might be so numerous in a portion of a valley in a given year that people would assemble from considerable distances to hold a communal hunt. Several years might then follow before it was worth while to hold another such hunt in the same place, whereas rabbits were ready for a hunt in an adjoining valley the next year. The same was true of antelope. A cooperative hunt would so reduce the antelope that it required eight or ten years for their number to be restored. Even such foods as grasshoppers and locusts, or "Mormon crickets," were unpredictable. In certain years locusts occurred in such numbers as to be a major source of food to the Indians—and a plague to the modern farmers—and then during several years they were of no importance.

A limitation of the value of animal products was the absence of preservation and storing techniques. Rabbits, antelope, and fish might afford more meat than the people who assembled to take them could eat, but after a few days or weeks, they spoiled. Fish, unlike other animal species, occurred with some annual regularity in fixed places. During runs, a considerable number of families came from far and wide to fish for a few weeks, after which they had to disperse in search of other foods. Had the Shoshoneans been able to dry and smoke fish, like the Northwest Coast Indians, it is possible that fairly large permanent populations might have developed along certain of the better fishing streams and lakes. In the absence of this possibility, the winter inhabitants of these areas were limited to the few families who used fish as a supplement to other foods. Consequently, the effect of fishing resources on social groups was like that of other foods: it permitted large aggregates of people to assemble for short periods and it helped tide a small number of local families over the winter.

Shoshonean society was affected not only by the erratic and unpredictable occurrence of practically all principal foods and by the limited technical skills for harvesting and storing most of them, but it was also shaped by the predominant importance of wild vegetable products, which put a premium upon family separatism rather than upon cooperation. Anyone who has gathered wild berries in a party knows that he can pick far more if he finds a patch of his own. Unlike certain forms of hunting—for example, collective rabbit drives or antelope hunts—participation of many persons in seed and root gathering not only failed to increase the per capita harvest, but it generally decreased it so greatly that individual families preferred to forage alone so as not to compete with other families.

The competitive aspect of seed and root gathering together with the erratic annual occurrence of practically all principal foods and the inability of the people to store foods in any locality in sufficient amount to permit considerable numbers of families to remain there for a major portion of the year, all contributed to the fragmentation of Shoshonean society into nuclear family units, which moved about the country seasonally and annually in an unpredictable itinerary.

PROPERTY

The concept of property rights among the Shoshoneans was directly related to their mode of life. These Indians assumed that rights to exclusive use of anything resulted from work expended by particular individuals or groups and from habitual use. This is a rather obvious, simple, and practical concept, and it seems to have entailed a minimum of conflict.

In most parts of the area, natural resources were available to anyone. The seeds gathered by a woman, however, belonged to her because she had done the work of converting a natural resource into something that could be directly consumed. If a man made a bow or built a house, these were his, although prior to making objects of them, the trees he utilized belonged to no one. Any family might fish in a certain river or stream, but if a group of families built a fish weir, it alone had the right to use that weir.

When a number of families came into potential conflict in the utilization of natural resources, the same principle held. In seed gathering, it was "first come, first served." The families which entered a seed plot or pinon grove selected the best portion and, by virtue of having started to work on it, had prior rights. Other families gathered pine nuts elsewhere, which was reasonable and necessary because if they gathered in competition with the first family, all would have harvested less. In rabbit drives, the person who clubbed or shot a rabbit or who owned the net which caught it had first claim. In deer or mountain sheep hunting, the man whose arrow first entered the game was entitled to the skin and the choice portions of the meat.

This principle of property rights was essential to survival in the Shoshonean area. Owing to the erratic annual and local occurrence of foods, the arbitrary exclusion of territorially delimited groups of families from utilization of other territories would have caused starvation and death. With few exceptions, the habitat of most families always provided such uncertain subsistence that the territorial inter-penetration of families living in different localities was necessary to the survival of all. The absence of property claims of local groups to delimitable areas of natural resources upon which work had not been expended was the corollary of the fragmented nature of Shoshonean society.

In a few portions of the Great Basin, such as Owens Valley in eastern California, which was occupied by Northern Paiute, the many streams flowing from the high Sierra Nevada Range afforded food resources which were comparatively so abundant and reliable that each family could be reasonably certain of finding enough to eat within one or two days' travel from a permanent village. Instead of wandering an unpredictable course determined by the vicissitudes of nature, these families were able to make forays from permanent headquarters. Habitual use of resources within readily accessible portions of the terrain led to the concept that each local village or group of villages had exclusive rights to resources within bounded areas. This economic stability and permanent residence of a particular group of families provided a basis for association, leadership, and organization in band groups.

COOPERATION AND LEADERSHIP AS INTEGRATING FACTORS

The typical Shoshonean family was independent and self-sufficient during the greater part of the year, perhaps during 80 or 90 per cent of the time. It subsisted and fulfilled most cultural functions with little assistance from other families. It probably could have survived in complete isolation.

But human history provides no instances in which nuclear families had progeny and perpetuated their culture without associating with and intermarrying with other families. Moreover, nuclear families have always cooperated with other families in various ways. Since this is so, the Shoshoneans, like other fragmented family groups, represent a family level of sociocultural integration only in a relative sense. It is relative in that most societies having a higher level of integration possess patterns of cooperation and leadership among a permanent membership. I classify the Shoshoneans as an exemplification of a family level of sociocultural integration because in the few forms of collective activity the same group of families did not cooperate with one another or accept the same leader on successive occasions. By another definition, however, it might be entirely permissible to view this ever-changing membership and leadership as a special form of suprafamilial integration. While the Shoshoneans represent a family level of sociocultural integration in a relative sense, their suprafamilial patterns of integration involved no permanent social groups of fixed membership despite several kinds of interfamilial cooperation.

COLLECTIVE HUNTING

The most important cooperation consisted of collective hunts. In these hunts, rabbits, antelope, deer, and mud hens were the principal species taken. Communal hunts could be held, however, only when there was sufficient game, when a considerable number of families could assemble, and when an appropriate leader was available. Under these circumstances, cooperation yielded many times the quantity of game that individuals, expending the same effort, could take alone.

The principal collective hunt was the rabbit drive. It could be held fairly often, and it yielded not only meat which could be consumed during a short period but furs which, cut into long strips and twisted, were woven into robes and blankets. The only distinctive technical feature of these drives was a net of about the height and mesh of a modern tennis net but often several hundred feet long. A number of these nets were placed end to end to form a huge semicircle. Men, women, children, and dogs beat the brush over a wide area, gradually closing in so that rabbits which were not clubbed or shot by the drivers became entangled in the nets, where they were killed.

Custom determined the several crucial aspects of the drive and the division of game. Experienced men—in recent years called rather appropriately "rabbit bosses"—were given supreme authority to coordinate all activities in this fairly complex operation. They chose the locality of the drive, directed disposition of nets, regulated the drivers, and divided the game according to customary understandings. Anyone who killed a rabbit with a bow or throwing stick in the course of the drive could claim it. Since, however, only a few families owned rabbit nets, net owners received a somewhat greater portion of the rabbits caught in the nets.

In spite of the rather rigid direction of these drives, there were several reasons why they did not bring about permanent integration or cohesion of territorial or social groups of fixed membership. First, drives were held only when rabbits were sufficiently numerous in a particular locality. Second, participants in the drive consisted of families who, because of the rather fortuitous annual occurrence of seeds and other foods in one place or another, happened to be in the locality where the drive was worth holding. Third, the drive was held only if an experienced leader and families owning nets happened to be present. Since the occurrence of these factors was rather haphazard, since the place, the participants, and the leaders were never quite the same in successive years, the drives provided only temporary bonds between independent families. A given family was under no obligation whatever to participate in a drive with a fixed group of families under a permanent leader. And, since the "rabbit boss" held authority only during the drive, the family paid little heed to him in other times, places, and contexts.

The communal antelope hunt had a social function like that of the rabbit drive. It was held in any given locality at intervals of several years and the participants consisted of those families which happened to be in the vicinity. It was held less frequently than the rabbit drive because it took much longer for the antelope herds to recover their number. A major difference in form rather than function between the rabbit drive and the antelope hunt is that whereas the former were led by men of experience and prestige—qualifications which anyone might develop—the latter were led by "antelope shamans." According to Shoshonean belief, these men were qualified less by their practical ability—though no doubt they were far from incompetent—than by their possession of supernatural power which enabled them to charm the antelope into a state of helplessness.

The practical procedures in the antelope drives were as appropriate to the situation as those in the rabbit hunts. The people built a brush corral from which wings, consisting of piles of brush or stones, extended outward a half mile or so. Drivers spread out several miles from the corral, formed a line across the valley, and slowly closed in, urging the antelope between the wings and into the corral. Antelope differ from rabbits in that they not only flee from something threatening but they are drawn by curiosity toward strange objects. The antelope shaman evidently became one of the chief functionaries in native Shoshonean culture because his role combined this peculiarity of antelope with a basic belief about sickness. It was thought by many primitive peoples, including the Shoshoneans, that sickness might be caused by loss of one's soul. While the antelope shaman was not a curer of human ills, he was thought to possess the power to capture the souls of antelope before the hunt began and thus irresistibly to draw them into the corral, where he stood during the drive.

The shaman's authority was very great during these drives, but he had no voice in other activities. Moreover, even this socio-religious leadership like the lay authority found in rabbit drives failed to integrate social groups of fixed membership.

The other hunting activities involved much less cooperation than rabbbit and antelope drives. Mud hen hunts were held only by small groups in the lake areas, while deer drives, held in the mountains, were infrequent and involved few persons.

DANCING, GAMBLING, AND VISITING

The interfamilial associations of the Shoshonean Indians had to be adapted, as previously shown, to the exigencies of obtaining food by means of the techniques known to them. Although these families foraged throughout most of the year in isolation, their contacts with other families over many generations had contributed certain social patterns which strengthened bonds between them.

Whenever groups of Shoshonean families were together, they carried out certain recreational activities, such as dancing and gambling. Dancing, although popular, was originally limited to the circle dance, a performance in which men and women formed a circle and sidestepped to the accompaniment of singing. Gambling games were extremely numerous and included several forms of dice, the hand-game, sports such as racing and hockey, and games of skill such as the hoop-and-pole game and archery. Both dancing and games, however, could be held only when local abundance of food, such as rabbits, locusts, antelope, or pine nuts, made large gatherings possible. After a rabbit or antelope drive, for instance, people might dance and gamble for several days until the meat supply was exhausted, when each family had to go its separate way in the unending food quest.

Interfamilial contacts were not limited to such formalized activities as hunting, dancing, and gambling. Visiting was an important integrating fact since people were always eager to associate with one another whether or not they danced and gambled. They preferred to visit with relatives, but when food was plentiful, a large number of unrelated families could assemble.

HOSTILITIES AND WARFARE

In aboriginal times most of the Shoshonean people had no national or tribal warfare. There were no territorial rights to be defended, no military honors to be gamed, and no means of organizing groups of individuals for concerted action. When war parties of neighboring peoples invaded their country, the Shoshoneans ran away more often than they fought.

Hostilities generally consisted of feuds, not organized military action, and they resulted largely from the suspicion of witchcraft and from woman-stealing. They were therefore as often intratribal as intertribal. Death was generally ascribed to supernatural causes, especially to shamans, whose normally beneficent power had turned bad, perhaps even without the shaman's knowledge, and it was avenged by slaying the suspect. Usually, the malignant shaman was identified either as the person who had treated the deceased or as a member of a somewhat distant group. Accusations of witchcraft were rarely directed against relatives because kinship relations were too important to be endangered. It was, in fact, one of the most important kinship obligations to avenge the death of a relative. Once revenge had been taken, a series of reprisals and counter-reprisals might follow. These were purely personal and could not involve definable suprafamilial groups, for such groups did not exist.

THE RISE OF PREDATORY BANDS

After the Shoshonean tribes acquired horses and the territory was occupied by white settlers, warfare of a collective nature developed. Under aboriginal conditions, horses had little value because they consumed the very plants upon which the Indians depended while contributing little to the hunting of rabbits, antelope, or deer. The few horses acquired in early times were eaten. When immigrant trains crossed the area and when white settlers introduced irrigation, crops, and livestock into the country, horses enabled the previously dispersed families to amalgamate and remain fairly constantly together in *predatory bands,* which lived somewhat parasitically by raiding the whites. Warfare involved in raiding and in defense against white reprisals was the principal if not sole function of these bands, and the chiefs had authority over little other than raiding activities. It was only among the Northern Shoshoni of Wind River. Wyoming, and of eastern Idaho and the Bannock, who probably acquired horses by 1800, that bison hunting and native warfare of the Plains type were also functions of the native bands. The Ute received horses sometime after 1820, and their bands were essentially predatory, first in raiding people outside their territory and later in raiding the Mormons and other white settlers inside it. The Western Shoshoni and Northern Paiute continued to be dispersed in family units until about 1845, after which mounted bands rapidly developed. Mounted bands were dissolved among the Shoshonean peoples by 1870 or soon thereafter when the United States Army defeated them.

In understanding the quite specialized nature of these predatory bands and the restricted authority of the chiefs, it is important to note that the bands probably never involved all the people of any region. During the early phases of band operations, there were many families which had no horses and continued to live according to the older pattern of family separatism while some of their friends and relatives engaged in raiding. Later, when the United States Army opposed the raiders, the Indians had to decide whether to continue to fight or whether to accept peace, relinquish certain territory, and live on reservations. At this stage, there were two kinds of chiefs. The first were leaders of predatory bands which were now on the defensive. The second were spokesmen for those who advocated peace and the signing of treaties.

After the Indians were defeated, the division between peaceful and warring factions soon faded and the functions of war leaders were eliminated. Thenceforth, the principal need for leaders was to deal with the white men, especially with the officials of the United States government.

RELIGION

Religion integrated families with one another only to a minor degree. Shoshonean culture lacked collective social and economic activities and common interests, except the communal hunts, dancing, and gaming previously mentioned. There was no functional need for ceremonialism dedicated to group purposes and led by priests holding a definite office. The communal antelope hunt was directed by a special shaman, but this leader did not serve any permanent group.

The relationship between human beings and supernatural powers was conceived largely as a matter of individual concern. Every person hoped to acquire a supernatural power or guardian spirit. This power, manifest in the form of animals, plants, clouds, mountains, and other natural phenomena, came to him in dreams and gave him special abilities, such as gambling luck, hunting skill, endurance, and others of benefit to himself alone. Shamans' powers differed from those of ordinary persons mainly in the ability to cure sickness in other people. The shaman did not lead group ceremonies. His curing performances might attract large numbers of families which happened to be in the vicinity because they liked not only to watch his singing, dancing, trance, laying-on-of-hands, and other rites but to visit other families. Shamans were influential because their curing abilities gave them prestige while their presumed capacity for practicing black magic made them feared, but they carried no specific authority.

A minor collective religious activity designed for the common good was the circle dance, which, according to the belief of some of the Western Shoshoni, promoted general fertility and benefited everyone. Harris reported that the Tosavits or White Knife Shoshoni of northern Nevada held group ceremonies for general welfare. It is more likely, however, that the principal feature of such ceremonies was the circle dance, which was held by whatever families came together at various stages of their food quest, and that the religious aspect was secondary and incidental to the recreational purpose. The "dance boss" was certainly not a religious leader. Similarly, the bear dance of the Ute was primarily recreational and only secondarily religious in heralding the spring season and providing protection against bears. Its leader, like that of the circle dance, was a layman.

WINTER ENCAMPMENTS

The only prolonged accessibility of families to one another occurred in the winter encampments. These winter quarters have sometimes been called villages, but they were not tightly nucleated settlements which constituted organized communities. Instead, family houses were widely scattered within productive portions of the pinon zone. The location of each household was determined primarily by its pine nut caches and secondarily by accessibility to wood and water. The scattered families were able to visit one another to dance, gamble, and exchange gossip, and the men occasionally cooperated in a deer or mountain sheep hunt. Although dances and collective hunts required coordination, the leaders had no authority outside the particular activity.

Other interfamilial and interpersonal relationships were determined by customary usage. Disputes and hostilities arising from such matters as murder, theft, wife-stealing, and other violations of custom were settled between families. None of these was a "crime" against the community, for the community did not exist in any corporate or legal sense. Violations of custom threatened families, not larger socially integrated units. Thus, the very concept of crime presupposes some kind of suprafamily level of integration, some collectivity, which has a common purpose that must be protected against antisocial behavior by its members.

In addition to the leaders of special activities, each village or local area of scattered winter houses usually had a man of some importance whom modern Shoshonean informants frequently call the "village chief." So far as "chief" implies permanent authority over an identifiable group, this term is a complete misnomer, for this man had no authority and he served only one funcion. This function, however, was extremely important. It was to act as a clearing-house of information about where foods could be found. Since the Shoshoneans were constantly on the verge of starvation, especially at the end of winter, knowledge of where greens, seeds, rabbits, insects, and other foods were to be had made the repository of such information the most important person in the village.

The winter village cannot be considered a genuine suprafamilial form of social integration because it lacked permanent membership and even permanent location. Each year, families came from a general area to a locality of abundant pine nuts. Leaders were accepted by common consent to control such collective activities as required coordination. It was only in the few regions of uncommonly abundant and reliable food that a group of fixed membership occupied one or more permanent villages throughout most of the year and had a true village chief and permanent leaders of other activities.

FOOD-NAMED GROUPS

Considerable confusion concerning the nature of groups named according to special foods is found in the literature starting with the early accounts of the Shoshoneans and perpetuated in modern ethnographic studies. It was the native custom throughout practically all of the area to name the people occupying different localities by some important or striking food found in them. Thus, several different and widely separated groups were called Rabbit Eaters and Fish Eaters. Other names were Pine Nut Eaters, Ground Hog Eaters, Grass Seed Eaters, and the like. These names, however, did not designate definable groups but were merely applied to whoever happened to be in the locality. Since there were no bands and no territorial limitations on movements in search of food, families frequently traveled from one food area to another and were known by the local name in each. Just as a Washingtonian today becomes a New Yorker upon living in New York, so a Ground Hog Eater of western Idaho became a Salmon Eater if he moved to the Snake River.

Most of the early accounts of the Shoshoneans were written after wars with the whites began and predatory bands developed. Sometimes these bands were named after their leaders and sometimes after the food area from which the leader and many of his followers came. Writers therefore assumed that the inhabitants of these food-named localities constituted aboriginal, territorial bands under overall chieftainship. Data previously cited show clearly that this could not have been the case. The food-named areas were far too large for a foot people to associate in collective activities, even had the nature of Shoshonean subsistence not precluded integration in bands. After the whites entered the country, the "chiefs" of predatory bands not only failed to enlist the support of the peace faction in their own place of origin but their followers included persons from many other food-named areas.

Throughout the greater part of the area, therefore, food-names were a designation of people in a certain large region and nothing more. They implied no economic, recreational, religious, social, or political cooperation that would require collective action and lead to suprafamilial forms of integration.

KINSHIP RELATIONS

The economic and social relations of Shoshonean families previously described may be likened to a net in that each family had occasional associations with families on all sides of it and these latter with families farther away and these with still others so that there were no social, economic or political frontiers. The entire area consisted of interlocking associations of family with family. So far as subsistence, recreational, and religious activities are concerned, however, the analogy of a net is not entirely apt because no family was necessarily and consistently associated with certain other families. The net lacked knots; each family was at liberty to associate with whom it please. Kinship relations, however, supplied the knots and made a fabric of what otherwise would have been a skein of loose threads, each of which shifted about somewhat randomly. This is not to say that Shoshonean society was based on extended ties of kinship which gave cohesion to any definable group. The activities of a given family month by month were dictated primarily by the food quest, which took precedence over every other consideration. But marriage bonds were fairly enduring, and they created a strong fabric of close relationships, which extended from one locality to the next. They also made interfamilial economic and recreational associations somewhat less random, for kin preferred to cooperate with one another when possible. Moreover, the very absence of socioeconomic unity among inhabitants of local areas made the kinship ties seem relatively more important.

The irreducible minimum of Shoshonean society was the nuclear or biological family. Isolated individuals could not well survive in this cultural-environmental or ecological situation, and unmarried or widowed persons generally attached themselves to a nuclear family. This family was able to carry out most activities necessary to existence, for husband and wife complemented each other in food-getting and together they procreated, reared, and socialized their children. Women gathered vegetable foods, made the baskets needed for this purpose, and prepared all food. Men devoted most of their time to hunting, which, though not very rewarding, was extremely important and time consuming. It was important not only because meat was a desired dietary item, but because hides and furs were needed for clothing. The scarcity of game and the difficulty of hunting is evidenced by the fact that few men were able to kill enough deer or antelope to clothe their families in skin garments or even to make moccasins. Many persons were naked and barefoot during the summer, and in winter had only a rabbit-skin blanket which served both as a robe and as bedding.

In the household, women maintained the home and took care of the children. Men also played an important part in child-rearing. In the absence of toys and games designed expressly for children, boys played with small bows and arrows and other objects used by men, while girls imitated their mothers. In this way, children quickly learned the rudiments of adult functions and absorbed the attitudes, values, and beliefs of their parents.

This learning was accomplished largely within the context of the family, for association with other families was limited.

In the course of the very uncertain wanderings and activities of Shoshonean life, the most frequent associates of the members of a nuclear family were members of families with which they had intermarried. These families were companions on seed and root gathering trips, when there was enough food for several families to travel together, and they cooperated in hunting. Relatives were the favored visitors, and often a few families would camp together and spend evenings gossiping and telling legends. Relatives were to be counted on for support if suspicion of witchcraft led to a feud. And they, more than others, were willing to share food in times of shortage.

These close interfamilial bonds were expressed in the marriage system. Marriage was more a contract between families than between individuals. The perferred arrangement was several marriages between the children of two families. When a young man married, it was desired that his wife's brother marry his sister. Several brothers and sisters might marry several sisters and brothers. Shoshonean culture permitted plural spouses, wherein the same principle prevailed. If a man took several wives, custom prescribed that they be sisters, and penalties were imposed for failure to follow this custom. If a man's wife died, he was obligated to take her sister as his next wife. In a parallel way, a certain amount of polyandry, or plural husbands, was permitted. A woman might take a younger brother of her husband as a temporary spouse until he found a wife. If the husband died, his family was obligated to furnish a brother of the first husband if possible.

It was, of course, biologically impossible that the number and sex of siblings in two intermarrying families should be such that this cultural ideal could be met. Moreover, marriages of the parental and grandparental generation extended marital ties to many families. While marital ties often linked the younger generation of two families to one another somewhat more closely than either was linked to other families, the general pattern was one of innumerable interfamilial linkages extending over a wide area. It meant that a family in a given locality could probably find consanguinal or marital kin of one kind or another among a large proportion of the families which ranged its own territory and among many families farther afield.

These interfamilial marital and kinship bonds were not unbreakable, for, despite the contractual nature of marriage, separations or divorces were common. Individual temperament, incompatibility, and other factors were not to be discounted. Nonetheless, the cultural ideal ascribed these arrangements considerable importance. And this importance derived largely from the fact that these kinship bonds were the principal integrating factors in a cultural-environmental situation where the subsistence pattern prevented the development of bands, villages, or other social units consisting of permanent members having prescribed relationships to one another.

These marital and kinship ties were the knots of the social fabric of the various peoples in the Shoshonean area, but they did not constitute sociocultural frontiers. Marriage was contracted most often between families in contact with one another, but it was not governed by territorial or political units. While it united strands in the netlike fabric of Shoshonean society, it could not consolidate or integrate local groups in a political, social, or economic sense. To the contrary, it cut across local boundaries, making interfamilial ties diffuse and thus actually militating against band or community development.

THE THEORETICAL SIGNIFICANCE OF THE SHOSHONEANS

In a classification of cultures based on the concept of area, the Shoshoneans should probably be included in the Greater Southwest, for more of their culture elements, especially their material culture or technology, seem to have been derived from the Southwest than from any other area. Their economic, political, social, religious, and hostility patterns—general configurations which are not reducible to culture elements—were, however, wholly unlike those of the Southwest. Owing to the cultural ecological processes—to the exploitation of their particular environment by means of the techniques available to them—families functioned independently in most cultural activities, and the few collective interfamilial pursuits did not serve to give permanent cohesion to extended families, bands, communities, or other higher levels of sociocultural integration as in the Southwest.

The Shoshonean peoples were not unique in having a family level of integraiton. This level is also represented in North America by the Eskimo and in South America by the Nambicuara, Guató, Mura, and perhaps other groups. But this similarity of level does not mean that these tribes belonged to the same cultural type. In all cases, the food quest was of overwhelming importance, but, owing to the differences in environment and exploitative techniques, it entailed very unlike activities and associations between families. Perhaps there have been people similar to the Shoshoneans in other parts of the world; for the present, however, the Shoshoneans must be regarded as typologically unique.

This typological distinctiveness makes the Shoshoneans unique in cultural evolution. If the predecessors of any people who later developed to a community or state level were like the Shoshoneans, we have no way of knowing it. Even if all groups of mankind had begun their cultural evolution with sociocultural units integrated only on a family level, which is doubtful and certainly unprovable, it would not follow that they all had the same cultural configuration, that is, the same cultural type, as the Shoshoneans. Paleolithic data suggest that there were several major areas which differed in lithic technology, and within these areas many distinctive local cultural ecological adaptations must have taken place. So far as present evidence is concerned, therefore, the Shoshoneans represent a distinctive and nonrecurrent line of development in a scheme of multilinear evolution.

The family type of organization found among the Shoshoneans should not be confused with that which developed after white contacts among several peoples in various parts of the world. For example, many Indians in the northeastern United States and Canada, who previously had some form of band organization, broke up into family groups after the fur trade had become virtually essential to their existence, and each family came to own a clearly delimited trapping territory. Social, economic, and religious patterns which had given cohesion to the bands were seriously disrupted or disappeared. This did not mean that the whole culture was actually reduced to a family level. The families ceased to be related to one another through band institutions and became partially integrated into the economic and to some extent into the religious and political institutions of the colonial or national states. These institutions were mediated to them through the trader, the missionary, and government officials.

The Mundurucú of the Cururá River in the Amazon Basin, according to Robert Murphy's . . . studies, have tended to lose their band and tribal organization and to split into family units for similar reasons. Since they have become gatherers of wild rubber, each family works the trees within delimited sections of the rivers. Family contacts are increasing with the rubber trader and to some extent with church and government officials rather than with one another. A similar pattern was found by Wagley among the rubber-gathering Caboclos on the lower Amazon, although social and religious ties were stronger among them owing to their access to more developed communities.

The Shoshoneans developed a higher level of sociocultural integration and a cross-culturally significant type only after the whites entered their country and horses were introduced. The multifamily, mounted, predatory bands depended upon raiding the new resources brought by the whites. In this respect they differed from the mounted Plains tribes, which subsisted by hunting bison, and resembled such peoples as the Apache, whose forays made them the scourge of the Southwest, the Puelche and certain tribes of the southern Gran Chaco in South America, and perhaps some of the Asiatic horse nomads, whose existence was at least quasiparasitic through raiding activities.

The full significance of the predatory band as a cultural type warrants detailed comparative study, for it is not now possible to say what people belong to this type. There is no doubt, however, that the type has conceptual validity. Moreover, it should be stressed that the cross-cultural significance of this type consists of form and function rather than element content. The Shoshoneans, Apache, Puelche, and Asiatics were very unlike in specific details of behavior. They belonged to different culture areas, but they had the same type of culture.

. . . When the Indian wars ended, the people who did not enter reservations rapidly adapted themselves to the new white society by working for ranches, mines, or taking odd jobs in the new towns. The very absence of aboriginal band or community institutions made this adjustment easier. The principal obstacle to rapid and complete assimilation into the subculture of the local white American communities was and still is race relations, which bar the Shoshoneans from full participation in many crucial aspects of the American way of life.

POSTSCRIPT

When the field work for this chapter was done, in the mid-1930's, all anthropologists seemed tacitly to assume that every hunting, gathering, and fishing society was organized in bands of some kind, and this assumption persists among some writers. My field work in the Great Basin began with the expectation that I would find patrilineal bands, like those of the southern California Shoshoneans. Some Great Basin people, such as the Paiute of Owens Valley and perhaps in western Nevada and possibly some of the Ute in areas of great fertility, had aboriginal bands, but they were not patrilineal.

Among the Western Shoshoneans in particular, I found no territorially delimited bands; emphasis therefore was placed on the nuclear or biological family. In retrospect, however, I think the independence of such families from one another was overemphasized. Research on hunting and gathering societies during the last decade and discussions in recent conferences on Man the Hunter, Bands, and the Great Bason have disclosed the widespread occurrence among Canadian Athapaskans and Algonkians, Bushmen, many Australians, and others of minimal social aggregates (primary subsistence groups, local bands, or task groups) of twenty to thirty individuals. These are clusters of closely related families that seem to represent the smallest group that can remain viable. On occasion I have referred to family clusters of Shoshoneans engaged in seed gathering. Although I could not obtain precise data on the size and composition of the aboriginal Shoshonean seasonal groupings, I incline to the belief that they were comparable to the primary subsistence bands or groups elsewhere.

The Shoshoneans differed from most other hunting and gathering societies in that larger aggregates did not comprise bands of fixed membership. In this respect they were similar to the Alacaluf of the Chilean archipelago. The Eskimo, however, had bands of a fairly distinctive type rather than small family clusters.

6. STEEL AXES FOR STONE AGE AUSTRALIANS

LAURISTON SHARP

Reprinted from Edward H. Spicer (Ed.), Human Problems in Technological Change: A Casebook *(New York: The Russell Sage Foundation, 1952). Lauriston Sharp is Professor of Anthropology and Asian Studies and Director of the Thailand Project at Cornell University. His principal field research has been in North Africa, Australia, and Southwest Asia; his major interests are political and applied anthropology, with emphasis on comparative social organization, ideologies, and symbolic systems. He is a co-author of* Siamese Rice Village, Handbook on Thailand, *and* Some Principles of Cultural Change.

■ The preceding selection was a masterful account of adaptation in a foraging group. In this selection we turn to another well-known study of a hunting-gathering culture, but with a focus on what I have called cultural adjustment. This adjustment occurred in the symbolic sphere of the culture; specifically, it affected the subjective meaning attached by the Yir Yoront of Australia to one of their basic implements, the axe. The substitution of steel for stone axes among these people did not materially affect the relationship they maintained with their habitat because they continued to rely on the use of muscular energy. But profound changes occurred in many of their social relations as a result of the new materials from which their axes were made.

Even the smallest or simplest artifact used by a group as part of its adaptation to a habitat has important symbolic value. We need only recall the symbolic values of different automobiles, household appliances, and dress ("blue" and "white" collars) in American society, the bowler hat and the umbrella in Britain, and watches and Parker pen caps in some emergent nations in Africa (where they are sometimes symbolic claims to educated and elite status) to realize that the attachment of symbolic-cultural meaning to material things is not found only in primitive societies. It is an intrinsic part of all cultures.

When we say an implement has symbolic value we mean it is so intimately tied to so many aspects of the culture that a change in the implement will produce reverberations in most of the social system. These reverberations are not always of the same order. In some instances, as when a new source of energy is harnessed, the consequences are adaptive, in the sense that a new balance is introduced into

man's relationship with his habitat. This provides him with a new measure of freedom from the limitations of the milieu. In other instances, as in the case discussed by Sharp, the consequences are adjustive, in the sense that the level of adaptation remained the same while new relationships among the elements of the culture were produced.

Although the Yir Yoront are nomadic hunter-gatherers, their habitat enables them to live in somewhat larger groups throughout the year than was possible for the Shoshoneans. Hence social relations among the Yir Yoront are considerably more stable than they were among the Shoshoneans. The materials in this selection point to another consideration the reader should keep in mind: the Yir Yoront are characterized by a very weak political system, and the elders of the group—try as they might—were unable to halt the intrusion of steel axes into the culture. If the elders had more power, they might not only have had more control over events but might have stimulated a more efficient use of steel tools for productive purposes, thereby moving the Yir Yoront into a slightly more advanced level of technological development.

There is considerable material in his own culture that the reader can consider to further his understanding of the relationships between artifacts and social institutions. The relationship between artifacts and social relations is explored in other cultures in *Traditional Cultures and the Impact of Technological Change,* by George M. Foster (New York: Harper and Row, 1962), and *Medieval Technology and Social Change,* by Lynn White, Jr. (New York: Oxford University Press, 1962). One of the principal concerns in White's book is the range of repercussions in medieval Europe as a result of the introduction of the stirrup. For our own culture the reader may refer to *American Life: Dream and Reality*, by W. Lloyd Warner (rev. ed.; Chicago: University of Chicago Press, 1962). ■

1. THE PROBLEM

LIKE OTHER AUSTRALIAN aboriginals, the Yir Yoront group at the mouth of the Coleman River on the west coast of tropical Cape York Peninsula originally had no knowledge of metals. Technologically their culture was of the old stone age or paleolithic type; they supported themselves by hunting and fishing, obtaining vegetable foods and needed materials from the bush by simple gathering techniques. Their only domesticated animal was the dog, and they had no domesticated plants of any kind. Unlike some other aboriginal groups, however, the Yir Yoront did have polished stone axes hafted in short handles, and these implements were most important in their economy.

Toward the end of the nineteenth century metal tools and other European artifacts began to filter into the Yir Yoront territory. The flow increased with the gradual expansion of the white frontier outward from southern and eastern Queensland. Of all the items of western technology thus made available, none was more acceptable, none more highly valued by aboriginals of all conditions than the hatchet or short-handled steel axe.

In the mid-1930's an American anthropologist was able to live alone in the bush among the Yir Yoront for thirteen months without seeing another white man. They were thus still relatively isolated and they continued an essentially independent economic life, supporting themselves entirely by means of their old stone-age techniques. Yet their polished stone axes were fast disappearing and were being replaced by steel axes, which came to them in considerable numbers directly or indirectly from various European sources to the south.

What changes in the life of the Yir Yoront still living under aboriginal conditions in the Australian bush could be expected as a result of their increasing possession and use of the steel axe?

2. THE COURSE OF EVENTS

In 1623 a Dutch expedition landed on the coasts now occupied by the Yir Yoront. All cultural items, although few in number) recorded in the Dutch log for the aboriginals they encountered were still in use among the Yir Yoront in 1935. To this inventory the Dutch added pieces of iron and beads in an effort to attract the frightened "Indians." They remained at this spot for two days, during which they were able to kidnap one and shoot another of a group of some hundred males. Today metal and beads have disappeared, as has any memory of this first encounter with whites.

The next recorded contact in this area occurred in 1864, and here there is more positive assurance that the natives concerned were the immediate ancestors of the Yir Yoront community. These aboriginals had the temerity to attack a party of cattlemen who were driving a small herd from southern Queensland through the whole length of the then unknown Cape York Peninsula to a newly established government station at the Peninsula's northern tip. As a result there occurred what became known as the "Battle of the Mitchell River," one of the rare instances in which Australian aboriginals stood up to European gunfire for any length of time, A diary kept by the cattlemen records the incident: ". . . ten carbines poured volley after volley into them from all directions, killing and wounding with every shot with very little return, nearly all their spears having already been expended. . . . About thirty being killed, the leader thought it prudent to hold his hand, and let the rest escape. Many more must have been wounded and probably drowned, for fifty-nine rounds were counted as discharged." The European party was in the Yir Yoront area for three days, then disappeared over the horizon to the north, not to return.

During the anthropological investigation some seventy years later, lasting almost three years, there was not one reference to this shocking contact with Europeans, nor anything that could be interpreted as a reference to it, in all the material of hundreds of free association interviews, in hundreds of dreams and myths, in genealogies, and eventually in hundreds of answers to direct and indirect questioning on just this particular matter.

The aboriginal accounts of their first remembered contact with whites begin with references to persons known to have had sporadic but lethal encounters with them beginning about 1900, and it may be noted that from that time on whites continued to remain on the southern periphery of Yir Yoront territory. With the establishment of cattle stations or ranches to the south, occasional excursions among the "wild blackfellows" were made by cattlemen wishing to inspect the country and abduct natives to be trained as cattle boys and "house girls." At least one such expedition reached the Coleman River, where a number of Yir Yoront men and women were shot, apparently on general principles. A stick of trade tobacco, the natives now claim, was left with each body; but this kindness was evidently unappreciated, for the leader of the excursion was eventually speared to death by a native fighting party.

It was about this time that the government was persuaded to sponsor the establishment of three mission stations along the seven hundred mile western coast of the Peninsula as an aid in regulating the treatment of natives. To further this purpose a strip of coastal territory was set aside as an aboriginal reserve and closed to further white settlement.

In 1915 an Anglican mission station was established near the mouth of the Mitchell River in the territory of a tribe neighboring the Yir Yoront on the south and about three days' march from the heart of the Yir Yoront country. Some of the Yir Yoront refused to have anything to do with the mission or to go near it, others visited it on occasion, while a few eventually settled more or less permanently in one of the three "villages" at the mission.

Thus, the majority of the Yir Yoront continued to live their old self-supporting life in the bush, protected until 1942 by the government reserve and the intervening mission from the cruder realities of the encroaching new order which had come up from the south. To the east was poor country, uninhabited. To the north were other bush tribes extending on along the coast to the distant Archer River Presbyterian mission with which the Yir Yoront had no contact. Westward was the expanse of the shallow Gulf of Carpentaria, on which the natives saw only a mission lugger making its infrequent dry-season trips to the Mitchell River. In this protected environment for over a generation the Yir Yoront were able to recuperate from former shocks received at the hands of civilized society. During the 1930's their raiding and fighting, their trading and stealing of women, their evisceration and two- or three-year care of their dead, their totemic ceremonies continued apparently uninhibited by western influence. In 1931 they killed a European who wandered into their territory from the east, but the investigating police never approached the group whose members were responsible for the act. In 1934 the anthropologist observed a case of extra-tribal revenge cannibalism. The visitor among the bush Yir Yoront at this time found himself in the presence of times past, in an essentially paleolithic society which had been changed, to the casual eye, chiefly by the addition of oddments of European implements and goods put to a variety of uses.

As a direct result of the work of the Mitchell River mission, all Yir Yoront received a great many more western artifacts of all kinds than they ever had obtained before. As part of their plan for raising native living standards, the missionaries made it possible for aboriginals at the mission to earn some western goods, many of which were then given or traded out to natives still living under bush conditions; or they handed out gratis both to mission and to bush aboriginals certain useful articles which were in demand. They prevented guns, liquor, and damaging narcotics, as well as decimating diseases, from reaching the tribes of this area, while encouraging the introduction of goods they considered "improving." As has been noted, no item of western technology that was available, with the possible exception of trade tobacco, was in greater demand among all groups of aboriginals than the short-handled steel axe. A good supply of this type of axe was therefore always kept in stock at the mission for sale; and at Christmas parties or other mission festivals steel axes were given away to mission or visiting aboriginals indiscriminately and in considerable numbers. In addition, some steel axes, as well as other European goods, were still traded in to the Yir Yoront by natives in contact with cattle stations established south of the missions. Indeed, such axes had probably come to the Yir Yoront along established lines of aboriginal trade long before any regular contact with whites had occurred.

3. RELEVANT FACTORS

If we concentrate our attention on Yir Yoront behavior centering about the original stone axe, rather than on the axe—the thing —we should get some conception of the role this implement played in aboriginal culture. This conception, in turn, should permit us to foresee with considerable accuracy some of the results of the displacement of stone axes by steel axes acquired directly or indirectly from Europeans by the Yir Yoront.

The production of a stone axe required a number of simple skills. With the idea of the axe in its various details well in mind, the adult men—and only the adult men—could set about producing it, a task not considered appropriate for women or children. First of all, a man had to know the location and properties of several natural resources found in his immediate environment: pliable wood, which could be doubled or bent over the axe head and bound tightly to form a handle; bark, which could be rolled into cord for the binding; and gum, with which the stone head could be firmly fixed in the haft. These ma-

terials had to be correctly gathered, stored, prepared, cut to size, and applied or manipulated. They were plentifully supplied by nature, and could be taken by a man from anyone's property without special permission. Postponing consideration of the stone head of the axe, we see that a simple knowledge of nature and of the technological skills involved, together with the possession of fire (for heating the gum) and a few simple cutting tools, which might be nothing more than the sharp shells of plentiful bivalves, all of which were available to everyone, were sufficient to enable any normal man to make a stone axe.

The use of the stone axe as a piece of capital equipment for the production of other goods indicates its very great importance in the subsistence economy of the aboriginal. Anyone—man, woman, or child—could use the axe; indeed, it was used more by women, for theirs was the onerous, daily task of obtaining sufficient wood to keep the campfire of each family burning all day for cooking or other purposes and all night against mosquitoes and cold (in July, winter temperature might drop below forty degrees). In a normal lifetime any woman would use the axe to cut or knock down literally tons of firewood. Men and women, and sometimes children, needed the axe to make other tools, or weapons, or a variety of material equipment required by the aboriginal in his daily life. The stone axe was essential in making the wet-season domed huts, which keep out some rain and some insects; or platforms, which provide dry storage; or shelters, which give shade when days are bright and hot. In hunting and fishing and in gathering vegetable or animal food the axe was also a necessary tool; and in this tropical culture without preservatives or other means of storage, the native spends more time obtaining food than in any other occupation except sleeping.

In only two instances was the use of the stone axe strictly limited to adult men: Wild honey, the most prized food known to the Yir Yoront, was gathered only by men who usually used the axe to get it; and only men could make the secret paraphernalia for ceremonies, an activity often requiring use of the axe. From this brief listing of some of the activities in which the axe was used, it is easy to understand why there was at least one stone axe in every camp, in every hunting or fighting party, in every group out on a "walk-about" in the bush.

While the stone axe helped relate men and women and often children to nature in tech-nological behavior, in the transformation of natural into cultural equipment, it also was prominent in that aspect of behavior which may be called conduct, primarily directed toward persons. Yir Yoront men were de-pendent upon interpersonal relations for their stone axe heads, since the flat, geologically recent alluvial country over which they range provides no stone from which axe heads can be made. The stone they used comes from known quarries four hundred miles to the south. It reached the Yir Yoront through long lines of male trading partners, some of these chains terminating with the Yir Yoront men, while others extended on farther north to other groups, having utilized Yir Yoront men as links. Almost every older adult man had one or more regular trading partners, some to the north and some to the south. His partner or partners in the south he provided with surplus spears, and particularly fighting spears tipped with the barbed spines of sting ray which snap into vicious fragments when they penetrate human flesh. For a dozen spears, some of which he may have obtained from a partner to the north, he would receive from a southern partner one stone axe head. Studies have shown that the sting ray spears become more and more valuable as they move south farther from the sea, being passed on in recent times from a native on one cattle station to a native on another where they are used during the wet season, when al-most all aboriginal employees are thrust into the bush to shift for themselves until the next cattle-working dry season is at hand. A hundred and fifty miles south of the Yir Yoront one such spear may be exchanged for one stone axe head. Although actual investi-gations could not be made, presumably still farther south and nearer the quarries, one

sting ray spear would bring several stone axe heads. It is apparent that links in the middle of the chain who make neither spears nor axe heads receive both as a middleman's profit simply for passing them back and forth. While many other objects may move along these chains of trading partners, they are still characterized by both bush and station ab-originals as lines along which spears move south and axes move north. Thus, trading re-lations, which may extend the individual's per-sonal relationships out beyond the bound-aries of his own group, are associated with two of the most important items in a man's equipment, spears and axes, whether the latter are of stone or steel. Finally, most of the ex-changes between partners take place during the dry season at times when the great ab-original fiestas occur, which center about initiation rites or other totemic ceremonials that attract hundreds and are the occasion for much exciting activity besides trading.

Returning to the Yir Yoront, we find that not only was it adult men alone who obtained axe heads and produced finished axes, but it was adult males who retained the axes, keep-ing them with other parts of their equipment in camp, or carrying them at the back slipped through a human hair belt when traveling. Thus, every woman or child who wanted to use an axe—and this might be frequently during the day—must get one from some man, use it promptly, and return it to the man in good condition. While a man might speak of "my axe," a woman or child could not; for them it was always "your axe," ad-dressing a male, or "his axe."

This necessary and constant borrowing of axes from older men by women and children was done according to regular patterns of kinship behavior. A woman on good terms with her husband would expect to use his axe unless he were using it; a husband on good terms with his wives would let any one of them use his axe without question. If a wo-man was unmarried or her husband was ab-sent, she would go first to her older brother or to her father for an axe. Only in extra-ordinary circumstances would she seek a stone axe from a mother's brother or certain other male kin with whom she had to be most circumspect. A girl, a boy, or a young man would look to a father or an older brother to provide an axe for her or his use, but would never approach a mother's brother, who would be at the same time a potential father-in-law, with such a request. Older men, too, would follow similar rules if they had to borrow an axe.

It will be noted that these social relationships in which the stone axe had a place are all pair relationships and that the use of the axe helped define and maintain the character of the relationships and the roles of the two individual participants. Every active relationship among the Yir Yoront involved a definite and accepted status of superordination or subordination. A person could have no dealings with any other on exactly equal terms. Women and children were dependent on, or subordinate to, older males in every action in which the axe entered. Among the men, the younger was dependent on the older or on certain kinds of kin. The nearest approach to equality was between brothers, although the older was always superordinate to the younger. Since the exchange of goods in a trading relationship involved a mutual reciprocity, trading partners were usually a kind of brother to each other or stood in a brotherly type of relationship, although one was always classified as older than the other and would have some advantage in case of dispute. It can be seen that repeated and widespread conduct centering on the axe helped to generalize and standardize throughout the society these sex, age, and kinship roles, both in their normal benevolent and in exceptional malevolent aspects, and helped to build up expectancies regarding the conduct of others defined as having a particular status.

The status of any individual Yir Yoront was determined not only by sex, age, and extended kin relationships, but also by membership in one of two dozen patrilineal totemic clans into which the entire community was divided. A person's names, rights in particular areas of land, and, in the case of a man, his roles in the totemic ceremonies (from which women are excluded) were all a function of belonging to one clan rather than another. Each clan had literally hundreds of totems, one or two of which gave the clan its name, and from any of which the personal names of clan members were derived. These totems included not only natural species or phenomena like the sun, stars, and daybreak, but also cultural "species": imagined ghosts, rainbow serpents, heroic ancestors; such eternal cultural verities as fires, spears, huts; and such human activities, conditions, or attributes as eating, vomiting, swimming, fighting, babies and corpses, milk and blood, lips and loins. While individual members of such totemic classes or species might disappear or be destroyed, the class itself was obviously ever present and indestructible. The totems therefore lent permanence and stability to the clans, to the groupings of human individuals who generation after generation were each associated with one set of totems that distinguished one clan from another.

Among the many totems of the Sunlit Cloud Iguana clan, and important among them, was the stone axe. The names of many members of this clan referred to the axe itself, or to activities like trading or wild honey gathering in which the axe played a vital part, or to the clan's mythical ancestors with whom the axe was prominently associated. When it was necessary to represent the stone axe in totemic ceremonies, it was only men of this clan who exhibited it or pantomimed its use. In secular life the axe could be made by any man and used by all; but in the sacred realm of the totems it belonged exclusively to the Sunlit Cloud Iguana people.

Supporting those aspects of cultural behavior which we have called technology and conduct is a third area of culture, including ideas, sentiments, and values. These are most difficult to deal with, for they are latent and covert or even unconscious and must be deduced from overt actions and language or other communicating behavior. In this aspect of the culture lies the "meaning" of the stone axe, its significance to the Yir Yoront and to their cultural way of life. The ideal conception of the axe, the knowledge of how to produce it (apart from the purely muscular habits used in its production) are part of the Yir Yoront adult masculine role, just as ideas regarding its technical use are included in the feminine role. These technical ideas constitute a kind of "science" regarding the axe which may be more important in relation to behavioral change than are the neurophysiological patterns drilled into the body by years of practice. Similarly there are normative ideas regarding the part played by the axe in conduct which constitute a kind of "morality" of the axe, and which again may be more important than the overt habits of social interaction in determining the role of the axe in social relationships. More than ideas regarding technology, ideas regarding conduct are likely to be closely associated, or "charged," with sentiment or value. Ideas and sentiments help guide and inform overt behavior; in turn, overt behavior helps support and validate ideas and sentiments.

The stone axe was an important symbol of masculinity among the Yir Yoront (just as pants or pipes are among ourselves). By a complicated set of ideas which we would label "ownership" the axe was defined as "belonging" to males. Everyone in the society (except untrained infants) accepted these ideas. Similarly spears, spear throwers, and fire-making sticks were associated with males, were owned only by them, and were symbols of masculinity. But the masculine values represented by the stone axe were constantly being impressed on all members of society by the fact that nonmales had to use the axe and had to go to males for it, whereas they never borrowed other masculine artifacts. Thus, the axe stood for an important theme that ran all through Yir Yoront culture: the superiority and rightful dominance of the male, and the greater value of his concerns and of all things associated with him. We should call this androcentrism rather than patriarchy, or paternal rule. It is the recognition by all that the values of the man (*andros*) take precedence over feminine values, an idea backed by very strong sentiments among the Yir Yoront. Since the axe had to be borrowed also by the younger from the older, it also represented the prestige of age, another important theme running all through Yir Yoront behavior.

Important for an understanding of the Yir Yoront culture is a system of ideas, which may be called their totemic ideology. A fundamental belief of the aboriginal divided time into two great epochs, a distant and sacred period at the beginning of the world, when the earth was peopled by mildly marvelous ancestral beings or culture heroes who in a special sense are the forebears of the clans; and a second period, when the old was succeeded by a new order that includes the present. Originally there was no anticipation of another era supplanting the present; the future would simply be an eternal continuation and reproduction of the present, which itself had remained unchanged since the epochal revolution of ancestral times.

The mythical sacred world of the ancestors with which time began turns out on investigation to be a detailed reproduction of the present aboriginal world of nature, man, and culture altered by phantasy. In short, the idea system expressed in the mythology regarding the ancestral epoch was directly derived from Yir Yoront behavior patterns—normal and abnormal, actual and ideal, conscious and unconscious. The important thing to note, however, is that the native believed it was just the other way around, that the present world, as a natural and cultural environment, was and should be simply a detailed reproduction of the world of the ancestors. He believed that the entire universe "is now as it was in the beginning" when it was established and left by the ancestors. The ordinary cultural life of the ancestors became the daily life of the Yir Yoront camps, and the extraordinary life of the ancestors remained extant in the recurring symbolic pantomimes and paraphernalia found only in the most sacred atmosphere of the totemic rites.

Such beliefs, accordingly, opened up the way for ideas of what *should be* (because it supposedly *was*) to influence or help determine what actually *is*. Dog-chases-iguana-up-a-tree-and-barks-at-him-all-night had that and other names because, so he believed, his ancestral alter ego had these same names; he was a member of the Sunlit Cloud Iguana clan because his ancestor was; he was associated with particular countries and totems of this same ancestor; during an initiation he played the role of a dog and symbolically attacked and killed certain members of other clans because his ancestor (conveniently either anthropomorphic or kynomorphic) really did the same to the ancestral alter egos of these men; and he would avoid his mother-in-law, joke with a distant mother's brother, and make spears in a certain way because his and other people's ancestors did these things. His behavior in these rather than in other ways was outlined for him, and to that extent determined, by a set of ideas concerning the past and the relation of the present to the past.

But when we are informed that Dog-chases . . . had two wives from the Spear Black Duck clan and one from the Native Companion clan with such and such names, one of them being blind; that he had four children with such and such names; that he had a broken wrist and was left-handed, all because his ancestor had exactly these same attributes, then we know (though he apparently did not) that the present has influenced the past, that the mythical world has been somewhat adjusted to meet the exigencies and accidents of the inescapably real present.

There was thus in Yir Yoront ideology a nice balance in which the mythical world was adjusted in part to the real world, the real world in part to the ideal preexisting mythical world, the adjustments occurring to maintain a fundamental tenet of native faith that the present must be a mirror of the past. Thus, the stone axe in all its aspects, uses, and associations was integrated into the context of Yir Yoront technology and conduct because a myth, a set of ideas, had put it there.

4. ANALYSIS

The introduction of the steel axe indiscriminately and in large numbers into the Yir Yoront technology was only one of many changes occurring at the same time. It is therefore impossible to factor out all the results of this single innovation alone. Nevertheless, a number of specific effects of the change from stone axes to steel axes may be noted; and the steel axe may be used as an epitome of the European goods and implements received by the aboriginals in increasing quantity and of their general influence on the native culture. The use of the steel axe to illustrate such influences would seem to be justified, for it was one of the first European artifacts to be adopted for regular use by the Yir Yoront; and the axe, whether of stone or steel, was clearly one of the most important items of cultural equipment they possessed.

The shift from stone to steel axes provided no major technological difficulties. While the aboriginals themselves could not manufacture steel axe heads, a steady supply from outside continued; and broken wooden axe handles could easily be replaced from bush timbers with aboriginal tools. Among the Yir Yoront the new axe never acquired all the uses it had on mission or cattle stations (carpentry work, pounding tent pegs, use as a hammer, and so on); and, indeed, it was used for little more than the stone axe had been, so that it had no practical effect in improving the native standard of living. It did some jobs better, and could be used longer without breakage; and these factors were sufficient to make it of value to the native. But the assumption of the white man (based in part on a realization that a shift from steel to stone axe in his case would be a definite regression) that his axe was much more efficient, that its use would save time, and that it therefore represented technical "progress" toward goals which he had set for the native was hardly borne out in aboriginal practice. Any leisure time the Yir Yoront might gain by using steel axes or other western tools was invested, not in "improving the conditions of life," and certainly not in developing aesthetic activities, but in sleep, an art they had thoroughly mastered.

Having acquired an axe head through regular trading partners of whom he knew what to expect, a man wanting a stone axe was then dependent solely upon a known and an adequate nature and upon his own skills or easily acquired techniques. A man wanting a steel axe, however, was in no such self-reliant position. While he might acquire one through trade, he now had the new alternative of dispensing with technological behavior in relation with a predictable nature and conduct in relation with a predictable trading partner and of turning instead to conduct alone in relation with a highly erratic missionary. If he attended one of the mission festivals when steel axes were handed out as gifts, he might receive one simply by chance or if he had happened somehow to impress upon the mission staff that he was one of the "better" bush aboriginals (their definition of "better" being quite different from that of his bush fellows). Or he might—but again almost by pure chance—be given some brief job in connection with the mission which would enable him to earn a steel axe. In either case, for older men a preference for the steel axe helped create a situation of dependence in place of a situation of self-reliance and a behavior shift from situations in technology or conduct which were well structured or defined to situations in conduct alone which were ill defined. It was particularly the older ones among the men, whose earlier experience or knowledge of the white man's harshness in any event made them suspicious, who would avoid having any relations with the mission at all, and who thus excluded themselves from acquiring steel axes directly from that source.

The steel axe was the root of psychological stress among the Yir Yoront even more significantly in other aspects of social relations. This was the result of new factors which the missionary considered all to the good: the simple numerical increase in axes per capita as a result of mission distribution; and distribution from the mission directly to younger men, women, and even children. By winning the favor of the mission staff, a woman might be given a steel axe. This was clearly intended to be hers. The situation was quite different from that involved in borrowing an axe from a male relative, with the result that a woman called such an axe "my" steel axe, a possessive form she never used for a stone axe.

(Lexically, the steel axe was differentiated from the stone by an adjectival suffix signifying "metal," the element "axe" remaining identical.) Furthermore, young men or even boys might also obtain steel axes directly from the mission. A result was that older men no longer had a complete monopoly of all the axes in the bush community. Indeed, an old man might have only a stone axe, while his wives and sons had steel axes which they considered their own and which he might even desire to borrow. All this led to a revolutionary confusion of sex, age, and kinship roles, with a major gain in independence and loss of subordination on the part of those able now to acquire steel axes when they had been unable to possess stone axes before.

The trading partner relationship was also affected by the new situation. A Yir Yoront might have a trading partner in a tribe to the south whom he defined as a younger brother, and on whom as an older brother he would therefore have an edge. But if the partner were in contact with the mission or had other easier access to steel axes, his subordination to his bush colleague was obviously decreased. Indeed, under the new dispensation he might prefer to give his axe to a bush "sweetheart" in return for favors or otherwise dispose of it outside regular trade channels, since many steel axes were so distributed between natives in new ways. Among other things, this took some of the excitement away from the fiesta-like tribal gatherings centering around initiations during the dry season. These had traditionally been the climactic annual occasions for exchanges between trading partners, when a man might seek to acquire a whole year's supply of stone axe heads. Now he might find himself prostituting his wife to almost total strangers in return for steel axes or other white men's goods. With trading partnerships weakened, there was less reason to attend the fiestas, and less fun for those who did. A decline in one of the important social activities which had symbolized these great gatherings created a lessening of interest in the other social aspects of these events.

Not only did an increase in steel axes and

their distribution to women change the character of the relations between individual and individual, the paired relationships that have been noted, but a new type of relationship, hitherto practically unknown among the Yir Yoront, was created in their axe-acquiring conduct with whites. In the aboriginal society there were almost no occasions outside the immediate family when one individual would initiate action to several other people at once. For in any average group, while a person in accordance with the kinship system might be superordinate to several people to whom he could suggest or command action, at the same time he was also subordinate to several others, in relation with whom such behavior would be tabu. There was thus no overall chieftainship or authoritarian leadership of any kind. Such complicated operations as grass-burning, animal drives, or totemic ceremonies could be carried out smoothly because each person knew his roles both in technology and conduct.

On both mission and cattle stations, however, the whites imposed upon the aboriginals thier conception of leadership roles, with one person in a controlling relationship with a subordinate group. Aboriginals called together to receive gifts, including axes, at a mission Christmas party found themselves facing one or two whites who sought to control their behavior for the occasion, who disregarded the age, sex, and kinship variables among them of which they were so conscious, and who considered them all at one subordinate level. Or the white might impose similar patterns on a working party. (But if he placed an aboriginal in charge of a mixed group of post hole diggers, for example, half of the group, those subordinate to the "boss," would work while the other half, who were superordinate to him, would sleep.) The steel axe, together, of course, with other European goods, came to symbolize for the aboriginal this new and uncomfortable form of social organization, the leader-group relationship.

The most disturbing effects of the steel axe, operating in conjunction with other elements also being introduced from the white man's several subcultures, developed in the realm of traditional ideas, sentiments, and values. These were undermined at a rapidly mounting rate, without new conceptions being defined to replace them. The result was a mental and moral void which foreshadowed the collapse and destruction of all Yir Yoront culture, if not, indeed, the extinction of the biological group itself.

From what has been said it should be clear how changes in overt behavior, in technology and conduct, weakened the values inherent in a reliance on nature, in androcentrism or the prestige of masculinity, in age prestige, and in the various kinship relations. A scene was set in which a wife or young son, his initiation perhaps not even yet completed, need no longer bow to the husband or father, who was left confused and insecure as he asked to borrow a steel axe from them. For the woman and boy the steel axe helped establish a new degree of freedom which was accepted readily as an escape from the unconscious stress of the old patterns, but which left them also confused and insecure. Ownership became less well defined, so that stealing and trespass were introduced into technology and conduct. Some of the excitement surrounding the great ceremonies evaporated, so that the only fiestas the people had became less festive, less interesting. Indeed, life itself became less interesting, although this did not lead the Yir Yoront to invent suicide, a concept foreign to them.

The whole process may be most specifically illustrated in terms of the totemic system, and this will also illustrate the significant role which a system of ideas, in this case a totemic ideology, may play in the breakdown of a culture.

In the first place, under pre-European aboriginal conditions in which the native culture has become adjusted to a relatively stable environment in which there can occur few, if any, unheard of or catastrophic crises, it is clear that the totemic system must serve very effectively to inhibit radical cultural changes. The closed system of totemic ideas, explaining and categorizing a well-known universe as it was fixed at the beginning of time, presents a considerable obstacle to the adoption of new or the dropping of old culture traits. The obstacle is not insurmountable and the system allows for the minor variations which occur about the norms of daily life, but the inception of major changes cannot easily take place.

Among the bush Yir Yoront the only means of water transport is a light wood log, to which they cling in their constant swimming of rivers, salt creeks, and tidal inlets. These natives know that forty-five miles north of them are tribes who have a bark canoe. They know these northern tribes can thus fish from midstream or out at sea, instead of clinging to the river banks and beaches, and can cross coastal waters infested with crocodiles, sharks, sting rays, and Portuguese-men-of-war without the recurring mortality, pain, or anxiety to which they themselves are constantly subjected. They know they lack any magic to do for them what the canoe could do. They know the materials of which the canoe is made are present in their own environment. But they also know, as they say, that their own mythical ancestors lacked the canoe, and therefore they lack it, while they assume that the canoe was part of the ancestral universe of the northern tribes. For them, then, the adoption of the canoe would not be simply a matter of learning a number of new behavioral skills for its manufacture and use. The adoption would require at the same time a much more difficult procedure, the acceptance by the entire society of a myth, either locally developed or borrowed, which would explain the presence of the canoe, associate it with some one or more of the several hundred mythical ancestors (and how to decide which?), and thus establish it as an accepted totem of one of the clans ready to be used by the whole community. The Yir Yoront have not made this adjustment, and in this case we can only say that ideas have for the time being at least won out over very real pressures for technological change. In the elaborateness and explicitness of the totemic ideologies we seem to have one explanation for the notorious stability of Australian cultures under aboriginal conditions, an explanation which gives due weight to the importance of ideas in determining human behavior.

At a later stage of the contact situation, as has been indicated, phenomena unaccounted for by the totemic ideological system begin to appear with regularity and frequency and remain within the range of native experience. Accordingly, they cannot be ignored (as the "Battle of the Mitchell River" was apparently ignored), and an attempt is made to assimilate them and account for them along the lines of principles inherent in the ideology. The bush Yir Yoront of the mid-1930's represent this stage of the acculturation process. Still trying to maintain their aboriginal definition of the situation, they accept European artifacts and behavior patterns, but fit them into their totemic system, assigning them as totems to various clans on a par with original totems. There is an attempt to have the myth-making process keep up with these cultural changes so that the idea system can continue to support the rest of the culture. But analysis of overt behavior, of dreams, and of some of the new myths indicates that this arrangement is not entirely satisfactory; that the native clings to his totemic system with intellectual loyalty, lacking any substitute ideology; but that associated sentiments and values are weakened. His attitudes towards his own and toward European culture are found to be highly ambivalent.

All ghosts are totems of the Head-to-the-East Corpse clan. They are thought of as white, and are, of course, closely associated with death. The white man, too, is white and was closely associated with death, so that he and all things pertaining to him are naturally assigned to the Corpse clan as totems. The steel axe, as a totem, was thus associated with the Corpse clan. But it is an "axe," and is clearly linked with the stone axe, which is a totem of the Sunlit Cloud Iguana clan. Moreover, the steel axe, like most European goods, has no distinctive origin myth, nor are mythical ancestors associated with it. Can anyone, sitting of an afternoon in the shade of a ti tree, create a myth to resolve this confusion? No one has, and the horrid suspicion arises that perhaps the origin myths are wrong, which took into account so little of this vast new universe of the white man. The steel axe, shifting hopelessly between one clan and the other, is not only replacing the stone axe physically, but is hacking at the supports of the entire cultural system.

The aboriginals to the south of the Yir Yoront have clearly passed beyond this stage. They are engulfed by European culture, in this area by either the mission or cattle station subcultures, or for some natives a baffling, paradoxical combination of both incongruent varieties. The totemic ideology can no longer support the inrushing mass of foreign culture traits and the myth-making process in its native form breaks down completely. Both intellectually and emotionally a saturation point is reached, so that the myriad new traits which can neither be ignored nor any longer assimilated simply force the aboriginal to abandon his totemic system. With the collapse of this system of ideas, which is so closely related with so many other aspects of the native culture, there follows an appallingly sudden and complete cultural disintegration and a demoralization of the individual such as has seldom been recorded for areas other than Australia. Without the support of a system of ideas well devised to provide cultural stability in a stable environment but admittedly too rigid for the new realities pressing in from outside, native behavior and native sentiments and values are simply dead. Apathy reigns. The aboriginal has passed beyond the reach of any outsider who might wish to do him well or ill.

Returning from the broken natives huddled on cattle stations or on the fringes of frontier towns to the ambivalent but still lively aboriginals settled on the Mitchell River mission, we note one further devious result of the introduction of European artifacts. During a wet season stay at the mission, the anthropologist discovered that his supply of tooth paste was being depleted at an alarming rate. Investigation showed that it was being taken by old men for use in a new tooth paste cult. Old materials of magic having failed, new materials were being tried out in a malevolent magic directed toward the mission staff and some of the younger aboriginal men. Old males, who had been largely ignored by the missionaries, were seeking to regain some of their lost power and prestige. This mild aggression proved hardly effective, but perhaps only because confidence in any kind of magic on the mission was by this time at a low ebb.

For the Yir Yoront still in the bush a time could be predicted when personal deprivation and frustration in a confused culture would produce an overload of anxiety. The mythical past of the totemic ancestors would disappear as a guarantee of a present of which the future was supposed to be a stable continuation. Without the past, the present would be meaningless and the future unstructured and uncertain. Insecurities would be inevitable. Reaction to this stress might be some form of symbolic aggression, or withdrawal and apathy, or some more realistic approach. In such a situation the missionary with understanding of the processes going on about him would find his opportunity to introduce religion and to help create the constitution of a new cultural universe.

7. VARIATION IN HABITAT AND CULTURE ON THE NORTHWEST COAST

WAYNE SUTTLES

Reprinted, with permission, from Proceedings of the 34th International Congress of Americanists (1960) *(Horn-Vienna, Austria: Verlag Ferdinand Berger, 1962). Wayne Suttles is Professor of Anthropology at Portland State College. He has done research on the Northwest Coast and elsewhere with North American Indians and also on Okinawa. One of his principal interests is the relationship between people and their habitats.*

■ As noted in Selection 3, it is necessary to distinguish hunter-gatherer-fishermen from nomadic foragers. This selection illustrates the hunting-gathering strategy to which fishing has been added, largely replacing hunting as a source of protein; it is a methodologically as well as substantively important article. Suttles carefully compares groups that are geographically very close to each other, a method that was alluded to by Steward in Selection 5. Even groups that are neighbors may experience what seem to be minor habitational differences that are nonetheless significant enough to set different limits and provide varying potentials for the organization of social relations. Habitational differences between neighboring groups are not the only source of variations in the organization of social relations. As will be seen in subsequent selections, different historical experiences also can play a strong role in giving rise to institutional variation.

In Suttles' examination of the American Northwest Coast—an area that is frequently discussed by anthropologists as though it were habitationally uniform—he points to the kinds of habitational factors that must be examined with the utmost care if we are to understand how they can affect the organization of social relations within the same level of adaptation. He focuses on two social variables that reflect habitational differences: language and political organization.

Suttles shows that the geographic distribution of two linguistic families, Straits and Halkomelem, closely parallel the migration routes of fish. Straits-speakers' settlements coincide with the routes taken by sockeye salmon, and these are the only people who use the reefnet to take fish. Straits-speakers live along the channels that lead to the Fraser River; the

Halkomelem-speakers live in the lower valley and delta of the Fraser. The two languages were not directly tied to fishing techniques, but using the notion that people who speak related languages are culturally more similar than people who speak disparate languages, we can assume that Straits-speakers represent one variation of a strategy of adaptation and that the languages of the Halkomelem family refer to another variation.

For the second variable of his study, variations in social organization, Suttles concludes that differences among groups in leadership and social ranking (what he calls "seriation") also must be examined in the context of habitational variation. His first comparison is between the Wakashan people and the Coast Salish people. Suttles observes that among the Wakashan (Nootka and Kwakiutl), leadership is strictly determined by descent, which is bilateral; productive resources are "owned" by means of inheritance; there are fewer leaders and their status is more clearly defined than among the Coast Salish; and stratification ("seriation") also is more clearly defined. Correlatively, Suttles notes that in the area inhabited by the Wakashan, there are fewer types of resources but a greater concentration of resources than among the Coast Salish. Similarly, the potlatch (an institution of ceremonialized feasting accompanied by competitive gift-giving) appears to be more important among the Wakashan people and it is an important means for maintaining rank and redistributing wealth.

Moving northward to the group of Northern people (Tsimshian, Haida, Tingit), Suttles superimposes a comparison of the Wakashan and Northern people on his comparison of the Wakashan and Coast Salish. Among the Northern people, in whose areas there are still fewer types of resources that are still more highly concentrated, social groups show even greater stability than among the Wakashan. Suttles maintains that matrilineal descent makes individual mobility very difficult, and kinship provides the most important form of social insurance in case of need. Suttles hypothesizes that the stricter definitions of group membership that appeared as he moved northward are intimately tied to the amount and concentration of resources.

There is considerable overlap between the organization of social relations among some Northwest Coast people (such as the Wakashan) and some horticulturists. This similarity can be attributed to the fact that the level of food productivity among the Northwest Coast people is comparable to that of many horticulturists, among whom domesticates make up about 50 percent of the diet.

The Northwest Coast has been well covered by anthropologists. A good general introduction to the area is *Indians of the Northwest Coast,* by Philip Drucker (Garden City, N.Y.: Natural History Press, 1963). Also worth consulting is *Indians of the Pacific Northwest,* by Ruth M. Underhill (Lawrence, Kansas: Indian Life and Customs Pamphlets, Vol. 5, 1944). *Fighting with Property: A Study of Kwakiutl Potlatching and Warfare, by Helen Codere* (New York: J. J. Augustin, 1950), is a thorough and sensitive examination of Kwakiutl culture that focuses on their custom of the potlatch. *North Alaskan Eskimo: A Study in Ecology and Society,* by Robert F. Spencer (Washington, D.C.: U.S. Government Printing Office, U.S. Bureau of Ethnology, 1959), is true to its title, and, like the paper by Suttles, it seeks to correlate variations in social organization with differences in habitat. A novel interpretation of the potlatch is presented in "Potlatch and Sagali: The Structure of Exchange in Haida and Trobriand Societies," by Paula G. Rubel and Abraham Rosman *(Transactions of the New York Academy of Sciences,* Series II, 32 [1970]: 732-42), in which the authors relate the custom of potlatching to rearrangements in structures of social relations that are required by the practice of father's-sister's-daughter marriage. Rubel and Rosman argue that the potlatch cannot be explained by reference to ecological considerations. For an opposing view, the reader should consult "The Potlatch System of the Southern Kwakiutl," by Stuart Piddocke *(Southwestern Journal of Anthropology,* 21 [1965]: 244-64). ■

"IN THE EARLY DAYS," writes Ruth Underhill, "the richest people in North America were the Indians of the Northwest coast."

Not rich in gold and silver! Even had they been able to dig those metals from the rocks where the White man finds them now, the Indians would have thought of them only as another ornament, like bear claws and abalone shell. To them, wealth was something a man could eat, wear or use to shelter him from the weather. And it was something he could give to his friends for these purposes. In this sense, the Northwest had everything. There were fish in the streams; game in the forests; berries and roots in the open places. There were trees large enough to build a banquet hall, yet splitting like matchwood. There was a climate so moist that plants grew as if in the tropics, yet so mild that few clothes were necessary.

People who lived in such a climate did not need to plant. They had more berries and roots than they could use, simply by going to the places where Nature had spread them. Most of them did not even hunt, unless they felt like a change of diet. Every year, they had only to wait until the salmon came swarming up the streams, "so thick," say the old settlers, "that you could walk across on their backs." In three or four months, a family could get food enough to last a year. The rest of the time they could give to art, to war, to ceremonies and feasting. And so they did.

In the chapter on economics in their text, *An Introduction to Cultural Anthropology,* Ralph L. Beals and Harry Hoijer present a brief sketch of "wealth and status among the Haidas." They begin with a few lines on the habitat, reading in part:

The region in which the Haidas live is mild and equable in climate throughout the year. ... Both land and marine fauna are exceptionally rich. ... Coastal waters and rivers teem with fish. ... *The potential food supply is consistent and dependable,* for though it is less in winter, there is no season when food is really difficult to obtain.

After discussing technology and kinship they continue:

The household is the producing unit and usually can find among its members all or most of the skills and labor it requires. Property is accumulated, not only by hunting, fishing, collecting, and manufacturing, but also by an elaborate technique of lending at 100 per cent interest and by trade and warfare with neighboring tribes on the mainland. Each household, *despite the ease of making a living in this rich environment,* works very hard to accumulate as large a surplus as possible, especially in storable foods, oils, furs, blankets, slaves, and shields made of native copper. The accumulations so made are not for trade, however. Indeed, *since there is little division of labor as between Haida households, such internal trade is not required; each household can amply supply its own wants.*

Instead the surplus accumulated by a household is consumed in lavish feasts and elaborate entertainments called potlatches.

Then after describing the potlatch and its relation to social status, they conclude with the following statement:

It is clear, then, that the potlatch provides an enormous incentive to hard work and the accumulation of property among the Haidas, *even though such accumulations are not really necessary to survival and have no outlet in trade. The patterns of the potlatch and its associated economic activities find their own logic in the total framework of Haida culture.* [All emphasis mine—W.S.]

In a recent essay on Boas's work on the Kwakiutl, Helen Codere writes:

The comparative view of Kwakiutl culture in relation to other Northwest Coast cultures seems to be based almost entirely upon studies of symbolic cultural materials, particularly those of mythology . . . probably because the Northwest Coast was an ecological and cultural area which shared fundamental technological and socioeconomic features. Boas even considered that "the material culture of the fishing tribes of the coast of northeastern Asia, of northwest America, and of the Arctic coast of America . . . (were) . . . so much alike that the assumption of an old unity of this culture seems justifiable." It would follow that his work in clarifying cultural relationships within the Northwest Coast area, and the relationships of that area to the Old World, would necessarily deal largely with symbolic materials, *since the most significant variation would be found at the nonmaterial pole.* [Emphasis mine—W.S.]

It is very difficult to generalize about ethnological writing on the Northwest Coast, especially since there have been wide differences of opinion on certain issues. However,

the statements just given, taken from a semi-popular ethnographic work, from an introductory text in anthropology, and from an essay by a specialist in the area on the foremost student of the area, seem to imply a set of propositions that are contained in much, though by no means all, that has been written on the Northwest Coast. These propositions are:

1. The Northwest Coast is ecologically a single area within which the natural environment is a constant, providing everywhere abundant and dependable sources of food.

2. This habitat permits the production of surpluses, which in turn permit the development of social stratification, art, and ceremony, and the manipulation of prestige goods culminating in the potlatch.

3. This "prestige economy" has little relation to the problems of subsistence but is largely an expression of cultural values.

4. Cultural differences within the Northwest Coast culture area are therefore due to the growth of differences in cultural values, to differences in cultural origins through migration or diffusion, or to combinations of these causes.

These propositions and the total argument that they make have perhaps never been set forth quite as explicitly as this, and perhaps not all writers who seem to have held any of them implicitly would accept them in this form. However, I do not think it is unfair to set them forth as possible implications of the writing I have quoted. I believe they should be set forth explicitly because they should be as explicitly questioned.

I have already questioned the first three of these propositions as applied to one portion of the Northwest Coast in an interpretation of the culture of the Coast Salish of Southern Georgia Strait and the Strait of Juan de Fuca which recently appeared in the *American Anthropologist.* In this interpretation several important features of native social organization and ceremonialism appear as parts of a total socio-economic system that enabled the native population to maintain a fairly high level of production and to reduce inequalities in consumption in a habitat characterized by a variety of types of natural resources, local diversity and seasonal variation in their occurrence, and year to year fluctuation in their abundance. In this portion of the Northwest Coast, the habitat was not a constant but a variable, and several aspects of native culture, including the potlatch, seem to have been adapted to its variability.

In the present paper I would like to present further evidence for qualitative and quantitative variation in natural resources on the Northwest Coast and to discuss some possible implications of my interpretation of the Coast Salish material for other areas on the Coast. This paper is to be then a sort of "view of the Northwest Coast as seen from the Coast Salish." And I should add that, while my discussion of the Coast Salish is based on a number of years of first-hand experience and what I believe to be fairly good evidence, my discussion of other portions of the Coast will be largely speculation. I say this merely to give fair warning, however, rather than to apologize, for I believe that speculation is quite proper in a symposium of this sort. Let me now first outline the Coast Salish cultural system as I see it and then discuss in more detail the features of habitat under which the system seems to be adaptive.

The term "Coast Salish" usually designates a large group of tribes occupying most of the area around Georgia Strait, the Strait of Juan de Fuca, Puget Sound, and extending to the Pacific between the Olympic Peninsula and Willapa Bay. Linguistically speaking, the Bella Coola and the Tillamook could also be called "Coast Salish," though they are culturally more distinct. Even among the contiguous group of tribes, however, cultural differences are great enough that generalizations about "the Coast Salish" are probably dangerous. I must make it clear therefore that here I am concerned with only one segment of the Coast Salish area, that occupied by the speakers of only two of the ten or more Coast Salish languages.

I am concerned here with the tribes that speak two closely related Salish languages, Straits and Halkomelem. The speakers of Straits are the Sooke, Songish, and Saanich on Vancouver Island and the Samish, Lummi, and Semiahmoo on the opposite mainland; the speakers of Halkomelem are the Cowichan, Chemainus, and Nanaimo on the Island and, on the mainland, the Musqueam, Kwantlen, Katzie, Chiliwack, and others along the Lower Fraser River. The Lower Fraser tribes have also been called "Stalo," and Wilson Duff has called those from Chilliwack to the canyon "Upper Stalo." Although these "tribes" so-called were not united in any sort of confederacy of the Wakashan type or by any system of clans and phratries as in the north, they were by no means separate "societies," but rather loosely bound groups of communities within a social and cultural continuum that extended northward and southward somewhat beyond the area of the two languages. Biologically the Straits and Halkomelem tribes were surely part of a single population and culturally of a single people. Unfortunately there is no way of designating these people other than with the cumbersome linguistic designation, so for convenience I will say simply "Coast Salish," hoping that the proper qualifications will be understood.

The aboriginal culture of this Coast Salish people may be seen as having these three components:

A. A primitive technology requiring complete dependence on hunting, fishing, and gathering—but providing sound houses and watercraft, a variety of weapons, nets, traps, and containers, and the preserving techniques of drying and smoking.

B. An ideology and enculturation process providing the individual with the incentive to strive to prestige through the display of supernatural power and the giving of property, the two being symbolically the same.

C. A socio-economic system containing the following—

1. Communities composed of one or more kin groups firmly identified with their locality by tradition.

2. Membership in kin group through bilateral descent, with alternate or even multiple membership possible, making the individual potentially mobile.

3. Preference for local exogamy, establishing a network of affinal ties among communities.

4. Preference for patrilocal residence, having the result that, within the community, most adult males are native and most adult females outsiders—though bilateral affiliation always makes for some exceptions.

5. Leadership within the kin group partly through seniority and partly through ability, kin group headmen having control (sometimes nominal, sometimes real) over especially productive resources within the territory of the kin group.

6. Sharing of access to resources among communities through affinal and blood kin ties—possibly leading to some change in residence.

7. Exchange of food for "wealth" (i.e., durable goods) between affinal relatives in different communities.

8. Redistribution of wealth through the potlatch.

The system of exchange and potlatching seems to have worked in this fashion. A kin or local group with a temporary surplus of any item of food, say the result of the run of some fish or the ripening of some berry, might take this surplus to an affinally related group in another locality and receive wealth in blankets or other imperishable items in return. Later the recipient in the first exchange might make a return visit with its own extra food and get back wealth for it. Any group that produced more food than its various affinally related neighbors would of course in time come to have more wealth. But any tendency for wealth to accumulate in a few places was controlled by the practice of potlatching, whereby the wealthy group converted its wealth into high status at the same time giving the other groups the means of continuing the whole process. Given the limitations of native technology, and operating under the stimulus of native ideology, this whole process was surely useful in the face of variation and fluctuation in natural resources.

Let us now look more closely at the natural resources of the territory of the Coast Salish people whose culture I have just outlined.

The Straits- and Halkomelem-speaking tribes occupied the southeastern shore of Vancouver Island from Sherringham Point, west of Sooke, to Qualicum, north of Nanaimo; the Gulf and San Juan Islands; the mainland from Deception Pass northward to Burrard Inlet; and the Lower Fraser Valley up as far as Yale at the lower end of the canyon. This territory thus includes portions of two large bodies of salt water, Georgia Strait and the Strait of Juan de Fuca, and the numerous channels connecting them; it includes the lower course and delta of a large river, several smaller rivers, and bodies of fresh water; and it includes marshes, low hills and valleys, and is fringed on both the island and mainland by snow-covered mountains.

Something of the variety of climate and of flora may be seen first of all from the fact that this territory lies mainly within two separate biotic areas and borders upon two more. The biologists Munro and Cowan have distinguished in British Columbia thirteen terrestrial and two marine biotic areas. Nearly all of the territory of the Straits-speaking tribes and the territory of the Halkomelem-speaking tribes on Vancouver Island lie within the "Gulf Islands Biotic Area," while the territory of the Halkomelem-speaking tribes of the mainland and a small part of that of the Straits-speaking tribes of the mainland lie within the "Puget Sound Lowlands Biotic Area." Straits territory is almost exactly coterminous with the Gulf Island Biotic Area in the south, but this biotic area extends northward beyond Halkomelem territory on Vancouver Island. Mainland Halkomelem territory is nearly coterminous with the Puget Sound Lowlands Biotic Area in the north, but this biotic area, as its name implies, extends to the south far beyond the territory of the tribes I am concerned with here. To the north of our territory on the mainland and again to the west on Vancouver Island is the "Coast Forest Biotic Area," except at higher altitudes where it gives way to the "Southern Alplands Biotic Area." There is then a partial but not a complete correspondence of biotic area and linguistic area. There are, however, other more precise correspondences of cultural and linguistic boundaries and ecological boundaries that I will point out later.

The Gulf Island Biotic Area is described as "moderate" in temperature and "mediterranean" in climate. Since it lies within the rain shadow of the Olympic Mountains and Island Range, it receives considerably less rainfall than the ocean coast of Vancouver Island to the west and appreciably less than the mainland shore to the east. Large areas are naturally half-open with Garry oak and madrona as the characteristic trees, with fewer of the usual conifers of the coast, and with "an abundance of spring flowering bulbous and herbaceous plants." In the Puget Sound Lowlands Biotic Area precipitation is greater—the average rainfall at New Westminster on the Fraser is 59.6 inches, as compared with 37.7 inches at Nanaimo and 26.7 inches at Victoria on the Island—and the range of temperatures is somewhat greater, but winters are still mild and summers cool. The native flora was characteristically Douglas fir, western red cedar, western hemlock, Sitka spruce, and a few other conifers, but also included broadleafed maple, red alder, flowering dogwood, vine maple, western birch, willows, and other smaller deciduous trees.

It should be mentioned here that the Douglas fir, which is the most common tree in the Puget Sound Lowlands and the most common conifer in the Gulf Islands Biotic Area, is not a climax type. To maintain a cover of Douglas fir the country must have periodic forest fires. If there were no fires the fir would presumably be gradually replaced by cedar, spruce, and hemlock, which are the climax trees and the characteristic cover of the areas of greater precipitation. Thus it is assumed that forest fires have periodically burned here and there throughout our area since remote prehistoric times, bringing a succession of types of cover from grasses and herbs, bush and deciduous trees, to Douglas fir again, and thereby providing even greater variability in natural resources.

As I indicated earlier, this environment was characterized by a variety of types of natural resources, local diversity and seasonal variation in their occurrence, and year to year fluctuation in their abundance. Let us briefly consider each of these characteristics.

1. Variety of types. Vegetable foods included the sprouts of several plants, the bulbs and roots of a dozen or so species, and the berries and fruits of about twenty species. Shellfish included ten different mollusks, two sea urchins, and a crab. More than twenty species of fishes were eaten; these included all five species of Pacific salmon, steelhead trout, halibut, herring, sucker, chub, and sturgeon, the last attaining a weight of 1,800 pounds. Two or three species of upland birds were eaten, and more than forty species of waterfowl and shore birds, ranging in size from little sandpipers to twenty-pound swans. Useful hand mammals included the elk, deer, mountain goat, black bear, and several smaller fur-bearers, and sea mammals, the seal, porpoise, and sea lion. Among these the bull elk may weigh up to 800 pounds and the bull sea lion more than a ton.

2. Local diversity. The occurrence and abundance of these plants and animals varied greatly from place to place depending on such general factors as precipitation, altitude, and salinity of water and on many other more particular factors as well. Camas and several other edible bulbs were found almost exclusively in the drier Gulf Islands Biotic Area while wapato grew only in ponds and sloughs along the Lower Fraser. Some of the berries also grew in quantity only on the bogs of the Fraser Delta. Blackberries, on the other hand, grow best on hillsides after forest fires.

All the shellfish are saltwater species except one, which was evidently not eaten much. But the very broken shoreline presents at one place a gravel beach, at another a spit of fine sand, and at a third a jagged face of rock. Each of these has its own types of shellfish and attracts different sorts of fishes and waterfowl. Some fishes are strictly salt-water species, but these may require different sorts of bottom. The halibut is found on banks of more than thirty fathoms; the lingcod and rockfish may be seen in shallow water off rocky shores; flounders prefer sandy bays near river mouths. Herring spawn in beds of eel grass. A few fishes, like the sucker and chub, live exclusively in fresh water. Still other fishes, and this group includes most of the really important species, are anadromous, spending part of their lives in fresh water and part on the sea. Some of these could be taken in both salt and fresh water, others only in fresh water. Sturgeon were taken in the Fraser and in the shallow bays along the mainland but rarely around Vancouver Island. Eulachon were not obtainable on the salt water but only at their spawning grounds of a few miles along the Fraser.

The habits of the five species of salmon especially limited the places where they could be taken. Two species, springs and cohoes, feed in the Straits and so can be taken in the salt water by trolling. The other three species do not feed after entering the Strait of Juan de Fuca and so cannot be taken in this way. The sockeye salmon move in fairly compact schools by the same routes each year on their way to the mouth of the Fraser and can be taken with the reef net at a limited number of locations along these routes. Sockeyes run only in the Fraser in this area; pinks and springs run largely in the Fraser. In the Fraser fish could be taken only with nets. Cohoes and chums, however, run in nearly all of the smaller streams on Vancouver Island as well as the mainland, and could be taken at weirs in traps or with gaffs or harpoons.

The habits of waterfowl also limit their availability in space. Diving ducks live on deeper water and many species live mainly on the salt water, but dabbling ducks must feed in shallow water or on land and so live along marshy shores or on lakes and streams. The mainland supported many more marsh-feeding ducks than the island.

Deer, elk, and black bear lived on both the mainland and the island. Deer were most plentiful in naturally half-open country as on the smaller islands and in areas recently burned, where feed was more abundant. Elk were most plentiful in flat country, bears probably near salmon streams. But mountain goats lived only on the mainland at higher altitudes. Porpoises and sea lions were found only in the salt water, but seals followed the salmon up the Fraser and had their hauling-out places and even breeding grounds in fresh water on Pitt and Harrison Lakes. They might be harpooned nearly anywhere, but at these places they could also be taken in greater numbers with nets and clubs.

3. Seasonal variation in abundance. Most of the vegetable foods could be harvested only in season—green sprouts in the early spring, camas bulbs in May when the blue flowers showed where they could be dug, berries of the different species from early summer to fall. Herring, smelt, eulachon, and most of the salmons could be taken only during spawning season, which might be of short duration. Some waterfowl, seals, and bears adjust their movements as well to those of the fish. Many of the waterfowl too are migratory. Some pass through this area on their way from the south to the northern interior, stopping only in spring and fall. Others winter here on the flats extending from the Fraser Delta to the mouth of the Skagit. At least nine species have been reported, even in recent winters, in flocks of thousands and even tens of thousands. Sea lions are also migratory, and were taken in this area by only a few communities in the Gulf Islands.

Besides seasonal differences in availability or abundance there were also, for some species, seasonal differences in desirability. Clams, it is said, could be dug most easily and were best at the time of the lowest tides in summer; at any rate this is the time of year when butter-clams and horse-clams were dug for preserving for winter. Weather for drying may have been an important determinant of the season. With deer, bucks are fattest and best in spring while does are best in fall. The flesh of the bear is least desirable in spring when they eat skunk cabbage, better in summer when they eat berries, and best in fall when they have fattened on salmon. The different species of salmon and even different races of the same species do not preserve equally well; weather and fat content may be the determinants.

4. Fluctuation from year to year. The various species and races of salmon also varied greatly in quantity from year to year. The

most spectacular regular fluctuations were in sockeye and pink runs. The pink salmon matures regularly in its second year and in this area the several populations are in the same cycle so that they all spawn every other year. It can be predicted then that pinks will arrive in great numbers in odd-numbered years and in even-numbered years not at all. Sockeye generally mature in their fourth year and as with pinks the various populations in the Fraser are mainly in the same cycle, with the result that every fourth year there is a run of sockeye several times larger than in any of the other three years. This four-year cycle in sockeye runs in the Fraser was recorded as far back as 1823 and presumably occurred in pre-contact times.

Besides these regular and predictable fluctuations, there are other less predictable fluctuations in number of salmon, caused probably by various factors such as precipitation, temperature, etc., during spawning season, changes in streambeds resulting from landslides, etc. Such factors may be especially influential in smaller streams—certainly estimates of fish runs in the smaller streams of southeastern Vancouver Island for recent years show a good deal of what appears to be random fluctuation. It should also be added that other animals whose lives are related to the salmon must fluctuate in numbers accordingly.

Another source of variability from year to year is the occasional burning that must have occurred. Blackberries and some other plants of economic importance to the Coast Salish grow best two or three years after a forest fire, and as the trees grow up again gradually lose out. Deer also find better fodder in the few years following a burn and are probably fluctuated in abundance in any single area depending upon the recency of fires. There is some reason for believing, incidentally, that the Coast Salish occasionally set fire to the woods in order to maintain the post-burn biota.

I pointed out earlier the partial correspondence of linguistic boundaries and the boundaries of biotic areas and mentioned that there were other correspondences of linguistic, cultural, and ecological features. The most striking of these are in the relationship between the Straits language and the migration route of the sockeye salmon. The territories of the various Straits-speaking tribes lie across the channels the sockeye take on their way to the mouth of the Fraser, and there the Straits tribes caught the sockeye in their reef nets. The International Pacific Salmon Fisheries Commission has recently compiled a map showing the routes taken by the sockeye. The reefnet locations of the Straits tribes, which I have mapped, fall very neatly along these routes. The reefnet was used by the Straits tribes only; it was their most important fishing device; and it seems to have been used wherever it was possible to take sockeye with it. The close correspondence of language, fishing method, and fish strongly suggests that we have here an ecological niche nicely filled by human beings culturally distinguishable from all others. This may surely be called "adaptation."

For the Halkomelem tribes there is no such precise correlation, but this group of tribes too has more in common than would appear at first glance. I identified earlier the Cowichan, Cheminus, and Nanaimo as living on Vancouver Island and the Musqueam, Kwantlen, etc. as living on the mainland on the Fraser. This identification refers to their winter residence, the sites of their largest permanent houses. But except for some of the Cowichan, who have a fair-sized salmon stream in the island, the Halkomelem-speaking people of Vancouver Island came across Georgia Strait each summer for the run of fish on the Fraser. Thus the Halkomelem tribes are essentially the people of the lower valley and delta of the Fraser as the Straits tribes are the people of the channels leading to the Fraser.

All of these data on the natural resources of the Straits and Halkomelem tribes should make it clear that I do not mean to say that this area was not well provided with useful plants and animals. It certainly was. What I do want to emphasize is that all things were not available everywhere at all times so that they could simply be had for the taking. On the contrary, everything useful was available more at one place than at another, and more in one season than in another, and often more in one year than in another. One may object that nobody has ever really said that this was not so, that Underhill, for example, shortly after her description of the richness of the habitat quoter earlier, describes how different foods were found at different places. But this is merely to introduce a discussion of the yearly round. So it is with much of the writing on the Northwest Coast; if spatial and temporal variation in resources get any consideration, it is in relation to technology and seasonal movements. The extent of these variations and their implications for social organization, however, are rarely considered. It is my position that the social organization and ceremonialism of the Coast Salish of the area I have studied is intelligible only in the light of these variations.

What about the rest of the Northwest Coast? Let us look first at the habitat to the northwest of the Coast Salish and then consider how the native cultures may be related to it.

The differences between the habitats of the Nootka, Kwakiutl, Bella Coola, and Tsimshian and even the Salish of Northern Georgia Strait may not be as great as the differences between the habitat of the Coast Salish that I have just described and the rest. The biologists have assigned all of Vancouver Island west of Sooke and north of Comox and all of the mainland north of Burrard Inlet to a "Coast Forest Biotic Area." This biotic area is characterized by a much greater precipitation and consequent differences in forest cover. The difference in precipitation between the Gulf Islands and Coast Forest Biotic Area is striking to say the least—Victoria receives 26 inches of rainfall, while Jordan River, a few miles to the west, receives 133 inches. The biologists assign the habitat of the Haida to a separate "Queen Charlotte Islands Biotic Area," which has a climate similar to that of the Coast Forest Biotic Area, but because of its isolation has a more restricted fauna.

In spite of the assignment of a large portion of the coast to a single biotic area, how-ever, there may still be less conspicuous differences between the territories of the different native peoples. The area within which the Douglas fir is the most abundant tree extends north of the Gulf Island and Puget Sound Lowlands Biotic Areas to the northern end of Georgia Strait to include just about the same area occupied by the Salish before the recent expansion of the southernmost group of Kwakiutl. To the west and north Douglas fir is replaced by the climax trees, cedar, spruce, and hemlock. This apparent correlation of Douglas fir and Salish speech should be given further attention.

Moreover, trees of the same species may differ in their useful qualities from one area to another. All cedar trees do not "split like matchwood." The Indian carvers working on the campus of the University of British Columbia have found some southern cedars unusable for reproducing Haida totem poles and prefer cedars from the Queen Charlotte Islands. The possibility that some regional differences in art style are related to regional differences in materials available should not be overlooked.

However, such possibilities notwithstanding, it must be granted that, more broadly speaking, the whole Northwest Coast is unquestionably a single ecological region. The principal differences between the habitat of the Coast Salish that I have described and that of the Nootka, Kwakiutl, Tsimshian, or Haida seem to be quantitative not qualitative. The habitats of each of these peoples, like that of the Coast Salish, are characterized by a variety of natural resources and by spatial and temporal differences in their abundance. But it seems to me that as we go northward along the coast we find less variety in types of resources, greater local and seasonal variation, and possibly less year-to-year fluctuation.

As soon as we leave the Gulf Islands and Puget Sound Lowlands Biotic Areas we find fewer species of edible bulbs and roots and less extensive areas where they can grow. The Kwakiutl, it is true, tended beds of cinquefoil and clover, but these could not have provided much as compared with Salish camas or wapato. Edible berries to the north may also be less plentiful. This is difficult to estimate, but we may consider that blackberries, which grow best after burns, would have less chance outside the Douglas fir area, and that in some parts of the Coast Forest Biotic Area the forest is so dense that there is no undergrowth at all, while in other parts salal and salmonberries grow profusely. Also, when we leave the Douglas fir area we find far fewer deer, perhaps less land game generally. In the Queen Charlotte Islands there were no deer at all in pre-white times, though caribou were found in a limited area.

Shellfish are certainly plentiful to the north, but the more rugged shoreline may mean fewer good beds per mile of coast than in the south, where there are more sand and gravel beaches. Waterfowl are very likely less abundant. There is nothing resembling the great expanse of flats offered to migrating and wintering waterfowl by the Fraser and Skagit deltas. Many of the winter residents in the Salish area fly inland as they migrate northward so that the northern coast is somewhat off the Pacific flyway. A few species, however, may be more numerous in the north, as for example the Western Canada goose in the Queen Charlottes. Sea mammals are certainly as numerous off the west coast of Vancouver Island and, farther north, some species undoubtedly are more numerous. At the present time 70 per cent of the sea lion population of British Columbia, which numbers 11,000 to 12,000, is concentrated each summer in two rookeries, one in Kwakiutl and one in Haida territory. In the past there may have been more rookeries, but the concentration was probably as great. Whales have no doubt always been more numerous in the ocean than in the more sheltered waters of Salish territory.

For some idea as to differences in fisheries resources of the different tribal areas we can consult some of the publications of the international, national, and local fisheries authorities. The Department of Fisheries of Canada issues each year a volume of *British Columbia Catch Statistics* in which the commercial salmon catch is given by species in each of 38 statistical areas within the province. These areas can be matched roughly with native tribal areas. The figures are for recent years and are for fish taken on modern gear, but they ought to give some hint as to what was available in pre-white times. It is evident from these figures that large numbers of fish are to be had in all areas, though less perhaps for springs than for the other species. But one difference between the Salish areas and the others is very obvious—the cycles in sockeye and pink salmon that are so pronounced in the Salish area are not perceptible farther north. . . . The reasons for the absence of regularity in the figures for sockeye and pinks farther north are probably two: the first sockeye are not on any cycle because they do not spawn as regularly in their fourth year as those of the Fraser, and second, the pinks for several populations are not in step with one another and so for the area appear regular. Fluctuation may also be seen in recent figures for herring spawning. I repeat, these are recent catches with modern equipment, but surely we can infer from them something of the variability of resources for the native peoples at an earlier time.

For other salt-water fishing, fluctuation in numbers of fish was perhaps not as significant a factor in productivity as the weather. Small-craft warnings are out often enough on Georgia Strait to suggest that under aboriginal conditions the Salish could not have fished for halibut as often as they liked, regardless of how the halibut were biting. This kind of limitation must have been even more severe on Queen Charlotte Sound or on the open ocean. Drucker mentions bad weather as a cause of famine among the Nootka. The passage is worth quoting in full for the implications it has for the thesis of this paper:

While the food resources were rich, now and then periods of scarcity occurred. Ethnographers have stressed nature's prodigality to the peoples of the Northwest Coast to the point that one is surprised by the thought they should ever have suffered want. But occasionally a poor dog salmon or herring run, followed by an unusually stormy winter or spring, as the case might be, that prevented people from going out to fish for cod and halibut, quickly brought privation. Those were the times when people walked the beaches looking for codfish heads, spurned by seals and sea lions, and storm-killed herring and pilchard. They collected and ate the tiny mussels of the inner coves and bays, and similar small mussels disdained in normal times. The spring of the year was perhaps more often a lean season than winter. Father Brabant reports two successive springs at Hesquiat when the pickings were lean and children cried with hunger, until the weather abated enough for the fishermen to go out. Family traditions of local groups who say they anciently lived the year around "outside," that is, on the outer beachers and islands, speak of hunger and even starvation that led them to make alliances with or make war on groups who had territories along the inner channels and owned salmon streams. Yet in general the periods of scarcity seem not to have been very frequent, and were periods of unpleasantly short rations but seldom real starvation. The specter of hunger was not constantly menacing, as it was to groups in the interior of the mainland. Most of the time food was available, and frequently it was so abundant that with the most extravagant feasting they could not use it all up.

Boas, in comparing the cultures of the Kwakiutl and the Tsimshian as reflected in their mythologies, notes that:

The difficulties of obtaining an adequate food supply must have been much more serious among the Tsimshian than among the Kwakiutl, for starvation and the rescue of the tribe by the deeds of a great hunter or by supernatural help are an ever-recurring theme which, among the Kwakiutl, is rather rare. One story of this type is clearly a Tsimshian story retold. . . . Starvation stories of the Kwakiutl occur particularly among the tribes living at the heads of the inlets of the mainland, not among those who dwell near the open sea, where seals, sealions, salmon and halibut are plentiful.

The data I have been presenting are fragmentary but sufficient, I believe, to suggest that, as compared with the Coast Salish, the more northern tribes rely on fewer kinds of plants and animals and get them at fewer places and for shorter times during the year, but in greater concentration, and with consequent greater chance for failure. At any rate, I would like to use this as a working hypothesis in looking at the relationship of culture to environment.

Now let us turn to the cultures of the peoples to the northwest of the Coast Salish.

Probably there is general agreement that these fall into two major types: Wakashan, which includes the Nootka and the Kwakiutl proper; and Northern, which includes the Tsimshian, Haida, and Tlingit. For the purposes of this paper I will ignore the transitional Bella Bella and Haisla and the Bella Coola.

Both the Wakashan and Northern cultures, it seems to me, have technological and ideological facets rather similar to what I have indicated for the Coast Salish; they have roughly the same technological limitations and the same individual motivations—though such detail as adz types and fish nets and concepts of the supernatural may vary. But in what I have described as the third facet of culture, the socio-economic system, there are some more important differences.

Looking first at the Wakashan peoples we find that as among the Coast Salish there are communities composed of one or more kin groups in which membership is through bilateral descent, with alternative membership and individual mobility possible but patrilocal residence preferable. The differences seem to be essentially in the addition of two features: (1) leadership is more rigidly determined by descent, that is, by hereditary "ownership" of productive resources, all of which are "owned" and leaders are fewer and more clearly defined; and (2) individuals and groups are ranked in an implicit numerical order, the principle of "seriation."

The first of these features may be related directly to the ecological differences just suggested. The fewer types and greater concentration of resources that I have postulated for both the Wakashan and Northern areas might increase the importance of the "owner" as a redistributor of resources within the local group and a representative of the local group in relation to other groups. This increase in importance of the role of the "owner" may be accompanied by an increased emphasis on differences in status throughout society.

The second new feature, "seriation," does not of course automatically follow the first, but may be encouraged by it. Once introduced within the group, it has the effect of more clearly defining membership; that is to say, the series has to exist for the individual to have a position; in contrast, among the Coast Salish the lack of any series means that the individual is less easily identified with a local group. And once introduced among local groups, seriation becomes the principle by which tribes and confederacies are formed. Among the Wakashans, the ranking of local groups in series replaces the Salish principle of establishing a network of affinal ties among local groups of relatively equal status. Thus among the Wakashan local exogamy is not as important as among the Salish, and in fact there was some slight tendency toward endogamy. The potlatch among the Waka-shan peoples is the means by which individuals and local groups establish and maintain rank within the series. Among the Salish the potlatch does not have this function.

Other points of similarity must also be mentioned. While seriation may make for more clearly determined groups among the Wakashan, bilateral descent, alternative membership, and individual mobility—perhaps especially for the lower ranks—all prevent the local groups from becoming rigid. This fluidity may operate advantageously for the whole population under conditions of gradually changing productivity.

Also, though local exogamy may not be as important, affinal ties are still used among the Wakashan peoples in the process of accumulating property for the potlatch. It may be that there is an underlying Northwest Coast principle here: that a man's affinals are his allies against his importunate blood kin. Perhaps a man can save better by giving to his affinals, who are honor-bound to return the gifts when he needs them for potlatching, than by keeping his food and wealth at home only to have it used up by his own blood kin, whom he is honor-bound to support.

I do not as yet fully understand the pot-latch outside the Coast Salish area. The Waskashan potlatch seems to differ from the Coast Salish potlatch in that it occurred more frequently but was of shorter duration, and the Wakashan potlatch may have had a greater importance in the redistribution of food. Generally there seems to have been a freer exchange of food and wealth among the Wakashan than among the Salish. Still I suspect that there too the potlatch may have served as a regulating mechanism within the total system, as among the Coast Salish. My colleague Dr. A. P. Vayda and several of our students have given some attention to this problem, as he is reporting elsewhere.

Moving on to the Northern peoples, we find even greater differences in the socio-economic system. Among the Tsimshian, Haida, and Tlingit, the social units have become even more stable. Membership is determined by the principle of matrilineal descent, making alternative affiliation and individual mobility less possible. At the same time, matrilineal descent with exogamy and cross-cousin marriage unites pairs of social units within a system that embraces the whole population. Such pairs of social units provide services for one another and potlatch with each other. Such units stand in an *affinal* relationship to one another.

In bilateral societies such as the Coast Salish and Wakashan, affinal ties in one generation lead to consanguineal ties in the next. If the incest prohibition is observed, marriage between two families in one generation reduces the number of potential mates in the next generation. To maintain affinal bonds between two communities for several generations requires that each community be composed of several family lines alternating with each other in their marriages. Among the Coast Salish each community usually contained enough people distantly enough related to each other so that they could maintain among them affinal ties with several neighboring communities without incestuous marriages. Since each community contained several "owners" of productive resources, there was no special advantage in marrying one rather than another among the good families of a neighboring community. On the contrary, the diversity of resources and variations in productivity gave some advantage to diversity of marriage ties. But if to the north we have less diversity and greater concentration of resources and greater control over them in the hands of fewer people, then marrying into the best family is best and the best families will hope to continue to marry best families.

Now unilateral descent is a means of legitimizing kin marriage. By defining our cross-cousins as non-kin, we can marry them without breaking the incest taboo. I suggest then that matrilineal descent in the culture of the Northern tribes may be seen as a sort of crystallization of two features already suggested for the areas to the south: (1) the preference for continued marriage between groups already enjoying a reciprocal relationship, and (2) the necessity of keeping consanguineal and affinal kin separate in order to continue that relationship.

The network of affinal ties among the Coast Salish, seriation among the Kwakiutl, and matrilineal descent among the Northern tribes may all have the effect of uniting different local groups in such a way that—assuming that the potlatching system operates elsewhere somewhat as it seems to among the Coast Salish—they can accommodate to variation and fluctuation in natural resources.

One further possible mode of accommodation should be mentioned. In the southern areas, if there were long-term shifts in productivity in the territories of different groups, people would probably have adjusted to them by a process of gradual individual movement from the less productive to the more productive territory through individual ties of kinship and marriage. In the north, on the other hand, individual mobility was probably far less usual, but group movements evidently did occur. In fact, one of the most striking differences between southern and northern mythology is in the origins of local groups; in the south most groups tell how they were either created or dropped from Heaven on the spot they now occupy, while in the north most groups tell how they migrated from somewhere else. Shifts in population probably occurred in both areas, but unilateral descent may encourage group rather than individual movements.

I have tried to show how the environment of the Northwest Coast cultures is neither uniformly rich and dependable within any tribal

area nor precisely the same from area to area. I have tried to show how some of the important features of Coast Salish culture may be adaptive under the conditions of Coast Salish environment. And I have suggested how some of the differences in culture along the coast may be related to differences in the environment. As I said in the beginning, this paper is a sort of "view of the Northwest Coast as seen from the Coast Salish" and when I leave the Salish area I enter the area of speculation. To make what I have said more than speculation, we would need much more work on the ecology of the Northwest Coast, on the relations of local groups to resources, and on the system of exchange of food and wealth among groups.

I believe this sort of approach would not only make each of the cultures of the Northwest Coast more intelligible but would also lead us to reconsider some of the existing hypotheses regarding their history. If it can be shown, for example, the matrilineal descent and its accompanying features are formalizations of tendencies present elsewhere on the coast and that these tendencies are themselves adaptive, then finding an extra-areal origin for the matrilineal principle becomes less urgent. We may then also question Boas's suggestion that the Kwakiutl social organization developed as a compromise between a patrilineal south and the matrilineal north (a position Murdock has already rejected on other grounds). We may not see the Northwest Coast as simply a series of centers of diffusion with matrilineal descent emanating from the north and self-aggrandizement emanating from the Kwakiutl. Nor may we see the greater individualism of the Coast Salish as simply the result of the survival of Plateau values. Seen in a framework that includes ecology, questions of migration, diffusion, and the persistence of values assume their proper places as parts of the larger whole, the study of culture change as an evolutionary process.

I am tempted to return to Kroeber's view (which has recently received some archeological support from Borden) that the development of culture on the Northwest Coast proceeded from a river-mouth, to an inland salt-water, to a maritime adaptation, with the center of development shifting from the Lower Fraser, to the Wakashan area, to the North. I am tempted to suggest that culture on the Northwest Coast has not only developed along the general course that Kroeber has charted, but that the more specific environmental features to which it has adapted have been the decrease in variety, increase in concentration, and continued spatial and temporal variation in abundance of resources that I believe we may find upon following that course up the coast. Abandoning now all caution, I would like to suggest further that a network of affinal ties, seriation, and matrilineal descent are each crucial features of three stages in the evolution of culture on the Northwest Coast.

8. FORMS OF KINSHIP

ELMAN R. SERVICE

Reprinted from The Hunters *(Copyright © 1966), by permission of Prentice-Hall, Inc., Engle-wood Cliffs, New Jersey. Elman R. Service is Professor of Anthropology at the University of California at Santa Barbara. His ethnological field work has been done mainly in South America and Mexico; his theoretical interests include problems of social and political organization and cultural evolution. Among his books are* Profiles in Ethnology *and* Primitive Social Organization.

■ In this selection we shift from descriptions of specific cultures to a general discussion of one of the most important features in the organization of social relations in human society: the system by which kinsmen are organized. At the moment of his birth every individual automatically acquires a host of relatives; when he marries, he acquires more. There is a kinship system in every society—a set of principles and rules that govern the behavior of kinsmen toward each other, the reciprocities in which they engage, the rights and duties they have with respect to each other, the terms by which they address each other, and the kinds of groupings into which they are organized. There is great variability among societies in regard to kinship, and the elements of a kinship system are an important aspect of the group's cultural adjustments.

Kinship systems are important because every social relationship—between parent and child, spouses, friends, strangers, and the like—must be governed by explicit rules. Furthermore, each set of rules has its own internal logic. Kinship has received, some people think, a disproportionate share of anthropologists' attention, but one of the main reasons for this preoccupation is that kinship generally plays a role of great importance in the pre-industrial societies that are most frequently studied by anthropologists. Another reason is the pervasiveness of kinship rules, many of which regulate social relations in ways that do not immediately appear to involve kinship relationships. The Anglo-American law that spouses cannot be forced to testify against each other in court is a kinship rule; laws or corporate rules against nepotism are kinship rules because they regulate ecomonic and other relations among kinsmen (even though they can be thought of as "anti-kinship" rules). National and state health-insurance programs must be viewed, in part, in terms of the kinship system because they connote the usurpation of traditional kinship roles by impersonal bodies; and the enforcement of schooling for children is, again in part, a rule governing kinship (parent-child) relationships in that it interferes with the traditional obligation of parents to educate their children.

Kinship systems also are aspects of a group's adaptation because they are part and parcel of the organization of social relations—which, as we have seen, is designed to enable a group to make efficient use of its energy system. This is illustrated by Service, who describes the social mold into which hunters and gatherers have placed kinship as an aspect of their strategy of adaptation.

The importance of kinship and its varieties will become apparent in many other case studies in this book. As we will see in Part VI, kinship plays a smaller role in post-agricultural societies than in earlier adaptive strategies. One of the conclusions that can be drawn from the study of kinship in the perspective of evolution is that the organization of social relations around considerations of kinship is maladaptive in an industrial society because it interferes with the efficient use of the energy systems on which industrial societies rely. The reason for this, as Service makes clear in this selection, is that even the most formal aspect of kinship—such as terminology—is inseparable from a group's ideological and value systems. The kinship systems discussed by Service are closely tied to ideologies of egalitarianism and to the social value that all the members of the group have rights of access to each other's wealth because they are related to each other. In an industrial society, on the other hand, people are (or in theory should be) recruited for occupational tasks according to their personal abilities, regardless of their kinship affiliations. There is striking harmony between the kinship systems described by Service and the social principle that no member of a group may go hungry when others have food; by contrast, hunger and affluence coexist in many modern industrial societies.

There is probably no other subject about which anthropologists have written as much as they have about kinship, and there have been several new developments in recent anthropological studies of kinship. A good, brief introduction to the mechanics of kinship organization (although it contains a few errors of fact) is *Manual for Kinship Analysis,* by Ernest L. Schusky (New York: Holt, Rinehart and Winston, 1965). It is a good companion to *Kinship and Marriage,* by Robin Fox (Baltimore: Penguin Books, 1967), which is a witty and well-written introduction to kinship. The advanced reader will profit greatly from *Matrilineal Kinship,* edited by David Schneider and Kathleen Gough (Berkeley: University of California Press, 1961). Also of great importance is *African Systems of Kinship and Marriage,* edited by A. R. Radcliffe-Brown and Daryll Forde (New York: Oxford University Press, 1950). *Explorations in Anthropology: Essays in Honor of George Peter Murdock,* edited by Ward H. Goodenough (New York: McGraw-Hill, 1964), contains several chapters that can serve as an introduction to some of the new developments in the study of kinship systems, as can the collection of articles in *Formal Semantic Analysis,* edited by E. A. Hammel (a special publication of *American Anthropologist,* [October 1965], 67[5], Part 2.) ∎

THE SMALL SOCIETY of hunters-gatherers is based entirely on kinship. Even when a complete stranger, like an anthropologist, comes to have some kind of consistent social relationship with the band, he should be adopted into it by means of a fictional tie of kinship.

A. R. Radcliffe-Brown says that "in a typical Australian tribe it is found that a man can define his relations to every person with whom he has any social dealings whatever, whether of his own or of another tribe, by means of the terms of relationship."

Once Radcliffe-Brown and his native guide approached a strange camp and the guide was unable to establish any bond of kinship, however distant, with anyone in the camp. "That night my 'boy' refused to sleep in the native camp as was his usual custom and on talking to him I found that he was frightened. These men were not his relatives and they were therefore his enemies. This represents the real feeling of the natives on the matter. If I am a blackfellow and meet another blackfellow, that other must be either my relative or my enemy. If he is my enemy I shall take the first opportunity of killing him for fear he will kill me."

In all societies the means by which interpersonal dealings are patterned are statuses of various kinds (the kinds depending on the nature of the society), but in a hunting-gathering society these statuses are nearly exclusively familistic—that is, they are kinship statuses. Hunting-gathering societies are all alike in that their social organization is formed in terms of kinship, although the kinds of kinship patterns vary.

But how can there be different forms of kinship from one society to another? Is not kinship simply genealogy, based on the biology of parenthood? The answer is that we know in fact that there *are* widely differing kinds of kinship—that is, there are varieties of ideological, symbolic ways by which people describe and categorize the people to be considered as relatives. Apes may have mothers and fathers but this is from *our* point of view only—the apes do not know it. On the other hand, many human societies label people mother or father who are not the procreators—a person may have several "mothers." It must be, therefore, that human kinship, the familistic social organization, is not simply genealogy, nor primarily based on the biology of parenthood at all.

(Incidentally, the elementary and apparently simple question of what kinship is and why there can be varieties of kinship systems from one society to another has plagued anthropologists from earliest times. Lewis H. Morgan, one of the founders of scientific anthropology, first posed the question and attempted to answer it in a monumental study called *Systems of Consanguinity and Affinity of the Human Family,* published in 1871. But after all that work he was still wrong; that is, his ideas are not accepted today, nor is any other theory widely accepted. This could be taken as a simple measure of the immaturity of anthropology, for surely the problem must be soluble.)

The different kinds of band organization and related systems of kinship nomenclature among hunters-gatherers have been divided into two major types: the *patrilocal band* and the *composite band,* with some intermediate cases, of course.

The patrilocal type of band organization is created by two related rules or customs pertaining to marriage. First is *band exogamy:* one marries someone from outside one's own band. Second is *virilocal marital residence:* the married couple join the man's band, not the woman's (which would be *uxorilocal residence* in anthropological parlance). Virilocality results in patrilocality: that is, children grow up in their father's band, not in the mother's original band. The band is thus also patrilineal; the members are all related through the male line because of the residence rule. But this is from our point of view; we understand it this way because we are accustomed to reckoning descent, even the pedigrees of dogs and horses. But hunting-gathering peoples do not normally do this, and the composition of the band is understood by them as being formed by the residence rule; hence patrilocal is a better name for the arrangement than patrilineal.

An interesting fact related to the above point is that some primitive peoples—the native Australians particularly—do not recognize the role of the father in procreation. One of the ancestral spirits that lives in the locality is responsible for inducing the pregnancy, thus the child is in part a reincarnation of some unspecified ancestor. We need not argue about whether the people *really* do or do not know about the relation of sexual intercourse to pregnancy. It is easily conceivable that they do not—the relationship is certainly not obvious—but the point is that "real" paternity is not relevant to the way the society is ordered. A person is a member of the band he is born into, and the band is in a place. It turns out to be the father's band and

place because that is where the married couple lives. But what does the word "father" mean if father's paternity is not comprehended? The answer is easy: The father is the husband of the mother (an answer, incidentally, that is also found in the *Code Napoléon*).

The composite band, on the other hand, does not follow regularized customs of band exogamy and marital residence. The band as a whole has a rather amorphous structure—neither patrilocal nor matrilocal—and lacks the affinal kinship relationship that is regularized in some other particular bands. "Composite" is a good name for this kind of band, because it seems to have been formed by the agglomeration of unrelated peoples after the catastrophic effects of contact with modern civilization. In many cases native peoples had no resistance to foreign diseases and were nearly wiped out and also were frequently forced to migrate to new areas as refugees. A usual consequence of either of these situations—and they often occurred simultaneously—was the formation of a composite group, sometimes quite large, out of the remnants of the bands. The nuclear families and the groups formed of brothers and their families tend to arrange marriages and the place of post-nuptial residence for expedient reasons of their own, without reference to group polity.

But if patrilocality is usual for hunting-gathering bands and if it is due to the virilocal residence rule, then the question naturally emerges: Why virilocality? And inasmuch as band exogamy is presupposed, we also wonder about that: Why exogamy? It is another of those deceptively simple questions, like that of the incest taboo, but in this case we seem to have the answer better in hand.

Let us first be clear about one thing that has caused considerable confusion in anthropological discussions of both exogamy and the incest taboo. Exogamy is a kind of rule about *marriage,* not just sexual behavior. The incest taboo has to do with *sexual behavior,* not marriage. Our own tendency to connect marriage with sex—as we do in our ideals, at least—is a very peculiar association that grew up in our very unusual society. In primitive society particularly, and in most societies generally, marriage is undertaken for a great many reasons, but "love" is irrelevant and sexual rights are almost incidental to it—in fact, in many societies the married couple might never have met, in others they may have been betrothed before they were born (promised by the parents).

Why *do* people in primitive societies marry? For one thing, people seem to want to establish themselves as adults, and there is no way to do this except by marriage. The economic division of labor in hunting-gathering societies is such that unless adult males and females share the work as husband and wife, each would remain a dependent, an appendage of another family—ordinarily that of their parents. Marriage is an economic necessity, whereas sex, however much a necessity, is easily satisfied in primitive society without marriage. But there are probably many other adult requirements that marriage does satisfy. Probably most people want children, others want to get away from their own parents or siblings, and so on. But all these are only reasons why various individuals might find the institution of marriage welcome, not why the institution exists in the first place, nor what its role is for the society as a whole.

In primitive society a certain kind of marriage rule results in a certain kind of system of relationship. Marriage is an economic institution from the point of view of the partners, perhaps, but for the parents of the couple, and especially for the band as a whole, marriage has very important *political* functions. The variations in the marriage rule have various political results, particularly with respect to the alliances created among bands, and they can be narrow and firm or extended and loose.

It seems obvious that the reason why the various rules of marriage are all different forms of exogamy is related to the matter of political alliance. It is frequently stated this way by the primitive peoples themselves, as well as being an obvious conclusion we might come to from witnessing its function. An early anthropologist, E. B. Tylor, put it this way:

Among tribes of low culture there is but one means known of keeping up permanent alliance, and that means is intermarriage. . . . Again and again in the world's history, savage tribes must have had plainly before their minds the simple practical alternative between marrying-out and being killed-out. Even far on in culture, the political value of intermarriage remains. . . . "Then we will give our daughters unto you, and we will take your daughters to us, and we will dwell with you and we will become one people," is a well-known passage of Israelite history.

That the marriage rule is a political device for the society rather than merely a convenience for the individuals is illustrated by the wide prevalence of two institutions closely related to it. These are the so-called *levirate* and *sororate,* which preserve a marriage arrangement even after the death of one of the partners. The levirate is the rule that obligates a man to marry the widow in case of the death of his brother. (*Levir* means "husband's brother" in Latin. The levirate was practiced by the ancient Hebrews [Deuteronomy XXV:5-20].) The sororate obligates a woman to marry the widower in case of the death of her sister. These are not merely reflections of the inclinations of individuals, clearly, for they are *rules,* widespread in primitive society, imposed on individuals by the society.

Exogamy, then, is comprehensible as a rule of marriage made by a group, and its function is to widen the network of kinship relations. And like typical political regulations it is explicitly end-oriented, consciously and intentionally. Endogamic (marrying *in*) restrictions are not usually so explicit, often being nothing more than a vague feeling on the part of individuals that they should not marry people too strange or distant, for they would not make good allies or adapt easily as family members. The latent function of endogamic restrictions would be, of course, to prevent the group of relatives from becoming too large and the kinship ties of alliance too attenuated. But mostly, primitive peoples have a rule of marriage that states that the specific group (or kinship category) must exchange marriage partners; the rule thus has simultaneous exogamic and endogamic aspects.

But why are the rules so often rigid about where the married couple should reside, and why, above all, should it be the husband's locality? A usual first-thought on this subject by anthropologists has been that in hunting-gathering societies the economic significance of the male's hunting is so great and his knowledge of his own territory is so important that he must stay in his own region. There are two things wrong with this idea, however.

One is that there is great variation in different societies in the economic significance of the males' activities. The Eskimo, for example, subsist nearly exclusively on the male hunters' catch, the only exception being the occasional fishing the women might do. The Yahgan of Tierra del Fuego, on the other hand, subsist mostly on the shellfish gathered exclusively by women. But if anything, the Yahgan have been more consistently given to virilocality than the Eskimo. In our sample of bands there is not, in fact, any correspondence between the significance of hunting and the strictness of virilocality.

The second difficulty is that while it may be true that hunters need to know their terrain, it is rare that they would not be equally familiar with the terrain of the neighboring bands that they would be likely to marry into. The band's "country" is normally set by the circuit of moves of the camps in their search for vegetable foods, whereas hunters go where the game leads them, except too deeply into territory that is clearly of enemies.

It seems likely that the importance of the cooperation of males in hunting and in warfare is a more significant factor. To hunt many of the animals, especially those in large herds, requires close collaboration of several men, just as does warfare. The women's gathering activities, whatever their economic significance to the society, ordinarily do not require the delicate coordination of several people. Thus women could be lost to their own band when they marry, and others gained, without weakening it so much as it

would be by breaking up the teams of brothers and male cousins who grew up together.

A much simpler explanation has sometimes been offered. Women are the "gifts" from one band to another, exchanged reciprocally as a form of alliance-making, simply because males are so dominant in hunting-gathering society—*they* make the rules. There are societies that are uxorilocal, however, but males are still dominant, still make the rules. These are horticultural societies and the gardening is don by women, and much of it is collaborative as well.

The virilocal-patrilocal band, at any rate, is the usual form of band society. It also has a typical marriage rule that anthropologists call cross-cousin marriage. Any kin group that is exogamous and of sufficient size to include cousins can have only half of the possible cousins, so-called *parallel cousins,* while the other cousins, the *cross-cousins,* are found in the group or groups which have intermarried with this group. In Figure 8.1, which illustrates this rule, cross-cousins are blacked out.

The parallel cousins, it is evident, are the children of Ego's aunts and uncles who, because of exogamy and the rule of residence, are likely to have remained in the band (*e.g.,* the father's brother) or to have come into it on marriage (*e.g.,* the mother's sister). The cross-cousins are the children of the aunts and uncles who have left the band after marriage (the father's sisters) or who were born away and remain there because of the rule of residence (the mother's brothers). This rule of marriage is the simplest, involving only two groups—conceptually, at least. More than two bands may be involved, actually, but there is a frequent tendency to form a dual organization, or *moiety,* as it is called in anthropology, arranging the several bands into two intermarrying sides.

There are a few instances of special permutations. Some Australian groups (the Northern Arunta are the best-known example) have a rule of second cross-cousin marriage—*i.e.,* one marries into the category of a mother's mother's brother's daughter's daughter rather than that of mother's brother's daughter. This rule has the effect of broad-

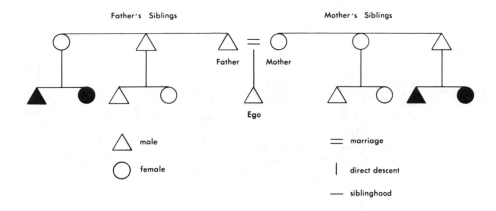

FIGURE 8.1

ening greatly the network of relatives. One cannot marry into the mother's group but must marry into mother's cross-cousin's group. Twice as many relatives are harvested this way but, of course, the relationships are only half as close.

A few Australian groups prescribe a form of cross-cousin marriage that anthropologists call *matrilateral cross-cousin marriage.* Ego must marry a cross-cousin from mother's group (*i.e.,* the category mother's brother's daughter) but cannot marry any of the other cross-cousins, the patrilateral (*i.e.,* father's sister's daughter). This rule results in a given band giving wives to one group and receiving them from another—at least three, usually more, therefore must be involved.

Related to the rules of marriage and residence are differences in the ways in which the kinsmen are categorized. The most common is the kind usually called the *bifurcate-merging system.* This categorization is closely associated with the cross-cousin marriage rule and moiety system, as can be easily suggested by taking the same diagram used in Figure 8.1 to show cross-cousin and adding the bifurcate-merging terms of kinship to it in Figure 8.2.

From our own pedigree-conscious point of view the bifurcate-merging system is most curious. How can a person have several

fathers and, above all, several *mothers?* How can certain cousins (the parallels) be "confused" with one's own brothers and sisters? The answer must be that people certainly will not really confuse their own siblings with cousins or their own mother with some other woman, so perhaps the questions are not being asked in the appropriate form. Let us assume for the moment that the people are not trying to state genealogical lines, but instead merely take a look at the social world of a member of a patrilocal band and see what categories of persons actually exist. These social categories we may call statuses, not meaning anything more special by this than that the category has to do with appropriate forms of interpersonal conduct. By leaving this definition so general and vague we avoid deciding in advance whether any particular terms are or are not genealogical. Any status in any given society *could* be genealogical, or based on strength, wealth, political office, skin color, or anything. We are thus permitted to investigate more freely.

But *this* we know for certain, without any argument: Whether a person is a male or female is a universally recognized and very important criterion of status. There is probably no need to discuss this point except to mention that whereas all societies recognize this set of related statuses, some give it much

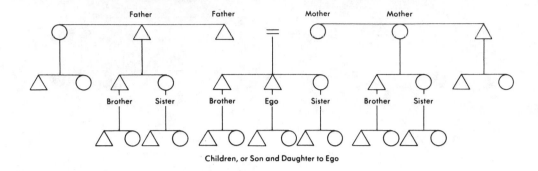

FIGURE 8.2

more significance in the etiquette of behavior than others. One of the characteristics of the urban U.S.A. and of modern cities in general is the considerable economic emancipation of women compared to older types of society, more social equality with men, and a much freer kind of social interaction—the statuses are more equal and therefore somewhat diminished in significance. But down the evolutionary scale the sex differentiation apparently increases. This conclusion is suggested, anyway, by the strictness and completeness of the division of labor by sex in a hunting-gathering society.

Another important social division is along the lines of generations. And again the significance of generational status and of age generally, like the sexual distinction, seems to be much more pronounced in primitive societies than in our own.

A third distinction involves affines. The kinship world of any person falls into two categories: "own" family group and "in-law" family group. In a patrilocal band this distinction corresponds to the difference between father's relatives and mother's relatives. Genealogically, both kinds of relatives are equally related to Ego, the individual. But they are not socially equal from Ego's point of view because of territoriality and exogamy. Father's group is his "own" group, the intimate one; mother's own kin are the "others,"

those actual and potential in-laws with whom more careful, restrained, formal kinds of conduct are the rule.

In all societies one behaves differently toward a brother-in-law than toward a brother, differently toward a mother-in-law than toward a mother. But just as in the case of sex and generational standing this status distinction between affinal moieties is more important in the more primitive societies. It is also much more broadly based, more highly generalized, in a society of patrilocal bands, in the sense that Ego conducts himself as a "brother-in-law" toward all males of his own generation in the *other* moiety or band or whatever the category he will marry into. This is the rule with all the other basic categories as well.

In essence, then, the bifurcate-merging kinship system is a nomenclature for only four kinds of social persons, each kind further subdivided by sex. These four basic categories are as follows: adjacent generation in own group, adjacent generation in affinal group, own generation in own group, own generation in affinal group. In genealogical terms we would discover that such people as mother's brother's children belong in the last-named category, father's brother's children in the third, mother's brother in the second, father's brother in the first, and so forth. Remember however, that this is *our* way of

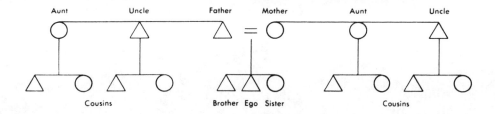

FIGURE 8.3

looking at the matter, because we are much more inclined to distinguish individual genealogical categories than are most primitive peoples.

The above kind of system seems to be standard among relatively undisturbed patrilocal bands. But not all the hunting-gathering peoples of the world were undisturbed at the time they were described. In some instances, modern influences, such as depopulation and the subsequent agglomeration of unrelated peoples, have caused the composite, unstructured band—which is to say, bands that do not exhibit group affinity.

Certain Eskimo villages offer a good example of one of the prevalent forms of composite organization, with a kinship terminological pattern that seems related to it. In most respects this terminology resembles the kinship system of the United States. This is related to the fact that the individual household of relatives, the nuclear family, is set apart from other relatives as a residential group. This means that Ego's brothers and sisters are terminologically distinct from all the cousins, and these cousins are not divided into cross and parallel categories.

Some of the Paiute Indians of the American Southwest illustrate another terminological pattern which itself seems to have resulted from, or at least to be related to, the lack of clear-cut band affinality or moiety distinctions. This is the so-called *generational system*. Ego's relatives in any generation are subdivided only in terms of sex—that is, no distinction is made between siblings and cousins, nor between mother's and father's siblings from others of that generation.

The Pygmy inhabitants of the Andaman Islands present an interesting case. These people live in territorial bands of a sort, but they are not clearly exogamous, with reciprocal marriage relations between specific bands, know nothing of moiety, and practice no clear-cut patrilocality. The Andamanese terminological pattern varies depending on whether the terms are being used in address or in reference. The terms used in address are simply status terms of respect and all they mean, apparently, is "older age" or "upper generation." This seems to be like our own usage of "sir" and "madam." Sometimes, also as in our own usage, this term is used along with a person's name. Other persons equal or lesser in status to Ego may be addressed directly by name alone. The Andamanese terms of reference—that is, the way in which they may refer to their relationship to another person who is not present—is similar to the Eskimo practice of isolating the individual nuclear family or household from other relatives in each generation.

II.
CULTIVATING

CULTIVATING WAS FIRST developed in sub-Saharan Africa, the eastern and south-western parts of what is now the United States, northern Mexico, tropical South America, southeastern and southwestern Asia, and Oceania (except Australia). There are, however, several different modes of cultivation, each with its own consequences in organizing of social relations. The first technique of cultivation developed in generally referred to as *horticulture*. In this mode, the farmer is largely restricted to the use of hand tools, the hoe or the digging stick. Thus confined to reliance on muscular energy, the horticulturist is limited in the amount of land that he can clear and on which food can be grown, and he must rely heavily on the cooperative labor of others in the heavy work of clearing land, digging local irrigation ditches, and harvesting. Horticulture represents the first stage in cultural evolution in which human intervention was used to sustain plant life.

More advanced cultivators, using plows or terraces and relying on large-scale and centralized irrigation networks, also require cooperative labor, but the natures of these cooperative relationships differ greatly. The reasons for this are both technological and political. Technologically, every advance in agriculture that reduces dependence on muscular energy increases the ability of the household to be self-reliant in productive activities. The instruments of production are more efficient—as is evident when we compare a plow with a hoe or digging stick—and they are associated with other technological advances that reduce dependence on cooperative labor. An excellent example is the introduction of commercial fertilizers which, though very expensive, enable one or two men to do the work of many.

Politically, farmers who rely on hoes or digging sticks are usually organized in autonomous local groups in which kinship serves as the major joining force in the organization of social relations, without the intervention of institutions outside the community, such as we find in state systems. We are now concerned with stateless cultivators whose life is often precarious and for whom kinship is therefore important in providing a pool of labor and food on which to draw when necessary. Kinship is the simplest principle around which to organize social relations because everyone shares in it to the same degree.

151

But kinship should not be assumed to be uniform in its patterns and consequences or used to organize stateless farmers in the same way in all societies. In some, kinship is an overarching force that serves to join people in all their activities, whether productive or ceremonial or recreational. In others, propinquity is more important than ties of blood or marriage, though most people in stateless farming groups tend to live alongside or near kinsmen.

Habitational and technological factors are the principal determinants of the nature and extent of kinship in the organization of social relations among horticulturists. An excellent example of this is provided in "Land Use and the Extended Family in Moala, Fiji" (American Anthropologist, 59 [1957]: 449-62; reprinted in Man in Adaptation: The Institutional Framework), where Marshall Sahlins compared people who are organized into extended families with those in nuclear family groups within a single society.[1] The former, he found, live distant from their lands, while those in nuclear families live close by them. Sahlins observes that an extended family constitutes a labor pool whose members produce and consume jointly. Because of its size, the extended family can release some of its members for several days to work on distant plots, while those remaining behind look after children, the aged, and the infirm. In contrast, people living near their garden plots have no reason to maintain an extended family system, and here we find nuclear families.

Clearing land for cultivation is the most arduous task for farmers, and since the soil is often depleted rapidly in primitive technologies, this recurrent activity—which requires the help of people from many households—often sets the tone for much of the group's way of life. The required labor pool has to be highly predictable because land clearance must often be carefully orchestrated with rainy seasons. Sometimes soil depletion requires villages to move their sites, but less often than anthropologists used to imagine. More characteristically, villages remain put for several years and new plots are cleared in wider and wider arcs.

If life is so precarious among stateless cultivators, why did they give up hunting-gathering? First, let us remember that while some foragers live in beneficent habitats, others live in very harsh milieus. But even that observation does not answer the question, because if "need" were the driving force, more hunter-gatherers would have sought alternative strategies of adaptation. As Carneiro observes in Selection 9, people settled down to horticultural strategies in areas where lakes and rivers were well stocked with fish. Protein is an indispensable nutrient; hunted meat can only be given up when fish can be substituted for it.

But the evolutionary changes that had to occur were not simple replacements of one source of protein by another. More fundamental changes had to take place in social organization—sometimes requiring thousands of years—and this is where the conservative aspect of culture is seen. As a result, in part, of the writings of V. Gordon Childe (Man Makes Himself [New York: New American Library, 1951], What Happened in History [Baltimore: Penguin Books, 1946], and other books), in which the phrase "Neolithic revolution" was popularized,

1. A nuclear family is the social group consisting of spouses and their offspring; an extended family is one that adds near relatives to these.

the emergence of farming is often spoken of as though it were to a single pattern, but this is a misconception. Furthermore, the concept of a neolithic development—or any other social change, aside from a violent political upheaval —as a "revolution" conveys an erroneous picture of what actually took place in the evolution of culture. There were no such revolutions, only a gradual emergence and unfolding.

Foragers did not stop hunting-gathering on Friday and begin cultivating on Monday morning so to speak. Fishing replaced hunting gradually; farming displaced gathering even more slowly. Not only does it take time to learn new techniques, but new concepts have to be developed for cooperation in new activities, for property, law, religion, the rearing of children for new conditions of life, and so forth. Here again we see that every technology is also a particular kind of social system. The members of a household must not only be fitted into a scheme for the division of labor, they also must know when and how to submit to authority and when and how to act independently. As Service showed us in Selection 8, relationships among households and families must be systematized for cooperation and for the regulation of competition.

These are some of the spheres in which the most fundamental cultural adaptations and adjustments have to be made after technological advance has become possible, and it is in these spheres that people in most societies exhibit their fundamental conservatism. As Sharp described in Selection 6, the elders among the Yir Yoront did not appear to object to the new steel axes as such but rather to their social consequences. One of the most important adaptations in the emergence and evolution of horticultural society is a change in the status and role of women that ensues with their deeper involvement in cultivation. In turn, the consequent adjustments that may occur in the rules of postmarital residence may lead to other cultural adjustments in rules of descent, in religion and sources of authority, and in modes of child-rearing. A change in the status and role of women connotes a change in the status and role of men. Such changes come slowly, not only because men generally make the rules but because women, like men, are generally reluctant to change their self-definitions.

It is necessary to remember the interrelationships among habitat, level of technology, physical relations among households, physical setting of the society, and political development. As Carneiro makes clear in Selection 2b. The degree of social complexity in any society cannot be understood without placing it in a habitational-spatial context. Carneiro maintains that strong, centralized political systems tend to develop in circumscribed regions, such as islands or deep valleys, from which it is difficult for subjugated people to escape. One of the conclusions that can be drawn from his analysis can be seen in a comparison of the Yako (Selection 13) with the Polynesians. Both were horticulturists, but the Polynesians developed a very advanced level of political complexity while the Yako did not.

One of the factors that may be responsible for this difference, on the basis of Carneiro's thesis, is that the Yako live in relatively open country while the Polynesians live on islands. When people live in open territory they can easily move elsewhere when an attempt is made to place them under a strong central authority. Obviously, it is easier to subjugate people politically when they live on islands or in narrowly bounded areas, because there is nowhere else for them to go. This does not guarantee that island societies will develop centralized political systems, but a highly circumscribed and naturally bounded habitat appears to be a precondition for complex political organization, at least in horticultural societies. Tight social boundaries can develop in open areas, but this is more easily achieved in physically bounded habitats. Another type of relationship between social organization and spatial factors is discussed by Sahlins in connection with "the segmentary lineage" (Selection 14).

I suggested in Selection 3 that statelessness constitutes a limitation on economic and technological development. It usually is difficult to exemplify these relationships among stateless cultivators because it is difficult to determine whether technological development has limited political development; or vice versa. One of the ways in which this puzzle can be solved is by comparing stateless and state societies with respect to one particular type of economic activity. To anticipate some of the materials discussed in Part II of this book, economic specialization provides an example of the limiting role of statelessness—and the stimulating role of state organization—in technological development.

There are specializations in cultivation and crafts in stateless societies, but they are qualitatively different from those generally found in state societies. In stateless societies, specializations are almost always tied to immediately available local resources and do not depend on the transportation and importation of raw or finished materials. Most items secured in trade are not essential to survival, although they may be important in spheres of cultural adjustment, such as ceremonial displays and competitions for prestige. (We will note an important exception to this rule in connection with long-distance trade in food among northeastern New Guineans.) Trading items are usually lightweight or scarce (hence valuable) commodities, such as salt, feathers, shells, and gold. Food is usually too heavy and perishable for transportation by foot over long distances. Most of these imported resources cannot form the basis of sepcialization in stateless societies because their importation is too undependable.

Trade that furnishes the raw materials for specialized production requires regulatory bureaucracies to negotiate treaties, assure safe passage, and establish equivalences in money, weights, and measures, and above all to insure the dependability of supply. Stateless societies cannot do these things. Without such mechanisms trade is subject to the accidents of personal whim among traders, to military interferences in trade routes, and to capricious fluctuations in monetary standards and weights and measures. Nor can stateless societies establish marketing systems or conquer territories that contain needed raw materials. These activities can be carried out only by state bureaucracies, and therefore only state-sponsored and state-regulated trade can provide raw materials that are not immediately and locally available for specialized activities.

Another limitation on the development of economic specialization in stateless societies is that it depends on the production of a surplus, defined as a gross deployable excess of wealth in the society at large, rather than as the margin between what each individual produces and consumes. As Orans observes in Selection 24, people need a good reason for producing more food than they personally need. Apparently, only states can provide such a stimulus and can mobilize and control the distribution of surpluses so that enough will be available to all specialized nonfood producers throughout the society. The autonomous groups of a stateless society have neither the coercive nor the regulatory mechanisms for accomplishing this. Thus, although a relatively advanced technology is necessary for the development of economic specialization, it is not sufficient; it must be accompanied by appropriate political institutions.

Although stateless cultivators are generally limited in the energy systems they can harness, they sometimes supplement their horticulturally appropriate system with others. An excellent example of this is provided in *Voyagers of the Vitiaz Strait,* by Thomas G. Harding (Seattle: University of Washington Press, 1967), which is a study of overland and relatively large-scale overseas trade in staple foods and other items among northeastern New Guinea horticulturists. Each of the small groups participating in this large-scale trading system specializes in what it produces, and these specializations, which are tied to immediately available local resources, are directly geared to the trading system. The people live in autonomous local units. Their trade involves locally grown foods such as taro, vegetables, dogs, and pigs, along with pots and shells that are used for ceremonial purposes, and the like.

This trade has provided the groups around the Vitiaz Strait with a strategy of adaptation—a nascent mercantilism—that is more advanced than many advanced but conventional horticulturists. These people are superb sailors and their outrigger canoes have provided them with an important measure of freedom from the restrictions of their local habitats. Their ships constitute a supplemental energy system. Thus Harding observes that there are small islands in this strait that could support about fifty people living by horticulture alone. The system of trading has freed them from the limitations of their habitats to the degree that some of these small islands can now support up to 500 people. In Harding's words, "By means of an elaborate cultural device—out-rigger sailing canoes—[they] are able to tap the productive capacity of dozens of small-scale societies lying far beyond their own restricted land and sea habitat."

The great majority of ethnographic monographs deal with stateless cultivators, but although the literature about individual societies is vast, there are few studies specifically of this strategy of adaptation. A very good introduction is *Tribesmen,* by Marshall D. Sahlins (Englewood Cliffs, N.J.: Prentice-Hall, 1968). *Politics, Law, and Ritual in Tribal Society,* by Max Gluckman (Chicago: Aldine, 1965), focuses on economic activities, as well as on "politics, law, and ritual." Most of Gluckman's analysis is based on African examples, and he tends to overlook habitational considerations. *Other Cultures: Aims, Methods, and Achievements in Social Anthropology,* by John Beattie (New York: The Free Press, 1964), also deals largely with horticultural societies and also ignores most problems of adaptation and cultural evolution.

A notable attempt to relate social organization to factors in the physical environment, especially in horticultural society, is "Environmental Limitations on the Development of Culture," by Betty Meggers (*American Anthropologist,* 56 [1954]: 801-24). Meggers suggests a "law of environmental limitations on culture" as follows: "The level to which a culture can develop is dependent upon the agricultural potentiality of the environment it occupies. As this potentiality is improved, culture will advance. If it cannot be improved, the culture will become stabilized at a level compatible with the food resources." Like many pioneering scientific attempts, this "law" stimulated considerable controversy and further research, but it is no longer accepted as tenable in this simple form. In addition to Carneiro's paper (Selection 21), the more important statements that were stimulated by Meggers' paper are "Environmental Limitation on Maya Culture: A Re-examination," by William R. Coe *(American Anthropologist, 59 [1957]: 328-35). "Meggers' Law of Environmental Limitation on Culture," by Richard I. Hirshberg and Joan F. Hirshberg *(American Anthropologist, 59 [1957]: 890-92); and "A Comparative Typology of New World Cultures," by James J. Hester *(American Anthropologist, 64 [1962]: 1001-14). Meggers has advanced her analyses in *Amazonia: Man and Culture in a Counterfeit Paradise* (Chicago: Aldine-Atherton, 1971); here she examines the relationship between different habitats and adaptational responses to them. It is a superb example of adaptation as a tool of analysis.

9. THE TRANSITION FROM HUNTING TO HORTICULTURE IN THE AMAZON BASIN

ROBERT L. CARNEIRO

Reprinted from Proceedings of the Eighth International Congress of Anthropological and Ethnological Sciences *(Tokyo and Kyoto, 1968, pp. 244-248). Robert L. Carneiro is Associate Curator of South American Ethnology, American Museum of Natural History, New York. He has combined field studies among the Kuikuru and Amahuaca Indians of the Amazon Basin with an interest in the role of ecological factors in the rise of complex societies. More recently, he has applied Guttman scale analysis to the study of cultural evolution. He is co-editor of* Essays in the Science of Culture *and editor of Herbert Spencer's* The Evolution of Society.

■ If hunting-gathering (especially in tropical climates) is an easy way to acquire a livelihood, why did many people give it up and adopt horticulture? The latter strategy not only may require harder work but is often a more precarious mode of existence. This has puzzled students of social evolution for many years, and in this selection Carneiro suggests a simple and ingenious solution to the problem. He finds that those who adopt horticulture live near fish-laden rivers, which provide ample protein, whereas those living far from such sources have to rely on hunting. Hunting requires nomadism, since even small numbers of people deplete animal resources quickly; fishing enables people to remain sedentary while filling their protein requirements. The sedentism permitted by fishing leads to longer occupation of an area and this favors the improvement and expansion of horticulture. Thus the presence or absence of well-stocked rivers or lakes—a purely environmental factor—will exert a strong influence on the type of settlements adopted and ultimately on the organization of social relations.

Carneiro's article (reprinted with his revisions) is a methodological as well as a substantive achievement, as evidenced in the measures of sedentism he has devised. I have stressed the growing importance of quantitative methods in anthropology, like calculating the number of hours worked and caloric yields or weighing people and estimating their numbers. Calculating the distance that people move or their distance from fish-bearing water are other examples. Such procedures may seem mundane at first, but their applications during the last few years have provided important lessons. Several accepted anthropological models have crumbled under the weight of these quantitative data, including many ideas about the nature of hunting-gathering; as a result, many more anthropologists are casting skeptical eyes at established models that are not supported by quantitative evidence. Building theories and models is an important activity, provided they grow out of hypotheses that are potentially disprovable. If one were to say that people shifted from hunting-gathering to horticulture because, say, of man's inexorable tendency to harness more efficient sources of nonmuscular energy, others would have to accept or reject it on faith alone because there is no way of disproving such a hypothesis. Carneiro's hypothesis is applicable to many parts of the world; if the evidence bears it out, our understanding of the evolution of adaptive strategies will be greatly enhanced. When I first described Carneiro's research to a group of students, one asked, "Can the causes of evolution be so simple?" I answered, "Sometimes, yes."

The reader who wishes to know more about the culture of a tropical forest society will be greatly rewarded by *Headhunter's Heritage,* by Robert F. Murphy (Berkeley: University of California Press, 1960), a study of the Mundurucu. (These people are the subject of Selection 16.) Two excellent surveys are *Native Peoples of South America,* by Julian H. Steward and Louis C. Faron (New York: McGraw-Hill, 1959), and *Handbook of Indians,* edited by Julian H.

Steward (7 vols.; New York: Cooper Square Publishers, 1963). Both surveys place very strong emphasis on the habitational factors in cultural development. ∎

THE EARLIEST INHABITANTS of Amazonia, who first entered the area around 10,000 years ago, lived entirely by hunting, fishing, and gathering. Of these three modes of subsistence, hunting was probably the most important, especially after the introduction of the bow and arrow. The natives of Amazonia continued to subsist on wild food sources exclusively until around 2000 B.C., when horticulture began to penetrate into the basin from the north and west. By the time the first Europeans arrived, 3000 years later, horticulture had been widely adopted throughout Amazonia, with only a few tribes continuing to rely solely on wild food.

From the time of its first introduction to the present day, horticulture has gained greatly in importance, while hunting, in turn, has declined. But the triumph of agriculture has by no means been uniform or unqualified. Even today, all Amazonian tribes who cultivate continue to hunt as well, many of them rather extensively. This fact gives rise to several questions: Why has hunting remained so entrenched? Why have Amazonian Indians not become more fully horticultural? And why do the various tribes of the basin rely on agriculture to such differing degrees?

Before attempting to answer these questions, let us examine the assumptions underlying them. The first assumption is that the productivity of horticulture, per unit of human labor, is greater than that of hunting. The second assumption is that this difference was large enough to have been clearly perceived by the natives themselves. The third one is that not only was agriculture substantially and perceptibly more productive than hunting, but that the Indians of Amazonia were free to change their subsistence practices to accord with this difference.

I would like to test these assumptions using data obtained during field work among two Indian tribes of Amazonia, the Amahuaca of the Peruvian Montana and the Kuikuru of the Upper Xingu basin in Brazil.

First of all, though, if we are to compare the relative productivity of hunting and horticulture, we must have some objective standard for measuring subsistence productivity generally. What is this standard to be? Some years ago I proposed and applied such a measure. It consisted of the number of man-hours required to obtain 1,000,000 calories of food from a given mode of subsistence. (Carneiro 1957: 169-170). The figure of 1,000,000 was chosen because it represents the annual caloric consumption of a person whose average daily intake is 2,750 calories, a figure close to the average for most human populations. Let us proceed to apply this index to hunting and horticulture among the Amahuaca.

The Amahuaca rely on horticulture for about 50 percent of their subsistence and on hunting for about 40 percent, with fishing and gathering together making up the remaining 10 percent. According to my calculations, the average Amahuaca hunter spends some 1,272.5 hours a year on hunting, an amount of labor that yields about 1,600,000 calories of meat. (See Appendix A for the details of this and subsequent calculations.) The index of productivity for Amahuaca hunting is thus 795 man-hours per 1,000,000 calories.

Turning to agriculture, we must first note that today all Amahuaca use steel tools to clear their garden plots in the forest. However, from accounts of older Amahuaca who had seen the stone axe in use or had heard about it from those who had, I was able to make a rough estimate of the time required to clear, plant, and harvest a garden before the introduction of steel tools. This estimate enables me to calculate that aboriginally about 603 man-hours were required to produce 1,000,000 calories from horticulture.

These figures throw a new light on our notions regarding the relative productivity of hunting and horticulture. The difference between 795 man-hours per 1,000,000 calories from hunting and 603 man-hours per 1,000,000 calories from horticulture does not appear to me especially great. Moreover, this difference is further reduced when we take account of the fact that an hour spent felling trees with a stone axe is much harder work than a hour spent hunting.

With the margin of productivity between hunting and horticulture thus narrowed, one is left to wonder if the Amahuaca, or indeed any Amazonian tribe, was really able to perceive this difference when they first took up cultivation. This is especially open to question since at that time, with horticulture more primitive, the margin must have been been even less. Factors other than productivity may well have determined their initial acceptance of agriculture as well as their subsequent increase in reliance upon it. It seems very likely that the possibility of accumulating relatively large amounts of food may have been just such a factor. The greater sedentariness permitted by a partly agricultural subsistence also may have served as an inducement to its adoption.

But the fact that present-day Amazonian tribes, after millennia of practicing agriculture, differ widely in their degree of reliance on it, indicates that the advantages of agriculture alone are insufficient to bring about its complete ascendancy. To account for this differential reliance on cultivation we must turn to ecology. Once the relevant ecological factors are grasped and applied, the problem finds a ready solution.

From a cultural-ecological point of view, the Amazon basin may be thought of as comprising two distinct types of habitat, one consisting of areas lying along the major rivers and the other of areas located away from them. These two types of habitat differ essentially in the amount of fish and other riverine food resources which they make available for human exploitation. In the small rivers and streams of the interfluvial areas, fish are relatively few in number and small in size. In such areas fishing can hardly serve as the major source of protein. For the Amahuaca, who live in just such a region, for instance, fishing provides no more than about 5 percent of subsistence.

In habitats of this type it is hunting, not fishing, which must be relied on for the bulk of protein in the diet. This fact is of special significance for settlement pattern, since a heavy reliance on hunting is incompatible with sedentary village life. Even communities as small as 15, which are characteristic of the Amahuaca, severely deplete the game in their vicinity in a year or two. After that, a village may need to be moved several miles away if the supply of meat is to continue to be met without an inordinate amount of walking time being required. The result is that a horticultural-and-hunting society living in such a habitat will be unable to take full advantage of the potentialities of agriculture for settlement size and permanence.

A marked contrast to this situation is provided by tribes living along the larger rivers. Since these rivers offer food in tremendous quantities, fishing comes more and more to displace hunting. Moreover, since the supply of riverine food is not only abundant but literally inexhaustible, tribes living on the major rivers seldom if ever face the need to move their villages because of a shortage of protein, as do tribes living away from the rivers and relying heavily on hunting. This longer occupation of a site permitted by fishing favors, in turn, the steady improvement and expansion of cultivation.

As an example of this second type of ecological setting, and of the adaptation made to it, I offer in evidence the Kuikuru of the Upper Xingu basin in central Brazil. The Kuikuru occupy a village close to a sizable lake, and are within a few miles of the Kuluene River. Both these bodies of water are most plentifully stocked with fish. While fishing supplies some 15 percent of Kuikuru subsistence, hunting has declined to the vanishing point, providing less than 1 percent of the diet. Agriculture, based on the cultivation of bitter manioc, accounts for fully 80 percent of subsistence.

The Kuikuru village has a population of 145, about 10 times that of an Amahuaca community. Furthermore, its locale has remained the same for the last 80 or 90 years. Three times during this period the village has been moved, but always for supernatural rather than ecological reasons, and over distances of only a few hundred yards.

In my opinion, the Amahuaca and the Kuikuru are not exceptional cases. Rather, they are typical of tribes living in the two types of habitat distinguished above. The adaptations that these two groups have made to their respective environments, other Amazonian tribes have undoubtedly also made, again and again, under similar circumstances. Interfluvial peoples, forced to maintain a relatively high reliance on hunting, adopted agriculture only to a limited extent, and remained small in size and semi-nomadic in settlement pattern. Riverine peoples, finding it possible to subsist heavily on fish and other river animals, became more sedentary, embraced agriculture more fully, and developed larger villages.

Differences between interfluvial and riverine peoples went beyond those of size and settlement permanence. Social, political, and ceremonial distinctions of considerable magnitude arose as well. Indeed, where riverine resources were most bountiful of all, on the Amazon River itself, tribes such as the Omagua, Manao, and Tapajó approached and even attained a Circum-Caribbean level of culture.

Let me restate my thesis once again. It is that in Amazonia strong reliance on agriculture and fishing promote sedentariness, while strong reliance on hunting and gathering deter it. This relationship, moreover, I see not only as general and qualitative, but as specific and quantitative. Degree of sedentariness and degree of reliance on contrasting modes of subsistence vary continuously with one another. And I would add, the relationship between the two, rather than being arbitrary and reciprocal, is deterministic and directional. Mode of subsistence is the independent variable, and degree of sedentariness is the dependent variable.

Having asserted this categorically, let me try to establish it empirically.

First of all, we need an objective numerical index of sedentariness. Since I am not aware of the existence of any such index, we will have to devise one of our own.

Sedentariness, as I see it, is not a simple factor. It cannot be measured adequately by means of its most obvious component, namely, the length of time a settlement remains in one place. Sedentariness involves more than this. It involves not only *how long* a settlement remains fixed, but also *how large* the settlement is. I would argue, therefore, that more sedentariness is manifested by a village of 500 persons staying in the same place for five years than by a village of 50 persons remaining in the same place for 10 years. The concept of sedentariness is thus a composite one, like that of momentum in physics, which is a product of the two factors, mass and velocity.

But sedentariness is more than just the product of the factors of size and length of occupancy. It involves a third factor. This third factor is the distance a village is moved when and if it is relocated.

The degree of sedentariness of a village is *directly proportional* to the first two factors, and *inversely proportional* to the third. In other words, the larger the village and the longer it remains in one spot, the more sedentary it is, while the greater the distance it is moved, when movement occurs, the less sedentary it is. Our Index of Sedentariness, in its preliminary form, is therefore:

$$\frac{PT}{D}$$

where P is the population of the settlement, T the average length of time, in years, between relocations of the village,[1] and D the average distance, in miles, between successive sites of the village. The index is so constructed that the higher its score, the greater the degree of sedentariness it shows.

[1]If the last movement of a village is beyond memory, then the numerical value used for T should be the length of time the village is known to have been located at its present site. If the village, or camp, is moved several times during the year, the number of such moves should be divided into 1, and the resulting decimal fraction used for T in the index. Thus, if a predominantly hunting group moved its camp once every week, the value of T would be 1/52 or .02.

Before proceeding to apply this index, however, I would like to modify it in one respect so that it reads:

$$\frac{PT}{D + 1}$$

By adding 1 to the factor D we obviate the possibility of having to divide PT by zero if a village is not known to have moved, and D thus equals zero.

Let us illustrate the use of this index by applying it to the settlement patterns of the Amahuaca and the Kuikuru. The population of an average Amahuaca community is, as we have seen, about 15 persons, the length of time it is occupied is about 1.5 years, and the distance between successive settlements is on the order of 15 miles. Substituting these numbers in the formula we have:

$$\frac{15 \times 1.5}{15 + 1} = 1.4$$

Now let us calculate the Index of Sedentariness for the Kuikuru. The population of their village is 145; the average length of time between relocations of the village is 27 years; the average distance between successive village sites is about a quarter of a mile. Thus we have:

$$\frac{145 \times 27}{.25 + 1} = 3,132$$

The marked difference in sedentariness we noted earlier between the Amahuaca and the Kuikuru is thus clearly reflected in the index. This difference between their scores, although perhaps not an exaggerated measure of the difference in their sedentariness, proves to be inconveniently large if we want to plot these scores on a graph, as we will. Accordingly, I propose that instead of using $PT/D + 1$ as our index, we take its square root. The Index of Sedentariness now becomes:

$$\sqrt{\frac{PT}{D + 1}}$$

When we extract the square root of the index scores computed above for the Amahuaca and Kuikuru we get 1.2 and 56.0 respectively. These figures still show a wide

margin in sedentariness, but keep this difference within convenient limits.[2]

Having devised a measure of sedentariness, we now need a measure of subsistence. This time we want an index which is based on those aspects of subsistence relevant to sedentariness. We have repeatedly stated that in Amazonia agriculture and fishing favor permanence of settlement,[3] while hunting and gathering discourage it. This suggests that a useful index would be the ratio which one of these sets of subsistence factors bears to the other. I therefore propose the following index, which we may call the Subsistence Quotient:

$$\frac{A + F}{H + G}$$

Here A is the percentage of subsistence derived from agriculture, and F is the percentage derived from fishing, while H is the percentage derived from hunting, and G the percentage derived from gathering. The higher the numerical value of the quotient, the greater the reliance on those subsistence activities favoring sedentary settlement.[4]

---

[2] The effect of taking the square root of $PT/D + 1$ is to decrease the size of index scores larger than one and to increase the size of those smaller than one. This compression of index scores toward 1 is greatest on scores furthest removed from 1, in either direction.

[3] At this point the objection might be raised that slash-and-burn agriculture in Amazonia should not be considered as falling entirely on the side of sedentariness. It is true that under certain conditions shifting cultivation may lead to the relocation of a village, but as I attempted to demonstrate elsewhere (Carneiro 1960), slash-and-burn is not the limiting factor in settlement permanence nearly so often as alleged. However, should it be decided that slash-and-burn did, in the long run, contribute to village movement, this influence could be accommodated in the Subsistence Quotient in the manner shown below:

$$\frac{.8\,A + F}{.2A + H + G}$$

Here we have assumed that 80 per cent of the effect of shifting cultivation is toward sedentariness, and 20 percent toward nomadism.

[4] When agriculture and fishing together exceed 90 percent of subsistence, the sensitivity of this index increases at a rapid rate. For example, while the 2-percent difference between $\frac{A + F = 49}{H + G = 51}$ and $\frac{A + F = 51}{H + G = 49}$ represents a difference in Subsistence Quotient of between .96 and 1.04, a 2-percent difference between $\frac{A + F = 94}{H + G = 6}$ and $\frac{A + F = 96}{H + G = 4}$ yields a difference in the quotient of 15.67 to 24. It seems unlikely that a difference in the degree of reliance on agriculture and fishing between 94 percent and 96 percent would have as much of an effect on sedentariness as the difference in the quotients would suggest. Accordingly, if one were to deal with a considerable number of societies having more than a 90 percent reliance on agriculture and fishing, one might want to consider using a subsistence index consisting simply of the percent of the total food supply derived from agriculture and fishing. This index, although perhaps less discriminating for intermediate values, would not rise so precipitously for extreme differences in subsistence ratio.

Using the Amahuaca and Kuikuru as examples once again, let us apply this index. According to my estimates, the Amahuaca rely on agriculture for 50 percent of subsistence, on fishing for 5 percent, on hunting for 40 percent, and on gathering for 5 percent. Their Subsistence Quotient is then:

$$\frac{.50 + .05}{.40 + .05} = 1.2$$

The Kuikuru, on the other hand, depend on agriculture for 80 percent of subsistence, on fishing for 15 percent, on hunting for 0 percent, and on gathering for 5 percent. Thus we have:

$$\frac{.80 + .15}{.00 + .05} = 19$$

Our indexes, then, objectify and quantify what we earlier found to be true, namely, that with regard to subsistence practices and sedentariness, a substantial difference exists between the Amahuaca and the Kuikuru.

We are now ready to put the two indexes together in such a way as to express the relationship between subsistence and sedentariness that we think they bear to each other:

$$\sqrt{\frac{PT}{D + 1}} = f \qquad \frac{A + F}{H + G}$$

That is to say, the degree of sedentariness of a society is a function of the ratio that modes of subsistence conducive to settlement permanence bear to modes of subsistence conducive to nomadism. Our final step is to calculate the two indexes for a number of Amazonian tribes, plot the obtained values on a graph, and observe how closely the expected relationship holds.

Because it is difficult to obtain the necessary quantitative information from most monographs on Amazonian tribes, and because the formulas were devised only recently, we have been able to graph only seven societies so far. But while limited in number, the data nevertheless show a very close relationship between the two classes of phenomena being studied (see Figure 9.1). A heavy reliance on agriculture and fishing does appear to foster sedentariness, while a heavy reli-

ance on hunting and gathering does seem to impede it.[5]

In closing, let us relate our findings back to the environment. The degree of reliance on one mode of subsistence or another is, as we have seen, largely determined by environmental factors. Habitats along the major rivers promote reliance on fishing and agriculture, while those away from the main rivers tend to engender reliance on hunting and gathering. The general evolutionary process by which some Amazonian societies have moved from a predominantly hunting to a predominantly agricultural mode of life, and which has seen them become progressively more complex, has not occurred in a vacuum. It has taken place only in those environmental settings favor it, and has failed to occur where the environment obstructed it.

Looked at from a distance, an evolutionary advance appears to be the logical unfolding of an inherent tendency. But examined more closely, it always proves to have been mediated by particular ecological conditions.

APPENDIX A

During the rainy season an Amahuaca man goes hunting every two or three days, but during the dry season he must spend

---

[5] I do not mean to imply that factors relating to subsistence are the only determinants of sedentariness. Warfare may also play a significant role. To an extent not possible for me to assess quantitatively, feuding among the Amahuaca may lead them to move their settlements more often than they otherwise would. On our graph, societies whose settlement pattern was significantly affected by warfare would be expected to fall below the regression line, since their sedentariness would presumably be less than that which their mode of subsistence would allow. However, a society forced by war to move more frequently than its normal subsistence practices required, would probably soon find itself altering its subsistence out of a need to conform to the exigencies of the new situation. Such a society might well begin to decrease its dependence on horticulture and increase its dependence on hunting. Thus, equilibrating forces might always be operative, tending to bring subsistence and settlement pattern back into congruity. For this reason, even societies frequently at war might turn out not to fall very far from the regression line after all.

We see then that the direction of causation, while generally that of "subsistence—settlement pattern," could, in circumstances such as this be reversed. War-induced changes in settlement pattern might, in such instances, lead to changes in the degree of reliance on the various subsistence activities.

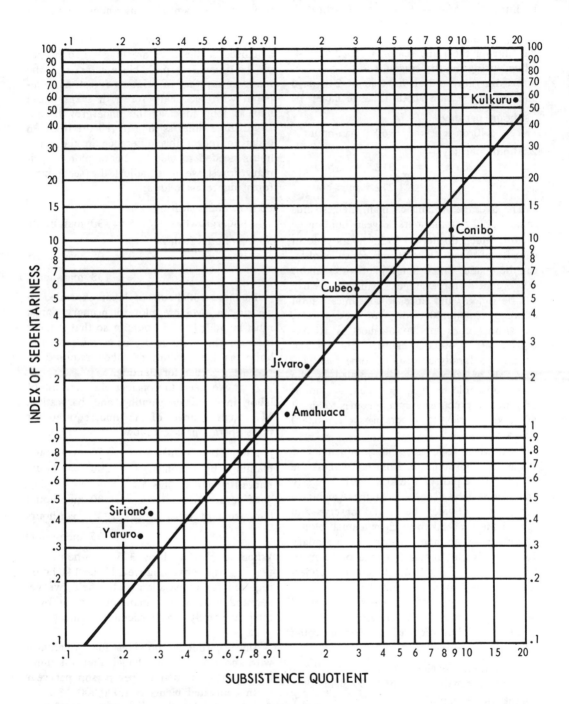

FIGURE 9.1

Index of Sedentariness plotted against Subsistence Quotient for seven societies of the Amazon Basin. Regression line fitted by eye.

considerable time clearing and planting, so he hunts less often—about every fourth day. A hunting trip lasts about 10 hours. Thus the average number of hours spent hunting per day during the rainy season is $10/2.5 = 4$, while during the dry season it is $10/4 + 2.5$. Since the rainy season lasts about 240 days and the dry season about 125, we have:

4 hours per day

    $\times$ 240 days $=$ 960   man-hours

2.5 hours per day

    $\times$ 125 days $=$ 312.5 man-hours

                       1,272.5 man-hours

The average Amahuaca man, then, spends some 1,272.5 man-hours a year hunting.

How much do these 1,272.5 hours yield in calories of meat? Only an indirect calculation can be made. Since hunting provides about 40 percent of the average Amahuaca's yearly caloric intake, and since he consumes a total of about 1,000,000 calories of food a year, his annual consumption of meat is $1,000,000 \times .40 = 400,000$ calories. The average Amahuaca family consists of some four persons, all of whose meat is supplied by the male household head, so that the total amount of game he procures annually comes to about 400,000 calories $\times$ 4 persons $= 1,600,000$ calories.

Next we have to assess the productivity of Amahuaca horticulture. I did not witness the clearing of a plot of average size in primary rain forest (the type of area the Amahuaca prefer to cultivate) but I did observe and record the time taken to clear a small plot—about ⅓ of an acre in size—in secondary forest. This plot required a total of 16 man-hours to clear: 10 hours to cut the undergrowth and 6 hours to fell the trees. Thus, had the plot been of average size (about 2 acres), but still in secondary forest, the amount of labor required to clear it would have been approximately:

10 man-hours clearing

    undergrowth $\times$ 6 $=$ 60 man-hours

  6 man-hours felling

    trees $\times$ 6 $=$ 36 man-hours

                       96 man-hours

However, in primary forest the proportion of work time spent clearing undergrowth and felling trees is considerably different because there is less undergrowth on the one hand, and because the trees are bigger and harder on the other. It is probably not far from the mark to say that in primary forest, as compared with secondary forest, it takes about half as long to clear the undergrowth, but about three times as long to fell the trees. In order to reflect this difference in the man-hours needed to clear a 2-acre plot of primary forest we must adjust the secondary-forest figure as follows:

60 man-hours clearing

    undergrowth $\times$ .5 $=$ 30 man-hours

36 man-hours felling

    trees $\times$ 3.0 $=$ 108 man-hours

                     138 man-hours

To these 138 hours of labor expended in clearing a two-acre plot in primary forest must be added the 3 hours or so that it takes to burn the plot, giving us a total of 141 hours as the amount of labor required to prepare a garden for planting.

Next we need to consider the amount of labor involved in planting' and harvesting. My rough estimate of the time required for these operations is as follows:

planting (by a man)   50 man-hours

planting (by a woman)   200 man-hours

harvesting and storing

  of corn   80 man-hours

harvesting of other crops   45 man-hours

                    375 man-hours

When to this total of 375 man-hours for planting and harvesting we add the 141 hours required for preparation of the field, we get a grand total of 516 man-hours spent by a nuclear family on horticulture during the year.

Since gardening provides the Amahuaca with about 50 percent of their diet, the number of calories obtained per person per year from cultivated plants is $1,000,000 \times .5 = 500,000$ calories. For an average-sized family of four the total number of calories from cultivated plants per year is thus 500,000 $\times$

4 = 2,000,000. Now if it takes 516 hours to produce these 2,000,000 calories, then producing 1,000,000 calories takes half as long, or 258 hours. This makes our index of productivity for Amahuaca horticulture 258 man-hours per 1,000,000 calories.

We are now in a position to compare the productivity of hunting and horticulture among the Amahuaca today. Since hunting requires 795 man-hours per 1,000,000 calories, while horticulture requires only 258 man-hours per 1,000,000 calories, horticulture is about 3 times as productive as hunting.

However, this calculation was based on present-day methods of clearing in which machetes and steel axes are used. The introduction of steel cutting tools to the Amahuaca came relatively late. As recently as about 1920 they were still relying heavily on stone axes and wooden clubs in clearing the forest. To compare the relative productivity of hunting and horticulture under aboriginal conditions, therefore, we must be able to estimate how much time was spent on gardening prior to the introduction of steel tools.

Replacing aboriginal cutting tools with machetes and steel axes has greatly shortened the time and reduced the effort required in clearing a garden plot in the forest. To judge from the accounts of older Amahuaca, it appears to have taken perhaps 10 times as long to cut down a tree with a stone axe as it does with a steel one.

However, in gauging the amount of labor spent in clearing garden plots aboriginally we cannot simply take the man-hours expended on this task today and multiply by 10. We must take into account the labor-saving effect of the driving tree fall. This involves felling a large tree in such a way as to have it bring down with it as many smaller trees as possible. By its use the Amahuaca were able to topple many of the smaller trees with an expenditure of labor probably not greatly in excess of that required today.

Clearing the undergrowth prior to felling the trees, now done with a machete, was formerly done with a heavy palm wood club which knocked over or buckled the smaller vegetation rather than cutting it. The replacement of wooden clubs by machetes in clearing brush has undoubtedly saved time, but proportionately less than is saved by the use of the steel axe in felling trees.

Taking these various factors into account, I would hazard a guess that aboriginally it took the Amahuaca about six times longer to clear a garden plot than it does today. Thus in computing the productivity of Amahuaca horticulture in aboriginal times we must begin by multiplying the 138 man-hours of clearing calculated for the present-day Amahuaca by a factor of 6. This gives us 138 × 6 = 828 man-hours. Thus, with a stone axe technology, it took the Amahuaca some 828 man-hours to fell the forest cover on a 2-acre plot. To this figure we must add 3 hours for burning and 375 hours for planting and harvest, figures unaffected by the change in technology. The grand total of man-hours required aboriginally to clear, plant, and harvest the average Amahuaca garden plot thus comes to 1,206.

Since these 1,206 man-hours yielded about 2,000,000 calories of plant food, we readily see that to produce 1,000,000 calories, or half that amount, required 603 man-hours. This figure of 603 is about 2⅓ times greater than the 258 man-hours now needed to produce the same amount of food from crop plants.

BIBLIOGRAPHY

Bertram, Kate, and Colin Bertram
1966 "The Sirenia: A Vanishing Order of Mammals." *Animal Kingdom*, (69): 180-184.
Carneiro, Robert L.
1957 *Subsistence and Social Structure: An Ecological Study of the Kuikuru Indians.* Ph.D. Dissertation. Ann Arbor: University of Michigan. University Microfilms.
1960 "Slash-and-Burn Agriculture: A Closer Look at Its Implications for Settlement Patterns." In *Men and Cultures; Selected Papers of the Fifth International Congress of Anthropological and Ethnological Sciences*, Anthony F. C. Wallace, ed., pp. 229-234. Philadelphia: University of Pennsylvania Press.
Ferreira, Jorge
1957 "Kuarup." *O Cruzeiro*, 29 (15), (January 27): 58-71.

Holmberg, Allan R.
1950 *Nomads of the Long Bow*. Washington, D.C.: Smithsonian Institution, Institute of Social Anthropology, Publication No. 10.

Hurt, Wesley R.
1964 "Recent Radiocarbon Dates for Central and South Brazil." *American Antiquity* (30): 25-33.

Lathrap, Donald W.
1970 *The Upper Amazon*. New York: Praeger.

Lowie, Robert H.
1948 "The Tropical Forests: An Introduction." In *Handbook of South American Indians*, Julian H. Steward, ed. Vol. 3: *The Tropical Forest Tribes*, pp. 1-56. *Bureau of American Ethnology Bulletin* 143.

Oberg, Kalervo
1953 *Indian Tribes of Northern Mato Grosso, Brazil*. Washington, D.C.: Smithsonian Institution, Institute of Social Anthropology, Publication No. 15.

Rouse, Irving, and José R. Cruxent
1963 *Venezuelan Archaeology. Caribbean Series*, 6 New Haven: Yale University Press.

Rubin, Meyer, and Sarah M. Berthold
1961 "U. S. Geological Survey Radiocarbon Dates VI." *Radiocarbon* (3): 86-98.

Simpson, George Gaylord
1940 Los Indios Kamarakotos. Translated by F. Villanueva-Uralde. *Revista de Fomento* (Caracas), 3 (22-25): 197-660.

Ursua, Pedro de
1861 The Expedition of Pedro de Ursua and Lope de Aguirre. Translated from Pedro Simón's *Sixth Historical Notice of the Conquest of Tierra Firme* by William Bollaert. Introduction by Clements R. Markham. *The Hakluyt Society, Publication* No. 28. London.

10. AN ETHNOECOLOGICAL APPROACH TO SHIFTING AGRICULTURE

HAROLD C. CONKLIN

Reprinted, by permission of the New York Academy of Science, from Transactions, *Ser. 2, 17 (1954): 133-42. Harold C. Conklin is Professor, Department of Anthropology, Yale University. He has done ethnographic and linguistic field work in the Philippines and other tropical areas. He is the author of* Hanunoó Agriculture; the Study of Shifting Cultivation, *and* An Ethnographic Atlas of Ifugao.

■ The Amazon Basin described by Carneiro in Selection 9 is of special interest because of the type of land clearance used there. This technique of soil preparation involves burning the brush and is variously referred to as "slash-and-burn" or "swidden." Considerable controversy exists among anthropologists over its consequences. Some feel that it destroys the nutrients in the soil and thus compels horticulturists to abandon their plots after two or three years—and, of course, this would have a strong effect on settlement patterns. Other anthropologists, like Conklin in this selection, maintain that it is not seriously detrimental to the soil.

Betty Meggers observes in *Amazonia* (Chicago: Aldine-Atherton, 1971) that slash-and-burn is a specialized form of land clearance that has emerged in response to the climate and soil conditions of the tropics. In this technique, vegetation is cut and burned on the plot, followed immediately by planting. Cuttings or seeds are inserted in holes made with a digging stick and the soil is moved over them with the foot; no other disturbance is made of the soil.

The tropical climate is the soil's greatest enemy; this can be seen in the rapidity with which a plot's productivity is diminished. What role does human intervention play? By leaving cut vegetation on the spot, the soil's surface is left with a cover that serves as a shield against the scorching sun. Burning the slash returns some nutrients to the soil and these become available to the sprouts. Decomposing slash returns nutrients to the soil at a slow and steady rate and diverts the attention of many pests and diseases from the growing crops. By contrast, the plowing techniques of temperate agriculture strip the soil and leave it bare to the tropical sun.

In this selection Conklin describes the basic technological procedures of horticulture that are most widely used in many parts of the world. His paper is based on a much more extensive report on the results of his investigations, in *Hanunoo Agriculture in the Philippines* (published by the Food and Agriculture Organization of the United Nations). The contrary point of view about the detrimental effects of slash-and-burn horticulture is effectively stated by Raymond Bouillenne in his article, "Man, the Destroying Biotype" (*Science,* 135 [March 2, 1962]: 706-12. The best detailed description of tropical horticulture, and especially of its techniques, is in *Subsistence Agriculture in Melanesia,* by Jacques Barrau (Honolulu: Bernice L. Bishop Museum, Bulletin 219, 1958). ■

METHODS OF SHIFTING cultivation, while unfamiliar to many of us living in temperate latitudes, are typical of vast areas in the tropics. Such methods account for approximately one third of the total land area used for agricultural purposes in southeast Asia today. In some countries, including the Philippines, it has been estimated that shifting cultivation produces food for up to 10 per cent of the total population. In these regions the economy of large segments of the upland population is based solely on such means. Nevertheless, shifting agriculture is still only inadequately understood. It is often categorically condemned as primitive, wasteful, or illegal, with little or no regard for such pertinent local variables as population density, available land area, climate, or native agricultural knowledge. For most areas, detailed field reports against which such statements might be tested are totally lacking. There is a definite need for ascertaining what are the real facts about shifting agriculture.

In this paper I shall attempt to throw some light on the nature of such methods of upland farming and to draw our attention to certain important problems in this area of research. First we shall review some of the more frequent statements made by writers on the subject. Then we shall examine the pertinent ethnographic data for a specific culture, emphasizing not only the local environmental conditions and their apparent modification, but especially the determination of how these conditions and modifications are culturally interpreted.

For our purposes we may consider shifting cultivation, also known by such designations as field-forest rotation or slash-and-burn agriculture, as always involving the impermanent agricultural use of plots produced by the cutting back and burning off of vegetable cover. We shall call such a field a *swidden*. This term, like its by-forms *swithen* or *swivven,* is an old dialect word from northern England (Northumberland, Yorkshire, Lancashire, and elsewhere) meaning "burned clearing" or "to burn, sweal, or singe, as heather." It has been revived recently, and in an ethnographic description, by a Swedish anthropologist. There are many vernacular terms for swidden, but few are widely known or used in the literature except in reference to limited geographical regions: *kaingin* (*caingin*) in the Philippines, *ladang* in Indonesia, *taungya* in Burma, and terms such as *djum* in India, *chitemene* in parts of Africa, and *milpa* in Central America.

Swidden agriculture, of course, involves more than is stated in our minimal definition, but before we attempt greater precision let us examine some of the characteristics which various authors have attributed to it. The following list is not intended to be complete, but does include the most frequent and problematic statements and assumptions I have encountered.

(1) Swidden farming is a haphazard procedure involving an almost negligible minimum of labor output. It is basically simple and uncomplicated.

(2) Usually, and preferably, swiddens are cleared in virgin forest (rather than in areas of secondary growth). Tremendous loss of valuable timber results.

(3) Swidden fires escape beyond cut-over plots and destroy vast forest areas. One author states that from 20 to more than 100 times the swidden area itself are often gutted by such fires.

(4) Swidden techniques are everywhere the same. Such features as the lack of weeding and the use of a single inventory of tools are practically universal.

(5) Stoloniferous grasses such as "notorious *Imperata*" are abhorred as totally useless pests by all groups whose basic economy is swidden agriculture.

(6) Swiddens are planted with a single (predominant) crop. Any given swidden can thus be said to be a rice or a maize or a millet field or the like. Hence, it is possible to gauge the productivity of a swidden by ascertaining the harvest yield of a single crop.

(7) Furthermore, it is possible to gauge the efficiency (*i.e.,* relative to some other method of agriculture) of a given swidden economy in terms of its one-crop yield per unit of area cultivated.

(8) Swiddens are abandoned when the main crop is in. "The harvest ends the series of agricultural operations."

(9) There is no crop rotation in swidden agriculture. Instead, soil fertility is maintained only by the rotational use of the plots themselves. The duration of the rotational cycles can be determined by the time interval between successive clearings of the same plot.

(10) Not only is fertility lost, but destructive erosion and permanent loss of forest cover result from reclearing a once-used swidden after less than a universally specifiable minimum number of years of fallowing (set by some authors at 25 years). It is claimed that "dangerous" consequences of more rapid rotation often result from native ignorance.

On these and many other points there is frequently an over-all assumption that the standards of efficiency in terms of agricultural economy in the United States or Western Europe are attainable and desirable among any group of swidden farmers.

FIELD OBSERVATIONS

From November 1952 until January 1954 I lived with the Yagaw Hanunoo of southeastern Mindoro Island in the Philippines. The Hanunoo, numbering approximately 6,000, are pagan mountaineers who occupy about 800 square kilometers of forest and grass-covered hinterland and whose primary economic activity is swidden agriculture. I was able to observe and participate in more than a full annual cycle of agricultural activities. Since most of my efforts during this time were directed toward an ethnographic analysis of the relation between Hanunoo culture and the natural environment, I was drawn toward an increasingly closer examination of Hanunoo concepts of the ecology of the Yagaw area and of Hanunoo methods of swidden farming.

The following brief statements summarize the preliminary results of my investigation of Hanunoo swidden agriculture. Except where otherwise noted, these remarks apply specifically to the Hanunoo on the upper eastern slopes of Mt. Yagaw. The six settlements in this area comprise an unstratified, unsegmented, neighborhoodlike community, which has a total of 128 inhabitants. The average population density for the entire Hanunoo territory is 10 per square kilometer, but in the more heavily settled areas, such as Yagaw, there are from 25 to 35 persons per square kilometer.

The Hanunoo do not have a general term for swidden or for swidden cultivation, but do employ a set of terms distinguishing developmental stages of potential, actual, or used swidden areas. These are based on changes—natural or artificial—in the vegetational cover. Swidden activities are best outlined by taking these stages in sequence, indicating the significant human activities and plant changes occurring at each.

FIRST YEAR

(1) Activities resulting in a slashed clearing, a *gamasun* (January-February). Possible swidden locations are discussed within the settlement group. Final decision depends on location augury, dreams, the local omens, as well as an intimate knowledge of the local forms of vegetation. The cultivator marks his plot with bamboo stakes and, using a large bolo, cuts down the underbrush and small saplings. Men and women participate in this initial clearing, family units making up the usual work teams. The average size of a Hanunoo swidden is two fifths of a hectare. This area averages about one hectare of cultivated swidden cleared each year for every eight people. The total area of productive swidden land in a given area, however, is always several times that of the most recently cleared fields, because of intercropping (see below). Forty-eight new swiddens (numbered serially for each settlement) were cleared in the Yagaw area in 1953. Of these only four were cut partly from virgin forest (amounting to less than 10 per cent of the total area cleared). Second-growth forest areas are preferred because the clearing of primary forest requires much more manpower for a given area, and demands a longer drying period before burning can take place than can profitably be allotted to such tasks.

(2) Activities resulting in a cut clearing, a *buklid* (February-March). Using the same bolos and a few single-bladed axes, men begin the more arduous task of felling large trees. Women continue to clear undergrowth and begin planting root crops (such as taro) which can survive the intense heat of swidden burning. Instead of being felled, a number of larger trees are pollarded, not only to remove unwanted shade branches, but also to provide firewood and promote seeding of other trees in the first fallow year. Smaller branches and cut underbrush are spread over the whole area so that complete burning will occur and exposed patches of earth will be protected from the dry season sun. These cutting, trimming, and drying activities may take more than a month, especially in a primary forest clearing. Group labor parties, repaid with feasts of rice, are usually needed to finish this stage.

(3) Activities resulting in a burned clear-

ing, a *tutud* (March-April-May). While the field dries, the Hanunoó farmer removes cut timber suitable for fence building or other construction purposes and clears a 4-meter-wide safety path around the entire clearing to prevent the fire from escaping into surrounding forest or fallow swidden areas. Firing starts at the upward and windward margins. A steep hectare of dry, second-growth vegetation will burn up in an hour or less, depending on the wind. While secondary burning is being completed, men begin fencing the entire swidden to prevent wild and domestic mammals (especially the zebu) from getting at young crop plants. Constant guarding against daytime animal marauders is facilitated by the construction of scarecrows of straw, wind-blown dangling objects, and small field houses from which children can jerk lines leading to distant parts of the swidden.

(4) Activities resulting in, and necessary for the maintenance of, a planted swidden, a *tanman* (May through October). Maize is planted soon after the swidden is burned. The main rice planting comes at the end of the dry season, in May or early June. It is an important social and religious event and involves special spirit offerings, large work parties in gala attire, feasting, and the participation of men, women, and children. Men make the seed holes (*ca.* 5 cm. deep and 25 cm. apart) with 2-meter-long pointed dibbles. Women and children follow, dropping a small handful of prepared seed (often from a mixture containing small quantities of pigeon pea, cucumber, melon, and sorghum seeds as well as rice). The Yagaw average for planted rice seed is 40 gantas (1-3/5 cavans) per hectare. Other important swidden crops are planted less ceremoniously (*e.g.*, sweet potatoes, in August), as are many secondary (*i.e.*, nonstaple) crops. During the rice-growing season, other swidden activities include completion of fences, continued guarding against destructive animals and birds, constant thinning and weeding (the entire swidden area being cleaned of weeds, shoots, and noncultivated vines at least three times), building of granaries, and the almost continuous planting

and harvesting of other crops in both new and old swiddens (see discussion of intercropping below).

(5) Activities resulting in a riceless field, a *dayamihan* (October-November). The most important harvest in a new swidden is that of short-growing-season maize (in July and August). This is usually performed (including minor magical rites) by the cultivator himself, with only one or two helpers. The main rice harvest, in late October and early November, involves elaborate arrangements for group labor, feasts, magical rites, and religious offerings. It is the most important agricultural event of the year. Harvesting rice is done by hand (usually without knives) by men, women, and older children. The normal yield in rice ranges from 25 to 40 times the volume of the seed planted. One hectare of swidden land may give more than 30 cavans of unhusked rice. After threshing, drying, hulling, cooking, and other preparations, a settlement-wide celebration is held, after which the rigid observance of many rice-connected taboos, such as that which forbids one to eat new rice from another's swidden, are removed.

(6) Activities resulting in a cleaned swidden, a *lumun baguhan* (November-December). After gleaning, all rice stalks are cut, piled, and burned. Group labor, with compensatory rice feasts, are necessary to finish this task in less than two months. Other cultigens, especially leguminous crops and sweet potatoes, are now the focus of attention.

Dry-season swiddens, always cut in second-growth areas, are cleared in September and October, planted in early November, and harvested unceremoniously in February, March, and April. They are usually small and are planted with corn and root crops only, never with rice. Some dry-season crops (including maize, certain beans, and sugar cane) are planted in main swiddens a few weeks before the rice harvest.

AFTER THE FIRST YEAR

(7) Activities resulting in a recleaned (used, but still productive) swidden, a *lumun*

daan. Fruit trees and other perennial cultivates planted in new swiddens continue to provide edible food products if the plot is systematically weeded and cleaned. By interplanting cultigens other than the principal grain staples, the Hanunoo practice a kind of limited crop rotation. Such intercropping results in successive harvests of different primary and secondary crops for at least two years, frequently extended to five or six years, especially where the cultivation of banana plants is continued. The many leguminous crops so interplanted, incidentally, return significant amounts of nitrogen to the soil. Single-crop swiddens are nonexistent. Up to 40 separate crops have been observed growing in one Hanunoo swidden at the same time. One informant drew a map of an "ideal" swidden containing 48 basic kinds of plants (over 250 subsumed specific types), including 41 cultigen crop foods (including varieties of rice, sweet potatoes, yams, taro, maize, squash, sugar cane, and beans); 1 noncultigen food plant (papaya); and 6 nonfood cultigens, namely tobacco, for chewing with betel, areca, and lime; betel vine, for leaves used in the betel chew; cotton, for spinning and weaving into garments; indigo, for dyeing cotton yarn; derris, for its fish-stupifying roots; and vetiver, for its scented roots (sachet).

Once productive cultivates give out—but usually not for two or three years after the main rice harvest—fallowing begins. After five years, fallow second-growth forest (*talun*) types are readily distinguishable by their predominant plant forms. The most common types are either some kind of tree or bamboo. Bamboo second growth is preferred for swidden making, because it dries uniformly and burns quickly and completely. If not recleared, of course, *talun* eventually reverts to primary forest (*puru*). Swidden areas are not recut before at least five years of fallowing—after the last cultigens give out—and this period is extended preferably to more than ten. In 1953, most Yagaw swiddens had been fallowed for more than eight years. The Yagaw area is in a rain belt and thus fallowing usually means the growth of replacement forest

and a continuing natural refertilization of the land. In areas where there is a long dry season—aided by frequent burning for hunting purposes—tough grasses tend to dominate the replacement vegetation. Without artificial manuring and draft animals, productive swidden cultivation then becomes difficult. Damper areas seem more suited to continued swidden making. Despite an apparently long history of occupation by swidden farmers—there are more than a dozen groves of coconut palms in the area—the Yagaw region today includes very little grassland. And *kugun* (*Imperata* spp.), the predominant grass, is highly valued for livestock pasturage and especially for roof thatching. It is a persistent weed, but in other respects it is an important economic necessity.

Swidden activities require from 50 to 1,000+ hours of work per year on the part of the average adult Hanunoo. In addition to swiddens, houseyard gardens are kept for experimentation with new cultigens, and for the individual cultivation of medicinal, ritual, aromatic, and ornamental plants.

The Hanunoo recognize innumerable natural and artificial factors as variables affecting swidden agriculture. Ecologically speaking, climatic factors, while closely observed, can be modified least by the Hanunoo. Edaphic factors, though not practically amenable to artificial change, can be dealt with in a more concrete manner. A study of Hanunoo soil classification and associated ideas regarding suitability for various crops—other variables being equal—checked well with the results of a chemical analysis of soil samples. Ten basic and 30 derivative soil and mineral categories are distinguished by the Hanunoo farmer. He may not know of the minute degree of lime disintegration and low pH value of *napunapu*, but he does know that certain beans and sugar cane (considered "high lime" crops, technically) will not thrive in such soil as they will in *baragan* (which has a higher lime content and pH value). Effects on soil quality of erosion, exposure, and over-swiddening are well understood. They are topics of frequent discussion, and preventive measures are often taken. Biotic factors are most subject to control and experimentation by the Hanunoo, and are of the greatest concern to them. More than 450 animal types and over 1,600 plant types are distinguished. The floral component is the more significant, especially in regard to swidden agriculture. Of some 1,500 "useful" plant types over 430 are cultigens (most of which are swidden-grown), existing only by virtue of the conscious domestication of the Hanunoo. Partly as a result of this intensified interest in plant domestication and detailed knowledge of minute differences in vegetative structures, Hanunoo plant categories outnumber, by more than 400 types, the taxonomic species into which the same local flora is grouped by systematic botanists.

CONCLUSIONS

Much of the foregoing is fragmentary and perhaps more suggestive than conclusive. There is certainly a need for continued research in other areas, and for field observations covering greater periods of time. However, by using what recent ethnographic materials are available, we may tentatively rephrase the statements made earlier, so that a more accurate picture of swidden agriculture will emerge. Most of the changes we shall make indicate that the swidden farmer sometimes knows more about the interrelations of local cultural and natural phenomena than ethnocentric temperate-zone writers realize.

(1) Swidden farming follows a locally determined, well-defined pattern and requires constant attention throughout most of the year. Hard physical labor is involved, but a large labor force is not required.

(2) Where possible, swidden making in second-growth forest areas (rather than in primary forests) is usually preferred.

(3) Swidden fires are often controlled by firebreaks surrounding the plot to be burned. Accidents happen, but greater damage may result from hunting methods employing fire in an area having a long dry season than from swidden clearing *per se*.

(4) Many details of swidden technique differ from area to area, and with changing conditions. Weeding is assiduously accomplished in some regions. Fencing is considered requisite if domestic cattle are kept, less so where such animals are rare. Wooden hand implements are very simple and are used only once. Metal cutting implements and harvesting equipment, however, vary greatly from region to region.

(5) Even the most noxious weeds, in one context, may serve the local economy admirably in another. *Imperata,* if dominant, restricts swidden opportunities, but its total loss causes similar hardships for those depending on it for pasture and thatch.

(6) Swiddens are rarely planted with single or even with only a few crops. Hence, the productivity of a swidden can be determined only partially by an estimate of the harvest yield of any one crop.

(7) It appears that the efficiency of swidden farming can be ascertained—relative to some other type of economy—only by taking into account the total yield per unit of labor, not per unit of area.

(8) Because of intercropping, the harvest of one main swidden crop may, serve only to allow one or more other crops to mature in turn. Plantings and harvests overlap usually for more than a full year, and frequently continue for several years.

(9) Swidden intercropping, especially if wet-season cereals are alternated with dry-season leguminous crops, amounts to a type of crop rotation, even if on a limited scale. Cycles of field "rotation" cannot be meaningfully assessed by merely determining the number of years which lapse between dates of successive clearings. The agricultural use of the swidden plot following initial clearing may have continued for one, several, or many years.

(10) It is difficult to set a minimum period of fallowing as necessary for the continued, productive use of swidden land by reclearing. Many variables are at work. A reasonable limit seems to be somewhere between 8 and 15 years, depending on the total ecology of the local situation. Swidden farmers are usually well aware of these limitations.

11. ECONOMIC ALTERNATIVES IN ARID LANDS: A CASE STUDY OF THE PIMA AND PAPAGO INDIANS

ROBERT A. HACKENBERG

Reprinted from Ethnology, *1 (1962): 186-95. Robert A. Hackenberg is Associate Professor of Anthropology, University of Colorado, and formerly research anthropologist with the Bureau of Ethnic Research, University of Arizona, and the National Institutes of Health. He has conducted comparative studies of ecological, demographic, and sociocultural change among the Pima and the Papago Indians, described in various articles.*

■ In this selection we can see, in stark perspective, some of the ways in which sociopolitical organization is inseparable from technology in a strategy of adaptation. Additionally, Hackenberg's comparison of two cultures in the American Southwest—the Pima and the Papago—illustrates the ways in which these cultural differences parallel habitational variations. This selection recalls the method of comparing neighboring groups that was used in Selection 7.

The neighboring Pima and Papago represent two different horticultural adaptations. Among the Papago, domesticated plants constituted a small proportion of the total diet; among the Pima, most of the diet was made up of domesticates. The Papago were not fully sedentary, relying to some degree on hunting, and they were dispersed in their farming activities. The Pima, whose reliance on hunting was much less, were permanently settled, and each village had several hundred people. Among the Papago, political organization was relatively unelaborated and headmen had little authority; among the Pima, there was much more complexity in village political organization and headmen had some measure of authority.

Correlatively, and consistent with the foregoing, when wheat was introduced to both groups by the Spaniards the Papago could not consolidate their multiple sources of water; the Pima, however, not only developed a more tightly integrated political structure but were able to construct an intercommunity water supply under a supravillage political structure. Moreover—and to illustrate the point that the histories of primitive societies contain ironies of their own—the Pima hired Papago labor.

The data discussed by Hackenberg also suggest that the acceptance of a centralized political system by a group depends in part on its earlier experience as a polity. Thus, and in contrast to the Papago, it is possible that one of the factors that made it possible for the Pima to unite politically under the stimulus of the Spaniards and to construct intercommunity hydraulic systems was their greater previous experience with a stronger political system.

It is sometimes said facetiously that there is one anthropologist to every Indian in the American Southwest, and it is true that our detailed knowledge of the cultures of these people is considerable. A good introduction to the traditional culture of the Papago is *Social Organization of the Papago Indians,* by Ruth Underhill (New York: Columbia University Press, 1937). Their contemporary culture is surveyed in *The Desert People: A Study of the Papago Indians,* by Alice Joseph, Rosamond B. Spicer, and Jane Chesky (Chicago: University of Chicago Press, 1949); this book has a strong psychological orientation. A good introduction to other societies in the American Southwest is *Social Organization of the Western Pueblos,* by Fred Eggan (Chicago: University of Chicago Press, 1950). It contains detailed accounts of the Hopi, Hano, Zuni, Acoma, and Laguna, but it does not provide much information on their sociotechnological adaptations. ■

IT HAS LONG BEEN the tendency of social scientists to catalogue the subsistence patterns of primitive peoples according to a simple categorical scheme as either hunters and gatherers, pastoralists, or agriculturists. Beyond agricultural beginnings, recent evolutionary schemes have indicated the processes through which simple farming societies have developed into states, and even empires. But, as Wittfogel observes, the post-agricultural phases of this developmental scheme are much better documented than the pre-agricultural ones. Little is known of the circumstances under which a group assumes the practice of agriculture, since this event is usually obscured by time and unrepresented by definitive archeological remains.

The circumstances of at least one primitive group's emergence as a farming society can be described from materials assembled by the author in the American Southwest. To understand this event, the assumption of farming practices will be described against the background of the logical economic alternatives available to a primitive people occupying an arid environment with a high agricultural potential. The manner in which selections and combinations of these alternatives have figured in the group's total pattern of environmental adaptation should further illustrate the dangers inherent in the oversimplified approach to primitive subsistence patterns referred to in the first paragraph.

The environmental setting for this study is the central and southwestern desert of Arizona, which receives between five and ten inches of rainfall per year, and is divided between river basins and poorly watered intermontane valleys. Soils are fertile, and gravity-flow irrigation has been possible for centuries from three sources: the Gila, Santa Cruz, and Sonoita rivers. The ground-water table has been adequate to support heavy pump irrigation for the past 25 years. Beyond its agricultural potential, the region produces an abundance of wild edible plants, and, during the aboriginal period, supported a variety of game, fish, and bird life. The nature of the plant cover and the types and distribution of animals have changed greatly since the beginning of the American occupation following the Civil War.

The aboriginal occupants of this area consisted of two groups, designated by different names but sharing many behavioral traits: the Pima and Papago Indians. The two groups had much in common in respect to language, physical type, and material culture. The reason for applying different names to them—a custom persisting since Spanish times—is to some extent environmental. The Pima have stayed largely within the valley of the Gila River, while the Papago have ranged widely throughout the other river valleys and across the drier intermontane regions.

Beyond this environmental difference, ethnographers separate the two tribes in terms of variant subsistence patterns, forms of political organization and types of village settlements. It will be a subordinate thesis of this presentation that these differences (1) consist of elements which are interdependent and (2) proceed from a choice of different economic alternatives.

This proposition, like the major question concerning the circumstances surrounding incipient agriculture, leads to a consideration of the economic alternatives themselves. These may be arranged along a gradient of increasing technological intervention to indicate the range of logical possibilities in subsistence typology, extending from pre-agriculture through several levels of agriculture. The alternatives will be discussed under the following rubrics: (1) hunting and gathering, (2) marginal agriculture, (3) pre-industrial agriculture, and (4) industrial agriculture. Each will be defined in connection with the discussion of its applicability to the Pima and Papago. Pastoralism has not been included as an alternative, since the grass cover of the Casa Grande Valley, Santa Cruz Valley, and the Papago country has always been very poor and few modern cattle-raising enterprises have succeeded in the area. The four categories, then, appear to exhaust the logical possibilities, though combinations can naturally occur.

Faced with these alternatives, how did the Pima and Papago choose? The answer may baffle those who are committed to notions of simple technological, cultural, or even economic determinism, for the Indians have shown such flexibility in their adjustment to the resources of their environment that it is difficult to assign them, throughout much of their history, to one or another specific position. To validate these assertions, let us consider some aspects of Pima and Papago history and ethnography in the light of the economic alternatives.

HUNTING AND GATHERING

The subsistence pattern of the Yavapai demonstrates adequately that small scattered groups could make a living in the area from wild food resources alone.

All writers on the Pima and Papago concede the important role played by wild plants and game animals in the diet of these tribes between the seventeenth century and the end of the nineteenth century. The rich resources of the desert region have been listed by Mark.

During the ethnographic present they used such foods as seeds, buds, fruits and joints of various cacti; seeds of the mesquite, ironwood, palo verde, amaranth, salt bush, lambsquarter, mustard, horsebean and squash; acorns and other wild nuts; screw bean; . . . the greens of lambsquarter, salt bush, canaigre, amaranth and pigweed; boxthorn and other berries; roots and bulbs of the sandroot (wild potato), covenas and others; and yucca fruit.

. . . Deer, antelope, mountain sheep and goats peccary, muskrats, bears, rabbits, quail, dove, mockingbird, wild ducks, geese, bittern, heron, snipe, wild turkey, rats, terrapin, lizards, grasshoppers, moth larvae, locusts, iguanas, snakes, toads, and beaver were used.

Since the crops cultivated aboriginally by both the Pima and the Papago were harvested by October and the stored products were consumed primarily during the winter, subsistence during the spring and summer depended largely upon hunting and gathering. Although both groups resorted to hunting and gathering, there was considerable difference in their relative degree of dependence upon them. The foods listed above provided the primary source of subsistence for the Papago, making up more than 75 per cent of their total annual food intake.

The Pima search for wild plants and animals was less intensive, since they often obtained an early corn crop in June. But they never dispensed entirely with wild foods,

which made up about 40 per cent of the annual diet of the Pima in the pre-Spanish period.

When cultivated crops were abundant, the Pima traded their surplus with the Papago for additional supplies of sahuaro syrup, cholla buds, and dried meat, which the riverine people regarded as delicacies.

Only in exceptionally dry years did Pima farm produce fail completely. About every fifth year, however, there occurred a drought of sufficient intensity to reduce the entire tribe to a diet of mesquite beans and jack rabbits. A serious famine was reckoned in terms of a failure of the mesquite beans to mature, of which several instances were recorded in the latter half of the nineteenth century. Nothing appears to have interfered with the proliferation of the rabbits.

The basic difference between the two groups, as we shall see, was the greater uncertainty of crop production among the Papago. This group was consequently more completely dependent upon foods obtained through hunting and gathering. The inadequacy of cultivated foods, together with the vagaries of their domestic water supply, forced many Papago to maintain several residences. These have been called "field villages" when they were adjacent to the locations used for flood-water farming (see below), and "well villages" when located near sources of a year-around domestic water supply in the mountains. Well villages, though smaller, were considered to be more permanent than field villages in aboriginal times. Since the "wells" were often merely seepage springs among the rocks, the mountain locations were often inhabited by only one or two extended families. There were, of course, more well locations than field locations.

The Papago spent part of their time in crop-producing activities at field locations, but the major portion of the year was consumed by activities for which the well village served as the base of operations. In moving between fields and wells, the Papago assumed a semi-migratory residence pattern, which had political implications as well as economic. Until the period of intensified Apache raiding, the organization of Papago villages was very loose, and tended to follow extended patri-family lines. Only in the field locations were suprafamily groups associated with each other under aboriginal conditions. The migratory tendency of the Papago reached its peak of development among the Sand Papago. This group, which occupied the extreme southwest of Papagueria, was entirely dependent upon hunting and gathering and had no field locations.

Hunting and gathering, in short, constituted the primary subsistence pattern for most Papago villages and the exclusive source of food for several of them. For the Pima villages, on the other hand, these activities provided only a supplementary source of subsistence, and were never relied upon exclusively except in times of drought.

MARGINAL AGRICULTURE

In this stage of elementary cultivation, maximum reliance is placed upon those environmental features which, without human intervention, are conducive to maturing a crop. Such features included the fertilization of the soil and the preparation of the land by natural floods. The tools employed are few and simple, produced by a pre-metal technology, and there is little organization of labor. Human technological intervention to either control or improve the environment is minimal, consisting of planting, occasional cultivation, and harvesting. If irrigation is required to supplement the natural floods, small ditches and temporary diversion dams suffice to serve this purpose. Even though marginal agriculture improves the environment as a human habitat, man does not secure himself against the loss of his advantage through flood disaster, drought, or crop failure. Hence marginal agriculture is still a precarious type of subsistence.

Like hunting and gathering, marginal agriculture was a pattern known to both the Pima and the Papago. In the pre-Spanish period the crops of both peoples were those of the traditional Southwestern maize, bean, and squash

complex. The difference between the Pima and Papago in their use of marginal agriculture was, again, largely one of emphasis.

Pima fields were laid out permanently, adjacent to either natural or artificial water courses, and the permanent houses making up the village settlement were located nearby. In early Spanish times the Pima were grouped in fewer than a dozen villages, extending 55 miles along the Gila River below the present site of the Casa Grande National Monument. The regularity of crop production in the Gila bottom lands enabled these villages to be sedentary. Pima villages were located at a considerable distance from each other, and each probably consisted of several hundred individuals. Because they were sedentary, and larger in size than the Papago villages, the Pima communities were more complex in their internal political structure, though there is some question about the precise nature of this structure for the first half of the eighteenth century. The Pima villages, like those of the Papago, were organized under a headman, but greater dependence upon agriculture gave the Pima chief more political authority. Direction of warfare and supervision of hunting were the village headman's responsibilities in both groups. In addition, the Pima leader initiated the construction and maintenance of irrigation ditches and diversion dams. He also figured in land clearing and apportionment. These activities comprised the bulk of Pima technological intervention in the modification of natural conditions.

Other forms of Pima collective labor did not necessarily depend upon the leadership of the headman. Planting and harvesting were organized cooperatively, though the total manpower of the village was seldom enlisted for these purposes. Less demanding tasks were discharged by individual families.

Papago flood farming tended to be more the affair of an individual family. Land suitable for cultivation appeared in small alluvial fans at the mouths of washes, and the fertility and irrigation of such patches resulted primarily from the flooding action of the washes themselves. Technological intervention on the part of the Papago was less than that of the Pima, consisting largely of placing earthen dikes to spread and collect the water, excavating tanks for water storage, and other minimal conservation measures.

The Papago, who were more dispersed in their farming activity, generally lacked a political and economic organization comparable to that of the Pima, but the difference, again, was one of emphasis. Diversion and canal irrigation, using river water, was primarily a Pima pattern, permitting a more intensive agriculture and a more complex social structure than among the Papago. Nevertheless, at San Xavier on the Santa Cruz River, the Papago had considerable land under cultivation using techniques analogous to those employed by the Pima, and several Papago communities in the valley of the Sonoita River, south of the present Sells Reservation, likewise made use of intermittent streams. Conversely, at several places in the Kohatk country on the northern periphery of the present Sells Reservation, along the lower portion of Santa Rosa Wash, villages were reported practicing flood-water farming of the Papago variety—settlements which several writers consider to have been Pima despite their desert subsistence pattern. The true affiliation of these people remains a historical problem.

To recapitulate, the Pima were predominantly irrigators, settled in sedentary communities along the Gila River, whereas the Papago were predominantly flood farmers strongly, but certainly not exclusively, dependent upon rainfall for growing their crops.

PRE-INDUSTRIAL AGRICULTURE

At the level of pre-industrial agriculture, man attempts to intervene with nature to secure more reliable productivity and to increase yields well beyond the potential of the undeveloped forces present in nature. These objectives can be achieved only through massive alteration of the "given" features of the environment, as through the construction of reservoirs, dams, and canals, the leveling and terracing of land, and related operations.

Without machines, these activities require the coordinated efforts of massed manpower. The social and political structure, which is the instrument of coordination, is consequently the key to successful agriculture at this level. Thus Wittfogel insists on the importance of the "hydraulic society" as a social instrument in areas of the world that are still struggling toward industrialization. Since human intervention of this sort tends to remove some of the aspects of risk from crop production, many disasters are averted, and, other things being equal, population continues to increase and the social and political structure becomes more complex.

A division occurs between the Pima and the Papago at this level. Tendencies toward advancement in the direction of a hydraulic society became manifest among the former, but not among the latter. These tendencies could have constituted a primary step in the socio-cultural evolution of an irrigation society among the Pima, had not other historical circumstances intervened. The essential event producing the Pima change in the direction of pre-industrial agriculture was the introduction of wheat by the Spaniards in the eighteenth century. The advent of this winter crop enabled them to augment their summer harvest of corn and achieve a year-around subsistence from agriculture. This freed the group completely from their previous dependence upon hunting and gathering.

The social and political consequences were even more important. The expansion in the scope of agriculture enabled the Pima to adjust to the challenge presented by the Apache wars. The year-around farming cycle permitted a greater population density to accumulate upon a reduced acreage, and this, in turn, fostered a more tightly integrated social and political structure.

The range of Pima village settlement contracted from 55 to 12 miles. Social integration was manifested in the growth of joint community dependence upon, and management of, a common water supply. Several villages came to rely upon a common canal system and arranged jointly for maintenance and water allocation through a supra-village structure. All villages, acting under a common chief, established a tribal system of defense, including lookouts, sentries, and patterns of mobilization to resist sudden surprise attacks. Some evidence of potential diversification in the Pima economy may also be seen. Surpluses of goods were produced and stored, and outlets were sought to trade them. The Pima hired Papago as laborers in the wheat fields, and there wos other evidence of the commencement of social differentiation.

The Papago received the same stimuli as did the Pima. They also obtained wheat from the Spaniards, and cultivated it widely as moisture permitted. However, they were unable to produce sufficient quantities to supplant hunting and gathering. They could not consolidate their farming areas since the multiple sources of water could not be united into a single adequate one. Consequently, though the Papago formed defense villages of a sort to ward off Apache attack, these were used more as fortifications than as residences. There was no tendency toward wider group consolidation, nor was a common chief appointed for all the Papago villages.

Wheat permitted the Pima to adopt preindustrial agriculture, to gain superior control over their environment, and to rise above the level of mere subsistence productivity. By the middle of the nineteenth century they were on the way toward the achievement of social and political integration at the tribal level. The Papago, on the other hand, because of their deficient environment, were unable to capitalize upon the new opportunity.

INDUSTRIAL AGRICULTURE

The alternative of industrial agriculture involves primary reliance upon nonhuman sources of energy as the instruments for transforming the productive capacity of the environment. While machines are vastly superior transforming agents, they maximize social structural demands even beyond those of the hydraulic society. The structure of finance, credit, transport, supply, communications, and maintenance needed for a machine technology has no parallel in complexity. This socio-technological complex, of course, permits the greatest known degree of mastery over the environment.

Industrial agriculture inevitably made its appearance with the intrusion of non-Indian farmers into the Pima and Papago country. Industrialized farm production was preceded by construction of a massive dam and reservoir system on the Salt River. Completed in 1905, this was followed within a decade by the introduction of a new cash crop for which there was a waiting market, namely, cotton.

Within the new environmental framework of flood control and managed water supply, non-Indian agriculturists brought vast desert tracts under cultivation. These were located on three sides of the Pima reservation, but the Indians did not participate as producers in this new economic challenge.

The Papago did not receive a similar opportunity since none of their lands lay within the zone of economic development. Despite their margin of superiority under aboriginal conditions, the Pima were no better equipped to participate as producers in the new controlled environment than were the Papago. The gap between their rudimentary irrigation society and the national level of socio-cultural integration required to operate and maintain hydraulic works, and to participate effectively in managed irrigation districts, was much too great, and it has not yet been closed.

Not all participants in industrial agriculture, however, need be landowning and operating producers. The Pima and Papago have found their place in the new system at the level of laborers. Here the Indian needed few technical or organizational skills that he did not already possess.

The Papago and Pima of today retain their aboriginal lands, but they are unable to put them to efficient economic use. Several attempts have been made through the Bureau of Indian Affairs to introduce both groups to the producers role within the newly defined farming situation of industrial agriculture. A pump irrigation project for the Papago at Chuichu and a much larger irrigation district on the Pima reservation have, however, yielded unsatisfactory results. Neither group of Indians is, as yet, capable of coming to terms with a new set of agricultural variables: credit, land preparation, fertilization, equipment rental, seed selection, strict water measurement, systematic irrigation, etc. Only when reservation lands have been leased to non-Indians have they been consistently and profitably productive. A recent, if somewhat uncertain, exception is the Gila River Pima-Maricopa Community Farm. A tribal enterprise, the Community Farm has successfully grown and marketed several thousand acres of cotton annually since 1952, but as yet it is largely a token effort.

INTERPRETATION AND CONCLUSIONS

The Pima alone made a promising start at pre-industrial agriculture. It began late in their aboriginal history—after 1750—and the trend lasted little more than a century. During this period, however, the Pima developed the following patterns unknown to the Papago:

1) Concentration of settlement pattern;
2) Cooperative intervillage water management;
3) Tribal-wide political leadership in war and mobilization for defense;
4) Production of surplus farm commodities for sale and trade;
5) Escape from the need for wild foods except in years of poor water supply;
6) Commencement of social differentiation, as seen in the employment of laborers and the accumulation of wealth.

The Pima never developed pre-industrial agriculture, however, to the point of gaining full environmental control. The drought of 1854 reduced them to eating mesquite beans, and the flood of 1868 destroyed three of their villages. Proper means of water conservation and flood control were never undertaken. After 1870 the social fabric of Pima life began to disintegrate, and the opportunity was lost to organize for such an output of group effort.

We may now summarize the relationship between the Pima and Papago and the several economic alternatives. Instead of a traditional designation within the unrealistic limits of a single type, the Papago appear to occupy an intermediate position between two alternatives which form the range of their subsistence pursuits: hunting and gathering, and marginal agriculture. The Pima, similarly, appear to occupy an intermediate position between marginal agriculture and pre-industrial agriculture, the alternatives which form the range of their subsistence activities. When combined, the subsistence patterns of both groups may be seen to form a continuum. This continuum is pure Papago at one extreme, represented by the Sand Papago with their exclusive dependence upon hunting and gathering, and pure Pima at the other, represented by the commencement of pre-industrial agriculture in the mid-nineteenth century. Since both groups developed and practiced forms of marginal agriculture, there is an area of overlap in the middle.

The institutions which have, in the ethnographic literature, served to differentiate the Pima from the Papago are those which the former group developed in consequence of its acceptance of wheat and its development of a year-around agricultural cycle. In the absence of these institutions, the differences between the two peoples seem to be largely of emphasis rather than of kind.

The question remains whether this discussion sheds any light on the problem of the assumption of the sort of agricultural productivity which leads to the establishment of the hydraulic society. One thing seems clear. Marginal productivity of the aboriginal Papago type, which also characterized Pima cultivation before the introduction of wheat, leads of itself to nothing significant in the way of social evolution. The management of small plots of farm land by individual families or extended families, whether under desert or riverine conditions, can produce a stable food supply which is marginally adequate. Socio-cultural stability is possible under such conditions, but there is no impetus to population growth or concentration, no unbearable strain on existing resources.

Among the Pima, two external stimuli destroyed this stability and appear to have started the group on an ascendant evolutionary sequence of changes: the adoption of wheat and the challenge of the Apache. In the absence of the motive power provided by the threat of annihilation, it is questionable whether the upward spiral would have been initiated. Some writers, indeed, feel that the Pima knew about wheat long before they began to cultivate it. We have already noted the social and political changes occurring as a result of their decision.

The failure of Pima society to survive the appearance of non-Indian industrial agriculture also deserves comment. There are two apparent reasons. First, the creation of a pre-industrial agricultural society appears to be an irrevocable commitment. The assumption of increased agricultural productivity, accompanied by growing population density, creates an environmental adjustment characterized by a reduction in the capacity of the area to produce wild foods and to support people in the absence or failure of their own productive activity. In the vicinity of the consolidated Pima villages, for example, timber soon became scarce, fish disappeared from the stream, and hunting parties ventured increasingly far away from their homes. Furthermore, the decision to attempt to control water through the creation of diversion dams and canal systems implies a commitment to co-operative effort. The effort required is usually beyond that of the single family or extended family to mobilize. Thus, should the pre-industrial society fail in its expanded agricultural attempt, retreat to marginal agriculture or to hunting and gathering becomes extremely difficult. If the society has been long established, and extreme environmental alteration has occurred, it becomes impossible. Faced with the non-Indian challenge, then, the Pima could not retreat to simpler patterns of subsistence.

This brings us to the second point. Other non-Western societies of irrigation farmers, such as the Burmese and Thai, are making the transition to Western agricultural productivity within an industrial framework and are achieving this without a breakdown in the social fabric. These peoples, however, have had long experience in meeting the requirements of a fully developed hydraulic society infinitely more complex than that initiated among the Pima. In Southeast Asia, for example, the following cultural and structural concepts were present:

1) Devotion of a portion of each year to labor on public works, with or without compensation;
2) Widespread use of writing and record keeping, with consequent calendrical knowledge of precision in the performance of timed activities;
3) Extreme social differentiation into managerial and working classes;
4) Authoritarian direction of economic activity by officials representing a remote central government.

While not directly comparable, each of these features has a parallel in the demands placed upon the peasant within the framework of industrial agriculture. He already accepts wage labor, timing of activities, supervision by remote and powerful social and political structures, and participation in parts of plans which he does not fully understand.

In the absence of these cultural and structural concepts, Pima Indian society had no chance to absorb and apply the technology and structure of industrial agriculture. The destruction of group life among the Pima was thus foredoomed by (1) their inability to retreat to previous patterns of subsistence activity, and (2) the insufficient development of the pre-industrial pattern of agricultural institutions, which, had they matured into a full hydraulic society pattern, might have protected them.

12. THE STRUCTURAL POSES OF 18TH-CENTURY CHEROKEE VILLAGES

FREDERICK O. GEARING

Reprinted from American Anthropologist, *60 (1958): 1148-56. Frederick O. Gearing is Professor of Anthropology, State University of New York, Buffalo. He has worked in contemporary North American Indian communities and, more recently, in contemporary Greece. He is the author of* Priests and Warriors: Social Structures for Cherokee Politics in the 18th Century *and* The Face of the Fox.

■ This selection illustrates the concept of seasonal variations in culture, which was briefly discussed in Selection 3. One of the themes that can be read in the evolution of culture is that there is a correspondence between direct dependence on seasonal cycles in productive activities and seasonal variations in the organization of social relations. Gearing refers to the latter as "structural poses." He uses this concept to draw attention to the fact that such variations (or alternating poses) in a culture are integral aspects of its organization of social relations. It is not Gearing's intent to examine the Cherokee in evolutionary perspective but only to describe them as they were in the eighteenth century. To his analysis we can add the hypothesis that as groups achieve increasing freedom from the limitations of their habitats there is a corresponding reduction in seasonal variation in the organization of their social relations.

Gearing's fuller report of Cherokee social organization, *Priests and Warriors: Social Structures for Cherokee Politics in the 18th Century (American Anthropologist, 64[5], Part 2, October, 1962),* should be consulted by the reader who wants to learn more about these people, and especially about the European-American impact on them.

Few anthropological studies have been made of seasonal variations in culture. As Gearing notes, references to such variations are generally perfunctory, if they are made at all. Franz Boas provides a very brief discussion in *Social Organization and Secret Societies of the Kwakiutl Indians* (in U.S. National Museum, Annual Report, 1895 [Washington, D.C., 1897], pp. 418 and 436), and one of the best descriptions of seasonal variations in culture is provided by Curt Nimuendaju in *The Eastern Timbira* (Berkeley: University of California Press, 1946). An interesting description of seasonal culture in medieval England is found in Chapter 22, "The Husbandman's Year," in George C. Homans' *English Villagers of the Thirteenth Century* (Cambridge, Mass.: Harvard University Press, 1941), from which Selection 30 is drawn. ■

THE NOTION OF structural pose, which is offered here, draws attention to the well-established fact that the social structure of a human community is not a single set of roles and organized groups, but is rather a series of several sets of roles and groups which appear and disappear according to the tasks at hand. The notion of structural pose elevates that known fact to a position of central importance in structural analysis. In every human community, a series of social structures come and go recurrently. A Cherokee village in 1750, faced with a community task such as holding a village council, divided that work and coordinated it by arranging all villagers into one social structure. Whenever the white flag was raised over a village council house to call the council, a young male villager assumed with little or no reflection a defined set of relations with every other villager. At the moment before, perhaps, his most engrossing relations had been with other men of his own age; now his mind's eye shifted to the old men of the village. Before, perhaps, his fellow clansmen had been dispersed and variously occupied with diverse interests; now they all came to sit together and were engrossed with him in a common task and were a corporate group among other like groups. Faced with another task, such as negotiating with an alien power, the community rearranged all villagers into still a different structure of roles and organized groups.

The notion of structural pose firmly fixes the mind of the student to that long-evident fact: human communities typically rearrange themselves to accomplish their various tasks. Orthodox studies of social structure do not. On most pages of the usual American structural studies, structural elements—clans, households, mother's brothers—are treated as if these groups and roles were ever-present. The usual operation is to elicit from observed events the shared understanding of the actors as to who is acting. The student sees one man speaking and other men listening. A participant, on questioning, reveals that the man speaks and is listened to because he is a man among men, because he is old among others younger, and because he is a fellow clansman. The student therefore knows that this society "has" these elements in its social structure. Having discovered the sundry elements of structure, the student usually proceeds to discover fit and ill fit—systematic interconnection—among the elements, treated as if ever-present. In obvious fact, all the elements are not operative all the time; one combination of elements operates, then another combination. When structural studies choose to give intensive attention to one or a few societies, the fact often intrudes that all elements are not operative at all times, but on the whole it remains in the background; when the studies move by drawing actuarial tables of correlation, the fact virtually disappears. British structural analyses of segmentary societies have, at the point where segmentariness itself is under discussion, given this temporal dimension of structure its deserved attention.

The thesis here is that the orthodox conceptualizations of social structures are a cumbersome reification of structural fact and that those conceptualizations hinder the articulation of structural studies with studies of personality and of ethos. I do not imagine that I here disclose a social fact which is new. Rather, I suggest here a less cumbersome and more profitable way of analyzing a known

fact. In a word, a human community does not have a single social structure; it has several. Put otherwise, the social structure of a society is the sum of the several structural poses it assumes around the year.

I will illustrate the notion of structural pose by describing the four recurrent structural poses assumed by the male population of any 18th-century Cherokee village as that village moved through its annual round of village tasks.

The aboriginal Cherokee kinship system was of the Crow type. Whenever any two Cherokee came together, the presence or absence of a kinship relation was a major fact determining their behavior and, among kin, behavior was patterned by the particular nature of that kinship connection. Gilbert has described the total set of relations among kin.

Differentiation according to age and sex also affected behavior whenever any two Cherokee came together. Two sex statuses were employed. Men hunted and warred; women tilled gardens, cooked, and raised infants. The sexual division of labor was rather complete, but certain phases of agricultural labor fell to the men, and female warriors apparently existed under rare circumstances. Both sexes participated in ceremonies, but men acquitted the major responsibilities. Male age statuses were boy, young man, and beloved man. Female age statuses were probably parallel. A boy joined his first war party in his teens, but between 25 and 30 years of age, probably after he had established a family, he would receive a war rank and thus pass into the status of young man. Between 50 and 60 years of age a young man would cease to join war parties and thus become a beloved man. The age status of beloved man carried much prestige and influence; young men were expected to speak their minds to beloved men, but decorously, and to defer to their judgments when disagreements arose.

The Cherokee kinship system and the sex and age statuses meshed and at no visible points were in conflict. Indeed, their separation is an intellectual act which would probably not occur to a reflective Cherokee. Fortes has termed this set of shared understandings which patterned the behavior of every villager toward any other villager the "woof" of society.

Beyond this, the Cherokee joined in organized groups, the "warp" of Cherokee village structure. These groups were 30 or 40 households which were ideally matrilocal but were often neolocal, the local segments of seven matrilineal clans, a body of elders which included all men over about 55 years of age, and a war organization.

In each such group, kinship relations and age and sex categories patterned behavior. But each kind of organized group brought together a different combination of relatives and nonrelatives and a different proportion of persons of the age and sex categories. While ideas about proper behavior between father and son were constant, father and son were not always together; hence that relationship was not always operative. Father and son were usually together whenever the household was together; they were necessarily apart whenever the clans were gathered; and they may or may not have been together, depending on their ages, when the body of elders or the war organization was acting.

The notion of structural pose points up the systematic, rhythmic way in which Cherokees joined in first one set of organized groups and then another. There were four structural poses. In each pose, different groups operated, singly or in combination. During every minute of the Cherokee year, villagers guided themselves by the set of relations of one or another of those four poses, or at least understood that they should. For the hunt and for other tasks, the Cherokee village was one structural pose, an aggregate of independent households. Beginning soon after the Cherokee New Year in October, young men in small parties, usually fewer than ten, left the village for the winter hunt. The principal prey was deer. Hunters stalked their prey; there was no premium on large parties, and success depended less on coordination of the group than on individual skill. Parties could be gone a full six months, but shorter trips were probably more common. They returned to the village in time for a festival in early April

which marked the end of winter and the beginning of summer. After the crops were in the ground and before the harvest, the young men again went out, this time for a shorter summer hunt. The division of labor—who would hunt and who would not—was an internal household matter. The relations among members of hunting parties was a household matter or at most a matter of voluntary association among men from a few households. The disposal of the catch and its preparation was a household matter.

A variety of other tasks fell to the aggregate of independent households. The household bore the major responsibilities connected with birth and the socialization of the child. It prepared food and provided shelter. In the event of illness, the household called in a priest-specialist and nursed the sick. In this first structural pose, the village was an aggregate of independent households.

Occasionally, and at no predictable time, the rhythm of such household activities was disturbed by a murder. For purposes of punishing a killer, the village assumed a second structural pose. For this task and others, the seven local clan-segments became the significant groups and the village became an aggregate of independent clan-segments. A murder was a signal; fathers left their wives and children, conceptually or physically, to join with their mother's brothers, their brothers, their sisters' sons, to accomplish the task at hand. Each clan-segment was for this task a corporate individual; all local clansmen were guilty if a fellow clansman had killed, and all male clansmen were responsible for revenge if a fellow clansman had been killed. The killer (or one of his clan) was usually killed if he had murdered intentionally; otherwise some other settlement was possible.

To the clan-segments fell also the regulation of marriage. That regulation included the selection of a clansman's mate outside the clan and preferably in his father's father's clan. Marriage was further regulated through the beating of widows or widowers who violated mourning regulations by clanswomen of the deceased, and through punishment of men who deserted or neglected their wives and children by clanswomen of the neglected women and children.

For the purpose of reaching certain decisions, the village became a third structure. Now it was not an aggregate of smaller independent groups, but a single organized whole. At the time of the New Year Festival in late October, the village met in its most important general council of the year. (Other village councils were called as needed; they probably tended to occur in conjunction with the annual cycle of religious festivals.) A white pole was raised with an eagle feather and a white flag at the top, and the whole population came into the council house; village council houses which could seat 500 were not uncommon. The variety of decisions a village made was probably not great. For example, public buildings might need repair or might have to be built. Or, since farming lands were limited in the mountainous sections and since slash and burn techniques sometimes exhausted the soil faster than the floods replenished it, villages were sometimes forced to move.

Villagers organized themselves into a single whole by again gathering the seven clan-segments and by adding another, cross-cutting, organized group—the body of elders. The body of elders contained all male villagers over about 55 years of age—the beloved men. The principal officials were four priests and one secular officer: the village priest-chief, his right-hand man, the keeper of the council house, the messenger, and the secular village speaker. These men lived near the council house and probably acted, during general councils, as if without clan affiliation. But a second order of officials were simultaneously clansmen and members of the body of elders. These were the priest-chief's seven-man inner council of clansmen; one man was drawn from each clan-segment and each was the voice of his segment during the councils. The remaining beloved men also acted during councils both as clansmen and as elders. The rest of the village, those not in the body of elders, sat with their fellow clansmen, women apart from men. All male villagers could speak to points under consideration. Decisions were reached along two structural axes: each clan-segment came to an opinion and those opinions were reconciled in the body of elders, though not in the simple two-phase manner implied. Decisions had the semblance of unanimity in the sense that they were delayed until overt opposition ceased.

The Cherokee village assumed this same structural pose in two other major activities. First, in religious festivals the village expressed its basic ideas about the nature of the relations between man and god, between man and nature, and between man and man; the beloved men, organized as the body of elders, served the clan-segments as the channel of that expression by leading the ritual acts. Second, to organize agricultural work, the village probably assumed the same structural pose. (However, in those parts of Cherokee country cut by mountains and narrow river valleys, as population expanded a new family was often forced to clear land apart from the clan land; possibly it might choose to do its agricultural work independently from the clan.)

To carry on offensive war, the Cherokee village assumed a fourth structural pose. When a general council decided for war, the red standard of the village was raised and a new combination of organized groups went into operation. The village became an order of command. The age status of beloved men remained organized as the body of elders, excepting four who removed themselves from the elders to assume major war roles. The age status of young men plus those persons from the age status of boys who had passed adolescence left their fellow clansmen; these joined warriors of their respective war ranks, became the village war organization, and left the village. Women, children, and young men not able-bodied acted as members of their several clan-segments through clan representatives in both the body of elders and the war organization.

The major village war commanders were four beloved men wth priestly esoteric knowledge necessary for war—the war priest, the war chief, the speaker for war, and the surgeon. The village war chief, and probably the other three top war officials, were elected by warriors. Those major war officials appointed four junior officers, probably ad hoc, from among the young men: a man with priestly knowledge to be flag bearer; a stand-in for the war priest to accompany the war party; two special war leaders, one a priest and one without priestly knowledge. There was also a seven-man council for war—probably a prominent warrior from each clan-segment— and a set of four scouts. The command functions were divided among those officers. Beneath the officials, the war organization was hierarchically stratified by four ranks which were earned through war deeds.

The day after a decision for war, the priestly war officials conjured; warriors fasted; a dance lasted through the night. Deeds were recounted to excite emulation. At dawn the young men went to the river and plunged seven times; again the priests conjured. The war speaker made a speech and the war party, carrying its standard and war ark, marched out of the village in a formal procession ordered by the offices and ranks of the war organization.

Three other village activities utilized this fourth structure. First, rather than decide for war with a particular tribe or colony, the village general council might decide to send a party to negotiate. Negotiations were handled by the war organization, and relationships among members of the negotiating party were the same relations that obtained among those persons during offensive war. The party carried instructions from the general council and, unlike war parties, usually maintained close communication with the body of elders during negotiations. Second, periodically during the summer, when warfare was rare, the young men joined for ball games with other villages. They assumed a set of relations with each other and with the village at large which duplicated the structure of the village for war. Third, in the event of attack on a village by an enemy, the village was organized under the war organization heirarchy.

To any Cherokee villager, each recurrent task was a signal to assume a certain set of relations with every other villager. For the variety of village tasks here reviewed, the male villagers organized themselves into four distinguishable structures. In other words, Cherokee village social structure was the rhythmic appearance and disappearance of those four structural poses.

For purely descriptive purposes, this notion of structural pose has no apparent advantage over the more usual conceptualizations found in structural studies. For certain theoretical purposes, it has significant advantages. I will briefly suggest two.

First, analysis in terms of structural pose provides an easier bridge to the individual, and hence an easier articulation with bodies of theory which deal with the individual and how he comes to be what he is. Structural pose holds the student's attention to the fact that individuals must move, recurrently and constantly, into and out of required relations with others. With analysis in terms of structural pose, a man's typical year, or typical lifetime, is immediately and concretely visible; his recurrent roles are laid out in the approximate sequence and frequency in which he must take them up and lay them down. A Cherokee young man, as he moved back and forth from the structural pose for war activities to the pose for village councils, shifted his loyalties and his relative status. Most importantly, he shifted from coercion-tinged war relationships, in which he feared the wrath of the prominent war leaders and perhaps was feared by warrior in ranks beneath him, to noncoercive deferential relations with gentle clan elders and village priest officials. The notion of structural pose reminds us and permits us to inquire in what way, and perhaps at what cost, the Cherokees could require any individual successfully to combine in himself the behavior required of warrior and young clansman.

The answers to that question cannot come from structural studies per se, but require help from disciplines which deal with psychologies of individuals—role theory and depth psychology. Role theory tends to assume great flexibility in men; it anticipates and explains well the frequently large degree of success in the conscious and purposeful adjustment of a man's behavior as he moves from one role to another; the major maladjustments are expected when contradictory roles are demanded of him simultaneously. In contrast, Freudian psychology tends to insist more on the limitations of human adaptability in virtue of inborn qualities and early childhood experience; it anticipates more frequent failure, and accounts for such failures. In order to see successful flexibility or unsuccessful inflexibility, both psychologies need an image of a man's movement through the variety of social niches his society lays out for him.

Both psychologies help illuminate Cherokee social behavior. The required ritual purification of warriors on their return to the village comes to be seen as a device which insisted that the young men lay down their coercion-tinged relations with fellow warriors and assume the proper noncoercive relations with their families, clans, and with villagers at large. Most young Cherokees, with the assistance of this ritual event, were successful in this recurrent adjustment. The more prominent warriors typically were not. These few remained improperly overbearing in their relations with fellow villagers, and suffered the displeasure of their fellows; they were given war honors, but otherwise avoided. Further, after prominent warriors entered the body of elders, they usually enjoyed little influence or honor. Role theory and depth psychology seem respectively best equipped to explain the usual successes and the less usual but recurrent failures. Both need structural data. Those data, in the form of structural-pose analysis, are immediately applicable to the problem; the same data, in the form of more orthodox structural analyses, are not.

Second, structural pose provides a more adequate backdrop for understanding ethos than do orthodox structural studies. It is common knowledge that human groups deem an act good in one relationship and bad or irrelevant in another. So much is easily seen in the usual structural studies. But a community also deems an act morally appropriate in one situation and inappropriate in another. Structural pose permits an easier

movement of the mind from structure to situation, and therefore from structure to the situational aspect of value. Situations evoke appropriate social groupings and, in and among those groupings, moral codes. Cherokee villagers valued personal freedom—or more accurately, they disvalued coerciveness. Yet Cherokee warriors were typically coercive. That social fact is not much illuminated by speaking of theory versus practice, or of a dual value system. It is, in the Cherokee instance, a complex matter of pervasive moral ideal, of certain allowed exceptions to that ideal, of certain characteristic violations of it, and of certain cultural devices for isolating those exceptions and violations into one corner of village life. In the event of war, the war organization formed; and the proper, allowed exceptions and the characteristic, expected, but improper violations both materialized in the relations within the war organization. The crisis situations in which war parties typically found themselves required command relations. Among the devices which bottled up that bothersome aspect of the Cherokee moral life was the custom of causing the war organization to disband when its immediate job was done. Cherokee value, situation, and structure were in reality of a piece.

Communities always divide their labor among social segments. The tasks require different operations of the different segments and the different operations can require different forms of leadership behavior within the different segments. Sometimes, the pattern of leadership within a segment unavoidably diverges from ideas about proper conduct because of the nature of the tasks that segment must perform. A society might conceivably exist where ethos floats evenly down over all tasks and all social segments, but assumptions of that condition have caused misinterpretations which are still accepted as truth. For example, Benedict put the Pueblo and the Plains groups at opposite poles of a continuum through this error. In effect, she compared the moral notions operative during a Pueblo general council with the partly immoral relations among a Plains war party. Yet some Pueblos had war parties which behaved not unlike Plains war parties, some Plains groups had general councils which behaved not unlike Pueblo general councils, and in both groups, the general council and related ritual were thought of as the clearest expression of the good life. Differences in emphasis surely existed, and those differences probably made for two quite different kinds of men. But the comparisons would more accurately begin with the basic pattern shared by both Plains and Pueblo societies. Structural pose allows us to leave value, situation, and structure interconnected, and therefore helps us to understand their interconnections.

Redfield argues that all of us should deem it worthwhile that some of us work toward conceptualizations that permit us to view the complex life of a human community as a single, systematic whole. Analyses such as social structure, personality and culture, and ethos grasp some aspect of that complex whole, but each grasps a different though overlapping aspect. I take it that a modification of one kind of analysis which allows an easier articulation with another kind is a good modification—in the sense that it allows us to hope that what was seen as two systems can now be seen as one. I believe that the notion of structural pose might be such a modification. It offers the possibility that things known from studies of social structure can be joined with things known from studies of personality and culture and from studies of ethos, and that all of them can be seen simultaneously and in their systematic interconnections.

13. LAND AND LABOR

C. DARYLL FORDE

Excerpted from Yako Studies *(London: International African Institute, 1964). C. Daryll Forde, Professor of Anthropology, University College, University of London, and Director of the International African Institute, has done ethnographic field research in the American Southwest and in eastern Nigeria. His publications reflect his special interest in ecology, economics, and pre-industrial social organization. His work on the Yako appears in a monograph,* Marriage and the Family among the Yako, *and his "Ethnography of the Yuma Indians" appeared in the University of California "Publications in Ethnology Series." He is the editor of* Africa *and* African Abstracts. *The several figures and tables that appeared in the original version of this article have been omitted here.*

■ Daryll Forde is one of the men most responsible for modern anthropological analysis of the relationships between culture and habitat. His book, *Habitat, Economy, and Society* (New York: Dutton), first published in 1934, helped establish this mode of inquiry in anthropology; it contains descriptions of more than fifteen cultures and their technological adaptations, and it continues to warrant careful study. In this selection Forde describes in careful detail the organization of labor among the Yako of southern Nigeria, a group of horticulturists who subsist almost exclusively on cultivated food and live in very heavily populated villages.

His description again demonstrates that a technology is a particular kind of social system, involving the distribution of village territories and a calendar of work (and therefore leisure and ceremonial activities) as well as principles of land tenure, kin groups, and work groups. The harvest of yams, for example, is more than a man "bringing home the bacon"; it is a complex set of social relationships—the product of technological activities that involve rights, duties, and privileges among husbands and wives and kinsmen related to each other by different principles of affiliation.

Despite their high productivity and density of population, the Yako have not developed a centralized political system. Although their social organization is relatively complex, each ward within their villages enjoys considerable autonomy. In an evolutionary perspective, it is intriguing to speculate whether the Yako would have developed a centralized political system if they had not been conquered by the Europeans. Such questions can rarely be answered definitively. However—the crucial variables of habitat aside—many of the Yako neighbors did create state systems, which suggests that the cultural potential for centralized political organization was widespread throughout the area.

Examples of southern Nigerian societies that developed state systems are described in *The Benin Kingdom and the Edo-speaking Peoples,* by R. E. Bradbury (London: International African Institute, 1957); *A Black Byzantium* (the Nupe), by S. F. Nadel (New York: Oxford University Press, 1942); and *Dahomey and the Slave Trade,* by Karl Polanyi (Seattle: University of Washington Press, 1966). A very good introduction to African societies generally can be found in *Peoples of Africa,* edited by James L. Gibbs, Jr. (New York: Holt, Rinehart and Winston, 1965]. ■

MY FIRST EXPEDITION to the Cross River country in Southern Nigeria in 1935 was made possible by the generosity of the Leverhulme Research Fellowships Fund and by the courtesy of the Nigerian Government, to both of whom my sincere thanks are due. I arrived at Calabar towards the end of July and proceeded up the Cross River by paddle boat to Obubra. After a short reconnaissance of the country lying on either side of the Cross River in the Obubra and Abakaliki Divisions, I decided to work in the Yako village of Umor. My main objective was the investigation of the economic life of a community of hoe cultivators in the West African forest zone, and I was concerned with the relations of this economy to both physical environment and social organization. For this purpose it would be necessary to select a group who would not only assent cheerfully to the sudden appearance of a European resident in their village but would also take kindly to detailed and persistent inquiries concerning that often difficult and dangerous topic—the land. I was also anxious to avoid in this instance a people whose economic life was deeply affected by an external market and whose agriculture and equipment had been extensively modified by the needs and opportunities of modern trade. These conditions were largely met in Umor, and to its people I owe a very great deal for their quick friendliness and their general freedom from suspicion. Although there were inevitable barriers of custom which made some lines of inquiry difficult, I was, so far as ease of human relations was concerned, particularly fortunate in my choice.

The Yako of the Middle Cross River area of Obubra Division live in five compact villages a few miles apart, each of which was formerly autonomous in its political as well as its ritual organization. They have a common tradition that their forebears all came from the east together with the people of Okuni, a settlement some fifty miles away up the Cross River. They were not a river people and had moved overland in several parties and over some years. A distinction is made between those villages in which the original migrants settled—that is, Idomi, where a section of the main group which founded Umor remained, Umor itself, and the separately settled community of Nko—and the remaining villages of Ekuri and Nkpani which are held to have been founded a generation or two later by local migrations, following dissensions, from Umor. Two of the Yako settlements, Umor and Ekuri which lie nearer the river, have grown considerably since the late nineteenth century during a period of increasing commerce and growing security. Umor had, by 1935, become exceptionally large for a single compact community having a population of nearly 11,000. My 1935 estimates of population for the Yako villages were Umor, 10,900; Ekuri, 7,100; Nkpani, 4,400; Nko, 2,600; Idomi, 1,900. A very high

degree of linguistic and cultural homogeneity has been maintained between the villages by a continual interchange of visitors and permanent migrants. But there is no centralized political organization and sporadic, short-lived fighting between villages, particularly between Umor and Ekuri, is said to have occurred in the past.

Yako settlement has been comparatively stable. In the larger and traditionally older villages of Umor and Ekuri the house sites of important ancestors four generations back are pointed out, and there are in places mounds several feet high said to have been formed by superposition of successive house floors. Of the smaller villages, Idomi and Nkpani are held to have been established by migrations from Umor, the latter after a bitter quarrel between two Umor wards. But despite a rapid increase of population over at least the past two generations and the growth of Ekuri and particularly Umor into very large and crowded settlements, there is a very strong tendency for men to remain with their own patrikin. When, as is increasingly common dwelling areas in the village become fully occupied, the pressure is relieved by building hamlets (sing. *kowu*) on the nearest tract of farming land belonging to the group and within half a mile or less of the village. The occupants of these hamlets continue to participate as fully as they can in the life of the main village. With the increase in size of settlements the areas appropriated for cultivation and the collection of forest products have been extended, but the overall density of population has not so far risen high enough to cause deleterious pressure on land. Even in the territory of Umor, where the density is highest, at about 230 per square mile there are still some tracts of unfarmed land.

THE VILLAGE TERRITORY

Umor (lat. 5° 50′ N. long. 8° 10′ E.) is called Ugep by the riverside peoples and is so named on maps and for administrative purposes. The village itself lies 7 miles east of the Cross River and, although only 70 miles north of Calabar in a direct line, is about 120 miles away by river. It is a large compact settlement covering an area of nearly a quarter of a square mile and, like the other Yako villages, is economically and territorially autonomous and has an independent native political organization. Approximately 11,000 people live in Umor, and the territory claimed by the village has an area of 47 square miles, so that the density of population in the village territory as a whole is approximately 230 per square mile. There are at least 4 or 5 square miles of continuous unfarmed forest on the eastern borders and a square mile of uncultivated swamp land in the north-west, but the remainder of the 40 square miles of territory is penetrated by a web of farming paths, which give access to periodically cultivated tracts of land on either side as well as affording routes to neighbouring villages. Farmed land appears rarely to extend to a distance of more than a quarter of a mile from these main paths while it is often restricted to a fringe only 200 yards on either side, so that there are at present numerous islands of uncultivated land between the more widely spaced farming paths. Thus, in accordance with my estimates, the aggregate area of land cleared for cultivation amounts to only 18 square miles, and of this, as will be seen later, a total of only 3 or 4 square miles is actually cultivated in a single year.

The village territory lies athwart a low undulating ridge of Cretaceous sandstone which never rises more than 200 or 300 feet above the level of the Cross River. It is crossed by a multitude of streams which drain broad open valleys aligned roughly parallel with the Cross River, and immediately east of the village a steep cliff face, descended by a precipitous path, overlooks a wide low-lying basin which is drained circuitously by the large Ewiden stream to the Cross River.

CLIMATIC CONDITIONS

The country lies in the northern part of the forest belt of Southern Nigeria, in which there is a clear distinction between wet and dry seasons. From early in April to the end of October there are heavy rains every few days, followed by a dry season of four months during the climax of which, in December and January, the rainfall is negligible. No climate records are available for Umor itself, but rainfall data for a period of thirty-one years down the 1935 are available for Afikpo, a Government station approximately 20 miles to the east. The Afikpo records give a mean annual rainfall of 80.12 inches, of which 71.65 inches fall during the seven rainy months and only 8.47 inches in the remaining months of the year. The rainfall normally rises to a maximum of about 15 inches in September, and in the period 1931-35, for which more complete data were available, there were on the average twenty-one rainy days in this month. In November the rainfall falls away abruptly, although there were at Umor, in 1935, several heavy falls accompanying the violent tornados that are characteristic at this season. December is a month of real drought, while in January and February only occasional light showers occur. Although this regime is normal there is an occasional break in the rains in the middle of the wet season. This was very marked at Afikpo in 1932, when only 1.67 inches fell in July, and it is a feature of the climate well known to the natives, who believe it to be very harmful to the yam crop.

Short-period data (9.0° a.m. and 3.0° p.m. shade readings for 1931-35) for Afikpo show a small annual range of temperature which rises to a 9.0° a.m. monthly mean of 79°F. in March at the end of the dry season with increasing insolation. There is a slight fall in April and May with moderate rains and a marked fall from June to August after the onset of the heavier rains. The mean daily range rises from little over 10°F. in the wet season to nearly 20°F. in the dry season (March 1931-35: 19.1°F.) The relative humidity is high throughout the year in the early morning, and at Afikpo the monthly mean at 9.0° a.m. is rarely below 85 per cent in any month, but 3.0° p.m. readings fall to around 60 per cent in the dry season.

This part of the Cross River region thus lies in the zone of heavy equatorial monsoon rainfall, but the length of the dry season and the period of two months of virtual drought in December and January are likely to affect the composition of the vegetation and the cycle of agricultural activities. The geological and soil conditions over the greater part of the territory of Umor are such as to intensify the effects of the marked dry season, for the Cretaceous sandstone is highly permeable and the soil weathered from it has very low water-holding qualities.

The natural vegetation is dense tropical forest which appears to be transitional from the evergreen forest to the mixed deciduous forest. This is indicated by botanical data from the general region collected by the Nigerian Forestry Department and by the composition of the dense forest tracts round Umor itself.

THE CYCLE OF CULTIVATION

The people of Umor are yam growers; practically every household is a farming unit and the sequence of agricultural tasks and rewards dominates the economic life of the village. The sharp seasonality of rainfall and the moderate natural fertility of the soil are clearly reflected in the agricultural cycle. There is only a single planting at the beginning of the rains each year, and since there is no effective fertilizing, farmland is usually rested for four years after a single harvest has been obtained. Yams, the large tubers of *Discorea* spp., which are the staple food cf the people, constitute by far the largest and most important crop. As all other cultivation is subordinated to the requirements of the yam harvest, the calendar of farm work can best be considered in connection with yam cultivation.

Early in January, after the second moon cycle of the dry season, clearing of the farm lands for the coming season begins. As these tracts have not been cultivated for four years they have grown up into a dense bush of saplings and undergrowth about 20 feet high.

This is cut down by parties of men, whose formation will be described later, and yam hills, mounds hoed up to an initial height of about 2 feet 6 inches and set close together, are made by women or foreign workers as the clearing progresses.

Planting, undertaken jointly by men and women, follows as soon as the first plot or section of hills has been prepared in each farm and it continues as clearing and hilling progresses until the end of April. A number of subsidiary crops such as coco yams (*Colocasia* and/or *Xanthifolia*), maize, okra, pumpkins, and less commonly beans and cassava (*Manihot*), are planted after the yams on the slopes of the yam hills. Small patches of ground nuts are also planted, and round the margins of the farm pepper bushes are transplanted from the previous farming site. The preparation and erection of the stakes and strings for the yam vines rest with the men, but all the subsequent tending of the farm, including the heavy task of a double weeding which continues throughout June, is done by the women.

In July the first crop of an early variety of yam (known as *lidjofi*), which is generally planted in every fifth row of yam hills, is available, but these may not be dug or eaten until after the performance of the First Fruits (*Liboku*) rites which are regarded as essential to the success of the main harvest. Early yams are said to be ready for eating from the middle of June as a rule, but before *Liboku* they can only be dug and brought into the village surreptitiously. From July onwards the women in their daily visits to the farms dig the early yams, as they are needed to feed the household until the main harvest begins in the last weeks of October.

This harvest is stored in great yam stacks, open air barns built on all the farm paths 2 or 3 miles from the village. The stacks are made ready for the harvest by the men in October, while the yams which the men and women have dug together are carried by the women to the streams for washing and then to the stacks. Here they are laid out to dry in the sun for a week or two before the men tie them in the stack. When the yam stacks have been filled the cycle is complete and there is a short lull in farm work until the clearing for the next year begins.

Farm crops are not the sole vegetable products obtained through the year. Supplies of bananas, plantains, kola nuts, native pears (*Pachylobis edulis*), pawpaws, and coconuts are obtained from groves of planted trees laid out along the farming paths, round the yam stacks, and in the village. The tending of these trees is entirely in the hands of the men, about half of whom are also daily engaged in exploiting the outstanding wild food plant of the forest—the oil palm, from which oil, kernel nuts and sap-wine are obtained.

PROBLEMS AND FIELD METHODS

The rhythm of agricultural activities just outlined will be recognized as characteristic of many parts of the forest belt of the Guinea coast, and my object here is not a detailed discussion of the technique of cultivation but a preliminary analysis of the organization of labour, and the consideration of that organization in relation to the resources of the territory and the production and distribution of the food supply and other wealth. In the course of my field work I made a census of the agricultural and other economic activities of about one hundred households, obtaining data on the composition of the household, the lands farmed, the crops grown, the division of labour, and the size of the harvest.

The effective study of the economic activities of primitive peoples demands more systematic and objective data than have hitherto been commonly obtained. Discussion of the efficiency of native methods and the limitations of physical conditions on the one hand, and of the relation between economic activities and social institutions on the other, cannot be securely based on general impressions or even on more detailed knowledge of a few individual cases, when such matters as division and intensity of labor, volumes of production, and accumulation and distribution of food supplies and materials are involved. But very real difficulties face the eth-

nographer here. He works alone in an area for which there has been no land survey, with maps, if any, that are only most approximate and small scale, among people whose numbers have been only most roughly estimated, if at all, and whose measures of time, value, and area are difficult to assess in objective terms. The people may be extremely suspicious of minute and systematic inquiries into their numbers, customary land rights, wealth, and property, and may refuse or falsify information. Data approaching the scope and accuracy of those obtainable for a western country could only be secured with the aid of a considerable party of surveyors and investigators; and such a procedure might well defeat its own ends by arousing suspicion and hostility, which would frustrate any investigation of other related problems in which everything depended on the good will and confidence of informants.

Nevertheless it is often possible with resourceful use of the local standards of value and knowledge, and with approximate, even if unorthodox, methods of survey to achieve reasonably accurate estimates in the economic and demographic field. I therefore devoted some considerable time to attempts to work out and employ methods for assessing quantitatively the economic conditions and activities in Umor, which would be feasible with the cooperation of the people themselves and would yield in a relatively short period results adequate for ethnographic and statistical analysis.

FARM AREAS

The farm lands in Umor are held by adult men individually and a man of middle age will have established and recognized rights to half a dozen sets of plots. Only one-fifth of the aggregate area is, however, cultivated in any one year while the rest remains in bush. One of my earliest tasks in Umor was that of finding a method of estimating with reasonable accuracy the size of these farm plots. Owing to the reluctance of their occupiers, the time required, and the difficulties of movement and sighting among the yam vines, it was impossible to make an instrumental survey of a sufficient number of farms to obtain adequate data on area and productivity. But the nature of the cultivation and the laying out of the farms in Umor permitted safe generalization as to the mean area and variation of farm areas. The process of clearing, hoeing, and planting farmlands proceeds piecemeal on each plot as the collective labour of a group of kinsmen becomes available to each individual in turn. A party of a dozen or so men clears a small stretch of bush day by day for each of their number in turn. These sections are hoed and planted by the women as they are cleared. The boundary between sections is marked and every man knows how many sections he has planted and the relative size of each. Further, the yam hills are made very methodically row by row across each section, forming an approximate rectangle, and since the number of yam hills on two sides in each section could be readily counted, an estimate of the number of hills could be quickly reached. The mean area of the individual farms of 97 adult able-bodied men of one patrilineal kin group (the Ndai *kepun*) obtained in this way was approximately 1½ acres (1.40), the equivalent of 2,440 yam hills. Thus a representative Umor household of a man, two wives, and three or four children is likely to have about 7 or 8 acres of farming land at its disposal, of which 1½ acres are cultivated each year. The estimated aggregate area of farm land in Umor (a minimum of 18 square miles, of which 3.6 are actually under cultivation in a given year) is obtained by the application of these results to the total adult male population. The Ndai kin group consisted of five sub-groups or lineages of closer kinsmen in which the number of farm holders ranged from 16 to 27. The means for the farms of these component lineages lie fairly close to the general mean, and some knowledge of conditions in other kin groups also indicated that a fair sample had been obtained. But the areas of individual Ndai farms cultivated in 1935 ranged widely from 0.25 to 8 acres. Although only five of the 97 were 4 acres or more and

only ten were less than 0.5 acres in area, there was a large group, about 40 per cent of the total and not confined to the farms of young recently married men, which lay well below the average (between 0.5 and 1 acre in area).

. . . The size of the farms of a few individuals, which appreciably raise the mean for the group, was very surprising. There were five farms of 4 acres or more and they were in some cases disproportionate to the size of the household. The larger farms were, as in the case of the exceptional 8-acre farms, those which provided most of the surplus sold outside the village and contributed to the considerable Cross River trade in yams. The adult strength of a household farming unit will obviously set limits to the area which can be cultivated, but the area of farms was found to bear no simple relation to the size of the household, whether considered as a farming unit of adults or a consuming unit including minors. Many other factors, such as interest in trading and hunting, seed yams available for planting, the capacity of the man and women, and the services of kinsmen, all affect the farm area of individual households. The people themselves are well aware of differences in farming capacity among both men and women. A youth is often told to choose as his wife a girl whose mother goes early to farm, while some of the elders often remarked that so-and-so did not care enough about seeing his yam stack grow bigger.

It is very significant, in view of the large stores of food that chiefs and leaders of social groups are said to accumulate among many peoples, that none of the very large farms in this kin group belonged to kin group leaders and priests or to heads of associations, who might be expected to have a special claim on the services of a wider circle of kinsmen or supporters. Indeed the priest-head of the Ndai group had a farm of only 1.2 acres, less than the average for the group as a whole, while that of his assistant was little above the average. It was clear from other instances that there is little tendency in Umor for men of prestige and authority to accumulate a large surplus of yams or other food supplies and marketable products, either by making large farms or by receiving gifts of these from others.

THE SIZE OF HARVEST

At the end of the farming season I undertook a census of the yam harvest of the ninety-seven farms whose area I had estimated. This was based on a native practice which lent itself to numerical estimation. At harvest-time the yams are stored in the stacks by tying them to raffia midribs or long stakes, each 10 or 12 feet high, set close together on the solid timber frame. The harvested yams, when they have been sunned, are graded according to size for greater ease in handling and are tied in neat, close-packed, vertical rows to the poles, so that they form a solid wall of yams 8 to 10 feet high. Every person refers to his yam harvest by stating the number of upright sticks which he has tied with yams. Such an estimate may be rather misleading because the actual size of the harvest will vary according to the height of the sticks and the bulk of the yams. In addition to the large yam tubers a number of small yams, sometimes attached to the neck of the main growth, are formed, and these small yams, often little larger than a big potato, are used extensively for planting in the ensuing year. At the harvest of 1935 I found that the greater part of the larger yams were between 9 inches and 12 inches long and that very few exceeded 18 inches in length, while the small yamlets ranged from 2 to 6 inches in length. A closer estimate of the bulk of the harvest was made possible by counting the number of sticks in each of three sizes (under 6 inches, 6 to 12 inches, and over 12 inches), and by obtaining at each harvest stack a mean value for the number of yams on the sticks in each size group. In terms of units of medium-sized yams the mean production for the 97 farms investigated was 2,545. The individual harvests ranged from a single exceptionally low value of 235 to a maximum of 11,410 units of medium-sized yams.

It will be observed that, while the harvest variation is of the same general character as that for farm area, an even larger percentage of farms falls in the lower class intervals, which suggests that a considerable number of farms of more than average size do not yield a correspondingly large harvest. This is to be expected, since yield will be considerably affected by care in cultivation, and the household data indicate that there are a considerable number of farms of more than average size with relatively low labour power as measured by the number of adult members. In such farms there would tend to be some falling off in efficiency of cultivation. This cannot, however, be directly concluded from the graph and must be determined from a consideration of all the data concerning the households.

As the size of the farms and the bulk of the harvest have been estimated independently, reliability of the estimates can be tested by investigating their correlation. Despite differences in fertility and in efficiency of cultivation, a high correlation between size of farm and bulk of harvest is to be expected for the series as a whole. . . .

KINSHIP BASIS OF FARMLAND RIGHTS

The farm and harvest data discussed above relate to one of the patrilineal kin groups in Umor through which men acquire rights to farmlands. Each patrilineal kin group or *kepun* (plural, *yepun*), which has collective rights to a delimited dwelling area in the village, has also rights to a number of tracts of farming land. The number and strength of the *yepun* in Umor cannot be stated definitely, for there are several quasi-*yepun* which lack one or more characteristic features, but from the point of view of farming rights there are about 30 kin groups ranging in size from 30 to nearly 200 adult men and their households. At the same time the *yepun* fall into larger territorial groups concerning which there is no principle of internal kinship. These larger groupings are wards (*yekpatu*) of the village, and it is on a ward basis that the village territory is primarily divided, since the patrilineal kin groups of the different wards as a rule share a number of common farming paths. . . . The people of the four wards thus farm lands lying in great blocks round the village; but the lands of the kin groups within a ward are as a rule considerably intermingled.

Large tracts of land, each a square mile or more in extent, lying along the farm roads are known by names usually referring to some natural feature, and their boundaries are known to all farming on these roads. But these named lands appear to be largely functionless with regard to property rights and are no longer the basis on which land is shared among the *yepun*. The control of land by the men of a particular kin group is subject to slow but continual change by processes of piecemeal accumulation or abandonment. For each farm road used by a *kepun* there is a 'farm path elder' (*oponotam eta*), who is expected to know the established rights of all individuals of his *kepun* on that road, to mediate in any disputes between those individuals, and to act as spokesman in disputes with other *yepun*. In general the majority of the men of a single lineage within a *kepun* farm on the same path—often in a cluster of contiguous plots in each year—and the path elder is often a leading member of the lineage which provides the majority of the *kepun* members farming from that path. He is thus a close kinsman of the majority of the kin group concerned.

The kinship basis of farmland tenure does not, however, completely circumscribe the farming rights of the individual. In the first place individuals or small groups of relatives are able, if welcomed, to migrate from their own *kepun* area in the village and go to live in the dwelling area of another *kepun,* and may, without formal adoption, be given farming sites in the lands of that *kepun.* A man may also obtain temporary rights to make a farm in the land of another kin group. This is fairly often done where the man's own *kepun* is short of lands of the particular road he has elected to farm. He visits a path elder of another *kepun* (generally on the same path)

which has a surplus and asks to be shown a tract which he may clear. A large gourd of palm wine must accompany such requests, when he visits the path elder in his house towards sundown. No other payment or gift is made for this right, but it can only be obtained by this formal recognition of the owning *kepun's* right and an appeal to its generosity. This is a very characteristic Yako attitude. Few economic opportunities are bought and sold, but there is great emphasis on correct form of procedure, and on open recognition of favour.

If serious pressure develops on the farming land, new and permanent farming paths are opened. These are as a rule only shallow loops from the main paths. Considerable labour is involved in opening up such paths and in keeping them clear of vegetation. Every year, as will be seen, large parties are formed to clear the farming paths at the opening of the new season, and despite the daily passage to and fro of people going to their farms a second clearing is often needed towards the end of the rainy season. Most of the old-established paths have been used so long that the daily passage of human feet has worn a gully in the soft sandstone 5 or 6 feet below the level of the surrounding ground which may become a torrent after heavy rains.

A man first takes up farmland when he marries: that is, when he first brings a wife to live with him in an independent household. Before this he has helped his father, and his prospective father-in-law. The provision of an elaborately coiled bundle of yam tying strings and a season's work in the farm is an important obligation of a youth to his prospective father-in-law. In his first year of farming the youth usually receives a part of his father's farm land. If the father needs to replace part of the ceded land he, not the son, goes to the path elder of his *kepun* to ask for and establish his claim to an unoccupied area.

In the first year the young man will probably farm only one or two sections of about one-quarter of an acre in total area. For the next two or three years he may continue to receive part of his father's farm plots as these are successively cleared for cultivation, while his father will as before recoup himself elsewhere if necessary; but after three or four years of farming he will endeavour to increase the area of his farm, both because there will by now, with average harvests, be a larger surplus of yams for planting in the coming year, and because he may already be taking a second wife. For his first year's farm the young man usually obtains his seed yams for planting from his parents, half a dozen sticks from his father and two or three from his mother. If his parents are poor or dead he will seek gifts from other close kinsmen. His wife will receive two or three sticks from her father and one or two from her mother, and she will get from her mother her supply of the early yams which belong entirely to women.

These two sources of planting yams—the man's and the wife's—are recognized as distinct, and the harvests they yield remain so throughout, for it is an important principle of Yako farming that the husband and wife each have their own yams. Yams although they are the staple food play no part in marriage payments and both parties to the new household thus bring their own farming capital.

It is necessary to emphasize here that, while the division of farm tasks is applicable to the farm as a whole, the yams of the man and his wives are planted and dug separately and are tied on distinct groups of sticks in the harvest stack. The husbands and wives have distinctive marks, which they incise on the base of their yams as they are dug at harvest time, and the yam harvest of both is used to maintain the family according to well-established rules. The husband's yams are usually completely dug, washed, and sunned first. He then proceeds to dig some yams for each of his wives every day that he is in the farm. During the period of digging, sunning, and tying, which lasts about two moons, food yams are taken from the husband's or the wives' supplies according to whichever is being handled at the time. When the yams are being tied each wife also takes the equivalent of one stick, say thirty medium-sized yams, equally from her own and her husband's

heaps. These are tied separately and are for food in the period immediately after the harvest, that is, from about the end of December, and when they are exhausted, the wife is expected to use two sticks of her own yams for household food, before asking for a stick of yams from her husband. These four sticks of yams (120 or so medium-sized yams) are considered to be sufficient for the wife, her children, and her share of the food provided for her husband for two moons (late December to late February). By this time bush-clearing for the new farm is well advanced, and before a wife asks her husband for another stick of his yams, she should have begun to make yam hills on the first section of the new farm. When this fifth stick is exhausted at the beginning of March, yam planting should have begun and the woman can then use the tips of the planting yams for food as well as the good parts of any decaying yams she may find on the sticks.

Hill making and planting generally occupy nearly two moons and after that, from late in April until the new yams may be dug in the latter part of July, the household must depend on a surplus of unplanted yams left in the stack. The area planted may therefore be limited by the minimum food requirements for these three moons, and inefficient cultivators find it hard to increase their farm areas on account of their very limited surplus after planting each year. In 1935 Ubi Okoi of Ndai, who had a farm of 2 acres with two wives, two young children, and one dependent relative (a youth who helped him in farm work and was fed by his senior wife), had tied 100 sticks of yams of his own at the previous harvest. His two wives had 40 and 16 sticks of harvest yams, a total of 156 sticks. Eighteen of these were used for food in January and February, 125 were used for planting and eating in March and April, and after planting he was left with eight sticks himself and his wives had three and two sticks for food until late July. Ubi gave four sticks to one wife, two to the other, and had two for feeding visitors during the three months before new yams were available.

While I heard nothing of serious famines in

the past among the Yako and most households are able to keep an adequate, if not lavish, supply of yams for food in the period after planting, only a small minority regularly have a considerable surplus beyond this. For these there is a ready market both in the village, among those who need more yams for planting, and also in the riverside villages of the lower Cross River and at Calabar itself. It should be noted that a man can sell only his own yams, and a wife's surplus is similarly her own.

The early yams, which provide food for three months from mid-July, are almost always the property of the women. A woman receives a small supply at marriage from her mother and she is entitled to plant them in every fifth row of hills in each section of the farm, including those sections that are otherwise planted with her husband's yams. From July to November about a fifth of the year's crop is thus removed from the farm. Although these early yams are normally the property of the women they are used to feed the entire household during this later part of the farming season.

GROUP LABOR IN FARM CLEARING

It is now necessary to review the farm cycle again and consider the special arrangement made for different phases of farm work. Both before the planting and the harvest each year the farm roads and the narrow paths leading to the lands have to be cleared. This is effected by obligatory co-operative labour. The path elders of the different kin groups farming on a road ask the ward heads to announce the day, and parties set out before daybreak working outwards from the village, cutting back the bush on the main road. These consist of all the able-bodied age-sets of the ward. When this has been done, smaller groups of men who propose to farm adjacent plots in different areas clear the branch paths giving access to their lands. Fines may be imposed on able-bodied men who refuse to

co-operate and one or two days is generally enough to complete the work.

The clearing of bush from the new farmlands is men's work, and it is also the occasion of cooperative labor. Farms are nearly always cleared and planted by stages in approximately rectangular sections, which vary according to the labour available from 200 or 300 up to 3,000 square yards, although exceptionally large sections made only by older men with numerous sons and helpers may extend to over 5,000 square yards. A party of a dozen men or more can clear a moderate section in a morning. Working parties are formed by the group labor of parties constituted within the *yepun*. Each man wanting a party to work on his farm goes to the *kepun* head bearing a calabash of palm wine and expresses his desire. This is generally done at an informal meeting in the compound of the *kepun* head or in the *kepun* assembly house at the opening of the farming season. All *kepun* members have an obligation to help for one day and they later go to the house of the applicant to make final arrangements. These *kepun* parties usually work only in the morning and on market, i.e. non-farming, days, and the man whose farm is being cleared provides a mid-day meal of baked yams in the farm. The Yako have a six-day week of which the second and fifth days are market and ceremonial days and the others farming days. It is a general rule that services in public and cooperative work and other group activities should not be demanded on farming days, and most rituals, whether of the *yepun,* clubs or other groups, are also generally confined to non-farming days.

The number of individuals taking part in the bush-clearing groups, in the farms of one Ndai lineage alone, ranged from 5 to 50, but the number usually lay between 12 and 30. A man who intends to make a farm of some three acres or more will need the services of four or more of these parties, but an attempt at fair rotation is made by the *kepun* head and the path elders. Claimants can be called on to give their own services or those of their older sons to those who have helped them on an equal number of occasions. At farm-clearing time there may be lively disputes as to priority in receiving parties and reciprocity of services. In practice strict reciprocity is not expected or obtained, and as a rule it only becomes a point in debate when disputes arise on some other head. *Kepun* bush parties are usually enjoyed for their own sake, and since a minority of farms greatly exceed the average area there are always a few men who will need more help than can be required of them in turn. But if they offer a meal and a generous supply of palm wine later, they will not as a rule lack helpers from among their kinsmen who have few yams. If a man requires more help than he can readily get from *kepun* parties, or if a man is at odds with his fellow *kepun* members concerning his rights and obligations either in the actual clearing or in connection with some quite different matter, and therefore refuses to take part in the *kepun* clearing parties, he has recourse to reciprocal parties of friends. These friends are as a rule farming a group of adjacent plots but are not necessarily members of the same kin group. Such a party generally numbers only about half a dozen men and successively clears sections of each member's farm, until the work is completed. Several instances occurred in Ndai of individuals who took little or no part on the *kepun* parties and relied on these parties of friends.

The clearing parties merely hack down the saplings and bush, and grub up the larger roots; the occupier often has to spend several farming days on a section of average size, digging out the mass of smaller roots and laying the land quite bare. Ten to fifteen days later he burns the dried vegetation which has been piled up in a number of heaps. Here again the services of a few helpers are needed, and men farming adjacent plots commonly help each other in starting and controlling the fires. Charred wood is cleared off and often carried back to the village, and the making of yam hills proceeds immediately after the ashes have been scattered over the section.

The hoeing of yam hills is traditionally women's work and in ordinary circumstances no Yako men undertake it. But for nearly a generation now parties of "strangers" visit Umor at this time and share in this work as paid labourers. These foreign labourers are Ezza Ibo living west of the Cross River, among whom a considerably greater share of the farm labour is done by men. Parties of young men arrive at Umor in January and may stay for two months or more. They are hired by individuals, usually in parties of from five to thirty, and may work on one farm for from two to ten days. In 1935 they were being given their food, shelter, and 2d. per day.

MINOR CROPS

After the yam planting—carried out jointly by the man and his wives in the intervals of clearing and hilling, and usually without help from outside—the farm work devolves almost entirely on the women. They plant between and on the sides of the yam hills the minor crops of maize, coco-yams, okra, pumpkins, and beans which are left entirely to their care. These minor crops afford welcome variety in a diet consisting so largely of yams. A capable wife is expected to be able to offer her husband dishes in which corn, okra, and other minor crops are used, and small supplies of most of these crops are stored—often in the house—after the harvest. On the other hand the people are aware that hills overloaded with minor plantings are likely to yield poorly in yams and fairly strict limits are set to this interculture.

From May to September the women work their way through the farm removing the weeds that rapidly spring up. The whole farm should be weeded twice and a third weeding is needed if a late ripening variety of bean, gathered a month or more after the yam harvest, is grown. Ground-nuts, which are also valued as a relish, gourds whose fruit cases are used to make a variety of receptacles, and cassava, which is generally regarded as a foreign and insipid yam substitute, are, however, planted by men. Ground-nuts often occupy a separate corner or the end of the last section of the yam farm and are planted in long wide ridges after the fashion of Hausa ground-nut cultivation in Northern Nigeria.

Although the amounts grown are small, most of these minor crops are raised on the majority of farms, and only cassava, sugar cane, the later ripening curly bean (*okpoma*) and the flat bean (*kekpomababali*), said to have been recently introduced, are absent from the majority of farms.

HARVEST LABOR

The labor involved at harvest in the digging, carrying, washing, and stacking of yams may be indicated by the actual numbers of yams tied in the stacks. In Ndai in 1935 the totals (for yams of all sizes) ranged from 350 in the case of a young man farming for the first time to 11,400, the harvest of an exceptionally large household from a farm of 8 acres. The mean was nearly 4,000 per household and the average number of yams handled was over 2,500 per acre of farm land.

OIL PALMS

While the farm plots are by far the most productive areas of the village territory and demand the greatest expenditure of labour, they are not the only economically productive areas. In addition to a wide variety of materials for food and crafts, collected on a small scale from the bush, the products of the wild oil palm are obtained regularly in large quantities throughout the year. About half the able-bodied men of Umor are daily engaged in obtaining palm wine and palm fruits, while the fronds are also collected in large quantities for house roofing. The oil palm grows abundantly throughout the territory and is left standing when land is cleared for farming. Rights to oil palms are acquired through patrilineal kin groups, each of which collectively claims the oil palms in tracts of territory reached from the farming paths. These tracts are not limited to the lands that are periodically farmed by the kin group but may extend into uncultivated areas, and there may apparently be considerable discrepancies between farming and oil palm rights. In detail the groups of palms actually exploited are constantly changing according to the yield and the convenience of their situation. Each man desires palms that are fairly easily accessible on his journeys to and from his farm, but side tracks have often to be kept open in the dense bush to reach them. Usually groups of two or three men co-operate to make a path into a promising and convenient area, settling their claims to particular palms by agreement.

A distinction is, however, recognized between palms tapped for wine and those from which fruit is collected. Palm wine—the fermented sap obtained by piercing the flower stalk and attaching a collecting calabash—has to be collected twice daily and considerable labor is involved in each tapping of an inflorescence which yields for only a month or so. To obtain about a gallon of palm wine some six to ten trees have to be climbed twice a day. Trees that are being tapped, have been prepared for tapping, or are being rested for three moons or so after tapping, are claimed by those who have worked on them and should not be interfered with by others. The owner generally places some leaves in a cut in the truck near the ground to indicate that it is reserved to himself. An individual can, however, cut palm fruits anywhere in his *kepun* palm land so long as he does not interfere with the tapped palms of others. In practice most individuals collect fruits in a tract round their current tapping area, and since there is a surplus of fruits there are few disputes. Surreptitious cutting of accessible palm fruits by men from other *yepun* is said, however, to be more frequent. Among 103 men of the Ndai kin group, 50 were tapping palms for wine and 48 were collecting fruit. In nearly all cases part of the product was sold in the village.

TRADE IN PALM OIL AND KERNELS

The preparation of palm oil is a household matter shared between men and wives. It is done at convenient intervals when a sufficient supply of fruits has been collected. Although the extraction of the oil is, apart from the pulping of the fruits, carried out by the wives, the oil, save for household requirements, belongs to the men alone. The wives receive as their share the nuts which they and the children crack to extract the kernels for sale.

The relatively small quantities of oil and kernels produced in the individual households are bought by one or other of the twenty or so men in the village who devote themselves to trading. Using kerosene tins with graduated dipsticks to measure the amount of oil, the traders endeavour to adjust their payments to the prices they are likely to receive at Ediba on the Cross River or in Calabar. In Umor oil trading is regarded as a specialized and somewhat risky business, and very few oil traders have practically given up farming to devote all their time to the trade. When traders think that the price offered at Ediba is too low they may have their oil carried by canoe to Calabar, where they can offer it to a number of competing firms.

Since nearly half the men of Umor are producing palm oil, which is their only important source of money, the fluctuations in wholesale prices, which have been very great in recent years, have had a considerable effect on the purchasing power of trade goods and on the tax-paying ability of the people. Ediba prices for a kerosene tin of oil ranged from 1/1d. to 3/3d. in the twelve months from November 1934, and the highest price was of course far below that of the boom period. It is difficult to estimate the amount of palm oil exported from Umor, but nearly 200 tons of oil reach the Cross River from this region and Umor is likely to produce some 60 to 70 tons a year, which at 1935 prices would have a value of only £400 to £500.

Trade in palm kernels is a more widespread venture and a considerable number of the younger men engage in it. They often get their wives and older children to go about the village offering to purchase kernels by the cupful. When a man has got together one or two bags he takes them to the river for sale. About 1,000 tons of kernels reach the Cross River from the Yako villages every year, and of this the likely share of Umor, 400 to 500 tons, was worth about £2,500. There are,

however, more women selling kernels than men selling oil in Umor and probably two or three times as many kernel traders.

There are approximately 1,500 households in Umor, so that their mean money income from the palm oil production of the village is probably slightly more than two pounds. This income is however very unequally distributed in the village.

The other forms of external trade are concerned both with an entirely native product— smoked bush meat—and with European trade goods, particularly cloth and cutlery. It should be noted that as the one involves long journeys into the forest of Agoi to the east where game is abundant, and the other frequent visits to Calabar and Port Harcourt for European goods, this trading is more specialized and time consuming than that in palm products. Although oil traders occasionally buy cloth in Calabar for sale on their return to Umor, this combination is not common, and the cloth and cutlery traders are for the most part young men who enjoy frequent visits to the coast and often return with an assortment of personal luxuries ranging from scented soap to cricket blazers.

HUNTING

A considerable number of Umor men hunt in the forest tracts and farm bush in the village territory. Game is taken in a variety of spring traps set along the paths and round the farms and is also shot with Dane guns—the long-barrelled flint locks that are widely used in Southern Nigeria. While a number of duiker and other forest buck and small game (of which the more common are lemurs, genets, civets, porcupine and the pangolin or scaly ant-eater) are obtained, this source of meat is very small in relation to the total population. Smoked bush meat brought in from Agoi is always available in the market, but the effective demand is apparently low, for only small quantities are usually displayed and it is only on the occasion of feasts of kin groups and associations that it is seen in large quantities. Organized hunting appears to have been more active a generation ago. There is still, however, an association of hunters in each ward which resorts periodically to a hunting camp in the bush and plays a part in ceremonials.

LIVESTOCK

Livestock do not contribute very substantially to the food supply. The Southern Nigerian dwarf cattle are found in Umor but there were only 32 head of cattle in the possession of 103 men of Ndai in 1935, which suggests that the entire village stock is little more than 500, and some of this is sold every year to Ibo who visit Umor to obtain cattle for their title feasts. Goats are more than twice as numerous and are a common food at feasts, the excellence of which is judged by the amount of meat provided. There are practically no sheep, although neighbouring villages have them, and the pigs which foul some of the other Yako settlements are not numerous in Umor. In fact the chickens and occasional ducks are the only livestock that are at all common: there were on the average nearly two per household in Ndai kin group. There is little doubt therefore that the Yako diet is poor in animal proteins, for meat is normally available only in minute quantities as a relish, and the local fish supply is negligible. Imported stockfish is however brought for sale to the village market.

LAND RIGHTS OF MATRILINEAL GROUPS

The land rights and labor services so far considered all take their rise from the collective claims and activities of the patrilineal kin groups—the *yepun*—and of their larger aggregations—the wards. But the patrilineal principle is not all-pervading among the Yako. There is also a matrilineal organization of great importance in the village government and responsible for rituals of greater prestige than those performed at the *yepun* shrines. Furthermore, while individual claims to eco-

nomic resources are usually established within the patrilineal kin group, the greater part of accumulated wealth and movable property is inherited by matrilineal kinsmen. This practice controls among other things the disposal of the yam harvests of men and women when they die and may involve matrilineal relatives in obligations to supply labor in a farm to complete the cycle of cultivation of a deceased kinsmen. The structure and significance of the groups of matrilineal kin groups thus formed are discussed below.

The economic rights of matrilineal kin groups may also, in certain circumstances, override those of the patrilineal groups, for the former lay certain claims to tracts of land which are at the same time cultivated and exploited by the *yepun*. At the funeral rites of an elder the dead man's matrilineal kinsmen can enter their tract and take wine from any or all of the tapped oil palms, despite the fact that these palms have been prepared by men who are not their kinsmen and who at all other times have exclusive rights to the palms, which they could defend in the village court. In these same tracts the valuable raffia palm may be planted in swampy ground by members of the matrilineal group, and these cannot be claimed either by the patrilineal kin group farming there or by patrilineal descendants of the planter. More recently the matrilineal groups have established a claim to the village share of the royalty fees which now have to be paid for felling within their lands certain valuable timber trees scheduled by the Forestry Department. As the patrilineal and matrilineal land rights coexist over the same territory, and the boundary lines of the divisions do not coincide, there is an intricate dual mosaic of established rights to the resources of the village territory.

Although no farming rights or duties normally derive from the matrilineal kin organization, that system is nevertheless closely associated with the general prosperity of agriculture. Three village rituals each year—the First Planting rites, the First Fruits or New Yam feast (*Liboku* rites), and the Harvest rites—are all performed by the priests at the spirits of the matrilineal kin groups, and it is the response of these which is sought for the prosperity of cultivation.

CONCLUSION

Although the basic economic activities in Umor operate within a framework of established rights of kin groups, these are not simple or comprehensive in character. Rights to farm land are acquired through member ship in the patrilineal *kepun*, but the area of the farm and the co-operation of the kinsmen are subject to but slight group control, and the farm once planted is regarded as household property into which a fellow *kepun* member will not lightly enter lest his motives be misconstrued. There are great contrasts in farming prosperity among the individual members of a kin group, which are reflected in the ability of individuals to pay for membership in the village associations. Similarly the establishment of rights to bush products within the *kepun* lands is left to the initiative of individuals or small groups. At the same time specific but more restricted claims are made to the resources of the territory by kin groups of an entirely different order.

The *kepun* organization of farming activities involves some obligation of mutual assistance in path and bush clearing but little or none in other farming activities. In times of misfortune, indeed, it is to the matrilineal kin as often as to the *kepun* that the distressed individual or household turns. A man who through sickness or absence cannot attend to his farm is likely to ask a younger matrilineal kinsman for help in caring for his farm. The rights of matrilineal kin to inherit the greater part of a man's movable property are but a partial explanation of this attitude. The sentiment of matrilineal kinship, perhaps because it is not subject, owing to territorial dispersion, to the day to day rivalries and differences within the *kepun*, is surprisingly strong. Within the *kepun* there is marked individualism, and except on ceremonial occasions few effective demands can be made on the individual for the benefit of *kepun* fellows outside his lineage.

There is not at present in Umor any severe competition for land or forest products, for the village has adequate territory. The continuance of the great increase in population that can be inferred from village expansion in the last two generations may eventually result in land hunger if other sources of wealth are not developed, but assuming no basic change in the present economy, the population could probably increase by another 50 per cent before severe strains would show. The need in Umor, however, are so generally in Southern Nigeria, is not a further increase in density of population but modifications in economy which will improve the quality and variety of the food supply of the West African, a need from which arise the most important social and scientific problems of the country.

14. THE SEGMENTARY LINEAGE: AN ORGANIZATION OF PREDATORY EXPANSION

MARSHALL D. SAHLINS

Reprinted from American Anthropologist, *63 (1961): 322-43. Marshall D. Sahlins is Professor of Anthropology, University of Michigan. His principal research interests are cultural ecology, primitive economics, and peoples of the Pacific. He is the author of* Social Stratification in Polynesia, Evolution and Culture *(with Elman R. Service and others),* Moala: Culture and Nature of a Fijian Island, Tribesmen, *and* Stone Age Economics.

■ As we have seen, the habitat to which people must adapt is multi-faceted. In this selection Sahlins expands the concept of habitat to include a social dimension: the presence or absence of neighboring groups. He contends that (all other things—such as technology and natural factors in the habitat—being equal) a group's organization of social relations will be strongly affected by having come as the first settlers in an area (and thus not being surrounded by other groups) or as intruders into the midst of other groups.

The organization of social relations that Sahlins examines is the "segmentary lineage" in tribal societies. By "tribal" Sahlins means a level of sociopolitical development that is midway between the band and the chiefdom; this level includes most stateless farmers and pastoralists. Segmentation, which Sahlins treats as an adaptation to specific pressures, refers to the fact that each segment of a society is an autonomous replica of all the others, without centralization of control. This replication denotes organizations of people, not necessarily numbers of people, which can vary greatly in each of the segments.

A tribal society, as Sahlins uses the phrase, is a collection of kinship and residential units larger than those found in bands; tribal segments are criss-crossed by other kinds of groupings, such as clans, age-grade associations, curing societies, war groupings, and secret societies. The segments are economically as well as politically autonomous.

Sahlins finds that the segmentary lineage is an adaptive form taken by a tribal society when it settles in an area that is already inhabited by other groups. Under these conditions, for reasons he discusses, the segment of a lineage becomes the decision-making unit. However, segments often unite to form larger decision-making and implementing units. The frequency with which segments unite depends on social rather than physical conditions in the habitat: the presence of habitually aggressive neighbors or the existence of a group on which it is possible to prey and at whose expense the segment can expand. If there is no pressure to establish a confederated defense or offense there will be little inclination on the part of the segments to unite. There are several types of lineage segmentation, but Sahlins concentrates on what he calls the "Tiv-Nuer segmentary lineage system."

Besides illustrating the concept that a group's organization of social relations is an integral aspect of its adaptation to social as well as physical pressures in the habitat, Sahlins points to another important lesson. It is not enough to say that a society is characterized by one or another type of organization to which we have given a name (clan, lineage, village, or social class); although these designations are not without value, it is also necessary to determine what people *do* with these groupings in their everyday lives. What we often designate as a "lineage," as Sahlins makes clear, does not operate in the same way in the lives of all people. This caution also should apply to those who use such terms as extended family, secret society, or initiation ceremony to describe modern industrial societies.

The reader who wants to learn more about Nuer culture should consult *The Nuer*, by E. E. Evans-Pritchard (New York: Oxford University Press, 1940). One of the best-known ethnographic monographs (and deservedly so), it provides a systematic attempt to relate the organization of social relationships to the total adaptation of a people. An excellent introduction to Tiv culture is *Return to Laughter*, by Eleanor Smith Bowen (Laura Bohannan) (New York: Harper, 1954), which is a fictionalized account by a contemporary ethnographer. In *Voyagers of the Vitiaz Strait: A Study of New Guinea Trading System* (Seattle: University of Washington, 1967), Thomas G. Harding applies Sahlins' basic concepts to show how intergroup relations intertwine with factors of the habitat to stimulate and also set limits on adaptations in northeastern New Guinea that are based both on horticulture and large-scale trading. ∎

THERE HAS BEEN A BROAD inclination in social anthropology in recent years to apply the designations "segmentary system" and "segmentary process" to a wide variety of societies. Only slightly narrower is the application of the concept to lineages or societies with lineages. While granting certain general similarities in all the organizations popularly called "segmentary lineage," it seems more useful to restrict the term to a very few societies, most notably the Nuer and the Tiv.

The argument can be made on purely formal grounds: Tiv and Nuer are in critical respects organized differently from other societies that have been placed in the category "segmentary lineage system." Thus, in *Tribes Without Rulers*, Middleton and Tait were moved to classify Tiv and Nuer—along with Lugbara, which seems inaccurate—as a *subtype* of segmentary lineage systems, at one point as the "classical" variety of such systems. But the type can also be considered in an evolutionary perspective: Tiv-Nuer, the segmentary lineage organization properly so-called, is a specific adaptive variety within the tribal level of society and culture. (The criteria of "tribal level" and the meaning of "specific adaptive variety" will be spelled out below).

This evolutionary perspective is adopted here because it furnishes a practical basis for distinguishing Tiv-Nuer from other "segmentary" societies and, at the same time, it has the power to suggest the circumstances which produce segmentary lineage organization, to "explain" it, at least partly. Conversely—and contrary to the vision of Radcliffe-Brown for a comparative-structural approach—formalism alone has only tended to obscure the salient characteristics of the segmentary lineage organization. Focusing on such general structural and functional resemblances as "segmentation" and "complementary opposition," the formal definition of "segmentary lineage" threatens to become as broad as the formal view of the "lineage" itself. For segmentation and complementary opposition are very widespread—nearly universal—features of human social organization. It is then no wonder that Tiv and Nuer have been lumped with societies that virtually run the evolutionary gamut from simple tribes to proto-states, such as the Alur. Our dissatisfaction with this procedure parallels Fried's discontent with the use of "lineage" in current social anthropology:

When the analytical framework which is so conducive to functional study is . . . transferred without modification to problems involving comparisons of greater or lesser scope, complications are sure to follow. . . . What happens when societies are classified together merely because they utilize kinship as an articulating principle without determining the nature of their particular kin relations or their quality, may be seen when Fortes links the Hopi with the Nuer, the Beduin, the Yako, the Tallensi, the Gusii, and the Tikopia on the basis of their common possession of unilineal descent groups. While this is correct, it is of little moment since we can also add, *inter alia,* the Northern Tungus and the Chinese, thereby giving a series that ranges from a simple pastoralist and hunting society to a sophisticated world power.

The argument for an evolutionary view of Tiv-Nuer segmentary lineage organization—and for the taxonomic distinctions drawn for the purpose of argument—does not rest simply on the existence of differences between Tiv-Nuer and other so-called segmentary lineage systems. The importance of perceiving Tiv-Nuer as a specific tribal form is that this leads to certain empirically testable conclusions about its genesis and incidence. The evolutionary perspective, moreover, does not supersede structural analysis, but complements it and adds to it certain understandings which structural analysis by itself seems incapable of producing. There is hardly need to repeat the oft-made observation that consideration of the relations between parts of a system does not account for the existence of the system (or its parts)—unless one is willing to accept the tautology that the system is what it is because that is the way it is. Yet without wishing to slight the magnificence of Evans-Pritchard's work on the Nuer—the position of *The Nuer* as an ethnographic classic is certainly secure—nonetheless, he does not break out of the circle:

Physical environment, way of livelihood, mode of distribution, poor communications, simple economy, etc., to some extent explain the incidence of [Nuer] political cleavage, but the tendency towards segmentation seems to be inherent in political structure itself.

Or, perhaps even more explicitly, Evans-Pritchard writes that ecological factors:

. . . to some extent explain the demographic features of Nuer political segmentation, but the tendency towards segmentation must be defined as a fundamental principle of their social structure.

In brief, Evans-Pritchard seems to reject the adaptive view as of limited value, leaving the impression that the Nuer have a segmentary organization because of the segmentary "principle" of their organization.

The alternative advanced here is that a segmentary lineage system is a social means of intrusion and competition in an already occupied ecological niche. More, it is an organization confined to societies of a certain level of development, the *tribal* level, as distinguished from less-developed *bands* and more advanced *chiefdoms*. Finally, the segmentary lineage is a successful predatory organization in conflicts with other tribes, although perhaps unnecessary against bands and ineffective against chiefdoms and states; it develops specifically in a tribal society which is moving against other tribes, in a *tribal intercultural environment.*

THE TRIBAL LEVEL OF CULTURAL EVOLUTION

The evolution of culture can be viewed as a movement in the direction of increasing utilization of the earth's resources, or, alternatively, of increasing transformation of available energy into cultural systems. This broad movement has two aspects. On the one hand, culture tends to diversify into specific cultures through selection and adaptation. This is specific evolution, the ramifying, diversifying, specializing aspect, from homogeneity to heterogeneity. On the other hand, higher cultural forms arise from, and surpass, lower. Culture produces successively higher *levels* of organization as new forms capable of harnessing increasing amounts of energy emerge. In popular terms, this is culture's movement toward complexity, the general, progressive aspect of evolution.

We are concerned here with the tribal level of general progress, and for comparative purposes with the preceding band level and succeeding chiefdom level. All of these are below the general level of state, or civilization, and are justifiably referred to as "primitive." The discussion focuses primarily on social and political matters, leaving aside other characteristics of general evolution; thus the designation of levels in social terms is particularly apposite.

In the general evolution of society there is movement in the direction of multiplication and specialization of social groups, parts of society, and increasing integration of the whole. In these respects, band societies are clearly least developed. Bands are small autonomous territorial groups of 20 to 50 or so people. They are undifferentiated, consisting of only two kinds of social units: families and the band of related families. They are relatively unintegrated. There is limited social control of the economy, relative economic and political autonomy of families, and for integration and direction there is no leadership beyond the "moral influence" exerted by elders and skilled hunters. Band society was the dominant type of the Paleolithic; it survived until recent times among marginally situated hunters and gatherers such as the Bushmen, Eskimo, Shoshoni, Semang, and others.

The tribal level may have emerged in a few exceptionally favorable environments in the food-collecting, Paleolithic era. However, it was the Neolithic Revolution that ushered in the *dominance* of the tribal form, that precipitated great sectors of the cultural world to a new level of general standing. Even in modern times tribes operating on a simple neolithic base have comprised a significant proportion of ethnographically known cultures. Well-known examples include most North American Indians—excluding bands of Canada and the Great Basin, and chiefdoms of the Southeast and the Northwest Coast— many groups of the South American forest, most Melanesian societies, most Siberian groups, peoples of highland regions of southeast Asia, and a number of African societies.

A band is a simple association of families, but a tribe is an association of kin groups which are themselves composed of families. A tribe is a larger, more segmented society. Without implying this as the specific course of development of tribes, we may nonetheless view a tribe as a coalescence of multifamily groups each of the order of a band. In this, the general evolution of society parallels overall biological progress: what is at one stage the entire organism (the cell, the band) becomes only the part of the higher organism (simple metazoa, the tribe).

A tribe is a segmental organization. It is composed of a number of equivalent, unspecialized multifamily groups, each the structural duplicate of the other: a tribe is a congeries of equal kin group blocs. The segments are the residential and (usually) proprietary units of the tribe, the people that settle or wander together in a given sector of the tribal domain and that separately exploit a sector of strategic resources. It is sometimes possible to speak of several levels of segmentation. Among Plains Indians, for example, the primary segments, small groups of relatives acknowledging a leader, wandered separately from fellow tribesmen some of the year, combined with like units into larger bands (secondary segments) in other seasons, and the whole tribe gathered briefly for annual ceremonies. "Primary tribal segment" is defined as the smallest multifamily group that collectively exploits an area of tribal resources and forms a residential entity all or most of the year. It is hazardous to speak of absolute numbers in view of the great specific diversity of tribal societies, but in most cases the primary segment seems to fall between 50 and 250 people. The structure of primary and higher (if any) tribal segments likewise varies. The primary segment may be a lineage (e.g., Iroquois), a nonlineal descent group (Malaita, Carrier Indians), or a loosely organized local kindred (Lapp, Iban, Plains Indians). This is another product of adaptive diversification, specific evolution. It is rather the general characteristics of tribal segments that concern us now.

Small, localized—often primary—tribal segments tend to be economically and politically autonomous. A tribe as a whole is normally *not* a political organization but rather a social-cultural-ethnic entity. It is held together principally by likenesses among its segments (mechanical solidarity) and by pantribal institutions, such as a system of intermarrying clans, of age-grades, or military or religious societies, which cross-cut the primary segments. Pan-tribal institutions make a tribe a more integrated social organism (even if weakly so) than a group of intermarrying bands, but tribes as such virtually lack organic solidarity. A tribe may well consider itself one people, often enough *the* people, but a system of order uniting the various kin segments and representing the interests of the whole rather than the several interests of the parts is at best only ephemerally achieved— characteristically it is never achieved.

The simple Neolithic mode of production is the key to the fragmented character of tribal polity. In most areas of the world the Neolithic did not immediately bring forth technology requiring intensive division of labor or socialization of the productive process over a wide region. Neolithic economic cooperation is generally localized; usually it is limited to cooperation within primary tribal segments. In addition, such common Neolithic techniques as shifting agriculture and simple pastoralism typically disperse a population and confine concentration ("nucleation") at a low level. Tribal unity suffers in consequence.

In many tribes the economic autonomy of primary segments is formally expressed by corporateness: the primary segment is a self-sustaining perpetual body exercising social control over its productive resources. The group manages its own affairs and is highly unified against the outside, acting as a collectivity in defense of its property and persons. But even where it is not expressed by incorporation, the small kin-territorial segments of a tribe tend to be self-sustaining economic and political bodies. Each has an equivalent organization; none is functionally dependent on another, but each does for itself what the others do for themselves.

Political solidarity is not necessarily completely confined to small tribal segments. Insofar as ecological conditions force segments into contact during certain seasons, a feeling of unity and of necessity to terminate feuds may develop over a wider or narrower range of the tribe. Thus secondary and higher segments may exist as territorially defined tribal sections (subtribal groupings). But this in itself rarely requires organized confederation in the sense that the subtribe has a structure which is more than the sum of its parts. Moreover, the subtribe is not normally the unit of political action.

At a matter of fact, considered as the territorial entity that collectively defends itself against the outside while maintaining the peace internally, the political unit of tribal society is typically variable in extent. The level of political consolidation contracts and expands: primary segments that unite to attack or repel an enemy at one time may fragment into feuding factions at another, quarreling over land or over personal injuries. Moreover, the degree to which political consolidation proceeds typically depends on circumstances *external* to the tribe itself. The existence of a well-organized predatory neighbor, or, conversely, the opportunity to prey

upon a nearby society, will give impetus to confederation. Local autonomy breaks down, on a greater or lesser scale, proportionate to the amount of—and during the extent of—concerted action possible against other societies. In an uncontested environment, on the other hand, the primary segments of a tribe will show little inclination toward consolidation. And if, at the same time, internal population growth places a premium on land, pasturage, or other vital resources, the tribe may exist in a virtual state of anarchy, of perpetual feud among small-scale segments.

We take the following then as fundamental facts of tribal political life:

1. Because small, equivalent tribal segments tend to be economically and socially self-sustaining, equal, and autonomous, the normal political state is toward disunity among them. There is no permanent organized confederation of these segments.

2. Small segments of a tribe will, however, consolidate to meet external competition. The specific nature of tribal structure of course permits greater or less consolidation in different cases. But disregarding this for the moment, the level of political consolidation within the tribe is generally proportionate to the requirements of external competition.

3. Yet a tribe will automatically return to the state of disunity—local autonomy—and remain there when competition is in abeyance.

It follows that leadership is weakly developed at the tribal level. Leadership beyond the small—normally, the primary—segment can only be ephemeral because organized action above this level is ephemeral. There is no need, and no field, for permanent tribal leadership. When the competitive objectives that induce confederation have been accomplished, the confederation *de facto* dissolves into its several segments, and leaders that had emerged now fall back into social oblivion, or at best retain only local influence. Once leadership is localized, moreover, it tends to become thereby superfluous. A primary segment is a face-to-face organization of kinsmen; good order here is largely achieved through kinship etiquette with its personal sanctions of ridicule, gossip, and ostracism. The typical leader in a tribal society is only the glorified counterpart of the influential elder in a hunting and gathering society. Like the latter, he achieves status by virtue of his personal characteristics, or to look at it another way, he builds a following on the basis of personally established ties. He creates loyalties through generosity; fearful acquiescence through magic; inclination to accept his opinions through demonstration of wisdom, oratorical skill, and the like. Leadership here is a charismatic interpersonal relationship. Since it is based on personal ties and qualities, it is not heritable. It is not an *office* within a definite group: It is not *chieftainship*.

An influential man can, of course, "build a name"—this expression is often encountered ethnographically at the tribal level—that is known beyond his local group. And if he has the special qualities selected for in times of confederation, such as skill in fighting, he will direct the confederation. But as soon as the confederacy dissolves, which is as soon as it can, he finds himself with few followers. The man might have little influence even within his primary segment because the very qualities which elevate him in times of confederation, such as fearless belligerence, would alienate him if displayed in the peaceful context of his circle of close kin. He may be without honor in his own camp.

The reader may have already inferred our distinction between tribes and chiefdoms. The latter, unlike the former, witness the development of a permanent political structure and socialization of the economic process over a wide area, embracing different local segments. The several segments of a chiefdom are not separate, equal, and autonomous. Rather, they are ranked relative to each other—and usually also internally ranked— and their leaders, true chiefs, hold offices accordingly in an extensive polity. In the more developed chiefdoms (many Polynesian societies, for example), this political structure becomes coterminous with social and cultural boundaries.

TIV-NUER SEGMENTARY LINEAGE ORGANIZATION

The significance of the preceding discussion lies in this: The Tiv and the Nuer are tribal societies, adaptive varieties of the general type. Their economies are Neolithic; the Tiv are small-scale shifting agriculturalists, the Nuer transhumant mixed farmers with a pastoral bias. Both have solidary, autonomous primary segments: the Nuer village and the Tiv "minimal *tar*" (a grouping of related compounds). Like many tribes, neither are permanently organized (integrated) above this level. Yet both are expanding, or rather, intruding into an ecological domain already occupied by other peoples. And success in this intrusive push for "living space" depends precisely and directly on ability to mobilize above the primary segment level, to deploy the concerted pressure of many local groups on the tribal borders. *The Tiv-Nuer segmentary lineage system is a mechanism for large-scale political consolidation in the absence of any permanent, higher-level tribal organization.* To use the Bohannans' apt phrases, it has the decisive function of unifying "within" for the purpose of standing "against." Evans-Pritchard viewed this, in its manifestation in feud, as a means of preserving equilibrium in Nuer society; yet in the larger and more revealing perspective of the intercultural milieu its significance is precisely that it disturbs equilibrium.

Because of the context in which the segmentary lineage system operates, and because of its singular function as a quasi-political structure, it is a distinctive kind of organization. But before examining the formal elements of the system in detail, it is well to present a brief general description of it.

Nuer is the type site, to to speak, of the segmentary lineage system. But the Tiv are a more perfect example. Among the Tiv, the men of the minimal tar are usually of the *focal* patriline, i.e., the line whose outside connections with other lines is the basis of alliance with other segments. In Nuer villages, only a minority—sometimes, none—

need be of the focal line (the "dominant" clans and lineages, in Evans-Pritchard's terms). The Tiv are also a more perfect example because their segmentary system expands through the whole tribe, embracing all Tiv in one patrilineage, whereas the Nuer system cuts off below the level of the Nuer as a people.

It should be stated at once that "lineage" does not describe the basic segment among either the Tiv or the Nuer. The "lineage system" is a set of relations between primary segments; the Tiv minimal tar and the Nuer village are themselves residential composites of different patrilines. Those lines of the local group other than the focal one are related to it cognatically or in other ways, which is the social rationale for their participation in the outside connections of the focal line.

The segmentary lineage system consists of this: the focal lines of primary segments can be placed on a single agnatic genealogy that accounts for much (all, in the Tiv case) of the tribe. The closer the genealogical relation between focal lines, the closer their respective segments are on the ground. Primary (or "minimal") segments whose focal line ancestors are siblings comprise a territorial entity of higher order, a minor segment, usually named after their common ancestor, the father of the siblings. They comprise an entity, however, only with reference and in opposition to an equivalent lineage segment, one descended from the brother of their common ancestor. In turn, minor segments comprise a higher-level entity, a major lineage, in opposition to the descendants of the brother of their common ancestor. The build-up of inclusive segments can proceed to the level of the tribe itself. Always the level of consolidation has a spatial counterpart; all segments of the same inclusive one form a geographical bloc. "Complementary opposition" and "structural relativity" should also be stressed: no entity above the primary segment exists as such, but it is only called into consciousness or being by reference to its genealogically equivalent segment.

To make this description more concrete, we quote extensively from one of Paul Bo-hannan's several lucid discussions of the Tiv, also appending one of his diagrams (Fig. 14.1):

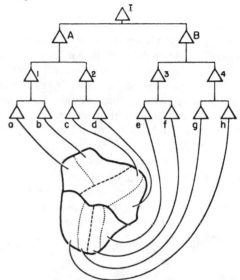

FIGURE 14.1

The lineage whose apical ancestor is some three to six generations removed from living elders and who are associated with the smallest discrete territory *(tar)* I call the minimal segment . . . it can vary in population from 200 people to well over a thousand. . . . The territory of a minimal segment adjoins the territory of its sibling minimal segment. Thus, the lineage comprising two minimal segments also has a discrete territory, and is in turn a segment of a more inclusive lineage, and of its more inclusive territory. In Fig. 1, the whole system can be seen: the father or founder of segment *a* was a brother of the founder of segment *b*. Each is a minimal segment today, and each has its own territory. The two segments taken together are all descended from *1*, and are known by his name—the children of *1*. In the same way, the territory of lineage *1*, made up as it is of the combined minimal territories *a* and *b*, combines with the territory of lineage *2*, made up of the combined minimal territories of *c* and *d*, to form territory *A*, occupied by lineage segment *A*, all descended from a single ancestor "A." This process is extended indefinitely right up to the apex of the genealogy, back in time to the founder who begot the entire people, and outwards in space to the edges of Tivland. The entire 800,000 Tiv form a single "lineage" (nongo) and a single land called *Tar Tiv*. The geographical position of territories follows the genealogical division into lineages.

The segmentary lineage system is a *complex* of formal-functional characteristics. Some of the elements of organization can and do appear singly or in various combination in other societies, which is the apparent cause of the popular tendency to apply "segmentary system" quite widely. It is our contention, however, that the full complement occurs only in expanding tribal societies. In other cases the segmentary tendencies remain incomplete, and because they are embedded in different social contexts, they have different "functional values," different roles in society.

We have separated out six salient elements of segmentary lineage organization: lineality, segmentation, local-genealogical segmentation, segmentary sociability, complementary opposition (or the massing effect), and structural relativity.

LINEALITY

Whereas a single segmented lineage extends through much or all of the tribe among the Tiv and the Nuer, lineality actually has comparatively limited functions. The Tiv and Nuer do not have corporate lineages, in the sense we take that term. The corporate groups are local aggregations of different agnatic lines. Lineality thus does not define the primary residential-proprietary segments but rather organizes relations between them according to genealogical ties between their focal lines.

One need not insist on the absence of local corporate lineages as an indicative characteristic of the segmentary lineage system, for it is the presence of a lineage superstructure uniting local groups that is critical. On the other hand, the mere presence of segmented lineages in a society is not sufficient for inclusion in the type. And failure to organize the polity on a unitary lineage model *does disqualify,* no matter how many other "segmentary" elements are present (e.g., the Tallensi and, in *Tribes Without Rulers,* the Dinka, Bwamba, and Konkamba).

Lineality suggests some general ecological preconditions for segmentary lineage development. Lineages and lineality are typically found with a mode of production involving repetitive or periodic use of restricted, localized resources, as in secondary forest or irrigation agriculture and many forms of pastoralism. The rule of descent that makes a lineage is one social aspect of long-term use of the same resources, another aspect being the development of collective proprietary rights in these resources. The rule of descent creates a perpetual social group linked to perpetually valuable strategic property; or, viewed another way, it allocates people with respect to their means of livelihood. Lineages do not form in the absence of long-term exploitation of restricted domains. They are lacking where resources (hence people) vary continuously in temporal and spatial distribution, as among buffalo-hunting Plains tribes or primary forest agriculturalists such as the Iban of Borneo. If ecological conditions preclude lineages (or lineality), they preclude the segmentary lineage system.

SEGMENTATION

A *segment* is, generically, "one of an indefinite number of parts comprising a whole in which one part is like another in structure, or composition, and function." A social group or a society as a whole is *segmented* (segmental, segmentary, exhibits segmentation) if composed of subgroups of this character. *Segmentation* also refers to the common process of growth by division into equivalent parts (fission). Tiv-Nuer organization is segmentary in the sense that higher levels of political organization are achieved through integration of equivalent, lower-level parts. It appears also to grow by segmentation.

But all kinds of societies and many varieties of social groups are segmentary in this generic sense. The University of Michigan has minimal, departmental segments (Anthropology, Chemistry, etc.), which are parts of semi-official divisions (Social Science, Natural Science), which are parts of colleges (Literary College, Engineering School, etc.), which together comprise the University—excluding the Administration (an oversight).

Obviously, the existence of segmentation alone does not qualify a society as a segmentary lineage system. And even if a unitary lineage system is the organization of political segmentation, it is not a segmentary lineage system unless certain other elements, especially structural relativity (see below), are present.

LOCAL-GENEALOGICAL SEGMENTATION

A political structure is often a system of local segmentation. That is, segments of the same order within the same inclusive political body are contiguous. Among the Tiv and the Nuer, local segmentation is simultaneously lineage segmentation (see Fig. 14.1). It is not simply that each territorial entity is identified with a lineage segment, but also that contiguous segments of the same inclusive territorial entity are identified with equivalent branches of the same inclusive lineage. Higher political levels are at the same time higher lineage levels. Thus the lineage system can be said to provide the structure for political consolidation—although there is plenty of evidence for the Nuer, at least, that *in origin* the process sometimes works the other way around, that the genealogy is fitted to political realities. (Among the Nuer, also local-genealogical segmentation is cut off at a high, subtribal level, but as there is rarely confederation beyond this level, political alliance consistently remains lineage alliance.)

A society may have local political segments and at the same time segmentary lineages. However, if genealogical segmentation does not consistently correspond to local segmentation, it does not have a segmentary lineage system.

SEGMENTARY SOCIABILITY (LOVE THY NEIGHBOR)

The closer the social position of two groups in a segmentary organization, the more solidary their relations; subgroups of the same inclusive group are more sociable than subgroups of different inclusive segments. This very general (and vague) sociological fact

can be applied in many contexts. However, segmentary sociability is particularly marked if segmentation is organized genealogically because kinship itself connotes sociability, and in many societies it more specifically connotes "peace." The closer the kin relation, the greater the sociability and peacefulness; the more distant, or more nearly unrelated, the less.

This is not to say that hostility is absent from close kin or close segmentary relations. It is probably easier to prove—considering interpersonal relations as such—that the closer the social bond, the greater the hostility. However, it not hostility that is at issue but the necessity to repress it or, conversely, the possibility of enjoining it. The closer the relationship, the greater the restraint on belligerence and violence, and the more distant, the less the restraint. Among the Tiv and the Nuer, given the kin quality of segmentation, segmentary sociability is particularly striking; it is virtually institutionalized. Hostility is put down effectively within the Nuer village and the Tiv minimal tar: if factionalism erupts the difficulty is either settled or one party will have to emigrate. These are groups of close kin who must maintain their integrity against the outside, and an unsociable action in this context is sinful. The moral injunction is accompanied by a prohibition on the use of dangerous weapons. But the greater the lineage-segmentary distance, the more dangerous the permitted means of violence—from fists, to clubs, to arrows, poisoned arrows, etc.—and the more difficult it becomes to repair a feud. Correspondingly, violence becomes more honorable in proportion to segmentary distance, reaching the extreme in dealings with foreign tribes. Here violence is an esteemed act—there are practically no holds barred on atrocity, and a state of war may well be the assumed normal relation. The value of segmentary sociability—or the lack thereof—for predatory expansion is obvious: violence is inhibited centripetally, among contiguous, closely related groups, but is directed centrifugally against distant groups and neighboring peoples.

Segmentary sociability of itself is a common political phenomenon. But it is outstanding in segmentary lineage systems because, in the absence of a permanent tribal political structure, it is the salient mechanism of the political process. Operating automatically to determine the level of collective political action, it is the built-in thermostat of a self-regulating political machine. The formal manifestation of segmentary sociability is complementary opposition.

COMPLEMENTARY OPPOSITION, OR THE MASSING EFFECT

Among the Tiv and the Nuer, segmentary sociability materializes in complementary opposition, the massing of equivalent segments in defense or extension of their respective privileges. In any opposition between parties A and B, all those more closely related to A than to B will stand with A against B, and vice versa. Segments are pitted against equivalent segments: any opposition between groups (or members thereof) expands automatically to opposition between the largest equivalent lineages of which the contestants are *respectively* members. The massing effect is self-limiting as well as self-expanding. It cuts off when sibling groups are joined because lineages equivalent to the inclusive one containing opposed sibling groups are equally related (or equally unrelated) to the contestants.

Evans-Pritchard describes complementary opposition among local-lineage segments of the Nuer in this way (Evans-Pritchard's "section" in this passage can be understood in lineage as well as territorial terms):

The principle of segmentation and the opposition between segments is the same in every section of a tribe [our "subtribe"] and extends beyond the tribe to relations between tribes. . . . It can be stated in hypothetical terms by the Nuer themselves and can be represented in this way. In the diagram . . . when Z^1 fights Z^2 no other section is involved. When Z^1 fights Y^1, Z^1 and Z^2 unite as Y^2. When Z^1 fights X^1, Y^1 and Y^2 unite, and so do X^1 and X^2. When X^1 fights A, X^1, X^2, Y^1 and Y^2 all unite as B. When A raids the Dinka, A and B may unite. [An accurate description of

segmentary opposition among the Tiv can be had by substituting the letters and figures from Fig. 1 in Evans-Pritchard's passage (Fig. 14.2).]

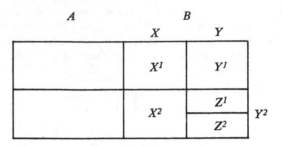

FIGURE 14.2

Among the Tiv and the Nuer, then, conflicts—even those resulting from personal injury—between individuals of equivalent primary segments call forth their respective primary groups en masse; it becomes a fight between segments. By the same logic, the logic of segmentary sociability, minor, major, and larger lineages may be pitted against each other. Thus does the segmentary lineage system operate as a political machine. The less the lineage-spatial distance between groups the more effectively peace is waged, not simply because of moral injunctions and felt obligations to settle, but also because the smaller are the opposed parties. However, the greater the segmental distance the more effectively war is waged because, in addition to use of dangerous weapons and disinclination to settle, the size of contending parties increases proportionately.

Complementary opposition is not peculiar to the Nuer and the Tiv—it occurs to a greater or lesser extent elsewhere. The uniqueness of Tiv-Nuer complementary opposition is that it *is* their political system. Complementary opposition *creates* the structure: without opposition the higher segments do not exist. Masses of people are not organized by social structures so much as organizations are made by massing. This leads us directly to the final and definitive characteristic of the segmentary lineage system, structural relativity. But one cannot refrain from noting beforehand the decisive advantages bequeathed by complementary opposition in intertribal warfare. War is effectively joined by the Nuer or the Tiv against neighboring tribes because, even if it has been initiated by a small lineage segment, it pits "all of us" against "them." More than that, the societies under attack do not form such extensive intratribal alliances; hence it is usually "all of us" against "a few of them."

STRUCTURAL RELATIVITY

Tiv-Nuer lineages do not come into existence except through the massing effect, in opposition to equivalent groups. They are not permanent, *absolute* social entities, but *relative* ones. Called into being by external circumstances, the level of organization achieved is in direct proportion to the social order of the opposition, and the lineage segment ceases to function as such when opposition is in abeyance. The lineage segment cannot stand alone but can only stand "against." Correspondingly, no lineage is more than the sum of its parts; it lacks internal structure, a skeleton, such as a system of segmentary chiefs. Lineage segments have only social exoskeletons; they are crystallized at one or another level by outside pressure of greater or less degree.

In a certain sense structural relativity is endemic in any social order that is segmental. At the very least it will be manifest in "relativity of reference," which comes into play to determine the respective status of interacting persons or groups. Thus in Figure 1 (above) a person speaks of himself as a member of group *a* relative to those of group *b*. But the same person is a member of *1* in reference to *c* or *d* (which are *2*) and of *A* in reference to those of *B*, etc. Evans-Pritchard is able to use a very familiar kind of example of such structural relativity, in one stroke thus demonstrating its generality in human societies as well as illustrating his Nuer material:

If one meets an Englishman in Germany and asks him where his home is, he may reply that it is in England. If one meets the same man in London and asks him the same question he will tell one that his home is in Oxfordshire, whereas if one meets him in that county he will tell

one the name of the town or village in which he lives. If questioned in his town or village he will mention his particular street, and if questioned in his street he will indicate his house.

Structural relativity among the Tiv and Nuer is more than a matter of status determination of individuals. Moreover, it is not simply a tendency to define "own group" by opposition in certain contexts; such tendencies exist in other societies with other organization. It is, if we may be permitted, *complete relativity*: the level of political organization that emerges as a collectivity is always relative to the opposition.

A comparison of Tiv-Nuer segmentary lineages with Polynesian ramages may be instructive. Polynesian ramages have many characteristics of segmentary lineage systems: lineality, segmentation, local-genealogical segmentation (or certain islands), segmentary sociability, and in internal political or jural matters they may show complementary opposition and relativity. But Polynesian ramages are permanent, absolute structures with continuous economic and political functions. Ramage segments are ranked, and the rank of the segment corresponds to its economic and political privileges and obligations. Ramage segments of every order have chiefs who represent and embody their groups and act for them. There is a political order of the whole operating in both internal and external affairs. A higher level of economic and political integration has been irreversibly established here, one that transcends the primary segment sphere. The Polynesian ramage system is an organization of the chiefdom level of general evolution.

But the segmentary lineage system is a tribal institution. It develops in the context of a comparatively restricted economy and polity, in the context of equal, autonomous, small localized kin groups. It may operate in the internal ordering of society (through segmentary sociability), but this is only derivative of the dominant function of consolidating otherwise autonomous primary groups for concerted external action. There are no permanent lineage segments beyond the primary group, but only temporary segments of different size, developing to the level they have to in order to meet opposition.

We [Evans-Pritchard] would . . . suggest that Nuer political groups be defined . . . by the relations between their segments and their inter-relations as segments of a larger system in an organization of society in certain social situations, and *not as parts of a kind of fixed framework* within which people live [emphasis ours].

Structural relativity in a segmentary lineage system is paralleled by relativity of leadership. A man may achieve some fame—personal and charismatic—beyond his primary group, enough perhaps to be influential among nearby, related segments. Insofar as these segments combine with his own in opposition to other groups, such a man may act as the spokesman and leader of the whole. But when his own primary segment stands against an equivalent, closely related one in feud or in a land dispute, then he is not heeded by the opposed segment but is only leader of his own. The Bohannans describe relativity of Tiv leadership very well:

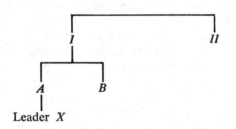

FIGURE 14.3

The same segmentary principle which allows very large units to appear in opposition to equivalent units make it impossible for any unit, from the internal viewpoint, to have unity. Thus in any affairs between *I* and *II*, *X* appears as the leader of *I*. In any affairs solely the concern of *I*, *X* appears as the leader of *A* . . . any account of Tiv leadership must discuss leadership in these two aspects: "against" and "within," or, if one prefers and will remember that the lineage level concerned is contextual, "foreign" and "domestic" affairs. However, the lineage structure itself, by an association of union with opposition, brings it about that emotively the feeling of "within" and of unity in any given segment is strongest when "foreign" affairs are concerned, and that the emergence of latent

cleavages is most prominent and the achievement of unity most difficult in "internal" affairs. That is, a leader wields his greatest influence "within" when he is a leader "against." This principle needs no modification if one remembers that the lineage span is variable. Only if one attempts to pin leadership to a definite lineage *(I)*, does it break down, unless one specifies that within *I*, *X* is the leader of *A*; within *A*, he is the leader of *"i,"* and so on, literally to the point at which he is himself "against" his full brother.

The Tiv and the Nuer, as many other tribal societies, are militantly equalitarian—a corollary of a fragmented kin economy and polity. The Tiv, in fact, have periodic purges of would-be tyrants. While the Tiv are capable of mass opposition to other tribes, even here the inherent weakness of their tribal polity shows through. Small clusters of close kin fight parallel to each other; there is no coordinated deployment, no master strategy, no division of military labors; and the scope of leadership thus remains restricted. As for the Nuer, the most influential men in the traditional system, the "leopard-skin chiefs," characteristically stand *outside* the lineage system. They are usually not agnatic members of the focal lines of their region and are not segment leaders. Theirs is ritual office, virtually without secular power, and their function is to compose feuds between lineage segments rather than to organize feuding factions.

Structural relativity reveals the tribal character of the segmentary lineage system. The one-sided function of the system, organization for external opposition, also suggests the specific adaptive circumstance which it meets: intertribal competition.

PREDATORY EXPANSION: "WE DON'T HAVE A BOUNDARY; WE HAVE AN ARGUMENT"

The Tiv are centered in the Northern Province of Nigeria, straddling both banks of the Benue River. According to traditions, the Tiv moved into this area from the southeast; their occupation of the plain north of the Benue is comparatively recent and Tiv intrusion in this sector is still progressing. Yet

Tiv expansion is not characterized so much by movement in one direction as it is by movement in *all* directions: "When seen from the periphery, and more especially when seen from the viewpoint of surrounding peoples, a centrifugal migration is the most important single factor about the Tiv." Only in the south has the Tiv advance been inhibited, and this by boundaries drawn by the British, not for lack of inclination on the Tiv's part to go farther.

Tiv migration has been accomplished specifically at the expense of a number of other peoples, who have either been rolled back by the Tiv or else have suffered infiltration of their lands by growing colonies of Tiv, sometimes to the point that these peoples now exist as isolated enclaves within Tivland. This fantastic predatory encroachment is more reminiscent of conquering nomad hordes than of a simple Neolithic peasantry:

To their east they are living intermingled with "Uke": the Hausa-speaking Abakwariga, Jukun, Jukunized Chamba and other peoples; they have even begun to push into Adamawa Province. To their north they are moving into (and leaving behind as enclaves) such groups as the Arago and Ankwe, who are linguistically related to the Idoma. . . . To the west they are exerting pressure on the Idoma and on the other groups called "Akpoto" by the Tiv; Tiv in adjoining areas say they dispossessed the Akpoto of the land on which they now live.

Many Tiv have migrated south into the Eastern Provinces and set up their homesteads among the various small tribes of Ogoja Province, known to the Tiv collectively as the Udam.

British administration encountered Tiv migra- almost as soon as they encountered the Tiv, in in 1912. As a result the "Munshi [i.e., Tiv] Wall" was built between Gaav of Jechira [a large Tiv lineage] and the contiguous people of Ogoja, a wall meant to "keep the Munshi in his place— north of the wall" but which "the Munshi merely climbs over."

The Tiv evidently intrude themselves wherever they can cultivate and where their opposition is weak. They now number over 800,-000 people, by far the largest pagan tribal grouping in Northern Nigeria. The decisive factor in this phenomenal success seems to be the Tiv segmentary lineage system: the

Tiv are able to exert mass pressure on their borders, while the peoples subjected to this pressure are incapable of defending their territories on a commensurate scale. Many of these hapless peoples are small tribal groups, the "broken tribes" of the north, for example, or the "congeries of small, semi-Bantu speaking tribes" to the south. Speaking of the Tiv's neighbors in general, L. Bohannan remarks:

Most of these societies seem to be made up of small descent groups—sometimes territorially distinct, sometimes dispersed—crossed and integrated by ties of reputed kinship, chiefship and religion. . . . In political organization the Tiv are in no way typical of the region in which they live.

Tiv expansive thrusts germinate at lower levels of the segmentary structure and develop upward through higher levels and outward toward the borders of Tivland. There are no natural or artificial boundaries between Tiv minimal segments (tar), as distinct from holdings under cultivation: "We don't have a boundary; we have an argument." Every year new plots are cleared, as used ones are left fallow, and, as P. Bohannan puts it, every compound headman within the minimal segment holds a right against the world to sufficient farming land. The existing fallow between adjacent minimal segments is likely to be disputed when such rights are exercised, and disputed by comparatively large groups at that. For the direction of expansion of cultivation is governed by tactical considerations: one moves against the bounding segment most distantly related to one's own, thus bringing the massing effect into maximal play.

Now when it is considered that lineage segments are at every level localized, it follows that an expansive push thus instigated may reverberate through a great part of the segmentary structure, inexorably building up intense centrifugal pressure. Minor, major, and higher-order segments are mobilized— through complementary opposition—against their equivalents. Those who are being pushed from the inside are induced to expand outward, which movement automatically allies both pushers and pushed, as companion

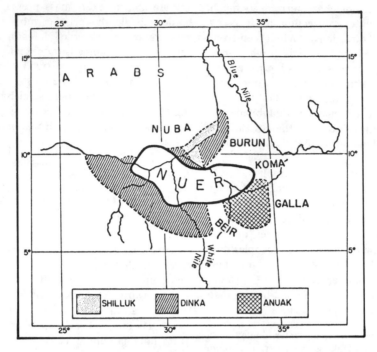

FIGURE 14.4

segments, against still higher-order Tiv lineages, and ultimately a large sector of Tiv are pressing foreigners. The Bohannans present an interesting hypothetical model of this process, too long to quote here, in which a man trying to expand holdings against companion segments is reminded at every turn that the segments are brothers and one should take land from the neighboring, higher-level equivalent lineage instead, until it becomes relevant that "All Tiv are brothers; you should take land from foreigners." The segmentary lineage system consistently channels expansion outward, releasing internal pressure in an explosive blast against other peoples.

A border lineage may be forced by internal pressure to move en masse against another tribe; the Bohannans aptly call this "steamroller expansion." A "long and bitter war" will follow. The concerted movement of a border village may be entirely against its will: the lineage is simply crowded out as the Tiv side of its land is consumed by the appetites of other Tiv. Of course, at the bor-

der internal Tiv lineages join their brothers in the good fight. Having advanced the border lineage, the internal lineages then fill in the vacated land, always keeping the same relative positions. Every lineage that does not bound foreigners knows "just which lineages they 'follow' (*chir*), and—though they are likely to push or shove (*kpolom*)—they will assist those in front to take over from foreigners." Steamroller expansion is most characteristic of Tiv expansion in the south, where there is intensive competition with neighboring tribes. In the north, "leap-frog" migration is more common: a group from an internal segment catapults over the border and infiltrates a new area. The invading nucleus is eventually joined by people of related segments and all distribute themselves according to genealogical distance, paralleling their original positions.

Across Africa, in the periodically flooded grasslands around the Upper Nile, a similar drama of expansion is played out. The principal protagonists in this arena are the Nuer and their principal victims, the Dinka. The Nuer invasion of Dinkaland—and also of Anuak territory farther east—can be described as a *Drang nach Osten*. This is the main trend, although there is a tendency to expand in other directions, especially against southern and western Dinka. If the tribal map of the area can be used to decipher its history, it appears that the Nuer have simply dismembered the Dinka, divided them into separate sections southwest and northeast of the Nile (Fig. 14.4).

The major outlines of Nuer incursions in the Upper Nile are summed up by Evans-Pritchard:

As far as history and tradition go back, and in the vistas of myth beyond their farthest reach, there has been enmity between the two peoples. Almost always the Nuer have been the aggressors. . . . Every Nuer tribe raided Dinka at least every two or three years, and some part of Dinkaland must have been raided annually. . . . The earliest travellers record that Nuer held both banks of the Nile, but it is probable that all the entire Zeraf Island was at one time occupied by Dinka and it is certain that the whole of the country from the Zeraf to the Pibor and, to the north of the Sobat, from the confines of Shillukland to the Ethiopian scrap, was, with the exception of riverain settlements of Anuak, still in their hands as late as the middle of last century, when it was seized by the Nuer. . . . The conquest, which seems to have resulted in absorption and miscegenation rather than extermination, was so rapid and successful that the whole of this vast area is today occupied by Nuer, except for a few pockets of Dinka. . . . Some Dinka tribes took refuge with compatriots to the south, where the Gaawar [Nuer] and Lou [Nuer] continued to raid them. The Western Nuer likewise persistently raided all the Dinka tribes that border them, particularly those to the south and west, obtained a moral ascendancy over them, and compelled them to withdraw farther and farther from their boundaries. . . . Of all the Dinka only the Ngok, to the south of the Sobat, were left in peace, probably on account of their poverty of stock and grazing.

Nuer expansion represents the successful conquest of a particular ecological niche: the true savannah of the Sudan. Nuer relations with neighboring peoples have been directly predicated on the potentialities of their areas for the Nuer mode of production. Thus, not only did the riverain Anuak and Ngok Dinka escape Nuer ravages, but the Nuer have had little to do with the powerful Shilluk kingdom because it is situated in poor pasture land. (Conversely, the Shilluk have probably tolerated the Nuer rather than moved against them because Nuerland is marginal to the Shilluk mode of production.) The Anuak were driven east into tsetse-infested forests; the Nuer wave then spent itself against this ecological barrier. The Dinka have been the consistent victim of Nuer predation precisely because "of all neighboring areas Dinkaland alone opposes no serious ecological handicaps to a pastoral people." (It may be then that the Western Dinka display considerable ingenuity in reconciling their fate, for they contrast themselves to the savannah-dwelling Nuer as primarily "a people of savannah-forest settlement.")

Nuer expansion is perhaps an outstanding instance of the Law of Cultural Dominance, the principle that the cultural system most effective in a particular environment will spread there at the expense of thermodynamically less effective systems. In any event it is clear that the Nuer have been able to expel the Dinka because of the superior military potential of the Nuer segmentary lineage system. While the Nuer and Dinka are alike in culture, there are differences in social organization. On the Dinka side these differences amount to the tragic flaw that has condemned them to a history of withdrawal.

The Dinka are, to use Lienhardt's terms, divided into a number of "tribal groups," each further subdivided into "tribes," "subtribes," and yet smaller segments. However, these are not genealogical segments—they cannot be placed on a single agnatic genealogy—nor are they disposed in local genealogical segmentation; in fact the "tribes" are not necessarily geographic blocs. Political units among the Dinka are not fixed by complementary opposition. Instead, subtribes, and even smaller segments, display a notable tendency to fragment into *absolute, independent* entities. Subtribes crystallize about two or more unrelated lineages, one a priestly group and another a warrior line, standing for and representing the subtribe, which is itself a camping unit in the wet season and is also concentrated (in one or two sites) in the dry period. The critical thing is that this divisive, segmenting tendency is not matched by fusion with lineage-equivalent segments in higher-order, relative groupings. The Dinka lack the thermostatic mechanism for massing against the outside, a deficiency that has been fatal.

In the 19th century, when much of Western Dinkaland was pillaged by slavers and adventurers, there was little wide-scale co-operation against the common enemies. It is known that neighboring tribes of Dinka harried each other in temporary alliances with the invaders until they began to understand the scale of the subjection which they were all inviting. *Even now, however, many Dinka recognize that Nuer are able to unite on a larger scale than are Dinka.*

This difference between Nuer and Dinka is, we think, related to differences attending their respective occupation of the Sudan. The Dinka appear to have spread without great opposition. *They were first.* They naturally grew by segmentation, and fissioning units could, in the absence of external threat, afford to organize as small, virtually self-contained entities. The Dinka themselves suppose that small settlements inevitably grow and break up into discrete groups, each able to stand by itself. Lienhardt remarks that "such a theory . . . could only develop among a people who know themselves free to move away from each other; *to occupy further tracts of empty or weakly occupied country, and to find new pastures*" (emphasis ours). There is no independent confirmatory evidence, according to Lienhardt. However, the enormous population of the Dinka—about 900,000—coupled with the weak, fragmented polity, certainly does suggest that they moved into a large uncontested domain.

The Nuer, by contrast, were invaders. They spread through an already occupied niche, one held by Dinka, and the very large Nuer population, over 200,000, is testimony of their success. The Nuer had different adaptive problems than the Dinka, precisely because *the Dinka were already there.* This selective circumstance placed a premium on

the ability to fuse as well as to segment, on complementary opposition. Nuer segmentary lineage organization was the adaptive response. The Dinka, whose development in an open environment had favored segmentation but minimized fusion, then found themselves socially ill-equipped to cope with Nuer predation.

The well known seasonal movements of the Nuer impose a particular form of expansion. The outward push seems to originate from dry season dispersal in search of water and pasturage. It is significant that lineage segments of relatively low level—Evans-Pritchard's "tertiary sections," composed of a number of villages, or else higher-order "secondary sections"—characteristically fan out in different directions in this critical period. On the one hand, of course, this minimizes competition for water and pasturage among equivalent segments of larger Nuer lineages. On the other hand, each Nuer segment is thus brought into juxtaposition with outsiders, typically Dinka. The Nuer are too scattered at this point in the cycle to take full advantage of the potential massing effect. But some fighting with foreigners during the dry season dispersal—or at the least something in the nature of a probe or reconaissance—is indicated.

Full-fledged wars and raids prosecuted by large sectors of Nuer (the component sections of a "tribe," in Evans-Pritchard's terms) occurred at the end of the rainy season. The Nuer chronically raided the Dinka for cattle and iron tools, but a raid might transform itself into an actual invasion. The raiders would settle in and systematically extend the sphere of terror until the Dinka were compelled to withdraw. The ranks of the invaders might be swelled by additional immigrants from their homeland, and also by Dinka captives and enclaved settlements. These Dinka were integrated into the lineage arrangement of the invading nucleus. (Conquest and absorption of this sort, as opposed to conquest and rule, seems typical of the tribal level, where political and economic means which would make the latter feasible have not yet been achieved.)

As a final note we might consider whether population pressure can be held responsible for Tiv expansion in Nigeria and the comparable Nuer incursions in East Africa. Certain resources, notably dry season water and pasturage, are evidently in short supply among the Nuer, and Evans-Pritchard is prepared to agree that Nuer expansion is due to overpopulation, which is also the Nuer explanation. Among the Tiv, population density is extreme and land has been subjected to dangerously intensive use in some parts of the south, evidently in consequence of modern checks on Tiv migration. But in the sector of rapid recent expansion, the northern frontier, population density falls to levels below one-half of the general Tivland average of 64 per square mile.

Perhaps population pressure in critical central locations gives impetus to both Tiv and Nuer predation. Yet it seems to us that a certain relativity is required in assessing land hunger among societies competing for occupation of a specific habitat. Because the success of one contestant is necessarily to the detriment of the other, neither has *enough* land until the other has been eliminated. The need for "living space" is built in: it becomes a cultural attitude and theory, particularly in that society which has the decisive competitive advantage. Among the invaders a natural increase of population beyond the carrying capacity of present resources will be taken for granted, and at least for them land hunger exists—the idea is adaptively advantageous— even if, by objective standards, there is enough land to support the present population. Thus, in northern and extreme southeastern Tivland, "where no land shortage exists," the search for more land is prominently articulated by Tiv as a cause for migration. From an adaptive viewpoint, this is no paradox.

CONCLUSIONS

The segmentary lineage system is an institution appearing at the tribal level of general cultural evolution; it is not characteristic of bands, chiefdoms, or the several forms of civilization. It develops among societies with a simple Neolithic mode of production and a correlative tendency to form small, autonomous economic and political groups. The segmentary lineage system is a social means of temporary consolidation of this fragmented tribal polity for concerted external action. It is, in a sense, a substitute for the fixed political structure which a tribal society is incapable of sustaining.

It will not, however, be found among all tribes. Certain social conditions are presupposed—for one thing, the existence of lineality or lineages. In turn, lineality is a product of repetitive, long-term use of restricted resources. If this ecological factor is absent, it seems unlikely that a segmentary lineage system will appear.

A segmentary lineage system develops in a tribe that intrudes into an already occupied habitat rather than a tribe that expands into an uncontested domain. Expansion in an open environment may well be accompanied by segmentation, the normal process of tribal growth and spread. But in the absence of competition small segments tend to become discrete and autonomous, linked together primarily through mechanical solidarity. These circumstances, in other words, favor fission but select against complementary opposition or fusion, and long-term occupation will eventually fix this structure, make it comparatively inflexible. By contrast, growth in the face of opposition selects for complementary opposition as a social means of predation. Thus the *first* tribe in an area is unlikely to develop a segmentary lineage system, but the *second* tribe in that area is more likely to.

That the segmentary lineage system occurs among intrusive tribal societies also suggests that, from a long-term view, it is likely to be ephemeral. Once a society has succeeded in driving competitors from its habitat, the selective force favoring fusion disappears and the fragmenting tendencies of the neolithic economy are free to express themselves. In other words, the segmentary lineage system is self-liquidating. It is advantageous in intertribal competition, but having emerged victorious it has no longer *raison d'etre* and the divisive tendencies of tribal polity reassert themselves. This helps to explain why segmentary lineage systems, contrary to the popular view, have a relatively limited ethnographic distribution.

Finally, the segmentary lineage system develops in a specifically *intertribal* environment, in competition between societies of the tribal level. Expansion of a tribe against small, weakly integrated band societies would normally not call for special mechanisms of tribal consolidation. And, on the other side, a segmentary lineage system would be ineffective in competition with chiefdoms and states. To oppose—let alone to prey upon—societies of this order requires large-scale, organic integration of economic and political, especially military, effort. Limited economic coordination, the relativity of leadership and its absence of coercive sanction, the localized, egalitarian character of the polity, the ephemerality of large groupings, all of these would doom a segmentary lineage system if brought into conflict with chiefdoms or states.

The Nuer themselves provide a convincing illustration. When faced with Arab aggression at the turn of this century and with later European intrusion, their segmentary system began to collapse, or rather it was transformed into something else. The Nuer were rallied against their common and formidable enemies by prophets who transcended the sectional oppositions of lineages, and acted, to use Evans-Pritchard's phrase, as "pivots of federation." A system of hereditary political leadership and extensive political unification began to emerge. If this revolution had not been checked by European dominance—and also if it had been able to muster adequate economic support—the Nuer would not simply have overthrown the segmentary lineage system, but catapulted themselves to the chiefdom level of evolutionary progress.

15. THE LELE OF KASAI

MARY DOUGLAS

Reprinted from African Worlds: Studies in the Cosmological Ideas and Social Values of African Peoples *(London and New York: Oxford University Press, 1954). Mary Douglas is Reader in Anthropology at University College in London. She has conducted field research on several occasions in the Belgian Congo. In addition to many articles, she is the author of* The Lele of Kasai, Purity and Danger: An Analysis of Concepts of Pollution and Taboo, *and* Natural Symbols: Explorations in Cosmology.

■ Man cannot survive without technology and institutions, without the organized social relations that enable him to make use of harnessed energy. Nor, apparently, can societies function effectively if their members are without established modes of thought, belief, and perception. These not only include the social definitions of objects (e.g., steel and stone axes), roles (e.g., kinship), and seasonally appropriate behavior e.g., "structural poses"), but also the religious ideas and beliefs that join people to the habitat they are exploiting and enable them to maintain a relationship with it. For people like the Lele of the Belgian Congo, the habitat is not a mere passive object for people to do with as they please. The Lele illustrate the principle that ideas and beliefs are integral parts of a group's adaptive strategy because they enable people to attribute meaning to their technological activities. Ideational and belief systems join with institutions in supporting a group's exploitation of its habitat.

The lives of people at the lower levels of sociotechnological development (such as the Lele) seem extraordinarily rich in symbolism. Everywhere are spirits, magical influences, nuances of meaning, unseen dangers, and unappreciated potential benefits. There is hardly a place in the habitat they feel to be free of the supernatural, and every human action— and especially aggressive actions—is thought to have an effect on the habitat.

At first, these notions may seem to us like heavy harnesses and we may wonder how people manage to get anything done within such belief systems. But stop for a moment and observe yourself in a crowded department store. Note the avoidances and the prescribed contacts, the tabooed places, the thousands of symbolic or arbitrary definitions that govern our behavior in such a milieu. As you wonder at the forest as a place that is taboo for Lele women, think of the many places and acts in our society that are taboo for each sex and for different age grades, in a department store, factory, hospital, school, street corner, or church. The relationships that people maintain with each other and with their physical habitat are definitions that enable them to get from one social (or physical) place to another with necessary orderliness and predictability.

We see in this selection many of the recurrent elements in the social maps of people like the Lele. Most notable are the commingling of social roles—such as divining and hunting—and the belief that people will suffer in the food quest if they fail to maintain harmony in their social relations. The Lele are farmers; yet, as Douglas observes, their greatest religious preoccupations seem to be with hunting. This should not occasion great surprise, since religious preoccupation usually concerns the areas of greatest uncertainty in people's lives; there seems little insecurity in Lele cultivation but quite a bit about getting adequate supplies of meat.

At several points in this selection, Douglas suggests that symbolism and ritual determine people's behavior in respect to the habitat. This point of view has many well-known proponents; Victor W. Turner may be considered their dean. His ideas are clearly spelled out in many writings, among which are *The Forest of Symbols* (Ithaca: Cornell University Press, 1967), *The Drums of Affliction* (Oxford: The Clarendon Press, 1968), and *The Ritual Process* (Chicago: Aldine, 1969). My own view is the opposite, that these beliefs serve to justify or give meaning to activities made necessary by an adaptive strategy. In either event, it is clear that people seem to need ideologies and rituals in maintaining their relationship with the habitat; without them these relationships may become meaningless. Is it possible that the recent concern with "ecology" in our society represents an attempt to inject more meaning into our relationship with our own habitat? If so, was this made necessary by a feeling that our earlier ideology—conquering nature—has outlived its own success? Now that nature has been conquered, what is left to be done?

The reader who wants to know more about the culture of the Lele should consult *The Lele of Kasai,* by Mary Douglas (London: Oxford University Press, 1963). An excellent brief introduction to the Lele with strong implications for the relationship between economic and political processes is Douglas' "Lele Economy Compared with the Bushong—A Study of Economic Backwardness," in *Markets in Africa,* edited by P. Bohannan and G. Dalton (Evanston, Illinois: Northwestern University Press, 1962). Many of the ideas in this selection are developed further by Douglas in "Animals in Lele Religious Symbolism," *Africa,* 27 (1957): 47-58. For those who wish to learn more of the ways in which anthropologists treat the study of symbolism, a good introduction is *Forms of Symbolic Action* (Proceedings of the 1969 Annual Spring Meeting of the American Ethnological Society), edited by Robert F. Spencer (Seattle: University of Washington Press, 1969). This collection of papers represents those anthropologists most actively engaged in such research; each of the papers has a very good bibliography for further reading. ∎

THE LELE ARE the western neighbours of the Bushongo in the southwest of the Belgian Congo. The population of 20,000 has a density of about four to the square mile, but the total density of the district they inhabit is doubled by recent immigrants of the Luba and Cokwe tribes. The region is bounded on the north and east by the Kasai river, whose tributary, the Lumbundji, divides it into eastern and western sub-regions, each a separate chiefdom. It is with the western sub-region, lying between the Loange and the Lumbundji, that I am familiar and from which my observations are drawn. However, what I have learnt in the west is probably true also of the easterly chiefdom, which shares similar ecological conditions. There is a third group of Lele living to the south, whose country is predominantly savannah,

instead of mixed savannah and forest. It is unlikely that my observations about the western Lele apply also to these southerners.

Lele country is at the extreme edge of the equatorial forest belt, hence the great change of scene in the 150 miles from north to south. The Nkutu, their northern neighbours on the other bank of the Kasai, inhabit dense forest. Their southern neighbours, the Njembe, live in rolling grassland. Lele country has thickly forested valleys separated by barren grass-topped hills.

It is useless to discuss any aspect of Lele religion without first summarizing the material conditions of their life. This is not because these seem to have determined the bias of their religious thinking. On the contrary, the manner in which they have chosen to exploit their environment may well be due to the ritual categories through which they apprehend it.

MATERIAL ENVIRONMENT AND ECONOMY

A straightforward account of Lele material culture would not give the impression that hunting is their most important activity. By comparison with the Cokwe hunters, who have immigrated from the Kwango district into Lele country, they even seem inefficient in this pursuit. On the contrary, the culture of the raffia palm would seem to be their most vital economic activity, and if their ritual values were derived from their social and economic values, then we would expect the Lele religion to be centred round the cultivation of the raffia palm. Yet this is not so. Again, assuming that a people long settled in their environment normally exploit it to the full, it is difficult to see why the Lele refuse to breed goats and pigs (which thrive locally), and why the cultivation of groundnuts is left entirely to the women. These problems find some solution, however, when they are seen in the context of their metaphysical assumptions and religious practice.

The Lele village, a compact square of 20 to 100 huts, is always set in the grassland. From each corner of the village, paths run down to the nearest part of the forest. They wind first through groves of palms which ring the village round, and then through the grass and scrub. The palm groves give shade to the men working at their weaving-looms. Each corner of the village belongs to one of the four men's age-sets, which has its own groves adjacent to its row of huts. Alternating with the men's groves are other groves used by their women-folk for pounding grain. Farther away still is another ring of groves where the women prepare palm-oil. The layout of the village shows a deliberate separation of the sexes. In all their work, feeding, and leisure, the women are set apart from the men. This separation of the sexes is a formality which they observe, a rule of social etiquette, not a natural principle derived from the nature of the work they perform, for in many of their economic activities there is a close collaboration between men and women. The separation and interdependence of the sexes is a basic theme of their social organization and ritual, and one which is reiterated in almost every possible context.

Their staple food is maize, cultivated in the forest by slash and burn methods. With such a scattered population no land shortage is recognized and no crop rotation is practised. Maize is only planted once in a forest clearing, and fresh clearings are made each year for the new crop. The original clearing is kept open for several years, until the other crops planted in it have matured. The most important of these is raffia palm, and in recent years manioc has become nearly as important as maize. Small quantities of pineapples, red peppers, and hill rice are also cultivated.

The palm takes four or five years to mature, and is very carefully cultivated. All its products are used; its main ribs for hut wall and roof supports, its fibres as string in hut building and basketry, its smaller ribs as arrow shafts, its outside leaves as thatching for the walls and roofs of huts. The inner cuticle of the young leaf is the material from which they weave their raffia cloths. Finally, one of the most valued products of the palm is the unfer-

mented wine, which forms the second staple article of diet. When the wine is all drawn off and the palm dead, its rotting stem harbours grubs which are a highly prized delicacy. When they have grown fat, and can be heard moving inside the stem, it is chopped open, and made to yield its last product.

This list of the uses of the raffia palm does not yet give an idea of its full importance in Lele culture. The Lele pride themselves on their skill in weaving, and despise the neighbouring Cokwe, Nkutu, and Dinga who are ignorant of the art, and who exchange their products for woven squares. The Dinga give fish, the Nkutu give lengths of red camwood, the Cokwe give meat in exchange. Although every Lele man can weave, they also use the woven squares among themselves as a kind of currency. There is no object which has not its fixed price in raffia squares—two for an arrow-head, two for a basket, one for a standard lump of salt. Moreover, they are required as marriage gifts, fifty to the father and forty to the mother of the bride. They are expected as mourning gifts, demanded in initiation fees, apprenticeship dues, fines, and payment for medical services. For diet, clothes, huts, and ceremonial gifts this is a culture heavily dependent on the raffia palm.

The palm and the banana are the only crops which, although they grow best in the forest's rich soil, are also planted around the village. Apart from these, and the groundnut, all good things come out of the forest: water, firewood, salt, maize, manioc, oil, fish, and animal flesh.

The division of labour is based mainly on two principles. The first is that work which relates to cookery and the preparation of food is performed by women. They draw water, gather firewood, cultivate fish-ponds in the marshy streams, cultivate salt-yielding plants, and prepare salt from the ashes. They are excluded from certain other tasks for which they are held to lack the necessary skill, strength, or courage. On these grounds hunting and everything to do with the weapons and medicines of the hunt are men's work, although women cook the meat. Women cannot climb trees, so cutting oil-palm fruits and drawing palm wine, and preparing all the products of the raffia palm are men's tasks. All the complicated process of preparing raffia and setting up the looms, weaving, and sewing is performed by men, although there is no prejudice against a man's wife or sister helping if she is able. The men cut down the trees for the maize clearings, and are aided by their women-folk who clear away the undergrowth, and later take on most of the work of keeping the crops clear of weeds. Women help with the planting and undertake all the harvesting of crops.

From this it is clear that the division of labour is based on practical considerations, men and women taking their appropriate share of the burden. Both are required to spend the major part of their time in the forest. Apart from the clearing and planting of crops there, which men and women share together, the time the men spend hunting and seeing to the raffia palms is paralleled by the time the women spend tending their salt and fish-ponds, chopping firewood, fetching water, and washing their manioc. If the women did not work in the forest the economic life of the village would collapse. Yet the Lele regard the forest as almost exclusively a male sphere, and women are frequently prohibited from entering it. On every third day they are excluded from the forest and must lay in their supplies of food, firewood, and water the day before. On all important religious occasions, such as mourning, birth of twins, appearance of the new moon, departure of a chief, in menstruation and childbirth, they are similarly excluded from the forest until proper rites have been performed by the men. This exclusion of women from the forest is one of the principal recurring themes of their religious practice.

THE FOREST

The prestige of the forest is immense. The Lele speak of it with almost poetic enthusiasm. God gave it to them as the source of all good things. They often contrast the forest with the village. In the heat of the day, when the dusty village is unpleasantly hot, they like to escape to the cool and dark of the forest. Work there is full of interest and pleasure, work elsewhere is drudgery. They say, "Time goes slowly in the village, quickly in the forest." Men boast that in the forest they can work all day without feeling hunger, but in the village they are always thinking about food. For going into the forest they use the verb *nyingena,* to enter, as one might speak of entering a hut, or plunging into water, giving the impression that they regard the forest as a separate element.

But as well as being the source of all good things the forest is a place of danger, not only for women at the specified times but often for men. No mourner may enter the forest, nor one who has had a nightmare. A bad dream is interpreted as a warning not to enter the forest on the next day. All kinds of natural dangers may hurt the man who disregards it. A tree may fall on his head, he may twist his ankle, cut himself with a knife, fall off a palm-tree, or otherwise suffer a fatal accident. These hazards exist at all times, but the risk on certain occasions is that inimical powers may direct them against him. The danger for a man is one of personal mishap, but a woman who breaks the injunction against entering the forest may endanger the whole village.

These risks, personal or general, can be warded off, or afterwards remedied, by means of sacred medicines, which give men power to dominate their environment, heal sickness, make barren women conceive, and make hunting successful. There seem therefore to be three distinct reasons for the great prestige of the forest: it is the source of all good and necessary things, food, drinks, huts, clothes; it is the source of the sacred medicines; and, thirdly, it is the scene of the hunt, which in Lele eyes is the supremely important activity. At this stage of description it would seem that two of these reasons are economic, not religious, but further examination shows that in reality the immense importance of the forest is derived from its role in Lele religion.

The attitude to hunting cannot be entirely ascribed to the importance of meat in Lele diet, although it is true that they have a craving for meat. Cooked maize, or manioc dough, would be unpalatable unless served with the appetizing sauces prepared daily by the women from vegetables, red pepper, salt, and oil. A purely vegetable diet is so much disliked that unless meat or fish can be served as well, people often prefer to drink palm wine and sleep unfed. Mushrooms, caterpillars, grubs, etc. are poor substitutes for fish, and even fish is second in their esteem to meat. In their ideal life the men would set traps and hunt regularly to provide their families with a daily supply of meat. To offer a vegetable meal to a guest is regarded as a grave insult. Much of their conversation about social events dwells on the amount and kind of meat provided.

The craving for meat has never led the Lele to breed goats and pigs, as do their southern neighbours, the Njembe. They profess to be revolted at the notion of eating animals reared in the village. Good food, they say, should come out of the forest, clean and wholesome, like antelope and wild pig. They consider rats and dogs to be unclean food, to which they apply the word *hama*, used also for the uncleanness of bodily dirt, suppurating wounds, and excreta. The same uncleanness attaches to the flesh of goats and pigs, just because they are bred in the village. Even plants which are used in sauces when gathered in the forest are left untouched if they grow near the village. This attitude does not seem to apply to poultry. Between men various social conventions cluster around the giving and receiving of chickens, but women are forbidden to eat their flesh or eggs. This prohibition, like most food taboos, is unexplained, but there may be greater danger to women from eating unclean food than for men, as in many contexts women are treated as if they were more vulnerable to pollution than men are.

Knowing of their craving for meat, and knowing that recent hunts had been unsuccessful, I was puzzled early in my visit to see a large pig carcass being carved up and carried some miles for sale to Luba and Dinga tribesmen. The Lele would not eat it. A few

go-ahead men keep goats or pigs, but not for food. They rear them for sale to the rich Luba lorry drivers and mechanics of the oil company at Brabanta. The Lele owners make no attempt to feed or control their livestock, which does much damage to the palms and bananas near the village. This carelessness does not result from total ignorance of rearing animals, for the Lele keep poultry and dogs successfully. In particular, the dogs are objects of an elaborate veterinary theory and practice. It seems that if they wished to make a success of goat herding they could do so.

Livestock is not the only source of meat which the Lele overlook when they declare that the forest is the source of all good things, for the grassland around the village harbours quantities of game. These duikers are eaten with relish when they are killed, but the Lele hunt them only at one season of the year— the short dry season when the grass is burnt, and the animals are slaughtered as they rush out of the fire. Their normal hunting techniques are not adapted to the pursuit of grassland game.

The way in which the Lele, in speaking of the forest, disregard other important sources of meat and food can be explained only in terms of the coherence of their religious concepts. To admit an alternative supply of meat, independent of the forest game, would be inconsistent with their attitude to the forest as the source of all the best things of life. Their view of the village as totally dependent on the forest is fundamental to their perception of the relation between human life and the natural and spiritual powers on which they depend. Ultimately, it appears that the prestige of the forest is entirely due to its place in Lele religion. It is the source of sacred medicines, but it need not be the only source of the material things of life. It is the scene of the hunt, but Lele hunting has primary religious functions which outweigh its economic importance.

The distinction of the village from the forest is one of the principal themes of their ritual, which is constantly emphasized and elaborated. There is also a subtle interplay between this theme and that of the separation of the sexes mentioned above. The separation of women from men, of forest from village, the dependence of village on forest, and the exclusion of women from the forest are the principal recurring elements of their ritual, on which minor variations are embroidered.

THE GRASSLAND

The appropriation of the forest by the men is balanced by treatment of the grassland as the exclusive sphere of women. The grassland has no prestige like the forest. It is dry and barren. The only crop which thrives there, the groundnut, is exclusively cultivated by the women. Ritual sanctions forbid a woman who has lifted the first sod of grass on her groundnut plot to have sexual intercourse until a month or six weeks later, when the seedlings are well established. No man must even set eyes on the work in progress, to say nothing of helping in the heavy work of cutting down the bushy trees on the plot. This is the only crop which women tend from start to finish, and the only crop which does not grow in the forest.

Most activities which custom allocates entirely to one or the other sex are similarly protected by sexual taboos, some lasting even longer than this example. No hunting expedition is undertaken without one night of continence being imposed first on the whole village. A man making pit traps may have to abstain from sexual relations for several months until certain specified animals have been caught. Most situations of ritual danger affecting the village as a whole are treated in the same way. The refrain "Tonight each woman her mat alone, each man his mat alone" is a regular announcement preceding important rites.

The groundnut crop is the most striking example of the appropriation of the grassland by the women as their sphere. They often manage to find in the grassland some substitutes for what they cannot get on days when they are excluded from the forest. When they

may not go fishing, other delicacies may be gathered in the grassland: grasshoppers in the dry season, caterpillars in the wet, or grubs from decaying palms planted near the village. A woman who has run short of firewood may collect in the grassland enough brushwood for the day's cooking. There are no ritual prohibitions connected with the grassland. As a neutral sphere between the two it is used again and again in the prohibitions which separate the village from the forest.

At first view I was tempted to find a natural explanation of the allocation of male and female spheres, the forest to the men, the grassland to the women. It is obvious that women, in spite of their economic tasks there, are at a disadvantage in the forest. Unarmed, and loaded with baskets, they are defenceless against strange men or wild animals. They are afraid of the dark. They do not understand the medicines which men find there and administer to the village. Hunting is a man's task. On the face of it there is something appropriate in regarding the forest as primarily the sphere of men, particularly if we associate the prestige and danger of the forest with male domination. But these considerations in themselves do not adequately explain the strict ritual exclusion of women on so many occasions.

A more satisfactory explanation can be given in terms of their religious concepts, according to which women hold a very complex status. Childbearing, their most vital function, is regarded as highly vulnerable. On the other hand, sexual intercourse and menstruation are dangerous to all male activities. These contrasted themes are handled with elaborate subtlety in the treatment of marital and extramarital relations, which do not concern us here. It is enough to remember the complex ritual status of women when trying to understand the separation of the sexes and the exclusion of women from the forest. As women are both highly vulnerable and highly polluting some separation of male and female spheres is indicated, and the very neutrality of the grassland makes its allocation to the women more appropriate.

MEDICINE

In Lele religion nearly all important rites are associated with the practice of medicine. The idiom of medical healing has so dominated their religious forms that it is often hard to distinguish two separate spheres of action. This is consistent with Lele speculations about life and death, which they consider to be controlled exclusively by God, *Njambi*. Such power of healing and curing barrenness as may be exercised by humans is derived only from God. Hence, the diviners must be at the same time healers and religious experts. Whether they are trying to cure a fever, or to set right the relation of a village to spiritual powers, the same vocabulary is used to describe the treatment, and the same personnel and resources are employed. To find the cause of the disorder they first use divination; then they prescribe and apply some herbal remedy with the proper formula, and impose a number of restrictions on the patient.

Although up to this point the vocabulary is the same, yet beneath the general similarity two categories are distinguished. The words used by the sick man to describe his symptoms are not used to describe the state of the village needing medical treatment. The man says he is feverish, sick, or weak, but of the village they say that it is bad (*bube*) or spoilt (*wonyi*). If the man is cured he says that he is strong (*bunono*) or that he has gained vigour (*manyin*). But a village in a sound condition is said to be soft (*bolabolu*) or peaceful, quiet (*polo*). The word for curing a sick man is *belu*; for setting right a disordered village, *ponga*, to mend, set straight, arrange in order. These important verbal differences show that there is a distinction between the two situations, and it may be only by analogy that they draw on the same vocabulary in describing the treatment given to a sick person or to a village.

The word for rites and medicines is *nengu*, which applies equally to healing and to village ritual. The practitioner who applies the medicine or performs the rite is in either case

ngang, which in its widest application means only "expert"; in its narrowest it refers to members of the group of diviners. As individuals they have each their own practice. As a body they have a public responsibility towards their village. They administer its *nengu* for it.

I prefer to translate *nengu* as sacred medicine, whether in its medical or its mainly religious sense, because the Lele themselves consistently identify rite and medicine. I should point out a distinction which they make between these sacred medicines and a range of simple remedies called *bilumbela,* which are used to treat minor ailments. The latter work by virtue of their natural properties, as wine intoxicates or food nourishes. They may be applied for headaches, constipation, coughs, and colds. Knowledge of them carries no prestige, for they are not worth a diviner's serious attention. Consistently with what has been said so far, these simple remedies are applied mainly by the women, not by the men, and significantly, they are to be found in the grassland. Sacred medicines, by contrast with women's remedies, are found in the forest. Diviners asking for a high fee remind their clients that their calling imposes on them arduous expeditions through the damp undergrowth.

Unlike simples, all sacred medicines, to be effective, require prohibitions to be imposed on the patient. Their power depends largely on the control the diviner has over them: according to whether he has undergone the correct initiation and paid for the power to apply them and followed the proper restrictions himself. It depends also on the recital of an address which adjures the medicine to do its work, and on the goodwill between the diviner and his client.

A man under medical treatment must accept restrictions on his way of living. He may be forbidden to drink palm wine, to eat certain kinds of fish, to enter the forest, etc. If a village is undergoing a course of medicines, it is similarly put under restrictions. The character of these gives us some further insight into Lele religious ideas. The favourite themes which are used over and over again have already been indicated: the separation of the two spheres, forest and village, the separation of the sexes, women's exclusion from the forest, the association of the forest with spiritual power, the neutrality of the grassland. To the Lele their rites do not appear as a series of disconnected and meaningless acts. The very economy and repetition of the themes they draw upon produces a kind of pattern which is intelligible in terms of their assumptions about the relation of God to men and animals.

SPIRITUAL BEINGS: GOD

In writing about God and the spirits, and the sacred medicines which draw their power from them, it is convenient to use the word 'spiritual', although I do not know of a Lele word to cover this single category of things which are not human and not animal. They frequently dwell on the distinction between humans and animals, emphasizing the superiority of the former and their right to exploit the latter. When they feel that too much is being required of them by the Administration, they like to exclaim; *"Cung bahutu i?"* "Are we animals then?" But there is no suggestion in their speech that God and the spirits belong to either of these categories.

Of God, *Njambi,* they say that he has created men and animals, rivers and all things. The relation of God to men is like that of their owner to his slaves. He orders them, protects them, sets their affairs straight, and avenges injustice. Animals of the forest are also under God's power, though they have been given to the Lele for their food. Game protection laws enforced by the Administration strike the Lele as an impious contravening of God's act, since he originally gave all the animals in the forest to their ancestors to hunt and kill.

The third class of beings under the power of God are the spirits, *mingehe.* In talking about them the Lele are careful not to speak in anthropomorphic terms. They insist that spirits are not and never have been men. They have never been seen by men. If one were

to set eyes on a spirit he would be struck blind, and die of sores. If pressed for more details they are forced to give analogies from human behaviour, but they do not like talking of the spirits. It is obvious that they are held in fear in spite of their benevolent powers.

The spirits inhabit the deep forest, especially the sources of streams. They sleep in the day, but roam about at night. Hence the need to avoid loud noises in the village at night, lest a spirit walking in the fringe of the forest hear, and be tempted to come near. The day of rest is the one time when the spirits roam abroad in daylight. Spirits suffer no death or illness. They control the fertility of women and prosper men's hunting. Or they may withhold the game, and turn aside the hunter's arrow. They may prevent women from conceiving. They can strike a village with sickness. In all their acts they do not behave capriciously. The study of their ways is the diviner's secret lore.

This is the official view of the spirits, held by the diviners, and which influences their practice of medicine. There are also popular fancies about them, told to children, or believed by the uninitiated. The thin wreaths of mist twisting up from the forest in the early morning are said to be smoke from the night fires of the spirits. A man walking alone in strange forest at night may find his hair stiffening, his body pouring with cold sweat, his heart beating madly. He suddenly comes on a clearing, where there was a bright light. He sees a smouldering fire, but no one there . . . a fire of the spirits.

The diviners regard the water pigs as the animals most highly charged with spiritual power, because they spend their days wallowing in the stream sources, which are the favourite haunt of the spirits. The ordinary man thinks of the pig as a sort of dog, owned by the spirits; he lives in his master's home, sleeps and feeds with him, obeys him like a hunter's dog. The spirits punish and reward hunters by giving or withholding game, but in the single act they control opposite destinies. For while they are rewarding a hunter with game, they are punishing the animal for some disobedience to their commands.

NATURAL OBJECTS
ASSOCIATED WITH SPIRITS

Certain animals and plants show signs that they are associated with the spirits in a particularly close way; the pig, as I have said, because he frequents the sources of streams. Certain bush bucks, because, like the spirits, they sleep all day and move at night, are spirit animals, and for that reason their flesh is forbidden to women. Fish also, because they live in streams, are associated with spirits, and are therefore prescribed or prohibited in different medicines. A pregnant woman must not eat fish. Crocodiles are the subject of some controversy among the experts. In the south they are classed with fish, because they live in water, and are therefore forbidden to pregnant women. In the north the fact that they inhabit water does not make them fish, and so here, crocodile flesh, since it can be bought and dried, is considered to be the food *par excellence* for pregnant women forbidden to eat fish.

Certain plants are either forbidden or recommended in medical treatment, because they are associated with the spirits. The banana, for example, is a plant of the spirits because, when it has been cut down, it does not die, as would a palm, but sprouts and lives again. Only spirits do not die, so this characteristic marks the banana as the proper ritual food on certain occasions. These few examples show how the animal and vegetable worlds are studied and classified according to religious categories.

Spring water and rain water are spirit things, because they are essential to life. The moon is called a spirit for two reasons. First, it seems to die, and to disappear completely, but always reappears. Second, it is associated with fertility, because by it a woman reckons the nine months of her pregnancy. They say, "The moon brings children." The moon therefore shares with the spirits their immortality and their control over fertility. The appear-

ance of the new moon is treated with characteristic rites. Sexual relations are forbidden, women are not allowed to pound grain, nor to enter the forest. No one may make loud noises in the forest, such as chopping trees. The next day the men go hunting and shed the blood of an animal. The hunt may be a pure formality, the death of one squirrel suffices. Then the restrictions are lifted. This rite is performed in order that the maize crop may thrive. It is highly characteristic of the bias of the Lele culture that the only rite which they perform to prosper their staple crop is a hunting rite. The taboos accompanying it are also characteristic: taboos on sexual relations, on women entering the forest, on noisy work. Further examples will make clear how the medical prescriptions draw constantly on the simple familiar themes which have been outlined above.

Fish, when freshly taken from the stream, are treated as if charged with spiritual power, or as if there were danger in their improper handling. They figure frequently in medical advice for this reason. There is a significant rite which must be observed before any fish can be brought into the village. A woman returning from her fishing expedition in the forest first sends a child ahead into the village to fetch a firebrand. The fish touched with the fire may then be carried into the village. Her fishing-baskets may not be brought in until they have been left for a night in the grassland outside the village. Special stakes are set up at the paths leading to the forest, on which fishing-baskets are always to be seen hanging. Similar rules apply to some other forest products, creeper-ropes and withies used in basketmaking, but not to meat, nor to planted products, maize, manioc, or palm wine. I do not know the basis of the distinction which treats fish and certain natural forest products as dangerous in this way, while exempting meat and planted products, but Lele ritual seems to be so consistent that deeper research would probably explain the distinction.

These are rules of everyday behaviour, but particular medicines also treat the grassland as if it were a ritually neutralizing element. For example, a woman in childbirth who confesses her adultery is held to be in mortal danger. The appropriate medicine for her case prescribes among other things that she be first carried out of the village, so that the difficult delivery takes place in grassland. When medicines are being used to establish a new village, there is a period between the setting up of the huts and the killing of certain game in the hunt, during which it is forbidden for villagers to eat in the village. They carry their food to be eaten in the grassland just outside. Examples could be multiplied.

RULES OF BEHAVIOR TOWARDS GOD AND SPIRITS

Some of the stock prohibitions concern noise. Noises associated with the day are always forbidden at night: for instance, women may not pound grain after dusk. Drumming, on the other hand, is a legitimate nighttime noise, and dancing does not usually take place in the day. On all important religious occasions, such as the day of rest, at the new moon, in mourning, and in villages undergoing certain medicines, pounding is completely forbidden. A mourning village goes hungry for three days, and the closest relatives of the dead may not pound grain for two or three months. Medicines sometimes forbid pounding to be done in the village, so the mortars are carried to the grassland outside. Other medicines forbid any kind of loud noise in the village at night. In such a case, were a man to let out a loud, yodelling call in the dark in the village, he would have to pay the maximum fine for spoiling the medicine. In one village a medicine required that the women should not carry their full load of firewood into their compounds, lest they drop it with a loud crash. They were obliged to drop the load in the grassland outside the village, then bring in the logs in armfuls, a few at a time.

Dance drums may not be beaten in periods of mourning. If a man dies his village does not dance for three months. On days of rest and other religions occasions, all work in the forest which involves what they call a drum-like noise is forbidden to men and women. No trees may be cut, no clearing of the forest, no chopping of wood, no opening of dead palm-trees to extract the grubs. Noisy work seems to bring the village into a dangerous relation with the forest, except on specified occasions. On ordinary days the spirits are sleeping in the farthest depths of the forest, and would not be disturbed, but on the day of rest they come out, and may be near the village. They would be angry to hear chopping sounds in the forest, or pounding in the village. On the day of rest the rules are in part reversed where drums are concerned. The spirits are then abroad in daylight as if it were night, so no workaday noise of pounding or chopping is allowed; but this is the only day when the drums may be beaten in full daylight, and everyone dances.

These examples sufficiently illustrate the themes on which the ritual idiom is based. The prohibitions are acceptable to the Lele because they relate in an intelligible way to what they know of the spiritual and natural worlds. They provide a code of behaviour for men towards God and the spirits. They introduce order into the universe; regulations distinguish the day from night, one month from another, the day of rest from working days, forest from the village, males from females. They place the whole environment in intelligible categories. These categories have unquestionable validity, because they have been proved, from the beginning of Lele times to the present day, by the working of the sacred medicines. Any particular medicine may fail, for a number of possible reasons, but the whole theory and practice of medicine is not thereby jeopardized. On the other hand, any little cure, any successful hunt, testifies to the soundness of the basic hypotheses. The rites contain in themselves the proof of their own efficacy and of the truth of the assumption on which they are based.

The various medicines bring before the mind the kind of good relations which ought to exist between the spiritual, the human, and the natural worlds. But they do more than this. As well as demonstrating order in the universe, they also provide for order in social relations. They insist on a high degree of harmony between the persons undergoing and performing the treatment.

HARMONY IN HUMAN RELATIONS

I have not said so far what kind of interest the spirits in the forest are thought to take in the affairs of men, what acts are meritorious, and what are transgressions to be punished. They uphold all the regulations which I have mentioned concerning men's relation to the spiritual: observance of the day of rest, of the food privileges of cult groups, the taboos on workaday noise at night-time, the distinction of the sexes, and of the forest from village. In the second place, they require all persons living in a village to be at peace with each other. The village faces its own forest, and through it the spiritual world, as a single whole. In this the ritual corresponds to the political situation, in which each village is autonomous and potentially at war with other villages. In religion the solidarity of each village is such that an offence by one member affects adversely the whole village, and the barrenness of a woman or the failure of an individual hunter may be attributed to the general condition of the village in which they live. This spiritual condition is constantly discussed in the terms I have given: the village is either *polo,* soft and quiet, or *bube,* bad. The exchange of greetings with a visitor usually includes a question; "Is your village quiet?" to which the answer may be that they are in mourning for a dead person, or that they are undergoing hunting medicine, or that all is well and quiet, wild pig having recently been killed.

Good hunting is the clearest sign that all is well with the village. The small amount of meat which each man, woman, and child may receive when a wild pig is killed cannot explain the joy which is shown in talking about it for weeks afterwards. The hunt is a kind of spiritual barometer whose rise and fall is eagerly watched by the entire village. This is one of the reasons why hunting carries more prestige than any other activity.

It is impossible not to be struck by the way in which child-bearing and hunting are coupled together, as if they were equivalent male and female functions. A village which has had a long series of bad hunts will begin soon to remark how few pregnancies there have been lately, or a village suffering from an epidemic or frightened by a recent series of deaths will send for a diviner to do medicines for them, saying that the village is spoilt, hunting has failed, women are barren, everyone is dying. Diviners themselves do not confuse the two symptoms. They perform distinct medicines for the separate disorders, but the grateful village whose hunting has been set on a sound basis will praise the medicine, saying, for example; "Our village is soft and good now. Since the diviner went home we have killed three wild pigs and many antelopes, four women have conceived, we are all healthy and strong." These are the accepted signs of a generally prosperous condition.

In a small village changes in the fertility of women are not easily observed. It is by watching the hunt, in the way that the Lele do, that we can see what kind of harmony between its members is rewarded by the spirits, and what dissensions are punished by hunting failure.

The concept of peace within the village receives a profound interpretation. The success of the hunt requires that internal solidarity be real in the fullest sense. Bloodshed, striking of blows, tearing of hair, scratching, or any violence spoils the village, but so also do hard words and insults. Whether the offender is a resident or a temporary visitor makes no difference. Villagers naturally resent violent behaviour by outsiders more acutely than they mind quarrels between residents. On the other hand, within the village itself the higher the ritual status of the persons quarrelling, the more fatal their ill will may be. The officially appointed diviner of the village may spoil it by a rebuke to his wife, whereas a more open show of anger from an ordinary man might escape notice. The village seems to be specially sensitive to any breach of marital peace. A wife who runs away in anger, even if she returns penitent the same evening, has spoilt the village, and both she and her husband owe a fine before hunting can be resumed. The anger of an old man, whether just or unprovoked, is highly dangerous. A simple rite performed usually before any hunt illustrates their interpretation of ritual peace. Each man, as he sets out, takes the matchet or knife from his girdle and gives it silently to his neighbour, who completes the exchange with his own knife. The meaning of this action is explained as if one were saying: "My age-mate, you take the matchet with which I may have been hitting my wife," and the other replying: "And you take my knife, in case I have struck my children with it." At the end of the hunt the weapons are returned to their owners, for the need for covering all secret breaches of peace is over.

ORGANIZATION OF VILLAGES

Village solidarity is evidently a major preoccupation. This is intelligible in view of the lack of strong internal village organization. Although the village is united politically against all other villages, and although it acts as a single unit in face of the supernatural, yet, apart from their religious institutions, it is difficult to see any underlying principle which is capable of producing this unity.

The men of the village belong to age-sets, but these do not perform any obvious function in regulating village life. They are the basis of a form of gerontocracy. Old men of the senior sets enjoy considerable prestige, but they only dominate the village in subtle, unformalized ways, through esoteric knowledge, and reputation as sorcerers. The principle of seniority is carried so far that it even prevents any strong leadership emerging in the person of the village chief. The man who carries this title is qualified by being the oldest man in the village. Since by definition he is approaching senility, he has little real power.

There is no centre of authority in the village and, moreover, it is customary to avoid public responsibility. Most men shun conspicuous roles for fear of exciting jealousy. The

Lele ideal of a man fitted to hold public office is not a dominating personality, but one who is modest, gentle, self-effacing. There are several posts in the village to which young men of this character are appointed, by the old men in some cases, by their age-mates in others, but they are junior executives of the village and not in any way its leaders.

To make internal cohesion more unlikely the population of the village fluctuates constantly. Of twenty or more men in the oldest age-sets, only two or three will have been born in the village. Every ten or fifteen years the village itself changes its site. There is no closely knit kin group forming the core of the village. The matrilineal clans are weak and scattered, and a man's tie with his father's people generally lasts only during the father's lifetime. From the standpoint of social organization alone it is surprising that such a heterogeneous collection of people can form a village highly conscious of its identity, and capable of carrying on historic feuds with other villages. Their very real corporate unity evidently derives from their religious institutions, and from the way these are related to the communal hunt.

HUNTING: A COMMUNAL ACTIVITY

It is the communal hunt, and not the private hunter's or trapper's success, which is the anxiously scanned indication of spiritual health. The method is to set a cordon of men armed with bows and arrows around a section of the forest, which is then combed by beaters and their dogs. Young boys and old men who can barely walk try to join the hunt, but the most valued members are the dog-owners, who have the heavy work of scrambling through the undergrowth, shouting to control and encourage their dogs. The game startled by them rushes out on to the arrows of the waiting hunters. This is probably the most effective method of hunting in dense forest. It depends on surprising the game and on quick shooting at very short range.

What is strange in a people proud of their hunting is the general lack of individual skills.

A man going into the forest for any purpose carries his bow and a few arrows, but these are intended for birds or squirrels. He does not expect to take large game by himself. They know none of the specialized techniques of the single hunter. They do not stalk, do not know how to imitate the calls of animals, do not camouflage or use decoys, seldom penetrate into deep forest alone. All their interest is centred on the communal hunt. I was often struck by the lack of confidence an individual hunter would have in his own aim. A range of 40 feet or more is outside their power, and they expect to hit at 10 or 15 feet. A man walking in the forest might come on a herd of pig wallowing in a marsh, creep up to them so close as to hear their breathing, then, rather than risk a long shot, he will tiptoe away agog to call out the village.

These weaknesses of the Lele style of hunting I attribute to their having specialized in techniques suited to the dense forest. Their inefficiency is noticeable by comparison with the Cokwe hunters, who are immigrants from true savannah country, and have what I suppose must be the characteristic skills of savannah hunting. They hunt in pairs or singly, stalk and call their game, and have such success that they decimate the animals of the forest in a few months. Admittedly, the Cokwe have for many generations been used to firearms, since the Portuguese used them as slave raiders, whereas very few Lele villages possess more than two or three guns.

The Lele have specialized in the communal hunt of the forest to such a degree that they only hunt the grassland when the same techniques are applicable, that is, in the dry season when they fire the grass. On this annual occasion several villages combine to ring around the burning countryside. This is the time when young boys expect to make their first kill, for the slaughter, I am told, is terrific. This is the only occasion when the hunting unit is more than the male population of one village, as it is in all forest hunting. Ultimately the village is a political and a ritual unit because it is a single hunting unit. It is

not surprising that the Lele think of theirs as a hunting culture first and foremost.

An account of a month's wet season hunting in one village will illustrate the points which have been discussed so far. Unfortunately, the period covered by the hunting journal gives a poor impression both of their skill in the hunt and of the efficacy of their medicine. It is only fair to mention that a party of Cokwe hunters had been for the previous three months staying in the village, killing the animals and selling the meat to the villagers at exorbitant prices. Finally, their funds of cash were as depleted as the game in the forest, and they chased the Cokwe away from the village when bargaining for lower prices had failed. However, for the purpose of illustrating an account of their ritual, a series of bad hunts is more illuminating than successful ones.

A village has sometimes to undergo a long course of medicine, extending over several months. At various stages of the performance a specified kill may be required. Until the pig or the right type of antelope is brought home and the dedicated parts eaten by the appropriate cult group, the medicines cannot be continued. An example of such a series of medicines is the one called *Kinda,* which is usually set up in a village after it has been moved to a new site. It ensures fertility for the women and good hunting. In these medicines the hunt becomes an essential part of the ritual which makes for the prosperity of the village.

HUNTING JOURNAL OF YENGA-YENGA.
FEBRUARY-MARCH 1950

18 February. Fruitless hunt. The failure was generally attributed to the refusal on the eve of the hunt of one of the diviners, Ngondu, a fiery tempered man, to cooperate with his colleagues. In the middle of their consultation he had suddenly burst out complaining that his wife's groundnuts had been stolen, and that when the Administration came to inspect the crop he would be sent to prison, though it was no fault of his that an enemy had stolen them. He flung out of the meeting and someone whispered: "See the diviner is spoiling the village." The hunt was fruitless, in spite of the medicines prepared.

19 February. The whole day was taken up in discussing the cause of failure. Ngondu's sister's son, who had overheard the whisper against his uncle, told him that he was suspected of having spoilt the hunt. Quarrelling went on in the centre of the village about this, Ngondu shouting with tears of rage that he was the injured party. He brought up all his old grievances: one of his wives had died the year before, allegedly killed by the poison of the catechist. Ngondu had actually been building her a new hut, and its unfinished framework still stood in the village. He declared that every time he saw it he felt bitter in his heart, for no food cooked by his remaining wives tasted so sweet to him as hers. This brought up all his concentrated dislike of the catechist. Now his other wife was in distress because her child had been beaten for playing truant from the catechism class. If this were reported to the missionary he, Ngondu, would be sent to prison, and for none of his own fault. And not for the first time. He could not speak the language of the white men, and did not understand their ways, so it was he, and no others who got sent to prison for avoiding road-corvée work, when others had been slacker than he. And so on. He brought up complicated histories reaching far back into the past. His friends tried to calm him, his enemies insisted that none of this was a reason for spoiling the hunting medicines; a diviner should feel more responsibility for his village. Finally, the matter was settled by a summing-up from a visitor, Bikwak, a famous diviner, who had been invited from another village to set up the *Kinda,* the fertility medicine which every new village should have. He suggested that the matter be dropped; Ngondu was in the wrong in having left the diviners' meeting in a rage, but he had been sorely provoked by the theft of his wife's groundnuts. No one knew who had stolen them. Perhaps it was some unthinking child. Let the matter rest there.

20 February. Bikwak, the visiting diviner, together with two important local diviners, Ngondu and Nyama, prepared the medicine for the next day's hunt. In the night Bikwak sang in a trance, during which he was visited by spirits, who told him where game would be found the next day.

21 February. The medicines were finished at dawn. Bikwak, as superintending diviner, directed the hunters where to go, but he had to stay in the village all day. Women were forbidden to pound grain or to cut wood until he gave the all-clear.

The kill was disappointing: one little blue duiker and one red duiker. In all, seven antelopes had been put up by the dogs, so the spirits had not deceived Bikwak. The village was undoubtedly spoilt, as they had only killed two instead of seven.

At night Bikwak sang again, and divined in his singing the cause of the failure to kill seven animals. The spirits were protesting at the prolonged absence of the *Kinda* medicine in the village. The village was over two years old, but after the *Kinda* had originally been set up with full rites by Nyama, it had been maliciously stolen by an unknown thief. The catechists and the young Christians of the village had been suspect. Bikwak learnt in the night's trance that it had been stolen by the men of Hanga, a rival village, which had been defeated in war many years ago by Yenga-Yenga and which, ever since, had been trying to be revenged by underhand means. Hunting would continue to fail so long as the *Kinda* was not set up. So they began at once to make preparations for it.

24 February. Bikwak sang again in the night, after announcing that men and women should sleep apart, as next day there would be hunting.

25 February. In the morning he streaked each man's leg with charcoal and white clay. But it rained, and the hunt was postponed. As the medicine for the new *Kinda* had been started, no visitors were allowed to eat in the village. A man and his wife from Mbombe were turned away, as, if they had taken food, they would have had to spend the night in the village. Taking food in the village brings the stranger under the full ritual prohibition affecting residents. Were he to eat, then go away, and have sexual relations while the village was still under the ban, he would be charged with having spoiled the medicine and be obliged to pay a heavy fine.

26 February. The hunt was successful. One blue duiker, one red duiker, and one big yellow-backed duiker. Bikwak ordered that the backs, heads, feet, and intestines should be set aside to be eaten by the cult groups of the village.

28 February. Bikwak still needed wild pig before he could proceed with the next step in the *Kinda* medicines. He announced that today everyone must get on with their usual work, for tomorrow he would send the men off on a hunt.

In the afternoon a bloody fight broke out between two road-menders and their wives. As the villagers gathered to watch the fight, the scratching and tearing of women's hair and head-wounds, nose-bleeding and insults, they were unanimous in their indignation: 'Fancy spoiling the village for other people! Disgusting! They are ruining tomorrow's hunt.' After the fight Bikwak, with the other diviners, ordered a fine of two raffia cloths and a chicken from the initiators of hostilities. They pleaded for time to pay. In order not to delay the hunt the village went bail for them, notching the ears of a goat in token of their payment. Bikwak did new medicine to cancel the effects of the fight, and announced in the evening: "Tonight each woman her mat, each man his mat. Tomorrow we hunt."

1 March. Rain. No hunt. The fighters were reported to the Tribunal, and taken away by the police. At night, Bikwak again announced: "Woman, her mat, man, his mat," etc.

2 March. Rain. No Hunt. Announced: "Woman, her mat, man, his mat," etc.

3 March. Hunt: killed three: one red duiker, one blue duiker, one bay duiker. No pig killed. At this hunt they drew cover four times:

1st draw. Blank. Consultation held. Agreed that the village must still be spoilt by the road-menders' fight. The fine asked could not have been heavy enough for so much violence. In token of a bigger fine, one man gave his matchet to another.

2nd draw. Blank again.

3rd draw. They put up an antelope, one man shot and wounded it, another fired his gun and killed it.

4th draw. One blue duiker killed, one bay duiker. End of hunt. Still no pig. At this stage, Bikwak, the diviner in charge, went away temporarily, and the medicines were suspended until his return.

5 March. A hunt without medicines, undertaken because they wanted to taste meat. One red duiker only killed. This time failure to kill more was not ascribed to moral or religious conditions. The two best dog-owners were absent, and neither of their two juniors knew the forest so well. Several animals had been put up by the dogs, but had slipped between the waiting hunters. Too many were missing for the communal hunt to be effective. A thunderstorm finally broke up the hunt, and they decided to postpone further attempts until the leading dog-owner returned.

10 March. The leading dog-owner returned, so they went hunting. Nothing to do with medicine, just to chase up some little blue duikers for food. No game.

16 March. Wild pig spoor reported very near the village. The men went off quickly. A fruitless expedition, the pig had passed by in the night. A few young men were in favour of going on in the hope of rounding up some little blue duikers. Then one of the dogs fell suddenly sick, and the owner had to prepare medicines for it. As the dog looked like dying, the hunt was abandoned.

18 March. Another impromptu hunt. A man reported fresh wild pig tracks. The men were called in from their work. They met at the grove of one of the chief diviners, Ngondu. The plan of the hunt was decided upon. Then a matter was raised by one of the other diviners. He mentioned the rumour that when

Bikwak, the visiting diviner, had been at work, he had not been given the help of his colleagues of the village. Was it right that he should have been left to collect medicines by himself? Was it true? In reply Ngondu asked scornfully, when was a visiting diviner ever left unaided? Of course they had all collaborated. Another diviner suggested that the rumor might have arisen because Bikwak had sent one of them to look for herbs in one direction, the other in another direction, and had set off himself in a third, so giving the impression of working alone. This settled the matter, and the man who had raised it took one of the dog bells, and breathed over it, in sign of goodwill. He then swopped his matchet with that of Ngondu and the hunt moved off.

No kill, as the herd of pig had escaped behind the place where the dogs were sent in.

23 March. Bikwak still absent. A local diviner, Nyama, prepared hunting medicines in the evening. He shouted his orders: no one was to sleep on Cokwe woven mats, but only on traditional Lele beds; no one to sleep in European blankets; no one to smoke European cigarettes or to wear European clothes, only Lele raffia loin-cloths; each man to sleep on his mat alone, each woman alone. Next morning at dawn, before the hunt, they were all to meet and to bring up their grievances, lest any secret grudge should spoil the hunt.

24 March. At the meeting, the first man called upon to speak was the village chief. A few days ago, on the morning of the impromptu hunt (18th), the tax-collectors and policemen were going away, and ordered him to provide men to carry their boxes. Just before the hunt the village chief went round pathetically pleading for volunteers. The young men laughed at his anxiety, and promised that after the hunt they would carry the luggage. But when they got back they said they were too tired, and would first sit down and rest. The village chief, though goaded by the police, could persuade no one. Finally, in despair, though so weak in the knees that he could hardly walk, he and his nearest agemate (nearly as decrepit as himself, and even

more a by-word for senility) prepared to lift the load themselves. Loudly complaining of aching backs, they staggered a few feet, and two young men were shamed into taking the load. This disrespect and indignity was felt to be very disgraceful to the village so the chief was asked to breathe out a blessing on the hunt, to show that he harbored no ill will.

The next to be asked for a blessing was Nyama, one of the principal diviners, and he who had prepared the medicines for that day. He said that he felt very bitter because, two years ago, he had made the *Kinda* medicine for the new village, and it had worked well: seven women in all had conceived, hunting had been good. Then someone had come in the night and stolen it away. It was useless their asking him to make it anew. Someone else could, but he felt too angry in his heart. However, he would not let his grief spoil the day's hunt, and he breathed out a blessing.

Then someone brought up the question of Nyama's wives who had been bickering for some time. On the previous day one of them, Ihowa, had been so stung by the taunts of her co-wife that she had run away to her mother's village. Was not this likely to spoil the medicine of the hunt? Nyama replied that the quarrel had not been serious, and Ihowa had not left in anger, she had merely paid a normal visit to her mother.

This completed the agenda, the meeting ended, and the hunters moved off. The first two coverts they drew were blank. They consulted and decided to swap matchets. In the next draw the dogs put up a duiker but it got away with a surface scratch. They consulted again, and decided that something should be done at once about Nyama's wife, in case her running off to her mother's village had been in anger after all. Nyama's sister's son, representing him, gave a knife to a man representing the village elders. At the next draw they put up a duiker again, but the arrow missed it altogether. The fifth draw was a blank. Decided it was useless to pursue the hunt. Someone must have been fighting secretly in the village. They would have to have an inquiry to find out what was wrong. No good hunting until it was set right.

24 March. Oracles were consulted. Nyama's wife was convicted of running away in anger. She was ordered to pay two raffia cloths and a chicken, and to destroy the skirt she had worn while running away. That evening all the diviners cooperated in a medicine for the next hunt.

25 March. They went hunting and killed two antelopes. Nyama's wife paid the fine, protesting her innocence.

30 March. Bikwak, the visiting diviner, came back at last, and took up again the series of medicines he had begun in order to replace the stolen *Kinda* medicine. Orders were given for men and women to sleep apart and stay in their huts next morning until the all-clear was given. At dawn next day all the men, lined up in single file, went slowly out of the village, the women behind them bent double sweeping the ground. At the diviner's grove he gave medicines to the men, smearing their chests with it. The women were sent back to their huts and told not to pound grain until the word was given. The hunt went off.

It was quite fruitless. The three gun owners fired and missed. Three arrows were shot, and three blue duikers escaped unhurt. All that was brought home in the evening was one half-grown duiker, which was reserved entirely for the cult group whose privilege it is to eat the young of animals. The rest of the village prepared to go to bed meatless again. Talking over the reason for the failure, Nyama was almost jubilant. He felt that the blank day proved that it had never been the quarrel between his wives which had spoiled the village in the first place. He kept saying, "Look, we paid a chicken and two raffia cloths, and Ihowa's skirt has been burnt. All in vain. They accused us falsely. Someone else has been fighting and has hidden it."

One theory was that Bikwak himself had been at fault. Medical convention required that after he had done the medicine he ought to have stayed in the village all day, ensuring by his presence there that the medicine worked successfully. But he had gone to set his wife and children on their homeward journey, about an hour's absence.

Another theory was soon circulated: that the official diviner of the village, who had been on bad terms with his wife for some time, had, on the day before the hunt, refused to eat what she had cooked for him. When her friends reproached her, she denied there had been a quarrel. Her husband had merely refused to eat because he could not stomach another vegetable meal. In spite of her denials she seemed to welcome the attention drawn to her domestic affairs. While she was sitting with her friends in the compound of the senior official diviner of the village, her husband came in. Without a word he gave a raffia cloth and two chickens to his colleague, who took them in silence. An official diviner cannot be even mildly annoyed with his wife without spoiling the village.

The journal ends at this point as I had to leave. Bikwak told me frequently that when he had finished the course of medicines and set up the *Kinda,* he would ask no payment for his services, but would simply take with him a haunch of meat to give to his wife. He had been born in the village, but had left it after his father's death. Now he belonged to a village to the north of Yenga-Yenga which had the same traditional name, Homba, and which recognized a common origin with it. As he counted himself a son of the village, and as he was resident in a "brother village," he felt he could not charge the usual fee for his medicines.

DIVINERS

The lending and borrowing of diviners is a very important aspect of inter-village relations, particularly when it takes place between villages which do not acknowledge a common origin. One of the obligations to each other accepted by "brother-villages" (i.e. those which have at some time split off from each other or from another parent village) is the supply of expert help in religious matters for a fee smaller than would be demanded from an unrelated village. But the borrowing of a diviner from a "brother village" is a much less interesting affair than a visit from a stranger village.

Any diviner imposes a ban on fighting in a village undergoing his medicines. But if he is only a local expert the village itself exacts fines for breaches of the peace and takes the proceeds into its own treasury. If fighting breaks out while a visiting diviner is at work it is he and his village which will demand payment for the spoiled medicine, and the fine will be much greater. He is temporarily a "chief" in the village which has invited him. A village which lends its official diviner or one of its Pangolin men to another village does not allow him to appropriate the whole of the fees paid. He should show his colleagues at home what he has been given, and a certain amount is taken from him as "things of the village." As few important village medicines can be completed in less than three months, the visiting expert is put to much inconvenience, and a fee of 100 raffia cloths and a bar of red camwood is not thought to be excessive.

If he brings the rites to a successful conclusion, after the last hunt, say when wild pig has been killed the specified number of times, his grateful clients send all their young men, dressed in finery and playing drums, to escort him to his home. He first sends word to his wife that on the day of rest after the next moon he will be returning. She then should spend all her spare time catching and drying fish against his arrival. The whole village is warned to expect the visitors, and the young men practise wrestling and summon their age-mates from other "brother-villages" of the same cluster. When the diviner's escort arrives, the two villages contest with each other in a wrestling match, the home team supported by all its "brother-villages." This wrestling match does not take place when the diviner has been lent by a "brother-village," for villages which have a common name and origin are not allowed to wrestle against each other. Then the visitors are feasted on fish provided by the diviner's wife, and he, to thank them for escorting him home, gives them a present of say twenty or thirty raffia cloths. If, however, something has gone wrong in the course of the expert's visit, if he is judged for some reason to have failed to achieve the results he promised, then he is sent home without pay, without escort, and is ridiculed by songs invented to mock his name. Some diviners acquire a countrywide fame and can list ten or more villages to which they have been called. Without doubt, this feature of Lele religious organization exercises a strong unifying influence on the scattered villages, for it is the most important form of friendly intercourse between them.

CULT GROUPS

The full role of the hunt in Lele religion is not made clear without a description of the cult groups. There are three of these, the Begetters, the Pangolin men, and the Diviners. The second and third have important duties in preparing medicines for the village, but the first seems to have no function more important than that of defending and enjoying its food privileges. Membership of all Lele cult groups is defined by a food privilege enjoyed by initiates, and forbidden to outsiders on pain of grave illness. The Begetters are entitled to eat the chest of game and the meat of all young animals. The Pangolin men are so called because only they are allowed to eat the flesh of the pangolin. The Diviners as a group may eat the head of wild pig and its intestines. The fact that in each case the cult privilege relates to the division of game gives the final clue to the religious importance of the hunt.

The Begetters' group is composed of men who have qualified by begetting a child, of either sex, and who have undergone a painful and expensive initiation. Within this group there is a subdivision of men who have begotten a male and a female child. From the latter are selected the candidates for the Pangolin group, the leading religious experts of the village, who are also diviners. Initiation into the Diviners' guild depends on other criteria altogether. They are supposed to be called to their status by spirit-possession or by a dream summons. A candidate has to undergo a novitiate of a year or more of restrictions on his life, and to pay crushing fees to his future colleagues. Once initiated he is bound to share the councils of the other diviners on village matters. One of the group is selected by the village to be its official diviner, a post to which various special functions are attached. He, together with the Pangolin men and the Diviners, performs all the rites of the village.

Nearly all major rites, such as those for setting up the *Kinda* for a new village, or for installing the official diviner, or for initiating a new diviner, require that the whole of the game taken in the hunt be reserved to the Diviners, or to the Begetters, or that certain additional parts be eaten by one of the cult groups. This very common practice could be regarded as simply derived from the interest of the cult groups in extending their gastronomic advantages. It is not clearly stated that these extensions of normal privilege are in themselves effective for the future of good hunting, and the enthusiasm with which breaches are punished could perhaps be attributed to the natural desire to protect privileged status. But similar practices in the field of gun and trap-medicines show more clearly the general implications of food taboos in Lele hunting rites.

HUNTING MEDICINE

A man who buys a medicine to make a trap more effective undergoes various restrictions on his life. He may have to refrain from sexual intercourse, avoid various foods, etc., until a certain number of animals have been killed in the trap. These restrictions are in the same spirit as those accompanying any medicine, but trap-medicines generally specify a particular treatment for the first three or five animals caught in the trap. In some cases certain parts, such as the head, liver, and feet, must be eaten by the trapper himself alone. In others these parts must be eaten by the trapper and his wives. After the given number of animals has been killed and eaten in this way, the medicine is completed, and the trap fully established to take game to which no further

restrictions apply. But if any other person were to steal and eat the parts indicated by the medicine, he would spoil the trap, and be made to pay a fine to the trapper for interfering with his medicine. In this case it is quite clear that the trap will not perform its work unless the food privileges are enjoyed by the owner of the medicine. The eating of the first meat, alone or with his wives, is itself a rite which completes the action of the medicine.

Guns are a relatively new weapon in Lele hunting. They replace bows and arrows, but no traditional medicine exists for rendering these more effective. They were assumed to profit from the general effects of the village medicines. The gun, therefore, has been treated as if it were in the same category as the trap. Trap-medicines have been adapted to guns, suitably enough in one way, as the gun is like the trap in being primarily the weapon of the individual hunter. However, unlike the trap, the gun is taken on the communal hunt, and hence arises a conflict of medicines. An uninitiated man who trapped a big animal would always give the chest to be eaten by an uncle or other relative belonging to the Begetters' group. No trap-medicine would require him to eat the chest of game, only the head, liver, or other parts not usually reserved to the Begetters except on special communal hunts. But the gun-owner, having bought a similar medicine for his gun, may find that the specified part of the game he has killed on a communal hunt has been reserved by village medicines to a cult group to which he does not belong. In such a case of conflicting medicines the gun-owner must give way to the village, but his medicine can be saved by payment of a fee to him by the village.

This is the situation which arose on 26 February in the hunt described above. A man who had bought a medicine for his new gun shot on the communal hunt the big yellow-backed duiker. The parts of the kill which the medicine prescribed should be eaten by himself alone, were reserved, by the village *Kinda* medicine, to the cult group of Begetters of which he was not a member. He was not paid for forgoing his rights. On 3 March he joined the hunt again, and a bay duiker was put up by the dogs. It came towards him, but not within what he considered to be the range of his gun. After it escaped the hunters consulted, and asked why he, usually so successful, was not shooting on that day; he replied that his gun-medicine had evidently been spoilt. After he had shot the yellow-backed duiker he had not eaten the meat reserved to him by his gun-medicine, nor had any of those who had eaten it paid him. His friends admitted the justice of his complaint, and then and there one gave him a franc in token for the part of the head which he had eaten. In the next draw they put up an antelope; one man shot and wounded it with his arrow, and the gun-owner fired the final shot that brought it down. He killed nothing else that day, and remarked that if only everyone had paid a fine to satisfy his gun-medicine he would undoubtedly have killed a whole beast by himself.

FOOD PRIVILEGES OF CULT GROUPS

The food privileges of the cult group demonstrate the same spirit as that shown in the eating of special parts of game prescribed by gun- or trap-medicines. The shared feast of cult initiates is in itself spiritually efficacious for the hunting of the village. It is not an object in itself, but a rite which brings to a climax the series of preparatory medicines and taboos which are undergone to ensure a variety of ends. Sometimes the object is good hunting, at other times the fertility of women, at others to establish a new village site, or to initiate a diviner. The dedication of certain parts of game has an aspect which completes the analogy between healing medicines and village rites. In the former case the private practitioner imposes on his patient food restrictions necessary for the working of the medicine. In the latter the body of diviners imposes on the uninitiated in favour of the cult members sacrifices which are necessary to the efficacy of the rites.

At first it seemed difficult to understand how a cult group so important as that of the Begetters should exist solely in order to enjoy its privilege of eating the chest of game and young animals. But as all cult privileges relate to the division of game, the result is that no big animal can be killed without being the object of a religious act. Only birds, squirrels, and monkeys are not counted as game and can be eaten by any man, woman, or boy. Of all animals the wild pig has most significance. The head and entrails are reserved to the Diviners, the chest to the Begetters, the shoulders go to the men who carried it home, the throat to the dog-owners, the back, one haunch, and one foreleg belong to the man who shot it, the stomach goes to the group of village-smiths who forge the arrows. This division is made for all animals except that the Diviners only claim the head of the pig.

RELIGIOUS SIGNIFICANCE OF THE HUNT

It is because it provides the feast of the cult groups that the hunt is the supreme religious activity, around which all the paraphernalia of medicines, divination, and taboos cluster. And it is to these religious aspects of the hunt that the forest owes its preeminent place in the Lele estimation of their environment. Without its central religious functions the hunt would not be able to sanction as effectively as it does the social solidarity of the village.

It is not difficult to account for the Lele tendency to regard hunting as the supreme male activity, more vital to the general prosperity than the equivalent female role of child-bearing. It provides the field in which Lele traditions are constantly validated. For when it is successful, and equally, as we have seen, when it fails, it shows that the relations of God and spirits to men and animals are in fact what the Lele ancestors have taught. It is the sign of the spiritual condition of the village, the test of orderliness in human relations, and in the relations of the village to God. It is itself an essential act in the rites which establish the desired religious condition in which the forest yields its products, and the fertility of women is assured.

16. TAPPERS AND TRAPPERS: PARALLEL PROCESS IN ACCULTURATION

ROBERT F. MURPHY and JULIAN H. STEWARD

Reprinted from Economic Development and Cultural Change, *4 (July, 1956): 335-53, by permission of the University of Chicago Press (copyright © 1956). Robert F. Murphy is Professor of Anthropology, Columbia University. His recent work has concentrated upon symbolic interaction processes but he has maintained his earlier interest in social change. This paper was written as a contribution to the University of Illinois Research in Cross Cultural Regularities and is partially based upon Murphy's ethnographic research in South America. Murphy also has conducted field investigations in western North America and West Africa. For a biographical note on Julian H. Steward, see Selection 5.*

■ People alter their organization of social relations not only to make effective use of the energy systems they have harnessed but also (as we saw in Selection 14) to adjust to the presence of surrounding and neighboring groups. While people like the Tiv and the Nuer set out to take the territories of others, they do not seek to subjugate the people whose lands they have aggrandized. Throughout history, however, many societies have expanded and subjugated other people in addition to seizing their land. In the minds of many, subjugation connotes passivity and abjectness. Although there is an element of truth in this, exclusive focus on subjection detracts from understanding a very important dimension of the lives of subjects: Their rulers constitute an aspect of the habitat to which they must adapt.

This selection deals with one kind of adaptive response to conquest. In their comparison of the horticultural Mundurucu and the hunting-gathering Montagnais (see Selection 8), the authors show that although the initial responses in both societies to invasion and conquest were different, their final adaptations were very similar. In both societies the nuclear family emerged as the most important and most autonomous unit. Because of the nature of their respective technologies in relation to the trading systems into which they were drawn, this was probably the only solution that enabled these societies to remain socially and economically viable.

The people in these two societies were not brought into the mainstream of industrial adaptation; they were, in a sense, in its backwash, and they continued to rely on muscular energy in supplying the fur and rubber for the traders on whom they became dependent. Why, then, did they not reintegrate themselves into a familistic band? One possible reason for this is that, despite their reliance on muscular energy, the products of their labor—fur and rubber—were not for their own consumption but were traded for the wherewithal of life.

In their interpretation of this evidence Murphy and Steward stress that the dispersal of fur-bearing animals among the Montagnais and of rubber trees among the Mundurucu are examples of the most important factors that underlie the adaptive autonomy of the nuclear family. To this can be added another consideration: If the Montagnais and Mundurucu had directly consumed the products of their labor, the familistic band would have been adaptive because individual families would have had to rely on each other for assistance; if a man fell ill or was injured, he could turn to other families for help, and he could reciprocate when they were in similar straits. Yet in a trading system in which each family is competing with the others, an ill or injured tapper or trapper could seek help only from the trader, who would extend credit, if he were so inclined, but not labor.

It would be a mistake to equate the autonomous nuclear family of these people with the family group in contemporary industrial society. In the latter, the family is part of a politically integrated society, and the society is the adaptive unit. Among the Montagnais and Mundurucu, the network of family and trader constitutes the adaptive unit. In an industrial society the nuclear family responds to—and often participates in—a coherent system of leadership; among the people described below there is no integrating leadership outside the network of nuclear family and trader.

Although there are many studies of acculturation and other types of culture change, there has been an unfortunate tradition in anthropology to treat change that results from conquest or other contacts as if it were something apart from the normal processes of cultural development. Because the development of culture must incorporate all types of change, this tradition contains some curious implications, one of which (if carried to its logical conclusion) is that the evolution of culture is something apart from the normal processes of cultural development. Robert Murphy deals with some of the consequences of this anthropological tradition in an important paper, "Social Change and Acculturation" *(Transactions of the New York Academy of Sciences,* Ser. 2, 26[7] [May, 1964]: 845-54). A good introduction to this topic, which tries to break away from the bias just discussed, is *Introducing Social Change: A Manual for Americans Overseas,* by Conrad M. Arensberg and Arthur H. Niehoff, 2nd ed. (Chicago: Aldine, 1971). *Social Life and Cultural Change,* by Don Martindale (Princeton, N.J.: Van Nostrand, 1962), deals with change in societies at much more advanced levels of adaptation—China, India, and ancient Palestine and Greece. ■

THE PROBLEM

THE PURPOSE OF this paper is to show how two cases of acculturation exemplify parallel processes of culture change, that is, cross-cultural regularities of function and causality, even though differences in outward form and substantive content are such that the acculturation might also be considered as convergent development.

As subsequent sections will show in detail, the Mundurucu of the Tapajos River in Brazil and the Northeastern Algonkians in Canada differed during pre-contact times in social structure, in the general nature of their culture, and in their cultural ecological adapta-

tions. The first were tropical forest hunters and horticulturalists living in semi-permanent villages and given to warfare. The second were hunters of large migratory game and were loosely organized in nomadic bands. Despite these differences, however, both represented roughly the same level of sociocultural integration. That is, individual families were related to one another through certain suprafamilial patterns—village activities in the one case and band functions in the other—but the local unit in each instance was politically autonomous.

Since this paper is essentially an illustration of methodology, it is important to stress that the concept of level does not classify cultures according to concrete and substantive form and content. Different cultures may be wholly unlike in their particulars in that they are the products of distinctive area histories or traditions and of local adaptations to environments. At the same time, the largest integrated and autonomous social units may be of a similar order of inclusiveness. While, therefore, similarity of level must underlie formulations of cross-cultural regularities, such similarity alone does not at all imply typological identity. The aboriginal tropical forest Mundurucu and the sub-arctic Algonkian hunters were wholly unlike in most cultural particulars and in social structure, although both were integrated on comparable sociocultural levels.

They were alike, however, in the acculturative processes to which they were subjected and in the final cultural types which is now emerging in both populations. The processes were similar in the special manner in which outside commercial influence led to reduction of the local level of integration from the band or village to the individual family and in the way in which the family became reintegrated as a marginal part of the much larger nation. The resultant culture type was similar in each case in that the local culture core contained the all-important outside factor of almost complete economic dependence upon trade goods which were exchanged for certain local produce and because the functional nature of local production, the family, and other features were directly related to this new element. The common factor postulated to have causal importance is a kind of economic activity—the collection of wild produce—which entailed highly similar ecological adaptations. While rubber production differs as greatly in particulars from fur trapping as the tropical forests differ from the sub-arctic barren lands of Labrador, the result of the acculturative processes in the two cases was the independent emergence of the same type of culture, as defined in terms of level of integration and culture core. We shall use the latter term to denote the structural interrelationships of the basic institutions of the culture.

This case study should also help clarify the heuristic concept of cultural ecology, and especially to illustrate how fundamentally it differs from environmental determinism. It will be shown that total environment is in no way the decisive factor in the culture-environment relationship. In analyzing the creative processes in the adaptation of culture to environment, it is necessary to determine the crucial features in the environment that are selectively important to a culture of a particular level and a particular area tradition. In this sense, it does not matter how different the sub-arctic and the tropical forests are in their totality. The primary fact is that each environment afforded a resource for trade purposes which could best be exploited by individual families controlling these products within delimited territories. These products did not achieve importance until the native populations became parts of larger sociocultural systems and began to produce for outside markets in a mercantilist pattern.

The process of gradual shift from a subsistence economy to dependence upon trade is evidently irreversible, provided access to trade goods is maintained. It can be said, therefore, that the aboriginal culture is destined to be replaced by a new type which reaches its culmination when the responsible processes have run their course. The culmination point may be said to have been reached when the amount of activity devoted to production for trade grows to such an extent that it interferes with the aboriginal subsistence cycle and associated social organization and makes their continuance impossible.

NORTHEASTERN ALGONKIANS

Our discussion of the acculturation of the Northeastern Algonkians assumes that the family-owned fur-trapping territories widely reported among these Indians were post-white in origin. The supposition of Speck, Cooper, and Eiseley that such territories were aboriginal lacks support in early historical documents. Moreover, indisputable cases of post-white formation of family territories have been reported by Leacock among the Eastern Montagnais, Jenness among certain of the Mackenzie Basin Athabaskans, and Steward among the British Columbia Carrier. Leacock's study deals with the processes of development of trapping territories in greatest detail and consequently provides the most illuminating material. We shall constantly refer to it in the following delineation of the aboriginal culture core and the subsequent changes in it.

According to Leacock, the Eastern Montagnais formerly possessed very loosely integrated bands. The basic aboriginal social unit was the "multi-family" winter hunting group consisting of two to five families. These groups were nominally patrilocal, but there was considerable deviation from this pattern, and individual families readily shifted from one group to another. The continual splits and reamalgamations of these winter groups depended upon the vicissitudes of the sub-arctic Labrador winter. Game, never abundant or highly concentrated, became thinly scattered during severe winters. Families then had to break away from the winter multi-family group in order to exploit the country extensively. In better times, they might reassemble with a different group of families. While each of these groups had a leader, his following was ill defined and fluctuating in membership.

Despite the frequent necessity for the winter group to split into smaller units, the Eastern Montagnais preferred to live in larger social groups, for collective hunting was generally more efficient for taking large game. Leacock's more conservative informants, in fact, regarded solitary or semi-solitary hunting as a white man's technique, and they expressly said that it was not appropriate for Indians. Moreover, in the absence of outside sources of food, which are available today, sharing of game was essential to survival since any family might be unlucky in hunting. The rigors of the environment necessitated a degree of social fluidity and amorphousness that was essential to physical survival. Owing to variations in environmental factors, especially in the quantity and distribution of game, crystallization of more rigid and permanent winter groups was impossible.

The Montagnais were, however, grouped into somewhat larger units during the summer season of fishing and caribou hunting. Each summer, several multi-family winter groups gathered together on the shores of the lakes and rivers, where they could obtain fish in some quantity. These groups, according to Leacock, did not maintain ownership of well-defined territories in native times. Each band had only a rough and generally recognized territorial locus of operations. But it would have been contrary to the interests of any one band to encroach upon the lands of other bands, for band areas represented an approximate division of resources in relation to population. But since local availability of game differed each year, it was customary that a temporarily favored band offer hospitality to one that was starving.

These "bands" had little or no formal organization. There were no band chiefs or definite mechanisms for integrating the band as a social entity. The bands existed principally upon the basis of economic reality. They had greatest functional significance during the season of hunting large, migratory animals. While both the Montagnais and the culturally indistinguishable Naskapi hunted caribou, the relatively greater reliance of the latter upon caribou probably accounts for the stronger development of band hunting territories in northern Labrador.

Leacock divides the development of the family trapping territory into three general phases. In the first stage, when the Indians were only slightly involved in the fur economy, the trapping of fur-bearing animals and trade for hardware and food-stuffs was secondary to native subsistence activities. In this stage, the Indians were only partially dependent upon the trader and could still subsist on the native economy. Since the small, nongregarious and nonmigratory fur-bearing animals were not killed in great numbers by the more primitive techniques of wooden traps and firearms and since they yielded inadequate meat, the primary winter dependence was upon deer and other larger game. The Indians could devote themselves to the luxury of securing trade articles only after assuring themselves of an ample food supply.

These marginal trappers, however, rapidly became so involved in the barter system that certain western goods, such as pots, pans, knives, axes, steel traps, and firearms became necessities to them. Since these available manufactured articles were much more efficient than the corresponding native implements, the latter were rapidly displaced and knowledge of their manufacture was eventually lost. The basic process therefore was one of increasing dependency upon trade, which eventually brought the loss of many useful arts. During this early stage of dependency, the customary use of ill-defined territories by amorphous bands was still the only approximation of land ownership to be found, and bonds of intra-group dependency were still tight.

In the second period of Montagnais acculturation, the same fundamental process continued to the point where certain basic readjustments became necessary. Dependency upon the trader increased to such an extent that fur trapping became more important than hunting for subsistence. The Indian was now forced to buy the major part of his winter's provisions from the trader, and game formed only a supplemental food source. Owing to the difficulties of transporting a supply of food adequate for the entire family, the men began to leave their families at the trading post during the winter while they trapped in the company of other men. Debt obligations and credit facilities had already linked Indians with particular trading posts. The practice of leaving families at the posts throughout the winter tightened these bonds. The families depended upon the store for subsistence, and the post became the center of the trapper's social world as well as economic world.

Leacock states that during this second stage, which is typified by the present-day Natashquan band of Eastern Montagnais, there is still considerable territorial shifting of fur trappers and that family trap line tenure is temporary and unfixed. Older informants expressed a preference for collective activity, which is exemplified today by trapping in groups, lack of definite proprietary rights in trapping territories, and the sharing among the men of the trapping groups of the fur from animals shot with guns. That animals trapped were claimed by the trap owner is probably also native.

The stages outlined by Leacock, however, are not presented by her as clearly distinguishable periods during which cultural stability was achieved. They are no more than transitory phases, and the Eastern Montagnais are now, in our terminology, moving toward the culmination of the processes of change. Certain men, says Leacock, show an increasing tendency to return to the same trapping territory year after year. Within these more limited precincts, usually no more than two trappers can work together. To a certain extent, the example for this pattern has been set by the white trappers, but the Indians follow it primarily because it is the most efficient working arrangement. When a single Indian enjoys the yield and has a vested interest in the vital resource of his territory, he attempts to protect and perpetuate it by practices of fur conservation which were not native to the culture. The more conservative Montagnais trappers do not wholly approve of the new mode of work followed by their compatriots, but they respect their tenure of exclusive trapping rights to a limited region. What emerges is a system of ownership by usufruct, a system also found among the Western Montagnais and, in fact, in many other areas of the world in which controls of law and government are loose and population density is low.

As more and more Eastern Montagnais adopt this new exploitative pattern, the group as a whole increasingly acknowledges family rights to delimited fur territories. Such rights will extend over much if not most of this area, and it will undoubtedly encroach seriously upon the semi-nomadism of the more conservative Indians. Ultimately, these latter, too, will have to change. What finally emerges will be the classical family trapping territory system in which definitely limited tracts are held by the head of a family and inherited patrilineally.

In order not to confuse or oversimplify theories of the origin and development of property rights, it is important to recognize that rights to fur-trapping territories mean merely customary or usufruct rights to the furs of animals within a defined area. They by no means give exclusive rights to control of and profit from the land itself and everything thereon or even to all its wildlife. Anyone may pursue and kill deer or caribou on any fur area. In some instances, another may kill and take the meat of a beaver, provided only that he give the pelt to the man having exclusive rights to the furs within the territory in question.

Two basically different concepts of rights to resources within the same area co-exist, each justifiable and explainable in its own way: the right to hunt large game for subsistence purposes practically anywhere and the right to monopolize fur-bearing animals within prescribed areas. In British Columbia the provincial government recognized these differences some years ago and registered family-owned trapping territories of the Carrier Indians and protected them by law while permitting moose hunting anywhere.

This end product of acculturation is substantially Leacock's third stage. The nuclear family now becomes the primary economic and social unit, and the old bonds of interfamilial economic dependency become attenuated. The new individualism has even penetrated the nuclear family. Among the Western Montagnais, the son of a trapper owns the beaver lodges which he discovers, whereas among the most acculturated of the Eastern group only the family head may own such a resource.

With the breakdown in inter-familial ties among the Northeastern Algonkians, the economic centers of gravity for the families are the trading posts. Leacock says:

The movement of trading posts has obviously been the most important factor determining recent shifts in the size and location of Montagnais bands. However, it would be wrong to infer from this that increasing dependence on trade has acted to destroy formerly stable social groups. The reverse seems to be closer to the truth—that the changes brought about by the fur trade have led to more stable bands with greater formal organization.

Leacock gives the Seven Islands band as an example of this post-contact development. This new "band," however, is of a different order entirely than aboriginal hunting bands, for the principal bond between the members is that they all trade at the Seven Islands trading post. They claim no band territory; in fact, all present trends are toward familial tracts and not band lands. The modern band has a chief whose principal function is to act as intermediary with the Indian Agent. Also, the Indians refer to themselves as the "Seven Islands" (derived from the name of the trading post) people, and are so called by other Indians. In the interest of taxonomic clarity it is best not to describe such an arrangement as a "band." Such a group is reminiscent of the post-white Shoshoneans of the Great Basin, who classify themselves principally by reservation, for example Warm Springs Paiute, Burns Paiute, Owyhee Shoshoni, and so forth. Prior to the Reorganization Act, the only basis for these groupings was common residence on a reservation and representation by a spokesman, who generally attained his position partly through prestige, but probably more importantly through recognition by the Indian Agent. Since the agents preferred "cooperative" men, the chiefs often did not truly represent the Indians. These reservation people, like Leacock's Seven Islands band, had little formal structure and a very limited *raison d'etre*. The stability of these groups is almost entirely a function of their linkage to the whites, an outside factor. Among the more acculturated Eastern Montagnais, the basic socio-economic unit appears to be the nuclear family.

THE MUNDURUCU

We shall discuss the Mundurucu in somewhat greater detail than the Algonkians not only because they are less known ethnographically but because the special problem of acculturation toward individual families has not been adequately described for South America.

The Mundurucu have been in active contact with European civilization for the last 160 years, of which only 80 years have been spent in rubber exploitation. The following description of the pre-rubber period Mundurucu does not purport to depict the *precontact*, or aboriginal, Mundurucu but refers to the middle of the nineteenth century. Earlier changes in Mundurucu culture form the subject of another paper.

The Mundurucu have inhabited the gallery forests and savannah lands east of the upper Tapajos River in the state of Para, Brazil, for at least two centuries. The savannah in this region is quite limited, and the predominant flora are the high forest and thick vegetation typical of the Amazon basin. The Mundurucu chose the open country for their villages because remoteness from the larger streams afforded some protection from river-borne enemy attack and relief from the swarms of insects which infest the river banks, while the absence of forests immediately adjoining the villages gave some security against the dawn surprise attacks favored by nearly all tribes of the region. These attacks were difficult to launch without cover. Since the Mundurucu used water transportation only slightly, isolation from the rivers was not a hardship.

It has been noted that the nineteenth-century Mundurucu and Northeastern Algonkians were on the same level of sociocultural integration. The simple, loosely structured nomadic hunting bands of the Algonkians were roughly equivalent to the semi-sedentary villages of the Mundurucu. In both instances, the local group consisted of a multi-family, autonomous community. Under certain circumstances, the various Mundurucu villages tended to integrate on a tribal level, but there were no permanent trans-village political controls. That no Mundurucu village could function in isolation, since there was inter-village marriage and periodic cooperation in warfare and ceremonialism, does not necessarily imply a higher level of integration in economic or political activities. Similarly, it can be argued that Northeastern Algonkian bands were autonomous but by no means isolated from other such units.

The Mundurucu and Algonkians were integrated on the same level, but their cultures differed structurally or typologically and in content. Patrilineal clans and moieties in Mundurucu society made kinship ties more extensive and pervasive. Village subsistence was based on slash-and-burn horticulture. Although the heavy work of clearing the forest was done by work groups consisting of all the village males, garden care and manioc processing were carried out by the women of the matrilocal extended family. The chief occupations of the men were hunting and warfare.

Leacock's reconstruction of the aboriginal society of the Eastern Montagnais shows the nuclear family to have had greater functional importance than among the Mundurucu. The Montagnais family was a relatively stable unit within the shifting and amorphous hunting bands, whereas the Mundurucu pattern was the converse. Each Mundurucu household was a stable unit composed of women and their female offspring. The Mundurucu had the seeming paradox of matrilocal extended families in a society of patrilineal clans and moieties. The men married into these extended families from similar units in the same village or from other villages. However, there was no need to integrate a husband into the extended matrilocal family of the household, because the focus of his activities was the men's house. All males upon reaching adolescence slept in the men's house, which was located on the western perimeter of the circle of houses composing the village. The females of each household prepared and sent food to the men's house to be eaten in a communal meal. The men's house was also the center of male work and relaxation. The most immediate economic tie of a man to his wife's house was that he brought his daily take of game there. Communal distribution of game, however, made this economically unimportant. Otherwise, the husband visited his household for purposes of sex, to play with the children, or to take a between-meal snack.

Marital break-ups caused no great social maladjustment. The woman and her children simply lived on in the household and took another husband. If the ex-husband was originally from the same village, he did not even have to move his hammock from the men's house. The husband and wife performed no economic tasks together, and the sexual division of labor operated mainly within the context of the village as a whole rather than the nuclear family.

The yearly cycle of activity of the pre-rubber period Mundurucu was not patterned by warm and cold seasons, as in Labrador, but by rainy and dry periods. At the end of each rainy season—April on the upper Tapajos River—the trees and vegetation in each projected garden were felled by a work party composed of all the men of the village and allowed to dry out. After clearing the forest, many families went in small groups to the larger streams where fishing was good during low waters and where they could hunt the many game animals which left the interior forests to feed and drink at the streams.

After two to three months it was necessary to return to the village to burn the felled vegetation in the garden clearings before the first rains wet the forests. After the early rains had sufficiently moistened the ground, individual gardens were planted to manioc by the cooperative efforts of all the men and women of the village. Other vegetables were planted by the women of the household of the man who initiated the gardens, and who was formally considered to own it.

Maize, squash, beans, and other vegetables were harvested by January or February and eaten immediately. The root crops, including bitter and sweet manioc, matured at the end of the rainy season in new gardens. A longer period of maturation was required for root crops in replanted gardens. Bitter and sweet manioc can be harvested as needed; this natural storage made these crops invaluable for year-around subsistence.

The bitter manioc, by far the most important garden product, required considerable labor to render it edible. The tubers were grated, the prussic acid was extracted by use of the *tipití*, or basketry press, and the pulp was then toasted either in the form of the native *beijú*, a flat manioc cake or *farinha*, the coarse Brazilian manioc flour. *Farinha* was sold to Brazilian traders. All phases of manioc processing were carried out by the women of the extended family household, who worked together under the direction of the oldest woman of the house. The labor was divided according to specialized tasks which, however, probably contributed as much toward making the operation pleasant as efficient.

Farinha was thus a collective product in that it involved the communal labor of the village in garden clearing and manioc planting, and the efforts of the women of the household in processing. Moreover, it was sold to the traders by the village as a whole and not by individuals. In this barter the hereditary village chief represented the village, and the proceeds from the sale were divided equally among the contributing households.

Bates, the British naturalist, describes the mode in which this trade was conducted in the mid-nineteenth century, when the first small quantities of rubber were traded by the Mundurucu along with larger amounts of other produce:

They [the Mundurucu of the upper Tapajos River] make large plantations of mandioca, and sell the surplus produce, which amounts on the Tapajos to from 3,000 to 5,000 baskets (60 lbs. each) annually, to traders who ascend the river from Santarem between the months of August and January. They also gather large quantities of salsaparilla, india-rubber and Tonka beans, in the forests. The traders on their arrival at the Campinas (the scantily wooded region inhabited by the main body of Mundurucus beyond the cataracts) have first to distribute their wares— cheap cotton cloths, iron hatchets, cutlery, small wares, and cashaca—amongst the minor chiefs, and then wait three or four months for repayment in produce.

When rubber became the major product of Amazonia the same pattern of trade was perpetuated among the Mundurucu. All of the rubber collected was turned over to the chief, who alone negotiated directly with the trader. The merchandise given for the rubber was, insofar as could be ascertained through contemporary informants, equitably distributed to each man in proportion to the rubber he had produced. But since chiefs were commonly more prosperous than other men, it can be assumed that they did not suffer in their role of middleman. The share taken by the chief, however, was never so great as to result in truly significant wealth differences. In fact, the traders usually managed to keep the Indians in debt, and this debt was charged against the chief as the representative of the village. Tocantins, who visited the Mundurucu in 1875, published a bill presented to one chief. If this bill is typical, the Indians' indebtedness was frequently very heavy. These debts were used to force the chief to extract greater production from his followers.

As the Mundurucu depended increasingly upon trade, the chief became more subordinate economically to the trader, who manipulated him accordingly. The trader eventually was able to appoint "chiefs" to carry on the trade. An appointed chief was usually known as the *capitao,* or "captain," as distinguished from the hereditary village chief, who was called *anyococucat* or *ichongop*. By using the "captains" as local trade representatives, the traders were able to increase their control over the villages. At the same time, by robbing the hereditary chiefs of their trade function, they weakened the entire structure of leadership. In time, the *capitao* displaced the hereditary chief almost entirely. To increase the prestige of the trader-appointed chief, the trader often took his protégé on his annual trip to buy supplies in Belém, where the chief's position was confirmed by the governor or some other official.

The Mundurucu dependency upon trade at first evidently increased the peacetime authority of the hereditary chief, for the villagers relied upon him to promote and secure their best interests in trading activities. The appointment of *capitoes* undermined the native chief, and initially increased the trader's control over the village. The people became confused, however, as to whether the *capitao* or the *anyococucat* should be regarded as "chief." Ill feeling toward and suspicion of the appointed chiefs began to develop, for the Indians were always aware of, although powerless to cope with, the sharp practices of the traders, and they usually assigned the *capitao* a share of the blame. Upon the latter fell the onerous task of goading the people to harder work in the rubber avenues. Since most Mundurucu do not even today consider rubber collecting a congenial occupation, the role of the *capitao* must have done little to increase his popularity. During the field research among the Mundurucu, the young, bilingual trader-appointed "chief" of the village of Cabitutu was in danger of losing his life. Distrust of the trader, whom the "chief" represented, was centered upon this young man and threatened his position so greatly that he was on the verge of flight.

In later years, as will be described subsequently, individual Mundurucu Indians have tended increasingly to deal with the trader directly rather than through the "chief." For this reason, village political organization has been effectively shattered.

The white-appointed Mundurucu "chief," unlike his Northeastern Algonkian counterpart, mediated trade relations between a group of followers and the whites. After individual trading had become strongly established among one section of the Mundurucu, however, "chiefs" were chosen by the Indian Agent and by missionaries in order to control the general behavior of the Indians, and not specifically for commercial purposes. This more nearly approximates the modern Montagnais situation, although it was reached through a different sequence of functional roles and from a different aboriginal base. In both cases, the Indians themselves were very conscious that these men were not genuine chiefs in terms of aboriginal leadership patterns, and both groups apparently suspected that the white-recognized chief was promoting the interests of the white men rather than those of his own people. The new leadership patterns never became fully established. While these patterns were functional in terms of white-Indian relations, they were dysfunctional in terms of the native sociocultural structure.

Among the Mundurucu, therefore, the integrity of the local sociopolitical groups was, in part, temporarily maintained by a change in the functional role of the chieftain. That the changed pattern of leadership eventually became dysfunctional resulted in part from the ecological adaptations necessary to rubber collection. These adaptations, however, did far more than contribute to the disintegration of political controls. They undercut the very economic basis of village life.

Hevea brasiliensis, the native and most common species of rubber tree, grows wild throughout the upper waters of the Amazon. It can be exploited only during the dry season, and, in the upper Tapajos River valley, the maximum length of the gathering season is from May to early December, approximately seven months. Since these trees are scattered throughout the low lands near the watercourses, they are reached by circuitous paths cut through the undergrowth. The spacing of the trees and the work involved in rubber collection generally limit the number of trees tapped daily by one man to 150 or less. Some collectors improved their yield per tree by maintaining two or three separate avenues which they visit only every second or third day. The distribution of rubber trees is such that each avenue gives access to trees within an area of about three to five square miles. The actual size of this territory depends, of course, upon the density of the rubber trees. In some sections of the Amazon drainage wild rubber is more abundant than are others.

One may travel ten to twenty miles on reaches of river where rubber is sparse without passing a single habitation, but, where rubber is more plentiful, one encounters houses at intervals of a mile or even a half-mile.

The rubber tapper must work in his avenue or avenues almost daily, and therefore must live near them. Since each tapper exploits a considerable tract of land, his physical remoteness from neighboring tappers is a matter of necessity. Thus, on the Tapajos River, which has a population of about 3,000, excluding the Mundurucu, there are only two Brazilian villages of any consequence. One of these has a population of about 700, and the other has only 150 people. The other settlements are merely hamlets consisting of a trading post and from two to seven houses. The majority of the population live in isolated houses on the river banks.

The exploitation of wild rubber is a solitary, individual occupation in that the tapping of the tree, the subsequent collection of the latex, and the final coagulation process are one-man jobs. The last phase, carried out at the end of the day, consists of solidifying the latex over a smoky fire. The simplicity and the daily time schedule of the entire rubber process in Amazonia is such that no one can profitably leave off collection to specialize only in tapping or collection or coagulation. For similar reasons, two men do not work in the same avenue. However companionable, it would not be a practicable means of increasing production.

This brief account of how wild rubber is exploited is necessary to an understanding of changes in Mundurucu society. In the earlier contact period, the Mundurucu traded chiefly in manioc flour and wild products, and rubber was of secondary importance. Chandless' observation that in 1860 the Mundurucu of the upper Tapajos "trade in salsa and sell provisions to the parties of India-rubber makers" indicates that important trade in articles other than rubber continued at least until 1860. Shortly after this date, however, the tempo of rubber extraction in the Amazon quickened, and in 1875, as Tocantins'

account shows, rubber was the most important Mundurucu product.

With the advent of the rubber trade, Mundurucu acculturation entered its second stage. During the first, when trade in manioc flour and certain wild products predominated, the hereditary chief mediated between the traders and his people, aboriginal social patterns were largely unchanged, and warfare was still vigorously prosecuted, frequently under the sponsorship of traders and colonial authorities. During the second stage, which lasted until 1914, warfare abated, the size of villages decreased owing to migration and European-introduced diseases, and the position of the hereditary chief was weakened by the imposition of appointed "chiefs." The period was characterized by a "loosening" of integration rather than by a change in mode of integration, or structure.

Work in the rubber avenues in the latter half of the nineteenth century did not upset the annual subsistence cycle as much as might be expected. Whereas many people had formerly left their villages during the dry season to hunt and fish along the streams, they now left to collect rubber. As in times past, they cleared their garden sites before leaving and returned to the village in time to burn them over and plant. The necessity to provide all their own subsistence limited the rubber-producing season to three months, mid-June to mid-September, out of a possible seven. This parallels closely the earlier phases of Northeastern Algonkian fur production, when the Indians' need to obtain their own meat supply by aboriginal cooperative techniques limited fur production and conflicted with their increasing desire for Western manufactures.

During the nineteenth century (and to the present day) the Mundurucu, like the Algonkians and in fact most aborigines, had been acquiring a seemingly insatiable appetite for the utilitarian wares and trinkets of civilization. Firearms increased their efficiency in warfare and hunting, especially the individual hunting carried on during the rubber season when one or two families lived in isolation adjacent to their rubber trees. In communal hunts, the game could be surrounded and the range and velocity of the weapons were not so crucial to success. Other items, too, became necessities to the Mundurucu. Contrary to popular belief that nudity is beneficial to tropical peoples, there are various reasons why clothing is desirable in the Amazon. Insect stings greatly annoy the Indians, and at night the temperature drops to from 55° to 65° F. Clothing, however, is expensive, and only in recent years has it been used consistently in some Mundurucu villages. The movement toward covering the body entailed the development within two generations of a sense of shame comparable to that of Europeans. The Mundurucu, especially the women, have also acquired a desire for finery for the sake of display. They have also developed a taste for many strictly non-utilitarian goods, such as the Brazilian raw cane rum and the beads and ornaments purveyed by the trader.

A full and adequate description of the growth of Mundurucu dependence upon trade would require a separate treatise, for reliance upon manufactured goods entailed further dependence upon many adjuncts of these goods. For example, firearms required powder and lead, while garments of factory-woven cloth had to be made and repaired with scissors, thread, and needles. The substitution of metal pots for native ones of clay and of manufactured hammocks for the native product has reached the point where many young women now do not know how to make these articles. The Mundurucu barely remember that their forebearers used stone axes and bamboo knives, and they would be helpless without the copper toasting pan used to make manioc flour.

Despite the flourishing trade in gewgaws, the allure of most trade goods lay more in their sheer utility than in their exotic qualities. The increased efficiency of the Mundurucu economy made possible by steel tools must have been enormous.

The parallels in these basic processes of acculturation between the Mundurucu and the Montagnais are probably to be found also among most aborigines. In the case of the Mundurucu, the displacement of aboriginal crafts by commercial goods better suited to meet local needs, both old and new, inexorably led to increased dependency of the people upon those who furnished these goods and therefore to a greater involvement in economic patterns external to their own culture.

The Mundurucu families, like those of the Algonkians, became dependents of the trading posts. More than a century ago, Bates related that Brazilian traders made seasonal expeditions to trade with the Mundurucu. After rubber became important in the Amazon, permanent trading posts were established on the upper Tapajos River. These posts, whether owned by individuals or companies, exercised such control over tracts of rubber-producing forest that they compelled the rubber collector to trade exclusively with them. They accomplished this by their power of dispossession and by holding the collector in debt. The traders among the Mundurucu were never able to obtain title of ownership to the rubber regions within Mundurucu country proper, but they made the Indians dependent upon them in a very real sense through their credit arrangements. In time, all of the Mundurucu villages came under the control of various traders, who were so influential by virtue of being necessary to the Indians that they were able to appoint the "chief," in violation of Indian tradition, and thereby intensified their control over the Indians.

The progressive weakening of the hereditary chief, whose authority was based upon aboriginal activities, was furthered by the decline in warfare. The postwhite warfare, although frequently mercenary in character and auxiliary to Portuguese occupation and expansion, continued the native pattern of authority. The Indians were paid in trade goods. When, at the end of the nineteenth century, the central Amazon region had been pacified, the military help of the Mundurucu was no longer needed. Meanwhile, rubber collecting had become the principal means by which the Indians acquired foreign trade articles. Since the Indians were important to rubber production in labor-starved Amazonia, they were pushed to greater efforts by the traders. Increased devotion of the Mundurucu to rubber production correspondingly interfered with their warfare, for in earlier times the rubber season was the time for war. When in 1914 a Franciscan mission was established in their midst, the earlier political and economic basis of Mundurucu warfare was so undermined that the admonitions of the priests that they live in peace were quite effective.

At the end of the second stage of Mundurucu acculturation, only bonds of kinship and economic collectivity in producing food for the group held Mundurucu society together. Much of the old structure was gone. The chieftaincy had been undermined, warfare had ended, and reliance upon the outside economy was taking effect. During the nineteenth century, increasing numbers of Mundurucu who had difficulties with their co-residents were able to leave their villages permanently. Many others left in order to participate more fully in the rubber economy.

Full dependency upon rubber collection is not compatible with village life. Since the aboriginal Mundurucu villages were located several days' foot travel from the rubber areas fringing the rivers, a family participating both in collective village life and the rubber economy had to migrate seasonally between its village and its house in the rubber area. Families living in this manner could spend only three to four months in rubber production. The only way the Indians can devote their full efforts to rubber tapping is to leave the villages of the interior savannah and live permanently near the rubber trees along the river banks. A large portion of the Mundurucu, whose increased need of and desire for trade goods could no longer be satisfied by the yield of only three month's work in the rubber avenues, have made this choice.

These families represent the third stage of Mundurucu acculturation. Their resettlement in the rubber regions, however, has occurred in two ways. The first is a direct and complete adaptation to rubber collection, which can be studied in many contemporary inland villages. People desiring to increase their income from barter improved their rubber

avenue house to make it more comfortable during the rains, plant gardens, and remain there. Although they maintain relationships with the inland villages, the loci of their social lives lie increasingly within the orbit of the communities of scattered families dependent upon the trading posts. The final step in their incorporation into the local Brazilian economy and the culmination of this acculturative process will come when they abandon horticulture to devote full time to work in the rubber avenues, and, like their Brazilian neighbors and the Western Montagnais, depend upon trade for the bulk of their food supply.

The second mode of readaptation to the rubber economy, while ending in the same type of settlement pattern and social organization as the first, involves passage through an intermediate stage. The previously mentioned mission on the Cururu River and an indifferent success in attracting the Mundurucu until the 1920s, when a policy of trading with the Indians was adopted. The missionaries were honest and generous in their commercial relations, and rubber tapping became more profitable to the Indians. Their intensified collecting activities resulted in a general movement to the banks of the Cururu River, and by the 1930s many interior villages had been abandoned.

The migrants settled so heavily on the river banks that they were able to nucleate in new villages. These villages, however, lacked the men's organization, division of labor, and collective patterns which structured the old-type villages. Although the population shift from the old to new villages was heavy, it involved individual families rather than whole villages. The new villages grew as additional nuclear families arrived from the savannah communities. During this period of growth, since the new villages consisted of families, many of which had not previously been connected with one another, each family had to carry on the subsistence activities which were formerly the function of the extended family and village. Gardens were cleared and planted by husband and wife with whatever aid their children were capable of giving. Fish, taken by family members from the nearby rivers, rapidly replaced game formerly taken in collective hunts as the major source of protein. Meanwhile, increased rubber production enabled the Indians to buy the hooks, lines, and canoes with which fishing was made more effective. As the new villages grew larger, the atomistic division of labor was perpetuated, and the nuclear family became the basic unit of production.

Political authority on the Cururu River was almost nonexistent. The migrants began to trade as individuals, first with the missionaries and later with the newly established Indian post. This economic trend stripped the "chiefs" of one of their last remaining functions, and their role was reduced to that of intermediary between the villagers and the priests and Indian Agent.

The amorphously structured villages which arose on the banks of the Cururu River represent a transition to the family level and are not the culmination of adaptation to the ecology of rubber collection. Most of the residents of the Cururu River still have to reside away from their villages during the rubber season, but the easy communication made possible by canoe transportation allows the majority to return to rubber production after planting their gardens.

The new individualism and fragmented division of labor, combined with facets of the old culture which had become dysfunctional in the new situation, contributed to the disorganization of Cururu River society. The political authority of appointed "chiefs" was now a means of extending the influence of the whites. The continuing migration of young men from the remaining primitive villages of the savannahs caused an oversupply of men on the Cururu River, and conflicts over women became rife. Owing to the endless squabbles in villages which had lost their aboriginal basis of integration, dissidents moved off to live at their rubber avenues or formed new and smaller villages. This fission process is still going on. Concomitantly, the mission and the Indian post are becoming more important as focal points in a new mode of integration of the Mundurucu. Over one-third of the Cururu River population make their rainy season homes at these agencies, which serve as centers of trade and of social and religious gatherings. It is from the post and mission, also, that the lines of authority now radiate.

COMPARATIVE SUMMARY

The accompanying table and chart present the major phases of acculturation in summary form, as abstracted from the historical continua. The basic acculturative factors in both cases exerted parallel influences, although the two societies were substantively different until the final culmination was reached. There were four causal factors common to each. First, both became involved in a mercantile, barter economy in which the collector of wild products was tied by bonds of debt and credit to particular merchants. Such involvement also occurred widely among native peoples who produced crops or livestock. This arrangement must be distinguished from cash transactions, in which, owing to the impersonality of money as a medium of exchange, the primary producer has greater freedom of choice as to with whom he will deal. In a pure credit-barter economy, all transactions are based on a personal relationship between the principals; the merchant must be able to rely upon the continued patronage of the primary producer whereby the latter liquidates past debts while assuming new ones. It seems to be a basic procedure that the pre-literate Indian is kept in debt by the trader. While the latter can manipulate accounts at will, and no doubt is frequently guilty of malfeasance, he usually allows the Indian to buy beyond his means. The debtor-producer is selling his future production, and the creditor will not extend payment unless assured of delivery. Where such an economy is found, it is common for merchants to refuse to deal with primary producers who are in debt to another merchant. This is a "gentleman's agreement" in the Amazon, although it is frequently violated by wandering traders. Second, the growing ties of dependency upon the traders

TABULAR COMPARISON

Mundurucu	*Montagnais*
1. Pre-rubber	1. Pre-fur

1. Pre-rubber

Village consists of men's house, matrilocal extended family households; population divided into patrilineal clans and moieties.

Village males form collective hunting and garden-clearing group.

Household females form the horticultural unit.

Intensive warfare for headhunting and as mercenaries allied to whites; partial dispersal of villagers in dry season for fishing and war.

Chief the war leader and representative of village in trade of manioc flour.

1. Pre-fur

Nomadic composite band hunts large migratory game animals.

Frequent band breakup during winter scarcity.

Amalgamation of several winter groups for summer hunting and fishing.

Chieftainship weak and shifting—leader of winter group; no summer band chief.

Residence bilocal; frequent shifts of winter group membership.

2. Marginal involvement

Chief continues as mediator with trader, but is now often trader-appointed—trader gains influence.

Dry-season population dispersal for rubber production rather than fishing and war—war continues, but lessened in importance.

Basic pre-rubber economy and settlement pattern unchanged.

Continuing displacement of aboriginal crafts.

2. Marginal involvement

Trade by family heads—leaders do not trade for followers.

Trapping secondary to subsistence hunting—subsistence still gotten traditionally, basic social patterns persist.

No trapping territory.

Linkage to trading posts.

3. Transitional

Further displacement of native crafts, increased need of trade goods, increased dependence on trader.

Chieftainship undermined due to new-type chiefs who now represent the trader.

Agricultural cycle and village life inhibit larger rubber production.

Trend toward individual trade.

3. Transitional

Further displacement of native crafts, increased need of trade goods, increased dependence on trader.

Increased fur production, interferes with subsistence hunting.

Individual trade conflicts with group solidarity.

4. Convergence and culmination

A. Intermediate

Move to new villages in rubber regions.

Chief now intermediary with Indian agent and missionaries.

Individual trade, individualized subsistence economy—end of men's house and traditional village—village held together only by weakening kin ties and sociability.

4. Convergence and culmination

Fur trapping now predominant; winter provisions purchased.

Winter groups not necessary with end of collective hunt—family or individual hunting gives greater efficiency, allows conservation.

Shift of economic interdependencies from group to trader.

Centripetal factors (e.g., sorcery, sexual rivalry) cause fission of these villages and result in *B*, below.

B. Dispersal (follow upon 3 or 4*A*)

Leadership no longer integrative.

Individual trade undercuts kin obligations.

Conflict with agricultural cycle resolved by moving to rubber avenue—family now in isolation except for trade bonds.

Emergence of a chief who serves as intermediary with Indian agents and missionaries.

Nuclear family basic unit at all times of year.

Trapper maintains and transmits right to a delimited hunting territory exploited only by his family.

---

are at the expense of collective bonds within the respective societies. Reliance upon individuals and institutions outside the native social system are intensified by a steady increase in demand and need for manufactured goods. This, as we have seen, goes beyond the mere initial allure of Western tools and ornaments. Luxuries soon became necessities—a process that can be found in our own culture. Third, while crude latex and animal furs are very unlike articles, they imply a common cultural-ecological adaptation. Both are natural products having a reliable occurrence in worthwhile quantity within an area which can be most efficiently exploited by one man. Both require conservation, for careless exploitation can seriously reduce the number of fur-bearing animals, or render rubber trees worthless. The producer has an incentive to maintain the productivity of his resources. Finally, both rubber trees and fur animals are sufficiently dispersed to require that persons exploiting them live or work at some distance from one another.

These factors of change were essentially the same among both Mundurucu and Montagnais, and they were introduced through contact with the outside world. Their initial effects upon the aboriginal cultures were somewhat dissimilar, owing to aboriginal differences between the two groups. Whereas the Mundurucu chief served at first as intermediary with the trader, this seems not to have been true of the Montagnais chief. Montagnais family heads, however, traded on behalf of their sons. For a short time, this pattern was followed by many Mundurucu during the period immediately after the Mundu-

rucu chief had ceased to act as intermediary with the trader. After the breakdown of extended kinship bonds in both groups, individuals traded completely on their own.

The native kinship organization persisted longer among the Mundurucu than among the Montagnais, and this has been a factor in perpetuating village life today among the less acculturated Indians east of the Tapajos River. Aboriginal Mundurucu kinship structure was more extensive and socially integrative than that of the Montagnais. Moreover, the aboriginal production of subsistence crops survives even among Mundurucu families living in isolation in their rubber avenues. The Mundurucu still produce all their own subsistence, although there are some changes in emphasis, technique, and organization.

The Brazilian rubber tapper—the white man who has gone into the forest or the Indian of mixed blood who is completely acculturated and enmeshed in the mercantile economy—usually buys all his food from the trader and devotes the season when he could be growing his own food to tapping rubber or to working off his debt to the trader by performing personal services. At present, we know of only one case of a Mundurucu who bought most of his food, but we can confidently predict that, as the population becomes more acculturated toward dependency in all ways upon the larger society, an ever-increasing number will buy food. When they are no longer able to feed themselves by their own efforts, they will have effectively become *caboclos,* or neo-Brazilian backwoodsmen.

The acculturative factors operated in two somewhat different ways among both the

Mundurucu and Montagnais. First, they created a succession of modifications in the native societies, which gradually converged toward typological identity in the final family level. Second, during this evolution of the total groups they produced deviant families which broke away from their fellow tribesmen to devote themselves entirely to tapping or trapping. It was not until the processes had nearly reached their culmination that the surviving but greatly modified native society began to disintegrate.

Among the Mundurucu the bonds of leadership and kinship had undergone a steady and slow attrition during 100 years. The end of warfare had robbed Mundurucu culture of a great deal of its vitality, and the chief was reduced to a mere figurehead, manipulated by the trader and the religious and governmental agencies. Work in the rubber avenues and dependence upon the trader had served to sever and weaken ties within the society. At the final point of transition to isolated residence, and total divorce from traditional communal life, the Mundurucu were not much more closely integrated than the Montagnais.

The culmination of the long acculturative processes shows a high degree of structural parallelism. Both Mundurucu and Montagnais populations are divided into loosely integrated and dispersed communities centering about particular trading posts with which the individual families have ties. The Indians still recreate, associate, and intermarry with one another, but the nuclear family is now the stable socio-economic unit. It is the highest level of integration found among the native population itself, but it is linked to the nation through the intermediary of a regional economy. The integration of the family with the national level is highly specialized and limited. These families do not yet share a substantial part of the common denominator of the national culture or even of the regional sub-cultures of their non-Indian neighbors.

There is a final phase, which, though occurring at different dates in the different localities, is characterized by assimilation of the Indians as a local sub-culture of the national sociocultural system and virtual loss of identity as Indians. At this point, the acculturational processes and results diverge, since the Indians participate to a much greater extent in the national culture. So long as the families maintain their marginal relation with the national society, they are quite unlike the basic populations of the nations in which they lived and much more like one another. When, however, they learn the national language, intermarry extensively with non-Indians, and acquire many of the non-Indian values and behavior patterns, they have to be classed with the special regional sub-cultures that have developed in portions of these nations.

It can be predicted that the drastic shift in mode and level of integration will do much to hasten the loss of cultural distinctiveness. Fortes has cogently expressed the relationship between social structure and formal culture content in such a situation.

I would suggest that a culture is a unity insofar as it is tied to a bounded social structure. In this sense I would agree that the social structure is the foundation of the whole social life of any continuing *society*. . . . The social structure of a group does not exist without the customary norms and activities which work through it. We might safely conclude that where structure persists there must be some persistence of corresponding custom, and where custom survives there must be some structural basis for this.

FURTHER COMPARISONS

We can delimit and refine the Mundurucu-Algonkian parallel by the cross-cultural examination of structural changes caused by acculturation in other areas. We will not seek further parallels, however, but will discuss cultures in which divergence appears manifest. One instance of such apparent divergence is the Northwest Coast, where the fur trade at first strengthened or intensified rather than weakened the aboriginal social structure. The florescence of the potlatch and class system on the Northwest Coast as a result of new wealth in trade goods is a thesis which has been ably expounded by a number of students. It would be very misleading, however, to consider *any* trade in furs as the crucial factor. What really matters is *individual trap-*

ping of fur-bearing animals. The sea otter was the principal fur bartered by most Northwest Coast tribes, and collection involved neither individual effort nor delimited territories. The amount of land trapping was probably fairly limited and in any event did not offset the cultural effects of the great salmon wealth which created surpluses rarely if ever paralleled by hunting, gathering, and fishing people.

The trapping activities of the Skagit of Puget Sound more nearly paralleled those of the Northeastern Algonkians, according to Collins' description:

The [trading] posts played an important part in altering the economy of the Indians. First, they encouraged a shift in their hunting habits. The skins in which the traders were most interested were beaver and land otter. These animals had small value in the aboriginal economy, since they were less desirable for food than deer or elk, for example. At the traders' behest, however, hunters pursued these animals eagerly. Another economic shift took place when the hunters, instead of killing game for meat, began to exchange skins for food.

The result of this trade was, however, quite different from its effects in eastern Canada.

The effects of these changes upon Skagit social organization were pronounced. Distinctions in social rank began to be more marked—a shift made possible since (though social mobility had always been within the grasp of any person of good descent who could acquire the distinction of wealth) new sources of wealth were now available.

The new wealth acquired by the Skagit was funnelled into the class structure and ultimately the potlatch. The difference, then, between the processes of change which occurred among Northwest Coast and northeastern Canadian groups is that the former integrated the new wealth into a *pre-existent* class structure created and perpetuated by a fishing economy. Among the latter, since there were no cultural means or goals promoting the concentration of surplus wealth in the hands of a select few, the benefits rebounded to all persons. The same was true of Mundurucu society which also was unstratified. The dif-

ferences between the Skagit on one hand as opposed to the Mundurucu and Montagnais on the other are attributable to the stratification of society among the former, which in turn in partially explainable by the greater aboriginal resources of the Skagit. In effect, this constitutes a difference of level of sociocultural integration.

The impact of trapping upon a pre-existing social structure can be even better appraised among the Carrier of the interior of British Columbia, where the wealth in salmon was far less than on the coast. The fur trade among the Blackwater River Carrier involved intimate interaction with Northwest Coast groups, especially the Bella Coola. Goldman summarizes the effects of this contact upon the simple, bilateral Carrier hunting bands:

Undoubtedly the Bella Coola, like all Northwest Coast tribes, became relatively wealthy as a result of this trade. And in Bella Coola where wealth was the decisive factor in building rank, the fur trade must have been particularly welcome. And the lowly interior Carrier who hunted for furs in order to trade with the Bella Coola, who traded them to the whites, became an important part of the scheme of elevating one's rank. Although a Bella Coola did not gain valuable prerogatives from a Carrier son-in-law, if he could get a monopoly upon his furs he could make enough wealth to purchase new prerogatives. And as the Bella Coola benefited by this trade, so did the Alkatcho Carrier. The latter took up products obtained on the coast and traded them to the Carrier villages eastward on the Blackwater River drainage. As they obtained guns and steel traps, economic productivity spurted so that they were able to build up the necessary property surpluses for potlatching. Potlatching obligations in turn stimulated economic activity, and the degree to which they were able to potlatch made possible the full integration of crests as honorific prerogatives.

Given our previous hypotheses, developments more or less parallel to those in eastern Canada might be expected. But these Carrier did not trade with European traders; they dealt instead with stratified Northwest Coast tribes in the context of an economic system, the rationale of which was the validation of rank by potlatch. As the following example of the Stuart Lake Carrier suggests, direct trade with the whites and the end of potlatching result ultimately in the family trapping territory system.

The effect of the fur trade among the Carrier of Stuart Lake to the north of the Blackwater River ran a similar course but culminated in family trapping territories, according to Steward's research. In pre-white times, the wealth of salmon fisheries, although far less than those of the coastal tribes, had provided some surplus, white contacts with the Tsimshian of the Skeena River had introduced a pattern for channeling this surplus to nobles who controlled the fishing rights of large territories in the name of matrilineal moieties. This wealth circulated through small scale potlatches. The fur trade, carried on directly with the whites more than through coastal contacts, created a new source of wealth and intensified the native pattern. Although furs were trapped by individual moiety members, a noble had rights to a certain percentage of the furs taken in his moiety's territory.

In the course of about 50 years, however, several processes combined to bring about individual trapping territories as among the Indians of eastern Canada. Most importantly, the new wealth in trade goods brought hardware that was of value to individuals. Pressures mounted to force the nobles to divide the trapping territories among their own children rather than to pass them on intact to their sisters' sons, who had traditionally inherited their titles and rights. This process was aided by the activities of the Catholic missionary-ethnologist Father Morice, who effectively undermined the native religious sanctions of the class of nobles, and by the government, which banned potlatching. The older pattern survives only in isolated localities, where it is carried on clandestinely. At Fort St. James on Stuart Lake, where there is located a Hudson's Bay Trading post and some few hundred whites and Indians, the processes have reached a culmination almost identical to that of the Montagnais.

Present-day Carrier society at Stuart Lake consists of individual families that have exclusive rights to certain trap-lines that are registered with and protected by the Provincial Government. The family is the kinship and economic unit.

It seems likely that the Blackwater River Carrier have not yet reached the final stage of acculturation. The same may be true of the Skagit. The critical consideration is whether wealth in salmon among these tribes was so great that it offset the importance of trapping. This was not the case at Stuart Lake. On the lower Skeena River, salmon are so important that canneries have been built, and the Tsimshian and Tlingit have given up fur trapping to become commercial fishermen and cannery laborers.

Certain Plains Indians in North America also engaged in the fur trade but developed in distinctive ways. This is another illustration of the need to examine specific features in the taking of furs. There is a significant ecological difference between the collection of fur on the Great Plains and in the coniferous forests of Canada that lies essentially in the difference between hunting and trapping. It is incomplete and misleading therefore to make comparisons simply on the basis of "fur trading." In the Great Plains, buffalo hides were the chief item traded, whereas in eastern Canada, small, nongregarious and nonmigratory animals were trapped. The trade on the Plains resulted in an emphasis upon the buffalo hunt beyond the needs of subsistence and served to strengthen the collective and cooperative techniques traditionally used in the pursuit of migratory herds. Moreover, band cohesion in the Plains was enhanced by acquisition of the horse and gun and by intensification of warfare, the latter carried on in part to obtain horses.

It is possible that a non-stratified society which acquires surplus wealth may develop a class structure, but this involves special conditions not ordinarily found among collectors of wild products. Some of the North American Plains Indians showed an incipient development of a class society in the late eighteenth and early nineteenth centuries, but the tribes were decimated by epidemics and overwhelmed by the advancing frontier when intensified wealth and significant prestige differences had begun to emerge. A parallel between the Plains and the Mundurucu can be found in the increased authority of chiefs owing to their functions as intermediaries between the traders and the Indians. Jablow notes such a florescence of political controls among the Cheyenne, and Lewis specifically states of Blackfoot trade:

In periods of monopoly [of the Indian trade by one company] the fur trade has a positive effect; that is, it increased the prestige and authority of the chiefs. In periods of competition it has a disruptive effect; that is, it weakened the power of the chiefs.

The Plains band chief traded a commodity which was obtained by collective effort. The Mundurucu chief served as middleman in the pre-rubber period when trade in manioc flour, which was also communally produced, was of primary importance. But he eventually lost his position when individually produced rubber became predominant. The Tenetehara Indians of northeastern Brazil have been in contact with civilization longer than the Mundurucu, but, according to Wegley and Galvao, the village chiefs and extended family heads still have a central role in the trading of collectively produced manioc flour and palm oils. It seems apparent that, lacking some other basis for political authority, it is difficult for leaders to maintain control over trade in individually produced goods.

Our formulations, in effect, state that when certain acculturative factors, defined functionally rather than formally, are present, the core of a culture will change in expectable and predictable ways. These formulations assume the constancy of certain other pre-conditions, which, though well worth investigation in themselves, can be regarded as given factors for methodological purposes.

This can best be exemplified in our present cases by reference to the basic, though incompletely explained, acculturative factor common not only to the Mundurucu and Naskapi but to most primitive peoples throughout the world. This factor can be stated simply as follows: *When goods manufactured by the industrialized nations with modern techniques become available through trade to aboriginal populations, the native people increasingly give up their homecrafts in order to devote their efforts to producing specialized cash crops or other trade items in order to obtain more of the industrially made articles.* The consequences of this simple though worldwide factor are enormous, even though they vary in local manifestation. The phenomenon is of such a high order of regularity that special explanations must be sought for the few departures from it.

The main hypothesis arising from the present study is: *When the people of an unstratified native society barter wild products found in extensive distribution and obtained through individual effort, the structure of the native culture will be destroyed, and the final culmination will be a culture-type characterized by individual families having delimited rights to marketable resources and linked to the larger nation through trading centers.* Tappers, trappers, and no doubt other collectors come under this general statement.

III.
PASTORALISM

STUDENTS OF CULTURAL evolution have long been interested in the question of the evolutionary status of pastoralism: Did it, for example, evolve out of different strategies of cultivation? The question is important because it goes to the heart of the problem of how readily people can move from one strategy of adaptation to another, but it cannot be answered at the present stage of theory. Pastoralism probably did not evolve out of a foraging adaptation, although this is not impossible; some North American foragers became pastoralists (see Selection 20), probably under the stimulus of cultivators who also became pastoralists.

There is growing conviction, however, that pastoralism represents a branch of the main line of social evolution rather than a stage along this line. This point of view is strengthened by the observation of Robert McC. Adams and Hans Nissen that pastoralism has often been part of a mixed economy in which herdings and settled cultivation are in reciprocal balance *(The Uruk Countryside* [Chicago: University of Chicago Press, 1972]). Adams and Nissen are speaking here primarily of pastoralists in a state society, but their statement also applies to stateless pastoralists who are almost always associated with settled cultivators for at least part of the year; herders provide the cultivators with meat and dairy products in return for cultivated food. If pastoralism represents a branch—rather than a stage—of the main evolutionary line, it helps to explain the fact that very few human societies have been pastoralist at any time and lends support to the impression of many anthropologists that history has passed by pastoralists.

In any case, pastoralism is a system of production devoted to gaining a livelihood from the care of large herds of animals. Like each of the other technological systems discussed thus far, pastoralism is a unique adaptation. It is based on transhumance: the cyclical movements from lowlands to highlands that are necessary for the year-round care of herds of domesticated animals. Although pastoralism is an adaptation to a particular habitat—semi-arid open country or grasslands—in which hoe or digging-stick cultivation apparently cannot be sustained, variations in pastoralists' habitats have profound consequences for their social organization. Most of the case studies in this section describe pastoralists who live in habitats in which, for the most part, resources are meager and unpredictable.

As Salzman observes in Selection 17, pastoralists living under such conditions are invariably stateless. In contrast, he notes, those living in habitats where resources are predictable tend to be organized under centralized controls.

In meeting their herds' needs, pastoralists do not move their camps in uninterrupted swings. Instead, they move from one camp to another in an orbit that extends elliptically from lowland to highland and back to lowland pastures. These shifts are made necessary by seasonal changes. Although a dry season may occur abruptly and unexpectedly, water holes and grazing lands are depleted gradually and in successive zones. Characteristically, pastoralists move their camps from one zone to the next and remain there until water and grass are depleted or until the tsetse flies invade. When habitational conditions change, they move their camps to the next zone.

Although pastoralists seem to resemble nomadic foragers in their seasonal movements, the resemblance is more apparent than real. Nomads generally have no fixed abodes but wander about—though not aimlessly—in search of available food. Pastoralists, however, move in orbits between relatively fixed points. This is not only a difference in patterns of migration but also in social organization. Salzman maintains that centralized control among pastoralists makes it possible for a group's chief to coordinate the movements of different units by apportioning access to water and pasturage. From an ecological point of view, he is able to maintain his authority because obedience to his directions results in a profitable payoff to the groups of herders: Each is assured that resources will be found in the areas to which they are directed. It is understandable that they will trade off a measure of autonomy in return for access to resources and the assurance that other groups will not compete with them for the same resources. But not only environmental pressures determine these moves and the organization of social relations appropriate to them; the presence of other groups (cultivators, towns, centralized states, and the like) also influence the nature of pastoralist movement. These other groups must also be regarded as habitational factors in pastoralists' lives.

In Selection 18, Bates concentrates on the social—and especially the political—forces in the pastoralists' habitats that underlie centralized controls. Bates' analysis focuses our attention on an important fact that might easily escape attention: Centralized political organization among pastoralists almost always occurs in the context of nation-states. In this framework, two elements predominate in the pastoralist milieu, in addition to those of the physical environment: the settled cultivators with whom they are associated and the central government itself. With these elements in mind, it becomes clear that centralized political and economic controls among herders are specific adaptations to particular habitational forces.

The juxtaposition of Salzman's ecological approach with Bates' sociopolitical framework—together with the other case studies in this section—now make it possible to expand the concept of adaptation to include more than ecological relationships. This broadened interpretation of the concept of adaptation enables us to understand variations within a single strategy of adaptation (such as pastoralism) or within a single ecological zone (such as northern Iran). It also provides us with conceptual tools for understanding rapidly changing adaptations to new social conditions in our own society, especially those stimulated by changing governmental policies.

Despite the fact that pastoralists control their animals' migrations, they are nevertheless very closely bound by the limitations of their habitats because they have no control over the availability of water, without which their herds cannot survive. Mitigating this dependence on the habitat is their ability to domesticate and herd large animals, which provides them with a more advanced adaptation than hunters and gatherers. Because of their dependence on the availability of water, pastoralists share an intimacy with nature and its cycles that characterizes most other pre-industrial people, and because their settlement patterns and productive activities are so closely attuned to changes in nature, their entire way of life also is responsive to these changes. An important aspect of this seasonality is that their group composition changes seasonally as a result of migrations in search of water. Also, as stated in Sahlins' paper (Selection 14), pastoralists are frequently characterized by lineage segmentation.

But group size, however important, is only a small part of the picture. The entire tenor of life changes seasonally among pastoralists. People's moods are transformed between rainy and dry seasons, and a new outlook on the world comes with changes in precipitation. Evans-Pritchard writes in *The Nuer* as follows:

Seasonal variation in quantity and kind of food is sociologically significant for several reasons. . . . Abundance of millet is the main reason for holding ceremonies in the rains, for ritual is seldom complete without porridge and beer and, since it consists of sacrifice, of meat also. Weddings, initiation rites, and religious ceremonies of various kinds take place in the rains and early drought, generally after the first millet harvest. This is also the main reason for raiding the Dinka [their traditional enemies]. Nuer say that hunger and war are bad companions and that they are too hungry to fight in the full dry season; and it is evident that they are then not so eager to come to blows over personal and community quarrels as they are in the rainy months when they are replete with grain and meat and, especially at wedding dances, sometimes slightly intoxicated. Nor do the young men find dancing so attractive in the drought, whereas in the rains they dance as much as possible and think nothing of traveling many miles to attend weddings, at which they dance from eventide until well into the morning. The tempo of village life is different from that of camp life.

Another illustration of the sensitivity of pastoralist adaptations to their milieus is the way in which stateless pastoralist groups usually fragment as a result of habitational pressures. This variation in group composition not only occurs seasonally but often from one region to another. As Gulliver shows in his comparisons of the Jie and Turkana of East Africa (Selections 21 and 22), these historically related people diverged sharply in their organization of social relations as a result of marked differences in their habitats. Households and other groups among the Jie are cohesive; they live in a very favorable habitat. The Turkana, however, live in a harsh desert-like region, and even their households have to split up to maintain their herds. These variations provide a baseline for understanding differences in political organization among pastoralists in more beneficent habitats and in complex national societies; these will be considered later in connection with centralized pastoralists.

Most pastoralists know about cultivation, and many of them practice it in a limited way. Cultigens play a small role in the diets of pastoralists, rarely constituting more than about 15 per cent of the food they consume. Cultivated plots are maintained at rainy-season settlements; they are generally poorly tended. What is more, as the papers in this section illustrate, pastoralists' organizations of social relations are vastly different from those of cultivators and are inseparable from their technology.

"The nomad, in fact, is a 'soldier born,'" wrote Marc Bloch in *Feudal Society* (Chicago: University of Chicago Press, 1960). Because pastoralists are mobile they have sometimes been able to exert an influence on history that has been disproportionate to their numbers or military strength. One of the greatest monuments in testimony to this is the Great Wall of China. Not only have pastoralists terrorized settled people for the past several thousand years, they are fond of warring upon and plundering each other. They have primarily sought movable goods, especially livestock; bravery in warfare has almost always been a main source of prestige among them. They are adaptively independent of lines of supply and home bases, whereas logistic problems have always plagued sedentary conquerors. Pastoralists have been able to wage war wherever their herds could graze, and their ease in segmenting has generally reduced their vulnerability to attack. As those who tried to destroy pastoralists have learned quickly—on the North American Plains, in East and Northwest Africa, Central Asia, and the far north of the U.S.S.R.—such people are difficult to defeat. Pastoralists are able to split up and still retain effective leadership, but Westernized armies often are unable to function when their centralized authority is destroyed.

Several of the selections in this section make clear that there are particular qualities of mind or personality that are especially suited to the pastoral way of life, at least in stateless groups: pugnacity and cooperativeness, the ability to make decisions and to act on them independently, the ability to operate in a large social context and to accept the absolute authority of others. Many students of pastoralist societies have also commented on the profound emotional attachment of these people to their animals; pastoralists are probably unique in their affection for their instruments of production. E. E. Evans-Pritchard speaks in *The Nuer*—a stateless group—of the Nuer's "love" for his cattle.

Start on whatever subject I would [in conversation with Nuer], and approach it from whatever angle, we would soon be speaking of cows and oxen, heifers and steers, rams and sheep, he-goats and she-goats, calves and lambs and kids. . . . This obsession—for such it seems to an outsider—is due not only to the great economic value of cattle but also to the fact that they are links in numerous social relationships. Nuer tend to define all social processes and relationships in terms of cattle. Their social idiom is a bovine idiom.

The maintenance of law and order and the elimination of conflict between groups (especially those that may compete over resources such as land and water) are among the primary concerns of those who speak in the name of the state. In an agrarian-based economy in which pastoralists are associated with settled cultivators, conflict between the two groups is an ever-present danger, given the temptations offered the pastoralists by the farmers' material possessions. Compared with the high mobility of pastoralists, farmers are sitting ducks.

No centralized government worthy of its name can tolerate even the possibility of such violence. As Bates shows, the central state is the principal mediator in peasant-pastoralist relations. A government cannot deal with whole groups, but only with their representatives, and this need for efficiency is all the more crucial when dealing with pastoralists. As Barth illustrates for the Basseri of southern Iran (Selection 26), herders cannot stay put long enough to participate in litigation and bureaucratic hearings like farmers, but their chiefs (serving as representatives) may do so.

In their day-to-day activities, pastoralist chiefdoms differ little from those without centralized controls. A man parachuted into a pastoralist camp would not know—without a lengthy stay and extensive questioning—whether he is among stateless or centralized pastoralists. He would be unable to determine this solely from their migrations, modes of subsistence, or patterns of mutual assistance. But this statement must be qualified. A stateless pastoralist group is entirely egalitarian; yet in many centralized pastoralist groups, important status distinctions emerge out of inequalities in the exercise of power and in wealth. But there are also many pastoralist chiefdoms in which status inequality is absent. William Irons observes that when central governmental influence among pastoralists is strong, stratification among the latter is increased; when governmental influence is weak, there is a greater tendency for the members of the pastoralist group to be equal in status among themselves (William Irons, "Variation in Political Stratification among the Yomut [northern Iran] Turkmen," *Anthropological Quarterly,* 44 [1971]: 143-56). Irons maintains that stratification increases when a government is able to increase a tribal chief's power by "putting him in a position to collect taxes and conscripts from the tribe he represented." This is illustrated by Barth's account of chieftainship among the Basseri of southern Iran (Selection 26) in which the chief's position in the group depends on his role as intermediary between his tribe and the farmers and government. Tribal headmen among pastoralist chiefdoms can be conceptualized as "boundary role players," a concept discussed by Robert Murphy in "Social Change and Acculturation" *(Transactions of the New York Academy of Sciences,* Series II, 26 [1964]: 845-54). A further illustration of boundary role-playing (also based on Iranian social organization) is "The Representative Mediator and the New Peasant," by Reinhold Loffler *(American Anthropologist,* 73 [1971]: 1077-91).

The influence pre-chiefdom pastoralists have exerted on history has not been confined to terrorization and conquest. Predation by pastoralists played an important role in stimulating the development of states in agricultural societies in ancient Mesopotamia, Africa, China, and eastern Europe. One of the most dramatic examples of this was the role played by the Hungarian nomads in establishing some of the earliest centralized political systems in Europe, around the tenth century; these played major roles in the history of medieval Europe. Similarly, sedentary people have performed an important role in helping to maintain pastoralists, even when the latter were predators; sedentary and pastoralist people have formed important parts of each other's environments.

Few comparative studies of pastoralism have been conducted. Two that may be consulted are "Nomadism: Middle Eastern and Central Asian," by Raphael

Patai *(Southwestern Journal of Anthropology,* 7 [1951]: 401-14) and "Ecology of Central Asian Pastoralism," by Lawrence Krader *(Southwestern Journal of Anthropology,* 11 [1955]: 309-26. Two other important works on pastoralism are Part III of *Habitat, Economy, and Society,* by C. Daryll Forde (New York: Dutton Paperback Edition, 1963) and *Inner Asian Frontiers of China,* by Owen Lattimore (London: Oxford University Press, 1940). For a good introduction to the political organization of segmentary pastoralists, the reader may consult "The Mandari of the Southern Sudan," by Jean Buxton, and "The Western Dinka," by Godfrey Lienhardt; both are chapters in *Tribes without Rulers: Studies in African Segmentary Systems,* edited by John Middleton and David Tait (London: Routledge and Kegan Paul, 1958). *The Nature of Nomadism: A Comparative Study of Pastoral Migrations in Southwestern Asia and Northern Africa,* by Douglas L. Johnson (Chicago: Department of Geography, University of Chicago, 1969), is an excellent analysis of transhumance and ecological relationships, but it is very short on social organization.

There have been many studies of individual pastoral societies. One of the earliest and best known is *The Chukchee,* by Waldemar Borgoras (New York: American Museum of Natural History, *Memoirs,* Vol. II, Pts. 1 and 2, 1904-09): this is a work of several volumes on a tribe of the northern U.S.S.R. Several similar works will be noted in the introductions to the selections that follow.

17. POLITICAL ORGANIZATION AMONG NOMADIC PEOPLE

PHILIP C. SALZMAN

Reprinted from Proceedings of the American Philosophical Society *(Vol. III, 1967, pp. 115-31). Philip C. Salzman teaches in the Department of Anthropology at McGill University. His principal interests are pastoralism, ecology, and political organization and he has conducted extensive field work among Iranian pastoralists.*

■ In this selection Salzman focuses on the correspondence between unpredictable resources and the lack of centralized authority roles, and predictable resources and centralized authority. When we combine these materials with Carneiro's (Selection 27), it is clear that political organization cannot be understood exclusively in terms of political processes. Applying the general scientific rule that, to avoid tautologies, every institution must be understood in terms of forces outside it, we must instead look to the limitations and potentials contained in the physical as well as the social milieu. Political systems do not develop in a vacuum or out of philosophers' theories alone.

To understand the kind of authority developed in pastoralist groups, Salzman concentrates on three variables: their dependence on livestock, their means for acquiring them, and the nature of transhumance. In connection with the latter, the degree of predictability of water and pasturage is important in setting limits and providing potentials for political development.

Salzman shows in this analysis that the nature of authority and the degree of stability in group composition are intimately related to ecological factors. However, he also argues cogently that his analysis is not mere ecological determinism. Ecological factors provide only a potential for political developments; they are a stage on which social and economic relations are enacted. The central point of his paper is that when resources are dependable a strong political system tends to develop, but this is not an inevitable causal relationship. Under these ecological conditions, the quality of resources are also likely to be great and sedentary people are also likely to be present as important elements in the habitat. When resources are dependable, economic activities can be coordinated, high population densities can occur, and surpluses can be developed.

More concretely, Salzman maintains that when resources are predictable, plans affecting many herding units can be made. When resources are unpredictable, the herding units have to respond to the smallest climatic changes that affect the welfare of their animals so planning is not possible. Under such conditions, resources tend to be scarce, and this creates a potential for competition among groups for water and pasturage and for uncoordinated movements. Apparently, unpredictable resources are also accompanied by lower population densities.

Salzman finds that when resources are predictable, pastoralist groups will be characterized by strong authority roles and stable group relations and composition. Those in authority not only coordinate the movements of different units with respect to resources but also regulate relationships with sedentary villagers. Salzman pays great attention to the latter factor and rightly regards settled people as important elements in the habitats of all pastoralists. His hypotheses are illustrated by sketches of six pastoralist groups, including the Jie and Turkana (described in Selections 21 and 22).

This paper concludes with a discussion of pastoralists in the modern world of nation-states. A very good book in this connection is *Bedouin of the Negev*, by Emanuel Marx (Manchester: Manchester University Press, 1967), which discusses pastoralists under Israeli political and military control, but which does not always succeed in remaining free of Israeli political ideology. In *The Samburu* (Berkeley and Los Angeles: University of California Press, 1965), Paul Spencer describes a Masai-speaking pastoralist tribe in arid northern Kenya. He analyzes the Samburu as a gerontocracy, a political system in which older men rigidly control the younger, especially those under 30. Though the latter strain at the leash, they unsurprisingly develop strong interests in the system when they become elders. ■

I. INTRODUCTION

ALTHOUGH MUCH excellent ethnographic work has been done on nomadic peoples, there has not been a great deal of discussion of the subject on a higher level of abstraction. Conceptualizations of nomadism and the analytic tools used are somewhat wanting in sophistication. And general conclusions about nomadism as a system of action are quite difficult to find.

The purpose of this essay is to contribute to the filling of these gaps. An attempt is made to sort out the empirical variables and to formulate a definition which delineates the field of inquiry without unduly limiting the empirical variables to be taken into account. Some dimensions of nomadism and relevant variables are discussed at different points in the paper. Empirical generalizations about the political organization of nomadism, based on an analysis of a limited number of nomadic peoples, are suggested. These generalizations stress the ecological factors which underlie differences of political organization, but also attempt to take into account the crucial factors of contact with non-nomadic peoples and ideological commitments.

II. THE CONCEPTUALIZATION OF NOMADISM

A. DEFINITIONAL DIFFICULTIES

The term "nomadism" has no generally recognized precise or technical meaning. Although derived from the Greek word *nomados*, which means "living on pasture," there seems to have been a shift in emphasis from what we would call "pastoralism" to "movement" as the class defining concept. A current dictionary definition of "nomad" is "a member of a tribe, nation, or race having no permanent home, but moving about constantly in search of food, pasture, etc."

(*Webster's New World Dictionary*). "Nomadism" is generally used in common language to indicate a continual movement on the part of persons or groups, and the usage in modern literature is similar. In anthropology the term has a number of rather more precise but conflicting and contradictory usages.

Briggs, in *Tribes of the Sahara*, implicitly uses movement as the class-defining concept. A group of hunters and gatherers who had no permanent home, the Nemadi, hunters and gatherers who have a permanent "settlement or central base," and the Imraguen, fishermen living along the Atlantic coast of the Sahara are discussed together under the rubric "non-pastoral nomadic life." He classes tribes of Arabs, Moors, Tuareg, and Teda as pastoral nomadic groups.

Fisher, in *The Middle East*, in describing the Bedouin indicates that nomadism is "regular movement in search of pasture for animals." He distinguished "true nomadism" from "transhumance"; the former being "Movement . . . from one district to another," the latter being "movement . . . in mountain regions (where) different levels in the same district are occupied successively." "True nomadism is, in effect, horizontal movement, transhumance is more a change in altitude."

Bohannan, in *Social Anthropology*, says that nomadism is movement in response to the demands of animals for pasture and water. Nomads follow a definite route over and over, although the cycle takes from three or four to fifty years to complete.

Transhumance differs from nomadism in that the cycle of movement is an annual one and follows the season, rather than a longer one requiring several years . . . annual movement between village and cattle camp is the most striking characteristic of the technology of societies that practice transhumance, just as temporary, moveable shelters are characteristic of nomads.

Kroeber, in *Anthropology*, says that "true pastoral nomads" are "people making their living wholly off their flocks without settling down to plant."

Bacon, in "Types of Pastoral Nomadism in Central and Southeast Asia," bases her detailed terminology on "degree of cultivation and permanence of dwelling."

"True" of full nomads are people who dwell the year round in portable dwellings and who practice no agriculture. In this usage sheep-breeders following a restricted orbit in their seasonal migrations may be as much true nomads as camel- or horse-breeders who travel hundreds of miles in the course of their annual migration. "Seminomads" plant a few crops at their base camp before moving out on the seasonal migration, but they normally live in portable or temporary dwellings the year round. "Semisedentary" has the connotation of people who dwell in permanent villages during a part of the year, where they plant crops, and move out in tents only during one season of the year.

. . . transhumance [is] applied usually to semisedentary or seminomadic peoples who move vertically into the mountains during the migratory season, [but, the term] does not appear to have wide applicability since it brings together two principles which are only accidentally found in association. Verticality in migration appears to be a matter of topography and climate, and may be found in association with any of the several kinds of nomadism—full, seminomadic, and semisedentary.

Patai, in "Nomadism: Middle Eastern and Central Asian," states that "Nomadism . . . is the mode of existence of peoples who derive their livelihood from tending herds of one or more species of domesticated quadrupeds and who wander to find grazing for their cattle." ". . . seminomads, or sheep-and-goat-nomads . . ." are distinguished from "true nomads" who have camels or horses as their main livestock. Transhumance is "a kind of 'vertical' nomadism, as against . . . 'horizontal' nomadism. . . . The nomads practicing transhumance spend the summer in the mountains and the winter in the lower level of the plateau or in the valleys within the area."

Stenning, in "Transhumance, Migratory Drift, Migration: Patterns of Pastoral Fulani Nomadism," is primarily concerned with functionally different types of movement. Among the Fulani, "transhumance" is "regular seasonal movement of cattle, southward in the dry season in response to shortages of pasture and water, northward in the wet season to avoid tsetse." "Migratory drift" is "gradual dis-placement of customary transhumance tracks and orbits, resulting even-

tually in a completely new orbit." "Migration" is "a dramatic shift to different transhumance orbits without the piecemeal abandoning of pastures which characterizes migratory drift."

It is natural to want to pick one of these definitions or sets of definitions and "side with it," or modify it to one's purposes. The criteria for such picking and modifying are neither precise nor easily applied in the short run, although they usually shape usage in the long run: (1) Our word usage contains our conceptual distinctions and agglomerations. In so far as our concepts and categories accurately represent differences and similarities in the world, we shall find them useful for making propositions and building theories which successfully predict the relations between categories of phenomena. (2) Even the crudest conceptual scheme must have certain kinds of logical consistency and efficiency. There should not be a proliferation of categories into which no examples fall, or too few categories, each based upon too many criteria, such that empirical cases overlap (such that a case with characteristic BC cannot be placed in a scheme with the two categories based upon AB and CD). (3) Common usage should be followed whenever possible, in order to avoid confusion and spare sensibilities.

At the present stage of the study of nomadism, what is needed is a general and flexible concept. This will allow consideration of similarities and differences and be conducive to the development of concepts which can be evaluated in terms of criterion (1). Distinctions which have been shown to have empirical importance can be incorporated into a more elaborate set of definitions of type and subtype.

Table 17.1 summarizes the class-defining concepts used for nomadism by the authors discussed above (with the exception of Stenning who was emphasizing types of movement rather than types of nomadism). Most notable is that out of seven defining concepts used, all of the authors with the exception of Briggs use a combination of "movement" and "pastoralism" in their definitions of nomadism, transhumance, seminomadism,

TABLE 17.1
CRITERIA FOR DEFINING NOMADISM

Author	Type	Movement	Pastoralism	Dwelling: temporary or portable only	Agriculture: absent	Movement: year-round only	Altitude Change: present	Livestock: horses or camels	Livestock: sheep and goats
Briggs	nomadism	X							
Fisher	nomadism	X	X						
	transhumance	X	X				X		
Bohannan	nomadism	X	X	X		X			
	transhumance	X	X						
Kroeber	true pastoral nomads	X	X		?				
Bacon	full nomadism	X	X	X	X				
	seminomadism	X	X	X					
	semisedentarism	X	X						
Patai	true nomadism	X	X		?			X	
	seminomadism	X	X		?				X
	transhumance	X	X		?		X		

and semisedentarism. Since this usage is "general and flexible," is almost unanimous, and follows the original Greek usage, it will be adopted here.

The five other defining concepts—agriculture, types of livestock, type of dwelling, seasonal movement, and altitude change—are all more or less of theoretical interest, and all probably co-vary to some extent. Given these variables, the important task is to study the dynamics of their relationships to each other, rather than to make a case for the *a priori* analytical primacy of one or two of them. However, a few comments about these variables might be appropriate here.

For Bacon, type of dwelling distinguished between full and seminomadism, on the one hand, and semisedentarism, on the other; for Bohannan, it is one of the factors distinguishing between nomadism and transhumance; and perhaps Kroeber would use it to distinguish true pastoral nomadism from other unspecified ways of life. This factor seems important from a theoretical point of view because types of association and ways of looking at the world, and certain types of ecological exploitation are associated with it.

"Absence of agriculture," advocated by Kroeber and Bacon, and perhaps Patai, to delineate "true pastoral nomads" and "full nomadism," seems on the face of it to be a useful variable. What could be more basic than the distinction between part-time nomad-farmers and full nomads? And does not the folk system of many nomadic groups, such as the Arabs, make such a distinction? However, there is a problem here: absence and presence of agriculture is too crude a distinction, for as Forde points out, "It is very doubtful indeed whether any of the higher pastoralists of Asia, from the Badawin to the Mongols of the Gobi, are completely non-agricultural. . . ." For example, it would be most odd to call seminomadic or transhumant the Saharan tribes whose on-the-run agricultural activities (such as sowing in wet spots and gathering from date palms) are described by Briggs. What needs examining here is the amount of time spent on such activities and the degree of dependence upon livestock.

Although it seems likely that Patai's emphasis on the type of livestock—camel and horse as opposed to sheep and goat—is important, he doesn't state exactly why it is important. However, it is possible that different types of culture are associated with the somewhat different ecological niches that are associated with these different animals. But from a logical point of view, his distinction between full nomadism and seminomadism is not clear. What is the characteristic of nomadism that makes horse or camel nomads "full" and sheep and goat nomads "semi"?

Patai's and Fisher's distinction between transhumance and nomadism on the basis of altitude change follows the French usage of "moving of flocks [to or from the Alpine pasture]" (Mansion's *Shorter French and English Dictionary*). It is by no means clear that this is an important distinction; it might well be obscuring more basic ones, as Bacon suggests: "Verticality in migration appears to be a matter of topography and climate, and may be found in association with any of the several kinds of nomadism—full, seminomadic and semisedentary."

Bohannan's distinction between nomadism and transhumance suffers from being based upon too many defining concepts. According to him, a group must either have a combination of temporary dwellings and year-round movement or permanent dwellings and only seasonal movements. To cite some cases which do not fit, most of the tribes of the Zagros have only temporary dwellings and migrate twice a year according to seasonal change. Another somewhat complicating factor is that all groups have seasonal movement, although there is variation in distance and goal (such as change in altitude, or concentration around permanent water), and there are cases of general movement in one seasonal area, and general stability in the other seasonal area. The significance of this variable is a result of its important correlates, which will be discussed below.

Nomadism, then, is a way of life at least partially based upon movement of people in response to the needs of their herds and flocks. The way of life of a particular group could be regarded as more or less nomadic than the way of life of other groups to the extent that it is "based upon movement . . . in response to the needs of . . . herds and flocks." How all of the important factors relevant to "extent" could be systematically weighed and evaluated is not clear; nor is the theoretical value of such a ranking immediately apparent. Perhaps it would be more fruitful to emphasize the construction of generalizations describing the relationships between the variables important within the nomadic way of life. In either case, some of the important variables are those suggested by various authors for definitional purposes (but rejected for those purposes here): extent of agricultural activity, types of dwelling, types of livestock, and patterns of movement.

B. SOME VARIABLES AND DIMENSIONS

An important variable in nomadic life is the extent of dependence upon livestock. Krader believes that herds are paramount in nomadic life and that such things as trading and carrying are secondary. But Downs says that "In the Old World pastoral peoples have combined trading and carrying with pastoralism and depend as much on the first two activities as they do on the last." Other authors have emphasized a somewhat different aspect of this problem. Kroeber states:

It is clear that without what they secure from the towns and traders of the farming country, the Bedouin would have so one-sided a culture that they could not survive by it: no clothing, shelter, weapons, few utensils, limited diet. In one sense, accordingly, their own culture is no more than a half-culture. . . .

To some extent, this condition of possessing a "half-culture" holds for most nomads. (i.e.) . . . peoples making their living wholly off their flocks without settling down to plant.

Along the same line, Barth says that "As far as the economic structure of an area is concerned, nomad and villager can therefore be regarded merely as specialized occupational groups within a single economic system. . . ." Although these discussions are valuable and important, none of these writers stress the variable nature of the extent of dependence upon livestock as one looks from group to group and perhaps from time to time. Nor do they stress the several dimensions of this variable. Just a bit of elaboration will be presented here.

First, the extent of direct dependence upon the livestock and their products for subsistence and maintenance varies from group to group. The percentage of caloric intake from produce of the livestock is an important index. Forde refers to "Bantu . . . pastoral freemen whose diet consists almost entirely of milk." Likewise the Masai and pastoral Somali depend to a greater extent upon products of their livestock than, for example, the Bedouin of Cyrenaica or the Basseri. Other groups depend to an even smaller extent upon their livestock. An example is the Mongol nomads who "set up their military camp in the heart of China . . . and from there made excursions into all four directions . . . they gave up cattle breeding and kept horses no longer for economic but only for military reasons." This group is an extreme example, and it is not clear to what extent they could still be called nomads. The point, however, is that their animals were necessary for their survival, but played no direct part in providing products used for subsistence or maintenance.

Second, the indirect dependence on livestock can be to a large extent ascertained by examining the products coming to the group through trade of livestock or products of livestock. This also varies from group to group. The Bedouin of Cyrenaica sent to Egypt eighty thousand sheep and goats and eighty-five thousand kilos of clarified butter per year, and in exchange received great quantities of foodstuffs and hardware. The Somali or Masai had no such extensive exchange relations and did not depend so much upon outside products. The Basseri, on the other hand, did depend upon a large quantity of foodstuffs and hardware for which they traded their animals and products of their animals.

Third, the source of stock and pasturage and water varies from group to group. Livestock can be obtained by purchase, trade, levy, raid, as payment for services rendered, and likewise for pasturage and water. The Baluci used to raid for livestock, as the Bedouin of Northern Arabia did, but this is not an important source for the Somali. The Bedouin of Arabia do not trade livestock among themselves, but the aristocratic tribes levy from their clients. While some nomads are provided pasture by farmers who value the fertilizing effects of the animal droppings, others, such as the Somali, have to fight among themselves for the use of pasturage.

Fourth, the source of nonpastoral goods, such as food, clothing, and hardware, varies from group to group. The Zagros tribes (Qashqai, Basseri, Bakhtiari) and the Bedouin of Cyrenaica trade large amounts of livestock and livestock products for nonpastoral goods. The Baluchi and Bedouin of Arabia raid for nonpastoral foodstuffs and hardware. According to Briggs, ". . . crop shares, trading, protection, and raiding [were] the four corner posts of Ahagger Tuareg economy." The Tuareg raided villages in the Sudan for captives to be sold as slaves (unless they were quite beautiful, and then they were kept), as well as running a protection racket for the caravan trade.

A second important variable is the pattern of movement. Although Stennings' notions of "migratory drift" and "migration" are important, attention is mainly given here to what he calls "transhumance," and which might be less confusing if called "year-long pattern." The dimensions of pattern of movement which have been emphasized in the literature are seasonal *versus* full-time movement (Bohannan) and movement within one altitude range *versus* movement between altitude ranges (Fisher, Patai). To some extent, seasonal movement and change of altitude are positively correlated, but by no means perfectly. The Zagros nomads are a good example of seasonal movement and change of altitude, and the Bedouin of Arabia are a good example of full-time movement and no change of altitude. But the Fulani and some of the Bedouin of Cyrenaica have important seasonal moves and little altitude change, and the Baluchi are more or less constantly moving although they move through different altitude ranges. The important factor here (climatic dependability, which is discussed below) is more closely associated with the seasonal *versus* full-time movement than with the altitude element, and so the former will be discussed further and no more will be said of the latter.

Coon, comparing the life of the villager with that of the nomad, suggests that ". . . the activities of the villager are repetitive and cyclical while those of the nomad are erratic." But this distinction could well be made in regard to the activities of different nomadic groups. For one can distinguish two basic kinds of spatial patterns of (year-long) movement: (1) the epicyclical, in which erratic and unpredictable movements are a "catch as catch can" response to the micro-climatic changes, and (2) the oscillineal, in which repetitive major movements are a response to gross seasonal climatic shifts. The epicyclical pattern is characterized by many short movements having no general direction, but rather heading in one direction and then in another. Throughout a year, there might be many score of such moves and thus the pattern of a year's movements is an irregular web of criss-crossing paths. The oscillineal pattern is often characterized by long migrations, up to several hundred miles from one seasonal camp to the other. And since the migrations are seasonal, there are in many cases only two per year. Both of these basic patterns are subject to a concentration and dispersion, a contraction and expansion, usually around wells in the case of epicyclical movement, usually during the seasonal encampment in the case of the oscillineal pattern.

The major factor influencing spatial pattern of movement is the degree of climatic dependability. For the pastoralist, water and pasturage are essentials for survival, and movement is a way of adjusting to the differential presence and absence of them. And the degree of dependability of presence and absence is the central factor in pattern of movement. How much, where, and when can pasturage and water be found? Can we know beforehand, and how much beforehand, so that we can count on these resources? is the question that determines the strategy of movement. Predictability, the cultural side of natural dependability, allows the long range and repetitive planning of the oscillineal pattern, and the lack of predictability determines the circumstantial adjustments of the epicyclical pattern.

III. POLITICAL ORGANIZATION OF NOMADISM

A. FUNCTIONAL AND INSTITUTIONAL ANALYSIS

In discussing political organization, one can approach the data under consideration from a "functional" or from an "institutional" perspective. The "functional" approach begins with specified results or effects and examines the empirical social unit in question to learn which part or parts of the social organization have contributed to the result and how these parts have done so. Aside from the occasional discussions of what the political function "really is," this is quite a useful approach, particularly in the analysis of individual systems. It emphasizes the multifunctional nature of different institutions of a society or parts of a social unit. And it shows that societies and social units of quite different types all have a number of important and similar tasks to carry out if they are to continue to exist.

Institutional analysis is the examination of specified roles and social relationships and their related symbol systems. With this approach, the specified institutions are examined in order to understand their inner workings, connections with other institutions, and functions.

In a sense, the institutional and functional approaches are two ends of the same process of analysis. It is a matter of choice whether one begins with function or institution, but no matter which one is the starting point, the other is the end point.

However, for certain purposes, the institutional approach is more feasible. One such purpose is comparative analysis with the goal of developing generalizations. Comparative analysis requires that (1) there are a limited number of variables, and (2) the variables can be made "operational," i.e., formulated so that their presence and characteristics or absence can be observed by publicly verifiable procedures. Functional analysis has great limitations here: on the one hand, contributions to such a broad function as the political come from many different parts of the society, particularly in the "simpler" societies where institutions are multifunctional, thus making for many variables to take into account. On the other hand, the procedures for determining the extent of contribution or lack of contribution of a part of a society to a given function are quite difficult to work out (at least for this student), thus making the variables less operational than is desirable for cross-cultural study with the goal of developing generalizations.

In institutional analysis, the number of variables is more amenable to manipulation. One can pick a role or a cluster of roles, and attempt to associate it or them with other variables. And it is possible to state with fair assurance that a role or relationship is present or absent, and its extent and circumstances. Institutional analysis, then, is the approach which is most suited to the purposes of this study, and so discussion will proceed in institutional terms.

Two constituents of what might be called the political institution will be given attention. The first is the presence and nature or absence of authority roles. Indices for authority roles include the ability to give orders and the extent of matters about which orders can be given, powers of positive and negative sanctioning, and powers of adjudication. The second is the extent of stability or instability of group parameters. Indices for this include recognition of authority roles over time, warfare within the group and peaceful settlement of disputes within the group.

B. POLITICAL ORGANIZATION
AND MIGRATION PATTERN

Perhaps more than peoples with other adaptations, nomads are limited and conditioned in their social organization and culture by ecological factors.

In those tribes who are wealthy in stock, from which a large proportion of subsistence is obtained (but also even in many tribes whose economy is predominantly agricultural), the mode and standard of living, material culture, kinship and community affairs, religion, ritual, law and war are not only set against a background of pastoral activities and necessities, but they are directly and continuously affected in a most intimate fashion.

On two bases, such an evaluation is not ecological determinism. First, recognition of the importance of ecological factors is not the same as asserting that they are the only causes of social organization and culture. And clearly, statements about the limitations and influences of ecological adaptation have to be demonstrated rather than be taken as given. Second, it is quite possible to assert that one adaptation, such as nomadism, limits and conditions to a greater extent than does another adaptation, such as agriculture. This seems to be the notion that Mair is expressing when she says ". . . the less a people are dependent on herding, the less significant is the connexion between their pattern of settlement and their political system." The areas in which nomadism exists can be placed upon a continuum of climatic dependability. Three factors are included in dependability: the amount, the time, and the location of precipitation. These factors determine the amount, time and location of pasturage, which is essential to the well-being of the flocks and/or herds and thus the people. (Although water is obviously just as essential to the general welfare, there are usually at least semi-permanent sources which can be counted on. For the most part, it is the dependability of pasturage that is the crucial factor.) The degree of latitude in evaluating an area as to dependability is quite small, for the matters under discussion are micro-ecological. A few score miles, several days, a fraction of an inch of rain can be of the utmost significance when transportation, communication, and economic reserve are close to the barest minimum.

Some areas can be counted on for a seasonal change, and the nature of the pasturage and water during each season is highly predictable. Other areas also have a seasonal change, but with little prediction possible about the different parts of that area. Usually pasturage is least dependable in the dry season, during which time the permanent or semipermanent sources of water are the only sources. In still other areas there is a minimal change of season, and the pasturage is unpredictable the year round. The permanent and semipermanent sources of water are virtually the only sources in such areas.

Setting aside those areas where there is no pasturage and almost no water (and which in a negative sense can also be called "dependable"), there is likely to be a second factor associated with dependability and predictability. The absolute amount of resources in a dependable area is likely to be greater than in an undependable area. The reason is simple: To be dependable an area has to have pasturage throughout (or none throughout), for climate cannot be nearly so micro-ecological as can nomads. And if an area has pasturage throughout, it will have more pasturage than an area that has some here and some there, quite aside from the problem of chasing about after pasturage.

Furthermore, in those areas where there is a greater amount of resources, it is much more likely that there will be non-nomadic peoples. The presence of agricultural villages is primarily dependent upon the presence of dependable rainfall, even with the small-scale irrigation that is often characteristic of such areas. Put in another way, agricultural villages can exist, often with the help of small-scale irrigation, in an area which for nomads has a large and dependable supply of rain.

The association of these factors with migration pattern has been mentioned above. The oscillineal pattern is a result of repetitive major movements in response to gross seasonal climatic shifts. The movement is from one area of dependable climate to another in response to a single predictable change in climate. As the resources within each of the seasonal areas are dependable, the area is likely to be one of relatively great resources. Non-nomadic peoples are likely to be present. The epicyclical pattern is a result of erratic and unpredictable adjustments to erratic and unpredictable micro-climate changes. The absolute amount of resources is likely to be low, and so agricultural villages are not likely to be present.

Climatic dependability and amount of resources are related, although in no simplistic way, to political organization. Among the intervening variables are coordination of interaction, population density, and economic surplus.

In an area where the resources are predictable, planning is possible. And plans can be implemented by coordination of the interacting social elements. Thus, herding camp units can through planning and coordination fulfill their requirements without unnecessarily competing and perhaps coming into conflict. And coordination between the nomads and the villagers can under certain circumstances be beneficial to the nomads.

In an area of unpredictable climate, planning is not possible. Movement for the herding unit must be in response to micro-climatic changes. Because of the lack of rapid transportation and communication, large-scale coordination is not possible. Rather, the unpredictability of climate combined with the relative scarcity of resources leads to differential scarcity of resources and concomitant social hardships, which result in competition between social units.

In an area of predictable climate and relatively great resources, a large population density can be supported. Thus the possiblity of coordination mentioned above becomes even more relevant. In an area of unpredictable climate and relatively scarce resources, the population density which can be supported is considerably lower.

In an area of predictable climate and great resources, the likelihood that an economic surplus will exist for the support of status and non-productive roles and activities is greater, especially if there is a relatively greater population density, than in an area of unpredictable climate and relatively sparse resources.

These primary and intervening variables can be associated with the two constituents of political organization mentioned above. In this preliminary and oversimplified model, it is hypothesized that nomads living in an area of predictable climate and relatively great resources will have political authority roles and stable group parameters. These roles will consist of powers to coordinate the movements and interactions of the constituent herding groups and the relationships between the herding groups and the villagers. Both positive and negative sanctions will be available for use by the individual or individuals in authority, and powers of adjudication will be included in the compass of the role. The role will have an associated income which provides a higher standard of living for the occupant. The group of herding units will have stable parameters, and will not break down into smaller units which are then independent or build into larger units and lose its independence and identity. It will not be a contingent polity or part of such a system.

In contrast, nomads living in an area of unpredictable climate and relatively sparse resources will have no political authority roles or at best weak and temporary ones, and have unstable group parameters. One or another kind of contingent polity will be the dominant form of organization, with groups combining and breaking apart as circumstances change. The contingencies in regard to which polities will form and break up will tend to be greatly influenced by ecological factors. Competition between groups as a result of differential scarcity caused by scarce and unpredictable resources will be the rule. Political authority roles and stable group parameters are possible in such groups only to the extent that they engage in non-pastoral activities which decrease dependence upon livestock for subsistence goods.

In the following sections, a number of nomadic peoples will be described. An attempt will be made to view them in the light of the variables formulated so far, and to use them to throw light on the model which has just been sketched. After the groups have been discussed, the model will be reexamined and discussed in terms of the data.

The Basseri is a Persian-speaking tribe of the Fars district of Iran. In 1958 there were 3,000 tents, approximately 16,000 inhabitants. The tribesmen are Shiah Muslims, but practice few religious duties other than the profession of faith. Homage is paid at the tombs of local saints, but there is no contact with Sufi brotherhoods which have in other places been so important, or for that matter

with any other carriers of the great tradition of Islam. The tribe is a member of the Khamseh confederacy with a number of Turkic- and Arabic-speaking tribes, but it is a politically autonomous unit in its own right.

Subsistence is derived from flocks of sheep and goats, through both the use of dairy products and meat and goods received from trade and sale of dairy products, hides, rugs, and wool. Other animals are used primarily for non-economic purposes: horses and donkeys for riding, dogs as watchdogs, and camels as burden animals. The sheep are a particularly large and productive strain, but especially lacking in tolerance of climatic extremes.

The area of migration extends from the southwestern edge of the Iranian plateau and the Zagros mountain range to the coast of the Persian Gulf. The summer and winter pastures are connected by the tribal *il-rah*, the tribal path. When the heat of the summer withers the pastures (2,000-foot altitude) bordering the Gulf, the Basseri gather together and, under the direction of the *Khan,* or chief, move along the *il-rah* a distance of three hundred miles, past Shirez to winter pastures at an altitude of thirteen thousand feet. Before the winter snows come, the tribe returns to its southern pastures. The *il-rah* is a usufruct right to a temporal-spatial location. Other tribes use the route and nearby routes in their migrations, and so it is imperative that the Basseri do not overlap their recognized space-time allotment. "The right which the Basseri claim to occupy any one locality is specific in time and duration; at other times that locality may be the 'property' of other tribes." With the following of one tribe after the other on a migration route and the delicate balancing of grazing resources

. . . it is necessary that each group stick very closely to its *il-rah* route and schedule. Any considerable deviation cannot but produce gigantic "traffic jams" with complete exhaustion of key grazing areas, flock famine, and inter-tribal anarchy.

This problem exists as well within the tribe; the numerous large sections and their flocks are spaced and coordinated in such a way that the tribe as a whole can move together without the sections being forced to compete for pasturage.

The migration is organized and run by the *Khan*. To understand how this is possible, it is necessary to examine rather closely what the *Khan* does and what he stands for. Although many of the subgroups of the tribe, the *tira* (sections) and *oulad* (herding groups), trace descent of their members through patrilineal ancestors and think of their unity in these terms, it is acknowledged that many of the groups come from different sources: different ancestors, different tribes, and even different ethnic-language groups. Their unity derives from the recognition of a common leader, a *Khan* from a noble lineage.

It is the fact of political unity under the Basseri chief which in the eyes of the tribesmen and outsiders alike constitutes them into a single "tribe" in the Persian sense.

The *Khan* is the "central, autocratic leader of the tribe." He has great power, and this power is seen by the tribesmen as emanating from him rather than as being instituted in him by them. "The outstanding feature of the chief's position . . . is his power of decision and autocratic command over his subjects." Under his command there are thirty-two headmen, one for each *oulad*. These men act as communicating links between their camps and the *Khan*, but they are not really an authority structure:

All Basseri are equal in their direct relation of subordination to the chief, who at any time may give any person an order which the latter must obey without regard to any pre-established organizational pattern.

Thus, there are chains of communication, but not chains of command.

The chief regularly exercises authority in allotting pastures and coordinating the migration of the tribe, settling disputes, and representing the tribe or any of its members in dealings with other tribes, villages, or outside authorities. It seems quite clear that without the *Khan's* direction of migration, the system of adaptation could not survive.

. . . a prerequisite for the development of a land use pattern such as this is a political form that ensures the disciplined and coordinated migration of large populations by regular routes and schedules. This requires . . . strong and effective coordinating authorities.

Although Barth does not mention such a usage, it is likely that the allotting of pastures is used as a method of sanctioning, as is done in other Zagros tribes (see below). In the tribal system, the *Khan* is the only source of adjudication. Disputes must be otherwise settled by custom, compromise, or diffuse sanctions in the herding camp. But once it is brought to the *Khan*, he decides the matter according to his own views, and is theoretically not hampered by custom, precedent, or *Shariat*. The *Khan* also acts as a representative of the tribe to other tribes or sedentary authorities of all kinds. Here again, his influence or withholding of influence can be

TABLE 17.2
THE FORMAL STRUCTURE OF THE BASSERI TRIBE

Group	Leadership	Estate
tribe (il)	chief	Basseri lands and *il-rah*
section (tira)	—	adjoining grazing areas same close migratory route similar migratory schedule
oulad	headman	joint grazing area joint migratory route and schedule

used as a sanction. Corporal punishment, usually in the form of a beating with a stout pole, can be ordered by the *Khan* and only by him. Any bystander who is a tribesman can be ordered to give the beating. There are no special functionaries for this purpose and no special segment for policing and coercion. Fines are used as a collective punishment to a camp or section held collectively responsible for a misdeed, such as trespassing on the pasture rights of others. This usually takes the form of an extra tithe on the flocks of the punished group.

The Basseri *Khan* and his close relatives are considerably more wealthy than his subjects. They own lands other than the *il-rah* and sometimes villages, and they have houses in Shiras. Sometimes they take part in a style of life completely different from the nomadic one. This can include extensive travel within and outside Iran, higher education, and participation in the activities of the national elite of Iran. The Chief's style of nomadic life indictates his status. His tent is large and his manner generous; sumptuous hospitality including gifts of weapons and stallions from his herds are offered to his guests. The expenses for these luxuries come from inherited properties, irregular taxes of one to three sheep in a hundred that are levied on the tribesmen, and annual taxes of clarified butter. In addition, visitors and supplicants to the chief bring gifts, usually of livestock.

The tribe's surplus of livestock and livestock goods is by no means completely expended in supporting the *Khan*. There is large-scale sale and trading in villages and town bazaars. Sheep and goats, clarified butter and cheese, hides and rugs and wool are exchanged for cash, clothes, various types of equipment and luxury items, and agricultural and industrial products. These transactions do not, however, take place collectively. Just as each tribesman has a relationship with the *Khan* so each tent is an independent economic unit. Mechanisms for support of tent units in economic difficulty are limited, and some tribesmen must drop out and become agricultural workers if their flocks remain below the subsistence minimum of sixty head. The average is about a hundred sheep/goats per tent. The standard of living is good on the average with a net annual income of over $500, not counting foodstuffs directly consumed.

The Bakhtiari is a Persion-dialect-speaking tribe of one-hundred thousand souls which resides on and off of the western edge of the Iranian plateau. As the Basseri, the Bakhtiari leave the plains to the west of the Zagros range when the summer temperatures dry up the pasturage and travel over three-hundred

miles up the mountains to their summer pasture where it is high and cool. Before the cold and ice kill the vegetation on the plateau, the trek down the mountains to the warm winter pasture takes place. Before each migration, the clans of the tribe gather together so that they can proceed *en masse*. With their flocks of sheep and goats, their horses and donkeys, they are led by the *Il-Khan*, or tribal Chief.

The *Il-Khan* is at the top of a hierarchical structure consisting of three levels. The many clans are led by elected *ketchuda*, and each of the Seven Tribes (*Haft Lang*) and Four Tribes (*Chahar Lang*) are led by *Khans*. At the top is the *Il-Khan*, the paramount chief and his deputy, the *Il-Begi*. According to one source, the job of the *Il-Khan* rotates from year to year among the princes, the *Khans*, and according to another source it is elective from certain highly placed families, subject to confirmation by the Shah of Iran. These two reports might accurately reflect social change between 1925 and 1964. In contrast the office of *Khan* is strictly hereditary.

Although there is no detailed account, it is quite clear that the *Il-Khan* and *Khans* have great power and prerogative. The *Il-Khan* is the chief administrator; he directs migration. The *ketchuda*, clan leader, "is responsible for the conduct of his contingent on the long and arduous route of the march, and he makes certain that his people take up their proper position in the great camp during tribal assemblies and also keep their sheep within their own pasture." His responsibility is to the *Il-Khan*, who has a large personal body-guard of armed riders for protection and sanctioning, as does each of the *Khans*.

The *Khans* not only receive taxes from the Tribesmen, but own villages.

. . . each Bakhtiari ruler, in addition to the 300 mile stretch of mountain valley over which the whole princely family rules as a unit, has his own villages, from which he receives private rents, taxing his people one third of their crops.

In addition, the *Khans* have castle-like structures in the Charar Mahal valley in which they reside, with large retinues of servants, when not with the tribes. When with the tribes, they live in elaborate tents and are surrounded by their servants and bodyguard. The *Il-Khan* acts as chief judge, presumably over the adjudicating powers of the *ketchuda* and *Khans*. There is little information on the function other than that "he hears complaints and renders justice."

The tribesmen sell wool in the villages and the money is used to buy tea, sugar, tobacco. Household goods include a few manufactured products and agricultural goods are among the staples.

The Qashqai is a Turkic-speaking tribe of the Fars district of Iran. Its forty-four constituent tribes include about four hundred thousand souls. With their flocks, they follow a migration pattern similar to that of the Basseri, and are usually just to the west of the Basseri in both summer and winter camps and in migration.

Under the *Il-Khan*, the head of the tribe, and his deputy, the *Il-Begh*, are the chiefs of the constituent tribes, the *Kalantara*. There are a number of headmen, called *Ketkhoda* under the *Kalantar*, and a number of *Rish-e-Safid*, white-beards, who are under the headmen, and who have only a little authority. The duties of the *Il-Khan* of the Qashqai are similar to the duties of the leaders of other Zagros tribes.

The problem of the migration preoccupies the Il-Khan. It is he who decides and plans it: he indicates the roads to be followed, the date of departure, the different grazing lands, the length of the stay in the various camping grounds.

During a stay with the *Il-Khan*, Nasser Khan Qashqai, and the *Il-Begh*, Nasser Khan's brother Malek Mansur Qashqai, Ullens de Schooten recorded their descriptions of their duties. Malek Mansur stated that " 'The migration is organized and controlled by the Chief.' " Nasser Khan described his duties as arbiter and judge: " 'When a quarrel starts, and a quarrel can flare up in the most united families, this dispute must not degenerate into a feud and be carried beyond our frontiers; it must be stopped and the problem solved among ourselves.' " He stated that his authority " 'must not be contested or discussed. . . .

Should I feel that, among all my men, five only were against me, I would abdicate without any delay. My role of Chief must be played with the agreement and help of all.' " Nonetheless, the *Il-Khan* has a bodyguard drawn from the forty-five thousand people of the Tribe of Amale. "These men are the *Khan's* escort and also his *executive power*. Nasser Khan is extremely proud of these youths, of their hunting prowess and of their valour as warriors" (emphasis added). Occasionally, the *Il-Khan* gives presents to members of this group of men as prizes for their services. These are regarded as the supreme mark of esteem. Negative sanctioning is best described by an actual case.

I then asked him (Maiek Mansur) if, in cases of disobedience, there would be some form of punishment? He replied by telling me the following story: A group of men had been ordered to join up Shiraz *(sic)* at an appointed hour. On the way they encountered very rough going and, delayed by a severe hail storm, had been forced to seek shelter. Consequently, they were late in arriving. Nasser Khan, who organizes every phase of the migration, decided that these men would be deprived for one season of their accustomed and excellent pasturelands, and would be sent, instead, to less favorable grazing grounds. This severe punishment was considered absolutely fair and was accepted without a murmur. "Those who are under the Chief's orders must know neither rain nor snow, nor storm, but must obey his word."

The Somali are a people of approximately three and a quarter million members located in the Horn of Africa. The majority live in the Somalia Republic, but with significant numbers in the adjacent provinces of Ethiopia and Kenya. The Somali have genealogical and historical ties with Arabia, and look toward Arabia culturally, especially in their strong commitment to Islam. The six large clan-families of the Somali which are tied together by a national genealogy do not all follow the same way of life: the clan-families which live in the southern area are agriculturalist; the clan-families of the north follow a nomadic existence. It is the northern Somali nomads that are of interest here, and therefore it is they who are described below.

Northern Somaliland is a harsh environment, consisting of semidesert with little rain and coarse grass and scrub bush as the predominant vegetation. The Somali distinguish between three zones: *Gubban, Ogo* and *Huad*. These zones differ somewhat in their offerings of pasturage and water, and the differences vary according to season, as does the usage which the nomads make of the zones. "... the sequence of displacement through the three zones ... corresponds to the seasonal distribution of pasturage and water." There are two wet seasons and two dry seasons (these being relative terms, for a wet season can consist of a few inches of rain) with concomitant (relative) abundance of water and pasturage. There are permanent wells in the *Ogo* highlands which are depended upon in the seasons of scarcity, and shallow more temporary wells are often possible elsewhere.

In some respects the migration·pattern is directly determined by the seasons. During the dry seasons, the lineage groups are concentrated around their home wells, although some sharing between lineages is common. During the wet seasons, the nomads are widely deployed in the pastures. There is thus a contraction-expansion pattern in response to seasonal variations. Other than this, however, movement is for the most part irregular, and has a "highly complex overall pattern." This is due to the temporal and spatial variation of rainfall and thus pasturage even within a given season. It is impossible to predict the time and place of pasturage. It comes as no surprise, then, that "scouts are sent out . . . to report where rain has fallen and where pasturage is plentiful." In response the migrating unit is the herding camp of a small number of agnates and the hamlet with flocks of sheep and goats.

. . . despite these fairly well-defined four seasons the annual rainfall varies considerably in both amount and distribution. The seasons are thus by no means constant and, with the small margin that exists between subsistence and famine, necessitates an exceedingly tight adjustment of the pastoral life to its environment.

The result of such adjustment is threefold: (1) "Men of different lineages and clans move with their stock where grazing and water are available. . . . Hence lineages are widely deployed in the pastures, intermingling with those of the same and other clans wherever water and grazing are plentiful." This mingling of small units resulting in interpenetration of lineages and clans means that migration does not take place as a collective activity of clan or lineage units. (2) The movement of a given lineage changes from year to year in response to the changing spatial and temporal location of pasturage, thus from year to year presenting "an entirely different pattern of distribution, although within the same general area." (3) "There is no strict localization of pastoral groups." It seems that the pasture area must be kept open, and not allotted to clans and lineages, for an allotment which has pasturage one year and none in another year is of no use. Ecological adaptation in a limited area must be based upon the minimal amount of productivity of the area. And this is the value of nomadism as an adaptation: it allows areas to be occupied during their maximum productivity and avoided during their minimum period.

Somali social organization is basically a segmentary lineage system, which is conceptualized by the Somali as *tol* or agnation. A person's membership in a lineage, clan and clan-family is established by a genealogy that links him through male ancestory to the eponym of the clan-family. Ancestory of lineage groups at various levels of segmentation are venerated as Muslim "saints." Probably largely because of their religious significance, the genealogies are regarded as history and manipulation does not take place. When fission and fusion, processes that separate and unify groups in times of conflict, take place, unification and division follow the lines of historical bifurcation. Because different lineages grow and wither differentially, and manipulating the genealogy to increase the size of one's segment is not permissible, other mechanisms are used. Alliances on the basis of uterine ties successfully cut across agnatic cleavages, and are used to redress the balance.

Heer, or contract, is conceptually superimposed upon *tol* by the Somali. Basically *heer* is a mechanism whereby a group of clan members bind themselves together for collective defense. Members are bound to protect each other from homicide, *dil*, wounding, *qoon*, and insult, *dalliil*, and to seek vengeance or compensation in any of these cases. If one member commits one of these offenses, then the rest are obliged to contribute toward compensation. These *dia*-paying groups are the fundamental political units of Somali society.

It is only through membership of a *dia*-paying group that one has political and jural status. An individual cannot himself act as a viable independent political unit.

It is within this group that conflicts are adjudicated and the decisions enforced. A group of elders directs such an inquiry and the other members combine to enforce the decision. Every Somali is a member of a widely ramifying series of lineages and *dia*-paying group which guarantees the security of life and property.

These affiliations have the potential to be activated at many different levels of segmentation, from clan-family down to primary lineages. ". . . structural relativity is rooted in the dynamics of the nomadic life where competition for sparse grazing and water continually arises at different levels of grouping." Pasturage is limited, and with members of different segments mixing, rivalry and hostility develop. When conflict breaks out, as it often does in an area where self-help is the rule, and the only protection for a group's rights is its willingness and ability to use force, alliances and splits develop at the point of bifurcation of the level or segmentation most relevant to the geographical area being disputed.

In this system, there are no authority roles, leaving aside the adjudicatory powers of the elders of the *dia*-paying group. Many clans have a Sultan, who acts as a symbol of the clan. He is usually a relatively wealthy man, and is expected to provide hospitality, but has no political power. He cannot give orders, adjudicate, or sanction, and he directs no activities. Attached to many lineages are Sheikhs. They are religious men (*wadaad*) and, following the Somali distinction between religious men and warriors (*waranich*), they are excluded from all political matters and not even allowed to participate in council as an ordinary *waranich* would.

The Jie is one of the tribes of the "Karamjong cluster" which is located on the border of northeastern Uganda and northwestern Kenya. The Jie had a population of 18,200 (in 1948) and is located in the Karamoja district of Uganda in a small area of about twenty-five by sixty-five miles. The environment is harsh and tropical, with one rainy and one dry season. The Jie economy is a mixed one, with the bulk of the staple food coming from cultivation of sorghum. Nevertheless, the cattle and sheep and goats are important economically and the cattle in particular for ritual and social usages.

Permanent settlement in the small agricultural area in the center of the district is surrounded by open pastures to the east and west. The few permanent water holes are located in the western region. In the wet season, the pastures to the east, with their temporary surface water, are used by the cattle camps. As the dry season approaches, the herding camps move to the western region, and as that area becomes more scorched, concentrate around the permanent water sources. The unit of migration is the camp of full brothers. In regard to movement, "the timing . . . is . . . entirely the concern of each owner, and so is the new location to which he moves."

No basis of control of general organization in pastoral affairs is provided by membership of extended family or clan, settlement or district. In the concentrations in the dry season and in the scatter at other times I have always found a tribe-wide intermingling of herds in any area. Neither does a herd, or camp, move in a fixed orbit each year, for the semi-nomadic movements vary from year to year according to the conditions of rainfall and vegetation and according to personal choices.

This is a result of the cultural principle that no specific pasture rights are attached to any individuals or groups, but rather belong to the tribe as a whole, and of the irregular condition of rainfall which results in the un-likelihood that pasturage and water will be found in the same place two years together. Jie never fight over pasture; pasture is open to all as they want it, and even previous pos-session and occupation of an area has no bearing.

There are no political authority roles in Jie. "Other than in ritual affairs, there are no acknowledged leaders of territorial groups, nor is coercive authority or decision-making responsibility ascribed to specialized roles and particular persons." Peace is maintained by the commonality of norms and recogni-tion of Jie unity. An individual who feels he has been hurt by another attempts to right the situation himself or with help of cattle-asso-ciates with whom he has personal ties (the activation of a "network" of relationships sur-rounding an individual) at first by peaceful means and by force if possible and neces-sary. Violence is, apparently, not a prominent part of Jie social life.

The Turkana, with a population of eighty thousand live in northwestern Kenya, just to the east of the Jie. The climate is similar to Jieland, but even less hospitable. There are mountains in Turkanaland which play an important part in the ecology, for the rain falls mostly there. As the Turkana depend completely on their flocks of sheep and goats and herds of cattle for subsistence, they have no permanent settlements, but build tem-porary thorn homesteads wherever they are camped. In the rainy season, they come down from the mountains to the pastures, digging shallow walls in the few water courses. In the dry season, they return to the mountainous area. Usually the flocks and herds are sepa-rated owing to the differential water needs and ability of the flocks to browse while the herds must graze, with the herds limited to the mountainous area.

Rainfall is not only small, it is irregular both in quantity and effectiveness. These considerable variations in rainfall—and thus in the supply of vegetation—are important in causing cor-responding variations in the movements and dispositions of the nomadic Turkana over the years.

The units of herding are the herds and flocks of one man. He chooses the time of move-ment and the next location. With the ex-ception of the general notion that less persist-ent pastures are to be used first and more persistent ones saved until later, there is no cooperation or coordination between herds in their movement.

Each man attempts to provide for his herds as best he can in the light of his experience and the needs of his animals. He must take into account the quantity and quality of vegetation, facilities for watering, distance between pastures and water, and future prospects of both.

It is characteristic for a group of temporary neighbors to agree that their area is ex-hausted and to move off in different direc-tions. In an actual case of seven temporary neighbors, five moved in different directions and the remaining pair moved in a sixth di-rection. When the same men returned to the general area during the next wet season, their homesteads formed parts of three separate neighborhoods.

In Turkanaland, the pasture is not owned but open to all. It is usual and predictable that in any area there will be "A complete intermingling and remingling of herds of many areas . . . [and] intermingling of the people also." The Turkana say, " 'We can move anywhere, everywhere. Are we not all Turkana? You own stock and things; you do not own the country.' " And yet, this ethic does not hold all of the time. Although such action is condemned in theory, movement is restricted towards the end of the dry season when pastures are becoming critically im-poverished.

A newcomer, especially a group of newcomers, may arouse inchoate public opinion to common opposition on the grounds that a further strain on available vegetational resources would ex-haust them before the next wet season . . . at these drastic times men are driven into tempo-rary alliance to protect their own welfare; and fights do sometimes occur. . . .

In this case, the temporary neighborhood group becomes a cohesive political unit, combined to protect its resources against outsiders.[1] There are no authority roles among the Turkana, and the only political unity other than the temporary group mentioned above is the raiding party which preys on herds of non-Turkana people.

CONCLUSION

The hypothesis suggested above, that nomads living in an area of predictable climate and relatively great resources will have political authority roles and stable group parameters, and that nomads living in an area of unpredictable climate and relatively sparse resources will have no political authority roles, or at best weak and temporary ones, and have unstable group parameters, seems to be borne out by the societies described above. The Zagros tribes—Basseri, Bakhtiari, and Qashqai—respond in their migration to gross seasonal changes, with minimal concern about micro-ecological variations of pasturage and water due to unpredictable climate. These tribes all have extremely strong authority roles, and in two cases hierarchies of authority roles. There are powers of positive and negative sanctioning and adjudication, broad areas in which orders are given and obeyed, and a large surplus provided for executive expenses. As suggested, these powers are used to coordinate the movements of the nomads and the relationships between

At any one time herdsmen who meet at one watering place will come from many different settlements, and no one will expect to meet the same people each year (in other words, the people who are in close contact during the dry season do not form a permanent social group). The Karimojong recognize this and say, 'The sun mixes us up.' They are most mixed up at the height of the drought, when a number of herds and their herdsmen combine to use the same water and grazing and to keep others out of it. If a conflict of this kind occurs, loyalties are clear. The 'insiders' in this temporary group must stand together against outsiders, whatever ties of kinship or neighborhood may bind them to the outsiders at other times.

1. Although Neville Dyson-Hudson's *Politics of the Karimojong* is not available to the author at the time of writing, Mair discusses some of the material from his (at that time) unpublished thesis:

the nomads and outside groups, including other nomads and villagers. The group parameters remain stable. The executive authority is ongoing and exists continually, and these tribes never break down into smaller political units. In contrast, the Somali and the tribes of the Karamojong complex are continually adjusting to micro-ecological variations as a result of undependable climate and having to face shortages of crucial resources. These groups do not have continuous authority roles. The only case of such powers is the adjudicatory powers of the *dia*-paying group elders of the Somali. The group parameters in the societies change, to the greatest extent in the Somali, to a lesser extent in the Turkana. (The Jie are discussed below.) The differences within this group are illuminating. On the one hand, the climate of northern Somaliland is more undependable than that of the Jie and Turkana. Where the Jie move from the east to west and back according to the seasons, and the Turkana move from the mountainous area to the plains and back according to the seasons, the Somali seem to have a much more vague pattern of concentration and expansion according to the seasons. This difference might to some extent account for the many levels of contingent organization of the Somali, and the lack of it in the others. For the level of segmentation and contingent organization of the Somali depends upon the size of the geographical area under dispute. (To some extent, the difference in number of possible contingent groups must be attributed to a cultural factor, that is, the lineage model which the Somali use to conceptualize their organization and which is not present among the tribes of the Karemojong complex.) At most, the Turkana have only two levels of contingent organization: the neighborhood protecting its resources during the worst part of the dry season (as do the Karamojong), and the groups which raid outside Turkanaland. The Jie do not even have the neighborhood contingent group, and so at most have the raiding group as the one contingent organization. This can be accounted for by a factor discussed in Part

II, that is, extent of dependence upon live-stock.[2] While the Turkana depend upon their stock for subsistence, the Jie get much of their staple foodstuffs from agricultural activities, and so are not pressed when there is a shortage of pasturage. Thus, if the hypothesis is limited to nomads completely dependent upon livestock, as it is meant to be, the Jie with their lack of contingent groups do not stand as a contravening case.

2. This is also an important factor in considering such groups as the Tuareg, for they also depend heavily upon other sources of wealth. It is likely that this has significant influences upon their political organization. Briggs describes the economic system of the Tuareg: "Pastoralism used to be the central column and crop shares, trading, protection, and raiding the four corner posts of Ahaggar Tuareg economy." The *Amanukal,* the supreme chief, had significant powers, particularly in regard to foreign affairs, and was chief judge, but his authority over his subjects was limited. There are few data on the authority roles of a lower level. Presumably, they would also be something close to true authority roles with effective powers. This type of political organization would not be expected in a nomadic group in the Sahara if it was entirely dependent upon livestock.

18. THE ROLE OF THE STATE IN PEASANT-NOMAD MUTUALISM

DANIEL G. BATES

Reprinted from the Anthropological Quarterly *(Vol. 44, 1971, 109-31). Daniel G. Bates is Assistant Professor of Anthropology at Hunter College, City University of New York. His major research interests are in ecology and intergroup exchange, economic organization, family structure and population in the Middle East. His principal research was conducted in Turkey and the Middle East between 1968 and 1971. He is the author of* The Yoruk of Southeastern Turkey: A Study of Land Use and Social Organization.

■ The previous selection concentrated on ecological forces in pastoralists' habitats that play a role in their political organization. In this selection Bates considers another set of forces in their milieus—social and political. Specifically, he examines the role of the central state in mediating relationships between pastoralists and cultivators. This political intervention by the central government, he suggests, is more important than ecological factors; politically, the intrusion of these political elements into the pastoralists' habitat has far-reaching consequences for their organization of social relations, in the wider milieu of the nation conceived as an adaptive unit.

Bates begins his analysis with the observation that these pastoralist-cultivator relationships involve more than one ethnically defined population. In other words, the members of each group interact with members of the other group as well as their own. An important aspect of these group interrelationships is the mutual dependence resulting from the agriculturists' need for meat and dairy products and the pastoralists' need for cultivated foods and manufactured goods. But both groups also are potential competitors for land; farmed land could be used for grazing while pasturage could be put to agricultural use. This competition may easily erupt into violent conflict that is difficult to control, especially when ethnically distinctive groups are involved. The state's intervention is the crucial factor in maintaining a balance of power.

This selection also suggests that transhumance cannot be understood solely within the pastoralist strategy of adaptation. Instead, it may be interpreted as an adaptive cycle of movement in response to the economic activities of a dominant society. As Bates shows, the pastoralists' movements are not only dictated by their needs for water and grasses but also by the farmers' cycles of planting, growing, and harvesting, and fallowing, and by the schedules of markets, fairs, and urban employment in which the herders participate.

The reader who wants to explore these relationships further should turn first to Robert McC. Adams and Hans Nissen, *The Uruk Countryside.* Interesting comparisons between the Middle East and Asia can be made by consulting also *Inner Asian Frontiers of China,* by Owen Lattimore (Boston: Beacon Press, 1962). A situation comparable to those discussed by Bates is presented in *The Kababish Arabs: Power, Authority and Consent in a Nomadic Tribe,* by Talal Asad (New York: Praeger, 1970). In his study of this camel-herding Sudanese tribe, Asad focuses on the role of individual choice in the management of household herds; this is a highly stratified society in which centralized authority grew directly out of external pressures, first British then Sudanese. ■

THIS PAPER WILL EXAMINE peasant-nomad interaction with respect to joint land-use and exchange, and will attempt to make explicit the primary conditions which a valid, comprehensive model of these relationships must fulfill. Specifically, this paper proposes to show that the relationship of a nomadic pastoral society to a sedentary population, where these are ethnically distinct, does not depend solely nor even predominantly upon factors of the local ecology. Rather, the interaction of societies pursuing specialized modes of production represents the resolution of external forces which engender local competition and cooperation. Any accurate representation of inter-ethnic exchange, quite apart from how it handles local social and economic processes, will have explicitly to account for external political relations—since the interaction of local entities in the Near East is often a function of how each articulates with such extra-local sources of political power as the state.

Processes which affect the distribution of populations over resources, such as intergroup exchange and the common use of a territory by nomadic pastoral and farming communities, are often best analytically framed as ecological systems (cf. Barth, Selection 25). In instances of interspecific exchange the concept of symbiosis can be usefully employed as a generic designator for all continued effects on population growth and survival arising from the interaction of two or more populations. Mutualism focuses on the beneficiality of these effects on both populations. This focus is appropriate to the analysis of exchanges between peasant and nomadic populations in systems of joint land-use where our concern is to evaluate the degree of reciprocity and value-equivalence. Available studies reveal a great diversity in the degree of mutualism characteristic of inter-population exchanges where groups, specialized in nomadic animal husbandry, acquire goods and services outside the limits of their own political economies.

Anthropological models of ecologic relationships usually focus on the material transfers (and concomitant social parameters) among one ethnically defined human population, animal populations and other biotic resources occurring within a circumscribed locality. However, many ethnographically interesting situations involve more than one culturally defined population. Often several communities are closely integrated in regional systems of land-use with ethnicity or other cultural markers distinguishing modes of production and delineating the resources to which social units will have access in a shared territory. Analytic models of land-use which are directed to spatially discrete human populations will not benefit investigations of eco-

logical relations in areas dominated by state political structures. Furthermore, models which focus on exchanges arising from one population's interaction with its immediate environment may well obscure the dynamics of overall resource allocation among specialized communities.

The approach suggested here argues that the relationship established in situations of peasant-nomad shared land-use is best analyzed as though it were predicated upon two distinct but closely related levels of interaction. The level immediate to the contact groups is the local ecological system, which includes the populations in question and their cultural adaptations together with the physical environment which they exploit. In this connection such factors as land tenure practices, local social and political organization, relative military strength, population size and density, modes of production and redistribution are relevant. The second level of interaction concerns how the local system relates to a wider economic and political milieu.

Ecological studies of nomadic pastoralism are not all narrowly cast. Barth, using an ecological idiom, analyzes the distribution of specialized ethnic groups and patterns of shared land-use involving nomads in Swat, West Pakistan. Treating Swat as an ecological system, he demonstrates that ethnic specializations in concentrating on selected portions of the "total environment," leave open other contiguous or even politically incorporated areas (niches) for other populations (including nomads) to exploit. In another study, perhaps the most comprehensive discussion of mountain nomadism available, Barth shows that throughout Southwest Asia ". . . nomads become tied in relations of dependence and reciprocity to sedentary communities in the area—their culture is such as to presuppose the presence of such communities and access to their products." Going on to describe the relations of a variety of nomadic adaptations to sedentary societies, he notes that the quality of exchange and joint land-use will be the outcome, in part, of the potential for expansion of the militarily dominant population.

Force alone, however, does not bear the

primary burden of determining the degree of mutuality achieved in peasant-nomad exchange systems, nor does it entirely set the distribution of ethnically defined modes of production in a region. In an analysis of Swat, in other discussions of nomadic pastoralism and with reference to the functions of ethnicity Barth proposes that stable patterns of co-residence expressed in niches (in ethnically heterogeneous systems) arise from differing but complementary modes of production. Each of these is delineated by political and social usages which establish the boundaries of the niche. With respect to the nomadic pastoralist niche, he states that ". . . there are no competing and more effective means of utilizing the seasonal pastures on which the nomadic adaptation is based; it remains the only economically viable form. Further, he stresses that the exchanges themselves generate this stable relationship, if they are phrased as value equivalent.

In areas where pastoral nomadism has been developed as a completely full-time specialization, and all agricultural and industrial goods are obtained in exchange for value equivalents in pastoral produce, a relatively peaceful and close market relationship is stablished between the two segments of the society, even without effective controlling mechanisms.

It is not the purpose here to give a critique of Barth's work. However, Barth raises a number of questions which are central to an attempt to specify the minimal conditions of peasant-nomad land-use mutualism; viz. the importance of relative power of the specialized ethnic groups in contact, the stability of the exchange system, and how the degree of exchange mutuality is related to other socio-economic variables within either political economy. Also, without faulting the overall thrust of the analysis quoted from above, it would seem that the logic of power in conjunction with the common need on the part of nomadic populations to secure grazing in potentially arable areas makes it tautological to posit value equivalent exchange as the independent variable and a close market relationship as the dependent one. Rather, as Barth himself suggests, reciprocity or value

equivalence in exchange is affected by the relative power of the groups engaging in the different modes of production.

Also, it must not be taken as given that ethnic specialization or even high land-use mutually makes for the most effective or efficient use of resources in a region, as is perhaps the case for Swat. This teleological aspect of the model is implicit in the general assumption that as a cultural system (like that of the Pathans) expands to the limits of its political economy, so these limits will coincide with the extremes set by the peak efficiency of that population's major mode of production due to the material requirements of the social organization. It is rare, however, in the Near East for any society to be organizationally so committed to one level or one mode of production that it cannot easily accommodate great variations in the basic adaptation without loss of its political coherence. Certainly the segmentary tribal structures, of all types, commonly associated with nomadic pastoral societies and many village communities lack this rigidity, and very often a tribal unit will encompass considerable diversity in modes of production.

This will be made clearer when we examine the concept of peasant-nomad mutualism in terms of the minimal conditions which must obtain for value equivalent exchange to be approached. The adjustment described by any set of inter-population relations is necessarily temporary. Each of the contiguous populations, agricultural or nomadic pastoralist, reacts dynamically to selective pressures internal as well as external to its socio-economic structure. Just as each group might react differently to changes in its external environment, so might each handle changes in its own domestic political economy differently. Demographic pressures, for example, are often treated differently among pastoralists than among their settled agricultural neighbors in the same ecosystem, reflecting the different limitations inherent in land and animals as property.

Although nomadic pastoralism as a full-time specialization has many requirements for non-pastoral products, and usually can offer products and services needed by sedentary populations in return, any such system of exchange or joint land-use represents the resolution of a number of potentially disruptive forces. These disruptive forces reflect the differences in the adaptations to animals and land as primary resources, and the nature of ethnicity as a boundary-keeping mechanism.

Foremost among processes which reduce the potential for high mutuality is direct competition for access to land. In any ecological setting, the farmer is exploiting land that would be, or could be utilized by nomadic pastoralists as pasture. There is usually a clear limit to the expansion of agriculture in a region, marked by such physical characteristics as soil or rainfall. The converse is rarely true. Rather political boundaries, the barriers erected by force or political convention restrict nomadic incursion into arable lands.

In virtually every area of peasant-nomad contact, crop damage due to nomad animals is a matter of local contention and the adjudication, if done at all, is a matter of conflict.

Demographic pressure on resources arising within either society, can dictate territorial expansion as an attractive alternative to a redistribution of resources already available in a given political economy. Ethnic distinctions often make the land of neighboring groups prime targets in the relieving of demographic imbalances. Also nomads whose herds fail to meet the minimum requirements for household self-sufficiency are often forced to settle. Often (as in Turkey) nomads who settle must interject themselves into ethnically different and initially hostile communities.

No ethnic economic specialization is immutable because a society can drastically vary its basic mode of production in an extremely short period. There are many instances where nomadic tribes have settled, displacing ethnically different agricultural populations. Ethnic stereotypes are not sufficient in themselves to reserve a mode of production from possible inroads by other groups. The much discussed nomadic antipathy for peasants is usually an expression of ethnic hostility. Should nomadic animal husbandry become economically a poor allocation of household capital, such hostility is rarely a substantial barrier to settlement and agriculture. Likewise, it is not at all unknown for sedentary communities to spawn nomadic pastoral households, even in areas where nomadic pastoralism is associated with a different ethnic group.

Furthermore, there is in most situations a marked inability to control inter-ethnic conflict. The segmentary political systems most often seen in the Near East tend to ramify external opposition through as wide a political network as possible, thus making conflict, once started, difficult to dampen. Similarly, there may be a tendency to emphasize short-term economic gain in transactions with cross ethnic or narrow community boundaries which again would mitigate against mutualism in systems without overarching political control directed to this end. Collectively the above are disjunctive factors which tend to lessen reciprocity, to put pressure on respective niche boundaries and thus to erode the economic basis for complementarity in production.

Exchange or mutuality is affected not only by divisive conditions mentioned above, but by the potential for complementary exchange between two specializations. Potential for reciprocal peasant-nomad exchange is, largely, inversely proportional to the self-sufficiency of each population with regards to the production or services of the other.

Peasant communities vary greatly in the amount of animal husbandry practiced in conjunction with agriculture, but most need not rely on external sources of animal products to meet minimum demands for protein and dairy goods. Probably more important are secondary nomadic services such as transportation of commercial crops to market as was the case in southeastern Turkey prior to World War II, in providing fertilizer for fallow fields and for protection from the predation of other nomads. In recent years, payment for grazing rights is a contribution to certain sedentary communities made by nomadic groups in Turkey.

However, the point to be stressed in this context is that peasant-nomad land-use and exchange systems are often less reciprocal or mutual than is potentially feasible. This is to say that actual relations do not represent a simple balance of *local* processes of economic adjustment, nor do they display a teleologic tendency for maximum efficiency in land-use systems involving ethnically different specializations. Each population, it may be assumed, is interested in increasing its own production and security as evaluated in the short-run. This renders the structure created by a system of peasant-nomad interaction extremely sensitive to shifts of power, whether instigated by forces outside the region or from pressures within either society. There is a potential or, perhaps, even a centrifugal tendency towards degrading the system, to reduce any region of shared co-exploitation to one where a single ethnic specialization dominates to the exclusion or restriction of others. Successful adaptations of one society are taken over by other groups, and security is often given precedence over production and profitable exchange.

The reasons for this devolve on the question of coordinating economic processes within the ecosystem, and how power from the outside affects these regulatory processes.

In the examples given by Barth for Swat it seems assumed that peasant-nomad exchange and land use tended to produce homeostasis; that regulation is located in the ecosystem itself. He makes reference to the absence of state authority (until 1917) and attributes the stability of the system to the fact that the fullest expansion of the dominant society had already occurred, and that there was little direct competition. At the same time sedentary agricultural communities could not raise sufficient animals to exploit distant pastures as relatively stationary herds are limited by the amount of grain and stored forage needed to carry them through the winter in the village.

However, although the nature of the terrain and the vegetational cycles establish the outer limits of migration and provide the direct economic impetus for mountain nomadic pastoralism, it is incorrect to view every schedule of migration as a predictable response only to available but marginal grazing land. Furthermore, it might with equal accuracy be interpreted as a political response of a community which is less powerful as it adapts its cycle of movement to the economic round of activities of a dominant society. Or, in some areas, the response itself may lie in dominating and restricting a weaker sedentary mode of production.

With an ecological approach to peasant-nomad interaction one must consider that high mutualism does not arise from the exploitation of non-competitive niches, but rather from the control of conflict generated by often antithetical social and economic processes associated with the different patterns of land-use. Such controls are often a function of how society articulates with extra-regional polities, including ethnically similar populations of which each is the local representative.

We have mentioned that the power of the state in most of the Middle East is of importance in determining local forms of interpopulation exchange. Somewhat more information is called for at this point. But before continuing, it is necessary to note that nothing more than a general outline can be provided, as not only is the ecology of the region complex, but also the forms of state or "national" authority vary greatly from place to place, as they have through history.

It is, I think, useful to distinguish as Coon does between sovereignty and suzerainty with regards to the Near Eastern state. Since very early historical times no area has fallen outside the claimed political borders of some central government. However, the amount of authority exercised by any state, or feudal kingdom, varies considerably. Often the political claims of erstwhile powerful governments amount to little in the day-to-day governing of distant or geographically inaccessible provinces. But no matter how tenuous the state's suzerainty, its formal claim to rule makes it amenable to manipulation by local political, often tribal, forces, each eager to tap what sources of power are available.

This is somewhat different than the traditional picture of state and local community relations, according to which the village or tribe is held to be the passive subject of the wider political aims of the central government. As often as not, the local power structures at a village or tribal level are concerned with transforming public force in the name of the state to personal or narrow community ends. When the state is able, there is little hesitation for it actively to intervene in the allocation of resources and territories among competing factions. But in every situation state power is a resource to be exploited by local contenders for supremacy or economic dominance.

It is difficult to generalize for an area as large and varied as is the Near East. What follows is only an attempt to suggest directions for possible detailed inquiry.

For example, in areas where the state's control is absolute, or nearly so, it is usually interested in maximizing total production and hence the tax base, in any region. This is done usually without regard to which ethnic group, if any, monopolizes the relevant modes of products.

The border reaches of Near Eastern states have witnessed virtually every strategem of political control or manipulation. For example, in those border regions which were difficult to control, Ottoman policy was aimed continually at shifting support among ethnic groups, allowing none to achieve supremacy or to establish stable exercise of authority which might jeopardize the claim of sovereignty of the state.

If the region controlled or secured lay on critical internal trade routes, such as across Syria in Ottoman times, the state might try to achieve stability at the expense of production by supporting the militarily dominant local political force. For example, agriculture was frequently sacrificed for security of communications as the government (Ottoman) allied itself with powerful Bedouin tribes. Such support was rarely consistent because the ultimate objective was always complete control. At the same time the government strived to prevent any tribe or ethnic group from setting up a reliable power base which could not be destroyed by shifting alliances.

The exercise of this power, even if through less than full control of local political apparatuses, has an important effect on the local ecosystem, as will be shown in the following examples.

IRRIGATION AGRICULTURE: LARGE-SCALE RIVER VALLEY

Irrigation plays a vital role in the agriculture of the Near East; more so where exotic rivers serve as the source of water. Everywhere such large-scale hydraulic works are associated with rigorous state control, high population density and labor intensive commercial cropping geared to a relatively efficient transportation system. Egypt, Sudan and Iraq supply traditional examples, with new developments in Syria and Iran soon to present similar aspects. Large-scale irrigation usually presents clear ecological boundaries between crop land and the desert. There is little fringe area capable of supporting nomadic small animal husbandry as found on the Syrian Steppe or Zagros foothills.

The camel pastoralists of the inner desert tend to articulate directly with the central government. The government is concerned always with presenting itself as a buffer between its peasant population and forces from the outside. The great disparity in population size makes the effects of nomadic demands for agricultural products negligible on the system. The peasant has slight need for pastoral products. His demands for meat are minimal, and he can supply animal traction better by stall feeding on grass grown intensively by irrigation. The nomad formerly did have a secondary impact on the peasantry in that defense against possible predation resulted in increased taxation or military levies.

When there is direct peasant-nomad contact it historically has resulted in the destruction or reduction of irrigation works, but not in an institutionalized system of exchange. The potential for complete mutuality is very low through shared use of land, although exchange via trader intermediaries is important for nomadic groups. An economic analysis would show that the peasant community requires little of what the nomad produces; irrigation leaves little of the arable landscape open to pastoralism. Nomadic requirements for urban goods are supplied through intermediaries.

However, as I shall point out for other areas, this lack of a close economic fit need not entirely preclude mutuality in land use. The crux of the problem seems to lie in the respective political structures of the two groups. Large-scale irrigation agriculture requires sufficient central control to maintain upstream canal systems. The segmentary tribal organization of the camel pastoralist facilitates the formation of large political groups in response to external threat, but stable groupings with strong leadership are not easily arrived at otherwise. Strong central control, if ever, is exercised only in times of war or raiding, and is of short duration. Although camel pastoralists can incorporate oasis settlements and isolated villages as tributary dependencies, the greater population size and administrative sophistication associated with states controlling large-scale irrigation systems is usually beyond the scope of descent based segmentary political integration. If they should militarily conquer such a state, they either rapidly acquire the accoutrements of an urban elite, or they maximize the short run benefits by destroying the system altogether. Here peasant-nomad mutualism falls at the negative end of the continuum since direct contact usually results in the destruction of the militarily weaker mode of production rather than its incorporation into a common polity, or the establishment of stable patterns of joint land use.

RAINFALL PLAINS AGRICULTURE: NORTH SYRIAN STEPPE

Although the Northern Syrian Steppe (ca. 8″ rainfall limits) marks the limits of grain agriculture to the peasant farmer, it also represents prime grazing to a variety of nomadic pastoralists. Mountain nomads such as the Kurdish and Türkmen tribes of southeastern Turkey and Syria use the steppes as winter grazing, while small-animal herding Arab tribes on the fringes of the Syrian desert approach the best watered foothill regions in times of summer drought and likewise for winter grazing. The much commented upon *tell*[1] remains of former villages give testimony to the historical ebb and flow of desert and sown land. This variation cannot be attributed to known climatic fluctuations, although periodic drought does make the agricultural economy more precarious.

Scholars dealing with the Levant have been careful to note the positive correlation between the strength of the sovereign central government and the expansion of grain agriculture into the desert periphery, paralleling the sedentarization of former pastoralists. This model might be further expanded to encompass the Bedouin of the inner desert. Musil states that during periods of increased governmental control and agricultural expansion, poorer segments of Bedouin camel herding tribes are sloughed off into sheep/goat pastoralism, thus replacing the former small animal herders absorbed by agriculture. Presumably a reverse trend is possible in times of government weakness, although it is little documented in the literature. There is adequate documentation that land under cultivation declined in the period following Ottoman conquest (1517) and that pastoral nomadic groups from elsewhere infiltrated the area.

Ottoman pashas sent out from Constantinople had a free hand in governing their districts during their short tenures and normally operated through local chieftains to collect tax levies in kind. However, frequently a tribe would be paid by the government to maintain security and trade. In the nineteenth century the Ottomans began a program of agricultural development and forced settlement of nomadic groups. Apart from Midhat Pasha, such governors as Dervish Pasha and

1. Mound or heap.

Cevdet Pasha were extremely effective in forcibly settling Kurdish, Arab and Türkmen tribes by bringing the full brunt of the military to bear on individual tribes while at the same time offering tribal leaders title to large tracts of land. Peasant groups from elsewhere, including Circassians, were settled in the area. The Mandate and subsequent regimes continued this policy. The present settlement pattern in northwest Syria and southeastern Turkey is one of interspersed tribal, non-tribal villages, and mixed villages.

Tell Toqaan, a village in this area, was established during the late nineteenth century and was non-tribal in political structure. Following the upheavals of the early Mandate era it was taken over by the elite of the Bu Layle tribe but continued sedentary agriculture as a "mixed" tribal village with non-tribal sections.

There are still nomadic pastoralists in the Tell Toqaan area and a high degree of mutuality obtained between them and both the tribal and non-tribal peasants at the time of Sweet's study. The peasant makes contractual arrangements whereby nomads herd village flocks. The village allows nomad flocks to graze on fallow fields and to pass through village lands during migration. Some grain and manufactured items are sold to the nomads, but the preferred payment for herding is in sheep. The contracts are considered equitable and are freely entered into. This situation is clearly related to the presence of the national gendarmerie adding to the local power of the sedentary population.

Formerly this was not the case. During times of pastoral nomadic dominance, such agricultural villages as remained intact either paid tribute to a pastoral tribe or were maintained as segments of a strong tribe. Village contacts with camel nomads were limited to sporadic raids, and formalized tributary relationships were mainly with sheep pastoralists.

In short, the equilibrium established between the two modes of production is a function of the manner in which power enters the system from the outside. In Tell Toqaan mutuality is not generated by the complementary nature of the two modes of production. The peasant is virtually self-sufficient and can provide for his own animal requirements. Nomadic demands for the products of agriculture can be supplied better through tribute and urban trade. Although at the time of Sweet's study the peasant-nomad pattern of land-use and exchange was highly mutual; this is a transitory state and can be expected to change to the further detriment of the nomad as the present government extends its control. The government views tribal power as a threat and normally takes steps to ensure the extension of a tax-paying body of peasantry in areas it can control. However, if it lacks sufficient strength to do this, it will treat with tribal leaders for a minimal condition of security.

The beneficiary of village-nomad relationship is largely determined by the nature of their articulation with the government, and the policies of the government. Where the government is forced to depend upon tribal force for the maintenance of security, the peasant sector of the area involved will suffer, and even the remaining tribal villages will be likely to become tributary to more powerful groups. Unlike inter-tribal warfare, raids against non-tribal village populations for territory are more sanguinary. As the pastoralists "represent" the government in such cases, there is little appeal for protection except to rival tribal groups. The existence of this option would seemingly encourage less stable and more predatory peasant-nomad relations. The upshot is that the limits of effective agriculture recede to the outer periphery of governmental control.

SOUTHEASTERN TURKEY: YORUK MOUNTAIN PASTORAL NOMADS

A final example, analogous to Barth's description of Swat, is that of the joint exploitation of the landscape in southeastern Turkey by peasant and nomadic communities. The following is from an area studied by me.

The area included in and lying between the winter and summer pastures of the Saçikara Yörük, and related tribes, represents a succession of ecological zones, each related to altitude as one proceeds upward from the inland Amik Plains. This zonal diversity is expressed in a series of village types. These range, roughly, from highly mechanized commercial wheat, cotton and rice growing villages in the lowlands which singularly or in aggregate are commonly dominated by large landlords, through foothill and middle slope communities which practice run-off irrigation and dry field grain agriculture and horticulture. At the highest altitudes, both in Maras and in Kayseri Provinces, villages at the upper limits of agriculture exploit a grain and mixed crop subsistence economy with limited irrigation, strongly supplemented by sedentary cattle and small animal pastoralism. Ethnic diversity is notable, but except when taken in the broadest sense does not correspond to differences in the local ecology. The lowlands are predominantly settled by Barakli Türkmen and Sunni Kurds who were forced to sedentarize in the 19th century. Villages through the middle slopes are again often Türkmen Avsar, Alevi and Sunni Kurds, Circassian and "Macar" (recent Turkish immigrants from Eastern Europe). No ethnically defined population has a monopoly of any mode of production except for the Yörük who are nomadic pastoralists.

Virtually all access to grazing is negotiated with non-Yörük, as there are only two Yörük villages, both of which are in the area of winter pasture and are open to grazing by members of the local lineages only. There is a certain amount of direct peasant-nomad exchange of foodstuffs, and nomads often purchase inexpensive manufactured products from village peddlers while in the higher summer pastures. More commonly, Yörük economic transactions take place in the market places along their migratory route, often with settled Yörük shopkeepers who extend credit.

The Yörük, quite like the mountain nomads discussed by Barth, have a migratory schedule that takes the herds through villages at times complementary to the agricultural cycle. Land for winter pasture (kislak) is rented

for cash payment from village landlords in the lowland plain, and the animals are put on fallow grain, cotton or rice following harvest in September and October. The migration north to upland pastures (*yayla*) starts concurrent with the impetus warm weather gives to nearly dormant winter wheat, and before the results of spring planting become as temptation to the sheep.

Yörük sheep, if unshorn, are driven early April up the route to summer pastures; those which have been shorn follow a few weeks later. In moving upward, the animals graze along the roadway, utilizing grass that is not used by the villagers, including fallow fields.

The summer pastures are owned by Avsar, Kurdish and Circassian villages, usually as village commons (*mer'a*). This land is let for cash payment at public auction supervised by governmental officials, although in practice direct, illicit, dealings arranged between village headmen (*muhtar*) and Yörük are the rule.

In fall, after harvest is nearly completed in the upland villages the longer, more leisurely migration to winter quarters in the Amik Plains begins. During this period the flocks graze on fresh stubble and fallow, when the chance of damage to crops is virtually nonexistent until the actual winter quarters are reached again in October.

It is clear that both the potential for exchange is great and that a high degree of mutuality in land use is evidenced during parts of the migratory schedule. Villages at either end of the migratory route cannot make full use of available grazing due to the necessity to maintain sedentary flocks through all seasons on the same grasslands, thus limiting herd size by the amount of forage available at the worst season. Furthermore, this pasture is rented annually to the nomadic herders for cash payment, which represents an income either for individuals or for village treasuries that would not otherwise accrue. The herds move in a schedule that corresponds with the harvest and planting cycles of the villages so that damage to crops is minimized. If there is damage, it is usually paid for.

This high degree of mutuality is not the consequence of strictly economic forces at work. The Yörük entered the area at the turn of the century and migration into the region continued through World War II. This was a result of pressure on traditional Yörük grazing lands along the southern Anatolian coast. Prior to the arrival of the Yörük, the forced sedentarization of Kurdish and Türkmen tribes starting in 1865, had been largely accomplished, a project which arose from the government's desire to bring politically threatening tribes under control. As in Iraq and elsewhere, the leaders of these tribes were given title to large tracts of formerly tribal land, and many of their descendents are found among the largest landlords of the region today. The Yörük, when they came into the region, filled an economic niche of pastoral nomadism which had been vacated for strictly political reasons. The grazing land still remained, as did open routes of access between summer and winter pasture.

The present high level of reciprocity in exchange is largely a matter of relative power. The Yörük were permitted to enter the region and to remain nomadic as they were never the threat to the state that the more powerful Türkmen and Kurdish tribes had been. The Yörük are in many ways representative of the adaptation of a politically weaker entity to the demands of a stronger one.

The Yörük migratory schedule is adapted to the agricultural cycles of the various villages, not because it is the optimum for grazing, or because it coincides with other productive requirements of the Yörük. It is a political adjustment.

The pasture fee is a similar matter, and represents the strength of local law enforcement agencies, together with village interest in making maximum use of lands to which they hold title. No household or group of tents can acquire access to grazing by force even though they might well be able to overpower an individual village or owner should violence occur.

Prior to 1949 grazing was, by all accounts, free in most areas, with payment, if any, consisting of inconsequential gifts of cheese or butter. Now grazing fees exacted with government assistance are a major form of capital outlay for the nomads, and the cash requirements of grazing payments have led to elaborate on-going credit transactions within the tribes. It has also raised the minimun herd size needed to support a family unit from ca. 50 in the previous generation to over 100 animals at the present time (average 268 sheep). This has pressured many families to settle. It is also likely that inflation of pasture fees will continue, and that the total nomadic herd production might well be impaired, and that fewer animals will be maintained than can be supported by the resources available.

Yörük animals would be often better served by staying longer in the lowlands than is presently possible due to the danger of crop damage. Grazing along the route to summer pastures is often poor, although it would not be if village agriculture were not so extensive. If government control was not as firm as it is now, it would be safe to say that much marginal agricultural land would revert to grazing as the risk of animal damage would make it unprofitable. Furthermore, pastures now rented would almost certainly be claimed by force.

Formerly, Yörük tribes if not clearly dominant, were strong enough and mobile enough to avoid paying grazing fees and fines for crop damage. At that time the amount of land under cultivation in the area of both summer and winter pastures was less, by local accounts, and that land which was cultivated was restricted to that of the best quality. Part of the increase in agriculture is due to technological advances and the reclaiming of swamp lands throughout the area. Another reason for pressure on grazing in the winter quarters is the increase in village population concomitant to the clearing of the land, and a rising birth rate due to the eradication of malaria within the last 20 years. But it is nevertheless true that if government control were not as effective as it is, the Yörük migratory schedule would be different in an attempt to make optimum use of grazing in each of the altitudinal zones through which they pass.

Optimal grazing times do not always coincide with harvest and fallow field cycles.

CONCLUSION

The sketches presented of different pastoral nomadic adjustments to sedentary village populations in shared geographic areas suggest that the degree of land-use mutuality, and the extent to which exchange is phrased in equivalent value depends on a balance of power. It is also the case that sources of power from outside the immediate system are important in determining the local equilibrium which often results in the political dominance of one or the other of ethnically specialized modes of production.

This is by way of saying that nomadic pastoralism is often best intelligible as a political response to other communities and the state. The migratory cycle, residental pattern and even aspects of internal organization often become clearer when approached from this perspective.

A more general albeit negative conclusion is that it is incorrect to equate stable patterns of mutuality and close equivalent exchange with the non-competitive nature of cultural niches using a shared environment. The type of mutuality achieved locally does not seem to have much to do with the potential for exchange offered by different modes of production.

Although my paper has discussed the apparent effects of external sources of power on local patterns of symbiosis, it has not sketched the local channels through which it flows, and other local organizational forms affecting the peasant-nomad structure. For example, variations in tribal structure might be a function of how different societies relate to the outside; however, many variations can also be correlated with the requirements of specific problems of herding and the economy. This organization itself affects the manner in which a community articulates with the external world thereby determining the sorts of culture brokerage which develop, and the individuals, be they chiefs, agas, mayors, saints or others,

who serve in this role to relate the local group to the outside.

The formal demands of a specific political and social structure not only shape the response of that society to new stimulae, but may also determine the limits of its territorial expansion and ability to maintain monopolies of production, or to adopt new ones. There are numerous examples of such non-economic specification of niche borders in the Near East. The Gypsies reserve a wide variety of tasks for themselves by virtue of their low caste status and the cultural definitions of the services in which they specialize. In areas of great ethnic heterogeneity involving nomadic pastoralists, even relatively minor distinctions of ritual, religiosity, language, and social usage are seized upon to channel economic cooperation, fix settlement patterns and circumscribe marriage systems. Ethnicity thus narrowly defines the limits of community. The ecological consequences of this behavior are clear: the resources are divided among social groupings which cultural values as well as economic processes tend to reinforce.

The total effects of these, however, extend beyond their purely regulatory function. Quite often the hostilities generated by group-defining cultural usages threaten the exchange networks they help to condition. Religion and ritual practices are good examples. On one level they may restrict or portion off certain modes of production, separating the nomadic pastoralists from the sedentary population by a cultural barrier. On another level, they simultaneously increase the chances of overt conflict which could disrupt the entire system.

Unlike those of animal populations, the boundaries of niches defined by cultural behavior are extremely elastic. Even the most specialized population can in whole or part change its adaptation rapidly in response to new conditions or in order to take over a more profitable mode of production. No monopoly on the production of either animal or agricultural goods is completely secure against outside encroachment. In parts of Southeastern Turkey, formerly nomadic populations have within one generation come to dominate certain types of commercial enterprises, as well as to compete successfully with long-established farmers in mechanized market-directed agriculture.

Numerous other factors condition on-going adjustment to other communities by any pastoral nomadic society. One is, perhaps, the length and variability of the migratory route. A nomadic mountain tribe normally has relations with a series of villages along its route. The existence of alternative routes, as well as variations in local production and defense, affects potential for symbiosis or conflict. One would suspect that relations with infrequently encountered villages would tend to be more predatory. Among the Saçikara Yörük more conflict arises between nomads and villagers closer to upper pastures where both the government's control is somewhat less and there is more direct competition for pastures between nomads and villagers. Villagers often try to make use of land which they own or have rented out to the nomadic herders.

All this makes it difficult to view mutualism as arising from the exploitation of non-competitive niches. It is often a result of how the groups in question relate to the central government, or otherwise establish a balance of power.

Furthermore, where symbiotic relations develop between ethnic groups, the structure is often so ridden with hostility, that should one community attain military dominance it might well use force to reduce mutualism,

even to the detriment of its own standard of living. The peasant-nomad relationships where each mode of production is ethnically defined, is normally so highly sensitive to shifts of power within it, that the threat of outside intervention encourages each group to maximize its short-run benefit. This is particularly exacerbated in frontier regions, the characteristic home of most mountain nomadism, where government control is the least consistent. It may also select for what Salzman terms "multi-resource nomadism," the combining of pastoralism with other modes of production within one tribal structure.[2]

The existence of most niches in the rural scene of the Near East is as much a creation by forces exterior to the immediate areas, as the niches themselves are inherent in the landscape, or even in the techniques of the people themselves. Whether specific economies are in competition or cooperation in using a shared area, depends as much upon how they relate to the outside world, as upon how much they would be able to supplement each other's diet.

2. The combining of sedentary agriculture and nomadic pastoralism within a common tribal political structure is quite common in the Near East. In such cases, not only can the requisite labor be easily assigned to the portion of the economy which needs it, but also, the two modes of production can present a common political front to the outside.

In Islahiye, southeastern Turkey, the nomadic lineages most likely to continue profitable animal husbandry are those which have lineage members in control of the two villages of settled Yoruk. The nomadic households are registered as village dwellers, and have free use of village commons (mer'a).

19. THEORY AND STRATEGY IN THE STUDY OF CULTURE ADAPTABILITY

Reprinted from American Anthropologist, *67 (1965): 402-07. Walter Goldschmidt is Professor of Anthropology, University of California, Los Angeles. In addition to the research described in the accompanying paper, Goldschmidt has studied California Indian groups and modern American communities. He is author of* Man's Way *and* Comparative Functionalism, *both theoretical treatises, and of a number of other works, including his most recent book,* Sebei Law.

■ This selection was originally published as the prefatory paper in a symposium of the members of the Culture and Ecology in East Africa Project, directed by Walter Goldschmidt. I am reprinting here only the papers by Goldschmidt and Edgerton (Selections 19 and 24; the other papers in the symposium, which deal with different tribes, should be consulted in their original form.

Goldschmidt's paper is important for several reasons. First, it presents a model of pastoralism, outlining its basic features as a unique adaptation. A model is a taxonomy, embodying a set of standards for comparing individual phenomena or occurrences within the class it represents. No model purports to be an exact replica of each event in the class. For example, it is possible to construct a model of the human circulatory system, but this representation is never meant to suggest that every person's circulation system will be identical with the model's. One of the purposes served by such a model is that it helps us determine the extent to which each event approximates the ideal, the nature of deviations from the ideal, and the conditions under which these happen. This is especially important in the study of cultural adaptation. Because cultures are constantly changing, none can ever conform exactly to a model. Furthermore, and as we have already seen, the subtlest differences in habitat (as well as other factors) can have profound consequences for people's social organization.

Another important purpose served by Goldschmidt's paper is in its description of the method of comparative field research. Although such a study might be undertaken by a single investigator, it is difficult for one person to achieve the same breadth and intensity of inquiry that may characterize research that is conducted by a team.

The reader who wants a further introduction to East African pastoralism should consult, in addition to *The Nuer*, by E. E. Evans-Pritchard (New York: Oxford University Press, 1951), *A Pastoral Democracy: A Study of Pastoralism and Politics among the Northern Somali of the Horn of Africa* (New York: Oxford University Press, 1961) and *Marriage and the Family in Northern Somaliland* (Kampala, Uganda: East African Institute of Social Research, 1962), by I. M. Lewis. A good comparison with the Nuer and the Somali can be gotten from *Savannah Nomads*, by Derrick J. Stenning (New York: Oxford University Press, 1959), a study of the Fulani of Nigeria. *Government in Zazzau*, 1800-1950, by M. G. Smith (New York: Oxford University Press, 1960), contains good descriptions of Fulani state organization. ■

THEORETICAL BASIS

THE THEORETICAL ORIENTATION of the Culture and Ecology Project stems from some of the considerations set forth in "Man's Way," which endeavors to join functional social anthropology with evolutionary theory. The following perhaps sets forth this thesis best:

This evolutionary theory is also a functional theory in the sense that it involves the basic functional thesis that (1) institutions are mechanisms of social interaction which serve the continued life of the society, and (2) all parts of the social system must form an integrated whole so that changes in one part require adjustments in others. In addition, the functional theory stresses the priority of some aspects of society over others. To translate a theme from George Orwell's *Animal Farm*, all social institutions are basic, but some are more basic than others. That is to say, some aspects of the situation have immediate, direct, and consistent influences on the total structure of society, whereas others are peripheral. We do not deny that art and economy are related, nor even that art might change the economy of a society; however, it is more likely and more frequent that the economy changes the art. Furthermore, certain areas of life activity lie closer to such external factors as environment or such internal ones as technical change and are therefore more vulnerable to their pressures.

In keeping with a certain underlying spirit of our research, each of us is here presenting material according to his own particular intellectual predilections and theoretical worries within the framework of the whole program. In this way it will be possible to appreciate the wide complexities that beset us in the task we have undertaken.

Our investigation is a study in cultural adaptation, in ecological analysis, in the character of economic influence on culture and behavior or in social micro-evolution— depending upon which of the currently fashionable terminologies one prefers. It is—or endeavors to be—all of these for the simple reason that they are different perspectives on the same thing. Let us use the framework of ecological adaptation.

If we take a broad look at sub-Saharan Africa—particularly the eastern or southern sectors—we find two basic economic life-modes (disregarding the remnant hunting peoples and the ancillary use of game). These are hoe farming and cattle pastoralism. One or the other may be followed exclusively but most peoples have both in some combination, here favoring farming and there favoring pastoralism. When we take a closer look at the economics of the area, we are impressed by the degree to which there was changing and shifting about; a pattern of continuing economic adjustment. Here the Turkana separate from the Jie to become nearly pure pastoralists; at Njemps and Arusha the Masai settle down to become farmers. The Pokot and the Kamba each have regions chiefly engaged in pastoralism, others engaged in farming, while the Sukuma and Tumbuka are acquiring cattle at the time of European contact. All of this can be seen as ecologic adjustment, a seeking out of a balance in the use of resources that is as efficient as possible in terms of existing technology.

But functional theory assumes that the institutions of a society are integrated wholes, that changes in one sector require adjustments in other sectors of the social system. This was the set of ideas which we are endeavoring to test. Let us put it this way: we treat environment as the independent variable; then, assuming a repertoire of techniques available, the pattern of economic exploitation becomes the intermediate variable, while the institutions of society, cultural attitudes and behavior patterns, become the dependent variables.

THE PASTORAL MODEL

Pastoralism is a very good subject for our investigation; being relatively confined into a narrowly defined environment and ecology, it has a more specific set of sociological requirements and a closer unity of institutional forms than most economic life-modes. The same cannot be said of hoe farming, which can be more variant and allows much more latitude in institutional behavior.

It would be possible to set forth certain central tendencies for particular kinds of hoe-farming societies, but these would be less sharply defined and would require far too extended a discussion for the limitations of this presentation. We may, for present purposes, simply assume that farming either (a) favors opposite forms or (b) allows for greater deviation from the elements suggested in this model of pastoralism. If we have cast our thinking in terms of the effect of pastoralism, this is only for efficiency of exposition; our thesis does not imply a direction of the actual historic shift, which clearly is variant.

Let me set forth some of the major elements in our model for pastoral life. This must be a logical model, a construct of institutional and behavioral relationships in terms of the requisites of the system. Pastoralism is a cultural adjustment to semi-arid open country or grassland in which the native vegetation will support large ruminants but in which hoe agriculture without advanced technologies cannot satisfactorily be sustained. Pastoralism requires, of course, the existence of domestic stock and adequate knowledge for their care and represents a higher use (in the economists' sense) of resources than the hunting and gathering economies which generally preceded it in areas where pure pastoralism is currently pursued. The technology of pastoralism requires that the life practices of the people be adjusted to the requisites of the animals; that is, movement to pasture, water and salt, as required, and protection from predators.

Some immediate consequences of pastoralism are: the people must remain mobile, they cannot invest heavily in personal goods, in houses or in land; both land, as such, and boundaries are unimportant, while permanent and essential resources—notably water—must be protected and shared.

Our model suggests that, in the absence of clear boundaries, spatial groups are relatively unimportant and another idiom must be found to unify the population. This must be flexible—able to bring together a large community for mutual defense, while allowing small units to operate independently when range conditions demand. Two mechanisms exist in Africa: segmentary lineages or Obok, and age-grades. The former, in its finest form, such as that of the Somali, can unify a large nation while preserving the independence of action of the individual household. The latter creates special institutional means for unifying a wide region for military action.

Stock must be cared for by the men; it can be no cultural accident that this is universally true of large-stock pastoralists. While the onerous work of hoe farming may be done by a pregnant woman, the handling of stock requires the masculine freedom from childbearing, and probably also the masculine kind of musculature. The male control of animals creates a predilection for patri-orientation—in residence, filiation and heritage. It also tends to reduce the social role of women, though not their value as females.

Pastoralists must early learn to make independent decisions and to act on them. Most herders (in Africa, at least) spend part of their time alone or in small groups; they must assess the grass available, the water problems, the dangers of overcrowding or overgrazing in handling of herds. At the same time, they must be able to operate within a larger context and even to accept the authority of others either when groups congregate or when military action is called for (suggestive of Gearing's "structural poses" though better integrated than he suggests). Youth is generally given responsibility for herds while still serving under an authoritarian father, thus combining both the independence of action and the acceptance of authority.

While both pastoral and farming people utilize kinship to form corporate groups, these tend to be differently constructed. Pastoral societies have a patrilineal basis, whereas hoe farmers can be more flexible, with perhaps some preference for a matri-bias. But the articulation of the system is more important than its sexual alignment: it is segmentary, without spatial ties but articulated into ever wider groups, as against the separation of independent units, with spatial ties, among hoe farmers. Stock requirements suggest the need for a multimale basic unit (household) and the collaboration of father and adult sons, which is non-advantageous to farmers.

Cattle are a volatile form of wealth. This makes for high status mobility; reinforces independence of action; reduces the importance of inherited offices in favor of leadership based on achievement, and favors direct legal action through retaliation and feuds over official courts.

Militarism, particularly agressive militarism, characterizes pastoral life. Several factors combine to cause this. The fact that livestock are goods that may easily be stolen provides constant temptation to raid and retaliation; the absence of boundaries and natural protection makes organization for defense requisite, while other factors of pastoral life tend to create and reward the type of personality given to overt hostile behavior.

The personality attributes of the ideal pastoralist may be summarized as follows: a high degree of independence of action; a willingness to take chances; a readiness to act, and a capacity for action; self-contain-ment and control, especially in the face of danger; bravery, fortitude, and the ability to withstand pain and hardship; arrogance, sexuality, and a realistic appraisal of the world.

The masculine orientation of the social system, together with aggressive independence, supports a pattern of sexuality in males which finds many recurrent expressions among pastoralists: the high incidence of polygyny, the overt sexuality of men, premarital sexual freedom, and jealous protection of wives. This emphasis on sexuality of males makes the acquisition of women a matter of prime importance, so that though women have low social status, they have a high social value. This is expressed in the institution of bride-price, polygyny, anxiety over adultery in the wives, and anxiety among males regarding their own sexuality, and it leads to aggressive, rather than warm, relations between the sexes.

The ready acting-out of hostility reduces the recourse to deviousness in interpersonal action. Thus we would not expect to find secret societies and would expect less sorcery and witchcraft accusation. On the other hand, the volatile and quixotic character of herd-building and depletion reinforce fatalism, with the consequent use of amulets, divination, etc. Ritual life will tend toward greater emphasis upon rites of passage, which focus on the individual and his status, rather than on rites of intensification, which reinforce group solidarity and, in so doing, tend to submerge the individual within the community.

RESEARCH STRATEGY

The basic strategy of our research design is simple enough: examine N cases where a single "tribe" is divided into regions in which pastoralism predominates in one, farming in the other; select a community within each region for detailed study, determining what features differ and whether the differences show a constant trend in accordance with our theoretical model.

Actually, we examined four tribes: the Sebei and Pokot, both Southern Nilotes

(Kalenjin), and the Kamba of Kenya and Hehe of Tanganyika, both Bantu speaking. Thus our research has a basic structure that fits into the following tabular form.

		Farmers	Pastoralists
Kalenjin	Sebei		
	Pokot		
Bantu	Kamba		
	Hehe		

The fact that the tribes divide into two language groups, with the reasonable presumption of common long-term historic background, not only gives us the opportunity to test differences in two separate basic "traditions," but also to examine the relative "force" of tradition and ecology.

A few tactical details should also be set forth. We included in our team a geographer (Porter), for inasmuch as our design treats environment as an independent variable, we wanted to know to what degree farming and pastoralism fit—as alternative life-modes— the regions in which they are in fact found. He obtained data for us on such items as temperature, precipitation, sunshine, topography, soils, soil moisture absorption, land use, crop yields, livestock numbers, size of landholdings and of herds. In his paper he offers some evidence of the complexity of environmental differentiation and suggests a means of reducing this to the most important single dimension from our sociological point of view.

The basic work on each of the four tribes was done by an ethnographer (Conant, Oliver, Winans, and Goldschmidt) who set up residence in each of the two communities of our respective tribes. In addition to more standard ethnographic information obtained through participant observation and from informants, we took schedules to obtain details on residence, demography, social status, economic levels, education, and degree of acculturation. Finally, the sixth member of the research team (Edgerton) took a series of 85 questions, Rorschach protocols, a picture values test and a set of photograph-induced responses from a sample of each community, minimally 30 adult males and 30 adult females.

SPECIAL PROBLEMS

The real world is an imperfect laboratory; there are large and cumbersome variables which intrude themselves upon the best laid field research plans. One must anticipate these insofar as possible and cope with them in such a manner as one's ingenuity allows.

There is the fact that we are not dealing with *pure* farming versus *pure* pastoralism, but varying degrees of each. In fact, the pastoral Sebei give as much importance to farming as the farming Pokot. We must, therefore, analyze our data in terms of range and degree. This we intend to do, but have barely initiated thus far.

Even more difficult is the fact of acculturation. We are attempting to analyze "aboriginal" adjustments, not modern ones. Yet we had no time machine, and our present investigations—especially of attitudes and on-going-behavior—had to be as of 1961-62. This situation is exacerbated by the fact that acculturation varies with our basic variable, for farmers are universally more drawn into modern life than are pastoralists. But we are not without our tools. We have a measure of individual acculturation and a measure of the degree of community acculturation and we shall examine each in terms of its relation to the variables in such a way as to evaluate the acculturation influences.

A closely related problem is the temporal aspect of ecological adjustment, the dynamics of the historical processes under which adaptation operates. A people's history takes place within a broader social context of other peoples; a most significant element in the environment of a society is the community of societies of which it is a part. This aspect of the "environment" is indeed influential in determining the institutional patterns of a society, as Winans' contribution to this symposium will demonstrate through an analysis of the geopolitics of the South Central Highlands of Tanganyika.

Spatial relations are also a factor. Each tribe is a unit, an interacting community in more or less close intercommunication; it is not a mere mosaic of independent villages. This fact means that our internal comparisons are not between separate and discrete social entities but between interdependent sectors of a larger whole. We shall see this clearly in the analysis that Conant makes of the Pokot *Korok,* where he shows the essential unity of the social system and the interdependence of its elements, but at the same time indicates that there are differences in emphasis and orientation.

BROADER IMPLICATIONS

Our investigation was ambitious in the extreme; it represents a rare effort to make a coordinated field investigation involving a comparison of whole cultures directed at a central problem in social theory. We endeavor to examine not only the patterns of ecological adjustments in four tribes and to find uniformities in these adjustments, but we are also concerned with broader theory, as indeed the very character of our study forces us to be. We must, for instance, concern ourselves not only with the character of culture in relation to environment, but with the whole phenomenon of cultural malleability. This is a problem which anthropologists have tended to neglect—except under the special conditions created by acculturation. Oliver makes a specific contribution to this in his discussion of the character and limitations of cultural commitment among the Kamba.

Another enduring problem in the theory of culture is the relation between institutional patterns and attitudes. Edgerton shows that attitude patterns tend to be quite consistent within communities—even as between the sexes—but do differ between communities of the same tribe under differing circumstances. If as students of society we treat psychological attitudes as intervening variables, perhaps it is possible to show that these are, in fact, the mediators of institutional adjustment.

20. ECOLOGY AND CULTURAL CONTINUITY AS CONTRIBUTING FACTORS IN THE SOCIAL ORGANIZATION OF THE PLAINS INDIANS

SYMMES C. OLIVER

Reprinted from University of California Publications in American Archaeology and Ethnology, *48(1) (1962): 13-18, 46-49, 52-68. Symmes Chadwick Oliver is Associate Professor of Anthropology, University of Texas. His primary research interests are in the nature of culture, cultural ecology, and sociocultural change. He has recently been a participant in the Culture and Ecology in East Africa Project. In addition to various works of fiction, he is the author of* The Kamba of Kenya.

■ This selection deals with the bison hunters of the North American Plains. Not only did these people use their herds of domesticated animals (horses) as instruments for hunting other animals, thereby developing an adaptation that differed considerably from most other pastoralist strategies, they also illustrate a very important concept: a group's history or antecedent culture, like the energy systems it has harnessed, sets limits and provides potentials for people's responses to their habitat. A modern example of this phenomenon is the variability in the industrial level of adaptation in the United States, England, France, Germany, Rumania, the Soviet Union, and China. Cutting across the similarities of these countries, each places its unique stamp on a single adaptive strategy; each develops slightly different institutions, establishes its own criteria for awarding livelihoods, generates its own motivational system, and evolves its own system of social control. Each of these cultures represents a special case of the strategy of adaptation in which it participates, varying in terms of its unique historical background.

Following the practice of several students of the North American Plains Indians, I am classifying these societies with other pastoralists, since their adaptation is based on the use of domesticated animals—in this case, horses used to hunt bison and conduct warfare. The most important pressure upon these Indians was caused by the wide dispersal of the bison herds during the winter and their dense con-gregation during the summer. Plains Indian groups split up and reunited in parallel fashion.

However, not all the societies that became known as Indians of the Plains had the same cultural background. Some had been nomadic foragers before the introduction of the horse; others had been sedentary horticulturists. Oliver here classifies the Indians of the Plains according to their cultural origins and shows that their historical antecedents profoundly affected their relationships to their habitat.

One of the principal tasks Oliver sets for himself in the major study from which the following excerpts are taken is to determine which elements in Plains pastoralist cultures were due to the demands of their particular system of food production and which were due to cultural-historical influences. To accomplish this he focuses on seven major variables in Plains Indian culture: (1) summer tribal congregations and winter dispersal in bands; (2) police organizations for the regulation of the summer hunt; (3) age-grade societies; (4) status and prestige acquired through warfare and hunting; (5) leadership; (6) councils; and (7) clans. He finds that the first four variables were primarily due to the introduction of the horse; the last three, as well as the presence of police the year round, are ascribable to antecedent cultural heritages. In addition, he finds that groups that had been hunters and gatherers before the introduction of the horse resembled each other more after the introduction of the horse than they resembled those who had been horticulturists; the different horticulturist groups resembled each other in the new adaptation more than they resembled the former foragers. But cutting across these differences were common features that stemmed from the new technology.

A good general introduction to this adaptation is *Indians of the Plains,* by Robert H. Lowie (New York: McGraw-Hill, 1954). Another, which includes a concise summary of Indians throughout the continent, is *Indians of North America,* by Harold E. Driver (Chicago: University of Chicago Press, 1961). *Changing Military Patterns of the Great Plains,* by Frank R. Secoy (Monograph 21, American Ethnological Society), is probably the best study of Plains Indian military organization; it is, to a large extent, a study of adaptation.

Classification of the Indians of the Plains as pastoralists is based on the writings of many students of this area, the most recent of which is "An Inquiry into the Nature of Plains Indian Cultural Development," by H. Clyde Wilson *(American Anthropologist,* 65 [1963]: 355-69). This paper also includes the relevant bibliography for this classification. For a description of bison hunting on the North American Plains about 8,500 years ago (that is, before the introduction of the horse) see "A Paleo-Indian Bison Kill," by Joe Den Wheat *(Scientific American,* 216[1] [January, 1967]: 44-52). Wheat's remarkable archeological excavation not only presents useful hypotheses about the organization of labor during a stampede and the ways in which the animals' meat was cut up after the kill, the author even surmises about the direction of the wind during the stampede.

There have been many studies of Plains Indian pastoralist cultures, of which the following can serve as good introductions: *The Gros Ventres of Montana,* by Regina Flannery; *Mandan Social and Ceremonial Organization,* by Alfred W. Bowers (Chicago: University of Chicago Press, 1950); *The Crow Indians,* by Robert H. Lowie (New York: Holt, Rinehart and Winston, 1935); *The Cheyennes,* by E. Adamson Hoebel (New York: Holt, Rinehart and Winston, 1960); "Personality Structure in the Plains," by Thomas Gladwin *(Anthropological Quarterly,* 30 [1957]: 111-24). A very good account of how one of these groups has fared under its European conquerors and the reservation system is *The Changing Culture of an Indian Tribe,* by Margaret Mead (New York: Columbia University Press, 1932); another, dealing with the Mandan-Hidatsa, is "Primary Group Experience and the Process of Acculturation," by Edward M. Bruner *(American Anthropologist,* 58 [1956]: 605-623).

The Indians of the Plains were not the only North American pastoralists. *The Navaho,* by Clyde Kluckhohn and Dorothea Leighton (rev. ed. [by Richard Kluckhohn and Lucy Wales]; Garden City, N.Y.: Doubleday, 1962), provides an excellent introduction to these famous sheep herders of the American Southwest. ∎

ECOLOGY AND CULTURAL CONTINUITY ON THE PLAINS

THE THEORETICAL IDEAS with which we are operating make it mandatory to have a distinction between the horticultural tribes and the hunting tribes. Therefore, going back in part to Wissler, we may define a "True" Plains tribe as one that carried on no horticulture, relied on the buffalo as its principal means of subsistence, and possessed the horse. Though it is certain that there were peoples on the Plains before the introduction of the horse, the period of Plains culture to which virtually all ethnological literature applies did include the horse; its inclusion is therefore necessary to a meaningful definition. All other contiguous or near-by tribes will be designated as "peripheral" tribes. It should be understood, of course, that this label has reference only to the purposes of this study; no implication is intended that the peripheral tribes were in any way less important that the True Plains tribes. It is only contended that the True Plains tribes form a distinct group with some unique characteristics.

Perhaps the central fact about the True Plains tribes is that most of them are relatively recent immigrants into the Plains. This is obvious enough for such tribes as the Comanche and the Cheyenne, and it can be demonstrated for most other True Plains tribes as well. It is a fact that some tribes were on the Plains a great deal longer than other tribes, and this is an important point to remember, but the fact remains that most of the tribes were newcomers. It can further be demonstrated that some of these tribes were hunters and gatherers before moving into the

Plains, whereas others were horticulturists. If culture does indeed come from culture, and if new sociocultural forms are built upon the base of the old, it is reasonable to expect that some of these differences in social structure would have persisted on the Plains.

What really seems to have happened on the Plains was that tribes of different cultural backgrounds moved into a similar or shared ecological situation. This seems to be a reasonable interpretation of the historic Plains situation. The fact that there were Folsom or other Early Man horizons on the Plains, and that they had a considerable time depth, does not alter the basic facts for the historic Plains tribes who were relative newcomers to the region. It may be granted that there were *resemblances* between the pre-horse Plains hunters and the later Plains tribes, or between the pre-horse and post-horse cultures of the same tribe. Both, after all, were hunting the same animal. But this is certainly not to say that these cultures were the *same*. The introduction of the horse created a different ecological situation which required new sociocultural arrangements.

No one questions the demonstrated facts of cultural diffusion on the Plains. The Plains tribes obviously borrowed heavily from one another. But diffusion cannot explain everything. And when one asks *what* diffused and *why,* it is difficult to avoid taking ecology into account.

The crucial investigation into the role of the horse in Plains culture have been very important, but they do not tell the whole story. To some extent, they shift the emphasis from the buffalo to the horse, which is misleading. Ecological studies must take into account the interrelationships between man and his culture and the environment in which he lives. The horse is one factor in the ecological equation, but it is not the only one. Horses have certain requirements which are in some ways similar to those of the buffalo. But there is a key distinction that perhaps has not been properly appreciated. For the most part, the horses that counted in the ecological situation on the Plains were not wild herds of mustangs but were the horses under the control of the Indians. Within limits, such as the condition of the grass and the need for shelter at certain times of the year, the horses adapted to the requirements of the Indians rather than the other way around.

Fundamentally, the horse was a means to an end. The horse was used to exploit the buffalo efficiently. And the buffalo was emphatically not under the control of the Indians. The Indians had to adjust themselves to the habits of the bison, or do without. The tie between the Plains Indians and the buffalo was an unusually close one. Their reliance on this animal for food and skins and sinews is too well known to require comment. The simple fact is that the Plains cultures could not have survived without the buffalo. In this situation, it is imperative that we examine the habits of the buffalo. Surely, any understanding of the Plains requires something more than the usual vague statement that Plains life was conditioned by the "movements" of the bison. What *was* the annual bison cycle?

In view of the recognized importance of the buffalo to Plains life, it is rather curious that anthropologists have not concerned themselves more with the habits of these animals. A great deal of folklore has insinuated itself into anthropological thinking about the buffalo, and in particular about the supposed vast annual migrations of the buffalo.

The popular notion that there was one organized herd of buffalo (*Bison bison*) on the Plains, and that millions of these animals charged south every winter into Texas and north every summer into Canada, has very little foundation in fact. Furthermore, the idea that the movements of the buffalo were precisely regular, following definite trails every year, is open to serious question. If this were true, it would mean two things. All the Indians would have to do would be to intercept the migrating herds as they galloped through their territories, on their way to Canada or Texas. Again, they would always know exactly where to find the animals; they could simply camp on the trail. As Frank

Gilbert Roe has noted, this was not the case. The Indians are described as "following the cows around" even before the coming of the horse. They did not "intercept" the migrating herds in any real sense. And if one thing is clear from the literature, it is that the Indians did not know exactly where the herds would be; they had to send out scouts to look for them, and the scouts were frequently gone for many days.

Virtually the first serious scientific study of the buffalo, made by J. A. Allen in 1877, clearly states the facts of the situation:

Doubtless the same individuals never moved more than a few hundred miles in a north and south direction, the annual migration being doubtless merely a moderate swaying northward and southward of the whole mass with the changes of the season. We certainly know that buffaloes have been accustomed to remain in winter as far north as their habitat extends. North of the Saskatchewan they are described as merely leaving the most exposed portions of the plains during the deepest snows and severest periods of cold to take shelter in the open woods that border the plains.

A moment's reflection will show that if the same animals only moved a few hundred miles north or south, then these movements could have affected seriously only the two extremes of the buffalo range. More to the point, perhaps, is the fact that for the bulk of the buffalo range the animals were present all year around. This seems to have been generally true. It is for the southern end of the buffalo range that we have the best evidence for significant movements of this type. Allen states: "That there are local migrations of an annual character seems in fact to be well established, especially at the southward, where the buffaloes are reported to have formerly, in great measure, abandoned the plains of Texas in the summer for those further north, revisiting them again in winter."

William T. Hornaday, whose classic study of the buffalo was published in 1887, has suggested that: "The movement north began with the return of mild weather in the early spring. Undoubtedly this northward migration was to escape the heat of their southern winter range."

In this connection, Martin B. Garretson has offered the following summary statement:

The buffalo is classed as a migratory animal. At certain seasons of the year there was a slight general movement north, east, south, and west. Many accounts of these movements are entirely misleading, because greatly exaggerated. There is no reason to believe that the buffalo which spent the summer on the Saskatchewan wintered in Texas. In one portion of the northern country bordering on the mountains there was a decided seasonal migration east and west, the herds tending in the spring away from the mountains while in the autumn they would work back again, no doubt seeking shelter in the rough broken country of the foothills from the cold west winds of winter. The correct explanation of this movement was best given by Dr. William T. Hornaday, who pointed out that the buffalo had settled migratory habits and that at the approach of winter, the whole great system of herds which ranged from the Peace River to Texas and the Indian Territory (Oklahoma), moved south from two to four hundred miles and wintered under more favorable circumstances than each herd would have experienced at the farthest north. This explains why buffalo were found on the range at all times of the year.

Roe takes a more extreme position on the question of regular migrations among the species as a whole. "The one resultant factor that emerges from our inquiry," he states, "is the direct antithesis of any conception of regularity; an imponderable, incalculable, wholly erratic and unreliable caprice."

We need not go this far; Roe overstates the case to prove a point. It is nevertheless true that the famous regular mass migrations of the buffalo are open to serious question. If we are to get at the heart of the matter we must look elsewhere.

Bearing in mind the fact that the buffalo were present in most of the range all year round, I believe that Hornaday has supplied us with the correct key to the situation. It relates not to the problem of migrations but to other features of the annual cycle of the buffalo.

Hornaday writes:

The history of the buffalo's daily life and habits should begin with the "running season." This period occupied the months of August and

September, and was characterized by a degree of excitement and activity throughout the entire herd quite foreign to the ease-loving and even slothful nature which was so noticeable a feature of the bison's character at all other times. The mating season occurred when the herd was on its summer range. . . . During the "running season" . . . the whole nature of the herd was completely changed. Instead of being broken up into countless small groups and dispersed over a vast extent of territory, the herd came together in a dense and confused mass of many thousand individuals, so closely congregated as to actually blacken the face of the landscape. As if by a general and irresistible impulse, every straggler would be drawn to the common center, and for miles on every side of the great herd the country would be found entirely deserted. At the close of the breeding season the herd quickly settles down to its normal condition. The mass gradually resolves itself into the numerous bands or herdlets of from twenty to a hundred individuals, so characteristic of bison on their feeding grounds, and these gradually scatter in search of the best grass until the herd covers many square miles of country.

There are several points here which merit emphasis. Despite questions of detail, it is important to remember that the buffalo only congregated into really large herds in the late summer and autumn. Moreover, at this time the surrounding country was virtually deserted as far as the buffalo were concerned. During the rest of the year, the buffalo were scattered into small groups that were spread out over a considerable expanse of territory. To put the matter simply, this means that the hunting methods that were appropriate for one time of the year were not appropriate for others, and that the dispersal or concentration of the Indians might be expected to follow seasonal patterns. When it is borne in mind that the buffalo sought shelter away from the open plains in the winter months, the picture becomes even clearer.

Garretson notes that Buffalo calves were born from April to June, and that the "running season" lasted from the first of July to the first of October. The buffalo sheds its coat in the spring, and is almost naked for a few weeks in early summer. Finally, as Roe notes, the late summer and autumn months were the ones when the grass was most plentiful and the buffalo coats had grown out

sufficiently to protect the animals to some extent from insect pests.

If the life of the Plains Indians was indeed adapted to the habits of the buffalo, then it is to this cycle that we must look for understanding. The essential fact does not concern vast annual migrations, but rather concerns cyclical patterns of concentration and dispersal.

Of course the buffalo was not the only animal available to the Plains Indians. Both rabbits and the pronghorn antelope lived on the Plains. But it must be understood that the Plains cultures were completely dependent on the buffalo; the other animals could not have supported either the population concentrations or the lifeways of the Plains Indians. As Walter Prescott Webb puts it, "In the Plains area lived one animal that came nearer to dominating the life and shaping the institutions of a human race than any other in all the land, if not in the world—the buffalo." More specifically, he writes: "They depended for their existence on the wild cattle or buffalo, and were often called buffalo Indians. The buffalo furnished them with all the necessities and luxuries of life."

How, then, were the sociocultural systems of the Plains tribes influenced by the total ecological situation? (1) The Indian tribes had to be dispersed in winter and concentrated in the summer. The buffalo were too scattered in the winter months to permit large numbers of people to band together, and the opportunities provided by the dense herds in the summer months were too good to miss, since food was stored at this time for the rest of the year. Moreover, the compact summer herds drew the Indians together for the simple reason that large parts of the buffalo range were without buffalo at this time. (2) The alternating patterns of concentration and dispersal made for a certain fluidity in social organization. A tribe that lives together in a unit requires a different sort of organization from one that is fragmented into wandering bands. Flexibility is required. It may be suggested that clans are less congenial to such a system than some less rigid principle of organization. (3) The communal type of buffalo hunting in the summer months would seem to demand a different kind of organization than the individual hunting of the winter months; we would expect to find more systematic controls in the large group situation. (4) Mobility was necessary for at least three reasons. The sedentary village was at a great disadvantage in military terms; frequent movements were required to hunt the buffalo; and the acquisition of horses by raiding put a premium on rapid mobility. (5) The presence of competing human societies put a premium on military skills. The tribes *had* to develop and reward warriors, since the very existence of the tribe depended on their skills. Finally, (6) the crucial role of the horse emphasized the value of raiding, as a means of getting horses, and tied in with the status system in two vital ways: the successful warrior who could steal horses was a man of high prestige, and the horse was a portable form of wealth particularly important in a nomadic society in which other types of wealth could not readily be transported.

In the problem of cultural continuity we have noted the recency of the historic Plains cultures, as well as the fact that the tribes that moved into the Plains came out of two contrasting backgrounds: some had been hunting and gathering peoples, whereas others had been horticulturists. It would have been remarkable, indeed, if all of these tribes had erased all vestiges of their former lifeways in a scant few hundred years. The problem is to identify instances of cultural persistence in the flux of the dynamic Plains situation.

Clearly, there are certain expectancies here. To put the matter simply, we would expect that horticultural tribes would be in general more highly organized than hunting and gathering tribes, and therefore we would expect to find that the True Plains tribes of horticultural origin would be more highly organized in some respects than True Plains tribes of hunting and gathering origin. No contention is made that *all* horticultural tribes are more highly organized than *all* hunting and gathering tribes; rather, we are asserting only that certain types of social systems are

more appropriate to one category than to another. Although there are exceptions, it is possible to speak of the general characteristics of hunting and gathering societies as opposed to horticultural societies. Goldschmidt has done this in considerable detail.

To be more specific, let us consider three aspects of sociocultural systems that should prove revealing. In the general area of authority and leadership, we would expect to find that the leaders of horticultural groups are more formally selected than the leaders of hunting and gathering groups, and that they have somewhat more authority. This may be expressed as the distinction between the charismatic headman and the chief who holds a well-defined office. In terms of formal social structure, we would expect to find clans frequently present in horticultural groups and rare in nomadic hunting and gathering groups. Finally, we would expect that status would often have hereditary implications in sedentary horticultural societies, though it would rest primarily on personal skills related to subsistence among hunting and gathering peoples. If these ideas have validity, it should be possible to identify these tendencies among the True Plains tribes.

It must be emphasized that we are dealing here with expectancies, not with infallible rules. In terms of the sample with which we are dealing, we would expect that most of the True Plains tribes would be similar in some respects owing to their shared ecological situation. We would also expect that the True Plains tribes that were formerly horticultural would resemble horticultural tribes to some degree, and the True Plains tribes that were formerly hunters and gathers would resemble the hunting and gathering tribes to some degree.

Any set of tables or series of correlations can but dimly reflect the richness and complexity of the changing lifeways on the Plains; they can only provide the tell-tale signs of the results of such changes, and direct our attention toward understanding the processes that produced these end products. The basic rationale for the attempted correlations that follow is a simple one. Whenever the True Plains tribes tended to share a pattern, the pattern has been referred to the shared ecological situation. When there was a break between the True Plains tribes of different origins, an explanation was sought by turning to the peripheral groups. If the True Plains tribes of hunting and gathering origin had the same pattern as peripheral hunting and gathering tribes, cultural continuity was assumed to be operative. Similarly, if the True Plains tribes of farming origin had the same pattern as peripheral farming tribes, cultural continuity was assumed to be operative. No claim is made that these are the only possible explanations for these phenomena. The only claim is that these correlations make sense in terms of the hypotheses with which we are working, and that they should provide valuable clues concerning the processes at work in the Plains situation.

The True Plains tribes share a basic pattern of tribes or linked bands in the summer months and dispersed bands the rest of the year. The only real exception to this statement would be the Comanche. (Most of the Teton Dakota bands came together in the summer, but apparently not all of them.) As a group, the True Plains tribes are distinct from either of the peripheral groups. It seems reasonable to relate this pattern to the shared ecological situation on the Plains.

The leadership pattern among the True Plains tribes shows a rather distinct break. All True Plains tribes of hunting and gathering origin shared a pattern of informal leadership. Four of the five True Plains tribes of farming origin had a formal or semiformal leadership pattern. The fifth tribe, the Crow, is an exception. This situation correlates neatly with the peripheral groups: the peripheral hunting and gathering tribes generally had an informal pattern, whereas the peripheral farming tribes all had a formal leadership pattern. Therefore, the difference in the leadership patterns among the True Plains tribes can be related to cultural continuity. (It must be noted that we are here speaking of *types* of societies—not continuity from one specific society to another specific society.)

In general terms, the council pattern follows the same lines as the leadership pattern. Again, we may relate the differences in council systems among the True Plains tribes to cultural continuity.

All True Plains tribes except one (the Comanche again are the exception) had police societies. Since this institution is nearly universal on the Plains, an ecological explanation seems to be called for. Moreover, among most of the True Plains tribes, the police functioned primarily in the summer months. The two partial exceptions to this, where the police were of some importance all year round, were both True Plains tribes of horticultural origin—the Cheyenne and the Teton Dakota. Most of the peripheral hunting and gathering tribes seem to have had no police at all; all of the peripheral farming tribes had police who were important all year round. Therefore, the differences within the police pattern may be tentatively correlated with cultural continuity.

All of the True Plains tribes had societies of some sort, with the exception again of the Comanche. There is no clear break within the True Plains group with regard to age-grades. It may be assumed that there is an indirect ecological explanation for the presence of societies among the True Plains tribes, just as there is for the peripheral farming tribes, all of which had societies. The data on peripheral hunting and gathering tribes are too fragmentary to be useful.

Most (10 out of 12) True Plains tribes had no clans. Therefore, the presence of clans cannot be attributed to the shared ecological situation. Moreover, there is a clear break between True Plains tribes of hunting and gathering origin and True Plains tribes of farming origin. None of the former had clans or evidence of the existence of clans in earlier times. With the exception of the Arapaho, all True Plains tribes of farming origin had either clans (Crow and possibly Gros Ventres) or some indication that clans had formerly been present (Cheyenne and Teton Dakota). This break correlates well with the pattern found in peripheral tribes. The peripheral hunting and gathering tribes had no clans, whereas all of the peripheral farming tribes did have clans. Cultural continuity would seem to be an important explanatory factor here.

With the partial exception of the Kiowa, all of the True Plains tribes determined status primarily on the basis of war honors, horses, and personal influence. An ecological explanation would seem to be called for here, bearing in mind that "ecological" is being used in a very broad sense. It should also be pointed out that hereditary factors were very important among the peripheral farming tribes, but not among the peripheral hunting and gathering tribes.

Finally, it may be useful to separate the two categories in a summary form.

RELATED TO ECOLOGY

The basic pattern of large tribal units in the summer months, and a dispersed band organization the rest of the year. Police societies for the summer tribal hunt. Societies. Status acquired by means of war honors, horses, and personal influence.

RELATED TO CULTURAL CONTINUITY

The pattern of leadership. Formal or informal councils. The importance of police all year round. Clans.

CULTURAL DYNAMICS OF THE PLAINS SITUATION

The story of man on the Plains of North America is a story of change. The story begins with men who managed a precarious existence by hunting the buffalo on foot. It continues through a phase of mixed horticulture and hunting. Its most dramatic chapter tells of the explosive development of the Plains cultures built around mounted buffalo hunting.

Throughout the story of the Plains, the influence of technological change is clear. It is a long step from the wandering pedestrian bands of the Paleo-Indians to the earth-lodge settlements of the horticulturists. It is another long step that converted the Plains Indians into hunters on horseback, and hunters with guns. Each successive technological development made possible a different kind of exploitation of the Plains environment.

Moreover, the story of the Plains is a story in which many different peoples have participated and interacted with one another. Tribes have moved into the Plains and out of the Plains. Tribes have made seasonal forays into the Plains. And the nature of life on the Plains has been influenced strongly by factors outside the Plains proper: the Spanish colonial policies, the English and French fur trade, the population pressure from displaced Indian tribes.

What really happened on the Plains in historic times? At first, the introduction of the horse seems to have stimulated the spread of horticultural peoples; this was certainly true of the Apache. But when the horse reached people who did not practice horticulture, the newly mounted tribes of nomadic hunters were too much for the farming peoples; the Ute and the Comanche virtually swept the Apache from the Plains. Secoy points out that:

the sedentary spring and summer phase of Apache life proved to be a great military liability when they were pitted against a foe always on the move. The Comanche quickly learned the location of the Apache horticultural rancherias and, at the appropriate season, could be almost certain of finding their foe there. With the element of uncertainty as to the location of the enemy ruled out, the Comanche could make telling use of the element of surprise, and thereby render the Apache war equipment and organization ineffective. The situation also allowed them to concentrate overwhelming numbers against the isolated rancherias and eliminate them one by one.

The introduction of the gun, largely in conjunction with the fur trade, greatly altered the balance of power among tribes. The Cree and the Assiniboine forced many of the Dakota out of northern Minnesota; this was the direct cause of the abandonment of horticulture by the Teton Dakota. Then, when the Dakota in turn got guns, they were in a position to apply pressure to such tribes as the

Iowa and the Cheyenne—sedentary horticulturists at this time (1680 to 1760) who lacked firearms. Ultimately, when tribes acquired both the horse and the gun, this changed the picture again, stimulating both raiding for horses and trading for guns and ammunition. Changes in military patterns are not the whole story, of course. People do not fight all the time, and people must eat. Whatever the ultimate causes, tribes of significantly different backgrounds found themselves on the Plains in historic times. Some, like the Cheyenne, had been horticulturists; they left their fields behind them and lived by hunting the buffalo. Others, like the Cree and the Comanche, had been hunting and gathering peoples; they too now lived by mounted buffalo hunting. Still others, as diverse as the Omaha and the Shoshone, made seasonal hunting forays into the Plains; they were "part-time" Plains tribes. All of these tribes, and particularly the True Plains groups, had to adapt to the varied aspects of the Plains situation: the crucial reliance on the buffalo, the mobility given by the horse and the nature of the treeless terrain, the competition with other tribes for horses, guns, land, and survival itself. It is in terms of such a dynamic situation that we must seek an interpretation of what happened to the social organizations of the Plains Indians.

It is generally true that all aspects of a sociocultural system tend to be interrelated; indeed, this is what is meant by the very word *system*. Still, it is both useful and necessary to isolate certain categories for purposes of analysis. In terms of this study, the basic categories are three in number: Groups, including the structure of groups; Authority and Leadership; and Status. Each will be considered in turn.

GROUPS

One basic key to the nature of the Plains groupings is that the True Plains tribes could not stay together as a unit all year round, and they could not stay in the same place. The Cheyenne are a classic example of this. They once tried to stay together as a tribe

throughout the year and nearly perished as a result. The Cree were able to hold large encampments together for less than a month, after which the bands had to separate in order to find food. We have previously indicated the severe problems faced by the Apache which were caused by the exposure of their horticultural settlements to the attack of the mounted nomads; the same dilemma was encountered by the farming tribes on the Missouri. As Newcomb puts it, the True Plains tribes had to be "constantly on the move following or seeking bison herds, and thus increasingly colliding with one another amalgamating, allying, and above all fighting."

Two important factors are at work here. Both of them, in broad terms, fall under the heading of ecology. First, there was the extremely heavy reliance of the Plains tribes on the buffalo. Without the buffalo, the Plains cultures could not have survived. Of necessity, the True Plains tribes had to adjust their lifeways to the cycle of the buffalo. Essentially, the buffalo were dispersed in small groups during the winter months, and they concentrated in large herds in the summer months. To hunt the buffalo effectively the Plains tribes had to be in a position to attack the large herds with concerted manpower in the summer months, and they had to break up into smaller units to hunt the dispersed groups the rest of the year. Moreover, the need for shelter and food for the horses led to much the same pattern. Also, the endemic raiding warfare of the Plains area put a premium on flexibility and mobility, for both offense and defense. A group that was tied down in one place was a sitting duck; what was needed was a reasonably large group that could move in a hurry and react quickly. There is also the possibility of a more direct environmental factor at work here: the aridity of the Plains may have in itself inhibited the persistence of sedentary horticultural groups.

The characteristic band organization of the True Plains tribes was a logical outgrowth of the ecological circumstances within which the tribes lived. The band organization did not "just happen." As Eggan states,

The conditions of Plains life demanded a local group small enough to subsist by hunting and gathering, but large enough to furnish protection against hostile war parties and raids. The extended family was adequate for the first condition but was at the mercy of any war party; the tribe, on the other hand, was too unwieldy to act as an economic unit for very long. The band provided an adequate compromise; this is perhaps the most important reason for its almost universal presence in the Plains area.

Still, there was one time during the year when the tribe *could* function as an economic unit: in the summer when the buffalo congregated in large herds. This was what happened; the True Plains tribes as a rule were tribally organized in the great camp circles during the summer months. The scattered bands came together and acted as a unit. This fact is of supreme importance in understanding the phenomenon of the Sun Dance. The Sun Dance characteristically was a *tribal* ceremony, and it emphasized tribal solidarity. It may be recalled that the first Comanche Sun Dance was a conscious attempt at demonstrating tribal unity among a people who had never before functioned as a united tribe. The Plains Cree are described as looking forward all year to the annual Sun Dance encampment. Lowie states: "to the Crow, the Sun Dance was precisely *not* an occasion for righting a private wrong but a public spectacle in which the whole tribe took part, as performer or spectator. . . ." Wissler has a perceptive comment to make on this. After noting the dispersal of the Plains bands in the winter, he states that in the summer:

the bands of each tribe came together and went upon a grand hunt. Then food was plentiful, feasting and social activities became the rule, as the great cavalcade shifted hither and thither with the bison. It is in the nature of things that such a grand picnic should culminate in a great ceremony, or religious festival, in which the whole group might function. This ceremony was the sun dance.

Leslie Spier has traced the diffusion of the Sun Dance on the Plains, pointing out that the complex seems to have spread from a nucleus of three tribes: the Arapaho, the Cheyenne, and the Teton Dakota. (It may be noted that all three of these tribes are of horticultural origin.) Spier also has noted that the Sun Dance usually occurred in the summer months when the whole tribe was united. The Sun Dance, he says, "stands alone at the focus of heightened ceremonial interest. Under such conditions the variations leading to elaboration may well develop." John Collier, I believe, has put the matter perfectly:

Viewed socially, the Sun Dance was the integrative and structuring institution of the Plains tribes. . . . The Sun Dance appears as an invention—an exquisitely perfect one—at the social level. With the acquisition of the horse, the life of the Plains tribes . . . became profoundly modified. No longer could the subgroups composing a tribe stay in continuous physical contact with one another. . . . Yet the significant and valued flow of life was tribal. The Sun Dance was the invention which met this dilemma. In the summer, at breeding season, the buffalo gathered in large herds; and in the summer, the grasses were lush, so that the concentration of the thousands of horses was possible. Therefore, at that time the scattered subgroups all drew together; and the Sun Dance was the celebration. The whole tribe camped in one immense circle; the circle of tepees symbolized tribal unity.

In other words, the Sun Dance was a rite of intensification; it "restored equilibrium for a group after a disturbance affecting all or most of its members."

In approaching the problem of clans among the True Plains tribes, it may be useful to compare briefly the types of social groupings that are characteristic of nomadic hunting and gathering peoples with the typical social groupings of horticultural peoples. Generally speaking, nomadic hunting and gathering peoples are organized into small (20 to 50 persons) bands. Neighboring bands interact with one another to some extent, and each band is part of what may be termed a "felt" tribe; that is, they share a feeling of belonging together but do not function as a unified tribe with a tribal system of organization. The band sometimes splits up into nuclear or extended family groups in search of widely dispersed food supplies. These bands may be either patrilineal or composite in type. As a rule, a person can change his band affiliation readily, even in the patrilineal type of band.

Horticultural peoples, as well as such sedentary hunters and food-gatherers as those of the northwest coast of North America, have different types of groups. Such societies are customarily divided into villages with relatively large (several hundred persons) populations. The villages are linked to one another by means of clans and/or secret societies. Generally, but not always, horticultural peoples lack true political unity. On the other hand, chiefs and councils frequently exist. Moreover, the tribe is a more important entity here than is usually the case among hunting and gathering peoples. The "felt" tribe of the Andamanese, for example, is a far more amorphous type of social grouping than the tribe among the Hopi, where the clan chiefs of the various pueblos met together occasionally to talk things over. The Iroquois tribes are also a case in point.

On the Plains, as we have noted, the basic pattern was one of dispersed bands throughout most of the year, with the bands coming together in the summer months. The data on the bands of most True Plains tribes emphasize the fact that the bands were extremely fluid; a person could switch bands without undue difficulty. Certainly, the band type of organization on the Plains was of value precisely because of its flexibility, and we have already indicated at some length the necessity for flexibility and mobility in the Plains situation.

Where, after all, do we usually find clans? They are most common and most important in the "middle range of social systems"; that is, between the hunters and gatherers and the state-organized agriculturists. Obviously, the clan is a very useful organizational device in certain kinds of relatively sedentary societies. As Goldschmidt states,

A fully functioning clan forms a kind of corporate group sharing territorial lands; it makes demands on the loyalty of its constituent members, each member being responsible to and for the whole. It may also be specially useful as a landholding entity, serving a broad basis for recognizing and protecting land rights. The clan in fact has some of the legal attributes of a modern corporation.

The clan is a technique for introducing continuity and stability into a social system. With specific reference to the peripheral farming tribes around the Plains, Eggan writes:

The increased density of population requisite for village life was made possible by the increased food supply resulting from combining maize agriculture with hunting and gathering. The utilization of fertile bottomlands along the Missouri and its tributaries made it possible for these villages to be both large and relatively permanent; the problems of integrating the population around common activities in connection with agriculture and hunting, with regard to both subsistence and rituals, made the development of a segmentary clan organization highly probable. Wherever it is essential to hold property in trust or to maintain rituals from generation to generation, unilateral organizations or "corporations" are far more efficient than bilateral ones. The clan gives a greater degree of stability and permanence but has in turn a limited flexibility and adaptability to new situations.

Elizabeth Bacon has made much the same point about the rigidity and lack of adaptability of clan systems.

The very essence of the Plains situation was that it demanded flexibility, adaptability, and mobility. People were constantly on the move; individuals who belonged to one band might not see individuals who belonged to another band but once a year. People shifted from one band to another. Land was not owned in the same sense as land was owned among farming peoples. Corporate responsibility would have been very difficult to maintain among people as dispersed as were those on the Plains. In short, the clan does not seem to be well suited to the necessities of Plains life.

We have noted that there are indications that two tribes, the Cheyenne and the Teton Dakota, seem to have abandoned their former clan systems as a response to the Plains situation. The Crow, who retained a matrilineal clan system on the Plains, seem to have been "in the process of changing from a more highly organized kinship system to a more diffuse type represented by the Cheyenne and Arapaho systems." Both the Pawnee and the Crow were "shifting from a clan toward a band type of organization and becoming more 'bilateral' in their kinship practices." Lowie has also noted the probability that the Crow abandoned a moiety system on the Plains. The case of the Gros Ventres is more puzzling. If they indeed had patrilineal clans, as reported, this may have been owing in part to the fact that the Gros Ventres groups were quite small and their hunting territories were fairly restricted. As Eggan has said, "the increase in band solidarity brought about by these factors may well have tended toward a more formal organization of the bands." (It is possible, of course, that the Gros Ventres did not have true clans at all. Kroeber states that "all the members of both the father's and mother's clan" were considered to be relatives. Flannery's evidence seems to indicate that residence was almost as important as descent in determining band affiliation, and it is the band that Kroeber equates with the clan. The definition of the clan with which we are operating, emphasizing descent in a unilineal line rather than residence, makes the existence of the Gros Ventres clans problematical.)

Still more revealing, perhaps, is the fact that no tribe of hunting and gathering origin developed clans on the Plains. The conclusion seems clear that most of the tribes with clans or traces of former clans had clans in their backgrounds before they moved into the Plains. The clan was not impossible in the Plains situation, but it certainly was not appropriate. As Eggan has noted, the tribes that moved into the Plains tended to develop similar types of kinship systems, and the Plains situation seemed to favor a flexible type of social organization that could adapt easily to changing conditions.

All of the True Plains tribes, with the apparent exception of the Comanche, had societies. We have defined societies as associations that are not based primarily on either territory or kinship. Among the True Plains tribes, most of the societies were not age-graded, but three tribes (Blackfoot, Gros Ventres, and Arapaho) had age-graded societies. Lowie has argued persuasively that the age-graded type of society spread by diffusion; this type of society originated among

the Mandan and Hidatsa, both horticultural village peoples, and spread to the Arapaho and Gros Ventres and, later, to the Blackfoot. He concludes: "The graded system is not the original form from which ungraded military organizations have developed, but arose through the grading of originally ungraded societies." Clearly, the age-graded type of society was useful on the Plains, and perhaps more efficient than the ungraded type of society, since it was adopted by tribes who seemingly already had nongraded societies. On the other hand, both types of societies must have functioned effectively in view of their almost universal presence among the True Plains tribes. The problem thus is one of accounting for societies in general.

Societies, like clans, are characteristic of the "middle ranges" of cultural systems. They are one technique of organizing such societies for action. We have already seen how the Plains situation tended to inhibit the development of large kinship units such as clans. In view of this, societies would seem to be an ideal alternative device for structuring the Plains tribes on a non-kinship basis.

There are also more specific factors at work here. Two of them are of crucial importance. First, the men's societies were intimately bound up with the military system. Characteristically, they are referred to almost always as *military societies*. Hoebel has presented an analysis of these societies that is very illuminating. With reference to the Cheyenne, he states that the societies are "social and civic organizations mainly centered on the common experience of the members as warriors, with rituals glorifying and enhancing that experience, and with duties and services performed on behalf of the community at large." Moreover, "Each club has four officers or leaders. The leaders are the main war chiefs of the tribe. . . ." Likewise, the societies were an important means of integrating the Plains tribes. As a rule, the societies only functioned fully when the tribe came together in the summer months. At this time, the societies were responsible for putting on *tribal* ceremonies. As Eggan has noted:

The larger tribal organization is reflected in the camp circle but finds its integration primarily in ceremonial and symbolic terms. The band system, which was primarily an economic organization, dominated most of the year, but when the tribes came together, the society organization, composed of males, was pre-eminent and overshadowed the band organization. The importance of tribal ceremonies in social integration can hardly be overestimated.

Finally, the military societies played an important role in maintaining order in the tribal assemblies and in policing the critically important communal buffalo hunts. These functions will be discussed under the heading of Authority and Leadership.

AUTHORITY AND LEADERSHIP

The use of such rubrics as "formal leadership" versus "informal leadership" doubtless makes for an oversimplification of the actual leadership patterns. It must also be admitted that the use of such opposed categories tends to mask certain similarities between them. However, the categories are not meaningless: they do point to some genuine differences in social organization.

What, precisely, do we mean by informal leadership and formal leadership? This can best be seen in terms of polar examples. The Blackfoot had a system of informal leadership. The "chiefs" were "leaders only by the consent and will of their people." They had no power except that of personal influence. A head "chief" was not formally selected; he "attained his position simply by a growing unanimity on the part of the head men of the bands as to who should hold the position." If the band headman opposed the desires of the members of his band, the band simply deserted him and got another headman. The tribal councils were likewise informal; they were just gatherings of the band headmen. It may be noted that warriors were supposed to get the permission of the band headman before going out on a raid. But if the warriors had reason to believe that the headman might object, they solved the problem by neglecting to tell the headman anything about it. Contrast this with the Cheyenne, who had a formal leadership pattern. A Cheyenne chief was an elected official. He was "chosen for a definite term of office—ten years—and ritually inducted as a member of the council." The formal tribal council of forty-four chiefs acted "as a judicial body in cases involving a criminal act." If a chief were still alive at the end of his term of office, he could pick his own successor from the members of his own band; each band as a rule had at least four representatives on the tribal council.

There are real differences here; the problem is to account for them. They cannot be attributed to ecology, since both of these True Plains tribes shared essentially the same ecological situation. The break in the data among the True Plains tribes of different backgrounds provides the clue: the tribes with formal leadership patterns were originally horticultural tribes, and the tribes with informal leadership patterns were originally hunting and gathering tribes. This correlates closely with the information from peripheral tribes. Most of the peripheral hunting and gathering tribes had a system of informal leadership, whereas all of the peripheral farming tribes had a system of formal leadership. The generalization may be broadened; it seems to be generally true that leadership patterns become more precise and formalized as one moves from nomadic hunting and gathering peoples to sedentary horticultural societies. The conclusion seems inescapable that the *differences* in leadership patterns among the True Plains tribes reflect differences in the types of leadership that they had when they first moved into the Plains. They certainly had to adapt to the new Plains situation, but they did this by modifying existing institutions.

How about the similarities in leadership patterns among the True Plains tribes? How did they adjust their institutions to the shared Plains situation, and what stresses appeared in the leadership patterns as a result? Here again we must turn to the two key points about the True Plains tribes: the basic pattern of a dispersal of the population in mobile bands for most of the year and the gathering of the bands in the summer months, and the crucial importance of warfare. The bands, after all, were the functioning social units most of the time. They had to be flexible, mobile, and rather loosely organized. A band, to put the matter simply, has to be organized as a *band*—not as a tribe. As a rule among the True Plains tribes, the band leaders were headmen, not chiefs. Even among the Cheyenne, who had what was probably the most formally organized leadership pattern on the Plains, a band leader was "a headman in exactly the same sense as the Comanche peace chief." Hoebel, the source of the above quotation, discusses the Comanche peace chief as follows:

The headman was a magnet at the core of the band, but his influence was so subtle that it almost defies explicit description. He worked through precept, advice, and good humor, expressing his wisdom through well-chosen words and persuasive common sense. He was not elected to the office or even chosen. "He just got that way." His role and status were only slightly more institutionalized than were those of the Eskimo headman. . . . Anyone who did not like his decision simply ignored it. If in time a good many people ignored his announcements . . . the chief had then lost his following. He was no longer chief, and another had quietly superseded him.

The point is that the band leader had to function as a headman while leading the band. Among the Cheyenne, though, the band headman was *also* a tribal official and functioned as such when the tribe came together in the summer. The Blackfoot had a similar pattern, although it was less formalized. As Ewers states, "The most influential band chief became recognized as the head chief of the tribe. Howver, his rank was of little significance except during the period of the tribal encampment in summer. Even then his role was more that of chairman of the council of chiefs than of ruler of his people." The True Plains tribes, in other words, tended to be band organized during most of the year and tribally organized during the summer months. This meant that among tribes with relatively formal patterns of leadership, the formal patterns could be largely retained in the tribal encampments but were displaced by the more fluid band leadership patterns the

rest of the year. Tribes that came into the Plains with a less formal system, on the other hand, adapted to the Plains situation by developing a kind of tribal leadership during the summer months but retained a somewhat modified band system the rest of the year.

The True Plains tribes depended on military skills for their very survival. It would be surprising indeed to find that their leadership patterns were divorced from military considerations, and quite the contrary was actually the case. A Plains leader had to be more than a hunter, and more than just a personable individual. He had to be a successful warrior —a tried and true military leader. To be sure, tribes frequently had "peace chiefs," known for their restraint and eloquence, in addition to war chiefs. But in order to *become* a peace chief, a man had to have an outstanding war record. Consider again the case of the Cheyenne. Hoebel states: "All the peace chiefs are proven warriors, but when a chief of a military organization is raised to the rank of peace chief, he must resign his post in the military society. He retains his membership, but not his position as war chief." Thomas Battey, who lived among the Kiowa, tells a most revealing story. Speaking of a man named Kicking Bird, he writes:

He might be considered the first chief of the tribe: although no chief is amenable to another, still there are, at the present time, no less than twelve chiefs who look to him for counsel in all matters of importance. His long-continued attachment to the whites at one time brought him into disrepute with his tribe, and they charged his friendship to cowardice, called him a woman, and refused to listen to his counsels. Finding his influence in the tribe nearly gone, he raised a force, conducted a raid into Texas, and had a severe engagement with the white soldiers. . . . The tribe, thoroughly convinced of his bravery, no more attribute his desire for peace to cowardice, and listen to his eloquent arguments. . . .

In some tribes, the connection between chieftainship and military prowess is quite explicit. What, for example, was a Crow chief? The native term for chief, according to Lowie, "denotes the standing that goes with military achievement, but need not imply any governmental functions. There were four normal types of creditable exploit: leadership of a successful raid; capturing a horse picketed within a hostile camp; being first to touch an enemy (the 'coup' in the narrower sense); and snatching a foeman's bow or gun." Any man who had performed each of these exploits ranked as a chief. "Such men formed a body of social leaders; on the other hand, to lack all these standardized points was to be a nobody." Among all the True Plains tribes, skill in military matters was an important factor in becoming a leader. The case of the Teton Dakota is particularly instructive, because it indicates a shift away from hereditary chiefs toward a leadership pattern based on military prowess as a result of the conditions of Plains life. When the tribe came together in the spring, four men termed *wakicunsa* were selected to take charge of the camp. Hyde states:

Not chiefs but prominent warriors were selected as *wakicunsa*. . . . The four *wakicunsa* had supreme authority over the people until the tribal circle was broken up in the autumn. . . . The real chiefs had no authority except in settling small matters which concerned their own camps alone. . . . Such a form of organization naturally thrust the prominent warriors to the fore and, in tribal affairs, prevented the hereditary chiefs (unless they were men of very strong character) from playing an important part.

In another revealing passage, Hyde writes:

When, about the year 1700, the Oglalas and other Tetons turned their backs on their old homeland along the Mississippi and started their long migration across the coteau toward the Missouri, they gradually lost touch with the Sioux of the East. . . . These wild Tetons of the coteau, constantly on the move, gaining a hard living by following the buffalo herds, had little in common with the Sioux bands settled along the Mississippi and the Lower Minnesota River, who spent much of their time in fixed villages and gained at least a portion of their support from the cultivation of the soil. As early as 1730 we find evidence that the Tetons had thrown off the authority of the Sioux chiefs. In their wandering camps each man was the equal of any of his fellows, and the chiefs were merely the heads of kinship groups and generally had no authority outside of the little group of kinsmen who recognized them as hereditary leaders.

There is a clear implication here that life on the Plains tended to decrease the importance of hereditary leaders. It is not only that "each man was the equal of any of his fellows," but more importantly that each man had to attain leadership on the basis of his personal ability. How could he become a leader? Horses were the most important form of property, and horses usually were stolen, not inherited. "The whole point of the war game was that a warrior took a long chance and risked his life that he might achieve status among his people." The most honored form of war exploit was stealing horses, and, significantly, "war insignia were standardized so that it was easy to tell what a man had achieved in war."

In the problem of authority and control, we must again take note of the basic ecological situation on the Plains. During most of the year, for reasons already noted, the True Plains tribes lived in fluid, scattered bands. As a rule, the band headman had very little actual authority; that is, he could not *compel* obedience to his wishes. This point has previously been noted with reference to such tribes as the Blackfoot, the Comanche, and the Cheyenne. The crucial question concerns *why* the band headmen had such limited authority. It may be suggested that there was only one time when strong social controls were needed within the band: on military raids. Generally speaking, the entire band did not participate in a raid, for obvious reasons. The usual pattern was for a group of warriors to detach themselves from the band, go out on a raid, and then return to the band after the raid was over. Therefore, it was not the *band* that had need of strong social controls, but rather the part of the band that actually made the raid. We would expect to find effective authority operable within the raiding party itself, and that is where we do find it. Among the Kiowa, for example, regardless of the size of the war party, "the war-leader was in absolute control, and far greater discipline was enforced here than elsewhere in Kiowa life." Even among the Comanche, who were probably the most determinedly individualistic of all the Plains tribes, the leader of a raiding party had a great deal of authority. Hoebel states:

On the raid the leader of the war party—the man who had organized it—had temporary dictatorial powers such as a peace chief never enjoyed. He determined the objectives of the raid; he appointed scouts, cooks, and water carriers; he set the camping places and the route of march; he divided the booty, if booty there was. In all his directives he was implicitly obeyed. If anyone seriously objected, he was free to leave the party and go his own way. Success on the raid demanded tough leadership, and the followers of a war chief submitted to it.

The other crucial band enterprise—hunting—was not communal hunting as a rule. It was a matter of small groups of hunters going after widely dispersed buffalo. In such a situation, there was no need for strong social controls, since the band was not hunting as a unit, and individualistic enterprise was what was required.

In the summer months, however, when the whole tribe came together, the entire situation was different. Many people were together in one place, and these were people who owed allegiance to different bands. There were important ceremonies to be organized. And, above all, there was the communal buffalo hunt to be undertaken, upon which so much depended. Order was necessary in the tribal encampment, to prevent disputes. Strict discipline was necessary on the hunt, because individual hunting was inefficient. (A single hunter who jumped the gun might get a few buffalo for himself, but he would alarm and scatter the herd in such a way that communal hunting techniques were not effective.) It was at this time that the police societies always functioned. Over and over again, the point is made that the most important job the police societies had was in policing the communal hunts. For most of the True Plains tribes, this was the only time when formal social controls were instituted. As long ago as 1927, Lowie pointed out the importance of the police societies as integrative mechanisms in the Plains tribes. He argued that associations could overcome the separatism of kin groups by bringing together men of different families, but that associations in themselves were not enough, since they could divide the community long associational lines. "Associational particularism can evidently be over-

come," he notes "if the several organizations are subject to the control of a single authority." (That is, if one of the societies was delegated to take charge in the summer, which was the customary pattern.) He states: "No other feature of Plains Indian life approached the buffalo police as an effective territorial unifier." It may be noted that the role of the police societies was integrative in another way. They not only were responsible for *punishing* offenders but also tried to *rehabilitate* the guilty persons by bringing them back within the tribal structure. As Provinse put it, "Conformity, not revenge, was sought, and immediately after a promise to conform was secured from the delinquent, steps were taken to reincorporate him into the society." For example, among the Plains Cree, "if a man evaded the Warriors and tried to make a kill before the proper time, they immediately advanced to the offender's tipi, slashed it to bits, and destroyed all his possessions." This sounds rather formidable. However, if the offender took his punishment well, the Warriers *replaced* all his property four days later.

The differences among the peripheral Plains tribes are instructive here. As a rule, the peripheral hunting and gathering tribes had no police at all. The peripheral farming tribes, on the other hand, had police who functioned all year round, both in the villages and on the hunts. The tendency for two of the True Plains tribes (Cheyenne and Teton Dakota) of horticultural origins to use police to some extent all year round may be a reflection of this former pattern. Certainly, however, the powers of the police were slight except in the summer encampments.

STATUS

It is a striking fact that, whatever the original differences among them may have been, almost all True Plains tribes ended up with a very similar method of determining status. In view of the marked differences between peripheral hunting and gathering tribes and peripheral farming tribes in this respect, the status systems of the True Plains tribes would seem to represent a classic example of the adjustment of social institutions to a shared ecological situation.

Three interrelated factors in the Plains situation directly affected status. First, there was the fluidity and mobility of the bands. As we have seen, this tended to reduce the importance of kinship as an organizing device; a status system based on kinship considerations was not well suited to the facts of Plains life. This point has been amply demonstrated in the preceding discussion. Other means of determining status were apparently necessary on the Plains. It is not suggested that kinship ties can never be a basic organization device among herding peoples. Indeed, the *Obok* type of segmented lineage seems to be characteristic of many herding societies. The Plains situation, however, is virtually unique. Although the Plains tribes resemble herders in many ways, the buffalo themselves were not herded. The constant movement of the Plains tribes, together with the fluid military situation partly induced by outside factors, prevented the development of precise patterns of land ownership. In any event, it is important to bear in mind the brief duration of the historic Plains cultures; on the Plains, "the opportunity for a final pattern to emerge was never fulfilled because new factors (traders, guns, settlers) were continuously introduced and constantly altered the balance of power and the character of opportunity."

Second, there was the military situation on the Plains. It is necessary to stress the point that the True Plains tribes were quite literally fighting for their lives. They were engaged in a fierce competition with other tribes and with outside powers for territory and for horses; both land to hunt in and horses to hunt with were crucial to survival. As Newcomb has pointed out, the "gaming" aspect of Plains warfare has been exaggerated or misinterpreted. The Plains cultures were warlike because they had to be, and the granting of high social status to warriors was a necessary part of the system. After all, a warrior must be rewarded somehow; he must have an incentive to fight. This does not mean, of course, that we must disregard the less directly utilitiarian aspects of warfare altogether. Mishkin has discussed this problem perceptively, stating:

The formalized deeds have a significant place in the practice of warfare and are prerequisites in the attainment of rank so far as the individual is concerned. In short, within the economic framework of war there functioned a system of warrior etiquette and formal accomplishment the successful performance of which was essential to rank.

Third, there was the crucial importance of horses in the Plains situation. A Blackfoot hunter on a good horse could kill four or five buffalo in a single chase, but a man on a poor horse couldn't kill any at all. Horses were quite clearly necessary in efficient buffalo hunting. In addition, it was the horse that made possible the rapid mobility of the Plains tribes, and this mobility was essential in Plains warfare. In a nomadic society, property has to be portable. The most important form of property was the horse which was ideally suited to these conditions: it could transport itself. It may also be noted that the horse was eight times more efficient than a dog as a bearer of burdens. The number of horses a man owned was a basic determinant of status. Among the Blackfoot, the introduction of the horse brought about a change from a relatively classless society to a society with three loosely defined social classes, and membership in one class or another was largely determined by horse ownership. Among the Comanche, as has been noted, the prestige of an individual was directly proportional to the size of his herd of horses. Similar examples could be cited for all of the True Plains tribes. Horses were bred and occasionally captured wild by some True Plains tribes, but the main way of getting horses was by raiding. Mishkin has stated:

But the supposition that wild horses ever constituted a primary source of the Indians' herds is unfounded. According to all the evidence, raiding was everywhere the principal method of acquiring horses. There is no reason to suspect that Indian horses bred poorly; nevertheless natural increase of the herds apparently did not satisfy the Indian's needs and he was ever impatient to replenish stock.

A Plains entrepreneur was essentially a horse thief; Grinnell notes that "there were many brave and successful warriors of the Cheyennes . . . who on their war journeys tried to avoid coming in close contact with enemies, and had no wish to kill enemies. Such men went to war for the sole purpose of increasing their possessions by capturing horses; that is, they carried on war as a business—for profit." Horses could be inherited, of course, and this gave a man valuable headstart in life. But the horse had to be used as well as owned; status had to be validated by performance as a warrior, generosity in giving horses away, and the like. This was true even among the Kiowa. And a fixed status system based on the inheritance of horses would have been difficult in view of the fact that any man could acquire horses for himself by raiding. There were other factors which entered into the situation as well. As Elkin states concerning the Arapaho:

The possession of wealth, other than it permitted one to gain a reputation for liberality, was thus not in itself a criterion for the ascription of prestige. The horse, however, under proper circumstances, might have allowed for social stratification on a property basis. Unlike other forms of property, it was the essential means of procuring a livelihood, was differentiated into relative values, and deteriorated slowly. Nevertheless, any development along this line was precluded by constant warfare. The frequency with which whole herds were won or lost served to prevent property ownership from becoming personally concentrated. The spoils of a successful raid, moreover, were equally divided among all participants, though those who acted most effectively received first choice.

It may also be noted that horses were frequently distributed outside the immediate family upon the death of the owner. Among the Teton Dakota, for example, a young man was expected to get his start in life by stealing horses, since he could not expect to inherit any horses from his father. Finally, the concentration of horses within family lines would have been difficult because a man who had a lot of horses was supposed to give horses away to less fortunate persons. Among the Teton Dakota, where horses were the most important form of property, "the only prestige attached to property was in giving it away." Among the Plains Cree, Mandelbaum states: "The possession of horses facilitated a rise in social status. Prestige could be acquired through the bountiful bestowal of gifts. A horse was the very best and most praiseworthy gift that could be given." Among the Kiowa, Richardson writes: "Generosity in giving horses was vastly more important than the possession of horses itself." It can be argued that both the custom of giving horses away and the custom of acquiring horses by raiding were effective techniques in Plains societies. In a culture so dependent on horses for efficient hunting, it was of obvious desirability to have all the hunters as well equipped with horses as possible. And the technique of stealing horses from other tribes offered a dual advantage: it increased the tribal horse holdings of the successful raider at the same time that it reduced the effectiveness of the competing society.

An obvious point, but still an important one, is that the True Plains cultures were decisively male-oriented. The ways of attaining status were involved primarily with male activities: hunting, raiding, and fighting. Rodnick states with regard to the Assiniboine: "Women had no rank or social status except the respect due them by relatives; the prerequisites of rank applied only to men. . . . As in all Plains societies, patterns of status were definitely masculine in form, with tendencies toward feminine traits being held in derision." Speaking of the Plains Cree, Mandelbaum notes: "Men who had not participated in warfare were derided and ridiculed. Their names might be given feminine endings and young warriors might summarily tell them to join 'their fellow-women.' " In other words, sex was one determinant of status. However, a man had to live up to his expected role as a warrior; his only real alternative was to become a transvestite.

To be sure, there were other ways of acquiring status in addition to those already enumerated. The ownership of medicine bundles was frequently important. Eloquence, ability as a shaman, and level-headed judgment were sometimes factors in the status system. Unquestionably, however, the crucial status determinants on the Plains were military skills and the possession of horses, and both of these were intimately related to the basic ecological patterns of Plains life.

CONCLUSIONS

This work has had two basic aims, which were interrelated. First, it has sought to clarify certain problems in Plains ethnology. It has related basic similarities in the social organizations of the True Plains tribes to their shared ecological situation, while relating basic differences between the social systems of these tribes to differences in their cultural backgrounds. Again, it has attempted to provide a test of a number of modern anthropological ideas concerning the development of social systems.

Let us now return to the specific propositions which we have tried to test. . . .

1. It has been demonstrated that the True Plains cultures were a late development. Such cultures, based on the mounted hunting of the buffalo, necessarily postdated the introduction of the horse into the Plains.

2. The True Plains tribes came into the Plains out of two fundamentally different economic backgrounds and from several distinct culture areas. It has been shown that a people like the Comanche had at one time been hunters and gatherers in the Basin-Plateau area, while a tribe such as the Cheyenne had at one time been a farming people in Minnesota.

3. The ecological situation on the Plains necessitated not only changes in material culture but also basic changes in social organization. It has been abundantly demonstrated, I believe, that the anual cycle of the buffalo necessitated common exploitative techniques. Moreover, the buffalo cycle necessitated a basic pattern of fragmented bands in the winter months and concentrated tribal units in the summer months. This in turn led to far-reaching adjustments in the social systems of the Plains tribes. The technological change which initiated the development of the True Plains cultures led to basic changes in the social organizations of these tribes. The ecological situation, involving the dynamic interrelationships between culture and environment, was a complex one of the Plains. An important part of the environment within which any Plains tribe lived was made up of *other* competing Plains tribes, as well as powers outside the Plains. The ecological situation, involving adaptations to the buffalo cycle and the existence of competing societies, influenced every aspect of Plains social organization: the patterns of leadership, the nature of social groupings, the determinants of status, and so forth.

4. There are abundant evidences of cultural persistence on the Plains. The exigencies of the changing Plains situation modified older cultural institutions, but these aspects of former lifeways did not vanish entirely. The tribal organization of the Cheyenne is only intelligible in these terms, as is the matrilineal clan system of the Crow. I believe also that the *absence* of certain institutions in some cases reflects cultural persistence or continuity. For example, the account of the first Comanche Sun Dance clearly reflects the influence of their loosely organized Great Basin heritage.

5. Despite their differing backgrounds, the ultimate similarities among the True Plains tribes in social organization are remarkable, and as a group they differ from peripheral tribes. They tended to share basic patterns of band systems during most of the year and tribal systems in the summer months. They tended to share the institution of the police societies on the communal buffalo hunts. The tended to share the high valuation of military skills as a determinant of status. There are many apparent similarities in the organization of their sociocultural systems. The data provide strong support for the idea that sociocultural systems are indeed adaptive systems; systems of social organization do not "just happen" without rhyme or reason.

6. The comparison of the True Plains tribes of different backgrounds with peripheral Plains tribes offers a strong evidence for the

fact that the *differences* among the True Plains tribes can indeed be related to what kinds of tribes they were before moving into the Plains. Wherever important differences in social structure have been found among the True Plains tribes, these differences have correlated with differences between peripheral hunters and gatherers as opposed to peripheral horticulturists. That is, the True Plains tribes which were originally hunters and gatherers tend to resemble peripheral hunting and gathering tribes in some respects, whereas the True Plains tribes which were originally farmers tend to resemble the peripheral horticultural tribes. In addition to shedding light on some of the diversity among the True Plains tribes, the distinctiveness of the two groups of peripheral tribes lends support to the idea that the hunters and gatherers are characteristically different from horticultural peoples in terms of social organization.

7. This work has been phrased in evolutionary terms. To the extent that it has been successful, it serves to emphasize the importance of the idea of cultural evolution in anthropology. The results indicate the validity of both multilinear and universal evolution as systems of explanation. We have demonstrated significant regularities in the process of culture change within a specific area. We have also tried to show, by means of a comparison of peripheral Plains tribes, that a taxonomy of cultures based upon the development of economic resources can yield rewarding results. Exceptions do occur, of course, but it is still broadly true that societies with different technological bases tend to have different types of social systems. In view of the known archeological sequence of cultural types, this fact supports the view that it is meaningful to speak of an evolutionary development of human culture, with increasing complexity through time.

This analysis of the Plains situation has suggested three basic conclusions. First, it has stressed the importance of viewing the Plains situation in dynamic rather than static terms. The story of man on the Plains is clearly a story of constant change. The movements of tribes, the interactions between tribes, the shifts in the balance of power, the influence of outside factors, the introduction of new cultural elements—the story of life on the Plains is unintelligible without an appreciation of these processes of change. The traditional trait-distribution approach to the concept of the culture area is grossly unsuited to the facts of the Plains situation and has led to a masking of many of the real problems posed by the Plains cultures. This point has been made by others, but it deserves restatement.

Second, the materials with which we have been dealing have underscored the crucial role of technology as a prime mover in cultural change. It was a technological change, the introduction of the horse, that made the historic Plains cultures possible. This basic technological change triggered a whole series of cultural modifications. However, it is not technology alone that is so important—it is rather the role played by technology in the total ecological system. The complex interrelationships between the technological systems and the environment of other men, other animals, and other societies were certainly key factors in the developing Plains situation.

Third, this work has emphasized the basic idea that sociocultural systems are indeed adaptive in nature. The "fit" of the Plains social systems to the character of the Plains situation is striking. Despite the differing backgrounds of the True Plains tribes, and despite the fact that the phenomenon of cultural persistence led to continuing differences among the Plains tribes, virtually every aspect of Plains culture adjusted efficiently to the requirements of the Plains situation. Indeed, it would be difficult to design a culture type that would be better suited to the exigencies of Plains life than the cultures which actually developed on the Plains. There was clearly a process of natural selection at work on the Plains: cultures adapted both by means of internal selection, by which institutions were brought into harmony with one another, and by external selection, by which the competition with other societies produced far-reaching changes in sociocultural institutions as the price for survival.

This study does not pretend to explain everything about the Plains Indians. It has been oriented toward a specific set of problems, and has perforce neglected many important aspects of Plains life. No claim is made that this type of work can serve as a substitute for other approaches to the complex Plains situation; rather, it is hoped that it will supplement investigations that have proceeded and will proceed from different points of view.

However, the interpretation herein presented has shown that there are important differences among the sociocultural systems of peoples who live in different ecological situations, and it does offer a reasonable explanation for the similarities among the Plains tribes, as well as the differences which persisted between them to the end.

21. THE JIE OF UGANDA

P. H. GULLIVER

From Peoples of Africa, *edited by James L. Gibbs, Jr. Copyright © 1965 by Holt, Rinehart and Winston, Inc. Reprinted by permission of Holt, Rinehart and Winston, Inc. P. H. Gulliver is Professor of African Anthropology, School of Oriental and African Studies, University of London. His major research interests have been in sociology and social anthropology, with special reference to East and Central Africa. He is the author of* The Family Herds, Labour Migration in a Rural Economy, Land Tenure and Social Change among the Nyakyusa, *and* Social Control in an African Society.

■ This introduction will serve for the next two selections, which are comparative studies of the Jie and the Turkana of East Africa. The Jie and the Turkana apparently were a single group which split up many generations ago. Whereas Plains Indians of diverse cultural origins came to resemble each other closely as a result of a common relationship to the habitat, the Jie and the Turkana diverged culturally in response to different habitats. We saw in Selection 20 how the historical backgrounds of the Indians of the Plains set limits on the degree to which they came to resemble each other. The Jie and the Turkana illustrate the corollary hypothesis, that common historical origins set limits on the degree to which people can diverge culturally from each other in their adaptations to different habitats.

Gulliver shows that both groups are characterized by the same basic social forms in household and kinship organization and in sodalities, but that the actual organizations of social relations—the content of these forms—vary considerably because of different habitational conditions. The Jie live in a much more beneficent environment than the Turkana; one result of this is that the Jie are able to supplement their pastoralism with horticulture and the Turkana cannot. Because of their harsher habitat, Turkana groupings constantly split up, and people are unable to maintain the solidary and cohesive relationships that are found among the Jie.

In terms of the concepts developed in this book, the Jie and the Turkana live in entirely different environments, in addition to different habitats. One of the concepts that is illustrated in the two selections that follow is the inseparability of technology and the organization of social relations in response to pressures of the habitat within a single strategy of adaptation. Although there are common themes in Jie and Turkana life—which can be attributed to the demands made on these people by their pastoral adaptation—there also are striking differences, which result from the pressures of their different habitats.

Pastoralists have played a dominant role in the evolution of social organization in Uganda, and the student can get a good introduction to this part of Africa by consulting the following works: *Bunyoro: An African Kingdom,* by John Beattie (New York: Holt, Rinehart and Winston, 1960); *The Baganda* (New York: Barnes and Noble, 1966) and *The Banyankole,* by John Roscoe (Cambridge: University Press, 1923); *Bantu Bureaucracy* (Chicago: University of Chicago Press, 1965) and *The King's Men: Leadership and Status in Buganda on the Eve of Independence* (New York: Oxford University Press, 1964), by Lloyd A. Fallers; *The Lugbara of Uganda,* by John Middleton (New York: Holt, Rinehart and Winston, 1965): *Alur Society,* by Aidan Southall (Cambridge: W. Heffer, 1956); and *The Western Lacustrine Bantu,* by Brian Taylor (London: International African Institute, 1962). ■

INTRODUCTION

LOCATION

THE JIE ARE A SMALL tribe, numbering 18,200 people in 1948, living in the north-central part of Karamoja District in northeastern Uganda. Culturally and linguistically they are part of the Teso Cluster, an eastern Nilotic group, which comprises a number of related peoples in contiguous territory in eastern Uganda, northwestern Kenya and the southern Sudan.

LANGUAGE

The dialects of this cluster of people are mutually intelligible, though clearly distinctive. They have conventionally been classified in the Nilo-Hamitic language group; alternatively the group is identified as the Great Lakes subdivision of the Nilotic branch of the Eastern Sudanic subfamily of African languages.

PHYSICAL APPEARANCE

The Jie have no outstanding physical characteristics to distinguish them from surrounding East African peoples. They are of average height and have a fairly uniform dark brown skin: only a few individuals have lighter or reddish skins. Hair and facial features are of the Negroid type. As a result perhaps of their well-balanced and generally adequate diet, the people have a good physique. Their children, who are always given priority in the distribution of milk, appear to be healthier than those in many African societies.

ETHOS

The life of the Jie is based on a mixed economy; but although agriculture provides the bulk of the staple food—sorghum for porridge—the Jie themselves give major importance to the care and value of their livestock, particularly cattle. From these animals they obtain additional food staples, and hides and skins. Unlike agriculture, livestock have a significance beyond food production. They have a notable aesthetic value, and they are essential to the rich complex of rituals that would be thought ineffective without the slaughter of oxen. Above all, livestock are the agents in all important social relations and transactions. For the Jie, every major bond of kinship or formal friendship creates a channel along which livestock may pass in either direction so that the two people may assist one another. For these reasons the herds are stores of value, economic and social capital, and the only capital the Jie have. Some prestige accrues to the owners of a large herd, but greater prestige accumulates from the proper use and disposal of animals in ongoing social life. Unlike some African pastoralists, the Jie ascribe little spiritual significance to their animals. Critically important though they are, cattle are not thought to have or to symbolize mystical qualities.

In all social transactions (including rituals) involving domestic animals, the "small stock" (goats and sheep) are used as the lesser units but for essentially the same purposes as cattle. In addition, most families have one or two donkeys for pack purposes—to carry water in the dry season, to carry loads on barter trips, to transport thatching grass, and so on. Little or no aesthetic value is attached to small stock or to donkeys.

ECONOMY

PASTORALISM

The Jie are comparatively wealthy in livestock, with an average of three to four cattle, and four small stock, per human being. Their cattle are the humped Zebu type, and they provide milk and blood, meat, and hides. Children are given preference for milk when it is in short supply toward the end of the dry season, but it is a favorite food of both adults and children. Blood, taken from the necks of living animals, is consumed fresh or mixed with other foods. The principal occasions on which meat is eaten occur when an animal is slaughtered for ritual purposes; beasts are rarely killed simply to provide meat. Jie do not normally milk she-goats and ewes, regarding their milk as much inferior, but children are permitted to take it if they wish.

Habitat and Climate

Because the Jie environment is harsh and tropical, it closely affects their subsistence economy. Jieland lies in the semiarid savannas of upland East Africa, at an altitude of about 4000 feet, with almost no higher land except on the extreme borders. There are two major divisions in the year: the rainy season, lasting from about late March to early August, with a dry spell of at least two or three weeks in about June; and the dry season, during which virtually no rain falls and when torrid conditions are exacerbated by hot, dust-laden winds from the semidesert lands to the east. Although Jieland is small—roughly sixty-five miles from each to west, and twenty-five miles from north to south—there are two fairly distinct ecological regions. In the eastern region, about one third of the country, rainfall is not more than about twenty-five inches in the season; here there is open, treeless savanna thinly covered with seasonal short grasses, and without water soon after the rains cease. In the western region rainfall is probably up to thirty-five inches, it is more reliable in both quantity and distribution, and the season tends to be more prolonged. Here are moderately dense bush and small trees with a thick cover of long perennial grasses; water is more plentiful, and there are a number of permanent watering places. The Jie attempt to make best use of their meager natural resources by pastoral transhumance between east and west regions, which they use for their herds in the rainy and dry seasons, respectively.

Settlement Pattern

Permanent settlement is limited to a small area in the middle of the country, in the borderland between the two regions. Here in fixed homesteads arranged in stable communities live some four fifths of the population—women, children, and most of the men—at a local density of about 130 persons per square mile; here, too, are all the arable lands. The bulk of the herds are kept in separate mobile camps in the pasture lands and are tended by youths and young men subsisting directly off the livestock. Only small dairy herds and a few small stock are kept at the homesteads, and even these are sent to the camps toward the end of the dry season when local pastures and water are exhausted. A camp is an easily built affair—a ring of brushwood often suffices to keep the animals enclosed at night. It may be divided into the kraals of the separate owners, but not

always. In the dry season herders usually sleep in the open under cattle hides; in the rainy season rough shelters are put up. A few essential utensils for milking, making butter, and storing blood and fat are all that are needed. Each herder has his own spears, necessary to protect the animals against hyenas, leopards, and lions. A camp can be abandoned and another made with ease. The pasture lands are dotted with deserted camps, for the Jie always build a fresh camp in a new location after a move.

Pastoral Cycle

The pastoral cycle is briefly as follows: by about the middle of the rainy season the stock camps are all located in the eastern region, where, by that time, new grass has grown sufficiently and surface water collects in pools and stream beds. Camps are scattered throughout the region. Dairy herds are at their largest in the homesteads, and milk supply is at its peak. As the dry season sets in, both grass and water quickly become exhausted and camps must shift westward. There is an irregular migration of the camps, for it is entirely the responsibility of each herd owner to determine the timing and direction of movement as he assesses the situation. At first in the western region water supplies are sufficient to allow a widespread scatter of camps, but as the time of the last rains recedes, surface water dries up and camps are compelled to converge on one or another of the half-dozen permanent watering places for the remainder of the season. The choice of watering place is a matter for each herd owner to decide, although usually he tends to put his camp near the same one each year. Nevertheless, some readjustment of locations does occur each dry season when some places tend to become overcrowded or when men decide to shift for personal reasons. With the onset of the next rainy season it again becomes possible for camps to scatter through the western region as fresh grass and water are available. Then there is a shift back to the east, where the rains come a little later.

In this pastoral cycle each camp shifts at least four of five times a year. No individual

Jie, nor any group, can lay claim to any particular part of the pasture lands, which are entirely communal. Environmental conditions are the only controlling force, with a single exception: intense public disapproval effectively prevents a camp from remaining in the western region throughout the rainy season (though this is physically possible). It is recognized that western pastures should be rested and allowed to reseed naturally, and it is also considered logical to leave those pastures for later use while taking advantage of the purely temporary pastures in the east. In addition, camps in the east are rather nearer the homesteads, and men like to have their herds as near as possible during the latter part of the rainy season, when animals are frequently required during that time of intense social and ritual activity. Also the young men at the camps are then able easily to visit and to participate in such activities.

Although the camps are the domain principally of youths and young men, older men visit their herds frequently, staying a week or two, in order to supervise arrangements and perhaps to make a decision on the spot regarding a move. Women make briefer visits, bringing some cereal foods for their sons and taking back milk and butter. The young men make visits to the homesteads, perhaps alternating with their brothers and cousins so that each can spend some time at home. As cows come into milk, some of them are transferred to the homestead; cows that go dry are sent to the camp; and some animals have to be fetched to the homestead for various purposes.

If the herds are large enough and if enough herders are available, small stock are put in a camp separate from the cattle. But usually only the wealthiest owners maintain camps of their own: generally the herds of two or three owners are kept in a single camp and herded together in the pastures, with duties shared by the younger brothers and sons of the owners. The commonest cooperators in this way are close agnates, but a man may choose to share a camp with friendly clansmen, maternal kin, or affines.

AGRICULTURE

Animal husbandry is preeminently the concern and dominating interest of the men in Jieland; female concern is mainly in domestic activities and agriculture. Although men often assist in milking, women and girls normally act as the dairymaids in the homesteads. But women cannot own livestock nor do they share in their management. There is a common saying that "sorghum is the cattle of women." As men acquire names based on their outstanding oxen, so women gain names from agricultural contexts. As Jie see it, only men can properly protect the herds from predatory animals (and formerly from raiders). Animals are closely associated with the solidarity and continuity of the family, with marriage and affinal relations, with ritual, and with law—and formerly with war making. All these are primarily men's concern, and therefore it is logical and appropriate that men should take the responsibility for the practical side of stock management.

Women own both the arable lands and the produce from them. Each married woman makes her own fields by clearing a patch of bush conveniently near the homestead. A field can be cultivated for three to six consecutive seasons before being allowed to lie fallow; there is no use of manure or other fertilizer. A woman aims to hold several sets of fields, one of which is in cultivation while the rest lie fallow. Rights over resting land are well established and a woman cannot use another's fallow without express permission. On her death, or in the infirmity of old age, a woman's land is taken over by her daughters if, after marriage, they live nearby; but most of it is taken by sons' wives as they come to live at the homestead. Small informal parties of co-wives and neighbors cooperate in the work of digging up each other's fields immediately after the onset of the rains. Then each woman plants, tends the growing crop, and harvests it on her own land. Over nine tenths of the crop is sorghum, which is best suited to the erratic rainy season and low rainfall. The remainder is finger millet (for beer) and tiny "luxury" crops of tobacco, peanuts, and gourds planted around the homestead. Each wife stores the produce of her own fields in large granary baskets in her own courtyard, and uses it as she herself sees fit—mainly, of course, to feed herself, her children, and her husband. Some of it, at her discretion, she may give to kinswomen in need, or she may use it in barter for small items she requires. She also makes beer occasionally and, nowadays, she profits from any cash sale of this.

The sorghum yield under simple hoe cultivation is low even in good years, for this is marginal country for cereal production. Occasionally there is an almost complete failure, but even in moderately good years sorghum supplies frequently do not last until the following harvest without stringent rationing. And yet scarcely a day passes when cereal porridge is not a main food in the homesteads, although it is variably augmented by milk, blood, some meat, and (in the rainy season) wild vegetables and fruits gathered in the bush.

TRADE

The additional grain needed is regularly obtained from neighboring agricultural peoples to the west: especially the Labwor, the southwestern neighbors, but also the Acoli, Lango, and Ngiangeya. It is acquired by barter: hides and skins, milk, butter, meat, small stock, and sometimes male calves. Men are chiefly responsible for this trade, which occurs mainly toward the end of the dry season and in the early wet season when Jie provisions and milk supplies are at their lowest. Each Jie man has one or more bond-friends among those peoples with whom he maintains a trading relationship. He obtains grain directly from his bond-friend, or uses him as an intermediary with fellow members of the tribe who have produce available. About one third of the men are likely to be away from the homesteads on barter expeditions at any time after the middle of the dry season.

The Jie also trade with the Labwor to obtain ironware (spears, knives, hoe blades, ornaments, bells), pots, and gourds. Still mainly by barter, this trade is conducted directly with the Labwor specialists in their own centers, or as they occasionally make trading journeys. These specialists are also often suppliers of cloth and beads (the remaining external needs of the Jie), although nowadays these articles are available in one or two local stores (alien-owned) in Jieland. Thus the Labwor barter trade is doubly important to the Jie because of the inadequacy of their agriculture and the poverty of their material culture, which contains no ironmaking and almost no potmaking.

MATERIAL CULTURE

On the other hand, Jie are able to provide themselves with a sufficient range of utensils for domestic and dairying purposes by the use of wood and leather—wooden troughs and bowls, leather and wood bottles, cups and jars, leather bags. Cowhide is used for thongs and thread, sandals, mats, and covers. Women continue to dress the skins of goats, sheep, and calves for their skirts and cloaks, although almost all the men have taken to calico cloth cloaks when they wear clothing at all. There are no drums or musical instruments. The main aesthetic expression occurs in the beaded decorations on women's clothing, in personal adornment with beads, wire, and fine wirework, and the fashioning of the horns of their oxen.

Traditionally, Jie men have gone naked, older men wearing a leather cover on the back. Nowadays most men wear a cloth cloak, but commonly this is thrown back over the shoulders, for the covering of nudity is still regarded with some suspicion. Few young or middle-aged men go far from home without their pair of long spears; invariably a man carries a stout stick and his wooden stool-headrest. Uninitiated men allow their hair to grow uncut, and they fashion it into a large bun that sticks out at the back of the head. Sisal string, dyed red, is wounded around this to give the appearance of a fez. After initiation a man wears a rather smaller bun covered with gray clay, which falls on the nape of the neck. The hair above the fore-head is covered with a mudded plate stretching from ear to ear, and decorated in six or eight different colored ochres. In both the mudded bun and the head plate small holes are made into which ostrich feathers can be set on festive occasions. Older men wear an intricate metal waistband; younger men wear bead necklets, earrings, and armlets; ivory armbands and lip plugs are common.

Unlike western Nilotic peoples women and girls never go naked. Girls wear a rather shapeless back-skirt and a short apron suspended from the waist. A wife's skirt is more elaborate: the hair is left on the animal skin and the skirt is flared and gored all around. A leather cloak is worn over the shoulders unless the woman is busily working. The hair is fashioned into a mass of ringlets, though the head is shaved above the ears, and some bead necklets and sometimes a metal or an ivory lip plug completes the ensemble.

KINSHIP ORGANIZATION

THE HOMESTEAD

In its physical construction, a Jie homestead is a series of contiguous enclosed yards roughly in the shape of a horseshoe, with the width of the open end—the entrance—varying according to the number of yards. In the middle of the homestead is an open space for one or more cattle and goat kraals. Although there may be some irregularity in the time and standard of construction and of the consequent abutment of yards, in general there is the appearance of a continuous, curving fence, whether viewed from outside or within the central kraal area. The fences are made of stout, tightly packed palisades six to eight feet high, with tiny doorways about three feet square leading into each yard from either side. This solid construction used to be necessary, say Jie, to safeguard the homestead against enemy raiders, but it serves a persisting purpose in making decisively clear the exclusive identity of the group of people within the fence.

Typically the homestead is the residence of an extended family. Ideally this comprises a group of men who are the descendants of one grandfather, together with their wives, sons, sons' wives and children, and unmarried sisters and daughters. On the average a homestead contains six to eight adult men, and about the same number of yards—thirty to forty people. There still exist some of the larger homesteads of traditional type that contain several extended families, all the members of one clan, the residents of which may number up to one hundred or more in fifteen or twenty yards. On the other hand, some extended families have now become divided residentially so that only some portion, two or three yards, occupies a single homestead.

Each yard is the household and home of a wife and her children. An unmarried mother, or a married daughter who has not yet gone to live with her husband, has her own small yard made by cutting off a corner of her mother's yard. On coming to her husband's homestead a wife has the right to her own yard (initially prepared for her by his womenfolk) and is responsible for maintaining its fences and keeping the bare earth floor clean and hard. In each yard is a small beehive-shaped house whose grass thatch scarcely rises above the fence and reaches more or less to the ground. It is used only for sleeping and for shelter during a storm—a simple, dark room with no window and a tiny doorway entered only on hands and knees. Another small hut, with rather higher walls and larger doorway, shelters the calves at night and often serves as a temporary kitchen in wet weather, though some women build an extra, open-sided hut for that purpose. Generally, cooking is done on an open fire at one side of the yard, and nearby, often hung on the fence, are cooking pots, bowls, gourds, and other domestic utensils. Each wife has several granary baskets of woven saplings (men's work) and shaped like gigantic pots about six feet tall, mudded, and mounted on low platforms.

THE HOUSE

The word *ekal* is used by Jie for both the physical yard and the group consisting of a wife and her children whose home it is. The yard in its social sense is, however, but a dependent unit within a larger, autonomous group. This is the "house"—again using the word in its social meaning—that is founded by a set of full brothers. Like a yard, a house focuses on a single mother, and Jie see the origin of a house in an earlier yard. The house contains all the yards established by the brothers' wives. Usually, though not invariably, all the yards of a house occupy a single segment of the family homestead, and often each house has its own kraals for its livestock. The house is vitally important in Jie society because it is the stock-owning and controlling unit, and it consistently acts as an integrated whole in its relations with the rest of the extended family and the outside world.

It is perhaps easiest to indicate the particular nature of the Jie house by saying that there is no domestic or nuclear family within it. Although a man may eat and sleep in his wife's yard he is not a member of it, for that is a subunit founded by her with her children. Structurally speaking, a child is the offspring of a house, rather than of a particular father, but he is marked off from his half brothers and cousins by maternal origin. He recognizes a group of fathers—his physiological father and the latter's full brothers—and ultimate authority comes from the eldest of these. The real father's death does not affect a son's status and social role so long as his father's full brother remains alive. A son commonly prefers his real father before the others, and a man takes a greater interest in his sons than in the sons of his brothers. He may well support his sons against his nephews, but he is limited in this because of his obligations to his brothers and the overriding unity of the house.

The Jie themselves think of a house primarily as the group of full brothers under the acknowledged leadership of the eldest, and they attach greater importance to the unity (in residence, cooperation, mutuality, and amity) of full brothers than to any other relationship. It represents the fundamental moral premise to these people and is directly connected with the control of a herd of livestock. A man does not possess a herd independently, but only in concert with his brothers. The leadership of the senior brother is chiefly exercised in relation to the administration and use of this herd that the house inherited as a group. Animals may not be used for any purpose whatever without at least the tacit approval of the senior brother, and it is he who formally accepts or disburses gifts of animals on behalf of the house. Younger brothers, even when old men, leave it to their senior to conduct transactions, although they do not refrain from influencing him in such matters. Ideally, and commonly in practice, the head of a house should manage the herd in the best interests of his juniors and the whole group; but so pronounced is the emphasis laid on his status that he can sometimes take advantage of it to act in his own interests and the possible detriment of the rest.

The preeminent unity of the house is generally reinforced by considerable affection among the brothers, which often goes to the extent of self-denial in the others' interests. These men spend a good deal of their time in each other's company. Even the more autocratic senior brothers continually consult with their juniors and are much influenced by their opinions and personal interests. Even where, nowadays, some extended families have become residentially divided, and where tensions and quarrels are common, it is exceedingly unusual when full brothers do not live together in a single homestead. It requires a catastrophe to cause this and even then is universally condemned by Jie. In other cases authority of the senior brother is sufficient to override potential dissension. This authority is buttressed by certain ritual prerogatives he exercises on behalf of the group, and by the belief that supernatural retribution follows deliberate flouting of his decisions. But despite this, the fundamental integrity of a house lies in its moral value, the values of cooperation, and the joint inheritance and use of the common herd.

Because of this joint ownership some conflict may occur over the divergent aspirations of the brothers and—when they become adult—their sons. Clearly one brother cannot plan to use many of the cattle for his son's marriage while another hopes to do the same for his son and a third is anxious to acknowledge and improve his relations with outside kinsmen by making a number of gifts of animals. There is an established regulation of the various claims and needs of different members, and here the control of the senior brother is paramount. There are two major allocations of the house's herds: for domestic economic purposes (as described below) and for bridewealth. Since a house must find about twenty cattle for each bridewealth this is a great strain on resources: not only can a house not tolerate the marriages of two members at the same time, other claims against the herd must be tempered by marriage needs and the necessity to leave enough animals to retain the nucleus of a herd and to ensure some milk. Allocation of animals for bridewealth, and therefore permission to marry, is made in strict order of seniority: first, by order of age among the full brothers; second, by a set order among their sons In this matter the wives (and thus their yards) of the full brothers are ranked by the order of their marriages. Sons of a single mother are ranked in order of birth. Then, as between sons of different mothers, where the difference in age is not large (less than about five years) the son of the senior yard has seniority over his half brother or cousin irrespective of age; where the difference in age is larger (more than five years or so) the older son is given seniority irrespective of yard ranking. Within a generation, men should marry in order of seniority; and a man should not marry a second time until all his juniors have married once, although this is sometimes ignored when no unmarried peer is of an age to marry. Sometimes, too, the senior full brother may take advantage of his position to marry again before a younger one—even though he is old enough to marry—takes a first wife.

LIVESTOCK DISTRIBUTION IN THE HOUSE

As far as outsiders are concerned, the group of full brothers controls its own single herd of animals. Within the house, although ultimate control remains with the brothers, many of the animals are allocated to particular wives and their children (that is, to yards) for domestic purposes. When a wife comes to live at her husband's homestead, to establish her new yard she is allocated a number of cows from the main herd, usually an ox or two, some small stock, and perhaps a donkey. The brothers retain a reserve of animals that are not allocated to any wife.

Domestic allocation to yards does not affect the legal and pastoral unity of the herd and transfers only limited rights and responsibilities to a wife and her yard. Adult animals, after allocation, remain in the central kraal and are herded and watered with the rest. Each wife has both the responsibility and the right to milk the animals attached to her yard (to obtain food for herself and her children) and to care for them (for example, to remove ticks). When animals are received by the house, as in bridewealth, each yard should receive a share. When the house makes a payment, animals are taken from each yard as determined by the full brothers, although the yard of a son who marries surrenders a few more than do the others. A wife herself cannot dispose of animals allocated to her yard.

On the other hand, there is a gradual, intensifying differentiation within a house as the founding full brothers grow older, and especially as their sons reach adulthood. As sons grow up they come increasingly to think of the yard's allocation as "our animals," in contrast to those of half brothers and cousins. Adult sons, therefore, begin to chafe when stock are taken for the benefit of men of another yard. There is an emotional aspect to this, for at least some of the animals have been tended as calves in the yard and cared for as they mature. The animals are bound up with the strong attachment to the mother by Jie sons who, even as young men, spend much of their leisure time in her yard.

Above all, there is their developing awareness that, sooner or later, when their fathers all die, they, the sons of one yard, will become the founders of a new house separate from their peers' houses. From early adulthood, sons' aspirations are strongly conditioned by the promise of ultimate autonomy. Other centrifugal forces are the separate matrilateral ties and, in due course, the separate affinal kin of each yard. Rivalry among yards is common, though it may be reduced by interpersonal affections that cut across yard lines, and by their fathers' attempts to preserve unity. Yet it is inevitable that sets of full brothers should diverge because of the practical and moral emphasis which the Jie sedulously give to the special unity of such men.

THE HOUSE LINE

It is only when the last of the fathers the founding full brothers—dies that their house dies. Until then, even though sons are mature, married adults, they remain subject to their seniors. After that each yard becomes a new, autonomous house. Strictly speaking, it is the set of full brothers who, with their wives and children, make a new house, but both the mother and their unmarried full sisters belong temporarily. At the death of the last surviving father, the single herd is divided and inherited by each successor house. Each new house takes the animals that were formerly only allocated to it—this is straightforward and rarely causes dispute. Any unallocated reserve of the old herd is then divided by the rule that the more junior houses should get a larger share, the more senior a smaller share. Jie justify this on the grounds that the more senior a yard is (and therefore usually the older the men in it), the more chance they will already have had to use animals for bridewealth.

The group of houses that together are the successors to a former single house may be called a house line. Jie themselves see this as the male patrilineal descendants (and their wives) of a common grandmother, and they use the same word—*ekal*—as for a yard and a house.

With the completion of inheritance and the simultaneous recognition of the full autonomy of the successor houses, the former rights and obligations between half brothers and cousins also come to an end. Each new house becomes principally concerned with husbanding its own herd for the benefit of its own members. But a house cannot normally afford to exist quite independently: few houses have the resources to make up a full bridewealth; hence, although other kinsmen are asked for help, it is to near agnates in other houses that men look first. In the early days after the dissolution of the old house, its former members still feel closer to one another than to other members of the extended family. Their past association and their division of the former single herd continue to be powerful factors. Thus, although the seniority order of marriage is no longer enforceable, it still guides men's actions. It is still thought that men *should* marry in that order, and any attempt to avoid it is likely to be disapproved in a practical manner: other houses may refuse to contribute cattle for the bridewealth of one who seeks to ignore precedence. There is a vital idea, too, that every man has the firm right to marry once, and to gain assistance to do so. But when some men begin to prepare to take a second wife conflict sets in, for men of other houses may desire to use their herds for their own additional marriages, (and other purposes also, of course) rather than assist the ambitions of others.

The autonomy of a house and the tendency of houses to conflict is here explained in terms of marriage and bridewealth payments, because that is how the Jie themselves perceive it. Marriage and the procreation of children are the main way of developing a house and account for the major nondomestic use of animals. The problems of gathering bridewealth are raised early each wet season—the time for negotiating marriages—and each successive year tends to show a growth of rivalry among houses, and increasing unwillingness on the part of each to give as generously as before to the others. Half brothers and cousins cannot refuse outright to assist a man and his house by denying the agnatic obligations to contribute to his bridewealth: such a refusal would be morally indefensible, and would invite isolation from the rest of the extended family. It is explicitly recognized that agnates should assist one another, both as a duty and in return for similar assistance, past or future. There is no authority whatsoever to compel these obligations, but the practical values of reciprocal assistance are self-evident to Jie. These obligations do not only concern bridewealth, for a house needs assistance and support at other times, both in livestock and otherwise.

Over a period of years, and by trial and error, relations among houses in the new house line come to find a rough balance at a level both tolerable and yet valuable to each house and every one separately. This level is not necessarily quite the same for each pair of houses in the house line, though Jie say that a "proper" bridewealth contribution is three to four cattle. Considerations of friendliness and trust, or alternatively of hostility and rivalry, clearly affect the situation. Houses with larger herds or fewer demands on them may be able to give more generously and therefore to make heavier demands in return. In any event, the Jie are specific that the principal factor is reciprocity—the idea of helping another house as much as that house helps yours. Jie are quite prepared to concede that at a particular time the state of a house's herds and the other legitimate claims of all kinds against the herds may prevent the men from giving as many animals as they had received earlier. But Jie stress not only the number of animals but the spirit of generosity that impels the gift. On the other hand, a house that is chronically unable to match the gifts it receives begins to find that assistance to it diminishes after a time.

THE EXTENDED FAMILY

A number of house lines make up the extended family. The *ideology* is that each line originates with a grandmother, and that all these grandmothers were the wives of the common grandfather who founded the family. This conception is associated with the notion that, although now separate stockowners, each of the constituent houses has acquired a part of the grandfather's original herd as that has been passed on by his sons to his grandsons and their children. Thus genealogical identity is reinforced by the exclusiveness of the family's herds. What is of practical importance, however, is the pattern of continuous cooperation, common residence in the homestead, relatively heavy commitment to mutual assistance in livestock, and the everyday contacts and interests that exist between the various houses of the extended family. There is usually a good deal of pastoral cooperation, for relatively few houses have both enough animals and enough youths and young men to tend them so that they can be entirely independent in day-to-day management. If the men of a house are unwilling to cooperate with other houses, they may be able to share a camp with, for example, a matrilaterally linked house; but Jie prefer if possible to restrict cooperation in these matters to their agnates who, they feel, are likely to be more trustworthy and also more easily kept under surveillance.

Conflict among houses is not uncommon, but it tends to be most marked among men of fairly new houses—that is, before a modus vivendi is reached between them. Among more mature houses, whose senior members are, of course, older men, the major emphasis is on collaboration for recognized mutual benefit, for such men have no longer to insist on their autonomy, which has come to be taken for granted.

THE KINSHIP NETWORK AND STOCK-ASSOCIATES

Each Jie man stands at the center of a particular network of formal, personal relations with certain other men. Some of these relations are established by birth (patrilateral and matrilateral kin), some by marriage—his own and those of his sisters and daughters (affinal kin), and some by deliberate pledge (bond-friends). A man looks to these people for friendship, sympathy, advice, and affection. He often visits them and he gives hospitality and assistance to them. More than this, they are the people with whom he maintains reciprocal rights to claim gifts of animals in times of need. While never neglecting the initial basis of the relationship—kinship—Jie always lay greatest stress on the exchanges of livestock at such times as marriage, shortage of milking animals, the desire for a particular kind of ox or goat, or the need to pay a judicial fine or to provide a specified animal for ritual purposes. For that reason I refer to these men as "stock-associates." A Jie refers to them collectively as "my people," but they do not form a corporate group since they act with respect to a particular individual, and seldom at all together. Every man is a stock-associate, in differing ways of course, to a number of men. Apart from his agnatic kin within the extended family, no two men's associates are quite the same—not even those of two full brothers who share the same matrilateral kin but have different affinal kin and bond-friends.

Jie recognize two kinds of stock-associates: those with whom reciprocal rights involve cattle, and those involving only small stock. In the first category come all agnatic kin, mother's full brothers and their sons, close affines (fathers and brothers of wives and sons' wives, sisters' and daughters' husbands and their brothers), and bond-friends. In the second category are more distant maternal and affinal kin and clansmen. The distinction is not precise and depends on the particular conventions established, but usual practice works out like that. The nature of reciprocal rights has already been discussed in connection with interhouse relations in the extended family, and the same general principles apply

in the case of other kin. In emphasizing the rights and obligations over animals, I am following Jie conceptions. I do not wish to ignore the many other kinds of assistance or affections, but, like the Jie, I stress the most vital aspects of the relationships.

Jie explain the potentialities of stock-association by saying that where animals have once passed a path is made along which other animals can travel in either direction. The initial path between agnates is created by inheritance; the passage of animals in bride-wealth establish future rights on each side between affinal kin and, in the subsequent generation, between a man and his matrilateral kin. With his mother's full brothers in particular a man feels especially warm affection and strong links. Friendly equality typifies relations between brothers-in-law, but a wife's father has a more distant and superior status.

Bond-friends are not kinsmen, though relations with them have a pseudo-kinship quality, setting those men off from unrelated persons. Essentially bond-friendship rests on an informal contract in which the element of reciprocity is paramount. Beginning usually in ordinary friendship, the two men agree to accept claims by each against the other for gifts of livestock. No formal pact is made—no witnessed agreement nor ritual act. A man is able by this means to extend the range of his stock-associates deliberately. Many of these bonds persist through a lifetime, and some are even inherited by the originators' sons; others founder as one of the men defaults, voluntarily or not, in his obligations against rights received. Most men continue to seek new bond-friendships—a wealthier man finds it easier, a poor one more difficult. Older men have at least one or two bond-friends outside their country, not only to gain rights there, but also in order to ensure a center of security and hospitality if travel is necessary. And every Jie man has a bond-friend in Labwor, and often other trading areas too, with whom he maintains the valuable barter relations previously described.

MARRIAGE AND BRIDEWEALTH

The significance of Jie marriage is twofold. First, there is union between a man and woman, leading to the procreation of children and their upbringing in a new unit (the yard) founded by their mother in the father's house; and second, vital affinal links are created between the husband and his wife's fathers and brothers, and between the close agnates of both parties. These conscious aims are accomplished over a period of not less than five years during which time the woman gradually advances from betrothed girl, to bride wife, to full wife; and affinal ties are progressively strengthened as the men change from relative strangers to close associates. In one way this period is measured by the rule that a wife does not shift to her husband's homestead and become a full wife and a member of his extended family until she has reared two children to the walking stage. Until then she remains at her father's homestead. In a different but related way, the period covers a number of chronological, ritual stages creating and strengthening the marriage, the fertility of the woman and the affinal link, and these culminate in her formal incorporation into her husband's family.

Wives become full members of their husbands' family, and they automatically lose membership in their natal group. They are little involved in the cooperative pastoral arrangements of their men, but, living in the same homestead, women cooperate in their own activities: expeditions to collect firewood or thatching grass, to gather wild fruits in the bush, to fetch water from a distant watering place in the dry season. Co-wives commonly form the nucleus of hoeing parties at cultivation time, and they accompany one another to the fields when going to work. There is a good deal of sharing and borrowing of food and utensils, and joining in leisure activities.

Marriage rules are straightforward: a man cannot marry a girl of his own clan (see below), nor of the clans of his mother, mother's mother, or father's mother. No man would receive help in building up a bridewealth or performing rituals were he to attempt to ignore these rules. But equally important in Jie eyes is the common-sense prohibition on marriage into a house that is already affinally linked to one's own. To do this would only confuse the reciprocal stock rights existing between the two houses, and it would also foolishly waste the opportunity to extend the range of kinship and stock-association. But most Jie prefer not to marry into any extended family with which there are even remote affinal links already. Other than this, there are neither prohibitions nor preferences in the choice of a wife: a man seeks the girl of his choice, subject to the approval of his father and hers.

Marriage is legalized by the transfer of bridewealth from the groom to the bride's kinsmen. An average bridewealth consists of about fifty cattle and one hundred small stock, and most of these are handed over on the day of the wedding, the remainder following very soon after. The house of the groom provides about twenty of the cattle; the rest are contributed by his various stock-associates, to each of whom he goes to gain approval of the marriage and to seek a gift of animals. Perhaps fifty people or more contribute in this way. On the receiving side, the animals are distributed among the stock-associates of the bride's father, his house retaining about twenty cattle. Other than the rare compensation payments for homicide or adultery, the transfer of brideweath (a common event each rainy season) is the most important occasion for the exercise of stock rights.

The size of bridewealth is a matter for negotiation between a man and his prospective father-in-law. The only prescription is that a man should give according to his ability—that is, the size of his house's herd and the number of his associates. This a Jie always attempts to do, both as a matter of prestige and in order to create the most favorable conditions for the new affinal bonds. Hard bargaining over the animals is quite antipathetic to Jie notions, for it seems to them irreconcilable with subsequent relations.

The transfer of brideweath gives the husband marital rights over his wife, but these are not wholly acquired in practice until she comes to live with him permanently as a full wife. All children she bears belong to his house and agnatic line, and they automatically gain rights in the herd and claims to support. But, say Jie, bridewealth alone cannot make a marriage: the subsequent ritual stages are essential for that. The whole marriage is completed when the wife and her first two children are ritually led through the main entranceway (the cattle entrance) into her husband's homestead.

There is no other form of marriage among the Jie. Divorce is so rare that I was unable to obtain full information on a genuine case. A widow does not remarry, but remains the wife of the dead husband. She may accept another man, preferably from her husband's house or at least an agnate, as pro-husband, but any children she bears by him are reckoned as members of their mother's yard within her husband's house.

CHILD TRAINING AND SOCIALIZATION

A Jie mother and father, and their adult kinsfolk, show unreserved affection toward babies and small children. Adults are markedly permissive toward them and rarely (ideally, never) are children chastised physically or verbally for their behavior. Jie say that small children have little sense and that they mean no wrong in what they do; therefore it would be wrong to punish them. Thus, if a small boy chases a calf round the kraal, causing commotion among the animals and perhaps upsetting utensils, and so on, he is the object only of tolerant amusement, to be picked up and put out of harm's way.

There is, however, a radical change as a boy grows older. By the age of about seven he is expected to begin helping with the herding of young animals around the homestead; and soon after he accompanies an elder brother or cousin with the dairy herd, which is absent all day from the homestead. Mothers now have

little to do with the training of their sons, and fathers become sharply disciplinarian toward them. The boy-herder who loses a goat is likely to be beaten rather severely; he who is clumsy in dealing with the animals is verbally castigated. When they get a little older (say, about eleven years) most boys spend much of their time in camps, away from the homestead and continuous parental control. Then they learn mainly from their peers and immediate seniors on terms of friendly equality. The particular timing of these stages for a boy depends on the need for herding labor and the supply of herdboys available in his house. Mothers are usually warmly affectionate toward their sons, but are separated from them in activities and interests (and often in residence) for long periods.

There is no corresponding change in the upbringing of girls. They remain continuously with their mothers until several years after marriage, as noted above, and gradually learn and share more and more of a woman's conventional work at home and in the field. A daughter might be beaten by an exasperated mother, but not often and not heavily. Fathers have little to do with their daughters' training. By puberty a girl should be capable of doing all of a woman's tasks and she is probably already cultivating her own arable plots more or less independently of her mother.

TERRITORIAL ORGANIZATION

As described already, the main part of Jieland consists of communal pastures where there is no permanent settlement. The settled area, about ninety square miles, is roughly in the center of the country. This area is divided into seven named districts, each containing a number of settlements that themselves comprise a number of clan-hamlets. The boundaries between these residential groups are not visible on the ground, and often there is a more or less continuous stretch of homesteads. The Jie cannot indicate specific boundary lines, but they are perfectly aware to which group any homestead belongs since determination of this is sociologically well established. These units at whatever level are groups of people kept together by important moral, economic, ritual, and general cooperative ties. Nevertheless, each unit is in effect a discrete territorial entity, and there is no geographical intermingling of the homesteads of two or more.

THE CLAN-HAMLET

The clan-hamlet contains all the members of a single clan: that is, the males born into it patrilineally, their unmarried sisters and daughters, and their wives and mothers who have been ritually incorporated into it on becoming full wives. Each clan, of course, is made up of a number of extended families, but in no case can the people trace any kind of genealogical link between these families. There is usually a dogmatic assertion of forgotten patrilineal links, but Jie see no particular importance in this and are content to affirm common clanship.

The clan is exogamous, and therefore there are no affinal links between members. To each clan are ascribed certain specific procedures that its members must follow in their ritual activities. The general pattern of Jie rituals (concerning marriage, death, illness, and so on) is common to all the people, but it is modified in its detailed observation by these clan prescriptions. Concomitant with this is the necessity for all (or at least as many as conveniently possible) of the clan members to participate in the clan-determined rituals of any of its families. In fact, differences in the ritual prescriptions of different clans are usually quite small, and they never affect the more significant acts; but for the Jie the minutiae of ritual observance are quite essential for efficacious results, and they perceive these distinctions between clans as crucial.

THE SETTLEMENT

Although because of the closeness of the homesteads to one another, there is much cooperation, gossip, and joint leisure activity among members of the hamlet, nevertheless this day-to-day and face-to-face contact is extended to all members of the same settlement. The hamlets of a settlement are located close together—perhaps strung along a low bridge—so that everyday contacts are easy and frequent. One or two settlements contain a single clan (clan-hamlet), but most comprise two or three hamlets, and some have four or five. There is no explanation why the constituent clans should be united in one settlement, though changes seem not to occur: there is no notion of putative kinship, nor is any clan considered to be superior to the rest. Exogamy does not extend beyond the clan, and therefore a network of affinal and matrilateral links reinforces the useful relations of neighborliness between families of different clans.

The men of a settlement associate together in all their informal activities, as well as in formal matters such as ritual. There are usually two or three popular shade trees where men collect to gossip and carry on their handicrafts, and where they can discuss their problems with friendly confidence. These men, and their wives also, know each other's lives intimately. The women only rarely gather together, but there is much visiting between homesteads as well as informal cooperation, such as collecting firewood or carrying water. Most of the arable land of the women lies in and around the settlement. There are no set boundaries within which women of a settlement must find their fields, and it is not unusual that the arable lands of adjacent settlements intermingle. But the Jie are able roughly to indicate the general cultivated area of each settlement, and often that area is identified by the use of the settlement name. When the dairy herds are at the homesteads, all or some of the men arrange a cooperative herding schedule, and they arrange to meet and help each other at watering time.

The sense of unity of a settlement is demonstrated by its possession of a rainy-season pond and a ritual grove. The pond is located in some dip in the land where water naturally collects and often a small dam wall is maintained to prevent runoff. The pond is cleaned when it has dried out, usually just before the rainy season, by the joint labor of all the men. It is used both for domestic supplies and for watering animals, and groups of youths and men gather there to bathe. Apart from pools left after a storm, there are no natural water supplies in the center of Jieland, and the maintenance of these ponds makes it unnecessary for people to go to one of the few streams that flow in the rainy season. Each settlement is therefore self-sufficient but responsible for its seasonal water supply. Members of one settlement do not take their livestock to the pond of another settlement when their own dries up, but must go to the only permanent watering place that lies beyond the western limits of the settled area.

The ritual grove of a settlement is a small clump of trees and bush adjacent to the homesteads. It is considered a sacrilege to cut these trees, which often are almost the only ones standing in the bare land created by agricultural clearing and heavy grazing. At the grove all rituals are performed that affect the settlement as a whole (rainmaking, warding off disease and misfortune, and so on), and also those public rituals of resident families that contain a regard for the welfare of the settlement even though chiefly concerning the particular family. The settlement is the primary *ritual* unit for the Jie, for even family rituals (whose specific form is determined by clan membership) are performed by members of the whole settlement under the leadership of the most senior male. Neighbors are therefore not only dependent on one another for their general welfare, but also for the efficacy of the rituals that personally affect them in life's crises. Since the Jie have a rich body of rituals, this means that the settlement is frequently assembling as a corporate group for purposive activity. It includes not only the ritual performance itself, but involves also the commensal feast from the slaughtered animal. This provides the main source of meat, for Jie do not approve of the slaughter of beasts merely for eating.

THE DISTRICT

A district is made up of several contiguous settlements; unlike the settlement, it is not a unit of everyday and general cooperation and contact, nor do members of different settlements have so close a knowledge of and concern for each other. Today the district is principally a ritual group; formerly it was important also as a military unit in that each had its own war leader and contributed its own contingent under that leader to the Jie offensive army. This no longer applies, although the memory of it persists and serves to activate a district (rather than the tribe or the individual settlements) in its relations with the central government.

The district is mainly concerned now with the rainmaking rituals, which are described later. But as an entity it also has responsibility at certain stages of the marriage process. Occasionally the district assembles in a ritual attempt to combat the more severe threats to social life—human and animal epidemics, locusts, and so on. Each district has its own ritual grove, separate from those of its settlements. In view of the ritual importance of the age group system, it is logical that the district is the major unit for its organization, as explained below.

THE TRIBE

The whole tribe, comprising the seven districts, is also significantly a ritual group, and there are at least three tribal groves at one or other of which tribal assemblies are held twice a year. In addition to this crucial activity, the Jie are markedly conscious of their tribal identity in a number of ways. The tribe was the largest unit of internal peace, except for the *Pax Britannica*, under the British protectorate. It is therefore a grave offense—and one believed to affect rainfall and fertility adversely—for one Jie to kill another, whether by intent or not. Homicide must be dealt with by compensation payment of livestock and by ritual purification; lesser offenses also have their limits at the tribal boundaries and should similarly be treated by regular judicial procedures. To kill a non-Jie, to take his cattle, or to seduce his daughter is not, by Jie evaluations, a crime or a sin; in fact, it is thought rather admirable. But Jie accept these as offenses nowadays insofar as the central government can compel them to do so. Finally, the tribe is recognized by its communal possession of the pasture lands, from which non-Jie are excluded.

Beyond the tribe and tribal land the Jie world reaches little more than thirty or forty miles. Beyond that there are few or no contacts and little interest in or knowledge about even the countries of their immediate neighbors. Peoples living farther off, even though culturally related (for example, the Teso of central Uganda), are but vaguely recognized. The local center of the government is some sixty miles from central Jieland (at Moroto in Karamajong country), and Jie are lightly administered. They have a poor understanding of this alien power except as it impinges directly on them at home through irregular visits of officials and through decisions of the local, appointed chief.

THE AGE GROUP SYSTEM

Among most Nilotic (or Nilo-Hamitic) peoples an age group system is of primary social importance, though there are many crucial differences between the various systems. That of the Jie is somewhat exceptional because it has only marginal significance in the political, judicial, or economic life of the people. Almost exclusively it provides the organizational basis for the performance of their communal rituals in two principal ways: first, it establishes the ritual efficacy of adult males through formal initiation in and membership of an age group; and second, by the order of seniority inherent in the system, it provides an established ranking and obligation of leadership at all levels of ritual activity, from the whole tribe down to the extended family. The system is concerned only with males; girls undergo a mild form of initiation but do not form groups, nor are

they able to participate in rituals outside the extended family.

Age Group Structure

All Jie males are ordered into fixed generations so that members of one generation are all the sons of the members of the immediately preceding one, irrespective of age. Usually there are two established generations in existence at any one time: the senior generation, all of whose members are initiated; and the junior generation, some of whose members are still too young to be initiated. Although male babies are considered to be born into a generation, the group of males is not inaugurated, named, and given formal recognition until all the members of the preceding generation have been initiated.

A new generation is publicly established at about twenty-five-year intervals by a ceremony held at a special tribal grove. This event should be administered by surviving members of the generation of grandfathers of the new group because it is necessary that the spiritual power of ritual efficacy be passed on by the old men to their grandsons. This is done by ritual anointing and blessing of the seniormost members of the new generation (the senior grandson of the seniormost member of the grandfathers' generation), who in turn passes the power to the senior man in each district. Later each district's senior man formally gives ritual power to the seniormost man in each new age group in each settlement. This power is therefore passed from the grandfathers and dispersed through the whole of their grandsons' generation; in due course the latter pass it on to their grandsons.

The intervening generations of the fathers of the new generation and, later, that of their sons play no part in this, for generations are linked alternately only. This grandfather-grandson link appears in a number of contexts among the Jie—for example, the whole complex of the extended family is ideologically based on the grandfather, and boys are personally named after a grandfather and obtain an ox-color from him. According to the Jie, the names of age groups are all taken from the grandfathers' generation and in the same order as they occurred there; this is not true in practice, although some of the earlier names are repeated.

The final inclusion of a man into his generation comes with his initiation into an age group. This occurs by the ritual spearing of an ox or he-goat, after which the initiate is anointed with the undigested stomach contents of the animal by the senior member of his settlement. His new ritual status is acknowledged by his participation, together with the other initiated men of his settlement, in a commensal feast of the meat.

When a new generation is permitted to begin initiations, a large number of men, some of whom are at least middle-aged, have had to await the end of initiations in the preceding generation. Thus, a single large group, which necessarily contains a wide age span, is quickly made up in the first year. Thereafter, age group membership gains a more truly coeval basis as males come forward periodically at about the age of eighteen to twenty. Initiations are held only in good rainy seasons —that is, about once in three years. Usually a new group is begun in each initiation year, though this is not essential.

The name of a new group is chosen by the seniormost men of the district, though there is consultation between districts so that most names have a tribe-wide application. As more groups come into being they become gradually arranged into three sets, which are named after the senior age group in each. This is a fairly loose arrangement that recognizes the principal age differences within the total age span of some fifty or more years within the single generation. Men invariably sit in their groups at all rituals, and groups of the same set cluster together. Later, in the senior generation, men tend to think in terms of the set rather than in terms of the age group. The generation itself takes the name of its most senior group, that name having been acquired at the inauguration of the generation at the tribal grove.

The Operation of the Age Group System

In this system relative seniority can easily be calculated between any two Jie men. First, men of one group are all senior to men of a chronologically junior group. Within a group a man is senior to all his fellow members whose fathers were junior to his father in the preceding generation. Seniority is not, then, a matter of physical age.

In communal rituals the age principle determines the patterns of seating and participation. Emphasis is always laid on the primacy of the most senior man of the unit involved. In some settlements, of course, he may perhaps not be a member of the most senior age groups; in others, or in a district, he is likely to be a very old man, often too infirm to do more than make a symbolic appearance, leaving the actual duties to his more active juniors. Senior men arrange rituals, determining the times, the donors of animals, and so on; at the rituals they supervise the proceedings and lead supplications to the High God. Junior men clear the ritual site, prepare branches and leaves for their seniors to sit on, bring firewood, tend the fires, and cook the meat. Men of middle seniority have a more passive role, no longer servants but not yet senior enough to take responsibility—except in their settlement where a smaller number of men are involved.

On ritual occasions, after the completion of the supplications, the meat is ordered to be cooked, and when ready it is distributed by the seniormost man to the age groups seated in order. Within each group, the meat is then distributed by the seniormost member to his juniors in strict order.

At the settlement level, in the small group of everyday cooperation, organizational responsibilities of ritual leadership are not heavy; rituals are arranged and carried out as part of the continuum of neighborhood life. At the district level, responsibilities are greater, for they require the cooperation of men of different settlements who are not in daily contact. It is necessary for the seniormost men of each settlement to meet in order to make arrangements for an assembly, and to ensure that men know what is expected of them. This is the duty of the district's seniormost man or, if he is too old, his immediate juniors. Because the districts are not large, the difficulties are not great; but the locus of responsibility is clearly determined. At the tribal level the problem is more serious, for then it is required to assemble all or most of initiated Jie men at the tribal grove on a certain day. Each district must have adequate warning so that its members may arrange to obtain an ox that they drove to the grove as their offering for ritual slaughter and subsequent feast. That this is successfully accomplished at least twice a year stands as a measure of the leadership pattern provided by the age group system in this noncentralized society, in which politically and economically the small kin and neighborhood groups are autonomous and without direct intercommunication. Because of its central location in the settled area, senior men of the Kotido District tend to act as a clearinghouse for information and arrangements on a tribal basis, irrespective of their particular seniority vis-a-vis the seniormost men of the other districts. This tendency has probably strengthened in recent times with the establishment of the chief's headquarters and the main store center in Jieland in that district, for people visit these from all other districts.

As is true of all men who achieve responsibility and influence in this society, those who by their seniority status begin to exercise ritual leadership begin simultaneously to acquire mystic power from the High God, whose agents they have become. Thus, the propitious grove, the right day, the color of the ritual animal, the name of the new age group are all dictated by the High God to one or more of these men in dreams. Such divine recognition is believed to give the old men sanctity and power. In ritual matters, more junior men should in any case obey their orders on pain of punishment and ritual impurity; but to disobey, say Jie, is also sacrilege against the High God, and it is met by supernatural punishment. A highly senior man should never be offered violence, physically or verbally, and because of this it is claimed that fights and quarrels can be stopped by the physical intervention of these men. Were this generally true, it would give an added political function to the age group

system; in fact, a senior man seldom concerns himself with mundane affairs that do not already affect him in his ordinary role as a kinsman. He may, by virtue of his ritual status, enunciate the accepted moral values of the people on some occasion when they have obviously been contravened. But, even then, he is content to point up the situation and does not himself initiate procedures to redress the matter. When a senior man uses his prestige to stop open violence, he is moved to act in this way primarily because the shedding of blood, or even the threat of it, is thought to prevent rain and spoil ritual efficacy until the pollution is removed.

Although the age group and seniority system is only marginally concerned with the nonritual aspects of Jie public life, it is the only large-scale organization they have. Settlements are united into functioning districts, and these again into the whole tribe, principally by ritual requirements and through the mechanism of the age group system. And although the age group is only a weak corporate group (as compared with some of the Nilotic peoples), nevertheless bonds of friendly equality between members of a group cut across the parochialism of clan and settlement to provide a wider network of personal links than kinship and neighborhood afford. Both district and tribe are significantly defined in ritual terms, but the unity obtained in this way spreads over into nonritual matters to give a general cohesion to the society.

RELIGION AND RITUAL

In such a region of meager and unreliable rainfall, each year's precipitation is of the utmost importance both for crops and for pastures. Jie know well how capricious the rains can be and the disastrous effects of a bad year—perhaps one in five years. Without rain, hunger is a stark reality: the land remains bare and unfruitful; human beings are made miserable and their children suffer; animals get in poor condition and their young are ill-nourished and susceptible to disease. In a moderate or good year, food is plentiful, grass is lush, and animals are in good condition. Rain has therefore come to be directly associated not only with a sufficiency of food, but with the welfare and fertility of the people and their livestock. Rainmaking rituals are consequently of the first importance, aiming not only at plentiful rain itself but also at general welfare and the absence of maleficent influences. The Jie explicitly recognize the necessity for cooperative and coordinated ritual efforts to these supreme ends.

Thus the first of the three main categories of Jie rituals is the annual cycle concerning rainmaking, fertility, and general welfare. In early March, before the rains begin, there is a tribal assembly of initiated men to ensure the coming of the new season and its fruitfulness. This is immediately followed by secondary assemblies in each district separately, both to bring the rain and to keep it when it arrives. If the rains are late or poor, further rituals are held in each settlement. In about June, during the normal dry spell between the May and July rainfall peaks, a second tribal ceremony occurs to bring back the rains and to seek good harvests, and this again is followed up by district rituals. In July, approximately, all initiated men and all livestock of each district assemble at their district's grove, where they are blessed and strengthened as the turn of the year is marked when all herds are finally in eastern pastures. Toward harvest time, rituals are performed in each settlement either to give thanks to the High God for good rains and abundant crops, or as a last-minute attempt to gain amelioration of a poor year. During the following dry season each district holds one or two assemblies to maintain contact with the High God, and to prepare the way for the next rainy season. On any of these occasions, should particular troubles have arisen (for example, a cattle epidemic), special attention is given to them in the ritual.

Second, a number of ad hoc rituals are aimed at promoting some particular public interest, or at preventing or mitigating impending misfortune. The opening of a new generation, the kindling of new fire when general misfortunes accumulate, or the prevention of an epidemic—all call for rituals at tribal and distinct levels—often followed up by lesser assemblies as each settlement attempts to safeguard its own special interests. At that level, too, there are occasional rituals to deal with local misfortune or threats to welfare—damage by fire or by the dust devil, violence in the settlement, witchcraft, and so on.

Third, there is the series of rituals connected with the marriage process. Although these are mainly of a private nature, all are performed by the initiated men of the settlement of husband or wife. One or two of them also require the attendance of initiated men of the district, although occurring in the homestead or at the settlement grove.

There are specified acts and observances in all these kinds of ritual, especially marked in those concerning marriage, but their main feature consists of appeals and requests to the High God, *Akuj*, who lives in the sky, where he has a vast homestead and huge herds. He is wholly a power for good, but chronically careless of human beings unless constantly exhorted; above all, he controls the rain. Although not thought of as the source of morals, he may punish wrongdoers, particularly if their disapproved conduct is brought to his notice by responsible or senior Jie.

At a ritual assembly, supplications are made by a leader, supported by the chorus of the other men present. The seniormost man present, holding a ritual wand, stands in the open space inside the cluster of seated men; he addresses *Akuj* directly, explaining the reason for the assembly and seeking benevolent assistance. Interspersed in the monologue are communal supplications led by the standing man, in which his specific pleas (for example, for rain, or for the fertility of a new wife) are echoed by the others' chorus. After the seniormost man, other seniors in turn take up the leadership. When a man begins to assume this role with the approval of his more senior associates he has achieved notable seniority.

The reinforcement of the role of a ritual leader by his recognition by the High God has been noted; the same reinforcement occurs in respect to the head of a family or of a house and, formerly, a war leader. Modern chiefs and headmen are not thought to have this supernatural support. In particular the High God gives power to diviners, one or two of whom live in each district. A diviner is visited by the High God in his dreams and given instructions on how to act and what agents to use to accomplish beneficent ends. Diviners are also skilled in the reading of entrails of ritually slaughtered animals in order to foretell the future and diagnose the past. They have some knowledge of herbs, but they tend to lay most emphasis on magical and ritual acts to effect cures and stimulate good fortune. They are able to detect witches and provide protection against them. Occasionally a diviner announces, by divine revelation, that a certain settlement or district must perform specified rituals in order to combat threatened misfortune. A diviner himself does not conduct rituals, nor does he lead communal supplications; often he does not attend ritual assemblies.

Apart from their beliefs in the High God and their actions relating to him, Jie have only vague ideas about the supernatural. Even he is so remote that he does not impinge on everyday life. There are thought to be witches, and they seem invariably to live in a settlement other than that of the victim. Jie are inclined to attribute death, disease, misfortune, and so on, to failure to reach *Akuj* properly, or to natural causes, rather than to the machinations of their fellowmen; on the other hand, they are inclined to think of non-Jie as powerful witches.

It is in keeping with this generally mundane attitude that Jie have no mystical practices in connection with economic or judicial affairs. Homesteads, camps, and kraals are not ritually established or maintained; cattle in themselves have no spiritual characteristics; agriculture is entirely a practical matter. The people seek to obtain the benevolence of *Akuj* to give favorable conditions (rain, fertility) in which they may apply their technology and their notions of human relations.

JUDICIAL AND POLITICAL AFFAIRS

The Jie have no centralized political system. The limits of kinship are relatively narrow, and beyond the settlement they are more or less peculiar to each individual. Other than in ritual affairs, there are no acknowledged leaders of territorial groups, nor is coercive authority or decision-making responsibility ascribed to specialized roles and particular persons. In modern times, by fiat of the colonial government of Uganda, there was established a chief, with subchiefs and headmen under him; the chief also heads the court of first instance. The authority of these officials is limited largely to the administration of government business—collection of the tax, enforcement of orders and edicts. They have little concern with the public or private affairs of the Jie, nor do the people look to them for responsibility. Although now constrained to accept court jurisdiction in certain major crimes (for example, homicide), Jie remain unwilling to use the courts in regard to their own affairs.

Where an injury is committed against the person, property, or interests of a Jie, it is entirely his own personal responsibility (or that of the head of his house) to initiate steps to obtain restitution, compensation, or other settlement. There are generally accepted norms that describe right behavior and that prescribe legitimate compensation in the case of their contravention. For example, it is commonly said that forty to fifty cattle are payable for homicide, and proportionately less for bodily injury; theft of animals should be compensated by the return of two animals for each one stolen; adultery calls for a fine equal to bridewealth. But these are only generalized norms and there is no one to enforce them in a particular instance.

An injured person often makes a direct contact with the offender and may be able to achieve some redress by moral argument and informal pressure. If the injury is serious, he does not work alone but seeks the support of his stock-associates—those individuals with whom he is personally linked, and who are bound to give him both material and moral assistance. If a man has to pay compensation, he looks to them for contributions of animals. Thus, the two parties to a dispute assemble as many of their associates as possible, and negotiations are held between the two groups. A man who belongs logically to both groups is often able to act as go-between by virtue of his joint acceptability—though the precise value of this service depends on the relative closeness of his bond to either party.

There are various courses open to an accused offender. He, with his associates, may admit to the offense and accept the demand for compensation. This seldom happens. Usually he may admit to the offense, but dispute the size of the compensation demanded. He may, however, deny the offense and thus any claim for compensation. Finally, he may ignore all demands and messages and refuse to recognize the dispute. If offense is admitted, then the two parties can concentrate on negotiating the compensation; this is done at a joint meeting, probably in the offender's settlement, where the whole matter is discussed and assessed and, with good fortune, an agreement reached. Except in the most blatant offenses, it is unusual for the eventual agreement to settle upon as large a compensation as the ideal norm allows, for the injured party must generally be prepared to temper his demands lest he risk further delay or get nothing at all.

Whether the offense is admitted or not, if compensation is denied, the injured party can accept the *fait accompli,* feeling unable or unwilling to do anything else because the difficulties are not commensurate with the gravity of the offense. On the other hand, he may threaten to use force by attacking the offender's homestead and seizing animals or by committing acts of vengeful violence against his person. This kind of threat is intrinsic to the situation; whether or not it is made with real intent depends on estimates of the relative strengths of the two parties and their chances of success. Jie clearly feel that an injured person has the moral right to resort to force if that is the only way open to him to gain a settlement. More peaceful pressures

are also exerted: for example, by using a go-between, by appealing to the need to restore amity in the neighborhood, or by arousing public opinion in favor of the injured. Where the offense is fairly clear, some of the offender's associates may be unwilling to support him in his refusal to negotiate, and others may become lukewarm in assistance. Conversely, the injured person's associates may be reinforced by righteous indignation and the expectation of success. On the whole, in so small a society where little happens that is not well known and widely discussed, it is usually impossible for genuine offenses to be persistently denied. An offender has to continue to live in his community, and his associates in theirs, and this is made difficult where there is flagrant contravention of others' interests.

When the two disputants are entirely unrelated and live at a distance from each other, such public opinion may be ineffective. The process of dispute settlement is not altogether efficient, and some offenders are able to deny or ignore the consequences of their acts. This is not common, for relations between any two men are likely to have some effect on a large number of other people. It is more probable that an offender, by his calculated recalcitrance, is able to avoid the full consequences of his act. The injured man must assess the degree of support both he and the offender can muster, the gravity of the offense, the difficulties of exerting persistent pressure on the offender, previous relations between the two men, and so on. Usually a balance can be struck somewhere so that some compensation is obtained—enough to satisfy the injured without completely alienating the offender.

It is only occasionally that some matter arises that affects the welfare of a number of people of different families, and in which it is inappropriate for particular individuals to initiate action. Most usually someone feels sufficiently threatened to act on his own behalf, with little or no thought for more general interests. For example, in one district a number of cases of alleged witchcraft occurred together. At first, persons who thought themselves involved took individual action against the accused woman; but as further misfortunes accumulated, and the rainy season turned out poorly, people began to see her as a general threat to the whole district. Eventually, with little formal organization, and led by some of those who felt themselves particularly injured, people of the district assembled at the woman's homestead. There she was compelled to admit to her misdeeds, and to declare that she would not use witchcraft again; and her husband provided an ox for slaughter to accompany ritual supplications to the High God.

The district is the usual level at which relations with outside world are ordered: offensive warfare formerly, and nowadays dealings with the central government. There is little or nothing of communal deliberations and decision making at the tribal level.

To sum up this aspect of Jie life: there is no continuously operating system of public administration outside the ritual sphere. Law and order are maintained by the common acceptance of the norms of conduct (that is, the unitary culture of the people), and these are declared and as nearly as possible enforced by any individual who is injured by their contravention. In this he is assisted by his stock-associates. The norms are also reiterated by ritual leaders on what are primarily sacred occasions, in order to bring generalized moral pressures to bear and to prevent the spoiling of ritual. Decision making is largely a matter for the individual, influenced more or less by his associates; but if enough people are seriously affected, public decisions can be reached at settlement or district levels. Finally, insofar as the ritual and age organization places persistent emphasis on the essential unity and interdependence of all Jie, on internal peace and the norms of right behavior, it powerfully reinforces mundane unity and cooperation and serves as the major integrative factor in the society.

CHANGE

There have been few changes in Jie society during the twentieth century, and Jie have remarkably little knowledge of or interest in preceding times. Colonial intervention began in the first decade of the century, primarily as a military operation to end ivory poaching by foreigners and to prevent intertribal warfare on the eastern borders of the then new Protectorate of Uganda. For the latter purpose, an important limitation was imposed on the Jie; not only were they compelled to abjure warfare but, to reduce the possibilities of conflict, the majority of the people were made to live permanently in the settled area in central Jieland. Previously, as the dry season advanced and milk and water supplies failed at the homesteads, the whole population had shifted into the stock camps, leaving the settled area deserted until the rainy season began. This compulsory change brought hardship, especially because of acute water shortage, until bored wells were introduced in the 1940s. It also exacerbated overgrazing and erosion in the settled area, as cattle have been retained there rather longer each dry season than hitherto. On the other hand, it is probable that the operative unity of both settlements and districts has been intensified now that most members of those groups no longer scatter for several months each year. Conversely, the district lost part of its *raison d'etre* since it had been the unit of military activity.

The colonial government appointed a chief and headmen over the Jie; their potential roles have not been understood by the people, who have passively accepted them as alien impositions. The first small mission and school opened in 1949; it has expanded since, but there are still few even partly educated Jie, and few who know or care about the outside world. On the whole, the colonial government remained remote, primarily keeping the peace, and interfering little in everyday life. Compulsory cattle sales began in the 1940s to reduce stock numbers, to supply meat to the more populous areas of Uganda, and to introduce cash into the Jie economy. Without compulsion it is doubtful that the Jie would have sold many animals, and they converted much of the money into goats and sheep purchased from their eastern neighbors. The one or two foreign-owned stores opened in the settled area have provided a source of foodstuffs alternative to the traditional barter trade, which, however, is still the more important. Ox plows, first introduced in 1951, have been enthusiastically welcomed; as a result cultivation is now primarily men's work, but in their wives' fields. There is no cash crop.

The population of Jieland has probably doubled during the twentieth century, increasing the dangerous pressure on meager natural resources. It seems possible, but not yet certainly demonstrated, that the increase in the numerical size of extended families has diminished their unity. This has been encouraged by the prevailing peace that has allowed the breakup of the old large homesteads, formerly thought necessary as a vital defense measure. Agnatic conflict can now be expressed and avoided by residential separation, and the overriding need to maintain unity is less evident.

The Jie are an example of the many peoples of the semiarid East African savannas for whom pastoralism and the economic and social values of livestock are all-important. Like so many of these peoples, and especially the Nilotes, they have thus far been relatively little affected by the impact of the outside world. In part their culture, and especially the strong individualism it fosters, is intrinsically unreceptive to change; more important, they inhabit country whose environmental limitations restrict the usefulness of Western ideas and techniques and the possibilities of change. The Jie socio-political system, typical in principle of the eastern Nilotes, is of a kind still relatively poorly studied. It has neither the centralized unity of traditional chiefdoms nor the particular integrity of the segmentary unilineal societies that have been so thoroughly examined by anthropologists in Africa.

22. THE TURKANA

P. H. GULLIVER

Reprinted from The Family Herds: A Study of Two Pastoral Peoples in East Africa, the Jie and Turkana *(New York: Humanities Press, 1955). For introduction and biographical sketch, see Selection 21.*

IN TURKANALAND THE mode of residence and the nature of all social activities are strongly affected by nomadism. Nowhere is any homestead permanent, nor under this particular nomadic system do groups of families necessarily move in concert. In any populated area at a given time there can be perceived three types of neighbourhood groups. Firstly, the primary neighbourhood is a small cluster of homesteads, geographically disparate from like clusters, and its inhabitants maintain for the time being daily-face-to-face relations. The secondary neighbourhood is a collection of two or three such groups of homesteads, often based on a common waterpoint, often using common pastures to the temporary, *de facto* exclusion of other people, and geographically near to one another and distant from others. The tertiary neighbourhood is a wider, more vague socio-geographical region, within which from time to time social intercourse is maintained, its frequency depending on personal inclinations and requirements and the attractiveness of the activities (e.g., feasts and ceremonies, dances and general visiting) available. The primary neighbourhood seldom consists of more than five homesteads, often two or three, and they are not necessarily very close together. The secondary neighbourhood comprises two to four such clusters spread over an area of several square miles—i.e., between five and twenty homesteads altogether. The tertiary neighbourhood is too vague to allow of numerical description, but in general it covers an area of some twenty miles around any given secondary neighbourhood which belongs to it. Such neighbourhoods are sometimes coterminous with natural regions, such as a river valley, a mountainside, etc. The point of chief significance is that social rela-

tions in a neighbourhood are principally based on mere temporary contiguity which allows a degree of economic and social co-operation. At any time they may break up as constituent homesteads, move away, or be added to as new families arrive. If a general move occurs, not all neighbours move together nor to the same destination, but they severally come to form parts of other neighbourhood groups in their new areas of residence. Neither do such groups re-form again at a later date—say, the equivalent time in the next year. A group of two or three families may sometimes move and keep together for a time, but such associations are always transitory, for the essence of Turkana nomadism lies in the individual freedom of each family under its own head. This will be described later.

The Turkana are loosely grouped into nineteen "territorial sections" (*ekitela,* pl. *ngitela*) which are merely geographical groups to which a few minor social distinctions attach —e.g., details of female clothing, dialect and types of ornamentation. A man and his family belong to that section in which they normally spend the wet seasons. Sections have no political, economic or ritual significance. There is an age-set system which is not particularly strong, endemically because of its subservience to the needs of nomadic pastoralism, and more recently because of the end of raiding. Unlike the Jie system, it provided the core of the primitive military organization. Today it exists mainly as a conservative continuation of the relations established by initiation, and by certain fraternity amongst contiguous age-mates exhibited in feasts, dancing and some ritual activities. . . .

In Turkanaland there is such a notably harsh and difficult environment that its effect on social life is all-pervasive, inescapable both for the people themselves and for the observer of their lives and activities. For a proper understanding of any facet of Turkana social organization it is necessary to begin with an appreciation of the environmental limitations rigorously imposed on all social activities. To a certain extent any study of the Turkana is also an ecological study.

I wish, also, to provide some data on the place and importance of domestic stock in the daily lives to these two peoples which may throw light on their conceptions of property rights in these animals. For, after all, cattle, camels, goats and sheep are not mere symbols in which rights are vested. They are, especially for the Turkana, but only to a lesser degree for the Jie, the principal means of life and livelihood. . . .

ECOLOGICAL SURVEY OF TURKANALAND

Turkanaland lies wholly within the eastern branch of the African Rift Valley. The general altitude at the base of the Rift escarpment is about 3,000 feet, and the land falls away gradually to 1,230 feet at Lake Rudolf. . . . Almost everywhere, from whatever vantage point, the observer is confronted with a continuous stretch of plains in which the mountains are but partial breaks. There are, indeed, large areas of plains altogether free of high land. The "black-cotton" plains in northwestern Turkanaland are quite unbroken for a distance of some eighty miles; central Turkanaland, as it slopes gently towards Lake Rudolf, contains only a few isolated hills. Elsewhere the vast plains make sharp contrast with the relatively small area of high land. This contrast is reflected in the ecology of the inhabitants. There is always the dichotomy— the plains and the mountains. The Turkana themselves are people of the plains who make use of the mountains unwillingly and only by necessity. . . .

Temperatures are uniformly high throughout the year, between 100°F. and 70°F., seldom lower, even at night. Whilst Turkana-land has not the excessive torridity of some more northerly desert lands, it has nevertheless a steady heat which is little relieved at any time.

The Turkana divide the year into two seasons—the dry season, *akumu,* and the wet season, *agiporo.* These two terms, in keeping with realities, are used in an extremely elastic manner, meaning only in a general way the division of the year into rainy and non-rainy periods. More precisely they refer to the times when the rains have been sufficient to produce new and fairly well-established vegetation—the wet season; or the times when rain is absent or quite insufficient to produce or maintain the vegetational cover of the land— the dry season. In the general way the wet season extends from about April to August and the dry season from about September to March; but the rains in any year may break any time between March and June, and may fall off between June and September—there is little correlation between Turkana's rainfall and that of the higher regions of British East Africa. Not infrequently the rains more or less fail altogether—even by Turkana standards—and the growth of vegetation is so poor that the people say that no wet season occurs in such years.

As a general statement, it may be said that the average annual rainfall in the plains is twelve to sixteen inches, falling to less than six inches in the central desert regions. The significant features of the rainfall are the wide range of variation over the years and the considerable degree of variation between successive years. Figures are misleading as they stand since they afford no indication of the nature and effectiveness of the rainfall. Where rainfall is so small, the way in which actual precipitation is received is of high significance. Rain usually comes in sharp storms which occur in the latter part of the day or persist intermittently for a day or two. There is a high degree of evaporation due to the constant heat; and owing to thin and sandy soil covers and poor vegetation there is a rapid run-off. Consequently water retention is low. A day or two of rainy weather in the wet season may well be followed by a fortnight or more of cloudless drought, when the earth becomes dried up, cracked and reduced to an infertile, dry, crumbled mass. Since the growth of vegetation depends almost entirely on rainfall, it is clear that an average fall, broken up into short periods of heavy precipitation separated by long periods of drought, is inimical to permanent and strong growth and seeding. An average fall may produce a poor, withered crop. The point of significance here is that in arid country the quantity and nature of the rainfall is quite critical. Variations of a few inches can have a considerable effect not known in more fortunate lands; similarly, a fairly concentrated rainy period during the year can have much more effect than an equal fall spread out over several months. Rainfall is not only small, it is irregular both in quantity and effectiveness. These considerable variations in rainfall—and thus in the supply of vegetation—are important in causing corresponding variations in the movements and dispositions of the nomadic Turkana over the years. Turkana say, with truth, that only about one year in four or five has a "good wet season," i.e., with rainfall well above the average paucity. . . .

The vegetation of Turkanaland, which is mainly a product of the distribution of rainfall, follows the same natural dichotomy. In the plains there is semi-desert bush which in the east-central regions deteriorates into almost sheer sandy or rock desert, and in the better regions in the northwest and northeast develops into semi-desert grasslands with relatively less bush. The typical state is one of bare sandy or rocky soil with a sparse, intermittent cover of low bushes, shrubs and scattered small trees in which acacias predominate. Most watercourses support some larger trees (mainly thorn), and over 3,000 feet there is much sanseviera and cactus. There is a virtual absence of permanent grass except in some better parts in the north, where nevertheless there is much bare ground. Much of this vegetation is dormant in drought, but, with the wet season temporary grass and herbage appear for longer or shorter periods according to the effectiveness of the rainfall. At this time useful grazing is provided along the banks of the larger water courses.

In the mountains above about 4,000 feet (sometimes lower) there is permanent grass which grows several feet high in the wet season. Bush is often thick and trees plentiful, and in many places they appear to be increasing at the expense of grass cover. In the better areas a thick grass cover grows, of the type usually associated with dry savannah lands. As the dry season progresses these mountain grasslands become increasingly arid and burnt up by sun and hot winds; nevertheless, grass of a kind does persist the whole year except in certain infertile parts and in the worst years. The bulk of the grasslands are between 4,000 and 5,500 feet. . . .

Water supplies are taken mainly from the watercourses. After the rains, ponds are formed, rock-pools are filled and local springs gush, but no more than about three weeks' drought exhausts them. Thereafter people find their water by digging in the dry beds of the watercourses; and the number of points where digging is fruitful diminishes as the dry season progresses. It appears most probable that the water table which these tap is largely a product of rainfall outside Turkanaland—to the west and south in eastern Uganda and the Kenya Highlands respectively. Thus contrary to what might be expected there are few areas which, by native standards, are seriously short of water. There are cases, but relatively few, where graze and browse outlast water. . . . Nevertheless, it must be emphasized that shortage of water scarcely reduces the effective use of available vegetation, and it does not primarily regulate or limit the movements and dispositions of these nomadic people. The cause of Turkana nomadism is poverty of vegetation. . . .

Stock must be herded in areas where there are both pasturage and water. Nomadic movements are largely the result of coventionalized attempts to maximize the supply of these necessities. From the foregoing description of the country it is obvious that at certain times of the year some areas are quite unable to contain herds, whilst the vegetation of other areas is such that only scattered, thinly distributed herds can live there. As vegetational resources become exhausted, movement must be made to areas where better conditions exist; conversely, as new resources become available following the rains, herds can be moved to hitherto barren areas. But this is by no means the whole case, for all types of animals have not the same dietary needs. At one extreme are cattle which must have grass (or certain types of herbage usually associated with grass); at the other extreme there are camels, which need browse (i.e., the leafage of bushes and trees) and which seldom graze if only because they are anatomically unfitted for it. Sheep and goats are capable of both grazing and browsing, though sheep fare better on grass.

To some extent these dietary requirements determine the areas in which the kinds of stock can be kept. Cattle are strictly confined to grasslands, which means the mountain areas all the year round and the banks of watercourses and the lower hills in fair wet seasons. In accordance with the Turkana traditions of living in the plains whenever possible, the cattle are driven down from the mountains as soon as the new rains have produced sufficient graze in the plains, and are moved back only when compelled by exhaustion of graze there at the beginning of the dry season. There tends, therefore, to be a distinct difference between the localities of cattle herding in the two seasons—a decisive movement from the mountains to the plains and back again. In the poorer wet seasons some of the cattle herds may not be able to move down to the plains at all since little or no grass grows there. At such times movement is restricted to leaving the better—usually the higher—parts of the mountains for those parts which had been grazed out earlier. Thus, whether the rains are good or poor, there is some movement in response to the appearance of new vegetational resources; and in any case, whether in the mountains or the plains, there are likely to be minor movements in adjustment to changing resources and changing demands upon them at any one time.

Browse, however, is ubiquitous, or almost so, in Turkanaland, varying only in quantity and quality. Even the worst of the central shrub desert region affords some browse in the wet season, whilst extensive areas of the plains provide some kind of supply right through the dry season. Thus the Turkana are usually able to keep their camels and goats in the plains, although some areas cannot maintain herds throughout the year. Camel and goat herds tend to make gradual movements, going from part of an area and then moving on elsewhere. The worst parts of the plains gradually empty as the dry season progresses, or perhaps a few widely scattered homesteads only may remain. There is a gradual concentration in the better parts of the plains and in the mountains. Probably less than half of the browsing herds reach the mountains, outside of the worst years. When the new rains break, bush leafage quickly returns and browsing stock are able to disperse again fairly soon.

These conditions mean that a family's herds must be split up—for all (or very nearly all) families own all types of stock. The typical arrangement is that the cattle are kept in one homestead and the goats and camels in another. If there are sufficient, the camels may occupy a separate homestead, or milch cattle may be separated from oxen and immature cattle. It is a matter of the convenience of herding, watering and general organization. In addition, an over-large herd may necessitate too frequent movements, as it more quickly exhausts local vegetation. The division of the family's herds is purely a practical measure and not socially conditioned, though it has of course important social consequences. For any single family this is not an absolute necessity, since the browsing herds could be kept along with the cattle in the mountains in the dry season; but it would not be possible for all families, since the mountain areas are restricted and could not maintain all of the Turkana stock throughout the dry season. The tradition of attachment to the plains serves to support and rationalize the system. Quite apart from this, however, the Turkana, realizing the general poverty of their natural resources, do not wish to leave any browse unused, and it is a firm principle that less persistent pastures should be utilized first and that more persistent pastures should be reserved until worse times of the year when the rest are more or less exhausted. Thus the goat and camel herds remain in the plains, apart from the cattle, whilst browse persists, moving to the mountains only when pastures in the plains can no longer contain all the herds. Similarly, the cattle can take advantage of new but purely temporary grasslands off the mountains in the wet seasons, thus leaving the latter pastures for intensive use in the dry season—and also, of course, allowing an interval in which the mountain areas may recuperate, free of stock, during the period of new growth.

Thus the natural dichotomy of plains and mountains is broadly followed in the pastoral organization. Cattle spend eight or nine months in the mountains each year (and not infrequently the whole of the year), whilst the camels and goats remain in the plains, although tending to shift towards the mountains by the end of the dry season. It may be convenient to speak of the cattle following a system of transhumance between mountains and plains, so long as that term does not obscure the movements within each region. This may be contrasted with the more truly nomadic movements of the browse homesteads, which tend to move about all the year in response to gradually changing conditions of vegetation . . . .

It must be emphasized that we are not dealing with a fairly straightforward system of transhumance such as that practised by the Jie and companion tribes in eastern Uganda, or by the pastoralists of the Nile basin in the southern Sudan; nor is it a migrational system controlled by strong, corporate territorial or kin groups as in the case of some of the North African camel herders. The irregular distribution and effectiveness of rainfall, the complex distribution of plains and mountains and the dietary needs of the different types of stock canot be reduced to a simple formula, nor is there any indigenous authority to enforce such a thing in practice. . . .

THE USE OF PASTURELANDS

In both tribal areas there are the same indigenous conceptions regarding the use of pasturelands. The first principle is that there are no specific pasture rights attached to any individuals or groups of any sort. All pasturage is common to all members of a tribe. A herd of stock can be moved anywhere at any time. The second principle is that movements are made primarily at the discretion of the "owner" of a herd, or of his agent in charge. Furthermore, a herd is not necessarily to be found in the same place at the same time of successive years; most importantly, particularly in Turkanaland, conditions of rainfall and therefore of grass and water are seldom the same two years together, and in any event there is no special reason why an owner should establish his herd in any one spot.

The principal reasons for the movements of herds are lack of grass or browse, lack of water, or both. Since, especially in the dry season, the relative adequacy of these at various places is a matter of opinion, there may well be a variety of opinion amongst owners. One man, for instance, may consider that his present area can no longer adequately support his animals and he moves to another area believed to be more satisfactory; another man, although he realizes the poverty of the area's resources, does not consider that sufficient advantage is to be gained by moving. Each man attempts to provide for his herds as best he can in the light of his experience and the needs of his animals. He must take into account the quantity and quality of vegetation, facilities for watering, distance between pastures and water, and future prospects of both. There are certain times when movement is essential, e.g., in the early dry season—in Jieland, herds must move westward as water supplies cease in the east; in Turkanaland, cattle must move to the mountains as the plains grasslands are exhausted. At other times movements are conventionally prescribed though not physically essential, e.g., when new pastures and water are available with a new wet season—in Jieland, herds scatter over the west and later move eastwards; in Turkanaland, flocks of goats and sheep scatter over the inferior plains areas, and cattle descend from the mountains. The timing of both essential and conventional movements is, however, entirely the concern of each owner, and so is the new location to which he moves. In addition to opinion on purely pastoral grounds, there may also be personal considerations. The availability of labour to an owner may limit movements. A man may prefer to go near to a kinsman or bond-friend when the decision to move has been made—though this must not be overemphasized. Some men appear to prefer to move as little as possible; others seem to like to shift at every opportunity. In all this there is no controlling authority to override personal choice and inclination. An owner may be influenced by the decisions of his kinsmen or even of casual neighbours; he may accede to the opinions of other owners with whom temporarily he shares a common camp (Jie) or homestead (Turkana), but such pastoral alliances are always a matter of mutual convenience, and strong disagreement causes their dissolution. There is no particular reason compelling kinsmen to cooperate, and very often in both tribes an owner asserts his independence of his near kin by deliberately following an independent course in pastoral affairs. . . .

It is to be expected, however, that men do not wander relatively aimlessly about the countryside. . . . On the whole, each man settles in an approximate, annual nomadic cycle. His detailed knowledge and experience of terrain, vegetation, water supplies, paths and passes, and so on, will apply only to a restricted territory, and the risks of moving elsewhere are increased by relative ignorance. The inertia of convention (though purely individual convention) is considerable, and if a certain territory is satisfactory there is little reason to change it. A man obviously does not wish to send his cattle to a mountain fifty miles away when there is an equally suitable area only thirty miles away. . . .

When a man becomes independent he tends to maintain an established routine which varies only in details—e.g., the time when the various moves are made each year, and the precise location of homesteads in an area. He may always move his cattle to a certain mountain area, but his homestead may in any one year be ten or fifteen miles away from its location the previous year. Again, a man may say that in the wet season he lives in a certain area, but his actual location in any year can vary considerably. This means that his homestead is likely to be found within a fairly wide field, and his stock watered at one of two or three waterpoints. One cannot locate a Turkana more specifically. These decisions of detail and the less frequent major changes in the cycle are fundamentally individual ones. Opinion can vary a good deal; needs vary also. A small flock of one hundred goats can manage in a rather poorer area than a large one of three hundred animals. When a move seems to be necessary there is often lengthy discussion amongst the neighbours, and there is, as I have frequently seen, a good deal of disagreement. . . .

It will be clear from the foregoing account that neighbourhood (i.e., residential) groups are only temporary associations, continually forming and breaking up. Two or three men and their families may keep together for a time because of ties of kinship or friendship and cooperation, but such collaboration is always liable to be broken off and there is no reason to believe that any Turkana goes through life bound to others in pastoral and nomadic activity. One informant put the situation thus: "A man lives next to his brother-in-law. They live together, perhaps they herd together; they move to one [part of the] country. Later the man wants to go this way—his affine wants to go elsewhere. They part and each moves to his [chosen] area. There are no [hard] words; it is finished."

In Jieland possession is not even "nine points of the law," and that principle holds in Turkanaland only during the worst time of the dry season and may in any case be set aside if a newcomer has the support of men already in the area (i.e., a kinsman or bond-friend). In the same way, water is considered a free good, a resource common to all tribesmen. Specific rights do, however, lie where water resources have been artificially developed. If there is a running spring, or an open, natural pool, anyone can water his stock there on the principle, "first come, first served." But such water is always scarce even in the wet season; soon after the last rains, holes must be dug in the beds of watercourses. This involves considerable initial labour, especially in view of the absence of proper digging tools, and a certain amount of upkeep is required. . . .

In Turkanaland, though there are wealthy men with up to 100 cattle and over 300 small stock, there is on the whole no great variation in wealth. An "average" family owns about 25 to 30 cattle and perhaps about 100 to 150 small stock. Very few men indeed have no stock or only a mere handful, for life is impossible, or almost so, without stock in that semi-desert land. Certain regions are probably more wealthy than others, but not to any great extent. . . . It is obvious that with a social system wherein cattle serve a multitude of non-economic ends and are thereby frequently passed from owner to owner (chiefly through the mechanism of bridewealth), any owner's wealth is liable to considerable fluctuations. A poor owner with unmarried sisters and daughters will in due course receive stock at their weddings; a wealthy man expends stock upon his own and his sons' marriages. In both tribes many wives or many animals are in practice synonymous with wealth; and it is a general principle that bridewealth is given according to the wealth of the bridegroom and his kin, so that a wealthy owner must surrender more stock at marriage, and, if his sons-in-law are relatively poorer, he will receive less at his daughters' marriages. We cannot therefore speak as if wealth in stock was an entirely fixed matter or only slowly changing. This is one of the most important respects in which property in animals differs from property in land. . . .

Under the Jie transhumantic system there is a contrast between the fixed homesteads (*ere*, pl. *ngireria*) and the peregrinating stock camps (*awi*, pl. *ngawie*). At the former live the older men, women and children, with a dairy herd for some ten months of the year; and there is the centre of agriculture and of social activities in general. At the camps live the young men and youths in charge of the stock. It is seldom nowadays that a wife or girl lives in a camp. A homestead is a permanent, firmly built structure, still bearing the stamp of the necessity for defense against raiders in its stout palisades. Internally, in its division into enclosed yards and kraals it is a material embodiment of the social structure of the family group which inhabits it. A camp is a transient affair, a mere ring fence of low bushwood. There is only a hut or shelter in the wet season, and no possessions that men cannot carry in their hands or on their shoulders. It is purely a subsidiary of the settled homestead.

Under the Turkana nomadic system the contrast is less obvious. No habitation is anywhere permanent. A family is typically divided, as we have seen, into at least two parts—one with the cattle, one with the browsing stock (camels and small stock). Owing to the nature of the distribution of vegetation and the different requirements of these two types of stock, the division is more fundamental. Each type of herd is kept at a homestead such that physically there is little or no difference between the two habitations. At least one wife (of the family head, a son or a dependent) should live at each homestead, and at least one adult male; these two supervise the domestic and watering, and the pastoral and herding sides of life respectively. Fences, huts, kraals, etc., are essentially similar at each homestead and there is but one word for both, *awi*. Each is the home of people of each sex and all ages. A wife keeps her utensils and property with her wherever she lives. Neither is like the "camp" of the Jie. On the other hand, there is always a "chief-homestead"—that at which the family head and his chief wife live. . . .

For present purposes the distinction to be drawn is between the Turkana situation, where the nuclear family is permanently (or nearly permanently) divided amongst at least two residential units, which may be many miles apart and subject to quite different conditions, but each is the home of its members; and the Jie situation, where home is quite specifically at the fixed homestead, with the stock camp a mere ancillary unit containing only the young men and boys, and in which the pattern of life is of a purely transitory nature. There is, of course, the similarity that both Jie homestead and Turkana chief-homestead are the natural centres of family activity by reason of the presence there of the men who are heads of the family groups and who are the owners of stock. . . .

STRUCTURE AND PASTORAL ORGANIZATION

In Turkanaland the basic family group which emerges in actual life as a legally independent, stock-owning, more or less self-sufficient unit will here be called the nuclear family. This may be described in a preliminary way as a man and his wives and children. A daughter leaves it when she marries and she then joins her husband's nuclear family. Sons remain within the group together with their wives and children, though they tend increasingly to achieve a considerable degree of autonomy together with physical and economic separation. The Turkana refer to this group by the general word *awi*, which means literally "a homestead" in the physical sense of thorn fences, huts, kraals, etc. By extension, *awi* also means the people who normally occupy the homesteads of an independent man and who join in the care and use of the domestic stock kraaled there.

Polygyny is not only the ideal but also the common practice. At the same time, married sons do not become entirely independent of their father until his death. The Turkana nuclear family therefore has elements both of a "polygynous family" and of a "patrilineal expanded family." My use of the term "nuclear" is different from the usage by Murdock and others. It is to be used in this present account to express in a convenient, shorthand way the basic position of the group in Tur-

kana society and in structural contrast with the "extended family." It is the smallest, independent, corporate kin group and is specifically identified by its ownership and use of a herd of domestic stock. The smaller groups contained within it are not legally independent and are only subsections in the structure of its internal organization. A number of nuclear families are linked together by a web of genealogically defined social bonds to form the more amorphous group, the extended family. . . .

Although Turkana speak of there being one *awi*, yet, except amongst the poorest people, few nuclear families occupy a single, physical homestead, for, as we have already seen, ecological and pastoral conditions normally necessitate at least two homesteads. From an external and also an economic point of view these two homesteads are similar. . . . Each, if possible, contains a wife of the head of the nuclear family or of one of his sons or of some other dependent, and she supervises the domestic and feminine side of life and work in the homestead, e.g., milking and watering the animals, fetching drinking water, collecting and preparing, building and repairing, etc.

The "chief-homestead" (*awi napolon*) is that in which, at any one time, the head of the family is living. A "secondary-homestead" is called *awi abor*. The composition of these has been briefly described earlier, and all that need be stated here is that the labour force of the family must be distributed between the homesteads, so that if possible an adult male and a wife live in each, together with youths, boys, and girls, to carry out the necessary routine work. In this is it by no means possible for brothers to keep together, nor for them to live with their mother. A shortage of womenfolk may require that an adolescent girl live apart from her mother. Except in the case of an elderly man who has several wives and many children, most families are perennially short of labour, though it may be pointed out that, on the whole, work for either sex is not particularly heavy. . . .

It is not possible to make a neat distinction between a main homestead and the cattle camp amongst many pastoralists. The chief-homestead at any time is the center of the family's life and organization, and here nearly all important social and ritual activities connected with the whole family are undertaken, under the direction of the family head. From the pastoral and economic viewpoint, a secondary-homestead often moves and lives in a completely different geographical region from that of the chief-homestead. Although the family head exercises ultimate control over movements and activities, yet he is commonly too far away to do more than lay down general policy. His representative, the senior adult man at the homestead, not only makes day-to-day decisions but decides when to move and where, his decision being based on his own judgment of the state of water and pastures and of future prospects. As will be seen later, an adult son assumes a good deal of independence in his control over the secondary-homestead, even to the point of direct disagreement with his father as to the general region in which that homestead is to operate. Despite a certain amount of visiting, a man may not see his cattle for months at a stretch, co-wives may not meet, nor sons be with their mother and brothers, for in the dry season a cattle homestead may be two or more days' journey away across rough country.

Though physically and economically divided, a nuclear family remains nevertheless a distinct and corporate group. This unity stems directly from the head of the family who legally owns the stock. . . . In actual life the nuclear family often does not exist alone as such, but is associated in the same homesteads with parts or wholes of other families. So far we have defined the nuclear family in purely structural and legal terms with direct reference to stock ownership, and Turkana do the same. In practice, however, a Turkana could also include people who, for the time being, join in the pastoral and economic activities of the group, and whose stock (if any) are not distinguished externally. A man welcomes additions to his family's labour force, and adult men are especially acceptable. A man with his nuclear family cannot achieve complete independence until he has sufficient labour to manage all the duties of nomadic, pastoral life. Consequently a young man or one of early middle-age, with perhaps only one wife, attempts to attract young male relations to help. Occasionally a poor, unrelated man, even a complete pauper, may become permanently attached to a family, acting as herdsman in return for food and shelter. Such a person becomes almost "one of the family."

If they possess stock of their own, such associates keep them in the relevant homestead of their adopted family. For many practical purposes—herding, watering, movements, even kraaling sometimes—their stock are merged into the herds of the family. Nevertheless, to some extent economically, but especially socially and legally, these stock are quite distinct from the herds proper of the family, and this is clearly recognized and acknowledged by the people involved. Later a man may wish to strike out independently, or before that time may shift his allegiance to some other man. In either case his animals go with him, together with all their offspring and all accretions by gifts, etc. Economically there is a good deal of give-and-take over the consumption of milk and blood, and even of meat, yet it is accepted that an associate has prime rights to the produce of his own animals. . . .

A son must accede to his father's desires and decisions; but he need not and often does not accede entirely gracefully. The idea of competition between father and son is begun, and it continues to grow. It grows slowly, especially at first, for men are brought up and culturally conditioned to the fact that they must give way to their father for many years. Immediately after initiation (at about the age of eighteen) and the recognized assumption of adult status, privileges and ambitions, a son does not expect to marry straight away, even though he might perhaps like to. Men with living fathers seldom marry before the age of twenty-five and frequently later. "Young men like to court the girls, go to dances and to play" [i.e., enjoy themselves freely], say Turkana. Typically, adult sons live at the secondary-homestead, relatively out of touch with important family affairs, centered as these are at the chief-homestead where the father lives. Neither is it very long ago since young adult men spent a large proportion of their time in raiding, roaming the countryside and engaging in age-set activities generally. This was the practice only a generation ago, and the tradition of relatively irresponsible youth persists. Another mitigating factor lies in the whole marital structure of the society. Since men tend to marry fairly late they are likely to be middle-aged or elderly by the time that their sons are wanting to marry and therefore competition for bridewealth stock may be correspondingly less as fathers desire less and less to marry again. Nevertheless, a son does begin to chafe at his father's restrictions in this matter, to the point of resentment against his father's use of stock which denies him the possibility of his own first marriage. When a father does eventually agree to his son's demands, he himself feels a certain resentment because it marks the end of his own marriage prospects; further, it marks the definite beginning or specific recognition of his approaching old age and of the diminution of his authority and of the tight unity of his nuclear family. A father is well aware that his son's marriage is but the prelude to the eventual autonomy of that son. Tension and the idea of competition between father and son does not necessarily reach a serious level, or at least not for many years. Elderly men, as they have told me, do genuinely recognize and respect their sons' desires to marry. The situation is regarded as more or less inevitable and therefore to a large extent must be gracefully accepted. Commonly, affection between father and son is enough to prevent the father persisting in too autocratic an attitude. It would be incorrect if I imply that father and son live normally in a state of hostility, even if suppressed below the surface of everyday relations. Affection betwen the men, and the common bonds established within the unitary nuclear family, permit the marriages of sons as alternatives to new marriage by the father. A new wife is brought into the group, more children may be born and new affinal links are established. Thirdly, in the case of an eldest son, at least, there is a valid reason why his marriage should not be too long delayed, and having once begun the process of sons' marriages it is difficult to revert back again to the old primacy by the father. An eldest son ought to marry fairly early in order to provide at least one settled line of succession to the father at his death. Turkana say that only a married man can properly inherit the father's position as head of the group and take over the herds. If a man dies and leaves only unmarried sons, the continuity of the group is believed to be threatened. People say that it would be necessary for some near agnate (the deceased's brother, for instance) to intervene, and that man's prime loyalty lies elsewhere, in his own nuclear family. There would be a possibility of the two sets of herds becoming mixed up, and that might negate the whole conception of the independence of the nuclear family as a man has established it during his lifetime. As will be seen later, there is a considerable distinction between even full-brothers, let alone other agnates, and their herds; for the whole trend of individual development in this society is towards the complete independence of a man and his own family. The continued independence and specific identity of a man's family is ensured by the existence of at least one married son. . . .

In addition to all this, there is the purely economic aspect to be considered. A family can scarcely afford a marriage each year, but, after the expenditure of stock in one bridewealth, must pause to rebuild its resources even though assisted, now more, now less, by the income received at the marriage of daughters. The question of marriage is doubtless perennially in the minds of the men of the family, but it cannot constantly come to a head in the course of actual events. The problem of marriage may also be postponed by poor wet seasons when most men prefer to await more favourable times. Unless the family head lives to a great age, or unless there is a high income of stock from daughters' marriages, there is often little cause to strain against the leash of his authority. Economic facts are against sons, and this is generally recognized and accepted philosophically. On the whole, Turkana men do not live to a great age, and even if a man has several sons of adult status it is unlikely that more than one or two of them can hope for marriage in his lifetime, however understanding and unselfish he may be. . . .

In all these matters there is no external agency to regulate intra-family relations. This is part of the significance of the independence of a nuclear family. Although a nuclear family is a part of the wider "house" and of the extended family, it is in no way part of those groups in an overall authoritarian structure. . . .

THE METAMORPHOSIS OF THE NUCLEAR FAMILY—INHERITANCE

With the death of the father the authoritarian unity of his nuclear family ceases, and it breaks down into a number of independent groups. These groups together still comprise the "family" (awi) of the father, but this, in the terminology used in the present account, is a "compound family." The constituent groups are of two kinds: firstly there are the "houses," each comprising a set of full-brothers with their wives and children—these are the primary units of inheritance; secondly there are, or in due course will be, the nuclear families of each independent son.

The principles of inheritance are similar to those already described when dealing with the Jie house. . . . Sometimes, however, the distribution of the "residual herd" may raise difficulties. Basically this should be divided up (as in Jieland) so that shares decrease inversely to the seniority of the houses. . . .

THE HOUSE

Ideally a set of full-brothers maintains a strong sense of corporate unity and loyalty which is in part at least expressed and thereby strengthened in the structural opposition to parallel sets of half-brothers, with whom they comprise the compound family. The eldest brother becomes head of the house. It is he who represents the group at inheritance dis-

cussions and who specifically takes over the house's portion of the herds. He may already be married, and may even have become already autonomous. In such a case he is joined by the rest of the house (including the mother) at his homestead. In any event there is a general and strong tendency for a new house to establish its own independent homestead as soon as possible; but at least until the time of the marriage of the eldest brother the empirical norm is that a house remains allied to one or more of its fellows which may already be headed by a married man. This does not affect the true status of the house, but does, however, temporarily limit the full-brothers' exercise of all their potential rights. In such cases the marriage of the eldest brother is speeded up, for in addition to this desire to independence the senior man is now controller of the house's herds and he himself can therefore initiate bridewealth negotiations. Here, however, legal property-owning independence is markedly tempered by the need for assistance from the other houses, for it is unlikely that at this stage a man can afford to marry without contributions of stock from his half-brothers. His desire for marriage at this early stage must therefore be regulated by common consideration of the whole range of sons of the dead father.

Sooner or later, however, a house leaves its fellows and establishes its own homesteads and its own pastoral-nomadic routine and becomes economically self-sufficient. This act, for the Turkana, is the supreme expression of a genuine legal independence. At this time the house is a quasi-nuclear family—a single stock-owning unit, with the conventional two homesteads under the authority of its head. This man, the eldest brother, is for the time being allowed prime authority by virtue of the status of birth, but he only exercises that power in the name of the whole group of brothers of which he is but one. At first the energies of the brothers are chiefly directed at the goal of separation from their half-brothers; but no sooner has this been achieved than the unity of the house begins to be threatened as each successive brother first seeks to marry and thereafter to become independent himself.

Whereas the son of a living father could only achieve a degree of autonomy, a younger brother aims quite consciously at complete independence from his elder brother. A nuclear family has an inviolate unity; a house has not that degree of unity because, unlike the nuclear family, it is not compulsorily kept together by the single authority of one man over his dependents by virtue both of paternity and his ownership of the herds. A house is an association of equals—subject to a certain reservation on account of seniority—and there appear to be no overriding reasons why they should make efforts to retain their unity, whilst there is a strong cultural convention amongst the Turkana which sets great store on individualism. The house is, as it were, but a holding unit, a temporary stage between the individual ownership of a man and that of each of his sons. Ultimately, in Turkana conceptions, property in animals is held only by a single man, who confers his ownership upon his nuclear family—his wives and children. In the end a man owes no legal property obligations to his full-brothers and half-brothers, although he accepts a certain fluid liability in respect both of near kinship and reciprocity. The whole structure of the house, and indeed of the compound family and the extended family, can be traced to this conception of ownership amongst the Turkana. Having accepted this axiom of individualism, the cleavages in agnatic kin groups can readily be understood. . . .

There are also certain ecological factors operating in the dispersion of the house which do not necessarily relate to the quality of fraternal relations. Owing to the poverty of vegetation and the vagaries of rainfall there is both an optimum size to the herds to be maintained at a single homestead and the number of homesteads that can exist together in a neighbourhood. Overcrowding of stock only leads to the speedy exhaustion of pasture resources and a larger number of nomadic movements. Further, it is easier to move a single homestead and a comparatively small herd than a group or a large herd. An important factor in the Turkana pastoral system is the flexibility of nomadic routines, and this comes directly from the principles of individual movement according to personal choice and opinion. Turkana dislike to cede their freedom of action for the doubtful value of membership of a fixed group. Thus local groupings of homesteads are almost always impermanent. A man does not wish to become tied to any territorial group, and a nomadic band based on agnatic kinship is but one possible form of this. Personal susceptibilities apart, as they see it, the total herds of a group of related men are best cared for by their dispersal over the country, each unit taking advantage of local conditions and the whole not jeopardized by any single calamity. Disease, though not rife in Turkanaland, is always a potential danger, but at least dispersed herds are unlikely to be affected simultaneously. Only a generation ago the dangers of raiding existed, and that has left its mark still on the present system of dispersal. Disastrous dry seasons are a permanent threat, and inadequacy of vegetation in local regions kills off stock nearly every year. If herds are kept in different regions this danger can at least be mitigated. . . .

THE PATTERN OF THE EXTENDED FAMILY

Internal relations within the extended family are principally those between the heads of independent nuclear families. . . . Cousins of all degrees do not have the same problems of readjustment which prove so difficult between brothers. They inherit, as it were, the pattern of relations previously established between their fathers in the previous generation. There is not in general, therefore, the same sort of tension between cousins as there is between brothers. Relations commence on a basis of reciprocal rights, which have already reached a level of stability. The common source of inheritance is relatively remote and the individual's history of personal development to independence only indirectly connected with that of his cousin. It is more or less fortuitous whether a man's cousin lives near to him at certain times of the year, whether or not they tend to use common pastures; but it is likely that they are geographically separated more often than not. Although the frequency of social intercourse permitted by such separation has its effect upon the strength and cordiality of relations, basically, between cousins, the important factor is the mutuality of stock rights accepted on either side. The notion of reciprocity is little affected by considerations of personal development. On the other hand, because of the relative indirectness of the kinship tie, reciprocal rights are weaker than they are between brothers. . . .

An underlying theme of Turkana social organization is the general difficulty of group activity on any large scale because of ecological conditions which cause a widespread dispersal of population together with diverse and frequent movement. Density of population is low everywhere, and in addition there is the cultural norm of strong individualism in connection with nomadic movements so that residential relations seldom become important over a period; and there is neither particular need nor opportunity for the frequent assembly of kinsmen. The only entirely corporate groups are nuclear families under the authority of their founders and heads. . . .

The general category of stock-associates can be divided into two classes—those with whom a man's relations are especially close and lasting and with whom reciprocal rights involve gifts of cattle, and those with whom a man's relations are relatively distant, and which tend to diminish through time if not die away altogether, and with whom reciprocal rights involve only the gifts of a goat or two. Cattle rights exist in reference to close agnates, close maternal kin (chiefly the mother's brothers), close affines (fathers-, brothers-, and sons-in-law) and bond-friends; goat (and sheep) rights exist in reference to other maternal and affinal kin, and to minor bond-friends, and, in Jieland, to clansmen. In practice this line of differentiation is not so precise or easy to demarcate, but the principle holds nevertheless. An especially friendly clansman or a wife's half-brother may on some occasion come into the cattle-giving class; for instance, a mother's brother may in a particular case fall into the goat-giving class. The cattle-giving class of stock-associates comprises of course those persons with whom relations are more intense, more important and more reliable, and which persist during a man's lifetime and may even be continued by his sons. It may appear a grossly materialistic concept of either the natives or myself to attempt, as it were, to measure social relations in terms of the nature and value of gifts made and received, but concerning this certain points must be made. In the first place I am adopting the native viewpoint here. If one asks a man which people seem most important to him as an individual, he will enumerate the cattle-giving class of stock-associates; and if one enquires why these people are so important, the ready answer is "They are the people who help me and give me cattle at certain times." The Jie and Turkana are a practical-minded people—as perhaps most Africans are in real life—and for them a relationship of significant value insofar as it allows the transfer of stock when required, remembering, however, that gifts of stock create reciprocal obligations. It is not only what an individual can obtain but also what he must give—rights are balanced by obligations. This constant process of giving and receiving stock is for the native dictated by the occurrence of social situations when a man has need of stock for which his own herd is sufficient. For instance, a man can not produce the whole of a normal bridewealth payment from his herd, or at least not without producing serious economic difficulties by removing the producers of milk, blood and meat supplies. He is, therefore, essentially dependent on his stock-associates for help, on the tacit understanding of the guarantee of his help to them severally in the future.

Stock-association is a form of cooperation and mutual insurance, and through it a man maintains a range of significant interpersonal relations within the wider society in which he lives. Stock-association is the core of social life through which an individual maintains himself as a full social being and not merely an isolated unit or even the member of a small, isolated group.

Whilst, like the people themselves, we may regard stock rights as a reliable index of the strength and importance of social relations, neither we nor they deny in any way the other values inherent in a person's closest relations. In Jieland, residential ties and the day-to-day cooperation in affairs large and small that results from intimate, face-to-face relations amongst close agnates (extended family) and within the small clan-hamlet are of real and considerable importance. Partly connected with such small-scale community relations, but extended also to the whole range of stock-associates, is the provision of hospitality and general assistance. A man can be sure of getting food and shelter and a welcome at the homestead of any of his stock-associates. He can attend their feasts as a guest. He or his wife can beg grain or seed or other foodstuffs when these are scarce. His wife can call upon their womenfolk to help her in gardening work in return for beer, milk and porridge. Of some importance in pastoral affairs is the right to ask permission to use a waterhole in the dry season. A poor man may put his cattle in the camp of some stock-associate when he has insufficient to warrant a separate camp of his own. Two or more stock-associates sometimes keep all or part of their herds in joint camps. In order to lessen the risks of disease (and formerly of raiding), men like to spread their stock amongst the camps of stock-associates, taking some of their animals in return. In judicial affairs the responsibilities of close relationship are not confined only to assistance in the payment of compensation, but under the indigenous system of self-help, including also the duty of lending verbal and, if necessary, physical support. An accused man might offer forcible resistance to the demands of his accusers and would expect his stock-associates to support him. On the other hand an injured person would back up his demands for compensation by actually going to seize the number of animals believed to be justified in the situation. Indeed, a man who could only put up a weak show of force was likely to be compelled to

submit to the opposite party; and in any case force, or the threat of it, was the only method of implementing the efficient resistance of unjust demands or the payment of just compensation. The support of a man's stock-associates in all this was partly a mattter of their friendliness with him, the allegiance they owe him; and partly it resided in the fact that if compensation had to be paid they themselves would be liable to contribute animals, and if compensation was to be received they were entitled to shares. Today in Jieland, with the abolition of self-help and the institution of native courts, the aspect of physical support has largely disappeared; nevertheless, the obligation to assist remains, both in contributing towards compensation and in giving moral and vocal support.

In Turkanaland, because of ecological conditions, the position is not the same. There are no permanent settlements, nor are there permanent, perambulating groups of families or other units. The ties of common residence, daily cooperation and face-to-face relations in the local neighbourhood always tend to be temporary and exiguous. A man's stock-associates are not linked to him by ties of a residential, economic or pastoral nature; his neighbours at any one time may not necessarily include any of his stock-associates, and seldom more than one or two out of the total category. He will not see many of them for lengthy periods, nor will he be aware of all their movements and activities, for they are likely to be scattered widely and arbitrarily over a large area, and both his and their locations change fairly frequently. The relationship of stock-association therefore consists primarily in mutual assistance on the more important occasions of individual social life. For much of the time relations are dormant, being reactivated as occasion requires. In this connection an aspect of the system peculiar to the Turkana is important. If a man receives a female animal as his rightful share in a stock-associate's in-payment (notably bride-wealth) or as a gift, a series of exchange gifts is begun which is ideally inextinguishable. If he receives a cow, he should later return one of its female calves; later again he himself may claim a female calf of that latter animal. These secondary claims are not necessarily made by a man because of a particular need at the time, although he has a strong right if he is in need. Often, however, it is a matter of "keeping the relationship going"—"keeping the pot boiling," as we might say colloquially. In this way a fairly constant and persistent series of exchange gifts is maintained additional to the exercise of rights at critical times of need. It is not, of course, a matter of the gifts as such, important though they are, but more significantly it keeps stock-associates in touch and helps to prevent relations fading out through prolonged inactivity. Not only are rights claimed and obligations accepted, but at the same time a certain amount of personal contact is maintained through visiting and accompanying hospitality. It provides a continuous reason for interest and concern in the state of the herds of a stock-associate.

Occasional pastoral cooperation may occur between stock-associates in a similar way to that in Jieland. The obligations of support in judicial affairs also exist; indeed, in Turkanaland, where there is no established court system yet, these obligations are rather more important as most disputes are settled in the traditional manner. . . .

Bond-friends are the only type of stock-associates whose ties are not coincident with kinship, but which in virtue of reciprocal stock rights have for both Jie and Turkana a "pseudo-kinship" quality. A bond-friend is a person with whom one informally contracts such rights for reasons of mutual convenience and trust. In Jieland there is usually a strong element of genuine and proved friendship, but not always so in Turkanaland. For both peoples there is something nearly approaching a business agreement. A bond-friend will give one a cow or ox (or camel) for some purpose on the tacit understanding that at another time he can obtain a return gift. There is no strictly formal basis of the relationship; it is not established by any legal or ritual act and consists primarily of this link of reciprocity. In this, of all stock-relations, if a man does not reasonably meet his obligations he will quickly forfeit his own rights and the association fails, for there is nothing at all to support it. Bond-friendship can be contracted with any man, irrespective of age, social position or residence. In Turkanaland especially, but also in Jieland, considerations of wealth enter into it, for a man does not wish to ally himself to someone considerably poorer than he is and from whom, therefore, he may find difficulty in obtaining his due return and a fruitful relationship in general. A wealthy man never finds it difficult to make new bond-friends, but a poor man is usually acceptable only to similarly poor men.

When a man is in need of stock for some important purpose he tends to approach anyone who be believes is likely to help him. If he has close friends he may attempt to persuade them to help. They have no compulsion to accede to his request, and some refuse on the grounds of insufficiency of the friendship, or current inability to afford help, or unwillingness further to extend the range of stock-association. Here and there, however, over the course of years some men will agree to give an animal. It is recognized by both men that the gift creates a reciprocal obligation and is in fact the beginning of a potentially unceasing chain of exchanges and other assistance. In Turkanaland, in many cases, however, the bond is begun when a comparative stranger seeks hospitality and later begs an animal.

With a firmly established bond-friend, one only gives and begs large stock, usually not more than one beast on any occasion. Within reason one can normally depend on such a person. Since the whole relationship rests on its obvious mutual convenience, care is needed not to overtax it by the too frequent exercise of rights nor by a one-sided exercise. Either party is entirely free to break off the bond, or to allow it to atrophy. On the other hand, many bonds persist throughout a man's lifetime and may even be continued by his sons. On the whole, a man is always seeking to establish new bonds, and even young unmarried men have at least two or three. Through these ties a man is able to extend the effective range of his personal relationships and his stock-associates beyond the relatively restricted and automatic ties of kinship. A man with many bond-friends becomes less dependent upon formal ties where these become irksome or are made difficult by tension and rivalry.

Today, with the disappearance of intertribal warfare, bond-friendship extends across tribal boundaries. In Jieland I met no man over the age of thirty-five who had not several alien bond-friends, and most Turkana had one or two in the tribes nearer to their own region. It is probable that even in the old days Jie had bond-friends amongst the Turkana, and vice versa. Some bonds are established for trading purposes primarily, especially by the Jie with the Labwor people to the southwest. Of course, no bond-friendship is entirely a matter of stock rights, for there is always much visiting, hospitality and assistance in general ways.

Amongst the Turkana, one of the main elements of bond-friendship is not directly connected with stock rights, but because of its importance in the pastoral system it inevitably affects and strengthens stock-association. Because of the unreliable nature of the rainfall and seasons, no Turkana ever feels quite secure in his dry-season pastures, most particularly his mountain grasslands. In any year he may have to quit his conventional area, exhausted of vegetation, and seek alternative pastures elsewhere. In the latter part of the dry season such movements are not easily made, and normally a man must go to an area where someone will stand surety for him in local, informal discussion. Kinsmen will serve this purpose, but their locations are fortuitous and do not necessarily cover all the alternative pasture areas. Through his bond-friendships a man endeavors to ensure that he has a potential supporter in most or all of the areas to which, in any year, he might wish to shift. This is a quite conscious policy, and each Turkana accepts the corresponding liability to help his bond-friends similarly. . . .

23. THE KAZAK: HORSE AND SHEEP HERDERS OF CENTRAL ASIA

C. DARYLL FORDE

From the book Habitat, Economy and Society, *by C. Daryll Forde. Dutton Paperback Edition (1963). Reprinted by permission of E. P. Dutton & Co., Inc., and by permission of Methuen & Co., Ltd. Acknowledgment is made to the author, the International African Institute (London), and Oxford University Press. This material was originally published in the Royal Geographical Society's* Geographical Journal, *90(1) (July, 1937). For biographical sketch, see Selection 13.*

■ Egalitarianism within the local group is a prevailing ideology among most foragers, horticulturists, and pastoralists. Cutting across this, but not contradicting it, is the fact that there is some measure of ranking in almost all societies. Even in the most egalitarian nomadic band, some people are looked up to and others are looked down on. Societies differ in the criteria by which individuals are ranked and accorded prestige (social influence). Furthermore, such ranking within the group always has consequences, which also vary from society to society. A person's prestige will affect his chances in getting a wife, in winning friends and followers, in being listened to, and in winning litigations.

But while ranking is present in all societies, not all are stratified into classes or castes—into groups that legitimately have different degrees of access to power, wealth, means of production, or the control of distribution. As we saw in Selection 7 and 8, the degree of elaboration and the form of social ranking are closely related to a group's productivity.

Pastoralists also vary in degrees and forms of ranking, generally in proportion to their productivity. One of the corollaries of a stratified pastoralist society is an efficient military organization. In this selection we read of the Kazak, a group that is representative of the social organization that enabled Asian pastoralists (the most famous of whom was Genghis Khan) to leave their mark thousands of miles from their home territories.

A number of works by Lawrence Krader are relevant here: *The Cultural and Historical Position of the Mongols: Kazakhastan and the Kazakhs (Asia Major,* 3, No. 2, 1953); "Principles and Structure in the Organization of the Asiatic Steppe-Pastoralists" *(Southwestern Journal of Anthropology,* 11 [1955]: 67-92); "Culture and Environment in Interior Asia," *Studies in Human Ecology* (Washington, D.C.: Anthropological Society of Washington and the Pan American Union, 1958); and "Ecology of Central Asian Pastoralism" *(Southwestern Journal of Anthropology,* 11[1955]: 309-326). Another important work on the nature of adaptation in Asia is *Inner Asian Frontiers of China,* by Owen Lattimore (London: Oxford University Press, 1940). ■

CENTRAL ASIA IS the traditional land of pastoral nomads who wander seasonally in search of pasture for their herds of sheep, cattle and horses. From time to time they have become the instrument of an organizing genius who has led them in rapid invasion over wide tracts of settled country and so given rise to the legend of the invincibility of the peoples of this nomad realm. Until the beginning of the nineteenth century this vast pastoral land had remained substantially unchanged since the times when the Scythians of its southwestern marches became known to the Greeks or when Marco Polo journeyed among the tribes tributary to Chingiz Kahn. It is only in the present century that the autonomy of the nomadic peoples has been seriously affected. And even today, although railways have been pushed across the lowlands of southern Siberia and Russian Turkestan and the herding peoples in some districts have been transformed into settled communities, large bodies of virtually independent pastoral nomads live in the less accessible parts of Russian Asia and in the Chinese territories beyond.

The heart of the great Asiatic continent is cut off by great mountain ranges from the rainy monsoons of the Indian and China seas, while the mountains and plateaux of Europe deplete the lighter store of moisture in the westerly winds from the Atlantic and Mediterranean. So it is that despite the enormous height of its mountain chains and the great elevation of the plateaux there is a vast track of country from the Volga river to the Hwang Ho and the Great Wall of China in which forests are found only as narrow girdles on the slopes of the higher ranges and rivers dwindle yearly after the melting of mountain snows.

But Central Asia is by no means a desert. Bare sands and gravels, although they cover wide tracts of the poorer country, make up only a small proportion of the total of this vast area. Save on the low-lying floors of a few mountain-hemmed basins, as to the east of the Caspian Sea and more strikingly within the great Tarim depression, sufficient rain falls at some season of the year to provide a rapid growth of grasses, the sprouting of many bulbs and the flowering of shrubs like the tamarisk and saxaul. The time and amount of the rainfall depend on the position in relation to the seasonal winds from the distant oceans, and on the elevation and exposure of the particular tract of country. In southern Siberia and in parts of the Turanian Basin of Russian Turkestan the moisture is brought by westerly winds from the Atlantic, the Mediterranean and the Black Sea. In eastern Mongolia and southern Tibet the last tongues of the summer monsoons from the east and south bring summer showers. Although precipitation on the plains and plateaux is light, the masses of the great ranges, the Hindu Kush, Karakorum and, above all, the Tian Shan and Altai receive more considerable amounts and accumulate the falls as snow during the winter season. While the snow-fields and glaciers of Central Asia are today remarkably small for mountains of such scale, they are adequate to provide a fringe of torrents which swell to great streams in spring and unite to form large rivers flowing

many miles before they end in inland lakes or slowly dwindle away in the porous sands and gravels of the dry lowlands.

Since it is so remote from the moderating influence of the oceans, the climate of western Central Asia is characteristically extreme or continental. In winter a great tongue of cold spreads to the very borders of the tropical lands, while in summer the great expanses of the interior heat rapidly under the high sun, and temperatures unknown in damp tropical lands succeed an arctic cold. Indeed, it is the intensity of the summer heat, with the consequently rapid drying out of the ground, which so decisively restricts the growth of trees and dense vegetation. The seasonal change is greatest on the lower lands towards the northeast.

The Kazak, often miscalled Kirghiz by the Russians to distinguish them from the European Cossacks, are the largest and most numerous division of Turki-speaking pastoral nomads. Their encampments range from the Caspian Sea and the Volga River for nearly two thousand miles eastwards to the Tarbagatai hills, the northern ranges of the great Tian Shan mountain system and the head waters of the Irtish. From the foothills of the Elburz Mountains in south Turkestan they extend over fifteen hundred miles northwards to the borders of the Siberian forests. Although some of the western Kazaks occupy high mountain pastures, and have an economy similar to that of the Kirghiz to be considered later, the great majority occupy the dry plains and foothill pastures of Turkestan and the smaller but richer area of the western Siberian steppe. In these two areas the people, who probably number about four millions, are about equally divided.

The Kazak are in general mongoloid in race. They are rather short in stature, heavily built, with yellow skin, and coarse and generally black hair. But when compared with the peoples farther to the northeast, including the Altai Kalmuck, the mongoloid element in the Kazak is seen to be frequently modified. The face is usually longer and more oval and the Mongolian eye-fold is quite often absent, while in many individuals the nose is large and prominent, the eyes are less narrow and slanting and the hair, brownish rather than black, may grow abundantly on the face. These characteristics suggest interbreeding of the Mongol type with members of the Alpine race, which is widespread in southwest Asia and Central Europe, and still constitutes the dominant stock in the mountain country to the south and the southwest of Russian Turkestan.

In origin the Kazak are probably a conglomeration of once-distinct Turkic tribes together with accretions of Mongols and Samoyeds. Since medieval times, when they formed part of the widespread but ephemeral Turkic empires, the main nucleus appears to have spread south and west from the region of the Jüs Steppe and the Abakan river. Their organization into three major political and territorial divisions, or "hordes," occurred in the thirteenth century. They have, however, remained unified in language and custom, although the formal organization and territorial separation of the hordes has, especially since the Russian control of the area, to a large extent decayed.

The main body of the "Great Horde" still occupies its traditional area south of Lake Balkash from the Ala Mountains, Lake Issik Kul and the northwestern Tian Shan as far east as Aulie-ata and Tashkent. The "Small" or "Young Horde" is found in the western steppe between the Aral Sea and the Caspian, while the greater part of Turkestan and Tashkent is occupied by the "Middle Horde." Although until the middle of the nineteenth century these Kazak hordes remained virtually free of all foreign control, they had no longer any knit organization of their own. For urgent defense alone would any considerable combinations be effected, and the Kazak polity is built up from small family units into a series of widening but progressively less coherent divisions.

The paternal kindred of father and sons with their wives and servants is the social nucleus. The father owns the greater part of livestock and decides the movements of the family. But a number of these families, many of them actually related in male line, form a clan which recognizes the head of the dominant family as its leader and negotiator with other clans. All men are necessarily members of their fathers' clan and must obtain their wives outside that body. Every clan has its crest, such as a bird's rib or a forked stick, which is branded on the live stock and marked on the belongings of members. The clan rather than the individual kindred is the unit for social and political relations. Traditional pastures belong to the clan, and contributions to the payment for a bride are often made by all clansmen. For the maintenance and defence of its members the clan is an effective unit. Its poor are fed when destitute by the richer members. Its livestock is branded with a single crest or symbol. But within the clan the leading family of the chief has considerable power and often controls the greater part of the wealth.

Clans (*taypas* or *ak-sakal*) which consider themselves to be ultimately related and may in many cases be the descendants of a once unified group, often migrate together as a group and form a wider unit (*sok*) or phratry. There is no formal leader and the unity of a phratry of clans depends on the concurrence of its separate clans as expressed by their chiefs. The phratries are less stable groups than their constituent clans and appear to have subdivided and reformed in new combinations according to the vicissitudes of migration and warfare and competition for pasture.

The tribal group (*uruk*) of several phratries comprising perhaps twenty or more clans appoints a chief (*bi*), but he has little effective political authority. Selected by the consensus of opinion of the clan chiefs, a man of personality and energy may, however, draw the tribal group into an unaccustomed unity.

The hordes are agglomerations of tribes which by territorial contiguity, and occasional combinations for attack and defence, have built up a tradition of solidarity. Leadership of the horde in any emergency falls to the chief of the dominant tribe, but the seasonal scattering of tribes and clans renders such authority ephemeral. In the great rising of the Kazak against the Russians in 1840 the "Sultan" of the Great Horde achieved this temporary control and endeavoured to reunite the three hordes in an independent and organized nation.

The members of the chiefly families of the tribes, who claim a quite imaginary descent from the Mongol ruler Chingiz Khan and the alleged descendants of the first converts to Mohammedanism in the *hodji,* constitute a superior class, the "White-bones," whose prerogatives to pastures are recognized by the commoners or "Black-bones." The White-bones thus form a wealthy noble class with larger herds and considerable social privilege. They refuse to marry their children to Black-bones, and noble families forming clans within the tribes or hordes cement their prestige and solidarity by the exchange of daughters in marriage.

While most of the commoners possess their own stock there is a poor cattleless group who through the ill success or misfortune of their forbears became dependants of richer men whose herds they tend. Until the middle of the nineteenth century slaves were found among the Kazak, but the majority were purchased to be sold again in the town markets of the settled areas.

Although conditions vary in different parts of lowland Kazak territory, according especially to the time of the more important rains, the two most critical seasons of the year are summer and winter. In summer the grasses, parched out in the heat, afford very poor pasture, so that localities in which moisture has accumulated during the rains are of great importance. Valley hollows and lake depressions and to some extent the windward slopes of the low plateaux yield the better pastures, but none lasts long. Summer must therefore be a period of constant movement. The families and clans do not lay claims to any stretch of country at this season, for the richness of the herbage in any place varies greatly from year to year; small groups with their herds pass from site to site, rarely able

to stay more than three or four days in one camp. This period of constant migration and of the greatest scattering of the population begins at the end of May. Among the more northerly tribes movement is generally northward towards the moister forest margins, while the tribes of southern Turkestan and those of the Great Horde in the east move up into the foothills of the mountain ranges to occupy valleys which have received more rain and may also be partly flooded by streams fed by the melting snows and heavier rains on the high ranges above. On the northern steppe rains revive the pastures in July, and autumn is an easier season, but by mid-October it is necessary to migrate rapidly once more to reach winter quarters.

The winter season is again critical, but conduces this time to a concentration of settlement. Protection against the severe cold and high winds of winter, even more dangerous to livestock than to man, is sought in stretches of deep river valley with a fringe of protecting woodland where the winter grass is more abundant. The winter and summer quarters of a group may be two hundred miles and more apart, and during the year a household may cover five hundred miles. The winter quarters alone are thought of as territorial possessions; these are essentially clan settlements, to be claimed and protected by the clan as a whole. For the rest of the year all pastures are free to those with the power to occupy them, and the family or clan which first occupies any tract is rarely interfered with. These winter sites are many of them impossible in summer on account of the plagues of insects which attack both men and beasts. Each kindred of a clan has its accustomed site marked out from those of its neighbors and competitors by natural boundaries—by hills, rocks and streams, or by cairns of stones and lines of stakes. Winter is the period of greatest competition, and if the year is very hard a weak group driven from its accustomed site may lose nearly all its stock and be reduced to dependence on the more successful. Effective control, therefore, depends on the solidarity and strength of the group, but there are obvious limits to the size of the group and of the stock which can occupy a winter site. When the pressure becomes too great the older sons are urged, and if necessary compelled, to move off to find another site.

A camp or *aul* in winter rarely consists of more than three to five huts, but the *auls* of a clan may be strung far along a valley bottom each only a few miles from the next. From November until mid-April the habitation remains fixed, although the pastures may change. Apart from a few riding animals the horses are not usually brought to the winter quarters; they remain with a few herders on the autumn pastures ten to fifteen or more miles away until the first snowfall, and are then taken back to the summer pastures, where, although the weather is inclement, the pastures which were waterlogged and infested with mosquitoes in summer now afford good feed.

In colder and more exposed places many groups replace their felt tents by more solid huts (*kstau*) in winter. The materials may vary from stone in the mountain foothill country to timber branches and bark on the forest border in the north, but the majority are built of turf. The floors of the huts are often sunk deeply in the ground, and walls nearly a yard thick are built up of sods to be roofed with timbers and willow branches and withes, which are again covered with layers of turf. In the more arid areas of southern Turkestan where no mat of turf is found hut frames are often built of reeds and withes and plastered with earth. These winter huts are usually rectangular. One or two small gaps left in the walls are covered with animal membranes to admit a little light. The low, narrow entrance is hung with heavy felts and the walls are lined with felt rugs hanging from pegs driven into the walls. Round a fire pit of beaten clay set towards the front late-born camels and calves huddle among the cooking materials and piles of harness, while at the back are the sleeping quarters of the household. Flanking the main dwelling are other huts for dependants, for young

and weakling sheep and stores. Round the whole camp a high wall of turf or reeds is built, against which a light roofing of reeds, supported on poles, is built on the inner side to afford shelter for the other livestock.

Towards the middle of April the spring migration begins. Households pack up and move off unostentatiously, each often concealing from others the plan of movement which has been formed from the reports of its horse herders on the outer pastures. Thus each group may hope to take first advantage of good pastures that are accessible. Since the grass remains short and scanty, for a few weeks migration is constant and as rapid as the reduced strength of the beasts will permit. But the six weeks of late spring and early summer, when the heaviest rains fall in the more northern half of Kazak territory, provide the richest pastures of the year. The stock fattens, milk is abundant. In favored areas along stream banks that are free of insect plagues many clans may concentrate in a single camp of fifty or a hundred tents. Towards the end of July, however, the intense heat parches the ground, grass and water become scarce and the households must again scatter, migrating every few days to find sufficient feed for their stock. In late September rains fall again, especially in the south, where the season is the most favourable of the year. The pastures improve and for about a month there is another respite and a chance for the animals to fatten against the winter, but by mid-October the cold begins to set in and the households move off rapidly to their winter quarters once more.

There are thus six phases in the yearly cycle. Their duration varies from district to district and from year to year while in exceptional years, both good and bad, the regime may be upset:

(1) The stationary period in winter quarters from November to about mid-April.

(2) The rapid spring migration in the direction of summer pastures until about the middle of May.

(3) A short stationary period on rich early summer pastures which lasts about six weeks until early July.

This phase is more characteristic of the northern steppes, where the summer rains are the heaviest of the year. In southern Turkestan it is often lacking and continuous migration is necessary throughout the summer.

(4) Frequent migration over parched pastures during the intense heat of late July and August.

(5) More leisurely migrations over the improved autumn pastures until mid-October. In the south where the autumn rains are the heaviest this is the richest season of the year.

(6) Rapid migration back to winter pastures during the later part of October.

The Kazak tent, or *yurt,* so well adapted to a migratory life with beasts of burden, is a circular felt-covered structure with vertical walls and a domed roof. The wall frame consists of a collapsible trellis set upright in a circle and standing about four feet high. It is constructed of willow rods held together with leather thongs passing through holes drilled where the rods cross, and when opened it has a mesh of about a foot. Half a dozen lengths of trellis are needed for the walling of a large yurt of about twenty feet in diameter. In a narrow small gap left in the circle a door frame of stouter poles is fitted. To the upper edge of the trellis willow rods eight to ten feet long are tied, about a foot apart. These curve upwards and inwards, like the ribs of an umbrella, to be lashed or socketed to a wooden hoop two or three feet across which crowns the dome. Lashings of horsehair rope which pass spirally down from the hoop and round the trellis strengthen the frame, and over it a number of large sheets of felt are stretched and lashed in position. The roof ring, which lies directly above the fire pit, is left uncovered as a smoke hole. In bad weather and at night when the fire has died down this too is covered with a sheet of felt. Across the door frame hangs a felt curtain which can be pushed aside. The floor is covered with felting, and the inner face of the trellis is often lined with reed matting decorated with wool, while woollen rugs are laid face down over the dome before the felt covers are put on so that their pattern may be seen from within. Similar rugs are laid on the floor. Over the central fire pit is set an iron tripod from which cooking-pots are suspended. In large yurts a space on the right side is screened off with reed partitions to serve as a kitchen, but the copper cauldrons, wooden platters and leather vessels often lie around the fire pit. The bedding, felt and skin covers and pillows of sheep's wool are rolled up under the walls. Sometimes a large couch, five or six feet wide, of raised planks covered with layers of felt nearly a foot thick is set at the back of the yurt where the family sleep. Married sons and children who share their parents' yurt sleep on the left, while poor relations, dogs and lambs lie still nearer the door. When honored guests appear well furnished couches are prepared for them at the rear. Leather and wooden chests containing stores of grain, sugar and tea and great leather bags containing milk products line the side walls of the richer yurts and indicate the wealth of the occupant.

The erection and dismantling of the yurt is the work of the women or poor dependents. Two or three camels or horses are needed to carry a large yurt when packed for migration and as many may be needed to bear its contents. When a party is moving frequently the whole yurt is often not erected; the domed roof alone is set directly on the ground to provide shelter for the night.

The clothing of the Kazak has been considerably influenced by the Moslem Tartars of the west, but the characteristic garment is the kaftan, a long, padded coat with wide sleeves and a narrow upright collar, reaching to the ankles. The coarse cotton and woollen cloth for the kaftan is usually traded from the cities, although the poor weave their own cloth from camel hair. In cold weather three or four of these wool-padded kaftans may be worn one over the other and with a shorter sheep skin jacket on top. Wide, thick woollen trousers are tucked in tall boots of heavy leather. These boots with pointed toes and sharp iron heels are adapted for riding but very difficult to walk in. When expecting to ride on a long journey heavy leather breeches are worn.

The Kazak horse herds graze separately from the other live stock. They will not eat the hard, strong-tasting herbage that is adequate for camels and sheep. A herd varies from fifteen to as many as fifty head led by a stallion which will permit no other stallion to join its herd. About half of the herd is mares, the rest young animals and a few geldings. If a wolf pack threatens the herd it huddles into a compact group, and the stallion will attack the wolves if they approach closely. A stallion is only used for a year or two for breeding and is then gelded to serve as a riding and draught animal. When a young stallion reaches maturity it must be driven out of the herd and grazed alone until a place is found for it in another. The relative poverty of the pastures limits the size of herds, and a rich Kazak who may have several hundred horses divides them into a number of small herds each on separate pastures. The mares foal in March and for the next four months provide a surplus of milk for human use. Foals are tied up round the yurt to ensure the return of their mares for milking, and since a mare gives little at one milking, they are often milked six or more times a day. A mare yields only about two quarts daily in addition to the considerable amount taken by the foals. If the winter snow is not heavy mares which foal in the autumn are kept near the yurt and milked in the same way, although they give still less at this season. Mare's milk is nearly always a luxury food. The greater part of it is made into *kumiss,* a slightly intoxicating and very nourishing drink, which will keep indefinitely. To make kumiss the fresh milk is poured unboiled into leather bags into which a wooden paddle is thrust. The bag is closed at the neck and the milk beaten to and fro with the paddle for several hours and left to sour for four days. Before festivities kumiss is accumulated in large numbers of these leather pouches which may fill almost the entire available space in a large yurt, and a rich Kazak makes enough to provide a limited supply for the rest of the year. In their second year horses are branded on the haunches with the clan mark, and the unwanted stallions are gelded for use as riding animals. Unlike the Arab, the Kazak and other central Asiatic pastoralists do not ride mares. The pastures

are sufficient for larger herds than in the poor Arabian steppe desert and the mares, valued highly for their milk, are spared other exertions. The majority of the riding and pack animals are geldings of four years and more.

At ceremonial races the winning horse is usually set aside as a sacred animal, its mane and tail decorated with ribbons. Such an animal is given the best of pastures but is never saddled or ridden again. At wedding, birth and other ceremonial feasts such races and contests are run, the most characteristic form being the *bagai.* A slaughtered calf or goat is provided by a giver of the feast and is thrown into the midst of a dense group of horsemen which includes all the active men available. Each man attempts to capture the carcass and to break away from the pursuing group in order to skin the animal before he is overtaken and has the carcass snatched from him.

Horseflesh, especially that of young fat mares, is the most prized meat. The paunch fat is a great delicacy and is salted and packed into lengths of gut and smoked for storage. The toughest leather straps and lines are made from horsehide, while the hair is braided into stouts cords for lassos, halters and yurt ropes.

Geldings are ridden, and although a man may have a favorite among his horses it is used only for short periods and is sent back to the herd to recuperate; for the riding horse is in constant use, and although it is often given a little hay and grain this small extra feed is not enough to maintain it in condition for any considerable time. Horse herds are rounded up by small parties of riders. Until bridled they are difficult to control, and when a particular horse is to be caught a long pole with a running noose of strong hide at the end is used. The pursuer overtakes and rides alongside his quarry until he is in a position to drop the noose and bring it to a standstill.

Poor families who have very few horses let them feed in common with their other stock. They do not milk their mares but reserve their strength for use as riding and baggage animals.

The horse saddle used by men is a light curved wooden frame set on felt blankets. It is held by two girths, and within the frame is set a riding pad covered with a saddle rug. Women's saddles are more massive. They have a pointed pommel and a cradle is attached in front when a young child has to be carried. The horse is ridden with a very short stirrup, the knees raised high and pressed against the front arch of the saddle; the bridle is held in the left hand and a long guiding rein several feet long is attached to the right-hand ring of the snaffle bit. With this trailing rein the horse is caught and tethered.

The superb horsemanship of the Kazak is of course famous, and many travelers in western Asia have remarked on the amazing contrast between the ungainly waddles of the Kazak on foot and the graceful and confident bearing of horse and rider.

Camels are used as supplementary beasts of burden by some Kazak, especially in the more arid southern areas. The Arabian camel, although it can carry heavier burdens, is rare, for the double-humped dromedary or Bactrian camel, which is probably native to southern Turkestan, is far better able to withstand the severe winters. The dromedary is hardly ever ridden. It is not often milked and its flesh is eaten only when it is the only meat available. But it will carry heavy burdens of several hundredweight some fifteen to twenty miles a day, while the hair of the winter coat which sheds in spring provides valuable fibre for the rough cloths woven on a crude loom by the poorer Kazaks. A rich man may keep as many as fifty camels if his establishment is large and his stores considerable, but the ordinary clansman will have but two or three and the poor often none at all.

Sheep form the largest single element of a Kazak's live stock and provide the main food supply. The majority of Kazak sheep belong to the fat-rumped breed, a large, rather goat-like variety derived from the wild Urial sheep of Asia. It is very strong and hardy, and has a thick coat of stiff wool mixed with coarser hair, and yellow, brown or white in colour. But the most remarkable characteristic is the large double cushion of fat which covers and hangs from the buttocks, obscuring the short tail; in a grown sheep after good feeding this fat hangs down in two great ropes dragging on the ground, and may weigh over thirty pounds. An adequate supply of plants such as wormwood bushes which are rich in soda salts seems to be essential for this development of fat, and it is greatest in autumn when little wooden trolleys are often fitted to prevent the hanging cushions from dragging on the ground. This fat-rumped breed of sheep is found from the Black Sea to China, but it is often mixed with other strains. True fat-tailed sheep are also found in Kazak herds, although these are more characteristic farther south and west; in this breed the fat is formed on the long tail itself, but is not usually so large and heavy.

Sheep are pastured in flocks of a thousand or more in the charge of boys. A horse is not wasted on sheep herding and the shepherd usually rides an ox. In the north a ram is kept for every fifty sheep. Since the winter is so severe that nearly all autumn-born lambs die felt aprons are strapped on the bellies of rams after the spring lambing in order to prevent further breeding that year. Where the winter is less severe in south Turkestan more rams are placed with the ewes, and late-born lambs after a few weeks in shelter may be safely left to themselves. All surplus rams are gelded and generally form a separate flock. The flocks are driven out from the camp in the morning and return often without guidance at midday. After milking they are driven out again to return before sundown for the evening milking. Alongside the yurts temporary stalls of stakes and ropes are set up, at which the ewes are tethered for milking. They give milk for three to four months after lambing, and although only half a pint may be obtained from a single ewe at one milking, the gross yield of large flocks is considerable. The milk is at once soured, or laboriously churned into butter in large leather pouches or made into cheeses. Butter is salted and packed into cleaned sheep paunches for storage. Soft cheeses are often kept to mash up in water at a later and less plentiful season as a substitute for milk, but most cheese is made to harden and it largely replaces meat as solid food in the winter and spring. In the autumn, after a spell of dry weather, the flocks are driven through a stream or lake to clean their wool and are then sheared; the fleeces taken off in one piece are packed into bales until required for felting or sold to traders from the oasis towns.

A large party is needed to make felt and many fleeces are required. The wool is first spread out in a thick layer over hides and beaten loose with pliant wooden laths by a group of young men and girls; it is then plucked out still further by hand, thoroughly damped and spread between two large straw mats between which it is rolled up and tightly bound. The felt-makers then divide into two groups and sit facing one another several yards apart while for an hour or more they push the roll to and fro over the ground between them with their feet. The matting is unrolled and the felted wool is now beaten with the hand several hours to compress it still further; it is finally bound at the edges with woollen thread, and if required for a special purpose may be colored with vegetable dyes or decorated with wool stitching.

The older sheep that are not likely to survive the winter are killed off at the end of autumn—a time of abundant if tough meat. Sheep are slaughtered in considerable numbers on many occasion during the rest of the year, but a meal which includes mutton is always, except among the wealthy, something of a feast. Milk products and wool rather than meat are the things for which the sheep is valued.

Goats are also kept in small numbers. They run in the sheep flocks and are milked with them. The goats are believed to protect the flocks from the attacks of wild animals and they afford soft leather for clothing and small bags.

Horned cattle are fewer than sheep and horses among the Kazak. They are less able to stand exposure to the severe winters, but cows give milk in greater quantities than ewes and for a longer season, and soured cows' milk (airan) is a favorite food. Moreover, increased markets for cattle in Russian settlements have led to a considerable increase in numbers in the last fifty years. The native breed has long, curving horns.

The cows will give milk only in the presence of a calf, but each yields about two and a half quarts a day for six months, and a small winter supply of milk can be obtained from those which calve in the autumn. Bullocks and cows are ridden by boys and servants on short leisurely journeys, and they are also used at need as auxiliary pack animals. Although the milk of sheep, goats and cattle is frequently mixed in the leather gourds for making butter, cheese and sour milk or airan, cows' milk is preferred for making the last. For airan the fresh milk is thinned with water, some airan from a previous making is added and the whole is poured into leather pouches to be stirred almost continuously for twenty hours. Airan will keep for long periods and is regularly mixed with small amounts of millet or wheat to make various broths. But other cattle products are largely neglected, beef is not liked and never eaten by the well-to-do, while the hides are also little used. Horned cattle have not been fully adopted into Kazak economy. They are less hardy and less tolerant of the dry salty pastures that are characteristic of the poorer steppes, and remain half foreign among the herds of sheep and horses.

To supplement the poor winter feed of the riding horses and late-born lambs every household attempts to collect a small amount of hay. Grass is not cut green for this purpose but small tracts in which good grass is found are left ungrazed, to cure naturally under the summer sun. Each aul tries to find a supply near its winter quarters and a small group goes back towards the end of summer to gather and store it for later use.

Extended travel everywhere involves the abandonment of herds, food stores and yurt so that the travelling Kazak is always dependent on the hospitality of other groups he encounters. But on this he can usually rely, for the monotony of the isolated encampments, the avidity for news of other districts and groups and the strong convention of hospitality ensure a welcome for the traveler; indeed he usually provides the occasion for a minor feast. When intending to cover a considerable distance the traveler receives a fresh horse from his host of the previous night in exchange for the one on which he arrived. On the return journey he brings back each horse one after the other to the camp from which it was taken and finally recovers his own at the last stage of the journey. On long journeys in empty country, food in the form of hard cheeses and dried flour or baked cakes can be packed away in surprising quantities in the leather bags which hang from the saddle.

Although the Kazak are essentially pastoralists, agricultural products are produced on a small scale. Whenever physical conditions suitable for the diversion of river water offer opportunities for irrigation, water channels and embanked plots are laid out for millet, wheat and rye and, in the far south, for rice. Much of this cultivation is undertaken by dependent peasants who are not Kazaks, and in former times slaves from the oasis settlements were used. But small groups of true Kazaks are also found engaged in cultivation and remain at work in the fields from spring to autumn. These are mostly poor families with little or no live stock of their own, who depend for their livelihood on service to richer families who provide them with meat and milk products.

Kazak agriculture is technically similar to that of the oases of central and southwestern Asia, although the standard of cultivation is often much lower. The stream or river used for irrigation is often embanked to protect the adjacent low-lying land on which the plots are made, and, in addition, must often be dammed back in summer with a strong wall of stones and brush so that the water will flow into the irrigation channels when the walling at the entrance to each is breached for the flooding. Where water cannot be made to flow directly over the plots, wooden water wheels are sometimes used to lift it into channels; it is often laboriously carried in leather skins. On the retentive soils of the northern steppes, where there is also more summer rain, a plot may need only one watering, but in southern Turkestan the sandy ground must be watered every week during the drought of summer.

The poorest cultivators may till the ground by hand with hoes, but more usually a simple plough, often merely an iron blade attached to a pole, is dragged by horses. The soil is not turned and the furrows are very shallow; the ground is not harrowed but merely smoothed down by dragging long poles across the field with horses, and the harvest, reaped by hand, is threshed by driving horses over the strewn ears. At the larger sites water-wheel grinding mills of central Asiatic type are erected and strong granaries built to hold the harvest.

Hunting has little importance in the economy of the Kazak, but falconry and coursing are favorite pastimes of the richer families, who may also keep specialist hunters to stalk larger game. Falcons and hawks are used to take wild duck, pheasant, hares and other small game, while boars, wolves and foxes are ridden down on horseback. Hunting greyhounds are used only by a few eastern Kazak groups in the Tian Shan. Moreover, the Kazak make almost no use of the dog for herding purposes, probably a result of the influence of Islam, which regards the dog as an unclean animal. Chamoix, mountain sheep and elk are stalked in the higher mountains of the northwest, but the majority of the Kazaks are lowlanders in a territory poor in valuable game.

The mobility of their life and the long-established contacts with oasis towns have limited the development of crafts among the Kazak. Much of their cloth and metalware is obtained from the settled peoples, and itinerant craftsmen often do the smithing and even the felt drying; the Kazak tinkers who repair horse bits and kettles are less skillful and self-reliant than the smiths of former days when access to markets and traded goods was less frequent and certain. The copper and silver smiths are still skilled craftsmen, but their products are mainly hammered ornaments for saddlery. Woodworking, the making of yurt trellises, chests, bowls, is done by men, while the women dress hides, do the stitchery and wool embroidery on felt and clothing on which much care is lavished to produce intricate patterns. They use very little pottery and make none themselves.

The Kazak have long been Sunnite Moslems, but they are extremely lax in many observances and many earlier beliefs and rites survive. Boys are circumcised and men usually shave their heads. Ramazan is kept to some extent and itinerant mullahs, usually Kazan Tartars from the west, wander from aul to aul reading the Koran and performing minor ceremonies while the aboriginal horse sacrifice has been adapted to symbolize the offering of Isaac by Abraham. But they have no mosques, and women are neither secluded nor veiled. Soothsayers divine the future from the marking on the shoulder blade of a sheep and magicians cure the sick.

24. "CULTURAL" vs. "ECOLOGICAL" FACTORS IN THE EXPRESSION OF VALUES, ATTITUDES, AND PERSONALITY CHARACTERISTICS

ROBERT B. EDGERTON

Reprinted from American Anthropologist, *67 (1965): 442-47. Robert B. Edgerton is Research Social Scientist and Professor of Anthropology at the Neuropsychiatric Institute, University of California, Los Angeles. His principal interest is psychological anthropology, particularly the comparative study of social deviance. In addition to research in East Africa, he has studied the Menominee Indians of Wisconsin and several ethnic populations in urban areas. He is the author of* The Cloak of Competence.

■ This selection is a discussion of some aspects of the values generated by pastoralism. There are many sources of a society's value system, its ideas and standards of the good life, of what is desirable, undesirable, and attainable. Goldschmidt noted some of the dominant values that are often characteristic of pastoralists in Selection 19. Edgerton, who also was a member of the Ecology in East Africa Project, begins his paper with an outline of some of the methods used in the attempt to elicit these aspects of culture.

We have seen that common habitational pressures and challenges can lead to great similarities in different groups and that differences in habitat can produce marked divergences in groups that once were similar. The problem Edgerton set was to learn whether parallels exist in four tribes between adaptations and the patterning of values and psychological processes. He found that there are common denominators between the pastoral and horticultural sectors of a tribe, and there also are significant differences that are best understood in terms of differences in habitat and levels of technological development. Psychological similarities among different tribes—the common denominators among the horticulturists or the pastoralists of the four different tribes—emerged as integral aspects of their strategies of adaptation.

A continuation of Edgerton's work appears in his paper, "Conceptions of Psychosis in Four East African Societies" *(American Anthropologist,* 68 [1966]: 408-425). My own point of view about culture-and-personality studies is spelled out in "On Alternative Views of the Individual in Culture-and-Personality Studies" *(American Anthropologist,* 68 [1966]: 355-61), and in my books, *Social Structure and Personality* (New York: Holt, Rinehart and Winston, 1961) and *The Transition from Childhood to Adolescence* (Chicago: Aldine, 1964). The principal source for my point of view is the work of A. I. Hallowell, especially his collection of papers, *Culture and Experience* (Philadelphia: University of Pennsylvania Press, 1957). ■

MY ROLE IN THE "Culture and Ecology Project" was first, to provide a systematic, objective investigation of values, attitudes, and personality characteristics among both the farming and herding sectors of all four tribes, and, second, to determine the extent to which differences in these matters might be accounted for by ecological variation.

It was obvious from the outset that if legitimate comparisons between tribal groups were to be made, that the data involved would have to be collected under rigorously standardized circumstances, and that further, these data must be at least minimally quantifiable. As all anthropologists are acutely aware, satisfying such conditions in field research is difficult in the extreme. However, following a series of conferences between project personnel and consultations with persons skilled in sundry interviewing and projective testing techniques, an interviewing program was decided upon that, with luck, had a chance to be successful.

The interviewing tactics as well as variety of forms of questions and a wide range of projective test stimuli were pretested in East Africa among the Sebei and Kamba. Following the pretesting experience and another conference of project staff, the final interview battery was determined. It consisted of: 1) 85 questions covering a great many subject areas, 2) 10 Rorschach plates, 3) 9 values-pictures (TAT-like pictures), and 4) 22 color slides. As you have already read, farming and herding sectors of each tribe were examined and areas particularly suited for our purposes were selected. Within each of these sites a systematic sample was drawn of at least 30 married men and 30 married women. In all, 505 persons were interviewed.

In each tribe an interpreter (who was a member of that tribe) was trained and all interviews were conducted in the native language through carefully supervised interpretation. Each person was interviewed in private and the place, circumstances, and format of the interview were rigidly standardized. Preselected respondents were induced to come to the interviewing place where all interviews took place. After the interview, which lasted between 60 and 90 minutes, each respondent was offered a gift (usually native beer). Despite assorted tribulations, both men and women in all tribes cooperated well and the refusal rate overall was less than 5% of the sample (the highest refusal rate for any of the eight communities was slightly under 8%).

The interview itself was conducted without notable difficulty and without conspicuous evasion or withholding of information. In order to establish the validity of the responses, however, in each of the eight communities follow-up verification sessions were conducted to ascertain any possible areas of misunderstanding, lying or withholding of information. By this procedure it was possible to omit suspected information and clarify answers whenever necessary. As a consequence, while I was in the field I was impressed by the face validity of the data

gathered. Analysis of these data has done nothing to shake my faith in the thoughtfulness and candor with which these many Africans responded to a strange and sometimes unwelcome interrogation.

What follows is an abbreviated report on the findings to date. Not all analyses are yet complete and obviously only a few of the available findings can be presented here. Nevertheless, I will attempt to provide a sense of some of the major findings by pointing to highlights and presenting a few examples.

CULTURAL DISTINCTIVENESS

Each of the four tribes gave an internally consistent and distinctive set of responses. Of course there are many ways in which the responses of all four tribes are alike, but despite a considerable amount of individual variation, there is for each tribe a characteristic response pattern that distinguishes it from each of the other tribes.

To mention but a few examples: the Kamba are marked by fear of poverty, extreme male dominance and restraint of emotions and motives; the Hehe are typified by impulsive aggression, concern with formal authority and profound mistrust and secrecy; the Pokot are characterized by intense interest in cattle, physical beauty, and sexual gratification; the Sebei are distinctively concerned with a fear of disease and death, the malignant power of women and remarkably profound interpersonal jealousy and hostility. I should add that these examples represent response differences that are statistically significant at the .01 level.

There are also clear similarities between the pairs of linguistically related tribes. Consistent response differentials exist between the Bantu-speaking tribes (Kamba and Hehe) and the Kalenjin-speaking tribes (Pokot and Sebei). The Pokot and Sebei are fairly close, linguistically and geographically, but the two Bantu-speaking tribes are far more distantly related. Nevertheless, there is a consistent Bantu response that is different from the Kalenjin pattern. For example, compared to the Kalenjin speakers, the Bantu are more concerned with sorcery-witchcraft; the Bantu value system is focused upon land rather than cattle; the Bantu want sons, the Kalenjin want both sons and daughters; the Bantu most respect a rich man, the Kalenjin respect a prophet; Bantu women look forward to old age as a period of security and relief from work duties while Kalenjin women tend to fear old age; and the Bantu are not shamed by the suicide of a relative whereas the Kalenjin are greatly shamed (again all these differences are significant at the .01 level).

The point of these examples is to demonstrate that the interviewing procedure employed here *was* capable of evoking response patterns that reveal consistencies of *cultural* emphasis. These patterns are clear and consistent for linguistically related tribes as well as for separate tribes. The question at issue is *whether these cultural response patterns can be shown to vary when ecological adjustments within the culture vary and if so is this co-variation predictable and meaningful?* Stated simply, does ecological change reshape basic cultural response patterns in values, attitudes, and personality characteristics?

Before this question can be considered directly it is necessary to sort out the effects that the sex, age, and acculturation of the respondent had upon the response patterns.

THE SEX OF THE RESPONDENT

In order to avoid an exclusively male-oriented study, equal numbers of men and women were interviewed. The sample size selected (never less than 30) was large enough to permit statistical comparison of men and women within both farming and herding sectors of all four tribes. The result of such a comparison is a surprise. In their responses to direct questions, in their detailed perceptions, and even in their Rorschachs, there is substantial agreement between men and women in each of the four tribes. This finding contradicts the general presumption (which we shared before this study) that men and women in the same society can be expected to

have considerable differences in values, beliefs, attitudes and personality characteristics.

For instance, of over 10,000 comparisons between the responses of men and women, only about 5% showed differences that were statistically significant. On most values, most attitudes, most beliefs, and most personality features, men and women do *not* differ. However men and women *consistently* disagree in matters concerning children, marriage, and relations between husbands and wives. To mention a few examples, Pokot herders insist that the best thing that can happen to a man is cattle; their wives, however, argue that the best thing that can happen to a man is a good wife. Men in most of the tribes believe that all women want to marry a rich man; women insist that they want to marry a man they love. And in every one of the eight communities men and women disagree on the following questions: "Do wives disobey their husbands?" and "Is it right for them to do so?"

It would appear then that the sex of the respondent is important principally where the questions directly involve relations between men and women. In summary, about 95% of the response variance is unaffected by the sex of the respondent.

ACCULTURATION

Dealing with acculturation was a difficult problem. Ideally, it was necessary to hold the acculturation of all eight communities equal despite the rapid changes in East Africa at that time and in the face of the inescapable fact that highland farmers were generally closer to acculturative influence than were lowland herders.

The first step in equalizing the acculturation of the respondents was to exclude from the sample persons with substantial European educations or greatly influenced by other tribal cultures, out of keeping with the norm in the community as a whole. This exclusion resulted in a sample without persons of conspicuously high acculturation but the sample that remained was nonetheless not homogeneous. Thus efforts were made to specify the relative acculturation of all respondents. Eventually an index of acculturation was constructed, comprised of 10 items concerning European education, religion, type and condition of clothing, travel, house type, wage work and involvement in cash economy. On the basis of this index, each male respondent was given a numerical score. There was insufficient information to permit quantification of the acculturation of women. However, it is apparent that the women in the sample were *uniformly* less acculturated than their husbands and consequently by omitting them in our estimates we do not distort the relative acculturation of the eight communities.

It should also be mentioned that while the young tend to be more acculturated than the old, each of the eight subsamples (both male and female) was selected to have the same age stratification, and thus age should not influence the comparisons between communities.

Attempts to analyze these data are not yet complete but considerable work has been done. First, each of the eight subsamples was split in half, with the most acculturated persons compared to the least. Then upper quartiles were compared with lower quartiles. Finally, tribe was disregarded entirely and persons were compared across tribes and sectors with the upper decile and quartile of acculturation from all tribes compared with the lower decile and quartile. These operations permit us a reasonably unobstructed view of the effect of acculturation upon response.

These analyses discovered few response differentials and even these few were not consistent across tribes. That is, a response that was sensitive to acculturation in one tribe was not sensitive to it in the others. The effect of acculturation in any given community was minor—the response differentials were few and rarely significant statistically. Overall, the influence of acculturational differences was similarly slight. Although conclusions must still be tentative, it now appears that *acculturative differences had no important effect upon response.*

"ECOLOGICAL" DIFFERENTIATION

It can now be said that, in general, the sex, age, and acculturation of the respondent have little to do with most responses. It is also clear that "culture" does make a difference— each tribe has its own distinctive response pattern. Let us then move to an examination of the effects of ecological differentiation— what happens when we compare our four herding communities with our four farming communities? Ideally each of these tribes would replicate the other; that is, the four herding communities would be highly similar and the same would be true of the four farming communities. We were not so innocent of African realities that we ever expected to discover four cases of identical farming-herding differentiation but even our most reasonable ethnographic assumptions were sometimes confounded by the reality of East Africa 1961-2.

Obviously any attempt simply to compare the responses in the four herding communities with the four farming communities could hardly be expected to be entirely satisfactory. And in fact this was the case. Many of our expected differences did not materialize and others were equivocal, holding in some tribes but not in others. However, even by such crude analytic means as comparing the four sets of herders with the four sets of farmers, some of our expectations are rewarded by statistically significant confirmation. Some of the confirmed expectations are relatively obvious—such as the fact that the farmers did indeed define wealth in terms of land whereas the herders did not. Others were more impressive: as we expected, the farmers divine and consult one another, the herders act individually; the farmers do value hard work, the herders do not; the farmers are indeed relatively more hostile and suspicious of their fellows than the herders. Some confirmed differences even extended as far as personality; e.g., the farmers tend to be indirect, abstract, given to fantasy, more anxious, less able to deal with their emotions, and less able to control their impulses. The herders, on the contrary, are direct, open, bound to reality, and their emotions, though constricted, are under control. It is apparent that even this crude analysis points to meaningful and predictable differentials between farmers and herders.

A preferred alternative is to recognize that our eight communities are ranged along a continuum, the poles of which are the ideal farming and herding types. Thanks to the availability of detailed geographic and economic data we can place our eight communities on this continuum with considerable objectivity. When we order the eight communities in this fashion, we find that certain responses are scaled in like manner. For example, our hypothesis concerning independence of action is strongly confirmed: that is, the more pastoral the economy the more that society will maximize and value independence of action for its male members.

We can, in fact, take this approach one step further with still more satisfactory results. In terms of our working models of pastoralism and farming, we set forth certain features that we considered to be characteristic of the two different socioeconomic adjustments. We refer here to the relative presence of such features as close and prolonged residence, warfare, land shortage, competition for power, women's economic importance, the potential for status mobility and the like. Though in our general model we treat these features as intervening variables, we can now set them up as independent variables and examine response patterns in relationship to them. Once again, we scale the eight communities in terms of each of our now independent variables and then determine if the responses scale in like fashion. For example, let us take the variable of warfare. We can rank the eight communities with respect to the extent that they are now, or were in the recent past, engaged in inter-tribal warfare. We then examine the responses in the eight communities to determine how well they relate to this ranking. To follow out this example, we find that responses dealing with the importance of bravery, the prestige of warriors, fear and hatred of the enemy, the

value of independence in young boys, etc., do in fact correlate with our warfare scale.

Another approach which is now being explored is multi-variate analysis, principally cluster and factor analysis. These techniques permit us to intercorrelate a great many variables concerning each individual in our sample irrespective of his tribal affiliation. For example, factors such as age, sex, acculturation, cattle wealth, land wealth, family composition, social status and economic practices can be intercorrelated with assorted interview responses concerning values, attitudes, and personality characteristics. Factors in the resulting correlation matrix may point to relationships which are invisible to ordinary analysis. Very preliminary factor analyses, for example, suggest an interesting but unanticipated relationship between 1) old age, 2) wealth, 3) intelligence, 4) fear, and 5) disturbed personality integration. That is, people who are old and wealthy are also intelligent, fearful, and disturbed.

CONCLUSION

In brief, I think it is clear that under certain circumstances of research design and careful cooperation survey research techniques can be applied even under difficult field conditions. The data that result can be highly instructive, especially when they can be buttressed by ethnographic investigations. More importantly, in this instance, the survey interview data confirm our underlying hypothesis that certain values, attitudes, and personality features do derive from the different economic adjustments of herders and farmers. This paper has necessarily abbreviated and simplified a large and complicated research undertaking, but when the analyses have been completed, I think it will be possible to conclude that while relationships between "ecology" and "culture" are complicated and reciprocal, at least some economic adjustments generate predictable and pervasive consequences in social organization, cultural content, and even in personality patterns.

25. ECOLOGIC RELATIONSHIPS OF ETHNIC GROUPS IN SWAT, NORTH PAKISTAN

Reprinted from American Anthropologist, *58 (1958): 107-189. Fredrik Barth is Professor of Social Anthropology, University of Bergen (Norway). Much of his field work has been done among tribal peoples in the Middle East, and one of his continuing research interests is the problems of ecologic analysis.*

■ In Selection 17, Saltzman outlined the ecological conditions that seem to underlie political centralization among pastoralists; in Selection 18, Bates concentrated on the social and political elements in the wider milieu. In the next selection, Barth—whose work has exerted great influence on students of centralized pastoralism—combines the two points of view. He examines three groups in North Pakistan in their relationships with the natural habitat and with each other: (1) The Pathans are plow agriculturists characterized by a caste system and various nonagricultural occupational groups; they live in the valleys of a fertile high-altitude region. (2) Kohistanis also practice plow agriculture, but on narrow artificial terraces and with lower productivity than the Pathans. In addition, however, they are also transhumant herders. Their habitat is an inhospitable mountain region, and the two technologies in combination enable them to adapt to their milieu. (3) Gujars are transhumant herders and true nomads who cut across the habitats of the first two groups; the latter are hosts to the Gujars. However, their distribution is not uniform; while they are found throughout Pathan territory, ecological barriers confine them to the western portion of Kohistan. Moreover, the Gujars have been assimilated as a specialized caste of herders into the Pathan caste system, caring for the Pathans' livestock.

Conforming to the principles explicated in Selection 18, the nomadic Gujars are under the political direction of a single leader who coordinates the movements of groups made up of lineages and clans; the small size of their units facilitates their bargaining for lower grazing taxes. Locally transhumant Gujars are tied individually to Pathan—not Gujar—leaders. In either case, the pastoralists are subject to political organizations more powerful than their own. Those who have been assimilated into the Pathan organization are politically subservient to Pathan leaders directly. Those who move back and forth across cultural and ecological borders are under the control of their own leader who mediates their relationships with their seasonal hosts.

A case study paralleling the one described by Barth is provided in "Adaptation and Political Organization in Iranian Baluchistan," by Philip C. Salzman *(Ethnology,* 10 [1971]: 433-44). One of the best-known anthropological studies of the relationships between habitat and the organization of social relations is *Political Systems of Highland Burma,* by E. R. Leach (Boston: Beacon Press, 1965). Closer to the area discussed in this selection is *The Social Organization of the Marri Baluch,* by Robert N. Pehrson (Chicago: Aldine, 1966), which was compiled and analyzed from Pehrson's field notes by Barth. The Marri Baluch are pastoralists and agriculturists of West Pakistan, and the analysis of the data is closely tied to the relationships between habitat and the organization of social relations. ■

THE IMPORTANCE OF ecology factors for the form and distribution of cultures has usually been analyzed by means of a culture area concept. This concept has been developed with reference to the aboriginal cultures of North America. Attempts at delimiting culture areas in Asia by similar procedures have proved extremely difficult, since the distribution of cultural types, ethnic groups, and natural areas rarely coincide. Coon speaks of Middle Eastern society as being built on a mosaic principle—many ethnic groups with radically different cultures co-reside in an area in symbiotic relations of variable intimacy. Referring to a similar structure, Furnivall describes the Netherlands Indies as a plural society. The common characteristic in these two cases is the combination of ethnic segmentation and economic interdependence. Thus the "environment" of any one ethnic group is not only defined by natural conditions, but also by the presence and activities of the other ethnic groups on which it depends. Each group exploits only a section of the total environment, and leaves large parts of it open for other groups to exploit.

This interdependence is analogous to that of the different animal species in a habitat. As Kroeber emphasizes, culture area classifications are essentially ecologic; thus detailed ecologic considerations, rather than geographical areas of subcontinental size, should offer the point of departure. The present paper attempts to apply a more specific ecologic approach to a case study of distribution by utilizing some of the concepts of animal ecology, particularly the concept of a *niche*—the place of a group in the total environment, its relations to resources and competitors.

GROUPS

The present example is simple, relatively speaking, and is concerned with the three major ethnic groups in Swat State, North-West frontier Province, Pakistan. These are: (1) *Pathans*—Pashto-speaking (Iranian language family) sedentary agriculturalists; (2) *Kohistanis*—speakers of Dardic languages, practicing agriculture and transhumant herding; and (3) *Gujars-Gujri*-speaking (a lowland Indian dialect) nomadic herders. Kohistanis are probably the ancient inhabitant of most of Swat; Pathans entered as conquerors in successive waves between A.D. 1000-1600, and Gujars probably first appeared in the area some 400 years ago. Pathans of Swat State number about 450,000, Kohistanis perhaps 30,000. The number of Gujars in the area is difficult to estimate.

The centralized state organization in Swat was first established in 1917, and the most recent accretion was annexed in 1947, so the central organization has no relevance for the distributional problems discussed here.

AREA

Swat State contains sections of two main valleys, those of the Swat and the Indus Rivers. The Swat River rises in the high mountains to the north, among 18,000 foot peaks. As it descends and grows in volume, it enters a deep gorge. This upper section of the valley is thus very narrow and steep. From approximately 5,000 feet, the Swat valley becomes increasingly wider as one proceeds southward, and is flanked by ranges descending from 12,000 to 6,000 feet in altitude. The river here has a more meandering course, and the valley bottom is a flat, extensive alluvial deposit.

The east border of Swat State follows the Indus River; only its west bank and tributaries are included in the area under discussion. The Indus enters the area as a very large river; it flows in a spectacular gorge, 15,000 feet deep and from 12 to 16 miles wide. Even in the north, the valley bottom is less than 3,000 feet above sea level, while the surrounding mountains reach 18,000 feet. The tributary valleys are consequently short and deeply cut, with an extremely steep profile. Further to the south, the surrounding mountain ranges recede from the river banks and lose height, the Indus deposits some sediment, and the tributary streams form wider valleys.

Climatic variations in the area are a function of altitude. Precipitation is low throughout. The southern, low-altitude areas have long, hot summers and largely steppe vegetation. The Indus gorge has been described as "a desert embedded between icy gravels." The high mountains are partly covered by permanent ice and snow, and at lower levels by natural mountain meadows in the brief summer season. Between these extremes is a broad belt (from 6,000 to 11,000 feet) of forest, mainly of pine and deodar.

PATHAN-KOHISTANI DISTRIBUTION

Traditional history, in part relating to place-names of villages and uninhabited ruins, indicates that Kohistani inhabitants were driven progressively northward by Pathan invaders. This northward spread has now been checked, and the border between Kohistani and Pathan territories has been stable for some time. The last Pathan expansion northward in the Swat valley took place under the leadership of the Saint Akhund Sadiq Baba, eight generations ago. To understand the factors responsible for the stability of the present ethnic border, it is necessary to examine the specific ecologic requirements of the present Pathan economy and organization.

Pathans of Swat live in a complex, multi-caste society. The landholding Pakhtun caste is organized in localized, segmentary, unilineal descent groups; other castes and occupational groups are tied to them as political clients and economic serfs. Subsistence is based on diversified and well-developed plow agriculture. The main crops are wheat, maize, and rice; much of the plowed land is watered by artificial irrigation. Manuring is practiced, and several systems of crop rotation and regular fallow-field rhythms are followed, according to the nature of the soil and water supply. All rice is irrigated, with nursery beds and transplantation.

Only part of the Pathan population is actively engaged in agriculture. Various other occupational groups perform specialized services in return for payment in kind, and thus require that the agriculturalists produce a considerable surplus. Further, and perhaps more importantly, the political system depends on a strong hierarchical organization of landowners and much political activity, centering around the men's houses (*hujra*). This activity diverts much manpower from productive pursuits. The large and well-organized Pathan tribes are found in the lower parts of the Swat valley and along the more southerly tributaries of the Indus, occupying broad and fertile alluvial plains. A simpler form of political organization is found along the north-ern fringes of Pathan territory. It is based on families of saintly descent, and is characterized by the lack of men's houses. This simplification renders the economy of the community more efficient (1) by eliminating the wasteful potlatch-type feasts of the men's houses, and (2) by vesting political office in saintly persons of inviolate status, thus eliminating the numerous retainers that protect political leaders in other Pathan areas.

Pathan territory extends to a critical ecologic threshold: the limits within which two crops can be raised each year. This is largely a function of altitude. Two small outliers of Pashto-speaking people (Jag, in Duber valley, and a section of Kalam) are found north of this limit. They are unlike other Pathans, and similar to their Kohistani neighbors in economy and political organization.

The conclusion that the limits of double cropping constitute the effective check on further Pathan expansion seems unavoidable. Pathan economy and political organization requires that agricultural labor produce considerable surplus. Thus in the marginal high-altitude areas, the political organization is modified and "economized" (as also in the neighboring Dir area), while beyond these limits of double cropping the economic and social system cannot survive at all.

Kohistanis are not restricted by this barrier. The Kohistani ethnic group apparently once straddled it; and, they were driven north by invading Pathans, they freely crossed what to Pathans was a restricting barrier. This must be related to differences between Kohistani and Pathan political and economic organization, and consequent differences in their ecologic requirements.

Kohistanis, like Pathans, practice a developed plow agriculture. Due to the terrain they occupy, their fields are located on narrow artificial terraces, which require considerable engineering skill for their construction. Parts of Kohistan receive no summer rains; the streams, fed from the large snow reserves in the mountains, supply water to the fields through complex and extensive systems of irrigation. Some manuring is practiced. Climatic conditions modify the types of food crops. Maize and millet are most important; wheat and rice can only be raised in a few of the low-lying areas. The summer season is short, and fields produce only one crop a year.

Agricultural methods are thus not very different from those of Pathans, but the net production of fields is much less. Kohistanis, however, have a two-fold economy, for transhumant herding is as important as agriculture. Sheep, goats, cattle, and water buffalo are kept for wool, meat, and milk. The herds depend in summer on mountain pastures, where most of the Kohistanis spend between four and eight months each year, depending on local conditions. In some areas the whole population migrates through as many as five seasonal camps, from winter dwellings in the valley bottom to summer campsites at a 14,000 foot altitude, leaving the fields around the abandoned low-altitude dwellings to remain practically untended. In the upper Swat valley, where the valley floor is covered with snow some months of the year, winter fodder is collected and stored for the animals.

By having two strings to their bow, so to speak, the Kohistanis are able to wrest a living from inhospitable mountain areas which fall short of the minimal requirements for Pathan occupation. In these areas, Kohistanis long retained their autonomy, the main territories being conquered by Swat State in 1926, 1939, and 1947. They were, and still are, organized in politically separate village districts of from 400 to 2,000 inhabitants. Each community is subdivided into a number of loosely connected patrilineal lineages. The central political institution is the village council, in which all landholding minimal lineages have their representatives. Each community also includes a family of blacksmith-cum-carpenter specialists, and a few households of tenants or farm laborers.

Neighboring communities speaking the same dialect or language could apparently fuse politically when under external pressure, in which case they were directed by a common council of prominent leaders from all constituent lineages. But even these larger units were unable to withstand the large forces of skilled fighters which Pathans of the Swat area could mobilize. These forces were estimated at 15,000 by the British during the Ambeyla campaign in 1862.

"NATURAL" SUBAREAS

The present Swat State appears to the Kohistanis as a single natural area, since, as an ethnic group, they once occupied all of it, and since their economy can function anywhere within it. With the advent of invading Pathan tribes, the Kohistanis found themselves unable to defend the land. But the land which constitutes one natural area to Kohistanis is divided by a line which Pathans were unable to cross. From the Pathan point of view, it consists of two natural areas, one containing the ecologic requisites for Pathan occupation, the other uninhabitable. Thus the Kohistanis were permitted to retain a part of their old territory in spite of their military inferiority, while in the remainder they were either assimilated as serfs in the conquering Pathan society or were expelled.

From the purely synchronic point of view, the present Pathan-Kohistani distribution presents a simple and static picture of two ethnic groups representing two discrete culture areas, and with a clear correspondence between these culture areas and natural areas: Pathans in broad valleys with a hot climate and scrub vegetation as against Kohistanis in high mountains with a severe climate and coniferous forest cover. Through the addition of time depth, the possibility arises of breaking down the concept of a "natural area" into specific ecologic components in relation to the requirements of specific economies.

Analysis of the distribution of Gujars in relation to other ethnic groups requires such a procedure. Gujars are found in both Pathan and Kohistani areas, following two different economic patterns in both areas: transhumant herding, and true nomadism. But while they are distributed throughout all of the Pathan territory, they are found only in the western half of Kohistan, and neither reside nor visit in the eastern half. The division into mountain and valley seems irrelevant to the Gujars, while the mountain area—inhospitable to Pathans and usable to Kohistanis—is divided by a barrier which Gujars do not cross. The economy and other features of Gujar life must be described before this distribution and its underlying factors can be analyzed.

Gujars constitute a floating population of herders, somewhat ill defined due to a variable degree of assimilation into the host populations. In physical type, as well as in dress and language, the majority of them are easily distinguishable. Their music, dancing, and manner of celebrating rites of passage differ from those of their hosts. Their political status is one of dependence on the host population.

The Gujar population is subdivided into a number of named patrilineal tribes or clans—units claiming descent from a common known or unknown ancestor, but without supporting genealogies. There are sometimes myths relating to the clan origin, and these frequently serve as etymologies for the clan name. The clans vary greatly in size and only the smallest are localized. The effective descent units are patrilineal lineages of limited depth, though there is greater identification between unrelated Gujars bearing the same clan name than between strangers of different clans. These clans are irrelevant to marriage regulations. There is little intermarriage between Gujars and the host group.

The economy of the Gujars depends mainly on the herding of sheep, goats, cattle, and water buffalo. In addition to animal products, Gujars require some grain (maize, wheat, or millet) which they get by their own agriculture in marginal, high-altitude fields or by trade in return for clarified butter, meat, or wool. Their essential requirements may be satisfied by two rather different patterns of life—transhumance and true nomadism. Pathans differentiate persons pursuing these two patterns by the terms Gujar and Ajer, respectively, and consider them to be ethnic subdivisions. In fact, Gujars may change their pattern of life from one to the other.

Transhumance is practiced mainly by Gujars in the Pathan area, but also occasionally in Kohistan. Symbiotic relationships between Gujars and Pathans take various forms, some quite intimate. Pathans form a multicaste society, into which Gujars are assimilated as a specialized occupational caste of herders. Thus most Pathan villages contain a small number of Gujars—these may speak Gujri as their home language and retain their separate culture, or may be assimilated to the extent of speaking only Pashto. Politically they are integrated into the community in a client or serf status. Their role is to care for the animals (mainly water buffalo and draft oxen) either as servants of a landowner or as independent buffalo owners. They contribute to the village economy with milk products (especially clarified butter), meat, and manure, which is important and carefully utilized in the fields.

In addition to their agricultural land, most Pathan villages control neighboring hills or mountainsides, which are used by Pathans only as a source of firewood. The transhumant Gujars, however, shift their flocks to these higher areas for summer pasture, for which they pay a fixed rate, in kind, per animal. This rent supplies the landholders with clarified butter for their own consumption. Gujars also serve as agricultural laborers in the seasons of peak activity, most importantly during the few hectic days of rice transplantation. They also seed fields of their own around their summer camps for harvest the following summer.

In Kohistan there is less symbiosis between Gujars and their hosts but the pattern is similar, except that the few fields are located by the winter settlements.

The transhumant cycle may be very local. Some Gujars merely move from Pathan villages in the valley bottom to hillside summer settlements 1,000 or 1,500 feet above, visible from the village. Others travel 20 to 30 miles to summer grazing grounds in the territory of a different Pathan tribe from that of their winter hosts.

Nomads travel much farther, perhaps 100 miles, utilizing the high mountain pastures in the summer and wintering in the low plains. While the transhumant Gujars place their main emphasis on the water buffalo, the nomads specialize in the more mobile sheep and goats. Nonetheless, the two patterns are not truly distinct, for some groups combine features of both. They spend the spring in the marginal hills of Pathan territory, where they seed a crop. In summer the men take the herds of sheep and goats to the high mountains, while the women remain behind to care for the buffalo and the fields. In autumn the men return with the herds, reap the crops, and utilize the pastures. Finally, they store the grain and farm out their buffalo with Pathan villagers, and retire to the low plains with their sheep and goats for the winter.

The true nomads never engage in agricultural pursuits; they may keep cattle, but are not encumbered with water buffalo. The degree of autonomous political organization is proportional to the length of the yearly migration. Households of locally transhumant Gujars are tied individually to Pathan leaders. Those crossing Pathan tribal borders are organized in small lineages, the better to bargain for low grazing tax. The true nomads coordinate the herding of flocks and migrations of people from as many as 50 households, who may also camp together for brief periods. Such groups generally consist of several small lineages, frequently of different clans, related by affinal or cognatic ties and under the direction of a single leader. Thus, though migrating through areas controlled by other political organizations, they retain a moderately well-defined organization of their own.

GUJAR DISTRIBUTION

The co-existence of Gujars and Pathans in one area poses no problem, in view of the symbiotic relations sketched above. Pathans have the military strength to control the mountainous flanks of the valleys they occupy, but have no effective means of utilizing these areas. This leaves an unoccupied ecologic niche which the Gujar ethnic group

has entered and to which it has accommodated itself in a politically dependent position through a pattern of transhumance. Symbiotic advantages make the relationship satisfactory and enduring. It is tempting to see the expansion of Gujars into the area as resulting from the Pathan expulsion of Kohistanis from the valley. The Kohistanis, through their own pattern of transhumance, formerly filled the niche and it became vacant only when the specialized agricultural Pathans conquered the valley bottom and replaced the Kohistanis.

But the co-existence of Gujars and Kohistanis poses a problem, since the two groups appear to utilize the same natural resources and therefore to occupy the same ecologic niche. One would expect competition, leading to the expulsion of one or the other ethnic group from the area. However, armed conflict between the two groups is rare, and there is no indication that one is increasing at the expense of the other. On the other hand, if a stable symbiotic or noncompetitive relationship may be established between the two groups, why should Gujars be concentrated in West Kohistan, and not inhabit the essentially similar East Kohistan area? The answer must be sought not only in the natural environment and in features of the Gujar economy, but also in the relevant social environment—in features of Kohistani economy and organization which affect the niche suited to utilization by Gujars.

EAST vs. WEST KOHISTAN

As indicated, Kohistanis have a two-fold economy combining agriculture and transhumant herding, and live in moderately large village communities. Although most Gujars also practice some agriculture, it remains a subsidiary activity. It is almost invariably of a simple type dependent on water from the melting snow in spring and monsoon rains in summer, rather than on irrigation, and on shifting fields rather than manuring. The Kohistanis have a more equal balance between agriculture and herding. The steep slopes require complex terracing and irrigation, which preclude shifting agriculture and encourage more intensive techniques. The size of herds is limited by the size of fields, which supply most of the winter fodder, since natural fields and mountain meadows are too distant from the winter dwellings to permit haying. Ecologic factors relevant to this balance between the two dominant economic activities become of prime importance for Kohistani distribution and settlement density.

There are significant differences in this respect between East and West Kohistan, i.e., between the areas drained by the Indus and the Swat Rivers respectively. While the Indus and the lowest sections of its tributaries flow at no more than 3,000 feet, the Swat River descends from 8,000 to 5,000 feet in the section of its valley occupied by Kohistanis. The higher altitude in the west has several effects on the economic bases for settlement: (a) Agricultural production is reduced by the shorter season and lower temperatures in the higher western valley. (b) The altitude difference combined with slightly higher precipitation in the west results in a greater accumulation of snow. The Indus bank is rarely covered with snow, but in the upper Swat valley snow tends to accumulate through the winter and remains in the valley bottom until April or May. Thus the sedentary stockowner in West Kohistan must provide stored fodder for his animals throughout the four months of winter. (c) The shorter season of West Kohistan eliminates rice (most productive per land unit) as a food crop and reduces maize (most advantageous in return per weight of seed) in favor of the hardier millet.

These features serve to restrict the agricultural production of West Kohistan, and therefore the number of animals that can be kept during the winter season. No parallel restrictions limit the possibility for summer grazing. Both East and West Kohistan are noteworthy for their large, lush mountain meadows and other good summer grazing, and are thus rich in the natural resources which animal herders are able to exploit. However, these mountain pastures are only seasonal; no population can rely on them for year-round sustenance. Consequently, patterns of transhumance or nomadism are developed to utilize the mountain area in its productive season, while relying on other areas or techniques the rest of the year. True nomads move to a similar ecologic niche in another area. People practicing transhumance generally utilize a different niche by reliance on alternative techniques, here agriculture and the utilization of stored animal fodder. There appears to be a balance in the productivity of these two niches, as exploited by local transhumance in East Kohistan. Thus, in the Indus drainage, Kohistanis are able to support a human and animal population of sufficient size through the winter by means of agriculture and stored food, so as to utilize fully the summer pastures of the surrounding mountains. In an ecologic sense, the local population fills both niches. There is no such balance in the Swat valley. Restrictions on agricultural production limit the animal and human population, and prevent full exploitation of the mountain pastures. This niche is thus left partly vacant and available to the nomadic Gujars, who winter in the low plains outside the area. Moreover, scattered communities of transhumant Gujars may be found in the western areas, mainly at the very tops of the valleys. With techniques and patterns of consumption different from those of Kohistanis, they are able to survive locally in areas which fall short of the minimal requirements for permanent Kohistani occupation. The present distribution of Gujars in Kohistan, limiting them to the western half of the area, would seem to be a result of these factors.

A simple but rather crucial final point should be made in this analysis: why do Koshistanis have first choice, so to speak, and Gujars only enter niches left vacant by them? Since they are able to exploit the area more fully, one might expect Gujars eventually to replace Kohistanis. Organizational factors enter here. Kohistanis form compact, politically organized villages of considerable size. The Gujar seasonal cycle prevents a similar development among them. In winter they descend into Pathan areas, or even out of tribal territory and into the administered areas of Pakistan. They are thus seasonally subject to organizations more powerful than their own, and are forced to filter through territories controlled by such organizations on their seasonal migrations. They must accommodate themselves to this situation by travelling in small, unobtrusive groups, and wintering in dispersed settlements. Though it is conceivable that Gujars might be able to develop the degree of political organization required to replace Kohistanis in a purely Kohistani environment, their dependence on more highly organized neighboring areas still makes this impossible.

The transhumant Gujar settlements in Kohistan represent groups of former nomads who were given permission by the neighboring Kohistanis to settle, and they are kept politically subservient. The organizational superiority of the already established Kohistanis prevents them, as well as the nomads, from appropriating any rights over productive means or areas. What changes will occur under the present control by the State of Swat is a different matter.

This example may serve to illustrate certain viewpoints applicable to a discussion of the ecologic factors in the distribution of ethnic groups, cultures, or economies, and the problem of "mosaic" co-residence in parts of Asia.

(1) The distribution of ethnic groups is controlled not by objective and fixed "natural areas" but by the distribution of the specific ecologic niches which the group, with its particular economic and political organization, is able to exploit. In the present example, what appears as a single natural area to Kohistanis

is subdivided as far as Pathans are concerned, and this division is cross-cut with respect to the specific requirements of Gujars.

(2) Different ethnic groups will establish themselves in stable co-residence in an area if they exploit different ecologic niches, and especially if they can thus establish symbiotic economic relations, as those between Pathans and Gujars in Swat.

(3) If different ethnic groups are able to exploit the same niches fully, the militarily more powerful will normally replace the weaker, as Pathans have replaced Kohistanis.

(4) If different ethnic groups exploit the same ecologic niches but the weaker of them is better able to utilize marginal environments, the groups may co-reside in one area, as Gujars and Kohistanis in West Kohistan.

Where such principles are operative to the extent they are in much of West and South Asia, the concept of "culture areas," as developed for native North America, becomes inapplicable. Different ethnic groups and culture types will have overlapping distributions and disconforming borders, and will be socially related to a variable degree, from the "watchful co-residence" of Kohistanis and Gujars to the intimate economic, political, and ritual symbiosis of the Indian caste system. The type of correspondence between gross ecologic classification and ethnic distribution documented for North America by Kroeber will rarely if ever be found. Other conceptual tools are needed for the study of culture distribution in Asia. Their development would seem to depend on analysis of specific detailed distributions in an ecologic framework, rather than by speculation on a larger geographical scale.

26. CHIEFTAINSHIP

FREDRIK BARTH

Reprinted from Nomads of South Persia: The Basseri of the Khamesh Confederacy *(Oslo: Universitetsforlaget. Copyright 1961, Oslo University Press). For biographical information see Selection 25.*

■ We have explored the principal ecological and political forces in pastoralists' habitats that underlie the emergence of centralized controls among them. In this selection we shift our attention to relationships within the centralized pastoralist group itself and examine in detail the role of the chief.

In this selection we consider the role of chieftainship among the Basseri of southern Iran. The Basseri are a tribe of the Khamesh confederacy *(khamesh* means "five"), but this larger grouping has all but lost its political and social meaning, undoubtedly due to central governmental pressures. The basic unit of a Basseri camp is a tent occupied by an independent nuclear family household; it is a unit both of production and consumption. These people herd camels (for wool and transport), sheep, and goats. Their pastures are rich. They are stationary during the winter and summer, and during the summer they work for wages in the villages. But even their transhumance is characterized by modern influences of the central Iranian government; during these migrations they cross rivers by means of bridges and ferries.

The chief (or *Khan)* of the Basseri is nearly omnipotent; the strength of his office is such as to militate against the emergence of strong leaders within the camps. The chief maintains his authority by threats of corporal punishment of subordinates and assassination of competitors. He has no formal administrative apparatus through which his commands may be issued and enforced; instead, he makes his wishes known through subordinates who are attached to him. When, for one reason or another, he wishes to have someone punished —say, by flogging—he can command any bystander to administer the punishment.

Because Basseri political organization is without a formal governmental apparatus, there are no ready successors to succeed a chief when he dies. This results in great precariousness in the tribe's political unity—which, I imagine, serves the interests of the central government admirably—and as Barth describes it, has produced periods of confusion in the tribe. Though the office is nominally inherited, anyone with a sufficiently large following may declare himself the tribe's chief.

We have seen that pastoralists respond sensitively to minute changes in climate and resources. With the introduction of central governmental pressures into the pastoralist milieu, the nature of the habitat changes for the herder, since he must now respond with equal sensitivity to shifts of power in the central government. This instability is itself an adaptation of sorts to the larger political system. Enough flexibility may be assumed in the Basseri system to permit the emergence of new leaders who can respond to shifts in the national political center of gravity. Otherwise, an entrenched Basseri dynasty might find itself at odds and out of favor with a new national regime, and this could result in a serious dislocation of government-pastoralist relations.

Interesting insights into Middle Eastern pastoralists are provided by "Nomadism: Middle Eastern and Central Asian," by Raphael Patai *(Southwestern Journal of Anthropology* 6 [1951]: 401-14). Centralized Mongol pastoralists are discussed by Lawrence Krader in "Principles and Structures in the Organization of the Asiatic Steppe-Pastoralists" *(Southwestern Journal of Anthropology,* 11 [1955]: 67-92). ■

The scattered and constantly shifting tent camps of the Basseri are held together and welded into a unit by their centralized political system, culminating in the single office of the chief. Though many tribesmen trace descent from common ancestors and thus validate their membership in larger groupings, some camp groups admit divergent origins, while others, outside the tribe, are regarded as close collateral relations. It is the fact of political unity under the Basseri chief which in the eyes of the tribesmen and outsiders alike constitutes them into a single "tribe" in the Persian sense.

The pivotal position then in the whole tribal organization is that of the chief. He is the central, autocratic leader of the tribe. In keeping with the historical forms of centralized leadership found elsewhere in the Middle East, he is traditionally granted a vast and not clearly delimited field of privilege and command, and power is conceived as emanating *from* him, rather than delegated *to* him by his subjects. In the following I shall attempt to analyse the effective fields and limits of his authority, and the sources from which this authority derives.

Among the nomads of South Persia, there are properly two distinct titles translatable as "chief," namely *Khan* and *Kalantar*. This reflects the organization of politically discrete tribes into larger confederacies, the former led by *kalantars,* subordinate to the *Khan* of their confederacy. But with the wide use of *Khan* as the proper term of polite address for all chiefs, and the political collapse of the confederacies, the title of *kalantar* tends to disappear; and the Basseri chiefs are today both addressed and referred to as *Khan*.

The chiefs of the Basseri belong to a branch of the Mahad Khan oulad of the Kolumbei. An authoritative genealogy including some of the important collateral members of the line is given in Fig. 26.1, as taken down from Mahad Khan Esvandiari. There is much confusion and disagreement over this

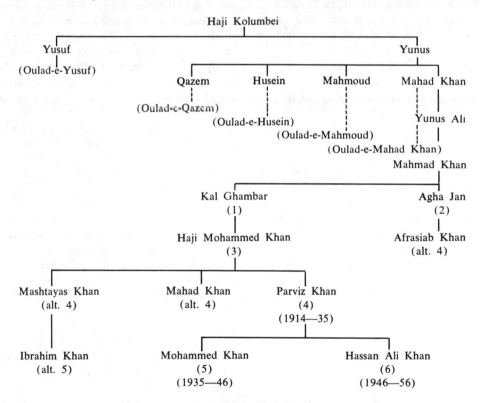

FIGURE 26.1.

Genealogy of the Basseri chiefs. The traditionally remembered chiefs are numbered consecutively from Kal Ghambar, and the main rival pretenders of the later chiefs are indicated as alternatives. Only reigning chiefs and important pretenders are shown in the genealogy.

genealogy, even with respect to the relationship of the chiefs marked (1) and (2) in the accompanying chart. Other versions were, however, largely simplifications of the one given here, and Mahad Khan was regarded by all as a genealogical/historical authority, who in discussions would convince others of the correctness of his version by marshalling further details of historical tradition.

The ruling chiefs are numbered in the chart from the first *kalantar* remembered by the general population; but there is no evidence that he was in fact the founder of the dynasty. It would appear that only the Weisi part recognized the earlier *kalantars,* and that they and the Ali Mirzai were united under one chief only during the reign of Haji Mohammed Khan. This expansion of the Basseri tribe was continued under Parviz Khan, who added the Ali Ghambari and Ali Shah Gholi, and under Mohammed Khan, who added Il-e-Khas, many Arab splinter groups, and the remains of the Nafar Turks.

Whereas the Kolumbei are generally regarded as forming the core of the Basseri today, it is notable that the dynastic line makes no claim to be the senior line of the Kolumbei. Yusuf is agreed by all to have been senior to Yunus; and Mahad Khan was the youngest of Yunus' sons. In fact it would appear that at least today, the genetic connection between the chiefs and the Kolumbei has no relevance to the legitimacy of the dynasty as chiefs of the Basseri tribe. It is, however, a source of some pride to the Kolumbei.

The chief and his immediate relatives belong in a category entirely apart from the rest of the Basseri, both in the minds of the tribesmen, and to an outsider. They are *Khavanin*, of the Khan's dynasty; they are shown respect and granted authority. Subject to the approval of the ruling chief, they are free to associate with any oulad and to utilize any of the Basseri pastures. Most of them, however, own lands and take little part in nomadic life. Particularly the chief and his brothers, one of them the former chief, are sophisticated members of the *élite* on a Persian national level; they maintain houses in Shiraz and travel extensively within and outside of Persia. In wealth they are also in a class entirely apart from other Basseri, each owning several villages as well as flocks of many thousand head of sheep and goats.

The position of the chief is one of great power and privilege. His tent must be large and his manner imperial; pettiness of any kind is inappropriate to him. His hospitality should be boundless—whereas the tribesmen tend to be parsimonious—and he should provide spectacular gifts of weapons, and stallions from his large herd of horses, to his more prominent subjects.

To support such a level of consumption, he has special sources of income in addition to his inherited property. The ruling chief has the recognized right to impose irregular taxes on the tribesmen, usually in the form of a tax of one sheep in a hundred *(sad-o-yek)* or sometimes even as much as three sheep in a hundred *(sad-o-seh)*. For the Basseri chief today, that would represent an income of nearly 8,000 sheep. In addition, each oulad pays a regular annual tax in clarified butter, and visitors and supplicants to the chief's tent are prone to bring gifts, usually of livestock.

The outstanding feature of the chief's position, however, is his power of decision and autocratic command over his subjects. Decisions governing collectivities among the Basseri are reached either by discussion or by command. I have described above how decisions governing camp groups are made by their members through a lengthy process of discussion and mutual persuasion. Apart from the authority occasionally exercised by the head of a household within his own tent, this is the only type of decision-making process in which the common Basseri participates. The right to command, to make decisions on behalf of persons in other tents than one's own, is a strictly chiefly prerogative. The monopolization by the chief of the right to command is a fundamental abstract principle of Basseri social structure. This idea was clearly expressed by informants, who were perhaps particularly aware of the chief's special position because of the disturbance caused by his formal deposition. All contemporary ills were explained by the resulting lack of a centralized coercive authority—the tribe without its chief was compared to a flock without its shepherd and a car without its driver. When I once tried to make some limited arrangements involving the movements of the camp in which I lived, stating that I would assume full responsibility for these arrangements, I was met with the objection that I was behaving like a chief and infringing on his rights.

However, though one may characterize the political organization of the Basseri by the abstracted principle of monopolization of coercive authority by the chief, such a formulation has in itself little meaning. One needs to have a picture of the organization in terms of how it maintains itself, and this is not given by distilling and abstracting its structural principle, even when the tribesmen themselves are aware of that principle. An analysis of the political organization calls for an analysis of the processes whereby the powers of the chief are exercised and defended. In the following I shall attempt to make such an analysis, first by describing the administrative apparatus at the chief's disposal and the fields in which his authority is exercised, and then by analysing his sources of power *vis-a-vis* the tribesmen, whereby his position of command is maintained.

The formal apparatus of the chief's administration is quite simple—rather surprisingly so in view of the difficulties of communication, and the apparent autocratic powers he exercises. Each oulad is, as we have seen, under a headman (*katkhoda*), of which there were properly 32 in the Basseri tribe at the time of the chief's deposition. These headmen act as the communicating links between their oulads and the chief when the chief is not himself present in their camp; but it is characteristic that the headmen do not represent a separate echelon of command: wherever his subjects are present, the chief deals directly with them and never through their headman, and in his decisions he does not take the opinion of the headman into particular account. All Basseri are equal in their direct relation of subordination to the chief, who

at any time may give any person an order which the latter must obey without regard to any pre-established organizational pattern. The hierarchy of organization consists of chains of *communication* from the central chief to all his scattered subjects, not of chains of *command*—which is another way of describing the monopolization of coercive authority noted above.

Associated with the chief is a special section of the tribe, the Darbar, known among most other tribes in Fars as the Amaleh. They travel with the chief and camp with him, and are without a formal headman. Among the members of the Darbar are found a personal valet, a master of the stores, a groom for the chief's riding horses, a scribe, and a hunting-and-drinking companion *cum* court jester. These offices were for explanatory purposes characterized by the common descriptive Persian terms for such offices; but since each is unique and personal in the tribe, the names of the office-holders were otherwise always used, and not their titles. Such office-holders, just like other members of the Darbar, each have their own flocks and tents and property, so in the absence of the chief the Darbar is indistinguishable from any other oulad.

In addition to these officers, the chief also has special contracts with persons who tend his flocks. At the time of my visit, the chief's sheep and goats were divided on several hands, one of them in the Darbar, his camels were herded by another member of the Darbar, while a herd of several hundred horses, predominantly mares and foals, was kept by some persons in a camp of the Jouchin.

The fields in which the chief regularly exercises authority, i. e. his main functions for the tribe, may be grouped in three: allotting pastures and co-ordinating the migrations of the tribe; settling the disputes that are brought to him; and representing the tribe or any of its members in politically important dealings with sedentary authorities.

It is mainly the co-ordination of tribal migrations that requires any ramifying administrative organization at all. The units involved in this are oulads, and orders regarding their movements pass mainly through the headmen, sometimes with the addition of a chief's representative and observer *(ma'umur)* assigned to each headman. These representatives were mainly drawn from the Darbar, and were particularly important some years ago, following the sweeping reorganization of migration routes and the distribution of pastures instituted by the last chief on his accession. Communications from the chief are relayed by word of mouth via messengers—a service to which any Basseri may be deputed—while much general information reaches the chief via the many visitors to his tent.

In the small and closely knit communities that constitute camps, most matters of law are governed by custom and compromise and regulated by diffuse sanctions. Where disputes cannot be settled informally, recourse may be had to the chief, who alone constitutes the only "court" in the tribal system. The chief is not bound by custom or precedent in his decision—the cases that are brought before him are precisely such as cannot be mediated within the framework of tradition, for reasons of their subject, or the personalities involved. Nor is he expected to give judgement according to the Shariat, which he does not claim to know and which runs clearly counter to important fields of custom. Quite explicitly, he is expected to make the decision which he feels is "best for the tribe"—he is expected to exercise his privileged arbitrary authority within a very wide area of free grace, unhampered by considerations of individual justice as derived from rules. Only in disputes over the division of an inheritance does he restrict his autocratic power—such cases he frequently refers for decision to a religious judge in a sedentary community.

The chief's "court" hearings are singularly lacking in formality. Any direction by the chief is an order, any definite statement is a decision, whether expressed as an aside in a conversation, or while washing his hands or taking his meal. Ceremony and pomp are only emphasized in "foreign" relations *vis-a-vis* non-Basseri visitors, particularly other chiefs and prominent men of the sedentary society.

Perhaps the chief's most important function is to represent the tribe in its relations with the Iranian administration, and in conflicts with sedentary communities or persons. This touches on a very fundamental problem in the organization of "plural" societies—societies composed of ethnically distinct groups in close interdependence in some fields of activity, while dissimilar and unconnected in other aspects of their social life. Where persons or groups belonging to such different parts of a plural society meet, there must be mechanisms mediating the relationship between them—within the limited situation of their interaction, they must be "comparable" in some appropriate framework. Usually, as in the case where the concept of plural society was first developed, this situation is the market place, where people meet as buyers and sellers, producers and consumers, and are equally subject to the "terms of trade" regardless of the differences in their backgrounds. So also in Fars, where the nomad meets the villager in economic transaction, the interaction is direct and relatively uncomplicated, governed by supply and demand in a monetary exchange system.

In the relations between groups of tribesmen and the organs of government, or where conflicts between a nomad and a sedentary are made the subject of judicial procedure, however, the situation is far more complex. Let us discuss the latter example first.

We have seen how a conflict between two Basseri nomads is settled, firstly by appeal to public opinion and the use of diffuse sanctions within the camp, and, if these fail, by the arbitrary decision of the chief. The persons or groups involved in such conflicts are homologous and fully comparable; their choices are subject to the same restrictions and actions directed against them have similar consequences for both parties.

Similarly, where two farmers in sedentary communities come into conflict, their positions are comparable: they are subject to the same public opinion, may appeal to the same or equivalent village headmen, or can go to the court of the subdistrict or district in which they live.

When, on the other hand, a conflict arises between a nomad and a farmer, e. g. because the former's herd has damaged the latter's crops, the position is different, and the problem of equivalence and comparability arises. In the case of the Basseri, this is not because of an extreme ethnic contrast—the language, religion, and major aspects of custom are shared. But pastoral nomadism by its technical requirements affects the position of the nomad and restricts the possible range of his actions in very determinate ways, which are very different from the restrictions implied by farming. The farmer's community and land are stationary; though his crops require attention, they readily survive a week's neglect. The nomad camp must move, for the sake of the herds; so to remain a member of his community the nomad can at most linger one or two days in any one locality. His property cannot be left in the charge of "neighbors," since it requires many hours of work each day to move it with the camp; his flocks are held together only by his constant shepherding, so his whole means of livelihood will be lost by a single day's neglect.

In other words, the opponents in a conflict between a nomad and a farmer cannot maintain contact for long; the difference in their modes of life precludes all the activities usually associated with mediation and the settlement of conflicts. Left to their own devices they can only mobilize their own communities and fight it out—and the prevalence of fortified villages in Southern Fars bears evidence to the frequency of this resort in the past, and its occasional practice today.

Alternatively, the farmer may take his grievance to the local court. But there the nomad cannot without great hardship even plead his case; while the farmer can readily sit for a week on the courthouse doorstep, the nomad is in practice unable to comply even with a court summons. If he succeeds in interesting the court at all, the farmer can thus mobilize a vast and powerful bureaucratic apparatus, the rules of which the nomad, because of his pastoral mode of life, is forced to break. On the other hand, internal tribal judicial mechanisms are equally unsuited for the farmer.

Between nomad and sedentary there are thus no mechanisms on the level of local communities for the regulation of social relations by law, and for the resolution of conflicts by other means than by violence; nor would it seem possible to develop other than very imperfect mechanisms on that level. A workable mechanism can only be achieved by channeling such conflicts through administrative superstructures which bridge this difference by transforming the interests and the social units concerned to a point where they become comparable and thus able to communicate.

Our primary interest here lies with the tribal side of this bridge. It is provided by the institution of centralized chieftainship. Whereas the common tribesmen from a sedentary point of view are elusive and irresponsible, the chief of a tribe is a known and responsible entity. It is in his interest to maintain stable and peaceful relations with the centres of power in sedentary society; and this he can do because he has the domestic staff that frees him from all pastoral and household duties. Where the common tribesman's relations with sedentary society are largely unstable and passing, his are continuous and permanent. His whereabouts in an area are always known, at least roughly; and since he maintains a house in Shiraz, he has a "permanent address." This places him on a par with the landowning *élite* of sedentary society, who also keep houses in Shiraz, but are occasionally, although less frequently, absent on tour of their villages. Where conflicts arise between tribesman and villager, the chief can represent the interests of his tribe, just as the landowner or local administrator can represent that of the villagers. They can meet as equals before the Provincial Governor, or in court, or directly. The two parties have thus on this level become comparable, and their conflicting interests amenable to negotiation and settlement in a political or a legal framework. Though the chief's influence in the provincial capital in large part derives from his *de facto* power as leader of a powerful tribe, the important fact here is that he is acceptable as a person and as an equal of the local *élite* because he is like them—he shares their diacritical symbols and can participate in their activities.

The chief's role in mediating relations with the sedentary society, in protecting the nomadic herders' interest *vis-a-vis* the often formidable and always confusing organizations that structure parts of their environment and encroach on their life, is correlated with a strong feeling of respect and dependence among the tribesmen. They explicitly recognize that without their chief they would be helpless in a number of recurring situations. Together with the chief's important role in directing the migrations and settling internal disputes, this might constitute a functional "explanation" of the great authority of the chief. However, the persistence of an institution is not exhaustively explained by a demonstration of its usefulness. The position of autocratic authority occupied by the Basseri chief can only be successfully maintained and defended if it is supported by enough coercive power to enforce discipline and suppress opposition from below, no matter how opportunistic and short-sighted such opposition may be. The fact that many tribesmen sooner or later in the course of their lifetime find themselves in a position where they desperately need the help of their chief cannot in itself serve him as a source of such power. The apparently poor development of formal groupings supporting the chief's coercive authority is thus surprising; and the Basseri political system requires further analysis, in terms of the political balance between its constituent groups, to be understood.

This means looking at the political system in its complete form as the "power household" of the tribe. In these terms, positions of authority can only be stable if the incumbent of such a position is able to mobilize enough force to counter any group that can form within the system to question his authority. The coercive requirements of the chief are thus not directly proportional to the extent of his authority, but depend on

the political constitution of his subjects, on the patterns of leadership and organization not directly under his control.

We must therefore return to the camps, as the basic spontaneous political groupings in Basseri society, and investigate their pattern of leadership and their possible interconnections from this point of view. As shown in the description of camps, the camp leader depends on influence for his position of leadership, and to prevent the fragmentation of his camp he is continually concerned to achieve unanimity, without access to coercive means. In this process, there is no crystallization of political "parties," since numbers are irrelevant: if *one* man remains adamant, the remainder of the camp does not constitute a majority party which can impose its decision on the group as a whole—there is no "majority" in terms of coercive power. The techniques of camp leadership are thus, as emphasized, those of compromise, persuasion, and a keen awareness of the drift of group opinion.

Clearly, this kind of leader can never serve as the rallying point of a strong faction or party; he is sensitive to all external as well as internal pressures and seeks to resolve them by accommodating them all, and by avoiding partisan commitments. Nor does any pattern of alignment of whole camps into two or more blocs develop, partly for this same reason, partly because of the prevailing suspicions and lack of intercommunication which isolate Basseri camps from one another. They are furthermore in a competitive relation to one another, since all camps by their presence restrict each other in the utilization of pastures and water.

The political subjects of the chief are thus organized in small, mutually hostile, and weakly led groups, each striving to maintain internal harmony and unanimity without coercive means. These are the only organized groups, and the only kind of leaders, within the Basseri system which can challenge the chief's authority and with which he must be able to deal. The poor development of centrally controlled coercive means reflects this impotence of any potential opposition. In most situations, camps and their leaders can be controlled merely by assertive and definitive orders from the chief; the mere pressure of such statements, backed by the chief's influence, prevents any disagreements from becoming explicit. Insubordination usually takes the form of verbal compliance with an order or instruction, but failure to execute it in practice; the sanction by which this is discouraged and punished is verbal abuse, and in more serious cases, corporal punishment. Orders are given in a form so that a particular person is responsible for their execution; and failure is punished unless it is reported and depends on some other person's refusal to comply. Thus no power is delegated even to persons who have duties and responsibilities foisted on them, except that power implicit in the right to report cases of resistance to the chief. Failure to execute an order from the chief can thus always be traced to one particular individual, who becomes liable to punishment.

Corporal punishment takes place in the presence of the chief and is specified by him —usually in the form of a certain number of strokes with a stout pole. Such punishment is painful and in more severe cases dangerous. The beating is not performed by any special category of functionary—any bystander who is a member of the tribe may be ordered to do it. The only collective punishment employed is a fine, levied as an extra tithe on the flocks belonging to the members of an oulad or section who are held collectively responsible for a misdeed, such as trespassing on the pasture rights of others. The collection of such fines is made the duty of a person unconnected with the group concerned —usually a member of the Darbar.

These characteristic features of the position of the Basseri chief are also apparent in the rules and practices in connection with succession. All close agnates of a chief are his potential successors, though usually only a few of them emerge as pretenders upon his death. Candidacy is by announcement, or rather assumption, since it is also marked by the person beginning to exercise a chief's authority; there is no previous appointment of an heir apparent, though sometimes one

son clearly points himself out as the one most likely to succeed.

As shown above, the Basseri political system does not produce strong opposed factions; so on the death of a chief, his potential successors stand without crystallized followings in the tribe, apart from their small retinue of personal servants and shepherds. Nor can the pretenders "seize the reins of government," since there is no formal administrative apparatus, the control of which might put a pretender in a position where he could effectively rule the tribe. Without social organs of an importance and dignity comparable to chieftaincy, there is not even any formal appointment or investiture of the successful pretender and *de facto* ruler— in a sense, he remains only *de facto* until he dies or is overthrown.

Almost at every point of succession, and occasionally in between, there appear among the Basseri to have been periods of confusion, when several "chiefs" have ruled simultaneously and vied for control of the tribe. The outlines of these internal dynastic turmoils are shown in Fig. 26.1. The last case of succession seems to have passed relatively unchallenged, and was unusual in that it involved a voluntary abdication, by Mohammed Khan, under strong external as well as internal pressure, in favour of his younger brother Hassan Ali Khan, who had always supported Mohammed Khan during his reign. The accession of Mohammed Khan, on the other hand, was far from untroubled. Though he was only 18 years old at the time of his father's death, he had exercised authority almost to the point of usurping his father's position for several years. Yet his cousin Ibrahim declared himself Khan and apparently exercised authority quite as successfully as Mohammed Khan for at least 6 months at the beginning of Mohammed Khan's rule, and again for a period while the latter was a prisoner of the Qashqai. The preceding rule of Parviz Khan was challenged several times by Parviz's brothers, and on his accession there was a period of confusion when not only they, but also Afrasiab Khan of a collateral line of the dynasty (FaFaBrSo of Parvis Khan) all tried to win control of the tribe. Similar rivalries appear to have taken place at previous points of succession, and to be common also in neighboring tribes.

The different informants' memories from these periods following the death of a chief, or a challenge to his authority, are highly contradictory and reflect the prevailing confusion at such times. Apparently, the several chiefs with their entourages move independently in the tribe, and each assert their authority, without building up a following of supporters in the tribe proper. The tribesmen respect all members of the dynasty, and comply with the orders of the chief's collaterals even in periods of stable rule. In periods of rivalry, they merely obey the orders last received, or from whichever pretender is present. Their impressions from such periods are thus various, depending on the contacts which their camp happened to have with different pretenders.

The clarification of successional disputes is a gradual process, and depends on the effects of the same kinds of control as those by which a ruling chief limits the authority of his dynastic collaterals. Through his stronger and more effective exercise of authority, one of the pretenders increasingly points himself out as the natural leader. In the words of the Basseri themselves, "the horse feels the rider's thigh"—the tribesmen sense and respond to willpower and assurance. Though the authority of other pretenders may not be directly challenged by the common tribesmen, people start dragging their feet and fail to act on the orders of other pretenders than one, until one day the whole edifice of administrative decisions and imperious manner built up by the unsuccessful pretender collapses, and nobody listens to him any more. Throughout such periods of confusion, the threat of assassination by the paid agent of a rival hangs over every pretender—increasingly so as his authority in the tribe wanes—so frequently the unsuccessful pretenders fear for their lives and escape to neighbouring, opposed tribes when they feel that the current runs against them. At a later point, when the new ruler feels secure in his position, they may be permitted to return and re-establish themselves as respectable members of the dynasty, as has, e. g., Mahad Khan, the uncle of the present chief (Fig. 26.1). Since few of the commoners take sides in the successional disputes, only a handful of followers accompany their chief in exile, or need to flee in the event of his death.[1] Defections from the tribe by larger groups of commoners are caused rather by the ruthlessness of strong chiefs, and thus occur during stable periods of rule, not as a sequel to successional disputes.

A chief thus achieves his position of authority by the same means as he maintains it: by its effective and continuous exercise, supported by the threat of corporal punishment of subordinates and assassination of competitors. Since in these activities he is independent of any formalized administrative machinery, his authority is not very closely delimited in the tribe—it extends to a variety of fields and gives him great personal latitude, or area of "free grace." Nor is it strictly delimited to a determinate social group. Nothing in the organization precludes a chief of strong will and personality from exercising authority over the subjects of another chief, if the two tribes have friendly relations. Unless a commoner is in a structural position which permits him to adopt a consistently hostile or violent attitude to a chief, he must show deference and thus becomes liable to that chief's influence and authority. Between friendly tribes, a division of authority over their component camps can thus only be maintained by a balanced opposition of the power centres represented by the chiefs themselves. In frequent cases, therefore, one chief is able to extend his sphere of control and encroach on, or even usurp, the authority of another. Among the Basseri, Mohammed Khan succeeded in this fashion in extending his authority over the Nafar Turkish-speaking tribe, only 40 years ago as numerous as the whole Basseri. Under the weak chief Yusuf Beg Nafar, this tribe experienced a decline, and when Mohammed Khan started directing the migrations of the

1. In the Darbar are found the descendants of a few such refugees from the Qashqai Amaleh who left upon the death of Chengish Khan, supposedly poisoned by his Br. and successor Saulat-e-Daulat, the father of Nasr Khan, who is the contemporary chief of the Qashqai.

remaining sections, Yusuf Beg was unable to assert any effective contrary authority, and the Nafar came under the sway of the Basseri chief.

The effects of this process of encroachment and usurpation of authority by one chief over the subjects of another are further magnified by the response it calls forth in the nomad population at large. Camps, oulads and sections seek out the strong chief and submit to him; from him they obtain better protection and by him their interests are best safeguarded. It was noted earlier that a "tribe" among South Persian nomads is a political concept; its unity is not ethnic, but depends on its allegiance to a chief. The processes whereby ethnic complexity persists in the tribes, and whereby rapid changes in their relative and absolute sizes take place, can now be better understood. Any imbalance between tribes in the effectiveness of centralized authority stimulates an extension of the stronger center's claims to authority, and a voluntary flow of commoners from the weaker to the stronger center.

Such movements are reversible and ever-changing, reflecting the balance of the moment. The Basseri, like most other tribes, have experienced both ups and downs. They were an independent, though relatively small tribe composed mainly of Ali Mirzai sections in the time of Nasr-ud-Din Shah (1848-96). In the next 20 years, there was a collapse of ordered government in the provinces, related to the constitutional struggles in Teheran; and in this period the Arab tribes became more powerful, dominating the Basseri and ruling many of its sections. Thus the Shaibani Khans of the Arabs assumed control of the Labu Musa and the Abduli (under Khan Baz Khan), and the Ali Ghambari (under his son Asgar Khan). During the chieftaincy of Haji Mohammed Khan (Fig. 26.1) the balance was reversed. His son Parviz Khan further married a daughter of the Shaibanis, as did also his son, Mohammed Khan. This close kinship connection with the Shaibani Khans facilitated the assumption of authority by the Basseri Khans over a number of sections of Shaibani subjects, not only those of Basseri origin but also increasingly those of

Arab stock. Before his abdication Mohammed Khan thus had direct or indirect control over about half the Arab tribes—those traditionally under Shaibani Khans—as well as a few splinters (e. g. the Safari) from groups traditionally under the other main Arab dynasty, the Jabbare. Present political circumstances, however, prevent the Basseri chief from exercising and consolidating this control.

The authority structure of the nomad camp and tribe also influences the form of the highest level of tribal organization: the confederacy. Though the Khamseh confederacy to which the Basseri belong is now practically defunct, it has till recently been of great importance, and requires some description.

The Khamseh (Arabic: "five together") contains five distinct tribes: the Arabs of Fars, under a medley of large and small chiefs, the Turk tribes of Ainalu, Baharlu, and Nafar, and the Persian-speaking tribe of Basseri. The confederacy is recent, only 90-

Mohammed

Mahmoud

Mohammed Hashem

Haji Ibrahim
Etemad-at-Dowleh

Ali Akbar
Ghavam-ul-Mulk

Ali Mohammed
Ghavam-ul-Mulk

Mohammed Reza
Ghavam-ul-Mulk

Habibullah
Ghavam-ul-Mulk

Ibrahim
Ghavam-ul-Mulk

FIGURE 26.2.
The heads of the Ghavam family from its founding to the present.

100 years old, and its origin must be traced, not to any of the constituting nomad tribes, but to the bazaars and governmental palaces of Shiraz.

The founders and rulers of the Khamseh confederacy are the Ghavam family. This family traces its origin from a merchant by the name Mohammed, who came to Shiraz from Kazvin, though his family supposedly was Shirazi by origin. His son Mahmoud became very prosperous, mainly from profits on trade through the southern ports of Kharak and Bandar Abbas, successors to the once fabulous Hormuz; and he thus laid the foundations for the family's great wealth, as well as their connections with the tribes in the South. His grandson, Haji Ibrahim, achieved political prominence as Minister of State to Karim Khan Zand and later to the first Qajars; in 1802 he was executed and the whole family exterminated by Fath Ali Shah, with the exception of one young son, Ali Akbar, who escaped and later returned and claimed his inheritance. The family quickly regained its political prominence in Shiraz, taking the title Ghavam-ul-Mulk. The building of the crystal palace which is an imposing sign of their wealth and prominence, and still the headquarters of the family, was started by Ali Mohammed and completed by his son.

As erstwhile Governors of Fars the Ghavam came into conflict with the increasingly important and powerful Qashqai confederacy; and it was as a counter-weight to the Qashqai, as well as to protect his caravans to and from the southern ports, that Ali Mohammed Ghavam-ul-Mulk caused the Khamseh confederacy to be formed, with himself as its chief.

For four generations, till Ibrahim Khan's deposition by Reza Shah in the early 30's, the Ghavam family of merchants thus served as leaders of one of the largest nomad confederacies of South Persia. Details of this organization are now difficult to unearth; but some of its general outlines are clear. The confederacy seems to have been without any special administrative apparatus, Ghavam visiting separate chiefs or calling them together in *ad hoc* meetings, and dealing di-

rectly and personally with them. The allegiance of the tribal chiefs was obtained by gifts of arms, of great importance to the receiving chiefs, and by the important services Ghavam could provide as a sponsor and protector of the tribes' interests *vis-a-vis* the Shah's government. Yet their allegiance was never secure, and he often had to resort to force to reduce various tribes or parts of tribes to submission, either by the seizure and execution of chiefs, or by relatively large-scale punitive expeditions. Though the Khamseh, according to Ghavam's estimate, numbered around 16,000-17,000 tents 50 years ago, they could not be readily mobilized in his support. Thus in the operations during the First World War, when Ghavam supported the British, the Khamseh supplied only a variable and relatively small fraction of the forces as his disposal.

The precariousness of the unity of the Khamseh confederacy, and of its control by the Ghavams, is suggested by the last case of succession, in 1916, which happened to take place in a Basseri camp in the presence of several of my informants. Habibullah Ghavam-ul-Mulk was travelling toward Shiraz at the time and staying with the recently acceded Parviz Khan of the Basseri when he fell from his horse during hunting and died. The fact of his death, however, was kept secret; he was reported to be ill while the body was kept in a tent under guard of his personal servants and a message was sent to Shiraz for his son Ibrahim to proceed to the spot; and not until the son had established himself among the nomad chiefs was the death of his father revealed.

In view of this weak point in the organization, connected with succession, the use of the name "Ghavam" is interesting, as it represents a pattern to my knowledge unique in the area. Not only is it used as a surname; without modifying personal names it is universally used as a term of reference and address to the ruling head of the Ghavam family. Even while giving the account of succession above, in the words of the tribesmen it was "Ghavam" who fell from his horse and "Ghavam" who announced his father's death. The continuity produced by this, in a situation where other persons do not even have surnames, is striking. Perhaps significant is the fact that when Ghavam decided to encourage and depend on the Basseri tribe, he bestowed the name "Zarghami" on Parviz Khan and his successors—a name which shows a tendency to be passed on and used in the same manner.

The development of a confederacy thus seems to be only a further elaboration of the pattern of centralized authority represented by the chiefs, and did not among the Khamseh depend on other sources of authority or elaborate any important organizational patterns of its own. It remained as a superstructure on the system, which could be fairly easily shattered by external intervention without greatly disturbing the fabric of tribal organization.

The main argument of this chapter might now be summarized. I have tried to analyze some of the political processes that play a part in producing the form of centralized organization found among the Basseri nomads. The resultant picture lacks the unity of a conventional "structural" description. This is inevitable, since phenomena historically unconnected and logically of different order appear to combine to produce this system.

Throughout the analysis, I have emphasized the relevance of certain aspects of the total environment in which the Basseri live, and their pastoral form of subsistence, to their forms of organization. Important in this chapter has been the fact that the Basseri travel thinly dispersed over areas with large sedentary populations entirely unconnected to the tribal organization. These towns and villages have for thousands of years been under some kind of centralized, bureaucratic administration—one in which authority is monopolized by a restricted class, vesting great arbitrary powers in some few persons. Any political body in South Persia, even if pastoral and nomadic, must deal with these persons by having a regular point of articulation with the sedentary hierarchy of authorities.

But there is also power flowing from other sources—here, from collectivities of free tribesmen, who for one thing constitute a mobile, ready-made cavalry force. My further point is that as a correlate to their pastoral adaptation, the communities in which these nomad tribesmen live have a composition and organization which militates against the emergence of strong leaders within camps.

This opens a niche for the political figure we have been concerned to analyse here: the omnipotent Khan or chief. Through him, as a bridge of communication, the nomads' relations with sedentary society may be mediated. By being the leader of tribesmen, a power factor in the province, he can become a member of the privileged urban *élite,* and is thus able to defend the interests of the tribe within the sedentary hierarchy of authority, from a vantage point which is unattainable to any active pastoralist. The tribal communities, by accepting such leadership, can obtain substantial benefits. But since they lack strong leaders on the level of their own communities, they lack mechanisms for delimiting and containing the powers of leaders on higher levels of tribal organization; and they thus become subjects of the chief on terms of autocratic dominance/submission. In the extreme case, as we saw in the Khamseh development, this power niche may even be invaded not from the tribes, but from the Persian side of the system, by a farseeing city financier.

PART TWO:
STATE SOCIETIES

INTRODUCTION

AUTHORITY AND FREEDOM—these two variables constitute the central problem in the analysis of nation-states. They are often regarded as mutually exclusive; actually, their interrelationships are very complex, and they are far from simple opposites.

We have seen that the salient features of a stateless group are egalitarianism, autonomy in making decisions about the allocation of resources, the predominance of kinship and other locally based bonds in the maintenance of order and conformity, and the absence of appreciable surpluses. The individuals who must directly affect a person's activities are known to him, and he to them, in direct and face-to-face relationships. This picture has great romantic appeal. However, in these groups pressures to conformity are very great and the most successful person is likely to be "the man in the gray flannel loincloth." It is precisely the direct and face-to-face relationships in such societies that underlie these pressures to conformity. The anonymity that is often experienced in contemporary nation-states may bring special problems in its wake; what is often overlooked, however, it that it provides the individual with an important measure of what is popularly called freedom, with the potential for donning different suits of varying colors.

One way of illustrating the profound qualitative difference between stateless and state societies is in an anecdote. A friend of mine, an architect of about 30, told me he recently realized that the two things that have affected most of his major decisions since leaving high school were, first, draft laws and then tax laws. As an aside (we were not talking about politics), I asked whether he knew the names of the people responsible for the policies and decisions that thus affected his life. He did not.

The basic concept of a nation-state is relatively simple, but the anthropological description and analysis of sociocultural processes in a nation are difficult, for two reasons. First, a stateless group can be simply described, since it is a self-contained and relatively undifferentiated unit, and this is not possible for life in a nation-state. The organization of social relations in a nation-state is characterized by systems of social stratification in which the members of each stratum participate in different technological activities and thus live by a different life style; correspondingly, each of these strata is distinguishable by its own symbolic systems, in religion, cognitive processes, political ideology, attitudes to

401

work, language, and art. Nevertheless, members of all strata are bound to each other—often in ways that are not immediately apparent—by a complicated technological and economic interdependence, overlapping life styles, and mutually shared cores of ideas and symbols.

Our second difficulty has to do with the nature of decision-making and implementation. People in a national society perform their daily activities in local communities and engage in social relations with known people in face-to-face interaction. These locally based groups are important in the maintenance of order, economic stability, and distinctive life styles and symbolic systems. Decision-making and implementation, however, in many areas of national life are ultimately in the hands of the society's ruling groups, who may be anonymous. These groups—which constitute the upper strata of the society—control the major sources of energy in the nation, and by virtue of these controls, are able to stimulate new industries and trades, monumental projects like pyramids, road systems and marketing systems (domestic and international). They compel the production of surpluses, write and enforce tax laws that enable them to mobilize and redistribute these surpluses, and control the organization of labor.

How do these groups come into being and how do they gain power over many communities that are widely dispersed and often have different economic bases? I assume from the historical record that every state system is imposed by force on previously autonomous local groups, using the term force in a technical sense and without value connotation. This hypothesis is explicated by Carneiro in Selection 27. As he shows, nation-states seem always to have been the products of military conquest under certain types of habitational conditions. States arose first in circumscribed areas (large islands, narrow valleys) where a conquered group's withdrawal and dispersal is difficult; in contrast, people who lived in unbroken expanses of land (plains) were able to move or disperse when military pressure was exerted on them. The first nation-states apparently were built up out of groups whose members relied primarily on hoe or digging-stick cultivation.

As in the Valley of Mexico, where the Aztecs established their centralized political system, and in England after the Norman conquest, nation-states were established when a small group invaded the territories of previously autonomous groups and brought them under control by force. The conquered groups had the choice of either fighting to the end or submitting. When they submitted, they became the lower classes in a nationwide system of social stratification. Atop the pyramid were the conquerors who enacted laws requiring surplus production and the payment of taxes, controlling mobility and the sale of land, imposing conscription and corvee, and the like.

But the political system of a nation-state is not one in which the ruling groups simply decree and those below them abjectly obey; neither rules nor local groups operate independently. For each, the other is an important element in its habitat which—like the physical habitat itself—sets limits and provides potentials. Those who govern and speak in the name of the state cannot easily ride roughshod over local groups in disregard of their existing organization of social relations and symbol systems; nor can local groups disregard centrally promulgated policies. These groups are in regular give-and-take, and each move in these interactions has profound consequences for the organization of social relations throughout the society. A dramatic example of such feedback is provided by Befu for Japan in Selection 28.

We cannot regard the loss of autonomy in decision-making among local groups as an all-or-nothing proposition. It is a gradual process in which those who speak in the name of the state try to concentrate decision-making in their own hands, while those who speak in the name of local groups try to retain as much autonomy as they can. Why, then, don't the members of local groups rebel or secede more often? Force, of course, plays a role in preventing such insurrections, but it is not the only element.

I offered the axiom in Selection 3 that the establishment of state systems represented a watershed in social evolution. The founding of nation-states marked a major advance over previous strategies of adaptation. Though the members of local groups may not be able to formulate the advantages of such change in these terms, especially among their lower classes, they are generally willing to trade their loss of autonomy for the adaptive advantages represented by the state. What are these gains? In strictly adaptational terms, state systems contribute to the freedom of local groups from an exclusive reliance on locally available resources in many ways: by stimulating the construction of large-scale irrigation projects, by setting up local specialization and marketing systems that enable groups in one region to benefit regularly from the products of other regions, by providing financial credits for new industries and trades, by embarking on wars and treaties and negotiations that open up new resources and markets, by establishing sophisticated educational systems, and the like.

An important consequence of these adaptive gains is a wide-ranging proliferation of roles in the occupational structure. The occupational diversity in a nation-state contrasts dramatically with that in a stateless group, in which a person invariably has only one role available (hunter, cultivator, herder, spouse, and parent) and in which there are no economic or social subgroups. As nation-states evolve, occupational roles become increasingly differentiated from kinship, religious, ethnic, and sex status; increasingly, the kind of work one does is not dependent on his kin connections, his religious beliefs, or his grandfather's origin. Freedom of choice in occupation, however limited it may be in particular nations and different groups, is practically unknown—even as an ideal standard—in stateless societies.

Occupational diversity underlies freedom. Although no nation-state has reached this point fully, such a political system at least embodies the potential for separating occupational roles (or the right to earn a livelihood) from social, political, and other beliefs. Such advances are invariably the results of policies and laws precipitated by the central government—and they are almost always opposed by people in local groups.

Equally important is the increase in legal egalitarianism seen in the development of nation-states. This too is a product of diversification of roles in the occupational structure, and it is most evident in the legal system. The state represents a great social advance in its replacement of customary law with formal law. Customary law is made up of established rules and procedures that are not codified, that remain informal and personal in application. In a system of customary law, the resolution of disputes takes place in the course of face-to-face relationships within the community. Justice—to the extent that it ever exists—emerges from the collective judgment of the community, often tacit rather than explicit. The force of law is in consensus, and the personalities and backgrounds of the disputants play an important part in the outcome. Formal law is administered through formal and often ritualized procedures. Lawyers and judges emerge as specialized technicians who study the law and rely on precedent and stereotyped actions in determining what it is and how it is to be applied. The specialized roles of lawyers and judges are part of the more elaborate division of labor that is generally found in national social organizations and especially in urban centers. A concern with precedent and ritualized procedure is intimately related to the use of impersonal criteria as ideal standards in the administration of law.

Developments such as the substitution of formal law for customary law are due neither to political nor technological factors alone. Rather, the two in combination make such social advances possible, though not inevitable. Advanced agricultural techniques increase the potential for producing surpluses that, in turn, enable large numbers of people to enter trades and other specialized occupations. Once a nation-state is established, the principles according to which social life is ordered are changed. By increasingly freeing large numbers from farming, every technological advance makes it possible for those who speak in the name of the state to extend and strengthen the policies that the state potentially represents, like the substitution of formal law for customary law.

In principle, conformity is best achieved by uniform laws and regulations, but it is clearly discernible from the study of the evolution of legal and political systems that unequal administration of the law persists, largely as a result of local vested interests. The Mississippi and Louisiana planters and their equivalents throughout human history have never been champions of uniform and equal application of the law. It is in the interest of those who control a nation's political apparatus, however, to achieve legal uniformity.

Current political rhetoric notwithstanding, there is probably less—and less painful—inequality in most advanced nations than in early nation-states. Without denying that even a little inequality is too much, the evolutionary record is clear, and it also points to a probable further reduction in inequality in future stages of development. In contemporary industrial nations, regardless of their political and economic ideologies, there is a pattern in the relationship between centralized political institutions and the society's major sources of energy. The greater the number of people who draw on a single source of energy, the greater the tendency to concentrate its control in the hands of the society's ruling groups, and this is always achieved at the expense of the autonomy of local groups and the people who control them, like local planters in Mississippi. For example, the control of steam to drive machines has almost always been localized, each factory maintaining and controlling its own power plant; generally, the worst legal horrors in an industrial society are committed in communities that are based on such localized energy systems. In contrast, a greater centralization of control of electricity has been produced by waterpower, and even more for electricity produced by nuclear energy. Each of these technological developments is accompanied by increasing equality in the administration of law.

A major political change occurs with the development of more advanced agricultural strategies of adaptation, such as those based on plow cultivation and centralized irrigation systems. Although reliance on muscular energy does not lessen, these techniques of farming also require nonmuscular sources of energy that are not freely and equally available to everyone; they are generally brought under the monopolistic control of the upper classes. The individual farmer cannot easily pick up his plows and draft animals (which he probably doesn't own anyway) and leave for other parts. Having become dependent on plows and draft animals and their associated institutions, on centrally distributed seed, fertilizer, and water, he is irrevocably tied to his small holdings. This monopolization of resources and means of production is the basis of systems of social stratification, by which we mean the unequal distribution of privilege and access to sources of energy. National societies differ in the amount of social mobility by which people can raise (and lower) their status, but each of the status groups in any society is characterized not only by a particular degree of access to sources of energy and means of production, but also it is marked by a particular lifestyle, or what is often called a "sub-culture."

As we read the case studies from different national societies in Part II, we may be led to wonder how and why previously autonomous groups allow themselves to become involved in the vortex that is set into motion by the establishment of a state system. Very few people living in the early stages of state formation can have foreseen the advantages in this new and qualitatively different strategy of adaptation. The repercussions of state formation and growth are not only political, they are also technological, as in the construction of massive irrigation networks and the stimulation of new industries, trades, and marketing systems. People almost always embrace more efficient means of production and distribution willingly; it is difficult if not impossible for them to foresee the consequences of technological advance for their traditional ways of life. Describing this process of social change in *Feudal Society,* Marc Bloch commented wryly, "Once get a finger trapped in the machine and your whole body may be drawn into it" (p. 246).

Before turning to the case studies of adaptation in state systems, it is necessary to note that just as nation-states represent a watershed in human social evolution, so do they require very different methods of study from those appropriate to stateless groups. In the latter, research is highly personalized, focusing on the face-to-face interaction of the anthropologist and those he observes; this parallels the fact that most significant social relations in stateless societies occur in the "structural poses" that people assume. In nation-states, however, where significant social relations are often affected—and sometimes precipitated—by the impersonal policies of the central state, research too must be less personal. For instance, if the anthropologist wishes to study the nation as a whole or any significant part of it, he cannot concentrate on individual and group behavior but must concern himself instead with laws, administrative regulations, and bureaucratic structures. This is not to say that he does not observe people in their face-to-face interactions at all. Instead, it means that he does not conduct his observations in any particular community; rather he focuses on one institution at a time—groups in which labor is organized (unions, professional, and trade associations), the legal sphere, schools, health institutions, marketing and trade, recreation—in sampling the types of communities that make up the nation and the various strata and other subgroups in each of these. Instead of looking at a community from within, the anthropologist studying a national social system must establish his perch outside particular communities to learn how people in different social and physical places respond to centrally generated pressures, that is, to the dominating elements in their habitat.

Indispensable for any overview of the development of state systems is *The Evolution of Urban Society,* by Robert McC. Adams (Chicago: Aldine, 1966). A good introduction to the relationship of the early period of nation-states and social stratification is "On the Evolution of Social Stratification and the State," by Morton H. Fried, in *Culture in History,* edited by Stanley Diamond (New York: Columbia University Press, 1960). The study of state systems necessarily involves the investigation of cities, and this too requires different research methods from those employed in small villages. In *The Pivot of the Four Quarters: A Preliminary Enquiry into the Origins and Character of the Ancient Chinese City* (Chicago: Aldine, 1971), Paul Wheatley maintains that the rise of the ceremonial center represents a major stage in urban development; he presents examples from China and six other regions. An excellent analysis of the relationship between state and local ideologies is "The Integrative Revolution: Primordial Sentiments and Civil Politics in the New States," by Clifford Geertz, in *Old Societies and New States,* edited by C. Geertz (New York: The Free Press, 1963). For a comparative study of the effects of central state policies on standards of sexual behavior, see my paper, "Ends and Means in Political Control: State Organization and the Punishment of Adultery, Incest, and Violation of Celibacy," *(American Anthropologist,* 71 [1969]: 658-87). For an analysis of the role of states in education, see my paper, "Schools and Civilizational States," in *The Social Sciences and the Comparative Study of Educational Systems,* edited by Joseph Fischer (Scranton: International Book Company, 1970).

IV.
CULTIVATING

TECHNOLOGICALLY, the advance in adaptation over hoe and digging-stick cultivation that is represented by strategies such as plow agriculture is one of kind rather than degree. The domestication of food, by whatever means, increases the range of habitats within which man can live and perpetuate his groups. It also increases the size and reliability of crops in proportion to the muscular energy expended and the amount of land used. But cultivation by advanced agricultural means, together with appropriate organizations of social relations, produces a qualitative rather than a merely quantitative advance over previous levels of adaptation.

One of the characteristics of cultural evolution is that each successive level of development is marked by greater heterogeneity than its predecessors. This is due largely to the fact that each new technology makes it possible to exploit a wider range of habitats, each of which may require different cultural adjustments within the level of adaptation. Furthermore, different historical backgrounds strongly affect the adjustments of different groups at the same level of cultural evolution. As more groups from different backgrounds come to terms with a greater variety of habitats, they exhibit increasing variety in their cultural patterns. (This contradicts the assertion by some anthropologists that increasing worldwide cultural uniformity is a consequence of evolution. Neither the spread of plows nor ballpoint pens makes people alike, any more than recorded music on magnetic tape makes Bach and The Beatles similar.) For these reasons there is much more heterogeneity among, say, plow agriculturists than among pastoralists and digging-stick cultivators, to say nothing of foragers.

This helps explain why it is increasingly difficult to write full ethnographies dealing with levels of adaptation as cultures become more and more complex and technologically advanced. It is not difficult to write a general ethnography of foragers because their similarities are greater than their differences. Most foraging societies tend to recapitulate each other in their basic organization of social relations, with variations corresponding to habitational factors. Furthermore, there are few differences within each foraging group; almost everyone tends to live the same kind of life. Differences in lifestyle also remain minimal in most groups relying on hoe and digging-stick cultivation. It is more difficult to generalize about advanced agriculturists because, in addition to the greater variety of habitats they exploit and the resulting variety of cultural adjustments, they tend to be highly stratified. Ruling groups and peasants usually live radically different lives and have different modes of thought.

Nevertheless, it is possible to generalize about advanced agricultural societies in evolutionary terms. Like each of the levels of adaptation discussed thus far, each type of advanced agriculture represents a unique social system. The energy systems harnessed by agriculturists provide them with a heretofore unparalleled measure of freedom from the limitations of their habitats, and these technologies require appropriate organizations of social relations within the local community and the society at large. Agriculturists organized in state systems made an unprecedented difference in human history because their political systems succeeded in stimulating the harnessing of sources of energy that are freeing man from his habitats.

Let us consider plow agriculture first. Plows, like digging sticks and large herds of domesticated animals, are more than implements or sources of food; they are inextricably tied to the use of draft animals (see Selection 31). Hence plows are inseparable from people organized into particular organizations of social relations that provide assurance for the care and provision of an adequate supply of draft animals. These livestock are often under the monopolistic control of one or a few individuals and must be borrowed, rented, or exchanged for other services or for food or money. Monopolistic control over sources of energy is intimately related to the development of systems of social stratification. Furthermore, because plowing seasons usually are short, provision has to be made for relatively quick and uniform access to draft animals by all the farmers of a community, and this requirement leads to the development of specific forms of social relations: standards of payment or exchange of services, priorities of access and determination of the periods when each person may use the animals, liabilities incurred in case of their injury or death, responsibility for their feeding, and the like.

Both agriculture and pastoralism involve the domestication of large animals, but the use of draft animals to draw plows denotes an entirely different strategy of adaptation from herding. There are entirely different relationships to the habitat in these adaptations that provided agriculturalists with a much greater degree of mastery over the habitat: Plow agriculturists get beneath the topsoil and turn it over, pastoralists rely more directly on their herds for food and generally practice a limited amount of gardening. The principal sources of food among pastoralists (their herds) are mobile and demand transhumant patterns of settlement and social relations; the principal sources of food among agriculturists (land) is fixed and immobile, and this—together with intensity of cultivation—underlies the establishment of permanent and year-round settlements. These patterns require entirely different organizations of society.

A variation on the agricultural strategy of adaptation is cultivation based on terracing. This too represents a particular kind of organizaion of social relations because terracing involves not only remarkable feats of engineering but a particular division of labor in the construction and maintenance of the terrace systems and the careful regulation of the water's flow to each terrace.

The regulation of the flow of water as a social—and not only a technological —system is illustrated by the Tokugawa Japanese village cooperative work group in paddy agriculture:

One function of the group that deserves special notice was to provide a single, large labor force for the spring planting. Even in the Tokugawa period, rice was not sown directly in the fields but was started in special beds from which the seedlings were later transplanted. This hard, slow work had to be performed within the exceedingly short period when the seedlings could be transplanted without dangerously interrupting their growth. Since enormous quantities of water were required to work the soil to the consistency of a thick paste preparatory to receiving the young plants, and since few fields could be given the necessary amount of water simultaneously, it was necessary to flood and plant fields one after another in rotation. This reduced the period allowed for planting any one field to a matter of a few hours. To accomplish the planting in the allotted time required a labor force far larger than the individual family could muster. And the various lineages in the village—main family, branches, and pseudo-branches—provided stable groupings for performing the critical work. Mobilizing all its adult members for the planting, the group moved with the water from field to field, without regard for individual ownership; not only did this permit fields to be planted in the extremely short time water was available to each, but it added to the sociability of this exhausting and otherwise wholly disagreeable task. Needless to say, the power to refuse a family this help and sign of solidarity gave the group enormous power over its members (Thomas C. Smith, The Agrarian Origins of Modern Japan, pp. 50-51, Stanford: Stanford University Press, 1959).

The importance of large-scale irrigation networks was discussed in Selection 3, and it need only be reiterated that these hydraulic systems are as much organizations of political relations in their construction, maintenance, and regulation as they are techniques. This is illustrated by Palerm in Selection 33. Also, it is necessary to distinguish between local and small-scale irrigation and centrally controlled large-scale hydraulic systems because each is associated with different organizations of social relations and, especially, political institutions.

Agriculture in state societies almost always is associated with an elaborate division of labor and with social specializations that proliferate throughout the entire society. Their repercussions are felt at almost every point in the society's institutional chains. The division of labor that characterizes agricultural state societies is found not only in the production of food but often in craft and bureaucratic specializations as well. In stateless societies the division of labor is based primarily on fixed (or ascribed) criteria, such as sex, age, and kinship. Although these criteria also are used as bases for role allocation in agricultural societies, advanced agriculturists emphasize criteria of achievement, such as social class, to an extent rarely found in earlier strategies of adaptation. Agriculture in a nation-state almost always entails specialization in food production to a much greater extent than in a stateless system. Regional specializations are most important and often are the basis of regional subcultural differences within a society. Craft specializations are almost important; farmers become dependent on craftsmen for farming implements, and craftsmen depend on farmers for food. When agriculture is accompanied by state bureaucracies, the people who fill these political roles also are specialists who have to be provided with food. Hence an important feature of agricultural adaptations in nation-states is a centrally regulated system of distribution by which nonfood-producing specialists can purchase food and regionally specialized farmers can buy from and sell to each other.

Are there any consistent relationships among the level of technological development achieved by a society and the degree of occupational specialization and regional diversification? Are these more complex institutional forms attributable to particular features of a strategy of adapation?

Anthropologists have long known that agricultural states are economically diversified and have believed—in the words of Meyer Fortes and E. E. Evans-Pritchard in their Introduction to *African Poltical Systems* (New York: Oxford University Press, 1940)—that "centralized authority and an administrative organization seem to be necessary to accommodate culturally diverse groups within a single poltical system, especially if they have different modes of livelihood" (p. 9). This hypothesis suggests that sociotechnological heterogeneity precedes political centralization. However, it now appears that the reverse may be true, that diversification may be the product of stimuli engendered by the political sectors of states. My illustrative comparison in the introduction to Section II (on stateless cultivators) suggested that occupational specialization and regional diversification that is not tied directly to immediately available local resources is attributable to the centralization of political controls rather than to the level of technological development as such. However, centralized states that produce these stimuli are more likely to develop under advanced agriculture than under hoe or digging-stick cultivation.

Many advantages accrue to a centralized and politically integrated society through specialization and economic diversification. The possibilities of gluts and shortages are reduced; the production of materials necessary for export and stockpiling can be planned; different parts of a country that are limited in particular resources or by other habitational factors can be supplied by other parts. Political advantages, primarily in terms of the maintenance of power and authority, also accrue to the political sector of the state from the stimulation of economic specialization.

Political power is often its own reward, and the holders of such power generally worry a great deal about being overthrown, sometimes with good reason. "Divide and conquer" is a useful strategy of domestic rulers as well as invading powers; when different groups in a centrally controlled society are stimulated to have different vested interests it is difficult for them to unite and overthow the established authorities. Alexander Hamilton (writing about an agricultural society in *The Federalist* papers) recognized this clearly when he said that political stability can be assured in a federal republic because an uprising in one state would fail for lack of support in another: However fierce a particular local economic interest, it was not likely to be embraced by the entire society. As history demonstrates, however, this is not impossible. Nor is this policy without disadvantages, especially when a society is invaded (as were the Aztecs and Incas) and communication among groups with different vested interests is found to be extremely difficult. Impediments to communication as a result of the diversity of local interests are among the serious vulnerabilities of totalitarian societies.

Cutting across regional and other differences in the organization of social relations in agricultural nation-states is the fact that they are almost always organized into social classes or castes, and sometimes both. One consequence of the development of social classes and castes is that all groups within the system of stratification (which cross-cuts the entire society, viewed as an adaptive unit) have their vested interests and values, and these are usually in competition. Thus one of the important sources of heterogeneity in an agricultural society is the confluence within the nation of occupational and regional specializations with the values and self-serving interests of different groups in the stratification system. The values of people of high status legitimate their occupations, privileges, positions of power, and control over production and distribution; correlatively, people of lower status hold to values that are appropriate to their own stations.

Which comes first, social stratification or the centrally controlling political institutions of the nation-state? There are passionate advocates of both positions, but much more research is needed before this question can be answered. It is clear, however, that control of sources of energy rather than control of instruments of production *per se,* underlies the stimulation, control, and redistribution of surpluses as well as the maintenance of political control by the ruling groups of a society. Control of the sources of energy is what enables these groups to maintain and extend their wealth and high standards of living.

Labor remains an important source of energy in every strategy of adaptation; hence, what people do with their labor is of paramount concern in social organization. The control of labor is an object of policy for all national rulers. A highly original and provocative example is given by Kurt Mendelssohn in "A Scientist Looks at the Pyramids" *(American Scientist,* 59 [1971]: 210-20). Mendelssohn, a physicist, speculates that the early Egyptian pyramids were built originally as means (or excuses) to organize Egyptian labor and bring it under centralized control. Their religious functions, he suggests, were secondary, if not incidental; this adds further support to the hypothesis (discussed below) that religion is an important means for legitimating existing social forms. Combining physical and archeological evidence, Mendelssohn maintains it was most unlikely that the pyramids were originally intended as tombs for the pharohs; instead, they seem to have been ingenious monumental works to bring a large proportion of laborers under central state control. Moreover, he argues, the ploy worked and, as a result, Egypt prospered economically. By such means the state becomes an important element in the habitat of local groups, to which they must adapt.

In contemporary industrial nations, regardless of their political and economic ideologies, there is a pattern in the relationship between centralized political institutions and the society's major sources of energy. The greater the number of people who draw on a single source of energy, the greater the tendency to centralize and concentrate its control in the hands of the society's ruling groups. For example, control of steam to drive machines has almost always been localized, each factory maintaining and controlling its own power plant. By contrast, there has been greater centralization of control of electricity produced by waterpower, and even greater centralization of control of electricity produced by nuclear energy is taking place. I do not think this is due only to the greater cost involved in producing higher and more efficient forms of energy. Many of the giant electric companies in the United States have the economic and technological wherewithal to construct nuclear power plants; nevertheless, the construction and use of nuclear power plants is under the control of the centralized state; in the United States it is through the Atomic Energy Commission. Increasing the centralization of control of new sources of energy tends to affect the relationship of the total society (not just one or another community or region) to the habitat. When the United States completes construction of its 73 proposed nuclear power plants, 30 million persons' power needs will be served by nuclear energy.

At the level of cultural development represented by agricultural nation-states the principles for the centralized control of sources of energy were first and firmly established. The specific modes and policies of this control of course are different in industrial and agricultural adaptations because they rely on different sources of energy. Industrial societies seldom maintain the same kind of control of the allocation of draft animals that we find in plow-agricultural societies; these animals, as sources of energy, have been superseded by other forms of energy that govern the group's relationship to the habitat.

The relationship of the individual to the sources of energy on which he relies is an important factor in the difficulty of establishing states under hoe and digging-stick cultivation. In the latter, each man controls his own muscular energy and his own hoe or digging stick; there is no extrapersonal source of energy that can be controlled and allocated. Only when land is in limited supply (as in the circumscribed regions described by Carneiro in Selection 27) or water available only in limited quantities is it possible for rulers to gain control of these resources and exchange access to them in return for conformity and allegiance. If a group cannot withhold resources and access to sources of energy, it generally cannot establish itself in political control. Only when an individual has exclusive control of the sources of energy on which he relies can he be free of centralized political control.

An important feature of life in all nation-states is an antagonism between local groups and those who speak in the name of the central government. The kin groups of pre-industrial societies provide the clearest focus of this antagonism. We have seen that these autonomous groups of kinsmen established the most significant social and economic bonds. As a result, kin groups invariably resisted the imposition of supra-community authority and control and the latter's demand that loyalty and allegiance be transferred from local groups to wider institutions, such as those of the state. When state systems were introduced, the new rulers imposed sets of laws and regulations that—whether by design or not—threatened to erode the autonomy of local groups. These groups and their chiefs were denied complete control over their lands; instead, the state claimed rights of eminent domain over all land in the nation. National religious cults and priestly bureaucracies were introduced to local regions. New taxes and mobilizations of labor (as for road building) were imposed. National legal systems were enacted, with the head of the state the highest court of appeal.

The existence of a peasantry is often an integral part of the status system of agricultural state societies. Peasants constitute a social stratum in these societies; in the words of Eric R. Wolf (in *Peasants* [Englewood Cliffs, N.J.: Prentice-Hall, 1966]), they are "rural cultivators whose surpluses are transferred to a dominant group of rulers that uses the surpluses both to underwrite its own standard of living and to distribute the remainder to groups in society that do not farm but must be fed for their specific goods and services in turn."

Peasants have proved difficult for anthropologists to characterize; students of peasant groups have had great difficulty in constructing models that fit all peasants, or even most of them. This is not surprising because, as I have noted, one of the correlates of an advance in the succession of strategies of adaptation is an increase in diversity within any given stage of development. However, the law" (from the capital to the most remote village) enforces the ultimate despite the diversity of peasants (which will become apparent in the selections that follow), they almost always tend to share the characteristics in Wolf's definition.

Because peasants are the food-producing specialists of their societies and because they occupy subservient sociopolitical status, they hold values different from those of their rulers and of other groups. Thus in studying peasants it is important not only to understand their ways of life but also the ways in which their local patterns relate to and are integrated with the total organization of social relations in their societies. The peasant subsystems of agricultural societies are aspects of agricultural adaptations.

But a system of social stratification is only one of the urban-dominated institutions that directly affect the peasant sector of society. Urban institutions intrude into peasant villages. In agricultural states, for example, schools develop. While in most societies schools were initially confined to the ruling classes, who lived in urban centers, there are instances (as in ancient China and Japan during the Tokugawa Period, from about 1600 to 1868) in which schools were established in rural areas. These were usually intended for the local nobility, however, and when an attempt was made to bring the peasants into the schools, an important step had been taken to identify them with national ideologies.

One of the first steps in a state's attempt to entrench itself is the establishment of courts; initially, these usually are circuit courts, but whether they are permanently established or make their appearances periodically, "the long arm of authority of the centralized state. A central concern of such courts is the enforcement of national laws on land tenure, which often are different from and in conflict with local village patterns. Not infrequently, as noted, centrally promulgated and enforced land laws are designed to benefit members of the ruling classes who want to add to their landholdings at the expense of the peasants. In some societies, laws are enacted that permit members of the nobility to buy land and deny this right to peasants.

Another important institution that affects the lives of a peasantry (generally neglected by anthropologists) is the nation's military organization. One source of the military's influence is that it recruits most of its foot soldiers among the peasants, and military training and indoctrination expose the conscripts to new values (such as allegiance and obedience to the state) that they communicate to their families and friends in one way or another. An excellent example of conscription as a means of introducing national institutions into peasant life and its consequences for marriage, household organization, and personal motivations, is to be found in *Proper Peasants*: *Traditional Life in a Hungarian Village,* by

Edit Fel and Tamas Hofer (Chicago: Aldine, 1969, pp. 365-70, 375-78). Professional militarists often are as much concerned with domestic policies as with guarding and expanding national borders, during the early stages of a state's development. Most states are born of conquest; therefore, militarism is one of the foundations of national social organizations. The social systems of states are intimately bound up with the maintenance of the integrity of territorial boundaries, and professional (differentiated) officers are of prime importance in this regard. Much the same can be said of the modern health and sanitation programs of national governments.

Another aspect of the complexity of agricultural societies is the wide range of social relations in which every individual engages. As Robert McC. Adams observes in *The Evolution of Urban Society* (Chicago: Aldine, 1966), every advance in adaptation is accompanied by an increase in the number and the types of groups with which each group interacts. Generally, a nomadic foraging group tends to interact primarily with other nomadic foraging groups; furthermore, the number of groups with which a band associates and on which it is dependent is very limited. This also tends to be the case among tribal cultivators, though there may be an expansion and elaboration of trade relationships among groups and an increasing mutual dependency between cultivators and nonculti- vators. In agricultural nation-states this dependency exists not only between people representing different adaptive strategies, as between agriculturists and pastoralists, but also between cultivators and artisans and other specialists within the society. However, urban and national influences sometimes fail completely to reach peasant groups, and this total insulation must also be regarded as an aspect of national social organization. An excellent example is provided in *Tonala: Conservatism, Responsibility and Authority in a Mexican Town,* by May Diaz (Berkeley and Los Angeles: University of California Press, 1966).

Urban centers depend on cultivators not only for food but also for personnel; until very recently in history, cities have not been able to sustain necessary population growth without recruitment from rural areas. Political bureaucrats, generally urban, interact with a wide variety of groups: other political function- aries, priests, warriors, artisans, traders, representatives of commercial interests, peasants, pastoralists, and often with members of other societies. Reciprocally, each group looks—and is forced to subscribe—to the legal and administrative rules of the state bureaucracy. Indeed, one of the accompaniments of cultural evolution is that the individual must at every successive stage learn to cope with an increasing variety of social categories. The most recent development of this aspect of evolution is to be seen in the range of social relations that characterizes the modern metropolis.

What roles are played by religious organization and ideology in agricultural nations? Many anthropologists (and others) have made much of the fact that centralized religious systems, represented by temples, elaborate priesthoods, monu- mental architecture, and the like, are important features of the evolution of agricultural states. Indeed, temples and priests have always played important roles in states, especially during the early stages of their development. Religious per- sonnel often supervised the distribution of seed and the collection of taxes; often they were also the principal administrators, in charge of human sacrifice where this was practiced, and the bureaucrats responsible for the stimulation of long-range trade. They were often the monopolizers of writing and books, and they have almost always had a hand in legal institutions, diplomacy, war, and other instruments of power, and the maintenance of conformity.

In complex state societies, religion appears to have played a unique and dominant role in the integration of politics. But in a comparative perspective, in the context of all societies at all stages of development, state religions are no more unique or dominant than the religions of lineage organizations, localized clan communities, or any other organization of social relations.

Religion is everywhere a political institution; in every society it provides an important source for the legitimation of the ideologies that contribute to the maintenance of order and conformity and validate the exercise of power and authority. Just as the head of a lineage invokes his ancestors in validating his leadership and authority, so does the head of a state invoke his deities. Just as a lineage or any other cohesive group is inconceivable without religious legitimation, national integration cannot be achieved without the stamp of the gods' approval. Counterpoised to the commingling of religious, political, economic, and kin roles in stateless societies, reflecting the general lack of role differentiation found there, is the presence of specialized priests in the bureaucracies of state societies, reflecting the specialization of labor and role differentiation characteristic there.

The political sectors of states use the temples and priesthoods they have created as indispensable crutches in gaining compliance with their policies. No peasant will toil for his masters unless he is convinced the gods have decreed he do so, and every head of state will proclaim that he is merely carrying out the will of the gods and that the temple is the central institution of society. Religion is thus an important element of every adaptation, but this ideology need not be incorporated into the study of adaptation itself. There is no basis for regarding religious institutions as the prime movers in the establishment of states; they only help provide legitimating ideologies for the political sectors.

The reader who wants to learn more about nations that have been based on agricultural technologies should consult works on the history of Japan (especially its Tokugawa Period, from about 1600 to 1868), China, India, Europe, and the United States (from about 1650 to 1870). An indispensable general introduction to the study of agricultural adaptations (on which I have drawn heavily) is *The Evolution of Urban Society,* by Robert McC. Adams (Chicago, Aldine, 1966). Another important book is *Peasants,* by Eric R. Wolf (Englewood Cliffs, N.J.: Prentice-Hall, 1966). Suggested readings for Japan will be given in connection with Selection 28. The reader who is interested in current studies of peasants will profit greatly by reading the *Peasant Studies Newsletter* (published by the University of Pittsburgh Press), a periodical that began publication in 1972.

For China, see *China's Gentry* (Chicago: University of Chicago Press, 1953), *Earthbound China* (Chicago: University of Chicago Press, 1945), and *Peasant*

Life in China (New York: Dutton, 1939), by Hsiao-t'ung Fei. *Fabric of Chinese Society,* by Morton H. Fried (New York: Praeger, 1953) is an excellent community study; *Ancient China in Transition: An Analysis of Social Mobility, 722-222 B.C.,* by Cho-yun Hsu (Stanford: Stanford University Press paperback, 1965) is a very good study of social change within an adaptational frame of reference; and *The Family Revolution in Modern China,* by Marion J. Levy, Jr. (Cambridge, Mass.: Harvard University Press, 1949) is an excellent study of change in family and household organizations.

For India, see *The Wonder That Was India,* by Arthur L. Basham (rev. ed.; Hawthorn Books, 1963); *The Twice-Born: A Study of a Community of High-Caste Hindus,* by G. Morris Carstairs (Bloomington: Indiana University Press, 1958); *Indian Village,* by Shyama Charan Dube (New York: Humanities Press, 1955); *Caste, Class, and Occupation in India,* by Govind Sadashiv Ghurye (4th rev. ed.; New York: Heinman Imported Books, 1961); *Village Life in Northern India,* by Oscar Lewis (Urbana: University of Illinois Press, 1958); and *Caste and Kinship in Central India,* by Adrian C. Mayer (Berkeley: University of California Press, 1960).

27. A THEORY OF THE ORIGIN OF THE STATE

ROBERT L. CARNEIRO

Reprinted from Science *(Vol. 169, 1970, pp. 733-38). For biographical information, see Selection 9.*

■ We saw in the descriptions of the !Kung Bushmen and the Shoshoneans (Selections 4 and 5) that when people rely exclusively on their own muscular energy and when resources cannot be controlled or appropriated by any person or group, people do pretty much as they choose in decision-making. This picture alters as soon as any of these variables changes; thus among the Northwest Coast Indians (Selection 7), chieftainship—however honorific and devoid of real power and authority—was elaborated in direct proportion to abundance and control over resources.

But it is a far cry from village chieftainship to the status of a chief of state. How are the resources of a wide area encompassing many communities brought under the control of a single political system? Carneiro suggests in this selection that a central state system can arise locally (disregarding cases where it is imposed by a colonial power) only under the particular habitational condition of circumscription. He suggests two types of circumscription: territorial (or environmental) and social. In the first, as in narrow valleys and other limited areas, a physical barrier prevents the escape of defeated groups. Under these conditions, a conquered group cannot withdraw or disperse, which sets the stage for their political subjugation. In unbroken expanses of land—plains—people can disperse as soon as military pressure is exerted.

"Social circumscription" refers to a situation in which a high density of population in an area produces effects on people like those of territorial circumscription. Defeated groups are prevented from dispersing by the presence of other groups, who constitute an impenetrable barrier. These boxed-in groups then become politically and economically subjugated.

Closely related to territorial circumscription is what Carneiro calls "resource concentration," which refers to the physical concentration of limited quantities of prized resources, for example, rich soil that can be cultivated

year after year. It is a kind of circumscription, and people are drawn to the areas where these resources are found. When war ends, losers have to submit to victors if they are to retain access to these resources—but they pay the price of becoming an economically and socially subordinate group.

Anthropologists have generally paid insufficient attention to the role of warfare in political evolution. It should be clear from Carneiro's analysis that this is myopic. Despite this gap, there are a few sources that the interested reader may pursue. There are good papers in *Systems of Political Control and Bureaucracy in Human Societies,* edited by Verne F. Ray (Seattle: University of Washington Press, 1958); *West African Kingdoms in the Nineteenth Century,* edited by Daryll Forde and P. M. Kaberry (London: Oxford University Press, 1967); and *Political Systems and the Distribution of Power,* A. S. A. Monographs 2 (New York: Praeger, 1965). Frederick Engels has played an important role in shaping modern ideas about the origin of the state, especially in his *The Origin of the Family, Private Property, and the State* (New York: International Publishers, 1942). In line with Carneiro's emphasis on population density in particular habitats and its conjunction with warfare in the rise of the state, see *Population and Political Systems In Tropical Africa,* by Robert E. Stevenson (New York: Columbia University Press, 1968). In this connection, however, one should bear in mind the caveat of Robert McC. Adams and Hans J. Nissen in *The Uruk Countryside* (Chicago: University of Chicago Press, 1972, ch. 6) that recent findings "prompt a reconsideration of the role of 'population pressure' as an important historical variable." ■

FOR THE FIRST two million years of his existence, man lived in bands or villages which, as far as we can tell, were completely autonomous. Not until perhaps 5000 B.C.

did villages begin to aggregate into larger political units. But, once this process of aggregation began, it continued at a progressively faster pace and led, around 4000 B.C., to the formation of the first state in history. (When I speak of a state I mean an autonomous political unit, encompassing many communities within its territory and having a centralized government with the power to collect taxes, draft men for work or war, and decree and enforce laws.)

Although it was by all odds the most far-reaching political development in human history, the origin of the state is still very imperfectly understood. Indeed, not one of the current theories of the rise of the state is entirely satisfactory. At one point or another, all of them fail. There is one theory, though, which I believe does provide a convincing explanation of how states began. It is a theory which I proposed once before, and which I present here more fully. Before doing so, however, it seems desirable to discuss, if only briefly, a few of the traditional theories.

Explicit theories of the origin of the state are relatively modern. Classical writers like Aristotle, unfamiliar with other forms of political organization, tended to think of the state as "natural," and therefore as not requiring an explanation. However, the age of exploration, by making Europeans aware that many peoples throughout the world lived, not in states, but in independent villages or tribes, made the state seem less natural, and thus more in need of explanation.

Of the many modern theories of state origins that have been proposed, we can consider only a few. Those with a racial basis, for example, are now so thoroughly discredited that they need not be dealt with here. We can also reject the belief that the state is an expression of the "genius" of a people, or that it arose through a "historical accident." Such notions make the state appear to be something metaphysical or adventitious, and thus place it beyond scientific understanding. In my opinion, the origin of the state was neither mysterious nor fortuitous. It was not the product of "genius" or the result of chance, but the outcome of a regular and determinate cultural process. Moreover, it was not a unique event but a recurring phenomenon: states arose independently in different places and at different times. Where the appropriate conditions existed, the state emerged.

VOLUNTARISTIC THEORIES

Serious theories of state origins are of two general types: *voluntaristic* and *coercive*. Voluntaristic theories hold that, at some point in their history, certain people spontaneously, rationally, and voluntarily gave up their individual sovereignties and united with other communities to form a larger political unit deserving to be called a state. Of such theories the best known is the old Social Contract theory, which was associated especially with the name of Rousseau. We now know that no such compact was ever subscribed to by human groups, and the Social Contract theory is today nothing more than a historical curiosity.

The most widely accepted of modern voluntaristic theories is the one I call the "automatic" theory. According to this theory, the invention of agriculture automatically brought into being a surplus of food, enabling some individuals to divorce themselves from food production and to become potters, weavers, smiths, masons, and so on, thus creating an extensive division of labor. Out of this occupational specialization there developed a political integration which united a number of previously independent communities into a state. This argument was set forth most frequently by the late British archeologist V. Gordon Childe.

The principal difficulty with this theory is that agriculture does (*not*) automatically create a food surplus. We know this because many agricultural peoples of the world produce no such surplus. Virtually all Amazonian Indians, for example, were agricultural, but in aboriginal times they did not produce a food surplus. That it was *technically feasible* for them to produce such a surplus is shown by the fact that, under the stimulus of European settlers' desire for food, a number of tribes did raise manioc in amounts well above their own needs, for the purpose of trading. Thus the technical means for generating a food surplus were there; it was the social mechanisms needed to actualize it that were lacking.

Another current voluntaristic theory of state origins is Karl Wittfogel's "hydraulic hypothesis." As I understand him, Wittfogel sees the state arising in the following way. In certain arid and semiarid areas of the world, where village farmers had to struggle to support themselves by means of small-scale irrigation, a time arrived when they saw that it would be to the advantage of all concerned to set aside their individual autonomies and merge their villages into a single large political unit capable of carrying out irrigation on a broad scale. The body of officials they created to devise and administer such extensive irrigation works brought the state into being.

This theory has recently run into difficulties. Archeological evidence now makes it appear that in at least three of the areas that Wittfogel cites as exemplifying his "hydraulic hypothesis"—Mesopotamia, China, and Mexico—full-fledged states developed well before large-scale irrigation.[1] Thus, irrigation did not play the causal role in the rise of the state that Wittfogel appears to attribute to it.[2]

This and all other voluntaristic theories of the rise of the state founder on the same rock: the demonstrated inability of autonomous political units to relinquish their sovereignty in the absence of overriding external constraints. We see this inability manifested again and again by political units ranging from tiny villages to great empires. Indeed, one can scan the pages of history without finding a single genuine exception to this rule. Thus, in order to account for the origin

of the state we must set aside voluntaristic theories and look elsewhere.

COERCIVE THEORIES

A close examination of history indicates that only a coercive theory can account for the rise of the state. Force, and not enlightened self-interest, is the mechanism by which political evolution has led, step by step, from autonomous villages to the state.

The view that war lies at the root of the state is by no means new. Twenty-five hundred years ago Heraclitus wrote that "war is the father of all things." The first careful study of the role of warfare in the rise of the state, however, was made less than a hundred years ago, by Herbert Spencer in his *Principles of Sociology*. Perhaps better known than Spencer's writings on war and the state are the conquest theories of continental writers such as Ludwig Gumplowicz, Gustav Ratzenhofer, and Franz Oppenheimer.

Oppenheimer, for example, argued that the state emerged when the productive capacity of settled agriculturists was combined with the energy of pastoral nomads through

1. For Mesopotamia, Robert M. Adams has concluded: "In short, there is nothing to suggest that the rise of dynastic authority in southern Mesopotamia was linked to the administrative requirements of a major canal system" [in *City Invincible*, C. H. Kraeling and R. M. Adams, Eds. (Univ. of Chicago Press, Chicago, 1969), p. 281]. For China, the prototypical area for Wittfogel's hydraulic theories, the French Sinologist Jacques Gernet has recently written: "although the establishment of a system of regulation of water courses and irrigation, and the control of this system, may have affected the political constitution of the military states and imperial China, the fact remains that, historically, it was the pre-existing state structures and the large, well-trained labour force provided by the armies that made the great irrigation projects possible" [*Ancient China, from the Beginnings to the Empire*, R. Rudorff, Transl. (Faber and Faber, London, 1968), p. 92]. For Mexico, large-scale irrigation systems do not appear to antedate the Classic period, whereas it is clear that the first states arose in the preceding Formative or Pre-Classic period.
2. This is not to say, of course, that large-scale irrigation, where it occurred, did not contribute significantly to increasing the power and scope of the state. It unquestionably did. To the extent that Wittfogel limits himself to this contention, I have no quarrel with him whatever. However, the point at issue is not how the state increased its power but how it arose in the first place. And to this issue the hydraulic hypothesis does not appear to hold the key.

the conquest of the former by the latter (11, pp. 51-55). This theory, however, has two serious defects. First, it fails to account for the rise of states in aboriginal America, where pastoral nomadism was unknown. Second, it is now well established that pastoral nomadism did not arise in the Old World until after the earliest states had emerged.

Regardless of deficiencies in particular coercive theories, however, there is little question that, in one way or another, war played a decisive role in the rise of the state. Historical or archeological evidence of war is found in the early stages of state formation in Mesopotamia, Egypt, India, China, Japan, Greece, Rome, northern Europe, central Africa, Polynesia, Middle America, Peru, and Colombia, to name only the most prominent examples.

Thus, with the Germanic kingdoms of northern Europe especially in mind, Edward Jenks observed that, "historically speaking, there is not the slightest difficulty in proving that all political communities of the modern type (that is, states) owe their existence to successful warfare."[3] And in reading Jan Vansina's *Kingdoms of the Savanna,* a book with no theoretical ax to grind, one finds that state after state in central Africa arose in the same manner.

But is it really true that there is no exception to this rule? Might there not be, somewhere in the world, an example of a state which arose without the agency of war?

Until a few years ago, anthropologists generally believed that the Classic Maya provided such an instance. The archeological evidence then available gave no hint of warfare among the early Maya and led scholars to regard them as a peace-loving theocratic state which had arisen entirely without war. However, this view is no longer tenable. Recent archeological discoveries have placed the Classic Maya in a very different light. First came the discovery of the Bonampak murals, showing the early Maya at war and reveling in the torture of war captives. Then,

excavations around Tikal revealed large earthworks partly surrounding that Classic Maya city, pointing clearly to a military rivalry with the neighboring city of Uaxactún. Summarizing present thinking on the subject, Michael D. Coe has observed that "the ancient Maya were just as warlike as the . . . bloodthirsty states of the Post-Classic".[4]

Yet, though warfare is surely a prime mover in the origin of the state, it cannot be the only factor. After all, wars have been fought in many parts of the world where the state never emerged. Thus, while warfare may be a necessary condition for the rise of the state, it is not a sufficient one. Or, to put it another way, while we can identify war as the *mechanism* of state formation, we need also to specify the *conditions* under which it gave rise to the state.

ENVIRONMENTAL CIRCUMSCRIPTION

How are we to determine these conditions? One promising approach is to look for those factors common to areas of the world in which states arose indigenously— areas such as the Nile, Tigris-Euphrates, and Indus valleys in the Old World and the Valley of Mexico and the mountain and coastal valleys of Peru in the New. These areas differ from one another in many ways—in altitude, temperature, rainfall, soil type, drainage pattern, and many other features. They do, however, have one thing in common: *they are all areas of circumscribed agricultural land.* Each of them is set off by mountains, seas, or deserts, and these environmental features sharply delimit the area that simple farming peoples could occupy and cultivate. In this respect these areas are very different from, say, the Amazon basin or the eastern woodlands of North America,

3. E. Jenks, *A History of Politics* (Macmillan, New York, 1900), p. 73.
4. M. D. Coe, *The Maya* (Praeger, New York, 1966), p. 147.

where extensive and unbroken forests provided almost unlimited agricultural land.

But what is the significance of circumscribed agricultural land for the origin of the state? Its significance can best be understood by comparing political development in two regions of the world having contrasting ecologies—one a region with circumscribed agricultural land and the other a region where there was extensive and unlimited land. The two areas I have chosen to use in making this comparison are the coastal valleys of Peru and the Amazon basin.

Our examination begins at the stage where agricultural communities were already present but where each was still completely autonomous. Looking first at the Amazon basin, we see that agricultural villages there were numerous, but widely dispersed. Even in areas with relatively dense clustering, like the Upper Xingú basin, villages were at least 10 or 15 miles apart. Thus, the typical Amazonian community, even though it practiced a simple form of shifting cultivation which required extensive amounts of land, still had around it all the forest land needed for its gardens. For Amazonia as a whole, then, population density was low and subsistence pressure on the land was slight.

Warfare was certainly frequent in Amazonia, but it was waged for reasons of revenge, the taking of women, the gaining of personal prestige, and motives of a similar sort. There being no shortage of land, there was, by and large, no warfare over land.

The consequences of the type of warfare that did occur in Amazonia were as follows. A defeated group was not, as a rule, driven from its land. Nor did the victor make any real effort to subject the vanquished, or to exact tribute from him. This would have been difficult to accomplish in any case, since there was no effective way to prevent the losers from fleeing to a distant part of the forest. Indeed, defeated villages often chose to do just this, not so much to avoid subjugation as to avoid further attack. With settlement so sparse in Amazonia, a new area of forest could be found and occupied with relative

ease, and without trespassing on the territory of another village. Moreover, since virtually any area of forest is suitable for cultivation, subsistence agriculture could be carried on in the new habitat just about as well as in the old.

It was apparently by this process of fight and flight that horticultural tribes gradually spread out until they came to cover, thinly but extensively, almost the entire Amazon basin. Thus, under the conditions of unlimited agricultural land and low population density that prevailed in Amazonia, the effect of warfare was to disperse villages over a wide area, and to keep them autonomous. With only a very few exceptions, noted below, there was no tendency in Amazonia for villages to be held in place and to combine into larger political units.

In marked contracst to the situation in Amazonia were the events that transpired in the narrow valleys of the Peruvian coast. The reconstruction of these events that I present is admittedly inferential, but I think it is consistent with the archeological evidence.

Here too our account begins at the stage of small, dispersed, and autonomous farming communities. However, instead of being scattered over a vast expanse of rain forest as they were in Amazonia, villages here were confined to some 78 short and narrow valleys. Each of these valleys, moreover, was backed by the mountains, fronted by the sea, and flanked on either side by desert as dry as any in the world. Nowhere else, perhaps, can one find agricultural valleys more sharply circumscribed than these.

As with neolithic communities generally, villages of the Peruvian coastal valleys tended to grow in size. Since autonomous villages are likely to fission as they grow, as long as land is available for the settlement of splinter communities, these villages undoubtedly split from time to time. Thus, villages tended to increase in number faster than they grew in size. This increase in the number of villages occupying a valley probably continued, without giving rise to significant changes in subsistence practices, until all the readily arable land in the valley was being farmed.

At this point two changes in agricultural techniques began to occur: the tilling of land already under cultivation was intensified, and new, previously unusable land was brought under cultivation by means of terracing and irrigation.

Yet the rate at which new arable land was created failed to keep pace with the increasing demand for it. Even before the land shortage became so acute that irrigation began to be practiced systematically, villages were undoubtedly already fighting one another over land. Prior to this time, when agricultural villages were still few in number and well supplied with land, the warfare waged in the coastal valleys of Peru had probably been of much the same type as that described above for Amazonia. With increasing pressure of human population on the land, however, the major incentive for war changed from a desire for revenge to a need to acquire land. And, as the causes of war became predominantly economic, the frequency, intensity, and importance of war increased.

Once this stage was reached, a Peruvian village that lost a war faced consequences very different from those faced by a defeated village in Amazonia. There, as we have seen, the vanquished could flee to a new locale, subsisting there about as well as they had subsisted before, and retaining their independence. In Peru, however, this alternative was no longer open to the inhabitants of defeated villages. The mountains, the desert, and the sea—to say nothing of neighboring villages—blocked escape in every direction. A village defeated in war thus faced only grim prospects. If it was allowed to remain on its own land, instead of being exterminated or expelled, this concession came only at a price. And the price was political subordination to the victor. This subordination generally entailed at least the payment of a tribute or tax in kind, which the defeated village could provide only by producing more food than it had produced before. But subordination sometimes involved a further loss of autonomy on the part of the defeated village— namely, incorporation into the political unit dominated by the victor.

Through the recurrence of warfare of this type, we see arising in coastal Peru integrated territorial units transcending the village in size and in degree of organization. Political evolution was attaining the level of the chiefdom.

As land shortages continued and became even more acute, so did warfare. Now, however, the competing units were no longer small villages but, often, large chiefdoms. From this point on, through the conquest of chiefdom by chiefdom, the size of political units increased at a progressively faster rate. Naturally, as autonomous political units increased in size, they decreased in number, with the result that an entire valley was eventually unified under the banner of its strongest chiefdom. The political unit thus formed was undoubtedly sufficiently centralized and complex to warrant being called a state.

The political evolution I have described for one valley of Peru was also taking place in other valleys, in the highlands as well as on the coast.[5] Once valley-wide kingdoms emerged, the next step was the formation of multivalley kingdoms through the conquest of weaker valleys by stronger ones. The culmination of this process was the conquest[6] of all of Peru by its most powerful state, and the formation of a single great empire. Although this step may have occurred once or twice before in Andean history, it was

5. Naturally, this evolution took place in the various Peruvian valleys at different rates and to different degrees. In fact it is possible that at the same time that some valleys were already unified politically, others still had not evolved beyond the stage of autonomous villages.
6. Not every step in empire building was necessarily taken through actual physical conquest, however. The threat of force sometimes had the same effect as its exercise. In this way many smaller chiefdoms and states were probably coerced into giving up their sovereignty without having to be defeated on the field of battle. Indeed, it was an explicit policy of the Incas, in expanding their empire, to try persuasion before resorting to force of arms. See Garcilaso de la Vega, *Royal Commentaries of the Incas and General History of Peru*, Part 1, H. V. Livermore, Transl. (Univ. of Texas Press, Austin, 1966), pp. 108, 111, 140, 143, 146, 264.

achieved most notably, and for the last time, by the Incas.[7]

POLITICAL EVOLUTION

While the aggregation of villages into chiefdoms, and of chiefdoms into kingdoms, was occurring by external acquisition, the structure of these increasingly larger political units was being elaborated by internal evolution. These inner changes were, of course, closely related to outer events. The expansion of successful states brought within their borders conquered peoples and territory which had to be administered. And it was the individuals who had distinguished themselves in war who were generally appointed to political office and assigned the task of carrying out this administration. Besides maintaining law and order and collecting taxes, the functions of this burgeoning class of administrators included mobilizing labor for building irrigation works, roads, fortresses, palaces, and temples. Thus, their functions helped to weld an assorted collection of petty states into a single integrated and centralized political unit.

These same individuals, who owed their improved social position to their exploits in war, became, along with the ruler and his kinsmen, the nucleus of an upper class. A lower class in turn emerged from the prisoners taken in war and employed as servants and slaves by their captors. In this manner did war contribute to the rise of social classes.

I noted earlier that peoples attempt to acquire their neighbors' land before they have made the fullest possible use of their own. This implies that every autonomous village has an untapped margin of food productivity,

7. The evolution of empire in Peru was thus by no means rectilinear or irreversible. Advance alternated with decline. Integration was sometimes followed by disintegration, with states fragmenting back to chiefdoms, and perhaps even to autonomous villages. But the forces underlying political development were strong and, in the end, prevailed. Thus, despite fluctuations and reversions, the course of evolution in Peru was unmistakable: it began with many small, simple, scattered, and autonomous communities and ended with a single, vast, complex, and centralized empire.

and that this margin is squeezed out only when the village is subjugated and compelled to pay taxes in kind. The surplus food extracted from conquered villages through taxation, which in the aggregate attained very significant proportions, went largely to support the ruler, his warriors and retainers, officials, priests, and other members of the rising upper class, who thus became completely divorced from food production.

Finally, those made landless by war but not enslaved tended to gravitate to settlements which, because of their specialized administrative, commercial, or religious functions, were growing into towns and cities. Here they were able to make a living as workers and artisans, exchanging their labor or their wares for part of the economic surplus exacted from village farmers by the ruling class and spent by members of that class to raise their standard of living.

The process of political evolution which I have outlined for the coastal valleys of Peru was, in its essential features, by no means unique to this region. Areas of circumscribed agricultural land elsewhere in the world, such as the Valley of Mexico, Mesopotamia, the Nile Valley, and the Indus Valley, saw the process occur in much the same way and for essentially the same reasons. In these areas, too, autonomous neolithic villages were succeeded by chiefdoms, chiefdoms by kingdoms, and kingdoms by empires. The last stage of this development was, of course, the most impressive. The scale and magnificence attained by the early empires overshadowed everything that had gone before. But, in a sense, empires were merely the logical culmination of the process. The really fundamental step, the one that had triggered the entire train of events that led to empires, was the change from village autonomy to supravillage integration. This step was a change in kind; everything that followed was, in a way, only a change in degree.

In addition to being pivotal, the step to supracommunity aggregation was difficult, for it took two million years to achieve. But, once it was achieved, once village autonomy was transcended, only two or three millennia were required for the rise of great empires and the flourishing of complex civilizations.

RESOURCE CONCENTRATION

Theories are first formulated on the basis of a limited number of facts. Eventually, though, a theory must confront all of the facts. And often new facts are stubborn and do not conform to the theory, or do not conform very well. What distinguishes a successful theory from an unsuccessful one is that it can be modified or elaborated to accommodate the entire range of facts. Let us see how well the "circumscription theory" holds up when it is brought face-to-face with certain facts that appear to be exceptions.

For the first test let us return to Amazonia. Early voyagers down the Amazon left written testimony of a culture along that river higher than the culture I have described for Amazonia generally. In the 1500's, the native population living on the banks of the Amazon was relatively dense, villages were fairly large and close together, and some degree of social stratification existed. Moreover, here and there a paramount chief held sway over many communities.

The question immediately arises: With unbroken stretches of arable land extending back from the Amazon for hundreds of miles, why were there chiefdoms here?

To answer this question we must look closely at the environmental conditions afforded by the Amazon. Along the margins of the river itself, and on islands within it, there is a type of land called *várzea*. The river floods this land every year, covering it with a layer of fertile silt. Because of this annual replenishment, *várzea* is agricultural land of first quality which can be cultivated year after year without ever having to lie fallow. Thus, among native farmers it was highly prized and greatly coveted. The waters of the Amazon were also extraordinarily bountiful, providing fish, manatees, turtles and turtle eggs, caimans, and other riverine foods in inexhaustible amounts. By virtue of this concentration of resources, the Amazon, as a habitat, was distinctly superior to its hinterlands.

Concentration of resources along the Amazon amounted almost to a kind of circumscription. While there was no sharp cleavage between productive and unproductive land, as there was in Peru, there was at least a steep ecological gradient. So much more rewarding was the Amazon River than adjacent areas, and so desirable did it become as a habitat, that peoples were drawn to it from surrounding regions. Eventually crowding occurred along many portions of the river, leading to warfare over sections of river front. And the losers in war, in order to retain access to the river, often had no choice but to submit to the victors. By this subordination of villages to a paramount chief there arose along the Amazon chiefdoms representing a higher step in political evolution than had occurred elsewhere in the basin.

The notion of resource concentration also helps to explain the surprising degree of political development apparently attained by peoples of the Peruvian coast while they were still depending primarily on fishing for subsistence, and only secondarily on agriculture. Of this seeming anomaly Lanning has written: "To the best of my knowledge, this is the only case in which so many of the characteristics of civilization have been found without a basically agricultural economic foundation."[8]

Armed with the concept of resource concentration, however, we can show that this development was not so anomalous after all. The explanation, it seems to me, runs as follows. Along the coast of Peru wild food sources occurred in considerable number and variety. However, they were restricted to a very narrow margin of land. Accordingly, while the *abundance* of food in this zone led to a sharp rise in population, the *restrictedness* of this food soon resulted in the almost complete occupation of exploitable areas. And when pressure on the available resources reached a critical level, competition over land ensued. The result of this competition was to

8. E. P. Lanning, *Peru Before the Incas* (Prentice-Hall, Englewood Cliffs, N.J., 1967), p. 59.

set in motion the sequence of events of political evolution that I have described.

Thus, it seems that we can safely add resource concentration to environmental circumscription as a factor leading to warfare over land, and thus to political integration beyond the village level.

SOCIAL CIRCUMSCRIPTION

But there is still another factor to be considered in accounting for the rise of the state.

In dealing with the theory of environmental circumscription while discussing the Yanomamo Indians of Venezuela, Napoleon A. Chagnon has introduced the concept of "social circumscription." By this he means that a high density of population in an area can produce effects on peoples living near the center of the area that are similar to effects produced by environmental circumscription. This notion seems to me to be an important addition to our theory. Let us see how, according to Chagnon, social circumscription has operated among the Yanomamo.

The Yanomamo, who number some 10,000, live in an extensive region of noncircumscribed rain forest, away from any large river. One might expect that Yanomamo villages would thus be more or less evenly spaced. However, Chagnon notes that, at the center of Yanomamo territory, villages are closer together than they are at the periphery. Because of this, they tend to impinge on one another more, with the result that warfare is more frequent and intense in the center than in peripheral areas. Moreover, it is more difficult for villages in the nuclear area to escape attack by moving away, since, unlike villages on the periphery, their ability to move is somewhat restricted.

The net result is that villages in the central area of Yanomamo territory are larger than villages in the other areas, since large village size is an advantage for both attack and defense. A further effect of more intense warfare in the nuclear area is that village headmen are stronger in that area. Yanomamo headmen are also the war leaders, and their influence increases in proportion to their village's participation in war. In addition, offensive and defensive alliances between villages are more common in the center of Yanomamo territory than in outlying areas. Thus, while still at the autonomous village level of political organization, those Yanomamo subject to social circumscription have clearly moved a step or two in the direction of higher political development.

Although the Yanomamo manifest social circumscription only to a modest degree, this amount of it has been enough to make a difference in their level of political organization. What the effects of social circumscription would be in areas where it was more fully expressed should, therefore, be clear. First would come a reduction in the size of the territory of each village. Then, as population pressure became more severe, warfare over land would ensue. But because adjacent land for miles around was already the property of other villages, a defeated village would have nowhere to flee. From this point on, the consequences of warfare for that village, and for political evolution in general, would be essentially as I have described them for the situation of environmental circumscription.

To return to Amazonia, it is clear that, if social circumscription is operative among the Yanomamo today, it was certainly operative among the tribes of the Amazon River 400 years ago. And its effect would undoubtedly have been to give a further spur to political evolution in that region.

We see then that, even in the absence of sharp environmental circumscription, the factors of resource concentration and social circumscription may, by intensifying war and redirecting it toward the taking of land, give a strong impetus to political development.

With these auxiliary hypotheses incorporated into it, the circumscription theory is now better able to confront the entire range of test cases that can be brought before it. For example, it can now account for the rise of the state in the Hwang Valley of northern China, and even in the Petén region of the Maya lowlands, areas not characterized by strictly circumscribed agricultural land. In the case of the Hwang Valley, there is no question that resource concentration and social circumscription were present and active forces. In the lowland Maya area, resource concentration seems not to have been a major factor, but social circumscription may well have been.

Some archeologists may object that population density in the Petén during formative times was too low to give rise to social circumscription. But, in assessing what constitutes a population dense enough to produce this effect, we must consider not so much the total land area occupied as the amount of land needed to support the existing population. And the size of this supporting area depends not only on the size of the population but also on the mode of subsistence. The shifting cultivation presumably practiced by the ancient Maya required considerably more land, per capita, than did the permanent field cultivation of say, the Valley of Mexico or the coast of Peru. Consequently, insofar as its effects are concerned, a relatively low population density in the Petén may have been equivalent to a much higher one in Mexico or Peru.

We have already learned from the Yanomamo example that social circumscription may begin to operate while population is still relatively sparse. And we can be sure that the Petén was far more densely peopled in Formative times than Yanomamo territory is today. Thus, population density among the lowland Maya, while giving a superficial appearance of sparseness, may actually have been high enough to provoke fighting over land, and thus provide the initial impetus for the formation of a state.

CONCLUSION

In summary, then, the circumscription theory in its elaborated form goes far toward accounting for the origin of the state. It explains why states arose where they did, and why they failed to arise elsewhere. It shows the state to be a predictable response to certain specific cultural, demographic, and ecological conditions. Thus, it helps to elucidate what was undoubtedly the most important single step ever taken in the political evolution of mankind.

28. VILLAGE AUTONOMY AND ARTICULATION WITH THE STATE: THE CASE OF TOKUGAWA JAPAN

HARUMI BEFU

Reprinted from The Journal of Asian Studies *(Vol. 25, 1965, pp. 19-32). Harumi Befu is Associate Professor of Anthropology, Stanford University. His Major interests have been in cultural evolution, the culture history of Japan, social organization and interpersonal relationships in Japan. He is the author of* Japan: An Anthropological Introduction.

■ I have stressed that in a nation-state, the central government is a dominant element in the local community's habitat and that the community must develop strategies for adapting to the pressures generated by those who speak in the name of the state. At the same time, however, the society is not a blank slate on which rulers may write whatever policies and laws they wish. Local communities are the relevant habitat for their rulers, and the social elements in this milieu set limits and provide potentials for the governing classes. Thus, there are inputs and feedbacks from the two; they must come to terms with each other and mesh (more or less) if they are to live in the same social system. They must, in the terms we have used earlier, adjust to each other.

In this selection we consider an example of this adjustment process in Japan during the Tokugawa period (from about 1600 to 1868). Although the country was governed by a military directorship during this period, the nation's rulers, as Befu shows, were compelled by local social conditions to create a governing bureaucracy within the villages rather than rely on the previously existing political organizations of rural villages for the maintenance of order. Befu shows us the points at which state and village goals conflicted, especially in respect to the promotion of village welfare. The members of each village thought of themselves as a corporate entity, concerned primarily with maintaining local harmony and efficient agricultural practices. In the rulers' eyes, the state existed for the benefit of the ruling classes, and the villages were merely means to that end; they could not rely entirely on them to further the state's interests.

At the same time, the government could not hope to rule by coercion alone; the nation's rulers therefore had to find institutions in village political organizations to which they could attach their bureaucratic machinery. Their solution was simplicity itself. The government used the local system of "traditonal authority"—vested by consensus in a village's oldest and most respected family—by appointing the village's senior member as headman, assisted by three or four other local elders. They were collectively responsible for the villagers' actions. But this local administration was not simply imposed on the village; Befu emphasizes that the peasants too were drawn into this by being forced to pay the headman's (and sometimes the elders') salaries from the farmers' crops. The peasants were further involved in the administrative machinery by being organized into five-family groups; each family was responsible for the actions and tax liabilities of the others, although these groups did not always function as they were intended to. This system of overlapping levels of collective responsibility exploited traditional patterns of mutual responsibility and cooperation, originally made necessary by the demands of paddy cultivation.

Prior to about 1600, the islands of Japan were composed of petty chiefdoms that were constantly at war with each other. Previous attempts at centralization had foundered in civil wars. Each of these attempts at centralization had weakened the powers of decentralized groups and no doubt contributed to the success of Tokugawa Ieyasu around 1600. But centralization is almost never achieved immediately; Japan was no exception. In theory the emperor held the central power; actual power, however, was in the hands of the *shogun,* the commander of the military and police. (The "shogunate" refers to his headquarters.) The *shogun* was also, in effect, the chief lord in a feudal hierarchy. Each domain—

more or less a remnant of the periods of decentralized authority—was governed by a powerful local lord, known as *daimyo,* and his vassals in a fairly typical feudal system. ("Daimiate" refers to these local centers of power derived from the shogunate.)

Befu's paper begins with the Tokugawa period well under way. In addition to using existing village patterns of authority and cooperation as building blocks in constructing its administrative machinery, the government imposed a system of village taxation, and it extended its elaborate divisions in social stratification to each village. These divisions were not only reflected in social and economic inequality but also in the limitation of membership in religious associations to members of the old and established village families. But at the same time that the government strengthened its controls by many of these means, its adaptive tradeoff with the rural village allowed the latter to retain many features of corporate life, especially in the maintenance of conformity. This aspect of village life during the Tokugawa period is reflected in the village codes, which are cogently described by Befu.

Japan's evolution is one of the best documented. *Village Japan,* by Richard K. Beardsley, John W. Hall, and Robert E. Ward (Chicago: University of Chicago Press, paperback, 1959) provides an excellent introduction to the social organization of rural Japan; *Tokugawa Religion,* by Robert N. Bellah (New York: The Free Press, 1957) concentrates on the national level from the point of view of religious change. *Education in Tokugawa Japan,* by R. P. Dore (Berkeley: University of California Press paperback, 1965) is, in my opinion, the finest study of a national system of education available together with unmatched insight into Tokugawa lifestyles. The reader should combine Dore's book with *The Agrarian Origins of Modern Japan,* by Thomas C. Smith (Stanford: Stanford University Press, paperback, 1959), which is a superb study of the Tokugawa Period as a state in Japan's evolution. An aspect of Japanese social organization that is rarely discussed is its caste systems; this was institutionalized during the Tokugawa period. An excellent introduction to it, along with many insights into American caste relationships, is *Japan's Invisible Race,* edited by George De Vos and Hiroshi Wagatsuma (Berkeley: University of California Press, paperback, 1967). ∎

WHEN VILLAGE COMMUNITIES exist in the context of a larger political system, understanding of the system of control at the village level requires analysis both of the system of control imposed on the village by the state and also of that which has evolved within the community through centuries of its existence. These two systems, of course, cannot operate altogether independently of each other but must somehow be articulated with one another. The specific ways in which the two systems articulate differ from society to society. Nonetheless a perusal of the literature suggests a solution to the problem of articulation which is common to many societies. The solution apparently is to maintain a relatively autonomous village community over which the higher authority exercises limited control through certain key agents or agencies, as is, for example, the case with Imperial China, Thailand, Ceylon, and Greece. And this was indeed the solution for Japanese villages of the Tokugawa period, in spite of the tight and rigid control of the military government over the peasantry which historians make much of. (Since our discussion will proceed at a general level at which differences in administration between the Shogunate and daimiate governments are minor, both types of government will be simply referred to as "the government" or "governments" without distinction.)

In what specific ways did the governments of the Tokugawa Shogunate and the daimiate articulate with the village polity?[1] More specifically, what areas of peasant life did these governments attempt to control and why? How was the indigenous political structure of the village organized in relation to the government? Questions such as these are not easy to answer. For most students of Tokugawa political structure have almost exclusively discussed the political institutions of the military government, ignoring the native village

1. It should be noted that for the problem under consideration, the villages of the Tokugawa period are not to be equated with the modern rural communities of Japan, commonly called *buraku.* For the mode of political articulation of the modern Japanese state to the *buraku* is vastly different—due to factors I cannot go into here —from that of the Tokugawa state.

political structure. And those who have analyzed the indigenous village political system have emphasized the autonomous and corporate character of the village, with little regard for the role of imposed government institutions. Consequently, how one is related to the other, how the powerful military government dealt with the supposedly semi-autonomous village has never been made clear.

The burden of this paper is to show that the government to a large measure depended for the implementation of its law on its own system of control which it instituted in the village, but at the same time utilized to a considerable extent the indigenous system of control. The village, on the other hand, relied primarily on its own machinery of control for the execution of regulations which evolved in the local scene, making relatively little use of the government-imposed control system.[2]

The administrative machinery of the Shogunate and daimiate governments consisted, at the village level, of the headman (generally called *shōya* in western Japan and *nanushi* in eastern Japan), the elders (*toshiyori, kumigashira*, etc.), the delegates (*hyakushōdai, yokome*, etc.), and the fiveman groups (*goningumi*). Among these the headman was without question the most important official both in terms of the power delegated and the responsibilities assigned by the government. The government held him responsible for keeping accurate and detailed records of the village census, reporting any changes in the village population (through birth, death, migration, marriage, divorce, etc.), apportioning to individual families rice tax levied on the village, collecting the tax in full and on time, maintaining public works in the village, adjudicating disputes arising within the village, reporting any violation of the law, and finally in general assuming the role of the father figure for the village. In addition, he

was responsible for the conduct of his villagers, i.e., punishable for their crimes.

There were three or four elders in most villages and it was their duty to assist the headman. The delegates were presumably representatives of ordinary peasants and according to Asakawa, they were supposed "to keep an eye on the conduct of the village officials, to give counsel and admonition, and generally guard and promote the best interest of the village."

That these officials were in fact held responsible and that these responsibilities were not merely on paper are clear if one examines such sources as the *Oshioki Reiruishu*, criminal records of the Tokugawa period, which list numerous cases in which the officials were punished either for wrong-doings of their own or of their villagers.

The power which the officials needed to execute their responsibilities was derived from the government and tradition of the village. The government empowered the officials to carry out their assigned duties and gave them the right to arrest and report to the magistrate any criminal offenders. But it is important to note at the same time, as Kodama points out, that the officials' ability to carry out their duties effectively was supported by the fact that they represented families which were respected by villagers because they were old, often being among the founding families of the village.

In compensation for their services, the officials received salaries. The headman's salary was roughly one percent or less of the village rice yield, other officials receiving, if anything at all, somewhat less than the headman. The officials' salaries were usually paid in rice, though sometimes a money payment was substituted. The headman's compensation might also have included free use of a piece of tax-exempt land provided by the government, and tax exemption on a certain portion of his own land plus free use of a specified amount of village labor. A point to be noted in this connection is that in whatever form officials were compensated, their salaries came from their own villages. That is, the village was obliged to provide the salaries of officials

2. As Thomas Smith has ably demonstrated in the *Agrarian Origins of Modern Japan* (Stanford, 1959), a great deal of change did take place during the Tokugawa period. Also, it is well known that there were important differences between the Shogunate and daimiate administration. We shall, nonetheless, attempt to generalize about the structure of control at a level of generality applicable throughout the period, both in the Shogunate and daimiate domains.

who were by and large representatives of the government and who did not perform functions important for the maintenance of the internal system of the village. This was one of the ways in which the village acknowledged the power of the state.

In addition, the headman and often other officials, too, were allowed certain privileges denied ordinary peasants, such as the use of surname and bearing of swords, both of which were generally prerogatives reserved for the military class. These officials were also allowed to live in larger and more sumptuously furnished houses and to wear better clothes than ordinary peasants. These privileges served as visible symbols of their status as government officials and of the authority of the government behind them.

As pointed out above, village officials were chosen from among the old and prestigious families of the village whose history often went back to the founding of the village. In some villages, their positions were hereditary; in others they were either selected through an informal agreement among the high ranking villagers or elected by propertied (and therefore (tax-paying) villagers (hombyakushō). Whatever the method of selection, officials were always of peasant origin, and almost invariably members of the village.

When a new headman was chosen, by whatever method, the choice had to be approved by the district magistrate—an official of the military class (known as gundai, daikan, etc.), who oversaw a large number of villages in an area. This approval was automatic in most cases. The choice of other officials did not require the magistrate's approval in most domains, though the choice had to be reported to him. It is significant that the officials were not outsiders ordinarily, and not warriors. A warrior, because of his superior class identification and because of the prerogatives and power that went with his class vis-a-vis the peasants, would have had a great deal more coercive power to rule than a peasant headman; but he would not have had the confidence of the people that a peasant headman had.

Although the headman was chosen by villagers, power was not delegated to him by villagers. For in the political philosophy of the time, power was reserved by the state and was delegated by the state to administrators.

In addition to the officers of the headman and his assistants, the government instituted the goningumi, or five-man group, system for additional security. Though called five-*man* group (go*ni*ngumi), the basic units of the group were always families rather than individuals. The size of the group, although supposedly five families, varied a great deal, from one or two to more than ten.[3] In most villages only the propertied peasants were the full-fledged members of the group, tenants and their families being usually included in the family of their landlord. All peasants were thus required to belong to one five-man group or another (with the exception of village officials, who were sometimes excluded from membership). The group had its head, generally called kumigashira. Whether his job was simply to act as the liaison man between the headman of the village and the group, or whether he was in fact held responsible for the conduct of members of his group, we do not know.[4]

The political significance of this institution for control of the peasantry is that it was the unit of group responsibility. A crime committed by a member was a crime of all the others, and concealment of a crime committed by a fellow member was also a crime of all the others. On the other hand, an informer who would report a violation of law by a fellow member of his five-man group

3. Such variation was inevitable, in part because of the constant fluctuation in the number of families in any village due to such factors as establishment of branch families, disolution of families through bankruptcy, and migration in and out of the village.
4. Because both the elders and the heads of five-man groups were sometimes called kumigashira in the same village, some writers have regarded these two positions as identical. In some places they were the same, at least in origin; but in some villages there were fewer elders than five-man groups. Also, it is not clear whether some of the heads of the five-man groups also served as elders, or whether the elders were an entirely different group of individuals. For these reasons, when we read in legal documents about kumigashira, we are not certain whether they refer to elders or to heads of five-man groups.

was given a lighter punishment than the others, or sometimes even rewarded.

The membership of the five-man group of a given village was written in a book, generally called *goningumicho,* one copy of which was sent to the district magistrate and another kept in the village. This membership book in most cases contained a preface (*maegaki*), which, varying a great deal in length and contents, listed official edicts and regulations handed down to the village from the Shogunate or daimiate government. The preface usually ended with an oath by all villagers to abide by the preceding regulations.[5] The preface also contained many clauses in which the headman, his assistants, and the five-man groups were explicitly mentioned—perhaps as additional reminders—as being responsible for specific misdemeanors. The government thus attempted to hold responsible not only individuals, but also groups to which they belonged, as well as village officials. Through such double and triple checks, the government attempted to control the peasantry.

By various methods the peasants were reminded of the regulations listed in the five-man group register, such as reading the preface periodically to assembled villagers or using the register as text for penmanship in village schools (*terakoya*). Some historians, such as Hozumi and Hosokawa, tend to interpret the records of the five-man group literally and would have us believe that the group functioned pretty much as was intended. It is, however, a simple truism of methodology that legal prescriptions do not necessarily reflect the reality. Nomura in fact takes an extreme position in this regard, declaring that "organization of the five-man group was almost a mere matter of record keeping, and in practice it scarcely had any meaning."

Though Nomura's scepticism seems too extreme, there are reasons to doubt that the five-man group functioned as effectively as

intended. The remoteness of many villages as well as their inaccessibility from the magistrate's office alone must have made effective surveillance difficult, if not impossible. Also, the strong feeling of solidarity of villagers vis-a-vis the ruling elite must have been an effective deterrent in many cases to what amounted to blackmailing of fellow villagers, in case, for example, a fellow *goningumi* member committed a crime against the state. There seems to have been variation in the effectiveness of this institution from domain to domain, also.

There is no doubt that the five-man group was sometimes useful in controlling the peasants. An examination of the above-mentioned *Oshioki Reiruishu,* for example, shows numerous cases in which members of five-man groups were punished for crimes committed by their fellow members.

These government-imposed institutions— the village officials and the five-man group— are predicated upon three concepts of responsibility. First is individual responsibility for one's own action. Second is the concept that the leader of a group is responsible for the action of the members. It is on the basis of this concept that village officials were punished for crimes committed by their villagers. The third concept is that of group responsibility, upon which the five-man group was organized. The concept of group responsibility was utilized in other contexts, too. For example, those living next door and in the three houses across the street from the house where a crime was committed were held responsible for certain crimes, regardless of whether they belonged to the same five-man group. In another application of the same concept the whole village was held responsible, rather than its individual members or five-man groups.

The government capitalized on the indigenous solidarity of the village in instituting group responsibility. For example, levying a lump sum tax on the village, as was usually done, was a far more effective way of collecting the full amount of tax than levying tax to individual families, some of which in any village were too poor to meet the quota. In

5. Although Sansom states that the document "was signed by the headman," it was more often "signed" by all members of all five-man groups of the village. Cf. Sansom, 1963, 102.

lump-sum taxation, wealthier peasants paid more than their share to help the poorer neighbors. Group responsibility, however had its negative effects, too. The same sense of solidarity—to help and protect one another—impeded the policing function of the group, because villagers were more likely to connive with one another against the government rather than blackmail a fellow villager.

It may be helpful to review briefly the regulations which the government imposed on peasants. To appreciate the types of regulations and their details, we should note several assumptions on which the Shogunate and daimiate governments based their philosophy of ruling the peasantry. First, the state manifestly existed for the benefit of the ruling class, and therefore other classes, including the peasants existed to support the ruling class. Hence the oppressive measures to keep the peasants at the bare subsistence level, taking away very bit of surplus they produced. Second, the peasants were considered by nature stupid, needing detailed regulations for conduct. Third, the society was conceived of in absolutely static terms in which the peasantry had a definite position defined by the ruling elite. Hence the numerous regulations aimed at maintaining and emphasizing the status relation of the peasants to other classes, especially to the ruling class. Fourth, as both Sansom and Asakawa observed, to Tokugawa administrators law and morals were both bound up in the concept of government. Hence the moralistic admonitions intermingled with legal codes and the moralistic tone of legal codes.

It is understandable, given these bases of government, that the Shogunate and daimiate law pertaining to peasants minutely spelled out prescriptions and prohibitions, and that it emphasized fiscal matters, status relations, policing, and morality.

Although Asakawa's claim that almost all administrative features were designed to facilitate the collection of taxes is probably an overstatement, we can understand many government regulations in terms of fiscal concern. It explains not only the quantity and detail of the regulations concerning tax assessment

and payment, but also the extensive body of law aimed at maximizing agricultural yields[6] and minimizing peasants' expenses beyond basic needs.[7] This is not to say that all prescriptions concerning agriculture were designed expressly to facilitate payment of the tax, but that a great many of them served this function.

Maintenance of status quo was another major concern of the government. Regulations prescribing peasants' behavior toward the warrior, particularly the district magistrate, with whom peasants came into periodic contact for official reasons like cadastral survey and payment of tax, served to define the superior position of the ruling class.[8] Sumptuary regulations mentioned above, which denied peasants the external symbols of well-being, served as much to keep peasants in an underprivileged position appropriate to their social status as to extract surplus wealth from them.

The government attempted to keep as tight a control over the peasants as possible, a third area of the ruler's concern. The five-man group was of course instituted for this very purpose. This policy is also manifested in the control of vagabond warriors (*ronin*), in the determined attempt to exterminate Christians,[9] in the minute records the headman was required to keep concerning the

6. For example, fields were never to be left fallow and rice fields never to be turned into dry fields or house lots; emigration of peasants was discouraged or prohibited for fear of decrease of crop yields; and severe restrictions were placed on growing luxury crops like tobacco, if it was not outlawed.
7. For example, ordinary peasants were not allowed to wear silk clothes or *kamishimo*, a formal dress for ceremonial occasions; peasants were to subsist as much as possible on grains other than rice, the premium crop of the state; and as for shelters, the size of house, number of rooms, kinds of furnishings, and materials to be used for construction were all minutely regulated.
8. The most obvious and visible regulation of this category was the universal law prohibiting peasants (except the village officials) from bearing swords and using surnames. In many domains, the warrior enjoyed the right to execute any peasant who did not behave properly toward him.
9. Each village was required to prepare a temple registry, called *shumoncho, shumon aratamecho*, etc., in which the names of the villagers were listed under the name of the temple of which they were parish members. This list, presumably brought up to date each year, was accompanied by an oath to the effect that none of the villagers espoused Christianity.

movement of his villagers, and in the detailed definitions of crimes.

Lastly, government considered itself responsible for moral exhortation. This sense of moral responsibility of the government is evidenced not only in specifically moral precepts—of a Confucian sort in most cases—but also as it pervaded the whole body of law.

The Tokugawa village, however, was not simply an artificial creation for purposes of political control from above. From the point of view of the government, it might indeed have been "an aggregate of peasant holdings and their fiscal values" or a "fictitious entity," as Asakawa and Nakamura, respectively, asserted. But from the point of view of village members, the village was a functioning unit which existed with its own raison d'etre. That the Tokugawa village was a corporation has been well demonstrated in Nakata's classic essay. The village was a corporate body, a legal entity which owned, bought, and sold property; loaned and borrowed money; and sued, was sued by, and entered into agreements with other villages. The fact that the village had such corporate qualities is important. It indicates the degree of commitment by village members toward the village as a unit and the degree of solidarity they expressed. It is this solidarity which enabled villagers to enforce their self-made laws and invoke sanctions against any members who transgressed them.

The solidarity of this corporate body is best expressed in village codes. These codes contain rules and regulations evolved in the village through centuries of collective living; their purpose was to maintain peace in the village by forbidding disruptive acts and requiring collective defense. The important point is that these codes are a pact agreed upon by all villagers and not something forced upon them from above. Village codes, written in the village codes book, are followed by a statement of oath by all members of the village assembly to abide by the codes.

Whereas the book of the five-man group generally included scores of clauses, sometimes more than one hundred, a book of village codes usually included approximately ten clauses and rarely more than twenty. The great length of the former resulted from the fact that government administrators simply piled edict upon edict, and most of them became incorporated into the book of the five-man group regardless of whether they applied to the village. The village codes, on the other hand, tended to contain only essential items of law.

The village codes are not to be equated with a constitution in the Western sense. They do not contain all the norms of the village in codified form, nor do they fully define the administrative machinery of the village. Inspection of individual books of codes thus gives only a fragmentary picture of the customary law of the village. When we examine codes of many villages, however, we see recurrent themes. In the following, on the basis of Maeda's excellent studies of village codes, we analyze the major characteristics of the codes, comparing them with those of government regulations. Such comparison will reveal functional division of the government and village law as well as overlap, the former complementing each other and the latter reinforcing one another.

Village codes covered such topics as taxation, agriculture, policing, adjudication, civil records (e.g., property transaction), sumptuary regulation, and inter-village agreement. This listing might give the impression that these codes simply reiterate regulations promulgated by the state. To a certain extent they do. For example, there are clauses dealing with handling of the tax levied by the government. Sumptuary regulations, too, seem to be almost direct copies of government edicts.

These regulations were included in the village codes because they were relevant to village life in one way or another. (We shall see later omission from village codes of certain government regulations which are irrelevant to village life.) This is obvious for the government tax. Sumptuary laws, too, made sense to peasants, simply as a means of making ends meet in their tight subsistence economy, although not as a means of maintaining and expressing status symbols as the government intended.[10]

In the areas of policing and security, again village codes overlap with government regulations. But in this case, the former are probably not simply copies of the imposed government regulations; instead they must have evolved independently in the village for its own sake. The reason for this duplication of government and village law regarding local security lies in the relative ineffectiveness of the government law in this regard for two reasons. One, already mentioned above, was the difficulty of reaching the magistrate because primitive transportation and communication made some villages inaccessible. Secondly, there was an implicit assumption in the political philosophy of the time that authorities were not to be disturbed for minor matters or with offenses which could not be definitely demonstrated to the authority's satisfaction.[11] These factors made it necessary for the village to take the law into its own hands, so to speak, even though formally such executions might have been illegal in that they were a prerogative of the state. In short, the village usurped the power of the state in handling matters which vitally affected its internal security or otherwise affected the village as a whole, such as public works and communal lands.

In addition to having regulations overlap with those of the government, village codes show different emphases. While the government law aimed to promote the welfare of the ruling elite, the village codes were designed primarily for the welfare of the village. For example, whereas government laws aimed primarily at increasing production, through encouraging reclamation, maximum use of land, etc., village codes aimed to reduce internal conflicts and disputes by regulating those

areas of village life (such as management of communal land, irrigation system, and property boundaries) in which disputes and conflicts were likely to occur. The corporate village is also of prime significance in codes concerned with external affairs. In dealing with higher authorities for such matters as filing of grievances against the district magistrate or in settling disputes with neighboring villagers, villagers were required to present a solid front; anyone who acted contrary to the interest of the village received the severest penalty. The corporateness of the village community is also clearly seen in the sanction system of *mura hachibu* to be discussed below.

Compared with the corporate welfare of the village, individual problems seem to have been relatively unimportant. Matters concerning families or individuals, such as marriage or inheritance, were not generally codified.

Although the government tended indiscriminately to regulate all spheres of life and sometimes even promulgated regulations which were completely irrelevant to a given village, the village codes, having evolved to meet local exigencies, did not include "waste" clauses. A case in point is the government law forbidding Christian worship. After the battle of Shimabara (1637-1638), there were no Christians in most parts of Japan. Yet the five-man group register rarely failed to include a clause about the prohibition of this alien religion. The temple registry, used as a means for controlling Christians, became an anachronism too, although the registry did serve as a convenient census record.

Also almost totally lacking in the village codes are regulations pertaining to relations with members of other classes, particularly warriors, and those having to do with morality. The government was concerned with maintaining a static, stratified society; for this end, the status segregation between classes had to be specified and enforced. Such concern was not shown in the village's indigenous system of law. Also, moralizing was the business of the stateman-philosopher of Confucian persuasion, which Tokugawa adminis-

---

10. It is interesting to note here that there are few sanctions prescribed in village codes against violations of sumptuary laws, indicating that economy and saving were virtues for peasants, but their opposite were not crime in their eyes.

11. In case a matter was brought to the attention of the magistrate and could not be proved to his satisfaction, the plaintiff was often punished for no other reason than having disturbed the authority without just cause.

trators invariably were. Peasants, with little or no education, were not concerned with moralizing.

Thus two bodies of law regulated the life of the peasant. But they did so in somewhat different spheres of life because their ultimate objectives were different. The state's objectives were maximum exploitation of the peasants and maintenance of a static and stratified society through both moral and legal legislation. The village wanted primarily to maintain internal peace and protect the village as a corporate entity. The village, of course, was subject to state regulations insofar as peasants were useful in helping the state achieve its goal. This meant that compliance to state law was most important in fiscal matters and status relations and of secondary importance in policing and morality. But the village codes emphasized policing as well as some other aspects of village life which the state did not stress. The next question is how the village executed its own law.

The major political institution for the enactment and enforcement of village codes was the village assembly. In addition, the elite families of the village and the age-grade organization performed important political roles in the village.

The village assembly was the governing body of the village. Although we are not always told who had the right and duty to attend the assembly, it seems that each family —at least the propertied familiets (*hombyakusho*)—was represented in it. The assembly met from time to time, though not at any regular intervals, for such purposes as drawing up new village codes, selecting village officials (if it had this function), indicting misbehaving officials, deliberating on violations of village codes, and discussing disputes with neighboring villages.

Punishments the assembly decreed varied according to the nature of the crime, but they also varied from village to village for the same crime. Those commonly mentioned in the village codes which Maeda examined are village ostracism, banishment, fine and the demanding of verbal or written apology to

the assembly. The best known to present day scholars of rural Japan is village ostracism, or *mura hachibu,* which is still in use. In *mura hachibu* villagers agree not to associate with the culprit's family except possibly in case of fire or death. In these cases villagers would help only in putting out the fire or in conducting funeral services. But in some villages even these occasions are not excepted. *Mura hachibu* was the punishment for such crimes as disclosing secret agreements made among villagers; supporting someone who had been purged from office; being incorrigibly intractable; or dissenting from a decision made by the village as a whole.

Banishment from the village probably was more severe punishment than *mura hachibu.* Village codes prescribed banishment for such crimes as stealing lumber from the communal land, stealing crops from the field, harboring gamblers, and committing arson. Punishment by property deprivation—monetary fine, property fine, or loss of the right of access to the communal land—was meted out for theft on communal or private land, theft of farm crops, refusal to provide labor for village corvée, violation of irrigation regulations, gambling, etc. Fines of money or rice were by far the most common form of punishment in Maeda's compilation. When the crime was not grave, the culprit was dismissed after having made a verbal or written apology. According to Takeuchi, confinement was used in some villages. For example, a man from whose house fire spread was required to confine himself in a temple for a certain period of time as an expression of apology for inconveniencing other villagers. Takeuchi lists several other modes of sanction, including corporal punishment, verbal abuse, and making the culprit perform menial tasks such as digging graves. Although Takeuchi's cases are by and large taken from the post-Tokugawa era, it is probably safe to assume that most of these modes of sanction were in practice during the Tokugawa period as well.

In addition to the corporate force of the village bearing on individual wrong-doers, one sees the influence of the government-instituted concept of joint responsibility being utilized by the village. The fellow members of a law-breaker's five-man group were usually, though not always, punished along with him for crimes such as gambling and theft. In another form of joint responsibility, the next-door neighbors on both sides and the three families directly across the street were held punishable in some villages for a crime such as gambling, regardless of whether these families belonged to the five-man group of the culprit.

Although village codes are an agreement of the entire village, a close examination reveals that the actual control, at least some of the time, lay with the elite of the village rather than among all members equally. Miyakawa's analysis of documents from a village in Echizen shows that various rules in the village codes are designed to protect the interests of the elite and to control the lower class peasants. Another illustration of the power elite is given by Ando. At Yuasa in Kinki, there was a group of elite families known as *Toshiyori Sujime Sanjurokunin* (the thirty-six elders). In this village if there were any disputes between a member of this group and a less privileged member of the village, the latter was judged wrong.

Elite families generally boasted long historical tradition going back sometimes to the founding of the village. They generally cultivated their own land and also often rented land to tenants in the village. Thus the elite position was defined in terms of historical depth of the family and its economic standing. These families composed the power elite of the village vis-a-vis less privileged families.

It is noteworthy that for the enforcement of village codes, the village headman and other officials did not seem to be empowered to take action, and apparently were not relied upon in internal matters. Rather, the sanction system seems to have operated through coercive power of the village assembly as a corporate body and through other indigenous systems of control.

Elite control of the village is best illustrated in the religious organization known as *miyaza,* or "shrine association." Its membership was limited to old, established families of the village. While *miyaza* was expressly a re-ligious association connected with the village shrine, its members enjoyed many privileges and exercised much power beyond religious functions. For example, it was this organization that chose the village officials; and officials had to be chosen from among its members. In economic spheres, too, members of the *miyaza* had privileges, for example, in possessing exclusive access to the village-owned land.

Miyaza then was a concrete and graphic expression of the power of the elite and served as a reminder for other villagers of the locus of power. I emphasize the fact that *miyaza* as an association functioned as a convenient seat of village power and that in villages where this association was absent, the same pattern of power structure existed.

It is important to note that the headman and other officials were members of the village rather than administrators sent into the village from outside, such as the warrior was, and that they were elite members of the community. The government, in other words, relied on locally influential individuals to enforce its law. From the point of view of the village, selecting as its head and its representative of the government a man who wielded influence in the village, entirely apart from whatever power he acquired as an agent of the government, meant a positive acceptance by the village of the unchallengeable authority of the government. Moreover, the fact that the village officials were normally chosen by the village elite—propertied peasants of the village—meant that the acceptance of the authority of the state could be forced upon the rest of the village through the indigenous political structure.

One last institution to be mentioned in connection with the internal system of control of the village is the age-grade system. Commonly one entered the group sometime in the teens and remained a member until he married or reached some set age in the late twenties or early thirties; membership was compulsory for all those of appropriate ages. Separate groups were organized for the two sexes, the female group being under the strict control of the male group.

The group had an internal hierarchy in which older members enjoyed higher status and much authority over younger members, demanding strict obedience from the younger ones. Just as the village elite, rather than the headman, held power in village politics, actual authority in the age group lay in a group of elder and more respected members, the leader of the youth simply being one among them. This council of elders arbitrated disputes among members, made all important decisions regarding activities of the group, and judged violations of group norms.

The youth group was a powerful control group. There were written and unwritten rules and regulations which everyone was to abide by. These codes concerned gambling, drinking, relations with the opposite sex, etiquette toward the elders, one's work habits, mutual help, and relations with outsiders, particularly women of other villages. The male group possessed exclusive sexual access to the unmarried women of the village. Neither the women themselves nor their parents had the right to deny this right to the group, and no men outside the village were to have access to these women. Conversely, no member of the youth group was allowd to flirt with or marry a woman of another village. Violators of these rules met with some of the severest sanctions. Any commission of severe crimes was publicly punished by the group as a whole, and in extreme cases the culprit was expelled from the group and members were forbidden to associate with him in any way whatsoever. It may be noted that this sanction parallels the *mura hachibu,* discussed above for here one sees the village youth practicing roles they were to play in adulthood. Incorrigible members of the age group were sometimes turned over to the village elders. For less severe cases, lighter punishments were meted out, such as temporary expulsion of the culprit from the group (the duration depending on the seriousness of the offense), temporarily seating him in the junior position, formal inquisition, monetary fine, corporal punishment, and written apologies.

Although the youth group was primarily concerned with internal discipline, they sanctioned outsiders, too—that is, villagers who were not members of the group. On certain nights of the year or month, the youth groups in some regions would gather in front of an offender's home or some other designated place in the village and enumerate all the wrong doings the family was responsible for, and shout abuse at the top of their voices.

It may be instructive to consider the basic reasons why the military government could not rely on the indigenous political system of the village and instead had to create its own legal and administrative structure which it imposed upon the village. The reasons lie in the differences in the goals of the two polities. Village goals were to maintain internal peace and to defend itself against external threat. The goals of the military government, on the other hand, consisted of economic exploitation of the peasants and maintenance of a static society in which the peasantry was given a well defined place. To the village, the welfare of the larger society, of which it was a part, was irrelevant; to the village, too, the exploitative state, represented external threat as much as, or even more than, say a neighboring village trying to steal water.[12] It is no wonder, seen in this light, that the indigenous village polity, whose goals did not coincide with those of the state, and whose instruments (political structure and codes (were either indifferent or hostile to the goals of the state, was not particularly useful for the implementation of state goals. For this reason the state had to create separate legal and administrative machinery within the village to achieve its goals.

But the government could not hope to rule the peasantry with coercion alone. It becomes all the more necessary for the state to articulate its political structure with the village structure. The government was success-

12. A threatening neighboring village could be dealt with either through appealing to higher authorities for arbitration or through armed conflict, illegal though the latter method might be. These means promised at least some chance of favorable resolution of the conflict. But the state offered no such chance; its law, its demands were absolute as well as unilateral.

ful in controlling the peasants because state-instituted machinery was in fact articulated with village institutions.

We have examined various modes of such articulation throughout this paper. Such artic-ulation is evident in the recruitment of the village officials, in that they had prestige in the village before they assumed government-appointed offices and that they administered at least in part through this "traditional au-thority." Another mode of articulation is seen in the fact that the village officials were able to perform their duties as government adminis-trators in part because they were chosen by the elite of the village and thereby given the stamp of village approval and promise of support.

On the other hand, this act of choice and approval meant that the village polity ac-knowledged the legitimacy of the military government's authority. This acknowledgment is symbolized in the village's payment of the tax and also of the salaries of these govern-ment officials.

Another mode of articulation is seen in the government's holding the whole village and the five-man group responsible. The concept of group responsibility made a good deal of sense to villagers of Tokugawa Japan. Since the village felt strong solidarity to begin with, and since such practices as mutual coopera-tion and labor exchange had been indigenous patterns of social organization, the govern-ment, by levying tax on the village as a whole and holding the five-man group responsible for any member's crime, was capitalizing on an accepted concept.

There was one area in which the state and the village saw eye to eye, so to speak; this was in the matter of maintenance of internal peace. Because both polities were concerned with peace and security of the village—for different reasons, of course—it appears on the surface that the village cooperated with the state in maintaining peace and punishing any criminal who disturbed the peace of the vil-lage. But because the village enforced the law, it usurped the state's prerogative to punish criminals.

The village polity, therefore was obliged to make a major concession in allowing the state to intrude. This meant that in matters of taxation, status relations and policing—areas most sensitive to the state—the village was forced to obey the law of the state. In turn, the state permitted the village to deal with internal matters as it pleased. The latter did adopt some of the institutions of the state, for example, in the concept of joint respon-sibility and made some use of the village offi-cials for sanctioning purposes. But the indig-enous political system by and large remained unaffected.

29. THE KINGDOM OF THE ZULU OF SOUTH AFRICA

MAX GLUCKMAN

Reprinted from African Political Systems *(London and New York: Oxford University Press, 1940). Max Gluckman was, for many years, head of the Department of Social Anthropology and Sociology at the University of Manchester in England. He is well known for his many books and articles on the peoples of South and Central Africa in which he established the highest standards for the anthropological study of law and other aspects of social organization. Among his many books are* The Judicial Process among the Barotse of Northern Rhodesia, Custom and Conflict in Africa, Order and Rebellion in Tribal Africa, The Ideas of Barotse Jurisprudence, *and* Politics, Law and Ritual in Tribal Society. *He is co-author of* Essays on the Ritual of Social Relations *and* Closed Systems and Open Minds: The Limits of Naivety in Social Anthropology.

■ The transformations in social relations that are precipitated by political centralization do not occur overnight or automatically. One of the aims of those who speak in the name of the state is to undermine the autonomy and cohesiveness of local groups—especially those based on kinship—and secure the transfer of the individual's allegiance from those local groups to the nation as a whole. In this selection we read about an early nation that was quite successful in this regard.

Prior to their unification into a single national entity, localized and solidary patrilineal clans provided the connective tissue for ongoing social relations among the Zulu. But those in control of the Zulu state were not able to destroy these groups immediately, probably for two reasons. First, the Zulu were pastoralists, practicing some hoe cultivation as well at the time they were welded into a nation, and as we have seen, solidary kin relations are especially well-suited to this technology. Second, rulers of new nations are themselves the products of the lineage or other local organizations they seek to subvert. This is the world they know; in most cases, they have no other models to substitute for traditional patterns. Furthermore, they seem to realize that too rapid a destruction of the previous way of life may lead to massive resistance and rebellion.

Gluckman's account of the early Zulu state is based on historical accounts and interviews with old men. He outlines the role of warfare in the origin of the Zulu state and its subsequent history. While the Zulu clans were not destroyed, they were widely dispersed; nevertheless, they remained the focus of powerful sentiment. Although the king owned the land, its allocation was in the hands of local chiefs who periodically mobilized labor for special projects. Similarly, although the king constituted the supreme court and was expected to maintain customary laws, the administration of the law was in the hands of the chiefs. An important aspect of the polarization of Zulu social organization is to be seen in the fact that while the chiefs had no control over the national regiments—this power was exclusively in the hands of the king—every man was considered to be attached to a local chief. In other words, during the period described by Gluckman, it seems that the central state had not succeeded in wholly gaining the obedience of the populace. But this may be an overstatement; it may be more correct to say that rulers as individuals had failed to secure this allegiance. As in many such kingdoms during their early stages, assassinations were frequent, due in large measure to kings' policies of terrorization; none of these *coups,* however, involved an attempt to change the political structure itself; they were not revolutions.

The Zulu state during its early stages also exemplifies another important feature of agricultural nations, especially (but far from exclusively) those based on rudimentary agriculture. Among the means by which the people were involved in the workings of the state were elaborate political rituals and ceremonies. (While the functions of these rituals are readily apparent, an intriguing [and unsolved] problem is why ceremonials, which are nearly universal features of political organization, are adopted

439

in the first place.) Similarly, the Zulu kings established early control over symbol systems (including magic) that had been integrating features of local groups in the maintenance of order and conformity.

The role of the economy in setting limits for lifestyles is illustrated by the fact that all Zulu had the same education—there were, indeed, no schools in our sense of the term—and all villagers (including chiefs) lived in much the same way. Within this type of economy, it was difficult to produce the wealth and material goods on which could be based different and stratified life styles. Even the wealthy men who controlled the cattle had to live like the rest of the populace, because there was little—other than local-level political power—into which these cattle could be converted or for which they could be exchanged.

The principal sources on which Gluckman relied—in addition to his personal knowledge of the contemporary people of the area—are *Olden Times in Zululand* and *Natal,* by A. T. Bryant (New York: Longmans, 1938) and *The Story of the Zulus,* by J. Y. Gibson (New York: Longmans, 1911). The reader who wishes to learn more about nation-states at this stage of technological development can compare the Zulu with two neighboring nations: *The Swazi: A South African Kingdom,* by Hilda Kuper (New York: Holt, Rinehard and Winston [Case Studies in Cultural Anthropology], 1963) and *The Basuto,* by Hugh Ashton (London and New York: Oxford University Press, 1952). ∎

I. HISTORICAL INTRODUCTION

I DESCRIBE ZULU political organization at two periods of Zulu history—under King Mpande and today under European rule. Zulu history has been well described by Bryant and Gibson, and I here give only a bare outline which can be filled in by referring to their books. I have used historical records partly to illustrate the functioning of the organization in each period and partly to discuss changes in the nature of the organization.

The Nguni family of Bantu-speaking people who later formed the Zulu nation migrated into south-eastern Africa about the middle of the fifteenth century. They were pastoralists practising a shifting cultivation. They

lived in scattered homesteads occupied by male agnates and their families; a number of these homesteads were united under a chief, the heir of their senior line, into a tribe. Exogamous patrilineal clans (men and women of common descent bearing a common name) tended to be local units and the cores of tribes. A tribe was divided into sections under brothers of the chief and as a result of a quarrel a section might migrate and establish itself as an independent clan and tribe. There was also absorption of strangers into a tribe. Cattle raids were frequent, but there were no wars of conquest. By 1775 the motives for war changed, possibly owing to pressure of population. Certain tribes conquered their neighbors and small kingdoms emerged which came into conflict. In this struggle Shaka, head of the Zulu tribe, was victorious; by his personal character and military strategy, he made himself, in ten years, master of what is now Zululand and Natal,[1] and his troops were campaigning far beyond his boundaries. He organized a nation out of all the tribes he had subjected. His chief interest was in the army and he made whole-time warriors of his men; he developed the idea of regiments formed of men of the same age, and quartered them, for most of the year, in large barracks built in different parts of his country. They trained there for war, herded the king's cattle and worked his fields. The men were forbidden to marry till the king gave them permission, as a regiment, to marry into a certain age-regiment of girls. Shaka's rule was tyrannous and he fought a war every year; therefore, when in 1828 he was assassinated by his brother, Dingane, the people gladly accepted Dingane as king.

During Shaka's life English traders settled at Port Natal on friendly terms with the Zulu. Later the Boers entered Natal, defeated the Zulu in 1838, and confined them north of the Tugela River. Dingane's rule was also tyrannous and his people began to turn from him to his brother, Mpande. Dingane plotted

1. An area of some 80,000 square miles, occupied, according to Bryant's estimate by about 100,000 people. I think this figure is too low. It may be noted that tribes fleeing from Shaka established the Matabele, Shangana, and Nguni nations.

to kill Mpande, who fled with his followers to the Boers in Natal; from there he attacked and routed Dingane and became king. The Zulu now entered on a period of comparative peace, for Mpande only occasionally raided the Swazi and Tembe (Thonga); to south and west were European states and the strongly entrenched Basuto. However, during his reign two of his sons fought for his heirship; Cetshwayo was victorious and he became king when Mpande died in 1872.

In 1880 the British defeated the Zulu, deposed Cetshwayo and divided the nation into thirteen kingdoms. Three years later they tried to reinstate Cetshwayo; for various rea- sons civil war broke out between the Usuthu (the Royal) section of the nation and tribes ruled, under the King, by the Mandlakazi Zulu house, which was united to the royal house in Mpande's grandfather. The king died but his son, Dinuzulu, with Boer help defeated the rebels who fled to the British. In 1887 the British established a magistracy in Zululand and restored the Mandlakazi to their homes. Dinuzulu resisted, was defeated and exiled. The Zulu were divided into many tribes and white rule was firmly established. Dinuzulu was later appointed chief over a small tribe (the Usuthu), but was again exiled after the Bambada Rebellion in 1906. He died

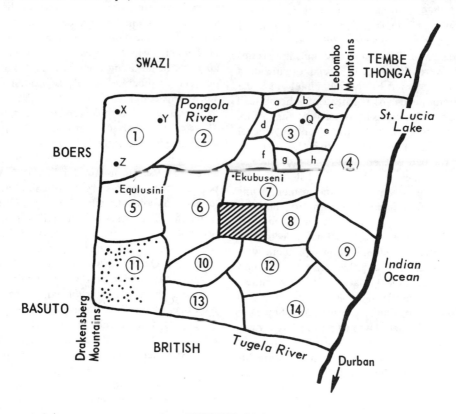

FIGURE 29.1

This is a sketch of the territorial organization of the Zulu nation under King Mpande. It is presented only as a plan, and not as a map.

The shaded area is the King's containing his capital, other royal homesteads, and military barracks (which are also royal homesteads). Numerals show tribal areas: there were many more than fourteen.

In tribe 3, of which Q is the capital, small letters show wards under indunas.

In tribe 1, X, Y, and Z are the homesteads of the chief and two of his important brothers: the men of the tribe are attached to these homesteads to constitute the military divisions of the tribe.

In tribe 11, the dots represent homesteads spread over the country. Equlusini and Ekubuseni are royal homesteads which were heads of national army divisions, though they lay outside the King's area.

in exile and his heir was appointed Usuthu chief; on his death he was succeeded by his full-brother as regent. The government has passed from Britain to Natal and in 1910 to the Union of South Africa.

II. THE ZULU KING AND THE STATE

Certain kinship groupings persisted through the devastating wars and the great change in political organization of Shaka's and Dingane's reigns. The clans had disappeared as units, and members of a single clan might by widely dispersed over Zululand: they retained their clan-name and their respect for the head of their senior line.[2] Pockets of clansmen were, however, still to be found in various parts. The important kinship groups which were the basis of social organization were still formed by the inhabitants of separate homesteads. At the head of a homestead was the senior male by descent of the group. Nearby there might be found homesteads of men of the same clan and they all acknowledged the heir of their senior line (the lineage-head) as their head. Some distance away there would perhaps be clan-kinsmen, living under a different political authority, but recognized as part of the group and therefore entitled to take part in affairs affecting it. Among these local agnatic groups there were often homesteads of other relatives by marriage or matrilineal relationship: then came a stretch of country occupied by members of another group, similarly constituted. Strangers might attach themselves to an important man, as his servants or dependants, and would be absorbed with their relatives into his kinship group as "quasikinsmen"; they retained their clan-name, but could not marry into their superior's own lineage, though they could marry into his clan. The second important change in Zulu family life was caused by the

2. Men and women with the same clan-name could not marry one another. No new clans have been formed in the period since the clans ceased to be local, political units, as in the past a chief desiring to marry a woman of his clan would split off her lineage and make of it a separate clan. Dinuzulu attempted unsuccessfully to form a new clan of a Mandlakazi lineage into which he married.

younger men having to serve at the king's military barracks, which kept them from home most of the year. In the homesteads the older men and the boys herded the cattle and the women worked the fields. Each homestead had its own fields and cattlefold. A demographic survey would show the homesteads scattered at some distance apart (a few hundred yards to a mile or two) along the hills which, intersected by deep bush-filled valleys, characterized the interior of Zululand. The fields were mostly along the ridges and the banks of streams; the low valleys, uninhabited because of fever, were winter-grazing and hunting grounds. The coastal tribes lived, similarly distributed, on the malarial sandy plain between the hills and the sea. Communication between different parts of Zululand was fairly easy; men went from all parts to the King's barracks and marriage between members of widely separated homesteads was common.

The Zulu nation thus consisted of members of some hundreds of clans, united by their allegiance to the king. The people belonged to the king and he therefore took the fine in cases of assault or murder. In the earlier period of Nguni history, political allegiance tended to coincide with kinship affiliation. Thus the Zulu tribe (*abakwazulu*) consisted originally largely of descendants of Zulu, a junior son of Malandela, as distinguished from the Qwabe tribe, the descendants of Qwabe, the senior son of Malandela. Today the term *abakwazulu* still means the members of the Zulu clan, but it has also the wider meaning of all the people who pay allegiance to the Zulu king. Collectively, whatever their clan names, they are politely addressed as "Zulu." Political and kinship affiliation came to be distinct also in the smaller political groups into which the nation was divided. These were composed of members of many clans, though they might have a core of kinsmen: members of a single clan might be found in many political groups. While the kinship basis of political groups disappeared, the new ones which emerged were described in kinship terms, for any political officer was spoken of as the father of his people, and his relationship to them was conceived to be similar to that of a father and his children. The territory of king or chief may be referred to as *umzi ka-Mpande* (the homestead of Mpande) or *umzi kaZibebu* (the homestead of Zibebu), as *umzi kabani* is the family homestead of So-and-So. The children of the king are not supposed to refer to him as "father," for, "is not the king father of his people, not of his family only."

The king also owned the land. All who came to live in Zululand had to acknowledge his sovereignty. *Abakwazulu* has two the meaning of the people of Zululand (*Kwazulu*) and the Zulu word *izwe* means nation, tribe, or country. The same rule applied to the smaller political groupings and to find out who a man's chief is, one asks either "Who is your chief?" or "Of whose district are you?" The relation of the political unit to land may be defined: any one coming on to land belonging to a political authority became subject to that authority, and all his subjects were entitled to land in his area.

The Zulu nation may therefore be defined as a group of people owing allegiance to a common head (the king) and occupying a defined territory. They combined under the king to attack or defend themselves against outside groups. In addition to controlling relations with other Bantu-speaking peoples and the Europeans, the king exercised judicial, administrative, and legislative authority over his people, with power to enforce his decisions. He performed religious ceremonies and magical acts on behalf of the nation. All the tribes which made up the nation spoke dialects of the same language and had a common culture.

The kings Mpande and Cetshwayo had no subjects directly under their control. They lived in a tract of land occupied only by royal homesteads and military barracks: [3]outside of this tract Zululand was divided into a large number of political groups. The inhabitants of the largest divisions of the nation

I call "tribes," and their heads I call "chiefs." The tribes were divided into smaller groups (wards) under relatives of the chief or men of other clans (*indunas*), responsible to the chiefs.

The king was approached with ceremonious salutations and titles of respect which, say the Zulu, increased his prestige. He was addressed as the nation. What tradition and history was common to all the Zulu had to be told in the names of the Zulu kings and it was largely their common sentiment about the king and his predecessors which united all Zulu as members of the nation. At the great first-fruits ceremonies and in war-rites, the king was strengthened and cleansed in the name of the nation. He possessed certain objects, inherited from his ancestors, and the welfare of the country was held to depend on them. This ceremonial position of the king was backed by his ancestral spirits. They were supposed to care for the whole of Zululand, and in the interests of the nation the king had to appeal to them in drought, war, and at the planting and first-fruits seasons. They were praised against the ancestors of other kings. The king was in charge of, and responsible for, all national magic. Shaka expelled all rainmakers from his kingdom, saying only he could control the heavens. The king possessed important therapeutic medicines with which he would treat all his ailing important people. All skilled leeches had to teach the king their cures. Finally, when people died and a person was accused of killing them by sorcery, no sentence was supposed to be executed unless the king's witch-doctors confirmed the verdict. These religious and magical duties of the king, in performing which he was assisted by special, hereditary magicians, were vested in the office of kingship; though a king might be killed, his successor took over these duties, and the spirits of tyrants were even supposed to become a source of good to the people who had slain them.

The ritual of these national ceremonies was similar to that of tribal ceremonies of pre-Shaka times, but Shaka militarized them and the men paraded for them in regiments. The

3. All military barracks were royal homesteads. They were built on the plan of ordinary homesteads but were very large, housing some thousands of men.

ceremonies were chiefly designed to strengthen the Zulu at the expense of other people, who were symbolically attacked in them. It was this military orientation of Zulu culture under the king which largely unified his people. A man was called *isihlangu senkosi* (war-shield of the king). The dominant values of Zulu life were those of the warrior, and they were satisfied in service at the king's barracks and in his wars. Today old men talking of the kings get excited and joyful, chanting the king's songs and dances, and all Zulu tend, in conversation, to slip into tales of the king's wars and affairs at his court.

The regiments belonged to the king alone. They lived in barracks concentrated about the capital; the chiefs had no control over the regiments and assembled their own people in territorial, not age, divisions. This organization probably persisted from the period before Shaka began to form "age regiments." In those times the chief of a tribe seems to have assembled his army in divisions which he constituted by attaching the men of certain areas to certain of his important homesteads. The tribes within the Zulu nation were (and today still are) organized for fighting and hunting on this basis. The king alone could summon the age regiments. The nation also was divided for military purposes in the same way as a tribe was divided. For the king attached certain groups of tribes to certain of his royal homesteads. I call each of these divisions and the royal homestead (*ikhanda*, head) to which it was attached a "head." Most of the homesteads which were "heads" were in the king's area; one or two lay outside it. Some were also barracks in which were quartered particular regiments. The division into "heads" was not purely territorial, for once a man was attached to a "head" he could not change his attachment even if he moved into a tribal area attached to a different "head." His sons inherited his attachment; when they were ready to be enrolled as soldiers, they went to the "head" to which their father belonged, and later from all the "heads" the king assembled all the young men and formed them into a new

regiment with its own barracks. Therefore each "head" contained members of all regiments and each regiment contained members of all the "heads." In a barracks or on parade, the "heads" within a regiment had set places according to the seniority of establishment of their respective royal homesteads. The members of a "head" supported the prince of their royal homestead; King Cetshwayo, therefore, when he succeeded to the throne, strengthened his own head by attaching to it more tribes. Each regiment had commanders who were usually princes, chiefs, or the brothers of important chiefs, but were sometimes brave commoners.

This centralization of the regiments in the king's area gave him a position in Zulu life entirely different from that of any of his chiefs. It continually brought the men close to his capital, where they lived on the bounty of his cattle and grain, supplemented by food sent from their homes. But though it brought the regiments under the king's control, it robbed him of personal followers, since all the men were attached to some chief. It may be noted that this centralization seems to have been effected when the Zulu were fighting few wars but maintaining a large standing army; Zulu prestige was so great that there was little likelihood of other Bantu raiding them, even though the Zulu troops were stationed far from the borders.[4]

The king was also the supreme court of the nation and appeals from the chiefs' courts went to him. He was called on to decide difficult cases. There were always in residence at his capital some *indunas* of cases (*izinduna zamacala*) who heard these cases and gave verdicts in the king's name. Most of these *indunas* were chiefs ruling areas of their own; others were sons, brothers, and uncles of the king, and there were commoners "lifted up" by the king for their wisdom and knowledge of law. In all the councils of men throughout

4. This organization may be contrasted with a lack of similar organization among the Tswana and Sotho and is perhaps a reflection of the scattered establishment of the Zulu. In the large Tswana towns the men could easily be summoned to the chief's home. But chiefs of tribes such as the Swazi and Thonga seem to have kept only one or two regiments near them: the concentration of the whole Zulu army about the king is unique in southern Africa.

the land, the *indunas* were supposed to mark men skilful in debate and law and their ability might get them into the king's council. Two of his *indunas* were more important than the others: the one was more specifically commander of the army and was a chief or prince; the other was called the "great *induna*" (prime minister) and had weightiest voice in discussing affairs of state. He was always an important chief, never a member of the royal family.

The king was supposed to maintain the customary law. Zulu have illustrated this to me by quoting a case in which Mpande had to decide against one of his favourites and then sent men to wipe out the successful litigant's family so as to make it impossible for the decision to be carried out. But he could not decide, against the law, for his favourite. Nevertheless, the king could in deciding a case create new law for what he and his council considered good reason.

The king was supposed to follow the advice of his council. If he did not, it is said that the council could take one of his cattle. The Zulu believed that the welfare of the country depended on the king's having wise and strong councillors ready to criticize the king. In council the king (or a chief) was supposed to put the matter under discussion before the council and himself speak last so that no one would be afraid to express his own opinion. The king might inform his close councillors of his views and they could put these to the council; he should not put himself in a position where he would be contradicted. But no councillor should express a strong opinion; he should introduce his points with some oblique phrase deferring to the king. The king ended the discussion and, if he were wise, adopted the views of the majority. The council could also initiate discussions on matters of tribal or national interest. It seems that in fact the king did consider his councillors' views and did not act autocratically. Sometimes he would excuse an action by saying that it had been done by his *indunas* without his authority, and this does seem to have happened; and in dealing with Europeans on occasion the kings said they were

willing to do something, and then backed out on the plea that their *indunas* had decided against it. The king's power and the councillors' insistence on their rights and jealousy of one another might all affect the course of discussion and the decision on any matter or case.

From his subjects' point of view, one may say that the main duty they owed the king was military service, including labour service. The king was also entitled to certain royal game, though he had to reward the hunters. In addition, it was customary to give him gifts of grain, beer, cattle and, some say, girls. As he also received most of the cattle and women captured in war and fines for certain offences, he was easily the richest man in the nation.[5] In return for this, he was expected to feed and help his people generously. He had to care for his regiments and give them their shields; in famine he was expected to help all his people and also at all times those in difficulties. Thus if the king ruled according to tradition, he was generous to his subjects, using his wealth for them; he gave them justice; he protected their interests; and through him they hoped to satisfy their ambitions on battlefield and in forum.

III. STATUS AND POLITICAL POWER

All the members of Shaka's family enjoyed a higher status as a result of his victories. Neither he nor Dingane had any children and it was the descendants of Mpande who came to form the royal family, though certain important collateral lines were regarded as princes. Any child of these lines, and the children of their daughters and adopted women, were referred to as *abantwana* (= children, but is equivalent to princes and princesses). They formed the superior rank in Zulu society, in status above even the chiefs; some of them also ruled as chiefs of tribes. Princes of the Zulu lines, and chiefs of other clan lines who were princes by royal women,

5. Shaka made all trade with Europeans pass through his hands; and later only important people were allowed to buy certain goods from traders.

were among the most powerful chiefs in the land. But the closer a royal prince was (and is) by birth to the reigning king the higher his social status, though he might exert less influence in the nation than other princes or even commoners. To a lesser extent the same rules applied to the reigning families within the tribes; the close relatives of a chief were the aristocracy in his tribe.

Any member of the Zulu royal family had to be greeted ceremonially by commoners, including chiefs. Any royal prince might also be greeted by some of the praise names of the king, such as "source of the country," if the king were not there, though the royal salute, *Bayede,* and the names *inkosi* (king), *ingonyama* (lion), should be strictly reserved for the king himself. This status of the princes brought some of them political power. Shaka's brothers became chiefs in the areas in which they settled. Mpande followed the practice of big, polygynous chiefs and settled his sons in various areas as chiefs there. The king was therefore head by descent of the powerful aristocratic Zulu lineage which was looked up to by all Zulu, and his position in the national organization was strengthened, since tribes scattered through Zululand were ruled by his close relatives, who were bound to him by strong kinship ties of mutual assistance and by their common membership of the royal lineage. Marriage between the royal family and families of chiefs established similar ties. The king would marry off a sister, a daughter, or even some girl belonging to him, to a chief, and her son (who ranked as a prince in the nation) should be heir. However, the princes might draw to themselves followers beyond those given them by the king, and as in the past brothers of tribal chiefs had broken away to establish independent tribes, so the princes within the nation were a potential threat to the king, especially if he misruled. They were ready to intrigue against him and take advantage of the people's dislike of him. Zulu custom says the king should not eat with his brothers, lest they poison him. His relatives on his mother's side and by marriage were said to be his strongest supporters, for their importance in national life came from their relationship to him, rather than their relationship to the royal lineage.

Zulu therefore state, on the one hand, that the king rules with the support of his brothers and uncles, and, on the other hand, that the king hates his brothers and uncles, who may aspire to the throne. In practice, it appears that more often the princes and chiefs competed for importance at court, i.e. they intrigued against one another, rather than against the king. While Mpande lived his sons also struggled for power. The most important of these struggles was for Mpande's heirship. The rule of succession is that the heir is born of the woman whom the king makes his chief wife. Mpande first appointed Cetshwayo heir, for Cetshwayo was born of a wife given him by Dingane. Then he began to favor Mbuyazi, son of his most beloved wife. Each son had his own following. Cetshwayo was supported by his most important brothers and the big chiefs, and he routed Mbuyazi: from that time he began to rule. Zulu succession has been very chequered: the first two kings were ousted by a brother, and Cetshwayo fought for the kingdom. When the British deposed him, his chief wife had had no children, so he appointed Dinuzulu, then about seventeen, heir. A son was born to the chief wife after Cetshwayo's death and was made a chief by the British; Dinzulu objected, as he feared his brother would come to be a rival.

Royal rank therefore tended to carry political power either in the form of a personal following or else of great weight in tribal and national councils. Otherwise high rank in the nation, with respect, was accorded to all political officers, whether they were chiefs or councillors of the king, and to his important servants and brave warriors.

One other principle also gave high rank—namely, kinship seniority within any kinship group. As stated above, Zulu, the founder of the Zulu clan, was the junior brother of Qwabe, the founder of the Qwabe clan. Today the Qwabe chief is one of the few chiefs who will not recognize the superiority of the Zulu king: he claims that he himself is superior by birth. People to whom I have put his claim consider that it is invalid: Shaka founded the Zulu nation and therefore his heirs are entitled to rule it. Nevertheless, they say, the king should "respect" the kinship seniority of the Qwabe chief. This principle worked through all the clans. Independently of political power or bundaries, the people continued to pay respect to the lineal head of their clan. They might take inheritance cases to him and assist him with the bridewealth for his chief wife, even if they lived under a chief of another clan line.

IV. THE TRIBES WITHIN THE NATION

Zululand was divided into a large number of tribes of varying sizes. In Zulu theory the chiefs (or their ancestors) of all these tribes were "raised up" by one or other of the kings. By this the Zulu mean that they held power subject to the king and that ultimately, at the time when the Zulu nation was being created and consolidated, Shaka or his succeeding brothers made their ancestors into chiefs, or allowed them to continue their rule in a particular area. The kings either recognized existing chiefs or sent some man with a following to colonize an uninhabited area. One of the important ways in which a man obtained political status was by royal birth, as described in the preceding section. Other men were the heads of the remnants of tribes which had been independent before Shaka's conquest and there were clanheads to whom, in the years after the initial wars had scattered their people, their followers returned. The kings on occasion also rewarded personal bodyservants, brave warriors, and learned councillors by putting them in charge of districts. But usually the chiefs were princes or the heads of clans. The lineal heads of certain clans had no political power; other clans were represented by chiefs in various parts of Zululand. It was even expedient for the kings to recognize clan-heads as chiefs since kinship affiliation was still a principle uniting people and cognizance had to be taken of the groups thus formed.

From the earliest times political officers had been succeeded by their sons and under the kings this rule continued to be recognized. Zulu still say that an *induna* or chief had his position because he was given it by the king; but if he died his heir, unless hopelessly incompetent, should succeed him. And, failing the heir, the king (or chief) should appoint a close relative to act as regent and the position return to the main line if possible. Zulu say the heir has a right to be appointed, but it depends on the king's will; yet it is recognized that if the heir is passed over he and his followers may cause trouble. For example, I heard an important chief discussing with two of his brothers the appointment of a successor to a recently deceased *induna* of the X——— clan. The brothers were against a descendant being appointed, as they held that the dead man had intrigued with the local magistrate to be recognized as independent. The chief replied that there was no proof that his sons would act in that way because he had; in any case, the area was thickly populated by the X——— people and he asked his brother how they would like it if a stranger were put in control of their own area? He concluded: "If we do that, we shall have trouble with the X——— people." (I need scarcely note that the magistrate was not party to this intrigue.) Nevertheless, in a small *induna*'s area the king (or chief) had power to appoint a parvenu: the king would hesitate to interfere directly in the succession to a large tribal chieftainship, or a chief with a powerful *induna*, for a number of the people might remain loyal to the man whom they considered the rightful heir. There were occasions, however, on which the king favored one or other claimant to a chieftainship to suit his own ends. If the homestead of an important son of the king or a chief (especially a Zulu clan chief) was built in a commoner *induna*'s area the prince became political head there and the *induna* became his *induna*. However when Mpande wanted to settle one of his sons as a chief, he asked a chief for land for him.

The chiefs had certain powers delegated to them by the king. Their most important duties were judicial and administrative. They tried cases coming to them on appeal from their *indunas'* courts and investigated breaches of the law. Though in theory all fines for bodily hurts went to the king, in fact the chiefs seem to have kept these; however, they periodically sent large herds of cattle as gifts to the king. They were supposed to forward difficult cases and cases involving important estates to the king. In their decisions they were bound to follow laws issued by the king and from them appeal lay to his court. They had power to execute judgment, but no power of life and death. In practice, some powerful chiefs were fairly independent and are said to have executed sorcerers and adulterers. As judicial heads in their districts, they had to report to the king all grave misdemeanors and they had to watch over the public weal. An example of how the king delegated administrative duties to his chiefs is Cetshwayo's appointing a coastal chief to facilitate the passage of laborers from Thongaland to Natal through Zululand, which he had agreed to do for the Natal Government. As the chiefs were often in attendance on the king, they could not perform these duties themselves, but delegated them to trusted relatives and *indunas*.

The king communicated with his chiefs by runners. To impersonate a king's messenger was punishable by death. Thus orders to mobilize at the capital, projected laws and matters of national import were announced to the people by the king through his chiefs, though many announcements were made at the first-fruits ceremony. When necessary, the chiefs passed on these orders to their *indunas* in charge of wards and these reported to the heads of lineage groups and homesteads. All the people were entitled to express their opinion on affairs and they did this through the heads of their kinship groups and then their immediate political officers. In addition, the chiefs and *indunas* had administrative duties within their own districts, including the allocation of land, the maintenance of order, trying of cases, watching over their districts' welfare, taking ritual steps to protect the crops, looking for sorcerers. Chiefs, like the king, received gifts of corn and cattle, but they levied no regular tribute. They could call out

their subjects to work their fields, build their homesteads, arrest malefactors, or hunt. In turn, they were expected to reward these workers with food and to help their people who were in trouble. Like the king, too, they were bound to consult and listen to a council composed of their important men.

Thus authority from the king was exercised through the chiefs, his representatives in various districts. They ruled through their brothers and *indunas* of smaller districts, under whom were the lineage- and homestead-heads. Zulu political organization may therefore be seen as delegated authority over smaller and smaller groups with lessening executive power. From inferior officers there was an appeal to higher ones; in theory the king's will was almost absolute. At the bottom were the heads of kinship groups who could issue orders and arbitrate in disputes within their groups, but who could not enforce their decisions, except over women and minors. On the other hand, as the groups became smaller the ties of community and kinship grew stronger, and as force lessened as a sanction other social sanctions increased in importance. The dependence of men on their senior relatives in religious and economic matters, as well as in trouble, was strong; even at the barracks they shared huts with their kinsmen and relied on them for food and support in quarrels. In kinship groupings the main integrating activities and social sanctions were based on reciprocity and communal living. Some kinship rules were backed by judicial sanctions, but when these obligations were enforced at law, force was used on the chief's judgment, not on the obligation itself.

I have described the tribes and smaller groups as part of a pyramidal organization with the king at the top in order to bring out the administrative framework which ran through the social groupings, but the position of the head of each group in the series was different, for he was related to the members of his group by different ties from those linking them to the head of the larger group of which it was part. Besides the ties of sentiment, homestead and lineage, heads exercised authority because of their kinship status and their importance in their inferiors' social and economic life; *indunas* and their followers shared in common social, and often economic, activities, as well as political affairs; tribesmen were attached to their chiefs mainly by political bonds; and all Zulu to the king by their military duties. The average Zulu's importance decreased the bigger the group of which he was a member. The king's position in the state was essentially his establishment in the "barrack area." He symbolized for the Zulu their identity as a nation as against the Swazi and other Bantu, and European, Powers. The nation was a federation of tribes whose separate identities were symbolized by their chiefs. The tribes were even autonomous within the national organization for on occasion many tribesmen supported their chiefs in quarrels with the king, though some were swayed by national loyalties.[6] However, it was in the relations between tribes that tribal tribal identities mainly appeared. There existed between the tribes a strong hostility which radically affected the course of Zulu history after the Zulu war of 1880; it was mirrored at court in the competition of the chiefs for power. For the people of any tribe of some strength were proud of their traditions and their chiefly line, were loyal to their chief and quick to resent any attempt by other chiefs to interfere in their tribal affairs. Occasionally, especially on the borders of tribes, this hostility broke out in affrays. It appeared most clearly in the people's attachment to their own chief as against other chiefs. Therefore, as will be seen in the next section, the chiefs tried by ruling well to win adherents from other chiefs. Nevertheless, the chiefs were often related to one another and on friendly terms. As part of the administrative machinery they served together on the king's council and they might even combine to constrain the king.

Within a tribe, there was a similar opposition between sections. The tribes were divided,

as described in the paragraphs on the Army, into sections attached to homesteads of the chief, his brothers, and his uncles; the adherents of each of these homesteads were very jealous of their "prince's" prestige and felt a local loyalty to him as against the adherents of other "princes." Before and after the death of a chief, these groups vied with one another to have their "prince" nominated as heir, and were even ready on occasion, despite their tribal loyalties, to support him against the heir when he assumed power. Faction fights between these sections continue today, often flaring up over trivial matters; and when Government assumed rule in Zululand it inherited a rich legacy of their feuds and of inter-tribal feuds. Even the members of wards under commoner *indunas* often came to blows, for at weddings and hunts they assembled as members of military sections or wards, and if a fight started between two men their fellow members would support them. Thus in every Zulu political group there was opposition between its component sections, often manifested through their leaders, though they cooperated in matters affecting the welfare of the whole group.

The opposed groups within the nation were united by the common service of their leaders in the council of the larger group of which they were part. The administration ran in separate threads from king to a particular chief, to a particular *induna,* to a particular lineage-head; all these threads were woven together in the council system. Though the group-heads were the main part of what bureaucracy there was in the simple Zulu social organization, their functions as bureaucrats and as group-heads were not entirely identical. In previous paragraphs some of their functions as group-heads have been reviewed. As administrators, they watched their people's interests and ruled them according to the orders of their superiors, and they also used their people's backing in their struggles for administrative power, perhaps against the people's interests. They and the officers about a court were the link between a ruler and his subjects, but frequently tended to become a barrier between them, for they were jealous

6. This is how Zulu describe it; in fact, they may have been moved by self-interest or other motives, but their actions are described in terms of tribal and national values.

of their rights, resented any encroachment on their privileges and sometimes acted independently of the ruler. The people had to consider these officials in approaching their rulers, the rulers were largely compelled to conduct their relations with the people through them. There was therefore an unstable balance of duties and interests between the group-heads acting as courtiers and other courtiers, and the rulers and the people.

V. SANCTIONS ON AUTHORITY AND THE STABILITY OF THE STATE

The king was bound to consider custom and his council. The Zulu king rarely called full meetings of the nation for discussion; he consulted their wishes through the chiefs. The people could not themselves criticize the king, but he might suffer if he disregarded their feelings entirely. The king was supposed to be just and generous and princes and chiefs were educated in, and conscious of, the tradition of good rule. The Zulu point to their history and show its lessons. Was not Shaka killed because he oppressed the people, so that Dingane did not fear to kill him? In turn, many people supported Mpande against Dingane. Mpande, the just and generous king, ruled long. I have been told that if a chief troubled his people, his family and *indunas* would poison him, but my informants could not give me a case in which this was done.

It required a long period of suffering before the people would turn against their rulers. Kings and chiefs were said to have many spies, and it was difficult to organize armed resistance to the king, though Zulu point out that all Shaka's spies did not save him from assassination. The king was backed with great force and a rebellion required that jealous chiefs and princes should unite. An early European visitor to Shaka records that his policy was to keep his chiefs at loggerheads with one another, and the Zulu admit this as a method of rule, pointing out that Government uses it today in dividing up Natal and Zululand into 300 chieftainships. Outside of the royal family there was no one who

could hold together the nation and this was recognized by the chiefs.

The people depended for leadership against an oppressive ruler on their nearer political officers. The Zulu had no idea of any political organization other than hereditary chieftainship and their stage of social development did not conduce to the establishment of new types of régime. Their only reaction to bad rule was to depose the tyrant and put some one else in his place with similar powers, though individuals could escape from Zululand to other nations' protection; that is, the people could take advantage of the princes' and chiefs' intrigues for power and the latter in intriguing sought to win the backing of the people. The king's policy was therefore to prosecute any one who threatened to be able to take his place: he had to meet rivals, not revolutionaries. The kings killed all brothers whose rivalry they feared. Uncles (fathers in the kinship system) were less likely to oust the king, and while the people should not complain against the king to his brothers they could appeal to one of his uncles. The kings, and all officers, were always on the watch for these threats to them. As the medicines of a ruler were believed to make him immune to the influence of his inferiors, if he felt ill in the presence of some person he could accuse the latter of sorcery.

The king had to treat all his brothers (and chiefs) carefully, lest they became centres of disaffection against him. The tension between the king and his brothers was a check on the king's rule because his subjects could shift their allegiance to his brothers. In addition, because the Zulu were strongly attached to their immediate political heads, the chiefs, and would even support them against the king, the chiefs had power to control the actions of the king. On the other hand, the chiefs remained dependent on the king. He could enlarge the powers of his favorites or assist the rivals of a recalcitrant chief.

Within tribes the chiefs held power under similar conditions. They could use armed force against disobedient or rebellious subjects though they had to inform the king that they were doing this. There were stronger checks on their rule. Their subjects could complain to the king if they were misruled. Though a man could in theory sue the king, he was not likely to do so; a chief could be brought before the king's court. Misrule by a chief would strengthen the hands of his brothers within the tribe and these brothers, unless the king intervened, might seize power. A quarrel with an important brother or subject might induce him to live elsewhere with his personal adherents. While misrule drove subjects to other chiefs a good and generous rule would attract followers. The Zulu have it that a chief should be free and generous with his people and listen to their troubles, then they will support him in war and "not stab him in his hut." The forces of fission and integration which marked the early political organization were still at work in the Zulu nation and to benefit by them it behoved a chief to rule wisely and justly in accordance with the wishes of his people.

The Zulu had loyalties to their various political heads. While these loyalties did not generally conflict, if king, chief, or *induna* abused his power the people would support one of their other political heads against him, and in their intrigues for power the political heads were ready to take advantage of this. Thus the potential conflict of these loyalties was a strong check on misrule and gave the people some control over their rulers.

VI. THE PEOPLE AND THEIR LEADERS

The working of these forces depended on the fact that political leadership was personal. In theory, any one could approach his superiors through their courtiers, though it might take some days. A chief (and even the king) was supposed to deal with his people himself and should not altogether delegate this duty. Chiefs and *indunas* knew most of their subjects, with their relationships and ancestry; if a stranger arrived at a capital all details about him were asked. To a lesser extent this applied to the king. The chief attended his people's weddings and sent his con-

dolences, or visited them, if a relative died. The Zulu sum this up by saying "the people respect their chief, but the chief ought to respect his people."

This intimacy between the chief and his people, despite the ceremonial which surrounded him, was largely possible because there was no class snobbery among the Zulu. The chief was still regarded and treated as the "father of his people;" "they are your father's people," he was told; "care for them well." And did not the chief belong to the tribe, especially if it had subscribed the bridewealth for his mother? There was no insurmountable barrier to marriage between his and any of his subjects' families. Though the courtiers had greater knowledge of affairs than the provincials had, the Zulu all had the same education and lived in the same way; and any one could take his part in the chief's council or assist in judging a case. Birth, age, courage, and wisdom all affected the attention a man would get; but every one could speak. Wealth brought a chief closer to, did not remove him from, his people. For under the conditions of Zulu life wealth did not give a chief opportunity to live at a higher level than his inferiors. He had more wives and bigger homesteads, but he could not surround himself with luxuries, for there were none. Wealth, in the form of well-filled granaries and large herds of cattle, gave a man power only to increase the number of his dependants and to dominate many inferiors. From the point of view of the chief, it may be said that he had to be rich in order to support his dependants; and besides this there was no use for wealth.[7] On the other hand, the wealth of a commoner attracted dependants and gave the rich man political status. Moreover, the kinsman of a wealthy man would not quarrel readily with him, so that there was little likelihood of his kinship group breaking up. However, there were few ways in which a commoner could acquire wealth: he might by magical practice, or as a reward from king or chief for some deed, or as booty in war. I

7. Today the position is different. Wealthy men can build European houses and buy motor-cars, clothes, ploughs, etc.

have been told that only important men owned cattle. The rich Zulu loaned out cattle to other people to herd for him; they could use the milk, and also the meat of animals which died, and this contract made them dependent on the cattle-owner because he could inflict great hardship on them by taking away his cattle. When the chief did this, it gave him a hold over his people and prevented them from easily changing their allegiance and going to some other chief.[8] Wealth therefore attracted followers, and as they increased and had children the wealthy man could collect about him a substantial group of dependants which was a poliitcal unit. Kinship alone, within a lineage, also created political units; even the head of a homestead had political duties. A notable feature of Zulu political organization throughout Zulu history is the creation of new groups as people moved about, settled and increased, and the heads of all these groups were minor political officers who might in time achieve prominence. Since leadership was personal, these groups were not merely absorbed into existing political groups; their leaders became officers within the organization.

There was thus a constant creation of new officials which, with the rise in rank of brave warriors and wise men, permitted of a high degree of social mobility. Any man, whatever his rank by birth, could become politically important if he had the ability, though those already established in high positions watched jealously over their rights and privileges. Thus it is said that sometimes if a chief became jealous of an inferior he would kill him on a trumped-up charge of sorcery, though it seems that more often these charges were brought by other men in the chief's court. They were (and are) frequent in court circles.

The Zulu say that today there is more security of life than in olden times, when a man might be killed for anything. Despite this, and despite accounts of lawlessness and favoritism, the old Zulu declare that they got justice from their chiefs and help in times of trouble.

8. A certain chief in Zululand today has a remarkable hold over his people: he has 16,000 cattle (out of a tribal total of 54,000) loaned out among them.

They deny that chiefs could be bribed. Mpande and Cetshwayo both gave decisions against important chiefs. The chiefs were undoubtedly cruel and capricious on occasion, but they were generous, though one old man who had been much at court said to me sadly: "There is no chief who is kind." The old Zulu generally shake their heads over the harsh rule of the past; and then speak of the glories under it. The life of the subjects seems to have varied with the character of their chief.

During the time of the kings, the State bulked large in the people's lives. In council and on the battlefield only could high ambitions be satisfied. In the smaller districts the men were always busy on administrative and judicial affairs when they were at home, especially after they retired from the active service, during which they had to spend a large part of their time at the military barracks. Here they starved for days, then feasted royally on meat. They lounged with their fellows, hunted, danced before the king, paraded for the national ceremonies. The king would sit and talk with his important men, discussing the law, mighty deeds, and history. Tribal and ward capitals were the centres of social life in their districts. The evolution of the barrack system affected Zulu social life considerably: it controlled marriages, and, though the old sexual labor division values remained, it was necessary for girls to assist in the work of herding and milking. The young men were not available for work at home and food had to be sent to them at the barracks. For the moment when they would be enrolled as warriors they waited eagerly, longing to join a regiment.

VII. THE PERIOD OF EUROPEAN RULE

Between 1887-8 the British Government finally took over the rule of Zululand, despite Dinuzulu's armed opposition. In a short time Government rule was confirmed. Today it is a vital part of Zulu life: of ten matters I heard discussed one day in a chief's council seven were directly concerned with Government. Fifty years of close contact with Europeans have radically changed Zulu life along the lines known all over South Africa. The military organization has been broken and peace established. The adoption of the plough has put agricultural labor on to the men, and they go out to work for Europeans in Durban, Johannesburg, and elsewhere. The development of new activities and needs, the work of various Government departments, missions, schools, stores, all daily affect the life of the modern Zulu. Communication has become easier, though pressure on the land is greater. Money is a common standard of value. The ancestral cult and much old ceremonial have fallen into disuse.

Zululand is divided into a number of magisterial districts, which are divided into tribes under chiefs, who are granted a limited judicial authority and who are required to assist the Government in many administrative matters. Within a district the magistrate is the superior political and judicial officer. He is the representative of Government. His court applies European law and is a court of first instance and of appeal from chiefs in cases between Natives decided according to Zulu law. He cooperates with other Government departments, and with the chiefs and their *indunas*. This, according to statute, is the political system: the chiefs are servants of Government under the magistrate, whom they are bound to obey. In Zulu life the magistrate and the chief occupy different, and in many ways opposed, positions.

The modern Zulu political system is ultimately dominated by the force of Government, represented in the district by the police. They are few in number, for the area and population they control, but behind them lies the overwhelming military power of the Europeans. The magistrate is backed by this power and he is vested with all the authority of the white upper class in the South African community. In the development of new activities which has marked the change in Zulu life, Government has played a leading role. It has established peace, encouraged men to go to work for Europeans, supported schools, started health, veterinary, and agricultural

services. The magistrate, therefore, not only applies Government regulations, but he is also the chief head of the organization which is bringing new enterprise and some adaptation to new conditions to the Zulu. He has to do many things which the chief cannot do for lack of power, organization, and knowledge. People go to the magistracy with questions and troubles. Thus the magistracy has come to stand for many of the new values and beliefs which today affect Zulu behavior.

However, while the Zulu acknowledge and use the magistracy, their attitude to Government is mainly hostile and suspicious. They blame it for the new conflicts in their community; they point to laws which they consider oppressive; they regard measures which Government intends in their interests as being designed to take from them their land and cattle, and cite in argument the encroaching of whites on Zululand in the past and what they regard as a series of broken promises to them. Moreover, many of these measures conflict with their pleasures, beliefs, and mode of life, as, for example, the forbidding of hemp-smoking and of sorcery trials, and the dipping of cattle and control of cattle movements. Therefore while Government requires the chiefs to support its measures, the people expect their chiefs to oppose them. And, indeed, the chiefs are usually opposed to them. This position was clearly emphasized in 1938, when a chief who opposed the building of cattle paddocks to prevent soil-erosion was praised by his people, but condemned by officials; a chief who asked for a cattle paddock was praised by officials, but condemned by his people. They complained against him to the Zulu king. For the people look to their native leaders to examine Government projects and "stand up for the people" against them.

The imposition of white rule and the development of new activities have radically curtailed and altered the chief's powers. He is subordinate to Government rule; he cannot compel, though he levies, labor service; he still owns the land, but it is less and subject to Government control; he has lost his relatively enromous wealth and often uses what he has in his own, and not his subjects' interests; he is surpassed in the new knowledge by many of his people. The men now have less time to devote to their chief's interests. A chief may try to enforce old forms of allegiance which some subjects will not render and this leads to conflict between them. If he tries to exploit or oppress a man, the latter can turn to the magistrate who will protect him. This last important point needs no elaboration, though it may be noted that as far back as the civil wars the different factions tried to persuade the British Government that they were in the right and should be helped. The chief can compel only that allegiance which Government, in its desire to rule through the chiefs, will make the people render, though his disapproval is a serious penalty in public life. Nevertheless, the chief still occupies a vital position in the people's life. Not only does he lead them in their opposition to Government, but he also has for them a value the magistrate cannot have. The magistrate cannot cross the barrier between white and black. He talks with his people and discusses their troubles, but his social life is with other Europeans in the district. The chief's social life is with his people. Though he is their superior, he is equal with them as against the whites and "feels together" with them. "He has the same skin as we have. When our hearts feel pain, his heart feels pain. What we find good, he finds good." A white man cannot do this, cannot represent them. The Zulu are ignorant of European history and it can have no value for them: the chiefs, and especially the king, symbolize Zulu traditions and values. They appreciate with their people the value of cattle as ends in themselves and of customs like bridewealth which are decried by Europeans. The chief is related to many of them by kinship ties and any man may become so related by marriage; the social and endogamous barrier between whites and blacks cannot be satisfactorily crossed. The Zulu acknowledge their chiefs' position largely through conservatism and partly because Government recognizes it. But a chief is usually chief by inheritance: "He has the blood and the prestige of chieftainship and they extend to his relatives; the magistrate has only the prestige of his office." By this contrast Zulu express the chief's position as it exists independently of Government's acknowledgement and rooted in the values and habits of the people. Chiefs and members of the royal family are greeted with traditional modes of respect. Their family history is retailed. Their capitals are centres of social life. They are given loyalty and tribute.

I have outlined the opposed positions of chief and magistrate: the balance between them is the dominant characteristic of the political system. However, it shifts from situation to situation in Zulu life. A certain minimum of allegiance to both magistrate and chief is legally enforced by Government; the influence of each may vary above that minimum with their characters and relations to each other, or according to the matter considered. A sympathetic magistrate who understands the Zulu will draw them to him, especially from a chief who is unsatisfactory; a harsh magistrate keeps people away from him and they go more to their chiefs. Even more the balance shifts for different individuals in different situations. A man who considers the chief to be biassed against him, favors the magistrate as impartial; but for him the chief is the source of justice when the magistrate enforces an unwelcome law. The people rally to the chief when they oppose measures such as the reduction of bridewealth. If the chief tries to force labor from people, they compare him unfavorably with the magistrate who pays for the labor he employs. Though in many situations it cannot be done, the Zulu constantly compare Native and European officers and switch their allegiance according to what is to their own advantage or by what values they are being guided on different occasions.

It has been necessary for this analysis to emphasize the opposition between chief and magistrate. It is strong, and appears in the jealousy each often has of the other's power. But in routine administration the system functions fairly well. Chiefs and *indunas* actively assist in the administration of law and the carrying out of certain activities. The magistrates, keen on their work and anxious to see their districts progress, may as individuals win the trust of their people, though it is never complete and the fundamental attitude to Government remains unchanged. They represent their people to Government, and the administration, in developing the Native reserves, seems to be coming into conflict with Parliament in so far as Parliament represents white interests. But though in general the system works, the opposition between the two sets of authorities becomes patent over major issues. Then ultimately the superior power of Government can force a measure through unless it depends on the willing cooperation of people and chief. The Zulu now have little hope of resisting Government rule and sullenly accept Government decisions. In the chiefs' councils, they vent their opposition in talk.

In evaluating this reaction to modern political institutions it is necessary to distinguish between two groups of Zulu, the pagan and the Christian (or schooled). Any schooled Zulu is in general much readier to accept European innovations than are the pagans. However, the majority of Christians have the same attitudes as the pagans, though their complaints against Government and whites may be differently formulated. Some better educated Christians measure the chief's value by the materialistic standard of the practical work done by Government and hold that the chiefs are reactionaries opposing progress and they favour a system like the Transkeian Bunga. They are possibly moved by desire for power themselves. In general it may be said that the most schooled Zulu regard the magistracy with more favor than do pagans, but among the best educated Zulu, who come most strongly against the color bar, there is a tendency to a violent reaction to their own people and culture and values away from the Europeans. Nevertheless, it is through the Christians that the Europeans introduce most new ideas into Zulu life. This is causing hostility between pagans and Christians and creating, on the basis of differences in education, adaptability, enterprise, and values, a new opposition in the nation. Aside from these Christians, there are the pagans who attend on whites, seeking some advantage and trying to profit from the political situation: thus Zulu unity against the whites is weakened. The people tend not to see a conflict in their own actions, though they feel and suffer under it, but often they criticize other Zulu for their allegiance to the whites, saying that they are selling their people to the white man.

Though all Zulu tend to be united against the Europeans, old tribal loyalties and oppositions are still at work and faction fights frequently occur. Tribes are often hostile to one another, but they are again beginning to support the Zulu king. He is recognized legally only as the head of a small tribe in Nongoma district, though Government recognizes his superior status and through him speaks to, and hears from, the Zulu people. He has been used on several occasions to settle disputes in other tribes and always gets precedence over other chiefs. The present Regent is Government's nominee to the Union Native Representative Council. Government thus recognizes the continued existence of the Zulu nation. The strength of Zulu nationalism is growing after a period of weakness. The head of the royal house is again the king (*inkosi*); other chiefs are *abantwana* (princes) or *abanumzana* (big people). He exercises influence, aside from what Government allows him, in other tribes. Nearly all the tribes of Zululand and Natal and some in the Transvaal acknowledge him as their king, though many of them were never ruled by the kings and fought in various wars for the whites against them. The king's present power is partly due to the fact that he symbolizes the great tradition of the Zulu kings, which gives the Zulu their greatness as against other peoples, such as the Swazi. Bantu national loyalties, pride, and antagonisms are still strong despite a growing sense of black unity. The king's power is also part of the reaction against white domination, for the Zulu feel that he has the ear of Government and therefore power to help them in their present difficulties, and that he has the courage and strength to oppose Government. Nevertheless, under Government each chief is independent. Jealousy and desire for power still divide the chiefs, but only the Mandlakazi and Qwabe chiefs are jealous of the king, though he could not get all the tribes to adopt his nominee to represent the Natal Natives in the Union Senate; but other chiefs, find that, as representatives of the king, their position among their people is stronger than it is as independent Government chiefs. As such, their people suspect them of being afraid to criticize Government. The allegiance they give the king varies from constant consultation to recognition when he travels. All Zulu crowd to see him when they can and heap gifts on him.

Within a tribe there remains the divisions into sections under brothers of the chief or *indunas* which sometimes leads to fighting. The chief must rule according to traditon or the tribe will support his brothers and weaken his court, though the magistrate is, as pointed out, the strongest sanction on misrule. If a chief palters to Government, his subjects may turn from him to a more obdurate brother, or sometimes if the chiefs say they approve of a measure, the people may accept it. The chief has to pick his way between satisfying Government and his people and has to control political officers over whom he has only slight material sanction, though, since these officials and the councils of the people are not legally constituted by Government, he may disregard them.

I am unable, for lack of space, to examine the way in which the political system functions in modern Zulu social and economic life; or the effect on the political situation of the division of the white color-group into Afrikaans-speakers and English-speakers, and other divisions within it. Briefly, it should be noted that the white group itself has contradictory values in approaching the Natives; though many Europeans are influenced by both sets of values, the missionaries, various other Europeans, and administrators, educationalists, and people in similar positions give more active expression to the Christian and liberal values. Many of these Europeans are on very friendly terms with Zulu. They fight for Zulu interests and the Zulu recog-

nize this to some extent, though they still regard them as whites and therefore suspect. In economic life the ties between Europeans and Zulu are strong. This may be seen in the traders who have to compete for Zulu customers and in the various labor employers competing with each other for the limited supply of labor. They attempt to get the goodwill of chiefs in their enterprises and at the Rand mines members of the royal family are employed to control Zulu workers as well as to attract them there. Meanwhile, the recognition accorded by these labor employers and traders, and also by missionaries, to the chiefs adds to their powers in the present situation, even while the labor flow and Christianity are weakening in other ways the tribal organization.

VIII. CONCLUSION

Zulu political organization has been twice radically altered. On both occasions the people quickly acknowledged their new rulers' power and the new organization functioned fairly well; but the old organization, which retained its values and significance, affected the functioning of the new one of which it was made a part. Meantime, despite the changes brought about by the centralization of authority and the regimental system under the kings, and today by the labor flow and the development of new social groups and values and modes of behavior, the smaller social groups have remained relatively constant.

The essence of both the systems described is the opposition of like groups and the potentially conflicting loyalties of the people to different authorities. The nation was a stable organization, for this opposition was principally between the tribes which were united in the king's position and his regiments. The circulation of the rulers' wealth was necessary to enable them to maintain their close relationship with their people. The conflict of loyalties to officials of different rank, often intriguing against one another, came into the open as a check on misrule. Therefore, despite the apparent autocracy of king and chiefs, ultimately sovereignty in the State resided in the people. However, though a ruler might be deposed, the office was not affected. In actual administration, the loyalties of the people and the competition of officers did not often conflict, since the administrative machinery worked through the heads of groups of different type: the main opposition was between similar groups, cooperating as parts of a larger group.

Today the system is not stable, for not only is Zulu life being constantly affected and changed by many factors, but also the different authorities stand for entirely different, even contradictory, values. The Zulu, with their strong political organization, have reacted against white domination through their political authorities, who were incorporated in Government administration. The modern political organization of Zululand is the opposition between the two color-groups represented by certain authorities. Each group makes use of the leaders of the other group if it can for its own purposes. The opposition between the two groups is not well-balanced, for ultimately it is dominated by the superior force of Government, against which the only reaction of the Zulu is acceptance or passive disobedience. The threat of this force is necessary to make the system work, because Zulu values and interests are so opposed to those of the Europeans that the Zulu do not recognize a strong moral relationship between themselves and Government, such as existed, and exists, between themselves and their king and chiefs. They usually regard Government as being out to exploit them, regardless of their interests. Government is now largely a sanction on oppressive chiefs, but the old

checks on the chiefs act to prevent them becoming merely subordinate tools of Government. Government, too, does much work that the chiefs cannot do.

The opposition is synthesized by cooperation in everyday activities; by the position that an individual white official wins in the people's esteem so that he comes even to stand for them against Government, i.e. he enters the black, as opposed to the white, color-group; and by the attempt of the people to exploit the opposed political authorities to their own advantage. In addition, divisions of each large group into political groups and opposed groups with conflicting ideals and interests act to weaken each group within itself and to lessen the main opposition. Members of dissident black groups, or individuals supporting Government in some matter, may be said to be supporters of the magistrate against the chief. In these ways social, economic, and other ties between Zulu and Europeans are bringing the Zulu more and more to accept white rule.

Within the one political organization there are officials, white and black, who have entirely different positions in the people's life and whose bases of power are different. These officials represent values which may be contradictory. By their allegiance in different situations the the officials representing each set of values, the people are prevented from being faced with a patent conflict of these values. Nevertheless, as the chief's material power is puny compared with Government's, the position he occupies is largely a centre for psychological satisfaction only and white domination is accepted by the Zulu, resignedly hostile.

30. CHARACTER AND VICISSITUDES OF THE TIE OF KINSHIP

MARC BLOCH

Reprinted from Feudal Society *(London: Routledge & Kegan Paul Ltd., 1961). Marc Bloch was born in Lyons, France, in 1886. After serving as Professor of Medieval History at the University of Strasbourg he was appointed in 1936 to the Chair of Economic History at the Sorbonne. In 1939, at age fifty-three, he volunteered for active service. After the fall of France in 1940, he went to the South where he taught at the University of Clermont Ferrand and Montpellier. When the South, too, was occupied, he joined the Resistance but was caught by the Gestapo, tortured, and finally shot in June, 1944.*

■ Because most anthropological studies of kinship have been conducted among tribal societies, many students are left with the impression that the analysis of kinship refers only to those societies and is irrelevant in our own history. Moreover, many of us are prone to assume that while corporate kin groups may have lurked in our remote past, they suddenly dropped out of sight. The way in which a society conceptualizes its history is an important part of its culture; the kind of history that most of us are taught rarely includes references to kinship. But as can be seen in Bloch's analysis of kinship in feudal western Europe, the evolution of kinship in our own history may be understood as an aspect of adaptive strategy as well as in tribal societies.

Bloch observed in his classic book that most people during the earliest stages of European feudalism lived as if they were members of stateless groups. An important feature of this situation was the predominance of extensive kinship relations in social and economic life. As a matter of fact, there were almost no social relations outside the framework of kinship; prior to about the twelfth century, the same words were used for "kin" and "friends" in France, Germany, Wales, and Ireland.

As kings began to entrench and extend their authority over their domains, the fabric of social and economic life began to change. How was this entrenchment and extension of power accomplished? Violence was a salient feature of life throughout the European feudal period, but it was at its worst prior to the thirteenth century. Its seeds were sown during the Viking, Islamic, and Hungarian invasions of western Europe from different directions,

beginning in the ninth century. One of the consequences was the destruction of hundreds upon hundreds of communities and districts and the resultant destruction of the institutional life in which they were embedded. Beginning in about the eleventh century, kings in western Europe began slowly and fitfully to make the countryside secure. The orbits in which they did so were at first very narrow, and it was a few hundred years before security in rural areas became normal.

But kings had very small armies in those days; their economies were insufficient to arm, feed, supply, and pay large forces. Instead, troops were mobilized when needed. But centralized authority, resources, and communications were insufficient even for this; most kings, for example, could not afford to provide armor for most of their forces. The social devices of what came to be known as feudalism—such as vassalage and serfdom—were among the most important instruments by which kings began to extend their authority by providing protection. To simplify what ended as an extraordinarily complex and diverse system, a king offered protection and land to a nobleman; in return, the latter paid tribute to the king and provided armed men whenever the king needed troops. This noble would then offer his protection—ultimately developing into control over land and labor—to villages and lesser noblemen within his orbit, with the same tradeoff. As Bloch wrote, "To be the 'man' of another man: in the vocabulary of feudalism, no combination of words was more widely used or more comprehensive in meaning."

These political relations were, however, incompatible with those of kinship. As Bloch describes in this selection, there was a process of replacement in which the nuclear family gained in importance at the expense of wider kin relations. Thus, the relationships that we observe in contemporary industrial society between the cohesiveness of the nuclear family and our attenuated kindred relations began more than 600 years ago. (See "Urban Families: Conjugal Roles and Social Networks," by Elizabeth Bott, reprinted in *Man in Adaptation: The Institutional Framework.*) The withering of extended kin ties, however, was not precipitated exclusively by political forces. It is noted in the next selection that after western Europe's recovery from the Viking and other invasions, new urban centers were erected on the most desirable lands, further breaking up communities in which kinship relations prevailed; in many places, kin groups held together in villages settled on the poorest lands. Even in industrial society there is a correspondence between poverty and reliance on kinship in the organization of social relations; Bloch's observations suggest that this too has a long history.

Anthropologists have paid little attention to this exciting period. One of the few exceptions is also one of the most important studies of change in kinship and its gradual replacement by ritual kinship: "An Analysis of Ritual Co-Parenthood (Compadrazgo)," by Sidney W. Mintz and Eric R. Wolf, *Southwestern Journal of Anthropology*, 6 (1950): 341-68. Henri Pirenne provided historical analyses that are potential sources for further anthropological insight in *Economic and Social History of Medieval Europe* (New York: Harcourt Brace, paperback, 1959) and *Medieval Cities* (Garden City, N.Y.: Doubleday Anchor, 1956). Six short biographies are offered in *Medieval People*, by Eileen Power (Garden City, N.Y.: Doubleday Anchor, 1954). Worthwhile vignettes of different institutions are offered in *Medieval Panorama: The English Scene from Conquest to Reformation*, by G. G. Coulton (New York: Meridan Books, 1955). A fascinating survey of violence during this period is to be found in *The Waning of the Middle Ages*, by J. Huizinga (Baltimore: Penguin Books, 1965). ■

1. THE REALITIES OF FAMILY LIFE

IN SPITE OF THE power of the family to give support to its members or impose restraints upon them, it would be a grave error to pic-ture its internal life in uniformly idyllic colours. The fact that the family groups engaged readily in blood-feuds did not always prevent the most atrocious intestine quarrels. Though Beaumanoir finds wars between kinsmen distressing, he obviously does not regard them as exceptional or even, except when waged between full brothers, as actually unlawful. To understand the prevailing attitude it is enough to consult the history of the princely houses. If, for example, we were to follow from generation to generation the destiny of the Angevins, the true Atrides of the Middle Ages, we should read of the "more than civil" war which for seven years embroiled the count Fulk Nerra with his son Geoffrey Martel; of how Fulk le Réchin, after having dispossessed his brother, threw him into prison—to release him only as a madman, at the end of eighteen years; of the furious hatred of the sons of Henry II for their father; and finally of the assassination of Arthur by his uncle, King John.

In the class immediately below, there are the bloody quarrels of so many middle and lesser lords over the family castle; as for example the case of the Flemish knight who, having been turned out of his home by his two brothers and having seen them massacre his wife and child, killed one of the murderers with his own hands. More terrible still was the affair of the viscounts of Comborn, one of those tales for strong stomachs that lose nothing of their flavor through being set down by the tranquil pen of a monastic writer. At the outset, we learn of the viscount Archambaud who, to avenge his deserted mother, kills one of his half-brothers and then, many years later, buys his father's pardon by the murder of a knight who had earlier inflicted an incurable wound on the old nobleman. The viscount leaves, in his turn, three sons. The eldest, who has inherited the viscounty, dies shortly afterwards, leaving a young boy as his only descendant. Mistrustful of the second brother, it is to the youngest, Bernard, that he confides the protection of his estates during the minority of his son. Arrived at the age of knighthood, "the child" Eble vainly claims the inheritance.

Thanks to the mediation of friends, however, he obtains the castle of Comborn though nothing else. He resides there, with rage in his heart, till one day his aunt (Bernard's wife) accidentally falls into his hands. He violates her publicly, hoping in this way to compel the outraged husband to repudiate her. Bernard takes his wife back and prepares his revenge. One fine day, he rides past the walls of the castle with a small escort, as if out of bravado. Eble, just rising from table, his brain clouded with drink, sets out madly in pursuit. After having gone a little way, the pretended fugitives turn, set upon the youth and wound him mortally. This tragic end, the wrongs which the victim had suffered, and above all his youth, so moved the people that for several days offerings were laid on his temporary grave at the spot where he was killed, as if it were the shrine of a martyr. But the perjured and blood-stained uncle and his descendants after him remained in undisturbed possession of both the castle and the viscounty.

None of this need surprise us. In these centuries of violence and high-strung emotions social ties could easily seem very strong and even show themselves frequently to be so, and yet be ruptured by an outburst of passion. But even apart from these brutal quarrels, provoked as often by greed as by anger, the fact remains that in the most normal circumstances, a strong sense of community was quite compatible with a pretty callous attitude towards individuals. As was natural perhaps in a society in which kinship was above all regarded as a basis of mutual help, the group counted for much more than its members taken individually. It is to the official historian employed by a great baronial family that we owe the record of a characteristic remark made one day by the ancestor of the line. John, the marshal of England, had refused, in spite of his promises, to surrender one of his castles to King Stephen. His enemies therefore threatened to execute before his eyes his young son, whom he had a short while beford handed over as a hostage. "What recks it me of the child," replied the good nobleman, "have I not still the anvils

and the hammers wherewith to forge finer ones?" As for marriage, it was often quite frankly a mere combining of interests and, for women, a protective institution. Listen, in the *Poem of the Cid*, to the words of the hero's daughters, to whom their father has just announced that he has promised them to the sons of Carrion. The maidens who, needless to say, have never seen their prospective husbands express their thanks: "When you have married us, we shall be rich ladies." These conventions were so strong that among peoples who were yet profoundly Christian they led to a strange conflict between social habits and religious laws.

The Church had no love for second or third marriages, although it was not expressly opposed to them. Nevertheless, from top to bottom of the social scale remarriage was almost universal. This was partly no doubt from the desire to place the satisfaction of the flesh under the shelter of the sacrament; but another reason was that when the husband had died first, it seemed too dangerous for the wife to live alone. Moreover in every estate that fell to the distaff side the lord saw a threat to the proper performance of the services due from it. When in 1119, after the defeat of the chivalry of Antioch at the Field of Blood, King Baldwin II of Jerusalem undertook the reorganization of the principality, he made a point both of preserving their heritage for the orphans and of finding new husbands for the widows. And, of the death of six of his knights in Egypt, Joinville naively remarks, "Wherefore the wives of all six of them had to remarry." Sometimes seignorial authority even went to the length of ordering that peasant women whom an untimely widowhood prevented from properly cultivating their fields or carrying out the prescribed labour services should be provided with husbands.

The Church proclaimed the indissolubility of the conjugal tie; but this did not prevent repudiations, especially among the upper classes, often inspired by the most worldly considerations. Witness, among a great many others, the matrimonial adventures of John the Marshal, narrated, always in the same level tone, by the *trouvere* in the service of his grandsons. He had married a lady of high lineage, endowed—if we are to believe the poet—with all the highest qualities of body and mind: "great joy had they together." Unfortunately, John had also an "over-mighty neighbor" whom prudence required him to conciliate. He got rid of his charming wife and married the sister of this dangerous personage.

But to place marriage at the centre of the family group would certainly be to distort the realities of the feudal era. The wife only half belonged to the family in which her destiny had placed her, perhaps not for very long. "Be quiet," says Garin le Lorrain roughly to the widow of his murdered brother who is weeping over the body and bemoaning her lot, "a noble knight will take you up again . . . it is I who must continue in deep mourning." In the relatively late poem of the *Nibelungen,* Kriemhild avenges on her brothers the death of Siegfried, her first husband—although it must be admitted that the justice of her action seems by no means certain; but it appears that in the primitive version of the story she pursued the blood-feud of her brothers against Attila, her second husband and their murderer. Both in its emotional climate and in its size, the family of those days was quite a different thing from the small conjugal family of later times. What then, precisely, was its scope?

2. THE STRUCTURE OF THE FAMILY

Vast *gentes* or clans, firmly defined and held together by a belief—whether true or false—in a common ancestry, were unkown to western Europe in the feudal period, save on its outer fringes, beyond the genuinely feudalized regions. On the shores of the North Sea there were the *Geschlechter* of Frisia or of Dithmarschen; in the west, Celtic tribes or clans. It seems certain that groups of this nature had still existed among the Germans in the period of the invasions. There were, for example, the Lombard and Frankish *farae* of which more than one

Italian or French village continues today to bear the name; and there were also the *genealogiae* of the Alemans and Bavarians which certain texts show in possession of the soil. But these excessively large units gradually disintegrated.

The Roman *gens* had owed the exceptional firmness of its pattern to the absolute primacy of descent in the male line. Nothing like this was known in the feudal epoch. Already in ancient Germany each individual had two kinds of relative, those "of the spear side," and those "of the distaff side," and he was bound, though in different degrees, to the second as well as to the first. It was as though among the Germans the victory of the agnatic principle had never been sufficiently complete to extinguish all trace of a more ancient system of uterine filiation. Unfortunately we know almost nothing of the native family traditions of the countries conquered by Rome. But, whatever one is to think of these problems of origins, it is at all events certain that in the medieval West kinship had acquired or retained a distinctly dual character. The sentimental importance with which the epic invested the relations of the maternal uncle and his nephew is but one of the expressions of a system in which the ties of relationship through women were nearly as important as those of paternal consanguinity. One proof of this is the clear evidence from the practices of name-giving.

The majority of Germanic personal names were formed by linking two elements, each of which had a meaning of its own. So long as people continued to be aware of the distinction between the two stems, it was the common custom, if not the rule, to mark the filiation by borrowing one of the components. This was true even in Romance-speaking regions where the prestige of the conquerors had led to the widespread imitation of their name system by the native peoples. Children took their names either from the father or the mother; there seems to have been no fixed rule. In the village of Palaiseau, for example, at the beginning of the ninth century the peasant *Teud-ricus* and his wife *Ermen-berta* baptized one of their sons *Teut-hardus,* another *Erment-arius,* and the third, by way of a double memorial, *Teut-bertus.* Then the practice developed of handing down the whole name from generation to generation. This was done again by taking the name from each side alternately. Thus of the two sons of Lisois, lord of Amboise, who died in 1065, one was named after his father but the other, who was the elder, was named Sulpice like his maternal grandfather and uncle. Still later, when people had begun to add patronymics to Christian names, they vacillated for a long time between the two modes of transmission. "I am called sometimes Jeanne d'Arc and sometimes Jeanne Romée," said the daughter of Jacques d'Arc and Isabelle Romée to her judges. History knows her only by the first of these names; but she pointed out that in her part of the country it was customary to give daughters the surname of their mother.

The double link had important consequences. Since each generation thus had its circle of relatives which was not the same as that of the previous generation, the area of the kindred's responsibilities continually changed its contours. The duties were rigorous; but the group was too unstable to serve as the basis of the whole social structure. Worse still, when two families clashed it might very well be that the same individual belonged to both—to one of them through his father and to the other through his mother. How was he to choose between them? Wisely, Beaumanoir's choice is to side with the nearest relative, and if the degrees are equal, to stand aloof. Doubtless in practice the decision was often dictated by personal preference. When we come to deal with feudal relations in the strict sense, we shall encounter aspects of this legal dilemma in the case of the vassal of two lords. The dilemma arose from a particular attitude of mind and in the long run it had the effect of loosening the tie. There was great internal weakness in a family system which compelled people to recognize, as they did in Beauvaisis in the thirteenth century, the legitimacy of a war between two brothers, sons of the same father (though by different marriages), who found themselves caught up in a vendetta between their maternal relatives.

How far along the lines of descent did the obligations towards "friends by blood" extend? We do not find their limits defined with any precision save in the groups that maintained the regular scale of compensation, and even here the customs were set down in writing only at a relatively late date. All the more significant is the fact that the zones of active and passive solidarity which they fixed were surprisingly large, and that they were, moreover, graduated zones, in which the amount of the indemnity varied according to the closeness of the relationship. At Sepulveda in Castile in the thirteenth century it was sufficient, in order that the vengeance wreaked on the murderer of a relative should not be treated as a crime, for the avenger to have the same great-great-grandfather as the original victim. The same degree of relationship entitled one to receive a part of the blood money according to the law of Oudenarde and, at Lille, made it obligatory to contribute to its payment. At Saint-Omer they went so far as to derive the obligation to contribute from a common founder of the line as remote as a grandfather of a great-grandfather. Elsewhere, the outline was vaguer. But, as has already been pointed out, it was considered only prudent in the case of alienations to ask the consent of as many collaterals as possible. As for the "silent" communities of the country districts, they long continued to gather together many individuals under one roof—we hear of as many as fifty in eleventh-century Bavaria and sixty-six in fifteenth-century Normandy.

On close examination, however, it looks as if from the thirteenth century onwards a sort of contraction was in process. The vast kindreds of not so long before were slowly being replaced by groups much more like our small families of today. Towards the end of the century, Beaumanoir felt that the circle of people bound by the obligation of vengeance had been constantly dwindling—to the point where, in his day, in contrast with the previous age, only second cousins, or perhaps only first cousins (among whom the obligation continued to be very strongly felt), were included. From the latter years of the twelfth century we note in the French charters a tendency to restrict to the next of kin the request for family approval. Then came the system under which the relatives enjoyed the right of redemption. With the distinction which it established between acquired possessions and family possessions and, among the latter, between possessions subject, according to their origin, to the claim of either the paternal or the maternal line, it conformed much less than the earlier practice to the conception of an almost unlimited kinship. The rhythms of this evolution naturally varied greatly from place to place. It will suffice here to indicate very briefly the most general and most likely causes of a change which was pregnant with important consequences.

Undoubtedly the governmental authorities, through their activities as guardians of the peace, contributed to the weakening of the kinship bond. This they did in many ways and notably, like William the Conqueror, by limiting the sphere of lawful blood-feud; above all, perhaps, by encouraging refusal to take any part in the vendetta. Voluntary withdrawal from the kindred group was an ancient and general right; but whilst it enabled the individual to avoid many risks, it deprived him for the future of a form of protection long regarded as indispensable. Once the protection of the State had become more effective, these "foreswearings" became less dangerous. The government sometimes did not hesitate to impose them. Thus, in 1181, the count of Hainault, after a murder had been perpetrated, forestalled the blood-feud by burning down the houses of all the relatives of the guilty man and extorting from them a promise not to give him succour. Nevertheless the disintegration and attenuation of the kindred group, both as an economic unit and as an instrument of the feud, seems to have been in the main the result of deeper social changes. The development of trade conduced to the limitation of family impediments to the sale of property;

the progress of intercommunication led to the break-up of excessively large groups which, in the absence of any legal status, could scarcely preserve their sense of unity except by staying together in one place. The invasions had already dealt an almost mortal blow at the much more solidly constituted *Geschlechter* of ancient Germany. The rude shocks to which England was subjected—Scandinavian inroads and settlement, Norman conquest—were doubtless an important factor in the premature decay in that country of the old framework of the kindred. In practically the whole of Europe, at the time of the great movement of land reclamation, the attraction of the new urban centres and of the villages founded on the newly cleared lands undoubtedly broke up many peasant communities. It was no accident if, in France at least, these brotherhoods held together much longer in the poorest provinces.

It is a curious but not inexplicable fact that this period, in which the large kinship groups of earlier ages began to disintegrate in this way, was precisely that in which family names first appeared, though as yet in a very rudimentary form. Like the Roman *gentes,* the *Geschlechter* of Frisia and Dithmarschen both had their traditional labels. So too, in the Germanic period, had the dynasties of chiefs, invested with a sacred hereditary character. The families of the feudal era, on the contrary, remained for a long time strangely anonymous, partly no doubt on account of the vagueness of their outlines, but also because the genealogies were too well known for anyone to feel the need of a verbal reminder. Then, especially from the twelfth century onwards, it became a common practice to add to the original single name—the Christian or given name we should call it today—a nickname or perhaps a second Christian name. The disuse into which many old names had fallen, together with the growth of population, had the effect of increasing the number of homonyms in the most troublesome way. At the same time, the increased use of written legal material and a generally growing desire for clarity made the confusions arising from this poverty of names less and less tolerable, and impelled people to seek distinctive labels.

But these were still purely individual appellations. The decisive step was taken only when the second name, whatever its form, became hereditary and changed into a patronymic. It is characteristic that the use of true family names first arose among the greater nobility, in which the individual was at once more mobile and more interested, when he went away from home, in retaining the support of his group. In twelfth-century Normandy people already spoke customarily of the Giroys and the Talvas; in the Latin East, about 1230, of "those of the lineage surnamed d'Ibelin." Next the movement reached the urban bourgeoisie, who were also accustomed to moving about and who because of their commercial interests were anxious to avoid mistakes over the identity of persons and even of families, which were often identified with business associations. The development eventually spread through the whole of society.

But it must be clearly understood that the groups which thus acquired definite labels were neither very stable nor of a size at all comparable with the old kindreds. The transmission of names, which sometimes, as we have seen, alternated between the paternal and the maternal lines, suffered many interruptions. The branches, in separating, often became known by different names. Servants, on the other hand, readily adopted the names of their masters. In short, what was here involved was not so much the clan-names as—in conformity with the general evolution of blood-relationships—the nickname shared by the members of the same household, the continuity of which was at the mercy of the slightest accident in the history of the group or the individual. It was not till much later that strict heritability of names was imposed by the authorities—together with civil status—in order to facilitate the work of police and administration. Thus in Europe, long after the demise of feudal society, the permanent family name, which today is held in common by men often devoid of any feeling of solidarity, was the creation not of the spirit of kinship, but of the institution most fundamentally opposed to that spirit—the sovereign state.

3. TIES OF KINSHIP AND FEUDALISM

It must not be supposed that from the remote tribal ages there was steady progress towards emancipation of the individual. On the continent at least, it appears that at the time of the barbarian kingdoms alienations were much less dependent on the consent of the near relatives than they were to become during the first feudal age. The same was true of arrangements for the disposal of property after death. In the eighth and even in the ninth century, it was possible, sometimes by will as in Roman law, sometimes under various systems developed by the Germanic customary laws, for a man to make his own arrangements for the devolution of his property with some freedom. From the eleventh century, this power was virtually lost except in Italy and Spain which were both, as we know, exceptionally faithful to the teachings of the old written laws. Gifts that were intended to take effect only after death thenceforward assumed exclusively the form of donations subject by the nature of the case to the approval of the relatives. This did not suit the Church, however, and under its influence the will properly so called was revived in the twelfth century. At first it dealt only with pious bequests; then, subject to certain restrictions for the benefit of the natural heirs, it was gradually extended. This was also the moment when the attenuated system of redemption (*retrait lignager*) replaced that of family consent. The blood-feud itself had been curtailed to some extent by the legislation of the states that sprang from the invasions. Once these barriers were removed, the feud took, or resumed, the foremost place in the penal law, till the time when it once more became the object of attack by the reconstituted royal or princely authorities. The parallelism, in short, appears in every respect complete. The period which saw the expansion of the relations of personal protection and subordination characteristic of the social conditions we call feudalism was also marked by a real tightening of the ties of kinship. Because the times were troubled and the public authority weak, the individual gained a more lively awareness of his links with the local groups, whatever they were, to which he could look for help. The centuries which later witnessed the progressive breakdown or metamorphosis of authentic feudalism also experienced—with the crumbling of the large kinship groups—the early symptoms of the slow decay of family solidarities.

Yet to the individual, threatened by the numerous dangers bred by an atmosphere of violence, the kinship group did not seem to offer adequate protection, even in the first feudal age. In the form in which it then existed, it was too vague and too variable in its outlines, too deeply undermined by the duality of descent by male and female lines. That is why men were obliged to seek or accept other ties. On this point history is decisive, for the only regions in which powerful agnatic groups survived—German lands on the shores of the North Sea, Celtic districts of the British Isles—knew nothing of vassalage, the fief and the manor. The tie of kinship was one of the essential elements of feudal society; its relative weakness explains why there was feudalism at all.

31. ENGLISH VILLAGERS OF THE THIRTEENTH CENTURY

GEORGE C. HOMANS

Reprinted by permission of the publishers from George C. Homans, English Villagers of the Thirteenth Century. *Cambridge, Mass.: Harvard University Press. Copyright © 1941, by the President and Fellows of Harvard College. George C. Homans is Professor in the Department of Social Relations at Harvard University. He is the author of* The Human Group, Social Behavior, *and* Sentiments and Activities *(a collection of essays), in addition to the book from which these selections are taken.*

■ This selection is a case study of plow agriculture as a particular kind of social system, that is, as a strategy of adaptation. One of the essential features of this strategy, especially in its organization of social relations, is an elaborate system of social stratification that controls production and distribution, the organization of labor, and land tenure.

Feudalism, in England as elsewhere, was a particular kind of political organization that in large part was a design for regulating the relationships of the land-owning class to be centralized state and of the peasantry to the landowners. Hence feudalism must be distinguished from the energy systems on which it rested; it is only one of the several political systems that can be built on an agricultural adaptation. But it is important to note that feudalism probably is incompatible with any other strategy of adaptation; agriculture does not always give rise to feudalism but feudalism can emerge only in an agricultural society.

Important in this strategy of adaptation, in addition to the distribution of cultivable land, was the assurance of the regular availability of draft animals. It will be readily apparent from many chapters in the book from which this selection is excerpted that draft animals and plows were among the main preoccupations in the proceedings of manorial courts (a society's court records often provide significant clues to its most sensitive problems).

Everyone who has studied the history of England during this period is familiar with such phenomena as the "enclosure movement" in East Anglia, "open field" manorial villages, and the "incorporated boroughs." These were different settlement patterns within the overall society and with the same level of adaptation, and each such spatial organization of households involved different organizations of social relations. The existence of these varying cultural uses of space and organizations of social relations in a society illustrates another important point in the study of adaptation: Just as there is increasing diversity among successive levels of technological development—that is, among societies at successive stages of their evolution—there also is increasing diversity among the societies within each successive level of adaptation. Almost everyone in a hunting-gathering society lives the same style of life and, to a large extent, by the same values. This is also the case—though to a diminished extent—in most horticultural and stateless pastoralist societies. But in an agricultural society, to say nothing of societies that participate in still more advanced strategies of adaptation, there are many styles of life within the society conceived as an adaptive unit. As we noted above, this variability is responsible for the difficulties experienced by anthropologists in attempting to construct models of the peasantry and other institutions of agricultural strategies of adaptation.

Plow agriculture is radically different from horticulture because these relationships to the land lead in each to unique organizations of social relations, different annual rhythms, larger and more stable concentrations of population, and wider ranges of exploitable habitats. Agriculturists cultivate their fields in the off season instead of confining themselves to one season, and there are two sides to this coin. One side shows that they do this to keep their fields free from overgrowth; the other shows that the advanced techniques of agriculture—compared to those of horticulture—make this practice possible. Unlike horticulturists, agriculturists crowd their harvest season into the end of the period of growth. Agriculturists fallow their fields; they do not abandon them like the horticulturists, who work marginally arable land and use only the most rudimentary plant technology. Agriculturists pasture their livestock on the stubble and fallow. Land that is unsuitable or not needed for crops is used as range land, on which livestock graze, under the care of herdsmen and herdsboys—an important element in the division of labor.

Several works can add greatly to an understanding of the cultures of England and other western European countries at this stage of evolution: *Medieval People,* by Eileen Power (rev. ed.; New York: Barnes & Noble, 1963); *Medieval Panorama: The English Scene from Conquest to Reformation,* by George G. Coulton (New York: Macmillan, 1957); *Feudalism,* by F. L. Ganshof (2nd ed.; New York: Harper and Row, 1961); *Medieval Feudalism,* by Carl Stephenson (Ithaca, N.Y.: Cornell University Press, 1956); and *Piers Ploughman,* by William Langland (New York: Sheed and Ward, 1945). Also important is *Plough and Pasture: The Early History of Farming,* by E. C. Curwen and Gudmund Hatt (New York: Abelard-Schuman, 1953).

I have not included in this book any case studies of mercantilism as a strategy of adaptation because of limitations of space, but the reader who wants to learn more about the evolution of European mercantilism will find it profitable to start with *Medieval Cities,* by Henri Piernne (Garden City, N.Y.: Doubleday, 1956), especially the last chapter, "Cities and European Civilization," or Pirenne's *Economic and Social History of Medieval Europe* (New York: Harcourt, Brace, 1956). A fascinating glimpse into the role of overseas explorations in the development of European cultures during the period discussed by Homans is "The Vikings," by Eric Oxensterna *(Scientific American,* 216[5] [May, 1967]: 66-78). ■

THE PEOPLE OF A village of England in the Middle Ages were divided not only into families, but also into social classes, of different degrees of wealth and consideration. In fact the notion that at any time in their history the Germanic tribes consisted of a mass of substantially equal freemen—a theory which was once a favorite—has gone the way of other similar theories, for instance that of primitive communism. In most villages the number of

the main social classes was two. There will be much more to say on this matter later, but a first sketch must be made now. The more substantial villagers were called the *husbonds,* or at least they were so called in north-eastern England. They were the bonds who had houses, in contrast with the villagers of the poorer sort, who were called cotters or cotmen, because their dwelling-places were only cots or cottages. In the thirteenth century a husbond was not simply a married man, but a man of a certain class, a substantial farmer. From this second meaning of the word we derive of course the word *husbandry.*

This division of villagers into two main classes seems to have been common in many parts of Europe under the old peasant social order and to have been determined fundamentally by an economic cleavage. In ancient France, for instance, the two classes were called the *laboureurs* and the *manouvriers.* The laboureurs were the substantial farmers, who had tenements large enough to enable them to keep plow-oxen; the manouvriers were the poorer peasants, who had only their hands with which to work. The laboureurs would lend the manouvriers their oxen for use in tilling the small holdings of the latter. And in return the manouvriers supplied the laboureurs with the spare hand-labor which the latter required on their larger lands. A considerable amount of mutual help between the two classes was maintained, together with a considerable amount of mutual distrust. The relation between the husbonds and the cotters of England may have been much like that between the laboureurs and the manouvriers of France.

One of the most interesting facts of the social order of medieval England must now be considered. In many a village the tenements of villagers fell into definite classes according as they were larger or smaller, and what is more, the tenements within each of these classes tended to be equal in size. There were standard tenement units, and we know that they were recognized as such by the villagers, since they were called by special names. In the first approximation—and in any exposition of something complex we must proceed by successive approximations— it is safe to say that there were two main classes of tenement units, as there were two main classes of villagers. These two main classes were also the two recognized in the first instance in the language of the people. To take first the terms used in champion villages[1] of the South of England, the large tenement units were called *yards* or *yardlands,* in Latin *virgatae terrae.* Though the size of the yardland varied from village to village—each village had its own standard yardland—a good average size to remember is thirty acres. The men who held each one yardland were often called *yardlings (vir gatarii).*

The smaller tenement units were the *cotlands.* These were of the order of five acres or less in size, each having little or no land in the open fields and in the village proper only the cot or cottage from which this class of holding took its name. The cotlands were held by the cotters, the cotsetles, the cotmen, as they were variously called—the poorer sort of villagers. Often there were sub-classes of tenements, as half-yardlands and quarter-yardlands, or the tenements were of irregular sizes—this is the correction which brings the first statement closer to the reality.

The yardland was the name for the standard tenement in champion villages in the southern part of England; the *oxgang (bovata)* was the name of the standard tenement in the North. (Scholars have got into the habit of using derivatives of the Latin names for the tenement units, of speaking of virgates and bovates, but there are old English names for them, yardlands and oxgangs, and the sense of being close to the villagers' point of view may be heightened by using the word they used themselves.) The oxgang tended to be smaller than the yardland; in other respects its position in the village economic organization was the same. The oxgang of one village might be larger or smaller than the oxgang of another, but within any given

village all oxgangs were of a size. Each of the more substantial villagers, the husbonds, would hold one oxgang, or more often each would hold two.

The yardland and the oxgang divided between them the part of England which in the Middle Ages was strictly champion country. If you plot on a map the area in which the documents show that the common tenement unit bore one name and the area in which it bore the other, the map will reveal that, upon the whole, the oxgang ruled in the country north of a line drawn from the Wash to the Mersey. Lincolnshire, northern Leicestershire, Derbyshire, and the shires north of them were oxgang country. The rest of champion England was yardland country. Between, a narrow debatable land was found, where there were both oxgangs and yardlands. The line between the two may go back to a boundary between ancient Anglo-Saxon kingdoms, but it is not important in later social history. Substantially the same social and economic system reigned in southern Leicestershire as in northern.

In the customs of land measurement in medieval England, the oxgang and the yardland were both fixed parts of larger units. In the North eight oxgangs made a *plowland (carucata),* and in the South four yardlands made a *hide.* Since the plowland and the hide were of the same order of magnitude—120 acres is a good average figure to remember— the oxgang tended to be about half the size of the yardland. Plow lands commonly went with oxgangs, and hides with yardlands, but not always. Sometimes plowland was simply another name for hide. The area assigned in different places to the plowland and the hide varied with a number of circumstances in a way which has never been satisfactorily worked out. The most important circumstance was probably that the plowland was the amount of land which one plow team was expected in custom to till in one year's work. Agricultural experts of the thirteenth century spoke as if this was the case, and the name of the plowland seems to confirm them. As such, the size of the plowland must have

1. Champion villagers were surrounded by grasslands on which herds were grazed, rather than plow land—ED.

varied with the character of the soil of a village and with the field system in force there, whether two-field or three-field. Perhaps its size also depended on fiscal considerations: it was a unit for the assessment of taxes and other charges. What is more interesting, *hide* may be derived from an old word meaning *family,* and before the Conquest the hide may have been thought of as the customary allotment of one family. But in the thirteenth century the hide and the plowland were important as measures of the size of large estates, not as holdings of individual villagers. Only a few wealthy villagers would hold so much land. The origins of these units may seem important to us; they were not to the townsfolk.

Disregarding for the moment the yardland and the hide, let us consider the oxgang and the plowland. The agricultural writers of the thirteenth century spoke of the plowland as the amount of land which could be properly tilled by one plow team in a year. And the commonest plow team of the thirteenth century was one of eight oxen. In view of these facts, is it not significant that the oxgang and the plowland bore the names they did and that there were eight oxgangs in every plowland? Early in the investigation of the champion husbandry, people suggested that the oxgang was that tenement which supported one ox and sent it to a common team of eight oxen, and that the plowland of eight oxgangs was tilled by this common team made up of one ox from each oxgang. The same sort of thing was said of the yardland, that each yardland sent two oxen, a yoke, to the common team of eight from the hide.

Whatever may have been the original dispositions, in point of fact in the thirteenth century such a neat regularity is almost never recorded, though there are sometimes hints of it. In an extent of the manors of Baldwin Wake, taken in 10 Edward I, the services due to the lord from his bondmen in Bransdale in Kirkby Moorside, Yorks., are detailed. There William Gondi held a messuage and two oxgangs of land. The entry continues as follows:

And his three neighbors with their oxen, joined to himself and his oxen, shall plow for one day at the winter sowing, and his work is worth a penny. . . . He shall plow at the Lent sowing for two days in the manner as above.

Each of William's three neighbors held two oxgangs, like himself, so that in this instance eight oxgangs in fact made up one plow team between them. Whether or not each of the neighbors sent just two oxen to the common team does not appear.

That one of the common village holdings, a yardland or an oxgang, could not usually support a full plow team, even if the team were of less than eight oxen, is plain, though there are exceptions even to this rule. A husbandman had to pool his oxen with those of his neighbors to make up a common team, or he had to borrow or hire oxen. All of these arrangements were common practice, and something must be said about each of them, in their many variations. But this must first be remembered, which is true of all sorts of information about villagers in the Middle Ages: the documents tell us for the most part what a villager was bound to do when he was working for his lord. That he worked in the same way when working with his neighbors or on his own account is an assumption. Occasionally, though only occasionally, it is supported by facts. For instance, there is no doubt that the standard set by a husbandman when he was working for himself was often the standard of what his work for the lord ought to be. He was expected to plow the lord's land only in the weeks when he was plowing his own, or to come to plow the lord's land with as many head of oxen as he yoked in plowing his own.

When a husbandman was unable to make up a plow team from the beasts of his own tenement, there was no rule about how many of his fellows he went into partnership with. Sometimes two, sometimes three, sometimes four, sometimes eight villagers formed a joint team. The evidence suggests that the commonest team was of eight oxen, but there was no regularity as to how the team was made up, no regularity as to the number of head furnished by each tenement. This is but natural. The accidents of husbandry would be likely to prevent a yardland from being able to send just one yoke, no more and no less, to the common team, year after year. An able yardling in a good year would be able to send more, a poor yardling in a poor year would not be able to send as many or would be unable to send any at all. The statement of the services of a yardling at Barton-in-the Clay, Beds., in a Ramsey inquest of 39 Henry III, puts the case:

Each Friday, however, in the aforesaid time [Michaelmas to Christmas], if he has his own plow team he will plow a half-acre, and when it shall have been sown, he will harrow it. If, however, he does not have a full plow team of his own, he will plow the land of the lord with as many beasts as he plows his own with. Four men or eight, if need force them, may indeed be joined at the plow, if their means reach no further, and they will be quit of the plowing of a half-acre as if said common plow was that of one man.

Sometimes when four tenements are making up an eight-ox team in the neatest possible way, it nevertheless turns out that they are not yardlings but half-yardlings, so that a plow team is being made up out of a half-plowland, instead of out of a whole plowland, as it should be to correspond with theory. Thus on one of the manors of the Bishop of Ely, Horningsea in Ditton, Cambs., one of the entries of the bishop's custumal of 1277 runs:

Roger Holdeye holds fifteen acres which make a half-yardland. . . . And furthermore he will plow within the same time [Michaelmas to August 1] every Monday until noon for one work, in such manner that he and three other men, his fellows, will make one plow team with eight beasts.

Lastly, on some of the manors of Ramsey Abbey, the number of men who pooled their plow beasts to make a common plow team varied with the season of the year. More men joined together in partnership in spring and summer than in winter, that is, the medieval winter, before Christmas. Perhaps after the cold weather, after a winter in the byre, the cattle were weaker and more of them had to be hitched to the plow. Perhaps, as winter came on, the husbandman slaughtered one or

more of his plow oxen, because he was not going to be able to feed them through the winter. Then he would have fewer oxen in the spring, and more men would have to join together to make a full team. These are speculations; what the real reasons were, whether these or others, we do not know. But the fact is plain. At Upwood, Hunts., for instance, among the services of a yardling in 1252 were these:

At wheat sowing he will plow one land alone without a fellow, for his yardland, and at barley sowing, as his plow team is joined with others, he wil plow one land and harrow it; and thus he himself and his partners will be quit of the plowing of said land.

The disputes which arose about joint plowing are often the means of revealing to us that joint plowing existed. Breaches of covenants men had made to plow jointly with their oxen or horses gave rise to suits before manorial courts. For instance, an entry in a court roll of 1338 of Alton, Hants., is this:

Nicholas Upechepyng was summoned to answer Henry Astil in a plea of covenant. And the same Henry complains therein that said Nicholas did not keep a covenant with him, in this that he agreed with Henry, in the village of Alton on Monday next after the Feast of All Hallows in the eleventh year of the reign of King Edward who now is, that he would find three horses for Henry's plow from the Monday aforesaid until the Christmas following in the same year, which covenant he broke to Henry's damage of 20 s., and thereupon etc. And said Nicholas defends etc. and wholly denies the aforesaid covenant and thereupon he wages his law six-handed.

So it was in the South, and so also in the North. At a court held at the Bridge of Rastrick, in the West Riding of Yorkshire, in 1286, among the proceedings were these:

It is found by an inquest of neighbors that Richard of Tothill was the companion of Roger of the Wood to plow jointly with his plow, and at the time of plowing cast him off, so that his land lies untilled. Therefore, let him make satisfaction to him for the damages, which are taxed at 10 s.

People were, as is natural, unwilling to plow with neighbors who did not bear a good character. In 1275, at the time of the taking of an inquest for the Hundred Rolls, John of

Fulbeck complained of injustices which had been done him by Geoffrey de Turnai, bailiff of the Isle of Axholme in Lincolnshire, saying, among other things:

Such hurt did he do him that this John could not find in the town of Belton a single neighbor who dared yoke one ox in a plow with him because of his [the bailiff's] forbiddance and power.

What happened to the poor wretches who had no plow cattle of their own and so could not join with neighbors in making a common team? Such might be those men whose holdings were not large enough, whose rights of common of pasture were not extensive enough to allow them to support plow oxen. But through misfortune or mismanagement even villagers who were potentially more wealthy might be in this case. Even yardlings were sometimes without plow oxen. An entry in the court rolls of 1293 of King's Ripton, Hunts., is this:

John William's son is attached by the pledges of John Dyke and Nicholas in the Nook because he does not come to the lord's plowing, which John comes into court and says that he has no beast of his own wherewith he can plow but only borrowed beasts, wherein he says and aleges that so long as he borrows beasts for plowing he is not bound to answer to the lord for any plowing, and thereupon he puts himself upon the Ramsey Register. And therefore let the Register be inspected before the next court.

The Ramsey Register was the book in which were entered all the rents and services owed to the abbot by his tenants. John William's son was appealing to it for confirmation of his claims, and other tenants are to be found doing the same thing. The Register has not survived, but some of the inquests, made by juries of villagers, from which the Register was compiled, were included in the Ramsey Cartulary, and this has come down to us. The reason why the tenants showed such confidence in the Register may have been that it was based on the sworn testimony of men of their own class.

Sometimes there were suits involving damages done to plow beasts while they were in the hands of a borrower. At a hallmote of Polstead, Suffolk, in 1292:

Robert le Coc comes and complains of the aforesaid Philip [Denelind] and says that the aforesaid Philip received a certain horse from him in a certain covenant, namely, that the aforesaid Philip should keep the aforesaid horse and pasture it and harness it in the plow. Moreover he says that Philip beat the aforesaid horse and bound a stone onto the ear of this horse, and he ought to render to the aforesaid Robert one day's work of plowing.

According to the last clause, either Philip had agreed to do some plowing for Robert in return for the use of the horse or he was bound to make up the damages by doing plowing. The fact that the amount of land a team was expected to plow in a day was everywhere fixed in custom made it easy to use plowing as a sort of payment in kind. Fines in manorial courts were often levied in the form of so many days' work in plowing. Why the rock was tied onto the poor horse's ear is dark to us.

Sometimes the borrowing of plow oxen was not with the consent of their owners, but without such consent and by stealth. An entry in the court rolls tof Newington, Oxon., for 1278 is the following:

They say [that is, all the villeins] that John Grug and Geoffrey his brother took without consent the beasts of good men by night on the eve of Michaelmas and plowed two acres and a half, that is, with three plows. An inquest is taken to find whether or not Richard of Berwick lent these two his plow, and the inquest says: not in that time.

How plowing was done successfully at night is again beyond those of us who are not dirt farmers, but other evidence confirms that people did plow at night and by stealth.

If a man could not borrow beasts of the plow, and had money, he could contract with other men to plow his land or even to do the plowing services he owned his lord. In its specification of the services owed by the tenants of Somersham, Hunts., the Ely custumal of 1222 laid down this rule:

And be it known that if by chance anyone holding a yardland has nothing in a plow team because of his poverty, he is bound to plow with his pence nine acres a year.

Even a yardling might be short of oxen. On the other side we are told of men who "take money for the plowing of other people's land."

But what, at last, of the man who was so poor that he was able neither to support plow oxen on his holding nor to hire them? Perforce he delved up his land with a spade. If a man's holding was small, he could prepare all of it for seed with a spade. Adam, who, as the father of mankind, stood in medieval mythology for the ordinary father of a family, was a delver. As usual we must guess, from what he did for his lord, what the husbandman did for himself when he lacked plow oxen. At Banstead in Surrey in 1325, the services due by villagers to the lord were such that:

if he does not have a plow team each tenant of a yardland ought to delve four dayworks.

The possibility is once again contemplated that even a yardling might not have plow oxen. The *daywork,* like the acre and the rood, was a measure of area, but it was a smaller area than these, because it probably represented the amount of land customarily delved, not plowed, in one day.

What certainly has not been established by all this evidence is that each oxgang sent one and only one ox to a common team of eight oxen for the plowland, each yardland one and only one yoke to a common team of eight oxen for the hide. Such a neat and seemly arrangement was found sometimes, but only rarely. In the thirteenth century, the varieties of common plow teams were many, whatever they may have been at an earlier age. But the important thing is the fact of common plowing, not the forms of common plows, and this fact cannot be contested. There were plenty of husbandmen, even the more substantial ones, who were not able to support on their tenements a full draught of oxen apiece. Such husbandmen, in groups of two or more, would become partners, or *marrows,* as men would have said in the North, and pool their oxen to form common teams, which then plowed the lands of all the partners. This was one of the practices which made it a matter of indifference whether a villager had his land in a single parcel or in scattered strips: the common plow team had in any case to move about from the lands of one of the partners to those of the others.

In any community where people are poor and the struggle to make a living is hard, mutual help must be a matter of course if the community is to survive. In a community of husbandmen, lending tools or animals and working in company with neighbors to get a job done which is beyond the resources of a single family are among the most familiar practices. In old New England, there was the custom of holding bees, according to which a man might call in his neighbors to help him do some heavy piece of work, such as raising the frame of a new barn. In the same way, in English villages of the Middle Ages, cooperation in farm work was the basis of village life. And inasmuch as plow beasts were the most important single means of carrying on husbandry, their hiring, borrowing, and the customs of joint plowing were a large part of this cooperation. A complicated code of borrowing obtains in most farming communities, even though it is formulated only half explicitly. For the loan of a tool, an animal, a day's work, a neighbor expects to be able to ask and receive at some later time a service to be done for him, not necessarily a service of the same sort. The reciprocities are not strictly measured, but are based on what is felt to be customary. Without these traditions of exchange of help, making a living from the soil would have been much harder than in fact it was. They must have been supported by strong sentiments of confidence and good will among neighbors—neighborhood (*vicinitas*) as the villagers of England called them. In champion country, the village was the social group on which these customs of mutual help were binding.

Spelsbury has been chosen not because it was a typical manor—there was no such thing—but because it failed of being typical in ways which make it a good example with which to begin the study of manors. Its structure was more simple than that of most manors. It had features which were common to many manors but would rarely have been found, as they were at Spelsbury, united in any one manor. Furthermore, Spelsbury was in the heart of the champion country of England, and its description is not an ideal reconstruction but is taken from a contemporary inquest. For these reasons, Spelsbury is a good point of departure, especially when social relations are to be studied rather than economic or legal arrangements.

In 1279, Angareta de Beauchamp held the manor of Spelsbury as her dower of the inheritance of the Earl of Warenne and Surrey. At her death, the manor was to revert to the earl. It was held of the Bishop of Worcester, and the bishop held of the king. Such was the chain of subinfeudation which bound Spelsbury, like any other piece of land in England, to the king. To the lady of the manor belonged the advowson of the parish church, that is, she had the right to name whatever priest she wished as parson of the parish. In the words of later centuries, she might present him to the living. She also exercised the rights of *waif*, that is, of appropriating abandoned property, and of *forefeng*, that is, of taking a reward for the rescue of stolen cattle, besides the rights of having her own gallows and holding the view of frankpledge. The jurors who took the inquest did not know by what warrant she exercised these rights, since they belonged to the king or to his officers unless specifically alienated. There was also woodland in the neighboring forest of Wychwood appurtenant to the manor.

Three plowlands of the manor were in demesne, that is, they were tilled under the direct management of the officers of the lady of the manor, by the work of her servants and of her villeins. The rest of the land was in the hands of her tenants. These, according to the classification used in the inquest, were of three kinds: freeholders (*libere tenentes*), villeins (*villani*), and cotters (*cottarii*). There were six freeholders. The most considerable of them was probably William of Colthurn, who held a mill and six acres of land, for which he paid a yearly rent of 20 s. 4 d., which freed him from all services except that of coming to the view of frankpledge on the two days a year when it was held. Next in

consequence after William was perhaps Thomas le Venur, who held three yardlands and a half, and did what was called suit and forinsec service, by which was meant suit at the manorial court and services due from the manor to the lord king, particularly suit at the royal courts of hundred and shire. John the Fraunckelein held two yardlands together with six acres of assart, likewise for suit and service. We must note his name, Frauncke-lein, and the fact that he was a substantial freeholder. There will be something to say later about franklins. Henry of Richel held one yardland for a rent of 3 s. and suit and service of the lord king. Thomas Smith also held one yardland, for which he was bound to make the irons—the coulters and the shares —for three of the lady's plows, out of her iron. He was free from all other services save suit to the hallmote. Lastly, Robert le Duk held a half-yardland, for which he rendered 4 s. 6 d. in rent, 6 d. worth of plowing, boon works in harvest worth 3 d. and four hens.

With the end of the list of freeholders and the beginning of that of villeins, the irregularity of the size of holdings ended and heavy labor services began. Thirty-three persons held each one yardland in villeinage. Three of them were widows and one of them was called Thomas Reeve. The reeve was a village and manorial officer whose duties will be described later. Each of the thirty-three had to do the following services: he had to do sixty works (*opera*) between Michaelmas (September 29) and the Gule of August (August 1). These works were in tilling the lady's demesne and in doing other labor for her profit. Beside this, each yardling had to do four special days' work of plowing on the lady's demesne wtih his own plow and one day's work of mowing her meadow. Between the Gule of August and Michaelmas, that is, in the harvest season, the rate of work was increased. In that time, a yardling had to do thirty-six works, and three bidreaps (*pre-carie*) besides. These bidreaps were days chosen by the lady when she had the right to call upon the villagers to come to reap her corn. Such were the yardling's services in farm work. He also had to collect nuts in the lady's wood for three days and render her a bushel of wheat at Martinmas. "Against Christmas" he was bound to give her a hen in return for having dead wood. That is, the hen secured for the yardling the right of gathering dead wood and windfalls in the lady's wood. We must remember that she held woodland appurtenant to the manor in the forest of Wychwood. He also gave her at Christmas a "present," worth one penny. What it was is not specified. On top of all these dues, a yardling was tallaged every year at the will of the lady. That is, she took every year what portion she pleased of the money and goods of her villeins.

Ten villeins held half-yardlands. Two of them were widows, and one was called Richard Bedell. The bedell was like the reeve a manorial officer, but one of lower rank. Each half-yardling had to do thirty manual works between Michaelmas and the Gule of August (half as much as the yardlings), three plowings, and five works in hay-making. In harvest time he did twelve works and came to three bidreaps. At Martinmas he gave the lady three hens. And he was tallaged.

The poorest class of Spelsbury people was that of the cotters, of whom there were six, three of them women. Each of them held a *cottagium*, the size of which is not specified. A cotter had to do forty works a year, plus five works making hay, plus three *precarie*. He had to give four hens. At this point the description of Spelsbury ends, with the information that the total yearly *valor* of the manor to Angareta de Beauchamp was £ 30, 19 s., 10 d.

If Spelsbury was a manor, what were the characteristics of a manor? In the terms of feudal law, it was a holding, a tenement, and was held *of* someone, but this statement is not of great significance, since any piece of land was a tenement or part of one. In particular Spelsbury was a free tenement, and not only was it a free tenement, but Angareta who held it was plainly a gentlewoman. It was also a compact tenement. The manor of Spelsbury was also the village of Spelsbury: there was none of Spelsbury that was not in the manor. There were two parts of the manor, a greater part, which was in the hands of tenants, and a lesser part, the demesne, which was managed by officers of the lady of the manor and tilled by her servants and her villeins. On this demesne there was probably a manor house and court, with farm buildings, and in the hall of the manor house the hallmotes would be held. According to the amounts of land they held and the rents and services they rendered in return for their land, the tenants were divided into classes, which were called by special names. Among the tenants also were men who held particular positions in the economy of the village or the government of the manor: the miller, the smith, the reeve, the bedell. Lastly, besides having her rents and services from her tenants, the lady exercised certain other rights over them, especially the right of holding a manorial court. They had to attend it, and she took the profits of its justice.

Spelsbury was not a typical manor, but it corresponded closely to what, thirty years ago, was conceived to be a typical manor. The typical manor was born of a study of the custumals of a few great religious houses. Later investigation of the organization of estates in all parts of England has allowed few of the characteristics of the typical manor to stand as typical. The typical manor was supposed to be coincident with a village. But there were manors which were larger than a village and manor which were smaller. Some estates which were called manors included several subordinate villages. An example is the Earl of Warenne and Surrey's manor of Wakefield in Yorkshire, the court rolls of which have often been quoted here. Sometimes two or more persons held manors in the same village—this arrangement was especially characteristic of the Danelaw—or there was a complicated structure of subinfeudated holdings. The typical manor was supposed to have both land in demesne and land in villeinage, that is, land held by villein tenants who owed labor services. Indeed, the size of the demesne and the number of labor services must have borne some relation to each other. More services cannot have been exacted than were needed for the cultivation of the demesne. But in the matter of the demesne any actual estate might differ from the typical manor in one of two ways. It might have no demesne but present a complex of free tenants holding of a lord and paying rent. On many manors, even when there was demesne land, parts of it from time to time would be rented out to tenants. Or the estate might consist entirely of demesne, without villein land.

Clearly we cannot specify, by any large number of characteristics common to all of them, what manors were. Estates which might have been called manors covered in the thirteenth century most of the land of England. They differed greatly in their composition, but the word was broad enough to include them all. Even now its meaning does not need to be defined strictly. People use the word *manor* not for complicated logical operations but only for convenience, to show that they are going to talk about one of a large and diverse class of things. But if *manor* is undefined, *village* is not. Whatever the complex of manors which divided its soil between them, a village was a distinguishable unit. It was a unit in that two or more great fields, submitted to the customs of the champion husbandry, surrounded it and belonged to it, that the houses of the villagers were clustered in one group, and that the villagers thought of themselves and behaved as a distinct social body. The royal government laid upon the village and not upon the manor its burdens of local police. We are interested here in manorial organization not for its own sake but only for its effect on village society.

But when all reservations are made, certain characteristics do remain to define a manor. That a manor was a free tenement still holds, and that it was a tenement of a certain order of magnitude. No one would mistake a yardland for a manor. It was also a tenement concentrated in one place, not scattered over several shires like some great honor. There were at least two classes of men on most manors: a lord, and tenants under him who owed him rents and services. It is true that even a yardling might have tenants, that is, undersettles. The difference lay not in the

tenants but in the control exercised over them. If the tenants of the lord of the manor were villeins, their goods were in the eyes of the law not their own but the lord's. They owned nothing but their bellies—so men said when they wanted to put the case as plainly and as brutally as they could. The lord might increase the rents and services of his villeins as he wished; they had no remedy. He might drive them penniless away from their homes. More important, the lord of the manor set up some kind of manorial government, and in particular held a court which most of his tenants were bound to attend, the lowest in the hierarchy of English courts. No court, no manor—that is a good rule, especially in a study which relies heavily on the information furnished by the rolls of manorial courts.

For the student of society, the most interesting question which can be asked about a manor is that of the relations between the lord and his tenants. The first thing to be said about these relations is that they were permanent. As long as he lived, the lord was likely to have the same families of tenants; as long as they lived, the tenants had the same line of lords. The two were bound together for better or for worse. A free tenant might leave the manor whenever he wished, a villein after paying a fine to the lord and agreeing to pay a small sum called *chevage* (head money) every year that he remained away, but no tenant would leave the manor without strong inducement, since leaving meant losing his land. The relations between lord and man were permanent but they were seldom a matter of face-to-face contact. If the lord held many manors, he probably would not reside at any one of them for more than a week or two during the year. The custumals always say that the tenant must render such and such rents and services to his lord and that the lord must give such and such benefits to his tenant, but this assumption of direct relations between the lord and his man was nothing more than a manner of speaking. Unless the lord was a very petty lord indeed, a steward or bailiff was an intermediary between him and his tenants. In the same way at the present time, the official documents often describe the relations between a workman and the company which employs him, when as a matter of fact his only face-to-face contact with the company organization is his contact with his immediate supervisor. This fact does not, of course, prevent the workmen and the upper members of the management from having strong feelings of loyalty or distrust towards one another.

Just as we must take into consideration at least two classes of men on a manor: a lord and his tenants, so we must begin by considering at least two factors determining their relationship: their interests and their sentiments. The economic and other interests of the two parties are obvious, as are most economic interests, and perhaps this obviousness is one reason why the science of economics is further advanced than the other social sciences. If his tenants did not render their rents and services, the lord would not have the wherewithal to keep up his household, pay his officers and retainers, dower his daughters. His state in the world was maintained by the income he received from his manors. He wanted to continue receiving it and if possible to increase it. But even when he had the legal right, as he did over his villeins, to exact what rents and services he pleased, he did not intend to press his tenants so hard that they would run away from the manor. Then the land would lie untilled and no revenue at all would derive from it. Even if the tenants did not leave the manor, oppression might drive them to a kind of passive resistance which would in the long run be just as damaging to the lord's interests. On the other hand, the tenant's possession of his means of livelihood, his holding, was dependent on his rendering to the lord the due and accustomed rents and services of the holding, and there was good positive reason for his remaining on good terms with the lord, since many favors were in the lord's power to confer. Finally, the tenant had the future of his family in mind and wanted to be sure that the tenement would descend to his son and heir.

But to think that the economic interests are the only factors involved in a relationship such as that between a lord and his tenant is always a mistake. Even when the two parties talk as if their economic interests were the only factors involved, when they talk about exploitation, a wise man will look for other forces at work. The situation may be revolutionary; it will seldom be revolutionary for the reasons envisaged by Marx. In point of fact, strong sentiments entered into the relations between landlord and tenant. To say what these sentiments were would be rash in anyone who had not been brought up in England and in the country. All that a historian can say is that for many, though not for all periods in English history, there is evidence in the behavior of landlords and tenants towards one another that the two parties felt much mutual loyalty and understanding. The landlord was not simply a landlord. He was in charge of local government and in some manner responsible for the general well-being of the people in his neighborhood. His duties demanded a traditional realism in looking at social relations, traditional because it was not a matter of study or clear expression but was born in the young men as they listened to their fathers talk and strengthened in them later by their own experience. It was realism because it never forgot, not even in the great age of economic theory at the beginning of the nineteenth century, that more than economic interest was involved in the constitution of society. This tradition was the one —we may call it the Tory tradition, though the Whig families were as well trained in it as the Tories—which led Disraeli to believe that the common people would rather trust their destinies to the landed gentry, the gentlemen of England, than to the new plutocracy of manufacturing. For centuries, in politics and war, the common people were in fact ready to follow the lead of their landlords. To be sure, the tradition did not prevent landlord and tenant from being very much alive to their special interests. Indeed they may both have taken the tradition so much for granted that they were seldom consciously aware that anything beyond economic interest was at stake. Furthermore, men of ill will on either side might violate the code. But if it were solidly enough established in the community, even such persons would be driven to conform. There is such a thing as being a gentleman in spite of oneself.

There is reason to believe that these non-economic factors in the relationship between landlord and tenant are old in England. As the French would say, the more the relationship has changed, the more it has remained the same thing. To describe it as it is today or was in the nineteenth century would be difficult enough. To describe it as it was in the thirteenth century, a man must cling to a few hints, a few inferences from the records, and these will tell him only about practices which had hardened into common customs; they will tell him little about the active attitudes of landlords and tenants. Nevertheless the description is worth attempting. Though the treatment of other matters may often obscure it, the importance of the non-economic factors in the relationship between lord and man is the theme which will be pursued in the pages to come.

32. TYPES OF LATIN AMERICAN PEASANTRY: A PRELIMINARY DISCUSSION

ERIC R. WOLF

Reprinted from American Anthropologist, *57 (1955): 452-70. Eric R. Wolf is Professor of Anthropology at the City University of New York, Lehman College. He has a longstanding interest in the study of peasantry, with special reference to Latin America and Mediterranean Europe. He is the author of* Sons of the Shaking Earth, Anthropology, Peasants, *and* Peasant Wars of the Twentieth Century.

■ Contemporary Middle and South America, containing a great variety of types of peasants, make up an important laboratory for the student of cultural evolution, from the level of foraging to modern industrialization. This area saw the development of great civilizations, which were destroyed in a moment of what is referred to as progress, and the annihilation of these civilizations produced new realities to which the inhabitants had to adapt. One aspect of this adaptation was a process of "devolution," in which new balances with the sociophysical habitat had to be sought, resulting in many variations of the basic agricultural adaptation.

Wolf describes two types of peasant communities in Latin America (but notes there are many others as well). Wolf first distinguishes an adaptation to "high highland" habitats; the second is found in humid "low highlands" and tropical lowlands. In its organization of social relations, the first type is designated "corporate"; it is relatively closed to outsiders and is stable. It is located on marginal land, its technology is traditional, and it is poor. It has a distinctive political-religious system.

The second type of community raises cash crops, such as bananas or cocoa, that require outside capitalization. The community in this variation of agricultural society is "open"; its membership is heterogeneous, in contrast to the homogeneity of the corporate peasant community.

Wolf seeks to relate the social organization of these types to their systems of production and, in turn, to the total society and the larger economic world. These larger economic forces require that the peasant in each type of community periodically make adjustments in his productive activities. Such adjustive shifts, Wolf shows, have important consequences in social organization.

An important companion piece to this selection is "Closed Corporate Peasant Communities in Mesoamerica and Central Java," by Eric R. Wolf *(Southwestern Journal of Anthropology,* 13 [1957]: 1-18. A good collection of papers is *Contemporary Cultures and Societies of Latin America,* edited by Dwight B. Heath and Richard N. Adams (New York: Random House, 1965). *The Plural Society in the British West Indies,* by M. G. Smith (Berkeley: University of California Press, 1965), explores aspects of the relationships between peasants and their wider societal memberships in the West Indies; Smith's formulations, which have aroused considerable controversy, are applicable to other areas as well. *The People of Puerto Rico,* edited by Julian H. Steward (Urbana: University of Illinois Press, 1956), presents a series of studies (including one by Wolf) of social subsystems on that island. A collection of valuable papers is entitled *Peasant Society: A Reader,* and is edited by Jack Potter, May N. Diaz, and George M. Foster (Boston: Little, Brown, 1967).

The following is a mere sample of studies of peasants in Latin America: *The Folk Culture of Yucatan,* by Robert Redfield (Chicago: University of Chicago Press, 1941); *Chan Kom: A Maya Village,* by Robert Redfield and Alfonso Villa (Chicago: University of Chicago Press, 1934); *A Village that Chose Progress: Chan Kom Revisted,* by Robert Rerfield (Chicago: University of Chicago Press, 1950); *Tepoztlan: A Mexican Village,* by Robert Redfield (Chicago: University of Chicago Press, 1930); *Life in a Mexican Village: Tepoztlan Restudied,* by Oscar Lewis (Champaign: University of Illinois Press, 1951), which presents a very different interpretation of life in this peasant community from Redfield's; *The Law of the Saints: A Pokoman* [Guatemalan] *Pueblo and its Community Culture,* by Ruben E. Reina (Indianapolis: Bobbs-Merrill, 1967); *The People of Aritama: The Cultural Personality of a Columbian Mestizo Village,* by Gerardo and Alicia Reichel-Dolmatoff (Chicago: University of Chicago Press, 1961); *Wealth, Authority and Prestige in the Ica Valley, Peru,* by Eugene A. Hammell (Albuquerque: University of New Mexico Publications in Anthropology No. 10, 1962); *The Social and Religious Life of a Guatemalan Village,* by Charles Wagley *(American Anthropologist* [N.S.,] 51[4], Pt. 2, October, 1949); *Moche: A Peruvian Coastal Community,* by John Gillin (Washington, D.C.: Smithsonian Institution, Institute of Social Anthropology, No. 3, 1947); *Cheran: A Sierra Tarascan Village,* by Ralph L. Beals (Washington, D.C.: U. S. Government Printing Office, 1946); and *Quiroga: A Mexican Municipio,* by Donald D. Brand (Washington, D.C.: Smithsonian Institution, Institute of Social Anthropology, No. 11, 1951). ∎

AS ANTHROPOLOGY HAS become increasingly concerned with the study of modern communities, anthropologists have paid increasing attention to the social and cultural characteristics of the peasantry. It will be the purpose of this article to draw up a tentative typology of peasant groups for Latin America, as a basis for further field work and discussion. Such a typology will of necessity raise more questions than can be answered easily at the present time. To date, anthropologists working in Latin America have dealt mainly with groups with "Indian" cultures, and available anthropological literature reflects this major interest. Any projected reorientation of inquiry from typologies based mainly on characteristics of culture content to typologies based on similarities or dissimilarities of structure has implications with which no single writer could expect to cope. This article is therefore provisional in character, and its statements wholly open to discussion.

There have been several recent attempts to draw a line between primitives and peasants. Redfield, for example, has discussed the distinction in the following words:

There were no peasants before the first cities. And those surviving primitive peoples who do not live in terms of the city are not peasants. . . . The peasant is a rural native whose long-established order of life takes important account of the city.

Kroeber has also emphasized the relation between the peasant and the city:

Peasants are definitely rural—yet live in relation to market towns; they form a class segment of a larger population which usually contains also urban centers, sometimes metropolitan capitals. They constitute part-societies with part-cultures.

Peasants thus form "horizontal sociocultural segments," as this term has been defined by Steward.

Redfield further states that the city was made "possible" through the labor of its peasants, and both definitions imply—though they do not state outright—that the city consumes a large part of what the peasant produces. Urban life is impossible without production of an agricultural surplus in the countryside.

Since we are interested less in the generic peasant type than in discriminating between different types of peasants, we must go on to draw distinctions between groups of peasants involved in divergent types of urban culture. It is especially important to recognize the effects of the industrial revolution and the growing world market on peasant segments the world over. These have changed both the cultural characteristics of such segments and the character of their relations with other segments. Peasants everywhere have become involved in market relations of a vastly different order of magnitude than those which prevailed before the advent of industrial culture. Nor can this expansion be understood as a purely unilineal phenomenon. There have been different types of industry and markets, different types of industrial expansion and market growth. These have affected different parts of the world in very different ways. The peasantries found in the world today are the multiple products of such multilineal growth. At the same time, peasants are no longer the primary producers of wealth. Industry and trade rather than agriculture now produce the bulk of the surpluses needed to support segments not directly involved in the processes of production. Various kinds of large-scale agricultural enterprises have grown up to compete with the peasant for economic resources and opportunities. This has produced a worldwide "crisis of the peasantry," related to the increasingly marginal role of the peasantry within the prevalent economic system.

In choosing a definition of the peasant which would be adequate for our present purpose, we must remember that definitions are tools of thought, and not eternal verities. Firth, for example, defines the term as widely as possible, including not only agriculturists but also fishermen and rural craftsmen. Others might be tempted to add independent rubber gatherers and strip miners. For the sake of initial analysis, this writer has found it convenient to consider each of these various kinds of enterprise separately and thus to define the term "peasant" as strictly as possible. Three distinctions may serve as the basis for such a definition. All three are chosen with a view to Latin American conditions, and all seem flexible enough to include varieties which we may discover in the course of our inquiry.

First, let us deal with the peasant only as an agricultural producer. This means that for the purposes of the present article we shall draw a line between peasants, on the one hand, and fishermen, strip miners, rubber gatherers, and livestock keepers, on the other. The economic and cultural implications of livestock keeping, for example, are sufficiently different from those of agriculture to warrant separate treatment. This is especially true in Latin America, where livestock keeping has been carried on mainly on large estates rather than on small holdings.

Second, we should—for our present purpose—distinguish between the peasant who retains effective control of land and the tenant whose control of land is subject to an outside authority. This distinction has some importance in Latin America. Effective control of land by the peasant is generally insured through direct ownership, through undisputed squatter rights, or through customary arrangements governing the rental and use of land. He does not have to pay dues to an outside landowner. Tenants, on the other hand, tend to seek security primarily through acceptance of outside controls over the arrangements of production and distribution, and thus often accept subordinate roles within hierarchically organized networks of relationships. The peasants generally retain much greater control of their processes of production. Outside controls become manifest primarily when they sell their goods on the market. Consideration of tenant segments belongs properly with a discussion of *haciendas* and plantations rather than with a discussion of the peasantry. This does not mean that in dealing with Latin America we can afford to forget for a moment that large estates overshadowed other forms of landholding for many centuries, or that tenant segments may exert greater ultimate influence on the total sociocultural whole than peasants.

Third, the peasant aims at subsistence, not at reinvestment. The starting point of the peasant is the needs which are defined by his culture. His answer, the production of cash crops for a market, is prompted largely by his inability to meet these needs within the sociocultural segment of which he is a part. He sells cash crops to get money, but this money is used in turn to buy goods and services which he requires to subsist and to maintain his social status, rather than to enlarge his scale of operations. We may thus draw a line between the peasant and another agricultural type whom we call the "farmer." The farmer views agriculture as a business enterprise. He begins his operations with a sum of money which he invests in a farm. The crops produced are sold not only to provide goods and services for the farm operator but to permit amortization and expansion of his business. The aim of the peasant is subsistence. The aim of the farmer is reinvestment.

In setting up a typology of peasant segments we immediately face the difficulty that peasants are not primitives, that is, the culture of a peasant segment cannot be understood in terms of itself but is a part-culture, related to some larger integral whole. Certain relationships among the features of peasant culture are tied to bodies of relationships outside the peasant culture, yet help determine both its character and continuity. The higher the level of integration of such part-cultures, the greater the weight of such outside determinants.

In complex societies certain components of the social superstructure rather than ecology seem increasingly to be determinants of further developments.

This is especially true when we reach the organization level of the capitalist market, where the relationship of technology and environment is mediated through complicated mechanisms of credit or political control which may originate wholly outside the part-culture under investigation.

We must not only be cognizant of outside factors which affect the culture of the part culture. We must also account for the manner in which the part-culture is organized into the larger sociocultural whole. Unlike other horizontal sociocultural segments, like traders or businessmen, peasants function primarily within a local setting rather than on an inter-local or nonlocal basis. This produces considerable local variation within a given peasant segment. It means also that the peasantry is integrated into the sociocultural whole primarily through the structure of the community. We must therefore do more than define different kinds of peasants. We must also analyze the manner in which they are integrated with the outside world. In other words, a typology of peasants must include a typology of the kinds of communities in which they live.

The notion of type also implies a notion of history. The functioning of a particular segment depends on the historical interplay of factors which affect it. This point is especially important where we deal with part-cultures which must adapt their internal organization to changes in the total social field of which they are a part. Integration into a larger sociocultural whole is a historical process. We must be able to place part-cultures on the growth curve of the totality of which they form a part. In building a typology, we must take into account the growth curve of our cultural types.

Here we may summarize briefly our several criteria for the construction of a typology of peasant groups. First, it would seem to be advisable to define our subject matter as narrowly as possible. Second, we shall be interested in structure, rather than in culture content. Third, the initial criteria for our types can be primarily economic or sociopolitical, but should of course include as many other features as possible. Fourth, the types should be seen as component parts of larger wholes. The typical phenomena with which we are dealing are probably produced principally by the impact of outside forces on pre-existing local cultures. Fifth, some notion of historical trajectory should be included in the formulation of a type.

TWO TYPES OF PEASANT PART-CULTURES

To make our discussion more concrete, let us turn to an analysis of two types of peasant segments. The first type comprises certain groups in the high highlands of Latin America; the second covers peasant groups found in humid low highlands and tropical lowlands. While these types are based on available field reports, they should be interpreted as provisional models for the construction of a typology, and thus subject to future revision.

Our first type (1) comprises peasants practicing intensive cultivation in the high highlands of Nuclear America. While some production is carried on to cover immediate subsistence needs, these peasants must sell a little cash produce to buy goods produced elsewhere. Production is largely unsupported by fluid capital. It flows into a system of village markets which is highly congruent with such a marginal economy.

The geographical area in which this type of peasant prevails formed the core area of Spanish colonial America. It supported the bulk of Spanish settlement, furnished the labor force required by Spanish enterprises, and provided the mineral wealth which served as the driving force of Spanish colonization. Integration of this peasantry into the colonial structure was achieved typically through the formation of communities which inhibited direct contact between the individual and the outside world but interposed between them an organized communal structure. This structure we shall call here the "corporate" community. It has shown a high degree of persistence, which has been challenged successfully only in recent years when alternative structures are encroaching upon it. Anthropologists have studied a number of such communities in highland Peru and Mexico.

The reader will be tempted immediately to characterize this type of community as "Indian" and perhaps to ask if we are not dealing here with a survival from pre-Columbian times. Since structure rather than culture content is our main concern here, we shall emphasize the features of organization which may make this type of community like corporate communities elsewhere, rather than characterize it in purely ethnographic terms. Moreover, it is necessary to explain the persistence of any survival over a period of three hundred years. As we hope to show below, persistence of "Indian" culture content seems to have depended primarily on maintenance of this structure. Where the structure collapsed, traditional cultural forms quickly gave way to new alternatives of outside derivation.

The distinctive characteristic of the corporate peasant community is that it represents a bounded social sysem with clear-cut limits, in relations to both outsiders and insiders. It has structural identity over time. Seen from the outside, the community as a whole carries on a series of activities and upholds certain "collective representations." Seen from within, it defines the rights and duties of its members and prescribes large segments of their behavior.

Fortes recently analyzed groupings of a corporate character based on kinship. The corporate peasant community resembles these other units in its corporate character but is no longer held together by kinship. It may once have been based on kinship units of a peculiar type, and features of kinship organization persist, such as a tendency toward local endogamy or in occasionally differential rights of old and new settlers. Nevertheless, the corporate community in Latin America represents the end product of a long process of reorganization which began in pre-Columbian times and was carried through under Spanish rule. As a result of the conquest any kinship feature which this type of community may have had was relegated to secondary importance. Members of the community were made co-owners of a landholding corporation, a co-ownership which implied systematic participation in communal political and religious affairs.

Several considerations may have prompted Crown policy toward such communities. First, the corporate community performing joint labor services for an overlord was a widespread characteristic of European economic feudalism. In trying to curtail the political power of a potential new landholding class in the Spanish colonies the Crown took over management of Indian communities in order to deny the conquerors direct managerial control over labor. The Crown attempted to act as a go-between and labor contractor for both peasant community and landowner. Second, the corporate community fitted well into the political structure of the Spanish dynastic state, which attempted to incorporate each subcultural group and to define its radius of activity by law. This enabled the Crown to marshal the resources of such a group as an organized unit, and to impose its economic, social, and religious controls by a type of indirect rule. Third, the corporate structure of the peasant communities permitted the imposition of communal as well as of individual burdens of forced labor and taxation. This was especially important in view of the heavy loss of labor power through flight or disease. The imposition of the burden on a community rather than on individuals favored maintenance of a steady level of production.

Given this general historical background, what is the distinctive set of relationships characteristic of the corporate peasant community?

The first of these is location on *marginal land*. Needs within the larger society which might compel the absorption and exploitation of this land are weak or absent, and the existing level of technology and transportation may make such absorption difficult. In other words, the amount of energy required to destroy the existing structure of the corporate community and to reorganize it at present outweighs the capacity of the larger society.

In the corporate peasant community marginal land tends to be exploited by means of a *traditional technology* involving the members of the community in the continuous physical effort of manual labor.

Marginal location and traditional technology together limit the production power of the community, and thus its ability to produce cash crops for the market. This in turn limits the number of goods brought in from the outside which the community can afford to consume. The community is *poor*.

Within this economic setting, the corporate structure of the community is retained by community *jurisdiction over the free disposal of land*. Needless to say, community controls tend to be strongest where land is owned in common and reallocated among members every year. But even where private property in land is the rule within the community, as is common today, the communal taboo on sale of land to outsiders severely limits the degree to which factors outside the community can affect the structure of private property and related class differences within the community. Land is thus not a complete commodity. The taboo on sale of land to outsiders may be reinforced by other communal rights, such as gleaning rights or the right to graze cattle on any land within the community after the harvest.

The community possesses a system of power which embraces the male members of the community and makes the achievement of power a matter of community decision rather than a matter of individually achieved status. This system of power is often tied into a religious system or into a series of interlocking religious systems. The *political-religious system* as a whole tends to define the boundaries of the community and acts as a rallying point and symbol of collective unity. Prestige within the community is largely related to rising from religious office to office along a prescribed ladder of achievement. Conspicuous consumption is geared to this communally approved system of power and religion rather than to private individual show. This makes individual conspicuous consumption incidental to communal expenditure. Thus the community at one and the same time levels differences of wealth which might intensify class divisions within the community to the detriment of the corporate structure and symbolically reasserts the strength and integrity of its structure before the eyes of its members.

The existence of such leveling mechanisms does not mean that class divisions within the corporate community do not exist. But it does mean that the class structure must find expression within the boundaries set by the community. The corporate structure acts to impede the mobilization of capital and wealth within the community in terms of the outside world which employs wealth capitalistically. It thus blunts the impact of the main opening wedge calculated to set up new tensions within the community and thus to hasten its disintegration.

While striving to guarantee its members some basic livelihood within the confines of the community, the lack of resources and the very need to sustain the system of religion and power economically force the community to enter the outside market. Any imposition of taxes, any increase in expenditures relative to the productive capacity of the community, or the internal growth of the population on a limited amount of land, must result in *compensatory economic reactions in the field of production*. These may be wage labor, or the development of some specialization which has competitive advantages within the marginal economy of such communities. These may include specializations in trade, as among the Zapotecs, Tarascans, or Collas, or in witchcraft, as among the Killawallas or Kamilis of Bolivia.

In the field of consumption, increases of expenditures relative to the productive capacity of the economic base are met with attempts to decrease expenditure by decreasing consumption. This leads to the establishment of a culturally recognized standard of consumption which consciously excludes cultural alternative. By reducing alternative items of consumption, along with the kinds of behavior and ideal norms which make use of these items of consumption, the community reduces the threat to its integrity. Moore and Tumin have called this kind of reaction ignorance with a "structural function."

In other words, we are dealing here not merely with a lack of knowledge, an absence of information, but with a *defensive ignorance*, an active denial of outside alternatives which, if accepted, might threaten the corporate structure. Unwillingness to admit outsiders as competitors for land or as carriers of cultural alternatives may account for the prevalent tendency toward community endogamy.

Related to the need to maintain a steady state by decreasing expenditures is the conscious effort to eat and consume less by "pulling in one's belt," while working more. The "exploitation on the self" is culturally institutionalized in what might be called a *cult of poverty*. Hard work and poverty as well as behavior symbolic of these, such as going barefoot or wearing "Indian" clothes, are extolled, and laziness and greed and behavior associated with these vices are denounced.

The increase in output and concomitant restriction of consumption is carried out primarily within the *nuclear family*. The family thus acquires special importance in this kind of community, especially in a modern setting. This is primarily because

on the typical family farm . . . the farmer himself cannot tell you what part of his income comes to him in his capacity as a worker, what in his capacity as a capitalist who has provided tools and implements, or finally what in his capacity as owner of land. In fact, he is not able to tell you how much of his total income stems from his own labors and how much comes from the varied but important efforts of his wife and children.

The family does not carry on cost-accounting. It does not know how much its labor is worth. Labor is not a commodity for it; it does not sell labor within the family. No money changes hands within the family. It acts as a unit of consumption and it can cut its consumption as a unit. The family is thus the ideal unit for the restriction of consumption and the increase of unpaid work.

The economy of the corporate community is congruent, if not structurally linked, with a marketing system of a peculiar sort. Lack of money resources requires that sales and purchases in the market be small. The highland village markets fit groups with low incomes which can buy only a little at a time. Such markets bring together a much larger supply of articles than merchants of any one community could afford to keep continuously in their stores. Most goods in such markets are homemade or locally grown. Local producers thus acquire the needed supplementary income, while the character of the commodities offered for sale reinforces the traditional pattern of consumption. Specialization on the part of villages is evident throughout. Regular market days in regional sequence making for a wider exchange of local produce may be due to the fact that villages producing similar products must find outlets far away, as well as to exchanges of produce between highlands and lowlands. The fact that the goods carried are produced in order to obtain small amounts of needed cash in order to purchase other needed goods is evident in the very high percentage of dealings between producer and ultimate consumer. The market is in fact a means of bringing the two into contact. The role of the nuclear family in production and in the "exploitation of the self" is evident in the high percentage of goods in whose production the individual or the nuclear family completes an entire production cycle.

Paralleling the mechanisms of control which are primarily economic in origin are psychological mechanisms like *institutionalized envy*, which may find expression in various manifestations such as gossip, attacks of the evil eye, or in the fear and practice of witchcraft. The communal organization of the corporate community has often been romanticized; it is sometimes assumed that a communal structure makes for the absence of divisive tensions. Lewis has demonstrated that there is no necessary correlation between communal structure and pervasive good-will among the members of the community. Quite the contrary, it would seem that some form of institutionalized envy plays an important part in such communities. Kluckhohn has shown that fear of witchcraft acts as an effective leveler in Navaho society. A similar relationship obtains in the type of community which we are discussing. Here witchcraft, as well as milder forms of institutionalized envy, have an integrative effect in restraining non-traditional behavior, as long as social relationships suffer no serious disruption. It minimizes disruptive phenomena such as economic mobility, abuse of ascribed power, or individual conspicuous show of wealth. On the individual plane, it thus acts to maintain the individual in equilibrium with his neighbors. On the social plane, it reduces the disruptive influences of outside society.

The need to keep social relationships in equilibrium in order to maintain the steady state of the corporate community is internalized in the individual as strong conscious efforts to adhere to the traditional roles, roles which were successful in maintaining the steady state in the past. Hence there appears a strong tendency on the social psychological level to stress "uninterrupted routine practice of traditional patterns." Such a psychological emphasis would tend to act against overt expressions of individual autonomy, and set up in individuals strong fears against being thrown out of equilibrium.

An individual thus carries the culture of such a community, not merely passively as a social inheritance inherited and accepted automatically, but actively. Adherence to the culture validates membership in an existing society and acts as a passport to participation in the life of the community. The particular traits held help the individual remain within the equilibrium of relationships which maintain the community. Corporate communities produce "distinctive cultural, linguistic, and other social attributes," which Beals has aptly called "plural cultures"; tenacious defense of this plurality maintains the integrity of such communities.

It is needless to add that any aspect relates to any other, and that changes in one would vitally affect the rest. Thus the employment of traditional technology keeps the land marginal from the point of view of the larger society, keeps the community poor, forces a search for supplementary sources of income, and requires high expenditures of physical labor within the nuclear family. The technology is in turn maintained by the need to adhere to traditional roles in order to validate one's membership in the community, and this adherence is produced by the conscious denial of alternative forms of behavior, by institutionalized envy, and by the fear of being thrown out of equilibrium with one's neighbor. The various aspects enumerated thus exhibit a very high degree of covariance.

The second type (2) which we shall discuss comprises peasants who regularly sell a cash crop constituting probably between 50 and 75 percent of their total production. Geographically, this type of peasant is distributed over humid low highlands and tropical lowlands. Present-day use of their environments has been dictated by a shift in demand on the world market for crops from the American tropics during the latter part of the nineteenth century and the early part of the twentieth. On the whole, production for the market by this type of peasant has been in an ascendant phase, though often threatened by intermittent periods of decline and depression.

In seasonally rainy tropical lowlands, these peasants may raise sugar cane. In chronically rainy lowlands, such as northern Colombia or Venezuela or coastal Ecuador, they have tended to grow cocoa or bananas. The development of this peasant segment has been most impressive in humid low highlands, where the standard crop is coffee. This crop is easily grown on both small and large holdings, as is the case in Colombia, Guatemala, Costa Rica, and parts of the West Indies.

Such cash-crop production requires outside capitalization. The amount and kind of capitalization will have important ramifications throughout the particular local adaptation made. Peasants of this type receive such capitalization from the outside, but mainly on a traditional, small-scale, intermittent and speculative basis. Investments are not made either to stabilize the market or to reorganize the apparatus of production and distribution of the peasantry. Few peasant groups of this type have been studied fully by anthropologists, and any discussion of them must to some extent remain conjectural until further work adds to our knowledge. For the construction of this type the writer has relied largely on his own field work in Puerto Rico and on insights gained from studies made in southern Brazil.

The typical structure which serves to integrate this type of peasant segment with other segments and with the larger sociocultural whole we shall here call the "open" community. The open community differs from the corporate peasant community in a number of ways. The corporate peasant community is composed primarily of one subculture, the peasantry. The open community comprises a number of subcultures of which the peasantry is only one, although the most important functional segment. The corporate community emphasizes resistance to influences from without which might threaten its integrity. The open community, on the other hand, emphasizes continuous interaction with the outside world and ties its fortunes to outside demands. The corporate community frowns on individual accumulation and display of wealth and strives to reduce the effects of such accumulation on the communal structure. It resists reshaping of relationships; it defends the traditional equilibrium. The open-ended community permits and expects individual accumulation and display of wealth during periods of rising outside demand and allows this new wealth much influence in the periodic reshaping of social ties.

Historically, the open peasant community arose in response to the rising demand for cash crops which accompanied the development of capitalism in Europe. In a sense, it represents the offshoot of a growing type of society which multiplied its wealth by budding off to form new communities to produce new wealth in their turn. Many peasant communities were established in Latin America by settlers who brought to the New World cultural patterns of consumption and production which from the outset involved them in relations with an outside market. Being a Spaniard or Portuguese meant more than merely speaking Spanish or Portuguese or adhering to certain kinds of traditional behavior and ideal norms. It implied participation in a complex system of hierarchical relationships and prestige which required the consumption of goods that could be produced only by means of a complicated division of labor and had to be acquired in the market. No amount of Indian blankets delivered as tribute could make up for the status gained by the possession of one shirt of Castilian silk, or for a small ruffle of Cambrai lace. Prestige goods as well as necessities like iron could only be bought with money, and the need for money drove people to produce for an outside market. The demand for European goods by Spanish colonists was enormous and in turn caused heavy alterations in the economic structure of the mother country. In the establishment of the open community, therefore, the character of the outside society was a major determinant from the beginning.

It would be a mistake, moreover, to visualize the development of the world market in terms of continuous and even expansion, and to suppose therefore that the line of development of particular peasant communities always leads from lesser involvement in the market to more involvement. This line of reasoning would seem to be especially out of place in the case of Latin America where the isolation and homogeneity of the "folk" are often secondary, that is to say, follow in time after a stage of much contact and heterogeneity. Redfield has recognized aspects of this problem in his recent category of "remade folk." Such a category should cover not only the Yucatecan Indians who fled into the isolation of the bush but also groups of settlers with a culture of basically Iberian derivation which were once in the mainstream of commercial development, only to be left behind on its poverty-stricken margins.

Latin America has been involved in major shifts and fluctuations of the market since the period of initial European conquest. It would appear, for example, that a rapid expansion of commercial development in New Spain during the sixteenth century was followed by a "century of depression" in the seventeenth. The slack was taken up again in the eighteenth century, with renewed shrinkage and disintegration of the market in the early part of the nineteenth. During the second part of the nineteenth century and the beginning of the twentieth, many Latin American countries were repeatedly caught up in speculative booms of cash-crop production for foreign markets, often with disastrous results in the case of market failure. Entire communities might find their market gone overnight, and revert to the production of subsistence crops for their own use.

Two things seem clear from this discussion. First, in dealing with present-day Latin America it would seem advisable to beware of treating production for subsistence and production for the market as two progressive stages of development. Rather, we must allow for the cyclical alternation of the two kinds of production within the same community and realize that from the point of view of the community both kinds may be alternative responses to changes in conditions of the outside market. This means that a synchronic study of such a community is insufficient, because it cannot reveal how the community can adapt to such seemingly radical changes. Second, we must look for the mechanisms which make such changes possible.

In the corporate peasant community, the relationships of individuals and kin groups within the community are bounded by a common structure. We have seen that the community aims primarily at maintaining an equilibrium of roles within the community in an effort to keep intact its outer boundary. Maintenance of the outer boundary reacts in turn on the stability of the equilibrium within it. The open community lacks such a for-

malized corporate structure. It neither limits its membership nor insists on a defensive boundary. Quite the contrary, it permits free permeation by outside influences.

In contrast to the corporate peasant community where the community retains the right to review and revise individual decisions, the open community lends itself to rapid shifts in production because it is possible to mobilize the peasant and to orient him rapidly toward the expanding market. Land is usually owned *privately*. Decisions for change can be made by individual families. Property can be mortgaged, or pawned, in return for capital. The community *qua* community cannot interfere in such change.

As in the corporate peasant community, land tends to be marginal and technology primitive. Yet functionally both land and technology are elements in a different complex of relationships. The buyers of peasant produce have an interest in the continued "backwardness" of the peasant. Reorganization of his productive apparatus would absorb capital and credit which can be spent better in expanding the market by buying means of transportation, engaging middlemen, etc. Moreover, by keeping the productive apparatus unchanged, the buyer can reduce the risk of having his capital tied up in the means of production of the peasant holding, if and when the bottom drops out of the market. The buyers of peasant produce thus trade increasing productivity per man-hour for the lessened risks of investment. We may say that the *marginality of land* and the *poor technology* are here a function of the speculative market. In the case of need, the investor merely withdraws credit, while the peasant returns to subsistence production by means of his traditional technology.

The fact the cash-crop production can be undertaken on peasant holdings without materially reorganizing the productive apparatus implies furthermore that the amount of cash crop produced by each peasant will tend to be *small,* as will be the income which he receives after paying off all obligations. This does not mean that the aggregate amounts of such production cannot reach respectable sums, nor that the amounts of profit accruing to middlemen from involvement in such production need be low.—

In this cycle of subsistence crops and cash crops, subsistence crops guarantee a stable minimum livelihood, where cash crops promise higher money returns but involve the family in the hazards of the fluctuating market. The peasant is always concerned with the problem of striking some sort of balance between subsistence production and cash-crop production. Preceding cycles of cash-crop production have enabled him to buy goods and services which he cannot afford if he produces only for his own subsistence. Yet an all-out effort to increase his ability to buy more goods and services of this kind may spell his end as an independent agricultural producer. His tendency is thus to rely on a basic minimum of subsistence production and to expand his cash purchases only slowly. Usually he can rely on traditional norms of consumption which define a decent standard of living in terms of a fixed number of culturally standardized needs. Such needs are of course not only economic but may include standardized expenditures for religious or recreational purposes, or for hospitality. Nor are these needs static. Viewing the expansion of the market from the point of view of subsistence, however, permits the peasant to expand his consumption only slowly.

In cutting down on money expenditures, he defers purchases of new goods, and distributes his purchases over a long period of time. The peasant standard of living is undergoing change but the rate of that change is slow.

The cultural yardstick enables him to limit the rate of expansion but also permits him to retrench when he has overextended himself economically. As in the corporate peasant community, the unit within which consumption can best be restricted while output is stepped up is again the *nuclear family*.

This *modus operandi* reacts back on his technology and on his ability to increase his cash income. The buyer of peasant produce knows that the peasant will be slow in expanding his demand for money. He can therefore count on accumulating his largest share of gain during the initial phase of a growing market, a factor which adds to the speculative character of the economy.

Peasants who are forced overnight to reorient their production from the production of subsistence crops for their own use to cash-crop production are rarely able to generate the needed capital themselves. It must be pumped into the peasant segment from without, either from another segment within the community, or from outside the community altogether. The result is that when cash-crop production grows important, there is a tightening of bonds beween town and country. Urban families become concerned with the production and distribution of cash crops and tie their own fate to the fate of the cash crop. In a society subject to frequent fluctuations of the market but possessed of little fluid capital, there are few formal institutional mechanisms for insuring the flow of capital into peasant production. In a more highly capitalized society, the stock market functions as an impersonal governor of relationships between investors. Corporations form, merge, or dissolve according to the dictates of this governor. In a society where capital accumulation is low, the structure of incorporation tends to be weak or lacking. More important are the *informal alliances of families and clients* which polarize wealth and power at any given time. Expansion of the market tends to involve the peasant in one or the other of these blocs of family power in town. These blocs, in turn, permit the rapid diffusion of capital into the countryside, since credit is guaranteed by personal relationships between creditor and debtor. Peasant allegiance then acts further to reinforce the social and political position of a given family bloc within the urban sector.

When the market fails, peasants and urban patrons both tend to be caught in the same downward movement. Open communities of the type we are analyzing here are therefore marked by the repeated "circulation of the elite." Blocs of wealth and power form, only to break up and be replaced by similar blocs coming to the fore. The great *concern with status* is related to this type of mobility.

Status on the social plane measures the position in the trajectory of the family on the economic plane. To put it in somewhat oversimplified terms, status in such a society represents the "credit rating" of the family. The economic circulation of the elite thus takes the form of shifts in social status. Such shifts in social and economic position always involve an urban and a rural aspect. If the family cannot find alternate economic supports, it loses prestige within the urban sector, and is sooner or later abandoned by its peasant clientele who must needs seek other urban patrons.

We are thus dealing with a type of community which is continuously faced with alignments, circulation and realignments, both on the socioeconomic and political level. Since social, economic, and political arrangements are based primarily on personal ties, such fluctuations act to redefine personal relationships, and such personal relationships are in turn watched closely for indices of readjustment. Relations between two individuals do not symbolize merely the respective statuses and roles of the two concerned; they involve a whole series of relations which must be evaluated and readjusted if there is any indication of change. This "overloading" of personal relations produces two types of behavior: behavior calculated to retain social status, and a type of behavior which for want of a better term might be called "redefining" behavior, behavior aimed at altering the existing state of personal relationships. Both types will be present in any given social situation, but the dominance of one over the other will be determined by the relative stability or instability of the economic base. Status behavior is loaded with a fierce consciousness or the symbols of status, while "redefining" behavior aims at testing the social limits through such varied mechanisms as humor, invitations to share drinks or meals, visiting, assertions of individual worth, proposals of marriage, and so forth. The most important of these types of behavior, quite absent in the corporate community, consists in the ostentatious exhibition of commodities purchased with money.

This type of redefining behavior ramifies through other aspects of the culture. Wealth is its prerequisite. It is therefore most obvious in the ascendant phases of the economic cycle, rather than when the cycle is leveling off. Such accumulation of goods and the behavior associated with it serves as a challenge to existing relations with kin folk, both real and fictitious, since it is usually associated with a reduction in relations of reciprocal aid and hospitality on which these ties are based.

This disruption of social ties through accumulation is inhibited in the corporate peasant community, but can go on unchecked in the type of community which we are considering. Here forms of envy such as witchcraft are often present, but not institutionalized as in the first type of community. Rather, fear of witchcraft conforms to the hypothesis proposed by Passin that

in any society where there is a widespread evasion of a cultural obligation which results in the diffusion of tension and hostility between people, and further if this hostility is not expressed in overt physical strife. . . . sorcery or related non-physical techniques will be brought into play.

Fear of witchcraft in such a community may be interpreted as a product of guilt on the part of the individual who is himself disrupting ties which are valued, coupled with a vague anxiety about the loss of stable definitions of situations in terms of clearcut status. At the same time, the new possessions and their conspicuous show serves not only to redefine status and thus to reduce anxiety but also as a means of expressing hostility against those who do not own the same goods. The "invidious" comparisons produced by this hostility in turn produce an increase in the rate of accumulation.

SUGGESTIONS FOR FURTHER RESEARCH

The two model types discussed above by no means exhaust the variety of peasant segments to be found in Latin America. They were singled out for consideration because I felt most competent to deal with them in terms of both time and field experience. Pleading greater ignorance and less assurance, I should nevertheless like to take this opportunity to indicate the rough outlines of some other types which may deserve further investigation. These types may seem to resemble the "open" communities just discussed. It is nevertheless important to conceptualize them separately. We may expect them to differ greatly in their basic functional configurations, due to the different manners of their integration with larger sociocultural systems, and to the different histories of their integration.

Thus, it seems that within the same geographical area occupied by the second type, above, there exists a third type of peasant (3) who resembles the second also in that a large percentage of his total production is sold on the market. This percentage is probably higher than that involved in the second case; between 90 and 100 percent of total production may go directly into the market. This peasant segment seems to differ from the second one in the much greater stability of its market and in much more extensive outside capitalization. Much of the market is represented by the very high aggregate demand of the United States, and United States capital flows into such peasant segments through organizations such as the United Fruit Company. In the absence of foreign investment, capital may be supplied by new-style local groups of investors of the kind found in the coffee industry of Antioqueno, Colombia. Anthropologists have paid little attention to this type of peasantry.

(4) A fourth type is perhaps represented by peasants who habitually sell the larger part of their total production in restricted but stable local markets. Such markets are especially apt to occur near former political and religious settlements in the high highlands which play a traditional role in the life of the country but do not show signs of commercial or industrial expansion. Outside capitalization of such production would appear to be local in scale, but a relatively stable market may offer a certain guarantee of small returns. Into this category may fit groups relatively ignored by anthropologists, such as many Mexican *ranchero* communities or the settlers of the Bogota Basin.

(5) The fifth group is perhaps represented by peasants located in a region which once formed a key area of the developing system of capitalism. This region is located in the seasonally rainy tropical lowlands of northeastern Brazil and the West Indies. Here sugar plantations based on slave labor flourished in the sixteenth, seventeenth, and eighteenth centuries. These plantations were weakened by a variety of factors, such as the end of the slave trade and the political independence movement in Latin America, and most of them were unable to compete with other tropical areas. Where the old plantation system was not replaced by modern "factories in the field," as has been the case in northeastern Brazil and on parts of the south coast of Puerto Rico, we today find peasant holdings as "residual bits" of former large-scale organizations which have disintegrated, as in Haiti or Jamaica. The economy of such areas has been contracting since the end of slavery, with the result that this type of peasant seems to lean heavily toward the production of subsistence crops for home use or toward the production and distribution of very small amounts of cash produce.

(6) A sixth group is perhaps represented by the foreign colonists who introduced changes in technology into the forested environment of southern Brazil and southern Chile. These areas seem to show certain similarities. In both areas, the settlers chose the forest rather than the open plain for settlement and colonization. In both areas, colonization was furthered by the respective central governments to create buffers against military pressures from outside and against local movements for autonomy. In both areas, the settlers found themselves located on a cultural ecological frontier. In southern Brazil, they faced cultural pressures from the Pampa and from the surrounding population of casual cash-crop producers. In southern Chile, they confronted the Araucanians. In both areas,

an initial period of deculturation and acculturation would seem to have been followed by increasing integration into the national market through the sale of cash crops.

(7) A seventh type is perhaps made up of peasants who live on the outskirts of the capitalist market, on South America's "pioneer fringe." This would include people who raise crops for the market in order to obtain strategic items of consumption, like clothing, salt, or metal, which they cannot produce themselves. The technological level characterizing this type of peasant seems to be low; his agriculture would appear to be mainly of the slash-and-burn type. His contacts with the market seem to be sporadic rather than persistent, and the regularity with which he produces a cash crop seems to depend both on uncertain outside demand and on his periodic need for an outside product.

Due largely to the requirements of the agricultural system, families live in dispersal, and the family level is probably the chief level of integration. Since there is no steady market, land lacks commercial value, and occupancy is relatively unhampered. A family may occupy land for as long as required and abandon it with decreasing yields. Such circulation through the landscape would require large amounts of land and unrestricted operation. Concepts of fixed private property in land would tend to be absent or non-functional. The land may belong to somebody who cannot make effective commercial use of it at the moment, and permits temporary squatting.

Once again I want to express the caution that the above list represents only suggestions. Further work will undobutedly lead to the formulation of additional or other types, and to the construction of models to deal with transitional phenomena, such as changes from one type of segment to another. Since segments relate with other segments, further inquiry will also have to take account of the ways in which type segments interrelate with each other and of the variety of community structures which such combinations can produce.

33. THE AGRICULTURAL BASIS OF URBAN CIVILIZATION IN MESOAMERICA

ANGEL PALERM

Reprinted by permission from Irrigation Civilizations in Mesoamerica *(Social Science Monograph 1, Pan American Union, Washington, D.C.), published by the Pan American Union and the General Secretariat of the Organization of American States. Angel Palerm is Professor of Ethnology at the Escuela Nacional de Antropologia e História de Mexico, and Director of the Escuela de Ciencias Políticas y Sociales at the Universidad Iberoamerican, Mexico City. One of his principal research interests has been the ethnography and ethnohistory of urban civilizations in the New World. Among his books are* The Tajin Totonac *and* La Agricultura y los Origenes de la Civilización en Mesoamérica.*

■ In this selection we consider some of the special factors involved in irrigation agriculture as a strategy of adaptation. I have assumed a particular point of view in this book toward large-scale irrigation networks—that they are the products rather than the causes of centralized political systems—but it must be reiterated that this is a point of controversy among anthropologists, many of whom hold the opposite view. In this selection (one of the sources for my point of view) Palerm presents the historical materials that support this contention and unravels the skein of political and technological factors it involves. He also points to many salient features of the organization of social relations within the local community that are aspects of this adaptation.

Palerm's discussion of the effects of large-scale irrigation networks on the development of urban centers points to another important feature of irrigation agriculture as a strategy of adaptation. Without these hydraulic systems, bringing water to warm and dry zones, urban concentrations would not be possible. Urbanization is a characteristic of state organization, not of a particular level of technological development as such. Urban centers are stimulated by the technologies that are made possible by the policies of centralized political systems. This hypothesis illustrates the idea that the appearance of a state in the course of cultural evolution is an adaptational development that significantly increases people's freedom from the restrictions of their habitats. The state makes it possible for urban centers to develop in regions that would otherwise be inhospitable to them.

Many of these ideas are explored in greater detail in the papers by Heizer, Sanders, Wolf and Palerm, Hole, and Adams in Section V of the companion volume to this book. There is an excellent discussion of the incomparable chinampa-system of Mexico in "The Chinampas of Mexico," by Michael D. Coe (*Scientific American,* 211[1] [July, 1964]: 90-98). An important report on the irrigated pre-Columbian city of Teotihuacan—which now seems to have been an urban center larger than imperial Rome—is provided by René Millon in "Teotihuacán" (*Scientific American,* 216[6] [June, 1967]: 38-48).

Counterpoised to Robert McC. Adams' *The Evolution of Urban Society* (Chicago: Aldine, 1966) is Karl Wittfogel's *Oriental Despotism* (New Haven: Yale University Press, 1957). The latter work presents a view contrary to Palerm's about the relationship between political organization and large-scale irrigation networks. Another relevant work is "Inca Culture at the Time of the Spanish Conquest," by John H. Rowe, in Volume 2 of *Handbook of South American Indians* (Julian H. Steward, ed.; New York: Cooper Square Publishers). A study in depth of pre-Hispanic Mexico is provided by Eric R. Wolf's *Sons of the Shaking Earth* (Chicago: University of Chicago Press, 1959).

An exciting prehistoric system of irrigation is described in "Ancient Ridged Fields of the San Jorge River Floodpain, Columbia," by James J. Parsons and William A. Bowen (*Geographical Review,* 56 [1966]: 317-43). The authors describe an extensive system of parallel ridges that served as cultivation platforms in a seasonally flooded plain; the parallel ridges were arranged in various patterns over an area of about 70 miles by 20 miles. This adaptation dates back to about 3090 B.C. More extensive archeological work will have to be conducted to learn the nature of the political system that was associated with this method of cultivation. ■

THE IDEA THAT a relationship exists between irrigation agriculture and the emergence of pre-Columbian urban civilization in Meso-america has been advanced by several writers. The introduction of irrigation agriculture creates the possibility of increased population density. This paper will be concerned with the classification of Mesoamerican agricultural systems in their relation to density of population and types of settlement patterns, rural and urban. Likewise the characteristics of Mesoamerican irrigation will be described and the importance of irrigation in Meso-america. Out of these considerations the circumstances which made the Valley of Mexico the core of the Central Area of Meso-america will be laid bare.

I. THE AGRICULTURAL SYSTEMS AND SETTLEMENT PATTERNS IN MESOAMERICA

The typology proposed here establishes three fundamental agricultural systems: slash-and-burn (*roza*), fallowing (*barbecho*) and irrigation (considering the *chinampas* as a specialized form of irrigation). Our description is based on historical sources and the techniques used today by some native groups. The data on productivity and demographic concomitants and settlement rely mainly on modern fieldwork, but can be checked against information obtained from historical documents.

THE SLASH-AND-BURN (ROZA) SYSTEM

This consists in clearing a section of the forest at a time propitious to the drying of the cut vegetation which is then set on fire. After the fire, the soil is seeded with a digging stick and later weeded periodically. After a varying but generally short time-span, the soil is exhausted and the yield decreases. The field is then abandoned to permit the regeneration of the soil and the return of the forest. A new section is then cut to continue the agricultural cycle. In a very general way, this is the slash-and-burn system typical of the tropical forest of Mesoamerica.

Tajin, a Totonac settlement of Veracruz, Mexico, gave us an opportunity to study the effects of such a system despite the modifications introduced since the Conquest. They are briefly summarized below.

On the average, each Tajin family cultivates a *milpa* of 1½ hectares, which yields two annual maize harvests. During the initial two or three years the yields are good. After that the *milpa* is frequently replaced by a vanilla patch which requires the growth of some selected trees. After ten or twelve years the field is abandoned and it enjoys a complete rest for ten or twelve additional years. We thus have a cycle: *milpa*—vanilla patch (with partial return of the forest)—complete rest. This cycle lasts twenty-four years.

The existence of this cycle implies that 12 hectares of cultivable land are needed for each hectare and a half in actual cultivation. These requirements would be smaller in the absence of the maize-vanilla rotation. On the other hand, the vanilla period also allows for the partial regeneration of the soil and the forest, and vanilla growing, by improving the economic condition of the cultivators, decreases the size of the *milpa* required per family.

The agricultural pattern functions successfully as long as the cycle is respected and there is sufficient land. If the cycle be contracted, the regeneration of the soil is not adequate. An increase of population is thus only tolerable up to a certain limit, beyond which land shortages appear. If the cycle is shortened, decreased productivity can be expected. The only solution consists in the emigration of some families in search of new lands.

Naturally, there is a direct relation between population density and the agricultural system, as well as the settlement pattern. The inhabitants can choose between two possibilities: scattered or concentrated settlements. If the latter be picked, the community will tend to cultivate first the land closer to town. In time, the cultivated area is farther and farther away and the distances to the maize fields are increasingly inconvenient. Eventually a process of disintegration through small migrations takes place, which may lead to the founding of a new town. Sometimes, again, the migration takes place in a body. Obviously such a system is possible only in the case of small communities. This situation apparently still prevails west of Tajin, in the spurs of the Sierra Madre Oriental.

If a scattered-type settlement be selected, the periodic "migration" of the maize fields takes place in a circle around the house, as it does in Tajin. The existence of a small residential nucleus which sometimes functions as a political, commercial and ceremonial center does not modify the dispersion pattern. One hundred sixty-seven families live away from the Tajin residential nucleus and only thirty-five within it.

THE "FALLOWING"
(BARBECHO) SYSTEM

This method of cultivation also begins with the clearing and burning of existing vegetation. The *milpa* planted on this field retains its productivity as long as the slash-and-burn maize patch, occasionally longer. The important difference consists in the fact that the fallow periods are incomparably shorter. Frequently it is enough for the rest period to match the number of years under cultivation. The main reason for the disparity is apparently environmental. The "fallowing" system is typically found in cool and temperate parts of Mexico.

We had the opportunity to compare this system with that of Tajin at Eloxochitlan, a Totonac town in the highlands of Puebla, in Mexico. . . .

We find two kinds of *milpa* in Eloxochitlan: the garden or *calmil* (the milpa of the house) and the milpa proper. Both yield only one crop a year. Productivity per harvest of a fallowed milpa is pretty much the same as that of a slash-and-burn milpa. It is cultivated usually for two or three years and left to rest for about the same period. The calmi is harvested annually; it is fertilized with garbage, the dung of domestic animals and with dry leaves and twigs. The yield per harvest from a calmil is double that of a slash-and-burn or fallowed milpa.

According to our figures (which naturally take into account annual yields as well as productivity per harvest), an Eloxochitlan family needs 2 hectares of milpa and a half-hectare of calmil in order to reach the annual yield of maize which can be harvested in Tajin from 1½ hectares. But while the cultivation cycle in Tajin demands 12 hectares of cultivable land per family, in Eloxochitlan it requires only 6½ hectares.

Obviously, the agricultural system of Eloxochitlan allows a greater density of population (almost double) than that of Tajin. In addition, the permanent nature of the calmil (which lives in symbiosis with the house and acts as its pantry) and the almost perennial "fallowed" milpa encourage, if they do not impose, a stability of residence. Almost the whole population of Eloxochitlan lives closely together, within or just outside the political and ceremonial nucleus which contains old, permanent buildings.

THE IRRIGATED SYSTEM

The third element in this comparison is Tecomatepec, a town in the south of the state of Mexico. Here we find, in addition to the fallowing system typical of cool and temperate lands, a recently built irrigation network. Despite such recency, Tecomatepec is located in a zone important for its pre-Hispanic irrigation, which still functions in some places. We found no significant differences between the pre-Hispanic irrigation techniques and those of present-day Tecomatepec.

The water is "bled" from the Calderon river (one of those descending from the

Nevado of Toluca), 36 kilometers away. A canal (*apantle*) was dug, 40 centimeters wide and 30 deep. This work took eleven years. A small dam was then built to intercept the river and redirect part of the water. Maintenance work on this system is continuous. Each rainy period clogs up or destroys a portion of the canal. In addition, some transversal "mouths" of the canal have to be opened, to facilitate the circulation of natural drainage.

Irrigation does not benefit all the inhabitants of Tecomatepec, but rather those who took part in the work. A group of cultivators from Yerbas Buenas, who cooperated with those of Tecomatepec, take part in the maintenance work and use some of the water. In addition to such cooperation between the two towns, special arrangements had to be made with the settlements whose lands are crossed by the canal and with others who share in using Calderon waters.

The need for firm leadership and authority among the irrigation-cultivators of Tecomatepec is evident. In addition to the slow and lasting excavation, the continuous maintenance, the need for formal agreements with other villages, insurance must be made of the equitable distribution of water between neighbors, who take turns at specified times. A system of sanctions for lack of discipline or abuses extends from deprivation of water for a specified period up to complete prohibition.

Productivity of irrigated agriculture (combined at Tecomatepec with a more consistent use of fertilizers) justifies these efforts. The yield is two and a half times greater than that of fallowed land. Also the same field can yield two crops annually: one with irrigation, the other without. Cultivation proceeds continuously; there is no need to "rest" the soil.

According to our figures, the 1½ cultivated hectares needed in Tajin and the 2½ required at Eloxochitlan can be reduced in Techomatepec to 0.86 hectares. The decrease is even more impressive if we compare the cultivable surfaces need per family: 12 hectares in the slash-and-burn system; 6½ in the fallowing-and-calmil areas; 0.86 hectares in

those where it is supplemented by irrigation. According to a communication in 1952 by W. Sanders, in a system relying exclusively on irrigation, like the *chinampas,* the requirements would fall to only 0.37 hectares for commercial cultivation, and to 0.6-0.7 for mixed subsistence and commercial cultivation.

The opportunities for a dense population are greatly increased through irrigation. The system also requires a settled home and the concentration of the residents in the irrigated zone. Like other towns in the irrigated region, Tecomatepec is "urbanized" and has permanent, well-planned buildings.

FINAL COMPARISON
AND CONCLUSION

We have reported on the relations between three traditional agricultural systems, population density and settlement patterns. A community of 100 families needs 1,200 cultivable hectares in a slash-and-burn system; 650 of fallowed land and calmil gardens; 86 hectares in a mixed system of fallowing and irrigation, and between 37 and 70 in a completely irrigated agriculture (chinampas). The corresponding settlement patterns are:

1). Dispersed or small migratory settlements, with frequently changing cornfields in both cases;

2). Stable residence, at times in hamlets, at times scattered; almost permanent cornfields; and

3). Concentrated and thickly settled communities and permanent cornfields (for the last two methods).

II. IRRIGATION AND THE NATURAL AREAS OF MESOAMERICA

The importance of irrigation in Mesoamerica as a fundamental factor in the emergence of an urban civilization can be stated even more emphatically. The earliest urban cultures of the Old World could follow (at least in theory) two alternatives in their agricultural development: either extensive "dry" cultivation or intensive planting with irrigation. Extensive agriculture requires three basic elements unknown in Mesoamerica: the plow, draft animals and adequate means of transport. Maybe one should also add the availability of a metallurgy more advanced than the Mexican. Only a favorable combination of these elements allows the clearance and cultivation of large areas with relatively little labor as well as the necessarily rapid transport of produce in sufficient quantities to feed an urban center.

It seems rather obvious that a rainfall agriculture, never extensive in Mesoamerica, could not accumulate an adequate and constant surplus to maintain the urban centers. It also seems incapable of creating the stimulus required for their development. Both requirements (productive capacity and stimulus) appear with an agriculture based on irrigation, which can develop with a rather primitive metallurgy and in the absence of plows, the wheel or draft animals. Their absence is made up by considerable emphasis on cooperation in work and a measure of political centralization.

CLIMATIC CONDITIONS

Our skepticism about the possible relation between rainfall agriculture and the impressively urban character of Mesoamerica increases when we consider the climatic conditions. Whetten has summarized the main difficulties: (1) two-thirds of the total surface of Mexico is mountainous; only one-third can be considered more or less a plain; of this third the greatest part is too dry for cultivation; (2) rainfall is inadequate for a flourishing, non-irrigated agriculture; 52.1% of the country's land cannot be cultivated without irrigation; on 30.6% the harvest is uncertain almost every year; 10.5% suffers from drought one year in four or five; only 6.8% of the land receives sufficient rain. To which we would add that a significant part of the latter is clad with tropical forests (where slash-and-burn agriculture is practiced).

OROGRAPHIC AND HYDROGRAPHIC CONDITIONS

Roughly speaking, the central part of Mesoamerica has the shape of a triangle. Its northwestern point rests on the mouth of the Santiago river, the northeastern at the mouth of the Panuco and the southern in the isthmian part of Chiapas. The greater part of this territory is made up of mountainous plateaus in which the major river systems originate. Its western and eastern limits are set by the mountains which descend toward the Pacific and the Gulf of Mexico. While the Gulf shore is lined with coastal plains of low elevation, the Pacific coast is close to the sharply rising mountains. This peculiar formation accentuates the torrential quality of the water courses. While the Gulf rivers eventually quiet down on the coastal plain (with occasional catastrophic floods), those flowing to the Pacific have no opportunity to even out; they flood regularly and reach the sea in turbulent fashion.

If we relate this situation to climatic conditions the conclusion is obvious. The waters which would be best for irrigation (those in the Gulf area) flow mainly through zones of rainy, tropical forests. The rivers on the Pacific side, where irrigation is frequently indispensable, are almost uncontrollable, in terms of pre-Hispanic technology. Sometimes, though, their periodic floods make possible some agriculture along their mundated banks.

Things are more propitious on the plateaus. Although the terrain is rough and craggy, there are also some flat surfaces. Even if the rivers are mostly torrential they could sometimes have been brought under control, even in the pre-Hispanic period. Irrigation is absolutely necessary in some places and highly desirable in others, because of climatic conditions. Two other reasons lead us to think that the plateaus are the most favorable locus in the Mesoamerican area for the development of civilization: (1) the existence of permanent water courses fed by the melting snows of the *sierras* and the accumulation of subterranean waters; (2) the presence of lakes which play the triple role of ways of communication, a source of food and the basis for the specialized agriculture of the *chinampas*.

This presentation claims no more than to outline a very general framework within which one can proceed to research and comparison. One could say that the coastal Mexican cultures played a minor role, particularly in the urban period. The key economic, political and military area was on the plateaus.

THE NATURAL ZONES
OF TOTONACAPAN

Wishing to add something more concrete to this discussion, we thought of commenting on a region well known to us. Totonacapan occupies a large part of the center of the state of Veracruz, the north of Puebla and the eastern part of Hidalgo. We can distinguish several natural areas: (1) a coastal zone, hot and dry, with flat grasslands, forming an arid wedge sunk into the rainy tropical forests of Veracruz; (2) a temperate, rainy belt of hills, lying between coast and sierra; (3) a hot and humid zone of tropical rain forests located mostly in the mountains; (4) a rainy, cold area in the highlands of the sierra; (5) another cold and high, but arid and semi-arid zone, sometimes reaching desert proportions, west of the sierra.

Examples of the sites characterizing each zone might be: (1) hot and dry: Cempoala; (2) temperate and rainy: Jalapa; (3) hot and humid: Papantla; (4) cold and rainy: Zacatlan; (5) cold and arid: Tulancingo and Perote, the latter a desert variant.

THE DEMOGRAPHIC AND URBAN
CONDITIONS OF TOTONACAPAN

Our study of population distribution in Totonacapan before 1519 indicates that the greatest density was found in the warm and dry area. We estimate 53-63 inhabitants per square kilometer for the two areas of Cempoala and Jalapa (warm and dry and temperate). Working independently, Sanders arrived at the figures of 75 per square kilometer

for Cempoala and 50 for Jalapa. In the northern part of Totonacapan (Papantla excepted), a hot and rainy zone, our figure was 52-56 inhabitants per square kilometer. Sanders, who includes Papantla, calculates 30.

Even more significant is the distribution of population centers. The sources ascribe 80-120,000 inhabitants to Cempoala; 24,000 to Colipa; 60,000 to Papantla; 120,000 to Jalapa; and lower figures, between 4,000 and 8,000 to Almolonga, Chapultepec, Chila, Jilotepec, Matlatlan, Miahuatlan, Naolinco, Tepetlan and Tlacolulan.

To what extent can we consider the four larger settlements to be true urban centers? It is quite probable that not all the population was completely urbanized and that the figures include the outskirts and even some none-too-well integrated hamlets. Yet it is evident that the 80,000-120,000 inhabitants of Cempoala are assigned to the city, not to the province, for which we have other figures (250,000 inhabitants). Also, the first descriptions of Cempoala portray a completely urbanized pattern: houses, palaces, temples, inner courts, streets, plazas, distribution of running water to private houses and gardens, etc. The evidence for Colipa is weaker as we have no data beyond the population figure: 24,000. This undoubtedly could be verified through excavation.

The case of Papantla is quite different. The source is ambiguous and the figure quoted could be attributed to either a town or a province; it is unlikely that a city of 60,000 inhabitants would have received so little notice from the chroniclers. Archaeological evidence is also negative. The pre-Hispanic culture of Papantla is not that of an urban society. The *Relación Geográfica* of Papantla describes a scattered population. It is almost certain that Papantla was the ceremonial and political center of a scattered people. It is well described by Torquemada. He indicates, first, that not all the ancient inhabitants of New Spain lived in cities; many lived dispersed and scattered, for example the Totonacs. "But one must notice that in some of these provinces the towns which were the capital or the metropolis of the nation or province were somewhat more ordered than the other towns or settlements subjected to them. . . . In this main agglomeration or capital they used to have their temples and worship. . . . The lord and king lived here and their houses were very luxurious: nearby were the houses of the important and noble folk; and although there were no actual streets, the houses were built with some alignment. . . . And such a settlement (somewhat confused and scattered) had one hundred and two hundred houses, sometimes more and sometimes less; the other folk (I mean the rest of the nation or county) who belonged to this capital lived everywhere, over hills and mountains, through valleys and ravines."

The case of Jalapa presents no greater difficulties. The figure quoted (120,000 inhabitants) must be attributed to both a center, with no more than a tenth of the total population, and a series of dependent rural communities and hamlets. Here again we find a description which is likely to be close to the truth. Written by Hernan Cortes, it refers to Jico, a town not far from Jalapa: "A well-fortified town, built in a strong place, because it is on the slope of a steep cliff . . . and on the plain are many villages and ranches of about five hundred and three hundred and two hundred cultivators, all in all about five to six thousand warriors."

The remaining places mentioned are more likely villages and towns and not true cities. With Armillas, we consider the town, *villa,* an intermediary form between village and city, a transition between rural and urban life.

To summarize: (1) True cities are found in Totonacapan apparently only in the hot and dry region; along with such urban developments we find considerable concentration of towns and the greatest population density. (2) There is no evidence of urban centers in the hot and humid areas; population density was low and settlements scattered with occasional ceremonial and political centers. (3) While we do not find urban centers in the temperate rainy zone, there is evidence of towns and well-planned ceremonial centers, frequently set up as fortresses. To all this we can also add: (4) the cold and rainy

area seems to present a situation similar to the temperate and rainy; (5) the pattern of settlement in the cold and dry zone is similar to that of the hot and dry one.

In conclusion, the greatest density of population and the only true urban development in Totonacapan (with its great variety of natural regions) is located in a warm and dry zone, where we also find the only irrigation system known from the Totonac area. One should also mention that irrigation in this zone benefited from some favorable conditions: (1) level terrain; (2) small rivers, an exceptional condition along the Gulf Coast; (3) permanent water courses, coming in part from snows, very infrequent along the Coast. Urban development may also have been stimulated through trade with the very distinct natural regions nearby, the proximity of the sea and the availability of water transport. In the cold and arid and semi-arid zones there may have existed another urban center in which the Totonac had apparently little or no part to play.

To what extent can these conclusions about Totonacapan be extended to include Mesoamerica? Our impression is that a measure of careful generalization is possible. We need a Mesoamerican framework which would combine natural areas with the cultural and which would formulate a systematic relationship between cultivation systems, population and urbanization, utilizing ethnographic, historical and archaelogical data.

III. IRRIGATION IN THE CENTRAL ZONE OF MESOAMERICA

It seemed quite obvious that irrigation agriculture provided optimum conditions for urban development in Mesoamerica. We then decided to study the early sources to determine the distribution of irrigation. The following sources were utilized: (1) *Anales de Cuauhtitlán;* (2) *Relación del origen de los indios* . . . ; (3) Ixtlilxochitl; (4) Tezozomoc; (5) Cortés; (6) Sahagún; (7) *Epistolario de Nueva España*; (8) Gómara; (9)

Suma de visitas; (10) Lebrón de Quiñones; (11) *Relaciones geográficas;* and (12) Ponce.

It is impossible to enumerate here all the villages with irrigation which we have identified. We have done so elsewhere. Here we will indicate only the overall results, grouping the villages within the various states of the modern Mexican republic. In Colima—10; Federal District—8; Guanajuato—1; Guerrero—34; Hidalgo—19; Jalisco—50; Mexico—34; Michoacan—24; Morelos—5; Nayarit—18; Oaxaca—54; Puebla—29; Queretaro—1; Veracruz—5; Zacatecas—2; a total of 294.

To this list one should add villages which are reported to have *huertas* (gardens). We assume that huerta implies some kind of irrigation. Armillas has argued in the same sense. The evidence is reinforced by the fact that in the majority of cases the garden under discussion was planted with *cacao* in regions where this plant needs irrigation (see below). In Colima—14; Federal District—3; Guerrero—8; Jalisco—9; Michoacan—1; Morelos—1; Nayarit—1; Oaxaca—2; Veracruz—1; a total of 40.

The distribution of cacao cultivation in Mesoamerica will help us to fill in the outline. Can one say with any certainty that a mention of this crop, even if no "garden" is reported, refers to irrigation? Armillas writes: "at least in the western part of Mesoamerica, when the historical sources refer to *cacao* grown by the natives there is either explicit mention of irrigation or the indirect reference to *huertas* of *cacao;* when we find a reference to *cacao* in this region which does not specify the techniques of cultivation we can be sure that it is accompanied by irrigation."

One must be careful in using such references to cacao when they refer to areas other than the ones where irrigation was indispensable. Father Ponce emphasizes that "the Indians [plant] their *cacao* orchards where there is water to irrigate them," but he also mentions the province of Yucatan as a place where cacao grew without irrigation "in valleys and in wet and shady spots, though there is little of it and it gives little fruit." We could add to Yucatan practically the whole coast of the Gulf of Mexico, although apparently cacao cultivation of any commercial importance extended only as far north as the Papaloapan river. We know, for example, that in Usila and Chinantla much cacao was grown, taking advantage of the humidity along the riverbanks. Villages where cacao was grown and irrigation seems certain: in Chiapas—4; Colima—7; Guerrero—11; Jalisco—9; Michoacan—1; Nayarit—7; Oaxaca—3; a total of 42.

A fourth possible list would include the villages where *acequias* (canals and ditches) are mentioned, though without any indication of their irrigating use. Actually acequias were used in Mesoamerica for various purposes (communication, defense, drainage, irrigation). Nevertheless, in the cases we have selected the evidence is impressive as they coincide with modern chinampas (which are probably also pre-Hispanic) or show some other indirect association with waterworks. Federal District—4; Mexico—2: a total of 6.

The overall total adds up to 382 different villages (duplications have been eliminated) —an impressive aggregate if we recall the number of sources used. With the exception of some cases culled from the list of acequias the others leave no doubt as to their association with irrigation.

IV. THE ANTIQUITY AND IMPORTANCE OF IRRIGATION IN MESOAMERICA

At least two important questions must be answered before we can definitely relate irrigation to the development of an urban civilization in Mesoamerica: How old is irrigation? What was the level of organization and the importance of these waterworks? We should like to present here some tentative data on this point.

ANTIQUITY

Armillas has suggested that the emergence of urban centers in the Classic Period in Mesoamerica is related to the transformation of agriculture, i.e. irrigation. Two main kinds of evidence seem to support this hypothesis (in addition to the reasons indicated above): (1) the geographic distribution of irrigation; (2) certain archaeological data.

The wide geographic distribution of irrigation may indicate considerable antiquity. Towns practicing irrigation can be found all over the central part of Mesoamerica, with the obvious exception of tropical forests and rainy areas. Outside the central part we find irrigation in the highlands of Guatemala and the Pacific Coast south of the Isthmus of Tehuantepec. Nevertheless, its concentration is greatest in the Valley of Mexico and the headwaters of the Tula, Lerma and Atlixco rivers and in some parts of western Mexico. This clustering and the few irrigated spots in the states of Michoacan and western Guerrero may suggest the possibility of two centers of diffusion: one in western Mexico, the other on the central plateau. This may be due to nothing more than the shortage of data for Michoacan and western Guerrero. According to a personal communication from Sanders in 1952, there may have been another center of diffusion in the highlands of Guatemala.

Other data seem to confirm the suggested relative antiquity of irrigation; Sears' studies of pollen indicate certain fluctuations in the climate of the Valley of Mexico. At the beginning of the Archaic (or Formative) Period the climate was humid, but towards the end of that period it grew progressively drier. This may well be the change which, through its effect on agriculture, stimulated the emergence or extension of irrigation on which the later development of settled centers was based. Another circumstance seems to strengthen the possibility; West and Armillas write that if the *tlateles* of Chalco and Xochimilco are fossil chinampas as has been thought, the age of this technique must be Late Ticoman-Teotihuacan I, which falls within the dry period outlined by Sears. Unfortunately, no archaeological excavation has yet been undertaken to determine the true nature of the tlateles.

The problem of dating the beginning of irrigation in Mesoamerica can be solved only by archaeological means. The historical sources apparently do not take it any further back than the Toltec era.

THE IMPORTANCE OF IRRIGATION

The written sources are somewhat more helpful in evaluating the importance of irrigation, not only insofar as its wide geographic distribution is concerned, but also with regard to its significance for particular localities. In writing about the Tacubaya and Coyoacan region, in the Valley of Mexico, Lopez says: "The natives have been seriously injured by being robbed and having been deprived of their estates, lands and water which supported them . . . particularly the inhabitants of Tacubaya and the Otomi of Coyoacan. . . . They had in ancient times taken some water which they brought along the foothills of the *sierra* . . . with which they irrigated their crops in sterile soil and through which they could cultivate many gardens and grow vegetables on which they subsisted, *which waters supported more than twenty thousand of your majesty's vassals*. These waters the President took away from them or damaged the canals, and near one drainage ditch he built three mills with 6 very powerful stones." In describing Cholula, Cortes says: "This city . . . is located on a plain and it has up to twenty thousand houses within the city proper and about as many on the outskirts. . . . It is a city rich in tilled fields as *it has much land and most of it is irrigated.*" Cortes also says that the valley of Izucar is *all irrigated* with very good canals, well traced and coordinated. We do not claim that irrigation was equally important everywhere. It is more likely that the most common variety was the one described by Mota y Escobar, who says that " they start ditches and small canals for water from the rivers, in some of the towns."

Once again, archaeology has been of little help so far in the solution of these problems. What do we know of the irrigation system of Cempoala which Garcia-Payon seems to have identified recently? And what of those in southern Hidalgo which made possible flourishing centers and a substantial population contrasting with their present poverty? Sauer has shown the importance of irrigation in the valley of Alima, but no archaeologist has followed in his footsteps. The great waterworks (canals, aqueducts, terraces) of the Tetzcutzingo, near Texcoco, Mexico, are still considered by many to have been a resort of King Netzahualcoyotl. Curiously enough, when Cook studied the demographic history of Teotlalpan he did not stop to consider the role of irrigation and its abandonment.

THE SITUATION IN THE
VALLEY OF MEXICO

If one uses historical sources, at the moment the Valley of Mexico is certainly the best place to study the techniques of irrigation. Despite its alluvial soils, the Valley is not very favorable to agriculture. Its climate has been described as semi-desert, with a relative humidity like that of Pachuca (Hidalgo), and with frequent frosts which add to the difficulties. The florescence of civilization in this arid valley, covered in part by lakes and swamps, was a genuine product of human effort comparable to that of other ancient civilizations.

The Valley was a closed basin, its bottom a series of lakes. Cortes described it: "On the ... plain there are two lakes ... and one ... is and the high *sierras*. ... And because this salt of fresh water and the other ... salt water. On one side they are separated by a small chain of very high hills located in the middle of the plain and at one end these lakes meet in a narrow plain found between these hills lake ... has flood and ebb times ... at flood time its water flows to the fresh lake as swiftly as an abundant river and at ebb times the sweet runs to the salt." Gomara adds that "one has nitrous, bitter and pestilent water and the other is sweet and good and fish breed in it. The sale lake ebbs and floods. ... The fresh is higher; and thus the sweet flows in the bad."

This means that whenever the lakes formed a single system the waters tended to flow toward Texcoco, the lowest point, until the "vessel" was full, when they flooded the rest of the basin. The peculiar character of this lacustrian system was due to the fact that some of the waters were fresh while others were nitrous, due to the "slow decomposition of sodic and potasic feldspar which abounds in the rocks of the mountains lining the valley." If this had been true of the lakes of Chalco and Xochimilco, and Zumpango and Jaltocan, the whole lake country would have been useless for agriculture, and particularly for the chinampas. As the high salinity was confined to the lowest part of the area, the useless section was limited to the eastern side of Lake Texcoco and those areas it reached when in flood, usually western Tenochtitlan.

In addition to topography, the river systems determined which would be the areas most likely to be threatened and damaged by the flood of nitrous waters. While Chalco had good-sized rivers of almost constant flow and Xochimilco used mainly springs, Texcoco was the victim of many strong streams of a torrential nature. This means that during drought the fresh water (by its altitude and constant supply) flowed toward the nitrous, but in rainy periods (given the torrents and flooding of Lake Texcoco's rivers) the nitrous waters violently flooded the fresh, threatening even the chinampa area of Xochimilco.

THE TECHNIQUES USED
TO CONQUER THE LAKE

The conclusion seems obvious. The use of chinampas in the fresh section of Lake Texcoco and even the irrigation of the lower reaches were impossible until a system was figured out and built to contain the flood of nitrous waters. Actually, the problem was even more complicated: the fresh waters also had to be kept at a more or less constant level to avoid the drying of the chinampas (which in fact happened after the Conquest) as well as to avoid their being flooded (this was a danger at all times). This applied not only to the sweet section of the central lake, but also to Chalco and Xochimilco and probably Zumpango and Jaltocan. Once the nitrous floods were contained within certain limits, one could start on the gradual conquest of the eastern section of the lake through draining, the rinsing of the nitrous soil, irrigation with fresh water (frequently brought by aqueducts) and the construction of chinampas. The latter were used as house sites, cultivated fields, and, where they crossed the lake, as supports for aqducts.

An outline of the techniques used can be sketched with the help of the sources. The Tenochca completed these remarkable waterworks but there is little doubt that the foundations had been laid by the *chinamperos* of Chalco and Xochimilco and by the Texcocans. We are dealing here with techniques whose roots are deep in the origins of civilization in the Valley. The description of chinampa construction has been made by West and Armillas and need not occupy us here.

THE CONQUEST OF THE LAKE BY THE TENOCHCA

When we first meet them, the Tenochca are established on their island using chinampa techniques to increase the available soil. This was also done by the Tlatelolcas. It is doubtful whether these early "chinampas" were cultivated fields in addition to being house sites. Tenochtitlan, along with the whole western part of the lake, was open to floods of nitrous water. Economic life during the reign of their early kings (Acamapichtli, Huitzilihuitl and Chimalpopoca) does not suggest agriculture (which they had practiced before, away from the lake). Torquemada states that they lived poorly and miserably, eating "seafood" and roots: some of this may be an exaggeration. Their main activities were fishing, hunting, canoe-building and war. The tribute to Azcapotzalco was made up of "those things which grow in this lake." Tezozomoc draws a similar picture. During a quarrel with Azcapotzalco, the Tepaneca chiefs said: "Let us see where they will get the wood which they burn there and the vegetables [crops] which go from our land to Mexico Tenochtitlan to support them."

During the reign of Itzcoatl things began to change. Torquemada mentions *sementeras*

(cultivated fields) as part of Tenochtitlan's tribute to the Tepaneca. The appearance of cultivated chinampas seems to be related to the construction of an aqueduct to bring water from the springs of Chapultepec. The decisive change took place after the defeat of the Tepaneca of Azcapotzalco, when Itzcoatl "had them call the Tepaneca of Axcapotzalco, those of Cuyuacan together with the Xochimilcas and told them: now you have to build, together, a paved highway and road, all of heavy stone, fifteen *brazas* wide and two *estados* high. After the order was heard, it was carried out and there resulted the present Xololco entrance to Mexico City." It seems as if this was the first major public work of the Tenochca, planned not only as a means of communication but also as a dike to detain the floods.

Actually, the measures taken by Itzcoatl were insufficient. In the ninth year of the reign of Moctezuma the Elder the city was flooded. The Tenochca appealed to the superior hydraulic skill of the Texcocans and under the leadership of Netzahualcoyotl a new dike was built of lumber and stone. The wall was more than four brazas wide and more than three leagues long; the stones had to be brought from three and four leagues away. Moctezuma had to put to work the people of Tenochtitlan, Texcoco, Tacuba, Culhuacan, Ixtapalapa and Tenayuca. The new construction "prevented the sudden blend of salty waters with those sweet ones." Another time, as during the reign of Itzcoatl, the building of a highway-dike was accompanied by the erection of an aqueduct to take fresh water to Tenochtitlan.

The volume of water thus transferred was soon inadequate and the new king, Ahuizotl, decided to build another aqueduct, from Coyoacan. It has frequently been said that the waters of the aqueduct were used only for domestic purposes. The thirst of the Tenochca seems incredible. The *Anales de Cuauhtitlán* report that when the aqueduct of Ahuizotl sprung a leak, Tenochtitlan was flooded and the waters reached Mixquic, Tlahuac and Xochimilco; even Texcoco was within the flood's radius. Another source indicates clearly that the waterworks were built "to increase the waters of the lake" (in other words, to maintain an adequate level). Tezozomoc tells us that during this period chinampas could already be found within the city of Tenochtitlan and that Ahuizotl ordered the chinamperos to plant maize, beans, squash, flowers, chile peppers, tomatoes and trees in "troughs" (*camellones*) so Mexico would "flourish" and the city "did not look like . . . a city . . . but a labyrinth, a flowering garden." This latter aqueduct (built of lime and stone) was erected by the natives of Texcoco, Azcapotzalco, Tacuba, Coyoacan, Xochimilco and "the other four *chinampa*-using towns." The crowd taking part in the work was so numerous "the Indians looked like ants." When the waters reached Tenochtitlan and Tlatelolco, Ahuizotl received them with the following greeting: "You will be used for human sustenance and as a result of the fruits produced by you, there will come many kinds of provisions and flying birds."

We feel there is little ground left for doubt. The cultivated zone was extended by the dike-highway which contained the floods and created reservoirs; fresh water was brought through aqueducts to "wash" the nitrous soil, for irrigation and to maintain the level of the lake in addition to domestic use. When the Spaniards arrived, the system was functioning. Gomara says that the paved road separating the fresh from the nitrous waters had "six or seven very large openings" through which fresh waters were channeled. He mentions no way of closing these holes which must have existed for use during the floods of nitrous water. This is confirmed by Cortes who, in describing a battle, explains that the Indians opened a "road or dike" from Ixtapalapa to Tenochtitlan and then "the water from the salt lake began to flow with violent force toward the fresh one." It is obvious that the inhabitants of the Valley had a method of controlling the water flow in both directions through openings in the dike-roads and this method was in active use. Most probably the Tenochca did no more than extend a system

used much earlier in Jaltocan and Zumpango, in Chalco and Xochimilco.

In conclusion, we view the development of irrigation in the Valley of Mexico not so much as the result of many small-scale initiatives by small groups, but as the result of large-scale enterprise, well planned, in which an enormous number of people took part, engaged in important antd prolonged public works under centralized and authoritative leadership. It is uncertain to what extent this was the general norm in Mesoamerica. We tend to think that usually irrigation was only of local importance, but in certain regions waterworks were built (even if with different techniques) which were similar to those in the Valley of Mexico. Among them are probably those of Cholula and the valley of Atlixco. Nor should one discard the possibility that local irrigation networks dependent on a common river basin would require the same conditions of cooperation, coordination, planning and authority. This may have been the situation in some parts of Colima, Oaxaca, Guerrero, etc.

V. SOME CHARACTERISTICS OF IRRIGATION AND THE HISTORY OF THE VALLEY OF MEXICO

The case of the Tenochca in the Valley of Mexico was presented as an easily available example, perhaps the culminating one, of the nature and importance of the public works serving irrigation agriculture in Mesoamerica. Nevertheless, it is obvious that the techniques employed were widely used and quite ancient in the Valley of Mexico. It is also obvious that other political units, like Texcoco, Cholula, the Tepanec empire, the Toltecs and certainly Teotihuacan, were in a position to gather and manipulate as considerable a labor force as that which was required by the Tenochca. The volume of human effort and the technical skill represented by the pyramids of Teotihuacan and Cholula are, no doubt, greater than those required for the construction of Netzahualcoyotl's dike. On the other hand, all during the same period when Itzcoatl began the Mexico-Xololco road, his neighbors of Cuauhtitlan were building a dam to deflect a river and excavating a new bed for it. The monumental structure of Tetzcutzingo, built by the Texcocans, dates from the same period.

Another characteristic to which Armillas has drawn attention is the "contrast between [the] relatively low technology and [the] highly developed socio-political structure and intellectual life." This is a real contrast, but not a contradiction. Actually, a strong sociopolitical organization seems to be the only way open to a people with a poorly developed technology to have and use large-scale public works. Human labor is the only substitute for advanced technology; the less technology the more human effort is required, which means greater coercive organization. The only possible way of constructing the great preHispanic public works (be they dike-highways, aqueducts, canals or monumental pyramids) in a limited amount of time is reflected for us by Tezozomoc's image, when he talks of large crowds working constantly "like ants."

We also have some additional, more detailed, references. The job of detaining the river of Cuauhtitlan and deflecting it into a new channel was assigned by the chiefs to the inhabitants of Tultitlan. The dam was made of beams, joined and upright; its construction lasted two years. To clean an old canal and make it fit for the new river bed took seven years. When Cortes asked for the help of Texcoco in order to widen a channel (so as to move the brigantines used in the siege of Tenochtitlan) 8,000 men from the Texcoco kingdom worked daily for fifty days. The finished canal was half a league long (about 2 kilometers), 2 *estados* (12 feet) wide, and about that deep. This required 400,000 mandays. We have seen above the number of villages moved to action by the Tenochca kings for their public works.

How can one mobilize such crowds, make them work in organized fashion and maintain them without a powerful and efficient social structure? In part, the socio political organization of Mesoamerica was the result or consequence of the low technology and it may be that the low technical development was perpetuated by a social organization which allowed the ready use of such supplies of human labor. In any case, the foundation of this complex relationship rested on irrigation agriculture, the only type capable, under Mesoamerican conditions, of producing the necessary crop surpluses required to feed the thousands who, from time to time, did not work at producing their own subsistence. These surpluses were necessarily also great enough to maintain the upper classes and the specialized urban population as well as keep up trading activities. The public works which increased the irrigated surface multiplied the surplus-producing capacity which in turn allowed the use of ever greater quantities of human effort for new works, new urban populations and the growing socio-political organization. Still, all this structuring and economic capacity were not used solely for developing irrigation. They could serve to make war, conquer one's neighbors and develop the historically known empires.

In the regions where irrigation did not acquire the importance it had in the Valley of Mexico, we find a different socio-political situation. Instead of the great concentration of power and the formation of empires we find "city-states" whose control reached rarely beyond a limited constellation of satellites. Coalitions sprang up sometimes but mostly they were at war with each other.

The process may be illustrated through a description of events at Yecapichtla, a town which, with its nine satellites, had about 20-25,000 inhabitants, about 10% of whom were *mayeques* and 1% chiefs. It had "many good irrigated lands, and in great amounts." Disputes with neighbors over water were frequent. In early colonial days they complained that if "they irrigated, it cost them a great deal of work as the water comes from Cuavecavazco . . . and many times it is taken away and shut off and not allowed to arrive." And elsewhere "and granted that it is irrigated with a bit of water which flows through the town of Jantetelco, it [the water] does not come from this town nor does it rise there, but in Tetela . . . and many times it is snatched away by the inhabitants of those towns; this causes great need, and through the loss of the said water they have lost and lose many times . . . some cotton and fruits which they plant."

These circumstances, which can probably be duplicated in many parts of Mesoamerica, may have pushed the "city-states" toward the development of a military organization, slowed down only by the imposition of an "empire" or the formation of temporary coalitions.

The explanation of how the Valley of Mexico could overcome this political situation may possibly be found, not only in the spectacular nature of the public works required for irrigation but also in the easily accessible water transport. The network of lakes made it possible for the Valley to become an economic unit before it was a political one, and to add to itself a part of the valley of Morelos. There are countless references in the sources to this special role of the lakes and to numbers and uses of canoes. Gomara thinks that there were 200,000 small boats (and perhaps more, as he mentions 50,000 in Mexico alone), carrying people and supplies. When the Texcocans evacuated their city at the arrival of the Spaniards, Gomara counted 20,000 canoes. Cortes states the most of the trade was carried by boat. Torquemada claims that there was nobody in and around the whole lake who did not have a canoe.

Much later, at the beginning of the eighteenth century, the lakes were still playing a most important role, although land communications had expanded and coaches, horses and mule trains were then in use. A document from Chalco, dated 1806, says: "In this province and town of Chalco, with grief I noted today the great hardships to be seen, it being market day—everywhere a shortage of victuals for survival this coming week; the peasants could not sell their grains and other seeds; the fruit and other precious things *grown in the hot country* could not be sent to the capital. . . . The greens and other foods which we lack and off which other towns live, are rotting near Tlahuac, the lumber of the Royal Factory [is] in the water but cannot move . . . *all this . . . occurs because for four days now the royal canal has been trafficless* as its sides have fallen" (italics ours). The following is said of Xochimilco: "since we are in the depths of destitution— not only we ourselves but also our unlucky families—this happening because the royal road is closed on which we communicate with the Capital, whence we receive our daily sustenance." The petition requests that a new *acalote* or waterway be opened as the old one had been closed by an earthquake. Earlier, Cortes had noted the existence of these waterways used for transport at Xochimilco.

This extraordinary coincidence of such different circumstances—some natural and ecological, other geographic, agricultural, technological, political and historic—allowed the Valley of Mexico to become the key area of pre-Hispanic Mesoamerica.

34. THE JAVANESE STATE AND ISLAM

ROBERT R. JAY

Reprinted from Religion and Politics in Rural Central Java *(Cultural Report Series No. 12, Southeast Asia Studies, Yale University, 1963). Robert R. Jay is Professor of Anthropology at Brown University. His principal interests have been in the social relationships of rural communities in Southeast Asia, especially their political and economic aspects. He is the author of* Religion and Politics in Rural Central Java *and* Javanese Villagers: Social Relations in Rural Modjokuto.

■ It is a truism that man does not live by bread alone. The ethnographic record for all societies at every stage of development demonstrates that religion, along with other ideologies, is an integral feature of every strategy of adaptation. While the facts are clear, students of society disagree over the reasons for this universality. But it is safe to assume that, for whatever reason, people seem to require ideologies that justify and validate the relationships they maintain with the habitat and with each other. Their social relations are not only interpersonal, however; they include the groups that serve as the society's building blocks, and such group relations are always among the subjects of a society's religion. To take a modern example, when the subservience of blacks in the caste system was an integral feature of American social organization, it was religiously justified and validated on religious grounds as the will of God. When, for political and economic reasons, the organization of American social relations was transformed and replaced with standards (or at least ideals) of egalitarianism, this too was religiously justified and validated, again as the will of God. Much the same kind of change is now occurring to reflect and validate changes in the status of women.

Most of the evolutionary changes that we have considered thus far were precipitated by local, intra-societal forces. However, as we move closer and closer to the contemporary world we find that not only must people adapt to forces precipitated within their own society but also to those whose source is geographically distant. Indeed, when we examine our own stage of cultural development, we may ask whether any strategy of adaptation within industrial society is free of such inter-societal pressures.

In this selection we read about the consequences in thirteenth- to fifteenth-century Java resulting from the harnessing by other societies of a new source of energy: long-distance navigation. Jay's focus in this chapter is on religious change, from Hindu-Javanese religion to Islam. It is clear from Jay's analysis that religious change does not occur in a vacuum and that it cannot be regarded as a self-contained ideological shift. Although a variety of interpretations may be made of Jay's material, I am using these data to illustrate the hypothesis that religious change results from political change.

Reminiscent of the politico-religious upheavals in Western Europe at the time of the Reformation and after, we observe here a transformation of Javanese religion paralleling the rise of a new mercantile class. But the latter's new body of interests were not solely economic; as Jay makes clear, they also entailed profound political changes. Moreover, their source was not within Javanese society but rather from without, namely, long-distance sea commerce initiated by other Asian societies. While Java was far from being homogeneous prior to the thirteenth century, the new mercantilism both represented and underlay a great increase in the society's heterogeneity. Religious affiliation always mirrors social status. In tribal societies, each of which is egalitarian and marked by a single religious system, the individual's subscription to his group's religious organization is one of the hallmarks of his membership in the group and his equal status with everyone else. In a more complex and heterogeneous society—Java after the thirteenth century—religious diversity mirrors diversity in social, economic, and political interests.

The social, political, and economic antagonisms involved in the conflict between local (especially rural) communities and urban-based groups representing the interests of the state are also expressed in religious schisms; as described by Jay, they may entail violence. But not only conflict characterizes relationships among groups in the heterogeneous society; corresponding to the idea that the nation as a whole replaces the small community as the adaptive unit, the histories of nations also exhibit attempted reconciliations of opposing lifestyles, symbolic systems, and economic and political interests. This is paralleled in the religious sphere; it is often observed that, especially among peasants, people will appear to adopt a new state-sponsored religion but quickly emerge with a mixture of traditional and inherited religious elements and those of the new religion. The resulting synthesis often resembles neither of its predecessors in "pure" form and is generally referred to as "syncretism." We see examples of such syncretism in this selection.

An excellent overview of Javanese religion is presented by Clifford Geertz in *The Religion of Java* (New York: The Free Press, 1960). Geertz also compares Islam in Java with that of Morocco in *Islam Observed: Religious Development in Morocco and Indonesia* (Chicago: University of Chicago Press, paperback, 1971). A striking parallel between the cognitive system embodied in Javanese religion, described in the next selection, and that of ancient Egypt, is to be found in Chapter 1 of *Before Philosophy: The Intellectual Adventure of Ancient Man,* by Henri Frankfort, H. A. Frankfort, John A. Wilson, and Thorkild Jacobsen (Baltimore: Penguin Books, 1949). A parallel between Javanese and English religious schisms can be traced in "Puritanism," by M. James *(Encyclopedia of the Social Sciences* [1st edition], Volume 13, 1930, pp. 3-6). For an excellent description of religious syncretism among a peasant population, the interested reader may consult Chapter 11 in *Life in a Mexican Village: Tepoztlan Restudied,* by Oscar Lewis (Urbana: University of Illinois, paperback, 1963.) ∎

THE JAVANESE STATE AND ISLAM

THE ROOTS OF THE historical sequence we are following here reach back to geographical factors operative in Southeast Asia around the beginning of the Christian period. At that time Southeast Asia found itself between the waxing strengths of the Sinitic and the Western worlds, with India a middle stage in

the sea routes connecting the two empires of Augustan Rome and Han China. Commerce increased significantly, much of it by way of the sea, and the inhabitants of Southeast Asian ports favorably situated on the east-west sea routes benefited directly. We have only circumstantial evidence of this great sea commerce—the existence of Malaysian trading populations in South India at this time, the Indonesian colonization of Madagascar probably not long after, and the discovery of Roman, Indian, and Chinese trade wares at certain coastal places. It seems clear, however, that the art of navigation had advanced so far—through development of indigenous elements and the introduction of hull design from China and sail design from the Near East—that long-range voyages to the coast of East Africa and back had become possible.

It is to be expected that under such stimulus there would have been substantial socioeconomic and sociopolitical development in those Southeast Asian societies sharing the profits of this commerce, that is to say initially those societies with harbors located on sea routes and with access to desirable trade goods. Of any such social evolution we have as yet no direct evidence, but it is improbable that such commercial developments would have left the societies participating in them unchanged.

A critical stage in their evolution apparently was reached when in the early centuries A. D. a new surge of Indian influences was transmitted, by means not yet clearly understood, to those societies. We know, in the main, what these novel elements were. The earliest to arrive (in southern Cambodia where we have the first evidence of them) were elements of Sanskritic learning, including conceptions of political office. Thereafter both Brahmanical and Buddhist religious elements were added, together with their monumental architecture. Early inscriptions suggest, moreover, that Indian techniques of irrigation and of land distribution were among those elements then imported, although indigenous systems of irrigation were almost certainly already present. Thereafter we find the rapid development of centralized states, evidently based upon a fusion of traditional leadership with Indian, mainly Brahmanical, theories of government.

The loci of these early Indian-styled states make clear their dependence upon sea trade. Minor states flourished on the Malay Peninsula near the Isthmus of Kra—across which goods were for a while transshipped—in north Sumatra, and along the northern and eastern coasts of Borneo. The major states which came to dominate commerce through Southeast Asia in a three-cornered contest had their origin in southern Cambodia near the mouth of the Mekong, on the east coast of Java near present-day Djakarta.

These harbor states drew, in part, upon their hinterland for trade resources and, in Cambodia at least, established a form of overlordship. By the eighth century, however, in both Cambodia and Java, inland states had developed that became more powerful than their coastal predecessors. In contrast to the harbor states, these inland states based their power more on the control of their population's manpower than upon control of the sea trade. Economic power came from the agricultural production of a dense population by means of intensive irrigated farming. Military power came more from a large land army than from sea power. The struggle between these two systems of state control—first in Cambodia, then for many centuries between Sumatra and Java, and finally in Java itself—characterized the history of Southeast Asia until the reduction of its states to European colonial rule. In each instance ultimate hegemony passed to an inland state.

Wherever broad areas of fertile and easily irrigable land were available—and large, dense populations had formed—such inland states rose to power. Here were located the great "Hinduized" kingdoms of Southeast Asia, with their massive armies, monumental architecture, elaborate courts, and highly developed music and dance, much of which remains to be admired or recreated as each nation's major classical art. As with central Burma, central Thailand, and the middle Mekong in Cambodia, central and eastern Java from Mount Merapi to the Malang highlands became one such area.

The theological supports of royal authority formed the core of a system of philosophy that represented a syncretism of Buddhist, Brahmanical, and indigenous religious elements. The essentially unitary and evolutionary process working upon these inland societies produced social and cultural forms which even today show remarkable similarities.

The philosophical system that emerged in Javanese society may be sketched in the following terms. The essential principle is that the inner self and the external cosmos are interdependent. The gradations between these two poles of being are conceived as layers about the inner self of increasingly externalized existence: through one's mental states and emotions to one's physical self, to one's society, to the entire world, and thence to the bounds of the cosmos. The states of being in these concentric layers reflect one another: what happens to one's inner self is reflected in one's physical condition, one's personal fortunes, the state of society, and ultimately the spiritual order of the universe cosmos—and, reciprocally, any one of these is a reflection of one's inner self.

The state of being most highly valued is an inner quietude, achieved through a stilling of one's affective thoughts and feelings. This reflects and is reflected in mental and physical health, a gently prosperous life with tranquil, well-ordered social relations, a peaceful society, and a harmonious cosmos.

There are certain propositions in the system that follow as corollaries of this principle. By achieving an inner stillness, a fixity of spirit, one gains coercive power over worldly and cosmic states of being. Intense mental fixation upon an end by itself brings about this end. Conversely, anyone exhibiting this power over external being shows himself able to reach great intensity in such inner fixity.

Inner fixity translates itself into spatial fixity in the physical world, and beyond that it connects the self with the power of a fixed cosmic center. Corresponding to the fixed center of the cosmos, then, is a fixed spatial center in this world—the residence of the ruler, who is the point of maximum spiritual intensity in human society. A universal axis is thus defined by the conjunction of three points: the ruler's inner self, his palace, and the center of the cosmos. The beneficent power of this universal axis radiates from the person of the ruler to each person in the surrounding population, who is then reciprocally joined with the ruler in gaining and maintaining individual and collective harmony and is thus his subject.

Various political and social characteristics of the society were consonant with this philosophical system. Proximity to the ruler through ties of kinship, marriage, or chance personal affinity, through royal office, or simply through residential proximity were believed to strengthen the material and spiritual benefits an individual secured for himself through the ruler's power. Correspondingly, there was a physical clustering of the population in the proximity of the palace.

The limits of a ruler's domain—that is, of his power—were indefinite. This power, while weakening as it spread out radially, was in theory capable of unlimited expansion if sufficiently intense at the center. International relations thus reduced themselves to contests of total strength, material and spiritual, between adjacent rulers to determine whose field of power should prevail. In this contest each ruler strove to maximize simultaneously his inner strength, the power developed by the spatial fixity of his residence, and his material power to command in the wider world, each reinforcing the other. This effort led to elaborate methods for spiritual control of the self through various modes of meditation and personal ritual. The mystical fixity of the palace complex was intensified through monumental architectural models of the universe that by symbolic magic fixed the ruler's residence as the actual center of the universe. Much emphasis was placed upon court and communal rituals which supported the reciprocal relations between the ruler and his subjects. Much diplomatic and military effort was spent in forcing symbolic submission to the ruler from surrounding autonomous rulers.

After death each ruler was ritually clad in the person of a major divinity by his successor and buried within a monumental complex that created, near the new ruler's palace, a divine pantheon which lent its spiritual strength to that of the new ruler. The dead ruler's royal spouse and his father and mother, and sometimes his parental siblings, were also thus apotheosized in death, to extend their spiritual aid reciprocally to that of the ruler as they had done, materially and spiritually, in life.

The ideal monarch was one who possessed such extraordinary inner control, demonstrated by various feats of magic and of outward calm under stress of great distractions, and such powerful worldly control, demonstrated by a large, contented, prosperous body of subjects and by impressive feats of monumental architecture, that other rulers thought fit voluntarily to come forward and submit to him in order to gain a share in his blessings.

Social rank was based on proximity to the ruler through the various kinds of affiliation: most powerfully, through kinship, extended more or less bilaterally; through voluntary submission; through royal administrative office; through royal service in other ways such as domestic and craft service; and, finally, through residence by living within the range of the ruler's spiritual strength. Other things being equal, the nearer a subject lived, the higher his rank, and the king's common subjects—the ordinary peasantry living out in the countryside beyond the circle of the court proper—represented the bottom of the social hierarchy. Position in one of the higher categories often carried with it a concomitant position in another, since kin relationship was translated into position in the official hierarchy and residential proximity to the ruler usually entailed some form of service at the court.

Standards defining the ideal man centered on control of personal emotions and of external situations through calm demeanor under all circumstances, on outward grace of movement and speech, and on control of the elaborate etiquette which served to express and fix relative individual rank. There was thus a strongly pragmatic rather than ethical emphasis in personal behavior, an emphasis on the empirical control of the external self and of external events through a combination of ritual and material means. Proper style and form were conceived to be the effectual modes for attaining personal and national ends, and their use in itself served partially to define success toward these ends.

Congruently there was an interest in the other world for the sake of this world, rather than the other way about. There was a marked lack of ethical interest in a heaven and a hell. Rather than the conception of a causal sequence in which ethically good action now leads to a state of reward in the other world, there was a conception that causal relations hold mutually here and now, along with stylistically proper action, a desirable state of affairs in this world, and a harmonious position vis-a-vis the other world. After death one's essential being removed itself to a fixed place of its own, there to maintain an ultimate stillness and quietude. This did not, however, mean a severing of ties with this world; on the contrary, the very stillness attained continued one's spiritual power among the living. It blessed those who had received blessings from the deceased reciprocally during his lifetime, and they in turn contributed their spiritual power to help maintain his spirit in its fixed state of quietude.

Finally, there was a conception according to which access to and control over cosmic forces were differentially distributed in the society and that this distribution was exhibited in differential rank, which it also served to define spiritually. Accordingly all social relations were conceived as necessarily hierarchical.

A sufficient number of these characteristics turn up in other Malaysian societies which were practically unaffected by Indian influences (and indeed appear in Malayo-Polynesian society generally) to make it clear that much of the social and political system sketched above, as well as the conceptions which supported it, evolved out of the pre-Hindu social order. The system, in any event, has for many centuries sunk deep roots into all levels of Javanese society.

A number of indigenous complexes which had been taken over more or less intact were accommodated to this system. Communal feasts, in which the participants jointly identify themselves with local spirits and assert their solidarity as a community, were elaborated into royal celebrations which identified the ruler as the temporal and spiritual head of his subjects. Familistic conceptions of community leadership were carried over to the relations between the ruler, the royal officials, and his subjects. The continuing spiritual bond of reciprocal support between a person and his deceased close relatives, especially his parents and grandparents, and that between a community and its members' collective ancestors became important elements in the royal eschatology. Other elements similarly retained were the mystical significance of location and direction, elaborated with calendrical systems both indigenous and Indian, and the sense of identity between the members of a community and the spirit of the original clearer of the land that served to define the community's joint rights of its exploitation. These indigenous cultural complexes were all woven one way or another into the philosophical system which came into being with the development of Hindu-Javanese civilization.

Conversion to Islam spread like a wave, from west to east, through the states of the archipelago. Its earliest successes were apparent in north Sumatra during the late thirteenth century. Thereafter, over a span of two centuries most of the major trading centers, including the ports of north Java, came under the control of local Moslem princes.

The political structure of conversion in Java is highly significant for the channeling of religious loyalties down to the present day. In essence, conversion to Islam ultimately came to accompany a break with the central power of Madjapahit (1292-1520), the last and greatest of the Hindu-Javanese kingdoms. Madjapahit had been established late in the thirteenth century in east Java, successfully uniting the inland interests of two rival predecessors—one centered at Kediri (Daha) and the other near Malang (Singasari)—with the maritime interests of the newly developing trading centers along Java's north-central and northeastern coasts.

During the following century the prosperity of these coastal trading centers caused them to increase greatly in size and power. Their serious conversion to Islam probably began as early as the fourteenth century, brought about by personal and commercial ties with trading centers farther to the west. This was not, however, simply the conversion of a trader class. The trading sector in commercial centers throughout Southeast Asia, as elsewhere in South Asia, embraced a wide social and economic range. The local rulers themselves in their role as merchant princes were at its head. In north Java the regents of the Madjapahit king drew most of their power as well as their living from trade. It was during the fifteenth century among the commercially oriented within this local political leadership, subordinate to the central power, that the most important converts to Islam were secured. In the hands of these leaders Islam became a political and economic weapon with which to free themselves from the overlordship of Madjapahit.

By the latter half of the fifteenth century a number of Javanese converts had risen to positions of political leadership in the north Javanese coastal towns of Ngampel (Surabaja), Bonang, Gresik, Demak, Tuban, Djapara, and Tjeribon. These were the famous *wali*—according to traditional sources the first generation of Islamic leaders in Java. The *Babad Tanah Djawi,* a traditional history available in various versions, recounts the troubles the reigning king of Madjapahit had with these leaders. They were all related by kinship or marriage to the local aristocracy, and a number of them, according to the traditional sources, owed their rise to power to the favor of the Madjapahit king. They moved toward independent sovereignty, however, at the same time that Madjapahit was shifting its center of power and interests increasingly toward the interior. These wali, according to the *Babad Tanah Djawi,* justified their renunciation of loyalty to the central throne by appeal to the superior authority of Islam.

The shift in power from Madjapahit in the interior to the coastal ports of north Java was complete by the beginning of the sixteenth century. Madjapahit itself was finally overthrown and its royal regalia formally transported to Demak around 1520. There followed some fifty years of Moslem hegemony in Java during which Islam was carried by conversion and by force of arms into west Java and over all but the extreme end of east Java. The old Hindu-Buddhist gods were forgotten, and to be Javanese began to mean to be Moslem. The first two generations of wali died, their religious and political unity—centered originally in the Sultan of Demak—was dismembered, and their power passed back and forth among their descendants.

It is extremely difficult to gauge how far, in more than a formal sense, Islamic theology and theories of government during this period replaced the Hindu-Javanese system sketched earlier. Even more difficult is it to guess what more profound changes in basic philosophical conceptions it may have stimulated among the "intelligentsia." Distinctions between orthodoxy and syncretism did appear in Islam locally, for we have the record of a certain Sheik Djenar being condemned to burning by his fellow wali during this period for propagating an Islamic doctrine that identified the Self with the Divine. Moreover, Near Eastern titles of royalty and certain religious officials would indicate the introduction of some Islamic legal and governmental theory. Together with the insistence that women marrying Moslems convert to Islam and the presence of certain surviving law books, Islamic *madrasah* were introduced, schools for higher religious education which while not differing greatly in form from earlier, traditional Javanese religious schools, would have been centers for disseminating some distinctly Islamic teaching. Pigeaud, further, considers that the Near Eastern cast of the popular music and drama, which even today is characteristic of the northeast coast area, had its beginning in this period. Certainly, also, mosques, with their distinctive personnel, ritual, and modes of preaching, replaced Hindu-Javanese sanctuaries.

Moslems were not content with *pro forma* conversion of local leaders for political purposes but proselytized with especial vigor among the Hindu-Javanese holy men, recluses, wandering teachers, and the like. The confrontations of Islamic and Hindu-Javanese learned men are recorded as leading to lengthy religious debates. It is true that according to the traditional sources, conversions were achieved by demonstrating the essential similarity of Islam with Hindu and Buddhist doctrines. Such identifications were undoubtedly used, although presumably for showing on theological grounds what there was to Islam that made it superior. The debates would otherwise scarcely have had any point.

The traditional historians chose to ignore those distinctions that may have been drawn. This insistence in the histories that the two teachings were "just the same" needs be read however in its Javanese context: "they are just the same" was and is an ubiquitous stock denial applied to socially distressful differences, especially differences between groups viewed as being closely related. Its assertion gives the audience much evident comfort but needs therefore to be taken with some skepticism. Moreover, the *Babad Tanah Djawi,* from which most of the available traditional sources for this period appear to derive, was composed during the succeeding Mataram period, at the court of Sultan Agung and his successors, by court intellectuals intent on syncretizing Islam with earlier Hindu-Javanese learning.

Schrieke, in a recently translated volume of important studies—some unfortunately left incomplete at his death—stressed the continuity between the Hindu-Javanese period and the Islamic kingdoms which succeeded it. This is surely valid. Historically, much of what followed the downfall of Madjapahit was a repetition of preceding Javanese history and culture. Certainly in court and presumably popular conception there was much satisfaction and power to be derived from demonstrating dynastic succession from the Madjapahit rulers as an essentially unchanging continuity. Yet both historically and in

the minds of contemporary Javanese much had changed. *Djaman buda,* the name given by the Javanese to the old Hindu-Javanese period, was completed and past; the *dewa-dewa,* the Hindu and Buddhist divinities, were no longer served by formal religious establishments. Royalty could not, without fear of heresy, seek to support their power through personal identification with the godhead. Royal power during the Demak period had in fact passed over to figures identified in the popular mind with the class of religious scholars, now no longer Hindu or Buddhist, but Islamic.

The most decisive change in the long run, perhaps, was that a new statement had been made of the relationship between the ruler and the Supreme God. The ruler, living or dead, was no longer of the gods, but a servant of God and, however powerful, a man. It does not matter that for most of the population the statement may have been incomprehensible. A community of religious sentiment was brought into being, centered around the new corps of religious learned men, that did understand and accept the statement. It was most powerful in the northeast coastal area but was also represented by local groups all over central Java. The loyalty of its members to Islam could, and during the succeeding period frequently did, call into question their loyalties to the ruler.

During the next period—the Mataram period that followed the Moslem hegemony of the northeastern coastal states under Demak —it came about that opposition to the Javanese ruler was focused most steadily in just this circle and that the standard of Islam, an Islam held to be purer than that supported at the ruler's court, was used time and again to rally forces against him. The ruler, in turn, encouraged the growth—the regrowth really —of old Javanese learning and ritual as theological supports for his power and used them as a weapon against his opponents.

It also does not matter that, judged by modern standards, the community of Islam during the period of Demak and subsequently until recent decades was itself perhaps more syncretist than orthodox. Schrieke makes the point, in another publication and context, that what is most important in considering social reactions to certain historical facts is not the historian's subsequent objective view of these facts but contemporary society's view. Relative to the times, more specifically to the alternate forms of Islam represented at the time in Javanese society, it is safe to say that the theological position of the Islamic leaders in the northeast coastal states, and of Islamic teachers elsewhere in central Java, was decidedly orthodox. More important, political and religious leaders on both sides of the argument acted as if this were so, and their mutual reactions presumably made it more so. There was without doubt much common ground between them, just as there is between present-day orthodox Javanese Moslems and those syncretist Javanese whom the orthodox consider to be superstitious peasants, infidels, or even atheists. As Clifford Geertz shows so vividly, it is a fact that a modern Javanese orthodox leader, in a talk to his own laity, may sometimes use an argument clearly more syncretic than orthodox, but this does not change his conviction or that of his audience that they themselves are all true Moslems and that the *abangan*, the syncretically oriented Javanese, are not.

Beginning in 1575 the new power of Mataram arose in the central interior of Java, near the present-day city of Jogjakarta, to dispute the power of the northeast coastal rulers. Mataram was of course also the name of a much earlier Javanese kingdom, located in this area during the eighth and ninth centuries, which had been responsible, among other things, for the building of the great Javanese-Buddhist monument, Boro Budur. The new Mataram, in its struggle against the northeast coastal states, used the military manpower and traditional organization of the Javanese agrarian state. The struggle recapitulated the earlier one between the coastal states and Madjapahit, with the opposite result. This time inland power won.

The Mataram rulers emphasized from the beginning their direct continuity with the lines of Madjapahit kings—which the coastal rulers had also not neglected to do. In addition, however, Mataram sought out members of the dispossessed Madjapahit inland aristocracy for royal alliances and for its bureaucracy. It reinstated traditional Javanese learning and state ritual. A religious synthesis incorporating Islam as simply a new frame for the earlier traditional religious system was gradually developed by the Mataram court scholars. This was made into something like a state religion, though not distinct from formal Islam. The practice of Islam at the court, accordingly, became deeply intertwined with much earlier, pre-Islamic ritual as part of the court scholars' new synthesis.

The syncretist character of their efforts shows through clearly in one version of the *Babad Tanah Djawi* in the following excerpt from its genealogical preface to the creation of the world.

This is the history of the kings of Java, beginning with the Prophet Adam, who had a Son, Sis. Sis had a son Nurtjahja [holy light]. Nurtjahja had a son Nurasa [holy taste, feeling, sensibility]. Nurasa had a son Sanghyang Wening [*sanghyang*, divine (Sanskrit); *wening*, clear pure fluid]. Sanghyang Wening had a son, Sanghyang Tunggal [*tunggal*, the one, unity]. Sanghyang Tunggal had a son Batara Guru [synonym for Siwa]. Batara Guru had five children, named Batara Sambo, Batara Brama, Batara MahaDewa, Batara Wisnu, and Dewi Sri [Javanese goddess of the harvest, especially of rice]. Batara Wisnu was king on the island of Java under the name of Prabhu Set. The kingdom of Batara Guru was called Sura-Laja [Hindu paradise].

The chronicle then goes on to describe quarrels arising between Batara Wisnu and his father Batara Guru, and to draw genealogical lines from these figures, especially Brama and Wisnu, to the various historical kings of Java. The whole is plainly inspired by Hindu-Javanese conceptions of the creation, with bare deference paid to an Islamic tradition.

The *Babad Tanah Djawi* went through various editions during the reign of Sultan Agung, each designed to justify and assist his current diplomatic and military endeavors. Berg shows that it was a court document evidently constructed and modified with care and deliberation in order to shape prevailing influential opinion throughout Java. Other more pedagogical works of the early Mataram court writers, such as *Serat Manikmaja* and *Serat Nitisruti,* have an even more uncompromising Hindu-Javanese character. The *pudjangga,* the court scholars, in contrast to contemporary Islam-oriented writers who spent their intellectual efforts on Koranic commentaires and narratives with Islamic themes and morals, seldom mentioned the Koran but drew instead on the Hindu epics *Ramayana* and *Mahabharata.*

This religious syncretism shocked the more faithful among the Islamic leaders and learned men. The coastal rulers in their struggle with Mataram invoked a religiously pure Islam as a rallying standard, especially against Sultan Agung (1613-1646) and his successors. Religious teachers traveled through villages in central Java preaching against the Sultan. The Mataram rulers in their turn invoked the glory of Madjapahit and at various times persecuted, even slew wholesale, numbers of local orthodox Moslem teachers. The fight was long and bitter and reportedly reduced large areas of east Java to near depopulation. Finally, in 1625, Sultan Agung of Mataram destroyed Surabaja, the last of the coastal ports to hold out. From being the major sea power in the archipelago, Java in a few decades was reduced to using foreign bottoms to transport rice from one place to another along its northern coast. The Mataram rulers seemed determined to profit from the lesson of Madjapahit.

This victory did not end the struggle between Mataram and east Java. Sultan Agung's successor continued his policy of assassination of the remaining east Javanese leaders as well as his persecution of local Mataram orthodox religious leaders. A rebellion against the oppressive rule of Mataram developed throughout east Java in 1675, the rebellion in which the famous Trunadjadja was involved, though he was by no means the sole leader. Again, Islam was an important rallying standard for the rebels against the syncretist rulers of Mataram. The rebellion was sub-

dued, but only by the military action of the Dutch East India Company, which therewith began its steady absorption of Mataram's power.

There followed the struggle with Sunan Giri, a remarkable figure of Islamic power, whom the Europeans termed the "Mohammedan pope of Java." He was a direct descendant of one of the early wali, in a line that had maintained a tiny, autonomous holy state outside Surabaja. The Sunan Giri exercised a powerful religious sway not only over east Java but also over other parts of eastern Indonesia and was naturally hostile, on both religious and political grounds, to the Mataram rulers. In 1680, again with the decisive help of the Dutch Company, the Mataram ruler finally extinguished the line.

Thereafter, from the end of the Surabaja War (1718-1723) in which the Mataram court, still in alliance with the Dutch Company, finally and definitely broke the power of the old ruling families of the northeast coastal states, there were major and minor uprisings directed against the Mataram ruler, the Dutch, or both—and sometimes supported by elements from within the Mataram court itself. Almost invariably the ideological standard of each uprising was the banner of Islam, and its leaders were also religious leaders in their supporters' eyes—more orthodox, more Islamic than the royal rulers. Increasingly, as the Dutch Company was drawn on other grounds more and more into the politics of the Mataram kingdom, it gave support to the ruler toward maintaining civil peace, and in the natural course of events came to inherit the court's position of chronic hostility toward orthodox Islam in Java. The last such uprising on a large scale was the Java War (1825-1830), in which the leader of the rebellion, Dipanegara, maintained the combined role of an aristocrat near the direct line of royal descent (he was a younger brother of the previous Sultan of Jogjakarta) and of a Moslem teacher-leader. He seems in fact originally to have held a position in court life close to the orthodox end of the religious spectrum in Javanese society.

Later uprisings were minor, local affairs although, again, almost always under the leadership of some relatively orthodox figure. Their nature may be illustrated by a story related to me in a village near Ngandjuk in central-eastern Java. The story explained the existence of a sacred shrine in the village, the burial place of a religious teacher who had lived there at an unspecified time in the past, apparently some time in the mid-nineteenth century. The teacher had become involved in a dispute with the local government official over some land rights and had killed him. In time a small force of government police came to investigate, and he routed them. The Bupati, the local regent, next came to put down the uprising, whereupon the teacher, having by that time gained a considerable body of suporters, killed the Bupati in battle. The Dutch colonial government finally sent in a troop of soldiers, and only then was the teacher defeated and killed. It may well be that his military successes have been magnified through the years, but the teacher's grave has become one of the village shrines which the traditionally oriented community honors with a yearly ritual feast and entertainment and to which during the year villagers come individually to seek his blessing. Birds allegedly fall dead to the ground if they fly over the grave.

The event as narrated parallels numerous other disturbances with which the Dutch administration had had to cope during the preceding two centuries, led in almost all cases by figures self-consciously Islamic—"religious fanatics," as the Dutch administrators called them. As late as 1919, in Garut, west Java, a similar occurrence gained wide attention: a certain Hadji Hasan defied a regular government rice requisition in order to sell rice privately at a higher price, arming and barricading himself in his large homestead together with a small number of "fanatical" fellow Moslems. The government police made a quick but bloody end of Hadji Hasan and his fellows as the government had been apprehensive about a wave of civil disturbance following the end of World War I. It is not likely that he has since been enshrined by his fellow villagers (though it is not impossible that this may happen in the course of time) but otherwise the parallel with the story told me in east Java is clear enough.

For our purposes the major concomitant of this history, beginning with the rise of Mataram, has been the alignment of the Javanese aristocracy and bureaucracy with the syncretic form of Islam, in cultural and political antagonism to those aligned locally with a relatively orthodox form of Islam. I attempt to causal argument for this development, any causal agents presumably being reciprocal and considerably tangled.

The social and cultural position of the aristocratic and bureaucratic elements does, however, show a close formal consistency with the philosopical and esthetic character of the syncretism, itself in most respects a carry-over from the pre-Islamic philosophical system sketched earlier. These formal connections, we may call them congruences, are apart from what appear as the obvious immediate or efficient cause of that alignment—personal commitment to the Mataram ruler and the state apparatus.

In the first place, the Javanese bureaucracy itself is intensely hierarchical. Each office is an element in a precisely defined chain of command and carries with it a precisely defined gradation of rank. Syncretist philosophy in its definition of personal spiritual power as reciprocally related to political and social rank, defined in turn as proximity to the ruler, is congruent with this hierarchy as well as with the social position of the bureaucracy as the aristocracy's junior partner at the pinnacle of society.

In the second place, grace of movement and refinement of speech, and the elaboration of these in literary and dramatic forms, are an obvious intellectual delight in Javanese culture—a distinctive "play element," in Huizinga's terms. The identification in syncretist philosophy of spiritual power with inner poise, calm, controlled movement, and social fixity is also in harmony with elaboration of these elements. As argued most recently by Burger, following Pigeaud and Rouffaer, there seems to have been a great increase during the eighteenth century in the elaboration of just these cultural elements, a late "Byzantine flowering" of traditional Javanese culture in its distinctive dimensions at the central Javanese courts of Mataram. This did not coincide with a sharpening of Mataram's political relations with its orthodox opponents; on the contrary, its power was then undergoing an eclipse behind the growing power of the Dutch. The latter were increasingly taking over the court's old struggle with orthodoxy. Burger argues, in fact, that it was precisely this loss in external interests that stimulated the courts to such heights of cultural refinement. Whatever the causal relations involved, it seems clear that, relieved of political responsibility, the Javanese aristocracy and bureaucracy chose to put their energies into further elaboration of traditional culture and its congruent syncretist philosophy rather than, let us say, into a shift toward more orthodox Islamic culture and theology. On the contrary, orthodox Islam in Java has been consistently and puritanically averse to cultural elaborations, while maintaining a relatively egalitarian bias in social relations.

Finally, in demonstrating his rank within the Javanese upper class, an individual depends to a significant extent on his ability to show unified control over the traditional culture in its manifold aspects—esthetic, social, linguistic, and philosophical. In contrast to the more single-minded emphasis upon religious learning in relatively orthodox circles, the superior man in syncretist circles must be a literatus, a dancer, a musician, a master of protocol and complex conversational language, and a philosopher, all at once. This itself is in keeping with syncretist philosophy in its emphasis upon the self, in all its dimensions, as the primary and ultimate point of reference. Control of the unified self—spiritual, mental, emotional, physical, and social—with the aid perhaps of some external doctrine, provided this requires absolutely no personal renunciation or submission, is the central teaching of the philosophy. Each individual must gain ultimate control for himself through separate control over all his various human faculties. None should be neglected; all must be kept in symmetrical balance.

It was also the nature of the synthesis that it contained no dogma, no rigid orthodoxy of its own. Beyond the requirements of certain formal ritual at the courts, each individual was free to seek salvation in his own way. The philosophy's pragmatic rather than dogmatic emphasis assisted individual variation. Its intellectuals have in fact consistently sought to synthesize various alien philosophical systems from a conviction that their own tradition was able to support any variant philosophy.

The synthesis, then, entered the wider Javanese society quite without discipline from the court. From the other side as well, orthodox elements continually entered the society also without discipline, for even if the orthodox leaders had the will, they had not the power. There emerged in the wide society, in the towns and villages of central and eastern Java, a broad spectrum of philosophy, religious ritual, and esthetics, nearly pure Hindu-Javanese at one end, nearly pure —for its time—orthodox Moslem at the other. The intermingling of formal elements toward practical ends allowed local intellectuals to pick and choose, to pull together elements from varying portions of the spectrum. The way in which a local figure, combining in himself the offices of local *kijai* and *pudjangga*, could unite disparately inclined individuals from his neighboring communities is illustrated by the lurah of Kebonsari, whose case is discussed below. With such a figure as a central spiritual focus, villagers could at random enter diverse activities in which varied Islamic and Javanese motifs were used without arousing cultural antagonisms among themselves.

In sum, the cultural landscape of the eighteenth and nineteenth century countryside came to be differentiated, though not discontinuously, by the varied inclinations of the locally dominant intellectuals. Certain landmarks were more distinctive than others.

More traditionally inclined Javanese intellectuals had unobtrusive circles of loosely organized students and followers, and they conducted no outstanding ritual. The more orthodox had mosques as centers for highly distinctive ritual and often had more formally organized boarding schools, *pondok* or *pesantren,* where advanced training in Islamic ritual and doctrine was given. Strongly Islamic centers thus made greater social and even economic impact on their rural communities than the simpler, less distinctively organized, traditional centers. The latter, however, provided more channels to urban society, for their intellectuals often had ties to the higher levels of syncretist society, which in most of Java dominated the towns and cities.

V.
INDUSTRIALISM

THE INDUSTRIAL STRATEGY of adaptation is the most difficult to analyze, for several reasons. It contains more diversity than any previous stage. There is hardly a single development in an industrial society that is unaffected in one way or another by political considerations. For instance, some people estimate that one-fourth of the jobs that will be available in another generation are nonexistent today, but the new industries and professions that will provide these jobs—and their accompanying lifestyles—will develop almost entirely as a result of direct or indirect governmental intervention in the economy. The rate of change in industrial societies is so rapid—more rapid than at any previous stage of development —that yesterday's bold and breathtaking innovation is tomorrow's antiquarianism.

Most important, however, is the partisanship and emotionalism that underly our every view of every feature of life in industrial societies. Negative values are often attached to phenomena that, when observed in pre-industrial societies, are treated dispassionately. But even the doomsday ethos has its analog in earlier historical periods. Evoking the rhetoric of modern times is the observation by J. Huizinga in *The Waning of the Middle Ages* (Baltimore: Penquin Books, 1955) that "in the fifteenth century, as in the epoch of romanticism, it was, so to say, bad form to praise the world and life openly. It was fashionable to see only its suffering and misery, to discover everywhere signs of decadence and of the near end—in short, to condemn the times or to despise them." My intention here is neither to praise nor condemn but to try to understand industrialization in the same framework that was applied to previous strategies. (I realize that even this position is regarded in some quarters as a form of partisanship.)

Because industrial societies are so heterogeneous, it is not possible to draw a summary profile of their way of life. Nor, in view of the complexity of political factors—which now include international relationships—is it easy to generalize about the roles of different institutions among different strata. A volume of at least this size would be required to analyze only the role of governmental policies in shaping the nuclear family household, for example, through tax laws, advocacy of family planning, educational policies, road building, price and credit controls, policies with respect to home construction and mortgages, child-labor laws, policies facilitating the employment of women, medical insurance and social security, and the like. Similar relationships obtain in connection with all other institutions. Hence, I am going to concentrate in this section on the social accompaniments of industrial technology and its correlates in the occupational sphere.

Like all the strategies of adaptation discussed, industrialism refers not only to a level of technological development but also to a particular organization of social relations. The industrial level of development is based on the machine, by means of which man maintains a viable relationship with his habitat. This relationship not only involves the production of clothing, shelter, furniture, books, and gadgets, but also food, the basic problem faced by every living organism that seeks to adapt. Drive through many of the fertile valleys of the United States (each of which claims to be the "breadbasket of the nation," if not the world) and you will notice an important transformation in the production of food. This transformation began with the plow and is now reaching a climax. More and more food is being planted, tended, harvested, packaged, and sold without being touched by human hands until it reaches the dining table. Land is prepared, fertilized, and irrigated, and food is grown entirely by use of machines. A newspaper dispatch from Canada a few years ago began with this statement: "By 1980, a farmer will be able to sit in the shade of his front porch while his tractor operates without him. A model of a driverless tractor, operated by magnetic tape fed into a special computer, has been built."

Here are a few other introductory paragraphs from newspaper reports, collected at random since 1965:

The country's biggest pipeline, stretching 1,531 miles from Houston to New York, is controlled by only one man. . . . Its network, which holds more than 14 million barrels of oil and can deliver 42 million gallons a day, is gauged, metered and monitored by an operator in Atlanta.

Final testing has begun on the historic [French] Rance River "Maremotrice"— a dam that will harness the giant Brittany coast tides to make electricity. Copying an idea that Breton farmers developed for milling grain seven centuries ago. . . . the $100 million "Maremotrice," or sea motor, will soon start generating enough electric power to fill the needs of a city the size of Boston.

Government by computer may not be just around the corner, but the Lindsay [New York City] administration may have taken a major step in that direction when it appointed . . . [an Israeli citizen] as deputy city administrator. . . . His major task will be to expand the authority of the electronic machines and gradually eliminate human error.

The temperature in the lower atmosphere has been raised by as much as 14.4 degrees Farenheit by experiments in manipulating the weather, Yevgeni K. Fedorov, a Soviet weather expert, has reported. In a paper prepared for the session . . . of the World Meteorological Congress, Dr. Fedorov said that this result had been obtained by experiments in dissipating clouds "over areas of several thousand square kilometers."

Israeli scientists have invented an engine that translates chemical energy directly into mechanical energy. Fibers made of material with large molecules alternately lengthen and contract as they pass through different liquids. Endless bundles of polymeric fibers, looped over pulleys, turn a crankshaft. . . . Expected applications include the operation and control of delicate instruments in meteorological ballons, space ships and satellites.

Dr. Glenn T. Seaborg, chairman of the U.S. Atomic Energy Commission, forecast today [August 10, 1970] that electrical power distribution would be organized in worldwide networks using satellites and possibly microwave or laser beams to send energy where it is most needed.

It may seem gratuitous for me to point out that man has come a long way from his relatively passive dependence on his habitats in earlier adaptations, but several noteworthy themes and implications run through these news items. First, it is becoming an everyday occurrence to read of such developments; we no longer have to wait decades or centuries for major technological breakthroughs. Second, these developments are taking place on a worldwide scale. This fact underlies the hypothesis stated in Selection 3 that the species as a whole, constituting a single community, is becoming the adaptive unit. Third, combinations and permutations of previously harnessed energy systems—and the development of new sources of energy—have almost freed man from reliance on muscular energy in productive activities. Fourth, man is on the brink of making new cultural uses of space, terrestrially and extraterrestrially, as accompaniments of many of these developments.

An important implication of such developments is that their new uses and new sources of energy will require appropriate organizations of social relations so that effective use can be made of them. The purpose of this section is to try to apply to the modern world what we have learned about the nature of human adaptation and to present some speculative hypotheses about the direction of man's adaptations and adjustments. Many of our organizations of social relations, such as the family and our political institutions, were designed during earlier levels of adaptation; present and future adaptations and adjustments may render them maladaptive.

Even if our current industrial innovations (and those of the future) prove to be adaptive, they may still contain disadvantages and problems for people. It has been suggested that one danger to man is that he may become accommodated to the disadvantages that result from modern adaptations: urban noise, overcrowding, pollution, supersonic travel and dislocations in body-clock mechanisms, monotonous work, centralized bureaucratic control, impersonal (automated) instruction, dull architecture, and the like. These are aspects of a more general question: How does man shape himself while he shapes his environments? Can man control the shapes he imposes on himself by controlling the shapes he gives his environments?

We do not know the full potentials of individual members of the species; hence we know what man is doing to his environments but we do not know what man's environments are doing to him, what they are helping him realize, and what they are thwarting. That the species has a future cannot be questioned; the increasing immunity to destruction achieved by groups at successive levels of adaptation is a prognosticator of this (which is not to say that we might not kill an awful lot of people in the process). But we know almost nothing about the future of—and for—the individual. This is one of the major challenges confronting our sciences.

There are any number of starting points for examining the appropriateness of organizations of social relations to the technological systems that are currently maturing. One of the most suggestive is the riderless tractor used in "factories in the fields." To regard this tractor as a climax is to take a myopic view of food production in the future. Once a computer-run tractor is put into operation, there is no basic reason why it should be run from an isolated farmhouse; it probably will be more efficient to have farms throughout the continent or even the world run by computer consoles centralized in Chicago or in Brussels. And even this tractor might one day be replaced by artificial food, produced by machines in factories.

Let us take the simplest plow agriculture as another starting point. This adaptation required a network of kinsmen to produce food; a man and his son (and possibly sons-in-law) usually worked a farm, together with kinsmen in other families who cooperated in their exploitative activities. Links of kinsmen and neighbors were an important segment of the adaptive unit; the availability of assistance, credit, access to seed and other resources, and marketing facilities depended on fairly close-knit social relations, bringing in its wake the pressures and responses to conformity that characterize agriculture life.

Because plow agriculture relied on muscular energy to an important degree, every farmer needed ready access to labor. If he could not purchase it—and hired labor itself involved a particular type of social organization—he had to be able to borrow and exchange labor in cooperation with his neighbors, suggesting an appropriate organization of social relations. In *The Polish Peasant in Europe and America* (New York: Dover, 1958), William I. Thomas and Florian Znaniecki provide a clear and dramatic picture of how the Polish peasant was constantly threatened by loss of credit and other marketing necessities if he deviated even slightly from local norms. One of these pressures was embodied in the saying, "He who learns written stuff casts himself into hell."

In contrast, the production of food by means of implements that are impersonally controlled by electronic (rather than muscular) energy implies more than the elimination of rural and hamlets and villages. The disappearance of these small communities also foretells the settlement patterns and organizations of social relations that will substitute for them, such as the metropolises.

In industrial society, the machine sets the intellectual standard not only for the organization of factories but for almost all other productive activities as well. Courts and lawyers' offices, operating rooms, universities, and military organizations all function by the same rational considerations as those of a factory. I have never met the man who signs my monthly paycheck; in fact, I do not even know his name without examining the checks. At a university where I once taught, a professor was brought up on disciplinary charges before a faculty-student committee for consistently holding his class after the bell sounded. Such norms not only denote a particular intellectual standard for the organization of productive activities, they have important consequences for the organization of social relations generally. They should not be evaluated by the standards of an agricultural society, as people often do in bemoaning the "impersonality" of contemporary life. They are the standards of an industrial society, of a particular strategy of adaptation, of a stage in cultural evolution. As increasingly efficient sources of energy are harnessed, still further changes will have to be made in the organization of social relations.

Industrialization highlights an important problem that has been alluded to throughout this book but has not been dealt with directly. We have seen that a group's technology and its appropriate organization of social relations mediate people's relationship to the habitat. But in addition to the fact that machines now mediate this relationship, man also maintains particular kinds of relationships to the machine, just as pastoralists are characterized by unique relationships to the animals that are their principal means of production (see the introduction to Section III). Industrial man is as dependent on the machine as agricultural man was dependent on the plow and irrigation networks or pastoral man on his animal herds.

The ambivalence that people often express about the machine may be due to its relative novelty. For technological as well as political reasons, industrial societies exhibit the fastest rate of change experienced thus far in human history. Rapid technological changes lead to rapid reorganizations of social relations, in (for example) labor organization, family and household, religion, and the criteria for distributing wealth, though political factors also play a role in complex societies. The same hostility was shown toward the railroad, the stethoscope, electricity and telephones and printed books, when these were first put into use, as we now see toward television and computers. The machine shapes values and motivations as did the bow and arrow, the hoe and digging stick, domesticated herds, and the plow. Each of these means of production is associated with a particular organization of social relations that is legitimated and rationalized by appropriate value systems.

We can only speculate about the consequences of the changes that will have to be made in a post-industrial stage of development, when very little human work will be necessary to sustain life and most productive activities will be done mechanically, and machines (like computers) will control other machines. We benefit from the perspective of history when we study previous levels of evolution, but the emergent adaptations of industrial and post-industrial societies compel us to pose problems rather than analyze the patterns that have emerged. Let us take a few examples of questions that are suggested by the changes that already are discernible.

Rules and criteria in every society govern the ways in which people will be provided with a livelihood (see Selection 37), and one such rule in many industrial societies is that everyone should benefit according to his productivity, with a day's wage for a day's work. As productive activities dispense with muscular energy and substitute less personal and more efficient energy systems, it appears that many people who are willing and able find no jobs in the conventional organization of labor. These people will still have to be provided with a livelihood, however, and the values of society therefore will have to be changed. Concepts that equate nonproductiveness with ungodliness will have to be banished and new ways will have to be found for evaluating people socially.

This is already becoming evident in our colleges and universities where grading systems are under serious attack. Grades serve to denote different degrees of competence and ineptitude, supposedly reflecting potential degrees of aptitude and failure in the economic sphere. If very little work will be available or necessary in the post-industrial stage, most people will not even have a chance to succeed or fail economically or occupationally. Since schools are principally intended to prepare people for future labor, the criteria of the factory and the marketplace now predominating in our schools will be—and are already beginning to be—regarded as irrelevent.

Any discussion of the challenges to society that asks what people without jobs will do with their time puts the computer before the tractor and overlooks a more fundamental problem. What will be the new standards, criteria, and ways of being human in this new adaptation, and in adaptations of the future? Generally, what people do with their time is determined in large part by their conceptualizations of how to be human. This is the fundamental consideration. The old ways of thinking about these issues, although appropriate to pre-modern adaptations (definitions of leisure and suggestions that people without jobs string beads, make lamps, play golf, or "be creative," whether or not they want to, or can), may be inappropriate to the new adaptations that are reaching fruition.

Another important question is the future of family organization. The nuclear family may well be maladaptive under modern conditions, and if this should prove to be the case, the household might substitute for it. The nuclear family is a kin group that is based on relationship by marriage and by descent, while the household is a residential and territorial unit; the two may in fact coincide, but they need not do so (see, for example, Selection 22).

Geographic (as well as social) mobility is one of the hallmarks of modern society. In an industrial adaptation the individual follows the machine or the job that will provide him with the best possible livelihood. This involves movement from one country to another as well as from region to region for an increasingly larger portion of society, and employment by governmental bureaucracies plays a major role in this mobility. The nuclear family's structure is designed to bind individuals to each other in marriage and biological kinship. Intimately related networks of nuclear families that lived in fairly close proximity to each other were adaptive necessities when people relied on the cooperative exchange of labor, but when reliance on muscular energy was no longer an important element in the group's adaptation, the stage was set for the atrophy of these social relations. Graphic evidence of atrophy is provided by the following notice, which appeared in *Drum,* published in Lagos, Nigeria, one of the better-known African news-weeklies. (It is here reproduced from *Atlas,* 13 [February, 1967]: 45.)

NOTICE

MR. GACHEGO DOES
NOT WISH TO SEE
ANY MORE OF HIS
'BROTHERS' ON
PAY DAY

Instead—and increasingly often under industrial condition—the primary social expectation is that each individual will rely on his own skills, which he sells on a nationwide or worldwide market, in gaining a livelihood. Thus, the loss of individual skills, the displacement of small businesses by large industrial enterprises and corporate giants, philosophical orientations that stress the "value of the individual," and geographic mobility must all be seen as threads in a single fabric. (It is difficult to avoid the observation that "hippies" adhere to these values in recruiting members as much as, if not more than, the supposedly conservative groups in the society, such as business corporations. This similarity can be seen in demands for conformity, for example, in modes of dress and hair styles, which have changed in the society at large under "hippy" influence.)

An important adjustment within this adaptation is a growing acceptance of divorce and a rising divorce rate. As bonds of kinship beyond the household become attenuated and cohabiting couples become increasingly socially isolated, relations between partners increase in intensity—there are fewer safety valves outside the marriage. When a marriage becomes unbearable the only direction to take is away from it entirely. As more people with children divorce, the remarriage of people with children increases correspondingly. Thus one of the many consequences of modern adaptation is an increasing discrepancy between family and household; more and more—at least in contemporary American society—the autonomous household contains segments of different nuclear families. The older, agriculturally based correspondence between family and household is beginning to disappear. Another of the growing pressures on the traditional family system is women's increasing economic independence.

This new adaptation will require many adjustments within household and family organization. To take but one example, entirely new premises and rules may have to be developed in connection with inheritance and taxation. One of our heritages from the agricultural past, in which the kin-group organization of labor was an important aspect of the adaptation, is the equation of lines of inheritance and tax liability with lines of kinship. But as generational relationships in household organization become less and less synonymous with biological kinship, the rules that govern inheritance and taxation will have to take this into account.

Of course, no legislator worth his votes would propose separating inheritance from biological kinship, and what is likely to happen is something along the following lines. A man dies intestate (as many do). He had children by his first wife, from whom he was divorced. She retained custody of their children (in accord with custom, not law) and remarried. The man in question also remarried, and the second wife, who also had children by her first marriage, brought them to her new household. She and her second husband then had children together. According to present law, if the man had not legally adopted the children of his second wife, they would not be entitled to inherit from him if he died intestate. But one of these days such a child will bring suit and demand that he be given the same inheritance rights as a biological offspring, on the grounds that the deceased man treated the plaintiff as his own in a social sense, and the biological kinship cannot be treated as the determining factor in the modern world. The first few times this happens the suits will be rejected by judges who will cite the letter of the law. Finally, sensing the support of public opinion, a judge will award inheritance rights to such a child on the ground that agriculturally based laws are not appropriate to modern conditions. And students in an anthropology class will some day study the quaint customs of people in transition to an industrial adaptation who continued to equate inheritance with biological kinship.

It has been suggested throughout this book, directly or indirectly, that an important aspect of man's attempts to free himself from the limitations of his habitats has been his search for rational and deliberate controls and planning. The sciences—including the social sciences—are important tools in modern adaptation. They have shown us that every alteration in a society's adaptation leads to the creation of a new environment—that man cannot change one aspect of his adaptation without producing changes in others. We also have seen that a faster rate of change is a prominent accompaniment of the succession of levels of adaptation. Hence, as the rate of change increases and as man exercises more rational and deliberate control over his environments, he can no longer let cultural nature take its course. We must ask new questions, for which the sciences are admirably suited: How rapid a rate of change can people tolerate? What are the minimal elements (if any) of family and household relationships that people need? How much ethnic heterogeneity is necessary or desirable for a nation's viability? Who will the decision-makers be in even more centralized nation-states? How—or can—an international adaptive unit be fashioned?

Before we can ask new types of questions about man we must know what he is, what he is capable of, and that is necessarily excluded by his constitution. For this, we have to know not only the principles that govern cultural adaptation and adjustment but more about the biological stuff of which man is made. His "genetically programmed" predispositions, limits, and potentials probably were established during his nonhuman past, and these constitute some of the most important perimeters within which he can function. Man must adapt not only to his habitats but also to his biological milieus. To what extent is man capable of freeing himself from his biological limitations, especially as they affect his family and household organizations, his stratification systems, and the like? Much more research must be done here.

Some of the questions posed above, together with the concept of "genetic programming," are taken from "The Zoological Perspective in Social Science," by Lionel Tiger and Robin Fox (*Man*, 1 [N.S.] [1966]: 75-81), and "Patterns of Male Association," by Lionel Tiger (*Current Anthropology*, 8 [1967]: 268-69). Some of these questions also are explored in *Man in Adaptation: The Biosocial Background. The Polish Peasant in Europe and America* (New York: Dover, 1958) is an excellent introduction to some of the initial adaptations and adjustments people have to make in the transition from an agricultural to an industrial adaptation. Along similar but more general and abstract lines is *The Secular City*, by Harvey Cox (New York: Macmillan, 1965), which explores the need for a new theology legitimating the impersonality and mobility of the modern world. *The Rise of the Meritocracy*, by Michael Young (New York: Random

House, 1959), is a satiric anticipation, in sociological terms, of life at the end of the twentieth century.

The reader who wants an empirical base for further exploration of changes in family and household organization will find the following a good starting point: "Types of Family and Types of Economy," by Meyer F. Nimkoff and Russell Middleton (*American Journal of Sociology,* 66 [1960]: 215-24; *After Divorce* (New York: Free Press, 1956) and *World Revolution and Family Patterns* (New York: Free Press, 1963), by William J. Goode; and Part II ("Marriage and the Family") of *Man in Adaptation: The Institutional Framework,* which traces the broad outlines of changes in household systems from hunter-gatherers to the present and speculates about post-industrial developments. A different kind of speculative look into the future is *The Year 2000,* by Herman Kahn and Anthony J. Wiener (New York: Macmillan, 1967).

For the challenge that faces modern societies in developing new ways of being human, the reader will find *Centuries of Childhood,* by Philippe Aries (New York: Alfred A. Knopf, 1962), very stimulating. Using paintings as a social document, the author of this fascinating book traces changes in the conceptualization of the individual from medieval times to the eighteenth century, with special emphasis on the treatment of children.

35. THE HUMAN RESULTS OF THE INDUSTRIAL REVOLUTION: 1750-1850

E. J. HOBSBAWM

Reprinted from Industry and Empire *(Baltimore and Harmondsworth: Penguin Books, 1969).*
E. J. Hobsbawm is Professor of Economic and Social History at Birkbeck College, University
of London. His books include Labouring Men: Studies in the History of Labour, Primitive
Rebels: Studies in Archaic Forms of Social Movements in the 19th and 20th Centuries,
Bandits, *and* Industry and Empire *(from which this selection is taken).*

■ Terms like "The Industrial Revolution" are in a sense, very unfortunate because they convey an impression of everything changing at once and for everyone. That this is untrue can easily be seen if we look around us today and watch our stumblings as we both inch and hurtle into what a myopic historian may someday refer to as "The Post-industrial Revolution." As Hobsbawm stresses early in this selection, the Industrial Revolution was anything but revolutionary for the advantaged classes who had been, and continued to be, placid and prosperous—and who wondered what all the fuss was about among the laboring and disenfranchised classes. Modifications in the advantaged classes' family organizations, religious and secular values, and attitudes toward the organization of labor had already taken place to make them adaptive to the demands of capitalism (which is not the same as industrialization) during the later stages of European agriculture. Moreover, factories employing hundreds of people had been in existence for more than a century before the advent of industrialism; what had changed was the sources of harnessed energy to drive machines, especially water power and steam and, later, electricity.

But no such prior or anticipatory adaptations had occurred among the proletariat, and it was they who bore the brunt of the demands of eighteenth century industrialization and urbanization. The large peasant family (which was a unit of production as well as consumption), their cooperative labor organizations, their habits of seasonal work, and their personal relations with agrarian employers, were, as Hobsbawm points out, maladaptive in industrial urban centers. Patterns of nuclear family relations had to develop, in which each person sold or bartered his own labor. New forms of cooperation among laborers—such as trade

unions and mutual aid societies—and new attitudes toward the routinized and monotonous round of factory work had to emerge. Relations between employer and employee became impersonal and bureaucratized.

Hobsbawm says that "the city destroyed society," but this is hyperbole. The industrial city—by which we mean a particular organization of social relations in a particular habitat using a particular technology—is more accurately viewed as an aspect of the adaptive changes that had to take place in the society as a whole (the adaptive unit) in response to the demands of industrialization. I do not think that the industrial city "destroyed society" any more than did the plow agricultural village that replaced the horticultural kin settlement; it was no more pernicious than the lineage which replaced the hunting-gathering camp. Another way of saying this is that the machine is no more inherently evil than a plow, digging stick, or bow and arrow.

Hobsbawm refers to the English Poor Law Act of 1834 as among man's most inhuman achievements. This legislation established three principles: (1) national uniformity—that is, identity in treatment of each class of destitute people throughout the kingdom; (2) a requirement that a pauper's condition be less desirable economically than that of the poorest employed laborer; and (3) the substitution of indoor for outdoor workhouse relief. Crosscutting these principles, the administration of the law was centralized by abolising the parochial (local) system of relief. This law remained in effect for nearly a century, though with frequent changes.

Every society must cope with the problem of people without a source of livelihood, and it must constantly attempt to adapt to new conditions. Tribal societies also have mechanisms for the care of the indigent, which are

528

aspects of the customary law of kinship relations rather than the formal law of a stratified and bureaucratized society. Retrospectively, the history of English "poor laws" illustrates man's fumblings and bumblings to evolve a system that will help him adapt to a habitat that changes with increasing rapidity, but for which there are no obvious precedents. This is equally true of other aspects of the legal system, marriage, household organization, education, religion, the arts, and so forth. Given the novelty of their problems in 1834, the lack of precedent and the speed of change, could the English have done any better? Can we?

A good starting point for the reader who wants to study this transitional period is *Economic and Philosophic Manuscripts of 1844,* by Karl Marx (New York: International Publishers, 1964), in which Marx spelled out the problem of the "alienation" of the industrial laborer. As an illustration of diversity within the industrial stage of development, see *Punishment and Responsibility: Essays in the Philosophy of Law,* by H. L. A. Hart (New York: Oxford University Press, paperback, 1968).

The writings of people who lived during the time discussed by Hobsbawm are invaluable sources of ethnographic data, especially in connection with emerging value systems. Good examples are *Self Help* (London: J. Murray, 1958) and *Life and Labor, or Characteristics of Men of Industry, Culture and Genius* (New York: Harpers, 1888), by Samuel Smiles; Smiles was an original purveyor of what we call today the Horatio Alger myth, and his books were runaway best-sellers in England in the second half of the nineteenth century. For the ideology of the first capitalist industrialists, see *On the Economy of Machinery and Manufactures,* by Charles Babbage, 4th edition (London: Chas. Knight, 1835) and *Principles of Sociology,* by Herbert Spencer (New York: Appleton, 1891). Perhaps the best documentation of the lives of the proletariat is the monumental (17 volumes) *Life and Labour of the People in London,* by Charles Booth and others (London: Macmillan, 1902-1903). I have found the novelists of this period to be among the best sources of data concerning emerging social patterns. One of the best modern sociological analyses of this period is *Social Change in the Industrial Revolution: An Application of Theory to the British Cotton Industry,* by Neil J. Smelser (Chicago: University of Chicago Press, 1959). ■

ARITHMETIC WAS the fundamental tool of the Industrial Revolution. Its makers saw it as a series of sums of addition and subtraction: the difference in cost between buying in the cheapest market and selling in the dearest, between cost of production and sale price, between investment and return. For Jeremy Bentham and his followers, the most consistent champions of this type of rationality, even morals and politics came under these simple calculations. Happiness was the object of policy. Every man's pleasure could be expressed (at least in theory) as a quantity and so could his pain. Deduct the pain from the pleasure and the net result was his happiness. Add the happinesses of all men and deduct the unhappinesses, and that government which secured the greatest happiness of the greatest number was the best. The accountancy of humanity would produce its debit and credit balances, like that of business.

The discussion of the human results of the Industrial Revolution has not entirely emancipated itself from this primitive approach. We still tend to ask ourselves: did it make people better or worse off, and if so by how much? To be more precise, we ask ourselves what quantities of purchasing power, or goods, services, and so on, that money can buy it gave to how many individuals, assuming that the woman with a washing machine will be better off than the one without (which is reasonable) but also (*a*) that private happiness consists in an accumulation of such things as consumer goods and (*b*) that public happiness consists in the greatest such accumulation by the greatest number of individuals (which is not). Such questions are important but also misleading. Whether the Industrial Revolution gave most Britons absolutely or relatively more and better food, clothes and housing is naturally of interest to every historian. But he will miss much of its point if he forgets that it was not merely a process of addition and subtraction, but *a fundamental social change.* It transformed the lives of men beyond recognition. Or, to be more exact, in its initial stages it destroyed their old ways of living and left them free to discover or make for themselves new ones, if they could and knew how. But it rarely told them how to set about it.

There is, indeed, a relation between the Industrial Revolution as a provider of comforts and as a social transformer. Those classes whose lives were least transformed were also, normally, those which benefited most obviously in material terms (and vice versa), and their failure to grasp what was troubling the rest, or to do anything effective about it, was due not only to material but also to moral contentment. Nobody is more complacent than a well-off or successful man who is also at ease in a world which seems to have been constructed precisely with persons like him in mind.

The British aristocracy and gentry were thus very little affected by industrialization, except for the better. Their rents swelled with the demand for farm produce, the expansion of cities (whose soil they owned) and of mines, forges and railways (which were situated on their estates). And even when times were bad for agriculture, as between 1815 and the 1830s, they were unlikely to be reduced to penury. Their social predominance remained untouched, their political power in the countryside complete, and even in the nation not seriously troubled, though from the 1830s they had to consider the susceptibilities of a powerful and militant provincial middle class of businessmen. It may well be that after 1830 clouds began to appear on the pure sky of the gentlemanly life, but even they looked larger and darker than they were only because the first fifty years of industrialization had been so golden an era for the landed and titled Briton. If the eighteenth century was a glorious age for aristocracy, the era of George IV (as regent and king) was paradise. Their packs of hounds (the modern fox-hunting uniform still reflects its essentially Regency origins) criss-crossed the shires. Their pheasants, protected by spring-guns and keepers against all who had not the equivalent of £100 a year in rent,

awaited the *battue*. Their Palladian and neo-classical country houses multiplied, more than at any time before or since except the Elizabethan. Since their economics, unlike their social style, were already adjusted to the business methods of the middle class, the age of steam and counting-houses posed no great problems of spiritual adjustment, unless perhaps they belonged to the backwoods of the lesser squirearchy, or their income came from the cruel caricature of a rural economy which was Ireland. They did not have to stop being feudal, for they had long ceased to be so. At most some rude and ignorant baronet from the hinterland faced the novel need to send his son to a proper school (the new "public schools" were constructed from the 1840s to civilize them as well as the rising businessmen's offspring), or to adjust to more frequent spells of life in London.

Equally placid and prosperous were the lives of the numerous parasites of rural aristocratic society, high and low—that rural and small-town world of functionaries of and suppliers of the nobility and gentry, and the traditional, somnolent, corrupt and, as the Industrial Revolution proceeded, increasingly reactionary professions. The Church and the English universities slumbered on, cushioned by their incomes, their privileges and abuses, and their relations among the peerage, their corruption attacked with greater consistency in theory than in practice. The lawyers, and what passed for a civil service, were unreformed and unregenerate. Once again the old regime probably reached its peak in the decade after the Napoleonic Wars, after which a few waves began to form on the surface of the quiet backwaters of cathedral close, college, inns of court and the rest. From the 1830 on change came to them, though rather gently (except for the savage and contemptuous, but not notably effective, attacks upon them by outsiders, of which Charles Dickens' novels are the most familiar example). But the respectable Victorian clergy of Trollope's Barchester, though very far from the Hogarthian hunting parson/ magistrates of the Regency, were the product of a carefully moderate adjustment, not of disruption. Nobody was as tender of the susceptibilities of weavers and farm-laborers as of parsons and dons, when it came to introducing them into a new world.

One important effect of this continuity—part reflection of the established power of the old upper class, part deliberate unwillingness to exacerbate political tensions among the men of money or influence—was that the rising new business classes found a firm pattern of life waiting for them. Success brought no uncertainty, so long as it was great enough to lift a man into the ranks of the upper class. He would become a "gentleman," doubtless with a country house, perhaps eventually a knighthood or peerage, a seat in Parliament for himself or his Oxbridge-educated son, and a clear and prescribed social role. His wife would become a "lady," instructed in her duties by a multitude of handbooks of etiquette which slid off the presses from the 1840s on. The older brand of businessman had long benefited from this process of assimilation, above all the *merchant* and financier—especially the merchant involved in overseas trade, who remained the most respected and most crucial form of entrepreneur long after the mills, factories and foundries covered the northern skies with smoke and fog. For him, too, the Industrial Revolution brought no major transformations, except perhaps in the commodities which he bought and sold. Indeed, as we have seen, it inserted itself into the powerful, worldwide and prosperous framework of trading which was the basis of British eighteenth-century power. Economically and socially their activities and status were familiar, whatever the rung on the ladder of success which they had climbed. By the Industrial Revolution the descendants of Abel Smith, banker of Nottingham, were already established in country seats, sitting in Parliament and intermarried with the gentry (though not yet, as later, with royalty). The Glyns had already moved up from a dry-salting business in Hatton Garden to a similar position, the Barings had expanded from the West Country clothing manufacture into what was soon to become

a great power in international trade and finance, and their social ascent had kept step with their economic. Peerages were already achieved or round the corner. Nothing was more natural than that other types of businessmen—like Robert Peel Sen., the cotton-master—should climb the same slope of wealth and public honour, at the peak of which there beckoned government, or even (as for Peel's son and the son of Gladstone, the Liverpool merchant) the post of Prime Minister. Indeed the so-called "Peelite" group in Parliament in the second third of the nineteenth century represented very much this group of business families assimilated into a landed oligarchy, though at odds with it when the economic interests of land and business clashed.

However, absorption into an aristocratic oligarchy is, by definition, available only for a minority—in this instance of the exceptionally rich, or those in businesses which had acquired respectability through tradition. The great mass of men, rising from modest, though rarely from really poverty-stricken, beginnings to business affluence, the even greater mass of those pressing below them out of the laboring poor into the middle classes, were too numerous to be absorbed, and in the early stages of their progress unconcerned about absorption (though their wives might often feel less neutral in the matter). They recognized themselves increasingly—and after 1830 generally—as a "middle class," and not merely a "middle rank" in society. They claimed rights and power as such. Moreover—especially when, as so often, they came from non-Anglican stock, and from regions lacking a solid aristocratic traditional structure—they did not possess emotional attachments to the old regime. Such were the pillars of the Anti-Corn-Law League, rooted in the new business world of Manchester—Henry Ashworth, John Bright of Rochdale (both Quakers), Potter of the *Manchester Guardian*, the Gregs, Brotherton, the Bible Christian ex-cotton-master, George Wilson, the starch and gum manufacturer, and Cobden himself, who soon exchanged his not very brilliant career in the calico trade for the function of the fulltime ideologist.

Yet, though the Industrial Revolution fundamentally changed their—or perhaps their parents'—lives, setting them into new towns, posing them and the nation new problems, it did not disorganize their lives. The simple maxims of utilitarian philosophy and liberal economics, broken down even further into the slogans of their journalists and propagandists, provided them with what guidance they needed, and if that was not enough, the traditional ethic—protestant or otherwise—of the aspiring and ambitious entrepreneur, thrift, hard work, moral puritanism, did the rest. The fortresses of aristocratic privilege, superstition and corruption, which had still to be razed to allow free enterprise to introduce its millennium, also still protected them against the sight of the uncertainties and problems which lay beyond their walls. Until the 1830s they hardly even had as yet to face the problem of what to do with more money than could be spent on a comfortable sufficiency and reinvested in an expanding business. The ideal of an individualist society, a private family unit supplying all its material and moral needs on the basis of a private business, suited them, because they were men who no longer needed traditions. Their efforts had raised them out of the rut. They were in a sense their own reward, the content of life, and if that was not enough, there was always the money, the comfortable house increasingly removed from the smoke of mill and counting-house, the devoted and modest wife, the family circle, the enjoyment of travel, art, science and literature. They were successful and respected. "Denounce the middle classes as you may," said the Anti-Corn-Law agitator to a hostile Chartist audience, "there is not a man among you worth a half-penny a week that is not anxious to elevate himself among them." Only the nightmare shadow of bankruptcy or debt sometimes lay over their lives, and we can still recognize it in the novels of the period: the trust in an unreliable partner, the commercial crisis, the loss of middle-class comfort, the womenfolk reduced to genteel penury, perhaps even emigration to that dustbin of the unwanted and the unsuccessful, the colonies.

The successful middle class and those who aspired to emulate them were satisfied. Not so the laboring poor—in the nature of things the majority—whose traditional world and way of life the Industrial Revolution destroyed, without automatically substituting anything else. It is this disruption which is at the heart of the question about the social effects of industrialization.

Labour in an industrial society is in many ways quite different from pre-industrial work. First, it is overwhelmingly the labour of "proletarians," who have no source of income worth mentioning except a cash wage which they receive for their work. Pre-industrial labor, on the other hand, consists largely of families with their own peasant holdings, craft workshops, and so on, or whose wage-income supplements—or is supplemented by—some such direct access to the means of production. Moreover, the proletarian whose only link with his employer is a "cash-nexus" must be distinguished from the "servant" or pre-industrial dependent, who has a much more complex human and social relationship with his "master," and one which implies duties on both sides, though very unequal ones. The Industrial Revolution replaced the servant and man by the "operative" and "hand," except of course the (mainly female) domestic servant, whose numbers it multiplied for the benefit of the growing middle class, for the safest way of distinguishing oneself from the laborers was to employ labor oneself.[1]

Second, industrial labor—and especially mechanized factory labor—imposes a regularity, routine and monotony quite unlike pre-industrial rhythms of work, which depend on the variation of the seasons or the weather, the multiplicity of tasks in occupations unaffected by the rational division of labor, the vagaries of other human beings or animals,

1. Certain categories of workers were, however, not totally reduced to the simple cash-nexus, such as the "railway servants" who paid the price of discipline and lack of rights for unusually good security, chances of gradual promotion, and even retirement pensions.

or even a man's own desire to play instead of working. This was so even in skilled pre-industrial wage-work, such as that of journeymen craftsmen, whose ineradicable taste for not starting the week's work until the Tuesday ("Saint Monday") was the despair of their masters. Industry brings the tyranny of the clock, the pace-setting machine, and the complex and carefully-timed interaction of processes: the measurement of life not in seasons ("Michaelmas term" or "Lent term") or even in weeks and days, but in minutes, and above all a mechanized *regularity* of work which conflicts not only with tradition, but with all the inclinations of a humanity as yet unconditioned into it. And since men did not take spontaneously to these new ways, they had to be forced—by work discipline and fines, by Master and Servant laws such as that of 1823 which threatened them with jail for breach of contract (but their masters only with fines), and by wages so low that only unremitting and uninterrupted toil would earn them enough money to keep alive, without providing the money which would take them away from labor for more than the time to eat, sleep and—since this was a Christian country—pray on the Sabbath.

Third, labor in the industrial age increasingly took place in the unprecedented environment of the big city; and this in spite of the fact that the most old-fashioned of industrial revolutions developed a good deal of its activities in industrialized villages of miners, weavers, nail- and chain-makers and other specialist workers. In 1750 there had been only two cities in Britain with more than 50,000 inhabitants—London and Edinburgh; in 1801 there were already eight, in 1851 twenty-nine, including nine over 100,000. By this time more Britons lived in town than in country, and almost one third of Britons lived in cities over 50,000 inhabitants. And what cities! It was not merely that smoke hung over them and filth impregnated them, that the elementary public services—water-supply, sanitation, street-cleaning, open spaces, and so on—could not keep pace with the mass migration of men into the cities, thus producing, especially after 1830, epidemics of cholera, typhoid and an appalling constant toll of the two great groups of nineteenth-century urban killers—air pollution and water pollution, or respiratory and intestinal disease. It was not merely that the new city populations, sometimes entirely unused to nonagrarian life, like the Irish, pressed into overcrowded and bleak slums, whose very sight froze the heart of the observer. "Civilization works its miracles," wrote the great French liberal de Tocqueville of Manchester, "and civilized man is turned back almost into a savage." Nor was it simply the steely unplanned concentration of those who built them on utility and financial profit, which Charles Dickens caught in his famous description of "Coketown" and which built endless rows of houses and warehouses, cobbled streets and canals, but neither fountains nor public squares, promenades and trees, nor sometimes even churches. (The company which built the new railway town of Crewe graciously allowed its inhabitants to use a locomotive roundhouse for divine service now and then.) After 1848 the cities tended to acquire such public furniture, but in the first generations of industrialization they had very little of it, unless by chance they inherited traditions of gracious public building or open spaces from the past. The life of the poor man outside work was passed in the rows of cottages or tenements, the cheap improvised inns and the cheap improvised chapels which alone recorded that man is not content to live by bread alone.

But more than this: the city destroyed society. "There is not a town in the world where the distance between the rich and the poor is so great or the barrier betwen them so difficult to be crossed," wrote a clergyman about Manchester. "There is far less *personal* communication between the master cotton spinner and his workmen, the calico printer and his blue-handed boys, between the master tailor and his apprentices, than there is between the Duke of Welington and the humblest laborer on his estate. The city was a volcano, to whose rumblings the rich and powerful listened with fear, and whose eruptions they dreaded. But for its poor inhabitants it was not merely a standing reminder of their exclusion from human society. It was a stony desert, which they had to make habitable by their own efforts.

Fourthly, pre-industrial experience, tradition, wisdom and morality provided no adequate guide for the kind of behavior which a capitalist economy required. The pre-industrial laborer responded to material incentives, insofar as he wanted to earn enough to enjoy what was thought of as comfort at the social level to which it had pleased God to call him, but even his ideas of comfort were determined by the past, and limited by what was "fitting" for one of his station, or perhaps the one immediately above his. If he earned more than the pittance he regarded as sufficient, he might—like the immigrant Irish, the despair of bourgeois rationality—take it out in leisure, in parties and alcohol. His sheer material ignorance of the best way to live in a city, or to eat industrial food (so very different from village food) might actually make his poverty worse than it "need have been"; that is, than it might have been if he had not been the sort of person he inevitably was. This conflict between the "moral economy" of the past and the economic rationality of the capitalist present was particularly clear in the realm of social security. The traditional view, which still survived in a distorted way in all classes of rural society and in the internal relations of working-class groups, was that a man had a right to earn a living, and if unable to do so, a right to be kept alive by his community. The view of middle-class liberal economists was that men must take such jobs as the market offered, wherever and at whatever rate it offered, and that the rational man would, by individual or voluntary collective saving and insurance make provision for accident, illness and old age. The residuum of paupers could not, admittedly, be left actually to starve, but they ought not to be given more than the absolute minimum—provided it was less than the lowest wage offered in the market—and in the most discouraging conditions. The Poor Law was not so much intended to help the unfortunate as to stigmatize the self-confessed failures of society. The middle-class view of Friendly Societies was that they were rational forms of insurance. It clashed head-on with the working-class view, which also took them literally as communities of friends in a desert of individuals, who naturally spent their money also on social gatherings, festivities, and the "useless" fancy-dress and ritual to which Oddfellows, Foresters and the other "Orders" which sprang up all over the north in the period after 1815 were so addicted. Similarly the irrationally expensive funerals and wakes on which laborers insisted as a traditional tribute to the dead and communal reaffirmation of the living were incomprehensible to a middle class which observed that those who liked them were often unable to pay for them. Yet the first benefit paid by a trade union and friendly society was almost invariably funeral benefit.

Insofar as social security depended on the laborer's own efforts, it therefore tended to be economically inefficient by middle-class standards; insofar as it depended on their rulers, who determined what little public assistance there was, it was an engine of degradation and oppression more than a means of material relief. There have been few more inhuman statutes than the Poor Law Act of 1834, which made all relief "less eligible" than the lowest wage outside, confined it to the jail-like workhouse, forcibly separating husbands, wives and children in order to punish the poor for their destitution, and discourage them for the dangerous temptation of procreating further paupers. It was never completely applicable, for where the poor were strong they resisted its extremes, and in time it became slightly less penal. Yet it remained the basis of English poor relief until the eve of the First World War, and the childhood experiences of Charlie Chaplin show that it remained very much what it had been when Dickens' *Oliver Twist* expressed the popular horror of it in the 1830s. And in the 1830s—indeed until the 1850s—a minimum of ten per cent of the English population were paupers.

Up to a point—as with the Georgian merchant and industrialist—the experience of the past was not as irrelevant as it might have been in a country leaping more radically and directly from a nonindustrial to a modern industrial age; and as in fact it was in Ireland or the Scottish Highlands. The semi-industrial Britain of the seventeenth and eighteenth centuries in some ways prepared and anticipated the industrial age of the nineteenth. For instance, the fundamental institution of working-class self-defense, the *trade union,* was already in being in the eighteenth century, partly in the unsystematic, but not ineffective, form of periodic "collective bargaining by riot" (as among seamen, miners, weavers and framework knitters), partly in the much stabler form of craft societies for skilled journeymen, sometimes with loose national links through the practice of assisting unemployed members of the trade tramping in search of work or experience.

In a very real sense the bulk of British workers had adjusted itself to a changing, industrializing, though not yet revolutionized society. For some kinds of labor, whose conditions did not change fundamentally as yet —again miners and seamen come to mind— the old traditions could still suffice: sailors multiplied their songs about the new experiences of the nineteenth century, such as the whaling off Greenland, but they were traditional folksongs. An important group had even accepted, indeed welcomed, industry, science and progress (though not capitalism). These were the "artisans" or "mechanics," the men of skill, expertise, independence and education, who saw no great distinction between themselves and those of similar social standing who chose to become entrepreneurs, or to remain yeoman farmers or small shopkeepers: the body of men who overlapped the frontiers between working and middle classes. The "artisans" were the natural leaders of ideology and organization among the laboring poor, the pioneers of Radicalism (and later the early, Owenite, versions of Socialism), of discussion and popular higher education—through Mechanics' Institutes, Halls of Science, and a variety of clubs, societies and free-thinking printers and publishers—the nucleus of trade unions, Jacobin,

Chartist or any other progressive movements. The agricultural laborers' riots were stiffened by village cobblers and builders; in the cities little groups of handloom weavers, printers, tailors, and perhaps a few small businessmen and shopkeepers provided political continuity of leadership on the left until the decline of Chartism, if not beyond. Hostile to capitalism, they were unique in elaborating ideologies which did not simply seek to return to an idealized tradition, but envisaged a just society which would also be technically progressive. Above all, they represented the ideal of freedom and independence in an age when everything conspired to degrade labor.

Yet even these were only transitional solutions for the workers' problem. Industrialization multiplied the number of handloom weavers and framework-knitters until the end of the Napoleonic Wars. Thereafter it destroyed them by slow strangulation: militant and thoughtful communities like the Dunfermline workers broke up in demoralization, pauperization and emigration in the 1830s. Skilled craftsmen were degraded into sweated outworkers, as in the London furniture trades, and even when they survived the economic earthquakes of the 1830s and 40s, they could no longer be expected to play so great a social role in an economy in which the factory was no longer a regional exception, but the rule. Pre-industrial traditions could not keep their heads above the inevitably rising level of industrial society. In Lancashire we can observe the ancient ways of spending holidays—the rush bearing, wrestling matches, cock-fighting and bull baiting—dying out after 1840; and the forties also mark the end of the era when folksong remained the major musical idiom of industrial workers. The great social movements of this period— from Luddism to Chartism—also died away: they had been movements which drew their force not merely from the extreme hardships of the age, but also from the force of these older methods of poor men's action. It was to take another forty years before the British working class evolved new ways of struggle and living.

Such were the qualitative stresses which

racked the laboring poor in the first industrial generations. To these we must add the quantitative ones—their material poverty. Whether this actually increased or not has been hotly debated among historians, but the very fact that the question can be put already supplies a gloomy answer: nobody seriously argues that conditions deteriorate in periods when they plainly do not, such as the 1950s.

There is, of course, no dispute about the fact that, *relatively,* the poor grew poorer, simply because the country, and its rich and middle class, so obviously grew wealthier. The very moment when the poor were at the end of their tether—in the early and middle forties—was the moment when the middle class dripped with excess capital, to be wildly invested in railways and spent on the bulging, opulent household furnishings displayed at the Great Exhibition of 1851, and on the palatial municipal constructions which prepared to rise in the smoky northern cities.

Secondly, there is—or ought to be—no dispute about the abnormal pressure on working-class consumption in the period of early industrialism, which is reflected in this relative pauperization. Industrialism means a relative diversion of national income from consumption to investment, a substitution of foundries for beefsteaks. In a capitalist economy this takes the form, largely, of a diversion of income from noninvesting classes like peasants and laborers, to potentially investing ones, namely the owners of estates and business enterprises, that is from the poor to the rich. In Britain, there was never the slightest general shortage of capital, given the country's wealth and the relative cheapness of the early industrial processes, but a large section of those who benefited from this diversion of income—and the richest among them in particular—invested their money outside direct industrial development or wasted it, thus forcing the rest of the (smaller) entrepreneurs to press even more harshly upon labour. Moreover, the economy did not rely for its development on the purchasing capacity of its working population: indeed economists tended to assume that their wages

would not be much above the level of subsistence. Theories advocating high wages as economically advantageous began to appear finally round the middle of the century, and the industries supplying the domestic consumer market—for example clothing and furniture—were not revolutionized until its second half. The Englishman who wanted a pair of trousers had the choice either of having them made to measure by a tailor, buying the cast-offs of his social superiors, relying on charity, going in rags, or making his own. Finally, certain essential requisites of life— food and perhaps housing, but certainly urban amenities—had the greatest difficulty in keeping pace with the expansion of the cities, or the population as a whole, and sometimes clearly did not keep pace. Thus the supplies of meat for London almost certainly lagged behind the city's population from 1800 until the 1840s.

Thirdly, there is no dispute about certain classes of the population whose conditions undoubtedly deteriorated. These were the agricultural labourers (about one million working men in 1851), at all events those in the south and east of England, and the smallholders and crofters in the Celtic fringe of Scotland and Wales. (The eight and a half million Irishmen, of course, mainly peasants, were pauperized beyond belief. Something not far short of a million of them actually starved to death in the Famine of 1846-7, the greatest human catastrophe of the nineteenth century anywhere in the world). There were further the declining industries and occupations, displaced by technical progress, of whom the half-million handloom weavers are the best known example, but by no means the only one. They starved progressively in a vain attempt to compete with the new machines by working more and more cheaply. Their numbers had doubled between 1788 and 1814 and their wages risen markedly until the middle of the Wars; but between 1805 and 1833 they fell from 23 shillings a week to 6s. 3d. There were also the nonindustrialized occupations which met the rapidly growing demand for their goods, not by technical revolution, but by subdivision and "sweating"—for example the innumerable seamstresses in their garrets or cellars.

Whether, if we were to add up all the hard-pressed sections of the labouring poor and set against them those who managed somewhat to improve their incomes, we would find a net average gain or loss is an insoluble question, for we simply do not know enough about earnings, unemployment, retail prices and other necessary data to answer it decisively. There was, quite certainly, no significant general improvement. There may or may not have been deterioration between the middle 1790s and the middle 1840s. Thereafter, there was undoubted improvement—and it is the contrast between this (modest as it was) and the earlier period that really says all we need to know. After the early forties consumption rose markedly—until then it had crawled along without much change. After the 1840s—still, and rightly, named the "Hungry Forties" even though in Britain (but not in Ireland) things improved during most of them—unemployment undoubtedly declined sharply. For instance, no subsequent cyclical depression was even faintly as catastrophic as the slump of 1841-2. And above all, the sense of imminent social explosion, which had been present in Britain almost without interruption since the end of the Napoleonic Wars (except in most of the 1820s), disappeared. Britons ceased to be revolutionary.

Of course this pervasive social and political unrest reflected not merely material poverty but social pauperization: the destruction of old ways of life without the substitution of anything the laboring poor could regard as a satisfactory equivalent. But whatever the motives, waves of desperation broke time and again over the country: in 1811-13, in 1815-17, in 1819, in 1826, in 1829-35, in 1838-42, in 1843-4, in 1846-8. In the agricultural areas they were blind, spontaneous, and, insofar as their objectives were at all defined, almost entirely economic. As a rioter from the Fens put it in 1816, "Here I am between Earth and Sky, so help me God. I

would sooner lose my life than go home as I am. Bread I want and bread I will have." In 1816, all over the eastern counties, in 1822 in East Anglia, in 1830 everywhere between Kent and Dorset, Somerset and Lincoln, in 1843-4 once again in the east Midlands and the eastern counties, the threshing machines were broken, the ricks burned at night, as men demanded a minimum of life. In the industrial and urban areas after 1815 economic and social unrest was generally combined with a specific political ideology and programme—radical-democratic, or even "cooperative" (or as we would say, socialist), though in the first great movements of unrest from 1811-13 the Luddites of the East Midlands and Yorkshire smashed their machines without any specific programme of political reform and revolution. Phases of the movement stressing political and trade-unionist agitation tended to alternate, the former being normally by far the more massive: politics predominated in 1815-19, 1829-32, and above all in the Chartist era (1838-48), industrial organization in the early 1820s and 1833-38. However, from about 1830 all these movements became more self-consciously and characteristically proletarian. The agitations of 1829-35 saw the rise of the idea of the "general trades union" and its ultimate weapon, which might be used for political purposes, the "general strike"; and Chartism rested firmly on the foundation of working-class consciousness, and insofar as it envisaged any real method of achieving its ends, relied on hopes of a general strike or, as it was then called, Sacred Month. But essentially, what held all these movements together, or revived them after their periodic defeat and disintegration, was the universal discontent of men who felt themselves hungry in a society reeking with wealth, enslaved in a country which prided itself on its freedom, seeking bread and hope, and receiving in return stones and despair.

And were they not justified? A Prussian official, travelling to Manchester in 1814, had made a moderately cheerful judgment:

The cloud of coal vapour may be observed from afar. The houses are blackened by it. The river which flows through Manchester, is so filled with waste dye-stuffs that it resembles a dyer's vat. The whole picture is a melancholic one. Nevertheless, everywhere one sees busy, happy and well-nourished people, and thihs raises the observer's spirits.

No observer of Manchester in the 1830s and 1840s—and there were many—dwelt on its happy, well-fed people. "Wretched, defrauded, oppressed, crushed human nature lying in bleeding fragments all over the face of society," wrote the American, Colman, of it in 1845. "Every day that I live I thank Heaven that I am not a poor man with a family in England." Can we be surprised that the first generation of the labouring poor in industrial Britain looked at the results of capitalism and found them wanting?

36. HUSBANDS AND WIVES

R. P. DORE

Reprinted from City Life in Japan: A Study of a Tokyo Ward *(Berkeley and Los Angeles: University of California Press, 1958). R. P. Dore is Professor of Sociology at the London School of Economics and Political Science. In addition to* City Life in Japan, *from which this chapter is taken, he is the author of* Land Reform in Japan *and* Education in Tokugawa Japan, *which is one of the finest studies ever conducted of the relationship between an educational system and the social organization of which it was a part.*

■ Many people, including some social scientists, say that industrial societies are confusing (and confused). If compared to relatively integrated pre-industrial societies, the industrial stage of development is certainly bewildering. The comparison is questionable because it is based on the assumption that modern industrial society has achieved the stable patterns of behavior and smooth mesh of its institutional gears that seem to characterize many pre-industrial groups. But the more or less stable societies that we have considered earlier developed their strategies of adaptation slowly and over hundreds of years. In most cases, what we observe in them can be regarded as the products of a long evolutionary process. Industrial societies seem confusing because they have only recently started to work out their adaptive strategies; they are like beginning toddlers who have not yet coordinated their activities and desires into a semblance of unified purpose.

The members of an American family with adolescent children of ten seem (and perhaps are) confused because constantly changing political and economic norms have rendered obsolete the goals and standards—not only economic and political, but also religious, sexual, legal, and recreational—around which their parents had organized their lives. No sooner did parents manage to re-orient themselves to the new pressures of the post-Korean era than they were told by their children that these goals and standards were not only currently inappropriate but would be worthless in the generation to come. These young people, especially those in the universities and colleges, may not speak explicitly of the post-industrial stage into which we have begun to move, but they sense it and are trying uncertainly to define the goals and standards that will be appropriate to it.

This selection is about the transition of the family in Japan from an agricultural stage to industrialism. The shift to notions of love as the basis of marriage, of relations between husband and wife in regard to money, sex, friends, and even such seemingly inconsequential matters as sending New Year's greeting cards, all attest to the fundamental changes characterizing all aspects of Japanese society. As Dore observes, the growing emphasis on love as a basis for marriage and equality between the spouses is achieved at the expense of traditional wider kin ties. Their implications for the organization of the whole society make it important for the anthropologist to know whether husbands change diapers, whether wives decide to whom greeting cards will be sent, or if household financial decisions are made jointly.

Shitayama-cho, where this research was conducted in 1951, is a densely populated and industrialized Tokyo suburb. There were about 1,225 people in the suburb in 1951, compared to 862 in 1930. The data for the study were collected largely by questionnaires administered by Japanese university students in 297 households. The questionnaire was made up of eight schedules covering basic data, domestic economy, kinship and neighborhood ties, leisure, education, religion, politics, and employment. Interviews lasted between 30 and 60 minutes for each of the schedules.

The reader who wants to learn more about the transition of the family to an industrial strategy should consult *Family and Social Network,* by Elizabeth Bott (New York: Free Press, 1972), one of the most important books on the subject. Her article, "Urban Families: Conjugal Roles and Social Network" (*Human Relations,* 8 [1955]: 345-84) summarizes the salient features of that book and is reprinted in *Man in Adaptation: The Institutional Framework.* Dore discusses changing attitudes toward sexual behavior as an aspect of changing conceptions of marriage; for a more detailed study of this in the United States, see *Family Design: Marital Sexuality, Family State, and Contraception,* by Lee Rainwater (Chicago: Aldine, 1965). Another Important point touched on by Dore is the role of international influences in legitimating the new directions taken by family organization in Japan; such intersocial influences are important aspects of modernization. In this connection, see *Political Modernization in Japan and Turkey,* edited by Robert E. Ward and Dankwart A. Rustow (Princeton: Princeton University Press, 1964) and *Changing Japanese Attitudes toward Modernization,* edited by Marius B. Jansen (Princeton: Princeton University Press, 1965); Dore has articles on Japanese education in both volumes. ■

THE GREATEST SINGLE CHANGE in Japanese family institutions lies in the increased importance attached to the emotional relationship between husband and wife, at the expense of the relationship between parents and children which was of overwhelming importance to the traditional family. . . .

In the large family the husband-wife relationship has to be fitted into a large number of other relationships of the same "personal," face-to-face type. Any excessive intensity of this one relationship would upset the equilibrium of the whole. This functional reason for not giving the husband-wife relation great institutionalized importance and for minimizing the overt display of affection between them disappears in the small conjugal family, and it is, as we saw before, the small conjugal family which is becoming the normal household type, at first by the mere mechanics of branch-family formation and later for various reasons including (circularly) changes in the ideal of the marriage relationship itself.

Not only is the need for restraint removed. In the traditional family there were many roles in which a bride could be successful. She could be a good daughter-in-law, a good sister-in-law, a good house-cleaner, a good rice-planter, a good link with another rich and influential family, an efficient performer of ceremonial duties *vis-a-vis* the ancestors or neighbours, as well as being successful as a

source of emotional and sexual satisfaction for her husband—if, indeed, the latter counted for much at all. In the new conjugal family she can still prove her worth as housekeeper, as mother and as maintainer of her husband's prestige, but the number of roles is whittled down. It is natural, then, that as the definition of wifehood becomes more circumscribed the function of providing emotional and sexual satisfaction for the husband should assume greater importance in it.

Along with this we must put the influence of ideas. Here, perhaps, is good support for the theory that a culture always selects its borrowings in the light of its predispositions or its needs. The Western ideals of marriage as the culmination of romantic love, a relationship the *raison d'étre* of which lies in the subjective feelings of two equal and independent individuals, might not so easliy have found favour had their introduction not coincided with the structural changes outlined above and with the aspirations of a sex whose traditionally submissive role had in other respects undergone some change with universal education and the growth of industry.

There was, as we have seen, considerable class variation in traditional values. One basic assumption, however, was that women are biologically inferior. "The five diseases of the female mind," says the Greater Learning for Women, "are disobedience, anger, slanderousness, jealousy and lack of intelligence. Seven or eight out of every ten women suffer from these faults. That is why women are inferior to men. In particular lack of intelligence is at the root of these other faults." Feminine inferiority was, of course, given more marked institutional expression in the upper classes, as also was the strict differentiation of male and female spheres—in the upper samurai class extending to the rigid division of the house into the master's quarters and the women's quarters. Sex was by no means sinful; it was a natural and pleasurable function, in the enjoyment of which, however, women, as part of the self-abnegating role imposed on them by the culture, were necessarily restricted. Chastity was expected of them, but men were permitted great freedom before and outside of marriage. The only form of affection towards women which the respectable man would permit himself, however, was the affection of a master for a domestic pet. A "love" which placed the woman on a footing of equality, much less on the pedestal of European romantic tradition, offended against the canons of masculine superiority. It was an effeminate emotion, for adoration of the superior being and the inability to control emotion were essentially feminine attributes. For the upper classes it was possible further to differentiate the functions of woman *qua* domestic manager and breeder of heirs, and of woman *qua* charming plaything, in the separate personalities of wife and concubine.

For the peasants and the urban commoners this was impossible. Moreover, economic factors prevented the same rigid division of male and female spheres, and the same extreme emphasis on feminine inferiority. The villages were characterized by freedom of pre-marital sex relations for women as well as for men, and by widespread phallicism often involving institutionalized periodic promiscuity. The novels and the drama of the towns portrayed with sympathy the man in the grip of passion, and the object of his passion (generally, however, a geisha or at least a girl with whom marriage was impossible) was a personality in her own right and not merely a negative plaything.

From the Meiji period until 1945 four separate trends in ideas can be distinguished.

1. A diffusion by deliberate government policy and via the schools and the police, of certain aspects of the samurai code—the insistence on the rigid division of male and female spheres, involving a taboo on social intercourse between the sexes, and an emphasis on the purity of womanhood, scorn of love as a detraction from masculine dignity, tacit approval of male sexual freedom, but a strict localization of the opportunities for sexual stimulation and enjoyment to brothel or semi-brothel districts whose existence was justified as an essential means of preserving the purity of the home. This entailed the cleaning up of rural phallicism and ritual promiscuity, and the control of obscene publi-

cations. Rigid educational segregation, separate youth clubs, even separate seats in cinemas, were part of the policy. Clandestine meeting with girls other than prostitutes was adequate reason for expulsion from high school; where factory organization made some contact between the sexes necessary, strict watch was enforced and (until the wartime pro-natalist policy brought a change) the man who fell in love with a fellow-employee and tried to marry her was liable to be dismissed. Husbands and wives lived separate social lives; it was a cause of shame to be seen walking together in the street. At one stage during the war police in some districts took it upon themselves to arrest 'abekku' (from the French *avec*, i.e. couples travelling together) once, by mistake, arresting a professor of an Imperial university travelling with his wife for the impeccable Confucian purpose of visiting his father's grave.

2. Coinciding to some extent with this in its effects, at least on rural customs, was the attempt, again by government policy, to enforce such modifications of traditional morality as were necessary to forestall the criticism and moral disapproval of foreigners, many of whom in the early days of Meiji had reported that Japan was a land of "nudity, rudity and crudity." This was of particular importance in the period when it was the overriding aim of Government policy to secure for Japan the prestige in the West which would earn for her the renunciation of extra-territorial rights. Numerous edicts and city by-laws of the period, forbidding nakedness in the streets or mixed bathing in public bath-houses, specifically state that although "this is the general custom and is not so despised among ourselves, in foreign countries this is looked on with great contempt. You should therefore consider it a great shame." Fukuzawa Yukichi, in an attack on the lewd behaviour of many of his contemporaries, reminds them that with the modern growth in communications, "sooner or later such conditions in our country will come to the ears of foreigners, exposing us to who knows what attacks and reproaches." The same sentiment is far from dead. In 1951, when a Tokyo haberdasher

filled his shop window with masculine models perpetually removing and replacing their trousers to display the merits of their underwear, the immediate newspaper comment was "what will foreigners think of us?"

This tendency had its more positive side. In the "Rokumeikan"—the "ballroom"— period, when officials sought to impress the foreign diplomatic community by throwing lavish fancy-dress balls, wives came out of their seclusion to dress as Venetian noblewomen, to learn to waltz and to be bowed to by their husbands. Foreigners' parties were an exception to the rule of segregated entertainment which affected a fairly wide section of the middle class (most towns had their missionaries, every high school had its foreign teachers), though defensive tactics were soon developed—women gathered at one end of the room and men at the other.

3. Deference to the values of foreigners inevitably ran the danger of admitting the intrinsic superiority of those foreign values, particularly at a time when Western industrial and social techniques were being deliberately adopted because no one doubted their superiority. Missionaries, too, had their sincere adherents.

Open concubinage was the first victim. Concubines, regarded as second degree relatives in the early Meiji period, disappeared from the Criminal Code in 1892 and from the Civil Code in 1898. The matter was finally clinched by a judgement of the Supreme Court in 1897. "Concubinage is a private relation between a man and a woman, and one which offends against the excellent principle of monogamy. It is therefore a relation to which the law cannot lend its recognition, and the status of concubine is one which we cannot recognize as a legitimate status. Hence all contracts in relations involving the status of concubine are null and void and the Court may not countenance their enforcement."

Strict monogamy, involving a single standard of marital fidelity, became an increasingly accepted ideal, and criticism of licensed prostitution grew. In the Legal Reform Committee of the early twenties, after a fierce debate, in the course of which the sacred symbol of the Imperial House Laws had been invoked by the traditionalists, a draft clause was passed making the wife's permission necessary before a husband could "recognize" a child by another woman and adopt it into his own family. The attempt was also made to make adultery by the husband a grounds for divorce equally with adultery by the wife. Most of the lawyers agreed that this was desirable, and it was only with the solemn expression of deep crocodile regret that they threw the proposal out as impracticable given the prevailing state of society. The chief upholders of this new morality were middle-class women; a writer who has analysed the middle-class women's-magazine serial novels of the pre-war period notes how consistent they were on this point. The growth of the ideal was largely a manifestation of feminist aspirations: unable to make the outrageous demand of equal freedom for themselves, women contented themselves with demanding equal restriction for men. The Christian terminology of "purity" and "soiling" which (male) educators of women had gratefully seized on in their inculcation of feminine chastity, recoiled on its users.

4. Allied with this was a change in attitudes to romantic love. La Rochefoucauld wondered "how many men would experience love if they never heard love spoken of." In translations of Western literature men came increasingly to hear love talked of, and to hear it talked of not as an effeminate sign of weakness, or as an inconvenient complication of the difficult business of getting married, but as a noble emotion, a fulfilment, an enrichment of the personality. Such ideas were most widespread among students and intellectuals, particularly in such periods as the twenties when the tide of samurai traditionalism was beginning to ebb. The result was sometimes the advocacy and practice of a Bohemian free love, but more often these ideas struck deeper at the roots of prevailing morality by combining with the ideal of monogamous marriage, and seeing marriage as the culmination of love, and love as a condition of marriage. A typical expression of these ideas was the series of essays by the

poet Kuriyagawa Hakuson which appeared in the Asahi daily paper in 1922 and were later issued as a separate work under the title *A Modern View of Love*. The English title of his first essay *(Love is Best),* his references to Romeo and Juliet, Pelleas and Mélisande, and Dante's Beatrice, to Browning, Stendhal, and Schopenhauer, and also to Freud, Havelock Ellis and Marie Stopes, show clearly the source of his inspiration. Such ideas certainly never gained widespread acceptance—the moral fury with which men like Kuriyagawa were attacked showed all the violence and irrationality of the "authoritarian personality" at its text-book best—but they achieved sufficient strength for it to be impossible for even the sort of guide to marriage which rated a preface from the President of the Patriotic Women's League to ignore them. "Nowadays," says one of these, "there are many people who say 'Love is the basis of marriage; for a woman to marry without love is to allow her purity to be soiled at the hand of a demon.' But these are extremely dangerous words. . . . This is not to say that love has never led to a good marriage. But to make this your object would be utterly reckless."

The prevailing morality was essentially an officially bolstered one. It is doubtful if there has ever been a totalitarian state with such a didactic flavour as that of pre-war Japan. Not even Victorian England produced such large numbers of moralizers, or gave them such complete control of the police forces, the means of education and the organs of public opinion. The paralysis of government which followed the defeat in 1945 removed the props of the old morality. It did more. The connection between the unique Japaneseness of Japanese family and sex morality, and the unique Japaneseness of Japan's military supremacy, her glorious traditions and her magnificent future destiny, had been too explicitly pointed out by the pre-war moralists for the discrediting of the latter not to have disastrous effects on the former.

The confusion which followed the defeat was catastrophic to the old morality. In some cases it was catastrophic to moral restraint of any kind. For many individuals, indeed,

patriotism was so predominantly the centre of their moral emotions, that defeat left them entirely disoriented. Crime of all sorts exacerbated by famine and shortage, rapidly increased. Prostitution, driven from the licensed quarters, became an expanding industry of the side-streets. The taboos which had maintained sexual segregation broke down, and promiscuity was a frequent result. A new school of literature arose called the "Literature of the Flesh" *(Nikutai-Bungaku).* It was ordinary poronography with streaks of sadism, but it was an interesting sign of the moral confusion of the times that its exponents could pose as the heralds of a new philosophy which aimed at the liberation of the instinctual human being from the artificial restraint of a feudal morality.

But the pattern of the future began to emerge. As local community pressures regained their strength and a more settled social order reduced the intensity of the immediate struggle for survival and began to hold some promise for the future, the more responsible of pre-war trends began to reassert themselves with a new force derived from the sweeping legal reforms of the Occupation. Coeducation was established in schools at all levels. Feminine equality was embodied in election laws, in labor laws and in the Civil Code; while the latter abolished house and householdheads, primogeniture and all the other legal supports of traditional "familism." Women became Diet members and civil servants. A new female-staffed branch of the Labor Ministry—the Women and Minors' Bureau—made it its business by research, by the organization of Women's Weeks and by public meetings to "fight feudalism" in workshop and home and, after the Occupation had ended, successfully weathered a campaign to make it the first victim of administrative retrenchment. In 1953, a translation of Simone de Beauvoir's *The Second Sex* was top best-seller for some months in succession.

The swing in public opinion has been unmistakable. Ten years ago, the questions asked in Shitayama-cho concerning living with parents and the choice of a mate would have produced very different answers. A few quotations from various sources will help to illustrate the change in opinion on the point which chiefly interests us here, the proper nature of husband-wife relations.

In Tokyo, nowadays, (1954) it is an absolute commonplace for husband and wife to be seen out together, and no one would any longer look askance.

In one of his newspaper essays, Takata Tamotsu tells the story of a diplomat who was found dead in mysterious circumstances in the late twenties. One of the reasons which finally persuaded the Court to give a suicide verdict was that a photograph of his dead wife was found in the man's pocket.

I don't suppose it would seem odd to anyone nowadays for a man to carry about with him a photograph of a dead wife whom he had loved. Today it is a commonplace and not in the least peculiar. But at the time this perfectly ordinary action was counted among the causes of the very extraordinary action of suicide. And this only twenty years ago. Was there ever a place where relations between husband and wife have changed as much as they have in Japan?

In 1953, the Asahi carried the following report of the ceremony at which an Oosaka Professor of Psychology was presented with the Asahi prize for research.

"There is one more thing I must say," the Professor said, and, after thanking the Asahi for the invitation to the ceremony addressed to Professor "and Mrs." Kurotsu, he went on, "For twenty years I have lived a life of research. The laboratory has practically been my home. Unitl I saw this invitation card it had never occurred to me to question my way of life—that was how things were. But when I came to the words 'and Mrs.' Kurotsu, I was brought up with a jerk. Looking back over these twenty years—there have been the children, there was the war with all its troubles and all the difficulties of the post-war period. Everything I have left entirely to those around me. When I read those words 'and Mrs.' I was suddenly overcome. Oh! I do not know what to say. Yes, . . . I . . . I . . . " Dr. Kurotsu suddenly gulped and dropped his eyes. Several times he tried to continue but the words would not come.

Below the platform, Fumiko, his wife (aged 46), who had at first been watching her husband with a very special sort of smile, looked down too. Then, as she raised her eyes filled with tears, her husband looked straight towards her.

The hall was filled with an immense silence. When the audience looked up again it was to see Mrs. Kurotsu, now all smiles again, make room for a weeping husband in the seat next to her—together on their first trip a *deux* in twenty years of married life.

A government-approved text-book, published in 1952 for use in the Social Studies course in secondary schools (ages 12-15) deals with the family. In the author's evolutionary historical presentation monogamy is represented as the product of "modern civilization" and as such is given all the authority of inevitability and all the associations surrounding the word "progress." The following extract will give an idea of the reformist tone of the book.

It cannot be said today that mistresses have entirely disappeared. Nor can it be honestly said that marriages no longer take place in which the wishes of the individuals concerned are ignored. . . . It is our task to build a real, and not simply a formal, system of monogamous marriage. . . . That men and women should be truly equal, that marriage should be guaranteed economic security, that marriage should be free—these are the foundations of a healthy and undistorted system of monogamous marriage. Only on such foundations can the union of two people who truly love one another be assured.

The change in the values now upheld by the organs of mass opinion is obvious, so is the change in the general nature of normative judgements of behaviour among the town population at large. But practice does not change so rapidly. Established patterns of marital relationships are not easily modified. One of today's standing jokes is the liberal intellectual who shouts "Oi!" to his wife. A newspaper leading article comments:

It is easy enough, today, to get up in meetings and in public places and expound the advantages of democracy. But how do the people who do this behave in matters which affect themselves? What sort of attitude do they take within the home towards their wives and children? Of course, there are exceptions, and particularly among the younger generations in the towns the changes have been immense, but in many cases the sad truth is that these "democrats" of the market place are the absolute despotic rulers of the home.

On the other hand, although the change in behaviour has not been so sudden as the change in opinion, it has been going on long-er. Whereas it now lags somewhat behind opinion, formerly it was some way ahead. . . . As far as concerns the way marriages are made, a change has been under way for a long time. Before going on further to discuss marital relations in Shitayama-cho, it may be useful, by way of elaboration of this table, to discuss the mechanics of getting married.

THE LOVE MARRIAGE AND
THE ARRANGED MARRIAGE

The word "love marriage" as it was used in the question to Shitayama-cho housewives, the results of which are tabulated below, implies that the initiative is taken by the couple themselves, and that their subjective feelings for each other are a prime condition of the match. In most cases in Shitayama-cho, as will be seen from the table, the parents' permission was obtained (a "good" girl might never allow her parents to know that it was all a put-up job when the go-between appointed by the groom's family came to ask for her hand). In such cases a go-between would then be appointed by agreement between the families to settle the details of the bride's trousseau, the size of the *yuinoo* money gift from the groom's family to the bride's, and the division of the expenses of the wedding feast. Sometimes the same go-between, but often someone else—someone who could stand in a fatherly position to the married pair and perhaps help the husband in his future career (the groom's employer is a frequent and obvious choice)—presided over the wedding ceremony. The presence of such a go-between is an essential for the social recognition of the marriage. A university professor about to be married during the war applied to the local borough office for the special wedding rice-wine ration. In the space provided on the form for name and address of go-between he wrote "none." The borough office held that a wedding without a go-between was not a proper wedding and refused to give him his ration until he invented one.

Several couples in Shitayama-cho had, as the table shows, dispensed with such social recognition. "Individualism by default," to borrow Marion J. Levy's phrase, is often the cause of their unconventional marriages rather than the "individualism by conviction" of the university professor. Themselves the children of impoverished disintegrated urban families, or single individuals separated from a provincial home, constrained by no bonds of kinship or local community pressure, propertyless and practically rootless, they have no status to lose. The women are often waitresses or members of the "water-trades," the entertainments industries which supply food, drink and sex in proportions varying with the type of establishment. Six of these marriages in Shitayama-cho started from acquaintances between waitress and customer in a "Milk Hall," spaghetti restaurant, or "social tea-house." Most of these couples lived in the one-room apartment blocks. In many cases they have children, the marriage appears to be stable and is perfectly respectable by Shitayama-cho apartment-block standards. Although the formalities of go-betweens and so on are dispensed with, the marriage may not go entirely unmarked and uncelebrated, a few friends may be called in for a small informal party. Other unions are less stable, never formalized either socially or legally, and for the woman little more secure than the only likely alternative for someone of rootlessness of its members, is not, how-mistress of a married man.

Such a marginal class existed in the Tokyo of Tokugawa times, and . . . shifting, socially unsanctioned unions were common within it. The size of this class, or at least the degree of rootlessness of its members, is not, however, as great as the speed and conditions of industrialization and urban growth might lead one to expect. Unlike the French industrial towns of the nineteenth century where, according to Le Play's description of the "anomic" state of their proletariat, it was "patrons not clients who were wanting," there has been no shortage of patrons in Japan. The employer's initiative lies at the origin of a number of arranged marriages in Shitayama-cho.

"Arranged marriage" (*mial-kekkon*) means that the parties were brought together expressly for the purpose of marriage on the initiative of parents, a friend of the family or a go-between. It means also that the initial criteria of selection were objective ones; not only the "family" considerations which were discussed in previous chapters—questions of status and lineage, of the value to the family of the new connections to be forged, the suitability of the bride as a preserver of family tradition and as a breeder of heirs—but also, and increasingly as "the family" declines in importance, the personal qualities of the individuals concerned—looks, health, intelligence, the bride's domestic abilities and her accomplishments (a girl's diplomas for the tea ceremony and flower arrangement would invariably be included in the go-between's recital of her virtues), the absence of leprosy or madness in the family's history, the man's earning power and also the suitability of their respective temperaments. In addition there are numerous horoscopic and geomantic considerations which have an important function since they are sufficiently complicated to forbid any match if "worked to rule" and therefore provided face-saving excuses for breaking off negotiations.

The first suggestion of a match may come from a common friend of the two families or from a go-between whose good offices have been requested. This initial "bridge-building" (*hashi-kake*) go-between performs essentially the functions of the English marriage bureau, though his services are requited not by a fixed fee but by a suitably large present of money on successful completion of the negotiations. Some people find in the work a rewarding, and even profitable, hobby. Many successful marriages were first conceived in Shitayama-cho by a widow who had a wide acquaintance among students to whom she often let rooms, and a friend who taught in a Girls' High School and visited her periodically with a sheaf of photographs and personal histories of her ex-pupils.

When a marriage is proposed, the first step is for both families to make discreet enquiries in order to substantiate the go-between's recital of the other party's virtues. Always maintain good relations with your neighbours, advises a pre-war guide to marriage, since it is always of your neighbours that the first enquiries will be made. In the impersonalized world of the city special detective agencies (*kooshinjo*) now exist to make the business easier.

The next stage of the process has undergone a considerable change. Within the framework of an arranged marriage, having ascertained that the objective conditions of a good match are fulfilled, the opportunities for the prospective partners to accept or reject the proposed marriage have increased. The development of the custom of holding a *miai*—a "mutual-viewing meeting"—among the merchants of the Tokugawa period was mentioned earlier. Photography later provided a chance for an initial eliminating process before the *miai* was arranged. Most of the couples in Shitayama-cho whose marriage was arranged were married on the strength of the *miai* without further meeting. Indeed, as some explained, to have met would have been bad manners towards the go-between in whose hands the whole conduct of the negotiations had been placed. Cousins who were known to each other before the marriage was proposed deliberately avoided meeting in order to prevent any embarrassment between the families. But nowadays it is not uncommon for the young couple to be packed off to the cinema together after the *miai,* or even for a period of some weeks or months of courtship to intervene before the intermediaries carry the final verdict. But withdrawal, once a *miai* has been held, requires some strength of mind to resist the pressure of parents and go-between who are convinced of the appropriateness of the match and would find extrication from the negotiations embarrassing—a strength of mind not often to be found in Japanese women. At that stage horoscopic excuses sound somewhat hollow, although no open unpleasantness will ensue provided that the fiction is politely maintained. Refusal after a *miai,* the more so after a *miai* followed by an unchaperoned cinema visit, can be a severe blow to self-esteem. One young man in Shitayama-cho was deeply hurt by such an experience, but blamed it all on his father's meanness in promising him as his *yuinoo* (money gift to the bride's family) a sum which he thought far smaller in proportion to his elder brother's than was justified by his position of second son.

The final decision having been taken, the subsequent steps of the process are identical with those for a "love marriage."

THE GO-BETWEEN

The injection into the business of marriage arrangement of the preferences of the individuals concerned—as a necessary and a sufficient condition of a "love" marriage and increasingly as a necessary condition of an "arranged" marriage—is having an effect on the functions of the go-between who is rapidly becoming as formal a part of the wedding ceremony as the striped trousers and frock coat which for every middle-school graduate bridegroom is *de rigueur*. Traditionally, the go-between (not the "bridge-builder" but the one who had handled the delicate negotiations and presided at the wedding ceremony) took some responsibility for the marriage. It was, after all, his handiwork. The couple would continue to visit him at New Year and in the summer; he would make ceremonial godfather-like gifts to their children, and when any trouble arose in the marital relationship it was to him that either of the parties, or preferably their families, took their complaints and their request that he should make the other side see reason. As individual choice, implying individual responsibility, is given more weight, such appeals to the go-between begin to seem inappropriate. For perhaps the majority of couples in Shitayama-cho the go-between still had not lost these functions; most were still keeping in touch, often by regular correspondence, although not many housewives when asked whether they had in the past or would contemplate in the future calling on the go-between's help, gave replies like "I went to him when I had trouble with my mother-in-law," or "I would if there was any question of divorce." There were only fifteen such replies (out of 200) which is not, however, a very reliable index since even in Japan many would hesitate to admit to such facts or possibilities to casual interviewers.

Three times as common, however, were references to economic help from the go-between—loans given, jobs found, business connections made, or worn clothes passed on—and it was clear that the help was reciprocated not only by traditional "service"—"if there is a marriage or a funeral at his house we all go along to help"—but also by financial help to go-betweens who have fallen on hard times, or to the go-between's children. Indeed, although the go-between's functions as a mediator decline in importance, the patron-client aspect of the relationship loses its importance more gradually, with the only slowly declining strength of such relations in the business, professional, educational and political worlds. Even now, a research student is well advised to get his professor to perform the office, a docker his labor-contractor boss, a young diplomat an Ambassador, or better still a rising Minister or Counsellor whose beneficent influence will continue longer.

THE "LOVE MARRIAGE" SINCE THE WAR

As emerged from the previous discussion of parents' views on their children's marriage, the "love marriage" which maximizes the importance of spontaneous individual choice is now the majority ideal in Shitayama-cho. Among the youth of the towns it is an almost universal ideal. This does not mean, however, that the romanticization of marriage has been carried very far. As an analyst of Japanese popular songs notes, golden dreams, blue skies, honeymoons, moonlit kisses and sultry palm beaches are symbols as yet imperfectly assimilated despite some years of education in American musicals. The institutionalized importance of the objective criteria of a good marriage in the old *miai* system has to some extent ensured that these factors are not ignored. Saikaku's seventeenth-century dictum that marriage is "a commercial transaction that only comes once in a lifetime" might still meet with agreement today. Women, in particular, are well aware that given the present constitution of society marriage is for them a means of livelihood. When asked to enumerate the desirable qualities in a husband 21% of factory girls and 27% of non-working girls mention "earning capacity" first.

There is another factor of importance. Despite the acceptance of the love-marriage ideal, there are no established patterns of courtship. Before the war opportunities for meeting members of the opposite sex were extremely limited. Of forty-one Shitayama-cho love marriages most developed from acquaintanceships struck up at work, between neighbours or with the relative of a friend of the same sex. The only exceptions were the six waitresses previously mentioned, one acquaintance which sprang from a "comforts letter" to the troops during the war, one started in a railway train after many months of traveling the same line to work, and two which began at youth meetings. Since the war, institutionalized segregation of the sexes has perforce broken down under the pressure of coeducation, and even in the villages joint youth clubs are now common. But although group mixing is now accepted, unchaperoned pairing off is still disapproved, particularly in middle-class society. A public-opinion survey sample 85% of whom saw nothing wrong in husbands and wives going out together, contained only 16% who thought it was all right for a young man and a young woman to walk the streets arm in arm. Moreover, there are no established patterns of behaviour in such relationships and embarrassment and frustration mixed with a sense of guilt is a frequent result. The new coeducated generation will doubtless find it much easier to manage its calf-loves and its flirtations but many now in their middle and late twenties are acutely conscious of, to use the terminology

of Merton's definition of *anomie,* the absence of "socially structured avenues . . . for realizing culturally prescribed aspirations." The solution of one university research assistant is interesting. He resigned himself to an arranged marriage, but went to his *miai* somewhat drunk on the grounds that it was giving the girl a fair chance by showing her the worst she could expect. In accepting the old, he nevertheless made a gesture of his ideological solidarity with the new.

One may note, in passing, that in Shitayama-cho both for men and for women "love" marriages are more common among the younger . . . and among the better educated. For both men and women, however, the younger are also the better educated. Partial correlation does not yield significant results with this size of sample, but it would appear that educational level has little independent relation with the form of marriage; the only group within which there might be a tendency for those with high school education to contract "love" marriages more frequently than those of the same age but of lower educational attainment is among men in their thirties.

HUSBANDS AND WIVES IN SHITAYAMA-CHO

The increased importance attached to subjective sentiment as a condition for entering marriage is part and parcel of changes noted earlier in ideals of the marital relationship. It is now time to offer what evidence there is of the nature of husband-wife relations in Shitayama-cho. That there was great variety was obvious. The persistence of traditional attitudes was made clear at the start of the survey. In the first meeting with ward leaders at which plans for the survey were discussed I was warned by one of them that interviewers should take care to call only when the husband was at home. "Otherwise you will never get the truth about Japan. Of course, nowadays we have feminine equality and I'm beginning by now to get used to the idea that my wife has the right to go out and vote. But the old ideas are still there and I should think a lot of women wouldn't have any opinions of their own and wouldn't know about the things you want to find out. Even if they did know, they wouldn't be sure if it was all right to tell you. . . ." (The advice was ignored, but the warning may be pertinent to the evaluation of interview replies.) That some men might have additional reasons for such a warning, other than a solicitous desire to ensure the accuracy of the survey, was apparent from some of the interviewers' experiences. There was, for instance, the woman who complained that "Japanese men are tyrants. A wife isn't allowed to do anything or to have any interests without her husband's permission.. I was fond of going to flower and tea classes, but one evening I got held up and it was ten o'clock before I got back. My husband was furious and for about six months he wouldn't let me go anywhere at all." There was the mother who explained that she brought her girls up to understand that "Men are beasts. If you grow up not to expect too much out of life you will be all right. Husbands are creatures who say that black is white, and all the wife has to do is listen in silence and say 'Yes, I see.' " There was the wife asked whether birthdays were celebrated in her household who said that they were, but added as the most natural thing in the world "but only my husband's of course." There were others who told interviewers who went enquiring for their husbands that he had not come home the previous night and as they had no idea where he might be they could not say when he would be back.

Equally there was plenty of evidence on the other side. The women who saw as the greatest improvement in the housewife's lot over the past generation the fact that "husbands are more cooperative" or "husbands and wives now do the worrying together" have already been mentioned. The gentle twigging by one young man of another on the grounds that he was an *aisaika*—in love with his wife—was certainly far from received as an insult or a reflection on a man's masculinity. There were husbands who did the washing-up and consented to be trailed on shop-ping expeditions, husbands who never went out to enjoy themselves without their wives; wives who expected to receive their husband's pay packet intact—and got it.

More systematically the attempt is made below to consider Shitayama-cho marriages, by means of necessarily somewhat superficial indices, in the light of three dimensions.

1. The extent of the wife's autonomous direction of domestic matters defined as a feminine preserve.
2. The extent to which the wife maintains her own personal social and economic relationships outside the home as an individual on an equal footing with her husband.
3. The extent to which there is a merging of personality and interests, a sharing of leisure activities and of domestic and social responsibilities.

1. DOMESTIC AUTONOMY

The control by the wife of the domestic economy—at least the consumption side of it—varied greatly as between classes and districts, as was noted before. In samurai families it was considerable and in the new urban middle classes it, for obvious reasons (the separation of the husband's employment from the home), became more so. The security and the satisfaction from the exercise of power which this provided was for many women adequate compensation for the lack of any emotional satisfaction from their relationship with their husband. It often gave them a quiet dignity, a certain confident self-sufficiency and inner serenity. The professor's wife in the post-war novel *Jiyuu-gakkoo* is well observed. She is telling her niece about her own marriage. Her husband, having been made Faculty dean, had become insufferably pompous, both inside and outside the home. One morning she reaches the limits of tolerance and attempts to quarrel with him. But he ignores her and begins to shave. She goes on:

I used always to soap his face for him when he shaved, but that morning I just sat there fuming and watched him. He tried to look dignified and began scraping away. Stretching his neck, pinching his nose, pulling the skin, making pop-eyes, pouting . . . Have you ever watched a man shaving? It is fantastic the faces they pull. Suddenly as I sat there I burst out laughing. It wasn't so much the funny faces he was making; all of a sudden it occurred to me what comic creatures men are. Their silliness, their gullibility, their unreliability, their childish boasting, their vanity, and on top of that their stinginess and pettiness and their fondness for you know what . . . Ever since that day, whatever Haneda did it didn't seem to make me so angry. I even came to see a certain quaint charm in him.

Most Shitayama-cho wives, too, had a secure basis for developing the same good-natured contempt for husbands who deserved it. In most cases their control over family expenditure was fairly complete. In no case, for instance, did any of the earning children in the ward hand over their wages to their father rather than to their mother. The replies to questions concerning what happened to the husband's wages were even more revealing. Seventy-eight wives (45% of all wage-earners' wives asked) said that they received the whole of their husband's wages and doled out their husband's pocket money. These results may represent some exaggeration of the truth —some housewives may have wanted to claim an authority which they did not in fact possess—but the frequent circumstantial details of how much the husband was given every morning as luncheon money or tobacco money were too convincing to leave any doubt that this is what often happens. In the other households the wife generally had a fixed housekeeping allowance either with or without the possibility of claiming more from her husband. In only seven (4%) households did the wife have to apply for money to her husband every time it was necessary. It was fairly common for wives to receive the whole of their husband's wages, but not his "side-earnings" of various sorts which remained his own. Some wives had no idea of what their husband's total income might be, but gave no indication that they thought this anything other than a proper state of affairs. "Of course, I've got a good idea how much he spends; I know the number of times a month he goes out to parties and I've a shrewd idea how much they cost, but I would never dream of asking him outright. He might start worrying about the housekeeping and he ought not to be worried." The possession of private undeclared funds by the husband permits him the private pleasures of male drinking parties and the like. This is nowadays more predominantly a part of white-collar than manual-worker culture (though well within the traditions of the old working class—the Edo artisan). It is not surprising, therefore, to find that the wife receives the whole of her husband's wages significantly more frequently in households of lower than in those of higher economic status. Provincial-born husbands are also significantly more likely to hand over their wages than those born in Tokyo or Yokohama.

2. RELATIONS OUTSIDE THE HOME

Three indices bearing on the second dimension—the extent to which the wife maintains economic and social relations outside the home on a footing of equality with her husband—were: whether the wife claimed any property of her own, whether the wife sent New Year cards in her own name to her own friends, and whether the wife had her own friends home to meals.

Only forty-six wives (23%) claimed to have any property, ten of them house property, ten of them "all that I brought with me when I was married," and seventeen some form of savings. There are two quite separate factors involved here, however. Modern notions of feminine equality may be one. Another is the tradition of rural society. Divorce (which was frequent) permitted the wife's family to reclaim all the trousseau—the clothes, chest of drawers, cupboards, etc.— which the bride had taken with her. That the latter factor may be dominant here is suggested by the fact that there is a noticeable tendency for provincial-born wives to claim to have property more often than those born in Tokya and Yokohama.

New Year cards were sent in their own name to their own personal friends by sixty-seven wives (34%). In 33% of households all were sent in the husband's name. In 20%

some were sent jointly in the name of both husband and wife. Here the wife's educational level has some importance. High-School graduates are very significantly more likely to send New Year cards than graduates of lower schools. A noticeably higher frequency of New Year card sending among the higher economic groups also supports the assumption that this is a predominantly middle-class characteristic. It is highly more frequent among younger wives.

The replies to the questions concerning visitors who were invited to meals in the home are best dealt with by a table. It will be seen that only about half as many wives had friends in to meals as husbands. We shall return to the small number of "equally friends of both of us" replies in the next section.

As indices of the third dimension—the extent to which there is a merging of personality and interests, and a sharing of leisure activities and of domestic and social responsibilities—there is first of all the answer "both of us" to the questions: "Who decides on the amount of the 'condolence money' gift?" (The gift made to neighbors when a death occurs in their family, the appropriate amount of which is a tricky thing to decide.) This

TABLE 36.1

FRIENDS INVITED TO MEALS IN THE HOME, SHITAYAMA-CHO

Reply	Number (%)
All visitors are equally friends of both husband and wife	6(3)
Both husband and wife have friends to meals	52(26)
Only the husband has friends to meals	59(29)
Only the wife has friends to meals	8(4)
The only visitors are relatives	22(11)
No visitors ever come to meals	33(17)
Not reported	20(10)
Total	200(100)

answer (from 38% of housewives) comes significantly more frequently from the younger and not quite noticeably more frequently

from the provincial born rather than from those born in Tokyo or Yokohama.

Secondly, questions were asked concerning the extent to which the husband helped with housework. Here is a case in which traditionally, in middle and upper class families at least, the differentiation of spheres was rigid, and for the husband to help in the home was as much a serious reflection on the wife's competence as it was on the husband's masculinity. One woman said that when she first came to live in their apartment block she had not fully recovered from an attack of pleurisy some two years before. Her husband used therefore to help her in the weekly communal cleaning. She discovered, however, that this was leading to a good deal of talk behind her back to the effect that she was lazy or that it was a household where "the wife wore the trousers (*kaka-denka*)." This made her so unhappy that she had to ask her husband to stop helping her.

However, according to housewives' reports, in only 32% of Shitayama-cho households (including 1% with domestic servants) did the husband never help. In another 24% he was said to be capable of turning to in an emergency but normally left everything to his wife. Regular help by husbands was often confined to spreading and rolling up the bed mattresses, others helped in cleaning and cooking, but only 3% ever helped with washing clothes. ("Minding the children"—the most common of male domestic activities—was entirely excluded to improve comparability.) Younger husbands help more frequently (to a noticeable extent) than older husbands, and clerical and managerial workers more than manual workers.

The small number of 'equally friends of both of us' replies shown in Table 36.1 is another indication that in sociable and leisure activities husband and wife traditionally moved in different spheres. Ruth Benedict's thesis that for the male, life was divided into the mutually exclusive "circles" of "duty" and "human feelings" is a good characterization of traditional attitudes. The family belonged to the former sphere; male friendships, usually involving alcoholic conviviality and hired feminine entertainment, belonged to the latter; and the two spheres were not allowed to overlap. The husband might do formal "duty" entertaining at his home, in which case his wife played the self-effacing role of waiting on the men at table (herself getting the left-overs in the kitchen afterwards) and speaking when she was spoken to. But boon companions would be entertained not in the home, but in a geisha house, at the house of a mistress in a restaurant, brothel or potato-wine bar according to economic resources. As, with changing views of marriage, the home tends increasingly to become a centre of the man's interests and emotional life as well as a means of performing his duty, it becomes more common for the husband to entertain his own friends at home.

THE EXPLANATION OF DIFFERENCES

Before going on to consider one or two other aspects of this third, or 'merging' dimension, it will be useful to summarize what has been said above concerning the relations between these various indices and other characteristics, such as age, education, birth-place and economic status of the husbands and wives concerned. . . . It is only deciding together about "condolence money" which shows a significant correlation with age. This suggests, what one might indeed expect, that the long-term trend of change in marital relationships is a change in the third of these dimensions. This is the only case where differences between households in Shitayama-cho easily lend themselves to interpretations in terms of "old" and "new" (and even here the explanation could be not that the younger generation manifests new characteristics which it will carry with it, but that the differences are characteristic of different phases of the marital relationship.) Many of these differences are likely to be due, not to changes in progress, but to personality differences, or to established and continuing class differences.

It has been suggested that change along the "merging and sharing" dimension is related to the increasing importance attached to love

as a condition of marriage, but . . . although the relation between the form of marriage of Shitayama-cho couples and these indices shows the same consistent tendency (i.e. the wives of "love" marriages are more likely to send their own New Year cards, have their husband's visitors to the house, get help from their husbands in housework, have more complete control over the husband's wages and say that "condolence money" amounts are decided jointly), the association is only a weak one. This suggests the qualification that the "love" insisted on for the "love" marriage is not necessarily a love between equals implying equal regard for the wishes of both partners and the sharing of responsibilities and interests which is the Western romantic ideal. It can be no more than an assertion by the man of the right of individual choice of the woman who shall be his bondmaid. A love marriage is not a precondition for greater sharing of interests and responsibilities; this trend affects the relations of couples married by arrangement too.

SEX AND MONOGAMY

It might be expected that the new role of love in marriage and the tendency towards greater sharing of responsibilities and pleasures between husband and wife would have an effect also on sexual relations in marriage. Something more nearly approaching the Marie Stopes ideal of "married love" might be expected to replace the idea that sexual enjoyment is the husband's prerogative, to be indulged by the wife on the same level as her indulgence of his needs for food and warmth (as implied by the professor's wife in the novel quoted above), or alternatively the more specifically upper-class definition of marital sex relations primarily in terms of breeding heirs, with the concomitant expectation that the husband seeks emotional and physical satifaction in relations outside marriage.

Fuufu-seikatsu—the word translated "married life"—is one commonly heard and has primarily sexual connotations. Taboos on the discussion of sex have always been much weaker in Japan than in Christian countries, and the removal since the war of police controls on the publication of works which discuss sex in the context of a romantic view of marriage has led to a great increase in their number. Stopes and van der Velde sell in large quantities, and they have many Japanese imitators. Such general notions as that the nature of a couple's sex relations have an important determining influence on their adjustment to one another in all other respects, seem to be widely diffused. Newspaper reporters interviewing famous divorcees regularly ask if they were dissatisfied with their sex life and, if they fail to get serious answers, invent them or substitute speculation, for the public expects such information. It seems also to be an accepted axiom that all marriages go through a "fed-up period" (the *kentaiki*)—generally around the seventh year—and that this is something to be consciously anticipated and provided against. The Japan *Woman's News,* in inviting essays from its readers, suggested as one of five topics "How I prevented a crisis in marital relations in "the fed-up period." "

There has also been a great increase since the war in the publication of pornographic magazines and books, some of which deliberately cash in on the boom in well-intentioned scientific works on sex in marriage. One monthly magazine, for instance, is called *Fuufu-seikatsu,* but its articles on Fifty Arts of the Bedchamber, and Virginity Old and New, leave no doubt of their pornographic intention. Although this particular magazine was taken regularly by one couple in Shitaya-ma-cho, literature of this sort is produced primarily for the male market. Long-distance trains generally arrive at their destination littered with such *ero-zasshi* ("erotic" magazines) which traveling businessmen buy to console the tedium of their journey but hesitate to take to their homes. It is significant that one sociologist whose post-war activities have been dedicated to the extirpation of feudalism and repression, particularly in the sphere of the family, and who generally welcomes all weakening of traditional restraints,

concludes a recent book by expressing concern at the hedonistic tendencies which provide such a ready market for such commercial sexual stimulation. In what he calls the "oversexualization" of contemporary Japanese culture he sees signs of a decadence which prompts him to invoke the parallel of the declining Roman Empire.

While it is true that this "hedonistic" tendency is leading on the one hand to a reduction of moral restraints on sex relations before marriage, in particular among young isolated individuals of the cities, there is a solid countervailing tendency in "respectable" society towards a strengthening of the ideal of monogamous fidelity within marriage. It may be worth considering in detail the replies given by a sample of a hundred in Shitayama-cho to the following questions:

Do you think it is all right for a married man to have a mistress?

No—74   Yes—20   Don't Know—6

But supposing the man looked after his wife properly and wasn't a particularly bad husband to her, would you still object to it?

Still objectionable—60   Then permissible—14

Implicit in the reasons and qualifications offered from both points of view in answer to this question is the assumption of three different motives which might prompt a man to keep a mistress.

1. As a luxury indulgence.
2. As a means of seeking sexual or emotional satisfaction not fully obtainable in marriage.
3. As a means of begetting children.

The replies showed that it was the first type of situation which the question immediately suggested to most people and it may be assumed that it was this which was being accepted by the majority of the twenty immediate and the fourteen reluctant approvers. According to one woman, "It's all right provided a man can afford it. I'm not one to worry much about these matters. It wouldn't matter to me in the least if my husband did it." Other women, however, while not being aware of any moral objections, thought themselves entitled to have emotional ones. "I don't see any objection to it, or at least, I don't mind saying so now when I know my husband couldn't afford it, but if it actually happened I'm sure I shouldn't feel so happy about it." As several, on both sides of the fence, agreed, "Women tend to be monopolistic about men."

"Higamous Hogamous, Woman is monogamous, Hogamous Higamous, Man is polygamous," dreamt the philosopher, and he would hardly have been hailed for the originality of his perception in Japan. It is sometimes on the basis of such a view of the nature of the man that the question is approached. "I suppose you have to overlook these things," said one woman, "provided a man doesn't ruin himself." Though a sign of weakness, it is a venial sin and, as the frequent qualifications of the "provided he can afford it" type indicate, much less reprehensible than failure to keep these indulgences within the limits appropriate to status and means.

By the same token, this form of indulgence can, in certain business circles, become almost an essential means of conspicuous consumption whereby a man demonstrates what his status and his means are. Business associates can be better entertained at the house of a mistress, particularly if, as is frequently the case, the mistress is a geisha or is set up with her own little restaurant or teahouse. There is, however, something which smacks of the sententious in this reply from a 33-year-old man. "To a certain extent it is necessary for a man's work, but he should always remember that his life is based on his home and he should always get his wife's permission first."

Others consider a mistress permissible only on one of the other two grounds listed above —when a man is unable to find adequate sexual or emotional gratification in marriage, or for the purpose of begetting children.

The latter receives only two mentions; one man considers it the sole justification, another is more doubtful, explicitly says "monogamy is best," but thinks a mistress preferable to the alternative expedient of adoption. The other reason is mentioned with greater frequency—"It is wrong except where a husband does his best for his wife and she fails to satisfy him in return." "If a man cannot find satisfaction in the home, then I suppose it can't be helped." "It is wrong unless a man's wife is ill or something." The assumption seems to be that no man can be expected to abstain from seeking other means of sexual gratification if he fails to find it in his home. This may apply equally when his failure to find adequate satisfaction can legitimately be blamed on the wife's remissness, or is simply due to the wife's illness. "We aren't made of wood and stone," said a young printer whose wife had tuberculosis, talking in another context about his visits to brothels.

Several add, from this point of view, that it is up to the wife; it is a test of her powers to keep her man. As the conception of a mistress as a legitimate piece of extra self-indulgence is replaced by the conception of a mistress as a remedy for a dissatisfied home life, so it becomes harder for a wife to accept the situation with equanimity. One woman in Shitayama-cho whose husband kept a mistress was noticeably nervous in the company of other women, and it was remarked that this change dated from the time of her husband's defection and she was very much to be pitied.

The majority of those who condemn the keeping of a mistress made it clear that their objection was a moral one. One man disapproved on the grounds that it destroyed the "fine virtues" of the "Japanese family system," though, as we have seen, the moralists of the Japanese family system have been somewhat ambiguous on this issue. Most, however, base their condemnation on the newer ideals of monogamous marriage, implying exclusive sexual rights for both partners and trust and confidence between them. The dreaming philosopher is explicitly repudiated, "It is impossible for a man to love two women at once." From which one man drew the conclusion that if a man did love someone other than his wife "he should do things properly and get a divorce." Another clearly rejected the double standard with the words, "If my wife had a lover, I know how I'd feel."

The sample was too small for significant

analysis, but as it stands the distribution of replies by both sex and age is fairly even.

Here again a caveat must be entered against assuming too readily that these replies can be interpreted in the context of a traditional-modern dichotomy. This sample was the same one as received the questions . . . presenting a choice between maintaining good relations with the mother or good relations with the wife. The latter questions immediately preceded those on keeping a mistress. It was expected that those who took a "traditional" view on the first question (i.e. evaluated the relation with the mother as the more important) would take a "traditional" view on the second (i.e. show tolerance of keeping a mistress). In fact, however, the tendency of association (though a weak one— .2 p .3) is in the opposite direction. If this association is not due to chance and would reach a higher level in a wider sample, the explanation might be that the relevant distinction is not between "traditional" ideas which give little importance to love between husband and wife, and "modern" ideas which give it great importance, but between what one might call a "hedonistic" attitude and "moral" attitude. That is, the hedonist might see the satisfactions of his relation with his wife as more important than fulfilling his duties to his parents, and the satisfactions of his relations with his mistress as not to be foregone in deference to his duties to his wife.

DIVORCE

The increasing importance placed on subjective factors in the definition of the husband-wife relation cannot fail to affect the nature and frequency of divorce. It is not only that the functions of the family are whittled down in reality, as was suggested at the beginning of this chapter. Of those which remain to it attention is increasingly directed to the emotional satisfactions of the marital relation itself, to the exclusion of the family's economic or child-rearing functions. As the whole *raison d'etre* of marriage is increasingly seen as the fulfilment of love, so the absence of love becomes sufficient grounds for divorce. We have already quoted the opinion that a man who loves someone else more than his wife, should "do things properly" and get a divorce. A newspaper writer commenting on the divorce of a member of the Japanese Royal Family reveals the same attitude when he remarks that Prince K in letting things slide and continuing the marriage after it became obvious that he and his wife were not suited to each other showed that he "was lacking in a serious attitude towards his own and his wife's human nature."

This is familiar ground; familiar also is the increase in divorce rates which it implies. It is a process, however, which has only just begun in Japan. From the beginning of statistical records to 1945, Japan was the only country in the world in which the divorce rate showed a steady and continued decline— from 1.4 per thousand in 1901 to about .6 per thousand at the beginning of the war. (Compared with an American increase from .7 in 1900 to 4.3 in 1946.) During all this period divorce was possible by the simple act of registering consent. To complete the reversal of the Western pattern, in 1930 the divorce rate was lower in towns with more than 50,000 population than in agricultural districts.

The probable reasons for this decline lie in later marriage, a more "responsible" attitude to marriage with the growth in education and the diffusion of new standards of respectability, and the effect of the whole complex of changes summed up in the words "improved status of women" on the traditional form of divorce, which amounted in fact to dismissal by the groom's family of a bride whom they found unsatisfactory.

Since the war, which has brought no legal changes except in the grounds for judicial divorce—which in any case accounts for only a small fraction of the total number of divorces—the divorce rate has risen from the pre-war .6 per thousand to a figure very close to 1.0 per thousand for each of the five years 1947-51. The new "Western" trend towards increased divorce would seem to be beginning to assert itself—and for the same reasons as in the West.

Nevertheless, it is still only beginning. More "realistic" conceptions of marriage still play a large part at least in feminine attitudes to marriage and divorce. We have already quoted the factory girl's concern to get a man "with earning capacity" for a husband. For women marriage is still a means of livelihood. The writer of a personal advice column in the newspaper, for instance, answers a woman with children whose husband is persistently and flagrantly unfaithful with a sympathetic denunciation of faithless husbands who "do not realize that equality of the sexes means equal recognition of the personality of each partner in marriage." But she concludes by advising the woman that with three children divorce might be the greater evil and her best course is to try to win back her husband with extra attentions.

Japanese feminists in their discussions of divorce are often concerned to point out that the equality which the law prescribes is a hollow mockery given the biological arrangement of reproduction and the existing economic and educational ordering of society which make it difficult for a woman to acquire a skill, or having acquired a skill to get a job, or having got a job to earn a living wage. Many divorces "by consent" are no more than the discarding by a selfish husband of a defenceless and dependent wife who is as yet unused to the idea that women in Japanese society have any rights to assert. Many feel that the remedy lies in making divorce by consent conditional on the approval of a Family Tribunal.

EXPECTED PERSONALITIES

The nature of the traditional expected personalities of men and women in Japanese society obviously bore an intimate relation to the expected relations of dominance and submission between husband and wife. With change in the latter one can expect change also in the former. Contrariwise, unless there is change in the former it is impossible for change in the latter to be complete. It may be worth considering here in some detail the answers from a sample of a hundred to the questions, "What sort of man (woman) do you admire most?"

The great diversity of expressions used in describing the ideal man shows that there is no accepted stereotyped form of words which springs readily to the tongue. The replies are not, however, devoid of pattern. Although each mentions only one or two or at the most four traits of character which they most admire, it is possible, by relating these to the hero type of popular films and novels, to the type of individual who acquires power and prestige in national and community life, and to the sort of evaluative judgements of character which are made in everyday life, to build up a composite picture of the admired type to which most of the answers may be deemed to be partial references.

Thus the ideal man is the leader type, the "manly" man, one who has suffered, a man of courage and endurance, strong-willed, quick, decisive and forceful in situations where lesser men would hesitate out of scrupulous regard for detail, frank in the expression of his opinion without excessive regard for etiquette or convention, disdainful of underhand scheming, direct in the expression of his emotions, a good loser, generously lacking in petty resentments, but ready to avenge insult whenever it is proffered, capable of deep passions but able to conquer them if necessary, a loyal friend, ready to act on the promptings of the heart, as a leader of men ready to give his life for his subordinates and chivalrous in his protection of the weak. In all, over half the respondents mention one or other of these traits and a just significantly greater number of such replies come from men than from women.

There is a tendency for women to favor what one might build up into a secondary pattern as the "safe-and-sound" type—the man who is faithful, loyal and sincere (11 respondents), who is punctilious in his personal relations (6), a man of integrity (1), a man of just dealings (2), thoughtful (1), a hard worker (6), a steady reliable man (3), to which should perhaps be added the "serious-minded man" mentioned by nine women and no men. This word *(majime na)* is the one recurring most frequently in these replies. It means specifically a man who does not spend his time and money on women and drink, particularly women—an eminently reasonable preference from the wife's point of view.

Two other groups of answers which do not fit into either of the above categories are gaiety and cheerfulness (7), and kindliness and consideration for others. It is noticeable that of the twelve people who mention this latter trait, ten are women.

The pattern of admired feminine types emerges more clearly than the masculine, which is perhaps an illustration of a general tendency for the lower statuses in any society to be more clearly defined than the higher. It is, for one tihng, generally those who occupy the higher statuses who do the defining. Moreover, the greater the restriction of choice which any role entails, the easier becomes its concrete definition and, perhaps, the greater the need for defining and enforcing it. Thus, in the writings of the Tokugawa moralists— Kaibara Ekken of the seventeenth century, for instance, or Nakamura Tekisai of the eighteenth—we get a very clear picture of what they expect of women, but a much vaguer picture of the ideal masculine character. The same is true of the ethics text-books on which the present generation was nurtured.

The essential qualities of womanhood stressed by Confucian moralists were especially those of loyal obedience and service, and it is these qualities which predominate in the replies. Twenty-six people out of a hundred used words such as "quiet," "reserved," "obedient," "submissive," "loyal," "modest," "quiet-mannered," "open and trusting" *(otonashii, juujun, ninjuu, chuujitsu, kenjo, odayaka, sunao)*. Eight mentioned "gracefulness" *(shitoyaka)*. Ten stressed the qualities of the ideal servant—"noticing" things (anticipating the wants of others), consideration, a woman who can look after people, gives of her best for others, devotes herself

to her home and her children. Eighteen used the word *yasashii* which has a wide range of meaning; graceful, gentle, tender, affectionate, qualities which hospitalized males in our society are expected to find epitomized in young nurses. Other traits mentioned which fit into this picture are lack of vanity, nonextravagance, lack of effectation, being a hard worker, not being "brainy," gaining the trust of neighbors. Each received one mention.

This does not, however, entirely complete the picture. Just as the heroine of the *kabuki* plays, for all her grace and submissive loyalty, nevertheless carries a short dagger in her bosom and is prepared to use it with grim determination (though most probably on herself) whenever the honor of her family or the life of her lord is at stake, so we find that eleven of those who mention one or several of the above characteristics add, "but on the other hand . . ." or "but combined with this . . ." a certain strength, spirit, solid reliability, a hard core, something positive about her, no weakling. The "but" is always there; the contrast is always pointed.

It is presumably this type of personality to which the six people who used the word "womanly" were referring. These qualities are the specific differentiating characteristics of the female sex. (In fact, only eight people used entirely the same terms and only nine others partially the same terms in describing both their ideal woman and their ideal man, though it must be remembered that the nature of the questions perhaps suggested that a contrast was expected.) It is interesting to notice the suggestion here (as in the case of the "Japanese family system") that such a pattern of feminine character is peculiar to Japan and (together, one suspects, with the *kimono,* the tea ceremony, the cherry trees and Mount Fuji) to be counted one of her chief glories. Five people, all men, in introducing one or other of the above traits said "a really Japanese type of . . ." or "a real Japanese woman." One even used the phrase *Yamato nadeshiko* which has about the same ring and if used in earnest would arouse about the same titter in sophisticated circles as "a true English rose," with the difference that the *nadeshiko* of fringed pink, is more slender, more pale and more modestly retiring than most roses. The belief that the Japanese woman was a unique and superior product was put forward explicitly by one man who quoted as evidence his experiences of the women of other parts of Asia during the war. There is an aphorism which the Japanese man of the world can rarely resist the temptation offered by the presence of a foreigner at a party to quote; it is to the effect that a man's physical wants are most adequately catered for by living in a Western-style house with a Japanese wife who can do Chinese cooking.

This ideal of what I shall call the Confucian pattern seems to be shared equally by both men and women. The only significant difference concerns the use of the word *yasashii* which women use more than men (fourteen to four). The reason may possibly be that the term implies a certain protectiveness, a positive tenderness springing from individual initiative, a role in which women like to picture themselves but which is hardly consistent with the subordination and the negative virtues of willing obedience which figure most prominently in the man's estimation of the ideal woman.

To that extent it might be doubted whether *yasashii* really belongs to the Confucian pattern or whether it is really part of another quality referred to by other respondents in such terms as "a capacity for love," "depth" or "delicacy" of feeling. (*Aijoo-yutaka, joo-bukai, joo ga komakai, ninjoo ga aru.*) One might point the distinction between the Confucian pattern proper and this emphasis on a loving nature in terms of Ruth Benedict's thesis that for the Japanese all social action falls into one of two mutually exclusive spheres, that of duty and that of "human feeling." ("Human feeling" is, indeed, a translation of one of these words, *ninjoo*.) Alternatively, and less abstractly, the Confucian pattern might be considered to belong to the samurai subculture and the warmly-feeling woman to the urban plebeian subculture of the Tokugawa period. The difference in heroine types is quite clear in the *kabuki* drama.

The heroines of the *buke-mono*—the dramas of intrigue and battle set mostly in the Kamakura and Muromachi periods—belong to the Confucian pattern. Rarely do they display emotional attachment towards a man. The "human feeling" which is allowed is almost entirely confined to their love for their children which, however, often serves only as a counterpoint to their duty of loyalty to lord or husband to which it often has to be subordinated. (The nurse who delivers up her own child to assassins who are searching for the heir of her master.) In the *choonin-mono*, however—dramas which reflect the culture of the town classes of Edo and Oosaka during the Tokugawa period—the wife of the merchant or artisan typically shows much greater freedom and independence of action and is allowed to express feelings of love and jealousy vividly and forcefully.

But although the Confucian pattern predominates in these replies, there is, nevertheless, a feeling that it rather belongs to the past. Two people spoke of the "old type" of Japanese woman. But though in decline the old norms are far from displaced, and those whose replies deviate from the above patterns frequently feel the need of explicitly pointing out, or even of justifying, their deviation. Thus one woman of 24 says "I dislike the old 'good-wife-and-wise-mother' type," and another, "I like someone who is not dependent on a man." "I don't like *even* women to be indirect and roundabout in their speech," said one man, and another, "It used not to be the thing for women to work, but as soon as I married my wife I set her to work. I treat her as an equal." (This particular man may be making the best of a bad job. He was the man previously mentioned who was so eclipsed by his wife in their business and social activities that he was falsely rumoured to be an adopted son-in-law.) There is too, a note of defiant overstatement in the replies of two young women who deviate from the traditional patterns. One used the word *jajauma*—"I like a woman to be a bit of a virago" and the other, "a woman who speaks her mind, even to the point of being cheeky."

The other character traits mentioned by the deviants are those which appeared as characteristics of the ideal man. *Sappari shita* —someone who is simple and direct, does not fuss or cry over spilt milk, *hakkiri shita* —someone who speaks her own mind, makes her intention clear and sticks to it, *hakihaki shita, tekipaki shita*—a sharp, bustling, managing type. Finally there are various odd remarks such as "someone with enough manliness about her to stand up for herself," "someone with as much ability as a man," a "thoughtful person," a "solidly reliable person." Altogether there are nineteen such replies. All of the eleven women who give them are under 35 (highly significant difference) and of the eight men, five are under 25. For the rest, ten were unable or unwilling to give replies, and seventy-one gave answers falling within the traditional pattern.

CONCLUSION

If the picture given above is one of confusion, it has done no more than reflect the confusion in normative ideals which exist in Tokyo today. There is not only the fumbling, experimentation and uncertainty which inevitably characterizes human relations in growing cities, cities which lack the established patterns of response to stock situations of the small local community and lack also the group pressures which give training in these responses, secure their enforcement and afford the individual the security which comes from the expectation of his group's approval.

To all this is added the sudden subversion of an official morality which was formerly inculcated at high pressure, the sudden release of tendencies which had been undermining the official morality for decades, and the sudden influx of Western ideas which in themselves present a confusion of ideals ranging from extreme individualistic hedonism at one end, to Catholic insistence on the indissolubility of the marriage sacrament and the predominantly procreative function of sex on the other. It is not surprising that the Don't Know group should be large for all questions in opinion-surveys about the family. Journalists, scholars and publicists of various sorts have exerted the whole weight of their influence to the destruction of "feudalism" in the family, a preoccupation which has prevented very careful consideration of the problems of the new nonfeudal family which is emerging. The ideal of marriage as the fulfilment of the mutual love of two independent and equal personalities is generally accepted, but how this ideal is to be fitted into the structure of the new conjugal family with its existing economic and child-rearing functions, is a question which has received scant attention. It will probably continue to be largely disregarded as long as the battle against the "remnants of feudalism" has still to be won, particularly in rural areas. But the rise in the divorce rate and the increase in juvenile delinquency suggests that the problems of the next stage are beginning to raise their head in the cities, and that the concern over family disintegration familiar to Western societies will increasingly occupy attention in the future.

37. LEGAL EVOLUTION AND SOCIETAL COMPLEXITY

RICHARD D. SCHWARTZ and JAMES C. MILLER

Reprinted by permission of the University of Chicago Press from American Journal of Sociology, *70 (September 1964): 159-69. Richard D. Schwartz is Dean of the Law School, State University of New York at Buffalo. Prior to that he was Professor of Sociology and Law, Northwestern University, where he also directed that university's Council for Intersocietal Studies. His principal research interest is the sociology of law. He has done field work in Israel and India on the origins and functioning of law and is currently engaged in an experimental study of tax-law enforcement. He is co-author of* Criminal Law *and* Unobtrusive Measures. *James C. Miller is Assistant Professor of Psychology, Yale University; he also holds a law degree. One of his major interests is the study of legal topics by means of social science research, particularly in sociolegal process and decision-making. He is co-author, with Myres S. McDougal and Harold D. Lasswell, of* International Agreements and World Public Order.

■ Few institutions in contemporary industrial societies arouse more emotionalism than those associated with the direct maintenance of law and order: police, judges, and prisons. One of the implications of the next selection is that a society's policies in the legal sphere are outgrowths of the adaptive strategy that characterizes it. Another is that the ferment surrounding legal institutions in the United States today is an aspect of the rapid change that is going on in almost all other institutional spheres; I interpret it as a feature of the transition to a post-industrial stage of development.

No society can exist without a legal system. This selection is a comparative study of the evolution of legal institutions, which can be regarded as examples of cultural adjustments within successive levels of adaptation.

A law is a rule that distinguishes the actions that will incur penalty—in threat or in fact—by a human agency as distinguished from penalty imposed by a supernatural agency. Legal penalties are predetermined, commensurate with the penalized action, and involve a specified loss of life, limb, freedom of movement, privilege, rights, or possessions. Societies vary greatly in the mechanisms they employ to enforce legal conformity and resolve disputes, and many societies enforce their laws without specialized legal personnel.

Schwartz and Miller explore the hypothesis that the development of techniques such as mediation, police, and specialized legal counsel is not random or fortuitous. Instead, they emerge as part of an overall evolutionary sequence: one development sets the stage for the next, although one level does not assure the emergence of the next. This can be regarded as an example of increasing role-differentiation, which in turn is an aspect of cultural evolution. Courts, for example, arise only in state societies. Prior to the development of states, established laws are enforced in face-to-face relationships within the community, and the force of law is in the feud or in the consensus of the community.

Schwartz and Miller show that there are several societies that have neither mediation, police, nor specialized counsel. Usually these are societies at the lower levels of socio-technological adaptation. Some societies use mediation but neither of the other two devices. With a few exceptions, societies that have police also employ mediation, although they may be without institutionalized counsel. Finally, a few societies have counsel, and these also and invariably have police and mediation. The authors note that specialized counsel are found only in advanced agricultural societies that are urbanized and literate.

To understand the role of specialized legal counsel (including judges) as an aspect of the level of adaptation represented in complex states, it must be remembered that it is virtually impossible for a judge in a national-urban context to know anything about the disputants in a case; he must evaluate the merits of the evidence in the light of precedent. Lawyers and judges are specialized technologists in an elaborate division of labor in urbanized state organizations who study the wording of the law with care and proceed according to precedent and stereotyped procedures. They administer the law according to impersonal criteria. It is partly in these terms that we can understand specialized counsel as an aspect of very advanced adaptations. As Schwartz and Miller note at the conclusion of their paper, many of these considerations carry important implications for the development of international legal systems.

Schwartz and Miller intended their paper to be as much a contribution to methodology as to substance in the study of legal evolution. Their methodological contributions, however, are largely in the footnotes to their paper, which had to be omitted here because of limitations of space. The reader who wants to learn more about such research should refer to the original version of the article.

The basic work in the anthropological study of law related to stages of cultural development is *Ancient Law: Its Connection with the Early History of Society and Its Relation to Modern Ideas,* by Henry Sumner Maine (New York: Oxford University Press, 1931); this book has been republished many times in various editions. *The Division of Labor in Society,* by Emile Durkheim (New York: The Free Press, 1947), is of great importance in the history of ideas in the anthropological study of law. Another basic work is *The Law of Primitive Man,* by E. Adamson Hoebel (Cambridge: Harvard University Press, 1954). A rebuttal to Hoebel's view of the relationship between law and kinship organization is offered in my own book, *The Transition from Childhood to Adolescence* (Chicago: Aldine, 1964). A stimulating collection of case studies is *African Law: Adaptation and Development,* edited by Hilda Kuper and Leo Kuper (Berkeley: University of California Press, 1965). An unfocused collection of case studies that nevertheless is worth consulting is *Law and Warfare: Studies in the Anthropology of Conflict,* edited by Paul Bohannan (Garden City, N.Y.: Natural History Press, 1967). ■

THE STUDY OF LEGAL evolution has traditionally commended itself to scholars in a variety of fields. To mention only a few, it has been a concern in sociology of Weber and Durkheim; in jurisprudence of Dicey, Holmes, Pound, and Llewellyn; in anthropology of Maine and Hoebel; in legal history of Savigny and Vinogradoff.

There are theoretical and practical reasons for this interest. Legal evolution provides an opportunity to investigate the relations between law and other major aspects and institutions of society. Thus Maine explained the rise of contract in terms of the declining role of kinship as an exclusive basis of social organization. Durkheim saw restitutive sanctions replacing repressive ones as a result of the growth of the division of labor and the corresponding shift from mechanical to organic solidarity. Dicey traced the growth of statutory lawmaking in terms of the increasing articulateness and power of public opinion. Weber viewed the development of formal legal rationality as an expression of, and precondition for, the growth of modern capitalism.

For the most part, these writers were interested in the development of legal norms and not in the evolution of legal organization. The latter subject warrants attention for several reasons. As the mechanism through which substantive law is formulated, invoked, and administered, legal organization is of primary importance for understanding the process by which legal norms are evolved and implemented. Moreover, legal organization seems to develop with a degree of regularity that in itself invites attention and explanation. The present study suggests that elements of legal organization emerge in a sequence, such that each constitutes a necessary condition for the next. A second type of regularity appears in the relationship between changes in legal organization and other aspects of social organization, notably the division of labor.

By exploring such regularities intensively, it may be possible to learn more about the dynamics of institutional differentiation. Legal organization is a particularly promising subject from this point of view. It tends toward a unified, easily identifiable structure in any given society. Its form and procedures are likely to be explicitly stated. Its central function, legitimation, promotes cross-culturally recurrent instances of conflict with, and adaptation to, other institutional systems such as religion, polity, economy, and family. Before these relationships can be adequately explored, however, certain gross regularities of development should be noted and it is with these that the present paper is primarily concerned.

This article reports preliminary findings from cross-cultural research that show a rather startling consistency in the pattern of legal evolution. In a sample of fifty-one societies, compensatory damages and mediation of disputes were found in every society having specialized legal counsel. In addition, a large majority (85 per cent) of societies that develop specialized police also employ damages and mediation. These findings suggest a variety of explanations. It may be necessary, for instance, for a society to accept the principles of mediation and compensation before formalized agencies of adjudication and control can be evolved. Alternatively or concurrently, nonlegal changes may explain the results. A formalized means of exchange, some degree of specialization, and writing appear almost universally to follow certain of these legal developments and to precede others. If such sequences are inevitable, they suggest theoretically interesting causative relationships and provide a possible basis for assigning priorities in stimulating the evolution of complex legal institutions in the contemporary world.

METHOD

This research employed a method used by Freeman and Winch in their analysis of societal complexity. Studying a sample of forty-eight societies, they noted a Guttman-scale relationship among six items associated with the folk-urban continuum. The following items were found to fall in a single dimension, ranging, the authors suggest, from simple to complex: a symbolic medium of exchange; punishment of crimes through government action; religious, educational, and government specialization; and writing.

To permit the location of legal characteristics on the Freeman-Winch scale, substantially the same sample was used in this study. Three societies were dropped because of uncertainty as to date and source of description or because of inadequate material on legal characteristics. Six societies were added, three to cover the legally developed societies more adequately and three to permit the inclusion of certain well-described control systems.

Several characteristics of a fully developed legal system were isolated for purposes of study. These included counsel, mediation, and police. These three characteristics, which will constitute the focus of the present paper, are defined as follows:

Counsel: regular use of specialized non-kin advocates in the settlement of disputes
Mediation: regular use of non-kin third-party intervention in dispute settlement
Police: specialized armed force used partially or wholly for norm enforcement.

These three items, all referring to specialized roles relevant to dispute resolution, were found to fall in a near-perfect Guttman scale. Before the central findings are described and discussed, several methodological limitations should be noted.

First, despite efforts by Murdock and others, no wholly satisfactory method has been devised for obtaining a representative sample of the world's societies. Since the universe of separate societies has not been adequately defined, much less enumerated, the representativeness of the sample cannot be ascertained. Nevertheless, an effort has been made to include societies drawn from the major culture areas and from diverse stages of technological development.

Second, societies have been selected in terms of the availability of adequate ethnographic reports. As a result, bias may have entered the sample through the selection of societies that were particularly accessible—and hospitable—to anthropological observers. Such societies may differ in their patterns of development from societies that have been less well studied.

Third, despite the selection of relatively

well-studied societies, the quality of reports varies widely. Like the preceding limitations, this problem is common to all cross-cultural comparisons. The difficulty is mitigated, however, by the fact that the results of this study are positive. The effect of poor reporting should generally be to randomize the apparent occurrence of the variables studied. Where systematic patterns of relationship emerge, as they do in the present research, it would seem to indicate considerable accuracy in the original reports.

Fourth, this study deals with characteristics whose presence or absence can be determined with relative accuracy. In so doing, it may neglect elements of fundamental importance to the basic inquiry. Thus no effort is made to observe the presence of such important phenomena as respect for law, the use fo generalized norms, and the pervasiveness of deviance-induced disturbance. Although all of these should be included in a comprehensive theory of legal evolution, they are omitted here in the interest of observational reliability.

Fifth, the Guttman scale is here pressed into service beyond that for which it was developed. Originally conceived as a technique for the isolation of uni-dimensional attitudes, it has also been used as a means of studying the interrelationship of behavior patterns. It should be particularly valuable, however, in testing hypotheses concerning developmental sequences, whether in individuals or in societies. Thus, if we hypothesize that A must precede B, supporting data should show three scale types: neither A or B, A but not B, and A and B. All instances of B occurring without A represent errors which lower the reproducibility of the scale and, by the same token, throw doubt in measurable degree on the developmental hypothesis. Although the occurrence of developmental sequences ultimately requires verification by the observation of historic changes in given units, substantiating evidence can be derived from the comparative study of units at varying stages of development. The Guttman scale seems an appropriate quantitative instrument for this purpose.

FINDINGS

In the fifty-one societies studied, as indicated in Table 1, four scale types emerged. Eleven societies showed none of the three characteristics; eighteen had only mediation; eleven had only mediation and police; and characteristics; eighteen had only mediation; eleven had only mediation and police and seven had mediation, police, and specialized counsel. Two societies departed from these patterns: the Crow and the Thonga had police, but showed no evidence of mediation. While these deviant cases merit detailed study, they reduce the reproducibility of the scale by less than 2 per cent, leaving the coefficient at the extraordinarily high level of better than 0.98. Each characteristic of legal organization may now be discussed in terms of the sociolegal conditions in which it is found.

MEDIATION

Societies that lack mediation, constituting less than a third of the entire sample, appear to be the simplest societies. None of them has writing or any substantial degree of specialization. Only three of the thirteen (Yurok, Kababish, and Thonga) use money, whereas almost three-fourths of the societies with mediation have a symbolic means of exchange. We can only speculate at present on the reasons why mediation is absent in these societies. Data on size, using Naroll's definition of the social unit, indicate that the maximum community size of societies without mediation is substantially smaller than that of societies with mediation. Because of their small size, mediationless societies may have fewer disputes and thus have less opportunity to evolve regularized patterns of dispute settlement. Moreover, smaller societies may be better able to develop mores and informal controls which tend to prevent the occurrence of disputes. Also, the usually desperate struggle for existence of such societies may strengthen the common goal of survival

TABLE 37.1
SCALE OF LEGAL CHARACTERISTICS

Society	Counsel	Police	Mediation	Errors	Legal Scale Type	Freeman-Winch Scale Type
Cambodians	x	x	x		3	*
Czechs	x	x	x		3	6
Elizabethan English	x	x	x		3	6
Imperial Romans	x	x	x		3	6
Indonesians	x	x	x		3	*
Syrians	x	x	x		3	*
Ukrainians	x	x	x		3	6
Ashanti		x	x		2	5
Cheyenne		x	x		2	*
Creek		x	x		2	5
Cuna		x	x		2	4
Crow		x		1	2	0
Hopi		x	x		2	5
Iranians		x	x		2	6
Koreans		x	x		2	6
Lapps		x	x		2	6
Maori		x	x		2	4
Riffians		x	x		2	6
Thonga		x		1	2	2
Vietnamese		x	x		2	6
Andamanese			x		1	0
Azande			x		1	0
Balinese			x		1	4
Cayapa			x		1	2
Chagga			x		1	4
Formosan aborigines			x		1	0
Hottentot			x		1	0
Ifugao			x		1	0
Lakher			x		1	2
Lepcha			x		1	3
Menomini			x		1	0
Mbundu			x		1	3
Navaho			x		1	5
Ossett			x		1	1
Siwans			x		1	1
Trobrianders			x		1	*
Tupinamba			x		1	0
Venda			x		1	5
Woleaians			x		1	0
Yakut			x		1	1
Aranda					0	0
Buka					0	0
Chukchee					0	0
Comanche					0	*
Copper Eskimo					0	0
Jivaro					0	0
Kababish					0	1
Kazak					0	0
Siriono					0	0
Yaruro					0	0
Yurok					0	1

*Not included in Freeman-Winch sample.

Coefficient of reproducibility = 1—2/153 = 0.987; coefficient of scalability = 1—2/153—120 = 0.94; Kendall's tau = + 0.68.

and thus produce a lessening of intragroup hostility.

The lack of money and substantial property may also help to explain the absence of mediation in these societies. There is much evidence to support the hypothesis that property provides something to quarrel about. In addition, it seems to provide something to mediate with as well. Where private property is extremely limited, one would be less likely to find a concept of damages, that is, property payments in lieu of other sanctions. The development of a concept of damages should greatly increase the range of alternative settlements. This in turn might be expected to create a place for the mediator as a person charged with locating a settlement point satisfactory to the parties and the society.

This hypothesis derives support from the data in Table 2. The concept of damages occurs in all but four of the thirty-eight societies that have mediation and thus appears to be virtually a precondition for mediation. It should be noted, however, that damages are also found in several (seven of thirteen) of the societies that lack mediation. The relationship that emerges is one of damages as a necessary but not sufficient condition for mediation. At present it is impossible to ascertain whether the absence of mediation in societies having the damage concept results from a simple time lag or whether some other factor, not considered in this study, distinguishes these societies from those that have developed mediation.

POLICE

Twenty societies in the sample had police —that is, a specialized armed force available for norm enforcement. As noted, all these but the Crow and Thonga had the concept of damages and some kind of mediation as well. Nevertheless, the occurrence of twenty societies with mediation but without police makes it clear that mediation is not inevitably accompanied by the systematic enforcement of decisions. The separability of these two characteristics is graphically illustrated in ethnographic reports. A striking instance is found among the Albanian tribesmen whose elaborately developed code for settling disputes, Lek's Kanun, was used for centuries as a basis for mediation. But in the absence of mutual agreements by the disputants, feuds often began immediately after adjudication and continued unhampered by any constituted police.

From the data it is possible to determine some of the characteristics of societies that develop police. Eighteen of the twenty in our sample are economically advanced enough to use money. They also have a substantial degree of specialization, with full-time priests and teachers found in all but three (Cheyenne, Thonga, and Crow), and full-time governmental officials, not mere relatives of the chief, present in all but four (Cuna, Maori, Thonga, and Crow).

Superficially at least, these findings seem directly contradictory to Durkheim's major thesis in *The Division of Labor in Society*. He hypothesized that penal law—the effort of the organized society to punish offenses against itself—occurs in societies with the simplest division of labor. As indicated, however, our data show that police are found only in association with a substantial degree of division of labor. Even the practice of governmental punishment for wrongs against the society (as

TABLE 37.2
DAMAGES IN RELATION TO LEGAL FUNCTIONARIES

	No Mediation	Mediation Only	Mediation and Police	Mediation, Police, and Counsel	Total
Damages	7	17	10	7	41
No damages	6	3	1	0	10
Total	13	20	11	7	51

noted by Freeman and Winch) does not appear in simpler societies. By contrast, restitutive sanctions—damages and mediation—which Durkheim believed to be associated with an increasing division of labor, are found in many societies that lack even rudimentary specialization. Thus Durkheim's hypothesis seems the reverse of the empirical situation in the range of societies studied here.

COUNSEL

Seven societies in the sample employ specialized advocates in the settlement of disputes. As noted, all of these societies also use mediation. There are, however, another thirty-one societies that have mediation but do not employ specialized counsel. It is a striking feature of the data that damages and mediation are characteristic of the simplest (as well as the most complex) societies, while legal counsel are found only in the most complex. The societies with counsel also have, without exception, not only damages, mediation, and police but, in addition, all of the complexity characteristics identified by Freeman and Winch.

It is not surprising that mediation is not universally associated with counsel. In many mediation systems the parties are expected to speak for themselves. The mediator tends to perform a variety of functions, questioning disputants as well as deciding on the facts and interpreting the law. Such a system is found even in complex societies, such as Imperial China. There the prefect acted as counsel, judge, and jury, using a whip to wring the truth from the parties who were assumed a priori to be lying. To serve as counsel in that setting would have been painful as well as superfluous. Even where specialized counsel emerge, their role tends to be ambiguous. In ancient Greece, for instance, counsel acted principally as advisors on strategy. Upon appearance in court they sought to conceal the fact that they were specialists in legal matters, presenting themselves merely as friends of the parties or even on occasion assuming the identity of the parties themselves.

At all events, lawyers are here found only in quite urbanized societies, all of which are based upon fully developed agricultural economies. The data suggest at least two possible explanations. First, all of the sample societies with counsel have a substantial division of labor, including priests, teachers, police, and government officials. This implies an economic base strong enough to support a variety of secondary and tertiary occupations as well as an understanding of the advantages of specialization. Eleven societies in the sample, however, have all of these specialized statuses but lack specialized counsel. What distinguishes the societies that develop counsel? Literacy would seem to be an important factor. Only five of the twelve literate societies in the sample do not have counsel. Writing, of course, makes possible the formulation of a legal code with its advantages of forewarning the violator and promoting uniformity in judicial administration. The need to interpret a legal code provides a niche for specialized counsel, especially where a substantial segment of the population is illiterate.

CONCLUSIONS

These data, taken as a whole, lend support to the belief that an evolutionary sequence occurs in the development of legal institutions. Alternative interpretations are, to be sure, not precluded. The scale analysis might fail to discern short-lived occurrences of items. For instance, counsel might regularly develop as a variation in simple societies even before police, only to drop out rapidly enough so that the sample picks up no such instances. Even though this is a possibility in principle, no cases of this kind have come to the authors' attention.

Another and more realistic possibility is that the sequence noted in this sample does not occur in societies in a state of rapid transition. Developing societies undergoing intensive cultural contact might provide an economic and social basis for specialized lawyers, even in the absence of police or dispute mediation. Until such societies are included in the sample, these findings must be limited to relatively isolated, slowly changing societies.

The study also raises but does not answer questions concerning the evolution of an international legal order. It would be foolhardy to generalize from the primitive world directly to the international scene and to assume that the same sequences must occur here as there. There is no certainty that subtribal units can be analogized to nations, because the latter tend to be so much more powerful, independent, and relatively deficient in common culture and interests. In other ways, the individual nations are farther along the path of legal development than subtribal units because all of them have their own domestic systems of mediation, police, and counsel. This state of affairs might well provide a basis for short-circuiting an evolutionary tendency operative in primitive societies. Then, too, the emergent world order appears to lack the incentive of common interest against a hostile environment that gave primitive societies a motive for legal control. Even though the survival value of a legal system may be fully as great for today's world as for primitive societies, the existence of multiple units in the latter case permitted selection for survival of those societies that had developed the adaptive characteristic. The same principle cannot be expected to operate where the existence of "one world" permits no opportunity for variation and consequent selection.

Nonetheless, it is worth speculating that some of the same forces may operate in both situations. We have seen that damages and mediation almost always precede police in the primitive world. This sequence could result from the need to build certain cultural foundations in the community before a central regime of control, as reflected in a police force, can develop. Hypothetically, this cultural foundation might include a determination to avoid disputes, an appreciation of the value of third-party intervention, and the development of a set of norms both for preventive purposes and as a basis for allocating blame and punishment when disputes arise. Compensation by damages and the use of mediators might well contribute to the development of such a cultural foundation, as well as reflecting its growth. If so, their occurrence prior to specialized police would be understandable. This raises the question as to whether the same kind of cultural foundation is not a necessary condition for the establishment of an effective world police force and whether, in the interest of that objective, it might not be appropriate to stress the principles of compensatory damages and mediation as preconditions for the growth of a world rule of law.

38. THE CONTROL OF CHURCHES BY MILLS

LISTON POPE

Reprinted from Millhands and Preachers: A Study of Gastonia *(New Haven: Yale University Press, 1942). Liston Pope is a clergyman who has been interested and involved in many aspects of education. He has been Stark Professor of Social Ethics at Yale University since 1947 and was Dean of the Yale Divinity School between 1949 and 1962 and has taught at many other universities. In addition to* Millhands and Preachers, *from which this chapter is reprinted, he is also the author of* The Kingdom Beyond Caste, *published in 1957.*

■ The organization of productive labor is an integral feature of a society's strategy of adaptation and an aspect of the maintenance of order and conformity. In an industrial nation, those who control the sources of energy and the means of production generally regard political harmony as a whole as requiring the passivity of hired labor; demands by employees for a larger share of the pie are seen as threats to the established order. Thus it is not surprising that religion plays an important role in the ideological legitimation of the established class relationships.

The subject of this selection is the use of formal religious institutions in the United States by factory owners as one means of insuring the smooth functioning of labor for profitably productive purposes. The mill owners of the 1930s described in this chapter opposed unionization and everything implied by it. As every student of this period of American history knows, hired thugs were often used to thwart unionization, but brute force is rarely sufficient to prevent change in complex societies; ideological legitimation is also necessary. Pope shows that in the mill city of Gastonia, North Carolina, the mill owners bought off the ministers and their churches to ensure that they would preach the holy—and not the social—gospel.

It may be thought that Pope's findings of more than 40 years ago are dated. In 1971, together with a group of students, I began a study of a small city in the Northeast that is dominated by a single factory; more than 75 per cent of the city's labor force is employed in it. No municipal programs are initiated in this city without prior consultation with the factory's directors, who are conspicuously involved in the city's churches, youth programs, and educational institutions. They are also very proud of "good labor

relations." There continue to be many such cities in the United States.

In concluding this chapter, Pope suggests that direct economic control over the churches was possible in Gastonia because it was a one-industry town; in larger urban centers, he notes, in which workers have more occupational choices open to them, the dominant group's influence on religious institutions are more indirect and subtle. This sheds light on the apparent paradox that religious institutions are not always rigidly conservative. One example was the role played by the black southern fundamentalist store-front churches in the civil rights movement. While many factors played a role in this activity, especially the 1954 Supreme Court desegregation decision, an important element was the growing industrialization of the South and the increase in occupational choices for blacks.

The fundamental work in the study of the relationship between theology and its social and economic context is *The Social Teaching of the Christian Churches,* by Ernst Troeltsch, 2 volumes (New York: Harper Torchbooks, 1960). The reader who wishes to know more about the connections between social and economic status and religious belief and practice in the United States will find an excellent introduction in *The Religious Factor,* by Gerhard Lenski (Garden City, N.Y.: Doubleday Anchor, 1963). The relationship between religious conflict and some of the major sources of change in the United States are explored in a set of papers in *Religious Conflict in America: Studies in the Problems beyond Bigotry,* edited by Earl Raab (Garden City, N.Y.: Doubleday Anchor, 1964). An excellent exploration of the rise of religious movements, with special reference to contemporary developments, is *Religious Sects: A Sociological Study,* by Bryan Wilson (New York and Toronto: McGraw-Hill, 1970). ∎

AS THE TEXTILE INDUSTRY grew in Gaston County, the wealth and power of its owners increased rapidly, and the relative number of its owners decreased. In the first three decades of industrialization, astute investors with small margins of available capital gathered the stock of the new mills increasingly into their own hands, and the ownership and control of a large percentage of the mills passed from a relatively broad community base into the hands of less than a dozen families. Large profits were realized from the new mills from the outset, providing capital for the construction and operation of additional mills.

Until recently it has been customary in the county to put new capital into a new mill instead of enlarging an old one; a number of chains, each containing several similar units, have been thereby created, with separate units having independent status but overlapping executive administration. Through this system a comparatively small number of employers came to control a large number of mills, each with its own mill village and other appurtenances of the village system. The degree to which concentration of administrative authority has proceeded during the last thirty-five years is indicated in Table 1; while the number of mills increased by 257 per cent from 1900 to 1935, the number of individuals holding offices in mill corporations increased only 23 per cent.

Control by mill owners over the total economic life was extended as the number of mills increased. Manufacturers estimated that about 45,000 people in Gaston County had become directly dependent upon the textile industry by 1925-26, of a total of about 65,000 persons. Mill workers and uptown citizens alike became heavily reliant for a livelihood upon the successful operation of the mills. Gaston County recapitulated the ante bellum economic policy of the South, putting all her economic eggs into one basket. Just as the Old South devoted its principal energies to the production of a single crop,

Gaston County after 1880 applied nearly all economic resources to the construction and operation of spinning mills. The whir of

TABLE 38.1

DISTRIBUTION OF CONTROL OVER MAJOR OFFICES IN GASTON COUNTY TEXTILE CORPORATIONS

	1880-1900	193E
Total number of mills	28	100
Total number of mill corporations	25	65
Total number of offices in corporations	112	187
Number of individuals holding offices	93	114
Average offices per individual	1.20	1.64
Number of individuals holding one office	77	85
Number of persons holding two offices	13	17
Number of persons holding three or more offices	3	12

spindles became a foundation and token of unprecedented prosperity, and little effort was made to diversify industry. In a pageant staged by Gastonia in 1924 to celebrate her civic achievements, a herald proclaimed:

O Gaston, you are rich in spindles,
And rich in other things;
We pass not by your other wealth,
We would not miss a single one,
But let the other industries
To spindles make obeisance
For sipndles make the county known
To all within the nation.

Command over economic structure carried over into all other spheres of social organization. Textile manufacturers became acknowledged leaders in every aspect of community life. They, or their representatives, were elected to many of the political and civic offices. They "set the pace" in houses and automobiles and leisure activities. They made the largest contributions to all "worthy causes." They became unchallenged arbiters of social policy and were regarded as praiseworthy guardians of community welfare.

Mill owners have been leaders in the churches of the county as in other institutions.

As already seen, they played an important part in church life and church extension dur-

TABLE 38.2
CHURCH AFFILIATIONS OF COTTON MILL EXECUTIVES IN GASTON COUNTY, AS BETWEEN 1880-1900 AND 1935

Denomination	Number of mill executives	
	1880-1900	193E
Lutheran	30	11
Presbyterian	28	32
Baptist	3	15
Methodist	15	21
Miscellaneous	3	5
Jewish	0	7
Nonchurchmen	2	3
No information	12	20
Total	93	114

ing the early days of the industry, and the role of leadership in religious institutions continued to be a tradition which few executives could ignore. Though denominational affiliations have shifted significantly, the percentage of major textile officials belonging to some church has changed very little as between 1880-1900 and 1935, as indicated in Table 38.2. In more recent years they have often expressed a desire to remain "in the background," lest ordinary citizens leave responsibility for the churches too largely in their hands, but at least half of the mill officials of the county hold important offices in their respective churches at the present time. Replies to a questionnaire in 1939 indicated that, of 78 mill officials from presidents down through overseers, 71 were church members, and 40 held some office in a church. A special study of 11 superintendents, with direct oversight of 15 mills, revealed that every one belonged to a church and 6 held at least one major office in a religious institution, while the 11 superintendents combined held a total of 15 offices in their respective churches.

Mill officials have supported the churches not only in membership and leadership but also through contributions to building funds and to the support of ministers. Financial support has often been interpreted as representing a means of control over the churches rather than a sincere desire to aid religious institutions as such. Mill owners explicitly deny any such intention. The attitude expressed by one mill president is typical of that almost universally advanced:

The mills regard churches as important in their villages, and support this regard with contributions. But the mills are interested in churches simply because the churches stand for decent and honest living. In one sense, of course, this is a selfish motive. The mills expect, however, to receive no direct returns; so far as I know, no effort has ever been made to dictate the attitudes of the churches toward the mills—not a word has ever been said. If any such direct effort was made, of course, the effectiveness of the churches would be crippled among the workers.

Despite disavowal of ulterior purposes, the fact that mills have almost universally contributed to the support of churches and ministers in their villages, whether or not any mill official belonged to those churches, justifies speculation on the real motives actuating such support. The degree to which textile managers have been conscious of an external purpose is a difficult and ambiguous question, to be sure, and is not as important as often assumed. It stresses motives to the neglect of structural relationships and results. Contributions by mills to churches are probably to be interpreted in the light of the general paternalistic background prevailing in the industry rather than as shrewd efforts to use the churches, in some diabolical way, as instruments of industrial policy. Most of the mill owners, under given cultural conditions, have not considered that they were using the churches in any way incompatible with the highest ideals of Christianity. The fact that churches have never challenged or refused their help, but have received it gladly, has confirmed them in their belief that they were philanthropists. Paternalism in industrial relations requires that they shall continue to be philanthropists, charged with the religious as well as the economic welfare of their workers. In playing this role, rationalizations have been made so subtly that neither mill owner nor church has questioned the essential sincerity of mill subsidies to churches.

The philanthropic mood has not prevented judicious discrimination by mill owners between the type of church to be supported and the type to be ignored. Direct subsidies have been allocated by the particular mill owner, almost without exception, to the churches attended by his own workers, whether or not these churches needed his help more than others in the vicinity. Concern simply for the religious welfare of the community has not resulted in an established policy for the support of Negro churches, though the need appears to be greater here than elsewhere. Further, the donor has often discriminated between the churches serving his own employees; until very recently, most employers discouraged establishment of the Church of God and similar groups in their villages, refusing to grant them space for the erection of buildings on mill property, and declining to render financial support to sect preachers. The personal affiliation of employers with older denominations may help to explain this discrimination—though many Presbyterian and Lutheran executives express a preference for Methodist and Baptist churches for their employees. On the other hand, it is well known in Southern mill villages that union organizers frequently obtain a following most easily from members of the newer sects, who have least to lose in an effort to improve their lot. Insofar as they "settle down" and become "stabilizing influences," according to employers, the Church of God and similar groups are receiving help from the mills. Otherwise, they are discouraged, and mill executives rationalize this policy by statements such as the following:

Our workers here in Gastonia are over 99 per cent pure Anglo-Saxon; they are intelligent, smart, educated. There is no use letting them get all stirred up emotionally. I'm a Methodist, but I don't like the old type of revivals, and naturally I express myself to that effect whenever any such question arises in regard to our mills. We don't care what road a man travels to get to heaven, just as we don't care whether a man travels the northern or southern route to get to San Francisco, but why should we let emotional sects get our people all stirred up?

More recently, a younger group of better-educated, more thoroughly secularized executives has begun to appear in the county, and at least a few of them see more clearly than have their predecessors the implications of their patronage of the churches. Most of them continue, nevertheless, to acquiesce in the system of subsidies. The infiltration of a number of executives from other regions of the country, including a few Jews from New York City, has also tended to increase self-consciousness on the part of their fellow executives: the Jewish managers help the churches quite as generously as do their Christian competitors, though they hold neither the same cultural presuppositions nor a common faith. Increasingly during the last two decades, and in a few instances even earlier, subsidies to religious institutions have been used as instruments of economic control—instruments the more effective because disguised in character. Paternalism in the county is becoming conscious of itself.[1]

Considerable debate has taken place as to whether financial support of churches by mill executives, and active leadership of many churches by them, has actually resulted in control of the churches by the mill owners, whatever their intentions may have been. A critic charged in 1929, after a wave of textile strikes in the South, that the churches were "undoubtedly owned and controlled by the mill owners," and that the clergy were "moral police for the industrial overlords." The charge was denied by mill owners and violently repudiated by many ministers in textile centers. The pastor of one mill church wrote:

May I give you some of my experience in this matter? First I was a student pastor at Spartanburg in the Glendale mill village, and lived just across the street from Mr. Lindsey, the president, and next door to one of the biggest

1. The end of this road may be foreseen in a feature appearing in the *Southern Textile Bulletin,* semiofficial journal of Southern mill superintendents. "Becky Ann's Own Page," appearing in a section designed for separate distribution to mill workers, is filled with religious admonitions, of which the following are samples:

"Those who have suffered most, serve best."

"God is good, friends are true, and somehow we get courage to 'keep on keeping on.' "

Mixed in with these mottoes are plaudits of the cotton mills, such as: "Today, those who have work in modern milles are the most fortunate people I know . . . nice homes . . . coal at reduced rates . . . educational advantages . . . hours are less and wages more . . . radios . . . daily papers . . . a car . . . insurance . . . fraternal orders. . . ." (August 28, 1930, March 5, 1936).

stockholders in the mill. Never for one time did they try to meddle in the affairs of the church that I was pastor of in their village.

At its meeting in October, 1929, the Western North Carolina Annual Conference of the Methodist Episcopal Church, South, openly acknowledged the system of mill supplements to some of its churches, and urged the extension of the system, recommending that manufacturers "should bear at least one-half the burden of maintaining religious worship in mill communities." The chairman of the committee which brought this recommendation to the conference was the presiding elder of Methodist churches in the Gastonia district, and another member of the committee became the new presiding elder of that district for the following year. When reminded a decade later of this overt appeal to mill owners for heavier subsidies, the chairman said:

Amen! I've always believed that. Mill churches serve the mill as much as they serve the folks; let the mill pay for the service. Churches help the mills to have a steadier and more intelligent supply of labor. Let the mills give more than they do, and let it all be perfectly above board. It's worth something to the mills to have churches work among their people. Why Mr.— [one of the largest textile manufacturers in North Carolina], a Jew, helps the preachers, and the first thing he does when a strike threatens is to call them up—and the strikers can't win with the preachers against them. So let Mr.—pay.

The Methodist appeal drew vigorous criticism from various sources. A correspondent wrote to the Raleigh *News and Observer*:

Pastors are very human. . . . They cannot bite the hand that feeds them. . . . In times of stress the employers and the employed clash. . . . What is a subsidized pastor and a subsidized church to do? . . . As a matter of fact they can do nothing. . . . Better have no church at all than to have one that is subsidized. . . .

The editor of the *News and Observer* agreed, writing that "if there is any institution that must be kept free, that ought to be kept above the faintest suspicion of taint, it is the church of Almighty God."

A similar debate over the implications of support of churches by mills has flared on other occasions, with very few of the dis-

putants being as frank (or cynical) as the sponsor of the Methodist recommendation. Ministers, almost without exception, resent the imputation involved in the question itself, and hasten to defend themselves and their colleagues. The standard formula, heard many times from mill pastors, insists that "the mill owners give our church the free use of a nice parsonage and make regular contributions to the support of the church, yet never have they said anything about the policy of the church." Many ministers in Gaston County aver that never, in all their experience, have they seen or heard any evidence that mills in any way have attempted to dominate church affairs.

Regardless of their own intentions and the protestations of ministers to the contrary, mill owners have held and exercised direct authority over many individual churches in Gaston County. It is very difficult to obtain information concerning explicit use of their power, as most pressures have been applied very subtly and quietly. Several incidents during the last sixty years indicate clearly, however, that on occasion particular mill officials have held determining power over particular churches. The following cases are representative:

The Presbyterian church at High Shoals, title to which had been retained in fee simple by the mill company there, was discontinued by the mill management in 1928 and transformed into a movie; the management said that the Baptists and Methodists had all the people, and there was no need for a Presbyterian church.

The Hebron Baptist Church was largely dependent on the Mountain Island Mill and when this mill was washed away by a flood in 1916 the church was forced to close for lack of support.

The mill management in one village is favorable to Baptists—at least workers think it is and they feel more secure in their jobs as Baptists than if they are Methodists. This feeling poses difficult problems for the Methodists.

In another mill village the management is decidedly pro-Methodist, and Baptists profess that they are discriminated against within the mill. The wife of the Baptist pastor in the vicinity says: "We face persecution worse than the Middle Ages."

Two brothers, each of whom was president of a cotton mill, quarreled over the distribution of offices in their particular church as between their respective sons, and a schism resulted in the church. Efforts have been made subsequently by denominational officials to heal the break, which has resulted in two separate churches only a block apart, but the mill presidents will not hear to it.

The most significant area for study of control by mill managers over churches is found in the mill churches, of course, as contrasted with uptown and rural churches. In churches located in mill villages the threat of domination by mill managers is always present, even if seldom exercised coercively. Several church buildings in the villages are owned outright by mill corporations, and a number of others contain in their deeds a retroactive clause, providing that the property shall revert to the mill by which it was given if it is ever used for nonreligious purposes. The system of direct subsidies by mill executives to salaries of mill ministers is a tool for overt control, if necessary. It is an instrument of covert control, in any case; given the low income level of mill churches, a gift of a few hundred dollars annually is necessarily a factor of influence in the determination of church policy, whether or not any stipulations or conditions accompany the gift.

Managerial authority over mill churches seldom needs to be made explicit, however, because it really inheres in the relations characteristic of mill villages. Description of these relations may best proceed through close analysis of two mill communities in Gaston County rather than through generalizations. Deviations from the patterns represented in these two samples are differences of degree only; most communities in the county are not so closely controlled, but comparable relations prevail in nearly all mill villages. Both villages represent the paternalistic system pushed to full development.

The first village, here called Milltown, is known through the South and nation as a "model mill village." Unincorporated, it is owned completely by the owner of the three mills that provide its economic base. The mill management is the direct and final authority on all matters of village administration, laying down rules and regulations for

the inhabitants and employing deputy sheriffs to control their infraction. Six hundred families, and a total population of about three thousand people, live there. Construction of the village, which is located on a semi-island between two rivers, cost about $1,500,000. Workers live in three- and four-room bungalows, which they rent at a rate of $1.25 a week for a four-room house with bath, with water and a minimum amount of electricity furnished. Neat lawns and landscaping have been designed and are maintained by the mill. A mill farm supplies eggs, milk, fowls, and vegetables to employees at cost. The village has a community hall, a golf course, two large school buildings, a boarding house, and several mercantile blocks, all built by the mill.

The mill owner also built the Baptist and Methodist churches in the village, expending $65,000 on the latter, and more recently has aided in the construction of a building for the Church of God. He provides parsonages, with all conveniences included, for four ministers who live in the village. The Methodist preacher receives a direct subsidy of $62.50 each month, is a total salary of $1,900, and an additional gift of $50 from the mill owner at Christmas. The mill retains title in fee simple to all church buildings and parsonages in the village, deeding them to their respective ecclesiastical bodies as "places of worship" but retaining title to them as pieces of real estate. The mill owner is not himself a churchman but has been interested in providing "adequate facilities" for the religious life of his workers. A son of the mill owner, himself secretary of the corporation, summed up as follows the philosophy underlying support of the churches by the mill officials:

We don't believe in overlapping or duplication here, even in the churches. In our organization every responsibility is graded by rank. We have officials corresponding to generals, majors, captains, lieutenants, and so forth right on down the line. We believe in efficiency. We believe in this in the churches, too. We want the churches we have to do a good job, instead of letting too many duplications ruin them.

But the mill keeps its hands off the church situation. It keeps its hands off everything except production. It leaves all welfare, religious, and other such matters in the hands of an informal committee composed of the four village pastors, two mill superintendents, and whoever else they may select. We don't even give the committee a name, as we want to keep it flexible. This committee distributes all welfare funds,[2] passes on applications for special religious services in the community, and in general looks after the common welfare, just as in Charlotte, in the crowd I run with, the country club is a rallying point. If a mill worker wants something, he goes to his preacher first.

We put all responsibility on this informal board and on the ministers in their own churches. We want them to stand on their own feet, to develop a sense of responsibility. The churches are vital as rallying points—we use them for that.

If a minister does a bad job we withdraw support, but we don't try to chase him off, as he will hang himself if we give him enough rope: that is, he loses members, his church begins to go down, and soon his church officials are coming to us and asking us what to do. We tell them to consider in what respects their minister is deficient, and then to find somebody who can meet their needs. If we can add inducements such as free rent to the new minister, we are glad to do so.

As for the Methodist church, the presiding elder often comes to see us regarding new ministers. If the last minister did not do a good job, we point out that his church lost members to other churches, that the Methodist Conference is obligated to us for sending such a poor man, and ought to send us a good one—one who will do a good job in his church, which is all that we require.

There is no support of the church as such by the mill as such; all support for several years now has been purely individual. Dad takes care of the Methodist church, my brother takes care of the Presbyterian church, our operating vice-president (who is an Episcopalian) takes care of the Baptist church, and I, not being especially committed to any church, take care of the Church of God. I do not go to see the Church of God preacher; he comes to see me, and we talk things over whenever he wishes. He is trying to hold his crowd down and seems to be doing it, but I don't see how he does it as well as he does—I tell him he can't get away with it. We had trouble with that crowd some years ago but they have settled down now.

Ministers in other mill villages in the county generally agree that the churches in Milltown are completely controlled by the mill owner and his executives. The Methodist

church there, they say, is a "one-man church," and "the preacher has to ask the mill owner when he can pray." As a specific example, they point out that the mill owner will not allow one of the churches to build a Sunday School building adjoining its worship auditorium, but says that it can use one of the mill houses, and that he will build a Sunday School annex himself when it is needed.

At least two of the ministers in Milltown are not happy about their situation. One of them reports that he yearns to get out of an industrial church and to have an independent church and freedom. "To work in a mill church," he says, "is to have a yoke around your neck continually. I have to call for my check every month at the mill office, and I have to consult them even about moving a piece of furniture. But the mill never attempts to dictate the policies of my church or to circumscribe its message—not a word has ever been said about that." Another minister in the village suspects, however, that the support of churches by the mill is designed to control internal religious policies. "The mill owners themselves are not church members," he says, "and I am beginning to wonder if their support of the churches is not hush money to keep us off the Social Gospel. They won't deed the church property to the churches, but I think they will have to if we are to get anything done. As for me, I want to move to a place where I can be independent and have some freedom."

A few miles away from Milltown lies another mill village regarded as one of the more exemplary manifestations of the paternalistic system. The mill was built in 1917, and it is reported that the builders, having the record of other mills in the country to profit by, set out to construct their community along ideal lines. Houses in the village, though of the same design, are painted different colors. A community house and picnic grounds, library, Boy Scout hut, baseball field, and an elaborate welfare program have been established and supported by the mill. One church has been erected there, and a parsonage. The total cost of church and

2. The fill is reported to have given $1,200 to one church recently, telling it to spend it wisely at its own discretion in relief work.

parsonage was $26,000, of which the mill contributed a total of $10,000.

The superintendent of the mill is habitually referred to in the vicinity as the "dictator" of the village. He exercises supervision over ownership of dogs by his workers, prohibits drunkenness, gambling, and immorality, and dominates all other aspects of life. His supervision of moral welfare extends to the churches. He organized and was superintendent of a small Sunday School which led eventually to the construction of the church in the village, and has remained superintendent of the Sunday School and treasurer of the church ever since their establishment. At one time or another he has held the following offices in the church, several of them at one time: chairman of the board of trustees, chairman of the Boy Scout committee, teacher of the men's Bible class, steward, and lay leader. He insists that his wife and children shall attend the village church also, from loyalty to it, though his wife is said to lament missing the cultural values of an uptown church.

The mill superintendent demands similar interest in the church from his employees. Overseers in the mill are affiliated almost automatically with the village church and Sunday School, and chiefly constitute its leadership. In hiring new workers the superintendent asks about church affiliation, and reports that he has had much better results from church members than from nonchurch members. He notices habitual absences from the services of the church, reminds absentees of their negligence, and instructs mill overseers to "keep an eye" on the wayward ones, to see if the quality of their work declines. He has discovered that it generally does. He also allows deductions from the pay envelopes of the workers, after their authorization, for the support of the village church, and about half of the total contributions to the church are secured in this manner. The mill adds $200 a year of its own, and the mill superintendent adds $200 privately, insisting that contributions from himself and the mill must not be mentioned lest the people "lay down" on their own contributions.

The superintendent declares that neither he nor any other official of the mill attempts any dictation to the minister or any stipulation of his message; they encourage and support the church, he affirms, simply for the general good of the community. He professes to belief in encouraging self-reliance on the part of churches, and points to the noncooperative attitude of many of the church members at Milltown as an example of the effect of too much open support by mills.

Despite his efforts at cooperation, the mill superintendent reports that he has had continual difficulty with pastors of the village church, and that he is disgusted with the denomination to which the church belongs, because of the poor caliber of the ministers it has provided. He was especially embittered by his experience with a pastor who served the church for one year recently. The minister, who may be designated as Mr. A, heard rumors before going to the parish of the support accorded to the church by the mill. On arrival, in his own words:

The superintendent of the mill told me that if my ministry pleased the mill officials they would give me $400 extra on my salary—that is, in addition to that reported in the Conference Minutes. I asked a Conference official about this, and he told me that the superintendent had more money than anybody else in the church and had been running it for fifteen years; he advised me to take the money, saying "Let him run it—what do you care?" I thought it over and told the mill superintendent that a straight salary increase would be all right, but that I didn't like two words in his proposition to me: "if" and "give." I had supposed, I said, that my ministry was to serve Jesus Christ, not mill officials.

There is a persistent rumor in the community that Mr. A stood in the pulpit on one of his first Sundays in the community and said that he had heard the church was a "one-man church." "If so," he added, "I expect to be that man." Mr. A himself denies that he made the statement publicly but admits that he told the chairman of the board of stewards, who was a worker in the mill, that the job of the mill superintendent was that of running the mill. He admits further that he challenged the prevailing arrangements within the church in several respects.

He differed with the mill superintendent on the system of deductions from pay envelopes for church support. He insisted that four members of the official board of the church were adulterers, and suggested that they should be left off the board, despite the fact that the mill superintendent objected.

The mill superintendent, in turn, began to bring pressure to bear against the new preacher. After sixty days he notified Mr. A that he was not satisfactory, and stopped coming to church. He required Mr. A to come, as previous ministers had done, to the mill office every Monday morning to get his check, paying him in private checks or in cash. He inspected the parsonage every week to make certain that it was being kept in good condition. He raised numerous questions about the use of facilities provided by the mill for church groups over which the new minister had assumed supervision. As treasurer of the church, he reduced Mr. A's salary to a small percentage of the previous level, explaining that income for the church had declined seriously; Mr. A reports that he investigated and found that income was up to the usual level and that all other bills were being paid in full. The superintendent insisted that the preacher should "preach the gospel, not rant." Mr. A had delivered only one sermon, according to his own testimony, that bore directly on industrial problems; in that sermon he had advocated collective bargaining, to which the mill was stringently opposed.

Mr. A claims that, in addition to direct harassment, the mill superintendent spread all sorts of charges against him to the effect that he had consistently refused to pay his bills in previous parishes, that he cursed in public, that he held the services of the church overtime, that he was overly familiar with women, especially in swimming parties, and that he had proselyted members from other churches. On such grounds the superintendent demanded that denominational officials investigate Mr. A's character. A committee was appointed to consider the matter; the decision stipulated that the accused must withdraw from the ministry at the end of the church year or else stand trial before his ecclesiastical body. Mr. A claims that the committee found no verification of the rumors emanating from the mill superintendent but ruled that he must withdraw from the ministry because the rumors were abroad, even if untrue. In the face of this ruling, Mr. A had no alternative; at the end of the church year he left the church, the community, and the ministry.

As indicated at several points in this record of altercation, Mr. A challenged existing arrangements by which the mill and its officials appeared to him to be exercising unwarranted control over the church of which he was pastor. His methods of protest were, indubitably, often tactless and, from the standpoint of expediency, ill-advised. There is also some evidence that at least one or two of the charges brought against him by the mill superintendent had foundation in suspicion, and perhaps in fact. With the exception of the mill superintendent, all parties involved in the dispute agree, however, that the crux of the matter lay in the refusal of Mr. A to cooperate without question, as his predecessors had done, with the mill management. Charges brought against his personal character were, at most, used to buttress and to mask deeper objections. As a brother minister observed: "If the mill officials 'get it in for you,' they will use any excuse to get rid of you."

Evidence of direct control by mills over churches in Gaston County is not limited to the two situations which have been described above. Interviews with pastors of mill village churches brought many statements such as the following:

The mill preachers' hands are tied. We know where we get our support, and can't say anything.

Mill preachers know where their bread is buttered (it generally is buttered on only one side), and do not talk of unions.

Mill officials never tell me what to preach, but on several occasions I have felt their pressure.

The X's [prominent textile manufacturers in a county near Gaston] match one dollar with four dollars for anything the church wants to do. I was pastor in their mill village and know.

They don't believe in the church no more than nothing; they are Jews, and they would as soon turn your church into a gymnasium or volley ball court as not if they wanted to. They help the church for the advertising—and the mill workers there don't appreciate it no more than they do here.

My relations with the mill officials are purely detached, but friendly. They do not want preachers to discuss labor questions with them: "Do not get yourself implicated one way or the other," they say, "as we do not want to tie strings on you."

A prominent official of an uptown church in Gastonia in the early 1920's was superintendent of three mills around the industrial church I was pastor over. He was a notorious whore-monger, and took girls from the night shift out into the grass nearly every night. Because I knew this, and he knew that I did, he undermined me with the uptown church, and I had to leave the pastorate.

Structural relations between churches and mills in Gaston County mill villages render control of churches and ministers by the mill officials almost inevitable, provided the latter wish to exercise that control. Control is seldom made explicit; it simply inheres in accepted relations. Its manifestation is almost always disguised in terms of the general welfare of the community, over which mill officials have final supervision. Positive and direct coercion appears very infrequently, because opposition does not demand it. When it does appear, the mill management has no difficulty in ridding itself of the troublemaker —for the good of the community.[3]

Control over religious institutions inheres not only in structural interrelations but also in the cultural setting in which mills and churches function. The traditions of mill villages include acceptance of mill executives as the final arbiters of all questions concerning community welfare, including questions that involve the policies of the churches. Pastors seldom protest seriously against these

traditions because they recognize the futility of their objections, and because they themselves derive benefits from existing arrangements. Their acquiescence is not habitually self-conscious and uneasy; more often than not, it is accepted as an axiom of ministerial workmanship in situations of this sort. In short, it is taken for granted that the dependence of the mill village church on the mill itself, structurally and culturally, largely circumscribes all possibility for independent action by the church or its minister.

It is sometimes suggested that the control exercised by mill officials over mill churches is no greater than that exercised by them over uptown churches to which they themselves belong, and of which they are the acknowledged leaders. The degree to which independent action is possible appears to be greater in uptown churches, however, than in mill churches. Uptown churches are not controlled by economic institutions as such. Influence over them is cultural and personal, rather than structural, in type. Further, they can lose the support of a few individuals without endangering their institutional life. In an uptown church, as compared with a mill village church, there is a relative heterogeneity of membership, and some diversification of economic foundations is represented; even if all economic activities center around a dominant industry, as in Gaston County, there is nevertheless some possibility for independent action by those not directly employed by the industry. In a mill village, however, the church is composed of persons with a single occupation—an occupation completely dependent upon the fortunes and decisions of textile managers. It has been inevitable that the high degree of social control associated with mill villages from the outset should have come to include, as a conspicuous feature, control over village churches.

For the most part, the churches and ministers have adapted themselves to the situation and serve as an arm of the employers in control of the mill villages. Ministers rationalize their position by equating paternalism (though they avoid the word) with

3. A well-known Southern sociologist tells of an interview he once had with a mill executive in South Carolina. The executive admitted that the mill contributed handsomely to the support of churches in the mill village, but averred that it did so only for the general good of the community. "We had a young fellow from an Eastern seminary down here as pastor a few years ago," he continued, "and the young fool went around saying that we helped pay the preachers' salaries in order to control them. That was a damn lie—and we got rid of him."

Christian principles. Does not the Christian gospel teach parental solicitude and admonish the strong to care for the weak, to practice generosity toward the less fortunate, and to extend the helping hand to mankind? Were not mill workers ignorant, diseased, and living in dirt and filth until the mills came along? Would they not be in the same condition today if the mills had not provided schools, welfare services, better housing, and all the advantages of life in proximity to cities and towns? Though a few younger ministers are beginning to ask whether Christianity does not demand that one shall be his "brother's brother" rather than his "brother's keeper," and to suspect that paternalism is a perversion of fraternalism, most preachers in Gaston County still ascribe untempered benevolence and Christian charity to the mill owners.

39. THE ROLE OF VOLUNTARY ASSOCIATIONS IN WEST AFRICAN URBANIZATION

KENNETH LITTLE

Reprinted from American Anthropologist, *59 (1957): 579-94. The thesis expounded in this article has been elaborated in Professor Little's* West African Urbanization: A Study of Voluntary Associations in Social Change *(New York: Cambridge University Press, 1965). Kenneth Little is Professor of Social Anthropology, University of Edinburgh. His principal research has been conducted in West Africa, and he is especially interested in problems of urbanization and social change in developing countries. In addition to his latest book,* West African Urbanization, *he is the author of* The Mende of Sierra Leone *and of a number of books on race relations, including* Negroes in Britain *and* Race and Society.

■ The transition from agriculture to an industrial adaptation involves the attenuation of kinship and other primary ties, but they do not disappear overnight. Transitions from one stage of development to another are always gradual, involving a series of readjustments in the use of energy systems and in their appropriate organizations of social relations,

We have seen in many case studies of pre-modern levels of development that the social relations in which people are organized are often relatively fixed, assigned to them at birth; correspondingly, people can substitute for each other in many social roles within the limits of their ascribed status. In industrially based societies, on the other hand, the nation-state becomes the adaptive unit, people achieve status for themselves and there is greater emphasis on the differentiation of social roles. The theme of this selection is the replacement of kin ties by voluntary associations in the transition to modernity.

Urbanization is not new to West Africa, but the growth of cities that are based on industrialization is a modern development. The traditional associations based on kinship quickly became inappropriate to this new habitat, and new associational forms had to be developed. Little here analyzes three types of voluntary associations in West Africa that emerged in response to the challenges of the new industrial cities. The three types he describes can be arranged along a continuum, from the most "traditional" to the most "modern"; between these extremes is what Little calls "traditional-modernized" associations. I suggest this interpretation of his data to underscore the idea that adaptation in a society does not affect everyone uniformly and immediately; different groups are affected at varying rates, which leads to different types of simultaneous adjustment. Some groups try to retain as much as they can of the traditional organization of social relations while making use of the new energy systems; others try to meet these challenges head-on and adjust their social relationships accordingly; still others try to live in both worlds.

The care of those members of the adaptive unit who are young, incapacitated, ill, or too old to work is an important feature of any adaptation. Little illustrates the struggles in making these adjustments in modern West Africa. Similar problems of caring for different population groups can be found in American society, in our social security program, relief programs for indigent groups, and (more recently) Medicare programs. The history of guilds in different parts of the world also reflect many of these processes.

Little has elaborated the thesis explored in this paper in his book, *West African Urbanization: A Study of Voluntary Associations in Social Change.* Also relevant is *Copper Town: Changing Africa, The Human Situation on the Rhodesian Copperbelt,* by Hortense Powdermaker (New York: Harper and Row, 1962); *Urbanization and Migration in West Africa,* edited by Hilda Kuper (Berkeley: University of California Press, 1965); and *Political Parties and National Integration in Tropical Africa,* edited by James S. Coleman and Carl G. Rosberg (Berkeley: University of California Press, 1964).

For discussions of the transition from kin groups to voluntary associations in Japan, the reader can consult "The Oyabun-Kobun: A Japanese Ritual Kinship Institution," by Iwao Ishino (American Anthropologist, 55 [1953]: 695-704); and Customs and Manners of the Meiji Era, edited by Kunio Yanagida (Tokyo: Obunsha, 1957). ■

INTRODUCTION

TAKEN AS A WHOLE, the West African region was relatively unaffected by the modern world until the end of the 19th century. Modern development of the hinterland began with the question of military manpower. colonial policy and with the British and French realization that these territories constituted an expanding market for imported goods as well as important sources of mineral and raw materials needed by the metropolitan country. The French were also concerned with the question of military manpower. These factors were finally crystallized by World War II and the events following it. The British war effort demanded greatly increased supplies of palm kernels, cotton, cocoa, and other locally grown products as well as hides, tin, iron ore, etc., which the colonial governments concerned were required to stimulate. Since the War there have been resettlement schemes, new industries and constructional projects have been instituted, and there has been a general improvement in communications by road, rail, and air. With the strategic implications of West Africa in the struggle against Communism also becoming manifest, political development has also gone on very rapidly, and there has been a corresponding expansion of education and the social services.

The consequence of all these technical and other changes is that there are now many more different modes of life and ways of earning a living than existed in West Africa some fifty years ago. It also goes without saying that its inhabitants have acquired a taste for the material elements of Western civilization, including consumer goods of every possible kind. In addition to new economic incentives, Western interests ranging from Christianity and nationalism to football and ballroom dancing have also been generated on a wide scale. In short, there has been produced the kind of phenomenon which anthropologists have customarily studied under the heading of culture contact, or acculturation. This term, however, is not precise enough for purposes of present analysis. First, many of the principal agents of cultural change nowadays are Africans themselves, and second, many Western ideas, practices, and procedures have already been fully assimilated to African culture. Africans became important as "acculturative agents" about the middle of the 19th century when Western-educated Creoles from Sierra Leone went off evangelizing and trading down the Coast. All the way from the Gambia in the west to the Congo in the south they constituted, in many cases, little oases of westernized culture. Consequently, although much of the traditional life was disintegrated, new forms of social organization have arisen out of the older structure. There are, moreover, considerable differences in the extent to which given peoples and groups of Africans have undergone so-called detribalization, and it is rare to find whole communities which have completely severed all traditional loyalties and obligations. More often is it the case, as I propose to show, that the African individual moving out of the tribal area continues to be influenced by tribal culture. In other words, instead of viewing the contemporary West African situation in terms of the juxtaposition of two entirely different cultures, we shall do better to conceive it as a process of adaptation to new circumstances and conditions. Cultural contacts still go on, but between westernized Africans and other Africans, as well as between Westerners and Africans; so that the changes occurring are no different in kind from those within a single society.

THE URBANIZATION OF WEST AFRICA

What, in effect, this transformation of West Africa involves is a social process somewhat analogous to the social changes that resulted in the urbanization of Western Europe during the 19th century. Western contact with Africa, like the Industrial Revolution in Europe, has created new social and psychological needs which life in the countryside is rarely able to satisfy. The consequence is a tremendous migration of men and women to the towns, and to places where money can be earned to pay taxes, to provide bridewealth, and to buy manufactured goods and appliances.

Many of these people are in search of a higher standard of living in the shape of the more up-to-date amenities and better housing as well as the higher income that the town can offer. But this is not the only motivation. A large number of the younger men are looking for further educational opportunities, or are hoping to start a fresh career. Others move as a means of escaping from the restrictions of village life, and some of the younger girls, as well as the boys, out of love of adventure and desire for fresh experiences. As Fortes has written in reference to the Gold Coast: "Labour, enterprise, and skill are now marketable in their own right anywhere in the country. . . . People feel that there is little risk in moving about, especially if, as appears to be the case with most mobile elements, their earning capacity is low. A clerk getting £2.10 a month feels that he cannot go much lower if he moves." The development of motor transport, in the shape of the ubiquitous lorry, is an important factor in these respects. Not only has it greatly increased local mobility between town and town, and between town and surrounding countryside, but it has created a new and influential social role—that of the lorry-driver, as a go-between between the urban labor market and the rural village.

Most of this migration is in the direction of towns already established as large centers of Western commerce and administration, of the rapidly growing ports, and of places where mining and other industries are being developed. Its effect has been to swell the population of such places far beyond their previous size, as well as to convert a good many villages into urban areas. For example, the principal towns of Senegal in French West Africa increased their populations by 100 percent between 1942 and 1952 and those of the French Ivory Coast by 109 percent during the same decade. In the Gold Coast there was an increase of 98 percent in the populations of the five largest towns between 1931 and 1948. Cotonou in Dahomey grew from 1100 in 1905 to 35,000 in 1952 and Lunsar, in Sierra Leone, which was a village of 30 inhabitants in 1929, has a population today of nearly 17,000.

Although urbanism in terms of "a relatively large, dense, and permanent settlement of socially heterogeneous individuals" is not a general characteristic of traditional life, it is far from being a unique phenomenon in West Africa. In 1931, some 28 percent of the Yoruba population of Western Nigeria lived in 9 cities of over 45,000 inhabitants, while a further 34 per cent lived in cities of over 20,000 inhabitants. However, what distinguishes the "new" African city—"new" in the sense, as George Balandier points out, that they were built by European colonists —from traditional urbanism is that a large part of its population is industrial, depending upon the labor market for a living. This is particularly evident in the case of towns of recent growth. In Cotonou, for example, some 10,000 persons out of a population of some 35,000 are in wage employment.

A further point is that the modern town is much more heterogeneous. It has groups of professionals, office workers, municipal employees, artisans, etc., and in addition to its indigenous political and social segmentation, it also accommodates a large proportion of "strangers." Not only do the latter frequently outnumber the native inhabitants of the town, but they include a wide diversity of tribes. For example, Kumasi, although the capital of Ashantiland, contains as many non-Ashantis as Ashantis; Takoradi-Sekondi contains representatives of more than 60 different tribes; and less than 10 percent of the inhabitants of Poto-Poto, one of the three African towns of Brazzaville, were born in that city. In the Gold Coast, as a whole, more than two-thirds of the inhabitants of the big towns have been there for less than five years. A further significant characteristic of these urban populations is the numerical preponderance of young people over old and, to a less appreciable extent, the preponderance of men over women. For example, only 2.4 percent of the population of Cotonou are over 60 years of age. In 1921, men considerably outnumbered women, but by 1952 the masculinity rate had dropped to 111. In an area of Poto-Poto, on the other hand, where the average age of the population is about 25, there are only 515 females to every 1000 males.

VOLUNTARY ASSOCIATIONS

(A) TRIBAL UNIONS

From the point of view of social organization one of the most striking characteristics of these modern towns is the very large number and variety of voluntary associations. These include a host of new political, religious, recreational, and occupational associations as well as the more traditional mutual aid groups and secret societies out of which some of these more recent organizations have developed. What generally distinguishes the latter kind of association is its more formal constitution and the fact that it has been formed to meet certain needs arising specifically out of the urban environment of its members. It is also more "modern" both in respect to its aims and the methods employed to attain them. One of the best illustrations of these points is provided by certain tribal associations of an extraterritorial kind, known in Nigeria and the Gold Coast as tribal unions.

These tribal unions range from little unions, consisting of a few members of the same extended family or clan, to much larger bodies like the Ibo State Union which is a collection of village and clan unions. In Nigeria, these associations were originally formed by Ibo and other migrants from Eastern Nigeria to protect themselves from the hostile way in which they were received when they took jobs as policeman, traders,

and laborers in the towns of the West and the North. Their aim is to provide members with mutual aid, including support, while out of work, sympathy and financial assistance in the case of illness, and the responsibility for the funeral and the repatriation of the family of the deceased in the case of death. The main raison d'etre, however, is that of fostering and keeping alive an interest in tribal song, history, language, and moral beliefs, and thus maintaining a person's attachment to his native town or village and to his lineage there. In furtherance of this sentiment, money is collected for the purpose of improving amenities in the union's home town and to provide its younger people with education. Social activities include the organization of dances on festival days and of sports meetings and games for their young people. Some of these unions also produce an annual magazine, called an Almanac, in which their members' activities are recorded.

Associations based upon membership of the same ethnic group also exist in French and Belgian Africa where they perform somewhat similar functions. In Cotonou, for example, such groups welcome and look after persons newly arrived from the country. They provide a means whereby both the old people and the "evolué" can keep in touch with their rural relatives and friends. Each such association has an anual feast and celebration which brings together everyone from the same region. It is also a means of helping the needy and aged members of the group.

In Nigeria there have also been developed home branches of the tribal union abroad; and as a final step, state unions have been created, comprising every union of members of the same tribe. It is not surprising, therefore, that these Nigerian tribal unions have obtained a power and influence far beyond their original objectives. The larger unions have played an important part in the expansion of education. They offer scholarships for deserving boys and girls and run their own schools. In some places, the monthly contributions of members for education are invested in some form of commercial enterprise, and appeals for money to build schools seem to meet with a particularly ready response. One observer claims that he saw an up-country union raise in six hours and in a single meeting over £16,000 for such purposes. Some higher education overseas has also been provided, and several leading members of the Nigerian Eastern House of Assembly owe their training in British universities to State union money. Even more ambitious plans have included the building of a national bank where people can obtain loans for industrial and commercial purposes. In this connection, some unions have economic advisers who survey trade reports for the benefit of members. These tribal unions also serve a number of important political purposes and are recognized as units for purposes of tax collection. In addition to pressing local authorities for better roads, dispensaries and hospitals, and other public amenities, they have been a powerful force in the democratizing of traditional councils; in the multi-tribal centers they were for many years the recognized basis for representation on Township Advisory Boards or Native Authority Councils. They have also provided a forum for the expression of national politics and for the rise to positions of leadership of the younger educated element.

(B) FRIENDLY SOCIETIES

In addition to the tribal union, there are also a large number of tribal societies where objectives are limited to mutual aid and benefit. One of the most complicated of these organizations is run by the wives of Kru immigrants in Freetown. This kind of society is divided into three classes. A member pays an admission fee of one guinea and enters the class of least importance. He or she may subsequently be promoted to a higher class and in this event will be expected to make members of that class a present of several pounds. On his or her death, the relatives receive a sum of money commensurate with the deceased person's status. These societies endeavor to develop a high esprit de corps and have been known to impose fines

of as much as £20 on members guilty of unfriendly conduct toward each other.

Kru men go to sea for a living and so the members of their societies are divided into "ships," named after various recent additions to Messrs. Elder Dempster's fleet [which serves the area], instead of classes. The Kru also have so-called "family societies" comprising the migrant members of a particular class, or *dako* (a small local federation of patriclans). These groups also provide bereavement benefits. In Freetown there are also a number of traditional organizations, including so-called secret societies and dancing groups, which provide funeral expenses, presents, and entertainment for members when they marry. The congregations of mosques, too, usually have what is loosely called a *Jama Compin* (Compin = Krio, "Company") whose members help each other over funerals. Up country, another Moslem group, composed of women, endeavors to intervene in domestic quarrels and to reconcile man and wife. In this case, a sixpenny subscription is collected every Sunday, and persons joining as new members have to pay the equivalent of what a foundation member has already paid in subscriptions. Some of this money is disbursed as alms, but most of it is used to provide sickness and funeral benefits.

A different kind of mutual aid group is the *esusu,* which is of Yoruba origin. Members of the group pay in at regular intervals a fixed sum and the total is given each time to one of the members. This is an important method for buying trading stock, expensive clothing, etc. In southeastern Nigeria, a somewhat similar kind of "contribution club" is divided into seven sections, each under a headman. Each member pays one or more weekly subscriptions. The headmen are responsible for collecting the shares from their members, and when the shares have all been collected, the money is handed over to a member nominated by the headman in turn. The recipient has a number of obligations, including that of supplying a quantity of palm wine for the refreshment of club members.

A further organization serves all three functions—providing funeral benefits, charity, and helping its members to save. This is the *Nanamei Akpee,* or "mutual help" society. It has its headquarters in Accra and branches in several other Gold Coast towns, including Keta. The Keta branch has well over 400 members, the great majority of whom are educated or semiliterate women traders. There is a monthly subscription of one shilling and when a member dies, the surviving relatives are given at least £ 10 towards the cost of funeral expenses. Money for loans is raised at weekly collections which begin with community singing. All the women present give as much money as they feel they can afford, and their contributions are written down in a book which also contains a list of the society's members, in order of seniority. When the collection is finished all the money is given to the member whose name takes first place; the following week it is given to the second, then to the third, and so on. Eventually, all members will in this way receive a contribution, though the process as a whole naturally takes a very long time. However, the man or woman receiving a collection is also given a list showing the amount of money contributed by other members. This determines, during later weeks, the amounts he must contribute himself. For example, if A has given B two shillings then B must raise the same amount when eventually A's turn arrives to receive a weekly collection. In effect, this arrangement means that senior members, i.e., those who have joined early, receive an interest-free loan, which they repay weekly by small contributions; those on the bottom of the list, on the other hand, are saving in a small way, for their own ultimate benefit. In a period of rising prices, those at the top of the list naturally have the advantage, but on the other hand those who wait longer may receive more because the society's membership will in the meantime have increased. There is an element of chance in all this which adds spice to the normally dull business of saving, and this partly explains the society's popularity. Finally, when a member falls ill he is visited in the hospital, given small gifts of money, and so on. At times the society also gives presents and small sums of money to old and sick people even if they are not members.

(c) OCCUPATIONAL ASSOCIATIONS

In addition to raising loans through such organizations as *Nanamei Akpee,* African market women also form associations in order to control the supply or price of commodities in which their members trade. Some of the larger markets have a woman in charge, and each of the various sections which women monopolize, such as the sale of yams, gari, cloth, etc., is also headed by a woman, who represents them in relation to customers and the market authorities. In Lagos market each such section has its own union, which discourages competition between women trading in that particular commodity. Another women's association is the Fish Sellers Union at Takoradi-Sekondi. The members of this association may club together to raise money to buy fishing nets. The group then sells the nets to fishermen on agreed terms. A fisherman who receives a net sells his catches during the fishing season to the creditor group, and the value of the fish is reckoned against the net. In this way, the members are able to obtain the fish on which their livelihood depends. Women also associate for industrial purposes. In southern Nigeria, for example, there are women's societies which run a bakery, a laundry, a calabash manufactory, and a gari mill. One of the most interesting of these associations, the Egba Women's Union in Abeokuta, claims a membership of 80,000 women, paying subscriptions of 13 shillings a year. It operates as a weaving co-operative, and runs a maternity and a child welfare clinic as well as conducting classes for illiterate women.

Other occupational and professional associations are concerned with the status and remuneration of their members as workers. Such groups include modern crafts such as goldsmiths, tinkers, gunsmiths, tailors, and barbers, as well as certain trade unions which, unlike Government-sponsored trade unions, have come spontaneously into being. One example of these is the Motor Drivers Union at Keta which is now a branch of a nation-wide union which negotiates freight rates, working conditions, and so on. Unlike European trade unions, this Motor Drivers Union is an association of small entrepreneurs owning their own vehicles rather than an association of employees. Its main purpose is to look after the interests of drivers generally and in particular to offer them legal assistance and insurance. When a driver is convicted, the Union tries as far as possible to pay his fine; and when a driver dies the Union provides part of the funeral expenses. There are also smaller sickness and accident benefits. The entrance fee is 14 shillings and there is a monthly subscription of one shilling. In addition, the Union organizes meetings and dances.

The organization of modern crafts, on the other hand, takes on the form of guilds resembling those of medieval Europe. The first rule of all these guilds in Yoruba towns, where many of them have developed, is that every craftsman, whether master, journeyman or apprentice, must be registered with the guild, must attend meetings, and must pay his dues. One of the guild's prime functions is to maintain a reasonable standard of work in the craft. It determines the rules of apprenticeship; fixes prices of workmanship; and settles disputes, whether between master and apprentice or between craftsman and customer. On the other hand, the guild does not undertake to care for its members in sickness or old age; neither does it function as a bank, lending money to members for tools. Most forms of social security are still organized by the lineage—in which the guild members still retain full membership—and not by the guild.

Unions of a different kind which are also concerned with the status and remuneration of their members are associations of prostitutes. These have been reported from Takoradi and also from Brazzaville. In the latter city, the members of such organizations try to improve their own social and economic position by insisting on a high standard of dress and deportment, and by ostracizing other

women who are too casual or too free with their sexual favors. Each group has its own name, such as *La Rose, Diamant,* etc., and is under a leader, an elderly woman, who can set a pattern of elegance and sophistication. Membership is limited and is regulated by a committee. There is also a common fund out of which members in financial straits are helped and their funeral expenses paid should they die. In the latter event, the association behaves as if it were the family of the deceased. Every girl goes into mourning, giving up her jewelry and finer clothes for six months, at the end of which there is a night-long celebration in some "bar-dancing" establishment hired for the occasion.

(D) ENTERTAINMENT AND RECREATIONAL ASSOCIATIONS

A large number of associations are concerned with dancing and musical forms of entertainment. Many of these, such as the drumming companies found in Ewe villages in the Gold Coast, still retain much of their traditional character. A number of groups in Brazzaville also perform traditional music, but on a commercial basis. These societies consist of young men who have formed themselves into an orchestra under the presidency of an older man whose compound they use for the purpose of staging an evening's "social" on Saturdays and Sundays. The public is charged for admission on these occasions and the "band," which goes by such appropriate titles as *Etoile, Jeunesse, Record de la Gaieté,* etc., undertakes outside engagements. The receipts are divided among the members according to their position in the society and anything left over goes toward the purchase of new instruments and the provision of further conviviality. Other such associations, which began as simple dancing societies, have developed under urban conditions into a relatively complex organization and set of modern objectives. A striking example of this kind of phenomenon is the dancing *compin* of Sierra Leone. This is a group of young men and women concerned with the performance of "plays" of traditional music and dancing and with the raising of money for mutual benefit. The music is provided mainly by native drums, xylophones, and calabash rattles, and is accompanied by singing. The dancing which, like the drumming, shows signs of Western influence, is somewhat reminiscent of English country dancing. A "play" is generally given in connection with some important event, such as the close of Ramadan, or as part of the ceremonies celebrating a wedding or a funeral. The general public as well as the persons honored by the performance are expected to donate money to the *compin* on these occasions. Money is also collected in the form of weekly subscriptions from the members.

In one of these organizations, which are particularly numerous among Temne and Mandinka immigrants in Freetown, this amount goes into a general fund to cover corporate expenses of the society's activities— rent of yard, provision of lamps, replacement of drum skins, etc. Then, when any member is bereaved, a collection is held to which all must contribute. However, quite an elaborate procedure is necessary before the money can be paid. The bereaved person must first notify the Reporter with a reporting fee. This is passed on to the company's Doctor, who investigates the circumstances of death, for the company will fine any member who has not notified them of a relative's illness so that they can see that the sick person receives attention. The Doctor washes the body and sends the Prevoe (Provost) round to the other members, telling them to gather that evening when they must pay their contributions. When anyone avoids payment without good cause, the Bailiff may seize an item of his property of equal value. The evening's meeting is organized by the Manager. He will bring the company's lamps, for members are under an obligation to take part in a wake which will last into the early hours. At the wake the bereaved person will provide cigarettes, kola nuts, bread, and coffee, and will employ a singer. Another duty of the Doctor is to examine members before admission, and to attend them if sick. The Commissioner or Inspector is the disciplinary officer and he

can arrest or eject troublemakers, the Prevoe acting on his orders. The Clerk or Secretary keeps accounts and writes letters, and the Cashier receives from the Sultan for safe keeping any money accruing to the society. The Sultan is the chief executive; his female counterpart, who has charge of the women members, is the Mammy Queen. For the dancing there is a leader who directs it, and a Conductor who supervises the band. There is also a Sister in charge of the Nurses, young girls who bring round refreshments at dances, often in white dresses with a red cross on the breast and the appropriate headgear. If there is no woman Doctor, an older Nurse or Sister may assist the Doctor with the invalids, or the washing of the corpse. There may also be further officials, such as an overseer, an M.C., a Solicitor, a Lawyer, Sick Visitor, etc. Many of these titles involve no work, but they can be given to honor even the least deserving member and to strengthen his identification with the group's company.

Other groups concerned with recreation range from Improvement Leagues and Women's Institutes to cricket and football clubs. Some of the latter are characterized by such colorful titles as Mighty Poisons, Hearts of Oak, Heroes, etc. Football teams are also run by associations of the former pupils of certain schools, known as Old Boys Associations, which also organize receptions and "send-offs" and sometimes hold evening classes. Most organizations of the latter kind are modeled rather closely on European lines, particularly the so-called "social club." This is constituted for dining and drinking purposes as well as for tennis, whist, billiards, ballroom dancing, amateur dramatics, and other European recreational and cultural activities. For the latter reasons, "social clubs" are mainly confined to the most Westernized section of the population, including well-to-do professionals and businessmen as well as teachers, clerks, and other white collar workers. Such clubs are open to persons of any tribe, but members are expected to conform to European patterns of social etiquette. Europeans themselves are frequently admitted either as members or as guests. Examples of this kind of institution are the Rodgers Club in Accra, the Island Club in Lagos, and the Bo African Club in Sierra Leone. In the latter association, all official business and proceedings, including lectures, debates, etc., are conducted in English. At the weekly dance, which is one of the club's principal activities, the general rule is for the women to wear print or silk dresses (without the head tie), and the men open-necked shirts with a blazer or sports jacket. On special occasions evening dress is worn by both sexes. In addition to its ordinary activities, this club undertakes a number of public functions, including special dances to honor visiting notables. It also entertains the teams of visiting football clubs, and its premises are used for such purposes as political meetings and adult education classes.

Women, too, have their social clubs which broadly complement those under the control of men. These are very often known as Ladies' Clubs and Women's Institutes. Many of the latter have been formed under the auspices of churches. A large number of literate husbands have nonliterate wives, and some of these women's clubs reflect the sociological situation in that they are divided into "literate" and "illiterate" sections which hold separate meetings. "Literate" activities consist mainly in sewing and crochet work, in practicing the cooking of European and native dishes, and in listening to talks about household economy. Individual literate women give instruction to these arts to the "illiterate" meeting, and in return nonliterate women sometimes teach the literate group native methods of dyeing, spinning, basketry, and traditional songs and dances.

Women's Institutes are primarily the result of the initiative of educated women. For example, the President and leading officers of the Keta Women's Institute in the Gold Coast are teachers, although the bulk of its membership consists of market women. It is principally a social club, but it has certain other more important interests. For example, it has acted as a "pressure group," intervening with the Urban Council in support of a plan for improving amenities at the local markets.

Among other local changes, the women achieved the provision of ambulance services, and the employment of a larger number of female nurses at the Keta hospital.

THE ORGANIZATION OF VOLUNTARY ASSOCIATIONS

Before we attempt to generalize about these voluntary associations, it is necessary to distinguish between three rather different types. The first is still basically concerned with traditional activities, although with some slight modification; in the second type, traditional activities have been deliberately modified or expanded to suit modern purposes; and the third type is wholly modern in organization and objectives. It will be convenient to term these three types, respectively, "traditional," "traditional-modernized" and "modern."

The function of the "traditional" association is generally limited to the organization of some particular religious, occupational, or recreational interest, such as a cult, a trade, or some form of dancing or drumming. Space unfortunately prevents description of religious associations in general. These exist alongside Islam and the ancestral cult, and according to Hofstra they may be divided into four categories: (1) Christian churches organized by missionaries, (2) so-called African churches, (3) looser, smaller groups of a syncretistic character, (4) irregularly organized movements of a messianic or prophetic kind. In the traditional type of association some provision may be made for mutual benefit, but this is incidental to the main purpose of the society. Membership in the group is usually confined to persons belonging to the same village or ward of a town and is often related to other traditional institutions, such as an age set. For example, drumming companies among the Ewe are organized on a ward basis, and usually there are three in every ward. The first comprises children up to the age of about fifteen; the second consists of the so-called "young men," ranging in age from about fifteen to thirty; and the third comprises "elders," i.e., the male population over thirty or so. The senior companies usually give themselves names such as Patience or U.A.C. (for United Africa Company), and some of these are, in effect, associations of semiprofessional entertainers who travel about the country in search of engagements. Although the organization of such "traditional" associations is generally quite simple and informal, a number of them have adapted to modern conditions by incorporating literate persons as officials and by widening the scope of their function. In the traditional economy of the Gold Coast, for example, each trade or occupation normally had a chief-practitioner who settled disputes and represented his associates in relation to outsiders. This is largely true today, but in addition some of these groups have turned themselves into local branches of a nationwide union. In the case of the goldsmiths, this involved appointing its chief-practitioner as Life-Chairman of the association, while an educated man who could deal adequately with its business affairs was elected President. Similarly, the semiliterate president of the Carpenters Union now has a literate secretary and treasurer to help him.

It goes without saying that the great majority of people who belong to "traditional" associations are unlettered. The number of persons who can read and write or speak a European language is larger in the "traditional-modernized" association, but what mainly distinguishes the latter is its syncretistic character, its relatively formal organization, and the variety of its functions. A particularly striking example of the latter point is *La Goumbé,* a Moslem and predominantly Dioula youth organization for both sexes in the Ivory Coast. This combines the functions of emancipating young women from family influence; assisting the process of marital selection; providing, on a contributory basis, marriage and maternity benefits (including perfume and layettes for the newborn); preserving the Dioula tribal spirit; running an orchestra; and acting as the local propaganda agent for *Rassemblement Démocratique Africain.* It also maintains its own police force. In addition to a written constitution which

embodies the declared aims and rules of the society, this kind of association sometimes has its own name and a special uniform of its own, and generally follows such Western practices as the holding of regular meetings, keeping of minutes, accounts, etc. The wearing of a uniform type of dress is probably more characteristic of women's societies than those formed by men. The women members of *Nanemei Akpee,* for example, all dress in white for meetings, and the practice of appearing in the same kind of dress, including head-tie, necklace, and sandals, is followed by other women's groups on formal occasions. Finance plays an important part in its affairs, and there is a regular tariff of entrance fees; weekly or monthly dues are collected and fines are sometimes levied. These funds are administered by a Treasurer or Financial Secretary, sometimes supervised by a committee which also conducts the everyday business of the association, including the sifting of fresh applications for membership, settlement of disputes, etc. Related partly to the wide diversity of functions performed is the large number of persons holding official positions in some of these societies. Many of these office-bearers, as exemplified by the dancing *compin,* have European titles, or, as in the case of the Kru women's societies, are known by the native equivalents of such titles. This enactment of European roles, as in the dancing *compin,* is a fairly common feature of associations of the "traditional-modernized" type. It has been termed "vicarious participation in the European social structure" by J. Clyde Mitchell, but as Michael Banton points out, this possibly places too much emphasis on the process of Westernization and too little on the independent process of change in the tribal group. An assistant official sometimes has the duty of conveying information about the society's activities to the general public as well as to members. *La Goumbé,* for example, has a number of town criers, members of the *griot* caste, to carry news through the town.

The organization of the "traditional-modernized" association is also rendered more elaborate by a tendency toward affiliation.

This ranges all the way from a fully centralized organization of individual branches to a loose fraternal arrangement between entirely autonomous branches of the same movement. Affiliation of individual branches sometimes seems to be the result of traditional conditions. Thus, the "village-group union" of the Afikpo Ibo of Nigeria is apparently modelled largely upon the indigenous age-set structure of the people concerned. The *Goumbé* movement comprises a number of local "cells" coordinated by a central committee, which settlets disputes between them and lays down general policy. The dancing *compin* movement, on the other hand, consists of a large number of separate societies which occasionally exchange visits and information and extend hospitality to each other's members, but are otherwise entirely independent. Finally, although membership of these associations tends to be tribally or regionally circumscribed, this is not invariably so. Even tribal unions sometimes have persons from more than one tribe among their members. The Benin Nation Club (Nigeria), for example, provides facilities for all natives of the Benin Province. Several occupational and other groups recruit their members on an intertribal basis, and this also applies to some of the societies run by women.

The "modern" association has already been briefly described in terms of the "social club," and so it will suffice merely to add that its organization is broadly the same as that of any European association of a comparable kind. Like its European counterpart, it is often a medium for social prestige.

Despite their wide variety, one objective common to all types of voluntary association is that of sociability and fraternity. Not only is the serving of refreshments, including such beverages as tea, palm wine, beer, or stronger drink, an integral part of any formal gathering of members, but the latter are expected and encouraged to visit each other's homes, especially in the event of illness or bereavement. Again, although some groups, including certain guilds and occupations, are confined to persons of the same sex, it seems to be a fairly common practice for women to be admitted into associations under the control of men, and for men to be members of certain associations in which women predominate. Some associations organized by men deliberately encourage the recruitment of female members but have them under a more or less separate administration, with the women's leader responsible to the head of the society. A further fairly common feature of all kinds of voluntary associations is the fact that most of their personnel are young people. Indeed, some societies expect their members to retire at the age of thirty, and it is rare for persons over middle age to play an active part in their affairs. This, however, is less typical of the "traditional" organizations than it is of the other types of association which, nevertheless, quite often like to have an elderly man or woman as an honorary president. The role of such a person is to uphold the association's reputation for respectability and to help its relations with the wider community. The fact that he is not infrequently a person of importance in tribal society is indicative of the desire of such associations to keep on good terms with the traditional authorities. The sizet of membership is a more variable factor. It ranges from a mere handful of individuals to several hundred or even thousands, in the case of the larger tribal associations. In the smaller societies, which are often very ephemeral, the amount of support given is probably bound up as much with the personality and personal influence of the leader as it is with the popularity of the institution.

VOLUNTARY ASSOCIATIONS AS AN ADAPTIVE MECHANISM

It was suggested earlier that the social changes resulting from culture contact may be seen as an historical process of adaptation to new conditions. Adaptation in the present context implies not only the modification of African institutions, but their development to meet the demands of an industrial economy and urban way of life. In effect, as Banton has shown in reference to Temne immigrants in Freetown, this sometimes amounts to a virtual resuscitation of the tribal system in the interests of the modernist ambitions and social prestige of the younger educated element concerned. The unpublished findings of Jean Rouch seem to give even greater emphasis to this kind of phenomenon, which he has labelled "super-tribalization." Some of the immigrants into the Gold Coast, whom he has studied, have gained sufficient solidarity through their associations and cults to dominate over the local population, achieving monopolies in various trades. A further important effect of this kind of development, as both Busia and Banton have pointed out, is to inhibit the growth of civic loyalty or responsibility for the town concerned. Modern urbanism, in other words, is the conditioning factor in contemporary African society as well as the culmination of so-called acculturation. West African urbanism of course differs from comparable Western situations in being less advanced, although it is probably more dynamic. It involves a particularly rapid diffusion of entirely new ideas, habits, and technical procedures, and a considerable restructuring of social relationships as a consequence of the new technical roles and groups created.

Voluntary associations play their part in both these processes through the fresh criteria of social achievement that they set up and through the scope that they offer, in particular, to women and to the younger age groups. Women, and younger people in general, possess a new status in the urban economy, and this is reflected in the various functions which these associations perform as political pressure groups, in serving as a forum for political expression, and in providing both groups with training in modern methods of business. Equally significant is the fact that women's participation in societies with a mixed membership involves them in a new kind of social relationship with men, including companionship and the opportunity of selecting a spouse for oneself. In particular, voluntary associations provide an outlet for the energies and ambitions of the rising class of young men with a tribal background who have been to school. The indi-

viduals concerned are debarred by their "Western" occupations as clerks, school teachers, artisans, etc., and by their youth from playing a prominent part in traditional society proper; but they are the natural leaders of other young people less Westernized and sophisticated than themselves. This is largely because of their ability to interpret the "progressive" ideas they have gained through their work and travel, and through reading newspapers and books, in terms that are meaningful to the illiterate rank and file of the movement.

It is, in fact, in relation to the latter group, particularly the urban immigrant, that the significance of voluntary associations as an adaptive mechanism is most apparent. The newly arrived immigrant from the rural areas has been used to living and working as a member of a compact group of kinsmen and neighbors on a highly personal basis of relationship and mutuality. He knows of no other way of community living than this, and his natural reaction is to make a similar adjustment to urban conditions.

This adjustment the association facilitates by substituting for the extended group of kinsmen a grouping based upon common interest which is capable of serving many of the same needs as the traditional family or lineage. In other words, the migrant's participation in some organization such as a tribal union or a dancing compin not only replaces much of what he has lost in terms of moral assurance in removing from his native village, but offers him companionship and an opportunity of sharing joys as well as sorrows with others in the same position as himself. (Probably an important point in this regard is the large number of offices available in some associations, enabling even the most humble member to feel that he "matters.") Such an association also substitutes for the extended family in providing counsel and protection, in terms of legal aid; and by placing him in the company of women members, it also helps to find him a wife. It also substitutes for some of the economic support available at home by supplying him with sickness and funeral benefits, thereby enabling him to continue his most important kinship obligations. Further, it introduces him to a number of economically useful habits and practices, such as punctuality and thrift, and it aids his social reorientation by inculcating new standards of dress, etiquette, and personal hygiene. Above all, by encouraging him to mix with persons outside his own lineage and sometimes tribe, the voluntary association helps him to adjust to the more cosmopolitan ethos of the city. Equally significant, too, is the syncretistic character of associations of the "traditional-modernized" type. Their combination of modern and traditional traits constitutes a cultural bridge which conveys, metaphorically speaking, the tribal individual from one kind of sociological universe to another.

The latter point is also indicative of various ways in which these voluntary associations substitute for traditional agencies of social control. Not only are positive injunctions to friendly and fraternal conduct embodied in the constitution by which members agree to bind themselves, but many associations have rules proscribing particular misdemeanors and what they regard as antisocial behavior. In this respect, the frequent inclusion of sexual offenses, such as the seduction of the wife or the daughter of a fellow member, is very significant. The association also sets new moral standards and attempts to control the personal conduct of its members in a number of ways. For example, the Lagos branch of *Awo Omama* Patriotic Union resolved not to marry any girl of their town so long as the prevailing amount of money asked for bride-wealth was not reduced. The dancing *compin* will withhold its legal aid from a member unless the company's officials examining the case feel that he is in the right. Also, there are women's groups concerning themselves specifically with the settlement of domestic quarrels, which expel members who are constant troublemakers in the home and among other women. More frequently, punishment takes the form of a fine, but the strongest sanction probably lies in the fact that every reputable association is at pains to check fresh applications for membership. In other words, a person who has earned a bad name for himself in one organization may find it difficult to get into another; and this form of ostracism may in some cases be as painful as exile from the tribe.

A final important point is the extent to which disputes of a private or domestic nature, which would formerly have been heard by some traditional authority such as the head of a lineage, are now frequently taken to the head of an association, even when the matter is quite unconcerned with the life of that particular body.

CONCLUSION

Theorists of Western urbanism have stressed the importance of voluntary associations as a distinctive feature of contemporary social organization. Wirth, in particular, has emphasized the impersonality of the modern city, arguing that its psychological effect is to cause the individual urbanite to exert himself by joining with others of similar interests into organized groups to obtain his ends. "This," wrote Wirth, "results in an enormous multiplication of voluntary organizations directed towards as great a variety of objectives as are human needs and interests." However, this thesis has not been strongly supported by empirical inquiry. According to Komarovsky, who studied voluntary associations in New York, the old neighborhood, the larger kin group, might have broken down, but they have not been replaced by the specialized voluntary groups to the extent usually assumed. Floyd Dotson, who conducted a similar investigation in Detroit, also failed to find a wholesale displacement of primary by secondary groups. He concludes that the majority of urban working class people do not participate in formally organized voluntary associations. Perhaps more significant for the present context is the fact that the same writer found even less participation in voluntary organizations among the working class population of Guadalajara, the second largest city of Mexico.

The quantitative methods used in obtaining the latter results have not as yet been employed in African towns, so it is impossible to make exact comparisons. Also, the investigations concerned appear to have been made among relatively stable populations. Further study is therefore needed of the two factors which seem to be largely instrumental in the growth of these African voluntary associations. The first of these factors is the existence of an urban population which is largely immigrant, unstable, and socially heterogenous. The second is the adaptability of traditional institutions to urban conditions. Possibly, it is the existence and interrelationship of these two factors rather than "anomic" which creates the essential conditions for the "fictional kinship groups," which, according to Wirth, substitute for actual kinship ties within the urban environment.

INDEX